American Casebook Series
Hornbook Series and Basic Legal Texts
Nutshell Series

of

WEST PUBLISHING COMPANY
P.O. Box 64526
St. Paul, Minnesota 55164–0526

ACCOUNTING

Faris' Accounting and Law in a Nutshell, 377 pages, 1984 (Text)

Fiflis, Kripke and Foster's Teaching Materials on Accounting for Business Lawyers, 3rd Ed., 838 pages, 1984 (Casebook)

Siegel and Siegel's Accounting and Financial Disclosure: A Guide to Basic Concepts, 259 pages, 1983 (Text)

ADMINISTRATIVE LAW

Davis' Cases, Text and Problems on Administrative Law, 6th Ed., 683 pages, 1977 (Casebook)

Davis' Basic Text on Administrative Law, 3rd Ed., 617 pages, 1972 (Text)

Davis' Police Discretion, 176 pages, 1975 (Text)

Gellhorn and Boyer's Administrative Law and Process in a Nutshell, 2nd Ed., 445 pages, 1981 (Text)

Mashaw and Merrill's Cases and Materials on Administrative Law–The American Public Law System, 2nd Ed., 975 pages, 1985 (Casebook)

Robinson, Gellhorn and Bruff's The Administrative Process, 2nd Ed., 959 pages, 1980, with 1983 Supplement (Casebook)

ADMIRALTY

Healy and Sharpe's Cases and Materials on Admiralty, 875 pages, 1974 (Casebook)

Maraist's Admiralty in a Nutshell, 390 pages, 1983 (Text)

Sohn and Gustafson's Law of the Sea in a Nutshell, 264 pages, 1984 (Text)

AGENCY—PARTNERSHIP

Fessler's Alternatives to Incorporation for Persons in Quest of Profit, 258 pages, 1980 (Casebook)

AGENCY—PARTNERSHIP—Continued

Henn's Cases and Materials on Agency, Partnership and Other Unincorporated Business Enterprises, 2nd Ed., 733 pages, 1985 (Casebook)

Reuschlein and Gregory's Hornbook on the Law of Agency and Partnership, 625 pages, 1979, with 1981 pocket part (Text)

Seavey, Reuschlein and Hall's Cases on Agency and Partnership, 599 pages, 1962 (Casebook)

Selected Corporation and Partnership Statutes and Forms, approximately 555 pages, 1985

Steffen and Kerr's Cases and Materials on Agency-Partnership, 4th Ed., 859 pages, 1980 (Casebook)

Steffen's Agency-Partnership in a Nutshell, 364 pages, 1977 (Text)

AGRICULTURAL LAW

Meyer, Pedersen, Thorson and Davidson's Agricultural Law: Cases and Materials, 931 pages, 1985 (Casebook)

AMERICAN INDIAN LAW

Canby's American Indian Law in a Nutshell, 288 pages, 1981 (Text)

Getches, Rosenfelt and Wilkinson's Cases on Federal Indian Law, 660 pages, 1979, with 1983 Supplement (Casebook)

ANTITRUST LAW

Gellhorn's Antitrust Law and Economics in a Nutshell, 2nd Ed., 425 pages, 1981 (Text)

Gifford and Raskind's Cases and Materials on Antitrust, 694 pages, 1983 with 1985 Supplement (Casebook)

Hovenkamp's Economics and Federal Antitrust Law, Student Ed., 414 pages, 1985 (Text)

List current as of April, 1985

Nelson & Whitman, Real Est.Fin. Law, 2d Ed. HB—1

I

T7202—1g

LAW SCHOOL PUBLICATIONS—Continued

ANTITRUST LAW—Continued

Oppenheim, Weston and McCarthy's Cases and Comments on Federal Antitrust Laws, 4th Ed., 1168 pages, 1981 with 1985 Supplement (Casebook)

Posner and Easterbrook's Cases and Economic Notes on Antitrust, 2nd Ed., 1077 pages, 1981, with 1984–85 Supplement (Casebook)

Sullivan's Hornbook of the Law of Antitrust, 886 pages, 1977 (Text)

See also Regulated Industries, Trade Regulation

ART LAW

DuBoff's Art Law in a Nutshell, 335 pages, 1984 (Text)

BANKING LAW

Lovett's Banking and Financial Institutions in a Nutshell, 409 pages, 1984 (Text)

Symons and White's Teaching Materials on Banking Law, 2nd Ed., 993 pages, 1984 (Casebook)

BUSINESS PLANNING

Epstein and Scheinfeld's Teaching Materials on Business Reorganization Under the Bankruptcy Code, 216 pages, 1980 (Casebook)

Painter's Problems and Materials in Business Planning, 2nd Ed., 1008 pages, 1984 (Casebook)

Selected Securities and Business Planning Statutes, Rules and Forms, 470 pages, 1985

CIVIL PROCEDURE

Casad's Res Judicata in a Nutshell, 310 pages, 1976 (text)

Cound, Friedenthal, Miller and Sexton's Cases and Materials on Civil Procedure, 4th Ed., approximately 1147 pages, 1985 with 1985 Supplement (Casebook)

Ehrenzweig, Louisell and Hazard's Jurisdiction in a Nutshell, 4th Ed., 232 pages, 1980 (Text)

Federal Rules of Civil-Appellate-Criminal Procedure—West Law School Edition, approximately 500 pages, 1985

Friedenthal, Kane and Miller's Hornbook on Civil Procedure, Student Edition, approximately 870 pages, 1985 (Text)

Hodges, Jones and Elliott's Cases and Materials on Texas Trial and Appellate Procedure, 2nd Ed., 745 pages, 1974 (Casebook)

Hodges, Jones and Elliott's Cases and Materials on the Judicial Process Prior to Trial in Texas, 2nd Ed., 871 pages, 1977 (Casebook)

Kane's Civil Procedure in a Nutshell, 271 pages, 1979 (Text)

CIVIL PROCEDURE—Continued

Karlen's Procedure Before Trial in a Nutshell, 258 pages, 1972 (Text)

Karlen, Meisenholder, Stevens and Vestal's Cases on Civil Procedure, 923 pages, 1975 (Casebook)

Koffler and Reppy's Hornbook on Common Law Pleading, 663 pages, 1969 (Text)

Marcus and Sherman's Complex Litigation–Cases and Materials on Advanced Civil Procedure, approximately 900 pages, 1985 (Casebook)

Park's Computer-Aided Exercises on Civil Procedure, 2nd Ed., 167 pages, 1983 (Coursebook)

Siegel's Hornbook on New York Practice, 1011 pages, 1978 with 1985 Pocket Part (Text)

See also Federal Jurisdiction and Procedure

CIVIL RIGHTS

Abernathy's Cases and Materials on Civil Rights, 660 pages, 1980 (Casebook)

Cohen's Cases on the Law of Deprivation of Liberty: A Study in Social Control, 755 pages, 1980 (Casebook)

Lockhart, Kamisar and Choper's Cases on Constitutional Rights and Liberties, 5th Ed., 1298 pages plus Appendix, 1981, with 1985 Supplement (Casebook)—reprint from Lockhart, et al. Cases on Constitutional Law, 5th Ed., 1980

Vieira's Civil Rights in a Nutshell, 279 pages, 1978 (Text)

COMMERCIAL LAW

Bailey's Secured Transactions in a Nutshell, 2nd Ed., 391 pages, 1981 (Text)

Epstein and Martin's Basic Uniform Commercial Code Teaching Materials, 2nd Ed., 667 pages, 1983 (Casebook)

Henson's Hornbook on Secured Transactions Under the U.C.C., 2nd Ed., 504 pages, 1979 with 1979 P.P. (Text)

Murray's Commercial Law, Problems and Materials, 366 pages, 1975 (Coursebook)

Nordstrom and Clovis' Problems and Materials on Commercial Paper, 458 pages, 1972 (Casebook)

Nordstrom and Lattin's Problems and Materials on Sales and Secured Transactions, 809 pages, 1968 (Casebook)

Nordstrom, Murray and Clovis' Problems and Materials on Sales, 515 pages, 1982 (Casebook)

Selected Commercial Statutes, 1389 pages, 1985

Speidel, Summers and White's Teaching Materials on Commercial and Consumer Law, 3rd Ed., 1490 pages, 1981 (Casebook)

Stockton's Sales in a Nutshell, 2nd Ed., 370 pages, 1981 (Text)

LAW SCHOOL PUBLICATIONS—Continued

COMMERCIAL LAW—Continued

Stone's Uniform Commercial Code in a Nutshell, 2nd Ed., 516 pages, 1984 (Text)

Uniform Commercial Code, Official Text with Comments, 994 pages, 1978

UCC Article 9, Reprint from 1962 Code, 128 pages, 1976

UCC Article 9, 1972 Amendments, 304 pages, 1978

Weber and Speidel's Commercial Paper in a Nutshell, 3rd Ed., 404 pages, 1982 (Text)

White and Summers' Hornbook on the Uniform Commercial Code, 2nd Ed., 1250 pages, 1980 (Text)

COMMUNITY PROPERTY

Mennell's Community Property in a Nutshell, 447 pages, 1982 (Text)

Verrall and Bird's Cases and Materials on California Community Property, 4th Ed., 549 pages, 1983 (Casebook)

COMPARATIVE LAW

Barton, Gibbs, Li and Merryman's Law in Radically Different Cultures, 960 pages, 1983 (Casebook)

Glendon, Gordon and Osakive's Comparative Legal Traditions: Text, Materials and Cases on the Civil Law, Common Law, and Socialist Law Traditions, approximately 1190 pages, 1985 (Casebook)

Glendon, Gordon, and Osakwe's Comparative Legal Traditions in a Nutshell, 402 pages, 1982 (Text)

Langbein's Comparative Criminal Procedure: Germany, 172 pages, 1977 (Casebook)

COMPUTERS AND LAW

Mason's An Introduction to the Use of Computers in Law, 223 pages, 1984 (Text)

CONFLICT OF LAWS

Cramton, Currie and Kay's Cases-Comments-Questions on Conflict of Laws, 3rd Ed., 1026 pages, 1981 (Casebook)

Scoles and Hay's Hornbook on Conflict of Laws, Student Ed., 1085 pages, 1982 (Text)

Scoles and Weintraub's Cases and Materials on Conflict of Laws, 2nd Ed., 966 pages, 1972, with 1978 Supplement (Casebook)

Siegel's Conflicts in a Nutshell, 469 pages, 1982 (Text)

CONSTITUTIONAL LAW

Engdahl's Constitutional Power in a Nutshell: Federal and State, 411 pages, 1974 (Text)

Lockhart, Kamisar and Choper's Cases-Comments-Questions on Constitutional Law, 5th Ed., 1705 pages plus Appendix, 1980, with 1985 Supplement (Casebook)

CONSTITUTIONAL LAW—Continued

Lockhart, Kamisar and Choper's Cases-Comments-Questions on the American Constitution, 5th Ed., 1185 pages plus Appendix, 1981, with 1985 Supplement (Casebook)—reprint from Lockhart, et al. Cases on Constitutional Law, 5th Ed., 1980

Manning's The Law of Church-State Relations in a Nutshell, 305 pages, 1981 (Text)

Miller's Presidential Power in a Nutshell, 328 pages, 1977 (Text)

Nowak, Rotunda and Young's Hornbook on Constitutional Law, 2nd Ed., Student Ed., 1172 pages, 1983 (Text)

Rotunda's Modern Constitutional Law: Cases and Notes, 2nd Ed., approximately 1055 pages, 1985, with 1985 Supplement (Casebook)

Williams' Constitutional Analysis in a Nutshell, 388 pages, 1979 (Text)

See also Civil Rights

CONSUMER LAW

Epstein and Nickles' Consumer Law in a Nutshell, 2nd Ed., 418 pages, 1981 (Text)

McCall's Consumer Protection, Cases, Notes and Materials, 594 pages, 1977, with 1977 Statutory Supplement (Casebook)

Selected Commercial Statutes, 1389 pages, 1985

Spanogle and Rohner's Cases and Materials on Consumer Law, 693 pages, 1979, with 1982 Supplement (Casebook)

See also Commercial Law

CONTRACTS

Calamari & Perillo's Cases and Problems on Contracts, 1061 pages, 1978 (Casebook)

Calamari and Perillo's Hornbook on Contracts, 2nd Ed., 878 pages, 1977 (Text)

Corbin's Text on Contracts, One Volume Student Edition, 1224 pages, 1952 (Text)

Fessler and Loiseaux's Cases and Materials on Contracts, 837 pages, 1982 (Casebook)

Freedman's Cases and Materials on Contracts, 658 pages, 1973 (Casebook)

Friedman's Contract Remedies in a Nutshell, 323 pages, 1981 (Text)

Fuller and Eisenberg's Cases on Basic Contract Law, 4th Ed., 1203 pages, 1981 (Casebook)

Hamilton, Rau and Weintraub's Cases and Materials on Contracts, 830 pages, 1984 (Casebook)

Jackson and Bollinger's Cases on Contract Law in Modern Society, 2nd Ed., 1329 pages, 1980 (Casebook)

Keyes' Government Contracts in a Nutshell, 423 pages, 1979 (Text)

CONTRACTS—Continued

Reitz's Cases on Contracts as Basic Commercial Law, 763 pages, 1975 (Casebook)

Schaber and Rohwer's Contracts in a Nutshell, 2nd Ed., 425 pages, 1984 (Text)

COPYRIGHT

See Patent and Copyright Law

CORPORATIONS

Hamilton's Cases on Corporations—Including Partnerships and Limited Partnerships, 2nd Ed., 1108 pages, 1981, with 1981 Statutory Supplement and 1985 Supplement (Casebook)

Hamilton's Law of Corporations in a Nutshell, 379 pages, 1980 (Text)

Henn's Cases on Corporations, 1279 pages, 1974, with 1980 Supplement (Casebook)

Henn and Alexander's Hornbook on Corporations, 3rd Ed., Student Ed., 1371 pages, 1983 (Text)

Jennings and Buxbaum's Cases and Materials on Corporations, 5th Ed., 1180 pages, 1979 (Casebook)

Selected Corporation and Partnership Statutes, Regulations and Forms, 555 pages, 1985

Solomon, Stevenson and Schwartz' Materials and Problems on Corporations: Law and Policy, 1172 pages, 1982 with 1984 Supplement (Casebook)

CORPORATE FINANCE

Hamilton's Cases and Materials on Corporate Finance, 895 pages, 1984 (Casebook)

CORRECTIONS

Krantz's Cases and Materials on the Law of Corrections and Prisoners' Rights, 2nd Ed., 735 pages, 1981, with 1982 Supplement (Casebook)

Krantz's Law of Corrections and Prisoners' Rights in a Nutshell, 2nd Ed., 384 pages, 1983 (Text)

Popper's Post-Conviction Remedies in a Nutshell, 360 pages, 1978 (Text)

Robbins' Cases and Materials on Post Conviction Remedies, 506 pages, 1982 (Casebook)

Rubin's Law of Criminal Corrections, 2nd Ed., 873 pages, 1973, with 1978 Supplement (Text)

CREDITOR'S RIGHTS

Bankruptcy Code, Rules and Forms, Law School and C.L.E. Ed., 602 pages, 1984

Epstein's Debtor-Creditor Law in a Nutshell, 2nd Ed., 324 pages, 1980 (Text)

Epstein and Landers' Debtors and Creditors: Cases and Materials, 2nd Ed., 689 pages, 1982 (Casebook)

CREDITOR'S RIGHTS—Continued

Epstein and Sheinfeld's Teaching Materials on Business Reorganization Under the Bankruptcy Code, 216 pages, 1980 (Casebook)

LoPucki's Player's Manual for the Debtor-Creditor Game, 123 pages, 1985 (Coursebook)

Riesenfeld's Cases and Materials on Creditors' Remedies and Debtors' Protection, 3rd Ed., 810 pages, 1979 with 1979 Statutory Supplement and 1981 Case Supplement (Casebook)

White's Bankruptcy and Creditor's Rights: Cases and Materials, 812 pages, 1985 (Casebook)

CRIMINAL LAW AND CRIMINAL PROCEDURE

Cohen and Gobert's Problems in Criminal Law, 297 pages, 1976 (Problem book)

Davis' Police Discretion, 176 pages, 1975 (Text)

Dix and Sharlot's Cases and Materials on Criminal Law, 2nd Ed., 771 pages, 1979 (Casebook)

Federal Rules of Civil-Appellate-Criminal Procedure—West Law School Edition, approximately 500 pages, 1985

Grano's Problems in Criminal Procedure, 2nd Ed., 176 pages, 1981 (Problem book)

Israel and LaFave's Criminal Procedure in a Nutshell, 3rd Ed., 438 pages, 1980 (Text)

Johnson's Cases, Materials and Text on Substantive Criminal Law in its Procedural Context, 3rd Ed., approximately 750 pages, 1985 (Casebook)

Kamisar, LaFave and Israel's Cases, Comments and Questions on Modern Criminal Procedure, 5th ed., 1635 pages plus Appendix, 1980 with 1985 Supplement (Casebook)

Kamisar, LaFave and Israel's Cases, Comments and Questions on Basic Criminal Procedure, 5th Ed., 869 pages, 1980 with 1985 Supplement (Casebook)—reprint from Kamisar, et al. Modern Criminal Procedure, 5th ed., 1980

LaFave's Modern Criminal Law: Cases, Comments and Questions, 789 pages, 1978 (Casebook)

LaFave and Israel's Hornbook on Criminal Procedure, Student Ed., 1142 pages, 1985 (Text)

LaFave and Scott's Hornbook on Criminal Law, 763 pages, 1972 (Text)

Langbein's Comparative Criminal Procedure: Germany, 172 pages, 1977 (Casebook)

Loewy's Criminal Law in a Nutshell, 302 pages, 1975 (Text)

CRIMINAL LAW AND CRIMINAL PROCEDURE—Continued

Saltzburg's American Criminal Procedure, Cases and Commentary, 2nd Ed., 1193 pages, 1985 with 1985 Supplement (Casebook)

Uviller's The Processes of Criminal Justice: Investigation and Adjudication, 2nd Ed., 1384 pages, 1979 with 1979 Statutory Supplement and 1983 Update (Casebook)

Uviller's The Processes of Criminal Justice: Adjudication, 2nd Ed., 730 pages, 1979. Soft-cover reprint from Uviller's The Processes of Criminal Justice: Investigation and Adjudication, 2nd Ed. (Casebook)

Uviller's The Processes of Criminal Justice: Investigation, 2nd Ed., 655 pages, 1979. Soft-cover reprint from Uviller's The Processes of Criminal Justice: Investigation and Adjudication, 2nd Ed. (Casebook)

Vorenberg's Cases on Criminal Law and Procedure, 2nd Ed., 1088 pages, 1981 with 1985 Supplement (Casebook)

See also Corrections, Juvenile Justice

DECEDENTS ESTATES

See Trusts and Estates

DOMESTIC RELATIONS

Clark's Cases and Problems on Domestic Relations, 3rd Ed., 1153 pages, 1980 (Casebook)

Clark's Hornbook on Domestic Relations, 754 pages, 1968 (Text)

Krause's Cases and Materials on Family Law, 2nd Ed., 1221 pages, 1983 (Casebook)

Krause's Family Law in a Nutshell, 400 pages, 1977 (Text)

Krauskopf's Cases on Property Division at Marriage Dissolution, 250 pages, 1984 (Casebook)

ECONOMICS, LAW AND

Goetz' Cases and Materials on Law and Economics, 547 pages, 1984 (Casebook)

Manne's The Economics of Legal Relationships—Readings in the Theory of Property Rights, 660 pages, 1975 (Text)

See also Antitrust, Regulated Industries

EDUCATION LAW

Alexander and Alexander's The Law of Schools, Students and Teachers in a Nutshell, 409 pages, 1984 (Text)

Morris' The Constitution and American Education, 2nd Ed., 992 pages, 1980 (Casebook)

EMPLOYMENT DISCRIMINATION

Player's Cases and Materials on Employment Discrimination Law, 2nd Ed., 782 pages, 1984 (Casebook)

Player's Federal Law of Employment Discrimination in a Nutshell, 2nd Ed., 402 pages, 1981 (Text)

See also Women and the Law

ENERGY LAW

Rodgers' Cases and Materials on Energy and Natural Resources Law, 2nd Ed., 877 pages, 1983 (Casebook)

Selected Environmental Law Statutes, 786 pages, 1985

Tomain's Energy Law in a Nutshell, 338 pages, 1981 (Text)

See also Natural Resources Law, Environmental Law, Oil and Gas, Water Law

ENVIRONMENTAL LAW

Bonine and McGarity's Cases and Materials on the Law of Environment and Pollution, 1076 pages, 1984 (Casebook)

Findley and Farber's Cases and Materials on Environmental Law, 2nd Ed., approximately 800 pages, 1985 (Casebook)

Findley and Farber's Environmental Law in a Nutshell, 343 pages, 1983 (Text)

Rodgers' Hornbook on Environmental Law, 956 pages, 1977 with 1984 pocket part (Text)

Selected Environmental Law Statutes, 786 pages, 1985

See also Energy Law, Natural Resources Law, Water Law

EQUITY

See Remedies

ESTATES

See Trusts and Estates

ESTATE PLANNING

Kurtz' Cases, Materials and Problems on Family Estate Planning, 853 pages, 1983 (Casebook)

Lynn's Introduction to Estate Planning, in a Nutshell, 3rd Ed., 370 pages, 1983 (Text)

See also Taxation

EVIDENCE

Broun and Meisenholder's Problems in Evidence, 2nd Ed., 304 pages, 1981 (Problem book)

Cleary and Strong's Cases, Materials and Problems on Evidence, 3rd Ed., 1143 pages, 1981 (Casebook)

Federal Rules of Evidence for United States Courts and Magistrates, 337 pages, 1984

Graham's Federal Rules of Evidence in a Nutshell, 429 pages, 1981 (Text)

LAW SCHOOL PUBLICATIONS—Continued

EVIDENCE—Continued

Kimball's Programmed Materials on Problems in Evidence, 380 pages, 1978 (Problem book)

Lempert and Saltzburg's A Modern Approach to Evidence: Text, Problems, Transcripts and Cases, 2nd Ed., 1296 pages, 1983 (Casebook)

Lilly's Introduction to the Law of Evidence, 486 pages, 1978 (Text)

McCormick, Elliott and Sutton's Cases and Materials on Evidence, 5th Ed., 1212 pages, 1981 (Casebook)

McCormick's Hornbook on Evidence, 3rd Ed., Student Ed., 1155 pages, 1984 (Text)

Rothstein's Evidence, State and Federal Rules in a Nutshell, 2nd Ed., 514 pages, 1981 (Text)

Saltzburg's Evidence Supplement: Rules, Statutes, Commentary, 245 pages, 1980 (Casebook Supplement)

FEDERAL JURISDICTION AND PROCEDURE

Currie's Cases and Materials on Federal Courts, 3rd Ed., 1042 pages, 1982 (Casebook)

Currie's Federal Jurisdiction in a Nutshell, 2nd Ed., 258 pages, 1981 (Text)

Federal Rules of Civil-Appellate-Criminal Procedure—West Law School Edition, approximately 500 pages, 1985

Forrester and Moye's Cases and Materials on Federal Jurisdiction and Procedure, 3rd Ed., 917 pages, 1977 with 1981 Supplement (Casebook)

Redish's Cases, Comments and Questions on Federal Courts, 878 pages, 1985 (Casebook)

Vetri and Merrill's Federal Courts, Problems and Materials, 2nd Ed., 232 pages, 1984 (Problem Book)

Wright's Hornbook on Federal Courts, 4th Ed., Student Ed., 870 pages, 1983 (Text)

FUTURE INTERESTS

See Trusts and Estates

IMMIGRATION LAW

Aleinikoff and Martin's Immigration Process and Policy, approximately 950 pages, 1985 (Casebook)

Weissbrodt's Immigration Law and Procedure in a Nutshell, 345 pages, 1984 (Text)

INDIAN LAW

See American Indian Law

INSURANCE

Dobbyn's Insurance Law in a Nutshell, 281 pages, 1981 (Text)

Keeton's Cases on Basic Insurance Law, 2nd Ed., 1086 pages, 1977

INSURANCE—Continued

Keeton's Basic Text on Insurance Law, 712 pages, 1971 (Text)

Keeton's Case Supplement to Keeton's Basic Text on Insurance Law, 334 pages, 1978 (Casebook)

Keeton's Programmed Problems in Insurance Law, 243 pages, 1972 (Text Supplement)

York and Whelan's Cases, Materials and Problems on Insurance Law, 715 pages, 1982, with 1985 Supplement (Casebook)

INTERNATIONAL LAW

Henkin, Pugh, Schachter and Smit's Cases and Materials on International Law, 2nd Ed., 1152 pages, 1980, with Documents Supplement (Casebook)

Jackson's Legal Problems of International Economic Relations, 1097 pages, 1977, with Documents Supplement (Casebook)

Kirgis' International Organizations in Their Legal Setting, 1016 pages, 1977, with 1981 Supplement (Casebook)

Weston, Falk and D'Amato's International Law and World Order—A Problem Oriented Coursebook, 1195 pages, 1980, with Documents Supplement (Casebook)

Wilson's International Business Transactions in a Nutshell, 2nd Ed., 476 pages, 1984 (Text)

INTERVIEWING AND COUNSELING

Binder and Price's Interviewing and Counseling, 232 pages, 1977 (Text)

Shaffer's Interviewing and Counseling in a Nutshell, 353 pages, 1976 (Text)

INTRODUCTION TO LAW

Dobbyn's So You Want to go to Law School, Revised First Edition, 206 pages, 1976 (Text)

Hegland's Introduction to the Study and Practice of Law in a Nutshell, 418 pages, 1983 (Text)

Kinyon's Introduction to Law Study and Law Examinations in a Nutshell, 389 pages, 1971 (Text)

See also Legal Method and Legal System

JUDICIAL ADMINISTRATION

Carrington, Meador and Rosenberg's Justice on Appeal, 263 pages, 1976 (Casebook)

Nelson's Cases and Materials on Judicial Administration and the Administration of Justice, 1032 pages, 1974 (Casebook)

JURISPRUDENCE

Christie's Text and Readings on Jurisprudence—The Philosophy of Law, 1056 pages, 1973 (Casebook)

LAW SCHOOL PUBLICATIONS—Continued

LEGAL RESEARCH AND WRITING—Continued

Rombauer's Legal Problem Solving—Analysis, Research and Writing, 4th Ed., 424 pages, 1983 (Coursebook)

Squires and Rombauer's Legal Writing in a Nutshell, 294 pages, 1982 (Text)

Statsky's Legal Research, Writing and Analysis, 2nd Ed., 167 pages, 1982 (Coursebook)

Statsky's Legislative Analysis: How to Use Statutes and Regulations, 2nd Ed., 217 pages, 1984 (Text)

Statsky and Wernet's Case Analysis and Fundamentals of Legal Writing, 2nd Ed., 441 pages, 1984 (Text)

Teply's Programmed Materials on Legal Research and Citation, 334 pages, 1982. Student Library Exercises available (Coursebook)

Weihofen's Legal Writing Style, 2nd Ed., 332 pages, 1980 (Text)

LEGISLATION

Davies' Legislative Law and Process in a Nutshell, 279 pages, 1975 (Text)

Nutting and Dickerson's Cases and Materials on Legislation, 5th Ed., 744 pages, 1978 (Casebook)

Statsky's Legislative Analysis: How to Use Statutes and Regulations, 2nd Ed., 217 pages, 1984 (Text)

LOCAL GOVERNMENT

McCarthy's Local Government Law in a Nutshell, 2nd Ed., 404 pages, 1983 (Text)

Michelman and Sandalow's Cases-Comments-Questions on Government in Urban Areas, 1216 pages, 1970, with 1972 Supplement (Casebook)

Reynolds' Hornbook on Local Government Law, 860 pages, 1982 (Text)

Valente's Cases and Materials on Local Government Law, 2nd Ed., 980 pages, 1980 with 1982 Supplement (Casebook)

MASS COMMUNICATION LAW

Gillmor and Barron's Cases and Comment on Mass Communication Law, 4th Ed., 1076 pages, 1984 (Casebook)

Ginsburg's Regulation of Broadcasting: Law and Policy Towards Radio, Television and Cable Communications, 741 pages, 1979, with 1983 Supplement (Casebook)

Zuckman and Gayne's Mass Communications Law in a Nutshell, 2nd Ed., 473 pages, 1983 (Text)

MEDICINE, LAW AND

King's The Law of Medical Malpractice in a Nutshell, 340 pages, 1977 (Text)

Shapiro and Spece's Problems, Cases and Materials on Bioethics and Law, 892 pages, 1981 (Casebook)

MEDICINE, LAW AND—Continued

Sharpe, Fiscina and Head's Cases on Law and Medicine, 882 pages, 1978 (Casebook)

MILITARY LAW

Shanor and Terrell's Military Law in a Nutshell, 378 pages, 1980 (Text)

MORTGAGES

See Real Estate Transactions

NATURAL RESOURCES LAW

Laito's Cases and Materials on Natural Resources Law, approximately 930 pages, 1985 (Casebook)

See also Energy Law, Environmental Law, Oil and Gas, Water Law

NEGOTIATION

Edwards and White's Problems, Readings and Materials on the Lawyer as a Negotiator, 484 pages, 1977 (Casebook)

Williams' Legal Negotiation and Settlement, 207 pages, 1983 (Coursebook)

OFFICE PRACTICE

Hegland's Trial and Practice Skills in a Nutshell, 346 pages, 1978 (Text)

Strong and Clark's Law Office Management, 424 pages, 1974 (Casebook)

See also Computers and Law, Interviewing and Counseling, Negotiation

OIL AND GAS

Hemingway's Hornbook on Oil and Gas, 2nd Ed., Student Ed., 543 pages, 1983 (Text)

Huie, Woodward and Smith's Cases and Materials on Oil and Gas, 2nd Ed., 955 pages, 1972 (Casebook)

Lowe's Oil and Gas Law in a Nutshell, 443 pages, 1983 (Text)

See also Energy and Natural Resources Law

PARTNERSHIP

See Agency—Partnership

PATENT AND COPYRIGHT LAW

Choate and Francis' Cases and Materials on Patent Law, 2nd Ed., 1110 pages, 1981 (Casebook)

Miller and Davis' Intellectual Property—Patents, Trademarks and Copyright in a Nutshell, 428 pages, 1983 (Text)

Nimmer's Cases on Copyright and Other Aspects of Entertainment Litigation, 3rd Ed., approximately 1000 pages, 1985 (Casebook)

POVERTY LAW

Brudno's Poverty, Inequality, and the Law: Cases-Commentary-Analysis, 934 pages, 1976 (Casebook)

POVERTY LAW—Continued

LaFrance, Schroeder, Bennett and Boyd's Hornbook on Law of the Poor, 558 pages, 1973 (Text)

See also Social Legislation

PRODUCTS LIABILITY

Noel and Phillips' Cases on Products Liability, 2nd Ed., 821 pages, 1982 (Casebook)

Noel and Phillips' Products Liability in a Nutshell, 2nd Ed., 341 pages, 1981 (Text)

PROPERTY

Aigler, Smith and Tefft's Cases on Property, 2 volumes, 1339 pages, 1960 (Casebook)

Bernhardt's Real Property in a Nutshell, 2nd Ed., 448 pages, 1981 (Text)

Boyer's Survey of the Law of Property, 766 pages, 1981 (Text)

Browder, Cunningham and Smith's Cases on Basic Property Law, 4th Ed., 1431 pages, 1984 (Casebook)

Bruce, Ely and Bostick's Cases and Materials on Modern Property Law, 1004 pages, 1984 (Casebook)

Burby's Hornbook on Real Property, 3rd Ed., 490 pages, 1965 (Text)

Burke's Personal Property in a Nutshell, 322 pages, 1983 (Text)

Chused's A Modern Approach to Property: Cases-Notes-Materials, 1069 pages, 1978 with 1980 Supplement (Casebook)

Cohen's Materials for a Basic Course in Property, 526 pages, 1978 (Casebook)

Cunningham, Stoebuck and Whitman's Hornbook on the Law of Property, Student Ed., 916 pages, 1984 (Text)

Donahue, Kauper and Martin's Cases on Property, 2nd Ed., 1362 pages, 1983 (Casebook)

Hill's Landlord and Tenant Law in a Nutshell, 319 pages, 1979 (Text)

Moynihan's Introduction to Real Property, 254 pages, 1962 (Text)

Uniform Land Transactions Act, Uniform Simplification of Land Transfers Act, Uniform Condominium Act, 1977 Official Text with Comments, 462 pages, 1978

See also Real Estate Transactions, Land Use

PSYCHIATRY, LAW AND

Reisner's Law and the Mental Health System, Civil and Criminal Aspects, 696 pages, 1985 (Casebooks)

REAL ESTATE TRANSACTIONS

Bruce's Real Estate Finance in a Nutshell, 2nd Ed., 262 pages, 1985 (Text)

Maxwell, Riesenfeld, Hetland and Warren's Cases on California Security Transactions in Land, 3rd Ed., 728 pages, 1984 (Casebook)

REAL ESTATE TRANSACTIONS—Continued

Nelson and Whitman's Cases on Real Estate Transfer, Finance and Development, 2nd Ed., 1114 pages, 1981, with 1983 Supplement (Casebook)

Nelson and Whitman's Hornbook on Real Estate Finance Law, 2nd Ed., Standard Ed., approximately 900 pages, 1985 (Text)

Osborne's Cases and Materials on Secured Transactions, 559 pages, 1967 (Casebook)

REGULATED INDUSTRIES

Gellhorn and Pierce's Regulated Industries in a Nutshell, 394 pages, 1982 (Text)

Morgan, Harrison and Verkuil's Cases and Materials on Economic Regulation of Business, 2nd Ed., 670 pages, 1985 (Casebook)

Pozen's Financial Institutions: Cases, Materials and Problems on Investment Management, 844 pages, 1978 (Casebook)

See also Mass Communication Law, Banking Law

REMEDIES

Dobbs' Hornbook on Remedies, 1067 pages, 1973 (Text)

Dobbs' Problems in Remedies, 137 pages, 1974 (Problem book)

Dobbyn's Injunctions in a Nutshell, 264 pages, 1974 (Text)

Friedman's Contract Remedies in a Nutshell, 323 pages, 1981 (Text)

Leavell, Love and Nelson's Cases and Materials on Equitable Remedies and Restitution, 3rd Ed., 704 pages, 1980 (Casebook)

McCormick's Hornbook on Damages, 811 pages, 1935 (Text)

O'Connell's Remedies in a Nutshell, 2nd Ed., 325 pages, 1985 (Text)

York, Bauman and Rendleman's Cases and Materials on Remedies, 4th Ed., approximately 1025 pages, 1985 (Casebook)

REVIEW MATERIALS

Ballantine's Problems

Black Letter Series

Smith's Review Series

West's Review Covering Multistate Subjects

SECURITIES REGULATION

Hazen's Hornbook on The Law of Securities Regulation, Student Ed., 739 pages, 1985 (Text)

Ratner's Securities Regulation: Materials for a Basic Course, 2nd Ed., 1050 pages, 1980 with 1982 Supplement (Casebook)

Ratner's Securities Regulation in a Nutshell, 2nd Ed., 322 pages, 1982 (Text)

LAW SCHOOL PUBLICATIONS—Continued

SECURITIES REGULATION—Continued

Selected Securities and Business Planning Statutes, Rules and Forms, 470 pages, 1985

SOCIAL LEGISLATION

Hood and Hardy's Workers' Compensation and Employee Protection Laws in a Nutshell, 274 pages, 1984 (Text)

LaFrance's Welfare Law: Structure and Entitlement in a Nutshell, 455 pages, 1979 (Text)

Malone, Plant and Little's Cases on Workers' Compensation and Employment Rights, 2nd Ed., 951 pages, 1980 (Casebook)

See also Poverty Law

TAXATION

Dodge's Cases and Materials on Federal Income Taxation, approximately 825 pages, 1985 (Casebook)

Dodge's Federal Taxation of Estates, Trusts and Gifts: Principles and Planning, 771 pages, 1981 with 1982 Supplement (Casebook)

Garbis and Struntz' Cases and Materials on Tax Procedure and Tax Fraud, 829 pages, 1982 with 1984 Supplement (Casebook)

Gunn's Cases and Materials on Federal Income Taxation of Individuals, 785 pages, 1981 with 1985 Supplement (Casebook)

Hellerstein and Hellerstein's Cases on State and Local Taxation, 4th Ed., 1041 pages, 1978 with 1982 Supplement (Casebook)

Kahn and Gann's Corporate Taxation and Taxation of Partnerships and Partners, 2nd Ed., 1204 pages, 1985 (Casebook)

Kragen and McNulty's Cases and Materials on Federal Income Taxation: Individuals, Corporations, Partnerships, 4th Ed., approximately 1200 pages, 1985 (Casebook)

McNulty's Federal Estate and Gift Taxation in a Nutshell, 3rd Ed., 509 pages, 1983 (Text)

McNulty's Federal Income Taxation of Individuals in a Nutshell, 3rd Ed., 487 pages, 1983 (Text)

Posin's Hornbook on Federal Income Taxation of Individuals, Student Ed., 491 pages, 1983 with 1985 pocket part (Text)

Rice and Solomon's Problems and Materials in Federal Income Taxation, 3rd Ed., 670 pages, 1979 (Casebook)

Rose and Raskind's Advanced Federal Income Taxation: Corporate Transactions—Cases, Materials and Problems, 955 pages, 1978 (Casebook)

Selected Federal Taxation Statutes and Regulations, approximately 1300 pages, 1985

Soboloff and Weidenbruch's Federal Income Taxation of Corporations and Stockholders in a Nutshell, 362 pages, 1981 (Text)

TORTS

Christie's Cases and Materials on the Law of Torts, 1264 pages, 1983 (Casebook)

Dobbs' Torts and Compensation—Personal Accountability and Social Responsibility for Injury, 955 pages, 1985 (Casebook)

Green, Pedrick, Rahl, Thode, Hawkins, Smith and Treece's Cases and Materials on Torts, 2nd Ed., 1360 pages, 1977 (Casebook)

Green, Pedrick, Rahl, Thode, Hawkins, Smith, and Treece's Advanced Torts: Injuries to Business, Political and Family Interests, 2nd Ed., 544 pages, 1977 (Casebook)—reprint from Green, et al. Cases and Materials on Torts, 2nd Ed., 1977

Keeton, Keeton, Sargentich and Steiner's Cases and Materials on Torts, and Accident Law, 1360 pages, 1983 (Casebook)

Kionka's Torts in a Nutshell: Injuries to Persons and Property, 434 pages, 1977 (Text)

Malone's Torts in a Nutshell: Injuries to Family, Social and Trade Relations, 358 pages, 1979 (Text)

Prosser and Keeton's Hornbook on Torts, 5th Ed., Student Ed., 1286 pages, 1984 (Text)

Shapo's Cases on Tort and Compensation Law, 1244 pages, 1976 (Casebook)

See also Products Liability

TRADE REGULATION

McManis' Unfair Trade Practices in a Nutshell, 444 pages, 1982 (Text)

Oppenheim, Weston, Maggs and Schechter's Cases and Materials on Unfair Trade Practices and Consumer Protection, 4th Ed., 1038 pages, 1983 (Casebook)

See also Antitrust, Regulated Industries

TRIAL AND APPELLATE ADVOCACY

Appellate Advocacy, Handbook of, 249 pages, 1980 (Text)

Bergman's Trial Advocacy in a Nutshell, 402 pages, 1979 (Text)

Binder and Bergman's Fact Investigation: From Hypothesis to Proof, 354 pages, 1984 (Coursebook)

Goldberg's The First Trial (Where Do I Sit?, What Do I Say?) in a Nutshell, 396 pages, 1982 (Text)

Haydock, Herr and Stempel's, Fundamentals of Pre-Trial Litigation, 768 pages, 1985 (Casebook)

Hegland's Trial and Practice Skills in a Nutshell, 346 pages, 1978 (Text)

Hornstein's Appellate Advocacy in a Nutshell, 325 pages, 1984 (Text)

Jeans' Handbook on Trial Advocacy, Student Ed., 473 pages, 1975 (Text)

McElhaney's Effective Litigation, 457 pages, 1974 (Casebook)

LAW SCHOOL PUBLICATIONS—Continued

TRIAL AND APPELLATE ADVOCACY—Continued

Nolan's Cases and Materials on Trial Practice, 518 pages, 1981 (Casebook)

Parnell and Shellhaas' Cases, Exercises and Problems for Trial Advocacy, 171 pages, 1982 (Coursebook)

Sonsteng, Haydock and Boyd's The Trialbook: A Total System for Preparation and Presentation of a Case, Student Ed., 404 pages, 1984 (Coursebook)

TRUSTS AND ESTATES

Atkinson's Hornbook on Wills, 2nd Ed., 975 pages, 1953 (Text)

Averill's Uniform Probate Code in a Nutshell, 425 pages, 1978 (Text)

Bogert's Hornbook on Trusts, 5th Ed., 726 pages, 1973 (Text)

Clark, Lusky and Murphy's Cases and Materials on Gratuitous Transfers, 3rd Ed., approximately 1200 pages, 1985 (Casebook)

Gulliver's Cases and Materials on Future Interests, 624 pages, 1959 (Casebook)

Gulliver's Introduction to the Law of Future Interests, 87 pages, 1959 (Casebook)—reprint from Gulliver's Cases and Materials on Future Interests, 1959

McGovern's Cases and Materials on Wills, Trusts and Future Interests: An Introduction to Estate Planning, 750 pages, 1983 (Casebook)

Mennell's Cases and Materials on California Decedent's Estates, 566 pages, 1973 (Casebook)

Mennell's Wills and Trusts in a Nutshell, 392 pages, 1979 (Text)

TRUSTS AND ESTATES—Continued

Powell's The Law of Future Interests in California, 91 pages, 1980 (Text)

Simes' Hornbook on Future Interests, 2nd Ed., 355 pages, 1966 (Text)

Turrentine's Cases and Text on Wills and Administration, 2nd Ed., 483 pages, 1962 (Casebook)

Uniform Probate Code, 5th Ed., Official Text With Comments, 384 pages, 1977

Waggoner's Future Interests in a Nutshell, 361 pages, 1981 (Text)

WATER LAW

Getches' Water Law in a Nutshell, 439 pages, 1984 (Text)

Trelease's Cases and Materials on Water Law, 3rd Ed., 833 pages, 1979, with 1984 Supplement (Casebook)

See also Energy Law, Natural Resources Law, Environmental Law

WILLS

See Trusts and Estates

WOMEN AND THE LAW

Kay's Text, Cases and Materials on Sex-Based Discrimination, 2nd Ed., 1045 pages, 1981, with 1983 Supplement (Casebook)

Thomas' Sex Discrimination in a Nutshell, 399 pages, 1982 (Text)

See also Employment Discrimination

WORKERS' COMPENSATION

See Social Legislation

XII

REAL ESTATE FINANCE LAW

SECOND EDITION

By

Grant S. Nelson
Enoch H. Crowder Professor of Law
University of Missouri-Columbia

Dale A. Whitman
Dean and R. B. Price Professor of Law
University of Missouri-Columbia

SECOND EDITION
HORNBOOK SERIES
STUDENT EDITION

St. Paul, Minn.
WEST PUBLISHING CO.
1985

COPYRIGHT © 1951, 1970, 1979 By WEST PUBLISHING CO.
COPYRIGHT © 1985 By GRANT S. NELSON & DALE A. WHITMAN

Printed in the United States of America

Library of Congress Cataloging-in-Publication Data

Nelson, Grant S.
    Real estate finance law.

    (Hornbook series student edition)
    Rev. ed. of Real estate finance law / by George B.
Osborne, Grant S. Nelson, and Dale A. Whitman.
    Includes index.
    1. Mortgages—United States. I. Whitman, Dale A.
II. Osborne, George Edward, 1894– . Real estate finance
law. III. Title. IV. Series.
KF695.N45 1985   346.7304'364   85–13589
ISBN 0-314-91412-9   347.3064364

To

Judy, Howard and Clara Nelson

Marjorie, Vern and Frances Whitman

*

Preface

Since our first edition of this book was published in 1979, the world of real estate finance has continued to change rapidly. It is no longer the staid, stable field it was in the 1960's and before. The law responds to the market, and the volatile economic conditions of the 1980's have demanded legal response.

We acknowledge our debt to the past, and in particular to Professor George Osborne, who wrote the original treatise in 1948 from which this book descended. Osborne's treatise was widely regarded as one of the finest works in the West hornbook series, and it has provided a superb base on which to build.

Even since our first edition in 1979, there have been immense changes. The law of due-on-sale clauses has been virtually revolutionized by Congress. The field of "alternative" mortgage instruments, which seemed complex enough in 1979, is far more so today. Bankruptcy continues (unfortunately) to be a staple commodity among real estate finance lawyers, but they are now confronted with new doctrines not even conceived of when we prepared our first edition.

Each of these matters is given enlarged space in this edition. We have also rewritten and expanded our coverage of deficiency judgments and the use of mortgages as security for other debts. Our treatment of the "clogging" doctrine is enhanced in response to the renewed interest lawyers have shown in it in the light of new forms of mortgages. The installment land contract, always a widely used substitute for the mortgage, is covered in much greater detail than heretofore.

In all respects we have tried to be as current and practical as possible, while at the same time providing the sort of theoretical underpinning which courts find of value, and which was such a characteristic strength of George Osborne's work. Within the inherent space limitations of a one-volume work, we hope we have provided a tool which all who work with the legal issues in real estate finance will find of value.

We express our appreciation to the University of Missouri-Columbia School of Law, where we both serve as faculty members, and especially to that school's law library staff for their excellent support of our research efforts. Some of our earlier work was done at the University of Washington and at the J. Reuben Clark Law School of Brigham Young University, and both of these institutions also deserve thanks for the help they have given us.

We have benefitted from the help of several research assistants, whom we wish to thank; they include Steve Gaunt, Karen M. Johnson, James Ritzen, N. Gregory Smith, Myrna South, and Grant Walker. Of course, any errors in this book must be laid at our feet, and not theirs, but their help was invaluable.

Our work together has strengthed our mutual respect and friendship and we hope we may have made some contribution to the profession we love. We express our gratitude to our wives, Judy Nelson and Marjorie Whitman, for the encouragement and patience they have shown during our long hours spent at the office and in the library.

G.S.N.
D.A.W.

August, 1985

WESTLAW Introduction

Real Estate Finance Law, Second Edition offers a detailed and comprehensive treatment of the basic rules and principles of real estate finance. However, law students and lawyers frequently need to find additional authority. In an effort to assist with comprehensive research of the law of real estate finance, preformulated WESTLAW references are included after each section of the text in this edition of the hornbook. The WESTLAW references are designed for use with the WESTLAW computer-assisted legal research service. By joining this publication with the extensive WESTLAW databases, the reader is able to move straight from the hornbook into WESTLAW with great speed and convenience.

Some readers may desire to use only the information supplied within the printed pages of this hornbook. Others, however, will encounter issues in real estate finance law that require further information. Accordingly, those who opt to go beyond the material contained in the textual format into WESTLAW can rapidly and easily access WESTLAW, an electronic law library that possesses extraordinary currency and magnitude.

The Appendix gives concise, step-by-step instruction on how to coordinate WESTLAW research with this hornbook.

THE PUBLISHER

*

Summary of Contents

Table of Contents

B. TORTIOUS INJURY TO LAND BY MORTGAGOR OR THIRD PERSONS

C. RIGHTS IN THE PRODUCT OF THE RES

D. ESCROWS OR RESERVES FOR TAXES AND INSURANCE

E. RIGHT TO RENTS

F. MORTGAGEE IN POSSESSION

G. RECEIVERSHIPS

CHAPTER 5. TRANSFER BY THE MORTGAGOR AND THE MORTGAGEE

A. TRANSFER BY THE MORTGAGOR

B. RESTRICTIONS ON TRANSFER BY THE MORTGAGOR

CHAPTER 7. FORECLOSURE

A. REDEMPTION FROM THE MORTGAGE

B. ACCRUAL OF THE RIGHT TO FORECLOSE

C. STRICT FORECLOSURE

D. JUDICIAL FORECLOSURE

E. POWER OF SALE FORECLOSURE

F.　DISPOSITION OF SURPLUS

CHAPTER 8.　STATUTORY IMPACTS ON FORECLOSURE

A.　REGULATION OF DEFICIENCY JUDGMENTS

B.　STATUTORY REDEMPTION

C.　THE SOLDIERS' AND SAILORS' CIVIL RELIEF ACT

D.　BANKRUPTCY

CHAPTER 9.　SOME PRIORITY PROBLEMS

CHAPTER 10. SUBROGATION, CONTRIBUTION AND MARSHALING

A. SUBROGATION AND CONTRIBUTION

B. MARSHALING

CHAPTER 11. GOVERNMENT INTERVENTION IN THE MORTGAGE MARKET

CHAPTER 12. FINANCING REAL ESTATE CONSTRUCTION

CHAPTER 13.   FINANCING CONDOMINIUMS AND COOPERATIVES

REAL ESTATE
FINANCE LAW

Chapter 1

AN INTRODUCTION TO THE LAW OF MORTGAGES

Table of Sections

§ 1.1 The Basic Mortgage Transaction

The material in this volume focuses upon, in a variety of simple and sophisticated factual settings, the use of real estate as security for obligations. In this connection, there is a substantial emphasis on the real estate mortgage and its functional equivalents. As the term is used in its modern context, a real estate mortgage involves a transfer by a debtor-mortgagor to a creditor-mortgagee of a real estate interest, to be held as security for the performance of an obligation, normally the payment of a debt evidenced by the mortgagor's promissory note.

It is analytically useful, initially, to distinguish the purchase money transaction from other mortgage transactions. As will be seen later in this volume, the distinction between purchase money and non-purchase money mortgages is especially important in determining lien priorities.[1] A purchase money mortgage arises where the mortgagor's acquisition of the mortgaged real estate is financed by the mortgagee-lender. Often a seller of real estate will take back a purchase money mortgage for part of the purchase price. More commonly, however, a third party lending institution will take a mortgage covering real estate acquired by the mortgagor with funds provided by the lending institution. In many states this is also treated as a purchase-money mort-

§ 1.1
1. See § 9.1 infra.

gage. Such transactions may be as simple as the purchase of a single family residence by a borrower-mortgagor or as complex and sophisticated as the construction and long term financing obtained by a developer to build a shopping center or an apartment building. In the non-purchase money situation the mortgagee-lender does not provide an acquisition loan but rather lends money on real estate already owned by the borrower-mortgagor. A corporation, for example, may often mortgage previously owned real estate to obtain money for expansion purposes. Or a long-time homeowner may give a mortgage to a lending institution on his home to secure a loan, the proceeds of which will be used to finance the college tuition of his children.

Today most mortgages are amortized or repaid over a substantial number of years. Until the 1930's most mortgages, however, were of the "balloon-note" type. Typically these were short-term mortgages for three or five years, and borrowers made only interest payments until the loan came due. Then if the borrower had not saved enough to pay the entire principal, he would expect the note to be renewed or would attempt to refinance it with another lender. However, during the depression period of the 1930's, many of these lenders were forced to demand full payment and to foreclose on properties when mortgagors could not pay. With the encouragement of the Federal Housing Administration and federal housing legislation, lenders during this period developed the amortized mortgage loan system under which mortgagors were permitted to repay loans over many years by making monthly principal and interest payments. Such loans are common today in both the housing and commercial real estate markets. However, as will be seen, much of the substantive law of mortgages developed prior to the advent of the long-term amortized real estate mortgage. In analyzing this substantive law, we should consider whether many of these principles do or should apply to modern long-term amortized mortgage loans.

Because the level-monthly-payment fully-amortized loan is so common in modern real estate financing, it is important to understand its characteristics. The monthly payment is set so that only a portion (though a large portion in the early years) is needed to cover the interest which has accrued since the last preceding payment; the remainder of each payment is applied to reduce the outstanding principal. Thus, the interest which accrues in each month will be less than the interest for the preceding month, since interest is being computed on a continually declining principal amount.

This is best understood by means of an example. Suppose a borrower signs a promissory note to repay $50,000 over a period of 30 years, with interest at the rate of 12% per annum. The loan is made on January 1, 1987, with level repayment installments to be made monthly by the borrower. Thus, the first monthly payment will be due February 1, 1987. Interest alone at the end of that first month would be $50,000 times 1% (the monthly equivalent of 12% per annum), or $500. However, consultation of a standard table of mortgage payments reveals that the full payment due (including both interest and amortization) is $514.31. The following schedule, known as an "amortization table", shows the effect of this payment and the next few which follow it.

Payment Date	Payment Amount	Credited to Interest	Credited to Principal	Principal Balance After Payment
Feb. 1, 1987	$514.31	$500.00	$14.31	$49,985.69
Mar. 1, 1987	$514.31	$499.86	$14.45	$49,971.24
Apr. 1, 1987	$514.31	$499.71	$14.60	$49,956.64
———	———	———	———	———
———	———	———	———	———
Jan. 1, 2017	$514.31	$ 5.09	$509.22	–0–

The last payment, made at the end of the 360th month of the loan, will be approximately the amount necessary to discharge entirely the small sum still remaining on the principal balance. Of course, filling in the entire table above is a tedious process unless you have a computer, but if you did so you would see that the amount we originally specified as the monthly payment, $514.31, is precisely the amount necessary to amortize the loan's balance fully over a thirty year period.

The amount of the regular payments necessary to amortize a loan over a given period of time depends on several factors: the frequency of payments (usually monthly for mortgage loans), the term or period of repayments, the interest rate, and the amount borrowed. The table below shows the monthly payments for each one thousand dollars borrowed at various interest rates and terms. You can apply the table to any principal amount simply by multiplying the factor shown by the number of thousands of dollars borrowed.

Interest Rate	Term of Loan		
	20 years	30 years	40 years
10%	9.65	8.78	8.49
11%	10.32	9.52	9.28
12%	11.01	10.29	10.08
13%	11.72	11.06	10.90
14%	12.44	11.85	11.71
15%	13.17	12.64	12.53
16%	13.91	13.45	13.36
17%	14.67	14.26	14.18
18%	15.43	15.07	15.01

Several observations can be made about the level-payment amortized loan. The principal balance declines very slowly during the early years. After five years of regular payments on the loan in the foregoing example, the principal would be reduced to $48,831.30, a reduction of only $1,168.70. Since principal amortization is in a sense a form of forced savings, some households might prefer to minimize, or even eliminate entirely, the amortization component. If the owner wishes to resell the house in our example after five years, it will probably be easier for a prospective buyer to "take over" the loan if its balance is still quite high. On the other hand, the lender will generally prefer a relatively more rapid reduction in principal, since the loan is seen as a safer investment if this occurs.

The monthly payments on the loan are affected by three factors: the amount borrowed, the term or duration of the loan, and the interest rate. The effect of higher interest rates on the payment can be quite startling. In our example, an interest rate of 13% (rather than the 12% we assumed) would raise the monthly payment by $38.79, to $553.10. These figures suggest something of the adverse impact high interest rates can have on the demand for housing. Lengthening the loan term can reduce the monthly payments, but beyond about 30 or 40 years, the impact is not very great. In our example (with a 12% interest rate), increasing the maturity from 30 to 40 years would lower monthly payments by only $10.05, to $504.25. Further increases in maturity would bring the monthly payments somewhat closer to $500 per month, the interest-only level, which forms a "floor" below which payments cannot go no matter how long the loan term.

The level-payment amortized loan is still widely used in single-family home financing, and quite commonly employed with commercial and industrial property as well. However, both Federal and state regulators of lending institutions authorize lenders to use other "innovative" loan repayment formats on home loans. Formats which permit modification of the interest rate during the life of the loan (with concomitant changes in maturity or monthly payment) are becoming increasingly common among lenders, who are seeking relief from the financial stress they have experienced as a result of holding portfolios of fixed-rate mortgages during recent periods of rapid fluctuation in their cost of funds. These new mortgage formats are discussed in detail later in this volume.[2]

When a mortgage loan goes into default, normally the mortgagee has the right to "accelerate," which has the effect of making the entire debt due and payable.[3] The mortgagee may, under some circumstances, simply decide to proceed against the mortgagor personally and forego reliance on the mortgage security. Usually, however, the mortgagee will choose or will be required by law to foreclose the mortgage first. Although methods of foreclosure differ widely, under most circumstances there will be a sale of the mortgaged premises. The proceeds will be used to pay off the mortgage debt and the surplus, if any, will go to any subordinate lien-holders and the mortgagor. If the sale does not yield enough to cover the debt, the mortgagee will often be able to obtain a personal judgment for the deficiency against the mortgagor.

2. See § 11.4 infra.

3. See § 7.6 infra.

Where more than one mortgage exists on the same property, questions of priority become paramount. Suppose, for example, the mortgagor gave a $65,000 long-term first mortgage to a savings and loan association on Blackacre, which then was worth $75,000. Assume that after paying the mortgage down to about $60,000, the mortgagor borrows $12,000 from another lender and gives that lender a mortgage to secure the $12,000 debt. This is a second mortgage. Suppose that the first mortgage is foreclosed. What will the purchaser get and what will she pay for it? Here it is important to remember one of the basic functions of foreclosure—to put the foreclosure sale purchaser in the shoes of the mortgagor at the time he executed the mortgage being foreclosed. Thus, the purchaser will obtain a title that is free and clear of all mortgages or other liens junior or subordinate to the mortgage being foreclosed. Accordingly, a sale purchaser, assuming that the market value of Blackacre free and clear of liens is still $75,000, will be willing to pay, at most, $75,000. For this she will get title free of the second mortgage. In other words, any junior liens are wiped out. If, however, the sale brings more than the $60,000 first mortgage debt, the second mortgagee should normally have a claim to the surplus superior to that of the mortgagor.[4]

Suppose, instead, that the first mortgage is not in default but that the second mortgage is and that the second mortgagee forecloses. What will the sale purchaser get and what will she pay for it? Again, remembering one of the basic functions of foreclosure discussed above, the sale should put the purchaser in the shoes of the mortgagor as of the time the mortgage being foreclosed was executed. Thus a purchaser will obtain fee title to Blackacre subject to the first mortgage. In other words, the foreclosure of a junior mortgage normally will not affect the status of a senior mortgage on the property.[5] Therefore, in calculating what a purchaser will bid, she will, at the very least, subtract from the market value of Blackacre free and clear of liens the amount of the first mortgage. Thus, assuming that this market value is still $75,000, the most the purchaser should bid is $15,000, the fair market value less the amount of the senior lien. Although the sale purchaser will not usually be personally liable on the first mortgage debt, if she does not pay it off she runs the risk that the first mortgage will be foreclosed and that she will lose title to Blackacre.

 WESTLAW REFERENCES
di mortgage
266k1
digest(mortgage /5 defin!)
di amortization

---

4. See §§ 7.31–7.32 infra.

5. For some instances where the foreclosure by a junior mortgagee may affect the senior mortgagee's options, but not its priority, see § 7.14 infra.

§ 1.2 The Impact of English History

An understanding of the modern real estate mortgage requires, at least, a limited consideration of its historical antecedents. Although the mortgage has its roots in both Roman law and in early Anglo-Saxon England, the most significant developments for our purposes are the English common law mortgage and the effects on that mortgage of the subsequent intervention of English equity courts. These developments not only substantially influenced the substance of American mortgage law, but they are responsible for much of its terminology as well.[1]

Although the common law mortgage as it developed in the fourteenth and fifteenth centuries varied, in form it was essentially a conveyance of fee simple ownership, but the conveyance was expressly on condition subsequent. For example, assume B loans A $1,000. A would convey Blackacre to B and his heirs, but on the condition that, if A repaid the $1,000 to B on a specified day, A would have the right to reenter and terminate B's estate. There were several important attributes to this transaction. B, the mortgagee, received legal title to the land and the normal incidents of that title. Perhaps the most important feature of this mortgage is that the grantee got the incidents of legal title even though unnecessary or even antagonistic to the sole purpose of the conveyance, namely, security for the performance of an act by the grantor. Thus the wife got dower until 1678;[2] the Rule in Shelley's case applied;[3] on the death of the mortgagee the property went to his heirs[4] or devisees;[5] creditors of the grantee could seize the property itself;[6] the mortgagee was entitled to all accretions to the property,[7] to compensation if the land was taken by eminent domain,[8] and to the title deeds;[9] he could bring actions against third parties and defend actions brought by them;[10] he might get the personal privilege of voting if he took possession;[11] his title would escheat;[12] and, most

§ 1.2

1. For a more complete analysis of the historical development of the modern real estate mortgage, see Osborne, Mortgages §§ 1–7 (2d Ed. 1970).

2. Nash v. Preston, Cro.Car. 190 (1632). This led to the practice of giving mortgages of long terms of years. Co.Litt., § 332 n.; 2 Blackstone, 158. One advantage of these was that on the death of the mortgagee the term vested in the personal representatives instead of the heir. A disadvantage was that on default by the mortgagor the mortgagee did not get the fee.

3. Simes, Future Interests, 2d Ed., § 20 et seq.

4. Ex parte Morgan, 10 Ves. 101 (1804); see 2 Coote, Mortgages, 9th Ed., 863. By statute the legal estate of a deceased mort-

gagor now vests in his personal representatives. 44 & 45 Vict. c. 41, § 30.

5. A general devise of lands, unless a contrary intention appears, passes the legal interest of the mortgagee. Co.Litt., 205a n. However, see Littleton's Case, 1 Vern. 3 (1681).

6. Turner, The Equity of Redemption, XXXV, 52.

7. Doe v. Pott, 2 Doug. 710 (1781).

8. Ranken v. East and West India Docks Co., etc., 12 Beav. 298 (1849).

9. 2 Coote, supra note 4, at 835.

10. Pomeroy, Eq.Juris. § 1182.

11. 2 & 3 Will. IV c. 45, § 23; 6 & 7 Vict. c. 18, § 74.

12. Y.B. 5 Ed. IV, 18 pl., 7 b. See Turner, supra note 6, at 55.

significant, he had the right to immediate possession.[13] Originally, the mortgagee used possession and the right to collect rents and profits as a method to get a return on his loan, since the charging of any interest was then considered to be usury and unlawful. Later the custom developed to leave the mortgagor in possession, although the mortgagee nevertheless retained the right to obtain possession. If he did obtain possession, however, he was required to account for the rents and profits on the mortgage debt.

The condition with provision for reentry was gradually displaced by a covenant by the mortgagee to reconvey upon full performance by the mortgagor. This covenant had a double operation. It was effective at law as a condition, and also was a promise which equity would enforce specifically. Its development apparently coincided with that of the equity of redemption referred to below, and its popularity was based upon the practical advantages of getting back by a reconveyance, instead of by reentry, the interest conveyed to the mortgagee. Regardless of which form was used, if the mortgagor failed to perform on the day set, the mortgagee's estate became absolute.

This common law mortgage was especially harsh on the mortgagor. The payment date was called the law day. Under the common law, if for any reason the payment was not made on that day, the mortgagor forfeited all interest in Blackacre. This was an absolute rule. It applied even if the mortgagor could not find the mortgagee to pay him. Time was strictly of the essence.

 WESTLAW REFERENCES
di equity of redemption
266k59* & redeem redemption /p equit!

§ 1.3 The Intervention of Equity

The excesses and harshness of the common law mortgage inevitably yielded to the moderating influence of English Chancery. Initially, equity intervened to aid the mortgagor who had failed promptly to perform on law day where the mortgagor could establish such traditional equitable grounds for relief as fraud, accident, misrepresentation, or duress. In other words, even though the mortgagee's rights at law were absolute, the mortgagor who had the financial capability to tender the amount due and owing could get his property back after law day so long as he could fit within the grounds described above. However, by the 17th century, the granting of such relief by equity became much more routine so that the mortgagor was able, as a matter of course and right, to redeem his land from the mortgagee if he tendered the principal and interest within a reasonable time after law day. It was no longer necessary to establish the more specific equitable grounds for

13. A thorough discussion of all the cases may be found in Turner, supra note 6, at 88 et seq.

relief. This right to tardy redemption was referred to as the mortgagor's equity of redemption and became recognized as an equitable estate in land.[1]

The mortgagor's right to tardy redemption obviously created a substantial problem for the mortgagee. Even though the mortgagor had defaulted, the mortgagee could never be reasonably sure that the mortgagor would not sue in equity to redeem. The mortgagee obviously needed to be relieved at some point of the threat of redemption. Thus, this same period saw the concurrent development in equity of the mortgagee's right to foreclosure. When the mortgagor failed to pay on law day or to bring a suit to redeem, at the request of the mortgagee in a bill setting forth the details of the mortgage and default, equity would order the mortgagor to pay the debt, interest and costs within a fixed period. Failure to comply with the decree meant that the mortgagor's right to redeem was forever barred. This type of foreclosure, which is little used today, is known as strict foreclosure because the land is forfeited to the mortgagee no matter what its value in relation to the original mortgage debt. No sale of the land is involved.

Whatever the original reasons for the chancellor's intervention, clearly the later equity view was that the mortgagee's interest was only security and intercession needed no other justification than to limit and protect it for that purpose. It is unlikely that the law courts did not recognize just as clearly as did the courts of equity that the parties intended the transaction to be one for security purposes only. The difficulty was that, although they saw it, they felt powerless to alter the design of the legal device chosen by the parties to achieve their purpose. So far as the law courts were concerned, since the parties had seen fit to have the entire legal title given as security (not absolutely, since the mortgagor could get it back by paying on a certain day), that was that. There were, however, no such limitations felt by the courts of equity, and consequently, they could superimpose upon the legal device various restrictions or additions so as to give to the mortgagee only that protection in regard to the property which they thought it necessary or desirable for the purpose of security. What this protection should be inevitably would be a mixture of conflicting economic interests, contradictory social ideals, business expediency, feelings of "fairness" in the particular case, and attempts at logical consistency with other legal rules, plus other miscellaneous considerations.

In developing this view of the mortgage as a security transaction the equitable theory of the nature and incidents of the mortgagor's interest in the property before default underwent considerable change. For one thing, the term "equity of redemption" which had previously and appropriately been applied to the mortgagor's right to get back his property after default was applied somewhat inappropriately to this

§ 1.3

1. For a more detailed consideration of the development of the equity of redemption, see Osborne, Mortgages, § 6 (2d Ed. 1970).

entirely distinct equitable ownership before default. This, however, is merely a matter of nomenclature. But the analytical nature of the interest itself was the subject of serious and important inquiry and decision.

Although at first the mortgagor's interest was looked upon as a purely in personam right against the mortgagee, it soon was perceived to be in rem, and finally was regarded as an equitable estate, a conception conforming to both popular and legal notions. For example, it could be cut into lesser estates; it had to be conveyed by a formal conveyance with formal limitations; it descended on to the heirs of the mortgagor; it could be devised, mortgaged, or entailed; and it prevailed against heirs, purchasers, and other successors of the mortgagee.

 WESTLAW REFERENCES
[no queries]

§ 1.4 The American Development

While strict foreclosure is theoretically available in a few states and in some relatively special situations in others,[1] the major method of foreclosure in the United States involves a public sale of the premises. There are two main types of sale foreclosure used in the United States today. The most common type is judicial foreclosure where a public sale results after a full judicial proceeding in which all interested persons must be made parties.[2] In many states this is the sole method of foreclosure. It is time-consuming and costly. The other method of foreclosure is by power of sale.[3] Under this method, after varying types and degrees of notice to the parties, the property is sold at a public sale, either by some public official such as a sheriff, by the mortgagee, or by some other third party. No judicial proceeding is required in a power of sale foreclosure. It is generally available only where the mortgage instrument authorizes it. As we shall see later in this volume, it raises serious constitutional problems.[4]

It is important to remember that, as a general proposition, an unwilling mortgagor cannot lose his equity of redemption (or equity of tardy redemption, as it is sometimes called) unless there has been a valid foreclosure of the mortgage. In other words, even though the mortgage is in substantial default, normally no agreement of the parties in the mortgage, or contemporaneous with it, can cut off a recalcitrant mortgagor's rights in the mortgaged property without the mortgagee resorting to foreclosure. This concept, which will be considered in greater detail later, is sometimes referred to as the *prohibition against clogging the mortgagor's equity of redemption*.[5]

§ 1.4

1. See §§ 7.9–7.10 infra.

2. See §§ 7.11–7.12 infra.

3. See § 7.19 infra.

4. See §§ 7.23–7.30 infra.

5. See §§ 3.1–3.3 infra.

Suppose, however, that there has been a valid foreclosure and that the mortgagor's equity of redemption has been cut off. Some states, by a variety of legislative methods, have created something called *statutory redemption*. This type of redemption becomes available *only* when the equity of redemption has been effectively cut off by a valid foreclosure. Statutory redemption, as we will see later, varies widely from state to state.[6] In general, however, these statutes permit the mortgagor and sometimes his junior lienors to redeem after the sale for various periods of time as short as a few months in some states to as long as 18 months or more in a few others. The statutory right of redemption was created, in part, to afford the mortgagor or other person entitled to exercise the right additional time to refinance and save his property, but also to put pressure on the mortgagee to bid the value of the property at the foreclosure sale, at least up to the amount of the mortgage debt. To enforce this purpose the redemption amount is usually the *sale price* and *not the mortgage debt*. A secondary purpose of these statutes in some states is to allow an additional period of possession to a hard-pressed mortgagor. The operation and effectiveness of these statutes will be analyzed in greater detail later in this volume. The important thing to remember at this point is that statutory redemption normally begins *only* after the mortgagor's equity of redemption has been validly terminated by foreclosure.

 WESTLAW REFERENCES
clog! /p equit! /p redemption

§ 1.5 The Title, Lien, and Intermediate Theories of Mortgage Law

Three "theories" of mortgage law exist today in the United States. One of these, the *title theory*,[1] has its roots in the English common law mortgage discussed earlier. Under this theory, legal "title" is in the mortgagee until the mortgage has been satisfied or foreclosed. While the states that recognize this theory have for the most purposes treated the mortgagee as simply holding a security interest, the mortgagee's "title" does appear to give him the right to possession. Under the more predominant *lien theory*,[2] however, the mortgagee holds no "title" but has security only. The mortgagor, accordingly, has the right to possession until there has been a valid foreclosure. The so-called *intermediate theory*[3] gives the right to possession to the mortgagor at least until default, and generally to the mortgagee after default. The lien theory states, with such exceptions as New York and South Carolina, tend to be west of the Mississippi, and the title and intermediate theory states

6. See §§ 8.4–8.7 infra.

§ 1.5

1. See § 4.1, infra.

2. See § 4.2, infra.

3. See § 4.3, infra.

in the east. Lien theory states have rejected the mortgagee's possessory rights, either by judicial decision or by statute.[4]

While the three theories have tended to interest academics more than practitioners, in certain situations they can prove to have important practical significance. It may come as a surprise that a mortgagee would want possession of the mortgaged premises prior to foreclosure. Most mortgagees, after all, are primarily in the lending business and do not view themselves as managers of real estate. Indeed, in every jurisdiction the mortgagor, at least initially, is in possession of the premises. Then why is the right to possession significant? Primarily because it carries with it not only the right to protect the premises against waste, but more importantly, the right to collect rents and profits. The mortgagee, however, must *account* for any such rents and profits on the mortgage debt.

There may be occasions when a mortgagee may wish to bring ejectment to obtain possession of the premises. Suppose, for example, that the foreclosure proceedings in a particular state are so lengthy that it may take up to three years to bring a foreclosure to successful culmination. Suppose further that a defaulted mortgage on commercial real estate is involved and that the mortgagor is so financially weak as to be judgment-proof. If the mortgagee can gain possession prior to foreclosure, deterioration or destruction of the security can be prevented and the mortgagee will be able to prevent the rents and profits from being diverted to purposes other than payment of the mortgage. Indeed, as we shall see later, the mortgagee may wish to have a receiver appointed to accomplish essentially the same purposes and, to some extent, the mortgage theory followed may influence availability of the receivership remedy. Moreover, many mortgagees attempt to draft around the lien theory by providing mortgage clauses which purport to give the mortgagee a present assignment of the rents and profits. As later material in this volume [5] will illustrate, the seriousness with which a particular jurisdiction views the lien theory may influence the validity of such provisions.

 WESTLAW REFERENCES
mortgage /p title lien intermediate /s theory

§ 1.6 The Deed of Trust as a Mortgage Variant

In many states the deed of trust represents the most commonly used mortgage instrument. This device normally involves a conveyance of the realty to a third person in trust to hold as security for the

---

4. For a consideration of the three theories, see Kratovil, Mortgages—Problems in Possession, Rents, and Mortgagee Liability, 11 DePaul L.Rev. 1 (1961); Gavit, Under the Lien Theory of Mortgages is the Mortgage Only a Power of Sale? 15 Minn.L. Rev. 147 (1931); Sturges and Clark, Legal

Theory and Real Property Mortgages, 37 Yale L.J. 691 (1928); Comment, Real Estate Mortgage Theory in Missouri, 6 Mo.L. Rev. 200 (1941).

5. See § 4.35 infra.

payment of the debt to the lender-noteholder whose role is analogous to that of the mortgagee. Deeds of trust will almost always contain a power of sale in the trustee to be exercised after a default at the request of the lender-noteholder. Such a deed of trust is essentially similar to a mortgage with a power of sale. Indeed, in many states the same statutes regulating foreclosure of power of sale mortgages are applicable to deeds of trust as well. Most courts today are inclined to treat a deed of trust like a mortgage for other purposes as well. However, this form of mortgage sometimes can create special problems which force courts into detailed analysis of the similarities and differences between the two types of instruments. The following language of the Supreme Court of California in Bank of Italy National Trust & Savings Association v. Bentley,[1] illustrates some of the problems the use of both the deed of trust and the normal mortgage can pose in a given jurisdiction:

> At common law and, in fact, in nearly every state in the United States, a deed of trust, both in legal effect and in theory, is deemed to be a mortgage with a power of sale, and differs not at all from a mortgage with a power of sale. * * * In Idaho, a state that has adopted nearly all of our Code sections on security transactions, it has been held that a deed of trust is a mortgage with power of sale. Brown v. Bryan, 6 Idaho 1, 51 p. 995. If California had followed this common law rule, there would be no dispute over the question now involved. It would necessarily follow that a deed of trust is a mortgage with power of sale. * * * The real difficulty is caused by the fact that the courts of this state have not followed the common law rule. Although, as already pointed out, this state, at an early date, adopted the "lien" theory of mortgages, it adopted the "title" theory in reference to deeds of trust. In the early case of Koch v. Briggs, 14 Cal. 256, 73 Am. Dec. 651, it was held that mortgages and deeds of trust were fundamentally different, in that in a mortgage only a "lien" was created, while in a deed of trust, "title" actually passed to the trustee. This distinction, although frequently attacked by counsel and often criticized by the courts, has become well settled in our law and cannot now be disturbed. * * * Thus we have in this state a type of instrument partaking of many of the characteristics of a mortgage, but for other purposes treated as a separate type of security. Two lines of authority have developed as a result, one group of cases emphasizing the distinctions between the two types of security, the other group emphasizing the similarity between the two. Thus it has been

§ 1.6

1.   217 Cal. 644, 20 P.2d 940 (1933), certiorari denied 290 U.S. 659, 54 S.Ct. 74, 78 L.Ed.2d 571 (1933).

held that a deed of trust differs from a mortgage in that title passes to the trustee in case of a deed of trust, while, in the case of a mortgage, the mortgagor retains title; that the statute of limitations never runs against the power of sale in a deed of trust, while it does run against a mortgage; and that a mortgagor has a statutory right of redemption after foreclosure (Code Civ.Proc. 702), while no such right exists under a deed of trust.   *   *   *

As opposed to these cases, there have been an increasing number of cases which, although recognizing that "title" passes in the case of a deed of trust, emphasize the fact that the function and purpose of the two types of security are identical, and, for that reason, apply the same rules to deeds of trust that are applied to mortgages. These cases hold that in legal effect, although perhaps not in theory, deeds of trust are similar to mortgages with a power of sale.   *   *   *

It is important not to overemphasize such problems, however, because in most important respects the substantive law of mortgages is equally applicable to deeds of trust. Thus, aside from the foregoing, consideration of deeds of trust will, for the most part, be integrated into our coverage of major problems of mortgage law rather than treated separately. On the other hand, where the substantive law is different from that governing straight mortgages or where there are important problems unique to the deed of trust, those areas will be considered specially.

 WESTLAW REFERENCES
synopsis,digest((deed /5 contract trust) /p mortgage /p power
   /5 sale)

§ 1.7   Mortgage Substitutes and Clogging the Equity of Redemption

From the mortgagee's viewpoint, the equity of redemption is irritating and undesirable; he would prefer, in the event of the mortgagor's default, simply to have the power to assert and keep fee simple title to the realty. Since the courts do not allow such "clogging" by mortgage language, mortgagees have sometimes resorted to other forms of documents, which we term "mortgage substitutes",[1] to achieve this result. Note, however, that the deed of trust was *not* developed for this purpose; a trustor under a deed of trust has the same equity of redemption as a mortgagor. The rise of the deed of trust is probably attributable to the desire of lenders for legal power to foreclose by power of sale, and simultaneously to be bidders, in effect, at their own

§ 1.7
1. See Chapter 3, infra.

sales; the latter power was often prohibited when an ordinary mortgage was foreclosed under a power of sale.[2]

The remainder of this section is concerned with devices which mortgagees do employ in attempts to avoid the consequences of the mortgagor's equity of tardy redemption. For example, a grantee-mortgagee may take an absolute deed on Blackacre from a grantor-mortgagor with the oral understanding that if the underlying debt is paid, there will be a reconveyance of Blackacre to the grantor-mortgagor. In the event the debt is not paid, however, the theory of this device is that the grantee-mortgagee retains title to Blackacre without the problems of foreclosure. This basic transaction may take numerous forms. There may, for example, be a written agreement to reconvey; "such a written agreement to reconvey may take the form of an option to repurchase, an unconditional contract obligating the grantee to reconvey and the grantor to repurchase, or a lease-back to the grantor with an option to repurchase at or before the end of the term."[3] As we shall see later in this volume,[4] however, courts have freely permitted the grantor-mortgagor to establish, by parol testimony or otherwise, that such transactions are actually mortgages, with the result that they are often of dubious value in circumventing the mortgagor's equity of tardy redemption and other substantive mortgage law rights.

The most commonly used substitute for the mortgage or deed of trust as a land financing device is the installment land contract. This device is also known variously as the contract for deed or the long term land contract. The installment land contract and the purchase money mortgage carry out the same economic function—the financing by the seller of the unpaid portion of the purchase price of the real estate. Under the installment land contract, the vendee normally goes into possession and agrees to make monthly installment payments of principal and interest until the principal balance is paid off. The vendor retains legal title until the final payment is made, at which time he has a duty to execute a deed to the land. Such contracts may be amortized over varying time periods as short as two or three years or as long as twenty years. During the period of the contract, the vendee will usually be required to pay the taxes, maintain casualty insurance and keep the premises in good repair.

The main advantage to a vendor under a land contract presumably is that upon the default of the vendee, the vendor, by summary proceedings analogous to strict foreclosure, may keep the land and all installments paid, and possibly even sue for future installments as they fall due if the contract so provides, with vendee having no equity of

---

2. See e.g., Dingus, Mortgages—Redemption After Foreclosure Sale in Missouri, 25 Mo.L.Rev. 261, 282 (1960); § 7.21, infra.

3. Cunningham and Tischler, Disguised Real Estate Security Transactions as Mortgages in Substance, 26 Rutgers L.Rev. 1 (1973).

4. See §§ 3.5, 3.17, infra.

tardy redemption. Because these devices are often perceived to be "pro-vendor," they are used a great deal, especially in states where foreclosure of a straight mortgage is cumbersome and time-consuming. However, as we shall see later in this volume,[5] because statutes and judicial decisions have substantially enhanced the rights of the defaulted vendee it is doubtful in many states that such contracts can achieve their intended purpose for the vendor, at least where there is a vendee actively asserting his rights.

 WESTLAW REFERENCES
266k591(3) forfeit*** waiv*** clog! /s equity /s redemption

---

5. See §§ 3.26–3.32 infra.

§§ 1.8–2.0 are reserved for supplementary material.

Chapter 2

THE NECESSITY AND NATURE OF THE OBLIGATION

Table of Sections

Sec.
2.1 Necessity of Obligation.
2.2 Nature of the Obligation.
2.3 The Necessity of Consideration.
2.4 Description of the Debt.

---

§ 2.1 Necessity of Obligation

While it is axiomatic that a mortgage is security for the performance of an act, it is not clear whether there must be a personal obligation by someone to perform the act. A personal obligation to perform the act was essential to the classical common law mortgage.[1] Moreover, there is today still substantial case authority holding or stating that a mortgage cannot exist without an obligation which it secures.[2]

§ 2.1

1. See generally Osborne, Mortgages, § 102 (2d Ed.1970).

2. See Morvay v. Drake, 325 So.2d 165 (Ala.1976) ("if there is no debt, there is no mortgage"); Bruckman v. Breitenbush Hot Springs, Inc., 271 Or. 1, 534 P.2d 971 (1975); Coon v. Shry, 209 Cal. 612, 289 P. 815 (1930); Kuhne v. Gau, 134 Minn. 34, 163 N.W. 982 (1917); Tyler v. Wright, 122 Me. 558, 119 A. 583 (1923); Cotten, Trustee v. Graham, 84 Ky. 672, 2 S.W. 647, 8 Ky. Law Rep. 658 (1887); Burr v. Beckler, 264 Ill. 230, 106 N.E. 206 (1914); Beck v. Sheldon, 259 N.Y. 208, 181 N.E. 360 (1932); Baird v. Baird, 145 N.Y. 659, 40 N.E. 222, 28 L.R.A. 375 (1895); Weich v. Graham, 124 N.Y.S. 945 (1910), affirmed 148 App. Div. 900, 132 N.Y.S. 1150 (1911) and 21 N.Y. 637, 105 N.E. 1102 (1914); McCourt v. Peppard, 126 Wis. 326, 105 N.W. 809 (1905); Bernheim v. Pessou, 143 La. 609, 79 So. 23 (1917); Perkins v. Trinity Realty Co., 69 N.J.Eq. 723, 727, 61 A. 167 (1905), affirmed 71 N.J.Eq. 304, 71 A. 1135 (1909). See also Smith v. Haertel, 125 Colo. 348, 353, 244 P.2d 377, 379 (1952). Cf. Standard Fire Ins. Co. v. Fuller, 90 U.S.App.D.C. 300, 195 F.2d 782 (1952), noted, 101 U. of Pa.L. Rev. 286 (1952), no mortgage interest under the "Standard Mortgage Clause" where note secured is invalid. And see Validity of a Mortgage Intended as a Gift, 39 Iowa L.Rev. 195 (1953), discussing De Penning v. Bedell, 242 Iowa 102, 44 N.W.2d 385 (1950); Sterling, Validity of "Myself" Notes and Deeds of Trust, 30 Rocky Mt.L.Rev. 195 (1958); Karesh, Security Transactions in Survey of South Carolina Law, 10 S.C.L. Rev. 114, 124 (1957), noting Johnston v. Farmers and Merchants Bank, 229 S.C. 603, 93 S.E.2d 916 (1956). See also § 6.11 infra.

Some of these cases, however, are explainable for collateral reasons. For example, some of the decisions that hold the mortgage unenforceable because the obligation is invalid for lack of consideration are explainable on the ground that the intention was that the mortgage should secure a certain note or obligation and, consequently, would not be enforceable if that note or obligation failed for want of consideration. The giving of a note or bond along with the mortgage, especially if coupled with the usual recital in the mortgage that it secures the note, or a similar recital in the note that it is secured by the mortgage indicates that this was the intention of the parties.[3]

The existence of a debt is also deemed vital in absolute deed as mortgage cases.[4] In these cases, since the central question is whether a mortgage is intended in spite of the transaction being cast in the absolute transfer or conditional sale format, there are considerations not present when the transaction takes the regular mortgage form.[5] In the former setting the courts might well insist more rigidly upon a debt as a guarantee of mortgage *intent*.[6] In the latter case, as between the parties, the intent of the transaction is clear and the questions are whether there can be a mortgage without a personal obligation, or whether, even if there can be, the parties intended this particular mortgage to be binding regardless of the validity of the personal duty. Both of these questions have been obscured in the cases by the entirely distinct one of whether, as between the parties, a mortgage requires consideration, and this, in turn, is confused with problems of validity against third parties, i.e., matters of priority, fraudulent conveyances, estoppel, and the doctrine of *bona fide* purchase. There is also a failure to separate the necessity of consideration for the transfer or creation of the security interest in the property from the necessity of consideration for the creation of the obligation secured.[7]

Moreover, the notion that the obligation secured must be "personal" is subject to several qualifications and modifications. "Thus, a mortgage to secure the debt of a third person, the mortgagor being

3. Among such cases are Hannan v. Hannan, 123 Mass. 441, 25 Am.Rep. 121 (1877); Saunders v. Dunn, 175 Mass. 164, 55 N.E. 893 (1900); Anderson v. Lee, 73 Minn. 397, 76 N.W. 24 (1898); Brooks v. Owen, 112 Mo. 251, 19 S.W. 723 (1892), reversed on rehearing 112 Mo. 315, 20 N.W. 492 (1884); Cawley v. Kelly, 60 Wis. 315, 19 N.W. 65 (1884).

4. Conway v. Alexander, 11 U.S. (7 Cr.) 218, 3 L.Ed. 321 (1812), (in holding the transaction a conditional sale rather than a mortgage Marshall, C.J., said: "It is * * * a necessary ingredient in a mortgage, that the mortgagee should have a remedy against the person of the debtor").

5. See generally §§ 3.4–3.16 infra.

6. See e.g., Ministers Life and Casualty Union v. Franklin Park Towers Corp., 307 Minn. 134, 239 N.W.2d 207 (1976).

7. See § 2.3 infra. Mortgages to secure future advances pose special problems. See Ladue v. Detroit & Milwaukee Railroad Co., 13 Mich. 380, 87 Am.Dec. 759 (1865) (" * * * the mortgage instrument, without any present debt, liability or obligation secured by it, can have no present legal effect as a mortgage * * * and it can make no difference in the result whether there has once been a debt or liability which has been satisfied, or whether the debt or liability to be served has not yet been created * * * as in this case. * * * "). For a detailed consideration of such mortgages, see § 12.7 infra.

subject to no obligation, is clearly valid." [8] It is also clear that an express provision in the mortgage that there shall be no personal liability for the debt on the mortgagor or any other person, is valid and effective.[9] Such mortgages are especially common in limited partnership rental real estate developments because under the federal tax law the mortgage loan must be "non-recourse" in order to enable the limited partners to enjoy the tax shelter benefits of that form of ownership.[10] Although it is possible to conceive of such a transaction as merely limiting the collection remedy to certain property or, perhaps, to regard it as creating a duty of imperfect obligation,[11] it is also possible to construe it as negating the existence of any independent obligation except insofar as the land itself can be looked upon as owing a "real" obligation.[12] Moreover, barring an action to enforce the personal liability of the mortgagor by the statute of limitations does not affect, in some states, the validity of the mortgage.[13] The same may also be true where antideficiency legislation not only bars a deficiency

8. Halderman v. Woodward, 22 Kan. 734 (1879); Garretson Investment Co. v. Arndt, 144 Cal. 64, 77 P. 770 (1904); Theodore v. Mozie, 230 S.C. 216, 95 S.E.2d 173 (1956), 10 S.C.L.Rev. 114, 123 (1957).

9. Seieroe v. First National Bank of Kearney, 50 Neb. 612, 70 N.W. 220 (1897); Weikel v. Davis, 109 Wash. 97, 186 P. 323 (1919); Wells v. Flynn, 191 Iowa 1322, 184 N.W. 389, 17 A.L.R. 710 (1921); Rice v. Rice, 21 Mass. (4 Pick.) 349 (1826), are typical. See 17 A.L.R. 717 (1922); Parks, Cas. on Mort., 96 n. 1. McKinney's Real Property Law of N.Y. § 249, provides that "A mortgage of real property does not imply a covenant for the payment of the sum intended to be secured; and where such covenant is not expressed in the mortgage, or a bond or other separate instrument to secure such payment has not been given, the remedies of the mortgagee are confined to the property mentioned in the mortgage." West's Ann.Cal.Civ.Code § 2928, is similar. See Van Brunt v. Mismer, 8 Minn. 232, Gil 202 (1863); Demond v. Crary, 9 F. 750, 752 (C.C.N.Y.1882). See also Restatement, Security, § 1(b). A mortgage to secure the obligation of a trustee limited to his liability *qua* trustee is good. In re Robinson's Settlement, 81 L.J.Ch.Div. 393 (1912). See Coote, Mortgages, 9th Ed., 11. In 1956 the Illinois Court of Appeals, in Bedian v. Cohn, 10 Ill.App.2d 116, 134 N.E.2d 532 (1956), commented on by Updike, Mortgages in 1956 Annual Survey of American Law, 32 N.Y.U.L.Rev. 789, 790 (1956), held that documents may effectively provide that the mortgagor shall not be personally liable without affecting the validity of the mortgage.

10. If any partner, general or limited, is liable on the mortgage loan, the limited partners will not be permitted to include in their basis their share of the mortgage amount. Under such circumstances the limited partners would largely be deprived of the deductions arising from the partnership's use of the borrowed funds (e.g., depreciation, mortgage interest and real estate taxes etc.). See I.R.C. §§ 465(c)(3)(d), 704(d), 705(a)(2), 752(a), 752(a); Treas.Reg. § 1.704–1(e); Weidner, Realty Shelters: Nonrecourse Financing, Tax Reform, and Profit Purpose, 32 S.W.L.J. 711 (1978).

11. See Williston, and Thompson, Contracts, Rev.Ed., § 16; Restatement, Contracts, § 14. Similar cases of personal substantive obligations recognized as existing but with remedies curtailed or unavailable are (1) quasi in rem actions against absent defendants who have property in the jurisdiction, (2) broad exemption statutes covering all of the debtor's property within the jurisdiction, (3) a non-assuming grantee of mortgaged property in the state with the mortgagor-transferor out of the state or with the remedy against him barred by statute of limitations, etc.

12. See 3 Tiffany, Real Property, 2d Ed. § 607 ("the debt being in such case regarded as due by the land itself"); Walsh, Mortgages, § 16 ("a mortgage * * * may create a real obligation in a business transaction with an express provision excluding any personal obligation on which the mortgagor may be held liable.").

13. See § 6.11, infra.

judgment, but any mortgagor liability on the underlying debt as well.[14] Nor will a bankruptcy discharge of a mortgagor normally affect the validity of the mortgage.[15] Finally, there is authority that a mortgage is valid as a gift where, because of lack of consideration, no personal obligation ever arose or where, for some other reason, it is clear there that no independent obligation for the mortgage to secure exists.[16] It has been argued that, regardless of theory and authorities, the existence of a personal obligation in most modern mortgages is of no practical importance and should be ignored.[17]

There is no reason why a mortgage without a personal obligation should not be permitted. However, it is useful to distinguish between (1) cases where the mortgage was attempted as a gift and no personal obligation ever arose because of lack of consideration, and (2) those cases in which a debt or other obligation is created with the property as security for it but there is (a) a limitation on the enforcement of the personal duty, by agreement or by rules of law, or (b) a release of the personal obligation with rights in the mortgaged property reserved by agreement.

In the gift cases, a suggested test of validity is whether the parties *intended* the mortgage to secure a debt or other personal obligation.[18] Almost universally that is the intent, and in such cases if the obligation does not arise the mortgage should not because that is the intention. A

14. See e.g., Ross Realty Co. v. First Citizens Bank & Trust Co., 296 N.C. 366, 250 S.E.2d 271 (1979); § 8.3 infra.

15. Bush v. Cooper, 26 Miss. 599, 59 Am.Dec. 270 (1853), affirmed 59 U.S. (18 How.) 82, 15 L.Ed. 273 (1855); Brown v. Hoover, 77 N.C. 40 (1877); Wilson v. Russell, 13 Md. 494, 71 Am.Dec. 645 (1859).

16. Goethe v. Gmelin, 256 Mich. 112, 239 N.W. 347 (1931) (note and mortgage intended as gift, note void for want of consideration. The court based the decision on the ground that no consideration is necessary for a mortgage and did not discuss the lack of an obligation to be secured). Cf. Cooklin v. Cooklin, 260 Mich. 69, 244 N.W. 232 (1932), in which the court said that "it is not necessary that a mortgage be accompanied by a note provided the mortgage itself contains a promise to pay" and treated the Goethe case, inferentially, as not involving any question other than the necessity of consideration for the mortgage which secures the debt. Other cases more clearly holding no obligation necessary are Cook v. Johnson, 165 Mass. 245, 43 N.E. 96 (1896) (instruction that transaction was a mortgage not inconsistent with verdict that no debt existed because conveyance extinguished the personal obligation); Matthews v. Sheehan, 69 N.Y. 585 (1877) (deed absolute with only an option to repurchase); Rice v. Rice, 21 Mass. (4 Pick.) 349 (1826) (deed absolute, no personal duty to pay); Mooney v. Byrne, 163 N.Y. 86, 57 N.E. 163 (1900) (deed absolute, no covenant to pay and agreement for no deficiency, but court said there was a debt); Niggeler v. Maurin, 34 Minn. 118, 24 N.W. 369 (1885) (deed absolute, no covenant for payment). See Pearson v. Mulloney, 289 Mass. 508, 194 N.E. 458 (1935) (dictum only, second mortgage "subject to" first mortgage estopped to deny validity of first mortgage); Campbell v. Tompkins, 32 N.J.Eq. 170 (1880) (dictum, want of consideration for bond secured held closed to inquiry); Fisk v. Stewart, 24 Minn. 97 (1877) (dictum, debt existed); Campbell v. Dearborn, 109 Mass. 130, 12 Am.Rep. 671 (1872) (dictum in deed absolute case; debt existed); In re Robinson's Settlement, 81 L.J.Ch. 393 (1912) (dictum); Ministers Life & Casualty Union v. Franklin Park Towers Corp., 239 N.W.2d 207 (Minn.1976) (dictum). See also Walsh, Mortgages, 75 n. 2; Coote, Mortgages, 9th Ed., 11; 2 Wis.L.Rev. 60 (1922) 14 Tex.L.Rev. 560 (1936); 31 Mich.L.Rev. 102, 105 (1932); 58 N.J.L.J. 1; 4 St. John's L.Rev. 276 (1930).

17. See Wiltsie, Mortgage Foreclosure, 5th ed., § 1.

18. Walsh, Mortgages, §§ 16, 17d.

court would never reach the question whether there *could* be a mortgage without a personal obligation. Further, since only an occasional case could not be decided on this reasoning, the ultimate question in this type of case should be regarded as of theoretical rather than practical importance. In the second group, the parties' intention usually is express and entirely clear. They intend the mortgage to remain valid in spite of restrictions upon the enforcement or even the complete extinction of the personal obligation which existed at the outset and which the property without question was intended to secure. It would be inflexible formalism at its worst to defeat that intention.

 WESTLAW REFERENCES
266 +1 k15 k25 k32(5) & underlying pre-existing prior valid legal
/s obligation debt indebtedness
266k15

§ 2.2 Nature of the Obligation

Any obligation capable of being reduced to a money amount may be secured by a mortgage.[1] Thus, unliquidated debts such as open book accounts and contingent obligations that are uncertain in amount, such as indemnity bonds, may be secured by a mortgage on real estate.[2] Moreover, promises to build a driveway and a sewer line on mortgagor's land and to build an apartment house have been held to be mortgagable.[3] In such cases, the cost of completion is prima facie evidence of the amount secured, absent evidence that the proof of expenditures offered is unreasonable.[4]

It is doubtful that an obligation that is incapable of reduction to a money equivalent can be secured by a mortgage.[5] There are several reasons for this. First, in the event of a foreclosure sale, the purchaser, of course, would presumably bid what the real estate is worth. Howev-

---

§ 2.2

1. Pawtucket Institution for Savings v. Gagnon, ___ R.I. ___, 475 A.2d 1028 (1984) (promise to construct an apartment building); Stub v. Belmont, 20 Cal.2d 208, 124 P.2d 826 (1942) (consignment contract); Cook v. Bartholomew, 60 Conn. 24, 22 A. 444, 13 L.R.A. 452 (1891) (promise to support during life); Dover Lumber Co. v. Case, 31 Idaho 276, 170 P. 108 (1918) (faithful performance of a contract to cut and deliver timber). See West's Ann.Cal.Civ. Code § 2920. Contra, Bethlehem v. Annis, 40 N.H. 34, 77 Am.Dec. 700 (1860) ("Wherever the condition, when broken, gives rise to no claim for damages whatever, or to a claim for unliquidated damages, the deed is not to be regarded as a mortgage in equity * * * ").

2. Merills v. Swift, 18 Conn. 257, 46 Am.Dec. 315 (1847); Emerson v. Knight,

130 Ga. 100, 60 S.E. 255 (1908); McDaniels v. Colvin, 16 Vt. 300, 42 Am.Dec. 512 (1844); Fidelity and Deposit Co. v. Oliver, 57 Wash. 31, 106 P. 483 (1910).

3. Jeffrey Towers, Inc. v. Straus, 31 A.D.2d 319, 297 N.Y.S.2d 450 (1969); Pawtucket Institution for Savings v. Gagnon, ___ R.I. ___, 475 A.2d 1028 (1984).

4. Pawtucket Institution for Savings v. Gagnon, ___ R.I. ___, 475 A.2d 1028 (1984).

5. See e.g., Pawtucket Institution for Savings v. Gagnon, ___ R.I. ___, 475 A.2d 1028, 1030 (1984). But see Jeffrey Towers, Inc. v. Straus, supra note 3 for the suggestion that a promise not capable of being reduced to a money amount may be secured by a mortgage so long as the mortgage "clearly refer[s] to the obligation which the realty is to secure".

er, unless the mortgage debt is reducible to a money amount, it would be impossible to determine a deficiency or to allocate surplus among junior lienors, if any, or to the mortgagor. Second, creditors of the mortgagor would face the same uncertainty in attempting to enforce a judgment against the mortgaged real estate. Third, mortgagees would have difficulty in assigning the mortgagee's interest. Finally, mortgagors would find it extremely difficult to obtain second mortgage financing. Because of the inability to ascertain the amount of the prior lien, lenders would have substantial difficulty in determining the value of the mortgagor's equity for loan purposes. Moreover, bidding at second mortgage foreclosure sales would be discouraged because a potential purchaser would be unable to determine how much to deduct from the land's fair market value in arriving at a rational maximum bid.

Mortgages to secure promises for support pose special problems. Two peculiarities of the normal agreement for support secured by a mortgage of land, i.e., that performance is to be by the mortgagor personally and out of the use of the property, make it inadvisable to apply to it all of the ordinary rules of mortgage law and have even raised some doubt as to whether it should be classified as a mortgage at all.[6] Moreover, courts tend to construe support mortgages liberally in favor of elderly mortgagees.[7] Some find an "implicit promise of peace, harmony and emotional well-being" in addition to the explicit promise of physical support.[8] Even if default is unintentional and causes no irreparable harm the mortgagor will not be permitted to redeem.[9] Although the mortgagee may obtain or accept damages in lieu of the promised support, he cannot be forced to take them.[10] The mortgagee

6. See Bethlehem v. Annis, 40 N.H. 34, 77 Am.Dec. 700 (1861); Soper v. Guernsey, 71 Pa. 219, 221 (1872). Typically the agreement is an intra-family one with the mortgagee elderly or physically dependent. And, since to permit the mortgagee to take possession would deprive the mortgagor of the means by which it was contemplated he was to carry out his obligation, the mortgagor is held to have the right to possession. Flanders v. Lamphear, 9 N.H. 201 (1838); Rhoades v. Parker, 10 N.H. 83 (1839); Colman v. Packard, 16 Mass. 39 (1819) (contra). The problem presented by these factors is also faced in cases where the consideration for an absolute conveyance is a promise to support which in many cases is oral. The majority of courts allow rescission by the grantor for failure of the grantee to perform. In such cases "courts are not so much concerned as to the proper theory upon which such contracts may be avoided, as they are that they must be set aside in order to prevent grave injustice and the imposition upon aged people, by unscrupulous persons, who pretend love, devotion, and friendship, where no one of such elements exists."

Anderson v. Reed, 20 N.M. 202, 215, 148 P. 502, 506, L.R.A.1916B, 862 (1915); Strock v. MacNicholl, 196 Va. 734, 85 S.E.2d 263 (1955); Sweeny v. Patton, 134 Va. 117, 113 S.E. 715 (1922). Contra: Conley v. Sharpe, 58 Cal.App.2d 145, 136 P.2d 376 (1943) discussed in note, 1944, 32 Cal.L.Rev. 191; Spangler v. Yarborough, 23 Okl. 806, 101 P. 1107, 138 Am.St.Rep. 856 (1909); Drake v. Drake, 148 S.C. 147, 14 S.E. 705 (1928).

7. See e.g., Thompson v. Glidden, 445 A.2d 676 (Me.1982).

8. See Thompson v. Glidden, 445 A.2d 676, 678 (Me.1982); Strock v. MacNicholl, 196 Va. 734, 739, 85 S.E.2d 263, 268 (1955); Annot., 112 A.L.R. 670, 708.

9. Bryant v. Erskine, 55 Me. 153, 157 (1867); Henry v. Tupper, 29 Vt. 358 (1857); Dunklee v. Adams, 20 Vt. 415, 50 Am.Dec. 44 (1848); Rowell v. Jewett, 69 Me. 293, 301 (1879).

10. Cook v. Bartholomew, 60 Conn. 24, 22 A. 444, 13 L.R.A. 452 (1891); Ridley v. Ridley, 87 Me. 445, 32 A. 1005 (1895); Tuttle v. Burgett's Administrator, 53 Ohio St. 498, 42 N.E. 427, 30 L.R.A. 214, 53 Am.St.

cannot assign the mortgage,[11] and not only is the mortgagor unable to transfer the property without the mortgagee's consent [12] but creditors of the mortgagor cannot reach it except subject to possession being retained by the mortgagor until the purpose of the mortgage has been fulfilled.[13]

WESTLAW REFERENCES
266   +1   k10 k25

§ 2.3 The Necessity of Consideration

There is substantial confusion over whether consideration is necessary to support a valid mortgage. Although there is contrary authority,[1] many cases state that consideration is an essential element of a mortgage.[2] Yet such statements are misleading. The legal mortgage itself is an executed conveyance and no more requires consideration than any other executed transfer of property.[3] This is obviously true of the common law mortgage conveying legal title, for if an owner may convey the whole title by deed of gift he surely may convey the lesser, security interest in the form of title subject to a condition subsequent.[4] No different rule need apply where the mortgage is in a lien theory jurisdiction, for, regardless of any controversy over the precise nature of the lien,[5] the transaction is executed.

Rep. 649 (1895); Austin v. Austin, 9 Vt. 420 (1837); Joslyn v. Parlin, 54 Vt. 670 (1881) contra.

11. Bryant v. Erskine, 55 Me. 153 (1867).

12. Bethlehem v. Annis, 40 N.H. 34, 77 Am.Dec. 700 (1860); Bryant v. Erskine, 55 Me. 153 (1867); Eastman v. Batchelder, 36 N.H. 141, 72 Am.Dec. 295 (1858); Flanders v. Lamphear, 9 N.H. 201 (1838).

13. Bodwell Granite Co. v. Lane, 83 Me. 168, 21 A. 829 (1891); Greenleaf v. Grounder, 86 Me. 298, 29 A. 1082 (1894).

§ 2.3

1. See e.g., In re Levine, 23 B.R. 410 (Bkrtcy.N.Y.1982); Campell v. Tompkins, 32 N.J.Eq. 170 (1880), affirmed 33 N.J.Eq. 362 (1880); Walsh, Mortgages 75 (1934).

2. See Huntingburg Production Credit Association v. Griese, ___ Ind.App. ___, 456 N.E.2d 448 (1983); Baker v. Citizens State Bank of St. Louis Park, 349 N.W.2d 552 (Minn.1984) (third party mortgage); Continental Bank of Pennsylvania v. Barclay Riding Academy, Inc., 93 N.J. 153, 459 A.2d 1163 (1983), certiorari denied ___ U.S. ___, 104 S.Ct. 488, 78 L.Ed.2d 684 (1983) (third party mortgage); Tiffany, Real Property, 2d Ed., § 606, n. 65 for a collection of cases so stating. See also 31 Mich.L.Rev. 102 (1932).

3. "Consideration has to do with contracts, not executed conveyances." National City Bank of Chicago v. Wagner, 216 F. 473, 132 C.C.A. 533 (1914), certiorari denied 235 U.S. 698, 35 S.Ct. 199, 59 L.Ed. 431 (1915). See also Perry v. Miller, 330 Mass. 261, 112 N.E.2d 805 (1953), commented on by Updike, Mortgages, in 1953 Annual Survey of American Law, 29 N.Y. U.L.Rev. 829, 830 (1954).

4. "There need not be proven, and there need not exist, as I understand it, any consideration between the mortgagor and the mortgagee for the defeasible conveyance manifested by the mortgage itself." Perkins v. Trinity Realty Co., 69 N.J.Eq. 723, 726, 61 A. 167, 168 (1905), affirmed 71 N.J.Eq. 304, 71 A. 1135 (1909). Actually, of course, mortgages of this sort existed prior to the development of any doctrine of consideration.

5. See Gavit, Under the Lien Theory of Mortgages is the Mortgage Only a Power of Sale? 15 Minn.L.Rev. 147; Durfee, Lien or Equitable Theory of Mortgage, 10 Mich.L. Rev. 587 (1912); Chapter 1, D, supra. See also 2 Wis.L.Rev. 59 (1922); 8 Wis.L.Rev. 184 (1933); 19 Ky.L.J. 146, 155 (1931).

Why then does this issue create confusion? Several plausible explanations may be given. Perhaps the most frequent source of confusion is the failure to differentiate between the mortgage and the obligation it secures.[6] "The mortgage itself is an executed conveyance, defeasible upon the carrying out of an executory contract. This executory contract is subject to all the laws applicable to contracts, and must, of course, be supported by consideration."[7] One reason for this failure to distinguish between the two disparate ingredients is the habit of using the word mortgage to refer indiscriminately to the debt, the property security, or the composite of the two.[8] More influential is the requirement that, either because it is the parties' intention or substantive law demands it, there must be an obligation for the mortgage to secure. This makes the validity of the mortgage depend indirectly upon consideration, not for the mortgage itself, but for the obligation upon which it ordinarily depends.[9] In some cases, flowing also from the conception of a mortgage requiring an obligation, the doctrine that a mortgage can be enforced only to the amount of the debt due regardless of the face of the note, etc., seems to be what the court means by its requirement of consideration.[10] Many other cases which say consideration is necessary are dealing with the validity of the mortgage as against third parties, a matter we consider later in this section.[11]

Based on the foregoing, one would suppose that the consideration requirement proves troublesome in situations involving mortgages to secure antecedent debts, the most common context in which the issue arises. In practice, however, this is generally not the case. Some courts suggest that consideration is unnecessary in such settings [12] or that the antecedent debt alone constitutes sufficient consideration for the mortgage.[13] Under this view, the "fact that [a] note and mortgage [are] given for antecedent consideration is of no importance. A valid

6. "Such confusion as exists with respect to the right to plead and prove no consideration arises, I think, out of the failure to distinguish between the mortgage and the debt which the mortgage is given to secure." Perkins v. Trinity Realty Co., 69 N.J.Eq. 723, 726, 61 A. 167, 169 (1905), affirmed 71 N.J.Eq. 304, 71 A. 1135 (1909). For an example of such confusion, see Barnes, Consideration in Mortgages, 19 Ky.L.J. 146, 148–151 (1931).

7. Perkins v. Trinity Realty Co., note 6 supra, at 727, 61 A. at 168. See Surety Life Ins. Co. v. Rose Chapel Mortuary, Inc., 95 Idaho 599, 514 P.2d 594 (1973).

8. A striking example of this is the conclusion of the court in Perkins v. Trinity Realty Co., note 6, supra, at 729, 61 A. at 169, that "there was consideration for the mortgage", i.e., the debt.

9. Chesser v. Chesser, 67 Fla. 6, 64 So. 357 (1914); Hall v. Davis, 73 Ga. 101 (1884); Conwell v. Clifford, 45 Ind. 392 (1873); Hannan v. Hannan, 123 Mass. 441 (1877); Saunders v. Dunn, 175 Mass. 164, 55 N.E. 893 (1900); Anderson v. Lee, 73 Minn. 397, 76 N.W. 24 (1898); Brooks v. Owen, 112 Mo. 251, 19 S.W. 723 (1892), reversed on rehearing 112 Mo. 251, 20 S.W. 492; Hughes v. Thweatt, 57 Miss. 376 (1879); Bradshaw v. Farnsworth, 65 W.Va. 28, 63 S.E. 755 (1909); Cawley v. Kelley, 60 Wis. 315, 19 N.W. 65 (1884).

10. E.g., Laylin v. Knox, 41 Mich. 40, 1 N.W. 913 (1879). See Barbour, History of Contract in Early English Equity, 4 Oxford Studies 89; 3 Tiffany, Real Property, 2d Ed. § 606.

11. See text at notes 15–18 infra.

12. See e.g., First National Bank of Omaha v. Kizzier, 202 Neb. 369, 275 N.W.2d 600 (1979).

13. Buffalo County v. Richards, 212 Neb. 826, 326 N.W.2d 179 (1982).

note may be given as security for a debt already owed by the party giving it, or by a third party." [14] Some courts, however, differentiate between debtor and third party mortgages. While an antecedent debt is sufficient in the former situation, in the latter "a stranger to the debt cannot issue a mortgage . . . without the passage of new and distinct consideration." [15] This latter position is based upon a suspicion "that a third party mortgage exacted subsequent to the creation of the debtor's liability may be prone to fraud, since the debtor's benefit will not have been bargained for by the mortgagor." [16] Yet in most cases, whether in the debtor or third party setting, consideration has rarely proved to be a stumbling block because it usually is present.[17] As the New Jersey Supreme Court recently explained, the "two most common forms of such consideration are (1) the creditor's forbearance in suing on an overdue debt and (2) renewal or extension of the debtor's original note. When a mortgagee forbears from exercising his right to collect another's debt, he incurs a legal detriment amounting to consideration." [18]

The foregoing, however, should not be interpreted to mean that mortgages to secure antecedent debts are immune from attack by a variety of persons who were not parties to the mortgage transaction. For example, under the recording acts, the absence of new "value" for a mortgage to secure antecedent debt may deprive the mortgagee of bona fide purchaser status and thus serve to subordinate his mortgage to prior unrecorded liens.[19] Moreover, where such a mortgage is given

---

14. Id. at 831, 326 N.W.2d at 182. See also Huntingburg Production Credit Association v. Griese, ___ Ind.App. ___, 456 N.E.2d 448 (1983).

15. Continental Bank of Pennsylvania v. Barclay Riding Academy, Inc., 93 N.J. 153, 164, 459 A.2d 1163, 1172 (1983), certiorari denied ___ U.S. ___, 104 S.Ct. 488, 78 L.Ed.2d 684 (1983). See also, Baker v. Citizens State Bank of St. Louis Park, 349 N.W.2d 552, 557 (Minn.1984). Cf. Westbrook State Bank v. Anderson Land and Cattle Company, 364 N.W.2d 416 (Minn. App.1985).

16. Continental Bank, supra note 15, 93 N.J. at 164, 459 A.2d at 1172.

17. See e.g., Safety Federal Savings and Loan Association v. Thurston, 8 Kan.App. 2d 10, 648 P.2d 267 (1982); Continental Bank of Pennsylvania v. Barclay Riding Academy, Inc., 93 N.J. 153, 459 A.2d 1163 (1983), certiorari denied ___ U.S. ___, 104 S.Ct. 488, 78 L.Ed.2d 684 (1983); In re Lowell, 20 B.R. 464 (Bkrtcy.Mass.1982). Zions First National Bank v. United Health Clubs, 533 F.Supp. 1127 (E.D.Pa. 1982), affirmed in part, reversed in part 704 F.2d 120 (3d Cir.1983).

18. Continental Bank of Pennsylvania v. Barclay Riding Academy, Inc., 93 N.J.

153, 164, 459 A.2d 1163, 1173 (1983), certiorari denied ___ U.S. ___, 104 S.Ct. 488, 78 L.Ed.2d 684 (1983). See Perkins v. Trinity Realty, 69 N.J.Eq. 723, 61 A. 167 (1905); Accord Kadish v. Kalloff, 3 Ariz.App. 344, 414 P.2d 193 (1966); Riddle v. LaSalle National Bank, 34 Ill.App.2d 116, 180 N.E.2d 719 (1962); Safety Federal Savings & Loan Association v. Thurston, 8 Kan.App.2d 10, 648 P.2d 267 (1982); Kessler v. Liberty Insurance Bank, 244 Ky. 73, 50 S.W.2d 43 (App.1932). Lortz v. Swartfager, 34 Cal. Rptr. 436, 221 Cal.App.2d 333 (1963); State Bank v. Criswell, 155 Kan. 314, 124 P.2d 500 (1942).

Intelligent drafting may also obviate consideration problems. For example, the Restatement of Contracts, Second, takes the position that a signed statement by the mortgagor identifying "one dollar" or similar "purported" consideration will be sufficient to sustain the validity of the mortgage. See Restatement, Contracts, Second § 88 and Comment (b).

19. See Manufacturers & Traders Trust Co. v. First National Bank, 113 So.2d 869 (Fla.App.1959); Salem v. Salem, 245 Iowa 62, 60 N.W.2d 772 (1953); Gabel v. Drewrys Limited U.S.A., Inc., 68 So.2d 372 (Fla. 1953); Brown v. Mifflin, 220 Ark. 166, 246

within 90 days of bankruptcy by an insolvent debtor who does not receive sufficient new value, to the extent that the new security would cause the creditor to realize more on his claim than he would otherwise receive in a straight bankruptcy liquidation, the mortgage may be set aside as a voidable preference.[20] Finally, irrespective of new consideration, to the extent that a mortgage to secure antecedent debt is given with the intent to defraud present or future creditors of the debtor, it may be avoidable as against those persons under state fraudulent conveyance law[21] or the bankruptcy code.[22]

 WESTLAW REFERENCES
266k25

---

§ 2.4   Description of the Debt

Under certain circumstances a mortgage, even though recorded, will contain such a defective description of the mortgage debt as to render it ineffective against subsequent claimants against the mortgagor. Cases involving the amount of the debt may be divided into two classes: those in which the amount is omitted entirely, or is expressed in general terms, or by way of reference; and those in which although specified, it is either overstated or understated. The objections to the validity of the first group are the possibilities afforded for the substitution of fictitious claims[1] and the burden of investigation to discover what could easily have been inserted in the mortgage. Nevertheless, most courts uphold them,[2] although there is a minority view requiring the amount of the debt to be stated as accurately as its nature permits on pain of having the mortgage held ineffective as to third parties.[3]

The divergence in the decisions reflects a judicial attempt to balance interests. The mortgagee wants to be protected as long as the

S.W.2d 567 (1952); Tripler v. MacDonald Lumber Co., 173 Cal. 144, 159 P. 591 (1916); Annot., 39 A.L.R.2d 1088 (1955); Cunningham, Stoebuck and Whitman, Property 785–786 (1984).

20. See 11 U.S.C.A. § 547(b); 4 Collier, Bankruptcy ¶ 547.14; §§ 8.12, 8.13, 8.16 infra.

21. See e.g., Uniform Fraudulent Coveyance Act § 7; Scholtz v. Yastremski, 247 App.Div. 823, 286 N.Y.S. 694 (1936).

22. See 11 U.S.C.A. § 548(a)(1); 4 Collier, Bankruptcy ¶¶ 548.01, 548.02; §§ 8.12, 8.13 infra.

§ 2.4

1. "The incumbrance on the property must be so defined, as to prevent the substitution of everything which a fraudulent grantor may devise to shield himself from the demands of his creditors." Pettibone v. Griswold, 4 Conn. 158, 10 Am.Dec. 106

(1822) cf. Pioneer Lumber & Supply Co. v. First Merchants National Bank of Michigan City, 169 Ind.App. 406, 349 N.E.2d 219, 222 (1979).

2. In re Truitt, 11 B.R. 15, 19 (Bkrtcy. Ga.1981); Equitable Building & Loan Association v. King, 48 Fla. 252, 37 So. 181 (1904); Hurd v. Robinson, 11 Ohio St. 232 (1860); Goff v. Price, 42 W.Va. 384, 26 S.E. 287 (1896). See Robinson v. Williams, 22 N.Y. 380 (1860). See also 145 A.L.R. 375 (1943).

3. Flexter v. Woomer, 46 Ill.App.2d 456, 197 N.E.2d 161 (1964) (statutory requirement to state amount of indebtedness); Pearce v. Hall, 75 Ky. (12 Bush) 209 (1876); Hart v. Chalker, 14 Conn. 77 (1840); Bullock v. Battenhousen, 108 Ill. 28 (1883). As to the description of an unliquidated debt, see Stoughton v. Pasco, 5 Conn. 442, 13 Am.Dec. 72 (1825).

description of the obligation is adequate to warn a person looking at it and to enable discovery of the truth by inquiry. The searcher of records, on the other hand, wants to be able to rely on them; she does not want to make any more inquiries outside the record than absolutely necessary. Even in the majority jurisdictions the claim must be described and defined with such accuracy as to make identification reasonably possible and certain.[4] Moreover, in all jurisdictions the mortgage will operate as security for only those obligations which are covered by the agreement of the parties and identified by it.[5] The problem of extending it to secure other existing or subsequently created debts or claims involves a consideration of mortgages to secure future advances, a matter dealt with in detail later in this volume.[6]

Where an amount is actually stated, but it is inaccurate, it can be argued that the mortgage should be invalid as to creditors and some other third parties. If the amount is overstated there is, in effect, a concealment of an asset to the extent of the overage; and an understatement may be misleading as to the debtor's affluence. In the absence of an actual intent to deceive, however, such mortgages are not invalid.[7] One reason for this is that the original amount stated, even though correct at the time, is seldom the amount actually due on the mortgage. Usually there will have been payments on the principal or accumulations of unpaid interest, installments, or taxes. Thus third parties, whether creditors or subsequent purchasers or encumbrancers would be unjustified in relying on the original statement.[8] Although this is true and although it is customary for purchasers from the mortgagor and subsequent encumbrancers to ascertain the exact amount of the prior mortgage, there seems little reason why they should not be entitled to depend on the expressly stated amount as the correct original indebtedness if there has been actual reliance and if an alteration would be disadvantageous to them. Ordinarily, of course, it will not harm purchasers or subsequent mortgagees to cut down the amount of an overstatement to the actual debt. An overstatement may, however, harm general creditors who fail to proceed against the mortgagor's property on the mistaken belief that it was fully encumbered.[9] This injury may be difficult to measure and not necessarily

---

4. See Harper v. Edwards, 115 N.C. 246, 20 S.E. 392 (1894). See also 145 A.L.R. 385 (1943); 49 Am.St.Rep. 207 (1896). See additionally Smith v. Haertel, 125 Colo. 348, 353, 244 P.2d 377, 379 (1952).

5. See, Pawtucket Institution for Savings v. Gagnon, ___ R.I. ___, 475 A.2d 1028, 1031 (1984) (quoting text).

6. See § 12.7, infra.

7. Nazro v. Ware, 38 Minn. 443, 38 N.W. 359 (1888). See Shirras v. Caig, 11 U.S. (7 Cranch) 34, 3 L.Ed. 260 (1812); Burnett v. Wright, 135 N.Y. 543, 32 N.E. 253 (1892). Cf., contra, Stearns v. Porter, 46 Conn. 313 (1878). See also Thompson,

What Description of the Debt is Sufficient in a Recorded Mortgage, 44 Cent.L.J. 490 (1897); Redfield, The Necessity of Describing the Security upon the Registry, 2 Am. L.Reg.,N.S., 1 (1862). If the debt is overstated with the intention of defrauding the mortgagor's creditors, the transaction will not be sustained. Holt v. Creamer, 34 N.J. Eq. 181 (1881). See Tully v. Harloe, 35 Cal. 302, 95 Am.Dec. 102 (1868).

8. See Bell v. Fleming's Ex'rs, 12 N.J. Eq. 13, 18 (1858), affirmed 12 N.J.Eq. 490.

9. "He [the creditor] finds an encumbrance on record for as much as the debtor's property is worth, and thinks it useless cured by revelation of the truth. The problem of an overstatement in the future advances context involves similar considerations but is considered later in this volume.[10] Where the amount is understated it cannot, of course, be enforced beyond the stated sum as against subsequent purchasers and encumbrancers, and, presumably, any creditors who actually rely on the incorrect amount.[11]

The date of maturity is of importance to transferees or creditors of both the mortgagor or mortgagee in order that they may know when a default may occur, and therefore it should be set forth in the mortgage. A failure to do so will not, however, ordinarily invalidate the mortgage but instead will be construed at least for purposes of foreclosure as merely making the debt payable on demand.[12]

The failure to include the maturity date in the mortgage may be significant under some statutes of limitation governing foreclosure. For example, under the Missouri statute, "[n]o suit, action or proceeding * * * shall be had or maintained * * * after the lapse of twenty years from the date at which the last maturing obligation secured by the instrument sought to be foreclosed is due on the face of such instrument * * *"[13] Under a subsequent statute, when that date "cannot be determined from the face of such instrument, the twenty year period * * * shall begin to run on the recited date of execution of such instrument, or if there is no recited date, the date of acknowledgment of such instrument, or if there is neither a recited date of execution nor a date of acknowledgment, the date of recording of such instrument, or if there is none of the above, the original date of the secured obligation."[14] Thus, in the case of a long term installment type mortgage, the failure to include the ultimate maturity date could mean that the statute of limitations could prevent foreclosure of the mortgage prior to the actual due date of some of the future installments.[15]

 WESTLAW REFERENCES
266k50

---

to take legal means to secure his debt; whereas, if the mortgage had truly expressed the debt actually due, the creditor might have secured his debt." Griffin v. New Jersey Oil Co., 11 N.J.Eq. 49, 53 (1855).

10. See § 12.7, infra.

11. Gilchrist v. Gough, 63 Ind. 576, 30 Am.Rep. 250 (1878); Burriss v. Owen, 76 S.C. 481, 57 S.E. 542 (1907). Look at Johns v. Church, 29 Mass. (12 Pick.) 557, 23 Am. Dec. 651 (1832) (personal property, actual amount enforcible against creditors).

12. Green v. Richards, 23 N.J.Eq. 32 (1872), affirmed 23 N.J.Eq. 536 (1872);

Cavanna v. Brooks, 97 N.J.Eq. 329, 127 A. 247, 37 A.L.R. 361 (1925); Ansorge v. Kane, 244 N.Y. 395, 155 N.E. 683 (1927), reargument denied 245 N.Y. 530, 157 N.E. 845; N.E.D. Holding Co. v. McKinley, 246 N.Y. 40, 157 N.E. 923 (1927). But cf. Williams v. Mathis, 186 Ark. 526, 54 S.W.2d 301 (1932). See 12 Cornell L.Q. 367 (1927).

13. Vernon's Ann.Mo.Stat. § 516.150. See Note, 19 Mo.L.Rev. 186 (1954).

14. Vernon's Ann.Mo.Stat. § 516.155 (applicable only to mortgages and deeds of trust recorded after January 1, 1979).

15. See § 6.14 infra.

§§ 2.5–3.0 are reserved for supplementary material.

Chapter 3

MORTGAGE SUBSTITUTES

Table of Sections

E. THE INSTALLMENT LAND CONTRACT

A.   RESTRICTING THE RIGHT TO REDEEM

§ 3.1 Clogging the Equity of Redemption

When the courts of equity created the equity of redemption, they did direct violence to the explicit intention of the parties. They did this by allowing the mortgagor to regain his property by performing the secured obligation after the legal title to the property had vested absolutely in the mortgagee—vested according to the express language of the parties in the mortgage deed and according to the effect the law courts gave to that language. Following their original intervention equity courts developed the doctrine *prohibiting the clogging of the mortgagor's equity of redemption.*[1] Under this doctrine, even though

---

§ 3.1

1. The first use of the term clog is in Bacon v. Bacon, Tot. 133–4 (1639): "Where the mortgagee will suddenly bestow unnecessary costs upon the mortgaged lands, of purposes to clog the lands, to prevent the mortgagor's redemption."

See Williams, Clogging the Equity of Redemption, 40 W.Va.L.Q. 31, 33 (1933) for various theories as to the origin and historical development of the doctrine against clogging. For other discussions of the problem or some aspects of it, see Wyman, The Clog on the Equity of Redemption, 21 Harv.L.Rev. 459 (1908); Coutts, Once a Mortgage Always a Mortgage—Stipulations in the Mortgage, 50 Cent.L.J. 464 (1900); Coughlin, Clogging Redemption Rights in Illinois, 3 John Marshall L.Q. 11 (1937); Falconbridge, Legal Mortgages in Equity, 54 Can.L.J.N.S., 1 (1918); Turner, The Equity of Redemption, 175–183; E.N.D., The Basis of Relief from Penalties and Forfeitures, 20 Mich.L.Rev. 646 (1922). Fratcher, Restraints upon Alienation of Equitable Interests in Michigan Property, 51 Mich.L.Rev. 509, 542 (1953). For a concise résumé of English decisions, see note, 136 L.T. 137 (1913). For an incorporation of the doctrine in a statutory enactment, see West's Ann.Cal.Civ.Code § 2889; Coursey v. Fairchild, 436 P.2d 35 (Okl.1967) (interpreting Okl.Stat.Ann. tit. 11: "All contracts in restraint of the mortgagor's the mortgage is in default, normally no agreement contained in the mortgage, or contemporaneous with it, can cut off a recalcitrant mortgagor's equity of redemption without the resort to foreclosure by the mortgagee. Stated another way, courts will not enforce attempts by a mortgagee to have the mortgagor at the inception of the mortgage transaction waive his right to be foreclosed in the event of a default.

While the prohibition against clogging has been characterized by a variety of labels, the most common characterization associated with the doctrine in the United States is "once a mortgage, always a mortgage." It has been pointed out that this "is only another way of saying that a mortgage cannot be made irredeemable." [2] The clogging doctrine, as a corollary of the original creation of the equity of redemption, was developed to prevent evasion of it by ingenious and determined mortgagees who utilized a wide variety of clauses which, while recognizing the existence of the equity of redemption, in practical effect nullified or restricted its operation.

One of the earliest and crudest of these attempts was the insertion in mortgages of clauses limiting redemption to a certain time after the law day.[3] Equity struck them down automatically. Moreover, when the same attempt took the form of a warranty by the mortgagor not to redeem after the law day [4] or a provision making time of the essence,[5] equity courts reached similar results. In addition, provisions that only the mortgagor himself, as distinct from his executor or heir,[6] or that only the mortgagor and the heirs male of the body [7] might redeem were held invalid, a restriction upon persons who may exercise the right to redeem being as offensive as a time limit within which it may be exercised. By a parity of reasoning, an agreement allowing the mortgagee to keep any part of the mortgaged property, redemption being

right to redeem * * * from a lien are void as against public policy"). There are cases both affirming and denying that the mortgagor's statutory right of redemption from a foreclosure sale may be waived. Nippel v. Hammond, 4 Colo. 211 (1878); King v. King, 215 Ill. 100, 74 N.E. 89 (1905), and Cook v. McFarland, 78 Iowa 528, 43 N.W. 519 (1889) hold that it may; Elson Development Co. v. Arizona Savings & Loan Association, 99 Ariz. 217, 407 P.2d 930 (1965); Mace v. Norwood, 155 Kan. 302, 124 P.2d 497 (1942); Parmer v. Parmer, 74 Ala. 285 (1883). See § 8.4 infra.

2. Lord Davey in Noakes v. Rice, A.C. 24, 32 (1902). See Fogelman, The Deed Absolute as a Mortgage in New York, 32 Fordham L.Rev. 299, 301 (1963). For an excellent discussion of Michigan authority, see Russo v. Wolbers, 116 Mich.App. 327, 323 N.W.2d 385 (1982).

3. Bradbury v. Davenport, 114 Cal. 593, 46 P. 1062, 55 Am.St.Rep. 92 (1896) (four months); Heirs of Stover v. Heirs of Bounds, 1 Ohio St. 107 (1853) (before a fixed date); Frazer v. Couthy Land Co., 17 Del.Ch. 68, 149 A. 428 (1929) (three years); Price v. Perrie, Freem.Ch. 258 (1702) and Floyer v. Lavington, 1 P.Wms. 268 (1714) (life of the mortgagor); Jason v. Eyres, Freem.Ch. 69 (1681) (three years "if the mortgagor so long lives"); Salt v. Marquess of Northampton, A.C. 1 (1892) (mortgagor dying in lifetime of his father). But Compare Newcomb v. Bonham, 1 Vern. 7 (1681). See Toomes v. Conset, 3 Atkyns 261 (1745).

4. East India Co. v. Atkyns, 1 Comyns 347 (1740); Cowley v. Shields, 180 Ala. 48, 60 So. 267 (1913).

5. Jackson v. Lynch, 129 Ill. 72, 21 N.E. 580 (1889), rehearing denied 129 Ill. 72, 22 N.E. 246. See note 2 supra.

6. Newcomb v. Bascomb, 1 Vern. 7 (1681).

7. Howard v. Harris, 1 Vern. 33 (1681).

limited to the balance, fails.[8] Similarly, the doctrine is violated when a mortgagee requires the mortgagor to deliver an executed deed to the mortgaged premises to the mortgagee at the time of the initial mortgage transaction, the mortgagee's purpose being, in the event of the mortgagor's default, to utilize the deed to obviate the need for foreclosure. For example, when an escrow was attempted in which the mortgagor executed a deed at the time the loan and mortgage was given and deposited it in escrow to be delivered to the mortgagee in payment of the debt in the event of default, the court held that the mortgagor still retained the right to redeem and that the arrangement violated the prohibition against clogging.[9]

Not quite so clear a case is a stipulation providing for an increase in the interest rate on nonpayment on a fixed law day.[10] The difficulty is that if the higher rate was stipulated for at the outset with a reduction for punctual payment the agreement is valid. Yet in both cases precisely the same amounts of money would be payable at exactly the same times.[11] Of course, situations could be envisaged where the jump in interest rate would be so enormous, or the provision for the payment of a bonus on default so huge, that as a practical matter, the mortgagor would be unable to pay it. This clearly would be recognized as merely a device to make the mortgage irredeemable and therefore in violation of the clogging concept. But quite apart from anything of this sort, and with a relatively mild jump in interest rate, (although any jump does, of course, make it more difficult to redeem), the decisions nevertheless seem based upon a principle which underlies relief from penalties and forfeitures.[12] That principle is that relief will be granted where there has been a misreliance upon a "mirage of hope". Ordinarily, the courts have talked in terms of granting relief because of solicitude for the "impecunious landowner"[13] or "necessitous men [who] are not, truly speaking, free men."[14] But another important factor is the mortgagee's tendency to play upon the mortgagor's natural optimism, the "overconfidence in one's own capacities and faith in a special providence [which] leads us to over-sanguine commitments."[15] Equity takes this human failing into account. Thus where the bargain is expressed in terms of a future increase in the amount due, for which

8. Salt v. Marquess of Northampton, A.C. 1 (1892).

9. Plummer v. Ilse, 41 Wash. 5, 82 P. 1009, 2 L.R.A.,N.S., 627 (1905). Also see Pollak v. Millsap, 219 Ala. 273, 122 So. 16, 65 A.L.R. 110 (1928). Cf. Kartheiser v. Hawkins, 98 Nev. 237, 645 P.2d 967 (1982).

10. Holles v. Wyse, 2 Vern. 289 (1693); Strode v. Parker, 2 Vern. 316 (1694). See Salt v. Marquess of Northampton, A.C. 1, 19 (1892); Firth, Freedom of Contract in Mortgages, 11 L.Q.Rev. 144, 153 (1895). See also Goodyear Shoe Machine Co. v. Selz, Schwab & Co., 157 Ill. 186, 41 N.E. 625 (1895).

11. See the dubious *quaere* in Strode v. Parker, supra note 10.

12. See note, 20 Mich.L.Rev. 646 (1922). Finger v. McCaughey, 114 Cal. 64, 45 P. 1004 (1896), held valid a jump in the interest rate on a mortgage if not paid, from ten percent to twelve percent.

13. "Impecunious landowner in the toils of a crafty money lender." Samuel v. Jarrah Timber & W.P. Corp., Limited, A.C. 52, 55 (1904).

14. Vernon v. Bethel, 2 Eden 113 (1761).

15. 20 Mich.L.Rev. 646, 647 (1922).

the mortgagor never expects to become liable, rather than a firm commitment to the higher rate at the very outset which he knows he has bound himself to pay but may reduce by future effort, the transaction is invalid. The same applies to a bonus to be paid to the mortgagee on redemption under certain conditions.[16]

Several forms of mortgage instruments which have become popular in recent years involve the capitalization, or adding to principal, of accruing interest. These include the graduated payment mortgage (GPM), in which the payment schedule is fixed at the outset so that payments will increase each year, but in the early years may be insufficient to cover accruing interest; the adjustable rate mortgage (ARM), in which interest varies with some external market index and may exceed the payments made by the borrower during some time periods; and the shared appreciation mortgage (SAM), under which a portion of the interest is computed on the basis of increases in the property's market value, and which may require that the interest thus computed be added to principal on some fixed date if the property has not been sold by the borrower.

Each of these mortgage types is discussed in detail in a later section.[17] Our purpose here is simply to inquire whether their characteristic of capitalizing interest (and thus, of computing interest on interest) violates the clogging doctrine. It has been argued that it may,[18] but the English authorities usually cited in support of this view turn out, upon close examination, to treat the practice as usurious or something akin to usury rather than as a clog.[19] We have found no case authority that interest on interest is a clog.

Nor can these mortgages be regarded as clogs under the policy analysis set forth above. The deferral of interest payments, and consequent adding of interest to principal, has been developed primarily as a means of easing the mortgagor's monthly payment burden and of making real estate purchases more affordable.[20] Its objective is by no means to penalize default or to make redemption more difficult. In this respect it must be distinguished from the provisions discussed above for higher interest upon default. Moreover, the operation of the instrument and the risks to the borrower are ordinarily disclosed in considerable detail before the transaction is entered into.[21] These new forms of mortgage instruments are socially useful and should not be discarded out of a misconceived or overstrict regard for the clogging doctrine. For most commercial lending institutions, the issue has

16. Chapple v. Mahon, Ir.R. 5 Eq. 225 (1870).

17. See § 11.4 infra.

18. See Comment, The Shared Appreciation Mortgage: A Clog on the Equity of Redemption?, 15 John Mar.L.Rev. 13 (1982).

19. Chambers v. Goodwin, 9 Ves.Jun. 254, 271, 32 Eng.Rep. 600 (1804); Waring v. Cunliffe, 1 Ves.Jun. 99 (1790).

20. See § 11.4 infra at notes 18 and 58.

21. For home loans by institutional lenders, applicable regulations typically require elaborate disclosure of the loan's terms and its practical operation; see, e.g., 12 C.F.R. § 545.6–2(7).

largely been preempted by federal law in any event; the Alternative Mortgage Transaction Parity Act of 1982 [22] provides that to the extent of any conflict between state law and federal regulations affecting such mortgages, the latter will prevail.

Attempts have been made to characterize the due-on-sale clause as an invalid clog of the equity of redemption.[23] Such clauses, which are treated extensively elsewhere in this volume,[24] afford a mortgagee the option to accelerate and foreclose the mortgage debt in the event the mortgagor transfers an interest in the mortgaged real estate without mortgagee permission. One commentator has suggested that such clauses violate the clogging doctrine because "[b]y preventing the transfer of the mortgagor's equity of redemption on the terms with which he acquired that equity, the value of the right diminishes and the equity of redemption is impaired."[25] Such an argument is plainly illogical. If the due-on-sale clause is contained in a purchase-money mortgage, it is, in fact, one of "the terms with which" the mortgagor acquired the property. If, on the other hand, a non-purchase money mortgage is involved, the argument is simply irrelevant because the clause is unrelated to the mortgagor's acquisition of the equity of redemption.

A somewhat more intriguing, but equally dubious, clogging argument was made in a recent Oklahoma case.[26] The mortgagor in that case relied on language from an earlier Oklahoma decision that stated "what is meant by a right to redeem is that upon discharge of the debt within the maximum permissible time, the mortgagor is entitled * * * to have the mortgaged premises relieved from the lien and his entire estate restored to that extent which he would have had if the transaction had never taken place."[27] The foregoing language, the mortgagor argued, afforded a mortgagor the right to make installment payments even after default. Any provision "giving the mortgagee the option to accelerate the [mortgage] debt therefore clogs both his and [a prospective grantee's] right to redeem because it prevents them from making installment payments over the life of the loan."[28] Interestingly, such reasoning not only would invalidate due-on-sale clauses but would also cast doubt on the universally-used acceleration clause that permits a mortgagee to render the entire mortgage debt due and payable if the mortgagor fails to make timely payment of the mortgage installments.[29]

The Oklahoma Supreme Court rejected this reasoning and held that due-on-sale clauses do not clog the equity of redemption. It noted

---

22. 12 U.S.C.A. §§ 3801 et seq. Note that some of the agencies' regulations issued under the Act may not apply to all types of mortgage loans.

23. See Comment, Due-on-Sale Clauses and Clogging the Equity of Redemption, 36 Wash. Lee L.Rev. 1121 (1979).

24. See §§ 5.21–5.26 infra.

25. Comment, supra note 24 at 1133.

26. Lincoln Mortgage Investors v. Cook, 659 P.2d 925 (Okl.1982).

27. Coursey v. Fairchild, 436 P.2d 35, 38 (Okl.1967).

28. Lincoln Mortgage Investors v. Cook, 659 P.2d 925, 928 (Okl.1982).

29. See § 7.6 infra.

that such acceleration clauses in general are valid and that the due-on-sale clause is simply a specialized form of acceleration clause. The earlier Oklahoma case relied upon by the mortgagor, the court reasoned, merely restated "the general principle that mortgagors in default have the right to tender the full unpaid amount of the mortgage debt" until a valid foreclosure has taken place. It "did *not* give a right to continued enjoyment of the benefits of a mortgage agreement to one who has breached its terms".[30]

Acceptance of a contrary analysis not only would have placed in jeopardy a pervasively used default remedy, but would also have ignored the historical context in which the clogging doctrine arose. Installment payment of mortgage principal was extremely rare at common law. Typically, common law mortgages provided for a lump sum payment of the entire debt on the law day.[31] It makes no sense to reason, from these early practices, that a modern mortgagor may cure his default merely by the tender of installment arrearages.[32] In any event, Section 341 of the Garn-St. Germain Depository Institutions Act, enacted by Congress in 1982 and considered in detail elsewhere in this volume,[33] makes most due-on-sale clauses enforceable notwithstanding contrary state law. With respect to mortgages covered by this federal legislative preemption, any attempt to employ the clogging doctrine as a weapon against due-on-sale clause enforcement is effectively foreclosed.

Provisions that the mortgagor shall pay the mortgagee's expenses in collecting the secured debt and that the mortgage shall secure this additional item have been upheld by some courts and disallowed by others.[34] The former seem preferable as the additional amount is merely fair compensation for extra trouble and expense by the mortgagee. Of course if an excessive sum is provided for, the effect of which is to interfere with the mortgagor's right to redeem, it will be disallowed and cut to a reasonable amount.[35]

30. Lincoln Mortgage Investors v. Cook, 659 P.2d 925, 928 (Okl.1982).

31. See §§ 1.2, 1.3 and § 6.6 infra.

32. Legislation in some instances allows a mortgagor to reinstate an accelerated mortgage debt by the payment of arrearages. See § 7.7 infra. Judicial decisions sometimes similarly limit strict enforcement of acceleration clauses, but general equitable principles of fairness and unconscionability, and not the clogging doctrine, have provided the rationale for such decisions. See Id.

33. See § 5.21–5.26 infra.

34. Valid: Clawson v. Munson, 55 Ill. 394 (1870); Baker v. Jacobson, 183 Ill. 171, 55 N.E. 724 (1899); Weatherby v. Smith, 30 Iowa 131, 6 Am.Rep. 663 (1870); Tholen v. Duffy, 7 Kan. 405 (1871) (but see Foote v. Sprague, 13 Kan. 155 (1874)); Gaither v. Tolson, 84 Md. 637, 36 A. 449 (1897); Pierce v. Kneeland, 16 Wis. 672, 84 Am. Dec. 726 (1863). See Voechting v. Grau, 55 Wis. 312, 13 N.W. 230 (1882). Invalid: Thomasson v. Townsend, 10 Bush 114 (Ky. 1873); Kittermaster v. Brossard, 105 Mich. 219, 63 N.W. 75, 55 Am.St.Rep. 437 (1895); Northwestern Mutual Life Insurance Co. v. Butler, 57 Neb. 198, 77 N.W. 667 (1899); Turner v. Boger, 126 N.C. 300, 35 S.E. 592, 49 L.R.A. 590 (1900); Miller v. Kyle, 85 Ohio St. 186, 97 N.E. 372 (1911); Daly v. Maitland, 88 Pa. 384, 32 Am.Rep. 457, 11 Lanc.Bar. 9 (1879).

35. Daly v. Maitland, 88 Pa. 384, 32 Am.Dec. 457, 11 Lanc.Bar 9 (1879).

The rule against clogging has occasionally been expressed by the twin concepts that (1) the mortgagee shall not have a "collateral advantage" and (2) there must be no stipulation in the mortgage which will "fetter" the property on redemption. The first concept has been expressed by the terminology that a person "shall not have interest for his money and a collateral advantage besides for the loan of it, or clog the redemption with any by-agreement." The second concept has been summed up as meaning "that the mortgagee shall not make any stipulation which will prevent a mortgagor, who has paid principal, interest, and cost, from getting back his mortgaged property in the condition in which he parted with it." [36] While these two aspects of the clogging doctrine have at times been important in England, they have never played a significant role in the United States and, accordingly, they are not considered in detail here.[37] To the extent that "collateral advantage" and fettering are valid concepts in modern American law, they will be relieved against only on general doctrines of oppression or unconscionability.[38]

 WESTLAW REFERENCES
266k591(3)

§ 3.2　The Option to Purchase as a Clog on the Equity of Redemption

Some courts have utilized the clogging concept to deny specific performance of an option to purchase, granted by a mortgagor to a mortgagee incident to a loan transaction.[1] Such an option can be viewed as a clog on the equity of redemption because it allows a mortgagee to acquire the mortgaged premises by means other than foreclosure. Thus, to the extent that such an option is enforceable, the land is rendered irredeemable. One court has used especially strong language to characterize its approach in this regard: "Where the option is a part of the original loan transaction, it is * * * absolutely void * * * regardless of whether there in actual oppression in the specific

---

36. Opinion of Lord Davey, Noakes and Co. Limited v. Rice, A.C. 24, 33 (1902); Smith v. Smith, 82 N.H. 399, 135 A. 25 (1926) (collateral advantage).

37. See Osborne, Mortgages, §§ 98–99 (2d Ed.1970).

38. Some recently-developed mortgage formats, such as the shared-appreciation mortgage (SAM) might conceivably be considered to create collateral advantages in the sense that the mortgagee's right to share in the appreciation is an advantage in excess of ordinary interest. Because these mortgages are accepted by many regulatory agencies and serve socially useful

purposes, it is highly unlikely that they will be held conceptually invalid.

§ 3.2

1. See Humble Oil & Refining Co. v. Doerr, 123 N.J.Super. 530, 303 A.2d 898 (1973); Smith v. Smith, 82 N.H. 399, 135 A. 25 (1926). Wilson v. Fisher, 148 N.C. 535, 62 S.E. 622 (1908); Hopping v. Baldridge, 130 Okl. 226, 266 P. 469 (1928); Barr v. Granahan, 255 Wis. 192, 38 N.W.2d 705 (1949); Lewis v. Frank Love Limited, [1961] 1 All E.R. 446. But see MacArthur v. North Palm Beach Utilities, Inc., 202 So. 2d 181 (Fla.1967).

case." [2] Moreover, the same court extended this principle to deny specific performance to a guarantor of the mortgagor who took an option to purchase the mortgaged premises as part of the original loan transaction.[3]

An overly dogmatic approach to such options may, however unduly discourage the flow of capital to a variety of socially useful projects. For example, the prospect of being able to share in the success of a corporate mortgagor may very well induce a mortgagee to consider use of a variety of techniques that afford the mortgage lender the opportunity to acquire equity ownership in the mortgagor is real estate.[4] In this connection, corporate mortgagors commonly grant their lenders warrants to purchase their stock. Conceivably a rigid application of the clogging principle could render such warrants unenforceable because they enable a mortgage lender to acquire an interest in the mortgaged corporate assets without having to resort to foreclosure. Even assuming that a court would be reluctant to apply the anti-clogging concept where the mortgagee acquires such an indirect interest in the mortgaged assets, it is not difficult to envisage its application in a variety of other settings where a mortgage lender is encouraged to provide capital by the prospect of sharing more directly in any future success of mortgagor. For example, suppose that part of the inducement to a mortgage lender to provide long term financing for several of borrower's shopping center developments is the prospect of being able later to acquire one or more of those projects or at least a significant interest in them, should the projects prove successful. A strict application of the anti-clogging doctrine could frustrate the use of options in such situations even though the lender's primary motivation is to share in the mortgagor's success rather than to avoid foreclosure when the mortgagor's venture proves to be a failure.

Moreover, the implications of the clogging concept for such options have been a significant concern for title insurors. It is not uncommon for lenders to seek endorsements to the standard mortgagee policy or separate policies that insure the enforceability and priority of such options.[5] However, title companies have been reluctant to issue such insurance unless the transaction contains an "unwind mechanism" enabling the mortgagor to repurchase the option for an additional fee and thereby to redeem the mortgaged real estate.[6]

Thus, it seems preferable to reject the inflexible position that all mortgagee attempts to enforce such options are invalid in favor of an

---

2. Humble Oil & Refining Co. v. Doerr, 123 N.J.Super. 530, 548–49, 303 A.2d 898, 907–08 (1973).

3. Id.

4. See e.g., Oharenko, Convertible Mortgages Gain Big League Attention, 44 Mortgage Banking 20 (No. 11, July 1984); Keyles, The Demise of the Long-Term Fixed Rate Mortgage: Legal Implications of Alternative Investment Techniques, Proceedings, 6th Annual Meeting, Legal Section, American Council of Life Insurance, 265, 270–71 (1981).

5. See Goode and Jordan, New Routes for Title Insurors, 44 Mortgage Banker 28, 32 (No. 6, March 1984).

6. Id.

approach where enforceability depends upon the nature of the parties, the terms of the option, and the circumstances under which the mortgagee is seeking to enforce it. Such an approach recognizes that the essence of the equity of redemption is the right of a mortgagor in default to insist that she be deprived of the mortgaged real estate only by a foreclosure process that tests its value at a public sale. In general, options should be deemed clogs on the equity of redemption when utilized as remedies for mortgagor default. For example, where the option language expressly ties exercise to mortgagor default, the option on its face is an attempt to circumvent foreclosure and probably should be unenforceable. Even where such express language is absent, an actual attempt to exercise the option after a mortgagor default should similarly be viewed as tainted by foreclosure avoidance motives and thus as invalid.[7] After all, in both of the foregoing settings, a mortgagee who desires to acquire a defaulted mortgagor's real estate may be tempted to utilize the option route in order to avoid the possibility that third party bidding at a foreclosure sale would make mortgagee acquisition more costly.

Moreover, it may be justifiable in extreme cases to protect even nondefaulting residential and small business mortgagors from inequitable attempts by mortgagees to profit by acquiring appreciated and improved real estate via the option route. Such mortgagors are more liable to be unrepresented by counsel and less commercially sophisticated than their more substantial business counterparts, and close judicial scrutiny is therefore probably justified. One Wisconsin case is illustrative in this regard.[8] There, mortgagee advanced approximately $8,500 to mortgagor, a good friend, to acquire a tavern property. Mortgagee took back a promissory note payable in six years secured by a mortgage on the tavern property. In addition, mortgagor, who was unrepresented by counsel, gave mortgagee, who had legal representation, a ten-year option to purchase the mortgagee's property for $8,000. The option was silent both as to refund of payments made by mortgagor on the indebtedness and as to reimbursement for improvements made on the property. Exercise was not tied to default. Two years later, after significant payments on the note and $3,000 in repairs and improvement, mortgagee exercised the option to purchase. Mortgagor was not in default on the note, and the mortgaged real estate at the time of exercise was worth between $14,000 and $18,000. The Wisconsin Supreme Court affirmed a denial of specific performance of the option. While the court's rationale was not entirely clear, it seemed to rely not

---

7. It is conceivable that a mortgagor could default intentionally solely to prevent a mortgagee from enforcing an option. We elsewhere consider the somewhat analogous problem of whether a mortgagor should be able intentionally to default and trigger a foreclosure proceeding in order to avoid payment of a prepayment charge. See § 6.2 infra.

We conclude that in such a case the equities favor the mortgagee, and would expect courts to reach a similar conclusion in the option setting.

8. Barr v. Granahan, 255 Wis. 192, 38 N.W.2d 705 (1949).

only on the anti-clogging concept, but also on its inherent discretion to deny equitable relief under harsh and unequitable circumstances. This latter ground is the preferable one in our view.

On the other hand, it seems anomalous to apply a doctrine that in large measure was designed to afford defaulting mortgagors the protections of the foreclosure process to shield all mortgagors, whatever the level of their commercial sophistication, against the consequences of their own success. For example, if our hypothetical shopping center developer was able to obtain a more favorable interest rate or other desirable loan terms because of a willingness to afford the mortgagee a favorable option, it hardly seems unreasonable to give the mortgagee the benefit of its bargain when the mortgagor's business venture proves to be successful. One Florida Supreme Court decision[9] is clearly sympathetic to this perspective. There a seller-mortgagee who sold land for a subdivision to the mortgagor and who provided financing to construct a sewer and water system for the subdivision also took back an option to purchase the system for its construction cost. Later the mortgagee sought specific performance of the option. Even though this enforcement attempt was unrelated to any mortgagor loan default, the trial court and District Court of Appeal applied the clogging principle to deny specific performance. The Supreme Court reversed and held the option enforceable. The court noted that the option was part of a complex business transaction and that both parties were represented by counsel. Accordingly, it held that neither the clogging doctrine nor equitable considerations should be a bar to enforcement of the option. To the court, the mortgagor simply made "a fair contract to resell for a valid consideration but refused to perform.[10]

The Uniform Land Transactions Act (ULTA) to some extent reflects the foregoing approach to the clogging problem. Under section 3–211, a 1983 amendment to the ULTA, an option to purchase granted to a mortgagee incident to a mortgage loan transaction is generally enforceable "if the right to exercise the option is not dependent upon the occurrence of default."[11] The ULTA amendment is somewhat less protective of mortgagors than the approach suggested above; under the ULTA, so long as the language of the option itself is not tied to mortgagor default, the mortgagee is apparently free to use the option as an alternative default remedy. States are free under the ULTA to choose whether to bar the application of the clogging concept to all mortgagee option situations or only those involving non-residential mortgage transactions.[12]

 WESTLAW REFERENCES
266   +1   k294 k591   &   clog!   /s   equit!   /s   redemption
clog!   /s   equit!   /s   redemption

---

9. MacArthur v. North Palm Beach Utilities, Inc., 202 So.2d 181 (Fla.1967).

10. Id. at 184.

11. ULTA § 3–211 (1983).

12. Id.

§ 3.3   Subsequent Transactions

The doctrine that the mortgagor's equity of redemption cannot be affected by any agreement contemporaneous with the mortgage is inapplicable to certain transactions subsequent to the creation of the mortgage. Thus, a subsequent sale of the equity of redemption to the mortgagee will not normally be considered an invalid clog on the equity of redemption.[1] Indeed, this transaction usually takes the form of a deed in lieu of foreclosure. While the majority of courts today permit the mortgagee to purchase the mortgagor's equity of redemption, they will scrutinize the transaction to insure that it is free from fraud or oppression on the part of the mortgagee and is based on an adequate new consideration, the burden of establishing these requirements being on the mortgagee.[2] Moreover, a deed in lieu of foreclosure may also sometimes be characterized as an "absolute deed as mortgage" and can create further problems for the mortgagee where there are intervening liens against the mortgagor. The deed in lieu of foreclosure and its attendant problems are considered in greater detail later in this volume.[3]

While the mortgagor, as noted above, may under some circumstances be permitted to sell his equity of redemption, "he cannot, even after the mortgage has been executed, bind himself by an agreement that, if he does not pay his debt by a certain time in the future, he will forfeit all right to the property."[4] In other words, courts will treat

§ 3.3

1. Cedarwood Associates, L.T.D. v. Trammell, 410 So.2d 50 (Ala.1982). See Smith v. Shattls, 66 N.J.Super. 430, 169 A.2d 503 (1961); Russo v. Wolbers, 116 Mich.App. 327, 323 N.W.2d 385, 390 (1982) (dictum); Bart v. Granahan, 255 Wis. 192, 38 N.W.2d 705 (1949) (dictum); See Note, 31 Mo.L.Rev. 312 (1966).

2. See Note, 31 Mo.L.Rev. 312 (1966); Gould v. McKillip, 55 Wyo. 251, 99 P.2d 67, 129 A.L.R. 1427 (1940) and cases there cited; Earle's Administrator v. Blanchard, 85 Vt. 288, 81 A. 913 (1911). Cf. Ferris v. Wilcox, 51 Mich. 105, 16 N.W. 252, 47 Am. Rep. 551 (1883) (mortgagor to be given the benefit of any doubt); Odell v. Montross, 68 N.Y. 499 (1877). But see Bailey v. St. Louis Union Trust Co., 188 Mo. 483, 87 S.W. 1003 (1905). Cf. Trull v. Skinner, 34 Mass. (17 Pick.) 213 (1835); Stone v. Jenks, 142 Mass. 519, 8 N.E. 403 (1886) (gift by mortgagor to mortgagee). If the price paid is inadequate, the sale will be set aside. Peugh v. Davis, 96 U.S. (6 Otto) 332, 24 L.Ed. 775 (1877). If the mortgagee buys on an execution sale under a judgment recovered by a third person, or upon a judgment recovered by the mortgagee on a debt other than that which is secured by the mort-gage, the same rule of scrutiny is not applied. This is "for the very good reason that, at this public sale conducted by an officer of the court, the mortgagee has no opportunity to overreach the mortgagor and take undue advantage of his economic weakness. *Per contra,* to permit to purchase on the same terms as any stranger adds one (and a most important one) to the potential market for the land, to the advantage of the mortgagor as well as the mortgagee." Wheeler and Durfee, Evasion of Mortgage Moratoria by Prosecution of Personal Remedies, 33 Mich.L.Rev. 1196, 1198 (1935). Farmers Union Trading Co. v. Wiggins, 127 Mont. 481, 267 P.2d 117 (1954), noted in Updike, Mortgages, in 1954 Annual Survey of American Law, 30 N.Y. U.L.Rev. 805, 806 (1955), upholds the deed where the consideration is fair and the debt is discharged.

3. See §§ 6.18–6.19, infra.

4. Holden Land & Livestock Co. v. Inter-State Trading Co., 87 Kan. 221, 227, 123 P. 733, 736, L.R.A.1915B, 492 (1912), appeal dismissed 233 U.S. 536, 34 S.Ct. 61, 58 L.Ed. 1083 (1914). Batty v. Snook, 5 Mich. 231 (1858); Tennery v. Nicholson, 87 Ill. 464 (1877); Cohn v. Bridgeport Plumbing Supply Co., 96 Conn. 696, 115 A. 328, *subsequent* executory agreements as uninforceable clogs on the mortgagor's equity of redemption, even though, under some circumstances, they will treat *executed* transactions as legitimate sales.

This distinction between subsequent executed and executory transactions has been criticized on the ground that a person should be able to contract to sell what he could dispose of at once. Nevertheless, it may be defended. The bases for the policy supporting the rule are the necessity of the borrower to obtain the loan coupled with an optimistic overconfidence in his capacities to surmount future difficulties. The two combine to lead to over-sanguine commitments. Both are present at the time the mortgage is entered into originally. When the transaction is subsequent to the mortgage and is consummated at once, neither exerts any influence. However, if it is a subsequent agreement for *future* forfeiture, the "mirage of hope" is sufficiently strong to bring it under the general ban against forfeitures due to "misreliance upon airy hope." [5] If the reasoning is valid, executory contracts to waive statutory rights of redemption from foreclosure sale should be unenforceable. There are, however, authorities holding such agreements good.[6] It has been suggested that the test should be whether the parties actually intended a sale agreement or whether it was merely an arrangement for additional security for the loan on different terms, one of which involved cutting off, by the agreement, the new equity of redemption which arose out of the new or modified mortgage agreement.[7] Since the real question is why such an agreement, whether it is to sell in futuro the redemption interest or to release it in satisfaction of the debt when it comes due and unpaid, should not be valid when it is not a part of the original mortgage, such a suggestion has little merit.

Because the mortgagor's equity of redemption and the prohibition against clogging that equity have become so firmly inbedded in the formal law of mortgages, mortgagees, as we have noted earlier, often

---

24 A.L.R. 808 (1921), accord. See notes, 13 Col.L.Rev. 170 (1913); 29 Mich.L.Rev. 757 (1931); 36 Mich.L.Rev. 111 (1937); 22 Harv.L.Rev. 295 (1909); 19 Va.L.Rev. 302 (1933). See also 55 Am.St.Rep. 100 (1897); 2 L.R.A.,N.S., 628 (1906); 65 A.L.R. 120 (1930) for discussions of and collections of cases on the problem presented in the principal case and some analogous situations. Bradbury v. Davenport, 120 Cal. 152, 52 P. 301 (1898) is usually cited as the leading case contra to the Holden case. See also Ravnaas v. Andrich, 60 S.D. 281, 244 N.W. 361 (1932), noted 19 Va.L.Rev. 302; Brockington v. Lynch, 119 S.C. 273, 112 S.E. 94 (1922). See additionally Durfee, Cases on Security, 1951, 167. See also Glenn, Mortgages, § 45, dismissing the rule as unsound in principle and contrary to more recent and better authority.

5. See note, 20 Mich.L.Rev. 646, 648 (1922), arguing that such misreliance is a basis for relief against forfeitures generally with the mortgage cases only one illustration.

6. Russo v. Wolbers, 116 Mich.App. 327, 323 N.W.2d 385 (1982); Nippel v. Hammond, 4 Colo. 211 (1878); Cook v. McFarland, 78 Iowa 528, 43 N.W. 519 (1889); King v. King, 215 Ill. 100, 74 N.E. 89 (1905); United States Bldg. & Loan Association v. Stevens, 93 Mont. 11, 17 P.2d 62 (1932) (clause in mortgage waiving right to possession during redemption period valid) semble. On the other hand there is authority that a waiver of such a right contained in the mortgage itself is invalid. Parmer v. Parmer, 74 Ala. 285 (1883); Lambright v. Bales, 139 Ark. 48, 213 S.W. 2 (1919).

7. See note, 13 Col.L.Rev. 171 (1913).

resort to other types of land security devices to avoid the consequences of those mortgage law doctrines. As Professor Durfee once aptly put it, "[T]he big idea is to find a form of a transaction that will have the practical effect of security, yet will be held not to be a security but to belong to a wholly different jural species and so be held immune from security law."[8] Commonly encountered mortgage substitutes include the absolute deed, together with its variations, and the installment land contract. A consideration of these devises and related concepts follows.

 WESTLAW REFERENCES
266 +1 k296 k297
266k591

B. THE ABSOLUTE DEED

§ 3.4 The Absolute Deed With Separate Instrument of Defeasance

The common law mortgage takes the form of a "deed conveying lands conditioned to be void upon the payment of a sum of money, or the doing of some other act."[1] This condition of defeasance was ordinarily tacked onto the end of what otherwise read as an ordinary straight deed of absolute conveyance. Although there are statutory forms of mortgages in many jurisdictions the language of the traditional deed of conveyance is still commonly used even in lien theory jurisdictions. When it is all put into one document no doubts are raised as to the effectiveness of the instrument to accomplish the intended result. Equity added onto the express terms of the transaction, for reasons which were examined earlier[2] a right in the grantor to tardy redemption even though the terms of the defeasance were not fulfilled and title had vested absolutely in the grantee, and gave a corresponding right to the grantee to foreclose that right of redemption—neither of these rights was founded on any expressed intention of the parties either explicit or implied in fact, and one of them at least, the redemption right, in flat contradiction to the stated terms of the instrument.

Sometimes, however, the defeasance is expressed in a separate instrument and the question arises whether the two can be read together so as to establish a legal mortgage. The practice has not gone uncriticised, one chancellor in the time of George II stating with vigor that "it will always appear with a face of fraud: for, the defeasance may be lost; and then an absolute conveyance is set up. I would discourage the practice as much as possible."[3] Nevertheless the well

---

8. Durfee, Cases on Security, 4 (1951).

§ 3.4

1. Lund v. Lund, 1 N.H. 39, 41, 8 Am. Dec. 29, 30 (1817).

2. See § 1.3, supra.

3. Cottrell v. Purchase, Cas.Temp. Talbot, 61, 64 (1732).

settled rule is that "the condition may be ✻ ✻ ✻ by a separate deed, executed, or at least taking effect, at the same time [as the deed of conveyance], so as to be part of one and the same transaction. It must be by deed, and cannot be by parol or instrument in writing not under seal. It must take effect at the time the deed of conveyance takes effect, and not at a subsequent time." [4] There is some authority that where the instruments are separate the result is not a legal mortgage but an "equitable" mortgage only. "Equitable" mortgage in this context is used to mean that the *mortgagor* has only an equitable interest which these courts seem to regard, even in title jurisdiction, as different from the redemption right of a mortgage executed as one document. This view seems illogical and undesirable even though the consequences are of little importance.[5]

The substitution of the proviso for reconveyance for the defeasance clause in the debtor's deed did not alter the fundamental character of the common-law mortgage. The proviso was given a double construction; it operated as a condition subsequent to the grant, and it also was specifically enforceable as a promise.[6] If, instead of one instrument being used, the transaction consisted of a deed of the land, absolute in form, given by the debtor to the creditor concurrently with the execution by the creditor of a bond of defeasance or a sealed promise to reconvey on payment of the debt, the two instruments were construed together and held to create a legal mortgage.[7] Although the requirement that the contemporaneous writing had to be of equal dignity and formality with the original conveyance, i.e., under seal if the deed were so executed, was the rule of the law courts; [8] in equity it was not

---

4. Lund v. Lund, 1 N.H. 39, 41, 8 Am. Dec. 29, 30 (1817); Sears v. Dixon, 33 Cal. 326 (1867), agreement for reconveyance executed, in accordance with terms of original agreement, after the absolute conveyance. "If the defeasance forms a part of the original transaction, it is not material that it be executed at the same time as the deed."; Cosby v. Buchanan, 81 Ala. 574, 1 So. 898 (1886), agreement subsequent to deed but made in performance of the original agreement by which the deed was executed; Erskine v. Townsend, 2 Mass. 493, 3 Am.Dec. 71 (1807); Waters v. Crabtree, 105 N.C. 394, 11 S.E. 240 (1887), agreement of defeasance made at time of deed but reduced to writing at subsequent time; Van Oehsen v. Brown, 148 Wis. 236, 134 N.W. 377 (1912); Teal v. Walker, 111 U.S. 242, 4 S.Ct. 420, 28 L.Ed. 415 (1884).

5. Williams v. Williams, 270 Ill. 552, 110 N.E. 876 (1915); Ferguson v. Boyd, 169 Ind. 537, 81 N.E. 71 (1907), rehearing denied 169 Ind. 537, 82 N.E. 1064 (1908). See note, 23 Ill.L.Rev. 80 (1928).

6. See Turner, The Equity of Redemption, General Preface, XXXII, XL–XLIV.

7. Sears v. Dixon, 33 Cal. 326 (1867); Ives v. Stone, 51 Conn. 446 (1883); Erskine v. Townsend, 2 Mass. 493, 3 Am.Dec. 71 (1807); Mills v. Darling, 43 Me. 565 (1857). See Williams v. Williams, 270 Ill. 552, 110 N.E. 876 (1915). Equity courts reached the same result. Edrington v. Harper, 3 J.J. Marsh. 353, 20 Am.Dec. 145 (Ky.1830); Hill v. Edwards, 11 Minn. 22, Gil. 5 (1866); Froidevaux v. Jordan, 64 W.Va. 388, 62 S.E. 686, 131 Am.St.Rep. 911 (1908); Williams v. Williams, supra, note 5. Semble, Brown v. Bement, 8 Johns. 96 (N.Y.1811); Dickinson v. Oliver, 195 N.Y. 238, 88 N.E. 44 (1909). See Holmes v. Grant, 8 Paige 243 (N.Y.1840). See also Turner, loc. cit. supra note 6. Here, also, some of the cases say that the transaction is technically not a legal mortgage. Furguson v. Boyd, supra note 5; Williams v. Williams, supra note 5.

8. Warren v. Lovis, 53 Me. 463 (1866); Kelleran v. Brown, 4 Mass. 443 (1808); Lund v. Lund, 1 N.H. 39, 8 Am.Dec. 29 (1817); Fitch v. Miller, 200 Ill. 170, 179, 65 N.E. 650, 653 (1902). See Illinois Trust Co. of Paris v. Bibo, 328 Ill. 252, 257, 159 N.E. 254, 256 (1928).

necessary for the separate instrument to be of an equal dignity with the original conveyance.[9]

Oral evidence can always be introduced to establish the fact that the two instruments really constituted one transaction; the parol evidence rule cannot be invoked to bar its admission since it is "not introduced to contradict or vary the writings, but as showing that the papers constituted one arrangement agreed upon at one and the same time." [10] Indeed, it has been held that, where the separate deed and the qualifying defeasance are one single transaction, parol evidence is inadmissible to show that the transaction was intended as a sale or a conditional sale.[11] And, of course, the Statute of Frauds is inapplicable since the defeasance is in writing.

The foregoing statements of law presuppose that the character of the separate instrument, whether it be in the form of a condition subsequent or a proviso for reconveyance as a clause of defeasance on the performance of a secured obligation, is clear.[12] In such cases the only problem is to show that the two instruments constitute one transaction and are to be construed together. When, however, the separate instrument is cast in the form of a written option or contract to repurchase, the issue is not merely whether the two instruments should be treated as though they had been embodied in one document and to be construed accordingly, but whether what has been stated as, for example, a resale agreement is in actual fact intended by the parties to be quite a different thing, namely, a defeasance clause in a mortgage. A later section deals with this and it suffices here to differentiate it from the simple question whether extrinsic evidence can be used to establish the unity in transaction of the two physically separate writings.

9. See Kelleran v. Brown, 4 Mass. 443 (1808). Cf. Emerson v. Murray, 4 N.H. 171, 17 Am.Dec. 407 (1827); Whitfield v. Parfitt, 4 De G. & Sm. 240 (1851) (a written defeasance on the back of the deed of conveyance, if there when the instrument was executed, will constitute a mortgage at law). See Cunningham & Tischler, Disguised Real Estate Security Transactions As Mortgages in Substance, 26 Rutgers L.Rev. 1, 13 (1972).

10. Reitenbaugh v. Ludwick, 31 Pa.St. 131, 138, 15 L.I. 101 (1858); Sears v. Dixon, 33 Cal. 326 (1867); First National Bank of Florida v. Ashmead, 23 Fla. 379, 2 So. 657 (1887); Cosby v. Buchanan, 81 Ala. 574, 1 So. 898 (1886), accord.

11. Woods v. Wallace, 22 Pa. 171, 1 P.L.J. 130, 2 Am.L.Reg. 186 (1853); Snyder v. Griswold, 37 Ill. 216 (1865). See Haines v. Thomson, 70 Pa. 434, 440 (1872). But see Gassert v. Bogk, 7 Mont. 585, 19 P. 281, 1 L.R.A. 240 (1888), affirmed 149 U.S. 17, 13 S.Ct. 738, 37 L.Ed. 631 (1893).

12. Where there is a conveyance by deed and a condition of defeasance in a collateral paper, any doubt whether the transaction is a mortgage will be resolved in favor of its character as a mortgage. Hennessey v. Rafferty, 326 Ill.App. 259, 61 N.E.2d 409 (1945). N.Y.—McKinney's Real Prop. Law, § 320: "A deed conveying real property, which by any other written instrument, appears to be intended only as a security in the nature of a mortgage, although an absolute conveyance in terms, must be considered a mortgage; and the person for whose benefit such deed is made, derives no advantage from the recording thereof unless every writing, operating as a defeasance of the same, or explanatory of its being desired to have the effect only of a mortgage, or conditional deed, is also recorded therewith, and at the same time." If the defeasance is oral such statutes have been held not applicable. Livesay v. Brown, 35 Neb. 111, 52 N.W. 838 (1892); Kline v. McGuckin, 24 N.J.Eq. 411 (1874).

WESTLAW REFERENCES
266k6081 /2 (absolute /s deed /p reconveyance
/p defeasance)

§ 3.5 The Absolute Deed Coupled With an Oral Understanding—Reasons for Frequent Use

Frequently a debtor will execute an absolute deed of conveyance to his creditor with only an oral understanding that the latter should hold it merely as security only and reconvey it to the grantor when the obligation has been satisfied. For the most part, such transactions are utilized to avoid the strict requirements of the law of mortgages. As our succeeding discussion will indicate, the advantages that are sought to be secured by using such transactions frequently are not obtained. Moreover, substantial dangers and disadvantages lurk in such transactions.

Perhaps the most important reason for utilizing such transactions is the desire to avoid what are perceived to be substantial costs and delays in certain types of foreclosure proceedings. Indeed, recent studies have indicated that judicial foreclosure, especially, can be both time-consuming and expensive.[1] However, the grantee runs the risk of a suit to establish that a mortgage was what was really intended by the parties and, if such a suit is successful, the grantee will be faced with the foreclosure difficulties he sought to avoid. Moreover, since the agreement is not in regular mortgage form, there is always the chance that some step in the foreclosure proceedings may encounter judicial disapproval, as well as the hazard of what the mortgagor may swear to, and the trier of fact believe, as to the terms of the oral mortgage. Finally, if the transaction is established as a mortgage and not an absolute deed, foreclosure inevitably must be judicial because the absolute deed will obviously not contain a power of sale.

The supposed ease of conveying the property to a purchaser if the mortgagor acquiesces in the sale and the capacity for informal enlargement of the mortgage to cover future advances are sometimes advanced as additional advantages for the absolute deed type transaction. As to the former reason, the advantage over usual methods is insubstantial. As to the latter reason, the law of future advances seems sufficiently simple and efficient in most jurisdictions to accomplish legitimate financing functions.[2]

Another reason for the absolute deed transaction hinges upon the deed operating to transfer legal title to the grantee. Grantees in lien theory states may utilize the absolute deed to gain the right to possession prior to default that would otherwise not exist in a normal mortgage transaction. As will be seen, the grantee may find that he

---

§ 3.5

1. See McElhone & Cramer, Loan Foreclosure Costs Affected By Varied State Regulations, Mortgage Banker 41 (December 1975).

2. See § 12.7 infra.

acquired neither title nor the right to possession. Moreover, even if he does get possession, it will not be free from the onerous duty to account in equity—a duty which usually is a substantial deterrent to exercising the right to possession in title jurisdictions where the mortgagee would get that right in a straight mortgage transaction.

Other miscellaneous reasons are sometimes advanced to justify the absolute deed as a financing device. For example, it is occasionally asserted that the absolute deed will enhance the mortgagee's rights to chattels severed from the realty. In addition, some grantees hope that the absolute deed will avoid the normal consequences of the statute of limitations running on the debt. When all of the foregoing reasons are evaluated it seems doubtful whether there are any substantial benefits to be obtained by the grantee-mortgagee in having the transaction framed in this fashion. Yet creditors in large numbers undoubtedly perceive such advantages. Because they do it is necessary to examine the law which governs these absolute deed situations.

Although the absolute deed transaction almost always occurs at the behest of the grantee, this is not uniformly the case. Occasionally, the grantor views such a transaction as an effective mechanism for concealing his equity of redemption from the claims of third party creditors. One Illinois case,[3] where an appellate court determined that an absolute deed constituted an equitable mortgage, is illustrative in this regard. There the grantor, who had experienced frequent financial distress, had borrowed small amounts of money from his brother that were never repaid. When the grantor's financial fortunes deteriorated further, he became fearful that the Internal Revenue Service was about to place a lien on his house and business for unpaid federal taxes. Consequently, he borrowed $1,000 from his brother, apparently in order to gain further forbearance by the IRS. When the brother suggested that the grantor and his spouse execute a mortgage on grantor's house to secure this "loan," the grantor stated: "I don't want to do it that way * * * I will sign the house over to you."[4] Accordingly, the grantor and his spouse executed and delivered a warranty deed to the brother, who promptly recorded it. Later the grantor died and the brother sought to perfect his ownership of his house against the claim of the grantor's surviving spouse that the conveyance was really a security transaction. Ultimately, the Appellate Court of Illinois concluded that "the deed was not evidence of a sale but [the grantor's] alternative way of handling the debt to his brother and dealing with the IRS at the same time."[5]

---

3. Beelman v. Beelman, 121 Ill.App.3d 684, 460 N.E.2d 55 (1984).

4. Id. at 57.

5. Id. at 59. The appellate court rejected the brother's clean hands defense based on the surviving spouse's admission that the deed was intended to conceal assets from the IRS. "Without approving such a tactic, we nevertheless find that the equitable doctrine of clean hands does not bar her claim. If in attempting to shield her property from a tax lien, she intended no harm to [the brother] * * * she may properly invoke the court's equity powers." Id. at 58. Interestingly, other courts have sometimes used the clean hands concept in a variety of contexts to deny retransfer relief where the original transfer was

WESTLAW REFERENCES
266 +1 k35 k36 k37 k38

§ 3.6 Parol Evidence—Admissibility

The case law in this country overwhelmingly establishes that parol evidence is admissible in equity to show that a deed absolute on its face was intended as a mortgage even though it was knowingly cast in that form and its execution was in no way effected by fraud mistake, ignorance, duress or undue influence.[1] In some states statutes authorize proof by parol testimony that such an absolute transfer was a mortgage even though the fact does not appear by the terms of the instrument.[2] Other states reach similar results through their statutory definitions of a mortgage.[3] On the other hand, a few states require that the plaintiff, in order to introduce evidence of the real purpose of the transfer, must allege and prove that the defeasance clause was omitted by reason of "ignorance, mistake, fraud or undue advantage" or some similar ground which would make out a case for reformation in equity.[4]

Moreover, in a few states there are statutory restrictions on the doctrine. Thus, for example, a Georgia statute provides that if the deed is absolute and accompanied by possession of the property, (a circumstance which is both very infrequent in real estate mortgages because ordinarily the reason for mortgaging instead of selling is that the mortgagor wants the use of the property), only "fraud in the procurement" will permit the deed to be established as a mortgage by parol

---

made with the intent to hinder, delay or defraud creditors. See, e.g., Haug v. Haug, 283 App.Div. 1107, 131 N.Y.S.2d 629 (1954); Pattison v. Pattison, 301 N.Y. 65, 92 N.E.2d 890 (1950).

§ 3.6

1. In Pierce v. Robinson, 13 Cal. 116, 125 (1859), a leading and typical case, the court said, "I consider parol evidence admissible in equity, to show that a deed absolute upon its face was intended as a mortgage, and that the restriction of the evidence to cases of fraud, accident, or mistake, in the creation of the instrument, is unsound in principle and unsupported by authority."

See Silas v. Robinson, 131 Ill.App.3d 1058, 87 Ill.Dec. 403, 477 N.E.2d 4 (1985); Havana National Bank v. Wiemer, 32 Ill. App.3d 578, 335 N.E.2d 506 (1975); Schultz v. Schultz, 117 Mich.App. 454, 324 N.W.2d 48 (1982); White v. Ford, 124 N.H. 452, 471 A.2d 1176 (1984); Kartheiser v. Hawkins, 98 Nev. 237, 645 P.2d 967 (1982); French v. Boese, 50 Or.App. 369, 623 P.2d 1070 (1981), review denied 291 Or. 1, 631 P.2d 340 (1981); Bown v. Loveland, 678 P.2d 292 (Utah 1984); Hansen v. Kohler, 550 P.2d

186 (Utah 1976); Burroughs v. Burroughs, 1 Ill.App.3d 697, 274 N.E.2d 376 (1971); Harris v. Kemp, 451 So.2d 1362 (Miss. 1984). Cf. Blumenthal v. Concrete Constructors Company of Albuquerque, Inc., 102 N.M. 125, 692 P.2d 50 (App.1984).

For an excellent consideration of the area, see Cunningham and Tischler, Disguised Real Estate Security Transactions As Mortgages In Substance, 26 Rutgers L.Rev. 1 (1972).

2. E.g., West's Ann.Cal.Civ.Code § 2925. West's Fla.Stat.Ann. § 697.01(1). See Workman Construction Co. v. Weirick, 36 Cal.Rptr. 17, 223 Cal.App.2d 487 (1963); Cinque v. Buschlen, 442 So.2d 1034 (Fla. App.1983); Smith v. Potter, 406 So.2d 1231 (Fla.App.1981).

3. E.g., see 46 Okl.St.Ann. § 1.

4. Poston v. Bowen, 228 N.C. 202, 44 S.E.2d 881 (1947); Jones v. Brinson, 231 N.C. 63, 55 S.E.2d 808 (1949). But see North Carolina's approach to the conditional sale. See § 3.18 infra. See Fogelman, The Deed Absolute as a Mortgage in New York, 32 Fordham L.Rev. 299, 302 (1963).

evidence.[5] Georgia courts, however, will admit parol testimony to establish an absolute deed as a mortgage in those cases where the grantor retains possession of the real estate.[6] The New Hampshire situation is more perplexing. Even though a statute provides that for an instrument to operate as a mortgage the agreement to that effect must be "inserted in the condition of the conveyance and made a part thereof" (thus apparently invalidating even a separate written defeasance),[7] a recent New Hampshire Supreme Court decision,[8] in affirming a trial court determination that a quitclaim deed was intended to be a mortgage, made no reference to the statute and relied on the traditional rule that parol evidence is admissible to establish such mortgage intent.

 WESTLAW REFERENCES
       266 +1 k37(2) k37(3)

§ 3.7 Burden of Proof

While a few decisions suggest that a mere preponderance of the evidence is the requisite burden of proof in establishing that an absolute deed is a mortgage,[1] most courts demand that the evidence be clear and convincing.[2] In the absence of such clear and convincing evidence

---

5. Official Code Georgia Ann. § 44–14–32. Accord, Miss.Code § 89–1–47.

6. See Haynes v. Blackwell, 232 Ga. 430, 207 S.E.2d 66 (1974).

7. N.H.Rev.Stats.Ann., ch. 479:1 and 479:2 (1968). Under the Pennsylvania approach, a separate defeasance "made at the time the deed is made and—in writing, signed and delivered by the grantee in the deed to the grantor" will be given effect although it must be acknowledged and recorded to be effective against any subsequent grantee or mortgagee for value. 21 Pa.S. § 951.

There is early authority that parol evidence can be used to establish an absolute deed as a mortgage only in equity and not in legal actions. Because of the merger of law and equity procedurally in most jurisdictions and other factors, the modern view is that such evidence is admissible whether the proceeding is characterized as legal or equitable. See Osborne, Mortgages, § 73 (2d Ed.1970).

8. White v. Ford, 124 N.H. 452, 471 A.2d 1176 (1984).

§ 3.7

1. Welch v. Thomas, 102 Mont. 591, 61 P.2d 404 (1936). See Campbell, Cas.Morts., 2d ed., 83 n. 1 for a collection of cases. Some of the decisions are not very clear and others are not in harmony with other authorities in the same jurisdiction, e.g., Schmidt v. Barclay, 161 Mich. 1, 125 N.W.

729, 20 Ann.Cas. 1194 (1910), preponderance of evidence is sufficient; Polokoff v. Vebb, 226 Mich. 541, 198 N.W. 194 (1924), "clear, irrefragable and most convincing proof." See Palmer v. Lundy, 293 Ala. 463, 305 So.2d 369 (1974); where the court states that "clear and convincing" is the test, but upholds the finding of a mortgage on a "preponderance of the evidence."

2. See e.g., Silas v. Robinson, 131 Ill. App.3d 1058, 87 Ill.Dec. 403, 477 N.E.2d 4 (1985); McGill v. Biggs, 105 Ill.App.3d 706, 61 Ill.Dec. 417, 434 N.E.2d 772 (1982); White v. Ford, 124 N.H. 452, 471 A.2d 1176 (1984); French v. Boese, 50 Or.App. 369, 623 P.2d 1070 (1981), review denied 291 Or. 1, 631 P.2d 340 (1981); Harris v. Kemp, 451 So.2d 1362 (Miss.1984); Kartheiser v. Hawkins, 98 Nev. 237, 645 P.2d 967 (1982); Bown v. Loveland, 678 P.2d 292 (Utah 1984). Havana National Bank v. Wiemer, 32 Ill.App.3d 578, 335 N.E.2d 506 (1975); Sorenson v. Olson, 235 N.W.2d 892 (N.D.1975); Fry v. D.H. Overmyer Co. Inc., 269 Or. 281, 525 P.2d 140 (1974). See Fogelman, The Deed Absolute As A Mortgage in New York, 32 Ford.L.Rev. 299, 303 (1963); Cunningham and Tischler, Disguised Real Estate Security Transactions As Mortgages In Substance, 26 Rutgers L.Rev. 1, 22–23 (1972). Additional cases attesting the heavy burden upon a claimant in establishing a mortgage transaction by clear and convincing evidence are noted by Updike, Mortgages, in 1956 Annual Surthe presumption that the conveyance is what it purports to be prevails.[3] Indeed, a few cases have required that the evidence of mortgage intent be "very clear" [4] or that it be established "beyond a reasonable doubt." [5]

The reason for the generally heavy burden of proof on the party attempting to establish the absolute deed as a mortgage is understandable. There is a general interest in enhancing the security of written real estate transactions and a particular interest in discouraging false swearing by unscrupulous grantors who regret their bargains and seek to avoid them by "redeeming" the property. Moreover, the prevailing burden of proof discourages debtors who wish to conceal their equity in the property from creditors by putting the apparently complete "title" in the name of the mortgagee. Finally, although the absolute deed intended as a mortgage is a frequent occurrence, the great bulk of absolute deed transactions are exactly what they purport to be, final and complete transfers. Consequently, the requirement of greater proof than is usually required in civil cases seems justified.

While most attempts to establish an absolute deed as a mortgage will be by the grantor-mortgagor, this is not universally the case. Occasionally, the grantee-mortgagee also finds it advantageous to have a deed declared a mortgage. For example, suppose that the value of the deeded land has dropped so significantly that its value is lower than the debt owing to the grantee-mortgagee. Moreover, suppose that the grantor-mortgagor has enough assets to satisfy any personal liability on a mortgage debt. In such a situation, the attractiveness of a deficiency judgment against the grantor-mortgagor may well encourage the grantee-mortgagee to establish that what appears to be an absolute conveyance is actually a debt transaction.

It may also sometimes be advantageous for a grantee-mortgagee to assert mortgagee status against third parties. Suppose, for example, a third party is injured on the "deeded" real estate and asserts that as a "landowner," the grantee either acted negligently or, in some other manner, failed to perform duties imposed by law upon an owner.[6] At this stage a grantee-mortgagee may well be eager to eschew ownership for the benefits of a mortgagee status because unless a mortgagee is a

---

vey of American Law, 32 N.Y.U.L.Rev. 789 (1957). See also Karesh, Security Transactions, in Survey of South Carolina Law, 8 S.C.L.Q. 122 (1955); Note, The Equitable Mortgage in Kansas, 5 U. of Kan.L.Rev. 114, 116 (1956); Young, Parol Evidence and Texas Deeds: Some Current Problems, 34 Texas L.Rev. 351, 360 (1956). See Stolk v. Lucas, 146 Cal.App.2d 417, 304 P.2d 33 (1956), and Evans v. Evans, 226 S.C. 451, 85 S.E.2d 726 (1955), which are in accord. So also are Howard v. Steen, 230 S.C. 351, 95 S.E.2d 613 (1956), noted in Karesh, Security Transactions, in Survey of South Carolina Law, 10 S.C.L.Q. 114, 115 (1957); Kohler v. Gilbert, 216 Or. 483, 339 P.2d 1102

(1959); Child v. Child, 8 Utah 2d 261, 332 P.2d 981 (1958).

3. See e.g., Peerless Construction Co. v. Mancini, 96 A.D.2d 666, 466 N.Y.S.2d 497 (1983), appeal denied 61 N.Y.2d 601, 471 N.Y.S.2d 1028, 459 N.E.2d 1291 (1983). Wile v. Donovan, 538 S.W.2d 906 (Mo.App. 1976).

4. See Schultz v. Schultz, 117 Mich. App. 454, 324 N.W.2d 48 (1982).

5. E.g. Rinkel v. Lubke, 246 Mo. 377, 152 S.W. 81 (1912).

6. See generally, Prosser Torts §§ 57–64 (1971).

"mortgagee in possession" or otherwise exercises dominion and control over the mortgaged premises, there normally will be no liability to third parties for unsafe conditions on those premises.[7]

Although there is authority to the effect that the same degree of proof is required whether the grantor or the grantee seeks to have the deed declared a mortgage,[8] it can be argued that a heavier burden of proof should be required of a grantee who seeks to establish the transaction as a mortgage. After all, it is the mortgagee who in all probability required that the transaction be framed in absolute deed terminology rather than in the traditional mortgage format. Thus it only seems fair that the mortgagee bear a heavier burden than would a grantor in establishing that the transaction was not what she made it appear to be.

 WESTLAW REFERENCES
266k38

§ 3.8   Factors Establishing an Absolute Deed as a Mortgage

The most important factor in determining whether an absolute deed is a mortgage is whether there is an indebtedness on the part of the grantor to the grantee left unaffected by the conveyance.[1] The debt may either have existed prior to the conveyance or have arisen from a loan made contemporaneous with the conveyance. As one excellent article has pointed out, "[p]roof of a pre-existing debt from grantor to grantee justifies concluding that the deed was given either in satisfaction of the debt or as security therefor. But where no written satisfaction of the debt has been executed and it can be shown that the parties

---

7. See Marcon v. First Federal Savings & Loan Association, 58 Ill.App.3d 811, 16 Ill.Dec. 253, 374 N.E.2d 1028 (1978). See generally infra § 4.26. For a recent example of grantee success in establishing mortgagee status as against a third party, see Smith v. Fried, 98 Ill.App.3d 467, 53 Ill. Dec. 845, 424 N.E.2d 636 (1981).

8. See e.g., Holman v. Mason City Auto Co., 186 Iowa 704, 171 N.W. 12 (1919). Cf. Downs v. Ziegler, 13 Ariz.App. 387, 477 P.2d 261 (1970).

§ 3.8

1. Palmer v. Lundy, 293 Ala. 463, 305 So.2d 369 (1974); Todd v. Todd, 164 Cal. 255, 128 P. 413 (1912); Anglo-Californian Bank Limited v. Cerf, 147 Cal. 384, 81 P. 1077 (1905), future advances as well as existing indebtedness; Holmberg v. Hardee, 90 Fla. 787, 108 So. 211 (1926); Beelman v. Beelman, 121 Ill.App.3d 684, 460 N.E.2d 55 (1984); McGill v. Biggs, 105

Ill.App.3d 706, 61 Ill.Dec. 417, 434 N.E.2d 772 (1982); Holman v. Mason City Auto Co., 186 Iowa 704, 171 N.W. 12 (1919) (retention in grantee's possession, without cancellation, of written evidence of debt raises strong presumption of mortgage) Thomas v. Klemm, 185 Md. 136, 43 A.2d 193 (1945); Dean v. Smith, 53 N.D. 123, 204 N.W. 987 (1924); Corey v. Roberts, 82 Utah 445, 25 P.2d 940 (1933); Bown v. Loveland, 678 P.2d 292 (Utah 1984); Hunter v. Bane, 153 Va. 165, 149 S.E. 467 (1929) ("a mortgage without debt to support it is a legal solecism"); Hofmeister v. Hunter, 230 Wis. 81, 283 N.W. 330, 121 A.L.R. 444 (1939). See Fogelman, The Deed Absolute as a Mortgage in New York, 32 Fordham L.Rev. 299, 305, 306 (1963).

See also When Is an Absolute Conveyance a Mortgage, 8 U. of Fla.L.Rev. 132 (1955), discussing Rosenthall v. LeMay, 72 So.2d 289 (Fla.1954).

have behaved as though the debt continued after the execution of the deed, it is clear that the deed was given as security not in satisfaction of the debt." [2] On the other hand, "[w]here there is no pre-existing debt and the grantee paid value for the land, the amount paid by the grantee can be regarded either as purchase money or as a loan. But where it can be shown that the parties thereafter behaved like debtor and creditor, it is clear that the transaction was a loan on security rather than an absolute sale." [3]

Another significant factor is the adequacy of the amount paid by the grantee as purported consideration for the transfer. If the value of the property is substantially greater than the amount advanced by the grantee this constitutes strong evidence that what was paid was a loan rather than purchase price and therefore there is a strong inference that the transaction was a mortgage.[4] On the other hand, if there is no great disparity between the value of the land and the amount paid, this tends to indicate that the transfer was a sale.[5]

Retention of possession of the land by the grantor also cuts in favor of finding a mortgage transaction.[6] While it is conceivable that a grantor could sell his interest in his real estate and retain possession as a lessee,[7] the retention of possession by the grantor at least indicates that he retained some interest in the deeded real estate. Moreover, when retention of possession is coupled with substantial improvements to the real estate, the grantor's case becomes even stronger. In any

2. Cunningham and Tischler, Disguised Real Estate Security Transactions As Mortgages in Substance, 26 Rutgers L.Rev. 1, 15 (1972).

3. Id. at 15.

4. Silas v. Robinson, 131 Ill.App.3d 1058, 87 Ill.Dec. 403, 477 N.E.2d 4 (1985); Harris v. Kemp, 451 So.2d 1362 (Miss. 1984); Horn v. Ketaltas, 46 N.Y. 605, 42 How.Pr. 138 (1871). Burroughs v. Burroughs, 1 Ill.App.3d 697, 274 N.E.2d 376 (1971); White v. Ford, 124 N.H. 452, 471 A.2d 1176 (1984); The authorities to this effect are numerous. For collections of authorities, see, 90 A.L.R. 1504 (1934); 129 A.L.R. 1504 (1940). See also Fogelman, The Deed Absolute as a Mortgage in New York, 32 Fordham L.Rev. 299, 307 (1963). So too, the negotiations and conduct of the parties which lead to the "deed" are significant in reaching a conclusion as to the character of the transaction. Ibid. The absence of disproportion between the value of the land and the expressed consideration is evidence that the transaction is not a mortgage. Howard v. Steen, 230 S.C. 531, 95 S.E.2d 613 (1956), noted in Karesh, Security Transactions in Survey of South Carolina Law, 10 S.C.L.Q. 114, 115 (1957).

5. See Baker v. Taggert, 628 P.2d 1283 (Utah 1981). Conway v. Alexander, 11

U.S. (7 Cranch) 218, 3 L.Ed. 321 (1812). So, too, if the grantor made a highly advantageous disposition of his interest by the transaction this indicates that the deed was intended to be absolute. Vinquist v. Siegert, 58 N.D. 820, 227 N.W. 556 (1929).

6. Harris v. Kemp, 451 So.2d 1362 (Miss.1984); White v. Ford, 124 N.H. 452, 471 A.2d 1176 (1984). See Fogelman, The Deed Absolute as a Mortgage In New York, 32 Ford.L.Rev. 299, 308 (1963) (discussing the significance of retention of possession by the grantor and miscellaneous factors in the transaction).

7. Hopper v. Smyser, 90 Md. 363, 45 A. 206 (1900), in which payment of taxes by the grantee together with transfer of possession to him, making improvements by him and no accounting of any income or recognition of any debt or payment of interest proved that no mortgage existed. Possession in the grantor may be explained by his having taken a lease back. Pancake v. Cauffman, 114 Pa.St. 113, 7 A. 67 (1886); Brickle v. Leach, 55 S.C. 510, 33 S.E. 720 (1899); Edwards v. Wall, 79 Va. 321 (1884). On the other hand, a lease back to the grantor is not conclusive that the conveyance is not a mortgage. See Rogers v. Davis, 91 Iowa 730, 59 N.W. 265 (1894); Bearss v. Ford, 108 Ill. 16 (1883).

event, when retention of possession is coupled with favorable evidence based on the two factors discussed previously, the grantor's case becomes strong indeed.

Several other factors provide evidence that the transaction was a mortgage: the grantee was a money-lender by occupation; [8] the grantee was not in the business of buying and selling property of the description conveyed; [9] the fact that the transferor was in financial difficulties at the time of the execution of the conveyance, (even though this might instead indicate a forced sale if it stood by itself); [10] prior negotiations for a loan from the grantee of approximately the amount paid; [11] payment of taxes by the grantor subsequent to the deed; [12] and the grantor was unrepresented by counsel. [13]

McGill v. Biggs, [14] a recent Appellate Court of Illinois decision, provides a poignant, as well as useful, illustration of the application of several of the foregoing factors. In that case, McGill, whose mother had just died, lacked sufficient funds to pay for her funeral. He asked Biggs, a half uncle, to accompany him in an attempt to borrow money from local lenders. This attempt failed, and after Biggs indicated that he would provide the funeral money, the two went to Biggs' attorney's office. There McGill executed a warranty deed conveying to Biggs a $15,000 house that McGill had just inherited from his mother. Biggs then paid the $1,473.75 funeral bill. McGill apparently believed that he could get the house back by paying Biggs 15 monthly installments of $115. After making one payment, McGill lost his job and suffered from frequent bouts of heavy drinking. Over the next two years, while McGill lived in the house sporadically, Biggs made no attempt to take possession. Ultimately when McGill discovered that Biggs was attempting to use a real estate broker to rent the house, he contacted an attorney for the first time and the latter filed suit to quiet title in the house in McGill. The trial court ruled that a debt relationship existed between the parties and that the warranty deed was intended to be a mortgage. It entered an order allowing McGill to redeem by paying the balance due on the amount advanced by Biggs for the funeral bill. The Appellate Court of Illinois affirmed and emphasized several factors: McGill clearly was in desperate financial straits at the time of the deed transaction; he had made previous unsuccessful attempts to borrow the money from others; he executed the warranty deed only after Biggs

---

8. Haggerty v. Brower, 105 Iowa 395, 75 N.W. 321 (1898).

9. Desloge v. Ranger, 7 Mo. 327 (1842).

10. White v. Ford, 124 N.H. 452, 471 A.2d 1176 (1984); Lewis v. Wells, 85 F. 896 (D.C.Alaska 1898); Smith v. Berry, 155 Ky. 686, 160 S.W. 247 (1913).

11. Couts v. Winston, 153 Cal. 686, 96 P. 357 (1908); Evans v. Thompson, 89 Minn. 202, 94 N.W. 692 (1903); Macauley v. Smith, 132 N.Y. 524, 30 N.E. 997 (1892).

12. McGill v. Biggs, 105 Ill.App.3d 706, 61 Ill.Dec. 417, 434 N.E.2d 772 (1982); King v. Crone, 114 Ark. 121, 169 S.W. 238 (1914); Hart v. Randolph, 142 Ill. 521, 32 N.E. 517 (1892). See Karesh, Security Transactions, in Survey of South Carolina Law, 10 S.C.L.Q. 114, 115 (1957).

13. Burroughs v. Burroughs, 1 Ill.App. 3d 697, 274 N.E.2d 376 (1971).

14. 105 Ill.App.3d 706, 61 Ill.Dec. 417, 434 N.E.2d 772 (1982).

told him that a deed would be required as "collateral"; Biggs testified that the parties came to an agreement that McGill would sell the house to Biggs for the amount of the funeral bill and then pay Biggs $115 per month for 15 months to get it back; the house was never advertised or offered for sale by McGill; McGill had been unrepresented by counsel; the house "sold" for ten percent of its market value; Biggs never took possession; and McGill continued to pay real estate taxes on the house. Under these circumstances, the appellate court concluded that "the trial judge was correct in finding that a debt relationship existed and that the warranty deed to Biggs was a mortgage." [15]

 WESTLAW REFERENCES
266k32 absolute /s deed /p mortgage

§ 3.9 Effect of Absolute Deed Between the Parties

Whenever an absolute deed is established as a mortgage, it will be treated, as between the parties, as if it were a mortgage executed in regular form. All the rights and obligations of the mortgage relationship bind the parties.[1] Thus the grantor may maintain an action to redeem.[2] Moreover, even though the grantee obtains possession he will be treated as a mortgagee in possession and be accountable as such.[3] Correspondingly, the grantee may maintain an action to foreclose the grantor's redemption right.[4] This result flows, of course, from the general doctrine that the right to foreclose, like the right to redeem or to compel an accounting, does not depend on any provision in the mortgage, but is simply one of the legal consequences flowing from the

15. Id. at 420, 434 N.E.2d at 775. Because the appellate court at one point states the issue as "whether the deed was absolute with a contract back to purchase, or whether it was intended as a mortgage to secure repayment of the funeral bill," the case is arguably susceptible of being classified as a "conditional sale" rather than a simple "absolute deed as mortgage" type case. See § 3.17 infra. However, at no point does the court refer to, much less analyze, an option to repurchase. Moreover, the thrust of the opinion itself not only repeatedly emphasizes the absolute deed as mortgage concept, the structure of the opinion is consistent with that mode of analysis. In any event, even if it is assumed that *McGill* is a conditional sale case, it is nevertheless worthy of emphasis here because the factors that influence finding a mortgage in both types of cases are substantially similar. See § 3.19, infra.

§ 3.9

1. Carr v. Carr, 52 N.Y. 251, 258 (1873). As to differences between a mortgage by deed absolute and a straight form mortgage, see Note, 28 Neb.L.Rev. 481 (1949).

2. Campbell v. Dearborn, 109 Mass. 130, 12 Am.Rep. 671 (1872). A large proportion of the cases brought to establish that the absolute deed was intended as a mortgage are cases of this sort and will be found in other footnotes.

3. Husheon v. Husheon, 71 Cal. 407, 12 P. 410 (1886); Murdock v. Clark, 90 Cal. 427, 27 P. 275 (1891); Miller v. Peter, 158 Mich. 336, 122 N.W. 780 (1909); Pratt v. Pratt, 121 Wash. 298, 209 P. 535, 28 A.L.R. 548 (1922). Cf., Barnard v. Jennison, 27 Mich. 230 (1873) (the duty to account is not so stringent as in the case of the ordinary mortgagee in possession).

4. Shadman v. O'Brien, 278 Mass. 579, 180 N.E. 532 (1932); Hughes v. Edwards, 22 U.S. (9 Wheat.) 489, 495, 6 L.Ed. 142 (1824). For other cases holding that a deed absolute intended as security may be foreclosed in equity as a mortgage, see, 22 L.R.A.,N.S., 572 (1909).

general mortgage relationship. Nevertheless, there is authority that this general doctrine will not apply to permit strict foreclosure of a deed absolute mortgage.[5] Moreover, since foreclosure by the exercise of a power of sale is permitted only when such a power has been expressly provided for in the mortgage itself;[6] and since a mortgage in the form of an absolute deed obviously does not contain such a power, this method of foreclosure is unavailable.

 WESTLAW REFERENCES
266k3* & absolute /s deed /p mortgage trust

§ 3.10   Grantee's Title

A difference of opinion exists as to whether the grantee under an absolute deed intended as a mortgage gets a "title" type interest in the property different from that received when the regular mortgage form is used. In title theory states the mortgagee gets legal title when the deed is in the form of a conveyance with a defeasance clause and *a fortiori* would get a like interest where the defeasance clause is omitted but nevertheless the conveyance is for security purposes.[1] On the other hand, if the jurisdiction follows the lien theory, it makes a difference in several contexts whether the deed absolute grantee gets title with the mortgagor having only an equitable interest or whether the result is precisely the same as though the conventional form of mortgage was employed. There is substantial authority for the view that the grantee under a deed absolute intended as a mortgage gets only a lien with the grantor retaining title.[2] Nevertheless, there are decisions to the effect

5. Libel v. Pierce, 147 Or. 132, 31 P.2d 1106 (1934). But cf. Northwestern State Bank of Hay Springs v. Hanks, 122 Neb. 262, 240 N.W. 281 (1932); and see § 7.10 infra. In Hermann v. Churchill, 235 Or. 327, 385 P.2d 190 (1963), in a suit to have a deed absolute declared a mortgage, the court decreed strict foreclosure in spite of ORS 88.010 providing that liens upon real property shall be foreclosed and the property sold by judicial sale.

6. See § 7.19 infra.

§ 3.10

1. Finlon v. Clark, 118 Ill. 32, 7 N.E. 475 (1886).

2. Jackson v. Lodge, 36 Cal. 28 (1868); West's Ann. California Civil Code §§ 2888, 2924, 2925, and 2927; Brandt v. Thompson, 91 Cal. 458, 27 P. 763 (1891); Shirey v. All Night and Day Bank, 166 Cal. 50, 134 P. 1001 (1913); Hulsman v. Deal, 90 Kan. 716, 136 P. 220 (1913); Flynn v. Holmes, 145 Mich. 606, 108 N.W. 685, 11 L.R.A.,N.S., 209 (1906); Shattuck v. Bascom, 105 N.Y. 39, 12 N.E. 283 (1887); Christy v. Camp-

bell, 57 Or.App. 491, 645 P.2d 573 (1982), review denied 293 Or. 483, 650 P.2d 928 (1982). Snyder v. Parker, 19 Wash. 276, 53 P. 59, 67 Am.St.Rep. 726 (1898); Clambey v. Copeland, 52 Wash. 580, 100 P. 1031 (1909); Pratt v. Pratt, 121 Wash. 298, 209 P. 535, 28 A.L.R. 548 (1922); Dobbs v. Kellogg, 53 Wis. 448, 10 N.W. 623 (1881). A deed absolute mortgage is not an alienation of the title within the meaning of fire insurance policies. Barry v. Hamburg-Bremen Fire Insurance Co., 110 N.Y. 1, 17 N.E. 405 (1888). Cf. Modlin v. Atlantic Fire Insurance Co., 151 N.C. 35, 65 S.E. 605 (1909). See note, 11 L.R.A.,N.S., 209 (1906) for a collection of additional cases as well as cases holding that the grantee gets legal title. See also 28 A.L.R. 554 (1924); Herron v. Millers National Ins. Co., 185 F.Supp. 851 (D.C.Or.1960); See Fogelman, The Deed Absolute as a Mortgage in New York, 32 Fordham L.Rev. 299, 310 (1963), on the effect of a deed absolute as creating only a lien in New York. Note, 43 Or.L. Rev. 350, 353 (1964).

that the mortgagee under a deed absolute in a lien jurisdiction does get title.[3]

In considering the merits of the question, the parties arguably should not be able to alter the legal character and incidents of the mortgage as developed in a lien jurisdiction simply by omitting the defeasance clause. When the defeasance clause remains in, the deed purports to pass the title but lien theory courts, as we have seen, refuse to recognize the passage of title. The same result should follow, regardless of the desires of the parties, once it is established that the intent was to create a mortgage. To hold otherwise would permit the parties to reinstitute the title theory in a lien jurisdiction by merely using a different form. On the other hand, a deed absolute intended as a mortgage and a regular mortgage should not always be treated alike. The latter sets forth the real nature of the transaction; it reveals on its face that there is a property interest—the redemption right—left in the transferor. The former falsely depicts the actual transaction, leaving the true situation to be revealed by oral testimony. They are therefore sufficiently different, certainly as to third parties and to some extent as between the parties, to justify the application of different rules. The straightforward way of dealing with the problem would be to focus on the extent to which and in whose favor the usual rights created by a mortgage should be modified by reason of the deceptive form in which the transaction has been cast. Instead, the courts have been somewhat inclined to adopt a mechanical attitude and let the solution flow from a determination of whether the grantee got "title" rather than a "lien," or whether the parol evidence would be admissible at law or only in equity. Since in most cases, a desirable result will be reached using this type of reasoning, the only criticism that can be leveled at the cases which concern themselves with whether a deed absolute intended as a mortgage conveys the legal title to the grantee is their mode of reasoning.

3. See Moore v. Linville, 170 Ind.App. 429, 352 N.E.2d 846 (1976), (grantee-mortgagee successful in an ejectment action to obtain possession against a grantor-mortgagor in possession); Woodson v. Veal, 60 Ga. 562 (1878); Gibson v. Hough, 60 Ga. 588 (1878); Shumate v. McLendon, 120 Ga. 396, 48 S.E. 10 (1904); Ferguson v. Boyd, 169 Ind. 537, 81 N.E. 71 (1907), rehearing denied 196 Ind. 537, 82 N.E. 1064 (1908); Burdick v. Wentworth, 42 Iowa 440 (1876); Baxter v. Pritchard, 122 Iowa 590, 98 N.W. 372, 101 Am.St.Rep. 282 (1904) (mortgagor's interest being purely equitable may be surrendered by parol); Lindberg v. Thomas, 137 Iowa 48, 114 N.W. 562 (1908); Williams v. Williams, 270 Ill. 552, 110 N.E. 876 (1915) (deed absolute with separate written agreement to reconvey, grantor's interest only equitable and therefore transferable without a deed). Illinois, however, is a hybrid state; First National Bank of Plattsmouth v. Tighe, 49 Neb. 299, 68 N.W. 490 (1896) (mortgagor's interest being equitable a judgment lien does not attach to it); First National Bank of David City v. Spelts, 94 Neb. 387, 143 N.W. 218 (1913); Northwestern State Bank v. Hanks, 122 Neb. 262, 240 N.W. 281 (1932), (mortgagee entitled to strict foreclosure since he had title); Hall v. O'Connell, 52 Or. 164, 95 A. 717, (1908), modified on rehearing 52 Or. 164, 96 P. 1070 (1908); dissenting opinion, Pratt v. Pratt, 121 Wash. 298, 209 P. 535, 28 A.L.R. 548 (1922) (conveyance from third party and therefore, if grantee got only a lien, it was argued that the third party would still have title, and the mortgagor would have an anomalous right); Beebe v. Wisconsin Mortgage Loan Co., 117 Wis. 328, 93 N.W. 1103 (1903).

The cases in which the courts have raised the question of title include actions for possession by the grantee-lender, assertion of rights in severed crops, timber or fixtures against third parties, the ability of creditors to reach the interest of the grantor by legal process, the formalities necessary for the transfer or surrender of the grantor's interest, and whether the running of the statute of limitations on the debt will prevent foreclosure of the property as a mortgage.[4] In a case of the last type the question was complicated by the fact that the deed absolute came to the creditor from a third party and thus present the difficulty in a lien state of getting title into the borrower-mortgagor who did not appear in the deed or on the record.[5] A separate section is devoted to this tripartite type of transaction [6] and the question of whether the running of the statute of limitations on the obligation secured should affect the mortgage is considered later and therefore will not occupy us here.[7] However it should be emphasized here that the question of whether the running of the statute of limitations on the debt should bar the enforcement of the mortgage should not depend upon any legalistic distinction as to whether the mortgagee got a lien or a title by using regular form mortgage, and even less upon whether in a lien jurisdiction a deed absolute gave the creditor a lien or title as security, but rather upon an examination of the desirability of permitting the enforcement of the security to survive the barring of a direct action to enforce the obligation secured. Upon this there are different views.[8] Moreover, since the security rests in an oral understanding, the remedy to enforce it, regardless of the effect upon it of the debt being barred, arguably may be governed by a different statutory period than where it is in writing.[9]

 WESTLAW REFERENCES
synopsis,digest(mortgag***) & deed /s absolute /p

§ 3.11 Rights of Grantor on Sale by the Grantee

Even courts in lien jurisdictions which, in other contexts, hold that a grantee under a deed absolute obtains only a lien, agree that a bona fide purchaser from the grantee will prevail over the grantor.[1] A

4. See cases cited in the preceding footnotes.

5. Pratt v. Pratt, 121 Wash. 298, 209 P. 535 (1922). See notes, 8 Cornell L.Q. 172 (1923); 71 U. of Pa.L.Rev. 284 (1923); 32 Yale L.J. 611 (1923). See also 28 A.L.R. 554 (1924); 11 L.R.A.,N.S., 209, 825 (1908). See also Coutts, Does a Mortgagee under Deed Absolute in Form Gain Rights Not Incident to an Ordinary Mortgage? 52 Cent.L.J. 360 (1901).

6. See §§ 3.20–3.25, infra.

7. See § 6.11, infra.

8. See note 6, supra.

9. Although there is some authority to the contrary, the general rule is that the equitable rule as to laches may bar the grantor from establishing that the deed absolute was a mortgage even though the delay on his part was short of the statute of limitations period. See 28 A.L.R. 554.

§ 3.11

1. Mooney v. Byrne, 163 N.Y. 86, 57 N.E. 163 (1900). See, 32 L.R.A.,N.S., 1046; L.R.A.1916B, 584 (1911). Macauley v. Smith, 132 N.Y. 524, 30 N.E. 997 (1892); Meehan v. Forrester, 52 N.Y. 277 (1873); Pancake v. Cauffman, 114 Pa. 113, 7 A. 67 (1886); Harrington v. Butte & Superior fortiori, in a title jurisdiction a purchaser from the grantee for value and without notice that the property has been conveyed for security will hold the land free from any equity of the grantor to redeem.[2] This result, apart from statute, rests upon the doctrine that a bona fide purchase of the legal title cuts off equitable rights. Thus, the cases preferring the bona fide purchaser are usually cited as establishing that the deed absolute gives to the grantee the full legal title and leaves only an equitable interest in the grantor.[3] In many states, statutes provide that the bona fide purchaser prevails unless a separate defeasance has been recorded.[4] Arguably, an equally valid basis for preferring the purchaser is that because the grantor apparently vested complete title in the grantee, she will be estopped to deny it as against the purchaser. Such an approach would have the virtue of avoiding the problem of whether the grantee acquired title rather than a lien.

Even though the mortgagor's rights in the land may have been cut off by the sale to a bona fide purchaser, he "is not prevented by that wrongful act from any form of redemption now practicable. * * * In order to prevent him [the grantee] from making a profit out of his wrong, the law raises the presumption that he now has the full value of the land as a separate fund in his hands, and, treating it as land, allows the plaintiff to redeem. * * *[5] Thus, the mortgagor's basic measure of recovery is the difference between the value of the land and the mortgage debt. However, the date of valuation of the land has been held variously to be the date of the sale,[6] the tender of payment[7] and the redemption action.[8] Arguably, the fairest approach is to afford the mortgagor the right to elect the date of valuation, "since any transfer of the land by [the mortgagee] which cuts off the mortgagor's right of redemption is a plain breach of [the mortgagee's] duty to hold it as security."[9] Finally, he is always entitled, at his election, to take the proceeds realized by the sale.[10] However, it should be noted again, that even though the action will bring only money to the plaintiff, it is an

Copper Co., 52 Mont. 263, 157 P. 181 (1916). The grantor's rights continue against a grantee with notice. Graham v. Graham, 55 Ind. 23 (1876); Hadley v. Stewart, 65 Wis. 481, 27 N.W. 340 (1886). Where the grantor under a deed absolute intended as a mortgage remains in possession, he may prove his equity by parol evidence against the grantee and also against a purchaser for value from him who had no actual notice of the occupant-grantor's equity and made no inquiry of him. Williamson v. Floyd C. Wildlife Association, Inc., 215 Ga. 789, 113 S.E.2d 626 (1960), noted by Smith, Security Transactions, 12 Mercer L.Rev. 182, 188 (1960).

2. Hogan v. Jacques, 19 N.J.Eq. 123, 97 Am.Dec. 644 (1868).

3. See Walsh, Mortgages, 37; 5 Pomeroy, Equity Juris., 5th ed., 587.

4. See, e.g., West's Ann.Cal.Civ.Code, § 2950; Carpenter v. Lewis, 119 Cal. 18, 50 P. 925 (1898); Payne v. Morey, 144 Cal. 130, 77 P. 83 (1904). See also Jones, Mortgages, 8th Ed., §§ 304, 631.

5. Mooney v. Byrne, 163 N.Y. 86, 95, 57 N.E. 163, 166 (1900).

6. Staples v. Barret, 214 Ala. 680, 108 So. 742, 46 A.L.R. 1084 (1926); Brimie v. Benson, 216 Ill.App. 474 (1920).

7. Clark v. Morris, 88 Kan. 752, 129 P. 1195 (1913). See note, 13 Col.L.Rev. 442 (1913).

8. Mooney v. Byrne, supra note 5; Boothe v. Feist, 80 Tex. 141, 15 S.W. 799 (1891).

9. Note, 13 Col.L.Rev. 442, 443 (1913).

10. Staples v. Barret, supra, note 90; Shillaber v. Robinson, 97 U.S. 68, 24 L.Ed.

action to redeem land from a mortgage and not to recover money. Consequently the statute of limitations fixing the time within which to bring an action to redeem governs.

 WESTLAW REFERENCES
synopsis,digest(mortgag it ***) & deed /s absolute /p grantee

§ 3.12   Creditors of Grantee

Where recording statutes are inapplicable, the grantor arguably should prevail over creditors of the grantee, the theory being that creditors merely stand in the shoes of their debtors.[1] Moreover, even where there is a statute requiring recordation of a defeasance when the mortgage is by deed absolute, there is authority that in the absence of an express provision that non-compliance will defeat the grantor as against creditors of the grantee, the statute will not be construed to so operate.[2] On the other hand, in some jurisdictions, where the absolute deed is accompanied by an unrecorded collateral defeasance, "creditors of the creditor-grantee obtaining judgments against him while he is record owner will obtain liens valid as against the debtor-grantor." [3]

 WESTLAW REFERENCES
(deed /s trust) (deed /s absolute /p defeasance) mortgage /p
grantee /p creditor

§ 3.13   The Absolute Deed as a Fraudulent Conveyance

Regular form mortgages are routinely set aside in a variety of contexts when they are used as a vehicle to defraud creditors.[1] Suppose, for example, there is no mortgage debt or it is smaller than the mortgage otherwise indicates. In either case, the extent of the mortgagor's true interest in the land is concealed and the mortgagor's other creditors may thus be unaware of their ability to proceed against it. However, when the mortgage format is used, cooperation by the mortgagee in fabricating or misstating the mortgage debt is usually necessary to accomplish the purpose and this may very well be difficult to obtain.

The absolute deed, however, unlike its regular mortgage counterpart, is almost always inherently deceptive vis à vis the grantor's other

967 (1877); Meehan v. Forrester, 52 N.Y. 277 (1873).

§ 3.12

1. Vallely v. First National Bank of Grafton, 14 N.D. 580, 106 N.W. 127, 5 L.R.A.,N.S., 387, 116 Am.St.Rep. 700 (1905). On the question of priorities of an equitable mortgagee against creditors of the mortgagor, an analogous problem, see Welton v. Tizzard, 15 Iowa 495 (1864).

2. See preceding footnote.

3. Cunningham and Tischler, Disguised Real Estate Security Transactions as Mortgages in Substance, 26 Rutgers L.Rev. 1, 26–27 (1972). See N.J.Stat.Ann. 46:22–1.

§ 3.13

1. See e.g., In re Colandrea, 17 B.R. 568 (Bkrtcy.Md.1982); Clarke v. Selben Apartments, Inc., 225 App.Div. 290, 233 N.Y.S. 22 (1929); Butts v. Peacock, 23 Wis. 359 (1868); Jones v. Third National Bank of Sedalia, 13 F.2d 86 (C.C.A.Mo.1926).

creditors. Particularly, where the grantor does not retain possession of the land, the recording of an absolute deed operates to conceal one of his assets from his creditors. Clearly, if such a device is used with the cooperation of the grantee to hinder, delay or defraud grantor's present or future creditors, it will be deemed void as to those creditors.[2] Some courts have held that a grantee who is a party to an actual fraudulent design in an absolute deed situation not only loses the property to the creditors of the grantor, but has no right to reimbursement for the amount loaned when the conveyance is set aside.[3] Usually, however, the grantee requires the use of the absolute deed without collusion with the grantor and for reasons unrelated to the concealment of assets from other creditors of the grantor. Nevertheless, some courts treat absolute deed mortgages as constructively fraudulent and, as a matter of law, void even as security, not only as to subsequent but also as to prior creditors.[4]

On the other hand, other courts take a more flexible approach. Some hold that the transaction cast in this form is a "badge of fraud," not conclusive, but capable of rebuttal by proof of the actual good faith of the parties.[5] Other decisions require actual fraudulent intent to be established as a fact.[6] In New Jersey, for example, the absolute deed is not fraudulent unless both the grantor and the grantee intended to use that device instead of a regular mortgage to conceal the grantor's equity of redemption from his creditors.[7] Finally, it should be noted that if the grantor had actual fraudulent intent, some courts, as we noted earlier,[8] may use the clean hands concept to deny the grantor the equitable remedy of redemption against the grantee.

 WESTLAW REFERENCES
mortgage (deed /s absolute trust) /s fraud! /p hinder delay defraud

§ 3.14 Recordation

There is diverse opinion as to whether and where a deed absolute mortgage may be recorded effectively. It has been held that it is unrecordable as either a deed or a mortgage and consequently is invalid

---

2. See Uniform Fraudulent Conveyance Act § 7.

3. Svalina v. Saravana, 341 Ill. 236, 173 N.E. 281, 87 A.L.R. 821 (1930).

4. Bryant v. Young, 21 Ala. 264 (1852). See Fogelman, The Deed Absolute as a Mortgage in New York, 32 Fordham L.Rev. 299, 312 (1963).

5. McClure v. Smith, 14 Colo. 297, 23 P. 786 (1890), and Hanneman v. Olson, 209 Iowa 372, 222 N.W. 566 (1928) (badge of fraud but not conclusive).

6. Capital Lumber Co. v. Saunders, 26 Idaho 408, 143 P. 1178 (1914); Hutchison v. Page, 246 Ill. 71, 92 N.E. 571 (1910). See note, 2 Am.L.Reg.,N.S., 1, 11 (1862). See also L.R.A.1916B, 576–580. See Glenn, Fraudulent Conveyances, rev.ed., § 299a.

7. See Kline v. McGuckin, 24 N.J.Eq. 411 (Ch.1874); N.J.Stat.Ann. 25:2–3, 25:2–4; Cunningham and Tischler, Disguised Real Estate Security Transactions as Mortgages in Substance, 26 Rutgers L.Rev. 1, 27 (1972).

8. See § 3.5 supra.

against creditors of the grantor.[1] Some authorities, however, hold it may be recorded as a deed; others hold that it may or must be recorded as a mortgage.[2]

 WESTLAW REFERENCES
deed /s absolute /p mortgage /p record!

§ 3.15   Objections to Parol Evidence

Although the authority permitting the use of parol evidence to establish that a deed absolute was intended on a mortgage is overwhelming, two objections have sometimes been raised to its introduction. One is the parol evidence rule; the other is the Statute of Frauds. The parol evidence bars extrinsic agreements which would vary the terms of the single written instrument or group of instruments which the parties have executed with the intention that it or they be the complete expression and embodiment of their entire agreement.[1] The Statute of Frauds, on the other hand, is a statutory requirement that certain agreements be in writing.[2] The explanations offered as to why the evidence should not be barred by one or the other of these two rules have varied significantly. While some of the same arguments may justify the admission of the evidence under either of the rules, the two are quite independent of each other in their operation and theory.

The simplest reason the admission of parol evidence does not violate the parol evidence rule is that the deed absolute did not embody, and was not intended to embody, the whole agreement of the parties. The oral agreement merely supplements the deed with respect to a matter on which the instrument is silent and with which it does not purport to deal.[3] As stated by Wigmore, "the act of transfer and the user of the property transferred are distinct legal ideas; or, put still differently, the kind of estate—according to the categories of fee simple, life estate, and the like—is a different thing from the quality of the

§ 3.14

1. Gulley v. Macy, 84 N.C. 434 (1881).

2. See, e.g., Livesey v. Brown, 35 Neb. 111, 52 N.W. 838 (1892). The following are a few representative authorities on the questions suggested above. Ives v. Stone, 51 Conn. 446 (1883) (agreement to reconvey construed as a defeasance); Clemons v. Elder, 9 Iowa 272 (1859); Marston v. Williams, 45 Minn. 116, 47 N.W. 644, 22 Am. St.Rep. 719 (1890); Kline v. McGuckin, 24 N.J.Eq. 411 (1874); Dey v. Dunham, 2 Johns.Ch. 182 (N.Y.1816), reversed 15 Johns. 555, 8 Am.Dec. 282, affirmed 16 Johns. 367, 8 Am.Dec. 323; In re Mechanics' Bank, 156 App.Div. 343, 141 N.Y.S. 473 (1913), affirmed 209 N.Y. 526, 102 N.E. 1106 (1913); Security Savings & Trust Co. v. Loewenberg, 38 Or. 159, 62 P. 647 (1900).

See L.R.A.1916B, 600; 1 Jones, Mortgages, 8th Ed. §§ 304, 631 (1928). See also White v. Moore, 1 Paige 551 (N.Y.1829). See Fogelman, The Deed Absolute as a Mortgage in New York, 32 Fordham L.Rev. 299, 311 (1963).

§ 3.15

1. See 3 Corbin, Contracts § 573 (1963); Calamari & Perillo, Contracts, 99–100 (1977).

2. For the historical connection between the parol evidence rule and the Statute of Frauds, see IX Wigmore, Evidence, 3d ed., § 2426.

3. See Cunningham & Tischler, Disguised Real Estate Security Transactions as Mortgages in Substance, 26 Rutgers L.Rev. 1, 9 (1972).

estate, i.e., trust or security. The simple question then is, whether the parties, under all the circumstances, appear to have intended the document to cover merely the kind of estate transferred, or to cover all possible aspects of the transfer, including that of the quality of the estate, i.e., its subjection to an equity of redemption. In the latter case, no extrinsic agreement can be considered." [4] A few cases have taken this latter view in the deed absolute cases, and if a court does conclude that the parties intended the document to cover the entire scope of the transaction it is difficult to see how parol evidence of a mortgage intent can be received, as one such court said, "without contradicting the instrument, for the reason, that the instrument and the parol testimony both assume to state the transaction; and as they differ, they must naturally be in contradiction. They both historically relate the same transaction, and the one says it was an absolute sale—the other, it was not such, but a mere mortgage, and is not this a plain contradiction? * * *" [5] That court also believed that logic in the matter was reinforced by sound policy: "* * * The general rule, that parol shall not be received to contradict written evidence, is founded in true policy, and in good sense. Why should parties state, in solemn instruments, that which is not true? These instruments assume to state the truth, and the whole truth; and if parties will state that which is untrue, should they not justly suffer the consequences? Is not the rule that parties must be held to mean what they say, the plain, honest, simple, and correct rule at last?" This argument ignores a policy factor which plays a decisive role in permitting the oral agreement to establish a mortgage and which is not present when the question is one of transforming a mortgage into something else. That policy factor is the traditional solicitude of the courts toward a mortgagor's redemption right, a matter which has been stressed earlier and which is a basic consideration in the problems considered in this chapter.

On the other hand, if the parties do not intend to cover all aspects of the transaction in the document, there is no objection to proof of an extrinsic agreement so far as the parol evidence rule is concerned.[6]

Nevertheless, the opinions of many of the cases seem to assume that the deed did contain and was intended to contain the parties' entire agreement, and then, because the evidence of the oral agreement for the mortgage is nevertheless let in, feel compelled to advance reasons why this can be done. These reasons can be boiled down to two: those that seek to allow it in on the ground that there are present

4. IX Wigmore, Evidence, 3d ed., § 2437. See also Scott, Trusts, § 38; I Bogert, Trusts, 2d ed. 410–412; Smedley and Blunk, Oral Understandings at Variance with Absolute Deeds, 34 Ill.L.Rev. 189, 198 (1939).

5. Lee v. Evans, 8 Cal. 424, 432 (1857). Accord, Gajewski v. Bratcher, 221 N.W.2d 614 (N.D.1974).

6. This same reasoning applies equally to a deed absolute with an oral agreement by the grantee to hold in trust. It has been suggested that the cases barring the oral trust do not do so because of the parol evidence rule but because of the Statute of Frauds covering trusts. See Wigmore, supra, note 4. This seems correct.

factors which will create an independent equity superior to the written agreement;[7] and those that seem to proceed upon the notion that the evidence comes in as an exception to the parol evidence rule. The first proceeds upon the theory that the written instrument can only be considered to be contradicted when the oral agreement is allowed in to enforce it according to its terms, and if it is allowed in to establish an equity arising by operation of law in the property, such use of the oral agreement is not in conflict with the other words used by the parties and put into the writing even though they intended that writing to be the sole repository and expression of their intention. The latter is based on the theory that the oral words are admitted to enforce them, that they do contradict or add to the document, but that this is permitted by a flat exception to the rule making it inoperative where certain factors are present.

The first of the standard explanations for admission of the oral agreement is that it is a virtual fraud upon the grantor for the grantee subsequently to refuse to perform his promise to treat the conveyance as security.[8] This fraudulent conduct by the grantee justifies making an exception to the parol evidence rule, or the Statute of Frauds, even if admission of the agreement does contradict the deed. Alternatively, it may be argued that the fraud warrants the imposition upon the grantee of a constructive trust founded upon the fraud itself, that the terms of the oral agreement are not being enforced, and, consequently, the parol evidence rule which would bar the oral agreement for the purpose of enforcing it is not involved at all. The problem with this explanation is that in effect the court is lifting itself by its own bootstraps because there is no fraud to justify the admission of the parol agreement unless there has been a breach of the parol agreement. And yet the parol agreement is first admitted in order to show a breach of it which will establish the fraud that justifies admitting it.[9]

To put the matter in a little different way, the fraud which will justify the admission of the parol evidence, if it is admitted for that reason, must occur when the transaction is entered into. The alleged fraud here consists in later insisting that it was intended as a sale when actually it was intended as a mortgage. The very question at issue before the court, therefore, is whether it was intended to be a mortgage or a sale. Until the court decides that it was intended to be a mortgage there would be no justification in saying that the defendant was fraudulent in insisting that it was a sale. What the court does is to

---

7. See, e.g., Pierce v. Robinson, 13 Cal. 116, 131 (1859), "The parol evidence is admitted * * * not for the purpose of contradicting or varying the written instrument, but to show facts *dehors* the instrument creating an equity superior to its terms."

8. Strong v. Stewart, 4 Johns.Ch. 167 (1819); Taylor v. Luther, C.C.R.I., 2 Sumn. 228, Fed.Cas. No. 13,796 (1835); Jenkins v. Eldredge, 3 Story 299, Fed.Cas. No. 7,267 (1845). See Newton v. Fay, 92 Mass. 505 (1865); 4 Pomeroy, Eq.Juris., 5th ed., § 1196.

9. See Smedley and Blunk, supra note 4, 197.

admit the parol evidence to discover what the intention really was, and then, having already admitted the evidence and determined the question in issue, it says that this determination makes the defendant's conduct fraudulent and consequently parol evidence is admissible to decide the question it had already decided, namely, that a mortgage was intended.[10] Another objection to this reasoning is that it treats the later breach of the agreement as establishing fraud in the entering into the agreement in the first place. Logically this amounts to converting a subsequent breach of contract into fraud in the inception of the contract.

But the basic objection, so far as the argument concerns the parol evidence rule is a fundamental fallacy in the reasoning. The assumption is that the parol evidence rule does operate to exclude the oral agreement that the property was to be held as security and returned on payment of the debt. If this assumption is true, it means that the court has concluded that the deed itself was intended by the parties to constitute the entire and complete transaction between the parties and consequently the oral agreement was not intended to have any legally operative effect and therefore is excluded from consideration. If this is so, it seems nonsense to predicate fraud upon the violation of an agreement which, by hypothesis, was barred from consideration initially on the ground that it was not intended by the parties to be a legally binding part of their agreement in the matter.

A second and similar explanation for admission of the oral agreement is that, even in the absence of fraud or undue influence, it is permissible to show an oral trust or contract for the purpose of preventing unjust enrichment. Here the transferee would be unjustly enriched if he were allowed to keep the property, and this unjust enrichment should be prevented by compelling the transferee to return the property on payment of the debt by the transferor.[11] But here also, if it is assumed that the parol evidence rule would bar the parol agreement because the parties did not intend that it should be any

10. A similar criticism was voiced in a leading case where the analogous question of allowing in a parol trust in the face of the Statute of Frauds was involved. The court said, "But it seems apparent to my mind to say, in such a case, it shall be admitted to establish the fraud, is equally a violation of the Statute. Because the fraud consists only in the refusal to execute the trust. The court, therefore, cannot say that there is a fraud, without first saying that there is a trust. And the parol evidence, if admitted, must be admitted to establish the trust, in order that the court may charge the party with fraud in setting up his claim against it." Rasdall's Adm'rs v. Rasdall, 9 Wis. 379 (1859).

11. See Scott, Conveyances upon Trusts Not Properly Declared, 37 Harv.L.Rev. 663

(1923). See also Stone, Resulting Trusts and the Statute of Frauds, 6 Col.L.Rev. 326, 339 (1906). "The substantive basis of the jurisdiction is the inequitable conduct of the grantee in receiving property for one purpose, and using it for another, and equity, consequently, imposes upon the grantee, an equitable obligation to restore the property to the grantor upon payment of the mortgage indebtedness. The inequitable conduct of the grantee in retaining the property for his own purposes is sufficient to give equity jurisdiction to declare the deed a mortgage, despite the parol evidence rule, and the provisions of the Statute of Frauds." Ames, Constructive Trusts Based upon the Breach of an Express Oral Trust of Land, 20 Harv.L.Rev. 549, 553 (1907).

binding part of their transaction, it is difficult to understand why the non-performance of such an agreement should be considered as establishing unjust enrichment and therefore justify the admission of it in evidence either for the purpose of enforcing it according to its terms or founding upon it a constructive trust or mortgage. On the other hand, if the parol evidence rule does not bar it, there is no need to talk unjust enrichment in connection with its admission unless the Statute of Frauds is urged as an obstacle. If the Statute is set up as a defense the argument seems sound. The only difficulty is that it would be just as applicable to an oral trust. But, as we shall see, the American authorities generally do not accept it in the latter case.

A third explanation, and one which is believed to be the correct one, is one rooted in the history of and policy of the courts toward the mortgagor's equity of redemption. As was pointed out by Field, J., in the leading case of Pierce v. Robinson,[12] which gives one of the best statements of this rationale, "The entire doctrine of equity, in respect to mortgages, has its origin in considerations independent of the terms in which the instruments are drawn. In form, a mortgage in fee is a conveyance of a conditional estate, which by the strict rules of the common law, became absolute upon breach of its conditions. But, from an early period in the history of English jurisprudence, Courts of Equity interposed to prevent a forfeiture of the estate and gave to the mortgagor a right to redeem, upon payment within a reasonable time, of the principal sum secured, interest and costs. * * * And when the right to redeem had been once established, to prevent its evasion, the rule was laid down and has ever since been inflexibly adhered to, that the right is inseparably connected with the mortgage, and cannot be abandoned or waived by any stipulations entered into between the parties at the time, whether inserted in the instrument or not. * * * It is against the policy of the law to allow irredeemable mortgages, just as it is against the policy of the law to allow the creation of inalienable estates. Under no circumstances will equity permit this end to be effected, either by express stipulation, or the absolute form of the instrument. * * *"

In creating the redemption right the courts clearly recognized that they were defeating the expressed intention of the parties as contained in the instrument. In other words, it involved as much or more of a departure from the terms of the instrument than the conveyance of an absolute conveyance executed as security. "The conveyance upon condition, by its terms, purports to vest the entire estate upon the breach of the condition, just as the absolute conveyance does in the first instance. The equity arises and is asserted, in both cases, upon exactly the same principles, and is enforced without reference to the agreement of the parties, but from the nature of the transaction to which the right attaches, from the policy of the law, as an inseparable incident. * * * Unless parol evidence can be admitted, the policy of the law

12. 13 Cal. 116 (1859).

will be constantly evaded. Debtors, under the force of pressing necessities, will submit to almost any exactions for loans of a trifling amount, compared with the value of the property, and the equity of redemption will elude the grasp of the Court, and rest in the simple good faith of the creditor." [13] This last point particularly, the notion that the mortgagor is in a weak economic position as compared with the mortgagee, and therefore the subject of special solicitude and protection of the chancellor, is frequently stressed and is a dominant consideration in mortgage law. Typical of this attitude is the much quoted statement of Lord Northington in Vernon v. Bethell that "necessitous men are not, truly speaking, free men; but, to answer a present emergency, will submit to any terms that the crafty may impose upon them." [14] This strong policy in favor of the mortgagor's redemption interest is sufficient to account for the letting in of parol evidence to establish it even if both the parol evidence rule and the Statute of Frauds logically apply to exclude it. It is also sufficient to outweigh any policy objections that the deed absolute opens an easy way to debtors to conceal their assets from their creditors, a possibility which in one instance was given as a bolstering reason for excluding the oral agreement.[15]

One final observation is appropriate. It may be that transactions of this sort are so common that the courts, recognizing this fact, have established a positive rule of law as an exception to the parol evidence rule, that when a claim of mortgage is made, the issue of whether the claim is borne out by the evidence shall go directly to the trier of fact without any preliminary inquiry by the court into whether the parties intended the written deed to constitute their entire agreement. The courts may well feel that such an exception is sufficiently safeguarded by the usual rule requiring clear and convincing evidence to establish the claim.

Statute of Frauds

The Statute of Frauds is a more substantial obstacle to the introduction of the parol agreement of defeasance than is the parol evidence rule. In the latter case, the easiest and soundest view is, as we saw, that the application of the rule does not operate to exclude the evidence. Further, upon the assumption that it did exclude the showing of the agreement, we looked at various justifications for admission in spite of the rule. Three of them—fraud upon the grantor, unjust enrichment of the grantee, and policy in favor of protecting the redemption inter-

---

13. Id. at 126. See also Glenn, Mortgages, 55; Walsh, Mortgages, 35.

14. 2 Ed. 110, 113 (1762). See also Russell v. Southard, 53 U.S. (12 How.) 139, 13 L.Ed. 927 (1851); Marshall, C.J., in Conway's Executors v. Alexander, 11 U.S. (7 Cranch) 218, 3 L.Ed. 321, 328 (1812), "lenders of money are less under the pressure of circumstances which control the perfect and free exercise of the judgment than borrowers", and they frequently make the effort "to avail themselves of the advantage of this superiority in order to obtain inequitable advantages."; Lord Chancellor Hardwicke in Toomes v. Conset, 3 Atk. 261 (1745); Thomas v. Klemm, 185 Md. 136, 43 A.2d 193 (1945).

15. Lee v. Evans, 8 Cal. 424, 432 (1857).

est—have been advanced as reasons for avoiding the prohibition of the Statute of Frauds. The second and third clearly are theories that afford rational grounds for admitting the evidence in spite of the Statute as well. Although the final criticism of the first explanation discussed above in relation to the parol evidence rule would be inapplicable where the Statute of Frauds is the obstacle, the other criticisms of it seem appropriate. Another reason closely connected with this first explanation frequently expressed is that rules of law designed to prevent fraud must not be used so as to produce fraud, and "that it would be a virtual fraud for the grantee to insist upon the deed as an absolute conveyance of the title, which had been intentionally given to him, and which he had knowingly accepted and therefore in reality as a mortgage." [16]

Perhaps the best reason advanced as to why the Statute of Frauds has not prevented showing that the transaction was a mortgage is that it is not violated.[17] "It is frequently and correctly stated that the statute of frauds has no application to parol proof of an equitable mortgage, but this is for the obvious reason that such proof by establishing an equitable mortgage does not transfer to the mortgagor an interest in land. The oral proof simply limits the effect of a conveyance absolute in form to the agreed effect—a transfer as security." [18] In other words, the parol evidence merely shows that the grantor retained a part interest in the property, namely the beneficial ownership of the property; and parol evidence showing that a person never even purported to part with the beneficial ownership of property does not constitute a transfer or creation of an interest in property.[19]

 WESTLAW REFERENCES
deed /s absolute /p "parol evidence" "statute of frauds" 266k37

---

16. See Smith v. Smith, 153 Ala. 504, 508, 45 So. 168, 169 (1907); Schultz v. Schultz, 117 Mich.App. 454, 324 N.W.2d 48 (1982). Pomeroy, Eq.Juris., 5th ed., § 1196. See also 15 Iowa L.Rev. 193 (1929).

17. De Bartlett v. De Wilson, 52 Fla. 497, 42 So. 189, 11 Ann.Cas. 311 (1906). See L.R.A.1916B, 71, 73.

18. Bennett v. Harrison, 115 Minn. 342, 355, 132 N.W. 309, 314, 37 L.R.A.,N.S., 521 (1911).

19. See Smedley and Blunk, Oral Understandings at Variance With Absolute Deeds, 34 Ill.L.Rev. 189, 198 (1940), where the argument was made that such an agreement did not, for this reason, violate either the parol evidence rule or the trust provision of the Statute of Frauds. However, even where there is a special statute, rather than § 4 of the English Statute of Frauds or a paraphrase of it, expressly requiring "mortgages" to be "created, renewed, or extended" by an instrument in writing it has been held that it would be no bar to the admission of oral evidence that a deed absolute was intended as a mortgage. Anglo-Californian Bank v. Cerf, 147 Cal. 384, 81 P. 1077 (1905). See Fogelman, The Deed Absolute as a Mortgage in New York, 32 Fordham L.Rev. 299, 303 (1963); Cunningham and Tischler, Disguised Real Estate Security Transactions as Mortgages in Substance, 26 Rutgers L.Rev. 1, 10 (1972).

§ 3.16   Parol Mortgage vs. Parol Trust Or Parol Condition Subsequent to a Written Contract

A further question arises as to whether an oral agreement to hold an absolute deed as a mortgage should be treated differently from an oral agreement to hold as trustee in so far as the impact of the parol evidence rule or the Statute of Frauds is concerned.[1] This is a potential problem because substantial authority holds that an oral express trust agreement by a grantee under a deed absolute cannot be established in favor of the grantor nor may a constructive trust be imposed.[2] With respect to the parol evidence rule no plausible distinction between the two types of cases has been offered. And, indeed, in spite of some respectable authorities[3] that imply, at least, that the parol evidence rule would bar it if there were no basis for an exception to it, the clearly preferable view, and the one accepted by most cases, is that the rule raises no barrier to the introduction of the oral agreement in either case.

The real hurdle, however, is the Statute of Frauds.[4] One reconciliation of the two groups of cases with respect to as the Statute of Frauds may be suggested initially. It is that trusts are specifically covered by two sections of the English Statute of Frauds, seven and eight,[5] whereas there are no sections specifically dealing with mortgages and, if they are covered, it is because the general language of section one or four is construed to apply. But there is authority for the view that establishing the mortgage only shows a reservation of an interest in the grantor and the Statute doesn't prevent doing this.[6] This distinction, however,

§ 3.16

1. For a thorough discussion of the whole problem see Smedley and Blunk, Oral Understandings at Variance with Absolute Deeds, 34 Ill.L.Rev. 189 (1939).

2. See Restatement (Second) Trusts § 44 (1959) and Reporter's Notes; Bottenfield v. Wood, 264 Ark. 505, 573 S.W.2d 307 (1978); Page v. Clark, 197 Colo. 306, 592 P.2d 792 (1979); Scott, Conveyances Upon Trusts Not Properly Declared, 37 Harv.L. Rev. 653 (1924); Ames, Constructive Trusts Based upon the Breach of an Express Oral Trust of Land, 20 Harv.L.Rev. 549 (1907); Costigan, Trusts Based on Oral Promises to Hold in Trust, to Convey, or to Devise Made by Voluntary Grantees, 12 Mich.L. Rev. 427, 515 (1914); Stone, Resulting Trusts and the Statute of Frauds, 6 Col.L. Rev. 326 (1906).

3. E.g., Pierce v. Robinson, supra § 3.15, n. 7.

4. See IX, Wigmore, Evidence, 3d ed. § 2437; Scott, Trusts, § 38; Bogert, Trusts and Trustees, 2d Ed., § 51.

5. In some states in the United States there is no provision in the Statute of Frauds applying to trusts. In these jurisdictions an additional reason exists why the parol evidence rule should not bar the oral trust, because if it did the courts "would be faced with the uncomfortable problem of having a valid oral trust with a destruction of the only means whereby the trust can be enforced. This would be in effect to add a trust provision to the Statute of Frauds by force of judicial decision." Smedley and Blunk, Oral Understandings at Variance with Absolute Deeds, 34 Ill.L. Rev. 189, 197 (1939). See Restatement (Second) Trusts § 39 (1959). The same argument would apply to an oral mortgage to which the Statute of Frauds did not apply.

6. See preceding section. But cf. Anglo-Californian Bank v. Cerf, 147 Cal. 384, 81 P. 1077 (1905), (holding that a Statute of Frauds explicitly referring to mortgages would not prevent showing the oral mortgage).

has seldom been pointed out [7] and, although some courts simply dismiss the apparent inconsistency by saying, without explanation that the oral mortgage cases are distinguishable from the oral trust cases,[8] more important authorities have stated flatly that they "can see no distinction between an express trust and a parol agreement making a deed a mortgage," [9] so far as the Statute is concerned. But, even assuming that both trusts and mortgages are governed by the requirements of the Statute of Frauds, there are several grounds upon which to reconcile the two lines of cases.

One approach is simply to say that the problem in the two cases is identical, that the mortgage cases are correct, and that in the oral trust cases the evidence should be let in also, not for the purpose of enforcing it, but to show unjust enrichment of the grantee and forfeiture of the grantor's interest in order to impose a constructive trust. Under this approach, the policy of the Statute against false claims and any other policy against a transaction which permits the concealment of assets is outweighed by the policy against allowing one person to be enriched at the expense of another as well as the general desirability of permitting the intention of the parties to a transaction to be enforced.[10] It has even been urged that the forfeiture in the trust case is greater than in the mortgage context and thus presents an even stronger basis for relief because in the latter "the party would get it for the money he had loaned, while in the latter he would get it for nothing." [11] This seems erroneous. The establishment and collection of the debt by the grantee would not be affected by the Statute of Frauds or the parol evidence rule. Moreover there is no reason to assume that if the court refused to admit the oral evidence of the mortgage that it would, because of this, prevent the collection of the debt. If so the amount of forfeiture would be the same in both cases.

The most important difference between the two cases is the one which best explains why courts, even though there may be strong objections in the mortgage case to letting in the evidence, nevertheless do allow it. That is the notion which has played such a part in the protection of the mortgagor's redemption interest, namely, that the mortgagor is an economic weakling who must be protected against his own agreements because he makes them under the pressure of necessi-

7. See, however, Smedley and Blunk, Oral Understandings at Variance With Absolute Deeds, 34 Ill.L.Rev. 189, 204 (1939).

8. E.g., Sturtevant v. Sturtevant, 20 N.Y. 39, 40, 75 Am.Dec. 371 (1859); Patton v. Beecher, 68 Ala. 579 (1872).

9. Rasdall's Adm'rs v. Rasdall, 9 Wis. 379 (1859), a leading case. See Restatement (Second), Trusts § 44, Reporter's Notes, Comment d. (1959); Stone, Resulting Trusts and the Statute of Frauds, 6 Col. L.Rev. 326, 341 (1906).

10. See Scott, Trusts, § 44; Stone, Resulting Trusts and the Statute of Frauds, 6

Col.L.Rev. 326, 339 (1906); Ames, Oral Trusts of Lands, 20 Harv.L.Rev. 549, 553 (1906).

11. Rasdall's Adm'rs v. Rasdall, 9 Wis. 379 (1859). See also Scott, Abridgment of the Law of Trusts, § 44.3: "Indeed, the unjust enrichment is greater in the case of an oral trust than in the case of an oral mortgage; for if no relief is given in the former case the whole of the property is lost, while in the latter case only the value above the amount of the debt is lost."

ty. The mortgagee has money and the mortgagor needs it. The mortgagee has the leverage to coerce the mortgagor into giving a deed absolute with its impact softened only by the oral agreement. And this strong policy in favor of the mortgagor's redemption right outweighs as we have suggested countervailing policies against both fraudulent claims and possible fraudulent concealment of assets.[12] In the case of the oral trust there is no similar reason to excuse the grantor. And the forfeiture and unjust enrichment, which exists in the mortgage case also, is not sufficient to overcome the opposing considerations.

This deference toward the mortgagor, if it is based upon the assumption that the owner of money is in a strong position, is illogical. A owns Blackacre and is in dire need of money. B has money. A can get money from B either by mortgaging Blackacre to B or by selling it to him. If A gives to B a deed absolute, the courts will allow A to show it is a mortgage and get back his property. But if it is a sale A cannot rescind the sale and get back the property on the ground that B drove a hard bargain when A was necessitous. Of course it can be answered that in the mortgage case equity is granting the relief to effectuate the executory intention of the parties as expressed orally while in the sale case it would be defeating an executed intention. Yet this seems only verbally to distinguish the cases for, in pursuance of its solicitude for the mortgagor, as, for example, in the original creation of the redemption right, equity did not hesitate to defeat a completely executed intention of both parties that title should be absolute in the mortgagee if the debt was not paid. Possibly the difference is psychological. In the mortgage case the mortgagee plays not merely upon the *necessities* of A but upon his *hopes* of getting the land back and his hopes lead him to make foolish bargains. In the case of the sale, however, the buyer plays only upon the needs of the seller.

There are other distinctions between the mortgage and the trust cases which may play some part in causing the divergent results. For one thing, there are no rules of law which prevent proving the existence of a debt which existed before or arose at the time of the conveyance and continued to exist after the conveyance. This observable and independent circumstance gives corroboration to the grantor's story that the conveyance was for security. There is no similar external guarantee for the grantor who claims an oral trust. Again, there were historical precedents permitting the oral mortgage to be established before the enactment of the Statute of Frauds whereas there was no similar power found in the case of oral trust. Courts may well have coupled the express provisions in the newly enacted Statute covering trusts, the lack of any such explicit coverage of mortgages, and the older mortgages cases to arrive at the conclusion that the oral trust was prohibited but the oral mortgage not.[13]

12. See Scott, Conveyances upon Trusts Not Properly Declared, 37 Harv.L.Rev. 653, 663 (1924); Scott, Abridgment of the Law of Trusts, § 44.3.

13. See Smedley and Blunk, supra, note 7 at 202–204.

It has also been suggested that the oral mortgage cases are inconsistent with the well settled rule that an obligor upon a written contract or a negotiable instrument cannot prove an extrinsic condition subsequent. It has been answered that the "distinction must rest on the assumption that A may very likely give an actual conveyance of Blackacre in absolute form when it is agreed that the transfer shall operate merely as a security, but that he is not so likely to make a written contract promising to transfer Blackacre in absolute form when the understanding of the parties is, as before, that the transaction shall be defeasible upon a certain contingency." This is an acute observation.[14]

 WESTLAW REFERENCES

parol /s evidence mortgage trust (statute +s fraud) /p absolute /s deed

C. THE CONDITIONAL SALE

§ 3.17 Nature of the Transaction

Where there is a conveyance by deed absolute on its face and, in addition, executed as part of the same transaction, a separate written agreement, there is no difficulty in construing the two instruments together. If the separate agreement provides by its terms that the deed is to be void on the payment of a debt which was part of the transaction, or that the grantee should reconvey on the same event, the whole transaction is clearly a mortgage. This we have already discussed.[1] But the written agreement may not disclose unambiguously that the property is to go back to the grantor on the payment of a debt, and likewise it may not clearly purport to be a contract or option for a resale of the property to the grantor. In such cases there is a question as to whether the separate writing was a mortgage defeasance or a contract of sale of some sort.[2] To answer this question, extrinsic evidence undoubtedly can be admitted to ascertain the true character of the writing.[3] But there are a large number of cases in which the separate instrument without ambiguity professes expressly to be a contract or option to resell to the grantor the property conveyed by the deed.[4] Indeed, some instances, in addition to spelling out the transaction, the parties may insert quite explicitly statements negating the

14. 3 Williston, Contracts, rev. ed., § 635.

§ 3.17

1. See § 3.4, supra.

2. There is authority that if the instrument leaves it doubtful, it will be construed a mortgage. Graham v. Mullins, 286 Ill.App. 393, 3 N.E.2d 723 (1936). See Smith v. Swendsen, 57 Idaho 715, 69 P.2d 131, 111 A.L.R. 441 (1937).

3. Keithley v. Wood, 151 Ill. 466, 38 N.E. 149, 42 Am.St.Rep. 265 (1894); Chase National Bank v. Tover, 245 App.Div. 615, 283 N.Y.S. 832 (1935), affirmed without opinion 271 N.Y. 518, 2 N.E.2d 674 (1936). See note, 111 A.L.R. 448, 455 (1937).

4. See cases cited in the following footnotes. For a collection of cases, see 79 A.L.R. 937 (1932); 155 A.L.R. 1104 (1945).

existence of a debt as the foundation of a mortgage or affirming the character of the undertaking as a contract.[5] When this is done the question of determining whether, nevertheless, the transaction is a mortgage presents more difficulty and is the subject of our present inquiry.

The historical origin of this type of transaction apparently lies in the social humiliation attached to being forced to mortgage the family estate and to resort to money lenders to do so. "The transaction, then, which will raise the needed money, will leave the way open for a winning back of the family inheritance when its fortunes have been regained, and will at the same time avoid the stigma of being forced by a pecuniary need, is the transaction which will commend itself as the desirable one, * * *. Such a transaction is the sale for repurchase."[6] In other words, it was the borrower historically who often desired this type of transaction.

Today, however, it is usually the lender who dictates this form of transaction and for at least three important reasons. First, as is the case with the absolute deed as a mortgage, the lender seeks to avoid the consequences of the mortgagor's equity of redemption and the accompanying rules of mortgage law.[7] Second, the lender often seeks to avoid the consequences of the usury law.[8] In other words, the lender will seek to characterize the difference between the "sale" price and the repurchase price as simply part of the repurchase price and not as interest. Finally, an income tax motive may be present. For example, the grantee may seek to mask the difference between the sale price and the repurchase price as a capital gain rather than as ordinary interest income.[9] This would, of course, be impossible in a regular mortgage transaction.

Such transactions today take many forms. The most frequent of them are "(1) a sale and conveyance of the land by R to E with option in R to repurchase it; (2) the same as (1) with the addition of a deed of reconveyance deposited in escrow * * *; (3) a sale and conveyance by R to E and a lease by E to R with option in R to repurchase; (4) a sale and conveyance by R to E with an unconditional contract by E to resell and by R to repurchase the land, that is, the creation of the relation of vendor and purchaser, rather than that of mortgagor and mortgagee, attended with a different right of foreclosure * * *; (5) the same as (4), with the addition of a deed of reconveyance deposited in escrow * * *; (6) a sale and conveyance by R to E with a written agreement

---

5. See, e.g., Downs v. Ziegler, 13 Ariz. App. 387, 477 P.2d 261 (1971).

6. Wigmore, The Pledge-Idea, 10 Harv. L.Rev. 389, 393 (1897).

7. See e.g., Swallow Ranches, Inc. v. Bidart, 525 F.2d 995 (9th Cir.1975).

8. See Schulte v. Franklin, 6 Kan.App. 2d 651, 633 P.2d 1151 (1981); Robinson v. Durston, 83 Nev. 337, 432 P.2d 75 (1967);

Kawauchi v. Tabata, 49 Hawaii 160, 413 P.2d 221 (1966); Bantuelle v. Williams, 667 S.W.2d 810 (Tex.App.1984), error refused n.r.e.; Booth v. Landau, 103 A.D.2d 733, 477 N.Y.S.2d 195 (1984); Kiar v. Brimley, 27 Utah 2d 411, 497 P.2d 23 (1972).

9. See, e.g., Robinson v. Durston, 83 Nev. 337, 432 P.2d 75 (1967).

that in the event of further sale the proceeds over and above a certain sum should be paid in whole or part to R * * *; (7) a sale and conveyance made by one already a mortgagor to the mortgagee, with a provision that the former should have the same privilege of redemption as would be given by statute in that state after a foreclosure sale." [10] The term conditional sale has been loosely applied to all such arrangements although frequently this description has been restricted to a sale with merely an option to repurchase.[11]

 WESTLAW REFERENCES
266 +1 k32 k33 reconveyance repurchase resale option /p (deed
/s absolute) mortgage

§ 3.18 Extrinsic Evidence

In all of these situations the question again arises whether extrinsic evidence can be introduced to show that the transactions, notwithstanding the terms of the agreements, are mortgages. In spite of some cases holding to the contrary,[1] the authorities in general again answer yes.[2] But there is one striking difference here from the case where the only written instrument is the deed absolute. Here the extrinsic evidence establishing the fact that the parties intended the transaction to be a mortgage contradicts the written agreement integrated with the deed as the full statement of the parties' agreement. It does not suffice to say that the oral agreement merely fills out a part of the transaction not covered, and intended not to be covered, by the part which was written. Also, although there are many authorities requiring the mortgage intent to be established by clear and convincing evidence [3] as in the deed absolute cases, others hold that a preponderance of evidence

10. Campbell, Cases on Mortgages, 2d ed., 109 n.

11. See Campbell, Cases on Mortgages, 2d ed., 97 n. 1. See also Sargent v. Hamblin, 57 N.M. 559, 564, 260 P.2d 919, 926 (1953); When Is an Absolute Conveyance a Mortgage?, 8 U. of Fla.L.Rev. 132 (1955).

§ 3.18

1. Thomas v. Ogden State Bank, 80 Utah 138, 147, 13 P.2d 636, 639 (1932); Carter v. Simpson Estate Co., 103 Or. 383, 388, 391, 193 P. 913, 203 P. 580, 581, 582 (1922) (alternative decision); McMurry v. Mercer, 73 S.W.2d 1087, 1089 (Tex.Civ.App. 1934), criticised, 13 Tex.L.Rev. 241 (1934). Cf. Fry v. D.H. Overmyer Co. Inc., 269 Or. 281, 525 P.2d 140 (1974).

2. See Downs v. Ziegler, 13 Ariz.App. 387, 477 P.2d 261 (1970); Robinson v. Durston, 83 Nev. 337, 432 P.2d 75 (1967); Orlando v. Berns, 154 Cal.App.2d 753, 316 P.2d 705 (1957); Hodges v. Hodges, 67 N.C. App. 290, 312 S.E.2d 703 (1984). McKinley v. Hinnant, 242 N.C. 245, 87 S.E.2d 568

(1955), noted in Third Annual Survey of North Carolina Case Law: Credit Transactions 34 N.C.L.Rev. 35 (1955); Cowles v. Zlaket, 167 Cal.App.2d 20, 334 P.2d 55 (1959), In re F & M Enterprises, Inc., 34 B.R. 211 (Bkrtcy.Fla.1983); Bantuelle v. Williams, 667 S.W.2d 810 (Tex.App.1983), error refused n.r.e. Cunningham & Tischler, Disguised Real Estate Security Transactions as Mortgages in Substance, 26 Rutgers L.Rev. 1, 13 (1972).

3. See Baker v. Taggart, 628 P.2d 1283 (Utah 1981); Bantuelle v. Williams, 667 S.W.2d 810 (Tex.App.1983), error refused n.r.e.; Fry v. D.H. Overmyer Co. Inc., 269 Or. 281, 525 P.2d 140 (1974). Parks v. Mulledy, 49 Idaho 546, 290 P. 205, 79 A.L.R. 934 (1930); Nitkey v. Ward, 199 Minn. 334, 271 N.W. 873 (1937), certiorari denied 302 U.S. 706, 58 S.Ct. 25, 82 L.Ed. 545 (1937), rehearing denied 302 U.S. 775, 58 S.Ct. 134, 82 L.Ed. 600 (1937); Sargent v. Hamblin, 57 N.M. 559, 260 P.2d 919 (1953); Cowles v. Zlaket, 167 Cal.App.2d 20, 334 P.2d 55 (1959).

will suffice.[4]   Further, in doubtful cases the courts will construe the arrangement as a mortgage [5] and some courts have ruled that if there is any agreement executed contemporaneously with an absolute deed whereby the grantor may, within a limited time demand a reconveyance the transaction is conclusively a mortgage.[6]   Indeed, in certain jurisdictions that limit the use of extrinsic evidence to establish a straight deed absolute as a mortgage to situations where a defeasance clause was omitted by reason of "ignorance, mistake, fraud or undue advantage," [7] such evidence is routinely permitted to be used without such limitations to show a mortgage transaction where such a deed is accompanied by some type of written option to repurchase.[8]

In other words the task of establishing the transaction to be a mortgage is distinctly easier than in the straight deed absolute case in spite of an apparently clear encroachment on the parol evidence rule. At first glance this seems curious and an apparent aberration.   As one court said, "* * * it seems illogical to hold that clear and convincing evidence is required to establish that the transaction is a mortgage, where the deed is absolute and there is no collateral writing, but that where there is a contemporaneous agreement to sell the property, less

4. Westberg v. Wilson, 185 Minn. 307, 309, 241 N.W. 315, 316 (1932). For cases on the quantum of proof, see Updike, Mortgages, in 1953 Annual Survey of American Law, 29 N.Y.U.L.Rev. 829, 830 (1954).

5. "In all doubtful cases a contract will be construed to be a mortgage rather than a conditional sale, because in the case of a mortgage the mortgagor, although he has not strictly complied with the terms of the mortgage, still has his right of redemption; while in the case of a conditional sale, without strict compliance, the rights of the conditional purchaser are forfeited." Matthews v. Sheehan, 69 N.Y. 585, 590 (1877). See, Russell v. Southard, 53 U.S. (12 How.) 139, 13 L.Ed. 927 (1851). See James v. Ragin, 432 F.Supp. 887 (W.D.N.C.1977) ("doubts as to whether the transaction is a sale or mortgage are to be construed in favor of a mortgage").

"A matter of intention is entirely one of fact to be determined by the trial court and a finding by it in this regard will not be set aside unless it is clearly or manifestly against the weight of the evidence." Nitkey v. Ward, 199 Minn. 334, 340, 271 N.W. 873, 876 (1937), certiorari denied 302 U.S. 706, 58 S.Ct. 25, 82 L.Ed. 545 (1937), rehearing denied 302 U.S. 775, 58 S.Ct. 134, 82 L.Ed. 600 (1937).

See also Fogelman, The Deed Absolute as a Mortgage in New York, 32 Fordham L.Rev. 299, 307 (1963) on the significance of the existence of a written defeasance.

6. Kerr v. Gilmore, 6 Watts 405 (Pa. 1837); Brown v. Nickle, 6 Pa. 390 (1847). Only slightly weaker than this is the attitude of a Canadian court expressed in Hawke v. Milliken, 12 Grant Ch. 236, 238 (1866), "when an obligation to purchase and pay the money is exacted from the grantor, that is sufficient to show the real character of the transaction to be a mortgage, though the form of it is a sale." It has been held that a *grantee* may establish that the transaction was a mortgage if he meets the requirements of proof which would be required of the grantor. Holman v. Mason City Auto Co., 186 Iowa 704, 171 N.W. 12 (1919); Goodbar & Co. v. Bloom, 43 Tex.Civ.App. 434, 96 S.W. 657 (1906); Baldwin v. McDonald, 24 Wyo. 108, 156 P. 27 (1916) (semble); Downs v. Ziegler, 13 Ariz.App. 387, 477 P.2d 261 (1971). See § 3.6, supra.

7. See Poston v. Bowen, 228 N.C. 202, 44 S.E.2d 881 (1947); Jones v. Brinson, 231 N.C. 63, 55 S.E.2d 808 (1949).

8. See Henderson v. Security Mortgage & Finance Co., Inc., 273 N.C. 253, 160 S.E.2d 39 (1968); McKinley v. Hinnant, 242 N.C. 245, 87 S.E.2d 568 (1955); James v. Ragin, 432 F.Supp. 887 (D.N.C.1977); High Point Bank v. Morgan-Schultheiss, Inc., 33 N.C.App. 406, 235 S.E.2d 693 (1977), certiorari denied 439 U.S. 958, 99 S.Ct. 360, 58 L.Ed.2d 350 (1979); Hodges v. Hodges, 67 N.C.App. 290, 312 S.E.2d 703 (1984).

evidence is required. * * *"[9] Yet the explanation is not difficult. The same solicitude for the redemption right is just as important here to prevent the summary ending of the grantor's right which would occur if he is held to be merely an optionee or vendee of a contract of purchase and to preserve to him the benefits of the mortgagor's right of redemption. This idea was stressed in a leading case, the court saying "it is not to be forgotten, that the same language which truly describes a real sale, may also be employed to cut off the right of redemption, in case of a loan on security; that it is the duty of the court to watch vigilantly these exercises of skill, lest they should be effectual to accomplish what equity forbids; and that, in doubtful cases, the court leans to the conclusion that the reality was a mortgage, and not a sale. * * * It is true [the mortgagor] must have given his assent to this form of the memorandum; but the distress for money under which he then was, places him in the same condition as other borrowers, in numerous cases reported in the books, who have submitted to the dictation of the lender under the pressure of their wants; and a court of equity does not consider a consent, thus obtained, to be sufficient to fix the rights of the parties."[10]

Moreover, since the grantor does have a written claim to reacquire the property from the grantee, the only controversy is whether it is to be by virtue of a contract of purchase or by a right to redeem as mortgagor. Thus, to permit the grantor to establish that the transaction is a mortgage clearly does not contradict the written documentation to the same degree as in the deed absolute situation where the successful grantor is allowed to take away real estate from a grantee who has an apparently indefeasible title to it. Also, there is a policy objection in the deed absolute cases both against permitting the grantor to conceal his assets by making a conveyance which does not reveal by a writing that the property can be pulled back, and, also, in favor of the grantee, against the possibility of false swearing to deprive her of the property. In the conditional sale getting on the other hand the written agreement minimizes both such policies. There is not only a written clue to the grantor's continued interest in the conveyed property for his creditors to follow up, but also no great hardship is going to befall the grantee if the amount the grantor is to pay is held to be a debt rather than a contract purchase price and his right, consequently, to be one of redemption instead of one upon the grantee's promise to reconvey. The chief injury the grantee suffers is in being deprived of her ability to end the grantor's right on default by means other than foreclosure. It

---

9. Johnson v. National Bank of Commerce, 65 Wash. 261, 275, 118 P. 21, 25, L.R.A.1916B, 4 (1911).

10. Russell v. Southard, 53 U.S. (12 How.) 139, 151, 13 L.Ed. 927 (1851).

"It may be premised that where upon the face of the transaction it is doubtful whether the parties intended to make a mortgage or conditional sale, courts of equity will always incline to consider it a mortgage, because by means of conditional sales oppression is frequently exercised over the needy, and they are too often made the vehicle of extortion." Earp v. Boothe, 24 Gratt. (Va.) 368, 375 (1874).

would be difficult to argue that this is of great seriousness; or, if it is, that it is not outweighed by the greater possible hardship on the grantor of the opposite result.

 WESTLAW REFERENCES

(266 +1 k35 k36 k37 k38) & parol extrinsic /s evidence /p mortgage (absolute /s deed)

§ 3.19 Factors Establishing Conditional Sale as a Mortgage

In determining whether the transaction is a mortgage, or an absolute or conditional sale, the problem is substantially the same as in the straight deed absolute case. Indeed, both types of cases focus on largely the same factors. It is the intention of the parties at the time the transaction is entered into, as gathered from the writings themselves and from relevant extrinsic evidence, which governs.[1] A good summary of some of these essential elements includes, "whether there was a debtor-creditor relationship created at the time of the transaction * * *; whether the grantor remains in possession * * *; whether the grantor was under distress and hard-pressed for money at the time of the transaction * * *; whether the transaction originated out of a loan * * *; and whether the purported sale price is less than the worth of the property."[2] Among other factors to be considered are: "the declarations and admissions of the parties; * * * the nature and character of the testimony relied upon; the various, social and other relationships of the parties; and the apparent aims and purposes to be accomplished."[3]

When the agreement gives the grantor only an option to repurchase and it is clear that he has no duty to pay the sum specified as "purchase" money, there is a question as to whether the transaction can be a mortgage. If, for example, a personal obligation is a condition

§ 3.19

1. Both parties must intend a mortgage. Douglass v. Moody, 80 Ala. 61, 69 (1885); Nitkey v. Ward, 199 Minn. 334, 271 N.W. 873 (1937), certiorari denied 302 U.S. 706, 58 S.Ct. 25, 82 L.Ed. 545 (1937), rehearing denied 302 U.S. 775, 58 S.Ct. 134, 82 L.Ed. 600 (1937); Ministers Life And Casualty Union v. Franklin Park Towers Corp., 239 N.W.2d 207 (Minn.1976); Fry v. D.H. Overmyer Co. Inc., 269 Or. 281, 525 P.2d 140 (1974).

2. James v. Ragin, 432 F.Supp. 887, 982–893 (W.D.N.C.1977).

3. Corey v. Roberts, 82 Utah 445, 452, 25 P.2d 940, 942 (1933). Another excellent summary of the evidence indicating the factors going into the finding is in Morton v. Allen, 180 Ala. 279, 286, 60 So. 866, 868, L.R.A.1916B, 11 (1912). See also Gray v. Frazer, 63 Idaho 552, 123 P.2d 711 (1942); Nitkey v. Ward, 199 Minn. 334, 271 N.W. 873 (1937), certiorari denied 302 U.S. 706, 58 S.Ct. 25, 82 L.Ed. 545 (1937), rehearing denied 302 U.S. 775, 58 S.Ct. 134, 82 L.Ed. 600 (1937); O'Briant v. Lee, 214 N.C. 723, 200 S.E. 865 (1939); Dean v. Smith, 53 N.D. 123, 204 N.W. 987 (1925) discussed in note, 2 Ill.L.Rev. 732 (1926); Selik v. Goldman Realty Co., 240 Mich. 612, 216 N.W. 422 (1927), discussed, 26 Mich.L.Rev. 821 (1928); notes, 16 N.Car.L.Rev. 416, 418 (1938); Robinson v. Durston, 83 Nev. 337, 432 P.2d 75 (1967); Downs v. Ziegler, 13 Ariz.App. 387, 477 P.2d 261 (1971); Kjar v. Brimley, 27 Utah 2d 411, 497 P.2d 23 (1972).

precedent to a valid mortgage,[4] then, of course, there could be no mortgage if the grantor has no such personal obligation. However, in those jurisdictions where a personal obligation on the part of the mortgagor may not be required to establish a valid mortgage,[5] its absence will not automatically bar the establishment of a mortgage in the option to purchase situation.[6] Nevertheless, the absence of a personal obligation in the latter situation is probably strong evidence that the parties did not intend a mortgage transaction.[7] On the other hand, evidence of the existence of a debt is strongly persuasive of a mortgage intent.[8]

As in the absolute deed situation, another significant factor cutting in favor of finding a mortgage transaction is great disparity between the price the grantor receives and the *value* of the land.[9] When a regular mortgage is used, the mortgagor is normally liable to pay the balance of the debt in the event that the mortgaged property is insufficient for that purpose. Where a sale with an option to purchase is used and the disparity referred to above is not great, if the land goes down in value, the grantor will not exercise the purchase option and the grantee will bear the loss. Where, however, the disparity is substantial, even if the value of the land subsequently drops, the grantee has substantial protection even though he has no personal action against the grantor.

It is also often necessary in these repurchase situations to consider the relationship between the amount received by the grantor and the *repurchase* price. For example, if the amount received is $10,000 and the repurchase price is $11,000 one year later, the 10% premium looks

---

4. See §§ 2.1, 2.3, supra.

5. See, e.g., Ministers Life and Cas. Union v. Franklin Park Towers Corp., 307 Minn. 134, 239 N.W.2d 207 (1976); § 2.1, supra.

6. See Robinson v. Durston, 83 Nev. 337, 432 P.2d 75 (1967).

7. "Neither that fund nor the option imposed any obligation to repurchase. It was entirely a matter of choice with the lessee. * * * That is a strong circumstance tending to prove that the conveyance was what it purported to be (see Dixon v. Wright, 175 Miss. 191, 166 So. 374) (1936), * * *." Nitkey v. Ward, 199 Minn. 334, 341, 271 N.W. 873, 877 (1937); Ministers Life and Casualty Union v. Franklin Park Towers Corp., 239 N.W.2d 207 (Minn.1976).

8. O'Briant v. Lee, 214 N.C. 723, 733, 200 S.E. 865, 871 (1939), "If there was a debt, either antecedent or presently created, the instrument must be construed to constitute a mortgage, unless a contrary intent clearly appears upon the face of the instrument." See Hawke v. Milliken, 12

Grant.Ch., Upper Can., 236 (1866). See note, 20 Ill.L.Rev. 732, 733 (1926).

In Investors' Mortgage Security Co. v. Hamilton, 51 Idaho 113, 4 P.2d 347 (1931), discussed in note, 2 Idaho L.J. 151 (1932), the fact that the grantee, who took a conveyance of mortgaged property in purported satisfaction of the grantor's mortgage debt to him, retained the original evidence of indebtedness was thought to be convincing evidence that the conveyance and option to repurchase constituted a mortgage.

9. Courts generally treat inadequacy of price as one of the important facts in determining whether a mortgage was intended. See Glass v. Hieronymus Brothers, 125 Ala. 140, 28 So. 71, 82 Am.St.Rep. 225 (1899); Rogers v. Davis, 91 Iowa 730, 59 N.W. 265 (1894); Daniels v. Johnson, 24 Mich. 430 (1872); Lawrence v. DuBois, 16 W.Va. 443 (1880); Carpenter & Carpenter v. Kingman, 56 Wyo. 314, 109 P.2d 463 (1941). See 155 A.L.R. 1109 (1945); 90 A.L.R. 953 (1934), for additional authorities.

a good deal like a normal interest return on a loan. If the repurchase price at the end of the one year is $14,000, the disparity could represent an attempt to mask a usurious loan and thus arguably could cut in favor of classification as a mortgage transaction. Suppose, however, that the repurchase price is $20,000. Here the substantial disparity could indicate a highly usurious loan or it may simply mean that the land was purchased at a distress sale and that there was no mortgage transaction.

Indeed, it is often necessary to consider all three "disparity" factors in repurchase cases or at least different combinations of them. For example, one court, in holding a transaction to be a loan, gave considerable weight to the fact that the value of the property conveyed greatly exceeded *both* the amount received by the grantor and the repurchase price.[10] In another case, the court was strongly influenced to find a mortgage because the repurchase price was exactly the amount owed by the grantors to the grantee at the time of the conveyance.[11]

 WESTLAW REFERENCES
conditional /s sale /p mortgage

D. TRIPARTITE TRANSACTIONS

§ 3.20 Purchase Money Resulting Trusts

Most American jurisdictions recognize the long-established rule that where one person pays the purchase price for land, but legal title is conveyed to another, a presumption is created that the grantee holds the land under a resulting trust for the person paying the purchase price.[1] "The real purchaser of the property is considered as the owner, with the right to control the title in the hands of the grantee, and to demand a conveyance from him at any time."[2] The same rule is applicable "if the money paid by the party taking the title is advanced by him as a loan to the other."[3] Thus, suppose that A desires to buy land from X, but lacks the cash to do so. He makes an agreement with B that the latter will lend A the money for the purchase price and that X should convey title to the land directly to B, the deed being security for the loan to A. "Thus A pays for the land just as truly as if he had

---

10. Orlando v. Berns, 154 Cal.App.2d 753, 316 P.2d 705 (1957).

11. Osipowicz v. Furland, 218 Wis. 568, 260 N.W. 482 (1935), discussed in note, 11 Wis.L.Rev. 118 (1935).

§ 3.20

1. See Nelson, Purchase-Money Resulting Trusts In Land In Missouri, 33 Mo.L. Rev. 552, 553 (1968); Restatement (second), Trusts § 440 ff (1959); Scott, Trusts, § 440

(3d Ed. 1967); Bogert, Trusts and Trustees, § 454 (2d Ed. 1964).

2. Campbell v. Freeman, 99 Cal. 546, 34 P. 113 (1893).

3. Campbell v. Freeman, 99 Cal. 546, 34 P. 113 (1893). See Grubb v. Delathauwer, 274 Pa.Super. 511, 418 A.2d 523 (1980); Bogert, Trusts and Trustees, § 455 (2d Rev. Ed. 1977). Accord: Kohler v. Gilbert, 216 Or. 483, 339 P.2d 1102 (1959).

had the money * * * from the start and had paid to the grantor the products of his labor or business."[4]

In all cases the burden of establishing the resulting trust is on the party asserting it. In the first type of case the alleged real purchaser "must prove not only that the consideration for the conveyance was paid by him or out of his funds, but also that the money was paid as the purchase price and not as a loan" to the grantee.[5] In the second case the fact of loan by the grantee must be clearly proved.[6] In both cases, however, when A establishes the fact that it was his money that paid for the land, regardless of whether it was his before the transaction or borrowed from B, the grantee, the burden of proof is met because the inference is then drawn that B does not take the beneficial interest and, therefore, that B holds on resulting trust for A. B may rebut this inference, but the burden of proof is upon him to do so.[7] Furthermore, in both cases, it is thoroughly settled that Statutes of Frauds do not prevent such trusts arising. It is sometimes stated that this is so because the trust arises by operation of law and therefore is within an express exception of the Statute of Frauds.[8] A better reason, given by an authority in the field, is that although such resulting trusts "arise out of the intention of the parties, that intention is evidenced by the circumstances of the transaction rather than by the language of the parties. There is not, therefore, as a practical matter the same danger of perjured testimony as in cases where the only evidence of intention is the oral language of the parties."[9] Quite obviously the parol evidence rule has no application: the only writing is the deed from the third party and it would not control as the sole memorial of the agreed upon rights between the grantee and the alleged purchaser.[10]

 WESTLAW REFERENCES
purchase /s money /s resulting /s trust

§ 3.21 Purchase Money Resulting Trusts—Security Agreements

Where the grantee of title under a purchase-money resulting trust has loaned the money, it is usual for him to stipulate that the land shall be security for the loan, and such an agreement, even though oral,

4. Bogert, Trusts and Trustees, § 455 at 648 (2d Rev.Ed. 1977).

5. Phillips v. Phillips, 81 N.J.Eq. 459, 461, 86 A. 949, 950 (1913), affirmed 83 N.J. Eq. 345, 91 A. 1070 (1914). See Scott, Cases on Trusts, 2d Ed., § 440 et seq. for a collection of authorities on purchase money resulting trusts. See also 42 A.L.R. 10, 21 (1926).

6. See Harnish v. Peele, 386 So.2d 8 (Fla.App.1980), review denied 394 So.2d 1153 (1981); McDonough v. O'Niel, 113 Mass. 92 (1873).

7. See Scott, supra note 1; Bogert, supra note 3 § 455.

8. Anonymous, 2 Vent. 361 (1683).

9. Scott, Trusts, 3315 (3d Ed. 1967). "This resulting trust depends for its existence on the actual intent of the creator, expressed in acts other than writing or on the spoken word". Bogert, Trusts and Trustees, § 454 at 633 (2d Rev.Ed. 1977).

10. See Williston, Contracts, Rev.Ed., § 647.

is recognized.[1] As one court stated, "In such a case the grantee holds a double relation to the real purchaser,—he is his trustee of the legal title to the land, and his mortgagee for the money advanced for its purchase, and, as in the case of any other mortgage which is evidenced by an absolute deed, is entitled to retain the title until the payment of the claim for which it is held as security; and he may also enforce his lien by an action of foreclosure. The conveyance is no less a mortgage because it was conveyed to him directly by a third party, to secure his loan to the purchaser for the amount of the purchase money, than if the conveyance had been made directly to the purchaser in the first instance, and the purchaser had then made a conveyance to him, as a security for the money that he had previously borrowed with which to make the purchase."[2]

Although the burden of establishing the resulting trust is on the alleged purchaser, including the proof that the money paid by the grantee was in fact a loan, the burden of establishing the mortgage agreement is a separate and distinct question and is on the party asserting its existence. Usually this is the purchaser and, when it is, the courts do not clearly differentiate between the tasks of establishing the resulting trust and the mortgage, saying that both must be proved by strong evidence. Since one element in the security agreement is the loan by the grantee, which must be proved to make out the resulting trust, it is understandable that the two problems are not segregated.[3] When the grantee is seeking to foreclose on the property there is a similar overlapping. His main task is to prove the fact of loan as an element in the mortgage; but when he does this he has made out the resulting trust. The additional part of his case, the agreement that the property be security for the payment of the loan, is treated either as controlled by the rules governing the creation of the trust, or as involving precisely the same problem raised in the case of a straight deed absolute from the borrower to the lender.[4] So far as burden and

§ 3.21

1. Miller v. Miller, 101 Md. 600, 61 A. 210 (1905). See Note, Equitable Mortgages in Iowa, 44 Iowa L.Rev. 716, 721–723 (1959).

2. Campbell v. Freeman, 99 Cal. 546, 548, 34 P. 113 (1893). Accord: Hicks v. Bridges, 152 Cal.App.2d 146, 313 P.2d 15 (1957). See Note, 13 Kan.L.Rev. 585 (1965), discussing Duncan v. Essary, 193 Kan. 241, 392 P.2d 877 (1964), in which the court held that equitable mortgages were created by a warranty deed from the defendant of property owned by it and also on property conveyed to the plaintiff from a third party grantor which had been bought by defendant with money loaned by plaintiff for that purpose. The note writer's thesis was that in the tripartite transaction it would be possible, and in some in-stances advantageous to either creditor or debtor, to choose between advancing the theory that the transaction was a purchase money resulting trust or an equitable mortgage. The Kansas statutes in respect to the existence in Kansas of purchase money resulting trusts was blamed by the writer for what he considered was confusion in the Kansas law on the tripartite problem. See also, Hergenreter v. Sommers, 535 S.W.2d 513 (Mo.App.1976); Scott, Trusts, § 448 (3d Ed.1967); Nelson, Purchase-Money Resulting Trusts In Land In Missouri, 33 Mo.L.Rev. 552, 576 (1968).

3. Hall v. O'Connell, 52 Or. 164, 167, 95 P. 717 (1908); Jackson v. Maxwell, 113 Me. 366, 94 A. 116, Ann.Cas.1917C, 966, 970 (1915).

4. Campbell v. Freeman, 99 Cal. 546, 34 P. 113 (1893).

standard of proof are concerned there is no objection to this approach. However, this tripartite situation is different from the two-party one with respect to the Statute of Frauds.

 WESTLAW REFERENCES
purchas*** /s money & result*** /s trust /p secur*** /s loan interest agreement

§ 3.22 Statute of Frauds in Tripartite Cases

Although the Statute of Frauds is no objection to the creation of the resulting trust interest in the purchaser in these cases, it is not so clear that the oral agreement between the parties that the grantee-trustee shall hold his title as security for his loan does not fall within its prohibition. It would seem clear that where T is an existing trustee under an express written trust and makes a loan to C, the beneficiary, with an oral agreement that T is to hold title to the trust property as security for repayment of the loan, the Statute of Frauds applies to prevent enforcement of the mortgage agreement by T. The same is true where T holds property as trustee for C under a purchase money resulting trust and later T loans money to C under an oral agreement that the property shall be security.[1] Whether in these cases the Statute would bar T from showing the agreement in case C brought an action to compel a conveyance seems to depend upon the purpose and use of the loan. If the borrowed money went into improvements or the clearing off of other liens, the court will invoke the principle that C must do equity in order to get the aid of the court of equity. As one court said in a case of this sort, "for equity to actively interpose its decree * * * denying to plaintiff all compensation for expenditures in improving and preserving the property is abhorrent, not only to a sense of natural justice, but to those fundamental principles upon which equity grants or withholds its peculiar remedies."[2] On the other hand, where the loan is made for purposes having no relation to the land, C may get the property from T without paying, the Statute of Frauds preventing T from showing the oral agreement.[3]

If the Statute of Frauds applies in the two foregoing cases, why does it not apply also to the case where T loans C the money with which to buy property from X, taking title in a direct deed absolute from X, but with an oral agreement at the time with C that T is to hold the property as security for the repayment of the loan? One answer is that the agreement is used only to rebut pro tanto the creation of the resulting trust. Parol evidence of the intention of C that T should have

§ 3.22

1. See Warner v. Tullis, 206 Iowa 680, 218 N.W. 575 (1928); Pierce v. Parrish, 111 Ga. 725, 37 S.E. 79 (1900).

2. Warner v. Tullis, supra note 1, 206 Iowa at 692, 218 N.W. at 580.

3. Pierce v. Parrish, 111 Ga. 725, 37 S.E. 79 (1900); Warner v. Tullis, supra, note 1, loan for funeral expenses not included in debts which must be paid as condition to compelling conveyance.

the beneficial interest for the limited purpose of security violates neither the Statute of Frauds nor the parol evidence rule. If resulting trusts arise because it is presumed from the facts that the payor of the money intended that the grantee should not have the beneficial interest, if it is shown that he intended that the grantee should have the complete or a limited beneficial interest, the foundation for raising the resulting trust does not exist.[4] On the other hand, if it arises by "operation of law," it is an interest independent of the intention of the parties and the parol evidence of what the payor's intention actually was is let in, not for the purpose of vitiating rights effectuating anyone's intention, but for the purpose of establishing by this proof that the law, for reasons other than effectuating intent, ought not to operate to create the right, or to create it only to a limited extent. Whichever of these views is accepted, there seems no reason why, on this rationale, the security agreement should not extend not only to the purchase money loan itself but to additional loans.

Another explanation invokes the "do-equity" rationale mentioned before. The idea is that the loan has paid for the property under an agreement that it be so used and, therefore, before the borrower should be allowed to obtain it from the lender under the resulting trust he should pay the loan just as he should have to pay off loans obtained for and used to make improvements. This explanation would confine the enforceable security agreements to those covering loans of purchase money.

A contributing influence, no matter which theory is followed, undoubtedly is the fact that in this sort of transaction there are normally present factors which minimize the evils at which the Statute aims.[5] These include the fact of the loan, the dealings with the third party (whose story is readily available) and the fact that the borrower-payor is frequently let into possession and pays taxes. On the other hand, the tripartite transaction differs from the straight deed absolute cases, in which it is clear that traditional concern for the hard pressed borrower who has to put his property at risk in order to get the money he needs plays a part. Here the borrower is acquiring new property, not risking old, and pledging as security only the property he never had before and for the money which enabled him to get it. Certainly no very convincing argument can be made for any special deference to the mortgagor in cases of this sort.

 WESTLAW REFERENCES
(390 +1 k6* k7* k8*) (resulting /3 trust) /p verbal oral parole
/s agreement contract /p (real /s estate) land house home

---

4. Scott, Trusts, § 441.1 (3d Ed.1967).

5. A good illustration is Miller v. Miller, 101 Md. 600, 61 A. 210 (1905), in which M, the borrower-purchaser, went into pos-session, made improvements, paid taxes, and not only paid interest on his loan from E, the grantee, but also the interest on the loan owed by E to T, the grantor.

§ 3.23   Continuing Equitable Ownership in the Borrower

In many cases the borrower-payor, instead of acquiring an interest in the property by way of resulting trust arising for the first time out of the transaction, had a prior equitable ownership.[1] Instances of this are contracts [2] or options [3] to purchase the property entered into by the borrower before the loan was made or the property conveyed to the lender by the contract vendor. On the question of showing the oral agreement for mortgage in such cases, an analogy to the two-party deed absolute cases can be invoked here, the prior equitable interest in the borrower giving her standing comparable to that of the legal owner-grantor. The fact that the conveyance is from a third party, but at the direction of the borrower, is insufficient to change the substance of the transaction. Indeed, the argument in favor of allowing the oral agreement is stronger here because the borrowed money was used to complete the payments necessary for the borrower to acquire the land. Moreover, it would seem that the reasoning in the purchase money resulting trust with oral security agreement cases is also applicable here. In both cases it is the borrower's money that pays for the property conveyed to the lender. It should be immaterial to the creation of a resulting trust by reason of this fact that the buyer had a prior equitable interest in the property because of an executory contract for its purchase and that the grantee, not being a bona fide purchaser, would take subject to it.

A still different approach may be suggested. The Statute of Frauds presents no obstacle where an oral agreement for a mortgage is made by one who borrows the money for the purpose of paying the vendor under a contract of purchase, if the money is so used and the conveyance made to the borrower.[4] It would be only a slight extension to apply this to our case in which the conveyance is made to the lender in accordance with the intention of the borrower. If this reasoning is accepted, the grantee-lender would be able to enforce an equitable security interest in the property to which he holds legal title. And, of course the borrower would have to do equity by paying the debt before she would be entitled to a conveyance in enforcement of either her preexisting equitable interest or her interest as beneficiary under a purchase money resulting trust.

§ 3.23

1. See generally, Cunningham & Tischler, Disguised Real Estate Security Transactions As Mortgages in Substance, 26 Rutgers L.Rev. 1, 22 (1972).

2. McConnell v. Gentry, 30 Ky.L.Rep. 548, 99 S.W. 278 (1907); Grout v. Stewart, 96 Minn. 230, 104 N.W. 966 (1905); but see Anderson v. Anderson, 81 Minn. 329, 84 N.W. 112 (1900). See also Logue's Appeal, 104 Pa. 136, 40 L.I. 485, 31 P.L.J. 116 (1883), in which A purchased land at a judicial sale and having borrowed from B the money with which to pay the sheriff, had conveyance made to B under an oral agreement for security. See note, 42 A.L.R. 10, 25 (1926).

3. Stitt v. Rat Portage Lumber Co., 96 Minn. 27, 104 N.W. 561 (1905); Welsh v. Griffith-Prideaux, Inc., 60 N.J.Super. 199, 158 A.2d 529 (1960).

4. See Osborne, Mortgages, Ch. 2 (2d Ed. 1970).

WESTLAW REFERENCES

equit! /s owner ownership /p property land /p mortgage
contract (option /s purchase) /p borrower payor vendee

§ 3.24 Effect of Statutory Abolition of Purchase Money Resulting Trusts

Statutes in several states have abolished the purchase money resulting trust.[1] In general, they provide that in the purchase money resulting trust situation, no trust shall be declared in favor of the payor unless the grantee takes title in his own name without the consent of the payor or the grantee in violation of some trust purchases the land with the money of another.[2] There is a presumption that such conveyances are fraudulent against the creditors of the payor, and unless such fraudulent intent is disproved, a trust results in favor of such creditors to the extent necessary to satisfy their demands.[3] Two states have provisions that purport to abolish purchase money resulting trusts, but these statutes are inapplicable where it can be shown that, absent any fraudulent intent, there is an agreement that the grantee hold the land in trust for the payor.[4] Such agreements need not be written. Essentially, these latter type statutes simply do away with the presumption in favor of a resulting trust and put the burden on the trust claimant to establish the trust intact.[5]

In theory, in those states that clearly have abolished the purchase money resulting trust, an oral agreement for a mortgage in tripartite cases will be invalid under the Statute of Frauds. This is so because, apart from the specific enforcement of the oral agreement, the alleged mortgagor has no interest whatsoever in the property either beforehand or arising out of the transaction, and to permit the purely executory oral agreement to create an interest would squarely contravene the Statute of Frauds.[6]

Some courts stick more closely than others to the language of the statutes barring resulting trusts. Thus, some courts have refused to permit the trust and, consequently, the mortgage, in cases where there is an oral agreement that the grantee shall hold the title as security for the purchase money loan and, subject thereto, for the benefit of the

§ 3.24

1. See Ky.Rev.Stat. § 381.170; Mich. Comp. Laws Ann. §§ 26.57–26.59; Minn. Stat.Ann. §§ 501.07–501.09; N.Y.—McKinney's Estates, Powers and Trusts Law § 7–1.3; Wis.Stat.Ann. § 701.04. On the other hand, four states have statutes expressly authorizing purchase money resulting trusts. See Mont. Code Ann. § 86–103; N.D.Cent. Code Ann. § 59–01–03(4); 60 Okla.Stat.Ann. § 137; S.D.Comp.Laws § 55–1–10.

2. See Nelson, Purchase-Money Resulting Trusts in Land in Missouri, 33 Mo.L.

Rev. 552, 605 (1968); Scott, Trusts, § 440.2 (3d Ed.1967).

3. See Nelson, Purchase-Money Resulting Trusts in Land in Missouri, 33 Mo.L. Rev. 552, 605 (1968).

4. See West's Ann.Ind.Code §§ 56–606—56–608; Kan.Stat.Ann. 58–2406—58–2408; Scott, Trusts, § 440.2 (3d Ed. 1967).

5. See Nelson, Purchase-Money Resulting Trusts in Land in Missouri, 33 Mo.L. Rev. 552, 605 (1968).

6. See In re Bennett, 115 Minn. 342, 132 N.W. 309 (1911).

borrower.[7] On the other hand, other courts have held that the resulting trust arises and the oral mortgage is good, the reasoning being twofold: (1) that the statute bars resulting trusts which would arise *solely* from the payment of the purchase money and have no other foundation. It therefore is inapplicable because there is another foundation in the oral agreement and the lending transaction. (2) That the transaction was purely one of oral mortgage.[8] The latter ground was justified on the basis that the title had been taken by the grantee "upon paying a balance due upon a contract of purchase" previously entered into by the borrower with the grantor;[9] in other words it was a case of a previously existing interest in the borrower claimant.

In many cases, even though no resulting trust can be established as an exception to the statutes prohibiting them, the borrower can establish a constructive trust in her favor which will satisfy the requirement of an interest in the property before or at the time of the mortgage transaction as effectively as would the resulting trust. An oral promise by the lender-grantee to hold it for the borrower should be sufficient.[10] Where there is an oral agreement with the borrower to bid in property about to be sold at foreclosure, execution, tax, partition or other judicial sale, coupled with forbearance on the part of the borrower, in reliance upon the agreement, to take steps to protect her interest, the courts have no difficulty in giving relief in spite of the fact the agreement was oral.[11] As one court put it, "where one of the parties to a contract, void by the statute of frauds, avails himself of its invalidity, but unconscientiously appropriates what he has acquired under it, equity will compel restitution; and it constitutes no objection to the claim, that the opposite party may happen to secure the same practical benefit, through the process of restitution, which would have resulted from the observance of the void agreement."[12] The same doctrine has been applied to oral agreements to redeem land for the owner after foreclosure or execution sales.[13] Similarly, if the purchase was made by one

7. Anderson v. Anderson, 81 Minn. 329, 84 N.W. 112 (1900), approved in Nelson v. Nelson, 149 Minn. 285, 288, 183 N.W. 354, 355 (1921); contra, alternative decision, Stitt v. Rat Portage Lumber Co., 96 Minn. 27, 36, 104 N.W. 561, 565 (1905).

8. Carr v. Carr, 52 N.Y. 251 (1873) (there was a prior oral contract of purchase between the borrower and the grantor as well as part payment of the purchase price and taking of possession by the borrower contemporaneously with the conveyance); Widmayer v. Warner, 192 App.Div. 499, 182 N.Y.S. 629 (1920) (alternative decision). See Bogert, Trusts and Trustees, 2d Ed., § 467 (1964); Scott, Trusts, § 440.2 (3d Ed. 1967).

9. Carr v. Carr, supra note 8.

10. See Scott, Trusts, § 440.2 (3d Ed. 1967).

11. Ryan v. Dox, 34 N.Y. 307, 90 Am. Dec. 696 (1866); Congregation Kehal Adath Jeshurun M'Yassy v. Universal Building & Construction Co., 134 App.Div. 368, 119 N.Y.S. 72 (1909); Widmayer v. Warner, 192 App.Div. 499, 182 N.Y.S. 629 (1920), alternative decision. If the borrower did not refrain from taking steps to protect himself no constructive trust will arise. Wheeler v. Reynolds, 66 N.Y. 227, 232 (1876); Southwick v. Spevak, 252 Mass. 354, 357, 147 N.E. 885, 886 (1925). See note, 42 A.L.R. 10, 78 (1926).

12. Ryan v. Dox, supra, note 11, at 319.

13. Wood v. Rabe, 96 N.Y. 414, 425, 427, 48 Am.Rep. 640 (1884). See note, 42 A.L.R. 10, 118 (1926); 54 id. 1207.

standing in a confidential relation to the borrower, or if the purchase was in breach of a fiduciary duty a constructive trust will be imposed.[14]

A preliminary inquiry in all of these cases is whether the arrangement between the parties was for a loan by the grantee to the claimant or whether it was for the grantee to buy the property and then resell it to the claimant. The latter clearly falls within the prohibition of the Statute of Frauds even in jurisdictions where purchase money resulting trusts are not abolished. Since this is so, it is not surprising that where the agreement is for a loan and security, but because of the abolition of purchase money resulting trusts the borrower gets no interest in the property, the courts should say that this is invalid because the Statute of Frauds prevents the enforcement of the oral agreement. In other words, it is treated as an oral agreement for purchase. This seems sound, for in both cases the claimant can acquire an interest in the property for the first time only by the enforcement of the executory oral agreement. And yet one cannot escape an uneasy feeling that the result may rest more upon adherence to what the courts consider the basic theory of a mortgage than concern with the Statute of Frauds. The usual mortgage involves a prior property interest in the mortgagor which is put up by him as collateral to obtain money and which will be lost if the mortgage is valid and is foreclosed. Starting with this as the norm, it is not difficult to see that courts might establish as an indispensable part of the mortgage concept that there must be a property interest in the mortgagor. Where the property interest in the mortgagor is acquired for the first time in and through the transaction which results in the mortgage, the concept still could be held to be satisfied even though the hazard the borrower runs in such a case is only that of losing what he acquired by the use of the loan. But where there exists only an executory right to get an interest in the property the mortgage concept will not stretch and the courts assimilate the case to that of a contract to sell.

 WESTLAW REFERENCES

purchase /s money /p resulting /s trust /p aboli! regulat!
    barr*** invalid /p statute /p land property (real /s estate)
court(mi mn wi nd sd) & 26.57 501.07 701.04 59–01–06(4) 55–1–10
court(ks ok mt) & 58–2406 (60 +s 137) 86–103
court(ny in) & 7–1.3 56–606
court(ky) & 381.170

§ 3.25 Contract or Option to Purchase

We saw in the two-party deed absolute case that the agreement between the parties may in form be one for an option or a contract to purchase, rather than an oral agreement that the property is to be

---

14. Foreman v. Foreman, 251 N.Y. 237, 241, 167 N.E. 428 (1929), is a leading case. See Peppard Realty Co., Inc. v. Emdon, 213 App.Div. 824, 209 N.Y.S. 5 (1925), affirmed 241 N.Y. 588, 150 N.E. 566 (1925). See note 42 A.L.R. 10, 28 (1926).

security. The same may be true here where the deed comes to the grantee from a third person.[1] Sometimes, indeed, the parties use the utmost care to adopt the form of a sale and purchase and not of a loan and mortgage.[2] When this is done the problem is similar to the two-party cases previously considered in which the deed absolute transaction was accompanied by an agreement or option to resell. In both the question is whether the transaction is what it purports to be or whether it actually is a mortgage. And in both there is no legal prohibition against resolving that question by any relevant evidence that is admissible. Plainly, in these tripartite cases those who would transform the expressed contract for sale into a different one carry a heavy burden.[3]

Two theories are used to justify treating such tripartite transactions as mortgages. First, it has been said that "if a transaction resolves itself into a security, whatever may be its form and whatever name the parties may choose to give it, it is, in equity, a mortgage." [4] Second, as two commentators have pointed out, "it can also be justified on the more complicated theory that the grantee-lender holds the legal title subject to a resulting trust based on the presumption that the lender was not intended to get the entire beneficial interest in the property conveyed to him, and that the security interest of the grantee-lender may be established by parol evidence." [5]

The factors which guide courts in the two-party transactions are much the same ones that will influence their decisions here. However there is one vitally important point to reiterate here: that to find a mortgage there must be in the mortgagor, either prior to, or arising through, the transaction otherwise than by the terms of the agreement that he should get it, an interest in the mortgaged property. As was stated in a penetrating opinion, "So far as we can find, every case in which the existence of an absolute promise by an ostensible vendee to pay the sum involved has been thought to indicate that the transaction was merely a loan instead of having the character in which it was made to appear, is a case where the contract vendee had parted with his recent title and was arranging to get it back again. In no case was the contract one for the purchase of property which he had never before owned." [6] Further, while in the two-party cases the tendency to find the transaction to be a mortgage was observed, the contrary is the

---

§ 3.25

1. See Pollak v. Millsap, 219 Ala. 273, 278, 122 So. 16, 20, 65 A.L.R. 110 (1929).

2. E.g., Stark v. Bauer Cooperage Co., 3 F.2d 214 (C.C.A.Ohio 1925), certiorari denied 45 S.Ct. 464, 267 U.S. 604, 69 L.Ed. 809 (1925).

3. Id. at 215. But cf. the following statement: "all doubts are resolved in favor of it being a mortgage, and not a conditional sale." Pollak v. Millsap, 219 Ala. 273, 278, 122 So. 16, 21, 65 A.L.R. 110 (1929).

4. Welsh v. Griffith-Prideaux, Inc., 60 N.J.Super. 199, 208, 158 A.2d 529, 534 (1960). See also, Miller v. Miller, 101 Md. 600, 61 A. 210 (1905).

5. Cunningham & Tischler, Disguised Real Estate Security Transactions As Mortgages In Substance, 26 Rutgers L.Rev. 1, 21 (1972). See Vreeland v. Dawson, 55 N.J.Super. 456, 151 A.2d 62 (1959). See also, Annot., 27 A.L.R.2d 1285 (1953).

6. Stark v. Bauer Cooperage Co., supra note 2, at 216.

general rule in this type of transaction. And the reason for this stems from the fact that in this sort of business deal the hazard is not of losing what the obligor had owned before, but only of failing to get for the first time what he had bargained for.

 WESTLAW REFERENCES
(option /10 buy) (sale /10 (contract agreement /5 condition))
    & equit! /s mortgage

E. THE INSTALLMENT LAND CONTRACT

§ 3.26 An Introduction to the Installment Land Contract

The installment land contract is the most commonly used substitute for the mortgage or deed of trust. This device is also sometimes referred to as a "contract for deed", a "long-term land contract," or a "land sale contract." The installment land contract and the purchase money mortgage fulfill the identical economic function—the financing by the seller of the unpaid portion of the real estate purchase price. Under an installment land contract, the vendee normally takes possession and makes monthly installment payments of principal and interest until the principal balance is paid off. The vendor retains legal title until the final payment is made, at which time full title is conveyed to the vendee. Such contracts may be amortized over time periods as short as a year or two or as long as twenty years or more. During the contract period, the vendee normally will be required to pay the taxes, maintain casualty insurance, and keep the premises in good repair.

It is important to distinguish the installment land contract from the ordinary executory contract for the sale of land, variously known as a "binder," a "marketing contract," or an "earnest money contract." This latter type of contract is used primarily to establish the parties' rights and liabilities during the period between the date of the bargain and the date of closing, usually only a month or two later, on which title passes to the purchaser and security agreements, if any, are consummated. In contrast, the installment land contract governs the parties throughout the life of the debt, while the earnest money contract is completed at closing when the purchaser either tenders the full purchase price of the land or enters into a separate security agreement. Indeed, it is not uncommon for parties to agree to enter into an installment land contract at the closing date of the earnest money contract.

Traditionally, the vendor has placed primary reliance on a forfeiture clause. This clause, found in virtually every installment contract, typically provides that "time is of the essence" and that when a vendee fails to comply with the contract, including the obligation to pay promptly, the vendor has the option to declare the contract terminated, to retake possession of the premises without legal process, and to retain all prior payments as liquidated damages. Generally, the clause also relieves the vendor from all further obligation under the contract.

As one commentator has aptly pointed out, "[i]f the contract is enforceable as written and if title will not be clouded ＊ ＊ ＊ [the installment land] contract gives the vendor a very favorable remedy, much more advantageous than would be available under a purchase money mortgage or deed of trust."[1] Indeed, under a mortgage or deed of trust, the defaulting mortgagor has a right to redeem (the equity of redemption) which the mortgagee can eliminate only by a foreclosure proceeding should the mortgagor prove to be uncooperative.[2] Moreover, in many states, this problem is compounded, from the mortgagee's perspective, by the existence of post-sale statutory redemption rights.[3] Thus, the forfeiture clause in an installment contract appears to give the vendor an efficient remedy unfettered by such equitable and statutory mortgagor protections. For our purposes, however, it is important to emphasize that if the vendee resists forfeiture the installment land contract is advantageous only if it *"is enforceable as written and if title will not be clouded."*

Installment land contracts have traditionally been used as mortgage substitutes in those states where the substantive law of mortgages and the procedural aspects of foreclosure are considered to be heavily pro-mortgagor. For example, in a substantial number of states, judicial foreclosure is the only method of foreclosing a mortgage.[4] This procedure requires a full court proceeding in which all interested persons must be made parties, and is often time consuming and costly. Against a mortgagor who contests the mortgagee's claims, it may take several years to conclude such an action. Thus, utilization of the installment land contract in such states, whatever its risks, is perhaps understandable. But the risks are high, as will be seen below.

 WESTLAW REFERENCES
land /5 long-term sale installment /5 contract deed /p defin!
    explain＊＊＊

§ 3.27 The Forfeiture Remedy—Some General Considerations

Traditionally, installment land contract forfeiture provisions were routinely enforced in favor of the vendor.[1] Enforcement of such provisions presumably was based on a desire to carry out the intent of the

§ 3.26

1. Comment, Installment Contracts for the Sale of Land in Missouri, 24 Mo.L.Rev. 240, 244 (1959). See also Comment, Forfeiture: The Anomaly of the Land Sale Contract, 41 Albany L.Rev. 71, 73–74 (1977).

2. See §§ 7.1–7.5 infra.

3. See §§ 8.4–8.7 infra.

4. See § 7.11 infra.

§ 3.27

1. See Note, Forfeiture and the Iowa Installment Land Contract, 46 Iowa L.Rev. 786, 788 (1961); Comment, Florida Installment Land Contracts: A Time for Reform, 28 U.Fla.L.Rev. 156, 159 (1975).

parties, even though forfeiture often resulted in a substantial loss to the vendee and in a windfall gain to the vendor.[2] Enforcement became especially burdensome on the vendee as the contract neared completion and the vendee's cash investment became increasingly substantial. Yet courts tended to ignore the mortgage substitute aspect of the installment land contract and to treat it instead as an executory contract for the sale of land.

However, during the past several decades, an increasing number of courts and legislatures have been focusing on the installment land contract and its forfeiture clause with a mortgage law analogy in mind. As one court recently asked, "if the absolute deed kind of forfeiture may not be enforced by the grantee according to the express terms of the agreement, why then, should a forfeiture under a land sale contract be so enforced?"[3] The foregoing process, however, has hardly produced either an analytical or practical concensus. Consequently, the law in this area is not susceptible to orderly analysis: "Not only does the law vary from jurisdiction to jurisdiction, but within any one state results may vary depending upon the type of action brought, the exact terms of the land contract, and the facts of the particular case."[4] The interplay of these various factors makes it extremely difficult to predict whether the buyer's interest will be forfeited. While forfeitures are still occasionally judicially enforced,[5] it nevertheless can be safely stated that in no jurisdiction today will a vendor be able to assume that forfeiture provisions will be automatically enforced as written.[6] This change is the result of both legislative and judicial intervention to ameliorate the harsh impact of automatic forfeiture.

 WESTLAW REFERENCES
installment /s land /s contract agreement /p forfeit***

§ 3.28 Statutory Limitations on Forfeiture

Several states have attempted to alleviate some of the harshness in forfeiture clauses by enacting legislation regulating the circumstances

2. Note, Forfeiture and the Iowa Installment Land Contract, 46 Iowa L.Rev. 786, 788 (1961).

3. Braunstein v. Trottier, 54 Or.App. 687, 635 P.2d 1397, 1382 (1981), review denied 292 Or. 568, 644 P.2d 1129 (1982).

4. Power, Land Contracts as Security Devices, 12 Wayne L.Rev. 391, 416 (1966) (footnotes omitted).

5. See Hamner v. Rock Mountain Lake, Inc., 451 So.2d 249 (Ala.1984); Bell v. Coots, 451 So.2d 268 (Ala.1984); Curry v. Tucker, 616 P.2d 8 (Alaska 1980); Ellis v. Butterfield, 98 Idaho 644, 570 P.2d 1334 (1977), review denied 98 Idaho 663, 572 P.2d 509 (1978); McEnroe v. Morgan, 106 Idaho 326, 678 P.2d 595 (App.1984); First National Bank in Alamo Gordo v. Cape, 100 N.M. 525, 673 P.2d 502 (1983); Jacobs v. Phillipi, ___ N.M. ___, 697 P.2d 128 (1985); Albuquerque National Bank v. Albuquerque Ranch Estates, Inc., 99 N.M. 95, 654 P.2d 548 (1982); Braunstein v. Trottier, 54 Or.App. 687, 635 P.2d 1379 (1981), review denied 292 Or. 568, 644 P.2d 1129 (1982); Stonebraker v. Zinn, ___ W.Va. ___, 286 S.E.2d 911 (1982). Cf. United States v. Winterburn, 749 F.2d 1283 (9th Cir. 1984).

6. Even in states that otherwise enforce forfeitures, courts may, for example, require that vendor provide notice of intent to forfeit and a reasonable period of time "to cure the default," even though such actions are not required by the contract. See e.g., Martinez v. Martinez, 101 N.M. 88, 678 P.2d 1163 (1984).

under which forfeiture is permitted. These statutes often incorporate a "grace period" within which late payments must be accepted. Perhaps the best example of this type of legislation is the Iowa statute.[1] It provides that installment land contracts may be cancelled only by following a specified procedure. The vendor must provide written notification to the defaulting vendee and to the person in possession of the real estate; the notice must identify the real estate, specify the terms of the contract that have not been complied with, and inform the vendee that he has thirty days in which to correct his default. If the vendee performs within this time period, the forfeiture is avoided. If he does not, the notice of forfeiture, together with proof of service, may be recorded to constitute constructive notice of the completed forfeiture. Several other states have statutes similar to that of Iowa;[2] the grace period varies from thirty days in Iowa to as long as one year in North Dakota. In Minnesota and Arizona the grace period depends on the percentage of the contract price the vendee has already paid.[3] Some of these statutes permit nonjudicial forfeiture, while others allow it only by judicial action. It should be emphasized, however, that the purpose of these statutes is not to prevent forfeitures, but to alleviate the harshness of their operation.[4] In this connection several observations should be made.

First, the statutory grace period approach, as a practical matter, is analogous to the mortgage law concept of strict foreclosure. This mortgage foreclosure method, rarely used in the United States, allows a judicial grace period during which the mortgagor either pays the mortgage debt or forfeits the land to the mortgagee.[5] Similarly, if a vendee under an installment contract fails to correct a default within the statutory grace period, he loses the land. It is perhaps ironic that in some respects the statutory contract forfeiture procedures are more "pro-vendee" than the strict foreclosure concept is "pro-mortgagor." Under strict foreclosure, the mortgagor must pay the *accelerated* debt or lose the land. On the other hand, in such states as Iowa and Minnesota, the defaulting vendee need only pay the *arrearages* within the grace period, rather than the accelerated debt, in order to reinstate the contract.[6]

Second, to some degree these statutes have institutionalized or formalized the forfeiture concept and, in so doing, may have tended to discourage judicial interference in those situations where the vendor

---

§ 3.28

1. Iowa Code Ann. §§ 656.1–.6.

2. See, e.g., Minn.Stat.Ann. § 559.21; N.D.Cent.Code 32–18–01 to 06, S.D.Comp. Laws Ann. §§ 21–50–01 to 07.

3. Minn.Stat.Ann. § 559.21 (90 days maximum); Ariz.Rev.Stat. §§ 33–741–742 (9 months maximum).

4. See Note, Forfeiture and the Iowa Installment Land Contract, 46 Iowa L.Rev. 786, 797 (1961).

5. See G. Nelson and D. Whitman, Cases and Materials on Real Estate Transfer, Finance and Development 481–482 (2nd Ed. 1981).

6. See Hampton Farmers Co-operative Co. v. Fehd, 257 Iowa 555, 559, 133 N.W.2d 872, 874 (1965); Needles v. Keys, 149 Minn. 477, 480, 184 N.W. 33, 34 (1921); 51 Iowa L.Rev. 488 (1966).

complies with the statutory forfeiture method.[7] It is true that courts in states having such statutes sometime suggest that judicial relief from an "unconscionable forfeiture" may be available.[8] Moreover, the Iowa Supreme Court has held that, notwithstanding vendee default and vendor compliance with statutory termination requirements, if the vendor himself was in default, "equity dictates a cancellation of the forfeiture."[9] Also, statutory forfeiture may be inappropriate for certain minor, non-monetary defaults.[10] Nevertheless, judicial intervention in such statutory termination settings tends to focus more on technical statutory compliance and interpretation than on an independent analysis of the fairness of forfeiture.[11]

Finally, one practical advantage of statutory regulation is that it encourages the stability of land titles. Whatever the defects in such statutory regulation, title examiners in many of these states apparently routinely approve of the titles derived through the statutory proceedings.[12] There are at least two reasons for this. First, the tendency of the courts to reject attacks on forfeitures on non-statutory grounds encourages reliance on a forfeiture proceeding that complies with the applicable statute. Second, many of these statutes provide for the recording of a written and formalized memorial of compliance with the statute.[13] As a result, the title examiner is able to rely on the record for evidence of a permissible forfeiture. This is true even where the original contract is recorded. On the other hand, in states that lack statutory control of the forfeiture process, the recording of a statement

7. Note, Forfeiture and the Iowa Installment Land Contract, 46 Iowa L.Rev. 786, 797 (1961). Comment, Remedying Inequities of Forfeiture in Land Installment Contracts, 64 Iowa L.Rev. 158 (1978).

8. See e.g., Jensen v. Schreck, 275 N.W.2d 374 (Iowa 1979) (court suggests that while relief from forfeiture may be appropriate in certain situations, forfeiture was not unreasonable where vendee's contract payments and other investment in the real estate were less than 5% of the contract price).

9. See e.g., Keokuk State Bank v. Eckley, 354 N.W.2d 785 (Iowa App.1984); Skubal v. Meeker, 279 N.W.2d 23 (Iowa 1979); Warren v. Yocum, 223 N.W.2d 258 (Iowa 1974).

10. See Lett v. Grummer, 300 N.W.2d 147 (Iowa 1981) (statutory forfeiture refused where failure to make minor repairs did not threaten security).

11. See Note, Forfeiture and the Iowa Installment Land Contract, 46 Iowa L.Rev. 786, 792 (1961); Dale v. Pushor, 246 Minn. 254, 75 N.W.2d 595 (1956); Conley v. Downing, 321 N.W.2d 36 (Minn.1982) (statutory termination valid notwithstanding misstatement of attorney's fees in notice of

cancellation); Miller v. American Wonderlands, Inc., 275 N.W.2d 399 (Iowa 1979) (upholds statutory forfeiture based on a $10.48 default on a $30,000 contract and vendee's allowing liens to be filed on the premises). But c.f. Keokuk State Bank v. Eckley, 354 N.W.2d 785 (Iowa App.1984) (waiver defeats statutory forfeiture).

12. Nelson, The Use of Installment Land Contracts in Missouri—Courting Clouds on Titles, 33 J.Mo.B. 161, 164 (1977).

13. The Iowa statute exemplifies such a provision: "If the terms and conditions as to which there is default are not performed within said thirty days, the party serving said notice or causing the same to be served, may file for record in the office of the county recorder a copy of the notice aforesaid with proofs of service attached or indorsed thereon (and, in case of service by publication, his personal affidavit that personal service could not be made within this state) and when so filed and recorded, the said record shall be constructive notice to all parties of the due forfeiture and cancellation of said contract." Iowa Code Ann. § 656.5.

that forfeiture has occurred may be regarded by a subsequent title examiner simply as a self-serving assertion that in itself may constitute a cloud on title.

The Maryland statute takes a substantially different approach from those described above.[14] Where an installment land contract for the sale of residential property to a noncorporate vendee is involved, forfeiture is prohibited. The vendor can utilize the land to satisfy the vendee's debt only through a foreclosure sale identical to that used for a mortgage.[15] The vendee is entitled to receive any surplus from the sale—that amount by which the sale price exceeds the unpaid balance of the purchase price. Since installment land contracts are treated like mortgages in residential transactions, there is apparently no incentive to continue their use in the residential setting. On the other hand, the common law rules as to forfeiture presumably still apply to nonresidential installment land contracts.[16]

The Ohio legislation governing installment land contracts is also somewhat unique. While it incorporates a grace period concept, it focuses on how long and how much the vendee has paid under the contract. Such contracts on "property improved by a dwelling", are categorized in two ways: those which have been in effect less than five years *and* on which less than 20% of the principal amount has been paid; and those which have been in effect five years or more *or* on which 20% or more has been paid. In the former setting, forfeiture, while subject to a 30 day grace period, is specifically authorized.[17] In the latter situation, the contract must be foreclosed judicially as a mortgage.[18] Installment land contracts that fall into neither of the above categories are governed solely by case law. Interestingly, those Ohio contracts on which forfeiture is statutorily authorized may be falling prey to the "institutionalization" process described earlier. According to one commentator, it is likely in such cases "that a court will grant forfeiture as a matter of law rather than exercise its equitable jurisdiction and consider factors normally used * * * in non-statutory forfeiture cases. * * * Unlike defaults on land contracts not covered by the Act, * * * [the vendee] subject to statutory forfeiture may find himself faced with a judge who either feels constrained by the statute from granting equitable relief or takes comfort in the simplicity of the statute and ignores the possibility of equitable action." [19]

---

14. Md.Code, Real Prop. §§ 10–101 to 10–108; Md.R.P. W79.

15. Md.R.P. W70 to W72, W77.

16. See also Mont.Codes Ann. §§ 52–401 to 417, in which the Montana Small Tract Financing Act of 1963 made possible an optional power of sale deed of trust mechanism for tracts of 15 acres or less. One commentator has suggested that this legislation makes the installment land contract in Montana unnecessary. See Lohn, Toward Abolishing Installment Land Sale Contracts, 36 Mont.L.Rev. 110 (1975).

17. Ohio Rev.Code §§ 5313.05, 5313.06 and 5313.08.

18. Ohio Rev.Code § 5313.07.

19. Durham, Forfeiture of Residential Land Contracts in Ohio: The Need for Further Reform of a Reform Statute, 16 Akron L.Rev. 397, 430 (1983).

Oklahoma legislation constitutes perhaps the most sweeping and decisive statutory regulation of installment land contracts. In one relatively short paragraph, an Oklahoma statute states that installment land contracts

> for purchase and sale of real property made for the purpose or with the intention of receiving the payment of money and made for the purpose of establishing an immediate and continuing right of possession of the described real property, whether such instruments be from the debtor to the creditor or from the debtor to some third person in trust for the creditor, shall to that extent be deemed and held mortgages, and shall be subject to the same rules of foreclosure and to the same regulations, restraints and forms as are prescribed in relation to mortgages.[20]

The effect of this statutory provision is to treat all installment land contracts entailing a transfer of possession to the vendee as mortgages and thus to make the forfeiture remedy unavailable to a vendor. Thus, installment land contracts presumably have been rendered obsolete in Oklahoma. This legislation is especially significant in view of the fact that Oklahoma permits only judicial, and not power of sale, foreclosure of mortgages.[21]

 WESTLAW REFERENCES
court(ia nd mn sd) & 656.1 32–18–01 559.21 21–50
court(az ok) & 33–741 (16 +s 11a 686)
court(md) & 10–101

§ 3.29 Judicial Limitations on Forfeiture

Absent statutory regulation, numerous state courts have in recent years refused to enforce against a defaulting vendee forfeiture clauses that the courts have deemed unreasonable or inequitable. These courts have employed several approaches to save the vendee from forfeiture. Some cases, for example, have in effect conferred on the vendee a mortgagor's equity of redemption, permitting him to tender the remainder of the purchase price (or even his arrearages) in a suit or counterclaim for specific performance of the contract. Where the vendee was unable or unwilling to redeem, courts have occasionally ordered the judicial foreclosure of the land contract. Finally, some courts, after determining that a particular forfeiture clause is unfair, have extended to the defaulting vendee the right to restitution—the right to recoup his payments to the extent that they exceed the vendor's damages caused by the vendee's default. Of course, many state courts have not consid-

---

20. 16 Okla.Stat.Ann. § 11A. See Panama Timber Co., Inc. v. Barsanti, 633 P.2d 1258 (Okl.App.1980), appeal decided 619 P.2d 872 (1980) (installment land contract deemed constructive mortgage).

21. 12 Okla.Stat.Ann. § 686. For an analysis of the statute, see Comment, The Decline of the Contract for Deed in Oklahoma, 14 Tulsa L.J. 557 (1979).

ered the forfeiture clause in all of the remedial contexts described above, nor have they always been theoretically precise. Some courts have utilized contract principles to protect the defaulting vendee from an inequitable forfeiture provision. Other courts have gone a long way toward simply treating the installment land contract as a mortgage—in much the same fashion as does the Oklahoma statute. Still others have employed a confusing amalgam of mortgage and contract law. The following headings examine these various approaches employed by state courts to mitigate the harshness of forfeiture.

Waiver By the Vendor As An Excuse for Delinquency

Frequently a vendor will accept one or several late payments from his purchaser without taking action to declare a forfeiture. When the vendor finally reaches the end of his patience and informs the purchaser that forfeiture has occurred, the purchaser may argue that the vendor's prior behavior constitutes a waiver of the time provisions of the contract and that the vendor is legally bound to accept the late payments. Often this dispute is presented to the court in the context of a purchaser's suit or counterclaim for specific performance of the contract. The vendee may be willing to tender the entire purchase price, or he may insist upon an opportunity to make up his arrearages and resume the original payment schedule.

Many cases have adopted the purchaser's position in this situation.[1] In effect, these cases hold that the vendor's waiver avoids the effect of the forfeiture clause and creates in the purchaser a right analogous to an equity of redemption. According to this view, if the vendor had given the purchaser clear notice that no further delinquencies would be tolerated, and if this notice had been given in adequate time to allow the purchaser to get back on schedule, the vendor might thereby have preserved his right of forfeiture as to future installments. Since he did not do so, the court itself will generally fix a reasonable time within which the purchaser must cure the delinquencies.

The courts of Missouri and Utah have been particularly inclined to employ this technique. One commentator aptly described the Missouri situation:

§ 3.29

1. See Shervold v. Schmidt, 359 N.W.2d 361 (N.D.1984); In re Northern Illinois Development Corp., 309 F.2d 882 (7th Cir. 1962), certiorari denied 372 U.S. 965, 83 S.Ct. 1090, 10 L.Ed.2d 129 (1963); Welch v. Cooper, 11 Ark.App. 263, 670 S.W.2d 454 (1984); Johnke v. Polomar Financial Corp., 22 Ariz.App. 369, 527 P.2d 771 (1974); Triplett v. Davis, 238 Ark. 870, 385 S.W.2d 33 (1964); Petersen v. Ridenour, 135 Cal. App.2d 720, 287 P.2d 848 (1955); Krentz v. Johnson, 36 Ill.App.3d 142, 343 N.E.2d 165 (1976); Woods v. Monticello Development Co., 656 P.2d 1324 (Colo.App.1982); Miles Homes, Inc. v. Mintjal, 17 Ill.App.3d 642, 307 N.E.2d 724 (1974); Pierce v. Yochum, 164 Ind.App. 443, 330 N.E.2d 102 (1975); Legg v. Allen, 72 Or.App. 351, 696 P.2d 9 (1985); Soltis v. Liles, 275 Or. 537, 551 P.2d 1297 (1976); Bailey v. Lilly, 667 P.2d 933 (Mont.1983); Stinemeyer v. Wesco Farms, Inc., 260 Or. 109, 487 P.2d 65 (1971); Bradley v. Apel, 531 S.W.2d 678 (Tex.Civ.App. 1975); Williamson v. Wanlass, 545 P.2d 1145 (Utah 1976); Paul v. Kitt, 544 P.2d 886 (Utah 1975); Keokuk State Bank v. Eckley, 354 N.W.2d 785 (Iowa App.1984).

Thus, Missouri courts today seem hesitant to give full effect to forfeiture provisions as measures of liquidated damages in installment land contracts. They are likely to find that such provisions have been waived by the vendor due to such acts as his acceptance of late payments of principal or of interest on late payments after the delinquency of those payments. Furthermore, waiver of forfeiture provisions is equally likely to be found in any of the following in which a land installment contract is involved: viz., an action for ejectment by a vendor, an action for specific performance by a defaulting vendee, a counterclaim for specific performance by a defaulting vendee who is defendant to an action for ejectment, or even a trespass action by a defaulting vendee against his vendor concerning the land that is the subject of the contract. The finding that such a forfeiture provision has been waived would be very likely if the value of the land subject to the forfeiture provisions substantially exceeded the amount still unpaid under the contract.[2]

The waiver cases tend to be variable and difficult to reconcile. In some cases rather innocuous forbearances by vendors have been translated into favorable holdings for purchasers,[3] while in others quite substantial leniency has been unavailing.[4] In one Utah case,[5] for example, the vendees under an installment land contract for the purchase of a house made sporadic late payments for the first two years of the contract. Some monthly payments were missed entirely. The vendor repeatedly demanded that the contract be paid up to date, but from time to time the vendees were assured that no forfeiture was contemplated "at that time." Finally, more than two years from the date of the contract, the vendor declared a forfeiture and after unsuccessful negotiation brought an unlawful detainer action to have vendees ousted and the contract forfeited. The trial court concluded that the vendor had waived the strict performance of the contract. The Utah Supreme Court reversed the trial court and upheld the forfeiture in the following language: "Under the circumstances of this case, we believe that the buyers * * * were given a reasonable length of time to clear themselves of default * * *. They had not paid the equivalent of the rental value of the property for the time they occupied it."[6]

The quoted language is quite telling. Obviously the amount of the payments in relation to the rental value has nothing at all to do with whether there was an effective waiver by the vendor. It is difficult not to conclude that the court was manipulating the waiver concept as a means of deciding whether, in terms of fairness and economic equity,

2. Note, 29 Mo.L.Rev. 222, 226 (1964) (footnotes omitted).

3. See note 2 supra.

4. See, e.g., Economy Savings & Loan Co. v. Hollington, 105 Ohio App. 243, 152 N.E.2d 125, 6 O.O.2d 61 (1957); Christy v. Guild, 101 Utah 313, 121 P.2d 401 (1942).

5. Pacific Development Co. v. Stewart, 13 Utah 403, 195 P.2d 748 (1948).

6. Id. at 409, 195 P.2d at 751.

the purchaser should have another opportunity to make up his missed payments.[7] Such decisionmaking may be entirely salutory, but it should not be disguised.

Recognition of An Equity of Redemption

A number of jurisdictions have taken the view that the purchaser, notwithstanding his default, should be granted a final opportunity to pay the balance owing on the contract or, in some instances, the arrearages, before losing his land. Some courts view this right, analogous to a mortgagor's equity of redemption, as unconditional, while others are inclined to recognize it only if the purchaser's prior payments add up to a substantial investment or "equity" in the property. Sometimes the existence of the right is made to turn on whether the purchaser's payments significantly exceed the property's rental value or some similar test. Moreover, some cases require the vendee not be guilty of gross negligence or bad faith. The critical point is that, unlike the cases discussed in the preceding paragraphs, these opinions do not rely upon a prior waiver by the vendor.

A typical case is Nigh v. Hickman,[8] decided by the Missouri Court of Appeals. There a vendee under an installment land contract covering farmland had paid almost 35% of the total purchase price. The vendee then defaulted on one payment by fifteen days, and the vendor refused to accept the late payment. The vendee sued for specific performance and tendered the balance owing on the contract. The appellate court held that the trial court correctly granted specific performance and that enforcement of the forfeiture clause would have been inequitable. Although the contract contained no "time of the essence" clause, the court indicated that the result would not have been different had such a clause been present.

A leading Hawaii Supreme Court decision, Jenkins v. Wise,[9] adopts the foregoing specific performance approach in less ambivalent fashion. In that case, vendees, prior to default, had made payments amounting to 16% of the total purchase price of $100,000 under installment land contracts on two parcels of land. Thereafter vendees defaulted on two semi-annual $4,000 installment payments due in March and April, 1972 respectively. During September, 1972 vendors, pursuant to the contracts, notified the vendees that the contracts had been cancelled. During October of the same year vendees contracted to sell the property to third parties for a $51,000 profit and, accordingly, vendees promised vendors that the original contracts would be paid in full on November 15, 1972. When payment was not forthcoming, vendors, in December,

---

7. The court may have been confusing the waiver concept with the principle of equitable relief from forfeiture. See text accompanying notes 31–45, infra.

8. 538 S.W.2d 936 (Mo.App.1976). See also Key v. Gregory, 553 S.W.2d 329 (Mo.

App.1977); Dill v. Zielke, 26 Wn.2d 246, 173 P.2d 977 (1946).

9. 58 Hawaii 592, 574 P.2d 1337 (1978).

1972, sought a judicial declaration of cancellation of the contracts and vendees counterclaimed for specific performance. The Hawaii Supreme Court reversed a trial court order cancelling the contracts and, notwithstanding "time of the essence" language contained therein, held in favor of vendees' claim for specific performance. According to the supreme court, "where the vendee's breach has not been due to gross negligence, or to deliberate or bad-faith conduct on his part, and the vendor can reasonably and adequately be compensated for his injury, courts in equity will generally grant relief against forfeiture and decree specific performance of the agreement * * * and a key factor in a trial court's determination is whether forfeiture would be harsh and unreasonable under the circumstances." [10] The court concluded that, notwithstanding the contract to resell, the vendees had acted in good faith. It pointed to the fact that the vendees had incurred architectual and building permit expenses. According to the court, the vendees "in good faith, were preparing to develop the property themselves, but, in the words of [one of the vendees], the [contract to resell] was 'too good a deal' ".[11]

The relationship between the granting of specific performance to a purchaser and more traditional mortgage concepts is illustrated by the Florida Court of Appeals' opinion in H & L Land Co. v. Warner.[12] There the vendee had made installment payments for about five years, but thereafter a four-year period elapsed during which no payments were made. During this period of nonpayment the vendor remained silent as to the vendee's default. The vendee ultimately sued for specific performance, tendering the balance of the purchase price; the vendor counterclaimed for removal of the contract as a cloud on the vendor's title. The court granted specific performance and stated: "[T]he vendor under a specifically enforceable installment land sale contract, who has received part of the purchase price and has given the vendee possession of the land and the benefits and burdens of ownership, is in essentially the same position as a vendor who has conveyed the legal title and taken back a purchase money mortgage * * *." [13] The court implicitly imposed at least three conditions to be satisfied in order to qualify for specific performance: (1) The vendee must be in possession or have a right to possession; (2) the contract must be specifically enforceable; and (3) the vendee must assert and exercise his right of redemption by tendering full performance.[14]

---

10. Id. at 597, 574 P.2d at 1341.

11. Id. at 602, 574 P.2d at 1344. *Jenkins* was specifically reaffirmed by the Hawaii Supreme Court in Kaiman Realty, Inc. v. Carmichael, 65 Hawaii 637, 655 P.2d 872 (1982), opinion supplemented ___ Hawaii ___, 659 P.2d 63 (1983) (the supplemental opinion suggests that *Jenkins* is probably applicable to installment land contracts and not Hawaii's equivalent of an earnest money contract). See also, K.M. Young & Associates v. Cieslik, ___ Hawaii App. ___, 675 P.2d 793 (1983). For

clear-cut case of a denial of specific performance to a grossly negligent vendee, see Curry v. Tucker, 616 P.2d 8 (Alaska 1980).

12. 258 So.2d 293 (Fla.App.1972). See also Huguley v. Hall, 157 So.2d 417 (Fla. 1963); Mid-State Investment Corp. v. O'Steen, 133 So.2d 455 (Fla.App.1961).

13. 258 So.2d at 295.

14. See Comment, Florida Installment Land Contracts: A Time for Reform, 28 U.Fla.L.Rev. 156, 168–70 (1975).

There are problems with these conditions, especially with the last two. Arguably, tying these latter two requirements together is an inconsistent blending of contract and mortgage law. It is axiomatic that a vendee in default does not have a right to specific performance of a contract. Yet under mortgage law the right to redeem is not exercised until there has been a default. In *Warner,* the second requirement was met because the court found that the vendor had waived the vendee's default. However, as has been pointed out, "By so holding, the court is going in circles. If one must tender the unpaid balance as a condition precedent to the vesting of the right of redemption, then one must exercise this right before one is entitled to it—an anomaly, to be sure. Thus, the rights of mortgagors will not be extended to purchasers in default who are either in straitened circumstances or unaware of the right of redemption—the very individuals whom the mortgage statutes were designed to protect." [15] Notwithstanding this apparent anomaly, more recent cases reinforce the argument that, in general, Florida installment land contracts will be treated as mortgages for redemption purposes. In *Hoffman v. Semet,* [16] a Florida District Court of Appeals held that a vendee *in default* under an installment land contract had an equity of redemption and that the vendee's successor was entitled to satisfy the total outstanding indebtedness due the vendor under the contract and to receive a conveyance of the real estate. The court cited *Warner* for the proposition that an installment land contract "must be deemed and held to be a mortgage, subject to the same rules of foreclosure and to the same regulations, restraints, and forms as are prescribed in relation to mortgages." [17] Unlike the situation in *Warner,* however, there had been no waiver of the default; therefore, the contract was not specifically enforceable within the implicit requirements of *Warner.* The *Semet* court did not deal with this difficulty. Instead, it simply repeated "equity of redemption" language in referring to the vendee's interest. Moreover, later appellate decisions,[18] while not arising in the context of a tardy vendee seeking to redeem, so pervasively assert that an installment land contract is a mortgage that there seems little likelihood that a Florida vendee will be denied mortgage redemption rights.

The Kansas case of *Nelson v. Robinson* [19] illustrates how a court can sometimes refuse to enforce a forfeiture provision and in addition can impose a remedy that treats the installment land contract involved as an equitable mortgage. The vendors in *Nelson* brought an action to cancel an installment land contract for the sale of farmland. The vendee was over $1,900 delinquent in back payments, but had paid nearly one third of the $48,000 purchase price and had made valuable improvements to the land. The trial court refused to permit forfeiture,

15. Id. at 170.

16. 316 So.2d 649 (Fla.App.1975).

17. Id. at 651.

18. See e.g., Parise v. Citizens National Bank, 438 So.2d 1020 (Fla.App.1983); Earnest v. Carter, 368 So.2d 428 (Fla.App.

1979); Cook v. Merrifield, 335 So.2d 297 (Fla.App.1976); Torcise v. Perez, 319 So.2d 41 (Fla.App.1975). Aycock Brothers Lumber Co. v. First National Bank of Dothan, 54 Fla. 604, 45 So. 501 (1907).

19. 184 Kan. 340, 336 P.2d 415 (1959).

but rather ordered strict foreclosure of the contract. Under the terms of the decree, the vendee was given six months in which to pay the entire amount remaining due on the contract. Failure to so pay within that period would result in forfeiture of the land and back payments to the vendor. If the vendee paid only the arrearages within ten days of the decree, however, the redemption period would have extended to eighteen months. Interestingly, the vendee, and not the vendor, appealed, and the Kansas Supreme Court affirmed this exercise of equitable discretion of the trial court. It is noteworthy that the court here imposed the relatively rare mortgage remedy of strict foreclosure which was sought by neither party, but in which the vendor acquiesced.[20]

The *Nelson* decision clearly does not mean that all installment land contracts in Kansas will henceforth be treated as mortgages. If, for example, the vendee's stake in the property had been substantially less, perhaps immediate forfeiture would have been ordered.[21] The case, however, does illustrate that Kansas vendors cannot rely on automatic enforcement of the forfeiture clause. Thus, in Kansas, courts may very well apply the law of mortgages to some installment contracts and contract law to others.

In California, the movement toward recognition of a right of redemption for a defaulting vendee has received a considerable impetus from general statutory provisions, although their application was somewhat uncertain until fairly recently.[22] In Barkis v. Scott,[23] the California Supreme Court reevaluated a long line of earlier precedents dealing with forfeiture. The court concluded that when a forfeiture would otherwise result, the vendee can be relieved under section 3275 of the Civil Code which provides that

> Whenever, by the terms of an obligation, a party thereto incurs a forfeiture, or a loss in the nature of a forfeiture, by reason of his failure to comply with its provisions, he may be relieved therefrom, upon making full compensation to the other party, except in case of a grossly negligent, willful, or fraudulent breach of duty.[24]

The vendor in *Barkis* sought to quiet title and to enforce a forfeiture after the vendees inadvertently overdrew their bank account with their monthly house payment. The vendees' later efforts at payment were refused by the vendor. The supreme court held that section 3275 should provide relief from forfeiture and that the vendees had established the right to keep the contract in force. Here the default was, at most, negligent and not "grossly negligent, willful, or fraudulent."

20. This mortgage remedy is apparently the standard method in Wisconsin for terminating a vendee. See Exchange Corp. v. Kuntz, 56 Wis.2d 555, 202 N.W.2d 393 (1972); § 3.32 infra.

21. For a discussion of the significance of the proportion paid, see Croft v. Jensen, 86 Utah 13, 40 P.2d 198 (1935).

22. See Comment, Reforming the Vendor's Remedies for Breach of Installment Land Sale Contracts, 47 S.Cal.L.Rev. 191, 205 (1973).

23. 34 Cal.2d 116, 208 P.2d 367 (1949).

24. West's Ann.Cal.Civ.Code § 3275.

In MacFadden v. Walker,[25] the California Supreme Court dealt with the "willful, but repentant defaulting vendee." There an elderly vendee had been in willful default over two years, but had paid over half of the purchase price. When the vendor sought to quiet title to the property, she counterclaimed for specific performance, tendering the full amount due and owing on the contract. The court held that the policy against forfeitures includes granting the right to specific performance even when the default is willful, reasoning that, when taken together, the prohibition against punitive damages contained in section 3294 of the Civil Code, the strict limitations on the right to provide for liquidated damages contained in sections 1670–1671, and the provision of section 3369 that "neither specific nor preventive relief can be granted to enforce a penalty or forfeiture in any case * * *" prevented a forfeiture having no reasonable relation to the damage caused by the vendee's breach even when that breach is willful. Although the court noted that "persuasive arguments" had been made by Professor Hetland that installment land contracts should be treated like mortgages and deeds of trust and that willfully defaulting debtors should therefore have the right to redeem, it concluded that because the vendee was entitled to specific performance, "we need not decide whether she might also be entitled to some other remedy under the law governing security transactions."[26]

The ultimate conclusion that a tardy vendee should be treated as a mortgagor for redemption purposes is still proving illusive for California courts. In Kosloff v. Castle,[27] a vendor under an installment land contract covering the sale of a house for $15,000 declared a forfeiture after the vendee had been in default on a final "balloon" payment of $11,400 for approximately a year and a half. A few months later, the vendor filed an action in unlawful detainer and to quiet title. The trial court refused to permit the vendee to tender the contract balance and granted the vendor his requested relief. The District Court of Appeal affirmed the trial court determination. In so doing, the court noted that *McFadden* had held that specific performance may be granted to willfully defaulting vendees "in proper cases." In *McFadden,* the *Kosloff* court emphasized, the vendee had paid over half of the purchase price prior to her default, whereas the *Kosloff* vendee had paid less than one-third of the price in the pre-default period. Moreover, the *Kosloff* vendee had not only been willful, but also "grossly negligent", whereas the *McFadden* default, while willful, was based on the vendee's belief that her actions in withholding payment were justified. Thus, the court concluded that there was substantial evidence to sustain the trial court's weighing of the equities.

25. 5 Cal.3d 809, 97 Cal.Rptr. 537, 488 P.2d 1353 (1971).

26. Id. at 816, 97 Cal.Rptr. at 541, 488 P.2d at 1357. See also Williams Plumbing Co. v. Sinsley, 53 Cal.App.3d 1027, 126 Cal. Rptr. 345 (1975) (where breach not intentional).

27. 115 Cal.App.3d 369, 171 Cal.Rptr. 308 (1981).

The court in *Kosloff* also refused to hold that the installment land contract is a mortgage under Section 2924 of the Civil Code, which states in part that "every transfer of an interest in property, other than in trust, made only as a security for the performance of another act, is to be deemed a mortgage * * * " Had the court so held, vendee would have been afforded the redemption of a tardy mortgagor. Rather, the court stated, "any reform in this area is more appropriately initiated by the legislature which is in a better position to effect and coordinate comprehensive answers to the many-faceted questions such a determination would evoke." [28]

From the viewpoint of vendors, the general trend toward recognition of an equity of redemption is rather frightening. In the absence of a statute, nothing but a court order can cut off an equity of redemption. In effect, this means that the vendor will be forced to litigate—precisely the thing he hoped to avoid by use of the installment contract. Even if the court will follow the example of the Supreme Court of Kansas, granting forfeiture in the event the purchaser is unable to redeem,[29] the vendor's situation as far less advantageous than he expected when the contract was signed.

Restitution

In a jurisdiction in which no equity of redemption is yet recognized, or in a case in which the purchaser cannot or will not redeem, traditional analysis would suggest that forfeiture should follow. But along this dimension, too, the courts have been actively reforming the law. Increasingly they are holding that forfeiture may not be "free" and that the vendor must return the payments he has received insofar as they exceed his actual damages.[30] Some courts, such as those of Utah, take this position only in cases in which they conclude that an outright forfeiture would be "unconscionable," [31] but this may simply mean that the purchaser would suffer a substantial net loss if no restitution were ordered.[32]

The Utah cases usually measure the vendor's damages as the fair rental value of the property during the period of the purchaser's occupancy, plus such incidental damages as repairs and a sales commission upon resale.[33] In most of the situations presented, courts have

---

28. Id. at 377, 171 Cal.Rptr. at 312. See also, Bartley v. Karas, 150 Cal.App.3d 336, 197 Cal.Rptr. 749 (1983) (vendee not entitled to reinstatement by payment of arrearages, but specific performance in vendee's favor appropriate where default not willful).

29. See notes 19–21 and accompanying text, supra.

30. See e.g., Moran v. Holman, 501 P.2d 769 (Alaska 1972); Randall v. Riel, 123 N.H. 757, 465 A.2d 505 (1983); Morris v. Sykes, 624 P.2d 681 (Utah 1981); Howard v. Bar Bell Land & Cattle Co., 81 Idaho 189, 340 P.2d 103 (1959); Jenkins v. Wise,

58 Hawaii 592, 574 P.2d 1337 (1978) (dictum). K.M. Young & Associates v. Cieslik, ___ Hawaii App. ___, 675 P.2d 793 (1983). Cf. Stevenson v. Owen, ___ Mont. ___, 687 P.2d 1010 (1984).

31. Jacobson v. Swan, 3 Utah 2d 59, 278 P.2d 294 (1954).

32. The Utah court has had difficulty in reaching a consensus as to what is "unconscionable." See Kay v. Wood, 549 P.2d 709 (Utah 1976).

33. See, e.g., Weyher v. Peterson, 16 Utah 2d 278, 399 P.2d 438 (1965).

concluded that these items exceed the purchaser's payments and that he is not entitled to restitution. For example, in Strand v. Mayne,[34] the vendees under an installment land contract for the sale of a motel had made payments of principal and interest of over $19,000 on a $41,500 purchase price. They also spent $9,500 on repairs on the premises. Upon default, the vendors obtained possession by an unlawful detainer action. The vendees subsequently brought an action to recover the payments made under the contract on the ground that retention by the vendor was unconscionable. The Utah Supreme Court affirmed a summary judgment for the vendor, noting that the fair rental value of the motel up to the date of forfeiture, when added to the down payment the vendees had received on a resale of the property to a third party, exceeded the total of their payments to the vendors. The court observed that "[t]his clearly shows that the amount they have lost under the forfeiture provision is not unconscionable. * * *"[35] Similarly, in Weyher v. Peterson,[36] the Utah court concluded, in affirming a judgment for a vendor under a forcible entry and detainer action based on a forfeiture clause, that the rental value and damages, totalling $10,505, exceeded the $9,387 the vendee had paid on the contract and found no inequity in refusing to allow the vendee to recover some of his payments.

Utah vendees have also encountered difficulties with the restitution theory where the focus was on the value of the contract land rather than on its rental value. In Park Valley Corp. v. Bagley,[37] the Utah Supreme Court reversed a trial court determination that a vendee, who had paid over $139,000 on a $1,080,000 installment land contract on 7200 acres of land, was entitled to almost half of that amount in restitution. After the vendee breach, vendors resold the land for $935,000, which was $145,000 less than the contract price. In calculating the restitution amount, the trial court allowed the vendors only $15,000 of the $145,000 as their loss of bargain. It did so on the theory that the contract price greatly exceeded the real value of the land. In reversing, the Utah Supreme Court stressed that it was not unconscionable to hold vendees to an improvident bargain and that, in calculating the amount of any recovery to the vendees, vendors' damages should be based on the $145,000 loss of bargain amount. Accordingly, since this latter amount exceeded vendees' payments under the contract, they were entitled to no restitutionary recovery at all.

Although vendees have generally not fared well in Utah litigation,[38] the reasoning of the above decisions indicates that complete vendor reliance on the forfeiture clause is probably misplaced. In the above cases, the court upheld forfeiture because it believed the vendor's

34. 14 Utah 2d 355, 384 P.2d 396 (1963).

35. Id. at 357, 384 P.2d at 398.

36. 16 Utah 2d 278, 399 P.2d 438 (1965).

37. 635 P.2d 65 (Utah 1981).

38. One factor contributing to this litigation record is that few Utah vendees appear to record their contracts. Those who do record and subsequently default can probably settle with their vendors for at least the nuisance value of the suit which would be necessary to clear the vendor's title, since the damages and restitution issues are always litigable.

actual damages exceeded the vendee's payments. In the few Utah cases in which the vendee's payments exceeded the vendor's damages, the court did approve of restitution to the vendee of the excess.[39]

Florida cases also appear to impose a burden of showing unconscionability upon a purchaser who prays for restitution. Unfortunately, Florida courts have been less than carefully analytic in articulating the relevant test and thus have made the availability of restitution quite unpredictable. In Chace v. Johnson,[40] for example, the vendee was one year in default and sued to recover money totalling 80% of the contract price. The Florida Supreme Court ordered the vendor to return payments to the vendee that exceeded the vendor's damages. On the other hand, in Sawyer v. Marco Island Development Corp.,[41] where a vendor brought suit to remove from the record the interests of several vendees, one of whom was one year in default and who had paid 90% of the purchase price, a Florida appellate court held that vendee's interest could be extinguished without return of the payments made. Title to thirty-six lots was involved in *Sawyer*. Other vendees were also involved but were represented by a guardian ad litem because they did not appear. None of the vendees so represented had paid over 25% of the purchase price. The vendee who had paid the 90%, however, was personally represented. Despite the special circumstances of this last vendee, the court enforced forfeiture as to everyone, observing:

> We see a substantial difference between the unjust enrichment which would result if a large deposit were forfeited within a short period of time and a situation where a vendor has removed his property from the market for several years while the vendee abandons the contract by ceasing to make further payments * * *.[42]

The purchaser's restitution remedy is perhaps best developed in California. It should be noted first that, under the rule of Venable v. Harmon,[43] a California vendor cannot receive a deficiency judgment regardless of his loss. Beyond this, California antiforfeiture cases also compel the vendor to return to the vendee any amount paid in excess of the vendor's damages. In Freedman v. Rector, Wardens and Vestrymen of St. Matthias Parish,[44] for example, the California Supreme Court held that it violated the public policies against forfeitures, penalties, and unjust enrichment to deny restitution, even to a vendee willfully in default. There have been problems, however, in determining the amount of restitution to which the vendee is entitled. Under the reasoning of the California Supreme Court decision in Honey v. Henry's Franchise Leasing Corp.,[45] the vendor apparently has the

---

39. Morris v. Sykes, 624 P.2d 681 (Utah 1981); Kay v. Wood, 549 P.2d 709 (Utah 1976); Jacobson v. Swan, 3 Utah 2d 59, 278 P.2d 294 (1954).

40. 98 Fla. 118, 123 So. 519 (1929).

41. 301 So.2d 820 (Fla.App.1974), certiorari denied 312 So.2d 757 (1975).

42. 301 So.2d at 821.

43. 233 Cal.App.2d 297, 43 Cal.Rptr. 490 (1965) (based on West's Ann.Cal.Civ. Proc.Code § 580b.

44. 37 Cal.2d 16, 230 P.2d 629 (1951).

45. 64 Cal.2d 801, 52 Cal.Rptr. 18, 415 P.2d 833 (1966).

option of measuring his damages by either the "rental value" (giving restitution of the amount by which the vendee's payments exceed the fair rental value of the property while the vendee was in possession) or the "difference value" (giving restitution of the amount by which the vendee's payments exceed the difference between the current market value and the higher original contract price).[46] Professor Hetland points out that "rarely over the past few decades has the value of the property dropped so that the vendor prefers difference value to his alternative measure—rental value." [47] The choice is the vendor's, according to *Honey,* because permitting the vendee to make it would in effect give all installment vendees an option to convert their contracts into leases—an advantage the court hardly thought appropriate to give to a defaulter.

It is interesting to note that the economic results of the "difference value" measure of restitution are roughly similar to those of a judicial sale, in the sense that the market value of the property is debited against the vendor's claim. Of course, the two approaches are distinct, since in a restitution case the property's value is measured by the court upon the testimony of witnesses, rather than by a sale.[48]

46. The court noted that since rescission was not sought by the vendor, the rental value standard was inappropriate; the court consequently held that the proper calculation involved the difference value.

47. J. Hetland, Secured Real Estate Transactions 52 (1974).

48. If the California Supreme Court's formulation of the "difference value" measure of restitution is taken literally, then it seems subject to serious criticism. The problem is illustrated by the following example.

Assume P buys property from V under an installment contract. The pertinent facts of the transaction are:

Purchase price   = $30,000
Down payment   =   2,000
Original debt   = 28,000,   8% interest, 25-year maturity
Monthly payments   =   216.11

Suppose default occurs after five years and that the value of the property has declined, so that:

Value of property = $25,000
Balance on debt   = 25,836.58 (based on standard mortgage payment tables)

If foreclosure by judicial sale occurs, and if the costs of foreclosure are neglected and the sale brings fair market value, the sale proceeds will be $25,000; V will be entitled

to a deficiency judgment of $836.58, assuming no antideficiency statute. (In California, no such judgment will be permitted if a one-to-four-family house is involved.) West's Ann.Cal.Civ.Proc.Code § 580b.

Suppose that V, instead of seeking foreclosure, elects to terminate P's rights under the contract and to make restitution, as he is permitted to do under *Honey.* V must restore to P all payments made in excess of V's loss. V elects the "difference value" measure of loss.

Payments made	= $14,966.60	($216.11 per mo. × 60 months) including $2000 down payment
(–) V's loss	= 5,000.00	($30,000 minus $25,000)
Restitution	= 9,966.60	

Thus, instead of being entitled to a deficiency judgment, V must pay back to P nearly $10,000. This is, to say the least, a strange result.

The problem is that the court, in computing the amount of restitution, has ignored the "time value" of money. In a short-term marketing contract for $30,000, if P breaches and V must remarket the property one month later for $25,000, it is reasonably accurate to say that V's damages are $5,000. See Jensen v. Dalton, 9

Foreclosure As a Mortgage

The trend of the cases discussed above is clearly toward application of mortgage concepts to aid defaulting purchasers. The logical conclusion of this trend would be an absolute equivalency of installment contracts and mortgages, with foreclosure becoming the exclusive means by which a vendor could realize upon his security interest in the property. For a court to take this position should hardly seem surprising, for the judiciary reached the same conclusion long ago with regard to other forms of mortgage substitutes.[49] In recent years, an increasing number of courts have indicated an acceptance of this view.

California cases actually include no direct holding that foreclosure is a proper remedy in an installment contract default. However, a California Supreme Court decision, Honey v. Henry's Franchise Leasing Corp.,[50] and an opinion by the Ninth Circuit Court of Appeals, Ward v. Union Bond & Trust Co.,[51] imply that a judicial sale would be appropri-

---

Cal.App.3d 654, 88 Cal.Rptr. 426 (1970). If, however, the period between contract and breach is five years (during which V has not had possession), the $5,000 damage figure is completely erroneous. Let us recompute V's damages, but in doing so translate all amounts involved to a single point in time by computing future values for each amount involved, using compound interest tables. We may select any point in time we wish, but a convenient reference point is the fifth anniversary of the sale—which happens to be the date of default. (This is convenient because nothing of financial significance happens thereafter, and whatever V's damages are on that date can easily be translated to their value on the date of judgment simply by adding interest.)

In order to make translations of values to any given date, we must assume some interest or discount rate. Let us use 8%, since it is the figure selected by the parties themselves when they initiated the transaction. Here is what actually happened:

Date

1-1-0	V gives up $30,-000 asset, receives $2,000 cash. Future value of $28,000, as of 1-1-5	=	$41,715.66 (+)
2-1-0 through 1-1-5	V receives regular monthly payments of $216.11. Future value of $216.11/mo for 60 months	=	$15,879.08 (-)

1-1-5	V receives back the property, worth $25,000	=	$25,000.00 (-)
Subtracting what V received from what he gave up, damages		=	$836.58

Thus the "difference value" approach to restitution, properly computed, yields results exactly equal to a foreclosure sale. Of course, under California law, V cannot actually recover the $836.58 deficiency. Venable v. Harmon, 233 Cal.App.2d 297, 43 Cal.Rptr. 490 (1965).

No California case appears clearly to recognize the foregoing problem. Perhaps the closest is Kudokas v. Balkus, 26 Cal.App.3d 744, 103 Cal.Rptr. 318 (1972), a "difference value" case in which the court refused to allow the vendees to claim, as part of their "payments," the interest they had paid prior or to default of deeds of trust they had assumed. *Id.* at 756, 103 Cal.Rptr. at 325. Even this holding does not address the problem systematically.

The "future value" problem is also raised in "rental value" restitution cases, but its impact is relatively slight if the vendee's payments have been fairly regular prior to default and if they approximate the rental value of the property.

49. See §§ 3.4–3.25 supra.

50. 64 Cal.2d 801, 52 Cal.Rptr. 18, 415 P.2d 833 (1966). One other decision by the California Supreme Court suggests the availability of foreclosure in the installment contract context. See MacFadden v. Walker, 5 Cal.3d 809, 97 Cal.Rptr. 537, 488 P.2d 1353 (1971).

51. 243 F.2d 476 (C.A.Cal.1957).

ate if at least one of the parties requests it. To date there appears to be no California appellate opinion in which either purchaser or vendor has sought a judicial sale, and thus the language in the cases mentioned must be regarded as dicta. Moreover, as our discussion of the *Kosloff* decision earlier in this section [52] indicates, not all California appellate courts are even willing to treat the installment as a mortgage for equity of redemption purposes. Nevertheless, as a practical matter, it seems safe to assume that, if the issue were squarely presented to it, the California Supreme Court would conclude that vendee and vendor alike have the right to foreclosure of a defaulted installment land contract.

In Indiana the case for judicial sale is both better defined and less dependent on the wishes of the parties. In Skendzel v. Marshall,[53] the vendor sought a judicial declaration of forfeiture of a vendee's interest where the vendee had already paid $21,000 of a $36,000 contract price. The Indiana Supreme Court applied the concept that "equity abhors a forfeiture" and held that enforcement of the forfeiture clause was "clearly excessive" and "unreasonable." More significantly, however, the court treated the installment land contract as a mortgage:

> The Court, in effect, views a conditional land contract as a sale with a security interest in the form of legal title reserved by the vendor. Conceptually, therefore, the retention of the title by the vendor is the same as reserving a lien or mortgage. Realistically, vendor-vendee should be viewed as mortgagee-mortgagor. To conceive of the relationship in different terms is to pay homage to form over substance.[54]

The court ordered that the contract be foreclosed judicially in accordance with Indiana mortgage procedure. While the court did not absolutely rule out forfeiture in all cases, it did limit application of forfeiture to cases of absconding or abandoning vendees or to situations in which a minimum amount has been paid and the vendee seeks to retain possession while the vendor is making expenditures for taxes, insurance, and maintenance.

Skendzel has been followed in several subsequent decisions by Indiana appellate courts. For example, in Tidd v. Stauffer,[55] a defaulting vendee sought to obtain specific performance by paying the remaining balance where $16,000 out of a $39,000 contract price had been paid. The Court of Appeals of Indiana noted that forfeiture was inappropriate and directed the trial court to order judicial foreclosure of the contract in the event that the vendees failed promptly to pay the balance of the contract price. In Fisel v. Yoder,[56] a vendee in default who had paid one-fourth of the purchase price was allowed to continue

---

52. See notes 27–28 supra and accompanying text.

53. 261 Ind. 226, 301 N.E.2d 641 (1973), certiorari denied 415 U.S. 921, 94 S.Ct. 1421, 39 L.Ed.2d 476 (1974), appeal after remand 264 Ind. 77, 339 N.E.2d 57 (1975).

54. Id. at 234, 301 N.E.2d at 646.

55. 159 Ind.App. 570, 308 N.E.2d 415 (1974).

56. 162 Ind.App. 565, 320 N.E.2d 783 (1974). See Johnson v. Rutoskey, ___ Ind. App. ___, 472 N.E.2d 620 (1984).

to make payments on the contract; the vendor's request for forfeiture was denied. On the other hand, in Donaldson v. Sellmer,[57] the Court of Appeals of Indiana affirmed a trial court's award of forfeiture to a vendor where the vendee had paid $7,000 out of a $23,158 purchase price. There the appellate court agreed that the case fell within an exception to *Skendzel* in that the vendee "had wholly failed to perform his obligation to acquire adequate insurance and had allowed the property to deteriorate to such an extent that substantial repair was necessary before the house would even be habitable." [58] Similarly, a trial court's forfeiture decree was sustained where less than 10% of the principal balance of $275,000 had been paid and the vendees had failed to keep the property insured or pay real estate taxes.[59]

Thus, in Indiana, in most instances where the defaulting vendee has a substantial equity, installment land contracts are now treated as mortgages. Because of the exceptions noted above, *Skendzel* does not go as far judicially as Oklahoma went legislatively in converting installment land contracts into mortgages. Nonetheless, the case remains one of the clearest judicial statements to date of that principle.[60]

The Indiana approach has been adopted by an intermediate New York appellate court in Bean v. Walker.[61] In that case, the tardy vendees had paid almost half of the original $15,000 principal amount on an installment land contract for the sale of a house. Moreover, vendees had made substantial improvements to the property. The New York Supreme Court, Appellate Division, perceiving "no reason why these vendees should be treated any differently than the mortgagor at common law", reversed a trial court forfeiture decree and held that the contract "vendors may not summarily dispossess the vendees of their equitable ownership without first bringing an action to foreclose the vendees' equity of redemption." [62] The court, however, qualified its holding by specifically adopting the *Skendzel* limitations on the availability of the foreclosure remedy.

Perhaps the most straight-forward acceptance of the view that the installment land contract should be deemed a mortgage for remedy purposes is Sebastian v. Floyd.[63] There, the Kentucky Supreme Court

---

57. 166 Ind.App. 60, 333 N.E.2d 862 (1975).

58. Id. at 866. In Goff v. Graham, 158 Ind.App. 324, 306 N.E.2d 758 (1974), forfeiture of an installment land contract was upheld because of evidence showing that the vendee had failed to insure as required by the contract, had committed waste, and had deliberately neglected the property. The vendee had paid a down payment of $1,950 and one monthly payment of $562.62 on a contract price of $61,750 amortized over 20 years.

59. Phillips v. Nay, ___ Ind.App. ___, 456 N.E.2d 745 (1983).

60. For analysis of the Indiana situation, see Bepko, Contracts and Commercial Law, 8 Ind.L.Rev. 116, 117–20 (1974); Polston, Survey of Recent Developments in Indiana Law—Property, 10 Ind.L.Rev. 297, 298 n. 4 (1976); Strausbaugh, Exorcising the Forfeiture Clause From Real Estate Conditional Sales Contracts, 4 Real Est.L.J. 71 (1975).

61. 95 A.D.2d 70, 464 N.Y.S.2d 895 (1983).

62. Id. at 898.

63. 585 S.W.2d 381 (Ky.1979).

reversed a trial court forfeiture determination where the defaulting vendee had paid $4300, or nearly 40% of the principal balance on an installment land contract for the sale of a house. The court noted a "modern trend * * * to treat land sale contracts as analogous to conventional mortgages, thus requiring a seller to seek a judicial sale of the property upon buyer's default." [64] Accordingly, the court was of the opinion "that a rule treating the seller's interest as a lien will best protect the interests of both buyer and seller. Ordinarily, the seller will receive the balance due on the contract, plus expenses, thus fulfilling the expectations he had when he agreed to sell his land. In addition, the buyer's equity in the property will be protected." [65] Although the court cited *Skendzel* with approval, its opinion contained none of the limitations on the foreclosure remedy suggested by the Indiana decision. [66]

The current Florida situation, while somewhat conceptually muddled, seems at a practical level relatively clear. While there appears to be no clear-cut holding of the Florida Supreme Court that installment land contracts must be treated as a mortgage or that a vendee has a right to insist on judicial foreclosure, Florida case law, whatever its analytical underpinnings, recognizes, as we noted earlier in this section, [67] a tardy vendee's right to redemption or specific performance. Not only do numerous Florida cases state, in a variety of contexts, [68] that the installment land contract is a mortgage, but vendors routinely seem to treat them as such by choosing to foreclose them as mortgages. [69] Consequently, it seems highly likely that Florida has joined the ranks of jurisdictions classifying installment land contracts as mortgages, at least for remedy purposes.

There is every reason to expect this movement to continue, particularly in states in which there is little or no statutory regulation of land contracts. The same factors that induced the courts to treat other mortgage substitutes as mortgages—particularly the necessitous borrower's willingness to sign anything presented to him and the potential for a harsh and unwarranted loss of his investment as a consequence of his default—should and will almost surely be increasingly persuasive in the installment and contract context.

64. Id. at 384.

65. Id. at 384.

66. Recent Idaho judicial attempts to apply mortgage law concepts to installment land contract are perplexing. Compare Ellis v. Butterfield, 98 Idaho 644, 570 P.2d 1334 (1977), rehearing denied 98 Idaho 663, 572 P.2d 509 (1978) (affirming a trial court forfeiture decree) with Thomas v. Klein, 99 Idaho 105, 577 P.2d 1153 (1978) (reversing a trial court decree of forfeiture and ordering the trial court to conduct a judicial sale of the contract property). See also McEnroe v. Morgan, 106 Idaho 326,

678 P.2d 595 (App.1984) (trial court determination that forfeiture was not unconscionable affirmed).

67. See notes 12–18 supra and accompanying text.

68. See cases cited in note 18 supra.

69. See e.g., Ricard v. Equitable Life Assurance Society of the United States, 462 So.2d 592 (Fla.App.1985); Ernest v. Carter, 368 So.2d 428 (Fla.App.1979); Parise v. Citizens National Bank, 438 So.2d 1020 (Fla.App.1983).

It is sometimes argued that this trend is undesirable and that it is socially advantageous for the law to provide an extremely quick and cheap method for a vendor to terminate his purchaser's interest in the real estate upon default. Such a procedure, it is said, encourages the extension of credit to individuals whose credit-worthiness is so poor that they would otherwise be unable to transact at all. There are, however, two errors in this argument. First, the cases discussed above illustrate that no vendor today can count on forfeiture under a land contract as being either quick or cheap; indeed, it is an invitation to litigation. Second, no procedure, however quick or cheap, can be justified if it amounts to foul play. The solution, of course, is not for the law to ignore the legitimate needs of installment contract purchasers, but to reform the modes of foreclosure commonly used for mortgages to make them as inexpensive and rapid as feasible, consistent with the requirements of fairness and due process. If this is done, land contracts (if they continue to exist at all) can be brought within the ambit of the more efficient mortgage foreclosure proceedings, and no one will have cause for complaint. Perhaps the growing tendency of the courts to treat land contracts as mortgages will bring pressure on state legislatures to accomplish the needed reforms of mortgage law.

In light of the judicial trend outlined above, we must ask why installment land contracts continue to be used. The question is particularly perplexing in those states in which relatively rapid nonjudicial foreclosure is available for mortgages or deeds of trust. The reason given several years ago by Professor Warren may still be applicable: "[T]he vendor continues to use the installment sale contract despite its deficiencies with regard to remedies because he is willing to gamble that the vendee's rights under this device will never be asserted and his own contractual advantages will not be challenged." [70] In addition, it is possible that neither most vendors nor most real estate brokers have an accurate concept of the risks of litigation that land contracts present today. Whatever the motivations of vendors, it is clear that the risks are inflating rapidly.

 WESTLAW REFERENCES

Waiver By the Vendor As An Excuse for Delinquency
installment /s land /s contract agreement /p forfeit*** /p
    waiv***

Recognition of An Equity of Redemption
land /s installment agreement contract /p specific /5
    performance /p default*** forfeit*** (equit! /s redemption
    redeem***)

Restitution
land /s installment agreement contract /p default*** forfeit*** /p
    restitution unconsciona! penalty (damage /s excessive exceed***
    unreasonable) (unjust** /s enrich!)

---

70. Warren, California Installment
Land Sales Contracts: A Time for Reform,
9 U.C.L.A.L.Rev. 608, 633 (1962).

§ 3.30   Constitutionality of Forfeiture

In recent years power of sale mortgage and deed of trust foreclosure procedures have been under increasing attack as violative of the due process clause of the fourteenth amendment. The constitutional questions presented by these attacks may be raised as well in the context of installment contracts. These cases are discussed in detail later in this volume,[1] but in essence they have focused on two aspects of the foreclosure process: notice and hearing. Many power of sale statutes do not provide for any notice, or only notice by publication or posting, to the debtor and to junior lienors.[2] In addition, the statutes usually make no provision at all for a hearing, either before or after the foreclosure. If the due process clause is applicable to the foreclosure process, it is very clear that many statutes violate the standard articulated by the Supreme Court in Mullane v. Central Hanover Bank & Trust Co.,[3] since the notice they provide is "not reasonably calculated to reach those who could easily be informed by other means at hand."[4] The hearing standard is not quite so clear, but there is a strong possibility that on the merits the total absence of a presale hearing would also be held unconstitutional.[5]

While the application of these due process standards to installment contract forfeitures is somewhat uncertain, several observations are appropriate. Many contract forms do provide for direct mail notice to the purchaser as a prerequisite to forfeiture, and this would certainly meet the *Mullane* standard.[6] However, as in the case of mortgages, a

§ 3.30

1. See §§ 7.19–7.30, infra. See Leen, Galbraith, & Grant, Due Process and Deeds of Trust—Strange Bedfellows?, 48 Wash.L.Rev. 763 (1973); Nelson, Deed of Trust Foreclosure Under Powers of Sale—Constitutional Problems—Legislative Alternatives, 28 J.Mo.B. 428 (1972); Pedowitz, Current Developments in Summary Foreclosure, 9 Real Prop.Prob. & Trust J. 421, 425–31 (1974); Comment, The Constitutionality of the California Trustee's Sale, 61 Calif.L.Rev. 1282 (1973); Comment, Due Process Problems of Mississippi Power of Sale Foreclosure, 47 Miss. L.J. 67 (1976); Comment, Notice Requirements of the Non-judicial Foreclosure Sale, 51 N.C.L.Rev. 1110 (1973); Comment, Power of Sale Foreclosure After Fuentes, 40 U.Chi.L.Rev. 206, 217–20 (1972).

2. See, e.g., D.C.Code § 45–615; Miss. Code Ann. § 89–1–55. Cf. Minn.Stat.Ann. § 580.03 (personal service on person in possession only).

3. 339 U.S. 306, 70 S.Ct. 652, 94 L.Ed. 865 (1950).

4. Id. at 319, 70 S.Ct. at 660. This conclusion has been reached in three mort-gage foreclosure cases. See Ricker v. United States, 417 F.Supp. 133 (D.Me.1976); Turner v. Blackburn, 389 F.Supp. 1250 (W.D.N.C.1975); Law v. United States, 366 F.Supp. 1233 (N.D.Ga.1973). See Mennonite Board of Missions v. Adams, 462 U.S. 791, 103 S.Ct. 2706, 77 L.Ed.2d 180 (1983) (notice by publication and posting fails to provide mortgagee with minimum notice required by the Fourteenth Amendment in a proceeding to sell mortgaged real estate for nonpayment of taxes).

5. See United States v. White, 429 F.Supp. 1245 (N.D.Miss.1977); Ricker v. United States, 417 F.Supp. 133 (D.Me. 1976); Turner v. Blackburn, 389 F.Supp. 1250 (W.D.N.C.1975); Garner v. Tri-State Development Co., 382 F.Supp. 377 (E.D. Mich.1974); Northrip v. Federal Nat. Mortgage Association, 372 F.Supp. 594 (E.D. Mich.1974), reversed on other grounds 527 F.2d 23 (6th Cir.1975). Contra, Guidarelli v. Lazaretti, 233 N.W.2d 890 (Minn.1975).

6. Junior liens may, of course, be created by contract vendees. For example, a vendee may mortgage his contract interest. If such an interest exists and is recorded or otherwise readily identifiable by the ven-

contract procedure that provided only publication notice or the like would not. The hearing issue is somewhat more difficult. Installment land contracts themselves almost never provide for a hearing. Moreover, state statutory termination procedures rarely require a pretermination hearing and those that do may still be constitutionally deficient. The Minnesota statute, for example, specifically authorizes a trial court, at the vendee's request, to issue, prior to contract termination, temporary injunctive relief against further termination proceedings.[7] The vendee may plead affirmatively "any matter that would constitute a defense to an action to terminate the contract."[8] If the constitutional hearing requirement is satisfied by legislation that authorizes the vendee to request a hearing, then the foregoing statute meets such a standard. On the other hand, the statute may still be constitutionally suspect if, as we consider in the power of sale context elsewhere in this volume,[9] the hearing must be triggered automatically by the contract termination itself.

Whether it will ever be necessary for the contract forfeiture process to withstand scrutiny on the merits of the due process clause is questionable, however. Two defenses raised, often successfully, by power of sale mortgagees appear to be similarly applicable to the contract situation. The first is waiver. If the contract itself contains language by which the purchaser authorizes a forfeiture by the vendor without notice or hearing, can the purchaser later be heard to complain that his constitutional rights were violated? In related contexts, the Supreme Court has held that the efficacy of such a contractual waiver depends on a variety of factors, including the specificity of the waiver, the relative equality of bargaining power of the parties, the sophistication of the waiving party and perhaps whether the waiver was part of a printed contract.[10] Obviously each case must be litigated upon its facts, but in the typical installment contract transaction the waiver is probably not very explicit, is part of the printed form, and is generally not a point of negotiation; the purchaser will often be able to make at least a colorable argument that the purported waiver does not bind him.

---

dor, failure of the vendor to provide notice to the junior lienor may raise the same due process issues as in the analogous first mortgage foreclosure situation. See Mennonite Board of Missions v. Adams, supra note 4.

7. Minn.Stat.Ann. § 559.211.

8. Id.

9. See § 7.25 infra.

10. Fuentes v. Shevin, 407 U.S. 67, 94, 92 S.Ct. 1983, 2001, 32 L.Ed.2d 556 (1972), rehearing denied 409 U.S. 902, 93 S.Ct. 177, 34 L.Ed.2d 165 (1972); Swarb v. Lennox, 405 U.S. 191, 92 S.Ct. 767, 31 L.Ed.2d 138 (1972), rehearing denied 405 U.S. 1049, 92 S.Ct. 1303, 31 L.Ed.2d 592 (1972); D.H. Overmyer Co. v. Frick Co., 405 U.S. 174, 92 S.Ct. 775, 31 L.Ed.2d 124 (1972). Mortgage foreclosure cases rejecting the mortgagee's waiver argument include Ricker v. United States, 417 F.Supp. 133 (D.Me.1976); Turner v. Blackburn, 389 F.Supp. 1250 (W.D. N.C.1975); Garner v. Tri-State Development Co., 382 F.Supp. 377 (E.D.Mich.1974); Law v. United States, 366 F.Supp. 1233 (N.D.Ga.1973). Cf. Huggins v. Dement, 13 N.C.App. 673, 187 S.E.2d 412 (1972), appeal dismissed 281 N.C. 314, 188 S.E.2d 898 (1972), certiorari denied 409 U.S. 1071, 93 S.Ct. 677, 34 L.Ed.2d 659 (1972) (provision in deed for foreclosure upon default found to constitute sufficient notice for due process requirements); 51 N.C.L.Rev. 1110 (1973).

The second defense that power of sale mortgagees have asserted in constitutional litigation is that no state action is involved in such foreclosures. State action is, of course, a prerequisite to applicability of the fourteenth amendment; if non-judicial foreclosure is deemed a purely private process, no due process standard need be met. The plaintiffs in these cases have sought to show the presence of state action, pointing out that in most states in which power of sale foreclosure is widely employed, it is authorized and regulated by statute. A few early cases found state action to be present,[11] but the clear trend of recent decisions is against such a finding.[12] There is no Supreme Court decision yet on the point, but the probabilities are that state action will not be found in the typical power of sale mortgage foreclosure.

While there are precious few state action cases in the installment land contract termination setting,[13] one federal decision is instructive in this regard. In Staley Farms, Inc. v. Rueter,[14] a contract vendee challenged the constitutionality of the Iowa statutory forfeiture procedure, discussed earlier in this chapter, on the ground that it failed to provide a hearing prior to forfeiture. The vendee argued that state action was present because the statute (1) "encouraged" the deprivation of constitutional rights and (2) delegated a traditionally public function to private parties. The United States Court of Appeals for the Eighth Circuit, in affirming a trial court determination that state action did not exist, rejected both vendee arguments. The encouragement theory lacked merit, according to the court, because the Iowa statute did not compel the vendor to use it. Likewise the "public function" concept was inapplicable because the statute did not constitute the exclusive method of resolving such contract disputes. Finally, the court noted that "there is no overt official involvement required by the Iowa statute."[15]

The *Staley Farms* result and reasoning have obvious implications for non-statutory forfeiture as well. While it is true that states through their court systems and case law superintend forfeitures generally, they surely are no less involved in the statutory termination

---

11. See Turner v. Blackburn, 389 F.Supp. 1250 (W.D.N.C.1975); Northrip v. Federal National Mortgage Association, 372 F.Supp. 594 (E.D.Mich.1974), reversed 527 F.2d 23 (C.A.Mich.1975). *Turner* relies heavily upon the rather peculiar participation of the clerk of the court in nonjudicial foreclosures under the then-applicable North Carolina statute.

12. See Northrip v. Federal National Mortgage Association, 527 F.2d 23 (C.A. Mich.1975); Barrera v. Security Building & Investment Corp., 519 F.2d 1166 (C.A.Tex. 1975); Bryant v. Jefferson Federal Savings & Loan Association, 166 U.S.App.D.C. 178, 509 F.2d 511 (1974); Y. Aleman Corp. v. Chase Manhattan Bank, 414 F.Supp. 93

(D.C.Guam 1975); Kenly v. Miracle Properties, 412 F.Supp. 1072 (D.C.Ariz.1976); Lawson v. Smith, 402 F.Supp. 851 (N.D.Cal. 1975); Global Industries Inc. v. Harris, 376 F.Supp. 1379 (N.D.Ga.1974); Federal National Mortgage Association v. Howlett, 521 S.W.2d 428 (Mo.1975), appeal dismissed 423 U.S. 1026, 96 S.Ct. 210, 46 L.Ed.2d 137 (1975), rehearing denied 423 U.S. 1026, 96 S.Ct. 471, 46 L.Ed.2d 400 (1975).

13. See Aldape v. Lubke, 107 Idaho 316, 688 P.2d 1221 (1984); Staley Farms, Inc. v. Rueter, 662 F.2d 520 (8th Cir.1981); Jensen v. Schreck, 275 N.W.2d 374 (Iowa 1979).

14. 662 F.2d 520 (8th Cir.1981).

15. Id. at 523.

setting. Thus, if no state action exists where state legislation specifically authorizes a contract forfeiture proceeding, it seems even more clearly absent where such contracts and their remedies are regulated exclusively by case law.[16]

 WESTLAW REFERENCES
(power /5 sale) /p notice hearing /p "due process"
land "real estate" /s forfeit*** (power /5 sale) /p "state action"
    notice hearing "due process"

§ 3.31 The Deed in Escrow as an Aid to Vendor Forfeiture Remedy

Vendors frequently attempt to avoid the pro-vendee implications of the case law considered earlier in this chapter and to obviate title problems incident to vendee recording of installment land contracts by utilizing a deed in escrow arrangement. Under this procedure, the vendee is typically required at the time of execution of an installment land contract to deliver to an escrow agent an executed quitclaim deed to the real estate. In the event of vendee default the vendor notifies the escrow agent and the latter, pursuant to the escrow agreement, is authorized to record the deed.[1] Ideally, from the vendor's perspective, the recording of the quitclaim deed not only terminates the vendee's interest, it also clears up any title cloud created by an earlier vendee recording of the contract.

The advantages of the foregoing procedure to the vendor may be more apparent than real. As we noted earlier in this chapter,[2] if, in a regular mortgage transaction, a mortgagor executes and delivers to the mortgagee, contemporaneous with the execution of the mortgage, a deed conveying the mortgaged real estate to the mortgagee, the deed will be deemed to be a clog on the mortgagor's equity of redemption and hence invalid and unenforcible. The clogging doctrine may be as readily applied where the financing device is an installment land contract rather than a mortgage. To the extent that a jurisdiction treats a contract for deed as a mortgage and the vendee as owning an equity of redemption, it may simply characterize the vendee's contemporaneous quitclaim deed as an invalid attempt to clog the vendee-mortgagor's equity of redemption. The fact that this escrow arrangement frequently succeeds is probably due less to its inherent substantive soundness than to the fact that defaulting vendees often fail to assert their rights and that many title examiners for subsequent purchasers from the vendor simply do not fully appreciate the implications of the anti-clogging doctrine in this context.

16. See e.g., Aldape v. Lubke, 107 Idaho 316, 688 P.2d 1221 (1984).

§ 3.31

1. See e.g., McEnroe v. Morgan, 106 Idaho 326, 678 P.2d 595 (1984); In re

Mancha, 35 B.R. 427 (9th Cir.Bktcy.App. 1983).

2. See § 3.1 supra.

WESTLAW REFERENCES
deed /s escrow /p default*** forfeit***

§ 3.32 Other Remedies for Vendors

If installment land contracts were governed exclusively by the law of mortgages, the vendor's remedies in the event of vendee default would be both clearly defined and relatively simple. The vendor could choose to foreclose the contract and, if less than the contract price were obtained at the foreclosure sale and anti-deficiency legislation [1] were not a problem, seek a deficiency judgment against the vendee for that difference. Alternatively, if the contract imposed personal liability for the contract amount on the vendee, vendor could sue on the contract debt and attempt to collect any judgment obtained from vendee's other assets, including from the contract land.

Unfortunately, in few, if any, jurisdictions will the vendor's remedies be that unambiguous. In some jurisdictions, the installment land contract is still largely regarded as a contract and, as such, is governed primarily by contract principles.[2] In others, courts apply an often-confusing amalgam of contract and mortgage law.[3] This "split personality" often exists even in those states that have taken the greatest strides [4] in treating the installment land contract as a mortgage because the courts in those jurisdictions have yet to confront the myriad issues and implications that the mortgage characterization ultimately creates.

Whatever the conceptual basis relied upon, vendors may well have a variety of non-forfeiture remedies against a defaulting vendee. While such remedies have traditionally received little attention because of pervasive emphasis on the forfeiture remedy, as the latter remedy becomes increasingly less reliable, alternatives will receive increasing attention. The following material explores the analytical underpinnings of certain non-forfeiture remedies and the practical considerations incident to their use.

Specific Performance for the Price

Under this remedy, the vendor chooses to treat the installment land contract like an earnest money contract and, consequently, tenders title to the land and seeks an order requiring the vendee to pay the remainder of the contract purchase price. While many courts will

§ 3.32

1. See §§ 8.1–8.3 infra.

2. See e.g., Stonebraker v. Zinn, ___ W.Va. ___, 286 S.E.2d 911 (1982); First National Bank in Alamogordo v. Cape, 100 N.M. 525, 673 P.2d 502 (1983); Nygaard et ux. v. Anderson, 229 Or. 323, 366 P.2d 899 (1961); Park Valley Corp. v. Bagley, 635 P.2d 65 (Utah 1981).

3. Compare Ellis v. Butterfield, 98 Idaho 644, 570 P.2d 1334 (1977), rehearing denied 98 Idaho 663, 572 P.2d 509 (1978) with Thomas v. Klein, 99 Idaho 105, 577 P.2d 1153 (1978).

4. See § 3.29 notes 49–69 and accompanying text, supra.

grant specific performance to the vendor under such circumstances,[5] a few, like the minority of courts in the earnest money contract context,[6] require the vendor to show that there is an inadequate remedy at law.[7]

However, it should be emphasized that the specific performance remedy is conceptually more problematical in the installment land contract setting than in the earnest money contract situation. This is because the latter contract typically contemplates the payment of the balance of the contract price on one closing date, whereas the installment land contract, as a financing device, is paid in installments over a long period of time. Thus, if an earnest money vendee defaults on the closing date, a suit for the full contract price seems conceptually uncomplicated. On the other hand, in the case of the installment land contract default, it is more difficult to envisage a suit for more than the installments actually in default. Consequently, it could be argued that a condition precedent to the granting of specific performance for the balance of the contract price should be an acceleration clause allowing the vendor to declare the entire contract amount due and payable upon vendee breach. In the absence of such a clause, the vendor conceivably could be left with the undesirable option of suing only for the past due installments plus interest. In any event, it clearly is prudent for the vendor to include such an acceleration clause in such an installment contract.

Where the specific performance remedy is available, a vendor normally would use it where the vendee has assets to satisfy a judgment for the price and the land is now worth less than the contract price. In this relatively rare situation, the forfeiture remedy, assuming it is otherwise available, should be avoided because of the election of remedies rule (which we consider later in this section), which may prevent any further relief against the vendee. Specific performance, on the other hand, would entail a judgment for the full price which would be collectible by a judicial sale of all or any of the vendee's assets, including the contract real estate.[8]

Foreclosure by Sale of the Vendee's Rights

This remedy, where permitted, allows the vendor to treat the installment land contract as a mortgage and results in a judicial sale of the land. If the sale brings more than the contract price, the surplus will go to the vendee. If the sale yields less than the contract amount, a deficiency judgment against the vendee often is available. It should

---

5. See e.g., Simon Home Builders, Inc. v. Pailoor, 357 N.W.2d 383 (Minn.App. 1984); SAS Partnership v. Schafer, __ Mont. __, 653 P.2d 834 (1982); Glacier Campground v. Wild Rivers, Inc., 182 Mont. 389, 597 P.2d 689 (1978); Renard v. Allen, 237 Or. 406, 391 P.2d 777 (1964).

6. See Centex Homes Corp. v. Boag, 128 N.J.Super. 385, 320 A.2d 194 (1974);

Suchan v. Rutherford, 90 Idaho 288, 410 P.2d 434 (1966).

7. See e.g., Williamson v. Magnusson, 336 N.W.2d 353 (N.D.1983).

8. See Glacier Campground v. Wild Rivers, Inc., 182 Mont. 389, 597 P.2d 689 (1978).

be noted that in those states that have opted to equate the installment land contract with the mortgage, the vendor may have little choice but to pursue the foreclosure remedy.[9] In those states where the mortgage status of the installment land contract is less clear, courts often indicate a willingness to allow the vendor to utilize the foreclosure remedy.[10] In still other jurisdictions, however, the vendor's ability to choose the foreclosure remedy seems more doubtful in that the vendor would be seeking a mortgage remedy under a device governed to a greater extent by the law of contracts. In such situations it is advisable to include in the installment land contract itself language specifically affording the vendor the foreclosure option.

Strict Foreclosure

A number of states, including some with no tradition of foreclosing installment contracts by sale, will award strict foreclosure [11] to a vendor.[12] The effect of this remedy is much like a judicial declaration of forfeiture: the contract is cancelled and the vendor's title to the land is confirmed.[13] However, it differs from forfeiture in that the court will fix a redemption period within which the purchaser and assignees [14] of the purchaser's interest may specifically enforce the contract by tendering the balance due.[15] Only if this is not done will the contract be cancelled. Because strict foreclosure, like forfeiture, deprives the vendee of any "equity" he or she may have accumulated in the property,

---

9. See § 3.29 notes 49–69 and accompanying text, supra.

10. See e.g., Ulander v. Allen, 37 Colo. App. 279, 544 P.2d 1001 (1976); Mustard v. Sugar Valley Lakes, 7 Kan.App.2d 340, 642 P.2d 111 (1981). Ryan v. Kolterman, 215 Neb. 355, 338 N.W.2d 747 (1983); Lamont v. Evjen, 29 Utah 2d 266, 508 P.2d 532 (1973). See generally, Annot., Vendor's Remedy by Foreclosure of Contract for Sale of Real Property, 77 A.L.R. 270 (1932).

11. For a more extended discussion of strict foreclosure in the mortgage context, see §§ 7.9–.10, infra.

12. See, e.g., Canterbury Court, Inc. v. Rosenberg, 224 Kan. 493, 582 P.2d 261 (1978); Ryan v. Kolterman, 215 Neb. 355, 338 N.W.2d 747 (1983); Swaggart v. McLean, 38 Or.App. 207, 589 P.2d 1170 (1979); Kallenbach v. Lake Publications, Inc., 30 Wis.2d 647, 142 N.W.2d 212 (1966). See generally Randolph, Updating the Oregon Installment Land Contract, 15 Wil.L.Rev. 181, 211–12 (1979); Vanneman, Strict Foreclosure of Land Contracts, 14 Minn.L. Rev. 342 (1930); Annot., supra note 10. Some courts routinely give strict foreclosure without calling it such; they simply award a "grace period" for the purchaser to pay the contract, and declare a forfei-

ture if he or she does not do so. See Jesz v. Geigle, 319 N.W.2d 481 (N.D.1982); Moeller v. Good Hope Farms, 35 Wn.2d 777, 215 P.2d 425 (1950) (grace period discretionary).

13. Some cases explicitly treat forfeiture and strict foreclosure as alternatives available to the vendor; see Zumstein v. Stockton, 199 Or. 633, 264 P.2d 455 (1953); Walker v. Nunnenkamp, 84 Id. 485, 373 P.2d 559 (1962).

14. See, e.g., Westfair Corp. v. Kuelz, 90 Wis.2d 631, 280 N.W.2d 364 (App.1979) (assignee of mechanics' lienor of vendee has right to redeem in strict foreclosure proceeding.)

15. There is a further distinction. If the vendor declares a forfeiture, and subsequently demands or accepts payments on the contract, the court may treat his behavior as inconsistent with the forfeiture and hence as waiving it. On the other hand, acceptance of payments is entirely consistent with a vendor's demand for strict foreclosure, since until the end of the redemption period fixed by the court, the purchaser has every right to attempt to pay off the contract. See Heisel v. Cunningham, 94 Id. 461, 491 P.2d 178 (1971).

some courts will award it only upon a showing that the land has no value in excess of the contract balance.[16] If there is excess value, some of the courts will decree a judicial sale instead.[17]

Suit for Damages

Another remedy arguably available to the vendor is an action for damages.[18] The vendor's damages will probably be measured by the difference between the contract price and the fair market value of the land as of the date of the vendee's breach, the standard normally applied in earnest money contract settings.[19] The pursuit of this remedy, however, is only possible where the vendee has abandoned the land. This is so because where the forfeiture remedy is necessary to regain the land the damages action will probably be barred by the election of remedies doctrine referred to earlier and next considered in this section. Moreover, the vendor faces the unenviable prospect of having to convince a court or jury that the land, as of the date of the breach, was worth less than the contract price. Obviously, if the vendee has assets to satisfy a judgment, vendor would be better off, where possible, suing for specific performance for the price or seeking to foreclose the contract as a mortgage. If the foreclosure sale yields less than the contract price, vendor can then usually obtain a deficiency judgment for the deficiency.[20]

Election of Remedies Problems

To the extent that a jurisdiction recognizes forfeiture as a valid remedy, a vendor faces an election of remedies problem. Once forfeiture has been accomplished, the vendor typically is barred from seeking to recover the mortgage equivalent of a deficiency judgment.[21] Suppose, for example, that under an installment land contract the total purchase price was $50,000, of which the vendee paid $5,000 in cash at the date of contract execution and agreed to pay the balance in nine equal annual installments of $5,000, together with accrued interest at 12% per annum. Suppose further that vendee never makes a further payment on the contract and that vendor chooses to invoke forfeiture. Later vendor discovers that the land is worth only $30,000. Because of the election of remedies doctrine, vendor will be unable to collect from

16. Ryan v. Kolterman, 215 Neb. 355, 338 N.W.2d 747 (1983); State Securities Co. v. Daringer, 206 Neb. 427, 293 N.W.2d 102 (1980).

17. Walker v. Nunnenkamp, 84 Id. 485, 373 P.2d 559 (1962); Blondell v. Beam, 243 Or. 293, 413 P.2d 397 (1966).

18. See Nemec v. Rollo, 114 Ariz. 589, 562 P.2d 1087 (App.1977).

19. See Nelson and Whitman, Real Estate Transfer, Finance and Development, 43 (2nd Ed. 1981). Note that the time value of money must be taken into account in order to avoid unfair results in computing damages. See § 3.29 supra at note 48.

20. See Glacier Campground v. Wild Rivers, Inc., 182 Mont. 389, 597 P.2d 689 (1978).

21. See Nemec v. Rollo, 114 Ariz. 589, 562 P.2d 1087 (App.1977); Langenes v. Bullinger, 328 N.W.2d 241 (N.D.1982); Butler v. Michel, 14 Ohio App.3d 116, 470 N.E.2d 217 (1984); Trans West Co. v. Teuscher, 27 Wn.App. 404, 618 P.2d 1023 (1980); Zirinsky v. Sheehan, 413 F.2d 481 (8th Cir. 1969). C.F. Novus Equities Corp. v. EM-TY Partnership, 366 N.W.2d 732 (Minn. App.1985).

the vendee the difference between the balance due on the contract ($45,000) and the fair market value of the land. Moreover, the same result will be reached even where the contract obligation to the vendor is evidenced by a separate promissory note.[22] Occasionally a state will reject the election of remedies doctrine, but reach the same result on the ground that it "flows from the fact that the contract between the parties has been terminated, thereby extinguishing any right to recover the unpaid purchase price."[23]

Some states ameliorate the vendor's election of remedies problem in a variety of ways. For example, the Ohio termination statute provides that even though a judgment for cancellation of the contract has taken place, a damage award may be entered against the vendee if the latter "has paid an amount less than the fair rental value plus deterioration or destruction of the property occasioned by the vendee's use."[24] In addition, a state may ameliorate the harshness of the election of remedies rule on the vendor by its determination of when the election took place. For example, the Michigan Supreme Court has held that "while the [vendor] may not accept or take possession and still seek money damages, he may, even after sending notice of forfeiture, refuse tender of possession and either commence an action for money damages or for foreclosure of the land contract."[25] Moreover, at least one court has rejected the election rule entirely in the installment land contract context and has substituted for it an estoppel concept.[26] Under this approach, "the proper inquiry should be whether the [vendee] has relied on [acts or statements by the vendor] and, therefore would be unfairly prejudiced by assertion of a different inconsistent remedy. If so, the [vendor] should be bound to the remedy earlier chosen. * * * Absent estoppel, he should be free to choose a different remedy."[27]

 WESTLAW REFERENCES

Specific Performance for the Price

358k66 (land "real estate" /s installment contract agreement /p forfeit*** default*** /p (specific! /5 perform! /10 price) (inadequate /5 remedy))

Foreclosure by Sale of the Vendee's Rights

land /s installment agreement contract /p default*** forfeit*** /p foreclos***

Strict Foreclosure

land /s installment agreement contract /p default*** forfeit*** /p strict /3 foreclos***

22. See Nemec v. Rollo, 114 Ariz. 589, 562 P.2d 1987 (App.1977).

23. Gray v. Bowers, 332 N.W.2d 323, 325 (Iowa 1983).

24. Ohio Rev.Code § 5313.10. For an interpretation of this provision, see Marvin v. Stemen, 68 Ohio App.2d 26, 426 N.E.2d 205 (1980). See also Durham, Forfeiture of Residential Land Contracts in Ohio: The

Need for Further Reform of a Reform Statute, 16 Akron L.Rev. 397 (1983).

25. Gruskin v. Fisher, 405 Mich. 51, 54, 273 N.W.2d 893, 896 (1979).

26. Keesee v. Fetzek, 106 Idaho 507, 681 P.2d 600 (App.1984).

27. Id. at 603–604.

Suit for Damages

land /s installment agreement contract /p default*** forfeit*** /p
    damag*** /s market /3 value

Election of Remedies Problems

land /s installment agreement contract /p default*** forfeit*** /p
    elect*** /3 redem***

Suit for Damages

land /s installment agreement contract /p default*** forfeit*** /p
    damag*** /s market /3 value

Election of Remedies Problems

land /s installment agreement contract /p default*** forfeit*** /p
    elect*** /3 remed***

§ 3.33   Title Problems for Vendees

When a person purchases property as a vendee under an installment land contract, the chances of title problems with respect to the vendee's interest are greater than if the transaction were cast in the purchase money mortgage setting. This is true, to a large extent, even in those jurisdictions that have reduced the impact of the forfeiture provision by statute or judicial decision.

In the usual purchase money mortgage situation, the chances are extremely high that the purchaser will examine the seller's title and require it to be marketable. Even if the purchaser is not sophisticated enough to have the title checked, any third party lender involved in the transaction will insist upon a title insurance policy or at least upon an attorney's title opinion as evidence that the seller's title is good. On the other hand, in installment land contract situations there is a strong possibility that the vendor's title will not be examined at the time the contract is executed. Here there usually is no third party lender to insist upon title examination—the vendor serves that economic function, and he is unlikely to insist upon an examination of his own title. Moreover, many contract purchasers have low incomes and either cannot afford a title examination or do not recognize the need for it. Accordingly, many purchasers may unknowingly execute the contract, go into possession, and make substantial installment payments when in fact the vendor's title is encumbered by mortgages, judgment liens, or other interests perfected prior to the execution of the contract.[1]

The recording act can also cause substantial problems for an installment land contract vendee. In the usual purchase money mortgage transaction, the deed to the mortgagor and the mortgage or deed of trust will be recorded almost immediately. If there is no third party lender, the purchaser will record his deed as a matter of custom. Any third party lender involved will insist upon and carry out immediate

---

§ 3.33

1. See generally Mixon, Installment Land Contracts: A Study of Low Income Transactions, With Proposals for Reform and a New Program to Provide Home Ownership in the Inner City, 7 Houston L.Rev. 523, 545–46 (1970).

recordation in order to protect itself against subsequent interests and encumbrances that may be created by or arise against the mortgagor. This recording by the mortgagee will also protect the mortgagor against any subsequent interests arising through the former owner of the land. On the other hand, in the installment land contract situation there is no third party stimulus for prompt recording. Many unsophisticated vendees do not record and, as we shall see later, may be prevented from recording by acts of the vendor.[2] Since vendors anticipate a high default rate among vendees, it is in the vendors' interest that the contracts not be recorded so that they may quickly resell to other purchasers without the necessity of a judicial proceeding to remove a title cloud posed by a recorded contract.[3] Suppose, for instance, that after executing the contract, a vendor either mortgages the land or sells it to another purchaser. While it is true in many jurisdictions that possession by the original vendee will constitute constructive notice to those dealing with the land thereafter and thus will be the equivalent of recording,[4] this is not universally the case.[5] Even if possession does constitute constructive notice, establishing the existence of that possession could require litigation,[6] while the fact of a recorded document would not.[7]

Recent bankruptcy law changes make vendor bankruptcy significantly less troublesome for the vendee than under prior law. Suppose, for example, that four years into a ten-year installment land contract, the vendor files a bankruptcy petition. Section 70(b) of the pre-1978 Bankruptcy Act (the "Prior Act") provided that "the trustee shall assume or reject an executory contract."[8] Because of the rule of In re New York Investors Mutual Group, Inc.,[9] this statutory provision pre-

---

2. See text accompanying notes 2–6, § 3.34 infra.

3. See Mixon, supra Note 1, at 547.

4. See e.g., Life Savings and Loan Association of America v. Bryant, 125 Ill.App. 3d 1012, 81 Ill.Dec. 577, 582–583, 467 N.E.2d 277, 282–283 (1984); Nelson and Whitman, Real Estate Transfer, Finance and Development, 194–95 (2d Ed. 1981).

5. See, e.g., Drey v. Doyle, 99 Mo. 459, 12 S.W. 287 (1889); Comment, Possession as Notice Under Missouri Recording Act, 16 Mo.L.Rev. 142 (1951).

6. See e.g., Beals v. Cryer, 99 Ill.App.3d 842, 55 Ill.Dec. 278, 426 N.E.2d 253 (1981) (vendee's mowing of grass and weeds insufficient "visible, open, exclusive and unambiguous" evidence of possession so as to be the equivalent to recording).

7. Failure to record an installment land contract may also cause problems for the vendee when the vendor goes into bankruptcy. This is because section 544(a) of the Bankruptcy Code authorizes a bankruptcy trustee in his status as a hypothetical lien creditor to take advantage of state recording statutes to defeat an unrecorded interest. If, under state law, such a contract is recordable (and they generally are) and an unrecorded interest is invalid against creditors who obtain a judgment lien without notice of the unrecorded interest, a bankruptcy trustee may be able under section 544(a) to avoid the contract. In re Sayre Village Manor, 120 F.Supp. 215 (D.N.J.1954); Lacy, Land Sale Contracts in Bankruptcy, 21 U.C.L.A.L.Rev. 477, 493–97 (1973); Lynn, Bankruptcy and the Land Sales Contract: The Rights of the Vendee Vis-A-Vis the Vendor's Bankruptcy Trustee, 5 Tex.Tech.L.Rev. 677, 694–99 (1974). Normally, however, possession will be the equivalent of recording. See Lacy, supra at 496. In some states where possession is not constructive notice, however, a nonrecording vendee in possession may be vulnerable under section 70(c). See note 5, supra.

8. 11 U.S.C.A. § 110(b).

9. 143 F.Supp. 51 (S.D.N.Y.1956).

sented serious problems for a vendee. In that case, a land contract vendee contended that he was entitled to specific performance against the bankruptcy trustee who had disaffirmed the contract under the above statute. The vendee contended that disaffirmance divested it of its equitable title to the land. The court, however, concluded that any rights of the vendee originated solely in the contract and that section 70(b) apparently did not exclude contracts for the sale of real estate from the trustee's power to reject executory contracts. Professor Warren commented that application of the *New York Investors* rule would leave an installment land contract vendee "with a claim for damages instead of a home." [10] Despite this criticism, subsequent decisions followed the *New York Investors Case.* [11] Although scholarly commentary emphasized that the contracts in the foregoing cases may have been executory or earnest money contracts rather than true installment land contracts,[12] there was a general concern that the principle of *New York Investors* was applicable to the latter type contract.[13]

Section 365(i) of the Bankruptcy Reform Act of 1978 [14] (the "Bankruptcy Code") resolved the above problem in favor of the installment land contract vendee. While the Bankruptcy Code continues to afford the trustee the right to assume or reject executory contracts,[15] where the vendee is in possession, the trustee's right to reject the contract is subject to the vendee's right to obtain legal title by completing the payments under the contract.[16] Where the vendee is not in possession, the trustee is able to reject the contract and leave the vendee with a claim for damages for breach.[17] While the vendee in this latter situation has a lien on the contract property to the extent of prior payments under the contract, he has the status of an unsecured creditor for purposes of recovering other damages.[18] Since most installment vendees normally are in possession, the Bankruptcy Code thus rejects the implications of *New York Investors* for most installment land contracts. On the other hand, with respect to the normal earnest money contract (where the seller retains possession) and the relatively uncommon installment land contract where the vendor retains possession, the Bankruptcy Code seems to codify the *New York Investors* result.[19]

10. Warren, California Installment Land Sales Contracts: A Time for Reform, 9 U.C.L.A.L.Rev. 608, 613 (1962).

11. See Gulf Petroleum, S.A. v. Collazo, 316 F.2d 257 (C.A.Puerto Rico 1963); In re Philadelphia Penn Worsted Co., 278 F.2d 661 (C.A.Pa.1960).

12. Lacy, supra note 7 at 483.

13. See Lacy, supra note 7 at 481; Power, Land Contracts as Security Devices, 12 Wayne L.Rev. 391, 413 (1966); Lynn, Bankruptcy and the Land Sales Contract: The Rights of the Vendee Vis-A-Vis the Vendor's Bankruptcy Trustee, 5 Tex.Tech.L. Rev. 677, 689 (1974).

14. 11 U.S.C.A. § 365(i).

15. 11 U.S.C.A. § 365(a).

16. 11 U.S.C.A. § 365(i). Interestingly, courts have held that an installment land contract is not an "executory contract" in situations where the vendee is the bankrupt. Thus vendors will not be able to compel the vendee-bankrupt to assume or reject the contract. See In re Adolphsen, 38 B.R. 780 (D.Minn.1983); In re Booth, 19 B.R. 53 (Bkrtcy.Utah 1982); Contra: Shaw v. Dawson, 48 B.R. 857 (D.N.M.1985).

17. Id.

18. Id. § 365(j).

19. Courts continue to experience difficulty with the meaning of "executory contract". See e.g., In re Summit Land Co., 13

Federal tax liens against the vendor should no longer be a problem for the prudent vendee who has title examined prior to contract execution and who has recorded the contract. If the vendor is delinquent in payment of federal taxes, the United States may obtain a lien on "all property and rights to property, whether real or personal, belonging to [the delinquent taxpayer]." [20] This lien is ineffective against "any purchaser, holder of a security interest, mechanic's lienor, or judgment lien creditor until notice thereof * * * has been filed" [21] in a designated place. Thus, for example, if a grantee recorded a conveyance of the taxpayer-grantor's property for adequate and full consideration prior to the filing of a tax lien and without actual knowledge of the lien, the grantee's title would not be encumbered by the lien. A fortiori, if the lien arose after the conveyance, the grantee is protected. Before the 1966 amendments to the Federal Tax Lien Act, however, there was case law indicating that a vendee who had taken possession under an installment land contract, but who had not received legal title, did not come within the statutory definition of a "purchaser" and thus was subject not only to preexisting unfiled tax liens, but also to liens for taxes arising against the vendor after the contract was executed and the vendee went into possession. [22] Now, however, that problem has been largely obviated by the rule which provides that a person who enters into a *written* executory contract to purchase property is afforded the protection of a "purchaser" with title. [23] Thus, in most situations the contract vendee who takes possession pursuant to an installment land contract is protected against unfiled tax liens arising against the vendor before the execution of the contract and against all such liens arising thereafter.

There is still, however, a potential pitfall for some vendees. Under the Federal Tax Lien Act, protection of the contract vendee as a "purchaser" is "conditioned upon his having taken whatever action is necessary under local law to protect his interest against subsequent purchasers without actual notice." [24] In most states the contract vendee's possession qualifies as constructive notice against such subsequent purchasers. However, in those states where possession does not so qualify, [25] recording is necessary. Thus, in view of the fact that many vendees do not record, it is conceivable that a vendee, after properly examining title at the time of execution of the contract and promptly going into possession, may nevertheless be vulnerable not only to

B.R. 310 (Bkrtcy.Utah 1981). For a consideration of the latter problem, what constitutes possession and other problems under section 365, see Comment, Installment Land Contracts and the Effect of Sections 365(i) and 365(j) of the Bankruptcy Reform Act, 49 Mo.L.Rev. 337 (1984).

20. I.R.C. § 6321.

21. I.R.C. § 6323(a).

22. See United States v. Creamer Industries, Inc., 349 F.2d 625 (C.A.Tex.1965), certiorari denied 382 U.S. 957, 86 S.Ct. 434, 15 L.Ed.2d 361 (1965); Leipert v. R.C. Williams & Co., 161 F.Supp. 355 (S.D.N.Y. 1957).

23. See I.R.C. § 6323(h)(6); Treas.Reg. § 301.6323(h)(f), Example 1; Plumb, Federal Tax Liens 73 (3d Ed. 1972).

24. Plumb, supra note 23 at 73.

25. See note 5 supra.

preexisting unfiled tax liens, but also to tax liens arising *after* the execution of the installment land contract.

 WESTLAW REFERENCES
land /s installment agreement contract /p (title /s market! problem) bankrupt** /p vendee purchaser buyer

§ 3.34 Title Problems for Vendors

As was pointed out earlier, there have been relatively few title problems for the vendor in those states that specifically regulate forfeiture by statutory procedure. In those states, of which Iowa and Minnesota are typical, the statutory procedure for termination has been institutionalized, and the statutes provide a mechanism for establishing record title in the vendor even if the vendee has recorded the contract. However, in states without such statutory mechanisms, and where the forfeiture clause is governed solely or largely by case law, there are potential title problems for the vendor. Indeed, in many such jurisdictions, the installment land contract "will provide the * * * vendor with an efficient and cheap method of regaining possession of the contract land and a merchantable title *only* if the vendee fails completely to assert his rights."[1] As one commentator has noted:

> Thus, if, after default, the vendee moves out of possession, without protest and without having recorded the contract, the vendor will be able to resell the land to a person who will probably qualify as a bona fide purchaser. In practice this probably often happens and may explain, in part, why the installment land contract is continually used. The thing to remember, however, is that *any* device is practical if the other party does nothing to protect his rights.[2]

On the other hand, suppose the vendee attempts to protect his rights by recording his contract and thereafter goes into default. Even assuming that a court will find that enforcing forfeiture would be valid under the circumstances, it will take a judicial proceeding to make that determination. A statement or affidavit that forfeiture has occurred, recorded by the vendor, will probably not suffice.

> Thus, the vendor is faced with the costly prospect of a quiet title action or some other judicial proceeding to regain a marketable title. The vendee, for settlement purposes, may very well be able to demand much more than what he has invested in the property as the price for a quit-claim deed.[3]

Some vendors try to eliminate such problems by attempting to prevent the recording of the contract. The most common method used

§ 3.34

1. Nelson, The Use of Installment Land Contracts in Missouri—Courting Clouds on Title, 33 J.Mo.Bar. 161, 164 (1977).

2. Id. at 165.

3. Id.

to accomplish this is to omit an acknowledgment of the parties' execution of the contract. For any vendee represented by counsel, however, this method is easily circumvented by recording an affidavit in which the vendee refers to the installment land contract and attaches the contract as an exhibit. Or, as a variation, the vendee could execute and record an affidavit that incorporates the essential terms of the contract, including the legal description, the parties, and the important terms. Occasionally, a vendor will attempt to prevent recording by keeping *all* copies of the contract. Again, however, it would seem that the vendee could use the second affidavit method described above. After all, if in fact a land contract exists, it would surely not be improper for a vendee to summarize the terms of that contract in an affidavit. In jurisdictions that do not permit recordation of affidavits or where state statutes prohibit the recording of land sale contracts unless acknowledged by vendors,[4] another possibly effective variant would be to record an acknowledged assignment of the purchaser's interest to a straw party and a reassignment back to the vendee.[5]

Vendors also occasionally attempt to discourage recording by the vendee by including a provision in the installment land contract that makes recording of the contract a ground for default and forfeiture. Such provisions may have a substantial deterrent effect because the risk of forfeiture should never be taken lightly. Nevertheless, such provisions probably violate the public policy of encouraging the recording of interests in real estate. Indeed, Professor Warren has indicated that it is doubtful that such clauses would be effective "to attain anything more than the hostility of the judge who has to interpret the contract."[6]

Stated simply, in states where the above title complications to the vendor can occur, the installment land contract can be a "pro-vendee" financing device. Where, for example, such contracts are used in a wholesale fashion as substitute financing devices in low income, low down payment situations, mass recording of such contracts by vendees could increase the vendees' practical economic interests in the involved real estate and possibly result in pervasive title clouds on substantial amounts of that real estate.

4. See West's Fla.Stat.Ann. § 696.01; Coggins v. Mims, 373 So.2d 964 (Fla.App. 1979).

5. Nelson, supra note 1 at 165–66. As we shall see, a vendee's interest is mortgagable. See text accompanying note 1, § 3.35 infra. Thus, even if a vendee does not record, a recorded mortgage from the vendee will similarly cloud the title. In any event, it seems unlikely that the recording methods referred to in the text would constitute slander on the vendor's title. See Nelson, supra note 1 at 166.

See also Ridgewood Utilities Corp. v. King, 426 So.2d 49 (Fla.App.1982) (where land contract which was recorded but not entitled to recordation because unacknowledged by vendor, vendor had no cause of action for slander of title where there was no showing that the contract as recorded was false and that vendor was damaged as a result of the recording).

6. Warren, California Installment Land Sales Contracts: A Time for Reform, 9 U.C.L.A.L.Rev. 608, 629 (1962).

The foregoing, of course, is not intended to deemphasize the risks for the vendee under installment land contracts. Many of these risks have been discussed previously. Where the vendee has paid a substantial amount of the contract and then defaults, the vendor may choose to go to court to seek enforcement of a forfeiture clause. Notwithstanding clouds on the vendor's title, what if the court determines that forfeiture is reasonable? In that event a vendee could lose his entire equity without a public sale. In addition, some local recorders may occasionally block attempts by vendees to record evidence of their contracts.[7] In other words, the installment land contract device means, at best, uncertainty for both sides.

It is perhaps understandable that, notwithstanding the above risks, installment land contracts would be used in states where mortgages must be foreclosed by a costly and time-consuming judicial action. This helps to explain why such contracts are popular in Iowa and Illinois where such a judicial proceeding is the only foreclosure remedy. On the other hand, in many states, of which Missouri and Utah are typical, where the power of sale mortgage or deed of trust is permissible and where foreclosure is efficient and relatively inexpensive, reliance on the installment land contract is difficult to understand or justify.[8] Several possible explanations may be suggested. First, the use of installment land contracts may spill over from states where they have been used successfully for the good reasons discussed above to adjacent states where such use is especially dangerous for vendors. Second, many vendors may use land contracts in low down payment situations and take their chances that the vendees will be too unsophisticated to record or to otherwise protect their interests. Finally, many vendors may simply want to feel assured that they will receive their land back in the event of a default by the vendee. With a mortgage or a deed of trust, of course, the mortgagee must ultimately foreclose against a defaulting mortgagor; a third party could purchase at the sale, and the mortgagee thus could be left with money and not the land. Nonetheless, in view of the uncertainty of the enforceability of the forfeiture clause in many, if not most, jurisdictions that do not regulate installment land contracts specifically by statute, reliance on the forfeiture clause to regain one's land is probably at best misplaced.[9]

There is a widely-held but erroneous notion that use of an installment sale contract, rather than a purchase-money mortgage, is necessary to qualify the sale for installment reporting under section 453 of the Internal Revenue Code. In fact, it is clear that the form of the

7. Such action on the part of the recorder may be unjustified or based on statutory restrictions. See note 4 supra.

8. While it is true that power of sale foreclosure has been under constitutional attack on fourteenth amendment due process hearing and notice grounds, those at-tacks have been meeting with diminishing success, primarily due to the reluctance of the courts to find state action in foreclosures by nongovernmental leaders. See § 3.30, supra.

9. See Nelson, supra note 1, at 167–68.

document is unimportant.[10] The confusion probably arises from the fact that the Code's terminology under § 453 is similar to that applied to real estate installment contracts.

There is, however, a more subtle reason why an installment contract might arguably be the preferred mode of sale. To understand it, some background information on Section 453's operation is necessary. Its objective is to tax each payment received by the seller in proportion to the fraction of the total gain which that payment represents; thus, the gain and the tax may be spread over several taxable years. Specifically, the gain taxed on each payment is the amount of the payment multiplied by the *gross profit ratio*. The *gross profit ratio,* in turn, is defined as the *gross profit* (in essence, the gain) from the sale, divided by the *contract price*.[11] Mathematically, the formula is:

$$\text{Gross Profit Ratio} = \frac{\text{Gross Profit}}{\text{Contract Price}}$$

Ordinarily, when the seller is taking installment reporting under § 453 and the purchaser assumes or takes subject to an existing mortgage on the property, the amount of the mortgage is treated as reducing the contract price.[12] But when the mortgage amount exceeds the seller's basis in the property, that excess of mortgage over basis does *not* reduce the contract price.[13] Instead, the excess is treated as being received by the seller in the year of the sale.[14] For properties with large mort-

---

10. See Internal Revenue Code § 453(b)(1), defining an installment sale as "a disposition of property * * * where at least one payment is received after the close of the taxable year in which the disposition occurs." Section 453 was extensively amended by the Installment Sales Revision Act, Pub.L. No. 96–471, 94 Stat. 2247 (1980), but its application to both installment contracts and purchase-money mortgages was unchanged.

11. See Int.Rev.Code § 453(c); Temporary Treas.Reg. § 15A.453–1(b)(2); Emory & Hjorth, An Analysis of the Changes Made by the Installment Sales Revision Act of 1980—Part I, 54 J.Tax'n 130 (1981).

12. Temporary Treas.Reg. § 15A.453–1(b)(2)(iii). This reduction of the selling price by the mortgage amount has the effect of increasing the gross profit ratio and therefore of taxing a higher percentage of each actual payment received by the seller.

13. Temporary Treas.Reg. § 15A.453–1(b)(2)(iii). If the full amount of the mortgage, including the part exceeding basis, were applied to reduce the contract price, the denominator of the fraction (the contract price) would be less than the numerator (the gross profit), and the gross profit ratio would be greater than 100%. This would be unfair to the seller, since he has

already been separately taxed at the closing on the excess of mortgage over basis.

To illustrate, assume a property with a basis of $20,000, a mortgage of $60,000, and a selling price of $100,000. If the full mortgage were applied to reduce the contract price, the gross profit ratio would be

$$\frac{\text{Gross Profit}}{\text{Contract Price}} = \frac{80,000}{100,000-60,000} = 200\%$$

However, since the amount of mortgage in excess of basis does not reduce the contract price, the gross profit ratio is instead

$$\frac{\text{Gross Profit}}{\text{Contract Price}} = \frac{80,000}{100,000-20,000} = 100\%$$

See Comment, Receipt of Payment in Installment Sales Transactions: Wraparound Mortgages and Letters of Credit, 61 Neb.L. Rev. 499, 506 (1982).

14. See Temporary Treas.Reg. § 15A.453–1(b)(3)(i). Thus, in the example in the preceding footnote, the seller would be treated as receiving the excess of mortgage over basis, or $40,000, in the year of sale (plus, of course, any actual cash payments received in that year.) This aspect of the regulations was even more important prior to the Installment Sales Revision Act of 1980, since under the preceding law installment reporting was disallowed if gages, but in which the seller has a low basis, this may be a very undesirable result, as it will tend to "bunch" more gain into the year of the sale.

In several cases the Tax Court held that this result would not follow if the sale is of the "wraparound" type, under which the seller continues to make the payments on the underlying mortgage. Under this arrangement the buyer makes payments only to the seller, and their amount is computed as if there is no prior mortgage on the property.[15] The court took the view that in a wraparound sale, the underlying mortgage is neither being assumed nor taken subject to in an economic sense; thus, there should be no reduction in the contract price to reflect the mortgage amount, and (most importantly) the seller should not be regarded as receiving the excess of mortgage over basis in the year of sale.[16]

In its most recent regulations the IRS has explicitly rejected this position of the Tax Court, and has held that wraparound transactions are no different than ordinary assumption or subject-to transfers for purposes of installment reporting.[17] However, there is no clear warrant in the statute or the legislative history for the Service's position, and the regulations might conceivably be held invalid.[18] Parties planning a transaction with this eventuality in mind might wish to structure it so as to qualify under the earlier Tax Court cases. Nearly all of those cases involved installment land contracts rather than purchase-money mortgages, and there is at least an argument that the retention of legal title by the seller was an important factor in the outcome.[19] The Tax Court has never clarified this point.[20] Thus, a cautious

---

the seller received more than 30% of the selling price in the year of sale. The amount of mortgage in excess of basis might well be enough to eliminate installment reporting.

15. See § 5.16 infra for a detailed discussion of wraparound mortgages.

16. See Stonecrest v. Commissioner, 24 T.C. 659 (1955); Estate of Lamberth v. Commissioner, 31 T.C. 302 (1958); United Pacific Corp. v. Commissioner, 39 T.C. 721 (1963); Comment, supra note 4, at 511–521. The rationale of these cases seems to be based on the seller's continuing personal obligation to make the payments on the underlying mortgage, so that the buyer cannot be regarded as having either assumed or taken subject to it in an economic sense. It is clear, of course, that whatever title passes to the buyer is encumbered by the mortgage, so that in real property terms it has been taken "subject to."

17. Temporary Treas.Reg. § 15A.453–1(b)(3)(ii), applying to installment sales after March 4, 1981. This regulation is consistent with the litigating position of the

IRS in the cases cited in the foregoing footnote. Under the regulations, it is immaterial whether title has passed to the buyer.

18. See Comment, supra note 13, at 525–30.

19. In two private letter rulings prior to the issuance of the present regulations, the IRS attempted to distinguish the Tax Court cases on the ground that they involved installment land contracts with no transfer of legal title; see Priv.Ltr.Rul. 7814011 (Dec. 29, 1977); Priv.Ltr.Rul. 7814010 (Dec. 23, 1977). The proposition that the tax treatment of the wraparound sale ought to depend on the location of legal title is, on its merits, very dubious. See Comment, supra note 4, at 528 n. 168. But see Gallagher, Wraparound Mortgages and Deferred Payment Sales of Real Property, 56 Taxes 400 (1978).

20. It explicitly refused to decide whether retention of title was relevant to its wraparound mortgage position in Goodman v. Commissioner, 74 T.C. 684, 712 n. 16 (1980).

planner designing a wraparound sale for the most advantageous installment sale reporting might conclude that the installment land contract
was preferable to a mortgage. In light of the Service's regulations,
however, the argument for use of the installment contract is an
attenuated one.[21]

 WESTLAW REFERENCES

court(fl)   &   696.01

land   /s   installment contract agreement   /p   default***   forfeit***
    /p   record!

headnote(i.r.c.   /s   453)   &   land   /s   installment contract agreement

§ 3.35   Mortgaging the Vendee's Interest—Problems for Mortgagees

As a vendee pays off his obligations under an installment land
contract and particularly if the land goes up in value, the vendee's
interest can become a significant economic asset. Thus, it is a relatively common practice for a vendee to seek to borrow money by using his
interest as security for the loan. Functionally, of course, a mortgage on
a vendee's interest is the economic equivalent of a second mortgage,
because the vendor holds an interest analogous to a first purchase
money mortgage on the land. Increasingly, the case law recognizes the
proposition that the vendee's interest is mortgageable.[1]

To state this latter proposition, however, raises some serious questions. The determination that the vendee has an interest which can be
mortgaged is of little use unless the mortgagee has some way to protect

---

21. Attempting to qualify the transactions under the Tax Court's cases is frus-
trating in another way as well. If the
seller in a wraparound transaction is not a
financial institution or a party of excellent
credit and solvency, the buyer is well advised to make each regular payment into
some form of trust, agency, or escrow arrangement, with the trustee or agent having authority to split the funds, pay the
amount due on the underlying mortgage
directly, and turn the remainder over to
the seller. This approach is good assurance against the possibility of the seller's
default in making the payments on the
prior mortgage. Unfortunately, the Tax
Court has held that if such an arrangement is used, the entire mortgage in excess
of basis must be realized as income in the
year of the sale, thus destroying the hoped-
for tax advantage of the wraparound sale.
See Goodman v. Commissioner, 74 T.C. 684
(1980).

§ 3.35

1. See Petz v. Estate of Petz, ___ Ind.
App. ___, 467 N.E.2d 780 (1984); Davis &

Son v. Milligan, 88 Ala. 523, 6 So. 908
(1899); Stannard v. Marboe, 159 Minn.
119, 198 N.W. 127 (1924); Fincher v. Miles
Homes, Inc., 549 S.W.2d 848 (Mo.1977);
O'Neill Production Credit Association v.
Mitchell, 209 Neb. 206, 307 N.W.2d 115
(1981); Shindledecker v. Savage, 96 N.M.
42, 627 P.2d 1241 (1981); Bill Nay & Sons
Excavating v. Neeley Construction Co., 677
P.2d 1120 (Utah 1984); Kendrick v. Davis,
75 Wn.2d 456, 452 P.2d 222 (1969). But
see Arkansas Supply, Inc. v. Young, 265
Ark. 281, 580 S.W.2d 174 (1979) (vendee
who had paid only $150 of a $15,000 purchase price under an installment land contract did not possess a mortgageable interest).

Such a mortgage typically is perfected
against third party claimants of the vendee
by recording it in the real estate records.
Perfection under Article 9 of the U.C.C. is
probably unnecessary. See In re Chimen-
to, 43 B.R. 401 (Bkrtcy.Ohio 1984). As to
perfection of a mortgage on a vendor's interest, see § 3.31 infra.

his interest against the vendor's declaration of forfeiture. Thus, cases generally hold that where the vendor has actual knowledge of the vendee's mortgagee, he cannot declare a forfeiture of an installment land contract without giving the vendee's mortgagee both notification of intent to forfeit and an opportunity to protect himself.[2] Furthermore, under the reasoning of some of the foregoing cases, even where the vendor lacks actual knowledge of the vendee's mortgagee, recording by the vendee's mortgagee constitutes constructive notice to the vendor of the mortgagee's existence and imposes a duty on the vendor to examine title to the land prior to a declaration of forfeiture in order to insure that notice can be given to any subsequent mortgagee of the vendee's interest.[3] On the other hand, there is also case law that holds that, absent actual knowledge of the mortgagee's existence, the vendor is under no obligation to notify the mortgagee of his intention to declare a forfeiture.[4] This latter approach relies on the notion that the recording of an instrument constitutes notice only to those acquiring interest in the land subsequent to a recording and not to those whose interest predated that recording. The practical effect of such reasoning will mean that a mortgagee, in order to protect himself, will be required to give actual notice to the vendor at the time the mortgagee takes his security interest.[5]

Assuming that notification of an intent to invoke forfeiture reaches the vendee's mortgagee, how may the latter protect himself? It has been suggested that notification would permit the mortgagee to fulfill the obligations of the vendee under the contract.[6] If this means that the mortgagee may take over the vendee's interest without foreclosure of the mortgage, it would seem to be clearly erroneous, since it would confer on a mortgagee of the vendee greater rights than those possessed by a second mortgagee in the normal mortgage situation. In the normal situation, the second mortgagee, when the senior mortgage goes into default, has two options. First, he may pay off or redeem the senior mortgage and stand in the senior's shoes as an assignee of that mortgage. At that point, the second mortgagee would own two mortgages on the land and would have to foreclose one or both of them in order to acquire either money or title to the land. Alternatively, the

---

2. See e.g., Lockhart Company v. B.F.K., Ltd., 107 Idaho 633, 691 P.2d 1248 (App.1984); Credit Finance, Inc. v. Bateman, 135 Ariz. 268, 660 P.2d 869 (App. 1983); Fincher v. Miles Homes, Inc., 549 S.W.2d 848 (Mo.1977); Stannard v. Marboe, 159 Minn. 119, 198 N.W. 127 (1924); Shindledecker v. Savage, 96 N.M. 42, 627 P.2d 1241 (1981) (dictum); Kendrick v. Davis, 75 Wn.2d 456, 452 P.2d 222 (1969). Contra: Estate of Brewer v. Iota Delta Chapter, 298 Or. 383, 692 P.2d 597 (1984). See also, Roberts v. Morin, ___ Mont. ___, 645 P.2d 423 (1982) (vendee who resells land on second installment land contract entitled to notice from the origi-

nal vendor prior to declaration of forfeiture of the first contract.)

3. See e.g., Stannard v. Marboe, 159 Minn. 119, 198 N.W. 127 (1924). See also Note, 45 Wash.L.Rev. 645, 646 (1970).

4. See e.g., Kendrick v. Davis, 75 Wn.2d 456, 452 P.2d 222 (1969); Shindledecker v. Savage, 96 N.M. 42, 627 P.2d 1241 (1981).

5. For a cogent criticism of this approach, see Note, Mortgages—Mortgage of a Vendee's Interest in an Installment Land Contract—Mortgagee's Rights Upon Default, 43 Mo.L.Rev. 371, 373–374 (1978).

6. See Note, 45 Wash.L.Rev. 645, 646 (1970).

second mortgagee could foreclose his mortgage, and the purchaser at that sale would buy the land subject to the first mortgage.[7] The foreclosing second mortgagee would get title only if he were the successful purchaser at the sale. Otherwise the second mortgagee would have his lien paid off. But in no event can the second mortgagee acquire title to the land without himself foreclosing.

In applying the mortgage analogy to the installment land contract situation, it would seem that the vendee's mortgagee should have no greater rights than a "normal" second mortgagee. In other words, the vendee's mortgagee should have two options. First, he could pay off the defaulted land contract and have all the rights of an assignee of the vendor under that contract. Assuming forfeiture is enforceable in his jurisdiction, the mortgagee-assignee presumably could then himself invoke the forfeiture rights under the contract.[8] But in no event should he be able to eradicate the vendee's interest without invoking the functional equivalent of foreclosure. Second, the mortgagee could choose to foreclose his mortgage on the vendee's interest. In that case the purchaser at the sale would buy the land subject to the vendor's rights.[9] The mortgagee would either purchase the land himself or be paid out of the proceeds of the sale. This second option is, of course, highly risky, because if the vendor is able to invoke forfeiture promptly, the purchaser at the vendee's mortgagee's foreclosure sale may simply be buying nothing.[10]

Very often, mortgagees of a vendee's interest make the mistake of taking an assignment of the vendee's interest and a quitclaim deed from the vendee as security for the loan to the vendee. This transaction, of course, will be treated substantively as a mortgage.[11] The problem is that the use of such documents means that the mortgagee's second option, foreclosure of his mortgage, must be accomplished by a costly and time-consuming judicial action. This is because the assignment and quitclaim deed will contain no power of sale, so that even if the particular jurisdiction permits nonjudicial foreclosure, the mortgagee could not utilize that remedy. Thus, if a mortgage on a vendee's interest is desired and if the applicable jurisdiction permits nonjudicial foreclosure, the mortgagee of the vendee should utilize a mortgage or deed of trust with an express power of sale instead of the assignment and quitclaim type documents.

7. See Nelson and Whitman, Real Estate Transfer, Finance and Development, 497–499 (2nd Ed. 1981).

8. Note, 43 Mo.L.Rev. 371, 376–377 (1978). But see Knauss v. Miles Homes, Inc., 173 N.W.2d 896 (N.D.1969).

9. Note, 43 Mo.L.Rev. 371, 376–377 (1978).

10. For a consideration of the vendor's rights vis a vis the vendee's mortgagee when the latter is not notified of the contract forfeiture proceeding, see Fincher v. Miles Homes of Missouri, Inc., 549 S.W.2d 848 (Mo.1977); Note, supra note 10 at 376–377.

11. Erickson v. First National Bank of Minneapolis, ___ Mont. ___, 697 P.2d 1332 (1985); O'Neill Production Credit Association v. Mitchell, 209 Neb. 206, 307 N.W.2d 115 (1981); Kendrick v. Davis, 75 Wn.2d 456, 452 P.2d 222 (1969); Cunningham & Tischier, Disguised Real Estate Security Transactions as Mortgages in Substance, 26 Rutgers L.Rev. 1 (1972).

WESTLAW REFERENCES
land /s installment contract agreement /p default*** forfeit***
/p mortgage /s vendee second

§ 3.36 Judgments Against Parties to Installment Land Contracts

In almost all states, a judgment creates a lien on the real, but usually not the personal, property of the judgment debtor.[1] While the mechanics of obtaining the lien and its effective date vary somewhat, typically the lien applies to all real estate of the judgment debtor in the county in which the judgment is docketed [entered by a court clerk in an appropriate docket book].[2] The time of docketing usually determines lien priority. Consequently, when the judgment debtor is either a vendee or vendor under an installment land contract, the characterization of the debtor's interest as real or personal property can be crucial in determining the rights of the judgment creditor.

Judgments Against Vendee

Most states hold that the vendee's interest is real estate for purposes of judgment lien legislation and that a judgment creditor of a vendee thus obtains a valid lien on the vendee's contract interest.[3] The practical implications of this rule can be illustrated by the following hypothetical: Suppose that a vendee has paid off $40,000 of an installment land contract price of $100,000. The land then has a fair market value free and clear of liens of $100,000. Vendee's creditor then dockets a $15,000 judgment against vendee in a county where the contract land is located. Vendee then borrows $30,000 from mortgagee and gives it a mortgage on the contract land, which mortgage mortgagee promptly records. Vendee then defaults on the mortgage and mortgagee forecloses. Because the judgment against the vendee is a valid lien on the vendee's interest and because it was docketed prior to the execution and recordation of the mortgage, the purchaser at the foreclosure sale will buy the vendee's interest subject to the judgment lien.

Courts justify the foregoing result either by application of the equitable conversion concept or as a matter of statutory interpretation. Under the equitable conversion theory, from the time an earnest money or installment land contract is executed, the vendee's interest is consid-

---

§ 3.36

1. See Epstein, Debtor-Creditor Law 46, 52–53 (2d Ed. 1980).

2. See e.g., Minn.Stat.Ann. § 548.09; Vernon's Ann.Mo.Stat. § 511.350; Utah Code Ann.1953, 78–22–1; Epstein, supra note 1 at 46.

3. See e.g., Mutual Building & Loan Association v. Collins, 85 N.M. 706, 516

P.2d 677 (1973); Fridley v. Munson, 46 S.D. 532, 194 N.W. 840 (1923); Utah Coop. Association v. White Distributing and Supply Co., 120 Utah 603, 237 P.2d 262 (1951); Bill Nay & Sons Excavating v. Neely Construction Co., 677 P.2d 1120 (Utah 1984); Cascade Security Bank v. Butler, 88 Wn.2d 777, 567 P.2d 631 (1977).

ered in equity to be real estate while the vendor's retention of legal title and the right to receive the balance of the purchase price is deemed primarily to be personalty.[4] Other courts eschew the equitable conversion approach and simply hold that the legislature intended that the vendee's interest be treated as real estate for purposes of judgment lien legislation.[5] This statutory construction approach is preferred by these courts because of a concern over the uncertainty of the equitable conversion concept and the implications its application would create for other areas such as devolution at death, wills and trusts.[6]

A judgment creditor of a vendee must sometimes cope with a related and potentially more troublesome issue. There is case law that holds that a judgment lien does not attach to equitable interests in real estate and, accordingly, that a contract vendee's interest, being equitable, is not subject to the lien.[7] Increasingly, however, courts are interpreting judgment lien legislation broadly so as to make equitable, as well as legal, interests subject to the lien.[8] Consequently, it is becoming substantially more likely that a judgment lien will attach to an installment vendee's interest notwithstanding its equitable nature.[9]

Judgments Against Vendor

The equitable conversion theory notwithstanding, the majority of courts treat the vendor's installment land contract interest as real estate for purposes of judgment lien statutes.[10] Thus, as one court stated, the judgment lien "extends to all of the vendor's interest remaining in the land and binds the land to the extent of the unpaid purchase price."[11] Under this approach, the vendor's real estate interest is grounded in the fact that she retains legal title to the land until the contract is fully paid and the deed is delivered to the vendee.[12]

---

4. Hume, Real Estate Contracts and the Doctrine of Equitable Conversion in Washington: Dispelling the Ashford Cloud, 7 U.P.S.L.Rev. 233, 240 (1984); Leavell, Love and Nelson, Equitable Remedies and Restitution 356–57 (3d Ed. 1980); Mutual Building & Loan Association v. Collins, 85 N.M. 706, 516 P.2d 677 (1973); Bartz v. Paff, 95 Wis. 95, 69 N.W. 297 (1896); C.f., Westfair Corp. v. Kuelz, 90 Wisc.2d 631, 280 N.W.2d 364 (1979).

5. Cascade Security Bank v. Butler, 88 Wn.2d 777, 567 P.2d 631 (1977); Joseph v. Donovan, 114 Conn. 79, 157 A. 638 (1931); Hoffman v. Semet, 316 So.2d 649 (Fla.App. 1975); Note, 47 Mo.L.Rev. 328, 321 (1982).

6. See e.g., Cascade Security Bank v. Butler, 88 Wn.2d 777, 567 P.2d 631 (1977).

7. See e.g., Warren v. Rodgers, 82 N.M. 78, 475 P.2d 775 (1970); Cheves v. First National Bank, 79 Fla. 34, 83 So.2d 870 (1920); FCX, Inc. v. Long Meadow Farms, Inc., 269 S.C. 202, 237 S.E.2d 50 (1977); Annot., 1 A.L.R.2d 717 (1948).

8. See Fridley v. Munson, 46 S.D. 532, 194 N.W. 840 (1923); Mutual Building & Loan Association v. Collins, 85 N.M. 706, 516 P.2d 677 (1973) (overruling Warren v. Rodgers, supra note 7); Eckley v. Bonded Adjustment Co., 30 Wn.2d 96, 190 P.2d 718 (1948).

9. See e.g., Mutual Building & Loan Association v. Collins, 85 N.M. 706, 516 P.2d 677 (1973).

10. See e.g., Chain O' Mines, Inc. v. Williamson, 101 Colo. 231, 72 P.2d 265 (1937); First Bank of Idaho v. Rogers, 91 Idaho 654, 429 P.2d 386 (1967); Bauemeister v. McDonald, 124 Neb. 142, 247 N.W. 424 (1932); Heider v. Dietz, 234 Or. 105, 380 P.2d 619 (1963); Heath v. Dodson, 7 Wn.2d 667, 110 P.2d 845 (1941); Note, 47 Mo.L.Rev. 328, 330–31 (1982).

11. First Security Bank of Idaho v. Rogers, 91 Idaho 654, 429 P.2d 386 (1967).

12. Note, 47 Mo.L.Rev. 328, 331 (1982).

Perhaps an equally plausible basis for the majority rule would be that the vendor has an interest in real estate to the extent of the unpaid purchase price.[13]

A minority of jurisdictions characterize the vendor's interest as personalty for purposes of judgment lien legislation.[14] This result is based not only on the fact that, for purposes of the equitable conversion doctrine, the vendor has personalty,[15] but also on the notion that, since courts overwhelmingly characterize the vendee's interest as real estate, it is illogical that the vendor should have it as well.[16]

Again, an example is helpful in understanding the implications of the majority and minority approaches: Suppose that an installment contract vendor was entitled to collect $50,000 over the next four years. X then docketed a $20,000 judgment against vendor in a county where the contract land was located. Y then docketed a $40,000 judgment against vendor in the same county. Y holds an execution sale on the judgment and he purchases at the sale for $40,000. Y clearly paid too much. Under the majority rule the vendor's interest is real estate and thus both judgments were liens on that interest. Their relative priority is determined by the date each judgment was docketed. Accordingly, since Y's judgment was docketed later than X's, Y purchased the vendor's interest subject to X's unpaid $20,000 lien. On the other hand, if the foregoing fact situation occurs in a minority jurisdiction Y is much better off. In such states the vendor's interest is personalty. As such, a judgment creditor can obtain no interest in it until it is levied upon by the sheriff pursuant to the issuance of a writ of execution.[17] The date of judgment docketing establishes no priority; rather, the first execution sale passes title to the personalty free and clear of any other judgment no matter when it was docketed. Thus, in our example, even though Y's judgment was obtained after X's, Y purchased at the execution sale a title free and clear of any lien in favor of X.

 WESTLAW REFERENCES
land /s installment contract agreement /p judgment /s lien creditor attach! equit! /s interest

§ 3.37 Mortgaging the Vendor's Interest—Problems for Mortgagees

The vendor's interest in an installment land contract is clearly mortgageable.[1] Traditionally, it has been a common practice for those

13. Lacy, Land Sale Contracts in Bankruptcy, 21 U.C.L.A.L.Rev. 477, 505 (1973).

14. See e.g., Marks v. Tucumcari, 93 N.M. 4, 595 P.2d 1199 (1979); Mueller v. Novelty Dye Works, 273 Wis. 501, 78 N.W.2d 881 (1956); Church, Equitable Conversion in Wisconsin, 1970 Wis.L.Rev. 405, 418–19 (1970).

15. See Marks v. Tucumcari, 93 N.M. 4, 595 P.2d 1199 (1979); Mueller v. Novelty

Dye Works, 273 Wis. 501, 78 N.W.2d 881 (1956).

16. Note, 47 Mo.L.Rev. 328, 331 (1982).

17. See Epstein, supra note 1 at 52–53.

§ 3.37

1. See e.g., Cain & Bultman, Inc. v. Miss Sam, Inc., 409 So.2d 114 (Fla.App. 1982); In re Freeborn, 94 Wn.2d 336, 617 P.2d 424 (1980).

who lend money on the security of a vendor's interest to treat the transaction as a simple mortgage on a fee interest in real estate. In other words, it has been assumed that because the vendor held legal title, he or she was the "real owner" of the land described in the contract until the contract was fully paid off. Consequently, the lender will take a regular mortgage and an assignment of the vendor's contract interest. The mortgage and, sometimes, the assignment are usually recorded in the real estate records. As a variant, instead of taking a mortgage, the lender may take a deed to the contract land together with an assignment and then record one or both in the real estate records.[2]

It has usually been assumed that the foregoing practice protects the lender's priority against both unsecured and subsequent lien creditors of the vendor. However, a Washington Supreme Court decision, In re Freeborn,[3] calls this practice and its underlying assumptions into serious question. In that case, the court held that to the extent that the vendor's lender desires to have a security interest in the vendor's right to receive the contract payments that will have priority over claims against those payments by subsequent lien creditors, including a trustee in bankruptcy, it must perfect that claim as a chattel security interest under Article 9 of the Uniform Commercial Code. The court's reasoning was premised on the notion that the vendor has both legal title to the land (which is realty) and the right to receive the contract payments (which is personalty), and that while taking and recording a mortgage or similar documents in the land records protects the lender against subsequent claims to the vendor's legal title, it does not similarly protect the lender with respect to subsequent claims on the vendor's right to receive the contract payments. Since only real estate recording had occurred, the security interests in *Freeborn* were deemed unperfected.

The *Freeborn* court found support for its conclusion that the vendor's right to receive the contract payments was personalty in an earlier Washington decision [4] that characterized the vendor's installment land contract interest as personalty for community property purposes. In addition, it relied on Cascade Security Bank v. Butler,[5] which, while rejecting the application of equitable conversion concept,[6] held that an installment vendee's interest was real estate for purposes of Washington's judgment lien statute. The *Freeborn* court also emphasized other Washington case law holding the vendor's contract interest to be personalty.[7]

2. See e.g., In re Freeborn, 94 Wn.2d 336, 617 P.2d 424 (1980).

3. 94 Wash.2d 336, 617 P.2d 424 (1980), noted 47 Mo.L.Rev. 328 (1982).

4. Meltzer v. Wendell-West, 7 Wn.App. 90, 497 P.2d 1348 (1972).

5. 88 Wn.2d 777, 567 P.2d 631 (1977).

6. Id. See Hume, Real Estate Contracts and the Doctrine of Equitable Conversion in Washington: Dispelling the Ashford Cloud, 7 U.P.S.L.Rev. 233 (1984).

7. Pierce County v. King, 47 Wn.2d 328, 287 P.2d 316 (1955) (vendor's interest personalty for inheritance tax purposes); In re Estate of Eilermann, 179 Wash. 15, 35 P.2d 763 (1934) (vendor's interest personalty for purposes of succession and administration).

More significant, however, is the *Freeborn* court's Article 9 analysis, which is grounded in a straight mortgage transaction analogy. The court cited an official comment to section 9–102(3) which states that although Article 9 is inapplicable to the creation of a real estate mortgage itself, "when the mortgagee pledges the note to secure his own obligation to X, this Article applies to the security interest thus created, which is a security interest in an instrument even though the instrument is secured by a real estate mortgage." [8] The court reasoned that the situation described in the comment—"where the mortgagee pledges the note to secure his own obligation to a third party"—was analogous to the [case before it.] "Here, the vendor and holder of legal title assigned the right to receive real estate contract payments in order to secure his obligation to a third party." [9] Finally, the court relied on a Florida federal trial court decision [10] for the proposition that Article 9 "applies to security interests in 'realty paper' and for its holding that Article 9 governed where installment land contracts were delivered to vendor's lender pursuant to a "Security Pledge Agreement."

The *Freeborn* approach has been followed by several other courts. [11] The court's basic thrust, which is to analogize installment contracts to notes secured by mortgages, is a trend we have already examined in other contexts earlier in this chapter, and which we applaud. Under this analysis, the case is correct in part and wrong in part. It is now becoming clear that Article 9 of the UCC is applicable to the perfection of security interests in mortgage notes. [12] On this point *Freeborn* is right. True, the method of perfection for notes, which is the transfer of possession to the secured party, is probably inapplicable to installment contracts, since they are evidently not "instruments" as the UCC employs the term. [13] Hence, an installment contract is correctly understood to be a "general intangible" in the Code's parlance, and a security interest in it must be perfected by the filing of a financing statement. [14]

---

8. U.C.C. § 9–102, Official Comment 4.

9. 617 P.2d at 428.

10. Hughes v. Russo, 20 U.C.C.Rep. Serv. 1349 (S.D.Fla.1976).

11. In re Shuster, 47 B.R. 920 (D.Minn. 1985) (Code filing necessary); Southwest National Bank v. Southworth, 22 B.R. 376 (Bkrtcy.Kan.1982) (both realty and Code filing necessary); S.O.A.W. Enterprises v. Castle Rock Industrial Bank, 32 B.R. 279 (Bkrtcy.Tex.1983) (Code filing sufficient); In re Equitable Development Corp, 20 U.C.C.Rep.Serv. 1349 (S.D.Fla.1976) (Code filing sufficient).

12. See First National Bank v. Larson, 17 B.R. 957, 965 (Bkrtcy.N.J.1982); Greiner v. Wilke, 625 F.2d 281, 284 (9th Cir.1980). See generally § 5.28 infra, especially at note 40.

13. See U.C.C. § 9–105(g), defining an "instrument" as a paper "of a type which is in the ordinary course of business transferred by delivery with any necessary indorsement or assignment." Customs vary from one area of the nation to another, but it would be difficult to say that there is a broad custom of transferring or pledging installment contracts by delivery of the original contract document. Perfection of a security interest in an "instrument" can be accomplished only by delivery; see U.C.C. § 9–304(1).

14. U.C.C. § 9–106. A security interest in a "general intangible" can be perfected only by filing a financing statement; see U.C.C. § 9–304, Comment 1. See cases cited at note 11 supra.

But it is with respect to the real property interest that *Freeborn's* attempt to assimilate installment contracts to mortgages breaks down. It is well recognized that an assignment of a mortgage note will carry the mortgage with it automatically,[15] and the cases are increasingly taking the view that, even when the transfer is for security purposes, the mortgage will attach to the note when it is delivered into the hands of the pledgee, and will be regarded as perfected irrespective of whether any assignment was recorded in the real estate records.[16] *Freeborn* displays no awareness of these cases, and instead insists on treatment of the realty interest as a separate species which must be perfected (by recording) in its own right.

Surely this is a waste of effort. Separation of the real estate interest from the payment stream may be conceptually possible, but it is meaningless in practical terms. If one holds the realty interest but has no right to the payments, his interest has no value. He obviously cannot sue for damages, specific performance, or any other money remedy. He cannot declare a forfeiture, for the reason that there is no debt owed to him. His "rights" are as empty and useless as those of a mortgagee when someone else holds the note; they are nugatory.[17]

Why, then, put the pledgee of the vendor's interest at risk of losing his security in the land if he does not record in the real estate records? Certainly one recording—in the financing statement files—is sufficient, once practitioners and the public know that they must search there. No policy is served by forcing everyone to use both belt and suspenders. The court, we suggest, should simply have carried the mortgage law analogy to its logical conclusion and held the Code filing sufficient for complete perfection. The only objection to this view is that it is contrary to long-established habits in many areas; but once the law is clarified, those habits can readily be changed.

One caution must be added. Installment contracts are not always recorded, and it is quite conceivable that a vendor will enter into one and later purport to mortgage the land as security for a loan, say from a bank, without disclosing the contract's existence. In a formalistic sense, such a mortgage is of the vendor's interest in the contract, and hence should be perfected under Article 9 as suggested above. But in practice this requirement makes no sense if the bank has no notice of the contract's existence. Indeed, the bank will have no reason to suppose that anything other than the land itself is serving as its security, and will have no idea that Article 9 is involved in any way.

In this situation, application of Article 9 would be manifestly unfair. The bank should be held to Article 9's perfection rules only if it is on actual or constructive notice (from the recorded contract or the

15. See § 5.27 infra at notes 5–13.   **17.** See § 5.27 infra.

16. See cases cited at note 13, supra; § 5.28 infra at note 40.

vendee's possession) that the contract exists. There is no extra burden to the bank in imposing constructive notice upon it in this setting; since it is being presented by its borrower with what purports to be a mortgage on fee simple ownership, it will normally search the realty records and obtain title insurance in any event.

Whatever its merits, *Freeborn* and its progeny exist and cannot be ignored. Until the law is further clarified, those who take security interests in the installment vendor's rights are well advised to record some appropriate instrument (a deed, an assignment of contract rights, or both) in the real estate records, and to file a financing statement as well. The added expense and inconvenience of following *Freeborn* seem a small price to pay for the enhanced protection the vendor's creditor will get as against third party claimants.

 WESTLAW REFERENCES

"real estate" land /s installment contract agreement payment /p title security /s equit! legal /p interest /p assign! convey! /p vendor seller

F. THE NEGATIVE COVENANT AS A MORTGAGE SUBSTITUTE

§ 3.38 The Negative Covenant and the "Coast Bank" Mortgage

Lenders occasionally, in otherwise unsecured loan transactions, exact a separate negative covenant from the borrower that certain separate real estate will not be encumbered or transferred by the borrower while the debt remains unpaid. Indeed, it has been suggested that such negative covenants have been used by some California creditors to retain the option, in the event of default, of choosing to proceed as either a secured or unsecured creditor.[1] If, for example, at the time of default, a borrower has sufficient assets to satisfy a judgment, the creditor may opt simply to sue as an unsecured creditor on the debt. In so doing, the creditor would presumably avoid the protections that the California mortgage law confers on the borrower. These protections include a "one-action" rule and significant anti-deficiency limitations.[2] Under the "one-action" rule, a debt secured by real estate must be foreclosed in a foreclosure action and any deficiency must be sought in that foreclosure proceeding.[3] On the other hand, if the defaulting borrower lacks other assets, the creditor will attempt to establish the negative covenant as a mortgage. As Professor Hetland has aptly pointed out, this use of a negative covenant represented an "attempted have-their-cake and eat-it-too device." [4]

§ 3.38

1. Hetland, Secured Real Estate Transactions, 73 (1974).

2. See §§ 8.2–8.3, infra.

3. Id.

4. Hetland, Secured Real Estate Transactions, 73 (1974).

Traditionally this type of negative covenant not to mortgage specified real estate has not created a security interest in favor of the creditor.[5] "The creation of a lien is an affirmative act, and the intention to do such an act cannot be implied from an express negative."[6] It seems probable that under certain circumstances the debtor might be enjoined from violating his promise and third persons with notice could be prevented from taking a mortgage.[7] This right, however, rests upon the protection of a purely in personam contract right rather than upon an equitable lien or mortgage theory.[8]

The 1964 California Supreme Court decision in Coast Bank v. Minderhout[9] suggested a break with the foregoing analysis. That case held that an equitable mortgage could be established based on a purely negative covenant. The agreement in *Coast Bank* was executed by the borrower together with a note covering some small loans and some contemplated future advances. The agreement provided that the borrower would not sell or encumber certain described real property until he had repaid all present and future advances. It also provided for acceleration of all indebtedness on default in payment or on breach of the property agreement. It gave permission to the bank to record the agreement at such time as the bank saw fit. The agreement was silent as to whether a lien on the property was created. The bank recorded and the borrower, while still indebted, conveyed the property. There was a default on the indebtedness and the bank accelerated and brought an action to foreclose the equitable mortgage that it claimed the agreement created. The defendant demurred generally and failed to answer the plaintiff's allegation that the parties intended to create a security interest in the property. The lower court decreed foreclosure and, on appeal, the judgment was affirmed.

The court based its holding in favor of an equitable mortgage on two grounds: (1) the parties intended to create a security interest, and (2) this intent was "reasonably susceptible" from the face of the executed instruments. While *Coast Bank* was a unanimous opinion by an influential court, much confusion resulted in the wake of that decision.

5. Palmeri v. Allen, 30 Conn.Sup. 56, 299 A.2d 552 (1972); Knott v. Shepherdstown Manufacturing Co., 30 W.Va. 790, 5 S.E. 266 (1888); Western States Finance Co. v. Ruff, 108 Or. 442, 215 P. 501 (1923), modified and rehearing denied 108 Or. 455, 216 P. 1020 (1923). See Kuppenheimer & Co. v. Mornin, 78 F.2d 261, 101 A.L.R. 75 (C.C.A.Iowa 1935).

6. Knott v. Shepherdstown Manufacturing Co., supra note 5 at 30 W.Va. at 796, 5 S.E. at 269.

7. See Kelly v. Central Hanover Bank & Trust Co., 11 F.Supp. 497 (D.N.Y.1935). See 49 Harv.L.Rev. 620, 627 (1936). Insolvency at time of suit rather than insolvency at time of breach seems the preferable test. See 36 Col.L.Rev. 319, 320 (1936). On the other hand, in the Kelly case an acceleration clause effective on breach was held to make the remedy at law adequate, the obligor being solvent at the time. See 49 Harv.L.Rev. 620, 623 (1936); 22 Va.L. Rev. 440, 448 (1936). Cf. 30 Ill.L.Rev. 487, 490 (1935); 46 Yale L.Jour. 97, 605 (1936).

8. Osborne, Mortgages, § 43 (2d Ed. 1970).

9. 61 Cal.2d 311, 38 Cal.Rptr. 505, 392 P.2d 265 (1964).

In 1971, the California Supreme Court again confronted the problem of negative covenants as security in the case of Tahoe National Bank v. Phillips.[10] In *Tahoe* the court clearly seemed uneasy with what it had created in *Coast Bank*. *Tahoe* involved an attempt by the bank to foreclose as a mortgage an "Assignment of Rents and Agreement Not to Sell or Encumber Real Property" that was very similar to the "Agreement Not to Encumber or Transfer Property" used in *Coast Bank*. The court ruled that *Coast Bank* was not controlling. In *Tahoe* the borrower had not conveyed or sold the property in question but had declared a homestead exemption on the property. The court also determined that the form used in *Tahoe* was not generally considered in the trade to be a security agreement.

The *Tahoe* court continued to use the somewhat general and confusing terminology of *Coast Bank* by stating that the language of the instrument was not "reasonably susceptible of interpretation" as a mortgage. This language obviously leaves the door open for an interpretation in favor of an equitable mortgage where the language is "reasonably susceptible" for that result.

The *Tahoe* court concluded that "to permit a creditor to choose an allegedly ambiguous form of agreement, and then by extrinsic evidence seek to give it the effect of a different and unambiguous form, would be to disregard totally the rules respecting interpretation of adhesion contracts, and to create an extreme danger of over-reaching on the part of creditors with superior bargaining positions. Since the bank was the party who selected the documents, it was required to "bear the responsibility for the creation and use of the assignment it now claims as ambiguous; it is only 'poetic justice' * * * if such ambiguity is construed in favor of the borrower. Legal alchemy cannot convert an assignment into an equitable mortgage, violating the customer's reasonable expectation and bestowing upon the bank the riches of an hypothecation of title." [11]

The confusion that resulted from *Coast Bank* and *Tahoe* is evident in two cases from different California Courts of Appeal decided in 1971 after the *Tahoe* decision. In Kaiser Industries v. Taylor [12] the court held that a letter of instructions containing an agreement not to encumber or transfer was sufficient evidence of the parties' intent to make a mortgage. The court followed *Coast Bank* and held that the letter of instructions was "reasonably susceptible" of interpretation as an equitable mortgage. It should be emphasized that because of California's "one-action" rule, the effect of this decision was "pro-debtor". The creditor had initially sued on the debt and secured a judgment against the debtor. On appeal, the Court of Appeal determined that an

10. 4 Cal.3d 11, 92 Cal.Rptr. 704, 480 P.2d 320 (1971).

11. 92 Cal.Rptr. at 711–712, 480 P.2d at 327–328.

12. 17 Cal.App.3d 346, 94 Cal.Rptr. 773 (1971).

equitable mortgage existed and that, because of the "one-action" rule, foreclosure was the only remedy permitted.

In Orange County Teachers Credit Union v. Peppard [13] an agreement admittedly similar to the ones both in *Coast Bank* and *Tahoe* was held not to be an equitable mortgage because it was not "reasonably susceptible" as such. The court attempted to follow both *Coast Bank* and *Tahoe* and discovered the problem that the Supreme Court of California had created when it failed to overrule *Coast Bank* in the *Tahoe* decision. The "reasonably susceptible" test had turned out to be no test at all, but instead, a source of confusion.

The Ninth Circuit Court of Appeals interpreted the California law of negative covenants in 1972 in Browne v. San Luis Obispo National Bank.[14] That court held that the document in that case was similar to the one used in *Tahoe* and that the facts indicated an equitable mortgage was not created. The court still used the language of intent, however, and ruled that there was no evidence of intent to create a mortgage.

The foregoing indicates, at least, that the California creditors will be foolhardy if they believe that such negative covenants will give them a "have-their-cake and eat-it-too" option. While courts may, at the creditor's request, occasionally determine that a mortgage exists, and thus give the creditor the advantage of being in a secured position, this advantage is offset by the fact that, if the creditor attempts to enforce the debt alone, the debtor may be able to invoke the "one-action" rule if the court is persuaded that the negative covenant is in fact a mortgage.

The Court of Appeals of Arizona, most likely aware of the confusion in California, specifically declined to follow *Coast Bank* and characterized the *Coast Bank* reasoning as "weak".[15] The Arizona court indicated that an equitable mortgage should be found only where the parties tried to create a mortgage but technically failed to do so. The court declined to apply the "reasonably susceptible" test.

Subsequent decisions reinforce this judicial unwillingness to permit negative covenants to become the vehicle for the creation of equitable mortgages.[16] Apparently Professor Gilmore's advice is still good: "Negative covenants should not, it is submitted, be allowed to operate as informal or inchoate security arrangements, even against third parties with notice. If a creditor wants security let him take his security in some recognized form: mortgage, pledge, Article IX security interest or what not. If he wants protection against third parties, let him take possession of the collateral or file. Nothing is to be gained by giving a shadowy effectiveness to informal arrangements which conform to no

13. 21 Cal.App.3d 448, 98 Cal.Rptr. 533 (1971).

14. 462 F.2d 129 (9th Cir.1972).

15. Weaver v. Tri City Credit Bureau, 27 Ariz.App. 640, 557 P.2d 1072 (1976).

16. Chase Manhattan Bank v. Gems-By-Gordon, 649 F.2d 710 (9th Cir.1981); Equitable Trust Co. v. Imbesi, 287 Md. 249, 412 A.2d 96 (1980); In re Friese, 28 B.R. 953 (Bkrtcy.Conn.1983).

recognized pattern." [17] According to Professor Gilmore, the "debtor's covenant not to encumber property, * * * should be treated, as on the whole the case law has done, as a covenant 'merely personal'—good enough to give rights against the covenantor for breach, to bring an acceleration clause into play, to constitute 'an event of default' under a loan agreement but not good enough to give rights, whether they be called legal or equitable, in the property." [18]

 WESTLAW REFERENCES

(negative /s covenant) (one-action +s rule) /p (equit! /s mortgage) (secur*** +s interest)

---

17. Gilmore, Security Interests in Personal Property 1017 (1965).

18. Id. For a thought-provoking contrary view, see Reichman, The Anti-Lien: Another Security Interest in Land, 41 U.Chi. L.Rev. 685 (1974).

§§ 3.9–4.0 are reserved for supplementary material.

Chapter 4

RIGHTS AND DUTIES OF THE PARTIES PRIOR TO FORECLOSURE

Table of Sections

A. THEORIES OF TITLE AND THE RIGHT TO POSSESSION

§ 4.1 The Title Theory

As mentioned earlier, three "theories" of mortgage law exist in the United States.[1] One of these theories, the title theory, has its origin in the English Common Law Mortgage. Under the title theory, legal "title" is in the mortgagee until the mortgage has been satisfied or foreclosed, whereas the lien theory regards the mortgagee as the holder of a security interest only and the mortgager as the owner of the land until foreclosure.[2] The intermediate theory, as we will observe later in this chapter, represents a compromise between the other two theories.

§ 4.1
1. See § 1.5, supra.

2. See Kratovil, Mortgages—Problems In Possession, Rents, and Mortgage Liability, 11 DePaul L.Rev. 1, 4–5 (1961).

Some consideration of English history is helpful in understanding the title theory. When the basic mortgage transaction became the conveyance of the fee on condition subsequent—defeasance being performance on the law day by the mortgagor—possession passed to the mortgagee upon the execution of the mortgage. There were two reasons for this. First, livery of seizen was necessary to the conveyance. Second, possession afforded the mortgagee a return on his investment during a period when the collection of interest was deemed usurious.[3] As late as the beginning of the seventeenth century it was unusual for the mortgagor to be left in possession and it was not until about the middle of that century that it became the general rule to do so. In all probability, the practice of leaving the mortgagor in possession was connected with the creation of the mortgagor's equity of redemption; certainly it coincided with it.[4] Indeed this was natural, for with the recognition of the mortgagor as equitable owner of the property, there was, of course, a corresponding understanding that the sole interest of the mortgagee in the property, regardless of his technical legal rights was that of security. With the acceptance of this view the mortgagee who exercises a right to possession was held to strict accountability to the mortgagor. This duty to account thus became an effective deterrent to mortgagees taking possession. As a result, this right to possession was resorted to infrequently and only in extreme cases.[5] Nevertheless, although seldom exercised, the right to possession, was as it still is, a fundamental incident of the mortgagee's legal title. The mortgagee could maintain ejectment against the mortgagor, or if he entered by self-help he could not be sued by the mortgagor in trespass.

The American states, at least initially, adopted the title theory as it had developed in England.[6] Even though it was the common practice for the mortgagor to remain in possession and although equity courts in both countries viewed the mortgagor as an owner in possession, law courts, because the mortgagee had legal title, attempted to fit the mortgagor into an established tenancy category. For example, when there was no agreement about possession, expressed or implied between the parties, there was some attempt to consider the mortgagor as having the status of a tenant at will. Under another mode of analysis,

---

3. See § 1.2 supra.

4. Turner, The Equity of Redemption, 89–91.

5. See Maitland, Equity, 274. In England, since 1936, actions by mortgagees for possession must be brought in Chancery. In such actions the judge, through the exercise of a discretionary power, not clearly defined, of adjourning the case, may afford a defaulting mortgagor an opportunity to delay or defeat the mortgagee. Robertson v. Cilia, 1 W.L.R. 1502 (1956), commented on in 73 L.Q.Rev. 17 (1957). See also id. at 300.

6. Trannon v. Towles, 200 Ala. 82, 75 So. 458 (1917); Brown v. Cram, 1 N.H. 169 (1818); Gilman v. Wills, 66 Me. 273 (1877) (trespass denied to mortgagor against mortgagee who took possession before default); Doe ex dem. Roby v. Maisey, 8 Barn. & C. 767 (1828) (ejectment by mortgagee against mortgagor); Jamieson v. Bruce, 6 Gill & J. 72, 26 Am.Dec. 557 (1834) (personal property; trespass denied to mortgagor against mortgagee who took possession before default). See Brown v. Loeb, 177 Ala. 106, 58 So. 330 (1912); Green v. Kemp, 13 Mass. 515, 7 Am.Dec. 169 (1816).

the mortgagor was "a tenant at sufferance."[7] In any event, both of the above attempts at characterization of the mortgagor seem anomalous. It is, after all, difficult to compare a mortgagor who in equity is considered the owner of a real estate and who was left in possession with the consent of the mortgagee, as being on the same basis as a tenant who was holding over wrongfully.

Normally, however, there was an express agreement permitting the mortgagor to stay on the property. If the agreement was that the mortgagor shall have possession until some specified date, a tenancy for a term was sometimes said to be established.[8] On the other hand, if the agreement provided for possession in the mortgagor until default, or without specifying any terminal date, a tenancy at will was said to result.[9] Moreover, even without an express stipulation, courts were quick to find an implied in fact agreement for the mortgagor to remain in possession from provisions of the mortgage or the nature and circumstances of the loan.[10] In any event, even in cases where there is an express agreement between the parties it would seem that the mortgagor in possession should be recognized in modern law as something more than a tenant of the mortgagee at will, at sufference, or even for a set term.

In any event, for the most part title theory states differ in few significant respects from their lien theory counterparts. Title theory states today generally recognize that the mortgagee holds title for security purposes only, and that, except as between the mortgagor and the mortgagee or one claiming under him, the mortgagor, for practical and theoretical purposes, is to be regarded as the owner of the land.[11] In the process of this recognition, title states have whittled away at incident after incident of legal title, although to varying extents in different jurisdictions and often inconsistently in the same jurisdiction. In many states this process diminished the title concept so far that the mortgagee's interest was called a chattel interest or even a chose in action.[12] Moreover, the title theory has also been tempered by two other developments. First, some title states by statute give possession to the mortgagor until default[13] and second, many commonly used mortgage forms in title states accomplish the same result.[14]

---

7. Thunder v. Belcher, 3 East 449 (1803); Doe d. Roby v. Maisey, 8 B. & C. 767 (1828). See Turner, The Equity of Redemption, 103.

8. Gibbs v. Cruikshank, L.R., 8 C.P. 461 (1873); Doe d. Parsley v. Day, 2 Q.B. 147 (1891).

9. Turner, The Equity of Redemption, 93.

10. Hartshorn v. Hubbard, 2 N.H. 453 (1822).

11. Turner, The Equity of Redemption, 103.

12. A good example of this, together with a résumé in the opinion of many of the normal incidents of legal title which are not accorded to the mortgagee's interest in states following the title theory, is Stevens v. Turlington, 186 N.C. 191, 119 S.E. 210, 32 A.L.R. 870 (1923).

13. See e.g., M.G.L.A. c. 183 § 26.

14. Kratovil, Mortgages—Problems In Possession, Rents, and Mortgagee Liability, 11 DePaul L.Rev. 1, 5 (1961).

Nevertheless, the title theory is hardly an obsolete concept. As the Connecticut Supreme Court recently reiterated, "a mortgagee * * *, both by common law and by statute is deemed to have taken legal title upon the execution of the mortgage. * * * As a titleholder, in the absence of any agreement to the contrary, the mortgagee has a right to immediate possession against the mortgagor." [15] This right to possession can be especially important where a lengthy foreclosure procedure could otherwise mean a substantial period during which a mortgagor in default would be able to divert rents from mortgage debt service and to forego normal maintainance of the mortgaged real estate. Moreover, while possession is almost always only sought by the mortgagee incident to foreclosure,[16] this is not universally the case.[17]

On the other hand, it should be emphasized that being a mortgagee in possession is certainly no bed of roses. As we will explore later in this chapter,[18] a mortgagee in possession is subject to a variety of burdensome obligations and potential liabilities to the mortgagor and third parties that may make possession undesirable. Indeed, there may be occasions when a solvent, but defaulting, mortgagor may be absolutely delighted to surrender possession to the mortgagee. This may be the case, for example, where being in possession may subject the mortgagee to building and health codes that impose obligations to repair and other liabilities to tenants and their invitees.[19] Such burdens may far outweigh any possible advantage that access to the rental payments would confer. Luckily for such a mortgagee, even though it may have the right to take possession in a title and, as we will discover shortly,[20] an intermediate jurisdiction, it cannot be compelled to do so unless and until it becomes a foreclosure sale purchaser.[21]

 WESTLAW REFERENCES
"title theory" /s mortgag***

§ 4.2   The Lien Theory

The substantial majority of states follow the lien theory of mortgages.[1] As the Wisconsin Supreme Court describes this theory, "the

---

15. Conference Center Limited v. TRC—The Research Corp. of New England, 189 Conn. 212, 214, 455 A.2d 857, 860 (1983). See also, First National Bank of Mobile v. Gilbert Imported Hardwoods, Inc., 398 So.2d 258 (Ala.1981).

16. See e.g., Olympic Federal v. Witney Development Co., Inc., 113 Ill.App.3d 981, 69 Ill.Dec. 684, 447 N.E.2d 1371 (1983).

17. See Araserv, Inc. v. Bay State Harness Racing & Breeding Association, 437 F.Supp. 1083 (D.Mass.1977) (mortgagee entitled to possession to race track concession even though it had no intent to foreclose on the real estate).

18. See §§ 4.24–4.32, infra.

19. See City Federal Savings & Loan Association v. Jacobs, 188 N.J.Super. 482, 457 A.2d 1211 (1983).

20. See § 4.3 infra.

21. See City Federal Savings & Loan Association v. Jacobs, 188 N.J.Super. 482, 457 A.2d 1211 (1983). See also, Marcon v. First Federal Savings & Loan Association, 58 Ill.App.3d 811, 16 Ill.Dec. 253, 374 N.E.2d 1028 (1978).

§ 4.2

1. Arizona, California, Colorado, Florida, Georgia, Idaho, Indiana, Iowa, Kansas, Kentucky, Louisiana (Civil Law), Michigan, Minnesota, Montana, Nebraska, Nevada, mortgagee does not have legal title in the [mortgaged real estate].   The mortgagor retains full ownership to the property, which consists of equitable and legal title, while the mortgagee's interest is that of a lienholder." [2]   Consequently, the mortgagor not only has full title, but also the right to possession until their has been a valid foreclosure.[3] For the most part, the development of the lien theory was the result of statutory enactments the earliest of which was in South Carolina.[4] This act provided not only that the mortgagee should not be entitled to maintain any possessory action for the mortgaged real estate even after default but explicitly said that the "mortgagor shall be deemed to be the owner of the land." [5]   Other statutes phrased in slightly different terminology accomplish the same result.   For example, some state that the mortgage shall not be deemed a conveyance so as to enable the mortgagee to recover possession without foreclosure and sale.[6]   Others provide that a mortgage does not entitle the mortgagee to possession unless there is an express provision to that effect; some are combinations of these two.[7]   Still others state that the mortgagee shall not be able to maintain an action of ejectment against the mortgagor, or that the mortgagor shall have the right to possession "regardless of the terms of the instrument." [8]

It was a provision denying the mortgagee the right to bring ejectment [9] that transformed New York into a lien state.   The history

---

New Mexico, New York, North Dakota, Oklahoma, Oregon, South Carolina, South Dakota, Texas, Utah, Washington, Wisconsin, and Wyoming are lien states. See Comment, Proposed Changes in Minnesota Mortgage Law, 50 Minn.L.Rev. 331, 339 (1965); Pomeroy, Equity Jurisprudence, § 1188 (1941). Missouri may also be a lien state. See § 4.3 infra.

2. Glover v. Marine Bank of Beaver Dam, 117 Wis.2d 684, 345 N.W.2d 449, 453 (1984). See Matter of Clark, 738 F.2d 869 (7th Cir.1984).

3. See Kratovil, Mortgages—Problems In Possession, Rents and Mortgagee Liability, 11 DePaul L.Rev. 1, 5 (1960); Martyn v. First Federal Savings & Loan Association, 257 So.2d 576 (Fla.App.1971). In some lien states, the right to possession remains with the mortgagor until the period of statutory redemption has run. See Mutual Benefit Life Insurance Co. v. Frantz Klodt & Son, Inc., 237 N.W.2d 350 (Minn.1975); Woodmen of the World Life Insurance Society v. Sears Roebuck and Co., 294 Minn. 126, 200 N.W.2d 181 (1973).

4. See Lloyd, Mortgages—The Genesis of the Lien Theory, 32 Yale L.Jour. 233, 241 (1922).

5. S.Car., Laws, pp. 32 and 33 (1791); Code §§ 45–51 (1962); Bredenberg v. Landrum, 32 S.C. 215, 10 S.E. 956 (1890).

6. West's Ann.Cal.Code Civ.Proc. § 744; Minn.Stat.Ann. § 559.17; Or.Rev.Stat. 86.010; West's Rev.Code Wash.Ann. § 7.28.230.

7. West's Ann.Cal.Civ.Code § 2927; Burns' Ann.Ind.Stats., § 56–701; cf. Ind. Rev.Stats., p. 459 (1843). See also 3 Tiffany, Real Prop., 2d Ed., 2427; Uniform Mortgage Act § 2.

8. Colo.Code Civ.Proc., § 281 (1921).

9. Revised Stat. of N.Y., Part 3, Ch. V, § 57 (1828): "No action of ejectment shall hereafter be maintained by a mortgagee, or his assigns, or representatives, for the recovery of the possession of the mortgaged premises."

N.Y.Civ.Prac.Act, Action to Recover McKinney's Real Prop., § 991: "A mortgagee, or his assignee or other representative, cannot maintain such an action to recover the mortgaged premises." Cf. Harlem Savings Bank v. Cooper, 199 Misc. 1110, 101 N.Y.S.2d 641 (1950) discussed in 52 Col.L. Rev. 150 (1952), holding that a mortgagor in possession was not a "tenant" entitled to protection against eviction under emergency rent laws as against purchaser at foreclosure sale. Since 1963, this provision in slightly different form is in Real Prop. Actions and Proc.Law, Art. 6, § 611, in 49½ McKinney's Consol.Laws of New York, Ann.

of the conversion is interesting and important because New York is not only a representative, but very influential exponent of the lien theory. An early decision limited the effect of the legislation by holding that the mortgagor could not oust the mortgagee who got possession peaceably after default because "he is still considered as having the legal estate after condition broken." [10] It took two later developments to establish without question that all that the mortgagee got at any time was a legal lien and that the mortgagor at all times prior to foreclosure was the legal owner. One was a change in the decision as to the circumstances and theory under which a mortgagee would be considered a "mortgagee in possession" entitled to hold as against the mortgagor, a matter which we will deal with in detail later in this chapter.[11] The other was a holding,[12] under the then New York statute which permitted levy of execution upon legal, but not equitable, interests in land, that a mortgagee who recovers a judgment against his mortgagor on a cause of action other than the mortgage debt, levies execution upon, sells, and buys in the mortgaged property gets the full title thereto which is not subject to redemption by the mortgagor. The reasoning of the court was that, since under the New York statutes the mortgagee had no right to possession, therefore the mortgage "gives the mortgagee no title or estate whatever," that "the mere right, when he goes into possession by consent of the mortgagor, to retain possession, is not an attribute of title" and since the mortgagee does not get legal title it must therefore remain in the mortgagor because title must be somewhere.[13]

In contrast to the doubts and difficulties that accompanied the establishment of the lien theory in New York, courts in many other states that enacted statutes similar to the New York legislation adopted the lien theory without hesitation. Michigan is a typical example.[14] Similarly, under the California legislation, in a leading case, Justice

---

10. Phyfe v. Riley, 15 Wend. 248, 256, 30 Am.Dec. 55 (1836). See also Mickles v. Townsend, 18 N.Y. 575, 584 (1859); Packer v. Rochester etc., Railway Co., 17 N.Y. 283, 287 (1858). And in holding that the right to redeem was limited by the section of the Code governing equitable actions generally, reasoning from the same decision on the mortgagee's right to defeat ejectment by the mortgagor after the mortgagee has possession, it was said that it can "hardly be said that such a mortgagee has no legal title." Hubbell v. Sibley, 50 N.Y. 468, 472 (1872).

11. See §§ 4.24–4.28, infra.

12. Trimm v. Marsh, 54 N.Y. 599, 13 Am.Rep. 623 (1874). Rev.Stats.N.Y., vol. 2, p. 368, §§ 31, 32 (1828); N.Y. Civil Pract. Act, Laws c. 925, §§ 710, 711 (1920), provided that the interest of the mortgagor, his heirs or assigns, should not be sold on execution levied thereon by virtue of a

judgment recovered on the mortgage debt. It was recognized that this statute would be applicable in Trimm v. Marsh, 3 Lans. 509, 511 (1874) affirmed 54 N.Y. 599, 13 Am.Rep. 623. The statute was applied in Delaplaine v. Hitchcock, 6 Hill (N.Y.) 14 (1843), and a similar one in Linville v. Bell, 47 Ind. 547 (1874).

13. See note 10, supra.

14. The 1843 Act in Michigan was substantially the same as the 1828 statute in New York. For the development of the law in that state see the following cases collected in Campbell, Cases Mortgages, 2d ed., 22, n. 3; Stevens v. Brown, Walk.Ch. 41 (1842); Mundy v. Monroe, 1 Mich. 68 (1848); Crippen v. Morrison, 13 Mich. 23 (1864); Ladue v. Detroit etc. Co., 13 Mich. 380, 87 Am.Dec. 759 (1865); Hogsett v. Ellis, 17 Mich. 351, 363 (1868); Newton v. McKay, 30 Mich. 380 (1874).

Field stated that "this section takes from the [mortgage] instrument its common law character, and restricts it to the purposes of security. It does not, it is true, in terms, change the estates at law of the mortgagor and mortgagee, but, by disabling the owner from entering for condition broken, and restricting his remedy to a foreclosure and sale, it gives full effect to the equitable doctrine, upon consideration of which the section was evidently drawn. An instrument which confers no right of either present or future possession, possesses little of the character of a conveyance, and can hardly be deemed to pass any estate in the land." [15]

In states where the lien theory is established the courts apply it even though the parties do not use the traditional mortgage format. Thus, under a deed of trust in a lien jurisdiction, the grantor-trustor has the right to possession until the trustee realizes on the security by a foreclosure sale.[16] The same is true of absolute deeds intended as mortgages.[17]

In some states adopting the lien theory it has been held that there is a statutory policy against possession in the mortgagee that invali-

15. McMillan v. Richards, 9 Cal. 365, 409, 70 Am.Dec. 655, 661 (1858).

16. Tyler v. Granger, 48 Cal. 259 (1874) (ejectment by the trustee against the grantor-trustor denied); Wisconsin Central Railway Co. v. Wisconsin River Land Co., 71 Wis. 94, 36 N.W. 837 (1888) (ejectment by grantor-trustor against third party allowed). See Sacramento Bank v. Alcorn, 121 Cal. 379, 384, 53 P. 813, 814 (1898): "* * * it would seem that, while we must say that title passes, none of the incidents of ownership attach, except that the trustees are deemed to have such estate as will enable them to convey." Although the California courts constantly state as fundamental that in a mortgage there is only a lien created while in a trust deed legal title actually passes (see, e.g., Bayer v. Hoagland, 95 Cal.App. 403, 273 P. 58 (1925)) nevertheless they also have repeatedly come to the conclusion stated in the extract from Sacramento Bank v. Alcorn. Bostwick v. McEvoy, 62 Cal. 496 (1882); McLeod v. Moran, 153 Cal. 97, 100, 94 P. 604 (1908) ("it is practically and substantially only a mortgage with power of sale"); Hollywood Lumber Co. v. Love, 155 Cal. 270, 100 P. 198 (1909); Curtin v. Krohn, 4 Cal.App. 131, 135, 87 P. 243 (1906); Wyser v. Truitt, 95 Cal.App. 727, 273 P. 147 (1928); Wasco Creamery & Construction Co. v. Coffee, 117 Cal.App. 298, 3 P.2d 588 (1931); Wilson v. McLaughlin, 20 Cal.App.2d 608, 67 P.2d 710 (1937); Pacific States Savings & Loan Co. v. North American Bond & Mortgage Co., 37 Cal.App.2d 307, 99 P.2d 355 (1940); C.A. Warren Co. v. All Persons, 153 Cal. 771, 96 P. 807 (1908) (the trustor has an estate of inheritance which may pass by devise or descent against all persons except the trustee); Aitchison v. Bank of America Association, 8 Cal.2d 400, 65 P.2d 890 (1936) (trustor has a legal estate which he may convey subject to the trust deed).

There is some authority drawing a distinction between trust deed mortgages containing a condition subsequent in the conveyance that it was to be void on payment by the trustor and those providing only that the trustee have power to sell on default; the former being construed to leave legal title in the trustor until sale and the latter to reserve only an equitable interest. Martin v. Alter, 42 Ohio St. 94 (1884); National Bank v. Tennessee etc., Co., 62 Ohio St. 564, 585, 588, 57 N.E. 450, 453, 454 (1900); City of Chicago v. Sullivan Machinery Co., 269 Ill. 58, 69, 109 N.E. 696, 700 (1915), all containing defeasance clauses. Morris v. Way, 16 Ohio 469, 479 (1847) (no condition subsequent).

17. A granted land to B by absolute deed to secure a debt. Held, B, as such grantee, not entitled to possession. Yingling v. Redwine, 12 Okl. 64, 69 P. 810 (1902). See also Hall v. Savill, Iowa, 3 G. Greene 37, 54 Am.Dec. 485 (1851); Flynn v. Holmes, 145 Mich. 606, 108 N.W. 685, 11 L.R.A.,N.S., 209 (1906).

dates agreements in the mortgage permitting the mortgagee to enter.[18] In other lien states, however, an agreement between the parties, giving the mortgagee the right to possession of the mortgaged premises, is valid.[19] Indeed, in some statutes such agreements are expressly contemplated.[20] Moreover, as we will see in detail later in this chapter,[21] if the mortgagee actually goes into possession with the consent of the mortgagor, or even, in many jurisdictions, without such consent but peaceably, or under color of legal right, he may hold onto possession until his debt is paid. The courts differentiate between an executory agreement for such possession and the executed transaction.[22] However, in the absence of such an agreement, wherever the lien theory prevails, a mortgagor, prior to foreclosure, may sue the mortgagee for any illegal interference with his possession of the mortgaged premises as freely as any owner of the land, under similar circumstances, may sue a wrongdoer.[23]

 WESTLAW REFERENCES
"lien theory" /s mortgag**

§ 4.3 The Intermediate Theory

Several states have adopted a compromise position between the lien and title theories. In these so-called "intermediate states" the mortgagee's right to possession accrues on default.[1] To justify this position courts have talked in terms of legal title being in the mortgagor until default, and then, "after the condition has been broken, the legal title is in the mortgagee."[2] Other courts more cautiously hold

---

18. Ganbaum v. Rockwood Realty Corp., 62 Misc.2d 391, 308 N.Y.S.2d 436 (1970); Teal v. Walker, 111 U.S. 242, 252, 4 S.Ct. 420, 28 L.Ed. 415 (1884); Hall v. Hall, 41 S.C. 163, 167, 19 S.E. 305, 44 Am.St.Rep. 696 (1893); Orr v. Bennett, 135 Minn. 443, 161 N.W. 165, 4 A.L.R. 1396 (1917); State ex rel. Gwinn, Inc. v. Superior Court, 170 Wn. 463, 16 P.2d 831 (1932), following Western Loan & Building Co. v. Mifflin, 162 Wash. 33, 297 P. 743 (1931); Rives v. Mincks Hotel Co., 167 Okl. 500, 30 P.2d 911 (1934). By statute in 1927, the Oregon policy was modified in certain instances. ORS 86.010. See a full discussion in Investors Syndicate v. Smith, 105 F.2d 611 (C.C.A.Or.1939).

19. Dick & Reuteman Co. v. Jem Realty Co., 225 Wis. 428, 274 N.W. 416 (1937); Penn Mutual Life Insurance Co. v. Katz, 139 Neb. 501, 297 N.W. 899 (1941); Hulseman v. Dirks Land Co., 63 S.D. 404, 259 N.W. 679 (1935); Kinnison v. Guaranty Liquidating Corp., 18 Cal.2d 256, 115 P.2d 450 (1941). Mich. Trust Co. v. Lansing Lumber Co., 103 Mich. 392, 61 N.W. 668 (1894); Rice v. St. Paul & Pacific Railroad,

24 Minn. 464 (1878); Kelly v. Roberts, 93 Mont. 106, 17 P.2d 65 (1932). See Geraldson, Clauses Increasing the Possessory Rights of Mortgagees, 10 Wis.L.Rev. 492 (1935).

20. E.g., West's Ann.Cal.Civ.Code § 2927.

21. See §§ 4.24–4.25, infra.

22. See §§ 4.24–4.25, infra.

23. See Rundle, Mortgages, 9 Wis.L. Rev. 40, 42, 43 (1933); Tiffany, Real Prop., 3d ed., § 1416.

§ 4.3

1. See Kratovil, Mortgages, Problems In Possession, Rents and Mortgagee Liability, 11 DePaul L.Rev. 1, 4, 6 (1960); Gutenberg Savings & Loan Association v. Rivera, 85 N.J. 617, 428 A.2d 1289 (1981); Wells v. Kemme, 145 Ga. 17, 88 S.E. 562 (1916); Cohn v. Plass, 85 N.J.Eq. 153, 95 A. 1011 (1915).

2. Bradfield v. Hale, 67 Ohio St. 316, 65 N.E. 1008 (1902). See also Taylor v. Quinn, 68 Ohio App. 164, 39 N.E.2d 627 (1941).

that the mortgagee's right to possession has been limited to cases where the condition of the mortgage has been broken.[3] In some states statutory provisions establish that rule.[4] Finally, it may be prudent to classify some states as "intermediate" where the commitment to the lien theory is not completely clear. For example, in Missouri, while the Supreme Court has referred to the " 'lien theory' of mortgages as the law of this state," [5] other lower appellate case law states flatly that "the general rule is that a mortgagee after default by a mortgagor has the right to possession of the mortgaged premises for the purposes of applying the rents and profits to the discharge of the mortgage debt." [6]

The intermediate theory has been vigorously attacked on the basis that the only correct and desirable view of the mortgage relation is that the mortgagor, not the mortgagee, is the legal owner and therefore is alone entitled to possession. Further, it is argued that it is completely indefensible to treat the mortgagor as owner before default and the mortgagee as owner after default since this would be combining two utterly inconsistent theories. Moreover, it has been stated flatly that the lien theory, under which the mortgagee has no right to possession, fully protects the creditor whose only interest should be recognized to be one of security.[7] In criticism of such arguments it may be suggested that the real issue is not whether it is desirable to accord to a mortgagee as part of his security interest the right to take possession at a particular time. If the question is posed in this fashion there is something to be said in favor of permitting a mortgagee to take possession after his debtor has defaulted. Certainly, it is difficult to argue that under no circumstances should the mortgagee be permitted to take possession. To reach this result upon the concept that the mortgagor has legal title is to reason as mechanically as do the title theory courts which allow the mortgagee to have possession. Moreover, the large number of situations in which the mortgagee may obtain possession or its benefits indicate that a rule permitting him possession cannot be dismissed as completely without merit. As one writer has pointed out "to establish the thesis that nature's livery of seisin pending foreclosure sale is to the mortgagor, [one] must struggle not

---

3. Kransz v. Uedelhofen, 193 Ill. 477, 62 N.E. 239 (1901).

4. E.g., 12 V.S.A. (Vt.) § 4772. "Every mortgagor shall, until condition broken, have, as against the mortgagee, the legal right to possession to the mortgaged premises, unless it is otherwise stipulated in the mortgage deed." Crahan v. Chittenden, 82 Vt. 410, 74 A. 86 (1909). See also Dickerson v. Bridges, 147 Mo. 235, 48 S.W. 825 (1898); Sanderson v. Price, 21 N.J.L. 637, 646 (1846); Shields v. Lozear, 34 N.J.L. 496, 3 Am.St.Rep. 256 (1869); Cohn v. Plass, 85 N.J.Eq. 153, 95 A. 1011 (1915); Mershon v. Castree, 57 N.J.L. 484, 31 A. 602 (1895); Stewart v. Fairchild-Baldwin

Co., 91 N.J.Eq. 86, 108 A. 301 (1919); Steinberg v. Kloster Steel Corp., 266 Ill.App. 60 (1932).

5. R.L. Sweet Lumber Co. v. E.L. Lane, Inc., 513 S.W.2d 365 (Mo.1974). See also, Belote v. McLaughlin, 673 S.W.2d 27 (Mo. 1984); Graham v. Oliver, 659 S.W.2d 601, 603 (Mo.App.1983).

6. Pine Lawn Bank & Trust Co. v. M.H. & H. Inc., 607 S.W.2d 696, 700 (Mo.App. 1981). See also, In re Stuckenberg, 374 F.Supp. 15 (E.D.Mo.1974), affirmed 505 F.2d 1250 (8th Cir.1974).

7. Walsh, Mortgages, 93

only with the ejectment cases that begot the 'title' and 'intermediate' theories but also with four other varieties of hostile decision. There are the cases that allow the mortgagee (a) to collect rent from tenants of the mortgagor; (b) merely by adding a few words to the mortgage agreement to obtain possession anytime he wants it; (c) to come in to possession by means of a receiver; and (d) if he has obtained possession peaceably but without valid foreclosure, to stay in until he is paid. Of these decisions at least the (b), (c), and (d) varieties are indigenous to so-called lien jurisdictions."[8] Given this tendency of many of the lien theory states to stray from a purely formalistic notion that a mortgagor always has the right to possession prior to foreclosure, the intermediate theory may come closer than the other theories to reflecting what courts do in practice.

 WESTLAW REFERENCES
No Queries

B. TORTIOUS INJURY TO LAND BY MORTGAGOR OR THIRD PERSONS

§ 4.4 Tortious Injury by the Mortgagor

The mortgagor in possession may do such acts on the mortgaged property in the same manner as such property is ordinarily used, or, in the common phrase, are "usual and proper in the course of good husbandry." She may do them even though they involve severance of fixtures or parts of the realty and result in a diminution of the value of the property.[1] In a lien state the ownership and possession being in the mortgagor should be sufficient justification of the rule. In title states it has been thought necessary to rest it upon the terms of a license. The license may be either express or implied from the relations of the parties and the consent of the mortgagee to the mortgagor's retention of possession.[2]

When the limits of permissible use have been exceeded the mortgagee has a right to recover damages for the injury he has suffered by the mortgagor's acts. There are, however, different theories as to the basis

---

8. McDougal, Reveiw or Walsh, Mortgages, 44 Yale L.J. 1278, 1280 (1935).

§ 4.4

1. Searle v. Sawyer, 127 Mass. 491, 34 Am.Dec. 425 (1879).

Cf. Ingell v. Fay, 112 Mass. 451 (1873). See Walsh, Mortgages, 113 and cf. McDougal, 44 Yale L.J. 1278, 1281 n. 15 (1935). A, a mortgagor, while in possession of the mortgaged premises, cut a reasonable quantity of wood. B, the mortgagee, thereafter evicted A. Held, A, upon quitting the land, was privileged to remove the wood for use elsewhere. Judkins v. Woodman, 81 Me. 351, 17 A. 298, 3 L.R.A. 607 (1889). On the exploitation of oil or gas resources of land by the mortgagor, or purchaser, or lessee subsequent to the mortgage as waste as against the mortgagee, see note, 9 Tulane L.Rev. 283 (1935). See also 95 A.L.R. 957 (1935).

2. Smith v. Moore, 11 N.H. 55 (1840); Page v. Robinson, 64 Mass. (10 Cush.) 99 (1852); Searle v. Sawyer, 127 Mass. 491, 34 Am.Dec. 425 (1879).

of the mortgagee's right and as to the proper measure of damages that he may recover.[3]

One view is that the mortgagor's conduct constitutes legal waste, or a tort in the nature of waste, the mortgagor in possession being treated as a tenant of the mortgagee.[4] "The right of action in such case is based upon the plaintiff's interest in the property; and the damages are measured by the extent of injury to that property. * * * It does not depend upon, and the damages are not to be measured by, proof of insufficiency of the remaining security."[5] Such a solution finds its logical grounding in the title theory of the mortgage but it also provides a simpler and more practical answer to the problem than do the decisions stemming from the lien theory. The mortgagor is protected, because any recovery by the mortgagee is applied on the debt or accounted for; and the mortgagee is fully protected in being assured the full benefit of the value of the security he bargained for.[6] Other cases, allowing the same recovery, have permitted the mortgagee to sue the mortgagor in trespass[7] for such acts as the removal of buildings although one court found it "difficult to see upon what principle, trespass, an action appropriate only to an injury to the possession of the plaintiff, can be maintained by a mortgagee who has never had possession of the mortgaged property against a mortgagor who is in possession of it, upon the ground that the former, by the cutting of the timber or the like, is exceeding his power over the mortgaged property." * * *[8] It has been suggested that waste committed by a tenant at will is regarded as ending the tenancy and making him liable as a trespasser.[9]

Other cases base the mortgagee's right to recover upon the impairment of his security interest, not upon the damage to the property

---

3. See Leipziger, The Mortgagee's Remedies for Waste, 64 Calif.L.Rev. 1086 (1976); Comment, Remedies for Waste in Missouri, 47 Mo.L.Rev. 295 (1982).

4. Delano v. Smith, 206 Mass. 365, 92 N.E. 500, 30 L.R.A.,N.S., 474 (1910). Since common law waste is limited to acts by tenants for life or years, unless the mortgagor were left in possession under a tenancy for years his conduct would not accurately be waste but a tort in the nature of waste for which either the action of trespass or case might be brought. Anon., 1589, Savile, 84; West v. Treude, 3 Croke, 187 (1630); Langdon v. Paul, 22 Vt. 205 (1850). Camden Trust Co. v. Handle, 132 N.J.Eq. 97, 26 A.2d 865, 154 A.L.R. 602 (1942) noted, 27 Minn.L.Rev. 407 (1942) allowed recovery for voluntary "waste" but denied it for permissive "waste" against a transferee of the mortgagor who did not assume payment of the mortgage debt.

5. Byrom v. Chapin, 113 Mass. 308, 311 (1873). See also Jaffe-Spindler Co. v. Genesco, Inc., 747 F.2d 253 (4th Cir. 1984); First National Bank of Gadsden v. Sproull, 105 Ala. 275, 16 So. 879 (1894); Scaling v. First National Bank, 39 Tex.Civ.App. 154, 87 S.W. 715 (1905). Cf. Ellis v. Glover & Hobson, Limited, 1 K.B. 388, 399 (1908).

6. The claim "when recovered applies in payment *pro tanto* of the mortgage debt, and thus, ultimately for the benefit of the mortgagor if he redeem." Gooding v. Shea, 103 Mass. 360, 4 Am.Rep. 563 (1869). See note, 10 Tex.L.Rev. 475, 476 (1932).

7. Stowell v. Pike, 2 Me. 387 (1823); Page v. Robinson, 64 Mass. (10 Cush.) 99 (1852); Pettengill v. Evans, 5 N.H. 54 (1829); Smith v. Moore, 11 N.H. 55 (1840); cf. Stevens v. Smathers, 124 N.C. 571, 32 S.E. 959 (1899); Hoskin v. Woodward, 45 Pa. 42, 3 Leg. & Ins.Rep. 27 (1863).

8. Waterman v. Matteson, 4 R.I. 539, 543 (1857).

9. Walsh, Property, 2d ed., 78.

itself.[10] They represent the lien theory view that the mortgagee, not having title, possession, or the right to possession, cannot maintain an action of trespass against a mortgagor who is guilty of acts of waste but can only recover in an action on the case for the damage to his security interest. It follows that the mortgagee's damages "would be limited to the amount of the injury to the mortgage, however great the injury to the land may be." [11]

Since that is the test, the chief problem is what constitutes an impairment of the security. One rule is the difference in value of the property before and after the wrongful acts.[12] Under this theory the measure of damages is almost identical with that in title states.[13] Another rule requires that the impairment of the security must go to the extent of reducing the value of the remaining mortgaged property below the amount of the debt secured.[14] This seems unfair to the mortgagee. The interest rate on the debt and mortgage initially are both determined in large measure by the amount of property securing the obligation and varies proportionately to the ratio between the debt and the value of the security. If a low rate of interest has been charged because ample security has been given, the mortgagee is forced to bear a risk he did not bargain for if part of the security can be taken away even though what is left still equals the debt.[15] And, also, the sale value of his debt and mortgage similarly will be reduced. Moreover, if the value of the remaining security is to be considered, so too should the solvency of the mortgagor. Although one early case,[16] later repudiated, so held, this clearly is a factor which should not determine the extent to which the mortgagee has been injured by wrongful reduction of the value of the property taken in mortgage.[17]

10. See Brown v. Critchfield, 100 Cal. App.3d 858, 161 Cal.Rptr. 342 (1980); Monte Enterprises, Inc. v. Kavanaugh, 62 N.C.App. 541, 303 S.E.2d 194 (1983); Heath v. Haile, 45 S.C. 642, 24 S.E. 300 (1898); Payne v. Snyder, 661 S.W.2d 134 (Tex.App. 1983), error refused n.r.e. (1984).

11. Van Pelt v. McGraw, 4 N.Y. 110 (1850).

12. President & Directors of Manhattan Co. v. Mosler Safe Co., 264 App.Div. 785, 284 N.Y.S. 145 (1935); Atlantic etc., Railroad Co. v. Rutledge, 122 Fla. 154, 165 So. 563 (1935); Ogden Lumber Co. v. Busse, 92 App.Div. 143, 86 N.Y.S. 1098 (1904).

13. Under the title theory the mortgagee may recover in trespass or trover the value of the severed property, e.g., gravel, which may either exceed or be less than the diminution in value to the land caused by its removal. Consequently the two measures are not always the same. Bates v. Humboldt County, 224 Iowa 841, 277 N.W. 715 (1938).

14. "The action must rest upon proof that, before the alleged injury, the mortgaged premises were of sufficient value to pay the plaintiff's mortgage, or a part of it, and that, by reason of such injury, they became inadequate for that purpose." Schalk v. Kingsley, 42 N.J.L. 32, 33 (1880). See Monte Enterprises, Inc. v. Kavanaugh, 62 N.C.App. 541, 303 S.E.2d 194 (1983); Payne v. Snyder, 661 S.W.2d 134 (Tex.App. 1983), error refused n.r.e. (1984); Carroll v. Edmondson, 41 S.W.2d 64 (Tex.Com.App. 1931), commented on 10 Tex.L.Rev. 475 (1932); Lieberman, etc., v. Knight, 153 Tenn. 268, 283 S.W. 450 (1925); Turrell v. Jackson, 39 N.J.L. 329 (1877).

15. Note, 10 Tex.L.Rev. 475, 478 (1932).

16. Gardner v. Heartt, 3 Denio 232 (N.Y.1846).

17. Ogden Lumber Co. v. Busse, 92 App. Div. 143, 86 N.Y.S. 1098 (1904); Toledo v. Brown, 130 Ohio St. 513 (1936). See Denton, Right of a Mortgagee to Recover

A further limitation, whichever rule of damages is followed, is that in no event can the mortgagee recover an amount in excess of the mortgage debt and expenses.[18] Most of the cases have arisen after maturity in connection with foreclosure proceedings [19] but there is authority, on the theory that the creditor is not injured until the foreclosure sale fails to raise enough money to pay his debt, that the mortgagee must first obtain a deficiency judgment.[20] When this is the case there is no difficulty in both limiting the mortgagee's recovery to an amount not to exceed his deficiency and in compelling him to apply it to his claim. However, this restriction, even more than the rule taking into account the value of the remaining property at the time of the wrong, deprives the mortgagee of the benefit of the security and substitutes for it not merely only so much of it as a court may consider adequate, but what the remaining property may bring at a foreclosure sale in the future.[21] Further, a judgment for damages against the mortgagor for taking or injuring the mortgaged property which cannot be brought before default is of no benefit to the mortgagee because he is then able to get a judgment for the entire debt or a deficiency after foreclosing on the remaining property. A second judgment at that time equal to a part or all of the mortgage debt or deficiency would be a completely useless duplication. The clearly preferable view, for which there is ample authority, is that the mortgagee may sue before default or foreclosure and recovery of a deficiency.[22] Although it is urged in such a case that the amount of damage to the security is difficult to ascertain and that it would be unfair to give it to the mortgagee before his debt is due, neither objection has great weight. Under any rule of damages, except the one requiring a foreclosure first, the amount can be ascertained. And, although the mortgagee could not be compelled to accept payment before maturity,[23] or the mortgagor to pay, the mortgagee should be permitted to take payment and the mortgagor, who has committed a wrong in injuring the security, ought to be estopped to

Damages from a Third Party, 3 Ohio L.J. 161, 164 (1936).

    "It certainly is not just, and cannot be lawful, to leave a mortgagee without redress for the destruction of that substantial security upon the strength of which he loaned his money, because he is unable to show the present insufficiency of that wavering staff, the solvency of his debtor, upon which he never expected to rely". Turrell v. Jackson, 39 N.J.L. 329, 332 (1877).

18. Lavenson v. Standard Soap Co., 80 Cal. 245, 22 P. 184, 13 Am.St.Rep. 147 (1889); Heath v. Haile, 45 S.C. 642, 24 S.E. 300 (1896); Cottle v. Wright, 140 Misc. 373, 251 N.Y.S. 699 (1931); Bowden v. Bridgman, 141 S.W. 1043 (Tex.Civ.App.1911); Edler v. Hasche, 67 Wis. 653, 31 N.W. 57 (1887).

19. E.g., Cottle v. Wright, 140 Misc. 373, 251 N.Y.S. 699 (1931), discussed 32 Col.L.Rev. 146 (1932); Heath v. Haile, 45 S.C. 642, 24 S.E. 300 (1896).

20. Taylor v. McConnell, 53 Mich. 587, 19 N.W. 196 (1884).

21. See 10 Tex.L.Rev. 479 (1932); 17 N.C.L.Rev. 291, 294 (1939).

22. President & Directors of Manhattan Co. v. Mosler Safe Co., 246 App.Div. 785, 284 N.Y.S. 145 (1935); Hummer v. R.C. Huffman Construction Co., 63 F.2d 372 (C.C.A.Ill.1933); Toledo v. Brown, 130 Ohio St. 513, 200 N.E. 750 (1936); Arnold v. Broad, 15 Colo.App. 389, 62 P. 577 (1900). Cf., however, Aggs v. Shackleford County, 85 Tex. 145, 19 S.W. 1085 (1892).

23. See § 6.1 infra.

object. Practically, the mortgagor will have little cause to complain because the debt will be reduced and along with it the amount of interest payments, and it is doubtful whether she could have used the amount she will have to pay to much better advantage. Even if she could, it should be no answer to the mortgagee's claim to redress for the mortgagor's tort.

Other damages rules for impairment of the mortgagee's security include: (1) the reasonable cost of restoring the land to its former condition when this is less than the diminution in market value of the whole property by reason of the injury; (2) as a minimum, the amount [24] received from the sale of wrongfully severed fixtures or part of the realty; [25] and (3) amount to be applied on the mortgage debt as will make the debt bear the same ratio to the mortgaged estate after the injury as the original debt bore to the mortgaged property before the injury.

WESTLAW REFERENCES

"good husbandry" (tort! trespass*** waste   /s   land (real   +1   estate
   property) realty)   /p   mortgagor

tort! trespass*** waste   /p   "security interest"   /p   mortgagor

tort! trespass*** waste   /p   damage*   /p   mortgagor

266k205

§ 4.5 Injury by Third Parties

While the authorities are sparse and unclear, it would seem that liability of subsequent grantees for waste normally should be the same as that of the original mortgagor.[1] Where a mortgagor's liability is based on tort or other noncontractual theories, a subsequent grantee's liability should be identical, whether the grantee assumed the mortgage debt or not.[2] Such a result is even more likely where a mortgagee's claim is to some extent buttressed by statute. For example, the California Supreme Court indicated that Section 2929 of the Civil Code, which prohibits any person whose interest is subject to a mortgage from doing "any act" that would substantially impair mortgage security, could be used to impose liability on nonassuming grantees.[3] On the other hand, because nonassuming grantees do not become personally liable on the debt or mortgage, to the extent that the mortgagee simply is attempting to enforce a specific mortgage covenant, only assuming grantees arguably should be liable.[4]

24. Hartshorn v. Chaddock, 135 N.Y. 116, 31 N.E. 997, 17 L.R.A. 426 (1892); Cedar Avenue Building etc. v. McLaughlin, 69 Pa.Super. 73 (1918). See Ogden Lumber Co. v. Busse, 92 App.Div. 143, 86 N.Y.S. 1098 (1904).

25. See Cottle v. Wright, 140 Misc. 373, 251 N.Y.S. 699 (1931). Note, 10 Tex.L.Rev. 475, 482 (1932).

§ 4.5

1. Leipziger, The Mortgagee's Remedies for Waste, 64 Cal.L.Rev. 1086, 1130 (1976).

2. Id. at 1129–1130.

3. Cornelison v. Kornbluth, 15 Cal.3d 590, 125 Cal.Rptr. 557, 542 P.2d 981 (1975).

4. Camden Trust v. Handle, 132 N.J.Eq. 97, 26 A.2d 865 (1942).

Where the action for injury to the mortgaged property is against other third parties, the authorities and theories follow substantially the same pattern as in the case against the mortgagor. Thus, in title states the mortgagee is allowed to bring trespass for injuries done to the land [5] and actions of replevin [6] or trover [7] to recover severed fixtures or parts of the realty or their value. On the other hand, in jurisdictions where the mortgagee can hold the mortgagor only for impairment of the security, he is similarly restricted against third parties.[8]

There seems little more objection to allowing the mortgagee to recover entire damages without regard to the measure of his own security, or the severed portion itself, and then crediting his recovery on the debt or accounting for it than there is in allowing a partial recovery limited to the extent his security interest is impaired and applying or accounting for it. Further, to restrict any relief of the mortgagee to holding the mortgagor and giving to the mortgagor the sole rights against third parties would pose practical difficulties in forcing the mortgagor to sue. In addition, such a view would permit settlements [9] between the mortgagor and the third party to preclude any recovery by the mortgagee, and, carried to a logical absurdity, deny relief to the mortgagee where the third party has acted to injure the property with the connivance of the mortgagor so that the latter has no action of his own.[10] Such considerations should not merely refute any argument that the sole desirable solution is to vest the right to full recovery against third parties exclusively in the mortgagor, but to lend support to the view that, as a practical solution, permitting the mortgagee not only the right to sue but to recover full damages has considerable merit. Indeed, the vitality of such a view is evidenced by legislation

5. Smith v. Goodwin, 2 Greenl., Me., 173 (1822); Frothingham v. McKusick, 24 Me. 403 (1844); Sanders v. Reed, 12 N.H. 558 (1842); Federal Land Bank of Columbia v. Jones, 211 N.C. 317, 190 S.E. 479 (1937) (after default by mortgagor); Jeffers v. Pease, 74 Vt. 215, 52 A. 422 (1902) (after condition broken); Harris v. Haynes, 34 Vt. 220 (1861) (after condition broken only).

6. Dorr v. Dudderar, 88 Ill. 107 (1878).

7. Searle v. Sawyer, 127 Mass. 491, 34 Am.St.Rep. 425 (1879). In Houle v. Guilbeault, 70 R.I. 421, 40 A.2d 438 (1944), noted, 25 Boston Univ.L.Rev. 149 (1945), a junior mortgagee in a title state was held unable to bring an action on the case against a third party for removal of fixtures without joining the first mortgagee.

8. Brown v. Critchfield, 100 Cal.App.3d 858, 161 Cal.Rptr. 342 (1980); Bates v. Humboldt County, 224 Iowa 841, 277 N.W. 715 (1938); Carroll v. Edmondson, Tex. Com.App., 41 S.W.2d 64 (1931), discussed, 10 Tex.L.Rev. 475 (1932); Federal Land Bank of Columbia v. St. Clair Lumber Co., 58 Ga.App. 532, 199 S.E. 337 (1938), discussed, 17 N.C.L.Rev. 291 (1939). The same conclusion has been reached in some title states on the ground that title is in the mortgagee only for security purposes and in relation to the mortgagor. McKelvey v. Creevey, 72 Conn. 464, 45 A. 4, 77 Am.St.Rep. 321 (1900); Verner v. Betz, 46 N.J.Eq. 256, 19 A. 206, 7 L.R.A. 630, 19 Am.St.Rep. 387 (1890); Cooper v. Davis, 15 Conn. 556 (1843). Some lien states, however, by statute permit the mortgagee to recover from third parties the full value of severed fixtures up to the amount of the mortgage debt. See, e.g., Ky.Rev.Stat. 382.350.

9. See cases cited Campbell, Cases Mortgages, 2d Ed., 152, n. 4.

10. See Sanders v. Reed, 12 N.H. 558 (1842).

in a number of states altering the rule that restricts him to recovery of the diminution of his security interest.[11]

There is early authority in lien jurisdictions that only intentional injury to the mortgagee's security will justify recovery against third parties.[12] Indeed, an early view was expressed in New York that not only must there be knowledge of the fact of the mortgage, but an actual fraudulent design to injure the mortgagee.[13] However, the present trend of the cases is based upon the principle that a person must be deemed to intend the necessary consequences of her voluntary act. This trend holds that such a third person is liable if she can be charged with knowledge of the mortgage and that her act impairs the mortgagee's security.[14] One California court of appeals decision exemplifies this approach.[15] There a mortgagee brought suit for damages against third party developers, designers and contractors who allegedly substantially impaired the mortgagee's security as a result of their work on a residential subdivision. The court rejected the "old" New York rule and recognized negligence as a valid basis for an action against such third parties. Moreover, the court imputed a broad knowledge of the existence of the mortgagee's interest to the third party defendants. According to the court, "it is common knowledge that the development of residential subdivisions is accomplished financially by means of loans secured by deeds of trust on the real property involved. Therefore, it was not only reasonably foreseeable that the alleged negligence of respondents would result in impairment of plaintiff's security; such a result was substantially certain to occur." [16]

 WESTLAW REFERENCES

tort! trespass*** waste /p land (real +1 estate property) realty
   "security interest" /p grantee (third +1 party person)
   transferee /p mortgag**
266k207

---

§ 4.6   Severed Property—Mortgagee's Rights

To what extent can the mortgagee follow and reclaim or subject to his mortgage fixtures, buildings or other things severed from the mortgaged real property? Here again title and lien theories have affected the law. Thus in Betz v. Verner,[1] the court summarized the two lines of reasoning as follows: "It seems that where the mortgage is

11. See, e.g., Ky.Rev.Stat. 382.350. See also, note, 53 Harv.L.Rev. 503 (1940).

12. Gardner v. Heartt, 3 Denio 232 (N.Y.1846); Wilson v. Maltby, 59 N.Y. 126 (1874).

13. Id.

14. U.S. Financial v. Sullivan, 37 Cal. App.3d 5, 112 Cal.Rptr. 18 (1974); Van Pelt v. McGraw, 4 N.Y. 110 (1850); Jackson v. Brandon Realty Co., 100 N.Y.S. 1005

(1906); Turrell v. Jackson, 39 N.J.L. 329 (1877).

15. U.S. Financial v. Sullivan, 37 Cal. App.3d 5, 112 Cal.Rptr. 18 (1974).

16. Id. at 37 Cal.App.3d 13–14, 112 Cal. Rptr. 22–23.

§ 4.6

1. 46 N.J.Eq. 256, 19 A. 206, 7 L.R.A. 630, 19 Am.St.Rep. 387 (1890).

regarded as a conveyance of the legal title to the property, giving the mortgagee the right of possession, his legal ownership, and actual or constructive possession, give him the right to follow and recover the property severed. The principle applied is that property severed from the realty, so as to become a chattel, belongs to the legal owner of the land; but where the mortgage is regarded merely as a lien for security, and the mortgagor has the right of possession until ejectment or foreclosure, there the mortgagee has merely the right to restrain the removal of the property by injunction, to protect his lien, or, after the removal, only a right to recover damages for the wrongful diminution of his security." Following this reasoning in title states, since the mortgagee has "legal ownership and right of possession, he may follow things severed from the mortgage lands without his consent wherever he can find them,"[2] and recover them by an action of replevin or through the appointment of a receiver, or, in the alternative, recover their value in trover.[3] On the other hand, the lien view has been followed to deny to the mortgagee any rights in things severed.[4] However, in a few title jurisdictions, the courts have decided that, because title was for the limited purpose of security, severance would divest the title so that no rights could be asserted in the severed article.[5] Conversely, there are several lien states that hold that the lien will continue after severance. It can be enforced even though in the hands of a third party provided he took with notice of the mortgagee's lien or acted in collusion with the mortgagor;[6] it will be cut off by

2. Betz v. Verner, 46 N.J.Eq. 256, 19 A. 206, 7 L.R.A. 630, 19 Am.St.Rep. 387 (1890).

3. Dorr v. Dudderar, 88 Ill. 107 (1878) (replevin); Burley v. Pike, 62 N.H. 495 (1882) (replevin); Waterman v. Matteson, 4 R.I. 539 (1856) (replevin against the mortgagor); First National Bank & Trust Co. v. Hagar Oil Co., 105 N.J.Eq. 62, 146 A. 878 (1929), noted 78 U. of Pa.L.Rev. 269 (1929) (receiver); Langdon v. Paul, 22 Vt. 205 (1850) (trover); Searle v. Sawyer, 127 Mass. 491, 34 Am.St.Rep. 425 (1879).

4. Cases denying the mortgagee a right to recover the severed chattel in actions at law are Vanderslice v. Knapp, 20 Kan. 647 (1878) (replevin denied against a purchaser from the mortgagor); Moore v. Moran, 64 Neb. 84, 89 N.W. 629 (1902) (replevin denied against a third party). Odell v. Buck, 5 A.D.2d 732, 168 N.Y.S.2d 756 (3d Dept. 1958) noted in 24 Brooklyn L.Rev. 372 (1958). An equitable lien on a leasehold does not extend to oil converted to personal property by severance. Onyx Refining Co. v. Evans Production Corp., 182 F.Supp. 253 (N.D.Tex.1960).

5. "If the mortgagee have the legal ownership and right of possession, he may follow things severed and removed from the mortgage lands without his consent wherever he can find them. If he holds title under the mortgage only as security for his lien, then the remedies appointed for preserving the security, and compensating for any loss sustained by its diminution, are such, only, as the mortgagee may use. The theory in the latter case is that, as to innocent third parties, the mortgagor is the owner of the property, and may sever and sell until restrained by injunction, or ejected by entry, or barred by foreclosure." Betz v. Verner, supra, note 2 at 267, 19 A. at 208; Cooper v. Davis, 15 Conn. 556 (1843); McKelvey v. Creevey, 72 Conn. 464, 45 A. 4, 77 Am.St.Rep. 321 (1900); Kircher v. Schalk, 39 N.J.L. 335 (1877) (replevin denied, his remedy being limited to an action for damages).

6. A mortgagor moved a house off the mortgaged premises onto other lands. Held, a decree of foreclosure sale, giving the purchaser leave to remove the house, proper. Turner v. Mebane, 110 N.C. 413, 14 S.E. 974, 28 Am.St.Rep. 697 (1892); Federal Land Bank v. Davis, 228 Ala. 85, 152 So. 226 (1934) (foreclosure), accord; Dakota Loan & Trust Co. v. Parmalee, 5 S.D. 341, 58 N.W. 811 (1894); Campbell, Cas.Morts., 153 n. 5; Hamlin v. Parsons, 12 Minn. 108

a bona fide purchase.[7] While a few cases allowing foreclosure on the severed part have been made conditional on the remaining property being insufficient to pay the debt others have ignored this requirement.[8] Here, as elsewhere, the rights of the parties should not flow from title or lien concepts but rather should be based upon considerations of how far a secured creditor should have protection. That the rule allowing the secured party to assert a security interest in the severed property as against all but bona fide purchasers is the preferable view in all jurisdictions, and that the test of how far constructive notice should be invoked to prevent there being such a claimant ought to depend, as previously suggested, upon the character of the severed property. Indeed, this seems to be the result of a majority of the cases, regardless of the reasoning by which they arrived there.

 WESTLAW REFERENCES
reclaim! reclamation remov*** severe* sever*n** /s building chattel
fixture improvement mortgagee

§ 4.7 Injunction Against Removal of Severed Property

Some authorities, influenced by the title theory, say that a mortgagor who wrongfully severs fixtures, buildings, or part of the land itself is liable for conversion because the mortgagee is deemed to have title to the severed product.[1] In these states the mortgagee normally can have an injunction against the mortgagor to restrain the conversion of the severed portion only if the mortgagor is insolvent or money damages would be inadequate.[2] On the other hand, in states in which severance from mortgaged land frees the severed part from the lien of the mortgage so that the mortgagee has no right to sue at law for it, it follows that the mortgagee would have no claim to an injunction to prevent the removal of the severed product. In these latter states even the insolvency of the mortgagor would not be sufficient to warrant an injunction.[3] The result is that in all states the mortgagee's only

(Gil. 59) 90 Am.Dec. 284 (1882) (foreclosure on house on land of a third person who took with notice); Mills v. Pope, 90 Mont. 569, 4 P.2d 485 (1931) (foreclosure permitted); Johnson v. Bratton, 112 Mich. 319, 70 N.W. 1021 (1897); Partridge v. Hemenway, 89 Mich. 454, 50 N.W. 1084, 28 Am.St.Rep. 322 (1891).

7. "So long as the mortgagor continues in possession, or when the property severed passes into the possession of a person in collusion with him to defeat the lien and security of the mortgagee, whether upon or off the mortgaged premises, it would seem that the rights of the mortgagee would be unaffected. But when the property is severed, and sold to an innocent purchaser, the lien in equity is gone, and the remedy of the mortgagee is an action at law

against the mortgagor, and those who act with him to impair or defeat the security of the mortgage." Betz v. Verner, supra, note 2 at 268, 14 A. at 208. In New Jersey, the court, although saying that the mortgagee has title, limits it to security purposes and, on the point involved here, follows the rule of lien jurisdictions.

8. See Tex.L.Rev. 481 (1932).

§ 4.7

1. See § 4.6, supra.

2. See, McClintock, Equity, 2d ed., §§ 45, 47.

3. Ames, Cas.Eq., 484 n. However, see American Trust Co. v. North Belleville Quarry Co., 31 N.J.Eq. 89 (1879); Chanango Bank v. Cox, 26 N.J.Eq. 452

reliable remedy is to prevent the commission of waste in the first place.[4]

Both lines of cases arguably are wrong. Regardless of whether the state is of lien or title theory persuasion, severance should not destroy the mortgagee's security interest in the severed article. Further, the criterion for issuing an injunction against a mortgagor should not be whether the subject matter of the mortgage is real or personal property, but whether after its disposal, there will be sufficient property left still subject to the mortgage to leave the plaintiff adequate security.[5]

WESTLAW REFERENCES

reclaim! reclamation remov*** severe* sever*n**   /s   building chattel fixture improvement /p   convert*** conversion enjoin*** injuncti** /p   mortgage*

§ 4.8 Injury by Third Persons—Mortgagor's Rights

A mortgagor in possession, even in title states, is treated as owner of the mortgaged property as to all persons other than the mortgagee or one claiming under the mortgagee, and this is *a fortiori* true in lien states.[1] It follows that he may recover from a third person for injuries done to the premises the full amount of damage done just as though the property were not subject to a mortgage.[2]

WESTLAW REFERENCES

No Queries

§ 4.9 Relation of Rights of Mortgagor and Mortgagee Against Third Parties

Another difficulty arises because of the fact that courts have recognized rights by both the mortgagor and the mortgagee against third parties who have injured the property. In states [1] where the mortgagee can have no action unless the value of the remaining property is less than the debt, if the injury has not reduced the security below that amount the mortgagor is the only one injured, and therefore

(1875); Ennis v. Smith et al., Del.Ch., 80 A. 636 (1911).

4. Watson v. Hunter, 5 Johns.Ch. 169, 9 Am.Dec. 295 (1821). See Cooper v. Davis, 15 Conn. 556 (1843); Vanderslice v. Knapp, 20 Kan. 647 (1878); Tomlinson v. Thomson, 27 Kan. 70 (1882). See note, 60 U. of Pa.L. Rev. 135 (1911).

5. Ensign v. Colburn, 11 Paige 503 (N.Y.1885); Hutchins v. King, 68 U.S. (1 Wall.) 53, 17 L.Ed. 544 (1862).

§ 4.8

1. Huckins v. Straw, 34 Me. 166 (1852), Campbell, Cases Mortgages, 2d Ed., 13; Cotton v. Carlisle, 85 Ala. 175, 4 So. 670, 7

Am.St.Rep. 29 (1887); Orr v. Hadley, 36 N.H. 575 (1858); Seaman v. Bisbee, 163 Ill. 91, 45 N.E. 208 (1896); Huckins v. Straw, 34 Me. 166 (1852).

2. Hamilton v. Griffin, 123 Ala. 600, 26 So. 243 (1898); Craig v. W.P. Carmichael Co., 271 Mo. 516, 197 S.W. 141 (1917); Watkins v. Kaolin Manufacturing Co., 131 N.C. 536, 42 S.E. 983, 60 L.R.A. 617 (1902); Van Dyke v. Grand Trunk Railway Co., 84 Vt. 212, 78 A. 958, Ann.Cas.1913A, 640 (1910).

§ 4.9

1. See Garrow v. Brooks, 123 N.J.Eq. 138, 196 A. 460 (1938).

he can recover for the entire damage done. The question of whether there must be two suits, one by the mortgagor and one by the mortgagee, or whether there may be a full recovery in one action by either party, is raised in two situations. (1) Where the injury has impaired the value of the remaining property to such an extent that it is insufficient to pay the debt. (2) In jurisdictions which permit the mortgagee to recover for the injury to the property itself.[2]

Assume the mortgagor sues first. In a jurisdiction in which the mortgagee's right to recover is a limited one, the mortgagor is allowed a complete recovery.[3] The defendant would be protected against an action by the mortgagee because such recovery would be a legal bar to further recovery by either.[4] However, the judgment recovered by the mortgagor would be subjected to the lien of the mortgage as substitute collateral "to the extent that it may be found the proceeds of the judgment represent the amount of damage sustained by the complainant under the rule as to the measure thereof",[5] i.e., the diminution in value of the security. In a title jurisdiction, the mortgagor's recovery would be subject, on a parity of reasoning, to a lien for the entire amount of the mortgagee's debt claim.

Suppose, however, the mortgagee is the first to sue. As one court has noted, the mortgagor "may still maintain an action for the injury, and the [defendant] can protect himself by giving in evidence the recovery by the mortgagee in mitigation of damages. The owner has suffered damage to the full extent of the injury, but his claim has been satisfied pro tanto by payment to the mortgagee for his loss."[6] Of course, if the mortgagee had been permitted to recover the entire amount of damage done, this should be a complete bar to the mortgagor's action.

 WESTLAW REFERENCES
266k217

---

2. See Turner Coal Co. v. Glover, 101 Ala. 289, 13 So. 478 (1892); Paine v. Woods, 108 Mass. 160 (1871). See also Ann.Cas.1913A, 652. Cf. Gooding v. Shea, 103 Mass. 360, 4 Am.Rep. 563 (1869); Jenks v. Hart Cedar & Lumber Co., 143 Mich. 449, 106 N.W. 1119, 114 Am.St.Rep. 673 (1906); Sanders v. Reed, 12 N.H. 558 (1842).

3. Delaware etc., Telephone Co. v. Elvins, 63 N.J.L. 243, 43 A. 903, 76 Am.St. Rep. 217 (1899); Garrow v. Brooks, supra note 92.

4. Id.

5. Garrow v. Brooks, 123 N.J.Eq. 138, 141, 196 A. 460, 462 (1938). "The mortgagee was entitled to the building as part of her security and is now entitled to look to the fund in the hands of the sheriff as converted into its original form." See American Savings & Loan Association v. Leeds, 68 Cal.2d 611, 68 Cal.Rptr. 453, 440 P.2d 933, n. 2 (1968).

6. Delaware, etc., Telephone Co. v. Elvins, 63 N.J.L. 243, 245, 43 A. 903, 76 Am.St.Rep. 217 (1899).

§ 4.10 Equitable Relief Against the Mortgagor For Threatened Injury

It is thoroughly settled that, under appropriate circumstances,[1] a mortgagee may have an injunction against a mortgagor in possession to prevent him from injuring the mortgaged property. This is true even though the mortgagee has the right to take possession of the mortgaged premises. The severe rules of accounting, that possession would trigger, make this such an inadequate remedy that it will not prevent the granting of equitable relief in appropriate cases.[2] There is some authority that equity will act to prevent the mortgagor doing any serious injury to the property over and above the normal use of it in the course of good husbandry, as by cutting down an undue amount of timber or the removal of buildings or fixtures.[3] This view makes sense. If five acres of land have been mortgaged the mortgagor could not sell off, free and clear of the mortgage, one acre even though what is left is more than ample to secure the debt. The mortgagee took the entire five acres and is entitled to keep all of it. He is not compelled to run the risk that though now the property that is left is ample, it might not be later when the debt is due. And so also in the physical injury setting. The mortgagee bargained for the greater amount of security and should not have to accept another's judgment on whether it, or what is left of it after the mortgagor does an act reducing its value, is adequate.

Most courts, however, follow the rule that the threatened injury must be one that will bring the value of the security down to a point where it might not be ample.[4] In one of the early and leading cases, the test was put this way: "It is rather a question of prudence than of actual value. I think the question which must be tried is whether the property the mortgagee takes as a security, is sufficient in this sense, that the security is worth so much more than the money advanced that the act is not to be considered as substantially impairing the value, which was the basis of the contract between the parties at the time it was entered into."[5] When such impairment occurs will depend in part on the nature of the property. A bigger margin of security must be left if the property is subject to wide and frequent fluctuations in value

---

§ 4.10

1. See generally, Leipziger, The Mortgagee's Remedies For Waste, 64 Cal.L.Rev. 1086, 1099–1100 (1976); Comment, Remedies for Waste in Missouri, 47 Mo.L.Rev. 288, 299 (1982).

2. See Glenn, Morts., § 211. See §§ 4.30–4.35 infra.

3. Nelson v. Pinegar, 30 Ill. 473 (1863); Williams v. Chicago Exhibition Co., 188 Ill. 19, 58 N.E. 611 (1900).

4. In re Tremblay, 43 B.R. 221 (Bkrtcy. Vt.1984); King v. Smith, 2 Hare, 239

(1843); Fairbank v. Cudworth, 33 Wis. 358 (1873); Fidelity Trust Co. v. Hoboken etc. R. Co., 71 N.J.Eq. 14, 63 A. 273 (1906); Coker v. Whitlock, 54 Ala. 180 (1875); Collins v. Rea, 127 Mich. 273, 86 N.W. 811 (1901); Hastings v. Perry, 20 Vt. 272 (1848); Brady v. Waldron, 2 Johns.Ch. 148 (N.Y.1816).

5. King v. Smith, supra note 4 at 243. See also In re Tremblay, 43 B.R. 221 (Bkrtcy.Vt.1984).

than if it is of stable value, but probably in no case would the security be considered adequate security by a prudent lender unless it is worth one-third more than the amount of the money lent at the time of the mortgage.[6] In no case would it be sufficient that the value of the property is barely equal to the mortgage debt.[7] Moreover, the insolvency of the mortgagor should be immaterial on this question. The mortgagee demanded the mortgage before making the loan so that he would not have to rely upon the general pecuniary condition of the mortgagor and it would be inequitable to take into account in granting relief a factor which the mortgagee took care to guard against by seeing to it that he was a secured and not a general creditor.[8]

The ability of the court of equity to protect the mortgagee from the commission of waste is not limited to the issuance of injunctions. Although "it is true that in general a receivership is ancillary or incidental to the main purpose of the bill, it does not follow that where a case is presented which demands the relief which can be best given by a receivership, such relief must be refused, because the time has not arrived when other substantial relief can be asked. For example, although as a rule, a mortgagee cannot ask for relief until his mortgage debt has become due, he can go into a court of equity before that time has arrived and ask for an injunction and a receiver to prevent the subject-matter of his mortgage from being impaired and wasted." [9] Nevertheless "the appointment of a receiver and authorizing him to take possession of property is the exercise of a higher and more far reaching power than the granting of an injunction, and should not be resorted to where an injunction will as well serve the purpose of the judicial proceedings, and to the same extent protect the rights of the complainant." [10] The foregoing attitude is not necessarily indicative of how a court will treat a request for a receivership by a foreclosing mortgagee. That problem is considered elsewhere in this chapter.[11]

6. King v. Smith, supra note 4; Moriarty v. Ashworth, 43 Minn. 1, 3, 44 N.W. 531, 532, 19 Am.St.Rep. 203 (1890). Perhaps a smaller loan to value ratio would be considered acceptable if the loan were originally a high-ratio one with mortgage insurance. See § 11.2 infra.

7. Moriarty v. Ashworth, supra note 4; Beaver Flume and Lumber Co. v. Eccles, 43 Or. 400, 73 P. 201, 99 Am.St.Rep. 759 (1903).

8. Fairbank v. Cudworth, supra note 2; Core v. Bell, 20 W.Va. 169 (1882).

9. Brassey v. New York & N.E.R. Co., 19 F. 663, 669 (C.C.Conn.1884). See also Farmers' Loan & Trust Co. v. Meridian Waterworks Co., 139 F. 661 (C.C.Miss. 1905); Davis v. Alton, Jacksonville & Pacific Railway Co., 180 Ill.App. 1 (1913). Cf. American Loan & Trust Co. v. Toledo, C. & S. Railway Co., 29 F. 416 (C.C.Ohio 1886).

But see, contra, Houston & B.V. Railway Co. v. Hughes, 182 S.W. 23 (Tex.Civ.App. 1916) (appointment of a receiver must be ancillary to foreclosure, and will not be made where the mortgagor has not defaulted in performance of obligation secured).

10. Schack v. McKey, 97 Ill.App. 460, 465 (1901). See also Original Vienna Bakery Co. v. Heissler, 50 Ill.App. 406, 413 (1893); Clark, Receivers, § 59.

11. See §§ 4.33–4.42, infra. Where the mortgagee has conveyed the mortgaged premises to a purchaser who assumes or takes "subject to" the mortgage, must the mortgagee bring a suit to enjoin waste by the grantee as a condition precedent to preserving his right to collect the debt from the mortgagor? While there is authority that indicates an affirmative answer, the better view is to the contrary.

WESTLAW REFERENCES
land (real + 1 estate property) realty /p damag*** destr! waste
    /s enjoin*** injucti** /s mortgage* % enjoin*** injucti**
    /4 foreclos***

§ 4.11 Enforcing Specific Covenants Against Waste

The mortgage theory followed by an individual jurisdiction, as we have seen, can substantially affect the mortgagee's remedies against waste. In a similar vein, the classification of waste as either "voluntary" or "permissive", when taken in the context of the lien or title theory, can prove significant in weighing the mortgagee's chances for recovery for waste. Voluntary waste entails such activities as excessive cutting of timber and removal or physical destruction of buildings, while permissive waste, on the other hand, consists of failing to repair or allowing the property to fall into disrepair.[1] While a mortgagee stands a good chance of recovering damages for voluntary waste in both title and lien jurisdictions, only in title theory states would recovery be possible for permissive waste.[2]

Thus, for a variety of reasons, mortgagees today generally include specific covenants against waste in the mortgage instrument. First, lien theory mortgagees seek to avoid the limiting consequences of the "substantial impairment" rule. Second, such mortgagees seek to be able to recover for permissive waste, a right their title theory counterparts sometimes enjoy as a matter of law. Similarly, the lien mortgagee seeks protection from "financial waste", such as failure to pay real estate taxes and senior liens. Moreover, both title and lien mortgagees use such covenants to establish that the commission of waste will be a ground for acceleration and foreclosure. While the use of covenants has to some extent enhanced the mortgagee's rights in the financial waste situation, in the other areas of concern referred to above they have not significantly increased the mortgagee's common law rights.[3]

While covenants against "financial waste" have generally been recognized judicially, practical enforcement methods are limited in both title and lien jurisdictions. There is almost no authority permitting the recovery of damages against the mortgagor who fails to pay real estate taxes.[4] Moreover, such a recovery may not be possible even after the mortgagee has paid the taxes.[5] As a practical matter, after such financial waste has occurred the only realistic option for the mortgagee is to protect the mortgage security by paying the delinquent taxes or

---

See Osborne, Mortgages, § 135 (2d Ed. 1970).

§ 4.11

1. Leipziger, The Mortgagee's Remedies For Waste, 64 Cal.L.Rev. 1086, 1087 (1976). Comment, Remedies for Waste in Missouri, 47 Mo.L.Rev. 288, 291 (1982).

2. Id. at 1103–1104.

3. Id.

4. Wiggin v. Lowell Five Cent Savings Bank, 299 Mass. 518, 13 N.E.2d 433 (1938); Camden Trust Co. v. Handle, 132 N.J.Eq. 97, 26 A.2d 865 (Ct.Err. & App.1942).

5. Glenn, Mortgages, § 91.1 (1943).

other liens, accelerate the debt, and then either attempt to sue on the entire debt, including advances, or foreclose on the mortgage. Most institutional mortgagees attempt to avoid the above predicament by requiring the mortgagor to make periodic payments into "reserve" or "escrow" accounts to provide a fund for the payment of taxes. Detailed consideration of this practice follows later in this chapter.[6]

Another type of covenant against waste is the "repair covenant". Under such covenants, mortgagees often agree "to maintain [the mortgaged property] in good condition and repair; not to remove or demolish any building or improvement [on the mortgaged property]; to complete promptly in workmanlike manner any improvement hereafter constructed thereon and to restore promptly in workmanlike manner any improvement thereon which is damaged or destroyed, and to pay when due all cost therefor or in connection therewith; to comply with all laws, ordinances, regulations, covenants, conditions and restrictions affecting the property; not to commit, suffer, or permit any waste thereof * * *"[7]

Mortgagors occasionally demolish or remove existing improvements to replace them with newer structures. Courts generally hold that repair covenants are unenforceable unless, after the improvements are made, the market value of the property is lower than prior to the demolition and new improvements.[8] Otherwise, no "damage" would be suffered by the mortgagee. Such cases do not distinguish between the breach of a repair covenant as a basis for a damage action and as a basis for acceleration of the debt and foreclosure of the mortgage. One commentator has criticized the reasoning of these cases as "shallow and unfair to the mortgagee" because while "the absence of damage to the property would indeed be fatal to a suit alleging waste and seeking to collect damages, * * * the mortgagee should have the right to accelerate the debt whenever any condition expressed in the note or the mortgage has failed. For it is reasonable to assume that the parties intended that the prohibition on demolition would give control over development of the property to the mortgagee. * * * If the covenant is not enforced, the mortgagee faces a real risk that the construction that was supposed to follow the demolition will never be completed or that, even if completed, the building will be uneconomic and provide less security than the original structure."[9]

Courts also construe narrowly and hesitate to enforce repair covenants either by a damage action or by foreclosure where the mortgagor's breach consists of a failure to make repairs.[10] For example one court has refused to permit foreclosure by a federal government mort-

6. See §§ 4.17–4.22, infra.

7. Krone v. Goff, 53 Cal.App.3d 191, 127 Cal.Rptr. 390, n. 1 (1976).

8. See e.g., Heller v. Gerry, 47 A.D.2d 697, 364 N.Y.S.2d 615 (1975); Bart v. Streuli, 5 Cal.2d 67, 52 P.2d 922 (1935).

9. Leipziger, supra note 1 at 1106.

10. See, e.g., United States v. Angel, 362 F.Supp. 445 (E.D.Pa.1973); Krone v. Goff, 53 Cal.App.3d 191, 127 Cal.Rptr. 390 (1975).

gagee where the mortgagor violated a covenant to comply with local building, health and other codes and to make all repairs and replacements necessary to preserve and maintain the value of the mortgage security.[11] Because the value of the mortgage property was seven times the mortgage debt, the court determined that the security had not been sufficiently impaired. Moreover, in damage actions for waste, other courts have indicated that security impairment will be required notwithstanding specific repair covenants.[12]

Finally, some repair covenants cases involve fact situations where the mortgagee has a right to compensation from a special fund. For example, where there has been substantial physical damage and the mortgagee is entitled to insurance proceeds, courts have refused to permit foreclosure even though the mortgagor refused to comply with a specific covenant to rebuild.[13] In one case, after substantial damage by fire, the property was not rebuilt and was vandalized notwithstanding some attempts by the mortgagor to prevent it. The mortgagee was a named insured under the insurance policy enforced at the time of the fire. The court refused to permit foreclosure, holding that the covenant language "to keep the property in good condition" required only normal maintenance and not rebuilding.[14] Moreover, the court determined that the mortgagor had not "permitted waste" within the covenant language because the mortgagor had attempted to protect the remains and obtain new insurance coverage for them.

 WESTLAW REFERENCES
repair waste /5 contract*** covenant** /p land (mortgaged real
   +1 estate property) realty /p deed foreclos*** mortgage*

C. RIGHTS IN THE PRODUCT OF THE RES

§ 4.12 Eminent Domain

Where mortgaged land is taken by eminent domain the mortgagee's rights in the land follow the award and attach to it.[1] "The underlying theory of the right of a mortgagee to part or all of the award is that, as the parties are powerless to prevent the taking of the property by the public and the mortgagee loses his lien on the part taken, the award equitably stands in the place of the land taken; and, as the mortgage does not cover the award in law, it is held to operate as

---

11. United States v. Angel, 362 F.Supp. 445 (E.D.Pa.1973).

12. See e.g., Krone v. Goff, 53 Cal.App. 3d 191, 127 Cal.Rptr. 390 (1975).

13. See Leipziger, supra note 1 at 1107.

14. Erickson v. Rocco, 433 S.W.2d 746 (Tex.Civ.App.1968).

§ 4.12

1. See e.g., People ex rel Department of Transportation v. Redwood Baseline Limited, 84 Cal.App.3d 662, 149 Cal.Rptr. 11 (1978); Department of Transportation v. New Century Engineering & Development Corp., 97 Ill.2d 343, 73 Ill.Dec. 538, 454 N.E.2d 635 (1983); Silverman v. State, 48 A.D.2d 413, 370 N.Y.S.2d 234 (1975); Nichols, Eminent Domain § 5.74 (1976).

an equitable lien thereon. This results in two separate encumbrances, the legal mortgage on the remainder of the land and the equitable lien on the award." [2] Where the entire property subject to the mortgage is taken, the mortgagee is entitled to the entire award, or so much of it as is necessary to satisfy his mortgage debt.[3]

Where there is only a partial condemnation, there are at least three views to the mortgagee's rights. One view gives the mortgagee the entire amount of the award without distinguishing whether the mortgage has been foreclosed or even whether it has matured.[4] According to a second view, the mortgagee in a partial taking situation is entitled to that amount of the condemnation award that will compensate him for the impairment of his security.[5] There are varying views as to what constitutes impairment of security. For example, some have said that if the value of the property after condemnation exceeds the amount of the mortgage debt, the entire condemnation award for a partial taking presumably belongs to the mortgagor.[6] On the other hand, it has been stated that "we do not agree that in a case where the mortgagee has bargained for a lien on property valued greatly in excess of the debt, his security may be whittled down in value by partial takings in condemnation ＊　＊　＊ to the point where it barely equals the amount of the debt, and there still be no impairment of his security." [7] One California appellate court has held that security impairment "is normally a question of fact [which] is to be determined in light of the circumstances of the particular case considering all of the relevant factors." [8] The Uniform Eminent Domain Code, approved by the Na-

2. Petition of Dillman, 276 Mich. 252, 258, 267 N.W. 623, 625 (1936). See cases cited in note 1 supra.

3. Calumet River Railway v. Brown, 136 Ill. 322, 26 N.E. 501, 12 L.R.A. 84 (1891); Chicago v. Gage, 268 Ill. 232, 109 N.E. 28 (1915); Connell v. Kakauna etc., Co., 164 Wis. 471, 159 N.W. 927, Ann.Cas. 1918A 247 (1916), rehearing denied 164 Wis. 471, 160 N.W. 1035 (1917). It is immaterial whether the mortgage debt is or is not due. Morgan v. Willman, 318 Mo. 151, 1 S.W.2d 193, 58 A.L.R. 1518 (1927); Federal Trust Co. v. East Hartford Fire District, 283 F. 95 (C.C.A.Conn.1922). See Teague, Condemnation of Mortgaged Property, 44 Tex.L.Rev. 1535, 1537–1939. (1966).

4. In re Forman, 138 Misc. 501, 240 N.Y.S. 718 (1930), noted 44 Harv.L.Rev. 1142 (1931); In re Public Park, 184 App. Div. 509, 172 N.Y.S. 50 (1918), dismissed, 224 N.Y. 697, 121 N.E. 356 (1918). If not mature, a rebate of interest on the debt must be given. See Teague, Condemnation of Mortgaged Property, 44 Tex.L.Rev. 1535, 1539 (1966).

5. Teague, Condemnation of Mortgaged Property, 44 Tex.L.Rev. 1535, 1540 (1966); Buell Realty Note Collection Trust v. Central Oak Investment Co., 483 S.W.2d 24 (Tex.Civ.App.1972), refused n.r.e. 486 S.W.2d 87 (1972); Swanson v. U.S., 156 F.2d 442 (9th Cir.1946), certiorari denied 329 U.S. 800, 67 S.Ct. 492, 91 L.Ed. 684 (1947).

6. Rayburn, Texas Law of Condemnation, §§ 79, 113 (1960).

7. Buell Realty Note Collection Trust v. Central Oak Investment Co., 483 S.W.2d 24, 27 (Tex.Civ.App.1972), refused n.r.e. 486 S.W.2d 87 (1972).

8. People ex rel. Department of Transportation v. Redwood Baseline Limited, 84 Cal.App.3d 662, 668, 149 Cal.Rptr. 11, 17 (1978). The following factors were identified by the *Baseline* court:

"whether the debt and security transaction resulted from a sale or a loan; whether or not a deficiency judgment is legally permissible; the terms for repayment; the interest rate charged compared with the prevailing interest rate in similar transactions; the original, tional Conference of Commissioners on Uniform State Laws in 1974, specifically provides that "notwithstanding the provisions of an agreement, if any, relating to a lien encumbering the property: (1) if there is a partial taking, the lien holder may share in the amount of compensation awarded only to the extent determined by the court to be necessary to prevent an impairment of the security * * * "[9] Whatever the exact parameters of the impairment of security approach, it will be followed even where the mortgage specifically confers on the mortgagee the option of releasing the proceeds of a condemnation award to the mortgagor or applying them to the mortgage indebtedness.[10] Still a third suggestion is that the court should allocate to the mortgagee a portion of the award measured by the ratio which the mortgage debt bears to the value of the whole mortgaged land, thus preserving the ratio of debt to security.[11]

Generally the mortgagee must be given notice of a condemnation proceeding and an opportunity to appear in that proceeding. In at least half of the states, this requirement is mandated by statute.[12] Although other state statutes provide that notice shall be given to the "owner" or "parties in interest", judicial interpretation of such statutes has generally resulted in the inclusion of mortgagees within the coverage of one or both of those terms.[13] Nevertheless, there may still be a few jurisdictions that hold, in the absence of express statutory requirements to the contrary, that the mortgagee need not be made a party or given notice of the condemnation proceedings.[14] This result seems in part to stem from the refusal of a few lien theory states to recognize, for purposes of interpreting their condemnation statutes, that the mortgagee has any interest in the mortgaged real estate other than a lien.[15] In such a situation, the mortgagee presumably must recover the award

pretake and posttake security to debt ratios; the length of time the transaction has been in effect; the amount of the debtor's equity and the amount actually invested by the debtor in the property constituting the security; the payment record of the debtor prior to the partial condemnation; the length of time the transaction is to continue in force after the partial condemnation; whether or not the partial condemnation necessitates repair to or reconstruction of the property; the amount of the annual taxes and assessments against the property; whether the debt is currently paid or is in default; facts bearing on the likelihood of default by the debtor; the nature of the security property; whether or not the security property is likely to be readily salable; and whether or not it is likely it can be sold at a foreclosure sale for a price approximating its fair market value."

Id. at 668, 149 Cal.Rptr. at 17. See Miller, Valuation of the Mortgagee's Interest Up-

on Partial Condemnation, 15 Loy.L.A. L.Rev. 227 (1982).

9. Uniform Eminent Domain Code, § 1014.

10. Milstein v. Security Pacific National Bank, 27 Cal.App.3d 482, 103 Cal.Rptr. 16 (1972).

11. Teague, Condemnation of Mortgaged Property, 44 Tex.L.Rev. 1535, 1543 (1966); Buell Realty Note Collection Trust v. Central Oak Investment Co., 486 S.W.2d 87 (Tex.1972).

12. Teague, supra note 11 at 1535.

13. See, e.g., Id. at 1535; Calumet River Railway v. Brown, 136 Ill. 322, 26 N.E. 501, 12 L.R.A. 84 (1891).

14. See, e.g., State Highway Commission v. District Court of the Thirteenth Judicial District, 499 P.2d 1228, 1234–35 (Mont.1972); Nichols, Eminent Domain, § 5.741 (1976).

15. See Nichols, Eminent Domain, § 5.741 (1976).

from the condemnor before it is paid to the mortgagor or from the mortgagor if it has already been remitted to him.[16] To the extent that any state law today still fails to require that both notice and an opportunity to be heard be afforded to the mortgagee in a condemnation proceeding, it must surely violate procedural due process requirements of notice and hearing under federal and state constitutions. Indeed, in a recent decision holding that notice by publication and posting provided inadequate notice to a mortgagee of real estate being foreclosed for failure to pay property taxes, the United States Supreme Court stated: "Notice by mail or other means as certain to ensure actual notice is a minimum constitutional precondition to a proceeding which will adversely affect the liberty or property interests of *any* party, whether unlettered or well versed in commercial practice, if its name and address are reasonably ascertainable."[17] If such notice is constitutionally required in a real estate tax foreclosure, it must surely be necessary in condemnation as well. After all, whether one characterizes the mortgagee's interest as an estate in land or as merely a lien, it not only is property, but an often economically substantial interest as well. So too should the mortgagee have a right to be heard in the condemnation proceeding. Frequently, the mortgagee will have a significant economic interest in convincing a fact finder that the condemnation award be as large as possible. Indeed, in a judicial era when procedural due process rights have been expanded to other areas of mortgage law,[18] it would seem unthinkable such protections should not be afforded to a mortgagee in a condemnation proceeding. In any event it seems undesirable to deprive the mortgagee of his bargained for security and leave him with inadequate protection. Indeed, after the award has been paid over to the mortgagor, the mortgagee is in the same position he would have been in had he never bargained for and obtained security.

When the mortgagee is a necessary party in a condemnation proceeding, what are the consequences of failure to join him? Some courts hold that the land condemned is still subject to his mortgage and the mortgagee can foreclose on it.[19] If the original award has not been paid to the mortgagor, the mortgagee may seek and obtain a revalua-

---

16. Whiting v. New Haven, 45 Conn. 303 (1877); Parish v. Gilmanton, 11 N.H. 293 (1840); Read v. Cambridge, 126 Mass. 427 (1879); Goodrich v. Commissioners of Atchison Co., 47 Kan. 355, 27 P. 1006, 18 L.R.A. 113 (1891); Thompson v. Chicago etc., Railway Co., 110 Mo. 147, 19 S.W. 77 (1892).

17. Mennonite Board of Missions v. Adams, 462 U.S. 791, 103 S.Ct. 2706, 77 L.Ed. 2d 180 (1983).

18. See §§ 7.23–7.30 infra.

19. Grigsby v. Miller, 144 Or. 551, 25 P.2d 908 (1933), giving, however, a reasona-

ble time to the condemnor to secure the property by new condemnation or purchase. See also Wilson v. European & N.A.R. Co., 67 Me. 358 (1877); Michigan Air Line Railway Co. v. Barnes, 40 Mich. 383 (1879); Morgan v. Willman, 318 Mo. 151, 1 S.W.2d 193, 58 A.L.R. 1518 (1927); Wade v. Hennessy, 55 Vt. 207 (1882); Stamnes v. Milwaukee etc., Railway Co., 131 Wis. 85, 109 N.W. 100 (1907), rehearing granted 131 Wis. 85, 109 N.W. 925 (1907), opinion modified 131 Wis. 85, 111 N.W. 62 (1907); North Coast Railway Co. v. Hess, 56 Wash. 335, 105 P. 853 (1909).

tion and new award and have this paid to him in amount sufficient to satisfy his mortgage claim.[20] Others hold that even though the full award has been made and paid to the mortgagor, the mortgagee is entitled as against the condemnor to so much of the original award as is necessary to compensate him for his interest in the property taken [21] or to have a new valuation of the property taken and be satisfied out of it.[22]

WESTLAW REFERENCES

lien /p condemn! "eminent domain" /p mortgagee

condemn! "eminent domain" /p mortgagee /s "due process"

hear*** notice notif! (join*** made +3 party)

§ 4.13 Insurance—Some General Considerations

Both the mortgagor and the mortgagee have an insurable interest in the mortgaged property.[1] Hence each may protect himself against loss by his own contract of insurance.[2] The insurable interest of the mortgagor is the full value of the property [3] while that of the mortgagee is limited to the amount of the mortgage itself, i.e., the amount of the debt secured.[4] Traditionally courts have insisted that insurance is a purely personal contract of indemnity against diminution in the value of the property; [5] the proceeds of the contract are not regarded as a substitute res for the destroyed property.[6] As a result, if the mortgagor

20. Seaboard All-Florida Railway Co. v. Leavitt, 105 Fla. 600, 141 So. 886 (1932), noted, 32 Col.L.Rev. 1240 (1932); Calumet River Railway Co. v. Brown, 136 Ill. 322, 26 N.E. 501, 12 L.R.A. 84 (1891); Stamnes v. Milwaukee etc. Co., 131 Wis. 85, 109 N.W. 100 (1907).

21. Stemper v. Houston County, 187 Minn. 135, 244 N.W. 690 (1932) noted, 17 Minn.L.Rev. 92 (1932); South Park Commissioners v. Todd, 112 Ill. 379 (1884); Sherwood v. City of Lafayette, 109 Ind. 411, 10 N.E. 89, 58 Am.St.Rep. 414 (1886); note, 58 A.L.R. 1534, 1539.

22. South Park Commissioners v. Todd, 112 Ill. 379 (1884); Gray v. Case, 51 N.J.Eq. 426, 431, 26 A. 805, 807 (1893).

§ 4.13

1. See e.g., Tech Land Development, Inc. v. South Carolina Insurance Co., 57 N.C.App. 566, 291 S.E.2d 821 (1982), review denied 306 N.C. 563, 294 S.E.2d 228 (1982); 495 Corp. v. N.J. Insurance Underwriting Association, 173 N.J.Super. 114, 413 A.2d 630 (1980), judgment affirmed 86 N.J. 159, 430 A.2d 203 (1981).

2. See e.g., Tech Land Development, Inc. v. South Carolina Insurance Co., 57 N.C.App. 566, 291 S.E.2d 821 (1982), review denied 306 N.C. 563, 294 S.E.2d 228 (1982);

Connecticut Mutual Life Insurance Co. v. Scammon, Ill., 117 U.S. 634, 6 S.Ct. 889, 29 L.Ed. 1007 (1885).

3. See Tech Land Development, Inc. v. South Carolina Insurance Co., 57 N.C.App. 566, 291 S.E.2d 821 (1982), review denied 306 N.C. 563, 294 S.E.2d 228 (1982); Florea v. Iowa State Insurance Co., 225 Mo.App. 49, 32 S.W.2d 111 (1930); Strong v. Manufacturing Insurance Co., 27 Mass. 40, 20 Am.Dec. 507 (1830).

4. Lockett v. Western Assurance Co., 190 Ark. 1135, 83 S.W.2d 65 (1935); Foster v. Van Reed, 70 N.Y. 19, 26 Am.Rep. 544 (1877); Grevemeyer v. Southern Mutual Fire Insurance Co., 62 Pa. 340, 1 Am.Rep. 420 (1869); Excelsior Insurance Co. v. Royal Insurance Co., 55 N.Y. 343, 14 Am.Rep. 271 (1873); Savarese v. Ohio Farmers' Insurance Co., 260 N.Y. 45, 182 N.E. 665, 91 A.L.R. 1341 (1932); Thompson v. National Fire Insurance Co., 48 S.D. 224, 203 N.W. 464 (1925).

5. See 1 May, Insurance, 4th ed. § 6.

6. There is occasional judicial recognition of the idea that insurance takes the place of the property destroyed. See Gordon v. Ware Savings Bank, 115 Mass. 588, 591 (1874). See note, 19 Va.L.Rev. 508 (1933) advocating the rule that insurance insures his interest in the property and there is a loss, he alone is entitled to payment. The mortgagee has no interest whatsoever in the proceeds in the absence of an agreement to insure for his benefit.[7]

So, too, on the same idea that the contract is a purely personal one of indemnity, a mortgagee who insures his interest at his own expense and with no understanding with the mortgagor, is entitled to recover even though the property remaining undestroyed is fully ample to cover his debt,[8] and the money paid belongs to him alone, the mortgagor being a stranger to the contract and entitled to no benefit under it. Consequently, in such a case, the payment to the mortgagee does not reduce the mortgage debt; but in order to prevent the mortgagee from getting double payment, the insurer, on payment of the loss becomes subrogated *pro tanto* to the mortgage debt.[9] The only result, so far as the mortgagor is concerned, is that his creditor is changed.[10]

Normally, instead of both mortgagor and mortgagee taking out separate policies, there is an agreement in the mortgage that only one policy shall be taken out but that it shall insure the respective interests of both parties. Usually it is the mortgagor who is bound to take out the policy. If in violation of the agreement the mortgagor only insures his separate interest, the mortgagee may impress an equitable lien on the amount due him under the policy.[11] The extent of the lien is the mortgagee's interest in the mortgaged property covered by the agreement to insure.[12] This equitable lien, it has been pointed out, arises as a consequence of the mortgagee's right to specific performance because of the inadequacy of money damages at law for breach of the contract to insure.[13] The amount realized by the mortgagee upon the lien must be applied in *pro tanto* satisfaction of the mortgage debt. Consequently, the insurer is not entitled to be subrogated to any rights that the

proceeds are a "new form of the old res." See, also, Gilligan, Insurance on Mortgaged Property, 88 U. of Pa.L.Rev. 347 (1940); Glenn, Mortgages, § 27.4.

7. See Walsh & Simpson, Cas. Security Transactions, 184 Note (1) citing, Niagara Fire Insurance Co. v. Scammon, 144 Ill. 490, 28 N.E. 919 (1891) affirmed 144 Ill. 490, 32 N.E. 914, 19 L.R.A. 114; Ryan v. Adamson, 57 Iowa 30, 10 N.W. 287 (1881).

8. Kernochan v. New York etc. Co., 17 N.Y. 428 (1858); Excelsior Fire Insurance Co. v. Royal Insurance Co., 55 N.Y. 343, 14 Am.Rep. 271 (1873); Aetna Insurance Co. of Hartford, Conn. v. Baker, 71 Ind. 102 (1880); Meader v. Farmers' etc. Association, 137 Or. 111, 1 P.2d 138 (1931).

9. Excelsior Fire Insurance Co. v. Royal Insurance Co., 55 N.Y. 343, 14 Am.Rep. 271 (1873); Foster v. Van Reed, 70 N.Y. 19, 26 Am.Rep. 544 (1877); Honore v. Lamar Insurance Co., 51 Ill. 409 (1851); Norwich

Fire Insurance Co. v. Boomer, 52 Ill. 442, 4 Am.Rep. 618 (1869); Gould v. Maine Farmers Mutual Fire Insurance Co., 114 Me. 416, 96 A. 732, L.R.A.1917A, 604 (1916); Leyden v. Lawrence, 79 N.J.Eq. 113, 81 A. 121 (1911) affirmed 80 N.J.Eq. 550, 85 A. 1134; Gainesville National Bank v. Martin, 187 Ga. 559, 1 S.E.2d 636 (1937); Le Doux v. Dettmering, 316 Ill.App. 98, 43 N.E.2d 862 (1942). Cf. King v. State Mutual Fire Insurance Co., 61 Mass. 1, 54 Am. Dec. 683 (1851).

10. See Gainesville National Bank v. Martin, 187 Ga. 559, 1 S.E.2d 636 (1937).

11. See Knapp v. Victory Corp., 279 S.C. 80, 302 S.E.2d 330 (1983).

12. Knapp v. Victory Corp., 279 S.C. 80, 302 S.E.2d 330 (1983). Nichols v. Baxter, 5 R.I. 491 (1858), Walsh & Simpson, Cas. Security Transactions, 180.

13. Walsh, Mortgages, § 25.

mortgagee had against the mortgagor.[14] On the other hand, even though the insurance is taken out by the mortgagee in his own name, if "it has been effected at the request or by the authority of the mortgagor, or under circumstances that would make him chargeable with the premium, the mortgagor, in case of loss, is entitled to have the proceeds of the insurance applied in liquidation of the mortgage debt pro tanto."[15] The consequence again is that subrogation will be denied to the insurer.[16] The same applies where the mortgagor takes out the insurance for the benefit of the mortgagee. The mortgagee is compelled to apply the proceeds insofar as the debt is due, and if he fails to do so, the law will make the application.[17]

 WESTLAW REFERENCES
insura! insure* /s mortgag** /p indemnif! personal subrogat***
217k581.1(1)

§ 4.14 Insurance—Types of Policies

Normally one insurance policy is obtained insuring the interests of both parties and, in this connection, one of two types of policy clauses is utilized. One is the older "loss payable" or "open" mortgage policy which is infrequently used today. The other is the "standard mortgage policy" or the "New York standard mortgage policy" which is in common use nationally.[1]

Loss Payable Policy

Under the loss payable policy, the courts were virtually unanimous in holding that the mortgagee is a mere appointee of the mortgagor to receive payment.[2] Therefore his right to recover is completely dependent upon the right of the mortgagor, so that a breach of the conditions

---

14. See Glenn, Mortgages § 27.5.

15. Le Doux v. Dettmering, 316 Ill.App. 98, 109, 43 N.E.2d 862, 867 (1942); Elliott v. Pendleton, 67 Mich. 496, 35 N.W. 97 (1887); see Honore v. Lamar Insurance Co., 51 Ill. 409, 413 (1851).

16. Waring v. Loder, 53 N.Y. 581 (1873), true although insurer took assignment; Kernochan v. New York Bowery Fire Insurance Co., 17 N.Y. 428, 441 (1858). See Pendleton v. Elliott, 67 Mich. 496, 498, 35 N.W. 97 (1887). There is authority that in a case of this sort, by agreement with the mortgagee, the insurer can reserve a right of subrogation. Foster v. Van Reed, 70 N.Y. 19, 26 Am.Rep. 544 (1877). As was succinctly observed, "This, however, does not make sense." 1 Glenn, Mortgages, 187, fn. 6. Imperial Fire Insurance Co. v. Bull, 18 Can.S.C. 697 (1889), denied subrogation in spite of a stipulation for it unknown to the mortgagor.

17. Thorp v. Croto, 79 Vt. 390, 65 A. 562, 10 L.R.A.,N.S., 1166, 118 Am.St.Rep. 961, 9 Ann.Cas. 58 (1905); Gordon v. Ware Savings Bank, 115 Mass. 588 (1874).

§ 4.14

1. See generally Appleman, Insurance Law and Practice, § 3401 (1970); Comment, Foreclosure, Loss, and The Proper Distribution of Insurance Proceeds Under Open and Standard Mortgage Clauses: Some Observations, 7 Valparaiso L.Rev. 485–487 (1973); Lev, Mortgagees and Insurers: The Legal Nuts and Bolts of Their Relationship, 12 Forum 1012, 1013 (1977); Fred v. Pacific Indemnity Co., 53 Hawaii 384, 494 P.2d 783 (1972); Hartford Fire Insurance Co. v. Associates Capital Corp., 313 So.2d 404 (Miss.1975).

2. Nassar v. Utah Mortgage Loan Corp., 100 N.M. 419, 671 P.2d 667 (1983); Hill v. International Indemnity Co., 116 Kan. 109, 225 P. 1056, 38 A.L.R. 362 (1924);

of the policy by the mortgagor, which would prevent a recovery by him, bars recovery by the mortgagee.[3] After loss, it has been held that the interest of the mortgagee becomes independent and is not affected by a breach of the policy by the mortgagor subsequent to the loss.[4] And the weight of authority clearly is that the mortgagee is not bound by any settlement of the loss or appraisal agreed upon between the mortgagor and the insurer to which he was not a party and did not consent.[5] However, since the mortgagee is only the appointee to receive what the mortgagor is entitled to under the policy, it follows that on receipt it goes in reduction of what the mortgagor owes on the mortgage debt just as though the mortgagor had paid him directly.[6] Consequently, even though there was a clause in the policy providing for subrogation of the insurer, it would be unavailing. The mortgagee would have no rights to which to subrogate him.[7] Or, to put it another way, to permit subrogation would nullify the mortgagor's insurance by preventing the payment of the insurance money from discharging his debt. If, however, the mortgagor's rights have been forfeited, but the policy is continued as to the mortgagee, since the only interest now insured is that of the mortgagee, a clause providing for subrogation of the insurer in case of payment to the mortgagee when no liability existed to the mortgagor will be honored.[8] The same has been held where there was no stipulation for subrogation in the policy.[9]

Standard Mortgage Policy

To have the mortgagee's right to collect insurance dependent upon the right of the mortgagor against the insurer, as it was under the older simple loss-payable policy, was unsatisfactory. So to it was added another clause: "and this insurance, as to the interest of the mortgagee only therein, shall not be invalidated by any act or neglect of the mortgagor." This is the standard mortgage insurance clause which is

Inland Finance Co. v. Home Insurance Co., 134 Wash. 485, 236 P. 73, 48 A.L.R. 121 (1925); St. Paul Fire & Marine Insurance Co. v. Ruddy, 299 F. 189 (C.C.A.Neb.1924). See 17 Cornell L.Q. 151 (1931). See also 48 A.L.R. 124 (1927); 38 A.L.R. 367 (1925) for collections of cases.

3. See authorities cited in note 2 supra.

4. McDowell v. St. Paul Fire & Marine Insurance Co., 207 N.Y. 482, 101 N.E. 457 (1913).

5. First National Bank of Duluth v. National etc. Co. of America, 156 Minn. 1, 194 N.W. 6, 38 A.L.R. 380 (1923). See 38 A.L.R. 383 (1923), for a collection of cases. Officer v. American etc. Co., 175 La. 581, 143 So. 500 (1932), noted, 7 Tulane L.Rev. 449 (1933), holding the mortgagee bound by an appraisal of which he had no knowledge represents a minority view. Of course if he does know and consent, he is bound.

Scania Insurance Co. v. Johnson, 22 Colo. 476, 45 P. 431 (1896).

6. Sisk v. Rapuano, 94 Conn. 294, 108 A. 858, 11 A.L.R. 1291 (1920). See 11 A.L.R. 1296 (1921) for a collection of cases.

7. Imperial Fire Insurance Co. v. Bull, 18 Can.S.C. 697 (1889); Burton-Lingo Co. v. Patton, 15 N.M. 304, 107 P. 679, 27 L.R.A.,N.S., 420 (1910); Milwaukee Co. v. Ramsey, 76 Or. 570, 149 P. 542, L.R.A.1916A, 556, Ann.Cas. 1917B, 1132 (1915); see Atlantic etc. Bk. v. Farmers' etc. Association, 203 N.C. 669, 166 S.E. 789 (1932).

8. Insurance Co. of North America v. Martin, 151 Ind. 209, 51 N.E. 361 (1898); Washington Fire Insurance Co. v. Cobb, 163 S.W. 608 (Tex.Civ.App.1914).

9. First National Bank v. Springfield etc. Co., 104 Kan. 278, 178 P. 413 (1919) (standard clause).

now in wide-spread use. The effect of the provision is to insure the mortgagee's interest as fully and to the same extent as if he had taken out a separate policy directly from the insurer free from the conditions imposed upon the mortgagor, at least to the extent that no act or neglect of the mortgagor which occurs subsequent to the issuance of the policy will defeat the mortgagee's right.[10] As to misconduct of the mortgagor at the time the policy is issued, the weight of authority protects the mortgagee even here.[11] This is in spite of the argument that, on agency principles, the insurance company should have a defense against the mortgagee, and, although in general it is abhorrent that the mortgagee should be at the mercy of the mortgagor as to whether his insurance is good, there would be no great burden upon him to make the mortgagee check on the mortgagor's conduct at the inception of the contract to make sure that it is valid.[12] The insurance being for the benefit of both the mortgagor and the mortgagee,[13] so long as the insurer remains liable to the mortgagor, any payments for loss made to the mortgagee under the policy must go in reduction of the mortgage debt as being in substance a payment from the mortgagor.[14]

10. See Neises v. Solomon State Bank, 236 Kan. 767, 696 P.2d 372 (1985); Hartford Fire Insurance Co. v. Merrimack Mutual Fire Insurance Co., 457 A.2d 410 (1983); General G.M.C. Sales, Inc. v. Passarella, 195 N.J.Super. 614, 481 A.2d 307 (1984); Starkman v. Sigmond, 184 N.J. Super. 600, 446 A.2d 1249 (1982); Nassar v. Utah Mortgage Loan Corp., 100 N.M. 419, 671 P.2d 667 (App.1983); Tech Land Development, Inc. v. South Carolina Insurance Co., 57 N.C.App. 566, 291 S.E.2d 821 (1982), review denied 306 N.C. 563, 294 S.E.2d 228 (1982); Fred v. Pacific Indemnity Co., 53 Hawaii 384, 388, 494 P.2d 783, 787 (1973); Savarese v. Ohio Farmers' Insurance Co., 260 N.Y. 45, 182 N.E. 665 (1932); Magoun v. Fireman's Fund Insurance Co., 86 Minn. 486, 91 Am.St.Rep. 370 (1902); Beaver Falls etc. Association v. Allemania Fire Insurance Co., 305 Pa. 290, 157 A. 616 (1931), noted 16 Minn.L.Rev. 597 (1932); American Building & Loan Association v. Farmers Insurance Co., 11 Wash. 619, 40 P. 125 (1895). See note, 11 Corn.L.Q. 553, 555 (1926). That it is not an independent contract between the insurer and the mortgagee but that it is a contract between the mortgagor and the insurer with the mortgagee as third party beneficiary, see Walker v. Queen Insurance Co., 136 S.C. 144, 134 S.E. 263, 270 (1926); see also Davis v. German-American Insurance Co., 135 Mass. 251, 256 (1883); Union Central Life Insurance Co. v. Codington County Farmers Fire & Lightning Mutual Insurance Co., 66 S.D. 561, 287 N.W. 46, 124 A.L.R. 1027 (1939), creditor beneficiary.

11. See Annot., 24 A.L.R.3d 431 (1969).

12. See 55 Can.L.J. 151 (1919); 17 Cornell L.Q. 151, 153 n. 4 (1931). Graham v. Fireman's Insurance Co., 87 N.Y. 69, 41 Am.Rep. 349 (1881), is the leading American case.

13. "The insurance was for indemnity to the mortgagor as well as to the mortgagee." Gordon v. Ware Savings Bank, 115 Mass. 588, 591 (1874). For an argument that one clause of such a standard policy, that providing for payment of premiums by the mortgagee in case of default by the mortgagor, is construed too favorably to the mortgagee, see Hartnett & Thornton, Is the Mortgagee a Free Rider, 1949 Wis.L. Rev. 714 (1949).

14. See Tarrant Land Co. v. Palmetto Fire Insurance Co., 220 Ala. 428, 125 So. 807 (1930). Reason also points to the conclusion that when a fire occurs the insurance company must pay the loss to the mortgagee in accordance with its contract with him. The mortgagor benefits by such payment as the insurance money reduces the amount of the mortgage debt. Waring v. Loder, 53 N.Y. 581 (1873). "The value taken out of the property by the fire is taken off the mortgage by the payment of the insurance money, and the parties remain in the same relative position after as before the fire." Savarese v. Ohio Farmers' Insurance Co., 260 N.Y. 45, 53, 182 N.E. 665, 667 (1932).

This seems an indirect admission that in this situation, at least, the proceeds do take the place of the destroyed property.

If, on the other hand, the policy has been forfeited as to the mortgagor, by reason of the violation of some provision not affecting the mortgagee, the mortgagor, since he is not entitled to recover under the policy, therefore is not entitled to have money paid to the mortgagee under the policy applied in satisfaction of his debt, but rather the insurance company is entitled to be subrogated to the rights of the mortgagee against the mortgagor.[15] This is true not only where the policy contains a stipulation for subrogation,[16] but also where there is no such agreement.[17] Where there is more than one mortgage on the property and the insurance includes only the first in the mortgage clause, the insurer, if not liable to the mortgagor, is entitled to subrogation not only to the rights of the first mortgagee against the mortgagor but to his priority over the subsequent mortgagee.[18] But when the second mortgagee also is included in the mortgage clause in the policy, the insurer's rights by subrogation are postponed to the second mortgagee's rights.[19] This is right because if the insurer were permitted, through subrogation, to enforce the first mortgage against the property left after the destruction it would result in making the property satisfy the first mortgage twice—once by the destruction of enough of it to justify the insurer in paying off the first mortgage, and again by enforcement of the assigned first mortgage on the property left—before the second mortgagee could enforce his claim. This would impair the second mortgagee's ability to collect his claim and thus violate the provision in a standard mortgage clause that the insurer's subrogation shall not impair the right of the mortgagee to recover the full amount of his claim.[20]

---

15. See cases in next two footnotes.

16. To permit the application of the proceeds of the policy to payment of the mortgagor's debt when the mortgagor has forfeited his rights to any benefit under the policy would render the insurer's declaration of non-liability to the mortgagor futile. The effect of the payment to the mortgagee is not to pay the mortgagor's debt but to give the insurer an equitable proportionate interest in the mortgage as a subsisting obligation. Grangers' Mutual Fire Insurance Co. v. Farmers National Bank, 164 Md. 441, 165 A. 185 (1933); Springfield Fire & Marine Insurance Co. v. Allen, 43 N.Y. 389, 3 Am.Rep. 711 (1871). See note, 52 A.L.R. 278 (1928).

17. First National Bank v. Springfield Fire & Marine Insurance Co., 104 Kan. 278, 178 P. 413 (1919); Hastings v. Westchester Fire Insurance Co., 73 N.Y. 141 (1878); see Tarrant Land Co. v. Palmetto Fire Insurance Co., 220 Ala. 428, 430, 125 So. 807 (1930). But see 19 Va.L.Rev. 508, 510 (1932).

18. Hare v. Headley, 54 N.J.Eq. 545, 35 A. 445 (1896); Tarrant Land Co. v. Palmetto Fire Insurance Co., 220 Ala. 428, 125 So. 807 (1930).

19. Mutual Fire Insurance Co. v. Dilworth, 167 Md. 232, 173 A. 22 (1934) discussed 19 Minn.L.Rev. 125, 83 U. of Pa. L.Rev. 273 (1934); Perretta v. St. Paul Fire & Marine Insurance Co., 106 Misc. 91, 174 N.Y.S. 131 (1919), affirmed 188 App.Div. 983, 177 N.Y.S. 923 (1919).

20. See 83 U. of Pa.L.Rev. 273, 274 (1934).

WESTLAW REFERENCES
266k201

Loss Payable Policy
"loss payable" open +4 insura! insure* /p mortgag**
217k581.1(4)

Standard Mortgage Policy
"new york" standard union +4 mortgage +4 clause insura!
   insure* policy
217k581.1(3)

§ 4.15 Insurance—Restoration of Premises

Today most mortgages in common use by institutional lenders specifically provide for the disposition of insurance proceeds in the event of a casualty loss. One commonly used form, for example, provides that "insurance proceeds shall be applied to restoration or repair of the property damaged, provided such restoration or repair is economically feasible and the security of this [mortgage] is not thereby impaired. If such restoration or repair is not economically feasible or if the security of this [mortgage] would be impaired, the insurance proceeds shall be applied to the sums secured by this [mortgage], with the excess, if any, paid to the [mortgagor]." [1] Moreover, even where such language is not contained in the mortgage instrument, mortgagors and mortgagees routinely agree, after a loss, to utilize the insurance proceeds to restore the premises.

However, in the absence of specific mortgage language governing casualty loss, to what extent, if any, will the mortgagor be able to compel the application of the insurance proceeds to rebuild the mortgaged premises? It could be argued that if rebuilding would restore the mortgaged premises to the pre-casualty condition, the mortgagee's security would be fully protected and that the proceeds therefore should be used to rebuild the premises. Moreover, this argument seems especially appealing where the mortgagee is simply using the casualty loss as a vehicle for compelling prepayment of a lower-than-market interest rate loan. Nevertheless, a significant number of cases give the mortgagee the option of applying the insurance proceeds to the mortgage debt or rebuilding the mortgaged premises.[2] Moreover, this right of the mortgagee is normally not conditioned upon a finding that rebuilding will jeopardize the mortgage security.[3]

§ 4.15

1. Federal Home Loan Mortgage Corporation Deed of Trust Form prescribed for use in Colorado. For background on this form, see Federal National Mortgage Association Public Meeting on Conventional Mortgage Form, Senate Banking, Housing and Urban Affairs Commission, 92d Cong., 1st Sess. (1971).

2. See e.g., English v. Fischer, 660 S.W.2d 521 (Tex.1983); General G.M.C.

Sales, Inc. v. Passarella, 195 N.J.Super. 614, 481 A.2d 307 (1984); Upham v. Lowry, 485 N.Y.S.2d 680 (1985) (contract for deed); Savarese v. Ohio Farmer's Insurance Co., 260 N.Y. 45, 182 N.E. 665 (1932); Walter v. Marine Office of America, 537 F.2d 89 (5th Cir.1976), rehearing denied 542 F.2d 1174 (5th Cir.1976). Cf. Loving v. Ponderosa Systems, Inc., ___ Ind.App. ___, 444 N.E.2d 896 (1983).

3. Id.

At least in the absence of mortgage provisions to the contrary,[4] it would seem that in the modern standard mortgage policy context where the mortgage is not in default, the mortgagor normally should be able, where rebuilding is practical, to insist upon the application of the insurance proceeds to rebuild the premises. To be sure, to permit the mortgagor to defeat the mortgagee's right of recovery by rebuilding may force the mortgagee to litigate the extent and sufficiency of the repairs.[5] On the other hand, it is almost always the mortgagor who is paying the premiums on the casualty insurance policy. Moreover, while permitting the mortgagee to utilize the insurance proceeds to pay the mortgage debt presumably benefits the mortgagor by rendering the property free from the mortgage lien to the extent of the loss, in many cases the mortgagor probably cannot afford to rebuild or is unable to obtain new mortgage financing for that purpose. Thus, on balance, it would seem more equitable in most cases to permit the mortgagor to rebuild and have the insurance applied to that purpose. Indeed, there is growing support for this point of view.[6]

Interestingly, a California decision[7] endorsed a presumption in favor of using insurance proceeds to rebuild even where the documents specifically gave the mortgagee the option to apply the proceeds to the debt. There, after a fire loss, the mortgagee refused to permit the mortgagor to utilize the insurance proceeds to rebuild and instead insisted on their application to the indebtedness. The mortgagors could not afford to continue to make mortgage payments and pay rent on an apartment. As a result they defaulted on the mortgage debt and foreclosure ensued. The mortgagors then sued the mortgagee for damages. The Court of Appeals held that "the right of a beneficiary to apply insurance proceeds to the balance of a note secured by a deed of trust must be performed in good faith and with fair dealing and that to the extent that the security is not impaired the beneficiary must permit those proceeds to be used for the cost of rebuilding.[8]

Where the loss occurs after the mortgage is either already in default or has matured, the equities probably favor the mortgagee. At that stage, the mortgagee, after all, has the immediate right to receive the mortgage debt and could foreclose to enforce that right. Moreover, by defaulting, the mortgagor arguably has created enough uncertainty

---

4. See e.g., First Federal Savings and Loan Association v. Stone, ___ Ind.App. ___, 467 N.E.2d 1226 (1984).

5. "Must the mortgagee litigate the extent and sufficiency of the repairs, or, if partially repaired, is his insurance to be reduced in proportion?" Savarese v. Ohio Farmers' Insurance Co., supra note 2 at 55, 182 N.E. at 668.

6. See e.g., Schoolcraft v. Ross, 81 Cal. App.3d 75, 146 Cal.Rptr. 57 (1978); Cottman Co. v. Continental Trust Co., 169 Md. 595, 182 A. 551 (1936); Starkman v.

Sigmond, 184 N.J.Super. 600, 446 A.2d 1249 (1982).

7. Schoolcraft v. Ross, 81 Cal.App.3d 75, 146 Cal.Rptr. 57 (1978).

8. Id. at 77, 146 Cal.Rptr. at 58. But see Giberson v. First Federal Savings and Loan Association of Waterloo, 329 N.W.2d 9 (Iowa 1983) (where clause allowed proceeds to be used for rebuilding "when authorized by the mortgagee," court refused to give summary judgment for mortgagors who sought the funds for rebuilding without the mortgagee's consent).

for the mortgagee to raise doubts as to the wisdom of continuing the mortgage relationship. Under these circumstances, allowing the mortgagee to apply the insurance proceeds to the mortgage debt may obviate the necessity for foreclosure proceedings.

 WESTLAW REFERENCES
rebuild*** reconstruct*** repair*** restor! /p mortgag** /p insura! insure*

§ 4.16 Insurance—Effect of Foreclosure Purchase By Mortgagee

Suppose that a mortgagee, either before or after a casualty loss, purchases the mortgaged premises at a foreclosure sale by bidding in the full amount of the debt. Where the insurance policy protecting the mortgagor and mortgagee is a loss payable type, the cases generally refuse to permit the mortgagee to collect on the policy.[1] Under the loss payable type policy, as we have noted, only the mortgagor's interest technically is insured, the mortgagee merely being an appointee to collect the proceeds. When the mortgagee bids in the full amount of the debt, the debt is extinguished and the mortgagee's interest in the policy is terminated.[2]

When the commonly used standard mortgage policy is in force, however, the mortgagee's rights to insurance proceeds depends largely on when the loss occurred. If the loss occurs after a foreclosure purchase by the mortgagee for the amount of the debt, courts permit the mortgagee to recover.[3] The reasoning of these decisions has been based on several factors. First, the cases emphasize that the standard mortgage policy creates an independent insurance contract between the mortgagee and the insurer.[4] Moreover, they note that the standard mortgage policy, unlike the loss payable type policy, which refers only to a property interest in the mortgagor, protects the mortgagee's interest in the property.[5] Finally, these courts have noted that "a change in status from mortgagee to owner through foreclosure and

---

§ 4.16

1. See Reynolds v. London & Lancashire Fire Insurance Co., 128 Cal. 16, 60 P. 467 (1900); Power Building & Loan Association v. Ajax Fire Insurance Co., 110 N.J.L. 256, 164 A. 410 (1933); Comment, Foreclosure, Loss, And The Proper Distribution Of Insurance Proceeds Under Open And Standard Mortgage Clauses: Some Observations, 7 Valparaiso L.Rev. 485, 490 (1973). Annot., 19 A.L.R. 44, 778, 788 (1983).

2. Comment, supra note 1 at 490.

3. Guardian Savings & Loan Association v. Reserve Insurance Co., 2 Ill.App.3d 77, 276 N.E.2d 109 (1971); Shores v. Rabon, 251 N.C. 790, 112 S.E.2d 556 (1960); 495

Corp. v. New Jersey Insurance Underwriting Association, 86 N.J. 159, 430 A.2d 203 (1981). See generally Annot., 19 A.L.R. 4th 778; 783–788 (1983). Moreover, mortgagees have been successful even where the loss occurred after a foreclosure bid, but prior to the expiration of a ten day upset bid period. See Tech Land Development, Inc. v. South Carolina Insurance Co., 57 N.C.App. 566, 291 S.E.2d 821 (1982), review denied 306 N.C. 563, 294 S.E.2d 228 (1982).

4. See, e.g., Shores v. Rabon, 251 N.C. 790, 112 S.E.2d 556 (1960).

5. See Comment, supra note 1 at 494.

purchase does not defeat the mortgagee-owner's right to the insurance proceeds because the provisions of the standard mortgage clause are designed to accommodate such change in status." [6]

When, however, the foreclosure purchase for the amount of the debt follows the loss, courts uniformly deny the mortgagee-purchaser recovery of the insurance proceeds.[7] A variety of reasons for this result have been advanced. One court, for example, believed that the independent contract of insurance under the standard mortgage policy was of limited scope and that the mortgagee's interest was based upon the mortgage debt rather than the mortgaged property.[8] Other courts have emphasized that the value of the property to the mortgagee was presumably reflected by his bid and that the recovery of the insurance proceeds in addition to his purchase for the full debt would be inequitable and result in double recovery for the mortgagee.[9] According to one court, this no-recovery rule was fair and practical because no one "disputes that the mortgagee is entitled to recover only his debt. Any surplus value belongs to others, namely the mortgagor or subsequent lienors. Indeed, it is not conceivable that the mortgagee could recover a deficiency judgment against the mortgagor if it had bid in the full amount of the debt at foreclosure sale. To allow the mortgagee, after effectively cutting off or discouraging lower bidders, to take the property and then establish that it was worth less than the bid encourages fraud, creates uncertainty as to the mortgagor's rights, and most unfairly deprives the sale of what ever leaven comes from other bidders.[10]

The time of loss distinction utilized in standard policy cases is probably reasonable. In the loss after foreclosure sale situation, it is unlikely that the bid is influenced by the possibility of a loss and insurance recovery. On the other hand, in the loss-purchase situation, as the court in the preceding paragraph pointed out, a mortgagee presumably could bid in the amount of the debt on the damaged premises intending to discourage lower bidders and, ultimately, to collect the insurance proceeds as well. To be sure, in view of the common practice for mortgagees to bid in the amount of the mortgage debt, the full debt bid in the loss-purchase situation may simply be the result of mere inadvertence. However, the prudent mortgagee in this situation can protect himself by bidding what the property is actually worth. If a third party bids more than the debt, the mortgagee will be

---

6. Id. at 494.

7. See e.g., Smith v. General Mortgage Corp., 402 Mich. 125, 261 N.W.2d 710 (1978); Northwestern National Insurance Co. v. Mildenberger, 359 S.W.2d 380 (Mo. App.1962); Rosenbaum v. Funcannon, 308 F.2d 680 (9th Cir.1962); Whitestone Savings & Loan Association v. Allstate Insurance Co., 28 N.Y.2d 332, 321 N.Y.S.2d 862, 270 N.E.2d 694 (1971).

8. Northwestern Insurance Co. v. Mildenberger, 359 S.W.2d 380 (Mo.App. 1962).

9. See Rosenbaum v. Funcannon, 308 F.2d 680 (9th Cir.1962); Whitestone Savings & Loan Association v. Allstate Insurance Co., 28 N.Y.2d 332, 321 N.Y.S.2d 862, 270 N.E.2d 694 (1971).

10. Whitestone Savings & Loan Association v. Allstate Insurance Co., 28 N.Y.2d at 336, 270 N.E.2d at 697 (1971).

made whole by the sale proceeds. On the other hand, if the mortgagee or the third party purchases for less than the debt, the mortgagee can normally obtain a deficiency judgment and have it satisfied out of the insurance proceeds.[11]

WESTLAW REFERENCES

foreclos*** /6 bought buy*** purchas*** /s mortgagee /p insura! insure*

D. ESCROWS OR RESERVES FOR TAXES AND INSURANCE

§ 4.17 Escrow Accounts—Some General Considerations

As we have seen, mortgagees are understandably insistent that mortgagors carry casualty insurance on the mortgaged real estate and that insurance premiums be paid promptly. Insurance, of course, provides protection against the partial or complete destruction of the mortgage security. Mortgagees, moreover, have special concern as to real estate taxes and assessments because, as Professor Durfee once aptly pointed out, "in most tax systems * * * the burden of the ordinary tax on land and the burden of special assessments for local improvements rests on both mortgagor and mortgagee in the sense that unless these charges are satisfied by someone before the axe falls the interest of both parties will be rubbed out. The state goes after the land and its claim overrides *all* prior interests whatever their character."[1] In other words, a "first" mortgage on real estate will be eliminated by a sale under a subsequently arising real estate tax lien. Thus, mortgagees are extremely cautious to protect their security and generally utilize mortgage clauses specifically imposing the duty to pay taxes on the mortgagor and making failure to pay a cause for acceleration of the mortgage debt.

An important additional protection device for the mortgagee today is the "escrow" procedure. Contemporary lending institutions commonly require that one-twelfth of estimated annual taxes and casualty insurance premiums be paid monthly together with the usual payment of principal and interest.[2] Such payments are usually credited to an account variously known as an "escrow," "reserve," or "impound" account. These accounts became widespread after the depression experience of the 1930's when substantial numbers of mortgagors lost their homes, and mortgagees some of their mortgage security, because of real

---

11. See Builders Affiliates, Inc. v. North River Insurance Co., 91 A.D.2d 360, 459 N.Y.S.2d 41, 43 (1983); Whitestone Savings v. Allstate Insurance Co., 28 N.Y.2d 332, 335, 321 N.Y.S.2d 862, 865, 270 N.E.2d 694, 697 (1971).

§ 4.17

1. Durfee, Cases on Security, 136 (1951).

2. Comment, Trusts: Requiring Mortgage Loan Escrow Holders to Account for Profits Earned on Tax and Insurance Prepayments, 28 Okl.L.Rev. 213, 213 (1975).

estate foreclosures.[3]   As a result, lending institutions adopted the escrow or impound requirement on the theory that mortgagors would have less difficulty paying monthly installments than a year-end lump sum tax payment.   This practice was accelerated because the Federal Housing Administration (FHA) made such escrow accounts mandatory for all loans it insured.[4]

While lending institutions do not require an escrow or impound account for all mortgagors, it is common practice as to most conventional loans which exceed 80% of value, and is currently required with respect to loans insured by the FHA.[5]   The Veterans Administration (VA) encourages the practice as to VA guaranteed loans [6] and requires it as to its direct loans.[7]   The Federal Home Loan Bank Board (FHLBB), which regulates all federally chartered savings and loan associations, authorizes such associations to escrow taxes and insurance,[8] and requires them to do so where the loan to value ratio exceeds 80%.[9]

There are three types of escrow procedures utilized by lending institutions today.[10]   First, a few mortgagees deposit escrow funds in a special savings account from which the mortgagee may withdraw to pay taxes and insurance premiums.[11]   The mortgagor, under this method, receives the prevailing savings account interest rate on the impounded funds.   Second is the capitalization method.   "Under this system, all payments, when received, are applied to decrease principal of the loan.   When payments * * * are made by the [mortgagee], the outstanding balance is accordingly increased." [12]   The net effect is that the mortgagor receives a return on the escrowed funds equal to the interest rate he is paying on the mortgage debt.   Since the latter rate is almost always higher than savings account interest rates, the capitalization method is highly advantageous from the mortgagor's perspective.   The third and most widespread method, however, is "to deposit escrow payments in noninterest bearing accounts which allow the lender to comingle funds with his own." [13]   Any income earned from these funds is retained by the mortgagee.

Because of its failure to pay mortgagors any interest return on escrow accounts, controversy over this last method has been substantial in recent years.   This has resulted in considerable litigation and some

3. Comment, The Attack Upon the Tax and Insurance Escrow Accounts in Mortgages, 47 Temp.L.Q. 352, 352 (1974).

4. Comment, Trusts: Requiring Mortgage Loan Escrow Holders to Account for Profits Earned on Tax and Insurance Prepayments, 28 Okl.L.Rev. 213, 213 (1975).

5. 24 CFR 203.23.

6. See V.A. Lender's Handbook § 4150 (1969).

7. 38 CFR 36.4512.

8. 12 CFR 545.6–11(b).

9. 12 CFR 545.6–1(4)(iii).

10. Comment, Payment of Interest on Mortgage Escrow Accounts, 23 Syracuse L.Rev. 845, 849 (1972).

11. Id. at 849.

12. Buchanan v. Brentwood Federal Savings and Loan Association, 457 Pa. 135, 142, 320 A.2d 117, 122 (1974).

13. Comment, Payment of Interest on Mortgage Escrow Accounts, 23 Syracuse L.Rev. 845, 850 (1972).

significant legislative response. The following material considers the major judicial theories of attack utilized thus far and some of the important legislative and regulatory impact on the problem.

 WESTLAW REFERENCES
di escrow account

§ 4.18 Judicial Scrutiny of Escrow Accounts

Several theories have been advanced to justify compelling mortgagees to account for escrow account profits. However, after a few notably successful judicial challenges during the mid-1970's, more recent attacks on mortgagee escrow practices have proved increasingly ineffective. This section focuses on the more important avenues of attack and their treatment by the courts.

The Express Trust Theory

The most common theory utilized in challenging noninterest-bearing escrow arrangements is based on breach of an express trust.[1] The most important early case to utilize this theory was Carpenter v. Suffolk Franklin Savings Bank [2] (*Carpenter I*), in which the Massachusetts Supreme Court determined that the mortgagor's complaint stated a cause of action in trust. The court chose as a standard the following language: "Where the mortgagor pays funds to a bank with an expressed purpose that the funds shall be used for a particular purpose, then the funds may be deemed to be held in trust * * *. We think it is clear from the bill that the tax payments were designated by the mortgagors for a specific purpose, namely, to pay real estate taxes." [3] The Massachusetts Supreme Court did not have the actual written instruments before it, but relied on what the parties pleaded as the legal effect of the documents. In Buchanan v. Brentwood Federal Savings & Loan Association,[4] the Pennsylvania Supreme Court had the written documents before it and reached a result similar to *Carpenter I* on the express trust issue. The court concluded that the mortgagors had alleged sufficient facts, together with the instruments, to afford them the opportunity to prove their claim that funds were paid to the mortgagee with the expressed purpose that they be used for tax payments.

Carpenter II [5] undid much of what *Carpenter I* created. When *Carpenter I* was returned to the trial court, the trial judge concluded that there was no manifestation of intention to create a trust on the part of either of the parties. The court noted that the written agreements were silent as to investment of the payments, as to profits

§ 4.18

1. Note, Tax and Insurance Escrow Accounts in Mortgages—The Attack Presses On, 41 Mo.L.Rev. 133, 133–34 (1976).

2. 362 Mass. 770, 291 N.E.2d 609 (1973).

3. Id. at 778, 291 N.E.2d 614.

4. 457 Pa. 135, 320 A.2d 117 (1974).

5. Carpenter v. Suffolk Franklin Savings Bank, 370 Mass. 314, 346 N.E.2d 892 (1976).

thereon, and as to intention to create a trust. The trial court also determined that the agreements established contractual relationships and not trusts and that the payments constituted general deposits for a special purpose, creating a debtor-creditor relationship, rather than special deposits creating a fiduciary situation. In *Carpenter II*, the Supreme Court of Massachusetts upheld the trial court as not being clearly erroneous. The court emphasized "the general understanding and practice in Massachusetts" over a forty year period that "the bank has the right to treat the tax payments as its own." [6] Thus, any attempt to establish a contrary arrangement required "a clear understanding to that effect" which mortgagors failed to establish.[7]

Other attempts to utilize the express trust theory have been notably unsuccessful.[8] These decisions emphasize the difficulty of establishing the express trust relationship. The Supreme Court of Illinois, for example, held that in the absence of express language by which a mortgagor retains an interest in the escrowed funds, and in view of the common practice for savings and loan associations to commingle escrowed funds with its other funds, there was insufficient evidence to create an express trust.[9] Another court [10] rejected the argument that the escrow payments are "deposits made for a special purpose" giving rise to a trust. While the court conceded that the escrow payments were "earmarked for a separate purpose," there was no indication that the funds "were to be kept separate . . . or that the [lenders] were to be precluded from using them in the regular course of business." [11] Moreover, one federal court [12] emphasized that even where, under the terms of agreement, the mortgagor paid the tax payment to the mortgagee "in trust," an express trust was not created. "[D]espite the scattered use of the words 'trust' and 'trustee' and the phrase 'in trust' the mortgagors do not transform a traditional debtor-creditor relationship into a fiduciary [one]." [13] Even where a court

---

6. Id. at 900.

7. Id.

8. See Judd v. First Federal Savings and Loan Association, 710 F.2d 1237 (7th Cir.1983); American National Bank & Trust of New Jersey, 166 N.J.Super. 216, 399 A.2d 663 (1979); Kronisch v. Howard Savings Institute, 161 N.J.Super. 592, 392 A.2d 178 (1978); Brooks v. Valley National Bank, 113 Ariz. 169, 548 P.2d 1166 (1976); Marsh v. Home Federal Savings & Loan Association, 66 Cal.App.3d 674, 136 Cal. Rptr. 180 (1977); Tucker v. Pulaski Federal Savings & Loan Association, 252 Ark. 849, 481 S.W.2d 725 (1972); Lathrop v. Bell Federal Savings & Loan Association, 42 Ill. App.3d 183, 355 N.E.2d 667 (1976); Surrey Strathmore Corp. v. Dollar Savings Bank, 36 N.Y.2d 173, 366 N.Y.S.2d 107, 325 N.E.2d 527 (1975); Richman v. Security Savings & Loan Association, 57 Wis.2d 358, 204 N.W.2d 511 (1973). But see, Abrams v.

Crocker-Citizens National Bank, 41 Cal. App.3d 55, 114 Cal.Rptr. 913 (1974). Cf., Buchanan v. Century Federal Savings & Loan Association, 306 Pa.Super. 253, 452 A.2d 540 (1982) (summary judgment for mortgagors improper where mortgagee sought to show a debtor-creditor relationship rather than a trust).

9. La Throp v. Bell Federal Savings & Loan Association, 68 Ill.2d 375, 12 Ill.Dec. 565, 370 N.E.2d 188 (1977), certiorari denied 436 U.S. 925, 98 S.Ct. 2818, 56 L.Ed.2d 768 (1978).

10. Kronisch v. Howard Savings Institute, 161 N.J.Super. 592, 392 A.2d 178 (1978).

11. Id. at 184.

12. Judd v. First Federal Savings and Loan Association, 710 F.2d 1237 (7th Cir. 1983).

13. Id. at 1239.

recognizes an express trust relationship, the mortgagor may nevertheless come up empty-handed. In a California appellate decision,[14] the court determined that the agreement of the mortgagee to pay taxes and insurance from the tax impound account, and the fact that the impound account was substantial, indicated a fiduciary situation rather than an ordinary deposit relationship. However, because the agreement between the parties expressly authorized commingling of the impounded funds with others of the mortgagee and provided that "no interest would be payable," the court felt compelled to deny a claim for interest, notwithstanding the presence of a trust relationship.

Not only are courts becoming more unwilling to find an express trust where the documents are ambiguous, but the express trust theory has become increasingly vulnerable to redrafted escrow and impound agreements which expressly negate a trust relationship.[15] Moreover, even if the agreement creates a trust relationship, the inclusion of "no interest" and "commingling permission" language will probably mean no recovery for a mortgagor. In this connection, it should be noted that the mortgage form utilized by those lending institutions that sell their loans on the secondary market to the Federal National Mortgage Association (FNMA) or the Federal Home Loan Mortgage Corporation (FHLMC), specifically provides that absent a contrary agreement, the "lender shall not be required to pay borrower any interest on the funds."[16]

Constructive Trust Theory

The *Buchanan* court is the only appellate court thus far to endorse constructive trust as well as express trust theories. Unlike an express trust, a constructive trust is not the creature of an express agreement or the intention of the parties, but is remedial in nature and is utilized to prevent the unjust enrichment of one person at the expense of another.[17] In this connection, *Buchanan* approved three possible constructive trust theories.

First, it was argued in *Buchanan* that a confidential relationship arose between the mortgagors and the mortgagee. The mortgagors claimed that the mortgagee's retention of profits from the escrow account had breached this confidential relationship. The court stated that "the existence, if proved, of a confidential relationship is sufficient justification for imposing a constructive trust, unless the dominating party can prove by clear and satisfactory evidence that the contract was not tainted by his overweening bargaining position."[18]

---

14. Marsh v. Home Federal Savings & Loan Association, 66 Cal.App.3d 674, 136 Cal.Rptr. 180 (1977).

15. Comment, Tax and Insurance Escrow Accounts in Mortgages—The Attack Presses On, 41 Mo.L.Rev. 133, 138 (1976).

16. FNMA/FHLMC Uniform Deed of Trust, 1 to 4 Family, par. 2.

17. Comment, note 1 supra at 136–137.

18. Buchanan v. Brentwood Savings and Loan Association, 457 Pa. 135, 143, 320 A.2d 117, 123 (1974), appeal after remand 306 Pa.Super. 253, 452 A.2d 540 (1982).

The *Buchanan* mortgagors also advanced a constructive trust-agency argument based on the alleged agency relationship between the mortgagors and the mortgagee. Under this theory, if an agent uses the principal's money without authority to his own advantage, a constructive trust may be an appropriate remedy. The court concluded that the mortgagors could prevail on this theory if they could prove on remand that the mortgage agreement envisaged an agency relationship.[19]

Finally, the mortgagors claimed that unjust enrichment was a proper basis for the imposition of a constructive trust. The court noted that a constructive trust is appropriate "whenever justice and fair dealing warrant it."[20] Accordingly, the court concluded that the mortgagors were to be given a chance to offer evidence to convince the "conscience of equity" that the mortgagee would be unjustly enriched if it were allowed to retain the profits on the escrowed funds.

Stating valid constructive trust claims and proving them are two significantly different matters. Moreover, while some courts recognize the possibility of proving a constructive trust theory in the escrow context,[21] others seem almost as a matter of law to reject the theory in the usual escrow situation.[22] For example, the trial judge in *Carpenter II* found no basis for the imposition of a constructive trust and the Massachusetts Supreme Court affirmed. While the supreme court admitted that the escrow agreements were "contracts of adhesion," they were not "unconscionable in aspects here in issue."[23] Nor did the supreme court believe that there was the unjust enrichment necessary for constructive trust. According to the court, "most of the unjust enrichment, if any, enriched the bank's depositors at the time."[24] Moreover, because the legislature had acted to require mortgagees to pay interest on escrow accounts at "a rate and in a manner to be determined by the mortgagee,"[25] the court noted that even the legislature was not prepared to say how much enrichment was too much; the court was unwilling to go further. Another court stressed that a constructive trust "is predicated upon a finding that one party has taken unconscionable advantage over another."[26] Consequently, "there must be clear proof of some wrongful act, such as fraud, undue influence or breach of a confidential relationship . . . " Such proof was "entirely wanting."[27] The Arizona Supreme Court, emphasized

---

19. Id. at 144, 320 A.2d at 124.

20. Id. at 145, 320 A.2d at 125. For a decision that seems to adopt such a rationale, see Derenco, Inc. v. Benjamin Franklin Federal Savings & Loan Ass'n, 281 Or. 533, 577 P.2d 477, 491 (1978), certiorari denied 439 U.S. 1051, 99 S.Ct. 733, 58 L.Ed. 2d 712 (1978).

21. See, e.g., Carpenter v. Suffolk Franklin Savings Bank, 370 Mass. 314, 346 N.E.2d 892 (1976).

22. See e.g., Brooks v. Valley National Bank, 113 Ariz. 169, 548 P.2d 1166 (1976);

La Throp v. Bell Federal Savings and Loan Association, 68 Ill.2d 375, 12 Ill.Dec. 565, 370 N.E.2d 188 (1977).

23. Carpenter v. Suffolk Franklin Savings Bank, 346 N.E.2d 892, 900 (Mass. 1976).

24. Id. at 346 N.E.2d 900.

25. Mass.Gen.Laws Ann. c. 183, § 61.

26. Kronisch v. Howard Savings Institute, 161 N.J.Super. 592, 600, 392 A.2d 178, 184 (1978).

27. Id.

freedom of contract: "The absence of a provision to pay interest on the impoundment funds is equivalent to an agreement that it should not be paid. A person is not entitled to compensation on the grounds of unjust enrichment if he receives from the other that which was agreed between them the other should give in return." [28]

Miscellaneous Theories

Noninterest bearing escrow accounts have also been attacked on a resulting trust theory. Unlike an express trust, which is created by a settlor's external expression of intention, "a resulting trust exists if the circumstances show an absence of intention on the part of a transferor to give the beneficial interest in property to one who has received legal title." [29] The closest analogy in the escrow area is the purchase-money resulting trust, in which property is purchased with A's funds, but legal title is taken in B. A presumption of trust in favor of A is created.[30] More particularly in point are "those purchase-money resulting trust cases in which two parties are intended to have a beneficial interest in the property, but where one party takes more than his intended share." [31] In the escrow situation, the mortgagor and mortgagee each intend to have an interest in the escrow funds. It could be argued that the mortgagee is intended to have an interest in the escrow payments sufficient to protect his mortgage security and that any other beneficial interest in the escrow payments belongs to the mortgagor.[32] Accordingly, where a mortgagee takes a profit in the form of interest from the escrow funds, he arguably is taking more than he was intended to have and, thus, a resulting trust should be imposed on those profits.[33] In *Carpenter II,* the only reported case in which this theory was advanced, however, the court tersely rejected the resulting trust theory. "The [trial] judge ruled that neither the nature of the transaction between the [mortgagors] and [mortgagee] nor their relationship now calls for the imposition of a resulting trust. We agree substantially for the same reasons that we uphold his finding that there was no express trust." [34] Moreover, since a purchase-money resulting trust is grounded on the presumed intent of the settlor, it would seem that future mortgage forms could obviate the purchase-money resulting trust argument by expressly providing that the mortgagee shall be entitled to have the beneficial interest in the profits from the escrow payments.

In Madsen v. Prudential Federal Savings & Loan Association,[35] a Utah Supreme Court decision, the mortgagors were successful in utiliz-

28. Brooks v. Valley National Bank, 113 Ariz. 169, 176, 548 P.2d 1166, 1171 (1976).

29. Comment, supra note 1 at 136.

30. See Nelson, Purchase-Money Resulting Trusts in Missouri, 33 Mo.L.Rev. 552 (1968).

31. Comment, Lender Accountability and the Problem of Noninterest-Bearing Mortgage Escrow Accounts, 54 B.U.L.Rev. 516, 527 (1974).

32. Id. at 527.

33. Id. at 527.

34. Carpenter v. Suffolk Franklin Savings Bank, 346 N.E.2d 892, 900 (Mass. 1976).

35. 558 P.2d 1337 (Utah 1977).

ing a pledge theory, a concept that had not previously been advanced to attack noninterest bearing escrow procedures. The deed of trust in *Madsen* provided for the usual monthly payments of one-twelfth of estimated annual taxes and insurance premiums, but further provided that "said *budget payments are hereby pledged to the beneficiary as additional security for the full performance of this deed of trust and the note secured hereby.*" [36] The mortgagors argued that the monthly escrow payments constituted a pledge and that the pledgee was liable to account to the pledgor for profits earned from the pledged property. The trial judge granted the mortgagee a summary judgment, ruling that the funds were not pledged property. The Utah Supreme Court reversed and held that the granting of the summary judgment in favor of the mortgagee was erroneous. The court determined that a deposit of money as security for the performance of a contract can be a valid pledge. Moreover, the court found that the deed of trust agreement established the essential elements of a pledge. In this connection, the court emphasized the existence of a debt and a transfer of property to the pledgee to be held as security and, if necessary, to be used to assure performance of the obligation. Moreover, the court noted that the mortgagee had the discretion to withdraw funds for taxes, insurance premiums or for *any* sum due under the deed of trust or note. The court then cited Section 9–207 of the Uniform Commercial Code (UCC) for the proposition that when collateral is in the secured party's possession, unless otherwise agreed,

> "The secured party may hold as additional security any increase or profits (except money) received from the collateral, but money so received, unless remitted to the debtor, shall be applied in reduction of the secured obligation; * * *." [37]

The opinion is somewhat ambiguous, and could reasonably be read either as holding that the pledge relationship had already been established or that mortgagors had simply properly pleaded a pledge theory and that proof of the pledge relationship was still necessary. However, on remand, the trial court placed the former interpretation on the case and stated that "if there is any 'law of the case' established by the decision of [the Utah Supreme Court] as contended by [mortgagors], it is that the [escrow payments] constitute 'pledged' property under the law and are to be so treated in the proceedings that must follow." [38] According to the trial court, the only further issue to be resolved was whether "profits" existed on the escrow accounts; if so, accounting of them to the mortgagors would be required.[39]

Although the Utah pledge theory is unique, there is some doubt whether it can have substantial impact elsewhere. First, the court emphasized the use of the "pledge" language in the deed of trust,

36. Id. at 1338.

37. Utah Code Ann. 1953, 70A–9–207(2).

38. Madsen v. Prudential Federal Savings & Loan Association, Memo Decision 3 (Dist.Ct., 3rd Dist.Utah 1977).

39. Id. at 3.

language that is probably not commonly used in other jurisdictions. In any event, just as other courts have rejected an express trust theory even where the words "in trust" are used in the mortgage instrument,[40] so also could another court hold that "pledge" language alone is not significant enough to create a pledge transaction. Finally, mortgagees in Utah and elsewhere will probably delete the pledge language and attempt to negate the pledge by doing what the UCC permits, namely, having the parties specifically agree that the profits from any "pledge"-escrow arrangement are for the benefit of the pledgee-mortgagee.

 WESTLAW REFERENCES

digest(153 +p mortgag**))

digest(266 +p escrow (impound reserve /4 account))

The Express Trust Theory

fiduciary interest (express /s trust) /p escrow (impound reserve
    /4 account) /p bank institution savings /p mortgag**

The Constructive Trust Theory

escrow (impound! reserve* /4 account fund) /56 bank institution
    savings /p mortgag** /p (constructive /5 trust) "unjust!
    enrich!"

sh 320 a2d 117

Miscellaneous Theories

No Queries

§ 4.19 Statutory and Related Regulation

Numerous unsuccessful attacks have been made on noninterest paying escrow arrangements under the Federal Truth in Lending Act.[1] Even though the Act specifically exempts escrow charges for insurance and taxes from disclosure as finance charges,[2] mortgagors frequently allege that interest on the impound or escrow accounts constitutes a "finance charge separately paid" and that failure by the mortgagee to disclose interest earned on such accounts violates the act.[3] In addition, mortgagors argue that the impounds or escrows are "required deposit balances" as to which disclosure under the Act is required.[4] However, courts have uniformly held that the impounds or interest thereon cannot be construed as a "finance charge separately paid" and that escrow and impound accounts are an exception to the concept of "required deposit balances."[5] In short, interest earned on escrow accounts seems to be exempt from the reporting requirements of the Act.[6]

40. See Brooks v. Valley National Bank, 113 Ariz. 169, 548 P.2d 1166 (1976); Judd v. First Federal Savings and Loan Association, 710 F.2d 1237 (7th Cir.1983).

§ 4.19

1. 15 U.S.C.A. §§ 1601–1665.

2. 15 U.S.C.A. § 1605(e)(3). See 12 CFR 226.4(e).

3. See Moore v. Great Western Savings and Loan Association, 513 F.2d 688 (9th Cir.1975).

4. Id.

5. Id.

6. See Stavrides v. Mellon National Bank and Trust Co., 487 F.2d 953 (3rd Cir. 1973); Moore v. Great Western Savings

Several states have enacted legislation regulating escrow accounts and generally requiring the mortgagees to pay interest to the mortgagors on escrowed funds.[7] The legislation varies considerably from state to state. In California, for example, mortgagees of single family, owner-occupied dwellings are prohibited from requiring, as a condition of their loans, an impound for taxes and insurance premiums except where such an impound is required by federal or state regulatory authorities, where the loan is made, guaranteed, or insured by a state or federal lending or insuring agency, where the mortgagor has previously defaulted on the payment of taxes, or where the original mortgage loan is for 90% or more of the sale price or appraised value of the mortgaged property.[8] Where impounds are used and authorized as to one to four family residences, the mortgagee must pay the borrower interest on the impound at the rate of at least 2% per annum.[9] Under the New York statute, the mortgagee is prohibited, as to one to six family owner-occupied residences, from charging a service fee for maintaining escrow accounts as to any loans after the effective date of the law, and mortgage lending institutions must pay interest on escrow accounts (except as to those mortgages existing prior to the date of the legislation which expressly provided for no payment of interest) at the rate of 2% or such rate established by the New York Banking Board, whichever is higher.[10] Minnesota, as to one to four family owner-occupied dwellings, prohibits the imposition of a service fee for escrow services and requires the payment of interest at the rate of 5% or such rate set by the state Commerce Commission, whichever is higher.[11] Massachusetts legislation requires the payment of interest on escrow accounts with respect to mortgage loans on one to four family owner-occupied households, but leaves the amount and manner of payment up to the mortgagee; a mortgagee can obtain from the Commissioner of Banks an exemption from the payment of interest during a particular year if that mortgagee can show that it lost money on escrow fund

and Loan Association, 513 F.2d 688 (9th Cir.1975); Umdenstock v. American Mortgage & Investment Co. of Oklahoma City, 495 F.2d 589 (10th Cir.1974); Foster v. Maryland State Savings and Loan Association, 369 F.Supp. 843 (D.D.C.1974); Bass v. Boston Five Cent Savings Bank & Trust Co., 478 F.Supp. 741 (D.Mass.1979); Kinee v. Abraham Lincoln Federal Savings and Loan Association, 365 F.Supp. 975 (E.D.Pa. 1973); Munn v. American General Investment Corp., 364 F.Supp. 110 (S.D.Tex. 1973); Graybeal v. American Savings and Loan Association, 59 F.R.D. 7 (D.D.C.1973); Buchanan v. Brentwood Federal Savings and Loan Association, 457 Pa. 135, 320 A.2d 117 (1974).

7. See West's Ann.Cal.Civ.Code §§ 2954, 2954.8; Conn.Gen.Stat.Ann. § 49–2(a); Mass.Gen.Laws Ann. c. 183, § 61;

Minn.Stat.Ann. § 47.20; N.H.Rev.Stat. Ann. 384:16–c; Neb.Rev.Stat. § 45–105.05–.06; New York—McKinney's Banking Law § 14–b; New York—McKinney's Gen.Obligations Law § 5–601; Or.Rev.Stat. 86.240, 86.245.

8. West's Ann.Cal.Civ.Code § 2954.

9. West's Ann.Cal.Civ.Code § 2954.8. See Marantz, Consumerism Reaches the Sacrosanct Trust Deed, 52 Cal.St.Bar J. 203 (1977).

10. New York—McKinney's Banking Law § 14–b; New York—McKinney's Gen. Obligations Law § 5–601.

11. Minn.Stat.Ann. § 47.20. See also Or.Rev.Stat. 86.240, 86.245 (Lender must pay interest on the escrow account at the bank passbook rate minus ¾ of one per cent, but in no event less than 4%).

investment during that year.[12]   Connecticut simply requires the payment of not less than 2% interest on escrow accounts,[13] while New Hampshire sets the rate at 2% below the rate for regular savings deposits in the mortgagee institution.[14]   Finally, some statutes merely regulate the method and amount of monthly payments into the escrow account, but do not require the payment by the mortgagee of interest on the account.[15]   Finally, others simply impose reporting responsibilities on the mortgagee as well as penalties for failure to make prompt tax payment from escrowed funds.[16]

Constitutional problems have arisen because statutes mandating the payment of interest on escrow accounts generally require the payment of interest after the effective date of the legislation on all mortgage loans in the mortgagee's portfolio, whether they were executed prior to or after the date of the legislation.[17]   The New York legislation was upheld by a three-judge federal court against a broadside attack in Jamaica Savings Bank v. Lefkowitz.[18]   The decision was affirmed without opinion by the United States Supreme Court.[19]   The bank argued that nonpayment of interest on escrow accounts, though not an express provision of prior mortgage contracts, was a term implied in fact that was unconstitutionally impaired by the legislation. The court rejected this contention, stating that the mere absence of a contract provision does not raise the implication of a term implied in fact, and held that since the escrow fund profits were not *specifically* allocated by contracts, the legislature possessed the authority to allocate those profits to "safeguard the vital interests of the people."[20] Further, the court rejected the bank's claim that payment of interest on escrow accounts constituted a "taking" without due process in violation of the Fourteenth Amendment as "not substantial."[21]   Finally, the bank argued that the legislation's distinction between pre-existing mortgage contracts which expressly excluded payment of interest and those which were silent as to such payment, violated the equal protection clause of the Fourteenth Amendment.   However, the court rejected this argument and noted that "where by express language mortgagors were made aware of the possibility of interest, and they expressly waived their rights to it, the legislature was entirely rational in not wishing to confront a potential constitutional problem."[22]

This decision did not deal with a situation in which escrow interest legislation attempts to reach mortgages, executed prior to the legisla-

12.   Mass.Gen.Laws Ann. c. 183, § 61.

13.   Conn.Gen.Stat.Ann. § 49–2(a).

14.   N.H.Rev.Stat.Ann. 384:16–c.

15.   Neb.Rev.Stat. §§ 45–105.05–.06.

16.   Mich.Comp.Laws Ann. §§ 565.161-163.

17.   See e.g., Conn.Gen.Stat.Ann. § 49–2(a);   Minn.Stat.Ann. § 47.20;   N.H.Rev. Stat.Ann. 384:16 c;   New York—McKin-ney's Banking Law § 14–b;   New York—McKinney's Gen.Obligations Law § 5–601.

18.   390 F.Supp. 1357 (D.C.E.N.Y.1975).

19.   423 U.S. 802, 96 S.Ct. 10, 46 L.Ed.2d 23 (1975).

20.   390 F.Supp. at 1362.   See Note, 11 Tulsa L.J. 124, 126 (1975).

21.   Id. at 1363.

22.   Id. at 1362.

tion, which by express language provide for no payment of interest on escrow funds. To be sure, the majority of older mortgages are probably silent as to payment of interest on escrow accounts. However, the FNMA and the FHLMC forms expressly negate the payment of escrow interest unless there is an express agreement to the contrary.[23] Thus, to the extent that there are pre-legislation mortgages outstanding using such forms, the constitutional argument based on impairment of contractual obligation would be stronger. Nevertheless, even in this situation it could be argued that the express contractual provision waiving any right to escrow account interest should be considered a year-to-year contract to correspond to its purpose of meeting annual tax and insurance requirements. Thus, any legislation arguably would impair no "existing" contracts because the previous years' contracts would have expired prior to the effective date of the legislation. Moreover, even actual impairment of existing contracts may be deemed to be reasonable and hence valid where an important enough state interest justifies the impairment.[24] In this regard, it could be argued that a legislature properly can conclude that because mortgagees possess an overwhelming bargaining position, such mortgage agreements were in all probability not bargained for. Thus, it would arguably be proper for a state legislature to exercise its power to correct an imbalance in the bargaining relationship.

While legislation has occasionally been introduced in Congress,[25] there is currently no federal law or regulation requiring mortgagees to pay interest on escrow accounts.[26] Indeed, as noted earlier, much of the federal or quasi-federal regulation in this area is aimed at encouraging or requiring the establishment of escrow accounts. The Federal Home Loan Bank Board, for example, requires federally-chartered savings and loan associations to pay interest on escrow accounts only if the loan is on an owner-occupied single family dwelling, was executed after June 15, 1975 and state law requires such payment.[27] Moreover, to the extent that state legislation imposes a more onerous interest payment burden on such federally-chartered institutions, it will be deemed preempted by the foregoing Bank Board regulation.[28]

When a new loan is made, it is usually necessary for the lender to require the mortgagee to make an initial deposit into the escrow account. At a minimum, this deposit must be large enough so that, when added to the amounts which will accumulate through regular monthly payments, it will result in enough money to pay the taxes and

---

23. See text at note 16, supra.

24. See El Paso v. Simmons, 379 U.S. 497, 85 S.Ct. 577, 13 L.Ed.2d 446 (1965), rehearing denied 380 U.S. 926, 85 S.Ct. 879, 13 L.Ed.2d 813 (1965).

25. See Comment, Lender Accountability and the Problem of Noninterest-Bearing Mortgage Escrow Accounts, 54 B.U.L.Rev. 516, 537 (1974).

26. See text at notes 12–15, supra.

27. 12 CFR 545.6–11(b).

28. First Federal Savings and Loan Association of Boston v. Greenwald, 591 F.2d 417 (1st Cir.1979). (Massachusetts statute preempted at least to the extent it requires payment of interest on escrow accounts for other than owner-occupied single family dwellings).

insurance premiums when they fall due. Many lenders prefer to require an initial deposit in a larger amount in order to provide a "cushion" against the possibility that the mortgagor will miss a later payment or that the taxes or insurance premiums will be more than expected. To curb the tendency of some lenders to require excessively large cushions (sometimes as much as a six months' tax and insurance payments), the Real Estate Settlement Procedures Act (RESPA) [29] limits the initial payment into the account to the minimum described above, plus a two-month cushion.[30] RESPA also provides that, after regular monthly payments on the loan have begun, the mortgagor cannot be required to pay more than one-twelfth of the annual taxes and other charges each month, unless a larger payment is needed to make up a deficit in the escrow account or to maintain the two months' cushion referred to above.[31]

 WESTLAW REFERENCES

"truth in lending" (15 +3 1601 1605) /p escrow (impound!
    reserve* /4 account fund) /p mortgag**

legislat*** statut*** /p escrow (impound! reserve* /4 account
    fund) /p mortgag** /p interest

E. RIGHT TO RENTS

§ 4.20 General Considerations

The rights to rents of mortgaged property are largely determined by (1) whether the lease precedes or follows the giving of the mortgage and, (2) as a matter of legal right, whether the particular jurisdiction follows the title or lien theory. The importance of this latter factor is minimized in actual practice, as will be seen later, (a) by agreements which are ordinarily entered into by the parties respecting possession, either permitting the mortgagor to remain in possession in title states [1] or the mortgagee to take possession in lien states; (b) by clauses assigning or pledging the rents; (c) by the appointment of receivers; (d) by the practical inefficacy of remedies by which a mortgagee may enforce his rights to possession against a non-cooperative mortgagor or his tenant; and (e) by the burdens and strictness of the accounting to which a mortgagee in possession is subjected.

When the lease precedes the mortgage it is clear that the tenant's term cannot be affected by the later mortgage.[2] In both title and lien

---

29. 12 U.S.C.A. § 2609.

30. HUD Guide, Settlement Costs, 35 (1976).

31. Id. at 36.

§ 4.20

1. See Tefft, The Myth of Strict Foreclosure, 4 U. of Chi.L.Rev. 574, 582 (1937).

2. American Freehold Land Mortgage Co. v. Turner, 95 Ala. 272, 11 So. 211

(1891). 1 Tiffany, Landlord and Tenant, § 146e. See Anderson, The Mortgagee Looks at the Ground Lease, 10 U. of Fla.L. Rev. 1 (1957); Boshkoff, Financing Construction on Long Term Leasehold Estates, 5 Buffalo L.Rev. 257 (1956). That a mortgagee in possession of the mortgaged premises of a lessee in a lien state is not an assignee of the lease and therefore not liable on a covenant for rent was held in jurisdictions the only interest the mortgagor is capable of mortgaging is reversion. Title to the reversion passes in one case and in the other the mortgagee gets only a lien upon it.[3] This difference is often vital, however, on the matter of the legal right to rents.

 WESTLAW REFERENCES
266k199(1)

§ 4.21 Lease Before Mortgage—Title States

In a title jurisdiction the transfer of the reversion carries with it the right to rent and creates a privity of estate between the mortgagee and the tenant of the mortgagor.[1] In the early law, due to the personal nature of the relation between landlord and tenant, there had to be consent by the tenant to be the tenant of the transferee before the relationship arose.[2] However, this requirement of attornment was dispensed with by the Statute of Anne[3] in England. The same result was reached in this country, either by similar statutes or by decision.[4] The tenant, by a saving provision, is always protected as to rents paid to his original landlord before notice to him of the transfer. Today, therefore, in title jurisdictions, the "mortgagee has by force of the conveyance a right, which he may exercise or not at his pleasure, to demand and recover all rent which becomes due and payable subsequently to the conveyance. To this end he may give notice, whenever he chooses to do so, of this right to the lessee, who will thereupon become bound to pay the rent to him. This liability however is limited to rent becoming due after execution of the deed of conveyance, and does not extend to that which was then already due, or to that which before notice of the conveyance has been paid to the lessor. For rent which is due and payable at the time when the conveyance is made is a mere chose in action; a debt which the lessee owes to the lessor, and which being disconnected from the reversion does not pass to the grantee by a conveyance of it."[5]

Amco Trust, Inc. v. Naylor, 159 Tex. 146, 317 S.W.2d 47 (1958) discussed in 58 Mich. L.Rev. 140 (1959).

3. Burden v. Thayer, 44 Mass. (3 Metc.) 76, 37 Am.Dec. 117 (1841), title state; Metropolitan Life Insurance Co. v. Childs Co., 230 N.Y. 285, 130 N.E. 295, 14 A.L.R. 658 (1921), reargument denied 231 N.Y. 551, 132 N.E. 885 (1921), lien state: "If a lease is prior to a mortgage, a sale under the latter is but a sale of the reversion."

§ 4.21

1. Moss v. Gallimore, 1 Doug. 279 (1779), a decision by Lord Mansfield is the leading authority.

2. See Litt. § 551; Co.Litt. 309a; 2 Sheppard's Touchstone, c. 13, 253–266.

3. 34 Anne, c. 16, §§ 9, 10.

4. 1 Tiffany, Landlord and Tenant, § 146.

5. Coffey v. Hunt, 75 Ala. 236 (1883); Baldwin v. Walker, 21 Conn. 168 (1851); Noble v. Brooks, 224 Mass. 288, 112 N.E. 649 (1916)—accord. But see St. Louis National Bank v. Field, 156 Mo. 306, 56 S.W. 1095 (1900). See also 14 A.L.R. 640 (1921); Russell v. Allen, 84 Mass. (2 Allen) 42 (1861); King v. Housatonic Railroad Co., 45 Conn. 226 (1877); Burden v. Thayer, 44 Mass. (3 Metc.) 76, 37 Am.Dec. 117 (1841)—accord.

As to rents which become due but unpaid after the mortgage but before notice by the mortgagee, it has been argued that the mortgagee should be entitled to them only if he asserts his right to them in connection with a foreclosure action,[6] in which case the mortgagor is in no moral position to object. Otherwise, according to this argument, the mortgagee should be entitled only to rents which are current or of later maturity than the notice.

The rule is otherwise,[7] however, and it seems correct. The mortgagee became entitled as transferee of the reversion to all rents accruing after the mortgage, although if paid to the mortgagor the tenant would be protected and the mortgagor would clearly be entitled to keep them. However, if they have not been paid over there seems no reason why the mortgagee should not be able to assert his right to them even though past due and, if the tenant pays the mortgagor thereafter, he should be liable again, for he is outside the protection of the statute.[8]

The tenant of the mortgagor, where the lease precedes the mortgage, is protected in paying his rent to the mortgagor before notice of the mortgagee's claim to it provided he pays in accordance with the provisions of the lease.[9] But he is not protected when he pays his rent in advance when it is not called for by the lease contract even though he did not know of the mortgage at the time.[10] His privilege to pay, and of the mortgagor to receive, rents is only to do so as they fall due. A fortiori it would be no defense to the tenant if he makes payment in advance of the date due after notice of the mortgage but before demand upon him by the mortgagee.

The foregoing rule is fair. The tenant can bargain for the payment of the rent to be made in any way he wishes at the time he makes the

6. Glenn, Mortgages, § 33.4, citing N.Y. Life Insurance Co. v. Fulton Development Co., 265 N.Y. 348, 193 N.E. 169 (1934), a receivership case in a lien state in which the court said the receiver might collect rents already accrued but not paid to the mortgagor.

7. King v. Housatonic Railway, 45 Conn. 226, 234 (1877), "he [the mortgagee] becomes entitled to all rents accruing after the execution of the mortgage and in arrear and unpaid at the time of the notice, as well as to those which accrue afterwards. But the rents in arrear at the time the mortgage was executed belong to the mortgagor." But cf., New Order Building & Loan Association v. 222 Chancellor Ave., 106 N.J.Eq. 1, 149 A. 525 (1930), receivership case; Stewart v. Fairchild etc., Co., 91 N.J.Eq. 86, 108 A. 301 (1919), receivership case.

8. Ex parte Wilson, 2 V. & B. 252, 253 (1813): "the mortgagor does not receive the rents for the mortgagee." Payment of rent to record senior mortgagee at a time when he no longer had title to the mortgage is not a defense to the claim of a second mortgagee in possession. Lamson & Co. v. Abrams, 305 Mass. 238, 25 N.E.2d 374 (1940), noted, 53 Harv.L.Rev. 1402 (1940); 26 Va.L.Rev. 1070 (1940). This would be true regardless of whether the lease preceded or followed the first mortgage. However, the decision emphasizes the dilemma of a tenant who must at his peril determine which party to the mortgage transaction he must pay in spite of possibly unascertainable facts and intricate questions of law.

9. Baltimore Markets v. R.E. etc. Co., 120 Pa.Super. 40, 181 A. 850 (1935).

10. De Nichols v. Saunders, L.R. 5 C. p. 599 (1870). For legislation in New York enacted to prevent mortgagors from "milking" the mortgaged premises by manipulating the terms of the lease and by prepayment of rent, see Norvell, 1959, Annual Survey of New York Law: Property, 35 N.Y.U.L.Rev. 1495, 1507 (1960).

lease. Prepayment of the entire rent may be a stipulation of the lease and, if so, the later mortgagee cannot complain. A mortgage cannot affect a prior lease except to make the lessee pay to the mortgagee rent accruing under the lease after the mortgage is given if the mortgagee demands it. Further, if a prepayment has been made, not in accordance with the terms of the lease, before the mortgage is taken and the mortgagee can be charged with notice of this deviation, the payment should be good against the mortgagee because he made the loan on that basis. However, in the absence of notice it is reasonable to charge the tenant with knowledge that the property might later be mortgaged, that the rent provisions of the lease would be relied on in part to determine whether the loan should be made, and consequently that a change would prejudice the mortgagee and should not be permitted.[11]

 WESTLAW REFERENCES
lessee tenant /s due paid pay! remit! rent! /s assign! transfer! /3
    mortgag**
topic(233 +p attorn!)

§ 4.22   Mortgage Before Lease—Title States

Where the mortgage precedes the lease the lessee's rights can rise no higher than those of his landlord, the mortgagor. "The mortgagor has no power, express or implied, to let leases, not subject to every circumstance of the mortgage. * * * The tenant stands exactly in the situation of the mortgagor."[1] It follows that if the mortgagee could take possession against the mortgagor, as he can in title states at any time in the absence of agreement to the contrary and in intermediate states after default, he has the same right against a tenant of the mortgagor. And if such a right is exercised the mortgagee can repudiate the lease and treat the tenant as a trespasser subject to eviction by an action of ejectment.[2] Moreover, like all interests in the mortgaged property attaching to it subsequent to the mortgage, the lease can be wiped out by foreclosure in all jurisdictions, title or lien. However, a mortgage transfers no reversion against subsequent tenants and therefore there is no privity of estate or contract between the mortgagee and the mortgagor's tenant. Consequently the mortgagee "cannot, by mere notice, compel the tenant to pay rent to him,"[3] nor exercise any of the

---

11. See Berick, The Mortgagee's Right to Rents, 8 Cin.L.Rev. 250, 263 (1934).

§ 4.22

1. Keech v. Hall, 1 Doug. 21, 22 (1778); Zimmern v. People's Bank, 203 Ala. 21, 81 So. 811 (1919).

2. Keech v. Hall, 1 Doug. 21 (1778); West Side Trust & Savings Bank v. Lopoten, 358 Ill. 631, 193 N.E. 462 (1934); City of Hagerstown v. Groh, 101 Md. 560, 61 A. 467 (1905); Brown to Use of Par Bond & Mortgage Co. v. Aiken, 329 Pa. 566, 198 A. 441 (1938); Guttenberg Savings & Loan Association v. Rivera, 85 N.J. 617, 428 A.2d 1289 (1981). See Randolph, The Mortgagee's Interest in Rents: Some Policy Considerations and Proposals, 29 Kan.L. Rev. 1, 27 (1980).

3. Kimball v. Lockwood, 6 R.I. 138, 139 (1859); Long v. Wade, 70 Me. 358 (1879); Winnisimmet Trust, Inc. v. Libby, 234 Mass. 407, 125 N.E. 599, 14 A.L.R. 638 (1920); Trask v. Kelleher, 93 Vt. 371, 107 A. 486 (1919).

remedies of a landlord against the tenant.[4] "Until there has been an actual entry, or some act equivalent thereto has occurred, the mortgagee can maintain no action against him for the recovery of rent, except upon an express promise to pay it."[5]

However, having the right to oust the mortgagor and his tenant, mortgagee may assert the right and compel the tenant to agree to pay the rent to him in order to avoid eviction. Such an agreement is commonly referred to as an "attornment" by the lessee.[6] Actually, however, it is the creation of an entirely new lease between the mortgagee and tenant.[7] Such new lease, or "attornment," is "no violation of the principle which estops a lessee from denying his lessor's title" for "by promising to pay the mortgagee upon the latter's rightful entry, the tenant saved the trouble and expense of eviction, which he could not lawfully prevent,"[8] and "only recognizes a title which his landlord has granted".[9]

Whether the new lease between the mortgagee and the tenant is for the balance of the original one upon the same terms as were contained in it is a question of fact in each case.[10] In most cases the parties would have in mind the terms of the original lease. Further, talking of the new lease in terms of attornment by the lessee, although technically incorrect, nevertheless probably is an accurate portrayal of the attitude of the parties toward the relationship they are entering into. Yet there is authority that the mere payment and acceptance of rent, without more, creates only a tenancy from year to year.[11]

When the mortgagee takes over possession of the property in the middle of the term of a lease, several questions arise. If the tenant stays on under an agreement with the mortgagee, that agreement usually is called an attornment and normally will provide for paying to

---

4. Burke v. Willard, 243 Mass. 547, 137 N.E. 744 (1923). See Teal v. Walker, 111 U.S. 242, 248, 4 S.Ct. 420, 28 L.Ed. 415 (1884).

5. Russell v. Allen, 84 Mass. (2 Allen) 42, 44 (1861); Peoples-Pittsburgh Trust Co. v. Henshaw, 141 Pa.Super. 585, 15 A.2d 711 (1940); noted, 89 U. of Pa.L.Rev. 679 (1941).

6. E.g., "the tenant of the mortgagor may attorn to the mortgagee, and by thus placing him in possession of the mortgaged premises, entitle him to the rents thereof." Kimball v. Lockwood, 6 R.I. 138, 139 (1859). See Anderson v. Robbins, 82 Me. 422, 19 A. 910, 8 L.R.A. 568 (1890).

7. See Berick, The Mortgagee's Right to Rents, 8 Cin.L.Rev. 250, 266 (1934).

8. Anderson v. Robbins, 82 Me. 422, 426, 19 A. 910, 911, 8 L.R.A. 568 (1890); Magill v. Hinsdale, 6 Conn. 464a, 16 Am. Dec. 70 (1827); Smith v. Shepard, 32 Mass. (15 Pick.) 147, 25 Am.Dec. 432 (1833)—

accord. See Towerson v. Jackson, 2 Q.B. 484 (1891); Reed v. Bartlett, 9 Ill.App. 267 (1881); note, 1 Harv.L.Rev. 255 (1887); note, 1918, 18 Col.L.Rev. 91; note, 80 U. of Pa.L.Rev. 602 (1932). See 14 A.L.R. 640 (1921); 105 A.L.R. 744 (1936); note, 70 Sol. J. 972 (1926). See also McDougal, Review of Walsh, Mortgages, 44 Yale L.J. 1278, 1280 (1935).

9. Kimball v. Lockwood, 6 R.I. 138, 139 (1889).

10. See Taylor, Landlord & Tenant, § 120; note, 1 J. Marshall L.Quar. 161, 168 (1935).

11. Gartside v. Outley, 58 Ill. 210, 11 Am.Rep. 59 (1871); West Side, etc., Bank v. Lopoten, 358 Ill. 631, 193 N.E. 462 (1934). By statute in Missouri the new tenancy runs from month to month. V.A.M.S. § 441.060; Roosevelt Hotel Corp. v. Williams, 227 Mo.App. 1063, 56 S.W.2d 801 (1933).

the mortgagee rent for the entire term, including that portion of it prior to the mortgagee's entry. Since the lease really is a new one beginning when the mortgagee enters, it would seem that it covers a period of time over which the mortgagee had no rights. The mortgagor, arguably should have a right to hold the tenant for the use and occupation during that portion of the term prior to entry by the mortgagee and this right should not be affected by the new agreement by the tenant with the mortgagee. That is not, however, the law. The new agreement, if it covers the entire term, will bar any recovery by the mortgagor.[12]

But the lessee may refuse to make an agreement with the mortgagee and in such case the mortgagee cannot hold him for rent as such for any period.[13] Rent falling due and paid to the mortgagor prior to taking possession may be kept by the mortgagor.[14] So, too, rent due but not paid to the mortgagor before the mortgagee takes possession belongs to the mortgagor.[15] But there is the portion of the term before the mortgagee entered during which the tenant was in occupation. The mortgagor cannot collect on the lease for this portion because rent is not apportionable.[16] The mortgagee has no claim to payment for it because his rights accrue only on entry and here he gets no payment for it by agreement with the tenant.[17] If the mortgagor brings a quasi-contractual action for use and occupation there are difficulties in allowing recovery. If the mortgagor had deliberately brought on the entry, or had not apprised the tenant of the possibility of such an entry, recovery should be denied. On the other hand, if the mortgagor did inform the tenant of the mortgage and the possibility of entry and did not do things to bring on the entry and it occurred prior to default, the mortgagor ought to be able to recover.

If the mortgagee enters because of default by the mortgagor the question is closer. Here the lease has been ended by the mortgagee because of the mortgagor's failure to pay and the lessee in such a case can escape any liability to his landlord, the mortgagor, because the

---

12. The cases uniformly hold that the tenant does not have to pay twice. Bulger v. Wilderman, 101 Pa.Super. 168 (1931); Magill v. Hinsdale, 6 Conn. 464a, 16 Am. Dec. 70 (1827); Hinck v. Cohn, 86 N.J.L. 615, 92 A. 378 (1914) are cases so holding in addition to Kimball v. Lockwood, supra note 9, and Anderson v. Robbins, supra note 8.

13. The mortgagee, in the absence of an "attornment" by the lessee, cannot enforce any of the terms of the lease against him. Evans v. Elliot, 9 A. & E. 342 (1838); Trask v. Kelleher, 93 Vt. 371, 107 A. 486 (1919); Moran v. Pittsburgh, C. & St. Louis Railway Co., 32 F. 878 (C.C.Ohio 1887); Bessemer Investment Co. v. Fell, 225 F. 13, 140 C.C.A. 473 (C.C.A.Pa.1915), discussed in

note 16 Col.L.Rev. 76 (1916); Mack v. Beeland Brothers Mercantile Co., 21 Ala.App. 97, 105 So. 722 (1925), certiorari denied 213 Ala. 554, 105 So. 725 (1925).

14. Kimball v. Lockwood, 6 R.I. 138 (1889).

15. Clarke v. Curtis, 1 Gratt. 289 (1844).

16. Anderson v. Robbins, 82 Me. 422, 19 A. 910, 8 L.R.A. 568 (1890).

17. "The lessee becomes liable to the mortgagee for rent accruing due after the latter's entry and the lessee's promise to pay, but not for rent due before such entry and promise, as prior thereto there would be no privity between them." Anderson v. Robbins, 82 Me. 422, 424, 19 A. 910, 911 (1890).

mortgagor was responsible for the loss of the lease.[18] In title states where the mortgagee could have entered prior to default and the tenant knew it, to let the tenant acquire such a windfall at the expense of the defaulting mortgagor seems undesirable, at least in cases where the mortgagee was willing to permit the lessee to stay on under the terms of the old lease, as is usually the case.

But suppose the tenant stays on after the mortgagee takes over, at the same time refusing to come to any agreement with him. The mortgagee may bring ejectment, which is slow and cumbersome,[19] or an action to foreclose, which is also time consuming. Equity may not help him to get possession,[20] as the legal remedy may be considered adequate. As a result, a recalcitrant tenant might well occupy the property for a considerable period of time without any agreement to pay rent. In such a case the mortgagee should be able to hold him for use and occupation of the premises from the time the mortgagee entered until the tenant departs and collect the fair rental value regardless of the rent reserved in the original lease.[21]

The foregoing doctrine that a mortgagee who takes possession cannot affirm the leases made by the mortgagor subsequent to the mortgage because of lack of privity between the mortgagee and the lessee is a most dubious one. The mortgagee, although he comes in by paramount title as a technical matter is quite unlike the ordinary third party who enters. This is because the mortgagor still continues to be the substantial owner of the property and the mortgagee has only asserted an additional security right, the right to possession, which carries with it the income. Whatever the merits of the rule permitting tenants to disaffirm leases in the ordinary case where his landlord's interest has been completely ended, to permit him to do so here impairs not only the mortgagee's security interest but the mortgagor's substantial interest as well.[22] It has been pointed out that the doctrine was

---

18. Where a receiver disaffirms a lease and demands payment of the value of the use and occupation, this constitutes a breach of the covenant of quiet enjoyment in a lease, releasing the tenant from liability under the lease. In re O'Donnell, 240 N.Y. 99, 147 N.E. 541 (1925); Casassa v. Smith, 206 Mass. 69, 91 N.E. 891 (1910). The tenant can also sue the mortgagor for breach of covenant of quiet enjoyment. Ganz v. Clark, 252 N.Y. 92, 169 N.E. 100 (1929) lease ended by foreclosure.

19. See Tefft, The Myth of Strict Foreclosure, 4 U. of Chi.L.Rev. 575, 583, n. 43 (1937), for authority that eight to eleven months would elapse before the plaintiff would be in possession in an ejectment action.

20. Seton, Decrees, 140, 143. This was true both before and after a foreclosure decree. After decree an order for posses-

sion is now obtainable. Keith v. Day, L.R. 39 Ch.D. 452 (1888).

21. Lucier v. Marsales, 133 Mass. 454 (1882). See 1 Tiffany, Landlord & Tenant, § 73a. On the other hand in Burke v. Willard, 243 Mass. 547, 137 N.E. 744 (1923), the mortgagee was denied recovery on the ground that the tenant was holding adversely to the mortgagee under the lease from the mortgagor. Most of the authorities allowing recovery are receivership cases, but the principle is the same. Rohrer v. Deatherage, 336 Ill. 450, 168 N.E. 266 (1929), fair rental value; Monro-King, etc., Corp. v. Ninth Avenue, etc., Corp., 233 App.Div. 401, 253 N.Y.S. 303, 32 Col.L.Rev. 144 (1931). A similar right was given to a purchaser on foreclosure sale in Harris v. Foster, 97 Cal. 292, 32 P. 246 (1893).

22. See Tefft, Receivers and Leases Subordinate to the Mortgage, 2 U.Chi.L.Rev.

extended to the mortgage cases only after considerable controversy and in the face of a line of cases that had held that the mortgagee by giving notice might affirm the mortgagor's leases.[23] A possible justification of the rule, apart from the argument that it is desirable to let the general real property rule as to privity operate mechanically to achieve certainty, is that it would be an additional deterrent to mortgagees' asserting their legal rights to possession and thus bolster the mortgagor's protection. This last reason would be inapplicable to receivership cases in which the same question arises and will be discussed later.

Where a mortgage precedes the lease even if the tenant pays his rent in advance according to the terms of his lease he may nevertheless be ousted by the mortgagee who enters. And, if he stays in possession, he must either come to terms with the mortgagee or be liable for the fair rental value from the time of the mortgagee's entry.[24]

 WESTLAW REFERENCES
lessee tenant /s attorn! eject! enter*** entry foreclos*** possess***
     /s mortgagee

---

§ 4.23 Lien States

Under the lien theory of mortgages the mortgagor remains the full legal and beneficial owner of the mortgaged property until his rights are ended by foreclosure sale. The mortgagee, having no right to possession prior to foreclosure except where he acquires the status of a "mortgagee in possession", a matter discussed later, is not entitled to rents from the mortgagor's tenants regardless of whether the leases preceded or followed the giving of the mortgage.[1] If the mortgagor has leased the property before giving the mortgage, the lien acquired on the reversion gives the mortgagee no right to the rents accruing under the lease. If a mortgagor leases the mortgaged premises subsequently to giving the mortgage, he is entitled to the rents until title passes under a decree of foreclosure.[2]

33, 41 (1934). See also note, 17 Wash.L. Rev. 37, 46 (1942).

23. See Tefft, supra note 22, 42 n. 35, citing Pope v. Biggs, 9 B. & C. 245 (K.B.1829); Waddilove v. Barnett, 4 Dowl. 347 (K.B.1835); Brown v. Storey, 1 Man. & G. 117 (C.P.1840); Underhay v. Read, 20 Q.B.D. 209, 1 Harv.L.Rev. 255 (1887). Cf. Evans v. Elliot, 9 Ad. & El. 342 (K.B.1838); Towerson v. Jackson, 2 Q.B. 484 (1891); 1 Tiffany, Landlord & Tenant, § 73a(6).

24. See note, 46 Harv.L.Rev. 491, 493 (1932). See also Berick, The Mortgagee's Right to Rents, 8 Cin.L.Rev. 250, 271 (1934).

§ 4.23

1. Wagar v. Stone, 36 Mich. 364 (1877). On the problem of a mortgagee's security interest in crops, with especial reference to California law, see Smith, Security Interests in Crops, 10 Hastings L.J. 23, 156 (1958). See Woolley v. Holt, 77 Ky. (14 Bush) 788 (1879) in which the mortgagor, who leased the property before mortgaging it, transferred the lease to X. Held, on foreclosure, X took free and clear of the mortgage lien.

2. See Mills v. Hamilton, 49 Iowa 105 (1878); Mills v. Heaton, 52 Iowa 215, 2 N.W. 1112 (1879); Orr v. Broad, 52 Neb. 490, 72 N.W. 850 (1897); Mason v. Lenderoth, 88 App.Div. 38, 84 N.Y.S. 740 (1903). The mortgagee of a lessee in possession in a lien state is not an assignee of the lease and thus is not liable on the covenant for rent. Note, 58 Mich.L.Rev. 140 (1959).

Foreclosure of the mortgage in lien states creates problems similar to those in title jurisdictions when the mortgagee before foreclosure asserts the right to possession against the mortgagor and seeks to reach the rents. If the lease preceded the mortgage and the latter was taken with actual or constructive notice of it, only the lessor's interest can be sold on foreclosure and the tenant's rights under the lease cannot be extinguished.[3] However the purchaser on foreclosure sale has rights analogous to those of a mortgagee in a title state who takes a mortgage on leased property. Where the mortgage precedes the lease, since title remains in the mortgagor until foreclosure, the lease by the mortgagor cannot be affected until foreclosure. Since it depends upon the mortgagor's interest it may, however, be foreclosed along with it if the tenant is properly joined in those proceedings.[4] The purchaser on foreclosure sale acquires rights to rents and in respect to the lease that the mortgagee did not possess.[5]

If the mortgagor puts the mortgagee into possession with authority to collect the rents this will not affect the leases apart from altering the person to whom the rents are to be paid. Although the leases are subject to the mortgage, the mortgagee cannot terminate them except by foreclosure unless the tenant consents or breaks some condition in the lease.[6] A foreclosure receivership in lien jurisdictions will also alter the simple general rule that the mortgagor is entitled to the rents before foreclosure.[7]

 WESTLAW REFERENCES
lessee tenant /p foreclos*** /s mortgagee /p lien

F. MORTGAGEE IN POSSESSION

§ 4.24 "Mortgagee-in-Possession" Rule

The mortgagee may lawfully acquire possession while the mortgage is still subsisting. The courts have developed the doctrine that if he does his security interest as mortgagee in possession generally entitles him to hold the premises until either the mortgagor redeems or the property is foreclosed.[1]

---

3. Possession by the tenant or recordation of the lease will give notice of it. Taylor v. Bell, 129 Ala. 464, 29 S.W. 572 (1900); Tropical Investment Co. v. Brown, 45 Cal.App. 205, 187 P. 133 (1920); Heaton v. Grand Lodge No. 335, IOOF, 55 Ind.App. 100, 103 N.E. 488 (1913).

4. For the effect of non-joinder in foreclosure proceedings, see § 7.15 infra.

5. E.g., a purchaser at a foreclosure sale may eject the mortgagor's tenant, or make a new lease. McDermott v. Burke, 16 Cal. 580 (1860). See 8 L.R.A.,N.S., 404; 1921, 14 A.L.R. 664 (1907).

6. Fidelity Bond and Mortgage Co. v. Paul, 90 Colo. 94, 6 P.2d 462 (1931).

7. The effect of foreclosure, of receiverships in foreclosure, and of agreements in respect to rents and possession in lien jurisdictions upon leases and the right to rents in those jurisdictions is dealt with in §§ 4.33–4.43 infra.

§ 4.24

1. See e.g., Properties, Inc. v. Brownsville Savings & Loan Association, 581 S.W. 2d 222 (Tex.Civ.App.1979). He may, however, be ousted for gross mismanagement, by the extinction of the mortgage through

As we have already seen, in jurisdictions following the title theory of mortgages, the mortgagee, in the absence of an agreement or a statutory provision to the contrary, is entitled as a matter of right to possession before or after default.[2] In the "intermediate" jurisdictions the same is true after default.[3] In both types of states, when the mortgagee exercises his right to enter, his possession is clearly lawful within the scope of the doctrine and he becomes a mortgagee in possession. On the other hand, this right to take possession under such circumstances does not normally, as we noted earlier,[4] impose an obligation to do so.

In lien states the mortgagor has the right to possession of the mortgaged premises both before and after default until foreclosure and, in many instances, the expiration of any statutory redemption period.[5] Consequently, it would seem that the doctrine of mortgagee in possession would have no place in them. Nevertheless, it has generally been accepted although there is a divergence of view especially as to what will constitute lawful possession. One line of cases reconciles it with the lien concept only upon the basis of consent, express or implied in fact, on the part of the mortgagor that the mortgagee be in possession of the mortgaged premises. As one of the leading cases expressed it, "it would seem to follow that when the legislature deprived the mortgagee of the only legal method by which he could get possession of the mortgaged premises without the mortgagor's consent, prior to foreclosure, there was no way left by which the mortgagee could acquire such possession except by the mortgagor's consent." [6] Further, this consent

tender, merger, or sale of the property by the mortgagee to a purchaser without notice, or by the assertion of a prior mortgage interest. For cases, see 35 Col.L.Rev. 1248, 1253 notes 31, 33, 34 (1935). The doctrine that a mortgagee in possession cannot be dispossessed by the mortgagor without payment of the mortgage debt applies although an action on the debt or the right to foreclose the mortgage is barred by the statute of limitations. Jasper State Bank v. Braswell, 130 Tex. 549, 111 S.W.2d 1079, 115 A.L.R. 329 (1938); Spect v. Spect, 88 Cal. 437, 26 P. 203, 13 L.R.A. 137, 22 Am. St.Rep. 314 (1891); Bulson v. Moffatt, 173 Cal. 685, 161 P. 259 (1916), noted in 5 Cal. L.Rev. 258; Kelso v. Norton, 65 Kan. 778, 70 P. 896, 93 Am.St.Rep. 308 (1902). Knight v. Hilton, 224 S.C. 452, 79 S.E.2d 871 (1954) noted by Karesh, Survey of South Carolina Law (1954): Security Transactions, 7 S.C.L.Q. 171. See Burns v. Hiatt, 149 Cal. 617, 87 P. 196, 117 Am.St. Rep. 157 (1906). Nor does a hostile reentry on the land by the mortgagor divest the rights of the mortgagee as mortgagee in possession. Finley v. Erickson, 122 Minn. 235, 142 N.W. 198 (1913); Cory v. Santa Ynez Land, etc. Co., 151 Cal. 778, 91 P. 647

(1907). On the ability of a mortgagee in possession to acquire title by adverse possession, see 6 Minn.L.Rev. 510 (1922), and Cory v. Santa Ynez Land Co., supra.

2. See § 4.1, supra; Cook v. Curtis, 125 Me. 114, 131 A. 204 (1925); Weathersbee v. Goodwin, 175 N.C. 234, 95 S.E. 491 (1918); Brown v. Loeb, 177 Ala. 106, 58 So. 330 (1912).

3. See § 4.3, supra.

4. See § 4.1 supra.

5. See Mutual Benefit Life Insurance Co. v. Frantz Klodt & Son, Inc., 237 N.W.2d 350 (Minn.1975); § 4.2 infra.

6. Barson v. Mulligan, 191 N.Y. 306, 315, 84 N.E. 75, 78, 16 L.R.A.,N.S., 151 (1908); Myers-Macomber Engineers v. MLW Const. Corp., 271 Pa.Super. 484, 414 A.2d 357 (1979); McClory v. Ricks, 11 N.D. 38, 88 N.W. 1042 (1902). Accord: 8 Col.L. Rev. 486 (1908); note by E.N.D., 15 Mich.L. Rev. 58 (1916). A few lien jurisdictions, it is true, invalidate executory agreements for the mortgagee to take possession. See Geraldson, Clauses Increasing the Possessory Rights of Mortgagees, 10 Wis.L.Rev. 492 (1935); Tiffany, Real Prop., 3d ed., must be to an entry by the mortgagee "under or by virtue of the mortgage," or, at least, "for purposes, or under circumstances not inconsistent with their relative legal rights under the mortgage." [7] Thus when the mortgagee gets possession in a capacity other than that of mortgagee, e.g., as a tenant of the mortgagor, he cannot, during, or after the expiration of his term as lessee, assert a right of possession as mortgagee, without the express or implied consent of the mortgagor. [8] So, too, if he enters as the agent of the mortgagor, he will not be a mortgagee in possession, only an agent with the liabilities of that relation.

The doctrine of mortgagee in possession in lien jurisdictions is not confined, however, to cases where the mortgagee entered with the consent of the mortgagor. [9] In some states a peaceable entry, in good faith, and under color of right, e.g., under a void foreclosure sale, is sufficient to make the possession lawful without any consent whatsoever by the mortgagor. [10] And in others it is enough that the entry was peaceable. [11] But in all such states, in order for the occupation of the premises to entitle him to the status of mortgagee in possession, he must assert his claim to have and to hold them under and by virtue of

§ 1416. This result, however, can be regarded as "an extension of the familiar view early developed in equity that the mortgagor shall not be permitted to bargain away his right to redemption as a part of his mortgage contract," Rundle, Work of the Wisconsin Supreme Court— Mortgages, 1933. 9 Wis. 33, 40, and thus distinguished from cases holding that a later actual entry with consent is valid. For a discussion of the development of the problem of lawful possession after default by a mortgagee in New York, where the doctrine originated, see note, 8 Col.L.Rev. 486 (1908). See also E.N.D., The Mortgagee in Possession in New York and in Michigan, 15 Mich.L.Rev. 58 (1916). A mortgagee may not be able to remain in possession, during a statutory redemption period, at least where the foreclosure sale yielded an amount equal to the mortgage debt. See Cross Co. Inc. v. Citizens Mortgage Investment Co., 305 Minn. 111, 232 N.W.2d 114 (1975).

7. Barson v. Mulligan, supra note 5, at 322, 84 N.E. at 81. See 26 Albany L.Jour. 526 (1882); 27 Albany L.Jour. 6 (1883).

8. Barson v. Mulligan, supra n. 35, Robinson v. Smith, 128 S.W.2d 27 (Tex. Com.App.1939), discussed, 24 Minn.L.Rev. 434 (1939); Russell v. Ely, 67 U.S. (2 Black.) 575, 17 L.Ed. 258 (1862), a mortgagee who obtains possession from the tenant of the mortgagor after his lease had expired is not lawfully in possession. See 8 Col.L.Rev. 486 (1908).

9. See 7 Tex.L.Rev. 170 (1928); 18 N.Car.L.Rev. 61 (1939).

10. Jasper State Bank v. Braswell, 130 Tex. 549, 111 S.W.2d 1079, 115 A.L.R. 329 (1938); Raggio v. Palmtag, 155 Cal. 797, 103 P. 312 (1909); Cameron v. Ah Quong, 175 Cal. 377, 165 P. 961 (1917); Pettit v. Louis, 88 Neb. 496, 129 N.W. 1005, 34 L.R.A.,N.S., 356 (1911); Caro v. Wollenberg, 68 Or. 420, 136 P. 866 (1913). In such states, a mortgagee who entered into possession under an agreement with his mortgagor that he should do so as additional security would be given, *a fortiori*, the status of a mortgagee in possession. Spect v. Spect, 88 Cal. 437, 26 P. 203, 13 L.R.A. 137, 22 Am.St.Rep. 314 (1891).

11. Stouffer v. Harlan, 68 Kan. 135, 74 P. 610, 64 L.R.A. 320, 104 Am.St.Rep. 396 (1903) same case, 84 Kan. 307, 114 P. 385 (1911); Burns v. Hiatt, 149 Cal. 617, 87 P. 196, 117 Am.St.Rep. 157 (1906); West v. Middlesex Banking Co., 33 S.D. 465, 146 N.W. 598 (1914); Pierce v. Grimley, 77 Mich. 273, 43 N.W. 932 (1889) (power of sale illegally exercised); Jaggar v. Plunkett, 81 Kan. 565, 106 P. 280, 25 L.R.A.,N.S., 935 (1910). But see State ex rel. Montgomery v. Superior Court, 21 Wash. 564, 58 P. 1065 (1899); Herrmann v. Cabinet Land Co., 217 N.Y. 526, 112 N.E. 476 (1916) (mortgagor not served with process in foreclosure action).

his lien, i.e., *qua* mortgagee.[12] If he enters as the result of a defective foreclosure sale, the most usual case, this satisfies the requirement.[13] But suppose that, although a mortgagee at the time, he enters peaceably in a capacity other than mortgagee and later claims to hold possession as mortgagee. Or, that he takes possession peaceably under an invalid claim derived from a third party and later, while in possession he thus acquires a subsisting mortgage and then claims as mortgagee in possession. It has been suggested that possession so acquired might be regarded as having been obtained by fraud and thus as illegal as though obtained by force.[14] However, the mortgagee's claim probably will be sustained.[15]

Where the mortgagee in possession is there with the consent of the mortgagor the doctrine of according him rights as such is not inconsistent with lien theory. When, however, consent by the mortgagor to the mortgagee's entry is dispensed with, it becomes more difficult to reconcile the doctrine with the lien theory.[16] One explanation of the extension is that "the old rule, existing when a mortgage actually passed the title to the property, kept its hold upon the later opinions when the reason which led to it was gone."[17] In other words, it is just an anachronistic survival of the title view of mortgages. While this may have been the origin of the rule, its vitality and wide acceptance demands a better rationalization. The one most commonly accepted is that the mortgagee's "right to retain possession does not depend upon an estate held by him. His possession is protected by his lien. It is certainly more simple and just that the mortgagee should be left in possession, and the mortgagor forced to redeem, than that the mortgagor should be permitted to recover the possession by an action at law, and be immediately liable to the consequences of a foreclosure suit in equity brought by the mortgagee."[18]

12. Daniel v. Coker, 70 Ala. 260 (1881); Anglo-Calif. Bank v. Field, 154 Cal. 513, 98 P. 267 (1908), in possession under deed of redemption right of mortgagor; Armistead v. Bishop, 110 Ark. 172, 161 S.W. 182 (1913) in possession as tenant; Compton v. Jesup, 68 F. 263, 15 C.C.A. 397 (1895). A mortgagee who, without the consent of the mortgagor, acquires possession after the mortgage lien has become extinguished cannot assert the rights of a mortgagee in possession. Faxon v. All Persons, 166 Cal. 707, 137 P. 919 (1913). See Tiffany, Real Prop., 3d ed., § 1419; Pomeroy, Eq.Juris., 5th ed., § 1215.

13. See note 10, supra. Even though the purchaser under a defective foreclosure sale taking possession under such sale is not the mortgagee himself, he succeeds to the rights of the mortgagee although the sale under foreclosure is void, and he is treated, therefore, as a mortgagee in possession. Bryan v. Brasius, 3 Ariz. 433, 31 P. 519 (1892) affirmed 162 U.S. 415, 16

S.Ct. 803, 40 L.Ed. 1022 (1896); Kaylor v. Kelsey, 91 Neb. 404, 136 N.W. 54, 40 L.R.A.,N.S., 839 (1912).

14. See note 15 Mich.L.Rev. 58, 60 (1916).

15. See, e.g., Jaggar v. Plunkett, 81 Kan. 565, 106 P. 280 (1910).

16. The extension of the doctrine beyond cases of consent by the mortgagor has been vigorously criticized. See Walsh, Mortgages, § 19, which in turn is criticized by McDougal, 44 Yale L.Jour. 1278, 1281 (1935); E.N.D., 15 Mich.L.Rev. 58 (1916); Tiffany, Real Prop., 3d ed., § 1415.

17. Stouffer v. Harlan, 68 Kan. 135, 74 P. 610, 64 L.R.A. 320, 104 Am.St.Rep. 396 (1903), attributing it to Howell v. Leavitt, 95 N.Y. 617 (1884). This basis is, however, older and was expressed in Phyfe v. Riley, 15 Wend. 248 (1836). See E.N.D., 15 Mich. L.Rev. 58 (1916).

18. Pomeroy, Eq.Juris., 5th ed., § 1189.

Both the doctrine itself and this last justification of it have been criticized on the ground that, under the lien theory, the right to possession before foreclosure "admittedly belongs to the mortgagor and his suit in ejectment by which he enforces it can hardly be called useless or unnecessary," and that the doctrine gives "the mortgagee a right to possession in fact though acquired without right, and forces the mortgagor to redeem long before he is required to do so under the general principles of equity applying to the action to redeem." The cases following it are called "anomalous, without explanation other than an undefined equity or feeling of abstract justice is the bases of it." [19]

Several answers may be made. First, in view of the strong judicial authority recognizing the right of the mortgagee to retain possession, it is difficult to say that "admittedly" possession belongs to the mortgagor under all circumstances before foreclosure is complete. These decisions are square holdings to the contrary, creating an exception to the general rule, and the only question ought to be whether the result is fair, taking into account not only the lien theory, but the practical situation involved in the particular problem. The interest of the mortgagor in having possession after default must be balanced against the mortgagee's interest in continuing in possession of the security. Before default, the mortgagor's interest outweighs any claim the mortgagee may assert. But when the mortgagee has acquired the right, through the default of the mortgagor, to realize on his security, his interest in having possession of the property and getting its proceeds to apply on the debt become very strong. As we shall see, he often can take possession away from the mortgagor by getting a receiver appointed and, although inadequacy of the security or waste are, in theory, essential requirements for this, in actual practice receivers are sometimes appointed pretty much as a matter of course.[20] The mortgagee in possession has advantages in keeping down costs and, under the requirement of strict accountability, of providing better management than a receivership affords.[21] Finally, when the mortgagor's action for possession can be immediately nullified by an action to foreclose by the mortgagee, it can properly be regarded as "useless or unnecessary" unless justified by substantial reasons.[22]

One of the chief arguments for allowing the mortgagor to have possession is that it is the source of his ability to get income with which to pay off the mortgage debt. However, the mortgagee in possession must account for all rents and profits, which will be applied to payment of the mortgage debt, thus accomplishing the same result and benefit-

19. Walsh, Mortgages, 100.

20. See §§ 4.33–4.34, infra.

21. See Note, 35 Col.L.Rev. 1248, 1260 (1935).

22. American Trust Co. v. England, 84 F.2d 352 (C.C.A.Cal.1936); where the mortgagee is in possession after a breach of the conditions in a mortgage, the mortgagor must show affirmatively that his possession is not lawful.

ing the mortgagor. There exists, of course, the possibility that the mortgagor could have made more out of the property had he been in possession, and thus, it should be assumed, have paid off more of the mortgage debt. But this overlooks the fact that the doctrine is seldom invoked except in cases where the mortgagor is in a precarious,[23] if not hopeless, condition, for it is applicable in lien jurisdictions only after default, and, practically, occurs most frequently, when consent to entry is not obtained, after a defective foreclosure. The dangers to the mortgagee, under such conditions, that the mortgagor will resort to "milking" the property if he regains possession, or at least fail to maintain it adequately are great and the ability of the mortgagee to protect himself is unsatisfactory. To allow the mortgagor to get back possession of the property under these circumstances would amount to a judicial exemption founded upon mechanical application of the lien theory at the expense of mortgagees. Such considerations serve both to explain and support the desirability of decisions accepting the doctrine of mortgagee in possession even in cases where there is no consensual basis for it.

 WESTLAW REFERENCES
mortgagee-in-possession /p consen! "good faith" permi! right /p
default*** enter*** entry
di mortgagee in possession

§ 4.25 What Constitutes Possession

In order to qualify as a mortgagee in possession, the mortgagee must have possession of the premises *qua* mortgagee. What constitutes such possession varies with the nature and condition of the property.[1] The words "possession" and "occupation" are not necessarily synonymous in this regard because a mortgagee can be a mortgagee in possession without actually occupying the premises.[2] Perhaps the standard is best expressed in terms of whether the mortgagee exercised "dominion and control" over the mortgaged real estate.[3] Nevertheless, because possession is a factual issue,[4] results are often difficult to predict. For example, in the case of urban rental real estate, while the collection of rent alone by the mortgagee may not create a mortgagee in

---

23. "The paucity of redemption cases points to the probability that possession is merely a prelude to foreclosure. In that event, continuation of possession in a mortgagee may be socially desirable, since it gives him control over his security without resort to receivership." 35 Col.L.Rev. 1247, 1254 (1935).

§ 4.25

1. See 35 Col.L.Rev. 1248, 1250 (1935).

2. See cases in 35 Col.L.Rev. 1248, 1250, notes, 14, 15, 16 (1935). Gandrud v. Hansen, 210 Minn. 125, 297 N.W. 730 (1941),

discussed, 26 Minn.L.Rev. 880, 887 et seq. (1942).

3. Strutt v. Ontario Savings & Loan Association, 28 Cal.App.3d 866, 881, 105 Cal.Rptr. 395, 405 (1973); Bank of America National Trust & Savings Association v. Bank of Amador Co., 135 Cal.App. 714, 28 P.2d 86 (1933); Stephens Investment Co. v. Berry Schools, 188 Ga. 132, 3 S.E.2d 68 (1939).

4. Nettles v. First National Bank of Birmingham, 388 So.2d 916, 920 (Ala.1980).

possession,[5] that factor combined with active management will probably suffice.[6] On the other hand, while mortgagee cultivation and harvesting of an orchard crop after mortgagor abandonment has been deemed sufficient to confer mortgagee in possession status,[7] active day to day advice and financial assistance to mortgagor in running a mortgaged factory was not.[8] Moreover, where a representative of the mortgagee "visited the property on three or four occasions, asked the tenant to 'keep an eye on it,' and arranged and paid for emergency repairs and cleanup work following the breaking of water pipes and the flooding of a building," such evidence was insufficient to establish that the mortgagee was "in possession." [9]

 WESTLAW REFERENCES

mortgagee-in-possession /48 control! dominion possess** possessing

§ 4.26 Liability of Mortgagee to Third Parties

When a mortgagee goes into possession questions as to his personal liability to third persons arise. By virtue of that possession, the mortgagee becomes personally liable in tort for injuries resulting either through his actionable fault in utilizing the property or by reason of his failure to perform duties imposed by law upon the owner of land.[1] Even more clearly he is liable for goods and services furnished to him during his occupancy on either an express or implied contract basis.[2]

The liability of a mortgagee in possession on covenants running with the mortgaged land presents some substantial problems. Normally, use restrictions are enforcible *in equity* as equitable servitudes

---

5. Ireland v. United States Mortgage & Trust Co., 72 App.Div. 95, 76 N.Y.S. 177 (1902) affirmed 175 N.Y. 491, 67 N.E. 1083 (1902); cf. Whitley v. Barnett, 151 Iowa 487, 131 N.W. 704 (1911). See 35 Col.L. Rev. 1248, 1250 (1935); 50 Yale L.Jour. 1427, 1431 n. 42 (1941).

6. Zisman v. City of Duquesne, 143 Pa. Sup. 263, 18 A.2d 95 (1941), noted, 7 Pitts. L.Rev. 345 (1941).

7. Nelson v. Bowen, 124 Cal.App. 662, 12 P.2d 1083 (1932).

8. Blackstone Valley National Bank v. Hanson, 15 Mass.App.Ct. 953, 445 N.E.2d 1093 (1983).

9. Id.

§ 4.26

1. See Restatement, Second, Torts, § 329, comments a, c. City of Newark v. Sue Corp., 124 N.J.Super. 5, 304 A.2d 567 (1973); Zisman v. City of Duquesne, 143 Pa.Sup. 263, 18 A.2d 95 (1941), noted, 7 Pitts.L.Rev. 345 (1941); Daniels v. Hart, 118 Mass. 543 (1875); Rogers v. Wheeler, 2 Lans. 486 (N.Y.1870); affirmed 43 N.Y. 598

(1870); Barter v. Wheeler, 49 N.H. 9, 6 Am.Rep. 434 (1869); Sprague v. Smith, 29 Vt. 421, 70 Am.Dec. 424 (1857). The liability is probably exclusive. See Sabiston's Administrator v. Otis Elevator Co., 251 Ky. 222, 229, 64 S.W.2d 588, 591 (1933). Exceptions to this may be based upon an agency relationship between the mortgagor and the mortgagee in possession as to third persons, Grand Tower Manufacturing & Transportation Co. v. Ullman, 89 Ill. 244 (1878), or in the case of a known dangerous condition existing at the time of transfer of possession to the mortgagee, at least if the transfer was consented to. Restatement, Second, Torts §§ 353, 354.

2. Essex Cleaning Contractors, Inc. v. Amato, 127 N.J.Super. 364, 317 A.2d 411 (1974) (quoting text with approval); First National Bank v. Matlock, 99 Okl. 150, 226 P. 328, 36 A.L.R. 1088 (1934). He probably can avoid such liability, as can a foreclosure receiver, by express stipulation in the contract with the third person. Cf. Knickerbocker Ice Co. v. Benson, 155 Misc. 738, 741, 279 N.Y.S. 86 (1935).

against non-fee holders such as lessees and even licensees.[3] Thus, mortgagees in possession presumably should be subject to equitable relief at least to the same extent as other non-feeholders.

Where, however, money damages are sought for violation of use restrictions, the problems are more complex. This is because "the contractual obligation attaches to the estate of the covenantor, and can run with the land only against one who succeeds to that estate. Succession of estate between the covenantor and his assignee is often essential to the running of the burden at law."[4] If this reasoning is applied to the mortgagee in possession, the title-lien distinction could theoretically become important. For example, in a title theory state it could be argued that the mortgagee in possession should be liable for damages on a covenant running with the land because the mortgagee, as the holder of legal title, has succeeded to the estate of the covenantor. On the other hand, the lien jurisdiction mortgagee in possession, since he holds only a security interest and not legal title, would not be similarly liable.

The few cases in this area have dealt for the most part with the liability of a mortgagee in possession for rent where the mortgaged property consists of a leasehold. There is title theory case law holding the mortgagee liable.[5] Two lines of cases are discernible in lien states. There are New York cases holding that the mortgagee will be bound because "when the mortgagee takes possession he then has all the right, title and interest of the mortgagor."[6] This, of course, runs counter to the usual lien theory concept that the mortgagee can acquire the title to the mortgaged real estate against a recalcitrant mortgagor only by foreclosure. However, there are other, preferable cases holding that the mortgagee never becomes liable even though he has taken possession. This result has been reached on the ground that the "mere act of the parties of going into possession, and consenting to or acquiescing in it can [not] have the effect to pass the mortgagor's estate to the mortgagee" and, therefore, just as he could not sue on a covenant running with the land "because he is not the owner of the land with which such covenants run" so he is not liable on them.[7] A preferable

---

3. American Law of Property, § 9.31 (1952).

4. Id. at 427. See Cunningham, Stoebuck & Whitman, The Law of Property § 8.17 (1984).

5. See Gibbs v. Didier, 125 Md. 486, 94 A. 100 (1915), Annot., 73 A.L.R.2d 1119, 1121 (1960).

6. Astor v. Hoyt, 5 Wend. 603, 617 (N.Y. 1830); Moffatt v. Smith, 4 N.Y. 126 (1850). Cockrell v. Houston Packing Co., 105 Tex. 283, 147 S.W. 1145 (1912), accord.

7. Cargill v. Thompson, 57 Minn. 534, 543, 59 N.W. 638, 640 (1894); Johnson v. Sherman, 15 Cal. 287, 76 Am.Dec. 481

(1860). Annot., 73 A.L.R.2d 1119, 1123–1134 (1960).

"We suspect the courts of New York would hesitate to hold that as soon as he gets possession he may sue upon or may release such covenants, which he certainly can do, if he has an estate that makes him the owner of them." Cargill v. Thompson, supra note 33, at 544, 59 N.W. at 640. The mortgagee in possession under an arrangement with the mortgagor to manage the mortgaged leasehold was held not liable to the landlord on the ground that he was acting as agent of the mortgagor in holding possession. Cleveland v. Detroit Trust Co., 264 basis, would have been that, whether technically the mortgagee has legal title or lien, his interest is for security purposes only and liabilities that are founded upon full ownership should not attach to it.

 WESTLAW REFERENCES
mortgagee-in-possession /p liab! responsib! /s contract covenant
goods negligen** service tort!

§ 4.27 The Mortgagee's Duty to Account—Nature and Scope

Once the mortgagee is in possession, he becomes entitled to the income of the property on the one hand and, on the other, he becomes subject to certain duties in respect to management of the property. These concepts apply equally in title and lien jurisdictions.[1]

The rules of accounting for a mortgagee in possession are harsh. While the parties to some extent may alter the impact of these rules by contract provisions [2] and courts of equity will vary them to avoid hardship,[3] the role of the mortgagee in possession is not an easy one. As was seen in examining the development of the lien theory and in other connections, there is a strong policy in favor of leaving the mortgagor in possession which is furthered by stringent rules discouraging mortgagees from taking over even when they have the legal right to do so. Realization by sale of the capital asset is the essence of the mortgagee's right. To take possession from the mortgagor is justified by the danger of "milking" by a hard pressed mortgagor, and the idea that the mortgagee is entitled not only to the capital asset itself but all it yields in the form of income from the time his right to realize accrues and he starts to exercise it; the time lag between starting and final realization should not defeat his rights. But on both counts possession is purely in the mortgagee's interest and deprives the mortgagor of a source of income and sometimes the means by which he has the best chance of saving his property. Further, the mortgagee in possession holding the property as security has it in its power to prolong the period of his responsibility or to shorten it by foreclosure proceedings. Finally, since the income of the property must be applied to the payment of the mortgage debt, the mortgagee who takes control of the source of that income should answer pretty strictly for any conduct that prevents income arising.

The mortgagee in possession is sometimes characterized in semifiduciary terminology. In this connection, cases have labeled him

Mich. 253, 249 N.W. 842 (1933), commented on in 32 Mich.L.Rev. 864 (1934).

§ 4.27

1. See Walsh, Mortgages, § 20

2. See, e.g., Johns v. Moore, 168 Cal. App.2d 709, 366 P.2d 579 (1959).

3. See 35 Col.L.Rev. 1248, 1251 (1935), citing as examples, Madison Avenue Baptist Church v. Baptist Church in Oliver St., 73 N.Y. 82 (1878); Walter v. Calhoun, 88 Kan. 801, 129 P. 1176 (1913).

as having the "quasi character of trustee or bailiff"[4] or of being a "trustee",[5] a "quasi trustee,"[6] a "constructive trustee"[7] or a "pledgee in possession."[8] Actually the mortgagee in possession is not a trustee and he is not truly a fiduciary, and invoking these designations is chiefly by way of analogy and for the purpose of ascribing to him certain rights and duties. It would have been better to have recognized that his position was *sui generis* and then determined what legal incidents should attach to it.

Whatever the label, the mortgagee in possession has a duty of conduct in respect to the mortgaged property which is substantially that of a provident owner—"to manage the property in a reasonably prudent and careful manner so as to keep it in a good state of preservation and productivity"[9] and to use the yield and rents of the property for no other purpose than to credit them on the mortgage debt.[10] However, the mortgagee in possession in the course of his management of the property, in addition to receiving income, will have incurred various expenses for which he is entitled to be reimbursed, or by his affirmative conduct or neglect have subjected himself to charges other than income actually received which will be assessed against him. It is only the balance, after these charges and debits have been cast up and set off against each other, that goes in satisfaction of the debt.

From the foregoing two things are apparent. One is that before it can be known how much of the income is to be applied to the mortgage debt there must be an accounting which can be made only in accordance with equitable theory and practice. The other is that the application in the accounting of the balance when ascertained is in the nature of an equitable set-off when the debt is being paid. This being so, it must be made in a proceeding or transaction directly involving the satisfaction of the mortgage debt.[11] Consequently an accounting can be called for only when the mortgagee enforces his debt by foreclosure or when the mortgagor seeks to pay it, either by voluntary agreement with the mortgagee or else in an action in equity to redeem.[12] Therefore, questions as to the accountability of the mortgagee in possession cannot be raised in actions at law for possession by the mortgagor[13] or

4. Hubbell v. Moulson, 53 N.Y. 225, 228, 13 Am.Rep. 519 (1873).

5. Toomer v. Randolph, 60 Ala. 356, 360 (1877); Anglo-Calif. Bank v. Field, 154 Cal. 513, 98 P. 267 (1908).

6. Myers-Macomber Engineers v. MLW Construction Corp., 271 Pa.Super. 484, 414 A.2d 357 (1979).

7. Real Estate-Land, Title & Trust Co. v. Homer Building & Loan Association, 138 Pa.Super. 563, 10 A.2d 786 (1940); Travis v. Schonwald, 131 S.W.2d 827 (Tex.Civ. App.1939).

8. Spect v. Spect, 88 Cal. 437, 26 P. 203, 13 L.R.A. 137, 22 Am.St.Rep. 314 (1891).

9. Myers-Macomber Engineers v. MLW Construction Corp., 271 Pa.Super. 484, 487, 414 A.2d 357, 360 (1979). See New York and Suburban Federal Savings & Loan Association v. Sanderman, 162 N.J.Super. 216, 392 A.2d 635 (1978).

10. Id.

11. Hubbell v. Moulson, 53 N.Y. 225, 13 Am.Rep. 519 (1873).

12. See 23 Harv.L.Rev. 301 (1910); Eisen v. Kostakos, 116 N.J.Super. 358, 282 A.2d 421 (1971).

13. Hubbell v. Moulson, 53 N.Y. 225, 13 Am.Rep. 519 (1873); Green v. Thornton, 8 Cal.App. 160, 96 P. 382 (1908).

by action and garnishment by a junior encumbrancer or any similar action not putting the payment of the mortgage debt directly in issue.[14]

It is elementary that the mortgagor is entitled to an accounting from any mortgagee in possession. So, too, are junior encumbrancers,[15] because they derive their interest from and participate in the mortgagor's right to redeem. And the same is true of transferees of the mortgagor's redemption interest.[16] Similarly, an assignee of the mortgagee in possession will be bound to render an accounting.[17] On the other hand, a senior mortgagee has no right to an accounting from either a junior mortgagee in possession [18] or a transferee of the mortgagor. This follows from the fact that they stand in the same position as the mortgagor and the mortgagee has no right to compel an accounting from the mortgagor in possession. Nor do unsecured creditors of the mortgagor normally have a right to an accounting against the mortgagee in possession.[19] "Such creditors must look to the mortgagor upon whose credit they relied." [20]

 WESTLAW REFERENCES
mortgagee-in-possession /p account conduct*** income manage! /s
    debt equit! mortgage set-off

§ 4.28   The Duty to Account for Rents

A mortgagee in possession may either rent the mortgaged property or occupy it himself. In any event, "with respect to accountability for rents and profits which the mortgagee in possession received or could have received, the general duty of the mortgagee toward the premises is that of an ordinarily prudent owner." [1] In the case where the property is rented the mortgagee must account for the rents and profits actually received.[2] Moreover, if he remits to a tenant part of the rent which he

14. Toomer v. Randolph, 60 Ala. 356 (1877). See note, 23 Harv.L.Rev. 301 (1909).

15. Landau v. Western Pennsylvania National Bank, 445 Pa. 217, 282 A.2d 335 (1971); Gaskell v. Viquesney, 122 Ind. 244, 23 N.E. 791, 17 Am.St.Rep. 364 (1890); Hirsch v. Northwestern Mutual Life Insurance Co., 191 Ga. 524, 13 S.E.2d 165 (1941); Mallalieu v. Wickham, 42 N.J.Eq. 297, 10 A. 880 (1886), holder of judgment lien. Thus it has been held that a mortgagee in possession is under a duty to a junior encumbrancer to refrain from permitting the mortgagor to receive the rents. Gandrud v. Hansen, 210 Minn. 125, 297 N.W. 730 (1941) discussed at length in note, 26 Minn. L.Rev. 880 (1942). But see McNicholas Appeal, 137 Pa.Super. 415, 9 A.2d 200 (1939).

16. Dicken v. Simpson, 117 Ark. 304, 174 S.W. 1154 (1915); Ruckman v. Astor, 9 Paige 517 (N.Y.1842); Elliott v. Brady, 172 N.Car. 828, 90 S.E. 951 (1916).

17. Strang v. Allen, 44 Ill. 428 (1867); Ackerman v. Lodi Branch R. Co., 31 N.J. Eq. 42 (1879).

18. Leeds v. Gifford, 41 N.J.Eq. 464, 5 A. 795 (1888), affirmed 45 N.J.Eq. 245, 19 A. 621 (1890).

19. Myers-Macomber Engineers v. MLW Construction Corp., 271 Pa.Super. 484, 414 A.2d 357 (1979).

20. Id. at 487, 414 A.2d at 360.

§ 4.28

1. Johns v. Moore, 168 Cal.App.2d 709, 336 P.2d 579, 581 (1959). See also, Shaeffer v. Chambers, 6 N.J.Eq. 548, 47 Am.Dec. 211 (1847). See Gerrish v. Black, 104 Mass. 400 (1870).

2. Gerrish v. Black, 104 Mass. 400 (1870).

could have collected with reasonable diligence he will be charged for it.[3] However, the standard itself permits some flexibility in bargaining with tenants as to amount of rent, subordination, extension of time for payment and length of lease and other similar matters [4] and the mortgagee will not be liable if the standard of provident owner is adhered to.[5] Even occasional vacancies will not be charged to him if he has used reasonable diligence to obtain tenants.[6]

When a mortgagee occupies the premises himself instead of leasing them several questions arise. One is whether there is any duty upon him to work or operate it in case he has tried with due diligence to rent it and failed. The answer should be yes and there is authority so holding, at least in the case of a farm.[7] If the mortgagee retains possession when he finds that he cannot rent the property, he should have to work it or, if he does not, he should be held for the fair rental value. Business property would present a more difficult case and it would seem undesirable to force a mortgagee to start a new business on it although there may be a duty to carry on an existing business.[8]

But when the mortgagee does operate it for how much should he be held accountable? The prevailing view is to charge him with the fair rental value no matter what he makes, letting him keep any excess and bear the loss if he makes less. In support of this it is argued that "The rule is founded in sound policy, for the reason that the particular items of expenditure, in labor or otherwise, as well as the profits received, are wholly within the knowledge of the mortgagee, and if he is not disposed to render a full and honest account, it would be impossible for the mortgagor to show them, or to establish errors in the mortgagee's

3. Carroll v. Tomlinson, 192 Ill. 398, 61 N.E. 484, 85 Am.St.Rep. 344 (1901); Miller v. Lincoln, 72 Mass. (6 Gray) 556 (1856), allowing "notoriously insolvent" tenant to remain in possession eighteen months made mortgagee chargeable for the lost rent.

4. Landau v. Western Pennsylvania National Bank, 445 Pa. 217, 282 A.2d 335 (1971) (voluntary subordination of mortgage to existing lease upheld even though junior lienor and mortgagor claimed that this would reduce the value of the premises on a foreclosure sale.); Chapman v. Cooney, 25 R.I. 657, 57 A. 928 (1904), 11% reduction to retain tenant who could not afford former rental; Wilmarth v. Johnson, 124 Wis. 320, 102 N.W. 562 (1905) rent remission to tenant "probably insolvent" when "times were hard" and mortgagor had consented; Eldriedge v. Hoefer, 52 Or. 241, 93 P. 246 (1908), modified 52 Or. 257, 94 P. 563 (1908), motion to recall mandate denied (1908) 52 Or. 241, 96 P. 1105, ten year lease; Hays v. Christensen, 114 Neb. 764, 209 N.W. 609 (1926), five year lease;

Brown v. South Boston Savings Bank, 148 Mass. 300, 19 N.E. 382 (1889), rent below value stated by expert testimony.

5. "The reasonableness of the mortgagee's action must be tested in light of general economic conditions, the character of the premises, the likely duration of his possession, and the extent of the mortgagor's residual interest." 50 Yale L.Jour. 1424, 1432 (1941).

6. Whitley v. Barnett, 151 Iowa 487, 131 N.W. 704 (1911), recognizing that vacancies might occur despite "the very best management obtainable"; Chapman v. Cooney, 25 R.I. 657, 57 A. 928 (1904); cf. McDonald v. Lingle, 199 N.C. 219, 220, 153 S.E. 848 (1930). Contra: Humrich v. Dalzell, 113 N.J.Eq. 310, 166 A. 511 (1933).

7. Shaeffer v. Chambers, 6 N.J.Eq. 548, 47 Am.Dec. 211 (1847).

8. Baumgard v. Bowman, 31 Ohio App. 266, 167 N.E. 166 (1928), mortgagee in possession must operate oil wells. But see Engleman Transportation Co. v. Longwell, 48 F. 129 (C.C.Mich.1880).

account." [9] Another possibility is to allow the mortgagor to hold the mortgagee for the fair rental value as a minimum but, in the alternative, the actual net rents and profits.[10] This would be fair enough in case it were established that the mortgagee had intentionally falsified his accounts. It seems unduly harsh to make the mortgagee liable for all he makes when successful but to hold him for a fair rental even when unsuccessful. The only possible justification for it would be a very strong policy of discouragement to mortgagees taking possession.

Where the mortgagee has entered believing that he is owner and not mortgagee, although in fact the latter is his status, he will be charged only with the rents actually received. The reason is the obvious unfairness of holding a person to a standard of responsibility based upon a conscious occupation of the property of another when no knowledge of the situation on which the liability is founded exists.[11] On the other hand if possession is taken wrongfully and with knowledge of the wrongfulness the least the mortgagee will be charged with is the rental value.[12]

 WESTLAW REFERENCES

mortgagee-in-possession /p account! /s (find*** /4 tenan**) (maintain! maintenance operat*** /4 business) rent!

266k199(3)

§ 4.29 Maintenance and Improvements

The duty of the mortgagee in possession to maintain the physical condition of the property reflects the fact that, however precarious his financial condition may be, the mortgagor is the beneficial owner of the premises and, as such, is entitled to protection against depletion of its value. Clearly any acts of destruction of the corpus of the property by the mortgagee will be waste for which he will be accountable.[1] Mis-

9. Sanders v. Wilson, 34 Vt. 318, 321 (1861); Barnett v. Nelson, 54 Iowa, 41, 6 N.W. 49, 37 Am.Rep. 183 (1880); Walter v. Calhoun, 88 Kan. 801, 129 P. 1176 (1913); Miller v. Peter, 184 Mich. 142, 150 N.W. 554 (1915); Liskey v. Snyder, 66 W.Va. 149, 66 S.E. 702 (1927)—accord. See, 46 A.L.R. 138, 153 (1927); 4 Am.St.Rep. 69 (1887). See also Shaeffer v. Chambers, 6 N.J.Eq. 548, 47 Am.Dec. 211 (1847), and Moshier v. Norton, 100 Ill. 63, 69 (1881) contra.

10. This seems to be what was done in Engleman Transportation Co. v. Longwell, 48 F. 129 (C.C.Mich.1880), for after an accounting for net rents and profits, of which there were none, the mortgagee was held for fair rental.

11. Parkinson v. Hanbury, L.R. 2 H.L. 1 (1867). Anglo-Cal. Bank v. Field, 154 Cal. 513, 98 P. 267 (1908); Morris v. Budlong, 78 N.Y. 543 (1879).

12. Sedlak v. Duda, 144 Neb. 567, 13 N.W.2d 892, 154 A.L.R. 490 (1944).

§ 4.29

1. American Freehold Land Mortgage Co. v. Pollard, 132 Ala. 155, 32 So. 630 (1902), timber removed; Smith v. Stringer, 228 Ala. 630, 155 So. 85 (1934), grapevines destroyed; Whiting v. Adams, 66 Vt. 679, 30 A. 32, 25 L.R.A. 598, 44 Am.St.Rep. 875 (1894), timber removed; Sandon v. Hooper, 6 Beav. 246 (1843), cottages torn down; Hansom v. Derby, 2 Vern. 398 (1700), wainscoting destroyed; Brown v. Daniel, 219 N.C. 349, 13 S.E.2d 623 (1941), timber removed. The measure of damages will be the diminution in the value of the estate caused by the destruction, Smith v. Stringer, supra; or, in case there is a severance and sale, either the proceeds or market value of the severed portion, Brown v. Daniel, supra.

management of the property is treated as akin to impairment of the property itself and the mortgagee will be charged with damage resulting from it.[2] But the mortgagee's duty goes beyond refraining from actively harming the property. He "is bound to use reasonable means to preserve the estate from loss and injury"[3] and one court has gone so far as to state that the mortgagee must "maintain the mortgaged premises in good condition to prevent its deterioration.[4] He must, therefore, conserve its value by making necessary repairs,[5] and this duty is recognized on the one hand by charging him for any loss that flows from his failure to act[6] and, on the other, by allowing him credit for expenditures in carrying it out.[7]

There are, however, limitations on this. For example, he is not bound to dig into his own pocket and so need not expend more than the rents and profits he receives.[8] Moreover, whatever the language of the general standard, there is some authority that, the mortgagee does not have to compensate for or prevent depreciation caused by ordinary wear and tear—"the silent effect of waste and decay from time."[9]

2. Baumgard v. Bowman, 31 Ohio App. 266, 167 N.E. 166 (1928). The mortgagee's irresponsibility or mismanagement may also be relieved against by the appointment of a receiver. Harding v. Garber, 20 Okl. 11, 93 P. 539 (1907); Brayton & Lawbaugh v. Monarch Lumber Co., 87 Or. 365, 169 P. 528 (1917), rehearing denied 87 Or. 365, 170 P. 717 (1917); Gibson v. Hamiltion & Rourke Co., 21 Wash. 365, 58 P. 217 (1899).

3. Barnard v. Paterson, 137 Mich. 633, 634, 100 N.W. 893 (1904); McCarron v. Cassidy, 18 Ark. 34 (1856); Woodward v. Phillips, 80 Mass. (14 Gray) 132 (1859); Eggensperger v. Lanpher, 92 Minn. 503, 100 N.W. 372 (1904)—accord. See Barthell v. Syverson, 54 Iowa 160, 6 N.W. 178 (1880); 1914, 49 L.R.A.,N.S., 122. Cf. Williams v. Rouse, 124 Ala. 160, 27 So. 16 (1899) (statute); Halbert v. Turner, 233 Ill. 531, 84 N.E. 704 (1908).

4. Landau v. Western Pennsylvania National Bank, 445 Pa. 217, 282 A.2d 335, 339 (1971).

5. Shaeffer v. Chambers, 6 N.J.Eq. 548, 47 Am.Dec. 211 (1847), "a mortgagee in possession is not at liberty to permit the property to go to waste, but is bound to keep it in good ordinary repair; and if it be a farm he is bound to good ordinary husbandry." Scherer v. Bang, 97 N.J.Eq. 497, 500, 128 A. 258, 259 (1925) "such repair as is absolutely necessary for the protection of the estate"; Hirsh v. Arnold, 318 Ill. 28, 148 N.E. 882 (1925).

6. Miller v. Ward, 111 Me. 134, 88 A. 400, 49 L.R.A.,N.S., 122 (1913); see S.P. Wragge v. Denham, 2 Younge & C. 117,

121 (1836); Hughes v. Williams, 12 Ves. 493 (1806); Dexter v. Arnold, 7 Fed.Cas. 597, 604 (1834).

7. Burns v. Williams, 147 Ark. 608, 228 S.W. 726 (1921); Hidden v. Jordan, 28 Cal. 301 (1865); Buettel v. Harmount, 46 Minn. 481, 49 N.W. 250 (1891); Mosier v. Norton, 83 Ill. 519 (1876); Miller v. Curry, 124 Ind. 48, 24 N.E. 219 (1889) rehearing denied 124 Ind. 48, 24 N.E. 374 (1889); Wise v. Layman, 197 Ind. 393, 150 N.E. 368 (1925); Gordon v. Krellman, 207 App.Div. 773, 202 N.Y.S. 682 (1924); Lynch v. Ryan, 137 Wis. 13, 118 N.W. 174, 129 Am.St.Rep. 1040 (1908).

8. Fidelity Trust Co. v. Saginaw Hotels Co., 259 Mich. 254, 242 N.W. 906 (1932); Carter v. McMillan, 68 Dom.L.R. 653 (1922). See Dexter v. Arnold, 7 Fed.Cas. 597, 604 (1834).

9. Dexter v. Arnold, 2 Sumn. 108 (1834), Fed.Cas.No. 3,858, Story, J.: Brown v. South Boston Savings Bank, 148 Mass. 300, 19 N.E. 382 (1889). See also Russell v. Smithies, 1 Austr. 96 (1792); S.P. Wragge v. Denham, 2 Younge & C. 117, 121 (1836).

"But where a mortgagee is guilty of wilful default or gross neglect as to repairs, he is properly responsible for the loss and damage occasioned thereby. * * * And there is the stronger reason for this doctrine because it is also the default of the mortgagor himself, if he does not take care to have suitable repairs made to preserve his own property." Dexter v. Norton, 7 Fed.Cas. 597, 604 (1834). Toole v. Weirick, 39 Mont. 359, 102 P. 590, 133 Am.St.Rep. 567

Indeed, a few cases describe the mortgagee's obligation in terms of "gross negligence" or "recklessness and improvidence." [10] In any event, the mortgagee's liability is governed by the condition of the property as of the time he went into possession. [11]

When it is a question, not of duty to make repairs, but of privilege of doing so, there seems to be considerably more latitude in determining what will constitute necessary repairs than when it is a matter of duty to do so. [12]

Normally a mortgagee in possession will not be allowed to make improvements on the property and to charge them to the mortgagor, a rule which is in sharp contrast with that governing repairs. [13] The reason for it is simple and sound. It "is a rule to protect the interests of the mortgagor, and to prevent the mortgagee from rendering it more difficult for the mortgagor to redeem the premises". [14] Otherwise, it might enable the mortgagee "to improve the mortgagor out of his estate." [15] But the line of demarcation between repairs and improvements is blurred. [16] Consequently, the rule against improvements is not inflexible. [17]

For one thing, if the improvements were made in pursuance of an agreement with the mortgagor or with his consent, either express or implied, there can be no question but that the cost is an allowable

(1909), mortgagee accountable for depreciation resulting from "the reckless or improvident management of the property."

Other cases laying down the test of "wilful default or gross negligence" include: Dozier v. Mitchell, 65 Ala. 511 (1880); Fidelity Trust Co. v. Saginaw Hotels Co., 259 Mich. 254, 242 N.W. 906 (1932); Mosier v. Norton, 83 Ill. 519 (1876). But in Burnett v. Nelson, 54 Iowa 41, 6 N.W. 49, 37 Am. Rep. 183 (1880), the court said the standard the mortgagee must use in keeping up the premises was ordinary care and he is not exonerated because not guilty of fraud or gross carelessness.

10. Barnard v. Paterson, 137 Mich. 633, 100 N.W. 893 (1904).

11. Gordon v. Krellman, 207 App.Div. 773, 202 N.Y.S. 682 (1924), in which new stoves and other items of a permanent nature put in to obtain tenants on advantageous terms was allowed as repairs. On the other hand, in Fletcher v. Bass River Savings Bank, 182 Mass. 5, 64 N.E. 207, 94 Am.St.Rep. 632 (1902), repairs made for the purpose of enhancing the sale price but not necessary to preserve it from deterioration for the short period it would be occupied by the mortgagee, although of such a nature as ordinarily would be credited to a

mortgagee in possession, were disallowed. Today in Massachusetts, by statute the mortgagee will be permitted to make "reasonable repairs and improvements." Mass.Gen.Laws Ann. c. 244, § 20; McFarlane v. Thompson, 241 Mass. 486, 135 N.E. 869 (1922).

12. Malone v. Roy, 107 Cal. 518, 40 P. 1040 (1895). See Roberts v. Fleming, 53 Ill. 196 (1870).

13. Sandon v. Hooper, 6 Beav. 246 (1843); Schuetz v. Schuetz, 237 Wis. 1, 296 N.W. 70 (1941), discussed, 40 Mich.L.Rev. 133 (1941). See also authorities cited in following footnotes.

14. Miller v. Ward, 111 Me. 134, 138, 88 A. 400, 402, 49 L.R.A.,N.S., 122 (1913).

15. Burns v. Williams, 147 Ark. 608, 228 S.W. 726 (1921); Kinkead v. Peet, 153 Iowa 199, 132 N.W. 1095 (1911); Cook v. Ottawa University, 14 Kan. 548 (1875); Moore v. Cable, N.Y., 1 Johns.Ch. 385 (1815)—accord.

16. See 35 Col.L.Rev. 1248, 1258 (1935).

17. "This rule [against improvements] is not inflexible, for the allowance may be regulated by the justice and equity arising out of the circumstances of each particular case." Wells v. Van Dyke, 109 Pa. 330, 42 L.I. 345, 16 W.N.C. 151 (1885).

item.[18] Credit will be given to a mortgagee who completes an unfinished building in order to make it tenantable, something most beneficial to the mortgagor and something he ought to want to have the mortgagee do.[19] However, the charge is justified, not on the ground of the mortgagor's acquiescence, but because the improvement was necessary to prevent deterioration on the one hand and to make it productive of income on the other, both essential to the protection of the interest of the mortgagor and for that reason chargeable to him as a matter of justice and equity. Similarly, the mortgagee may make reasonable improvements which are fairly and competently undertaken for the maintenance or increased income yield of the property.[20] But the character of the property cannot be altered. It cannot be made into a new and different thing rather than a better and more productive version of the premises taken over. Still another group of cases in which the mortgagee is allowed credit for improvements is where he is in possession believing in good faith that he is the owner, or at least free from the possibility of redemption by the mortgagor, whereas in truth all he has in his security interest and therefore has, even though he does not know it, only the rights of a mortgagee in possession.[21]

These cases, in addition to pointing to the mortgagee's good faith,[22] the beneficial character of the improvements and their reasonableness,

18. Shellnutt v. Shellnutt, 188 Ga. 306, 3 S.E.2d 900 (1939); Fort v. Colby, 165 Iowa 95, 144 N.W. 393 (1913); McGuire v. Halloran, 182 Iowa 209, 160 N.W. 363 (1917) rehearing denied 182 Iowa 209, 165 N.W. 405 (1917); Lynch v. Ryan, 137 Wis. 13, 118 N.W. 174, 129 Am.St.Rep. 1040 (1908). See 49 L.R.A.,N.S., 122, 128 (1913).

19. Miller v. Ward, 111 Me. 134, 88 A. 400, 49 L.R.A.,N.S., 122 (1913); Gilpin v. Brooks, 226 Mass. 322, 115 N.E. 421 (1917).

20. Hays v. Christiansen, 105 Neb. 586, 181 N.W. 379 (1921) new boiler; Gordon v. Krellman, 207 App.Div. 773, 202 N.Y.S. 682 (1924), new ranges and other items of permanent nature to keep tenants and attract new ones, the court classifying them as "repairs"; Wells v. Van Dyke, 109 Pa. 330, 42 L.I. 345, 16 W.N.C. 151 (1885) new improved machinery to enable mill to compete successfully with other mills; McFarlane v. Thompson, 241 Mass. 486, 135 N.E. 869 (1922), new cesspool, but statute covered case; Shepard v. Jones, 21 Ch.D. 469 (1882), deepening of well increase sale value although purchaser did not use water supply, mortgagee allowed for increased value.

21. Such cases include those in which the mortgagee purchased at a defective foreclosure sale. McSorley v. Larissa, 100 Mass. 270 (1868); Hicklin v. Marco, 46 F. 424 (C.C.Or.1891), affirmed 56 F. 549, 6

C.C.A. 10 (1893); Bradley v. Snyder, 14 Ill. 263, 58 Am.Dec. 564 (1853); Poole v. Johnson, 62 Iowa 611, 17 N.W. 900 (1883). See Martin v. Ratcliff, 101 Mo. 254, 13 S.W. 1051, 20 Am.St.Rep. 605 (1890) (defective exercise of power of sale); Freichnecht v. Meyer, 39 N.J.Eq. 551 (1885); Green v. Dixon, 9 Wis. 532 (1859) (statute). Cf. McCumber v. Gilman, 15 Ill. 381 (1854). Also those in which he was a grantee under a deed absolute given as security, so that by the form of the transaction he has reason to believe he is owner. Gillis v. Martin, 17 N.C. 470, 25 Am.Dec. 729 (1833); Harper's Appeal, 64 Pa. 315 (1870); Liskey v. Snyder, 66 W.Va. 149, 161, 66 S.E. 702, 708 (1909). Miller v. Curry, 124 Ind. 48, 24 N.E. 219, 374 (1889), contra, in spite of good faith by the mortgagee. Cf. Wilson v. Fisher, 148 N.C. 535, 541, 62 S.E. 622, 624–5 (1908), in which it was held that the appreciation was merely deductible from the charge for rents and profits.

22. Where the mortgagee takes possession wrongfully, claiming to be owner although he knows of the mortgagor's claim, there is an absence of good faith and no allowance will be made. Mahoney v. Bostwick, 96 Cal. 53, 30 P. 1020, 31 Am.St.Rep. 175 (1892); Malone v. Roy, 107 Cal. 518, 40 P. 1040 (1895); Bradley v. Merrill, 88 Me. 319, 34 A. 160 (1896); Dougherty v. McColgan, Md., 6 Gill & J. 275 (1834); Sedlak v.

stress the fact that the mortgagor stood by in silence without asserting his rights while the improvements were being made. This makes the injustice of permitting him to redeem without paying anything for the value added to his property so clear that the ordinary rule against allowances for improvements will not be followed.[23] This conduct by the mortgagor, it should be observed, is the foundation for imposing a nonconsensual obligation upon him to prevent unjust enrichment rather than the basis for inferring an implied in fact contract to pay for the improvement. Indeed, in an extreme case, the mortgagor's continued passivity over a long time may be so reprehensible in view of the mortgagee's reliance upon it as to estop the mortgagor altogether from redeeming.[24] And, finally, in some states there are statutory provisions making changes in the rule. Thus in Massachusetts improvements which are "reasonable" may be made and charged to the mortgagor.[25] An Alabama statute permits the mortgagee to charge for improvements up to the amount of rents charged against him.[26]

Suppose, after improvements, the property is sold to a third person against whom the mortgagor no longer has the right to redeem. As we have seen, the major reason for the "no reimbursement for improvements" rule is to avoid making mortgagor's redemption more burdensome. Consequently, it hardly seems unfair to give the mortgagee that

Duda, 144 Neb. 567, 13 N.W.2d 892, 154 A.L.R. 490 (1944); Shelley v. Cody, 187 N.Y. 166, 79 N.E. 994 (1907); Cookes v. Culbertson, 9 Nev. 199 (1874); Witt v. Trustees of Grand Grove of United Ancient Order of Druids, 55 Wis. 376, 13 N.W. 261 (1884). By the weight of authority, constructive notice from a record of the existence of a paramount title or interest does not prevent an occupant from being an improver in good faith. See 68 A.L.R. 288 (1930).

23. Hadley v. Stewart, 65 Wis. 481, 27 N.W. 340 (1886); Morgan v. Walbridge, 56 Vt. 405 (1883); Mickles v. Dillaye, 17 N.Y. 80 (1858). Also, basing the allowance on the fact that the mortgagor had permitted a long period to elapse without asserting his rights, see Roberts v. Fleming, 53 Ill. 196 (1870); Montgomery v. Chadwick, 7 Iowa 114 (1858); Miner v. Beekman, 50 N.Y. 337 (1872). See also Morris v. Budlong, 78 N.Y. 543 (1879). There are, however, some cases that require only that the mortgagee believe that he is the owner and make beneficial improvements in good faith. Hicklin v. Marco, 46 F. 424 (C.C.Or. 1891) affirmed 56 F. 549, 6 C.C.A. 10 (1893); Ensign v. Batterson, 68 Conn. 298, 36 A. 51 (1896); Liskey v. Snyder, 66 W.Va. 149, 162, 66 S.E. 702, 708 (1909); Green v. Dixon, 9 Wis. 532 (1859).

24. Ferguson v. Boyd, 169 Ind. 537, 81 N.E. 71 (1907), rehearing denied 169 Ind.

537, 82 N.E. 1064 (1908); Purcell v. Thornton, 128 Minn. 255, 150 N.W. 899 (1915). That mere silence by the mortgagor should not work an estoppel, see Glenn, Mortgages, § 220.1, criticizing Purcell v. Thornton, supra. The estoppel in cases of this sort is against showing that the right of redemption exists, either because the foreclosure was defective or because the transaction, although not in form a mortgage, was so intended by the parties, and not against asserting a redemption right already established. It does not, therefore, violate, technically at least, the rule safeguarding the exercise of the equity of redemption once it has been shown to exist. See Glenn, Mortgages, § 220.1.

25. Mass.Gen.Laws Ann. c. 244, § 20; McFarlane v. Thompson, 241 Mass. 486, 135 N.E. 869 (1922).

26. Dozier v. Mitchell, 65 Ala. 511 (1880). For the statutory rule requiring payment for improvements by a redemptioner from a foreclosure sale, Ala.Code 1958, Tit. 7, §§ 732, 740; Rudisill v. Buckner, 244 Ala. 653, 15 So.2d 333 (1944); Ladd v. Parmer, 278 Ala. 435, 178 So.2d 829 (1965). "Betterment" statutes have been enacted in many states protecting the improver in good faith of another's property. See 30 Col.L.Rev. 575, 576 (1930), on the requirement of good faith under "betterment" statutes.

part of the sale proceeds that represents the excess over what the property would have sold for without the improvements. Moreover, there is case law supporting this position.[27]

Where improvements are allowed, how should the credit to the mortgagee be calculated? Where they are allowed because of consent by the mortgagor [28] or in order to make or keep the property tenantable or productive, the amount reasonably expended is the criterion, just as in the analogous case of necessary or authorized repairs.[29] However, where the mortgagee acted under an honest belief that he was the owner, or that the redemption interest was barred or would never be exercised—a belief to which the mortgagor's conduct usually contributes—an entirely different principle is operative. Its purpose is the prevention of unjust enrichment due to justifiable misreliance because of mistake. Consequently the value added to the property by the improvement, not to exceed its actual cost, is the proper measure of recovery and the one recognized by the courts in such cases.[30]

Where the mortgagee is not allowed any charge for improvements, it seems unfair to charge him for rent other than for the property without the improvement, and this has been held to be the rule.[31] When, however, the mortgagee is charged with the full rental value of the property as improved, he will be entitled to interest upon the cost of the improvement as an offset.[32] Indeed, there is authority that, although the full value of the improvement cannot be allowed, the mortgagee will be able to recoup so much of its value as will be covered by the net income of the property for which he is chargeable.[33] Finally, where the mortgagee is permitted to charge for the improvements, "no interest should be allowed the [mortgagee] appellant on the value of his improvements, as he has had the use of them, and, under the rule of

---

27. Halbert v. Turner, 233 Ill. 531, 84 N.E. 704 (1908).

28. Lynch v. Ryan, 137 Wis. 13, 19, 118 N.W. 174, 176, 129 Am.St.Rep. 1040 (1908), "where the making of the improvements was authorized or consented to * * * the legitimate basis is the reasonable cost, the same as in repairs. * * *".

29. E.g., Miller v. Ward, 111 Me. 134, 139, 88 A. 400, 402, 49 L.R.A.,N.S., 122 (1913), "the money expended * * * was a proper charge"; Hays v. Christiansen, 105 Neb. 586, 181 N.W. 379 (1921); Gordon v. Krellman, 207 App.Div. 773, 202 N.Y.S. 682 (1924).

30. See Ladd v. Parmer, 278 Ala. 435, 178 So.2d 829 (1965); Hadley v. Stewart, 65 Wis. 481, 485, 27 N.W. 340, 342 (1886), "the sum the improvements enhanced the value of the whole premises, and not their cost, in case the cost exceeds the value which

they have added to the premises."; Mickles v. Dillaye, 17 N.Y. 80, 93 (1858), "he should be required to make equitable compensation for the benefits he will receive from the improvements."; see quotation, s.c., supra, § 169 note 26. Merriam v. Goss, 139 Mass. 77, 28 N.E. 449 (1885); Halbert v. Turner, 233 Ill. 531, 84 N.E. 704 (1908); Moore's Guardian v. Williamson's Executor, 201 Ky. 561, 257 S.W. 711 (1923); Howard v. Clark, 72 Vt. 429, 48 A. 656 (1900); see 49 L.R.A.,N.S., 122, 129.

31. Bradley v. Merrill, 91 Me. 340, 40 A. 132 (1898); Gresham v. Ware, 79 Ala. 192; see 49 L.R.A.,N.S., 122, 130 (1885).

32. Lynch v. Ryan, 137 Wis. 13, 118 N.W. 174, 129 Am.St.Rep. 1040 (1908).

33. Dozier v. Mitchell, 65 Ala. 511 (1880); Montgomery v. Chadwick, 7 Iowa 114, 7 Clarke 114 (1858); Wilson v. Fisher, 148 N.C. 535, 62 S.E. 622 (1908).

estimating the rent * * * he will not be charged any rent for the use of his improvements."[34]

 WESTLAW REFERENCES

mortgagee-in-possession /53 deplet*** injur*** loss mismanage! repair*** waste

mortgagee-in-possession /s improv!

§ 4.30 Compensation for Services

If the circumstances are such that an owner would be reasonable in employing someone to take care of the premises and do such things as collecting the rents, the mortgagee in possession may hire it done and charge the expense to the mortgagor.[1] However, there is significant authority that even though the situation is such that the mortgagee could have hired someone else, he cannot do the job himself and charge the mortgagor compensation or commissions for so doing.[2] One reason advanced is that the mortgagee in possession is comparable to a trustee,[3] and the courts do not want the fiduciary relation which exists under such circumstances to be permitted with the mortgagee having a selfish interest adverse to that of the mortgagor. The interest of the mortgagor is in having the work done for as little as possible; the interest of the employee, is in getting paid as much as possible. The rule as to trustees, however, has been changed either by statute or decision, and since admittedly the mortgagee situation is a weaker one for imposing the restriction, it should also be abandoned.[4] Another reason given for denying the mortgagee compensation is that he is in possession solely for his benefit and consequently there is no foundation for implying in fact any agreement to charge or to impose a quasi-contractual obligation on the mortgagor.[5] But an answer to this is that

34. Hadley v. Stewart, 65 Wis. 481, 27 N.W. 340 (1886); Howard v. Clark, 72 Vt. 429, 48 A. 656 (1900); Poole v. Johnson, 62 Iowa 611, 17 N.W. 900 (1883); see Lynch v. Ryan, supra note 30, 49 L.R.A.,N.S., 122, 130.

§ 4.30

1. Turner v. Johnson, 95 Mo. 431, 7 S.W. 570, 6 Am.St.Rep. 62 (1888); Johnson v. Hosford, 110 Ind. 572, 10 N.E. 407 (1887), rehearing denied 110 Ind. 572, 12 N.E. 522 (1887); see Harper v. Ely, 70 Ill. 581 (1873). But in American Freehold Land Mortgage Co. v. Pollard, 132 Ala. 155, 32 So. 630 (1902), although the mortgagor had voluntarily given possession to a non-resident corporation mortgagee, the court refused to recognize that fact of non-residence as sufficient reason to allow payment of agents to collect the rents.

2. Barnard v. Paterson, 137 Mich. 633, 100 N.W. 893 (1904); Lynch v. Ryan, 137 Wis. 13, 118 N.W. 174 (1908); Wadleigh v.

Phelps, 149 Cal. 627, 87 P. 93 (1906); Shaw v. G.B. Beaumont Co., 88 N.J.Eq. 333, 102 A. 151, 2 A.L.R. 122 (1917); Moore v. Cable, 1 Johns.Ch. 385 (N.Y.1815). His own out of pocket expenses incurred in management and collection do not fall under the ban. Harper v. Ely, 70 Ill. 581 (1873); Turk v. Page, 64 Okl. 251, 167 P. 462. See 170 A.L.R. 181 (1917).

3. Bonithron v. Hockmore, 1 Vern. 316 (1685). See Green v. Lamb, 24 Hun 87, 89 (N.Y.1881), "the mortgagee in possession is classed with a trustee; and it is said that neither was entitled to commissions. Plainly the law is changed as to a trustee."

4. In re Hemphill's Estate, 157 Wis. 331, 147 N.W. 1089 (1914); see Green v. Lamb, note 35, supra; Scott, Trusts, § 242.

5. Benham v. Rowe, 2 Cal. 387, 408, 56 Am.Dec. 342 (1852), "his care and trouble are bestowed for the furtherance and protection of his own interests."; Barnard v.

the care and management of the premises is also necessary to preserve the value of the mortgagor's redemption interest.[6]

Other courts permit compensation to the mortgagee. Massachusetts and a few other states allow the mortgagee a reasonable commission for his services.[7] Still others leave the setting of compensation to the discretion of the court.[8]

 WESTLAW REFERENCES

mortgagee-in-possession /p care-taker job manager work /s
compensat*** h**self hir*** service

§ 4.31   Reimbursement for Insurance and Taxes

Today the usual mortgage contains a clause requiring the mortgagor to keep the premises insured for the benefit of the mortgagee, or, more commonly, as their interest shall appear. If there is such a contractual duty and the mortgagor fails to insure, the mortgagee is privileged to do it and charge the expense thereof to the mortgagor as an addition to the mortgage debt.[1] In the absence of such agreement or an authorization by the mortgagor, some older cases hold that a mortgagee may not insure the mortgaged premises and charge the mortgagor.[2] It has been pointed out, however, that some of these authorities represent an attitude toward insurance out of harmony with present day notions, while others are those in which the mortgagee insured only his own interest.[3] Trustees today have a duty to keep trust property insured and are surcharged in their accounts if they do not do so and a loss occurs.[4] The same duty should apply to a mortgagee in possession. As was pointed out in a leading case, "in the light of modern ideas in respect to the reasonable care of property by one in possession thereof in the nature of trustee for another, having a

Paterson, 137 Mich. 633, 100 N.W. 893 (1904).

6. See 24 Col.L.Rev. 318, 319 (1924).

7. See MacNeil Brothers Co. v. Cambridge Savings Bank, 334 Mass. 360, 135 N.E.2d 652 (1956); Van Vronker v. Eastman, 48 Mass. (7 Met.) 157 (1843); Barry v. Dow, 240 Mass. 419, 134 N.E. 367 (1922); Barry v. Harlowe, 242 Mass. 159, 136 N.E. 105 (1922), possession by consent does not alter the rule; Waterman v. Curtis, 26 Conn. 241 (1857); Bradley v. Merrill, 91 Me. 340, 40 A. 132 (1898).

8. Walter v. Calhoun, 88 Kan. 801, 129 P. 1176 (1913); Massari v. Girardi, 119 Misc. 607, 197 N.Y.S. 751 (1922).

§ 4.31

1. Baker v. Aalberg, 183 Ill. 258, 55 N.E. 672 (1899); Jehle v. Brooks, 112 Mich. 131, 70 N.W. 440 (1897); Sanford v. Litchenberger, 62 Neb. 501, 57 N.W. 305 (1901);

Hays v. Christiansen, 114 Neb. 764, 209 N.W. 609 (1926). See 20 St. John's L.Rev. 59 (1945).

2. Curtis v. Curtis, 180 Ala. 70, 60 So. 165 (1912); Barnett v. Nelson, 54 Iowa 41, 6 N.W. 49, 37 Am.Rep. 183 (1880); Saunders v. Frost, 22 Mass. (5 Pick.) 259, 16 Am. Dec. 394 (1827); Faure v. Winans, N.Y., 1 Hopk.Ch. 283, 14 Am.Dec. 545 (1824); see United States Trust Co. v. Miller, 116 Neb. 25, 29, 215 N.W. 462, 469 (1927).

3. See Glenn, Mortgages, § 213. Miller v. Ward, 111 Me. 134, 88 A. 400, 49 L.R.A.,N.S., 122 (1913), policy in mortgagee's own name; Wise v. Layman, 197 Ind. 393, 150 N.E. 368 (1926), no showing that payment would be other than to mortgagee's personal favor.

4. Restatement, Second, Trusts § 176; Scott, Trusts, § 176.

duty or authority to preserve the same, reasonable expenditures for insurance are as legitimate as such expenditures for repairs and to prevent loss by decay or destruction or otherwise." [5]

It has been urged that the duty or privilege of insuring should extend beyond that against the hazard of fire to any kind that a reasonable person [6] in charge of his own property would take out. In this connection, some courts have allowed the mortgagee reimbursement for premiums on "property owners liability" insurance.[7]

A mortgagor in possession has the duty of paying all taxes on the mortgaged property.[8] If he fails to do so the law is well settled that the mortgagee may pay them to protect his security interest in the land.[9] If the property has been sold for taxes, the mortgagee may redeem it from the tax sale. In either event he may add the amounts so expended to the mortgage debt.[10] If the mortgagee is in possession, there is a duty upon him, at least to the extent of rents and profits received, to pay taxes.[11] But, since the payment nevertheless inures to the benefit of the mortgagor, the beneficial owner of the property, he can in such cases also demand credit for the payment and add it to his claim.[12] Consequently, whether the payment is made by a mortgagee in possession or out of possession the right clearly is one for reimbursement on quasi-contractual principles because of the benefit conferred

5. Lynch v. Ryan, 137 Wis. 13, 23, 118 N.W. 174, 178, 129 Am.St.Rep. 1040 (1908). cf. Land Finance Corp. v. Giorgio, 280 N.Y.S. 924 (1935).

6. Glenn, Mortgages, § 213.

7. See e.g., State Realty Co. of Boston Inc. v. MacNeil Brothers Co., 334 Mass. 294, 135 N.E.2d 291 (1956); MacNeil Brothers Co. v. Cambridge Savings Bank, 334 Mass. 360, 135 N.E.2d 652 (1956).

8. Dayton v. Rice, 47 Iowa 429 (1877); Pines v. Novick, 168 App.Div. 155, 153 N.Y.S. 891 (1915).

9. See, e.g., Eisen v. Kostakos, 116 N.J. Super. 358, 282 A.2d 421 (1971).

10. Eisen v. Kostakos, 116 N.J.Super. 358, 282 A.2d 421 (1971); see collection of cases, 60 A.L.R. 425 (1929); 84 A.L.R. 1366 (1933); 123 A.L.R. 1248. The rule extends to cases where taxes were paid in the mistaken belief, bona fide, that the payor held a mortgage on the land. Central Wisconsin Trust Co. v. Swenson, 222 Wis. 331, 267 N.W. 307, 106 A.L.R. 1207 (1936); see 84 A.L.R. 1366, 1371, 1372 (1933); 123 A.L.R. 1248, 1250, 1252, 1253 (1939). A first mortgagee who pays taxes can add the amount paid to his debt in priority to a second mortgagee. Wiggin v. Lowell Five Cent Savings Bank, 299 Mass. 518, 13 N.E.2d 433 (1938). Additional authorities

include Redic v. Mechanics & Farmers Bank, 241 N.C. 152, 84 S.E.2d 542 (1954), discussed in Third Annual Survey of North Carolina Case Law: Credit Transactions, 34 N.C.L.Rev. 36 (1955); Crofts v. Johnson, 6 Utah 2d 350, 313 P.2d 808 (1957). Although the mortgaged property becomes security for the right to reimbursement for delinquent taxes paid by the mortgagee, this right of repayment is separate and apart from the original mortgage debt. Equitable Life Assurance Society of the United States v. Bennion, 81 Idaho 445, 346 P.2d 1053 (1959).

11. Brown v. Simons, 44 N.H. 475 (1863); Shoemaker v. Commonwealth Bank, 15 Pa. 297, 11 W.N.C. 284, 39 L.I. 81 (1881); Ten Eyck v. Craig, 62 N.Y. 406 (1875). Cf. Eisen v. Kostakos, 116 N.J. Super. 358, 282 A.2d 421 (1971).

12. Eisen v. Kostakos, 116 N.J.Super. 358, 282 A.2d 421 (1971); Hays v. Christiansen, 114 Neb. 764, 209 N.W. 609 (1926); Wise v. Layman, 197 Ind. 393, 399, 150 N.E. 368, 371 (1926); Brown v. Berry, 89 N.J.Eq. 230, 236, 108 A. 51, 54 (1918); Johns v. Moore, 168 Cal.App.2d 709, 336 P.2d 579 (1959); United States v. Bond, 172 F.Supp. 759 (E.D.Va.1959), reversed 279 F.2d 837 (C.A.1960), certiorari denied 364 U.S. 895, 81 S.Ct. 220, 5 L.Ed.2d 189 (1960).

upon the mortgagor in relieving his property of the charge upon it for taxes.[13]

However, it is also the clear weight of authority that "this claim must be enforced as a part of the mortgage debt, and cannot be made the basis of an independent action against the mortgagor, as for money paid to his use, ＊ ＊ ＊ or ＊ ＊ ＊ by virtue of the law of subrogation." [14] In other words, the mortgagor is limited to reimbursement as part of the action of foreclosure or redemption. The explanation given for this rule is that the amount due for taxes, together with the amount due on the mortgage, constitutes a single, indivisible debt, and "could become a lien only in connection with and because of the mortgage, and could not exist independent of it" and consequently, mortgagees "could not at pleasure split up their demand and make the parts the subjects of separate suits." [15] The plain answer to this is that the debt claim itself is a contract claim and the mortgage securing it is the result of a consensual transaction, while the claim for reimbursement for taxes paid is clearly nonconsensual as is the lien on the property to secure it. It is true that the mortgage must exist, or be honestly thought to exist, at the time of payment in order for the mortgagee not to be classed as a volunteer and denied recovery altogether. But the existence of the mortgage as a necessary condition to the creation of the non-consensual right to restitution obviously does not make the right so created an integral part of his mortgage debt claim. Rather, the rule would seem to rest upon the practical ground that it is so intimately, if not indissolubly, connected with the mortgage debt that the whole matter should be, as a matter of expediency and fairness to the mortgagor, settled in the one suit in which the mortgage debt is enforced; the mortgagee should not be permitted inexcusable tardiness in not presenting his demand at the time the entire transaction was in issue.

So viewed, the rule seems a sound one, certainly as to all taxes paid before the foreclosure decree. If this is the proper basis it should not be applied mechanically. Independent recovery should be and has been permitted where payment is made (1) after entry of a foreclosure

---

13.　See Note, 90 U.Pa.L.Rev. 90 (1941).

14.　Home Owners' Loan Corp. v. Joseph, 306 Ill.App. 244, 28 N.E.2d 330 (1940); Criswell v. McKnight, 120 Neb. 317, 232 N.W. 586, 84 A.L.R. 1361 (1930); The Praetorians v. State, 53 S.W.2d 334 (Tex.Civ.App.1932); Vincent v. Moore, 51 Mich. 618, 17 N.W. 81 (1883); Eblen v. Major's Administrator, 147 Ky. 44, 143 S.W. 748 (1912); Stone v. Tilley, 100 Tex. 487, 101 S.W. 201, 10 L.R.A.,N.S., 678, 123 Am.St.Rep. 819, 15 Ann.Cas. 524 (1907). See 1907, 10 L.R.A.,N.S. 679. But see Childs v. Smith, 51 Wash. 457, 99 P. 304, 130 Am.St.Rep. 1107 (1909). Cf. Hill v.

Townley, 1891, 45 Minn. 167, 47 N.W. 653 (1891); 84 A.L.R. 1366, 1387 (1933); 123 A.L.R. 1248, 1256 (1939). And, it has been reasoned, that since the mortgagee cannot have an independent action against the mortgagor, even more clearly he should be denied independent relief against a non-assuming grantee of the mortgagor. Citizens Savings Bank v. Guaranty Loan Co., 62 R.I. 448, 6 A.2d 688, 123 A.L.R. 1236 (1939); cf. Conaty v. Guaranty Loan Co., 62 R.I. 470, 6 A.2d 698 (1939), noted and criticized, 53 Harv.L.Rev. 144 (1939).

15.　Vincent v. Moore, 51 Mich. 618, 17 N.W. 81 (1883).

decree;[16] (2) after the debt claim has been barred by a statute of limitations or non-claim;[17] or (3) in other situations where hardship on the mortgagee justifies departure from the rule.[18]

 WESTLAW REFERENCES
mortgagee-in-possession /s insur! tax

§ 4.32 Annual Rests

Rents received by a mortgagee in possession are not automatically applied on the mortgage debt or the interest on it. Before any of the income received by him is appropriated to such a purpose there must be, as was seen, an accounting in which the mortgagee's allowable expenses and charges are first set-off against what he has taken in, and such an accounting is had only when there is either an action to foreclose or to redeem.[1] Consequently the mortgagor cannot omit payments of interest or installments of principal on the ground that the mortgagee has in his hands income from the property more than sufficient to cover them.[2] However, an accounting is a matter of equitable set-off. So when it is taken there is no inherent difficulty in balancing off as of a prior date, if that be desirable, the net rents as they would have been at that time in payment or reduction of principal and income. Indeed, it would be unfair to the mortgagor if, in any one year, the mortgagee has in his hands a surplus of income over outgo which might be used to pay interest and also to reduce part of the principal debt so that the interest on it for the ensuing year would be less, and it were not so credited. One way to handle such a situation would be to compute on the one side, interest on the debt for the entire period without annual rests together with interest on the various items of expenses allowed to the mortgagee as they accrued, while on the other he would be charged interest on the rents and profits as and when received down to the date of the accounting.[3] Most courts, however, when an account is taken, meet the problem by ordering

16. Hogg v. Longstreth, 97 Pa. 255, 10 W.N.C. 95 (1881); New Haven Savings Bank v. Atwater, 51 Conn. 429 (1883); Mutual Life Insurance Co. v. Newell, 78 Hun 293, 28 N.Y.S. 913 (1894), affirmed without opinion, 144 N.Y. 627, 39 N.E. 494. See 90 U.Pa.L.Rev. 90, 93 (1941).

17. Federal Land Bank of Columbia v. Brooks, 139 Fla. 506, 190 So. 737 (1939) noted with approval, 17 N.Y.Univ.L.Q.Rev. 295 (1939), subrogation to lien of state for taxes paid; Catlin v. Mills, 140 Wash. 1, 247 P. 1013, 47 A.L.R. 545 (1926), quasi-contractual recovery; Hill v. Townley, 45 Minn. 167, 47 N.W. 653 (1891), contra.

18. White v. First National Bank, 24 F.Supp. 290 (D.C.Pa.1938); Dunlop v. James, 174 N.Y. 411, 67 N.E. 60 (1903). See cases in two preceding footnotes. See

also 123 A.L.R. 1248, 1256 (1939); 17 N.Y. Univ.L.Q.Rev. 295, 297 notes 16, 17 (1939); Restatement, Restitution, § 104, comment a, illustration 3.

§ 4.32

1. Eisen v. Kostakos, 116 N.J.Super. 358, 282 A.2d 421 (1971); Onderdonk v. Gray, 19 N.J.Eq. 65 (1868); Landau v. Western Pennsylvania National Bank, 445 Pa. 217, 282 A.2d 335 (1971).

2. 4 American Law of Property § 16.105 (1952) (quoted in Eisen v. Kostakos, supra note 1).

3. Keeline v. Clark, 132 Iowa 360, 106 N.W. 257 (1906); Morrow v. Turney's Administrator, 35 Ala. 131 (1859); Walter v. Calhoun, 88 Kan. 801, 129 P. 1176 (1913); cf. Green v. Westcott, 13 Wis. 606 (1861).

annual rests in all cases where the net income is in excess of the annual interest.[4] A frequently quoted statement of this method is as follows: "1. State the gross rents received by the defendant to the end of the first year. 2. State the sums paid by him for repairs, taxes, and a commission for collecting the rents,[5] and deduct the same from the gross rents, and the balance will show the net rents to the end of the year. 3. Compute the interest on the note for one year and add it to the principal, and the aggregate will show the amount due thereon at the end of the year. 4. If the net annual rent exceeds the year's interest on the note, deduct that rent from the amount due, and the balance will show the amount remaining due at the end of the year. 5. At the end of the second year go through the same process, taking the amount due at the beginning of the year as the new capital to compute the year's interest upon. So to the time of judgment."[6]

 WESTLAW REFERENCES

mortgagee-in-possession /s account! "annual rest" balanc*** set-off
/s (gross net /3 rent) income interest principal

G.   RECEIVERSHIPS

§ 4.33   General Considerations

An equitable receivership normally entails the judicial appointment of a third party to take possession of the mortgaged property to repair or preserve the property and to collect rents.[1] As the following sections will indicate, the grounds for the appointment of a receiver and the scope of a receivership vary substantially from jurisdiction to jurisdiction. Nevertheless, mortgagees generally prefer a receivership over attempting to obtain possession of the mortgaged premises as a mortgagee in possession, even where the latter remedy is available.[2]

The reasons for this preference are not difficult to understand. A title state mortgagee, as we have seen, in theory may successfully obtain possession by an action at law for ejectment. However, this action may sometimes be drawn out and time consuming whereas a

---

4. See, e.g., MacNeil Brothers Co. v. Cambridge Savings Bank, 334 Mass. 360, 135 N.E.2d 652 (1956).

5. In Massachusetts commissions are allowed. See supra, § 4.33. Of course where not allowed this item would not be deducted.

6. Van Vronker v. Eastman, 48 Mass. (7 Metc.) 157, 163 (1843). Gladding v. Warner, 36 Vt. 54 (1863); Adams v. Sayre, 76 Ala. 509 (1884); MacNeil Brothers Co. v. Cambridge Savings Bank, 334 Mass. 360, 135 N.E.2d 652 (1956). For further consideration of problems incident to annual rests, see Osborne, Mortgages §§ 175–176 (2d Ed. 1970).

§ 4.33

1. In certain infrequent instances the receiver may be the mortgagee rather than a third party. See United States v. American National Bank & Trust Co. of Chicago, 573 F.Supp. 1317 (N.D.Ill.1983); United States v. St. Paul Missionary Public Housing, Inc., 575 F.Supp. 867 (N.D.Ohio 1983). See note infra.

2. See Randolph, The Mortgagee's Interest in Rents: Some Policy Considerations and Proposals, 29 Kan.L.Rev. 1, 38 (1980).

receiver may usually be appointed incident to a judicial foreclosure suit. Moreover, by utilizing a receivership, a mortgagee avoids some of the strict accounting responsibilities that, as we have previously noted,[3] are associated with being a mortgagee in possession. While a "mortgagee in possession must credit on the mortgage debt not only all the net rents received, but also all the rents that he might have received by the exercise of reasonable diligence," [4] the mortgagee under a receivership need not shoulder that burden. Moreover, the receivership generally will insulate the mortgagee from tort and related landowner-type liabilities that, as we have seen,[5] are normally imposed on the mortgagee in possession. Finally, of course, in lien theory states, the availability of a receivership may be even more important to the mortgagee because of the unavailability of ejectment as a possessory remedy.[6]

 WESTLAW REFERENCES
di receiver

§ 4.34 Basis for Appointment—Title and Lien Jurisdictions

In states following the title theory, and in the intermediate states on default, no question arises as to the right of the mortgagee to take possession and with it the fruits of possession, the rents and profits of the land. Both the corpus and the income from it are part of his security by the creation of the mortgage, and no additional agreements are necessary either to give him the right to possession or the rents of the land that go with it. Earlier we saw that equity, although it would enjoin acts by the mortgagor that would imperil the adequacy of the

3. See §§ 4.24–4.32, supra.

4. Kratovil, Mortgages—Problems in Possession, Rents, and Mortgagee Liability, 11 DePaul L.Rev. 1, 7 (1961).

5. See § 4.26 supra.

6. While, as we noted earlier in this section, the receiver is usually a third party, recent case law suggests that the United States, as mortgagee, may act as a receiver. See United States v. American National Bank & Trust Co. of Chicago, 573 F.Supp. 1317 (N.D.Ill.1983) (appointment of United States as receiver permissible in the absence of mortgagor objection.). Moreover, it is not always clear whether the United States is taking possession as a receiver or as a mortgagee in possession. In one federal decision a district court granted a request by the United States, the mortgagee, to be put into possession as a "mortgagee in possession." See United States v. St. Paul Missionary Public Housing, Inc., 575 F.Supp. 867 (N.D.Ohio 1983). However, because the court applied traditional receivership standards and cited receivership case law, it probably viewed the mortgagee's petition as a request for a receivership rather than as one to become a mortgagee in possession.

It may be argued that the appointment of a mortgagee as receiver is objectionable because, as a party, it cannot act impartially. However, this concern is probably misplaced. Mortgagees, whether private or governmental, in some jurisdictions frequently become mortgagees in possession and probably carry out their accounting obligations to their mortgagors fairly and efficiently. In such settings, it would seem to be of little consequence to the mortgagor whether the mortgagee is designated a mortgagee in possession or a receiver. In any event, the United States as receiver is arguably less likely to short-change the mortgagor than would its non-governmental counterpart. Moreover, to the extent that some of the costs of the receivership may be borne by the taxpayers, the mortgagor may actually benefit from mortgagee-receivership.

mortgagee's security before foreclosure and in extreme cases might appoint a receiver, nevertheless took this latter step with the greatest reluctance. In general, equity courts took the position that either the legal remedy of obtaining possession or equitable remedies [1] restraining harmful conduct by the mortgagor were sufficient protection to the mortgagee.[2]

Under early title theory decisions, receivership was denied even as an incident to a judicial foreclosure action. The mortgagee was left to his remedies at law. Such remedies were deemed adequate despite the facts (1) that ejectment was so far from expeditious that the foreclosure action might well be concluded first, (2) that when pursued it had the unfortunate consequence of destroying leases subordinate to the mortgage and saddling the mortgagee with the hazard and burden of making new agreements for keeping the premises productive of income, and (3) that it subjected the mortgagee to an intentionally severe and strict accounting.[3]

What then will induce a court in a title jurisdiction to appoint a receiver of rents and profits in a foreclosure action? The clue to the solution may be found in the reason invoked in lien jurisdictions to give to the mortgagee a claim to the rents and profits prior to the sale on foreclosure. That reasoning has been expressed by an able court thus: "There can be no doubt, that in a proper case where a bill was filed for specific performance of a contract to convey land, the court might appoint a receiver of the rents accruing during the pendency of the action, for equity treats that as done which ought to be done, and, therefore, considers a conveyance as made at the time when it ought to have been made, and the rents as belonging in equity, to the vendee from the time when he became entitled to the conveyance. On the same principle it may deem the foreclosure of a mortgage completed as of the time when the mortgagee becomes entitled to it. The legal right to the rents, as well as to the possession, continues in the mortgagor until foreclosure and sale, as it does in a vendor until conveyance. But when default has been made in the condition of the mortgage, the mortgagee at once becomes entitled to a foreclosure of the mortgage and a sale of the mortgaged premises. *This process requires time,* and on general principles of equity, the court may make the decree, when obtained, relate back to the time of the commencement of the action, *and where necessary for the security of the mortgage debt,* may appoint a receiver of the rents and profits accruing in the meantime, thus anticipating the decree and sale." [4]

§ 4.34

1. See § 4.10, supra.

2. That the chancellor would not appoint a receiver to sequestrate rents and profits preceding foreclosure, Cortelyeu v. Hathaway, 11 N.J.Eq. 39, 64 Am.Dec. 478 (1855); Williams v. Robinson, 16 Conn. 517 (1844); Morrison v. Buckner, Fed.Cas.

9,844 (C.C.Ark.1843). Cf. the early New York rule. Bank of Ogdensburgh v. Arnold, 5 Paige (N.Y.) 38 (1835).

3. See Tefft, The Myth of Strict Foreclosure, 4 U. of Chi.L.Rev. 575, 582, 591 (1937).

4. Hollenbeck v. Donell, 94 N.Y. 342, 347 (1884), (opinion by Rapallo, J. The

That sort of reasoning, of course, is just as applicable in a title jurisdiction as in a lien jurisdiction. Moreover, that reasoning is not necessary in title jurisdictions to establish the mortgagee's right to the rents and profits for he has that right as part of his security from the outset, as was previously noted. But apart from the question of the right to the income the property produces it nevertheless is relevant in securing the aid of equity in reaching all the property he is entitled to reach, and in getting it in the foreclosure action itself, i.e., on whether his legal remedy is adequate. It should be as true in a title state as in a lien state that, on default and the beginning of a foreclosure action, the mortgagee is entitled to have applied to his claim as of the date of the beginning of his action all of the property to which he has a right as security, regardless of how that right originated, provided that property is *necessary* to the satisfaction of his claim. To obtain the appointment of a receiver the mortgagee must show that there is a genuine danger that the security will be inadequate without the rents and profits. Such a showing will be sufficient to make the court undertake the preservation of the entire security through a receivership.[5] When there is a real need for equity's aid the adequacy of mortgagee's remedies at law is either ignored or recognized as unimportant.

While inadequacy of the security without the rents and profits should be a sufficient basis for the appointment of a receiver in a title jurisdiction, title states in fact often impose additional requirements such as mortgagor insolvency and "some additional, distinct, equitable ground, such as danger of loss, waste, destruction, or serious impairment of the property." [6]

In lien jurisdictions the main obstacle to the appointment of a receiver is the mortgagor's right to possession until foreclosure. This right is founded upon a policy so strong that a few states even strike down agreements permitting the mortgagee to have possession.[7] On the other hand, the argument that the mortgagee's right to take possession constitutes an adequate legal remedy is inapplicable because the lien mortgagee has no such right.

order of the quotation has been altered. The italics are the author's); Bank of Ogdensburgh v. Arnold, 5 Paige 38 (N.Y.1838), was the earlier New York case relied upon. To the same effect is the opinion of Groner, J., in Totten v. Harlowe, 67 App.D.C. 132, 90 F.2d 377, 111 A.L.R. 726 (1937).

5. See Tefft, Receivers and Leases Subordinate to the Mortgage, 2 U. of Chi.L. Rev. 33 (1934).

6. Grether v. Nick, 193 Wis. 503, 508, 213 N.W. 304, 306 (1927). Although the quotation is from a decision in a lien state, it states correctly the requirements which

are usually expressed to be essential in all jurisdictions. First National Bank of Joliet v. Illinois Steel Co., 174 Ill. 140, 51 N.E. 200 (1898); Cortelyeu v. Hathaway, 11 N.J. Eq. 39 (1855) (inadequacy and insolvency not sufficient); Broad etc., Bank v. Larsen, 88 N.J.Eq. 245, 102 A. 265 (1917); Totten v. Harlowe, 67 App.D.C. 132, 90 F.2d 377, 111 A.L.R. 726 (1937), are other cases laying down requirements beyond inadequacy of the security.

7. See Geraldson, Clauses Increasing the Possessory Rights of Mortgagees, 10 Wis.L.Rev. 492 (1935).

The first problem is to find a right in the lien state mortgagee to have the rents and profits of the land. This right must be found in spite of the conflicting right of the mortgagor to have them until foreclosure. As was seen, the mortgagee's strongest argument is based on the time lag between the commencement of foreclosure and its completion. Another argument stresses wrongful conduct by the mortgagor in impairing the *res* to which the mortgagee is entitled, or threatening to do so by active misconduct or neglect. Such wrongdoing arguably makes it reasonable to give the mortgagee the yield of the *res* as a compensatory substitute.

The question arises as to why, if the mortgagee has a right on one or the other or both of these lines of reasoning, the lack of a legal remedy to enforce the right should not be sufficient to invoke the desired aid of equity. Normally if there is a right but no remedy at law, equity will supply the deficiency. But here something more is required. Generally, just as in title states, the courts in lien states find that additional something in inadequacy of the security in relation to the debt.[8] Not only does the receivership fly in the face of policy favoring the mortgagor but it imposes a heavy administrative burden upon chancery which it undertakes reluctantly. Furthermore, receiverships are more costly than if the mortgagor manages the property.[9] Consequently it is understandable that equity will not grant the relief unless it is *necessary* to the mortgagee's payment, i.e., unless there is actual or threatened inadequacy of security to meet the debt.

However, inadequacy of security is not the only condition precedent to the appointment of a lien state receiver. Some courts, for example, maintain that "a mortgagee is not entitled to a receiver if the security is adequate and no waste is threatened."[10] Other jurisdictions specify three requirements. For example, Minnesota decisions require proof that "(1) the mortgagor is insolvent; (2) the mortgagor was committing waste; and (3) the value of the security is inadequate to cover the mortgage debt."[11]

---

8. See Title Insurance Co. v. California Development Co., 164 Cal. 58, 127 P. 502 (1912).

9. For an example of the difference of cost of administering the property by a receiver as contrasted, for example, with a mortgagee in possession, see Wolkenstein v. Slonim, 355 Ill. 306, 189 N.E. 312 (1934). See also Folk v. United States, 233 F. 177, 147 C.C.A. 183 (Okl.1916); 50 Yale L.Jour. 1424, 1447; Carey and Brabner-Smith, Studies in Realty Mortgage Foreclosures: Ill. Receiverships, 27 Ill.L.Rev. 717, 753 (1933).

10. Dart v. Western Savings & Loan Association, 103 Ariz. 170, 438 P.2d 407 (1968).

11. Mutual Benefit Life Insurance Co. v. Frantz Klodt & Son, Inc., 237 N.W.2d 350, 353 (Minn.1975). In reaction to such decisions, the Minnesota legislature abolished the three part test in most non-homestead and non-agricultural mortgage settings and substituted for it a variety of less rigorous statutory standards for the appointment of a receiver. See Minn.Stat. Ann. §§ 559.17, 576.01(2). See also Brown v. Muetzel, 358 N.W.2d 725 (Minn.App. 1984) (applying three part test to contract for deed vendor request for receiver). Cf. Little Earth of United Tribes, Inc. v. United States Department of Housing and Urban Development, 584 F.Supp. 1301 (D.Minn.1983).

These additional requirements need closer examination. While insolvency of the mortgagor is often stressed in the cases as a condition precedent to a receivership [12] a good argument can be made that it should be irrelevant. The creditor who takes security is entitled to rely upon it exclusively for the payment of the entire debt without resorting to other assets of the mortgagor, if he so wishes, because that is why he took it in the first place. It is quite true that a solvent mortgagor will pay the debt to save the property if it is worth more than the mortgage debt. And it is equally true that a solvent mortgagor usually will pay the debt even though the property is worth less than the mortgage debt, for in this latter case he would face a deficiency judgment for the difference. Consequently it would be an extraordinary case in which the question of receivership would arise unless the mortgagor was insolvent. Nonetheless it arguably ought to be no part of the mortgagee's case to have to establish insolvency as a condition to his relief.

The waste requirement is subject to a variety of interpretations.[13] For example, to the extent that waste simply means conduct that impairs the mortgagee's security, it really is not a separate requirement. Moreover, courts sometimes will characterize as waste the failure to pay taxes or insurance premiums.[14] Also, mere neglect that causes rapid deterioration of the property has been classified as waste.[15] On the other hand, the concept of "committing waste" could very well require proof of affirmative destruction of the property by the mortgagor.

Where a lien mortgagee meets the requirements for a receivership, the receiver generally will be permitted to collect rents and profits and apply them to the mortgage debt.[16] However, there is isolated lien state authority that, once appointed, the receiver may be limited to preserving the security *res* against waste by the mortgagor.[17] Under this view the *res* to be preserved is just the property itself and not its yield. The waste, or threatened waste, does not justify giving the mortgagee any additional security but only sanctions the preservation

12. E.g., Chase Manhattan Bank v. Turabo Shopping Center, Inc., 683 F.2d 25 (1st Cir.1982); Minnesota Building & Loan Association v. Murphy, 176 Minn. 71, 222 N.W. 516 (1928).

13. See Annot., 55 A.L.R.3d 1041 (1974). A few cases take the position that waste is the *sole* ground for a receivership. See, e.g., First Federal Savings & Loan Association of Coffeyville v. Moulds, 202 Kan. 557, 451 P.2d 215 (1969). This approach, however, seems to be equating waste with inadequacy of security and, in any event, the receiver may be limited to protecting the property as opposed to collecting rents.

14. Grether v. Nick, supra note 75; Shepherd v. Pepper, 133 U.S. 626, 10 S.Ct. 438, 33 L.Ed. 706 (1890); Title Insurance & Trust Co. v. California Development Co.,

164 Cal. 58, 127 P. 502 (1912); Larson v. Orfield, 155 Minn. 282, 193 N.W. 453 (1923); Dart v. Western Savings & Loan Association, 103 Ariz. 170, 438 P.2d 407 (1968); American Medical Services, Inc. v. Mutual Federal Savings & Loan Association, 52 Wis.2d 198, 188 N.W.2d 529 (1971).

15. Little Earth of United Tribes, Inc. v. United States Department of Housing and Urban Development, 584 F.Supp. 1301 (D.Minn.1983); American Medical Services, Inc. v. Mutual Federal Savings & Loan Association, 52 Wis.2d 198, 188 N.W.2d 529 (1971).

16. See, e.g., Federal Farm Mortgage Corp. v. Ganser, 146 Neb. 635, 20 N.W.2d 689 (1945).

17. Wagar v. Stone, 36 Mich. 364 (1877).

of that security which the mortgagee took originally. It would follow logically from this that the receiver in taking over the *res* should allocate the rents and profits, not to the mortgagee, but to the mortgagor and his general creditors.[18] As one court noted in denying the right of the receiver to collect rents and profits, "The rents and profits of land do not enter into or form any part of the security. At the time of giving the security both parties understand that the mortgagor will and the mortgagee will not, be entitled to the rents, issues or profits of the mortgaged premises, until the title shall have become absolute upon a foreclosure of the mortgage. * * * It would be a novel doctrine to hold that the mortgagee had a right incident to ownership, and yet that he had neither a legal title nor right to possession. The legislature, in depriving him of the means of enforcing possession, intended thereby also to cut off and deprive him of all rights which he could have acquired, in case he obtained possession before acquiring an absolute title. To deprive him of this particular remedy, and yet allow him in some other proceeding to, in effect, arrive at the same result, * * * would not be securing to the mortgagor those substantial rights which it was the evident intent he should have." [19]

Many jurisdictions have statutes or other regulations governing the appointment of receivers.[20] For example, California provides for the appointment of a receiver "where it appears that the mortgaged property is in danger of being lost, removed, or materially injured, or that the condition of the mortgage has not been performed, and that the property is probably insufficient to discharge the mortgage debt." [21] Absent a receivership provision in the mortgage, the effect of which we will consider in the next section, California courts strictly adhere to the requirements of the above rule.[22] Minnesota, on the other hand, enacted legislation that discarded the three part test considered earlier in this section in many commercial mortgage situations and substituted for it a variety of alternative and less rigorous requirements for the appointment of a receiver.[23]

---

18. Ibid. See Rundell, Work of the Wisconsin Supreme Court: Mortgages, 9 Wis. L.Rev. 40, 43 (1933). There is some authority that the rents may be used, however for preserving the premises. See American National Bank v. Northwestern Mutual Life Insurance Co., 32 C.C.A. 275, 89 F. 610 (1898), certiorari denied 172 U.S. 650, 19 S.Ct. 883, 43 L.Ed. 1184 (1899).

19. Wagar v. Stone, 36 Mich. 364, 366 (1877). In accord with this view, look at Teal v. Walker, 111 U.S. 242, 4 S.Ct. 420, 28 L.Ed. 415 (1884), applying Oregon law; Investors' Syndicate v. Smith, 105 F.2d 611 (C.C.A.Or.1939), reviewing and applying Oregon law; American Investment Co. v. Farrar, 87 Iowa 437, 54 N.W. 361 (1893); Moncrieff v. Hare, 38 Colo. 221, 87 P. 1082, 7 L.R.A.,N.S., 1001 (1906).

20. See e.g., West's Ann.Cal.Code Civ. Proc. § 564(2); West's Ann.Ind.Code 34–1–12–1; Minn.Stat.Ann. § 576.01(1); Reissue Neb.Rev.St. § 25–1081.

21. West's Ann.Cal.Code Civ.Proc. § 564(2). See also West's Ann.Ind.Code 34–1–12–1; Johnson v. LaPorte Bank & Trust Co., ___ Ind.App. ___, 470 N.E.2d 350 (1984).

22. See Barclays Bank of California v. Superior Court, 69 Cal.App.3d 593, 137 Cal. Rptr. 743 (1977); Turner v. Superior Court, 72 Cal.App.3d 804, 140 Cal.Rptr. 475 (1977).

23. Minn.Stat.Ann. § 576.01(2). Under this statute the failure of the mortgagor to pay real estate taxes or insurance premiums constitutes an independent basis for the appointment of a receiver notwith-

WESTLAW REFERENCES

mortgage* /p equit! ground justif! necess! reason /s receiver! /s
    appoint! authoriz! engage!

mortgage* /p destruction impair! inadequa! insolven** loss #security
    waste /s receiver! /s appoint! authoriz! engage!

§ 4.35 Agreements for Rents, Profits, and Receiverships

To enhance the mortgagee's rights, mortgagees normally include in the mortgage two types of clauses. One conveys, pledges, or assigns the rents and profits of the mortgaged land and empowers the mortgagee on default to take possession and collect them.[1] The other provides for the appointment of a receiver on default to collect rents and profits and apply them to the secured debt.[2]

These clauses have two purposes. One is to give the mortgagee a right to the rents and profits as part of the security, distinct from the capital asset, the land. The other is to provide an additional basis for the appointment of a receiver to capture them, or, in the alternative, the privilege of taking possession to achieve the same end. The mortgagee wants this right not only to be able to reach and apply the rents and profits of the land to the debt as against the mortgagor but, also, in priority to other mortgagees and general creditors. Moreover, the mortgagee normally wants the right to exist either completely independent of taking possession or incident to acquiring possession either by his own act or through a receivership.

It is often said that a court will not enforce a receivership clause where it would, in its absence, deny the appointment of a receiver.[3] Indeed, as one authority has emphasized, "the answer is that no such contract provision should force a court of equity to exercise its discretion in favor of a party who stands in no need of aid."[4] On the other hand, the fact that the mortgagor consents to a receivership is sometimes considered by courts to be a relevant factor and, in some instances, may favorably influence the appointment of a receiver.[5] As

standing the absence of other evidence of security impairment, mortgagor insolvency or waste.

§ 4.35

1. See May, The Effect and Operation of a Pledge of the Rents and Profits of Real Estate, 21 N.Dame L. 225 (1946).

2. See 50 Yale L.Jour. 1424, 1426 n. 10 (1941); 45 Harv.L.Rev. 902, n. 9 (1932).

3. "Where a court has no authority under the law to appoint a receiver, such authority cannot be conferred by consent or stipulation of the parties." Baker v. Varney, 129 Cal. 564, 565, 62 P. 100, 79 Am.St.Rep. 140 (1900); Hubbell v. Avenue Investment Co., 97 Iowa 135, 66 N.W. 85 (1896); Hazeltine v. Granger, 44 Mich. 503,

7 N.W. 74 (1880); Aetna Life Insurance Co. v. Broecker, 166 Ind. 576, 77 N.E. 1092 (1906). Cf. Moncrieff v. Hare, 38 Colo. 221, 87 P. 1082, 7 L.R.A.,N.S., 1001 (1906); Dart v. Western Savings & Loan Association, 103 Ariz. 170, 438 P.2d 407 (1968); Barclays Bank of California v. Superior Court, 69 Cal.App.3d 593, 137 Cal.Rptr. 743 (1977).

4. 2 Glenn, Mortgages § 1.75.1

5. See Israels & Kramer, The Significance of the Income Clause in a Corporate Mortgage, 30 Col.L.Rev. 489, 492 (1930). See discussion of cases to this effect in Barclays Bank of California v. Superior Court, 69 Cal.App.3d 593, 601, 137 Cal. Rptr. 743, 747 (1977).

one court emphasized, "although a recital that upon default the [mortgagee] shall be entitled to the appointment of a receiver is not binding upon the courts, such a recital nevertheless has some evidentiary weight * * *. It reasonably follows that it presents a prima facie, but rebuttable, evidentiary showing of the [mortgagee's] entitlement to appointment of a receiver."[6] In addition, state statutes sometime provide for the enforcement of such clauses.[7] Finally, a receivership agreement is even more likely to be enforced if it was executed subsequent to the mortgage.[8]

Where the receivership clause is utilized in a federally insured mortgage, it tends to be much more influential. For example, federal courts have indicated that such clauses alone may justify the appointment of a receiver in situations where the mortgagee is unable to meet the traditional requirements for the appointment.[9] It should be emphasized however, that these cases are largely the product of applying a "federal common law" instead of the traditional mortgage rules of the forum state, a problem considered elsewhere in this volume.[10]

The "rents and profits clause," has received varying interpretations but they boil down to three.[11] A few states hold them unenforcible on the ground that they violate a fundamental policy of the law of the state as expressed in statutes banning ejectment, confirming possession in the mortgagor, or declaring mortgages to be liens.[12] On the other hand, some jurisdictions treat such clauses as transferring the legal right to the rents of the land *in praesenti* subject to a condition

---

6. Barclays Bank of California v. Superior Court, 69 Cal.App.3d 593, 602, 137 Cal. Rptr. 743, 748 (1977).

7. Under New York—McKinney's Real Property Law § 254(10), where the mortgage so provides, the mortgagee may have a receiver appointed on default as a matter of right. See Febbraro v. Febbraro, 70 A.D.2d 584, 416 N.Y.S.2d 59 (1979) (no showing of need required of mortgagee proceeding under such provision). See Minn. Stat.Ann. § 559.17 (Subd. 2) (as to mortgages of $500,000 or more.).

8. In some states statutes specifically state that agreements as to the possession of the mortgaged property may be made subsequent to the date of the mortgage. West's Ann.Cal.Civ.Code § 2927; N.Dak. Century Code 35–02–13; Rev.Code Mont. 1947, § 52–107; Ariz.Rev.Stat. § 33–703.

9. See United States v. Mountain Village Co., 424 F.Supp. 822 (D.Mass.1976); United States v. Queen's Court Apartments, Inc., 296 F.2d 534 (9th Cir.1961). Cf. United States v. St. Paul Missionary Public Housing, Inc., 575 F.Supp. 867 (N.D. Ohio 1983).

10. See § 11.6, infra; View Crest Garden Apartments, Inc. v. United States, 281

F.2d 844 (9th Cir.1960), certiorari denied 364 U.S. 902, 81 S.Ct. 235, 5 L.Ed.2d 195 (1960).

11. Decisions holding that the inclusion of the words "together with the rents, issues and profits thereof" in the description of the property mortgaged does no more than describe the lands should, perhaps, be put into a still different category. Myers v. Brown, 92 N.J.Eq. 348, 112 A. 844 (1921) affirmed 93 N.J.Eq. 196, 115 A. 926 (1922); In re Foster, Fed.Cas. No. 4,963, 6 Ben. 268, 10 N.R.B. 523 (D.C.N.Y.1872), affirmed C.C.N.Y., Fed.Cas. No. 4,981, 10 N.R.B. 523 (1872).

12. See Comment, the Right to Rents of Mortgaged Property in Oklahoma, 37 Okla. L.Rev. 605, 610 (1984); Hart v. Bingman, 171 Okl. 429, 43 P.2d 447 (1935); Comment, Proposed Changes in Minnesota Mortgage Law, 50 Minn.L.Rev. 331, 339–347 (1966); See also Geraldson, Clauses Increasing the Possessory Rights of Mortgagees, 10 Wis.L.Rev. 492 (1935); note, 50 Yale L.Jour. 1424, 1426, 1427 (1941); Israels & Kramer, The Significance of the Income Clause in a Corporate Mortgage, 30 Col.L.Rev. 488, 493 (1930).

precedent that it shall become effective upon default by the mortgagor.[13]

This is not to say that all courts purporting to follow this second approach have done so enthusiastically. A few courts have been reluctant to find that there actually was an assignment.[14] Some courts stress the language used and differentiate between an "assignment" and a "pledge" to arrive at the result. As the court in a leading case said " * * * an examination of the cases cited as authority for the statement that the mortgagor [sic] is not entitled to the rents until he takes possession, or until a receiver is appointed, convinces me that the word 'pledge' was there used as distinguished from the word 'assigned.' There is a marked difference between a pledge and an assignment. Ordinarily a pledge is considered as a bailment, and delivery of possession, actual or constructive, is essential, but transfer of title is not. On the other hand, by assignment, title is transferred although possession need not be. There may, of course, be pledges accompanied by an assignment where both possession and title are transferred to the pledgee; and there may also be a qualified assignment where neither possession nor complete title passes." [15] As has been pointed out, to achieve such a great difference in result upon such a distinction seems "to place an inordinately high premium upon the phraseology of the instrument. If the rents are available in one case without the requirement of obtaining possession, no policy ground is perceivable for denying them in the other." [16]

---

13. See Comment, Assignment of Rents Clauses under California Law and in Bankruptcy: Strategies for the Secured Creditor, 31 Hast.L.J. 1433, 1434–1435 (1980); Kinnison v. Guaranty Liquidating Corp., 18 Cal.2d 256, 261, 115 P.2d 450, 453 (1941); Granniss-Blair Audit Co. v. Maddux, 167 Tenn. 297, 69 S.W.2d 238 (1934); New Jersey National Bank & Trust Co. v. Morris, 9 N.J.Misc. 444, 155 A. 782 (1931); East Grand Forks Federal Savings and Loan Association v. Mueller, 198 N.W.2d 124 (N.D.1972). Cf. Aetna Life Ins. Co. v. McElvain, 363 N.W.2d 186 (S.D.1985). But see Smith v. Grilk, 64 N.D. 163, 250 N.W. 787 (1933). Such assignments may be made either by a clause in the mortgage contract or by a separate instrument. Paramount Building & Loan Association v. Sacks, 107 N.J.Eq. 328, 152 A. 457 (1920), clause in mortgage; Harris v. Taylor, 35 Ap.Div. 462, 54 N.Y.S. 864 (1898), separate clause. That such a clause when it appears in the granting clause of the mortgage is ineffective, being only an extended description of the land, Myers v. Brown, 92 N.J.Eq. 348, 112 A. 844 (1921), affirmed 93 N.J.Eq. 196, 115 A. 926 (1922). That it does operate to transfer a right, see Randal v. Jersey Mortgage Investment Co., 306 Pa. 1, 158 A. 865 (1932).

14. See Fisher v. Norman Apartments, 101 Colo. 173, 72 P.2d 1092 (1937).

15. Paramount B. & L. Association v. Sacks, 107 N.J.Eq. 328, 331, 152 A. 457, 458 (1930). For other discussions of the effect of an assignment or pledge of rents and profits to the mortgagee or third persons, see note, 43 Yale L.J. 107 (1933); note, 47 Yale L.J. 1000 (1938); Israels and Kramer, The Significance of the Income Clause in a Corporate Mortgage, 30 Col.L. Rev. 488 (1930); Abelow, An Historical Analysis of Assignment of Rents in New York, 6 Brooklyn L.Rev. 25, 52 (1936); note, 31 Mich.L.Rev. 1124 (1933) (discussion of Michigan statute permitting the assignment of rents and profits to a trustee under a trust deed mortgage); note, 18 Iowa L.Rev. 251 (1933); note, 21 Iowa L.Rev. 646 (1936); note, 50 Harv.L.Rev. 1322 (1937); note, 50 Yale L.Jour. 1424 (1941); note, 21 Notre Dame Law. 225 (1941); Berick, The Mortgagee's Right to Rents, 8 U. of Cin.L.Rev. 250, 283 (1934); Leesman, Corporate Trusteeship and Receivership, 28 Ill.L.Rev. 238, 239 (1933); 4 A.L.R. 1405 (1919); 55 A.L.R. 1020 (1928); 87 A.L.R. 625 (1933); 91 A.L.R. 1217 (1934).

16. 50 Yale L.Jour. 1424, 1428 (1941).

Moreover, several objections have been raised to the automatic operation of such clauses. Some have claimed that if the clause operated automatically to transfer the right to rents, logically the mortgagor would be held subject to the imposition of a constructive trust upon all rents collected and expended by him after default, a result which would "impose unworkable restrictions upon industry." [17] In addition it has been argued that, since the clause imposes no duty upon the mortgagee to collect rents, to permit these clauses to give automatic accrual would both deprive the mortgagor of his rights to the rents and use of them and give him no assurance that the mortgagee would collect them and apply them to the debt.[18] Even if this were true, as a practical matter the mortgagor would not have to worry that a mortgagee, after default by the mortgagor, would fail to collect any rents if they were available and apply them in payment.[19] But it is not true, as was pointed out by a court in giving one of the best reasons for construing the agreement as stopping short of an assignment. The court said, "the question before us is not dependent upon the power of the parties to the mortgage to contract as to the rents and profits of the mortgaged property, but upon the intention of the parties as expressed by them in the mortgage instrument. We do not think that the parties * * * intended * * * to make an absolute and unqualified assignment of the rent of the mortgaged property * * *. If so, the mortgagee should be charged with the amount of the rents accruing after default, at least if they could have been collected with reasonable diligence." [20] Probably most important of all is the policy of protecting the mortgagor's possession prior to foreclosure sale. But the validity of even this reason has been challenged. A defaulting mortgagor is usually insolvent and beset by creditors. Therefore, it has been pointed out, the most likely result of the policy is to deny the mortgagee priority on this contracted for asset—priority to which he should be entitled against general creditors by virtue of foresight in demanding it.[21]

A third, and probably predominate, approach holds that the rents and profits clause creates in the mortgagee only a security interest in the rents and profits and one which requires some further affirmative action by the mortgagee before it becomes effective.[22] Some courts

17. Prudential Insurance Co. of America v. Liberdar Holding Corp., 74 F.2d 50 (C.C.A.N.Y.1934).

18. Kidd's Estate, Re, 161 Misc. 631, 292 N.Y.S. 888 (1936).

19. See 50 Yale L.Jour. 1424, 1427 (1941).

20. Sullivan v. Rosson, 223 N.Y. 217, 223, 119 N.E. 405, 407 (1918).

21. 50 Yale L.Jour. 1424, 1427 (1941). 18; Storke and Sears; Colorado Security Law, 135–145 (1952).

22. See e.g., Bevins v. Peoples Bank & Trust Co., 671 P.2d 875 (Alaska 1983);

Bornstein v. Somerson, 341 So.2d 1043 (Fla.App.1977), certiorari denied 348 So.2d 944 (1977); In re Southern Gardens, Inc. 39 B.R. 671 (Bkrtcy.Ill.1982); Taylor v. Brennen, 621 S.W.2d 592 (Tex.1981); Wuorinen v. City Federal Savings & Loan Association, 52 Wis.2d 722, 191 N.W.2d 27 (1971); In re Matter of Village Properties, Limited, 723 F.2d 441 (5th Cir.1984), certiorari denied ___ U.S. ___, 104 S.Ct. 2350, 80 L.Ed. 2d 823 (1984), In re Colter, Inc., 46 B.R. 510 (Bkrtcy.Colo.1984). Kratovil, Mortgages— Problems In Possession, Rents, And Mortgagee Liability, 11 DePaul L.Rev. 1, 11 (1961).

have asserted that a rents and profits clause is ineffective "until the mortgagee obtains possession of the property, or impounds the rents, or secures the appointment of a receiver, or takes some other similar action." [23] Others have required that the mortgagee either take possession of the property or obtain the appointment of a receiver.[24] What constitutes "taking possession" is not entirely clear. As one commentator has noted, "possession is an illusive quality and * * * there is no uniform method which is certain to accomplish the desired end.[25] Some decisions hold that a refused demand for possession of property suffices.[26] Finally, in some states, the "affirmative action" required is much less significant. Some courts suggest "the request for the appointment of a receiver is enough to vest the right to rents and profits and it is not the actual appointment by the court that vests rents and profits".[27] Still other courts state that, if the mortgagee notifies the mortgagor of a default and "demands payment of rent, the [mortgagee] is entitled to the rents accruing after such notice as against the [mortgagor] * * * until the mortgage is paid in full." [28]

Once triggered, one would assume that a rents and profits clause remains effective until a valid foreclosure takes place.[29] Suppose, however, that a jurisdiction has statutory redemption and the mortgagee insists on enforcement of the clause during the redemption period. Where the property was sold for the full amount of the mortgage debt, there is authority that the assignment of rents and profits terminates with the foreclosure sale.[30] This result is sensible because it would seem both illogical and unfair to allow the mortgagee to collect further rents under such circumstances. After all, if redemption occurs the mortgagee will receive its debt plus a statutory rate of interest on it. If no redemption takes place, a mortgagee-purchaser will wind up owning land that, based on the foreclosure sale, is worth at least the amount of the debt. On the other hand, to the extent that the foreclosure sale results in a deficiency, the assignment should remain effective during

23. Taylor v. Brennen, 621 S.W.2d 592, 594 (Tex.1981). See In re Matter of Village Properties, Limited, 723 F.2d 441 (5th Cir. 1984), certiorari denied __ U.S. __, 104 S.Ct. 2350, 80 L.Ed.2d 823 (1984).

24. Matter of Gotta, 47 B.R. 198 (W.D.Wis.1985); Wuorinen v. City Federal S & L Association, 52 Wis.2d 722, 191 N.W.2d 27 (1971); Vecchiarelli v. Garsal Realty, Inc., 111 Misc.2d 157, 443 N.Y.S.2d 622 (1980); Freedman's Savings & Trust Co. v. Shepherd, 127 U.S. 494, 502, 8 S.Ct. 1250, 32 L.Ed. 163 (1887).

25. 43 Yale L.Jour. 107, 112 and cases cited (1933).

26. See e.g., Long Island Bond & Mortgage Guarantee Co. v. Brown, 171 Misc. 15, 11 N.Y.S.2d 793 (1939).

27. In re Flower City Nursing Home, 38 B.R. 642 (Bkrtcy.N.Y.1984). See In re Matter of Village Properties, Limited, 723 F.2d 441 (5th Cir.1984), certiorari denied __ U.S. __, 104 S.Ct. 2350, 80 L.Ed.2d 823 (1984).

28. Bevins v. Peoples Bank & Trust Co., 671 P.2d 875, 879 (Alaska 1983). See In re Southern Gardens, Inc., 39 B.R. 671 (Bkrtcy.Ill.1982); Miners Savings Bank v. Thomas, 140 Pa.Super. 5, 12 A.2d 810 (1940).

29. See Cross Co., Inc. v. Citizens Mortgage Investment Trust, 305 Minn. 111, 232 N.W.2d 114 (1975).

30. Id.

the statutory redemption period so long as the deficiency remains unsatisfied.[31]

To what extent does the presence of a rents and profits clause affect the mortgagee's ability to get a receiver appointed? There is authority that the pledge of rents and profits is sufficient by itself, without showing inadequacy or waste of the security or insolvency of the mortgagor, to entitle the mortgagee to a receiver.[32] On the other hand, other cases take the position that apart from giving to the mortgagee a clear right to the rents and profits as part of his security,[33] thus clearing the hurdle that faced lien theory states where there was no clause covering them, the same considerations should govern the appointment of the receiver where there is a pledge agreement as where there is none.[34] In other words, if the mortgagee's security, including the right to rents and profits which his agreement gave to him, is adequate, equity should not grant a receivership even though his bargain also expressly purported to give him a right to one. But although it is recognized that a mortgagee can claim no absolute right to a receiver and cannot bind a court by stipulations in the mortgage or separate agreement for the appointment of one, nevertheless, the presence of rent assignment or pledge and receivership clauses in the mortgage increases the chances of a receiver being appointed.[35]

 WESTLAW REFERENCES

mortgage /s agree! clause covenant provi! recital /s receiver!

synopsis,digest(mortgage /s agree! clause covenant provi! recital /s profit rent!)

266k467(3)

§ 4.36 Ex Parte Receivership—Constitutional Problems

Variations of the two clauses discussed in the previous section can have a significant impact on a related matter—the appointment of receivers by *ex parte* order. Ex parte receivership involves the appoint-

31. G.G.C. Co. v. First National Bank of St. Paul, 287 N.W.2d 378 (Minn.1979).

32. Howard v. Burns, 201 Ill.App. 579 (1916) affirmed 279 Ill. 256, 116 N.E. 703 (1917); Ohio Mutual Savings & Loan Co. v. Public Construction Co., 26 Ohio N.P.,N.S., 371 (1926); Rhinelander v. Richards, 184 App.Div. 67, 70, 171 N.Y.S. 436, 437 (1918); Cf. Turner v. Superior Court, 72 Cal.App. 3d 804, 140 Cal.Rptr. 475 (1977); Barclays Bank of California v. Superior Court, 69 Cal.App.3d 593, 137 Cal.Rptr. 743 (1977). See generally, Berick, The Mortgagee's Right to Rents, 8 Cin.L.Rev. 250, 290 (1934); 45 Harv.L.Rev. 902 n. 10 (1932); 27 Iowa L.Rev. 627 (1933); 43 Yale L.Jour. 112 (1933).

33. "All authorities agree that a pledge of rents and profits vests in the mortgagee a right thereto which equity will recognize and enforce in a proper manner." Grether v. Nick, supra note 20.

34. See e.g., Mutual Benefit Life Insurance Co. v. Frantz Klodt & Son, Inc., 237 N.W.2d 350 (Minn.1975); Aetna Life Insurance Co. v. Broecker, 166 Ind. 576, 77 N.E. 1092 (1906); Althausen v. Kohn, 222 Ill. App. 324 (1921). But see notes 91 and 98 supra.

35. Martorano v. Spicola, 110 Fla. 55, 148 So. 585 (1933); Pizer v. Herzig, 121 App.Div. 609, 106 N.Y.S. 370 (1907).

ment of a receiver, usually pending judicial foreclosure, without providing either notice or an opportunity to be heard to the mortgagor.[1]

Standing alone, the practice of appointing receivers *ex parte* arguably violates the constitutional principles of both Mullane v. Central Hanover Bank & Trust Co.[2] and Fuentes v. Shevin[3] and their progeny. The Supreme Court in *Mullane* noted that "where the names and post office addresses of those affected by a proceeding are at hand, the reasons disappear for resort to means less likely than the mails to apprise them of its pendency."[4] Implicit in this, at least, is that *some* notice is required before a court may deprive a person of a significant property interest. In *Fuentes,* the Supreme Court struck down certain state replevin statutes because they did not provide for an opportunity to be heard before chattels were taken from the possessor, even on a temporary basis, pending a trial on the merits. On the other hand, in Mitchell v. W.T. Grant Co.,[5] the Supreme Court upheld the constitutionality of a Louisiana sequestration statute which required the secured creditor to come before a judge who, based on a verified complaint delineating the specific facts supporting the claim, could then issue a writ of sequestration. There was no right to a hearing prior to the seizure of the chattel, but the procedure did provide for an immediate right to a hearing thereafter and dissolution of the writ if the plaintiff failed to establish adequate grounds for its issuance.

Prior to applying the foregoing standards in the ex parte receivership context, one must first find that "state action" is present to invoke the protections of the 14th Amendment. In general, courts have been unwilling to find state action present in nonjudicial foreclosure and in related nonjudicial creditor remedy contexts, a matter we examine in detail later in this volume.[6] Nevertheless, *ex parte* receivership, like replevin, is a judicial proceeding and, as such, is inextricably intertwined with the judicial system. Consequently, there is a stronger argument for state action in the ex parte receivership setting than in a variety of other creditor proceedings that do not directly entail judicial intervention.

Assuming that state action is present, the merits of the constitutional challenge against *ex parte* receivership must be confronted. While a more detailed consideration of *Mullane* and *Fuentes* and their progeny is provided elsewhere in this volume in the nonjudicial foreclosure context,[7] certain observations are nevertheless appropriate at this point. In the *ex parte* receivership situation the mortgagor can lose

§ 4.36

1. See e.g., Tweitman v. Lampman, 60 A.D.2d 667, 400 N.Y.S.2d 207 (1977).

2. 339 U.S. 306, 70 S.Ct. 652, 94 L.Ed. 865 (1950).

3. 407 U.S. 67, 92 S.Ct. 1983, 32 L.Ed.2d 556 (1972), rehearing denied 409 U.S. 902, 93 S.Ct. 177, 34 L.Ed.2d 165 (1972).

4. 339 U.S. at 318, 70 S.Ct. at 659.

5. 416 U.S. 600, 94 S.Ct. 1897, 40 L.Ed. 2d 406 (1974).

6. See § 7.27 infra.

7. See §§ 7.24–7.25 infra.

both possession of the mortgaged real estate and the ability to direct the disposal of its rents with *no* prior notice or opportunity to be heard. Nevertheless, this practice is probably justifiable in emergency situations such as where a mortgagor is engaged in removal or destruction of the real estate.[8] Moreover, one New York decision[9] has sustained the constitutionality of *ex parte* receivership against a 14th Amendment hearing challenge. The court emphasized that the receivership procedure was based on sworn documents under "judicial supervision" and that upon the appointment of the receiver, the mortgagor was entitled to "an immediate hearing on the validity or the probable validity of the underlying claim."[10] Consequently, while further litigation will be needed to resolve all constitutional ambiguity, courts probably will be inclined to sustain the validity of *ex parte* receivership practice.

Of course, even if ex parte receivership is constitutionally deficient as to notice and hearing, such rights, in theory at least, are capable of being waived. *Fuentes* and other cases recognize the possibility of waiver, at least where the parties were aware of the significance of the waiver and there was bargaining over contractual terms between parties who were equal in bargaining position.[11] Receivership clauses often provide that a receiver may be appointed "without notice" to the mortgagor for purpose of taking possession of the mortgaged premises and collecting rents and profits therefrom. Recent decisions have upheld waiver based on such clauses.[12] However, these cases have involved sophisticated real estate mortgagors who were deemed to have acted knowingly and from a bargaining position relatively equal to that of the mortgagee. Suppose, however, that the transaction does not involve commercial real estate and that the mortgagor lacks the sophistication, understanding and bargaining position incident to the usual commercial mortgage transaction. In such situations the waiver concept will be much more difficult to sustain.

 WESTLAW REFERENCES

receiver! /6 "ex parte" /p mortgage /p constitution** "due process" "14th amendment" hearing waive*

---

8. Cf. Ewing v. Mytinger & Casselberry, Inc., 339 U.S. 594, 70 S.Ct. 870, 94 L.Ed. 1088 (1950), rehearing denied 340 U.S. 857, 71 S.Ct. 69, 95 L.Ed. 627 (1960); North American Cold Storage Co. v. Chicago, 211 U.S. 306, 29 S.Ct. 101, 53 L.Ed. 195 (1909). See Elliot and Smith, 1 West's Texas Forms, § 1.4 (1977).

9. Friedman v. Gerax, 100 Misc.2d 820, 420 N.Y.S.2d 247 (1979). One other case seems to have upheld the constitutionality of ex parte receivership, although it did not consider *Fuentes* and waiver seems to have been an alternative ground. See Security National Bank v. Village Mall at Hillcrest, Inc., 79 Misc.2d 1060, 361 N.Y.S.2d 977 (1974).

10. Id. at 822, 420 N.Y.S.2d at 248.

11. See Nelson, Constitutional Problems With Power of Sale Real Estate Foreclosure: A Judicial Dilemma, 43 Mo.L.Rev. 25, 33–34 (1978).

12. See United States v. Mountain Village Co., 424 F.Supp. 822 (D.Mass.1976); Massachusetts Mutual Life Insurance Co. v. Avon Associates, Inc., 83 Misc.2d 829, 373 N.Y.S.2d 464 (1975), noted in 28 Syr.L. Rev. 379, 416 (1977); Security National Bank v. Village Mall at Hillcrest Inc., 79 Misc.2d 1060, 361 N.Y.S.2d 977 (1974).

§ 4.37 Effect of Receivership on Rents—General Considerations

When a receiver has been appointed in a foreclosure action many questions arise as to his rights to rents and profits. One concerns what rents the receiver is entitled to collect. Another is whether he may disaffirm leases and, accompanying this, how far a tenant may be bound on his lease when a receiver has been appointed, or be held liable upon any other basis. Although the most difficult problems have arisen in respect to leases made subsequent to the mortgage, there is also the question of the right of the receiver to rents of leases prior to the mortgage. Still a different matter is involved when the mortgagor himself is in possession and the receiver seeks to hold him for income actually earned or for an occupational rental. Indeed, this goes back to the question of whether a receiver is justified at all in such a case, a point which was not covered in the earlier discussion of the basis for receiverships. Priorities on rents and profits between various mortgagees and other creditors form still another area of controversy. Conduct of the mortgagor, generally classified as "milking" the mortgaged property, also becomes important especially in times of depression. And in all of these cases there is the inquiry as to whether title and lien theories as well as rents and profits and receivership clauses affect the solutions.

More complex problems arise when the mortgagor is involved in a federal bankruptcy liquidation or reorganization. For example, there are often competing claims to both possession and rents of the mortgaged real estate between the judicially appointed receiver and the trustee in bankruptcy. A detailed consideration of these problems follows later in this volume.[1]

 WESTLAW REFERENCES
266k471

§ 4.38 Receivership—Lease Prior to Mortgage

Where the lease is entered into prior to the mortgage both theory and practice are fairly clear. As was seen earlier,[1] such leases are superior to the mortgage and will not be affected by foreclosure. The purchaser at a foreclosure sale is bound by them. "It is entirely clear that if a lease is prior to a mortgage a sale under the latter is but a sale of the reversion."[2] It follows that the receiver has no power to disaffirm such leases; all that she can do is to collect the rents from the tenants.

§ 4.37

1. See § 8.17, infra.

§ 4.38

1. See § 4.21, supra.

2. Metropolitan Life Insurance Co. v. Childs Co., 230 N.Y. 285, 290, 130 N.E. 295, 297, 14 A.L.R. 658 (1921).

The only question is as to what rent the receiver is entitled, and even this narrows down to rent which had accrued but was unpaid at the time of her appointment, since it is clear that rent accruing between the date of appointment and the date of sale belongs to her.[3] Thus, for example, a receiver who is appointed before a judgment creditor actually levies on the rents by attachment, has priority over the judgment creditor.[4] While the receiver's claim is generally held to vest at the time of her appointment,[5] there is authority that it relates back to the commencement of the foreclosure action if a receiver is then requested and, if not, to the time in the action when a petition for one is made.[6] This latter rule has the merit of not penalizing the mortgagee by delays in appointment beyond his control after he has done all that he can to make his claim to the rents and profits operative.[7]

Where there are no rent clauses in the mortgage, in title jurisdictions the mortgagee may assert his right to possession even before default and the rule gives to the mortgagee accrued and unpaid rent on the date that the mortgagee asserts his right.[8] The receiver, it is true, does not take possession or collect rents under the rights of the mortgagee but as an officer of the court.[9] However, she stands in a stronger position than the mortgagee because she is not appointed until the mortgagor is in default and the mortgagee has started to realize upon his security, which in title states by virtue of the mortgage itself includes not merely the legal title to the reversion carrying the rents but the right to collect them, absent an agreement to the contrary, at any time. The defaulting mortgagor has no standing to insist that he be allowed to collect and keep any part of the property which was subject to the mortgagee's security claim.[10]

The same result should follow in a lien jurisdiction. There the right to collect the rents and profits, as was seen, does not come from the mortgage even though leases prior to the mortgage, being attached to the mortgaged reversion, are part of the mortgagee's security in the

3. Argall v. Pitts, 78 N.Y. 239 (1879); Johnston v. Riddle, 70 Ala. 219 (1881); Noyes v. Rich, 52 Me. 115 (1862); Stewart v. Fairchild-Baldwin Co., 90 N.J.Eq. 139, 106 A. 406 (1919), affirmed 1919, 91 N.J. Eq. 139, 106 A. 406.

4. See Connolly v. Plaza Cards & Gifts, 54 A.D.2d 553, 387 N.Y.S.2d 5 (1976).

5. Rankin-Whitham State Bank v. Mulcahey, 344 Ill. 99, 176 N.E. 366 (1931); Rohrer v. Deatherage, 336 Ill. 450, 168 N.E. 266 (1929); Greenwich Sav. Bank v. Samotas, 17 N.Y.S.2d 772 (1940). But see Morris v. Davis, 219 N.Y.S.2d 279 (1961), the court held that the receiver, although duly appointed, was not entitled to collect rents accruing prior to his qualification as receiver.

6. Kooistra v. Gibford, 201 Iowa 275, 207 N.W. 399 (1926).

7. See 27 Iowa L.Rev. 626, 635 (1942).

8. See § 4.21, supra.

9. See First National Bank of Chicago v. Gordon, 287 Ill.App. 83, 4 N.E.2d 504 (1936).

10. "Being in default upon the obligation which his mortgage secures, the debtor who starts a quarrel over this point is met by the answer, 'Well, if you pay up, of course you can have the rent. But since you refuse to do that, you are not in a position to demand the rent.'" Glenn, Mortgages, § 181.

sense that they will be subject to foreclosure in the same way that the land itself is. Nevertheless, on equitable considerations previously examined,[11] receivers are appointed to collect rents and profits which otherwise belong to the mortgagor up to foreclosure sale or even to the end of a post-sale redemption period. Those equitable considerations apply as much to accrued but unpaid income from the property as to that which accrues after appointment. A clause pledging rents and profits should not alter the situation because such a pledge gives no rights to collect rents prior to the receivership.[12]

Whether an assignment of the rents and profits would affect the question depends upon what rents were covered by the assignment. If it covered rents accruing prior to the receivership, even payment to the mortgagor, if with notice of the assignment, would not save the tenant from having to pay again to the mortgagee; and consequently, insofar as the rents have not been paid over to the mortgagee,[13] the receiver should be able to collect them from the tenant dating from the time the assignment transferred the right to them to the mortgagee. On the other hand, if the assignment by its terms were to be operative on the appointment of the receiver, it would confer upon the receiver no rights to rents accruing before that date whether paid or unpaid.[14]

Unfortunately the cases are not as clear on this point as the above analysis would indicate.[15] While there are cases to the effect that the receiver will be entitled, without the aid of rents and profits clauses, to rent accrued but unpaid prior to his appointment,[16] other cases stress the presence of rent clauses in giving the receiver the right to such rent as against the mortgagor [17] and junior mortgagees,[18] and there is still another authority that, in the absence of a clause pledging or assigning the rents, she would have no such right.[19] There is, also, authority that

11. See § 4.34, supra.

12. See Paramount Building & Loan Association v. Sacks, 107 N.J.Eq. 328, 331, 152 A. 457 (1930). See § 150, supra.

13. See §§ 4.34–4.35, supra.

14. Paramount Building & Loan Association v. Sacks, 107 N.J.Eq. 328, 152 A. 457 (1930).

15. See 33 Col.L.Rev. 1211, 1216 (1933); 50 Yale L.Jour. 1424, 1440 (1941).

16. Codrington v. Johnstone, 1 Beav. 520 (1838); Russell v. Russell, 2 Ir.Ch.R. 574 (1853); Palmieri v. N.Y. Prep. School, 248 N.Y.S. 934 (1931); see Wychoff v. Scofield, 98 N.Y. 475, 477 (1885); New Way Building Co. v. Mortimer Taft Building Corp., 129 Misc. 170, 171, 220 N.Y.S. 665, 666 (1927); Lofsky v. Maujer, 3 Sandf.Ch. 76, 78 (1845).

17. Touroff v. Weeks, 155 Misc. 577, 278 N.Y.S. 867 (1935); cf. Watts' Administrator v. Smith, 250 Ky. 617, 63 S.W.2d 796, 91 A.L.R. 1206 (1933).

18. New York Life Insurance Co. v. Fulton Development Corp., 265 N.Y. 348, 352, 193 N.E. 169, 171 (1934), "When the senior mortgagee has a receiver appointed, the lien of the senior mortgagee immediately attaches not only to future rents but also to past rents due and uncollected. As between the equitable liens of the senior and junior mortgagees, that of the senior is superior."; Paramount Building & Loan Association v. Sacks, 107 N.J.Eq. 328, 152 A. 457 (1930), prior mortgagee holding an assignment clause may have receiver appointed who will be entitled to unpaid rent as against junior mortgagee in possession.

19. New Order Building & Loan Association v. 222 Chancellor Ave., 106 N.J.Eq. 1, 149 A. 525 (1930). See also Paramount Building & Loan Association v. Sacks, 107 N.J.Eq. 328, 152 A. 457 (1930), indicating that a pledge of rents would be insufficient.

prior attaching creditors of the mortgagor will prevail over the receiver as to back rent.[20]

 WESTLAW REFERENCES
receiver! /p amass*** amount collect*** receive /s lease profit
rent! /p mortgage

§ 4.39 Receivership—Lease Subsequent to Mortgage

A receiver is appointed in order to conserve and prevent injury to property in which the mortgagee has a security interest. Consequently, in determining the rights of a receiver to rents and profits, there is always the question whether those rents and profits constitute a part of the mortgagee's security which he is entitled to have preserved and protected. Where the lease is subsequent to the mortgage both title and lien theories have played a part in the reasoning of the courts in answering this question. In such a lease the tenant's rights are dependent upon those of his landlord, the mortgagor, as against the mortgagee, and this marks the starting point in both types of states. In title states the mortgagee, at least on default, gets the right to possession and with it all of the rents and profits of the land as part of his security. However, while he can assert his right by evicting the mortgagor or his tenant, he does not acquire the mortgagor's rights under the lease against the tenant because he is not in privity with him. His only right against the tenant in such cases is either to come to a new agreement with him or, failing that, to hold him for the occupational use of the property as to such period as the tenant stays on after the mortgagee asserts his rights. And, reciprocal to the right of the mortgagee to oust the tenant, is the tenant's privilege of vacating the property, treating the mortgagee's assertion of rights as an eviction justifying his action and, also, giving him a right to sue the mortgagor for breach of covenant of quiet enjoyment.

Should the mortgage contain an assignment of the rents and profits, this can operate as an automatic transfer in equity of the future leases made by the mortgagor. It gives them to the mortgagee according to the terms of the assignment, usually upon default by the mortgagor, quite independent of rights in the capital asset or flowing from them.

As we have seen, rents and profits clauses often are inoperative until either the mortgagee takes possession or a receiver is appointed. When such an event occurs the agreement can be regarded as giving to the mortgagee at that moment an independent right to the mortgagor's rights against the lessee. It would be the same as though at the time the mortgagee determined to take over he had made an arrangement with the mortgagor whereby the mortgagor then assigned his leases to

20. Peoples Trust Co. of Binghamton v. Goodell, 134 Misc. 692, 236 N.Y.S. 549 (1929); In re Barbizon Plaza, 3 F.Supp. 415 (D.C.N.Y.1933). Contra: Donlon & Miller Manufacturing Co. v. Cannella, 89 Hun 21, 69 St.R. 8, 34 N.Y.S. 1065 (1895).

the mortgagee. Only the most artificial and mechanical sort of reasoning would hold in such an event that the mortgagee's entry into possession necessarily destroyed the interest of the mortgagor in the property and, along with it, the leases dependent upon it so that they could not be preserved to the mortgagee by agreement.[1] The mortgagee really occupied a dual position: (1) he is an assignee of the mortgagor's reversionary interest;[2] (2) he is a mortgagee who has taken possession. He should have his option as to which set of rights he will assert.

What is the effect of these principles upon the rights of a receiver when he is appointed? The chief difficulty in title states will be in giving the receiver a right to affirm leases in spite of the lessee's desire to disaffirm them. On the other hand, there will be no trouble in permitting the receiver to disaffirm leases regardless of the wishes of the tenant. In lien states, as we shall see, the chief problem is whether the receiver can disaffirm leases by the mortgagor subsequent to the mortgage.

In title states there is no doubt that the receiver may disaffirm all leases subsequent to the mortgage and collect from the tenant the reasonable rental value of the premises for occupancy after the receiver's appointment.[3] This is a conservation measure where the reserved rent is less than a fair market rental and the mortgagee's security interest is endangered by the lower yield. Often, however, the lease rental is higher than such a market rental and the receiver consequently wants to hold the tenant to the existing lease.[4]

Two difficulties confront the receiver in such a case if the tenant wants to avoid the lease. One is that there is no privity of estate between the receiver and the tenant any more than there is between the mortgagee who takes possession and the tenant the receiver being the equivalent of a mortgagee in possession.[5] The other is that since the receiver is not bound by the mortgagor's leases and may hold the tenant for a market rent if that be higher than the amount reserved in

---

§ 4.39

1. There is good authority that the mortgagee will succeed to the mortgagor's lease rights against the tenant on this reasoning in spite of claiming the rents "as mortgagee." International Paper Co. v. Priscilla Co., 281 Mass. 22, 183 N.E. 58 (1932). Chicago City Bank & Trust Co. v. Walgreen Co., 272 Ill.App. 434 (1933) also gave the mortgagee the right to collect rents from the mortgagor's tenant on the ground that he was a transferee of those rights and claiming them did not constitute an eviction ending the lease.

2. See Note, 17 Wash.L.Rev. 37, 41 (1942).

3. Rohrer v. Deatherage, 336 Ill. 450, 456, 168 N.E. 266 (1929); Rankin-Whitham

Bank v. Mulcahey, 344 Ill. 99, 176 N.E. 366 (1931); Henshaw, Ward & Co. v. Wells, 28 Tenn. 568 (1848); Lord Mansfield v. Hamilton, 2 Sch. & Lef. 28 (1804).

4. "Not only will the foreclosure ordinarily be commenced when real estate values are depressed, but the receiver's leases will of necessity be forced transactions negotiated under most unfavorable circumstances." Tefft, Receivers and Leases Subordinate to the Mortgage, 2 Chi.L.Rev. 33, 37 (1934).

5. See First National Bank of Chicago v. Gordon, 287 Ill.App. 83, 4 N.E.2d 504 (1936), noted, 4 Chi.L.Rev. 151, 504 (1936). Walgreen Co. v. Moore, 116 N.J.Eq. 348, 349, 173 A. 587 (1934).

the lease, it is only fair that the tenant have a reciprocal power to disavow the lease and either vacate the premises or, if he stays on without a new agreement, be liable only for the fair value of the use and occupation.[6]

A short answer to the first argument is that it is inconsistent with the fundamental nature of mortgage receiverships. Rent receivers are appointed as officers of the court to preserve the security interest of the mortgagee.[7] And, in the fulfillment of this purpose, the court has the power to direct the receiver to disaffirm the mortgagor's leases in cases where the mortgagee's margin of security cannot be preserved adequately without avoiding them. If the mortgagee's margin of security can be preserved without cancelling the mortgagor's leases, they should continue until wiped out by foreclosure sale.[8] The theory that the appointment of the receiver is the equivalent of entry by the mortgagee, amounting therefore to an eviction of the tenant of the mortgagor and for this reason ending the lease, is so foreign to the true basis of the receivership that it has been characterized as "both novel and startling."[9] As the same court pointed out, "if that argument were sound no mortgagee would ever take possession of mortgaged premises under the clause giving him a right to do so, nor would any receiver of rents ever be appointed in foreclosure proceedings, as upon such appointment the rental income would cease. But while the possession of a rent receiver has been likened to that of a mortgagee in possession, it is the possession of the court and not of the mortgagee. Such possession does not *terminate* the rights of any party to the proceeding, much less those of one not a party. They are merely held in abeyance and preserved pendente lite. And, moreover, the title of the mortgagor is not 'terminated' until final decree and sale."[10] Furthermore the contention that the appointment of the receiver is really the equivalent of the entry by the mortgagee into possession is not only at variance with an imposing array of decisions dealing with the appointment of receivers,[11] but is also disadvantageous to the mortgagor.[12]

6. See Holmes v. Gravenhorst, 263 N.Y. 148, 157, 188 N.E. 285, 288, 91 A.L.R. 1230 (1933). Crouch, J., dissenting.

7. Desiderio v. Iadonisi, 115 Conn. 652, 163 A. 254, 88 A.L.R. 1349 (1932); Chicago Title & Trust Co. v. McDowell, 257 Ill.App. 492 (1931).

8. See Tefft, Receivers and Leases Subordinate to the Mortgage, 2 Chi.L.Rev. 33, 35 (1934) citing, In re Newdigate Colliery, Limited, 1 Ch. 468 (1912); In re Great Cobar, Limited, 1 Ch. 682 (1915); Stamer v. Nisbitt, 9 Ir.Eq.R. 96 (1846); Murtin v. Walker, Sau. & Sc. 139 (1837); American Brake Shoe & Foundry Co. v. N.Y.R. Co., 278 F. 842 (D.C.N.Y.1922).

9. Walgreen v. Moore, 116 N.J.Eq. 348, 350, 173 A. 587, 588 (1934). Quoted with approval in First Nat. Bank of Chicago v. Gordon, 287 Ill.App. 83, 4 N.E.2d 504 (1936). See comment, 2 Chi.L.Rev. 487 (1935).

10. Id.

11. See Tefft, Receivers and Leases Subordinate to the Mortgage, 2 Chi.L.Rev. 33, 38–42 (1934).

12. The mortgagor is damaged not only because he loses a valuable lease, but also because he will be liable for breach of covenant to the tenant who is evicted. Mack v. Patchin, 42 N.Y. 167, 1 Am.Rep. 506 (1870); Ganz v. Clark, 252 N.Y. 92, 169 N.E. 100 (1929); B.F. Avery & Sons Plow Co. v. Kennerly, 12 S.W.2d 140 (Tex.Com. App.1929).

The second argument is more plausible. First, the lessee's plight is the consequence of a risk he voluntarily assumed and could have guarded against. A lessee who takes a lease when there is a prior mortgage on the land knows that his lease may be wiped out by a foreclosure of the mortgage, or, in title states, by entry by the mortgagee. And such a lessee can find out whether there is such a mortgage by examining his lessor's title. If he knew of the mortgage at the time he made the lease, he could have insisted that the mortgagee become a party to the lease [13] or have asked the mortgagee to agree, as part of the consideration for the lease, not to evict him in case of foreclosure. He might even have obtained an agreement subordinating the mortgage to the lease. Further, even if the receiver does reject the lease, the hardship on the lessee is mitigated by the rule that the receiver must decide promptly; [14] and, if he does renounce it, the tenant is then free to vacate [15] without liability other than for a fair market rental during the period he has stayed on.[16]

Second, if the receiver is allowed to preserve the lease, the tenant's position is in no way jeopardized or made more burdensome than was his expectation when he entered into it. His rights and obligations are the same as they would have been had there been no default by his landlord-mortgagor, and no resulting foreclosure action. The fact that the risk he voluntarily assumed has been realized would seem no sufficient reason to give him the option of avoiding his bargain.

Third, the tenant's argument of fairness is inconsistent with the rule recognized in many states [17] that the mortgagee, at his option, may have the property sold subject to the lease or free and clear of it. The mortgagee exercises this option by joining or not joining the tenant in the foreclosure action.[18] If the tenant is not joined his lease is unaffected by the foreclosure sale and the purchaser may enforce the lease as a transferee of the reversion.[19] If he is joined, the purchaser takes the

13. Flynn v. Lowrance, 110 Okl. 150, 236 P. 594 (1924).

14. Central Republic Trust Co. v. 33 South Wabash Building Corp., 273 Ill.App. 380 (1934).

15. "It would be manifestly unjust to permit a receiver to disaffirm the lease and put new obligations on the tenant without giving the tenant the reciprocal privilege to treat these demands as an interference with his title and equivalent to a constructive eviction." Monro-King & Gremmels Realty Corp. v. 9 Avenue-21 St. Corp., 233 App.Div. 401, 404, 253 N.Y.S. 303, 307 (1931).

16. Sager v. Rebdor Realty Corp., 230 App.Div. 106, 243 N.Y.S. 314 (1930).

17. See § 7.12 infra.

18. See notes, 14 A.L.R. 664 (1921); Ann.Cas.1915A, 397; 42 Harv.L.Rev. 280 (1928); 13 Col.L.Rev. 553 (1913); 21 Minn. L.Rev. 610 (1937); 42 Wash.L.Rev. 37 (1942).

19. See Metropolitan Life Insurance Co. v. Childs Co., 230 N.Y. 285, 130 N.E. 295, 14 A.L.R. 658 (1921) reargument denied 231 N.Y. 551, 132 N.E. 885 (1921); Commonwealth Mortgage Co. v. De Waltoff, 135 App.Div. 33, 119 N.Y.S. 781 (1909); Dundee Naval Stores v. McDowell, 65 Fla. 15, 61 So. 108 (1913); Markantonis v. Madlan Realty Corp., 262 N.Y. 354, 186 N.E. 862 (1933). Contra: McDermott v. Burke, 16 Cal. 580 (1860); really a dictum since the lease was after suit was started and therefore subject to the decree under the doctrine of *lis pendens;* Dolese v. Bellows-Claude Neon Co., 261 Mich. 57, 245 N.W. 569 (1932), discussed in 32 Mich.L. Rev. 119 (1933). See 17 Wash.L.Rev. 37, 41 et seq. (1942).

property title as it existed at the time the mortgage was entered into, i.e., free of the subsequent lease, and may therefore evict the tenant.[20]

In lien states the mortgagor remains the owner and is entitled to possession, hence to rents and profits, until foreclosure. Therefore, any leases subsequent to the mortgage are also binding as against the mortgagee until then. The logical consequence of this is that the rents and profits of the land where they are subsequent to the execution of the mortgage form no part of the mortgagee's security by virtue of the mortgage alone. Clauses assigning or pledging the rents and profits can, as we have seen, operate to bring them under the security of the mortgage, although often not without the mortgagee taking "affirmative action" such as taking possession or getting a receiver appointed.[21] Further, even without any such agreement, the mortgagee under proper conditions is generally held to be entitled to have them collected by a receiver appointed in foreclosure suit even though the mortgagee himself would not have been entitled to them. Also, as was just seen, the mortgagee has the option to determine whether the lease shall survive foreclosure in the sense that if the mortgagee omits the tenant from the foreclosure action, the lease remains in full force in the hands of the purchaser on the foreclosure sale who buys the reversionary interest carrying it.[22]

From the foregoing it is apparent that, in contrast to title states, the chief problem in lien states is not whether the receiver can affirm these leases. Rather it is whether she can disaffirm them and hold the tenant for the reasonable rental value of the property. It should be scarcely necessary to say that if the mortgagee, or his receiver, cannot repudiate the mortgagor's leases prior to foreclosure sale, the tenant will not be able to do so. And the same is true, even though there might be a power in the mortgagee to reject the lease, if he has acted to preserve it by omitting the tenant from the foreclosure action.[23] In such cases, all the receiver can do is to collect the rents reserved in the leases.

Suppose the mortgagee joins the tenant in the foreclosure suit and thus sells the property free and clear of the tenant's interest. Then the question arises whether the receiver, for the period from his appointment to the foreclosure sale, is entitled only to the rent reserved in the

---

20. The tenant, as a holder of an interest in the property subject to destruction by foreclosure sale, would have the privilege of redeeming from the mortgage and being subrogated to the mortgagee's rights. In this way he is able to protect his interest from destruction. See Glenn, Mortgages, § 181.1.

21. See § 4.35, supra.

22. Metropolitan etc. Co. v. Childs Co., 230 N.Y. 285, 130 N.E. 295, 14 A.L.R. 658 (1921), reargument denied 231 N.Y. 551, 132 N.E. 885 (1921).

23. Metropolitan etc. Co. v. Childs Co., supra note 74; Hewen Co. v. Malter, 145 Misc. 635, 260 N.Y.S. 624 (1932); Markantonis v. Madlan Realty Corp., 262 N.Y. 354, 186 N.E. 862 (1933); Knickerbocker Oil Corp. v. Richfield Oil Corp., 234 App.Div. 199, 254 N.Y.S. 506 (1931) affirmed 259 N.Y. 657, 182 N.E. 222 (1932); Lynch v. Harrer, 146 Misc. 493, 261 N.Y.S. 565 (1933).

lease or whether he may disaffirm it and either make a new lease with the tenant or hold him for the fair value of the use and occupation. In New York, the doctrine has been established that, barring the presence of fraud and collusion, the receiver on foreclosure sale could not disaffirm the leases entered into by the mortgagor subsequent to the mortgage, but could collect only the rent reserved in the lease itself. The Court of Appeals stated that "Though, during the pendency of the action, a court of equity has power to issue interlocutory orders for the protection of an asserted lien, such orders must be auxiliary to the right to foreclose the lien, and cannot deprive any part of a title or a right, which, though subordinate to the lien of the mortgage, survive and are valid until the lien is foreclosed by a sale under a judgment of foreclosure. * * * Until the lien of the mortgage is foreclosed, the mortgagee has no paramount title which would justify eviction of the occupants or abrogation of the agreements. The order of the court directing the occupants to vacate the premises or pay to the receiver the reasonable value of the use and occupancy deprives the occupants of a right which they have obtained by agreement. It does more than protect the security of the mortgage debt. It gives to the mortgagee a security beyond the stipulations of the mortgage and deprives the occupants of their enjoyment of rights secured by contract." [24]

 WESTLAW REFERENCES
topic(323)   +p   lease   /s   affirm! disaffirm! (fair reasonable   +1
    market rent! value) privity
323k91

§ 4.40 Receivership—Mortgagor in Possession

Closely related to the foregoing is the question whether a receiver may be appointed when the mortgagor remains in possession of the mortgaged property and uses it as a home or for other non-income producing purpose. There is scattered early authority not only that a receiver may be appointed to take over such property but that the mortgagor can be compelled by the receiver to pay a fair market rental.[1] This was also the law in New York until Holmes v.

---

24. Prudence Co. v. 160 W. 73 St. Corp., 260 N.Y. 205, 211, 183 N.E. 365, 366, 86 A.L.R. 361 (1932). The court was also moved by the unfortunate situation of the tenants under the decisions in New York, pointing out "that, if they vacate they not only lose the rights acquired under their agreements, but remain subject to its obligations, at least until there is a sale under a judgment of foreclosure, and even after that date, if the plaintiff should decide to discontinue the action as to them; if they do not vacate, they can be put out, unless they pay more than they agreed to pay."

§ 4.40

1. Yorkshire Bank v. Mullan, 35 Ch.D. 125 (1887); Pratchett v. Drew, 1 Ch. 280 (1924); Astor v. Turner, 3 How.Pr. 225 (N.Y.1848); Public Bank v. London, 159 App.Div. 484, 144 N.Y.S. 561 (1913). In New Jersey if the premises are in the possession of the mortgagor, especially if they are occupied by him as a home, the court will be most reluctant to appoint a receiver; and, in such a case will demand a clearer showing of the existence of the reasons for which receivers are appointed. See Rehberger v. Wegener, 107 N.J.Eq. 391, 152 A. 700 (1930), for a review of early

Gravenhorst [2] was decided. In *Holmes* the court heavily stressed the fact that the receiver was appointed under a receivership clause covering rents and profits, and not under the general equity jurisdiction of the court, and the additional fact that there were no rents and profits for the receiver to take under the terms of the contract.

The distinction stressed by the court makes it possible to distinguish the *Holmes* case from one in which the receiver is appointed on general equity principles. Where the receiver is appointed by virtue of the receivership clause alone there is no necessity for compelling the mortgagor to furnish additional security by way of rent. If the security is not shown to be inadequate, the result normally will be that any rents that the mortgagor is forced to pay as additional security will eventually be returned to him after the foreclosure sale. The imposition of the duty upon him to make payments under such circumstances is unwarranted. Where, however, the receiver is appointed under the general equity jurisdiction of the court because of the inadequacy of the security, the rent exacted from the mortgagor will go in payment or be a guaranty against a threatened deficiency. In such a case the justification for imposing the duty on the mortgagor is the same as that discussed in the preceding section in connection with tenants of the mortgagor. So long as the mortgagor is not in default he is privileged to keep the mortgaged property without regard to whether it produces any income of any sort. When he defaults, however, the mortgagee is entitled to enforce his security and, through the appointment of a receiver, have it produce income from the time he starts to realize on it, provided the security is inadequate without that income. Consequently the mortgagor, if he stays on, arguably should have to pay rent. If he does not wish to do so, he thus should vacate the premises and allow the receiver to obtain income by renting to someone else or utilizing the premises in some other profitable way.

In any event, some New York mortgagees seem to have avoided the *Holmes* problem by drafting. Such mortgagees seem commonly to include in their receivership clauses a provision that the mortgagor pay the receiver a reasonable rent for the mortgagor's occupation of the premises. While one lower New York appellate court cited *Holmes* and held that such a provision was unenforcible, at least where the clause

---

and unofficially reported cases on the point. There was no showing that there was any possibility of a deficiency in the foreclosure suit and the receivership was denied. However, it was indicated that in a proper case one would be appointed and the mortgagor ordered to pay occupational rent or vacate. See 91 A.L.R. 1236 (1934), for a collection of cases.

2. 263 N.Y. 148, 188 N.E. 285, 91 A.L.R. 1230 (1933), expressly overruling Citizens Savings Bank v. Wilder, 11 App.Div. 63, 42 N.Y.S. 481 (1896). The case is discussed in Abelow, The Doctrine of Holmes v. Gravenhorst, 3 Brooklyn L.Rev. 212 (1934); note, 11 N.Y.Univ.L.Q.Rev. 480 (1934); note, 20 Cornell L.Q. 366 (1935); note, 8 U. of Cin.L.Rev. 213 (1934); note 33 Col.L.Rev. 1211 (1933) (a general discussion of the receiver of rents and profits in New York, covering the situation after the decision in the Prudence case and the Appellate Division decision in the principal case); 91 A.L.R. 1236 (1934).

did not also grant the receiver the right of possession,[3] other decisions have found such rental language effective.[4]

 WESTLAW REFERENCES
receiver! /p mortgagor /s (fair reasonable +1 market rent! value) home lease residen!

§ 4.41 Receivership—Mortgagor Conducting Business

Where the mortgagor conducts a business on the mortgaged premises instead of renting them or occupying them as a home the first problem is whether the business is subject to the mortgage either by virtue of its being a product of the land or of an express inclusion under the terms of the mortgage.[1] This is so because it is clear that a mortgage foreclosure receiver cannot take into his possession or control property not covered by the mortgage, and a "mortgage covers the land and building—not the business enterprise housed".[2] The type of business ought to and does make a difference. Where the mortgagor has rented the property—a clear case for receivership—it is nevertheless true that the mortgagor, as landlord, engages in activities that come under the description of business, such as repairs, taking out insurance, paying taxes, getting tenants and executing leases with them and then collecting the rents, or, ousting them if they violate the conditions of the lease.[3] Notwithstanding the contribution to the income from these activities, the entire amount of the rent is regarded as issuing out of the land itself and there is no attempt to allocate the share of the total due to the work and abilities of the landlord-mortgagor. When a mortgagor conducts a business of any sort on his own land, the rental value of that land, whether explicitly recognized or not, is one of the elements comprising the gross income of the business, along with other factors such as price of materials, management, and interest on capital. Attempts to segregate from gross income that portion earned by the mortgaged real property can be little more than an arbitrary estimate in most cases.[4] It is not surprising, therefore, to find the courts appointing receivers in cases where the rent element clearly predominates and the services of the mortgagor are essentially the same in kind

3. Carlin Trading Corp. v. Bennett, 24 A.D.2d 91, 264 N.Y.S.2d 43 (1965); noted in 17 Syr.L.Rev. 774 (1966).

4. See Union Dime Savings Bank v. 522 Deauville Associates, 91 Misc.2d 713, 398 N.Y.S.2d 483 (1977); Bein v. Mueson Realty Corp., 17 Misc.2d 661, 184 N.Y.S.2d 246 (1959).

§ 4.41

1. "We have, therefore, in the first instance, to ask, before appointing a manager to manage a business whether the business is included in the security." Whitley v. Challis, 1 Ch. 64, 70 (1892).

2. Abelow, The Doctrine of Holmes v. Gravenhorst, 3 Brook.L.Rev. 212 (1933); Scott v. Farmers' etc. Co., 69 F. 17, 16 C.C.A. 358 (N.D.1895); Smith v. McCullough, 104 U.S. 25, 26 L.Ed. 637 (1881); Thomas v. Armstrong, 51 Okl. 203, 151 P. 689, L.R.A.1916B, 1182 (1915). See 14 St. Louis L.Rev. 315. Cf. Muss v. Bergman, 55 A.D.2d 894, 391 N.Y.S.2d 115 (1977) (no authority in receiver to operate business in absence of evidence of waste or impairment of security.)

3. Glenn, Mortgages, § 185.

4. See 50 Yale L.Jour. 1427, 1440 (1941); 44 Yale L.Jour. 701, 704 (1935).

as those of any landlord, even though accentuated in degree, and the contribution to the income of other conveniences furnished is small.[5] This would cover apartment houses and, probably, a garage or parking lot.[6] Where, in addition to the land and buildings, the business utilizes considerable amounts of chattels, good will is a substantial factor and the part that management plays is large, the propriety of permitting the mortgagee to take over the business through a receiver is dubious. Of course, if the chattels and good will are also given in mortgage, the receivership has more justification.[7] But even without such inclusion, receivers have been appointed for hotels,[8] although there is some authority to the contrary,[9] and one case limited the receivership to that portion of the revenues derived from rent actually paid for rooms occupied.[10] On the other hand a receiver of mortgaged premises on which the mortgagor conducted a dance hall, restaurant and ice cream parlor was denied on the ground that there were no rents and profits within the meaning of the *Holmes* case.[11] Nor is it surprising to find a receiver appointed of property on which the mortgagor has a tree nursery, the trees being treated as part of the realty.[12] Whether or not when the premises are used for a mixed purpose, e.g., a doctor using part of his home as an office, a receiver could compel the payment of some rent has been mooted but not answered by the courts.[13]

A California decision illustrates the problems presented where receivers attempt to exercise jurisdiction over the mortgagor's business and chattels.[14] There a rents and profits receiver appointed for a multi-million dollar motel complex attempted to take possession of a liquor license, food and beverage inventories, the furniture and television sets and certain other personal property. The California Court of Appeals

5. See 44 Yale L.Jour. 701, 703 (1935).

6. Garage: Fairchild v. Gray, 136 Misc. 704, 242 N.Y.S. 192 (1930); Title etc. Co. Belgrave Motor Sales Co., Inc., N.Y.L.J., Jan. 27, 1934, at 932, col. 4. Parking lot: City Bank Farmers Trust Co. v. Mishol Realty Co., N.Y.L.J., Jan. 27, 1934, at 441, col. 5.

7. See Cake v. Mohun, 164 U.S. 311, 17 S.Ct. 100, 41 L.Ed. 447 (1896), "furniture, equipment and other personal property" of hotel; Knickerbocker v. McKindley Coal & Mining Co., 172 Ill. 535, 50 N.E. 330, 64 Am.St.Rep. 54 (1898); Pacific N.W. Packing Co. v. Allen, 109 F. 515, 48 C.C.A. 521 (Wash.1901), tools, stock, and "outfit" of cannery. See 44 Yale L.Jour. 701, 702 (1935).

8. Lowell v. Doe, 44 Minn. 144, 46 N.W. 297 (1890); Warwick v. Hammell, 32 N.J. Eq. 427 (1880); Fidelity Trust Co. v. Saginaw Hotels, Inc., 259 Mich. 254, 242 N.W. 906 (1932); see Makeel v. Hotchkiss, 190 Ill. 311, 60 N.E. 524, 83 Am.St.Rep. 780 (1901).

9. Chatham-Phoenix Bank v. Hotel Park-Central, 146 Misc. 208, 261 N.Y.S. 490 (1931), receiver denied, not because the property was a hotel, but because the court thought a receivership could not accomplish the purpose of conservation and preservation any better than well advanced reorganization plans.

10. Stadtmuller v. Schorr, N.Y.L.J., Nov. 3, 1934, at 1633, col. 4.

11. Bartels v. Fowler, 160 Misc. 584, 290 N.Y.S. 908 (1936).

12. Heller v. Amawalk Nursery, Inc., 253 App.Div. 380, 2 N.Y.S.2d 196 (1938), affirmed 278 N.Y. 514, 15 N.E.2d 671 (1938), noted, 23 Cornell L.Quar. 614 (1938).

13. See Abelow, The Doctrine of Holmes v. Gravenhorst, 3 Brook.L.Rev. 212, 223 (1934).

14. Turner v. Superior Court, 72 Cal. App.3d 804, 140 Cal.Rptr. 475 (1977).

noted that the above property was not covered by the deed of trust on the real estate and held that, absent mortgagor consent, the receiver was not authorized to take possession of such property. Having determined that the receiver lacked authority to take possession, it followed that a sale by the receiver of such property without mortgagor consent was prohibited. The court quoted with approval the first paragraph of this section and emphasized the limited role of the mortgage receivership as opposed to the "general" or "equity" receivership. The general or equity receiver often "takes possession of all of the debtor's assets and attempts to satisfy creditors out of those assets"[15] for the purpose of the liquidation or reorganization of the debtor. On the other hand, in characterizing the mortgage receivership, the court used the words of Justice Cardozo to show that "the rents and profits are impounded for the benefit of a particular mortgagee to be applied upon the debt in the event of a deficiency. The [mortgagor] retains its other property, if it has any, unaffected in its power of disposition by the decree of sequestration."[16]

The cases reflect a conflict between penalizing the mortgagor for conducting a business on his property by taking from him the entire profits instead of just that part which represents the share properly allocable to rents, an allocation that cannot be made, as was pointed out, except by arbitrary estimate, and penalizing the mortgagee who, if the property were rented, would be entitled to collect the rents. The policy of the court toward protecting one or the other, as well as its attitude in regard to the desirability of receiverships as a remedy are factors that help explain the decisions.[17]

 WESTLAW REFERENCES
receiver! /p mortgagor /s business chattel corporation enterprise

§ 4.42 Receivership—"Milking" by the Mortgagor

When a mortgagor becomes resigned to the eventual loss of the mortgaged real estate, he frequently attempts to squeeze as much money out as possible before surrendering it. This process is often referred to as "milking." The chief devices by which such mortgagors attempt to "milk" the property are leases which require payment in advance for the entire term, the execution of a lease at an inadequate rental in return for a present cash consideration, the assignment of future rents to a third person, and the cancellation of a long term lease favorable to the lessor in exchange for a cash payment to the mortgagor.[1] As one commentator has aptly described the situation, such

---

15. Id. at 815, 140 Cal.Rptr. 481.

16. Duparquet Huot & Monevse Co. v. Evans, 297 U.S. 216, 221, 56 S.Ct. 412, 80 L.Ed. 591 (1936).

17. See, 44 Yale L.Jour. 701, 704–705 (1935).

§ 4.42

1. See Remedies Against "Milking" of Property by Mortgagors, 46 Harv.L.Rev. 491 (1933); Cancellation of Leases by Mortgagor as Affecting Mortgagee, 12 N.Y. Univ.L.Q.Rev. 501 (1935). There are other ways in which the mortgagor can milk the devices are used by hard-pressed mortgagors to "pocket the future earning capacity of the land and deliver to the mortgagee the empty shell of the mortgaged asset." [2] While the "milking" problem pervades more than receivership cases, the problem is commonly found in the receivership context. Accordingly, receivership situations often provide a useful vehicle for analysis and understanding of the milking concept.

The problem of preventing such undesirable practices necessitates reconciliation of three conflicting interests; safeguarding the mortgagee's security against impairment; protecting a tenant who made a lease in good faith from hardship; and preserving to the mortgagor the benefits of ownership.[3] It is, of course, bound up with the question whether the mortgagee or his receiver may affirm or disaffirm leases made by the mortgagor.[4]

Where the lease is executed prior to the mortgage, if it provides for prepayment, then prepayment in accordance with the terms of the lease is binding on the mortgagee for the simple reason that he took his mortgage subject to that very provision. However, prepayments not in accordance with the terms of the lease, if made with notice of the mortgage, will not be binding on the mortgagee or receiver even in the absence of proof of an actual fraudulent intent by the mortgagor or participation in it by the lessee.[5] This is true even though put in the form of an agreement altering the terms of the original lease.[6] Indeed such cases in most instances might well rest upon a theory generally more difficult to establish factually, that of setting aside a collusive agreement to defraud the mortgagee. As has been pointed out, any arrangement for prepayment of the rent for the whole term or a large portion of it is abnormal and, if made after a mortgage has attached to the property, indicates clearly a design to defeat the mortgagee's assertion of claim to it on default and foreclosure.[7] Since this is so, the tenant who agrees to such an arrangement must be charged with collusive acquaintance with the scheme [8] and, on this ground, the courts are justified in giving no validity to the prepayment, provided, of course, the tenant knew of the existence of the mortgage at the time.[9]

---

property. He may collect the rents and use them at the same time failing to pay taxes, keep up insurance, make repairs, etc.

2. Kratovil, Mortgages—Problems in Possession, Rents, and Mortgagee Liability, 11 DePaul L.Rev. 1, 13 (1961).

3. See 50 Yale L.Jour. 1427, 1437 (1941).

4. See § 4.39, supra.

5. See § 4.21, supra. Boteler v. Leber, 112 N.J.Eq. 441, 164 A. 572 (1933).

6. Colter Realty Co. v. Primer Realty Co., 262 App.Div. 77, 27 N.Y.S.2d 850 (1941).

7. See Glenn, Mortgages, § 183.1.

8. See Glenn, Fraudulent Conveyances and Preferences, rev. ed., §§ 299–299b.

9. "The court will take care of a sharper, as landlord, who leases premises for a long term, with rent payable in advance, and lets the mortgagee take the 'empty shell.'" Nerwal Realty Corp. v. 9th Avenue-31st St. Corp., 154 Misc. 565, 278 N.Y.S. 766 (1935). But where the lease is untainted by dishonesty payment in advance will be valid and the lease will stand. See 22 N.Y.Univ.L.Q.Rev. 731 (1947).

The cancellation of a favorable lease antedating the mortgage, or a reduction in the rent of such leases for a cash payment to the mortgagor might also be treated as fraudulent conveyances, if, in fact, such was the case.[10] Here, however, there is not present the abnormality of the transaction to charge the tenant with collusion as in the prepayment case, and difficulties of proof would make it an ineffective remedy. However, such acts do constitute a clear injury to the mortgagee's security because they deprive the mortgagee or his receiver of the rents they would be able to collect on entry into possession or on appointment. It is an injury which, looking at the mortgagor's responsibility, may be considered as waste insofar as it threatens to impair the security.[11] However, the mortgagee's remedies against the mortgagor for such a wrong would not be very satisfactory. An action for damages against him, would probably be worthless since he is likely to be insolvent.[12] An injunction should be allowed, but only against a particular threatened cancellation, and consequently constant vigilance and a series of suits by the mortgagee might be necessary.[13] To be able to hold the tenant on his original lease would give the mortgagee what he really wants. Notice to the tenant of the existence of the mortgage on the reversion should be sufficient to restrict his ability to enter into agreements with the mortgagor that will reduce the value of the security. Proof of actual fraud is unnecessary.[14]

Where the lease is subsequent to the mortgage, in those jurisdictions, chiefly title states, in which the mortgagee or a receiver in foreclosure may disaffirm the mortgagor's leases, neither a prepayment of the rental, even if in accordance with the terms of the lease, nor a lease calling for an inadequate rental will be binding. In the event that it is disregarded, other questions arise. One is whether the tenant may be held to pay a reasonable rental for the period of his use and occupation from the time that the mortgagee or the receiver takes over rather than being allowed to assert the terms of his agreement with the mortgagor as setting the bounds of his liability.[15] Another is whether, if the prepayment of inadequate rent was by an agreement changing the terms of a previous lease, also subsequent to the mortgage, the tenant could be held to the higher terms of the original lease or

10. Sager v. Rebdor Realty Corp., 230 App.Div. 106, 243 N.Y.S. 314 (1930).

11. See 46 Harv.L.Rev. 491, 494 (1933); 50 Yale L.Jour. 1427, 1438 (1941).

12. See § 4.4, supra.

13. See 50 Yale L.Jour. 1424, 1438 (1941); 46 Harv.L.Rev. 494 (1933).

14. Bank of Manhattan Trust Co. v. 571 Park Avenue Corp., 263 N.Y. 57, 188 N.E. 156 (1933) noted, 11 N.Y.Univ.LQ.Rev. 480 (1934). Cf. Colter Realty, Inc., v. Primer Realty Corp., 262 App.Div. 77, 27 N.Y.S.2d 850 (1941). Both cases involved leases subsequent to the mortgage with clauses making the rents and profits security for the debt. In holding that agreements lessening the yield of the property were invalid the court did so on the ground that, even short of fraud and collusion, the mortgagor and his tenant could not impair the mortgagee's security, with notice of the mortgagee's rights, even though the agreement was made before those rights had become operative. The case of a lease antedating the mortgage would be an *a fortiori* one.

15. Rohrer v. Deatherage, 336 Ill. 450, 168 N.E. 266 (1929).

whether he could treat the entrance by the mortgagee or appointment of the receiver as an eviction releasing him from his lease.[16]

Where the mortgagee or receiver seeks to take advantage of such a favorable lease by voiding the cancellation of it, lack of privity of title between the mortgagee and tenant together with the notion of eviction of the tenant by superior title are relied upon to block such action. If the cancellation or other agreement altering unfavorably the terms of such a lease can be established to have been effected in anticipation of foreclosure with the intent of defrauding the mortgagee it generally will be set aside. But, as was noted above, proof of this is ordinarily too difficult to make the rule of practical benefit. If the latter is the case, relief from milking operations of this sort may be illusory. If the tenant is unwilling to come to terms on a new lease, at most he can be held only for use and occupation of the premises from the time the rights of the mortgagee or receiver accrue until he moves out, and then a new tenant must be found.

While some lien states hold that the mortgagee or a receiver in foreclosure is bound by the terms of the mortgagor's subsequent leases and cannot disaffirm them, an order appointing a receiver "may [not] be frustrated by a collusive or fraudulent lease for an inadequate rental or advance payment of rent in anticipation of a foreclosure action." [17] Further, since the mortgagee may preserve favorable leases subsequent to the mortgage and have them sold as part of his security on foreclosure sale, cancellation of such leases can be regarded as an impairment of the mortgagee's security on the same reasoning as in the case of a lease prior to a mortgage, and the same consequences should attend it. In other words, notice of the mortgagee's rights should suffice to prevent a valid agreement being made even though no fraudulent design to defeat his claim can be adduced. This clearly ought to be, and apparently is, true where the milking agreement surrendering or changing the subsequent lease occurs after the date when an assignment or pledge of such rents has become operative.[18] It is also true where it is made after an action for the foreclosure of the property and appointment of a receiver has been begun and notice of *lis pendens* has been filed although the receiver is not appointed until after the agreement and prepayment.[19] It should further be true of agreements made

---

16. First National Bank of Chicago v. Gordon, 287 Ill.App. 83, 4 N.E.2d 504 (1936). See supra, § 4.39.

17. Prudence Co. v. 160 W. 73d St. Corp., 260 N.Y. 205, 213, 183 N.E. 365, 367, 86 A.L.R. 361 (1932), Hanna, Cas.Security, 983. Webber v. King, 205 Iowa 612, 218 N.W. 282 (1928), Gaynor v. Blewett, 82 Wis. 313, 52 N.W. 313, 33 Am.St.Rep. 47 (1892), might be explained on this same ground although the intent to defraud would have to be based on constructive notice of *lis pendens* of the suit to foreclose.

18. "After the mortgagors' release to the mortgagee of their right to rents under the lease became operative, the landlord had no right to modify the lease or enter into any agreement of modification that would bind the mortgagee without the latter's consent or approval." Franzen v. G.R. Kinney Co., 218 Wis. 53, 57, 259 N.W. 850, 852, 105 A.L.R. 740 (1935).

19. Gaynor v. Blewett, 82 Wis. 313, 52 N.W. 313 (1892).

before that time but with notice that under certain contingencies the mortgagee would become entitled to the rent stipulated for in the lease with the mortgagor.

This has been so held in New York where the mortgage contained a pledge of rents and profits, the operative contingency in such a case being the appointment of a receiver. The court, while still affirming its ruling that a "receiver could not require a tenant in occupation under a lease to pay any sum for use and occupation beyond the sum which the lease called for," pointed out that it had not intended by its earlier decision [20] to hold that the mortgagor's agreement was conclusive upon the mortgagee where such agreements were in contravention of the express covenants and the necessary implications of a recorded mortgage prior in lien. The court held that where a mortgagor's agreement is made surrendering the right to receive rent for the mortgaged premises, or for the assignment of rents collectible therefrom, it was an impairment of the lien of the mortgage upon the rent. "The court also held that it was not necessary to find collusion in the making of such an arrangement; that it was beyond the power of the parties to appropriate the pledged rents to a different indebtedness, or defeat the pledge by leasing the premises rent free." [21] The result of such a decision is the recognition of an equitable lien on the rents and profits at least sufficient to prevent arrangements between the mortgagor and the tenant with notice, made prior to the date when the pledge would become operative by the appointment of a receiver, which would impair the mortgagee's security.

On the other hand, in Grether v. Nick,[22] the Wisconsin court, in spite of the presence of a valid pledge of the rents and profits, held that a prepayment of rent by a subsequent lessee was valid against the receiver in foreclosure and the tenant could not be made to pay again. The case, however, can be distinguished from the New York cases even though in its opinion the court emphasized the rule that a pledge of rents and profits does not create any rights in them until a receiver is appointed or the mortgagee takes possession. The right of a receiver to collect rents and profits rests upon the theory that they form part of his security either by express agreement or by equitable considerations extrinsic to the mortgage language.[23] Further, the power of a receiver to disregard various sorts of milking arrangements, or, more broadly, to affirm or disaffirm leases of his mortgagor, rests upon the idea that his action is justified to prevent the security to which the mortgagee is

20. Prudence Co. v. 160 W. 73d St. Corp., 260 N.Y. 205, 183 N.E. 365, 86 A.L.R. 361 (1932).

21. Colter Realty, Inc., v. Primer Realty Co., 262 App.Div. 77, 80, 27 N.Y.S.2d 850, 852 (1941), summarizing Bank, etc. Co. v. 571 Park Avenue Corp., 263 N.Y. 57, 188 N.E. 156 (1933), and holding that the same reasoning invalidated a prepayment arrangement under a lease subsequent to the mortgage in which there was a pledge of the rents, the prepayment occurring before the receiver was appointed and, therefore, before the pledge became operative.

22. 193 Wis. 503, 215 N.W. 571, 55 A.L.R. 525 (1927).

23. See § 4.34, supra.

entitled from being impaired. Applying this to the case of prepaid rents, if the mortgagor used them to improve the mortgaged property instead of diverting them to his own pockets, then "the mortgagee enjoys the full benefit of the advanced payment, and * * * a court of equity should not work oppression by requiring its payment a second time." This was the express rationale of Grether v. Nick, the prepaid rent having been used to complete a building on the mortgaged premises.[24]

 WESTLAW REFERENCES

mortgagee receiver! /p (cancel! inadequa! prepay! reduc! /s lease rent!) milk*** /p mortgagor tenant

§ 4.43 Priorities Between Mortgagees as to Rents

Frequently there is a race between different mortgagees to obtain for themselves the rents and profits of the mortgaged property through the appointment of a receiver. When this happens how are the priorities to be determined? The general rule is clear that a first mortgagee, even without a rents and profits clause, who obtains a receiver or takes possession, will prevail as to all rents thereafter[1] to the exclusion of any other claimant whether junior mortgagee,[2] judgment creditor[3] or general creditor.[4] This includes accruing and uncollected back rents. This rule is understandable because, after all, to the extent that the rents reduce the senior lien, the status of the junior lienors often improves. To be sure, there can be situations where the total value of the liens against the property is so high in relation to the value of the property that reduction of a senior lien will have little

---

24. See Glenn, Mortgages, § 183.1. Grether v. Nick was also differentiated from the sort of case in which prepayments of rent were made to enable the mortgagor to appropriate them in fraudulent contravention of the rights of the mortgagee to them. Gaynor v. Blewett, 82 Wis. 313, 52 N.W. 313 (1892), was distinguished on this ground.

§ 4.43

1. Both as to income earned prior to default and after default, "it is usually stated as an elementary proposition of law that the mortgagee or trustee [in a trust deed mortgage] has no right to income unless and until he either makes a demand for possession of the mortgaged premises, applies to the court for the appointment of a receiver, or intervenes in a proceeding brought by a junior mortgagee or a general creditor." Israels & Kramer, Income Clause in a Corporate Mortgage, 30 Col.L. Rev. 488, 498 (1930).

2. Last v. Winkel, 86 N.J.Eq. 356, 97 A. 961 (1916), affirmed 86 N.J.Eq. 431, 99 A.

1070 (1916); Metropolitan Life Insurance Co. v. Tash-Lap Realty Corp., 138 Misc. 68, 245 N.Y.S. 281 (1930).

3. Central Trust Co. v. Chattanooga Rome & Columbus Railroad, 94 F. 275, 36 C.C.A. 241 (C.C.A.Ga.1899).

4. Hayes v. Dickenson, 9 Hun 277 (N.Y. 1876). See Israels & Kramer, Income Clause in Corporate Mortgages, 30 Col.L. Rev. 488, 503 (1930). The mortgagee's ability to obtain the rents of mortgaged property after bankruptcy of the mortgagor is considered in note, 45 Harv.L.Rev. 901 (1932); 50 Yale L.Jour. 1424, 1445 (1941); 18 Col.L.Rev. 91 (1918); Berick, The Mortgagee's Right to Rents, 8 Cin.L.Rev. 250, 292 (1934); 56 Harv.L.Rev. 305 (1942); 75 A.L.R. 1526 (1931); Cf. In re Hotel St. James Co., 65 F.2d 82 (C.C.A.Cal.1933). For his right to rents and profits during an agricultural composition proceeding, see note, 11 Rocky Mt.L.Rev. 65 (1938).

economic meaning to junior lienors. Even in that situation, however, there seems to be no compelling reason to depart from the consequences of normal priority rules.

A junior mortgagee who obtains a receiver is generally entitled to all rents and profits collected by the receiver prior to the time the senior mortgagee obtains the appointment of his own receiver, is ordered included in the junior receivership or acquires possession of the mortgaged real estate.[5] Similarly, a junior mortgagee who takes possession instead of obtaining the appointment of a receiver will prevail as to rents collected prior to the appointment of a senior mortgage receiver.[6] This result rewards the diligent junior mortgagee for had it not been for his action, the rents up to the time the senior mortgagee asserted his rights, would have gone to the mortgagor-landlord. To put the matter differently, a senior mortgagee who has done nothing to capture the rents arguably should be in no better position than he would have been in had the mortgagor continued in possession.[7] Nevertheless, there is, some authority that even though the junior mortgagee obtains a receiver first, if the senior mortgagee intervenes, all of the rents and profits collected by the receiver will be allocated in the order of the priorities of the mortgages, thus depriving the junior mortgagee of his advantage as to the part already collected.[8]

5. See Waible v. Dosberg, 83 A.D.2d 983, 443 N.Y.S.2d 621 (1981); Vecchiarelli v. Garsal Realty, Inc., 111 Misc.2d 157, 443 N.Y.S.2d 622 (1980); Yoelin v. Kudla, 302 Ill.App. 413, 24 N.E.2d 67 (1940); Detroit Properties Corp. v. Detroit Hotel Co., 258 Mich. 156, 242 N.W. 213 (1913); Post v. Dorr, 4 Edw.Ch. (N.Y.) 412 (1845); Sullivan v. Rosson, 223 N.Y. 217, 119 N.E. 405, 4 A.L.R. 1400 (1918) noted, 27 Yale L.Jour. 1085 (1918); N.Y. Life Insurance Co. v. Fulton Development Corp., 265 N.Y. 348, 193 N.E. 169 (1934); Goddard v. Clarke, 81 Neb. 373, 116 N.W. 41 (1908); Longdock Mills & Elevator Co. v. Alpen, 82 N.J.Eq. 190, 88 A. 623 (1913); Bermes v. Kelley, 108 N.J.Eq. 289, 154 A. 860 (1931); Re Metr. Amal. Ests., 2 Ch. 497 (1912); Re Belbridge Prop. Trust, 165 L.T.Rep. 170 (1941). See 50 Yale L.Jour. 1424, 1442 (1945); 43 Yale L.Jour. 107, 108 (1933); 95 A.L.R. 1050 (1935).

6. Federal Deposit Insurance Corp. v. Briarwood Holding Corp., 54 A.D.2d 750, 387 N.Y.S.2d 712 (1976).

7. "His [the senior mortgagee's] failure to take any action would, or might have been as serious to him if the receiver had never been appointed as he now claims it will be if the money in the hands of the receiver is not paid to him as mortgagee. He is not now entitled to appropriate the proceeds of the diligence of a junior mort-

gagee." Sullivan v. Rosson, 223 N.Y. 217, 225, 119 N.E. 405, 408 (1918). See Tefft, Receivers and Leases Subordinate to the Mortgage, 2 U.Chi.L.Rev. 33, 41 (1934); 33 Col.L.Rev. 1211, 1218 (1933).

8. Bergin v. Robbins, 109 Conn. 329, 146 A. 724 (1929); Wolkenstein v. Slonim, 355 Ill. 306, 189 N.E. 312 (1934) noted 2 Chi.L.Rev. 149, possibly is susceptible to the same interpretation because the receiver was ordered to pay over to the first mortgagee all of the rents and profits collected by the receiver appointed in the foreclosure action by the second mortgagee. However, the first mortgagee, although he did not know at the time of the prior action by the second mortgagee, began his own foreclosure action on the day that the receiver was appointed in the prior suit and there is nothing in the facts to indicate that any rents had been collected by the receiver before the first mortgagee petitioned to have the receiver turn over to him all of the rents and profits. See, also, N.J. Title & Guarantee Co. v. Cone & Co., 64 N.J.Eq. 45, 53 A. 97 (1902), in which the first mortgagee, who began his foreclosure before the second mortgagee began his and obtained a receiver, was held entitled to all rents and profits, the second mortgagee being denied any priority as to them by securing the appointment of the receiver.

The effect upon these general rules of clauses assigning or pledging the rents and profits has not been definitively settled. Since the first mortgagee without a rents and profits clause will generally prevail as to uncollected rents and profits accruing from the time he intervenes to assert his rights, *a fortiori* the same would be true if it contained such a clause.[9] It would also seem clear that if the first mortgage contained an assignment of rents and profits which operated to give rights to the mortgagee prior to the appointment of a receiver or taking possession, the first mortgagee should be entitled as against a receiver appointed on the application of a second mortgagee to all rents accruing after the date the assignment become effective even though collected by the receiver prior to intervention by the first mortgagee.[10] On the other hand, if the clause is construed to be only a pledge of the rents and profits any inchoate equitable lien which may be raised by it before being made effective through action by the mortgagee [11] is insufficient to give him any claim to rents and profits collected by the receiver of a later mortgagee prior to that affirmative action.[12]

What is the effect on a senior mortgagee of rents and profits clauses in a subsequent mortgage? Where the first mortgage contains no clause and the later one contains a pledge clause, the general rule is that the prior one will prevail as to rents and profits from the time of intervention.[13] The same has been true where there was an assign-

---

9. Sullivan v. Rosson, 223 N.Y. 217, 119 N.E. 405, 4 A.L.R. 1400 (1918) noted, 27 Yale L.Jour. 1085 (1918), as against junior mortgagee; Atlantic Trust Co. v. Dana, 128 F. 209, 62 C.C.A. 657 (Kan.1903), as against judgment creditor; Newport etc. Co. v. Douglas, 75 Ky. (12 Bush.) 673 (1877) as against judgment creditor; Re Banner, 149 F. 936 (D.C.N.Y.1907), as against general creditor; First Savings, etc., v. Stuppi, 2 F.2d 822 (C.C.A.M.1924), as against general creditors.

10. Harris v. Taylor, 35 App.D. 462, 54 N.Y.S. 864 (1898), assignment by separate instrument; John McMenamy Investment & Real Estate Co. v. Dawley, 183 Mo.App. 1, 165 S.W. 829 (1914); Paramount Building & Loan Association v. Sacks, 107 N.J. Eq. 328, 152 A. 457 (1930), clause in mortgage.

11. See § 4.35 supra. Normally this action consists in asking for a receiver, or for the extension of an existing receivership.

12. Sullivan v. Rosson, supra note 91; Abrahams v. Berkovitz, 146 App.Div. 563, 131 N.Y.S. 257 (1911); Prudential Insurance Co. v. Liberdar Holding Co., 74 F.2d 50 (C.C.A.N.Y.1934), clause "assigning" rents and profits on default gave no rights against prior equity receiver for benefit of creditors as to rents collected by the receiver prior to the appointment of the mortga-

gee's receiver in foreclosure. That a "rents, issues, and profits" clause combined with a receivership clause gives to the mortgagee an inchoate lien valid in Kentucky against general creditors but not against subsequent assignees or specific liens, see Francis, Mortgages on After-Acquired Property in Kentucky, 35 Ky.L.J. 320, 327 (1947). See 50 Yale L.Jour. 1427, 1443 (1941); 30 Col.L.Rev. 488, 503 (1930); 43 Yale L.Jour. 107, 108 (1934).

13. Fidelity Mortgage Co. v. Mahon, 31 Ohio App. 151, 166 N.E. 207 (1929). In McBride v. Comley, 204 Iowa 622, 215 N.W. 613 (1927), where both a prior and subsequent mortgagee applied for a receiver, the junior mortgagee was given the prior right to the rents and profits on the ground that it contained a receivership clause while the earlier one did not but based its right to a receiver solely on the ground that the security was inadequate and the mortgagor was insolvent. The court's reasoning was that a receiver appointed on the latter grounds had no power to use the rents to pay the debt of the mortgagee. If the prior mortgagee had obtained a receiver on the ground of waste or impairment of the security, this would carry the right to have the rents applied to the debt, and the court intimates the prior mortgagee would then prevail over the latment of rents and profits in the later mortgage.[14] It would follow that if the prior mortgage contained a pledge of rents and profits the same result would be reached. Where both the earlier and the later mortgages contain clauses that are construed to be pledges only of the income, although the first mortgagee will be entitled to priority as to rents and profits from the time he effectively asserts his rights by having the receivership extended to him, a junior mortgagee who previously obtains a receiver is entitled to all rents collected up to the time of the first mortgagee's intervention.[15]

 WESTLAW REFERENCES

receiver! /p first junior later second senior +1 mortgagee /p profit rent!

H. ACQUISITION OF TITLE IN BREACH OF DUTY

§ 4.44 Acquisition by Mortgagor

A mortgagor is under a duty to the mortgagee to discharge the secured obligation. Hence he cannot fail to do so, buy the property in on foreclosure, and hold it free of the mortgage. He can do this neither directly nor through intermediaries.

Thus, where there are covenants of title and to defend by the mortgagor in a second mortgage, he cannot acquire title on the foreclosure sale of a defaulted first mortgage so as to cut off a second mortgage by direct [1] purchase or through collusion with another.[2] The same has

---

ter one with a clause in it calling for a receiver or pledging the rents.

14. Wiggins v. Freeman, 174 App.Div. 304, 160 N.Y.S. 448 (1916).

15. Sullivan v. Rosson, supra note 9.

§ 4.44

1. Third National Bank in Nashville v. McCord, 688 S.W.2d 446 (Tenn.App.1985); Dixieland Realty Co. v. Wysor, 272 N.C. 172, 158 S.E.2d 7 (1967); Home Owners Loan Corp. v. Guaranty Title Trust Co., 168 Tenn. 118, 76 S.W.2d 109 (1934); Hilton v. Bissell, 1 Sandf. Ch. 407 (N.Y.1844).

2. See Dorff v. Bornstein, 277 N.Y. 236, 242, 14 N.E.2d 51 (1938), motion granted 278 N.Y. 566, 16 N.E.2d 105 (1938); Wood & Oberreich, Revival of a Second or Subsequent Mortgage upon Reacquisition of Title by the Original Mortgagor after Foreclosure of a First Mortgage, 11 Ind.L.J. 429 (1936). See White, Revival of Mortgages, 10 U. of Cin.L.Rev. 217 (1936). 44 Harv.L. Rev. 128 (1930). The doctrine of estoppel has been invoked in behalf of a foreclosing

first mortgagee to refasten the lien of his mortgage upon a title obtained by the mortgagor from a third party when the original mortgage given by him was defective. Yerkes v. Hadley, 5 Dak. 324, 40 N.W. 340, 2 L.R.A. 363 (1888). So, too, where a mortgage contained a warranty of title, but before the execution of the mortgage the property, unknown to the mortgagor, had been sold for taxes, a reacquisition by the mortgagor of the title from the state will inure to the benefit of the mortgagee. Jacobsen v. Nieboer, 299 Mich. 116, 299 N.W. 830 (1941), noted, 26 Va.L.Rev. 101 (1941). The doctrine has been held inapplicable in such a situation where the mortgage is given to the vendor for the purchase money. The mortgagee in such a case having first conveyed the defective title to his mortgagor has no standing to invoke the rule. Florida Land Investment Co. v. Williams, 84 Fla. 157, 92 So. 876, 26 A.L.R. 171 (1922). Butterfield v. Lane, 114 Me. 333, 96 A. 233 (1915) accord. But see Clark v. Baker, 14 Cal. 612, 76 Am.Dec. 449 (1860); Toms v. Boyes, 50 Mich. 352, 15 been held to be true even though the second mortgage was expressly subject to the first mortgage, such a clause being construed as mere identification of a lien already existing and superior from the standpoint of priority on foreclosure but in no way affecting the covenant between the parties.[3] The same rule has been applied to a grantee from the mortgagor who assumed the payment of the mortgage debt,[4] but not to one who merely [5] took "subject to" it. The distinction is that in the latter case there is no duty on the nonassuming grantee to pay off the mortgage.

Suppose, however, the mortgagor reacquires title from an independent third party rather than by purchasing at the foreclosure sale. Some courts hold that the mortgagor is still subject to the lien of the subsequent mortgage.[6] Others hold that he will take free and clear in the absence of any contract duty or fraudulent conduct by the mortgagor toward the second mortgagee.[7] Courts follow this approach are influenced by a policy that favors a bona fide purchaser being able to convey good title to any subsequent grantee, the mortgagor included.[8]

N.W. 506 (1883). See 26 A.L.R. 173 (1923). See Note, 29 N.D.L.R. 50 (1953), reviewing the different theories on which the courts hold that junior liens revive.

3. Martin v. Raleigh State Bank, 146 Miss. 1, 111 So. 448, 51 A.L.R. 442 (1927). See 51 A.L.R. 445 (1927); 111 A.L.R. 1285 (1937); Merchants National Bank of Fargo v. Miller, 59 N.D. 273, 229 N.W. 357 (1930). Contrast Huzzey v. Heffernan, 143 Mass. 232, 9 N.E. 570 (1887); Sandwich Manufacturing Co. v. Zellmer, 48 Minn. 408, 51 N.W. 379 (1892); Chamberlain v. Forbes, 126 Mich. 86, 85 N.W. 253 (1901). Federal Farm Mortgage Corp. v. Larson, 227 Wis. 221, 278 N.W. 421 (1938), prior mortgage excepted in covenant of warranty; Zandri v. Tendler, 123 Conn. 117, 193 A. 598, 111 A.L.R. 1280 (1937).

4. Beitel v. Dobbin, 44 S.W. 299 (Tex. Civ.App.1898).

5. Searles v. Kelley, 88 Miss. 228, 40 So. 484, 8 L.R.A.,N.S., 491 (1906).

6. Federal Land Bank of Columbia v. Bank of Lenox, 192 Ga. 543, 16 S.E.2d 9 (1941) discussed, 27 Iowa L.Rev. 482 (1942); Kerr v. Erickson, 24 S.W.2d 21 (Tex.Com. App.1930), noted, 30 Col.L.Rev. 742 (1930); Jensen v. Duke, 71 Cal.App. 210, 234 P. 876 (1921), statute; Johnson v. Clark, 7 Cal.2d 529, 61 P.2d 767 (1936), statute; Jones v. Kingsey, 55 N.C. 463 (1856); Martin v. Raleigh State Bank, 146 Miss. 1, 111 So. 448 (1927) with aid of statute; Merchants National Bank of Fargo v. Miller, 59 N.D. 273, 229 N.W. 357 (1930); Baird v. Chamberlain, 60 N.D. 784, 236 N.W. 724 (1931). See Wood & Oberreich, Revival of a Second or Subsequent Mortgage upon Reacquisition of Title by the Original Mortgagor after Foreclosure of a First Mortgage, 11 Ind.L.J. 429 (1936).

7. Zandri v. Tendler, 123 Conn. 117, 193 A. 598, 111 A.L.R. 1280 (1937); Dorff v. Bornstein, 277 N.Y. 236, 14 N.E.2d 51 (1938) noted, 13 St. John's L.Rev. 182; cf. Schultz v. Cities Service Oil Co., 149 Kan. 148, 86 P.2d 533 (1939) noted, 52 Harv.L. Rev. 1176 (1939). Cf. also McDonald v. Duckworth, 197 Okl. 576, 173 P.2d 436 (1946) criticized 60 Harv.L.Rev. 658 (1947). See also 30 Va.L.Rev. 496 (1944).

Florida courts seem to be having an especially uneasy time with this issue. One court has stated: "If a mortgagor suffers foreclosure of a first mortgage on property which is also subject to a second mortgage, the second mortgage is extinguished and the second is left 'holding the bag'. Subsequent acquisition of one or many other parcels of property does not inure to the benefit of the second mortgagee." County of Pinellas v. Clearwater Federal Savings & Loan Association, 214 So.2d 525, 527 (Fla.App.1968). On the other hand, a subsequent Florida appellate decision, showing clear discomfort with the foregoing language, held it inapplicable when a foreclosure sale purchaser reconveys to the mortgagor after foreclosure, but prior to the issuance of the final foreclosure certificate of title to the foreclosure sale purchaser. See Webb v. Verville, 434 So.2d 360 (Fla. App.1983).

8. See 13 St. John's L.Rev. 182, 183 (1938).

Purchase of the mortgaged premises by the mortgagor at a tax sale provides another illustration of the general doctrine. "If a tax deed always conveyed title clear of all past encumbrances, it would be possible for delinquent owners to extinguish outstanding encumbrances by a repurchase of their property at a tax sale."[9] To prevent such manipulation, one who owes to another the duty of paying taxes cannot, as to that other at least, default in that duty and then better his title by purchase at the tax sale resulting from his breach of duty.[10] The mortgagor in possession, being bound to pay the taxes as between himself and the mortgagee cannot, therefore, default in that obligation, allow the property to be sold for taxes, which constitute a paramount lien, and then buy in at the tax sale free and clear of the mortgage.[11] He cannot base a title on the violation of his duty [12] and his purchase, so far as the mortgagee is concerned, will be considered a payment of the taxes.[13] The doctrine extends even to the case where the tax sale is held after the foreclosure of the mortgage,[14] for, even though at the time of purchase the mortgagor-mortgagee relation no longer existed, his title would still be based upon a failure of duty during the time it did exist. Moreover, because the land was sold at the foreclosure sale subject to the tax lien and not free of it, the sale proceeds that would otherwise accrue to the benefit of the mortgagee were reduced.[15] Further, the great weight of authority holds that a transferee of the mortgagor, whether he assumes the payment of the mortgage debt or merely takes subject to it cannot defeat the lien of the mortgagee any more than could the mortgagor.[16]

 WESTLAW REFERENCES

acquir*** bought buy*** purchas*** /3 forclos*** /s mortgagor
        /s land property "real estate" realty

tax +1 sale title /s mortgagor /s land property "real estate"
        realty

---

9. 46 Yale L.J. 334 (1936).

10. 3 Cooley, Taxation, § 1437. It has been pointed out that, since it seems inequitable to permit one to profit by buying in a tax title after neglecting the duty to pay them, regardless of to whom the duty ran, a broader statement is desirable. See 46 Yale L.J. 334, n. 2 (1936).

11. Dayton v. Rice, 47 Iowa 429 (1877); Woodbury v. Swan, 59 N.H. 22 (1879). Cf. Allison v. Armstrong, 28 Minn. 276, 9 N.W. 806, 41 Am.Rep. 281 (1881). See 16 L.R.A.,N.S., 121 (1908).

12. Pines v. Novick, 168 App.Div. 155, 153 N.Y.S. 891 (1915).

13. Waring v. National Savings & Trust Co., 138 Md. 367, 114 A. 57 (1921); Allison v. Armstrong, 28 Minn. 276, 9 N.W. 806, 41 Am.Rep. 281 (1881). See 90 U.Pa.L.Rev. 90, 94 (1941).

14. Adams v. Sims, 177 Ark. 652, 9 S.W.2d 329 (1928), noted, 42 Harv.L.Rev. 583 (1929). See also 52 L.R.A.,N.S., 877, 878 (1914).

15. Barnard v. Wilson, 74 Cal. 512, 16 P. 307 (1888).

16. See 16 L.R.A.,N.S., 121, 124 (1908); 1914, L.R.A.,N.S., 877, 878, (1941) for collections of cases. See also 90 U.Pa.L.Rev. 90, 95. Zuege v. Nebraska Mortgage Co., 92 Kan. 272, 140 P. 855, 52 L.R.A.,N.S., 877 (1914), is against the great weight of authority in holding that a purchaser from the mortgagor subject to the mortgage debt may buy a tax title free of the mortgage and seems incorrect. Ownership of the redemption interest, not personal obligation to pay the mortgage debt, is the criterion of duty to pay taxes. And it is the failure of the duty to pay the taxes that prevents the founding of a title on the tax sale purchase.

§ 4.45 Acquisition of Tax Title by Mortgagee

A mortgagee in possession has the duty to pay the taxes and cannot, therefore, after failing to pay them purchase the property at a tax sale caused by his default and hold the property free of the mortgagor's claim to redeem.[1] Where the mortgagee is not in possession there is a split of authority.[2] Some let the mortgagee buy at the tax sale and cut off the rights of the mortgagor. They argue that the mortgagee had no duty to pay the taxes and stood in no fiduciary relation to the mortgagor. A denial of the privilege would let the mortgagor—who did have the duty to pay taxes—force the mortgagee still to hold only as a security claimant. This would allow the mortgagor to take advantage of her own default.[3] Further, the rule does not operate harshly against the mortgagor since, under tax statutes, she can redeem from the tax sale.[4] Moreover, the incentive to the mortgagor and other mortgagees to pay taxes promptly and to purchase at the tax sale would be increased.[5] The clear weight of authority, however, will not permit the mortgagee thus to shake off the claim of the mortgagor.[6]

Suppose, instead that the mortgagee acquires a tax title in order to cut off a senior mortgage, rather than the mortgagor. While there is

§ 4.45

1. Schenck v. Kelley, 88 Ind. 444 (1882); Dusenberry v. Bidwell, 86 Kan. 666, 121 P. 1098 (1912); Howze v. Dew, 90 Ala. 178, 7 So. 239, 24 Am.St.Rep. 783 (1889); Brown v. Simons, 44 N.H. 475 (1863); Hall v. Westcott, 15 R.I. 373, 5 A. 629 (1886). See also Moore v. Titman, 44 Ill. 367 (1867). Cf. Beckwith v. Seborn, 31 W.Va. 1, 5 S.E. 453 (1888); Ten Eyck v. Craig, 62 N.Y. 406, 422 (1875). See 140 A.L.R. 294, 318 (1941), for a collection of cases. A mortgagee in possession under an invalid foreclosure sale purchase has been held to be barred from acquiring a valid tax title as against the mortgagor. National Surety Co. v. Walker, 148 Iowa 157, 125 N.W. 338, 38 L.R.A.,N.S., 333 (1910).

2. See 90 U.Pa.L.Rev. 90, 95 (1941).

3. Jones v. Black, 18 Okl. 344, 88 P. 1052, 11 Ann.Cas. 753 (1907); Price v. Salisbury, 41 Okl. 416, 138 P. 1024, L.R.A., 1917D, 520 (1914); Williams v. Townsend, 31 N.Y. 411, 415 (1865), "A mortgage is a mere security for a debt; and there is no such relation of trust or confidence between the maker and holder of a mortgage as prevents the latter from acquiring title to its subject matter, either under his own or any other valid lien. The defendant [mortgagee] had no duty to perform to the plaintiff, or toward the mortgaged premises, that precluded her from buying at the tax sale; she was under no obligation to pay the taxes."; McLaughlin v. Acom, 58 Kan. 514, 50 P. 441 (1898), noted 1898, 11 Harv.L.Rev. 343; Reimer v. Newel, 47 Minn. 237, 49 N.W. 865 (1891). Cf. First National Bank of Rapid City v. McCarthy, 18 S.D. 218, 100 N.W. 14 (1904); see Waterson v. Devoe, 18 Kan. 223 (1877); Beckwith v. Seborn, 31 W.Va. 1, 5 S.E. 453 (1888). See also 140 A.L.R. 294, 311 (1941).

4. 4 Cooley, Taxation, 4th ed. § 1565 (1924).

5. See Baird v. Fischer, 57 N.D. 167, 185, 220 N.W. 892, 899 (1928), Christianson, J., dissenting.

6. Koch v. Kiron State Bank, 230 Iowa 206, 297 N.W. 450, 140 A.L.R. 273 (1941); Hadlock v. Benjamin Drainage District, 89 Utah 94, 53 P.2d 1156, 106 A.L.R. 876 (1936), discussed, 46 Yale L.J. 334 (1936); Eck v. Swennenson, 73 Iowa 423, 35 N.W. 503, 5 Am.St.Rep. 690 (1887); Porter v. Corbin, 124 Mich. 201, 82 N.W. 818 (1900). See Shepard v. Vincent, 38 Wash. 493, 80 P. 777 (1905); Burchard v. Roberts, 70 Wis. 111, 35 N.W. 286, 5 Am.St.Rep. 148 (1887); note, 46 Yale L.J. 334 (1936). See also 11 Ann.Cas. 750 (1909); 38 L.R.A.,N.S., 333 (1912); L.R.A.1917D, 522; 140 A.L.R. 294, 302 (1941); Stallings v. Erwin, 148 Mont. 227, 419 P.2d 480 (1966); National Bank of Washington v. Equity Investors, 86 Wn.2d 545, 546 P.2d 440 (1976).

some authority to the contrary,[7] most cases hold that a junior mortgagee cannot assert a tax title against a senior mortgage where both mortgages are outstanding.[8] Several reasons have been advanced for the majority approach. Occasionally it is said that the mortgagee is like a trustee and therefore is debarred from founding a title on the tax sale in opposition to the mortgagor or other mortgagees.[9] But the mortgagee may buy at even his own foreclosure sale and, consequently, even if it were true that he is a trustee, it is difficult to see why purchase at a tax sale would be a breach of any fiduciary obligation owed to the mortgagor and to other mortgagees. Sometimes the analogy of joint tenants is invoked.[10] But each joint tenant has a duty to pay the taxes and therefore as to them the general principle applies that one cannot profit by failing to do his duty. There is no such duty on a mortgagee not in possession, in the absence of an express contractual obligation in favor of the mortgagor or another mortgagee, to pay the taxes.[11] Still other courts stress the community of interest of the parties in preserving the estate by the payment of taxes and conclude that it would thus be inequitable conduct to acquire and assert a tax title against the others, or that presumably it is paid for the common protection.[12] Just why it is inequitable when there is neither a contractual duty or one arising out of their relationship to pay the taxes is not explained. Moreover, the common derivation of their interests in the land does not create a common interest but rather antagonistic inter-

---

7. Security Mortgage Co. v. Herron, 174 Ark. 729, 296 S.W. 363 (1927); see 140 A.L.R. 294, 329 (1941). Security Mortgage Co. v. Harrison, 176 Ark. 423, 3 S.W.2d 59 (1928).

8. Connecticut Mutual Life Insurance Co. v. Bulte, 45 Mich. 113, 7 N.W. 707 (1881); Chrisman v. Hough, 146 Mo. 102, 47 S.W. 941 (1898); Oregon Mortgage Co. v. Leavenworth Securities Corp., 197 Wn. 436, 86 P.2d 206 (1938), 14 Wash.L.Rev. 231 noted (1939); Baird v. Fischer, 57 N.D. 167, 220 N.W. 892 (1928), 13 Minn.L.Rev. 623 noted (1929); 38 Yale L.J. 263 (1928); 29 Col.L.Rev. 93 (1929). See notes, 14 Wash. L.Rev. 231 (1939); 11 Harv.L.Rev. 343 (1897). See also 11 Ann.Cas. 759 (1909); L.R.A.1917D, 522; 140 A.L.R. 294, 322 (1941); 90 U. of Pa.L.Rev. 90, 96 (1941). That a prior mortgagee cannot cut off a subsequent mortgagee, Anson v. Anson, 20 Iowa 55, 89 Am.Dec. 514 (1866). The junior mortgagee obtains his position in this respect as holder of a security interest in the redemption right of the mortgagor. There is a difference of opinion as to whether the fact that the title had become absolute and irredeemable in the hands of a third person when the mortgagee acquires it alters the result. Safe Deposit and Trust Co. v. Wickhem, 9 S.D. 341, 69 N.W. 14, 62 Am.St.Rep. 873 (1896), rehear-

ing denied 9 S.D. 515, 70 N.W. 654 (1896). Contra: Chrisman v. Hough, 146 Mo. 102, 47 S.W. 941 (1898).

9. See, e.g., Finlayson v. Peterson, 11 N.D. 45, 89 N.W. 855 (1902); Ten Eyck v. Craig, 62 N.Y. 406, 422 (1875), mortgagee in possession: "A mortgagee is often called a trustee, and in a very limited sense this character may be attributed to him."

10. E.g. Connecticut Mutual Life Insurance Co. v. Bulte, 45 Mich. 113, 122, 7 N.W. 707, 710 (1881), "It is as just and as politic here as it is in the case of tenants in common, to hold that the purchase is only a payment of the tax."

11. "It certainly cannot be said that the second mortgagee owes any duty to the first mortgagee to protect his lien against tax sale. Neither, on the other hand, does the first mortgagee owe any such duty to the second mortgagee, or to the owner. To the state each one of the three may be said to owe the duty to pay the taxes; and the state will sell the interest of all if none of the three shall pay." Connecticut Mutual Life Insurance Co. v. Bulte, 45 Mich. 113, 121, 7 N.W. 707, 710 (1881).

12. Fair v. Brown, 40 Iowa 209 (1875); Woodbury v. Swan, 59 N.H. 22 (1879); Hall v. Westcott, 15 R.I. 373, 5 A. 629 (1886).

ests, certainly as between two mortgagees. The courts may be disturbed by the possibility that one who merely had a lien on the property might obtain a tax deed for a small sum and by it destroy the liens of other mortgagees and the mortgagor. If the payment were viewed as a redemption, "the mortgagee, acquiring a prior lien on the property to the amount expended in that redemption would be placed in a position no worse than that which he occupied prior to the delinquency, while at the same time the other lienors would be materially benefitted." [13] Another argument is that the rule preventing tax title purchase by one who owes a duty to another person to pay them should be broadened to include all who owe a duty to the public to pay taxes. Such a duty is then found in the fact that the mortgagee, if he does not pay them, will lose his entire interest in the property.[14] Probably the same idea, but more broadly based, is expressed by saying that it is against public policy to allow the mortgagee to purchase at the tax sale and gain an advantage by so doing in that it would encourage him to fail to take advantage of his privilege to pay taxes. It is to the interest of the state that taxes be paid promptly, and since the mortgagee is fully protected by his privilege of paying when they are due, he should not be encouraged to fail to take advantage of that privilege.[15] But this is an argument that cuts both ways [16] and the incentive in any event is speculative and dubious.

 WESTLAW REFERENCES

tax   + 1   sale title   /s   mortgagee   /s   land property "real estate" realty

§ 4.46   Tax Payment by Subsequent Mortgagee—Effect on Prior Mortgagee

If a second mortgagee pays off the paramount tax lien of the taxing authority, it is quite clear that he can add that amount to his own mortgage debt or be subrogated to the lien of the taxing power as against the mortgagor.[1] Whether he can be subrogated to that paramount lien as against a prior mortgagee is a more difficult question. In

13. 46 Yale L.J. 334, 338 (1936).

14. 46 Yale L.J. 334, 337 (1936). See quotation from Connecticut Mutual Life Insurance Co. v. Bulte, 45 Mich. 113, 7 N.W. 707 (1881), supra note 75. But judgment creditors, who also have a security interest in the property, are not subject to the rule. Wilson v. Jamison, 36 Minn. 59, 29 N.W. 887, 1 Am.St.Rep. 635 (1886). "The recognition of a disability to purchase an unencumbered tax title, an issue of policy and not of legal rules, depends on a balancing of social interests that are far from clear; certainly there is no basis for a

blanket disqualification of all such lienors." 46 Yale L.J. 334, 337 (1936).

15. See 3 Tiffany, Real Prop., § 616; Baird v. Fischer, 57 N.D. 167, 185, 220 N.W. 892, 899 (1928), Christianson, J., dissenting.

16. See supra, text, where the possibility that one mortgagee might acquire a clear tax title is cited as an incentive to other mortgagees and the mortgagor to see to it that taxes are paid.

§ 4.46

1. See § 4.31 supra.

Laventall v. Pomerantz,[2] the first mortgage contained a clause accelerating the right to foreclosure on nonpayment of taxes. The New York Court of Appeals held that payment of the taxes by a holder of a subordinate mortgage would give him no right to be subrogated to the priority of the tax lien over the first mortgage. There are, however, cases giving subrogation to the second mortgagee even where there is an acceleration clause permitting foreclosure on default by the mortgagor in paying taxes, although most of them do not mention whether the mortgagor had such a right.[3] In these latter cases there may have been no such right; or it is possible that there was one but it had been so neglected that it could not be and was not seriously urged.[4] In a few jurisdictions the taxpaying junior encumbrancer is given a prior lien by statute.[5]

Where there is an acceleration clause in the first mortgage allowing foreclosure on non-payment of taxes by the mortgagee, the strongest argument against giving subrogation to the paramount lien for taxes as against the first mortgagee is that such payment destroys a most valuable right of the first mortgagee.[6] The right to foreclose on tax default is a valuable one because it is an effective means of forcing the mortgagor to pay the taxes and, also, because it provides a remedy at the first signs of financial irresponsibility of the mortgagor.[7] Consequently a junior mortgagee who destroys that recourse to the detriment of the earlier mortgagee should have no claim to be elevated to priority over the first mortgagee but should be remitted to adding the amount paid to his own mortgage debt,[8] at least in the absence of unreasonable refusal or delay of the prior mortgagee to act for the protection of his own interest. But other reasons have been advanced. It is said that the first mortgagee is not unjustly enriched because he merely got a benefit to which he was entitled, and to grant subrogation would deprive him of a part of the security upon which he based his original loan.[9] The tax lien is the obligation of the mortgagor and if paid by someone else it should not detract from the mortgagee's security any more than if paid by the mortgagor himself.[10] Furthermore, the payment should be considered voluntary because it is made for the

---

2. 263 N.Y. 110, 188 N.E. 271 (1933), discussed in notes, 19 Cornell L.Q. 487 (1934); 11 N.Y.Univ.L.Q.Rev. 655 (1934); 1 U. of Chi.L.Rev. 813 (1934); 29 Ill.L.Rev. 123 (1934); 20 Va.L.Rev. 914 (1934). See also notes, 46 Harv.L.Rev. 1036 (1933); 42 Yale L.J. 971 (1937); 17 Tex.L.Rev. 352 (1933).

3. See e.g., Smart v. Tower Land & Investment Co., 597 S.W.2d 333 (Tex.1980), appeal after remand 635 S.W.2d 615 (1982), error refused n.r.e. (1982). Marks v. Baum Building Co., 73 Okl. 264, 175 P. 818 (1918), acceleration clause; Noeker v. Howry, 119 Mich. 626, 78 N.W. 669 (1899), "usual tax clause"; Ringo v. Woodruff, 43 Ark. 469 (1884); Fiacre v. Chapman, 32 N.J.Eq. 463

(1880). For collections of cases holding both ways, see 84 A.L.R. 1366, 1393 (1933); 123 A.L.R. 1248, 1261 (1939).

4. See 1934, 29 Ill.L.Rev. 123.

5. Ky.Rev.Stat. 134.080; La.Stat.Ann.—Civ.Code art. 2161; see Timken v. Wisner Estates, 153 La. 262, 95 So. 711 (1923).

6. Laventall v. Pomerantz, supra note 2.

7. See 29 Ill.L.Rev. 123 (1934).

8. Sidenberg v. Ely, 90 N.Y. 257, 43 Am.Rep. 163, 11 Abb.N.C. 354 (1882).

9. See 42 Yale L.J. 972 (1932).

10. 20 Va.L.Rev. 914 (1933).

purpose of keeping the senior mortgagee from foreclosing, not for the purpose of relieving the estate of any tax liens,[11] and the *quid pro quo* he received was the extinguishment of the prior mortgagee's power to foreclose.[12] Also, where the mortgagor is liable, subrogation cannot be given as against another mortgagee because subrogation cannot be invoked against a third party not liable for the indebtedness discharged.[13] And in any event, a subordinate mortgagee stands in the mortgagor's shoes and gets no better rights than does the mortgagor, his rights being thus limited by reason of his position as mortgagee of the redemption interest. Since it was the mortgagor's duty, owed to all mortgagees, to pay the taxes, although he can add the tax to his claim against the mortgagor, he has no more power to be subrogated to a lien prior to that of the senior mortgagee than would his mortgagor.[14] To grant subrogation would encroach upon the privileges of sovereignty by according to a private individual the privilege of the taxing body's methods of collection.[15]

The chief arguments advanced in favor of permitting subrogation are that it would encourage payment of taxes,[16] a socially desirable result;[17] prevent the conferring of an unjust enrichment on the prior mortgagee because the second mortgagee, by discharging the tax lien, has to that extent increased the proceeds available to the prior mortgagee; the first mortgagee is not injured because otherwise he would be subordinate to the lien of the taxing authority[18]; and not only is the prior mortgagee not injured but he is benefited positively by the prevention of accrual of tax penalties and a sale of the land for taxes[19] and this benefit offsets the value to the prior mortgagee of the right to foreclose under an acceleration clause.[20] Further, there is some doubt whether payment by anyone other than the mortgagor would prevent the acceleration clause from becoming operative.[21] Additionally it is pointed out that subrogation to the lien of the taxing power can be *pro tanto* for the purpose of priority only and need not include granting the state's methods of collection which might be considered a delegation to

11. Pearmain v. Massachusetts Hospital Life Insurance Co., 206 Mass. 377, 92 N.E. 497 (1910); Fiacre v. Chapman, 32 N.J.Eq. 463 (1880), contra. For a brief discussion of the subrogation of a volunteer, see 40 Mich.L.Rev. 133 (1941).

12. Laventall v. Pomerantz, supra note 2.

13. Lawyers' Title & Guaranty Co. v. Claren, 237 App.Div. 188, 260 N.Y.S. 847 (1932). But see 46 Harv.L.Rev. 1036 (1933); 1 U.Chi.L.Rev. 813, 814 (1934); 42 Yale L.J. 972 (1932).

14. Glenn, Mortgages, § 39.2.

15. Sperry v. Butler, 75 Conn. 369, 53 A. 899 (1903).

16. But it should not go unnoticed that one of the purposes of an acceleration clause is to compel the mortgagor to pay taxes, and encouragement of other mortgagee to pay lessens the pressure on the mortgagor.

17. See 46 Harv.L.Rev. 1037 (1933); 11 N.Y.Univ.L.Q.Rev. 655 (1934); 19 Cornell L.Q. 487 (1934). See also preceding section.

18. See 46 Harv.L.Rev. 1037 (1932); 19 Cornell L.Q. 487 (1934).

19. 11 N.Y.Univ.L.Q.Rev. 655 (1934).

20. See Noeker v. Howry, 119 Mich. 626, 78 N.W. 669 (1899); Fiacre v. Chapman, 32 N.J.Eq. 463 (1880); 1 U.Chi.L.Rev. 813, 814 (1934); 29 Ill.L.Rev. 123 (1934).

21. See 46 Harv.L.Rev. 1037 (1932); 1 U.Chi.L.Rev. 813, 814 (1934).

a private individual of functions reserved to the public government.[22] The absence of personal liability of the prior mortgagee is no bar for the subrogation is to the lien, and not to a right *in personam* against a third party; and further, it is arguable that there is a [23] duty on all mortgagees to pay taxes and the subsequent one therefore is performing that duty.[24] And finally, the motive of the junior encumbrancer in paying to avoid foreclosure by the first mortgagee rather than of the tax lien ought not to be the test for granting subrogation. Even if the primary purpose were to avoid such foreclosure, that is insufficient cause for conferring so substantial a benefit on the prior mortgagee at the expense of the subordinate lienor.[25]

 WESTLAW REFERENCES

first junior later second senior　+1　mortgagee　/s　tax　/p　pay! subrogat***

---

22. 42 Yale L.J. 971, 972 (1932); 1 U.Chi.L.Rev. 813, 814 (1934).

23. 42 Yale L.J. 972 (1932); 19 Cornell L.Q. 487 (1934).

24. See Connecticut Mutual Life Insurance Co. v. Bulte, 45 Mich. 113, 7 N.W. 707 (1881); 46 Yale L.J. 334, 337 (1936).

25. See 46 Harv.L.Rev. 1037 (1932); 11 N.Y.Univ.L.Q.Rev. 655.

§§ 4.47–5.0 are reserved for supplementary material.

Chapter 5

TRANSFER BY THE MORTGAGOR AND THE MORTGAGEE

Table of Sections

A. TRANSFER BY THE MORTGAGOR

B. RESTRICTIONS ON TRANSFER BY THE MORTGAGOR

C. TRANSFER BY THE MORTGAGEE

A. TRANSFER BY THE MORTGAGOR

§ 5.1 Transferability of Mortgagor's Interest

It is axiomatic that a mortgagor's interest in real estate is normally freely transferable.[1] In lien states he is the legal owner subject only to the legal lien of the mortgagee.[2] In title states, regardless of the technical legal title being in the mortgagee, the mortgagor is recognized as the owner in substance.[3] On the other hand, the mortgagor cannot transfer to another the duty of performance. He remains bound by the debt unless it is discharged by payment or by agreement with the mortgagee[4] or, in limited circumstances, by other contractual or suretyship principles.[5]

The transfer, of course, can take place in a variety of ways. "Voluntary inter vivos transfer of the mortgagor's interest is ordinarily effected by a deed of conveyance in the usual form. At the mortgagor's death transfer of his interest may be effected either by a duly executed will or by the statute of descent if he dies intestate. Successive transfers of the mortgaged land may take place in any of these ways or by various modes of involuntary transfer, such as foreclosure, execution, or bankruptcy sale."[6]

§ 5.1

1. See e.g., Bermes v. Sylling, 179 Mont. 448, 587 P.2d 377 (1978); Young v. Hawks, 624 P.2d 235 (Wyo.1981)

2. See § 4.1, supra.

3. See § 4.2, supra.

4. See Berg v. Liberty Federal Savings & Loan Association, 428 A.2d 347 (1981); Yasuna v. Miller, 399 A.2d 68 (D.C.App. 1979); Davis v. National Homes Acceptance Corp., 523 F.Supp. 477 (N.D.Ala.1981); Hernandez v. Leiva, 391 So.2d 292 (Fla. App.1980); See Prudential Savings and Loan Association v. Nadler, 37 Ill.App.3d 168, 345 N.E.2d 782 (1976); United States v. Glass, 298 F.Supp. 396 (D.Ala.1969); Adair v. Carden, 29 L.R.Ir. 464, 481 (1892), the mortgagor "cannot get rid of his personal liability as between him and the mortgagee, where such liability exists, in the absence of anything amounting to a complete novation of the contract."

5. See §§ 5.19–5.20, infra.

6. Cunningham and Tischler, Transfer of the Real Estate Mortgagor's Interest, 27 Rutgers L.Rev. 24, 25 (1973).

The following sections will focus mainly on a variety of voluntary transfers. Indeed, because of the generally rising interest rates of the past two decades, it has become increasingly common for purchasers of land to "take over" the mortgagor-sellers' existing lower than market interest rate mortgage loans. The following material will focus in detail on the methods and implications of "taking over" such existing mortgagees. Many mortgagees often are displeased with the implications of the mortgagor's common law freedom to alienate his interest.[7] Some mortgagees, for example, may believe that particular transferees threaten the security of the mortgage. Many other mortgagees simply want to be able to "call in" existing mortgage loans when there is a transfer in order to facilitate reloaning the money at higher interest rates. Thus we will closely examine the extent to which the mortgagee, by including appropriate language in the mortgage documents, may defeat or at least discourage the transferability of the mortgagor's interest.

 WESTLAW REFERENCES
alienat*** assign! transfer! /s (interest real /3 estate property)
    performance /s mortgagor

§ 5.2 Methods of Sale of Mortgaged Land

There are three basic methods by which a mortgagor sells mortgaged real estate and the purchaser "takes over" the existing mortgage:

1. The purchaser may pay to the mortgagor only the agreed upon value of the redemption interest, i.e., the difference between the amount of the mortgage debt and the amount set by the parties in their sale agreement as the total value of the land.[1] She may not, however, assume any personal liability for the payment of the mortgage debt. She takes, as it is said, "subject" to the mortgage. The effect of such a transaction is considered later.[2]

2. The purchaser may pay to the mortgagor, as in the first transaction, only the value of the redemption interest. In addition the purchaser may promise the mortgagor to pay off the mortgage debt. Such promises are referred to as assumptions of the mortgage and ordinarily the language used says that the transferee "assumes" the debt. The promises do not relieve the mortgagor of his duty of payment to the mortgagee. In addition to giving the mortgagor a personal right against the transferee to have her instead of the mortgagor pay the mortgage debt, it also operates to make the land in the hands of the transferee "subject" to the mortgage debt as in the first

7. See § 5.21, infra.

§ 5.2

1. This amount has been aptly termed the "basic bargain price." See Storke and Sears, Transfer of Mortgaged Property, 38 Corn.L.Q. 185, 187 (1953). See also, Cunningham and Tischler, Transfer of the Real Estate Mortgagor's Interest, 27 Rutgers L.Rev. 24 (1973).

2. See § 5.3, infra.

case. The promise of the transferee to pay necessarily eliminates any claim between the parties that the transferor should pay instead of having the debt satisfied out of the land. The rights such an assumption gives to the mortgagee are considered in later section.[3] So, too, in more detail, are the rights of the transferor against an assuming grantee.[4]

3. The purchaser may pay the full value of the land, as agreed upon, free from the incumbrance. The mortgagor in return agrees to pay off the mortgage debt when it comes due.[5] This transaction reverses the situation as it exists in the second situation. The land in the hands of the transferee is likened to a real surety with the mortgagor having the primary duty, as principal, to discharge the debt. This transaction normally is unwise from the purchaser's perspective because, while the latter has paid the whole purchase price, she runs the risk that the mortgagor will fail to discharge the mortgage. Of course, if the mortgagor breaks his contract to pay, the transferee has rights against him which will be examined later.[6] However, the mortgagor may not be good for the money personally and since the purchaser is already out of pocket for the mortgage amount, she may not be financially able to prevent foreclosure of the mortgage and loss of the land.

The relationship between the mortgagor and the land in the hands of such a transferee will also affect possible subsequent action by the mortgagee, another matter for subsequent elaboration.[7]

Which one of these three transactions was the one actually entered into presents questions which are considered in the following sections.[8]

 WESTLAW REFERENCES
topic(mortgag**) +p buyer purchaser /s assum! redemption-
interest (subject /3 mortgage) takeover

§ 5.3 Transfer "Subject To" the Mortgage

Mortgagors commonly transfer real estate "subject" to an existing mortgage. This language goes beyond its apparent meaning that the land in the hands of the transferee can be reached by the mortgagee on default in priority to any right of the former in it. This is always true

---

3. See §§ 5.11–5.15, infra.

4. See § 5.10, infra.

5. "Ordinarily, where the owner of lands subject to a mortgage to secure his debts conveys the mortgaged premises, or any part of the same, to a purchaser, without any express provision with reference to the mortgage debt, such purchaser takes the same subject, of course, to the mortgage, but so far as the rights of the mortgagor and his grantee are concerned with reference to such mortgage debt the mort-

gagor will be regarded as the principal in such debts, and the land conveyed standing as his surety therefor * * *." Kinney v. Heuring, 44 Ind.App. 590, 596, 87 N.E. 1053, 1055 (1909). See also Van Valkenburg v. Jantz, 161 Wis. 336, 154 N.W. 373 (1915); Wadsworth v. Lyon, 93 N.Y. 201, 45 Am.Rep. 190 (1883).

6. See Chapter 10, infra.

7. See §§ 5.9–5.10, infra.

8. See §§ 5.3–5.8, infra.

regardless of any agreement by the parties. What it means in this connection is that the transferee agrees, as between her and her transferor, that the debt is to be satisfied out of the land. Or, as it is frequently put, the land is the principal and the transferor is only in the position of a surety or one secondarily liable.[1] Stated in another and perhaps more basic way, the grantee does not become personally liable, without more, to either the mortgagor or the mortgagee.[2] Nor does it affect the obligation of the mortgagor to the mortgagee.[3] But the mortgagor has no obligation to the transferee to pay it for the purpose of relieving the land in the hands of the transferee. And, although he may not be able to compel the mortgagee to proceed first against the land before seeking payment from him,[4] he does have a right against the grantee that the land be first exhausted in payment of

---

§ 5.3

1. "When the grantee merely takes subject to the mortgage, while it is true that the grantee assumes no personal liability whatever, nevertheless the security in his hands is liable for the payment of the mortgage debt, which liability as between the grantee and the mortgagor is primary. Therefore, to the extent of the value of such security properly applicable to the mortgage debt, the original mortgagor and the grantee subject to the mortgage stand in a relation one to another, which, while not a true suretyship, is nevertheless equitably analogous thereto and subject to the operation of the same principles." Zastrow v. Knight, 56 S.D. 554, 229 N.W. 925, 72 A.L.R. 379 (1930). Accord: North End Savings Bank v. Snow, 197 Mass. 339, 83 N.E. 1099, 125 Am.St.Rep. 368 (1908); Johnson v. Zink, 51 N.Y. 33 (1873); Howard v. Robbins, 170 N.Y. 498, 63 N.E. 530 (1902), Campbell, Cases on Mortgages, 2d ed., 407; King v. Whitely, 10 Paige 465 (1843); see Wright v. Anderson, 62 S.D. 444, 451, 253 N.W. 484, 487, 95 A.L.R. 81, L.R.A.1917C, 592, 593 (1934). If the land is sold "on execution against the mortgagor or under a second mortgage the purchaser acquires only the equity of redemption and the land becomes the primary source from which the mortgage must be satisfied, not the personal responsibility of the mortgagor." Howard v. Robbins, 170 N.Y. 498, 502, 63 N.E. 530, 531 (1902). The concept of a suretyship relation as between the mortgagor on the one side and the land and the transferee on the other is frequently invoked. Both the validity of the concept and its consequences will be considered in later sections, especially in those dealing with the effect of extensions of time and other actions by the mortgagee. See § 5.19, infra.

2. See Cassidy v. Bonitatibus, 39 Conn. Sup. 188, 473 A.2d 350 (1984); Life Savings and Loan Association of America v. Bryant, 125 Ill.App.3d 1012, 81 Ill.Dec. 577, 467 N.E.2d 277 (1984); Trauner v. Lowrey, 369 So.2d 531 (Ala.1979); Scafidi v. Puckett, 118 Ariz. 589, 578 P.2d 1018 (1978); Fye v. Cox, 263 N.W.2d 725 (Iowa 1978); Del Rio Land, Inc. v. Haumont, 110 Ariz. 7, 514 P.2d 1003 (1973); Brice v. Griffin, 269 Md. 558, 307 A.2d 660 (1973); Howard v. Clardy, 29 N.C.App. 570, 225 S.E.2d 149 (1976); Tom Kus v. Parker, 236 Ga. 478, 224 S.E.2d 353 (1976); Andrews v. Robertson, 177 Cal. 434, 170 P. 1129 (1918); First Trust Joint Stock Land Bank of Chicago v. Cuthbert, 215 Iowa 718, 246 N.W. 810 (1933); Chilton v. Brooks, 72 Md. 554, 20 A. 125 (1890); Flynn v. Kendrick, 285 Mass. 446, 189 N.E. 207 (1934); Malcolm v. Lavinson, 110 N.J.Eq. 63, 164 A. 318 (1933); Johnson v. Davis, 146 Okl. 170, 293 P. 197 (1930); Hylands' Estate v. Foote's Estate, 106 Vt. 1, 168 A. 925 (1933); Shepherd v. May, 115 U.S. 505, 6 S.Ct. 119, 29 L.Ed. 456 (1885); see J.H. Magill Lumber Co. v. Lane-White Lumber Co., 90 Ark. 426, 430, 119 S.W. 822, 823 (1909); Comstock v. Hitt, 37 Ill. 542, 548 (1865); Crawford v. Nimmons, 180 Ill. 143, 54 N.E. 209 (1899); Fourth National Bank in Wichita v. Hill, 181 Kan. 683, 314 P.2d 312 (1957).

3. Conway Savings Bank v. Vinick, 287 Mass. 448, 192 N.E. 81 (1934); Stevenson v. Black, 1 N.J.Eq. 338 (1831); Syracuse Trust Co. v. First Trust & Deposit Co., 141 Misc. 603, 252 N.Y.S. 850 (1931); In re May's Estate, 218 Pa. 64, 67 A. 120 (1907).

4. See cases in note 17, supra. But see § 5.9, infra.

the debt.[5] Likewise, if the mortgagor pays, he will be entitled to reimbursement out of the land.[6]

The transferee for her part, although under no personal duty to pay the debt, has the privilege of doing so. If she fails to exercise this privilege she runs the risk of losing her land by having either the mortgagee or the mortgagor apply it to the indebtedness. If she does pay, the mortgage is extinguished and she will hold the land free and clear. She will not, however, be able to obtain any reimbursement from her grantor.[7]

There are cases in which the conveyance in terms is only "subject" to the mortgage where the courts have held that the grantee should be regarded as having assumed the payment of the mortgage debt. They will be considered later in a section dealing with implied personal obligations.[8]

WESTLAW REFERENCES

land /p buyer purchaser transfer** /p subject /3 mortgage /p duty obligat*** privilege*
266k278

§ 5.4 Assumption of the Mortgage—In General

When a purchaser "assumes" an existing mortgage, she becomes personally liable to pay off the mortgage debt.[1] Whether an assumption has actually taken place, however, depends in general on contract principles. The contract need not be formal.[2] The agreement may be contained solely in the deed of conveyance.[3] On the other hand it "may be made orally or in a separate instrument; it may be implied from the transaction of the parties, or it may be shown by circumstances under which the purchase was made, as well as by the language used in the

5. Syracuse Trust Co. v. First Trust & Deposit Co., 141 Misc.Rep. 603, 252 N.Y.S. 850 (1931).

6. Braun v. Crew, 183 Cal. 728, 192 P. 531 (1920); Harvey v. Lowry, 204 Ind. 93, 183 N.E. 309 (1932), discussed, 42 Yale L.J. 798 (1933); Johnson v. Zink, 51 N.Y. 333 (1873); Murray v. Marshall, 94 N.Y. 611 (1884); Marsh v. Pike, 10 Paige 595 (N.Y.1844). But see § 5.9 infra.

7. See Wright v. Anderson, 62 S.D. 444, 450, 253 N.W. 484, 487, 95 A.L.R. 81 (1934).

8. See § 5.8, infra.

§ 5.4

1. Cassidy v. Bonitatibus, 39 Conn.Sup. 188, 473 A.2d 350 (1984); Ruther v. Thomas, 43 Colo.App. 435, 604 P.2d 703 (1979); Ellickson v. Dull, 34 Colo.App. 25, 521 P.2d 1282 (1974); Nutz v. Shepherd, 490 S.W.2d 366 (Mo.App.1973).

2. Howard v. Robbins, 67 App.Div. 245, 73 N.Y.S. 172 (1901), affirmed 170 N.Y. 498, 93 N.E. 530 (1902).

3. See § 5.5, infra.

agreement."[4] It must, however, be established by clear and unequivocal proof.[5]

 WESTLAW REFERENCES
buyer grantee purchaser /s assum! /s mortgage /p establish!
proof prove unequivocal**

§ 5.5 Assumption of the Mortgage—Deed Provisions

Where the parties intend to create an assumption agreement, it is most commonly found in the deed of conveyance itself. The language will refer to the mortgage and recite that the grantee "assumes and agrees to pay said mortgage according to its terms." The grantee does not have to sign such a deed for him to be bound by the provision.[1] However, assent to the assumption clause must be established as a fact.[2] Consequently the plaintiff must show that the grantee accepted the deed,[3] either with knowledge of the assumption clause in it[4] or under such circumstances as would raise a presumption of knowledge of its existence.[5]

4. Hopkins v. Warner, 109 Cal. 133, 138, 41 P. 868, 871 (1895). For New York legislation broadening the requirement that the assumption of the mortgage indebtedness by a grantee of the mortgage must be in writing, see Curtiss, The Commission and the Law of Real Property, 40 Cornell L.Q. 735, 742 (1955). On the other hand, Rosenberg v. Rolling Inn, Inc., 212 Md. 552, 129 A.2d 924 (1957), noted in 18 Md.L.Rev. 138 (1958), held that the Statute of Frauds does not apply to an assuming promise. And Manget Foundation, Inc. v. White, 101 Ga.App. 239, 113 S.E.2d 235 (1960), noted by Smith, Security Transactions, 12 Mercer L.Rev. 182, 188 (1960), held that the Statute of Frauds does not prevent the showing of an oral assumption by a grantee who accepts a warranty deed reciting that the grantee agreed to pay the grantor's debt as part of the consideration. In Barkhausen v. Continental Illinois National Bank & Trust Co., 3 Ill.2d 254, 120 N.E.2d 649 (1954), reversing 351 Ill.App. 388, 115 N.E.2d 640 (1953), noted in 33 Chi.-Kent L.Rev. 83 (1954), the beneficiaries of a trust were not liable upon an assumption of a pre-existing mortgage by a trustee as trustee, that being the intention of all parties to the transaction.

5. Heggen Construction Co., Inc. v. Turalba, 88 Wn.2d 711, 565 P.2d 420 (1977); Perkins v. Brown, 179 Wash. 597, 38 P.2d 253, 101 A.L.R. 275 (1934). See Note, 101 A.L.R. 281 (1934) as to what language amounts to an assumption.

§ 5.5

1. Thomas v. Home Mutual Building Association, 243 Ill. 550, 90 N.E. 1081 (1910); Jager v. Volliger, 174 Mass. 521, 55 N.E. 458 (1899); Furnas v. Durgen, 119 Mass. 500, 20 Am.Rep. 341 (1876); Sparkman v. Gove, 44 N.J.Law 252 (1882); Schley v. Fryer, 100 N.Y. 71, 2 N.E. 280 (1885); South Carolina Insurance Co. v. Kohn, 108 S.C. 475, 95 S.E. 65 (1918); Thacker v. Hubbard & Applby, 122 Va. 379, 94 S.E. 929 (1918); Bishop v. Douglass, 25 Wis. 696 (1870); Keller v. Ashford, 133 U.S. 610, 10 S.Ct. 494, 33 L.Ed. 667 (1889).

2. McFarland v. Melson, 323 Mo.App. 977, 20 S.W.2d 63 (1929); see Perkins v. Brown, 179 Wash. 597, 600, 38 P.2d 253, 256, 101 A.L.R. 275 (1934). See also 13 N.Y.Univ.L.Q.Rev. 486 (1936); 9 Wash.L. Rev. 118 (1934); Acceptance of the conveyance without knowledge of the assumption clause does not bind the grantee who repudiates it on discovery of its presence in the deed. Blass v. Terry, 156 N.Y. 122, 50 N.E. 953, 6 N.Y.Ann.Cas. 79. See L.R.A.1918A, 1003 (1898).

3. Papamechail v. Holyoke Mutual Insurance Co., 8 Mass.App. 849, 397 N.E.2d 1153 (1979); Nutz v. Shepherd, 490 S.W.2d 366 (Mo.App.1973).

4. Hamilton Co. v. Rosen, 53 R.I. 346, 166 A. 691 (1933); Magallon v. Schreiner, 97 Wash. 15, 165 P. 1048 (1917).

5. Blass v. Terry, 156 N.Y. 122, 50 N.E. 953, 6 N.Y.Ann.Cas. 79 (1898).

However, the deed itself is sometimes silent as to assumption. For example, it may be in the form of a quit claim deed [6] or it may contain covenants of warranty not only of title but against encumbrances. It may also, whether a quit claim or warranty deed, contain a statement that the conveyance is "subject to" the mortgage. In such cases whether there has been an assumption of the mortgage depends upon establishing it by evidence extrinsic to the deed. That evidence may consist of either a separate written or oral express agreement. Or it may consist of the circumstances accompanying the transaction, the most important of which is the amount paid by the grantee for the property. These situations present at least two questions. One is whether any or all of this kind of extrinsic evidence is barred by either the Statute of Frauds or the parol evidence rule. Another is, if the evidence is admitted, whether the language used or the facts proved establish that an assumption by the transferee was intended.

 WESTLAW REFERENCES
buyer grantee purchaser /s mortgage /p assum! /s assert**
deed "extrinsic evidence"

§ 5.6 Assumption of the Mortgage—Statute of Frauds

Although there is some authority to the contrary,[1] under the overwhelming majority of decisions, the Statute of Frauds will not be an obstacle to establishing an assumption agreement because the assumption of a mortgage debt is not within that provision of the Statute covering promises to answer for the debt or default of another.[2] The reasons usually advanced are that the promise is to pay the transferee's own debt, or that the promise is not to the creditor, the mortgagee, but to the debtor, the mortgagor. Unless taken out by some doctrine of part performance, it would seem that such a promise would be under that section of the Statute of Frauds relating to contracts not to be performed within a year.[3] The cases, however, have given little consideration to the point. Additional but untenable explanations are that the acceptance of a deed with an assumption clause in it is equivalent to an execution of it by the grantee,[4] or that, by reason of such acceptance, the law imposes an "implied" obligation identical in scope

6. E.g., Howard v. Robbins, 170 N.Y. 498, 63 N.E. 530 (1902).

§ 5.6

1. Cassidy v. Bonitatibus, 39 Conn.Sup. 188, 473 A.2d 350 (1984).

2. White v. Schader, 185 Cal. 606, 198 P. 19, 21 A.L.R. 499 (1921); Herrin v. Abbe, 55 Fla. 769, 46 So. 183, 18 L.R.A.,N.S., 907 (1908); Lamb v. Tucker, 42 Iowa, 118 (1875); Neiswanger v. McClellan, 45 Kan. 599, 26 P. 18 (1890); Strohauer v. Voltz, 42 Mich. 444, 4 N.W. 161 (1880); Langan v. Iverson, 78 Minn. 299, 80 N.W. 1051 (1899);

see Enos v. Anderson, 40 Colo. 395, 93 P. 475, 15 L.R.A.,N.S., 1087 (1907); 15 L.R.A.,N.S., 1087 (1908); 25 L.R.A.,N.S., 1202 (1910). Cf. Rooney v. Koenig, 80 Minn. 483, 83 N.W. 399 (1900).

3. See Tiffany, Real Prop., 3d ed., § 1437; Enos v. Anderson, 40 Colo. 395, 93 P. 475, 15 L.R.A.,N.S., 1087 (1907).

4. Foster v. Atwater, 42 Conn. 244 (1875); Schmucker v. Sibert, 18 Kan. 104, 26 Am.Rep. 765 (1877); Baldwin v. Emery, 89 Me. 496, 36 A. 994 (1896).

with the provision in the deed.[5] Mere acceptance of the deed seems insufficient to invoke the doctrine of part performance; and the obligation on the transferee is contractual, not non-consensual.

Although cases holding that contracts of assumption are not within the provisions of the ordinary Statutes of Frauds seem correct, there are good reasons why a writing should be required.[6] Such contracts are long term ones with several of them being created during the existence of a mortgage as the mortgaged land is sold to successive buyers. The question of whether there has been an assumption is frequently raised years after the alleged event at a time when recollection is uncertain and intermediate grantees[7] may well have lost their copies of the contracts and memoranda. Consequently it is not surprising to find a few statutes explicitly dealing with the matter. For example in California the contract of assumption must be in writing signed by the transferee unless it is specifically provided for in the conveyance of the property.[8] Moreover, in New Jersey no assumption agreement can be effective unless contained in the deed or in a separate written instrument.[9] New York has similar legislation.[10]

 WESTLAW REFERENCES
mortgage /s assum! /p "part performance" "statute of fraud"

---

§ 5.7 Assumption of the Mortgage—Parol Evidence Rule

Where the conveyance from a mortgagor is by quit claim deed with a recital of a nominal consideration and no other evidence is presented, the presumption is that the land is to be charged primarily with the payment of the mortgage.[1] Since the presumption arises only where there is no other evidence as to intention, if there is a clearly expressed intention in a separate agreement it will control.[2] In such a case there is no question of the extrinsic agreement varying the terms of the deed. The deed neither contained any part of the terms of the contract

5. Pike v. Brown, 61 Mass. (7 Cush.) 133 (1851); Urquhart v. Brayton, 12 R.I. 169 (1877). See 14 Bost.U.L.Rev. 692 (1934).

6. See Glenn, Mortgages, § 257.

7. The mortgagee may not only maintain an action against the mortgagor and his assuming grantee, but also against one or all of successive grantees who assume and agree to pay the mortgage. Baber v. Hanie, 163 N.C. 588, 80 S.E. 57 (1913); Wright v. Bank of Chattanooga, 166 Tenn. 4, 57 S.W.2d 800 (1933); Hofheimer v. Booker, 164 Va. 358, 180 S.E. 145 (1935). An assuming grantee cannot escape liability by transferring it to another. Central Life Insurance Co. v. Thompson, 182 Ark. 705, 33 S.W.2d 388 (1931); McLeod v. Building & Loan Association of Jackson, 168 Miss. 457, 151 So. 151 (1933). But

contra, Brinton v. Davidson, 308 Pa. 371, 162 A. 905 (1932).

8. West's Ann.Cal.Civ.Code § 1624(7). See note 11 So.Cal.L.Rev. 109 (1937).

9. N.J.Stat.Ann. 46:9–7.1. See Cunningham and Tischler, Transfer of the Real Estate Mortgagor's Interest, 27 Rutgers L.Rev. 24, 29 (1973).

10. N.Y.Civ.Prac.Act, § 1083c, added by N.Y.Laws 1938, c. 502. See note, 13 St. John's L.Rev. 215 (1938).

§ 5.7

1. See Howard v. Robbins, 170 N.Y. 498, 93 N.E. 530 (1902); Scribner v. Malinowski, 148 Mich. 447, 111 N.W. 1032 (1907).

2. Society of Friends v. Haines, 47 Ohio St. 423, 25 N.E. 119 (1890).

governing the sale nor was meant to cover the question whether the transferee did or did not assume the mortgage debt. The separate agreement is the sole expression of the contract and supplants the presumption which exists in the absence of affirmative evidence of intent.

However, the deed may contain covenants of warranty against incumbrances without any express provision in respect to the mortgage on the property and without any other evidence as to the parties' intent. In such a case the inference is that as between the grantor and grantee the former is to pay the debt to the exoneration of the land.[3] If, in addition to the covenant against incumbrances, the deed also contains a statement that the conveyance is "subject" to a certain mortgage or other explicit statement of intention that the covenant is not to apply to the mortgage specified, the covenant will be nullified as to it.[4] The terms of the deed dealing directly with the mortgage will govern as they would had there been no covenant against incumbrances in the instrument.

Where the deed contains only the covenant against incumbrances the question arises whether extrinsic evidence, in the form of a written or oral agreement or of accompanying circumstances, may be introduced in spite of the covenant to show that the grantee assumed the mortgage. Prima facie such a deed seems to cover exactly the subject with which the extrinsic evidence, if let in, also deals. And the provision in the deed apparently is directly varied and contradicted by the evidence.[5] Nevertheless the evidence is often admitted,[6] although the reasons advanced for doing so have not escaped criticism.[7] Some cases say it is admissible to show the consideration.[8] Others feel that the parol agreement is an independent contract neither at variance with the deed nor merged in it.[9] Finally, some admit the evidence

---

3. Maher v. Lanfrom, 86 Ill. 513 (1877); Wadsworth v. Williams, 100 Mass. 126 (1868); Hooper v. Henry, 31 Minn. 264, 17 N.W. 476 (1883); Barnes v. Mott, 64 N.Y. 397, 21 Am.Rep. 625 (1876).

4. King v. Whitely, 10 Paige 465 (N.Y. 1843); Drury v. Holden, 121 Ill. 130, 13 N.E. 547 (1887); Hopper v. Smyser, 90 Md. 363, 45 A. 206 (1900); Brown v. South Boston Savings Bank, 148 Mass. 300, 19 N.E. 382 (1889); Fuller v. Devolld, 144 Mo. App. 93, 128 S.W. 1011 (1910); Belmont v. Coman, 22 N.Y. 438, 78 Am.Dec. 213 (1860); Gerdine v. Menage, 41 Minn. 417, 43 N.W. 91 (1889); Calkins v. Copley, 29 Minn. 471, 13 N.W. 904 (1882).

5. In Simanovich v. Wood, 145 Mass. 180, 13 N.E. 391 (1887) parol evidence was excluded on this reasoning; Hicks v. Sullivan, 127 Miss. 148, 89 So. 811 (1921); Patterson v. Cappon, 125 Wis. 198, 102 N.W. 1083 (1905), accord.

6. Bolles v. Beach, 22 N.J.L. 680, 53 Am.Dec. 263 (1850); Hays v. Peck, 107 Ind. 389, 8 N.E. 274 (1886); Laudman v. Ingram, 49 Mo. 212 (1872); Deaver v. Deaver, 137 N.C. 240, 49 S.E. 113 (1904); Johnson v. Elmen, 94 Tex. 168, 59 S.W. 253, 52 L.R.A. 162 (1900).

7. See notes, 12 Wis.L.Rev. 405 (1937); 78 U. of Pa.L.Rev. 432 (1929).

8. Hays v. Peck, 107 Ind. 389, 8 N.E. 274 (1886); Bolles v. Beach, 22 N.J.L. 680, 53 Am.Dec. 263 (1850); Deaver v. Deaver, 137 N.C. 240, 49 S.E. 113 (1904); Johnson v. Elmen, 94 Tex. 168, 59 S.W. 253, 52 L.R.A. 162, 86 Am.St.Rep. 845 (1900). See 50 A.L.R. 1216, 1228 (1927); 84 A.L.R. 347, 358 (1931).

9. Laudman v. Ingram, 49 Mo. 212 (1872); Bolles v. Beach, supra note 6. See 50 A.L.R. 1216, 1229 (1927); 84 A.L.R. 347, 360 (1931).

when the mortgagee is plaintiff on the ground that the parol evidence rule is inapplicable to strangers to the deed.[10] The real reason for admission seems to be that if it is excluded the grantee would be unjustly enriched. Under such circumstances, the evidence should be admitted, not to enforce the agreement to assume, but to recover the amount of enrichment which would otherwise accrue unfairly to the grantee.

A less difficult case is where the deed itself says that the conveyance is "subject" to the mortgage and extrinsic evidence is offered that the grantee assumed the mortgage. The parol evidence rule clearly does not[11] and should not exclude this evidence. The term "subject" to the mortgage deals with and is meant to be limited to part only of the transaction, i.e., the relationship between the grantor and the land. The extrinsic agreement of assumption concerns an entirely separate and independent matter, the personal liability of the transferee to pay the mortgage debt.[12] It does not in any way vary or affect the terms of the instrument of conveyance. It merely creates a quite distinct contract obligation. Other grounds for admitting the evidence are those relied upon where there is only a covenant against incumbrances in the deed, i.e., that it may come in to show the consideration,[13] or, when the mortgagee is suing, that the exclusion rule does not apply to strangers to the deed.[14]

On the other hand, suppose that the deed clearly spells out an assumption agreement. To what extent may extrinsic evidence be used to establish a contrary understanding? Generally, if the deed contains such assumption language and it was known to the grantee, it cannot be contradicted by parol evidence, at least where the grantor sues the grantee.[15] On the other hand, where the mortgagee sues, there is

---

10. See 50 A.L.R. 1216, 1226 (1927); 84 A.L.R. 347, 358 (1931).

11. Consumers Savings Bank v. Coven, 8 Mass.App.Ct. 594, 395 N.E.2d 1331 (1979); White v. Schader, 185 Cal. 606, 198 P. 19, 21 A.L.R. 499 (1921); Herrin v. Abbe, 55 Fla. 769, 46 So. 183, 18 L.R.A.,N.S., 907 (1908); Strohauer v. Voltz, 42 Mich. 444, 4 N.W. 161 (1880); Lamb v. Tucker, 42 Iowa 118 (1875); Langan v. Iverson, 78 Minn. 299, 80 N.W. 1051 (1899); Gustafson v. Koehler, 177 Minn. 115, 224 N.W. 699 (1929); Gilmer v. Powell, 256 S.W. 124 (Mo. App.1923); Ordway v. Downey, 18 Wash. 412, 51 P. 1047, 63 Am.St.Rep. 892 (1898). See Warm, Rights and Liabilities of Mortgagee, Mortgagor and Grantee, 10 Temple L.Quar. 116, 121, 3 Mercer Beasley L.R. 113 (1935); 9 Tex.L.Rev. 453 (1930); 25 L.R.A.,N.S., 1202 (1910); 50 A.L.R. 1220, 1222 (1927); 84 A.L.R. 355, 356 (1931); Hood v. Young, 178 Ark. 439, 11 S.W.2d 767 (1928); Wayne International Building & Loan Association v. Beckner, 191 Ind.

664, 134 N.E. 273 (1922), contra. See 78 U.Pa.L.Rev. 432 (1930), criticizing the grounds of admission.

12. Strohauer v. Voltz, 42 Mich. 444, 4 N.W. 161 (1880); McFarland v. Melson, 323 Mo. 977, 20 S.W.2d 63 (Mo.App.1929); Ordway v. Downey, 18 Wash. 412, 51 P. 1047, 63 Am.St.Rep. 892 (1898).

13. White v. Schader, 185 Cal. 606, 198 P. 19, 21 A.L.R. 499 (1921); Brosseau v. Lowy, 209 Ill. 405, 70 N.E. 901 (1904); Swarthout v. Shields, 185 Mich. 427, 152 N.W. 202 (1915); Morgan v. South Milwaukee Lake View Co., 97 Wis. 275, 72 N.W. 872 (1897); Wayne International Building & Loan Association v. Beckner, 191 Ind. 664, 134 N.E. 273 (1922), contra.

14. McFarland v. Melson, 323 Mo. 977, 20 S.W.2d 63 (1929) noted, 78 U.Pa.L.Rev. 432 (1930). See 12 Wis.L.Rev. 405 (1937).

15. See Muhlig v. Fiske, 131 Mass. 110, 113 (1881); Clark v. Henderson, 62 N.D. 503, 244 N.W. 314, 84 A.L.R. 347 (1931).

authority that such evidence is admissible, apparently on the theory that because the mortgagee is the plaintiff, the parol evidence rule is inapplicable to strangers to the deed.[16] In any event, such evidence must be clear and convincing.[17]

 WESTLAW REFERENCES
infer! intend** intention presum! /s assum! /s mortgage /p deed (extrinsic parol /5 agreement evidence)

§ 5.8 Implied Personal Obligations

While the general rule is that a conveyance "subject" to a mortgage creates no personal obligation on the part of the grantee, there are deviations. In Pennsylvania, for example, while such a conveyance creates no direct obligation to the mortgagee on the part of the grantee, the grantee is obligated to indemnify the grantor from the mortgage obligation.[1] This implied obligation has been spoken of variously as "founded on principles of equity and fair dealing," as "purely contractual in nature", and as "impliedly contractual."[2] The Pennsylvania doctrine has been explained as arising out of a misconstruction of early cases in that state in which the conveyance was subject not to the mortgage but to "the payment" of it, a form of expression which understandably could be construed as amounting to an assumption of payment.[3]

Where in addition to a conveyance subject to the mortgage, the full value of the land is agreed on[4] as the purchase price and from it the purchaser has deducted the amount of the mortgage and has paid the balance, there are a good many cases holding that the purchaser has become personally liable.[5] This has been explained on the ground that "His [the grantee's] retention of the vendor's money for the payment of the mortgage, imposes upon him the duty of protecting the vendor

16. See Nissen v. Sabin, 202 Iowa 1362, 212 N.W. 125, 50 A.L.R. 1216 (1927); Stowers v. Stuck, 131 Neb. 409, 268 N.W. 310 (1936); Page v. Hinchee, 174 Okl. 537, 541, 51 P.2d 487, 491 (1935); Nutz v. Shepherd, 490 S.W.2d 366 (Mo.App.1973). But see Kozan v. Levin, 50 A.D.2d 663, 374 N.Y.S.2d 829 (1975). For a criticism of the distinction, see 12 Wis.L.Rev. 405 (1937).

17. See McFarland v. Melson, 323 Mo. 977, 985, 20 S.W.2d 63, 66 (1929) If the clause was inserted by fraud or mistake there may be relief. See 26 A.L.R. 528; 100 A.L.R. 911; 22 Va.L.Rev. 355 (1935).

§ 5.8

1. See Heaney v. Riddle, 343 Pa. 453, 23 A.2d 456 (1942); Masgai v. Masgai, 460 Pa. 453, 333 A.2d 861 (1975).

2. See Moschzisker, C.J., in Dobkin v. Landsberg, 273 Pa. 174, 180, 116 A. 814, 816 (1922).

3. See Tiffany, Real Prop., 3d ed., § 1435.

4. This agreement frequently appears in the deed of conveyance. See cases in note 66, infra. It may, however, be established by admissible extrinsic evidence. E.g., Canfield v. Shear, 49 Mich. 313, 13 N.W. 605 (1882); Hawn v. Malone, 188 Iowa 439, 176 N.W. 393 (1920). See § 5.7 supra.

5. Brice v. Griffin, 269 Md. 558, 307 A.2d 660 (1973). Townsend v. Ward, 27 Conn. 610 (1858); Drury v. Holden, 121 Ill. 130, 137, 13 N.E. 547, 548 (1887); Lamka v. Donnelly, 163 Iowa 255, 143 N.W. 869 (1913); Canfield v. Shear, 49 Mich. 313, 13 N.W. 605 (1882); Sanderson v. Turner, 73 Okl. 105, 174 P. 763, 2 A.L.R. 347 (1918); Parlette v. Equitable Farm Mortgage Association, 165 Okl. 155, 25 P.2d 300 (1933).

against the mortgage debt. This must be so * * * for it would seem
to be almost intolerably unjust to permit him to keep back the vendor's
money with the understanding that he would pay the vendor's debt,
and still be free of all liability for a failure to apply the money
according to his promise." [6] The personal liability so created generally
is held to be an assumption of the debt, but in some instances it is one
of indemnity as in Pennsylvania.[7] In end result there is little difference between a personal obligation to pay the debt and one to reimburse another person who has had to pay it.

Many states, on the other hand, have specifically rejected the
validity of such "implied assumptions." New Jersey, for example, since
1947 has prohibited the concept by statute.[8] Other jurisdictions have
reached similar results by judicial decision.[9]

The "implied assumption" decisions have been vigorously criticized.[10] It is a fair enough inference from the fact that the conveyance
is subject to a mortgage that the purchaser paid only the value of the
redemption interest.[11] And it is a further proper inference that the
grantee in such a case, as between him and the grantor, assumes the
debt as a charge upon the land he has acquired.[12] Such an interpretation exposes the grantee only to the risk of losing the property and to
no additional loss should it prove to be inadequate security for the debt.
But to impose upon such a grantee, whether on grounds of implication
of fact or ideas of fairness,[13] a duty to recoup his vendor when he has
had to pay the mortgage irrespective of the value of the land seems
unwarranted.[14] Such a risk should not be imposed upon him in the

6. Heid v. Vreeland, 30 N.J.Eq. 591, 593
(1879). See Dimmitt v. Johnson, 199 Iowa
966, 969, 203 N.W. 261, 263 (1913), for a
similar statement of rationale.

7. Lamka v. Donnelly, 163 Iowa 255,
143 N.W. 869 (1913); Hawn v. Malone, 188
Iowa 439, 176 N.W. 393 (1920); Friedman
v. Zuckerman, 104 N.J.Eq. 322, 145 A. 541
(1929); Britton v. Roth, 313 Pa. 352, 169 A.
146 (1933).

8. See N.J.Stat.Ann. 46:9–7.1; Cunning-
ham and Tischler, Transfer of the Real
Estate Mortgagor's Interest, 27 Rutgers
L.Rev. 24, 29 (1973).

9. See Yasuna v. Miller, 399 A.2d 68, 73
n. 11 (D.C.App.1979). Belmont v. Coman,
22 N.Y. 438, 78 Am.Dec. 213 (1860); Equitable Life Assurance v. Bostwick, 100 N.Y.
628, 3 N.E. 296 (1885); Fiske v. Tolman,
124 Mass. 254, 26 Am.Rep. 659 (1878), (but
otherwise if *payment* of the mortgage is
stated to be part of the consideration, Jager v. Vollinger, 174 Mass. 521, 55 N.E. 458
(1899), and cf. Flynn v. Kenrick, 285 Mass.
446, 189 N.E. 207 (1934), noted 14 Bost.U.L.
Rev. 692 (1934); yet see 101 A.L.R. 281,
283); McFarland v. Melson, 323 Mo. 977,
20 S.W.2d 63 (1929); Redhead v. Skidmore

Land Credit Co., 194 Wis. 123, 215 N.W.
937 (1927). For discussions and additional
authorities, see Warm, Rights and Liabilities of Mortgagee, Mortgagor, Grantee, 10
Temple L.Quar. 116, 119 (1935); Friedman,
Creation and Effect of Personal Liability of
Mortgage Debts in New York, 50 Yale L.J.
224, 226 (1940); Walsh, Mortgages 209.

10. See Warm, supra note 9; Walsh, op.
cit. supra note 10; Tiffany, Real Prop., 3d
ed., § 1435; Glenn, Mortgages § 256.

11. See Adair v. Carden, 29 L.R.Ir. 469,
482 (1892).

12. See Adair v. Carden, note 11, supra;
Glenn, Mortgages, § 252.

13. That the obligation is not based upon an implication of fact as to the parties'
intention, see Farwell, J., in Mills v. United Counties Bank, 1 Ch. 231 (1912), commented on in 28 L.Q.Rev. 122 (1912); Adair
v. Carden, 29 L.R.Ir. 469, 482 et seq. (1892).

14. Additionally, it has been suggested,
that if the obligation is imposed at all it
should be to pay the debt, not merely to
recoup the transferor to the extent he has
had to pay it. See Tiffany, Real Prop., 3d
ed., § 1435. This may be correct if the

absence of clear and explicit evidence of an intention to do so.[15] And the same criticism applies to cases which rest the result upon the terms of the agreement as to the purchase price which must be established in addition to the fact of taking subject to the mortgage.[16] As has been pointed out: "In actual fact there is not the slightest difference between a sale of the equity subject to the mortgage for a stated price to be paid for the equity and a sale of the same property by a contract which states the price at the full value of the property unencumbered and provides for payment to the amount of the mortgage by taking subject to the mortgage, the balance to be paid in cash. * * * To say that the purchaser has retained the vendor's money to pay the mortgage is simply contrary to the fact." [17]

The practical solution in those states that recognise one form or another of "implied assumptions" is proper drafting. For example, where an assumption is not intended the drafter could include after the "subject" to language, the following language: "Said mortgage is *not* being assumed by the Grantee."

 WESTLAW REFERENCES
implication implied** imply*** /s assum! oblig! /s mortgage

§ 5.9 Rights of Transferor—Non-assuming Grantee

As against a non-assuming grantee the mortgagor or other transferor has no personal claim to have him pay off the debt.[1] However, as we have seen, the land in the hands of such a grantee becomes the principal fund for payment and the mortgagor stands in the position of a surety.[2] When the debt comes due the mortgagor may pay it and then be subrogated to the rights of the mortgagee in the mortgage.[3] The mortgagor may then reach the land by using the mortgagee's right to foreclosure. Since the grantee's duty is limited to having the land in his hands go to pay the debt, this remedy gives the mortgagor adequate relief.

There are difficulties in such a course due to the rule that, technically, payment of the mortgage debt discharges it and releases

---

obligation rests upon an implication of fact as to the parties' intention. If however, the basis is unjust enrichment at the expense of the transferor, limiting recovery to the amount of loss established by him can be defended.

15. See Warm, supra note 9, 121; Glenn, op. cit. supra, note 12 § 256.

16. See note 9 supra.

17. Walsh, Mortgages, 209 note 16. See also, Warm, supra note 9, 120.

§ 5.9

1. See § 5.3, supra. Cf. Fitzgerald v. Flanagan, 155 Iowa 217, 135 N.W. 738,

Ann.Cas.1914C, 1104 (1912); Locke v. Homer, 131 Mass. 93, 41 Am.Rep. 199 (1881); Hall v. Morgan, 79 Mo. 47 (1883); Woodbury v. Swan, 58 N.H. 380 (1878); Hoy v. Bramhall, 19 N.J.Eq. 563, 569, 97 Am.Dec. 687 (1868); Faulkner v. McHenry, 235 Pa. 298, 83 A. 827, Ann.Cas.1913D, 1151 (1912). But cf., Glenn, Purchasing Subject to the Mortgage, 27 Va.L.Rev. 853, 865 (1941).

2. See § 5.3, supra and § 10.2, infra.

3. University State Bank v. Steeves, 85 Wash. 55, 147 P. 645, 2 A.L.R. 237 (1915). See 2 A.L.R. 242, 243 (1919); see § 5.3, supra and § 10.2, infra.

the mortgage.[4] Consequently, as an alternative, the mortgagor may sometimes ask that the mortgagee assign both the debt and the mortgage to a nominee of the mortgagor so that the lien clearly will be kept alive for his benefit. Since the mortgagee cannot be injured by such action and it is important to the mortgagor's protection, equity will grant specific performance of such a request.[5] A court could, of course, treat such a transaction as ineffective based on a "form over substance" argument. However, it would seem that if the reasons for giving the mortgagor subrogation rights in the first place are persuasive, those rights should not be impaired by an overly technical application of the "no debt, no mortgage" rule.

The above concept of the mortgagor's subrogation rights, however, was rejected by the Arizona Supreme Court in Best Fertilizers of Arizona, Inc. v. Burns.[6] In that case A conveyed land to B, who took "subject" to an existing mortgage in favor of E–1. B then gave a second mortgage to E–2. The E–1 mortgage went into default. A then paid the mortgage debt to E–1, who endorsed the note and assigned the mortgage to A. Several years later, A sold the note and mortgage to D. D then brought foreclosure proceedings. E–2 counterclaimed for foreclosure of its mortgage and for a declaration that its lien had first priority. The Supreme Court of Arizona found in favor of E–2. It held, first, that under Section 3–601(3) of the Uniform Commercial Code (UCC), which provides that "The liability of all parties is discharged when any party who has himself no right of action or recourse on the instrument * * * reacquires the instrument in his own right * * *,"[7] the note and all liability thereon was discharged. Thus, since the debt no longer existed, the mortgage and all rights thereunder were destroyed. Second, and seemingly alternatively, the court rejected the argument that A was, in any event, subrogated to the rights of E–1. It reasoned that there cannot be subrogation rights in a "subject to" situation where the debt paid was the obligation of the person who paid it.

The first part of the Best Fertilizer case needs further analysis. Suppose that instead of taking the note and mortgage directly, A had simply directed that the note and mortgage be endorsed and assigned to a third party. In that event, technically at least, the application of the UCC would arguably not have resulted in the destruction of the debt. However, even if the court had been confronted such a situation and had rejected it as a sham transaction placing form over substance, it still can be argued, in any event, that the UCC should not be utilized as the basis for denying equitable subrogation. To be sure, there was a basis under the Negotiable Instruments Law, the predecessor to the UCC, for the argument that suretyship and subrogation principles had

---

4. See § 5.3, supra.

5. E.g., Johnson v. Zink, 51 N.Y. 333 (1873); Howard v. Robbins, 170 N.Y. 498, 63 N.E. 530 (1902); see 1919, 2 A.L.R. 242.

But see Lamb v. Montague, 112 Mass. 352 (1873).

6. 116 Ariz. 492, 570 P.2d 179 (1977).

7. Ariz.Rev.Stat. § 44–2568(C)1.

been abrogated with respect to negotiable instruments.[8] However, such sweeping generalizations do not apply to the UCC.[9] Moreover, if the above UCC provision is applicable to destroy subrogation rights of the mortgagor in the "subject" to situation, its language is also literally applicable to destroy the debt and mortgage in the case of an assumption transfer. In both instances, the "liability of all parties is destroyed" when the mortgagor reacquires the note. Surely the UCC provision was not intended to destroy the mortgagor's subrogation rights against an assuming grantee. In any event, the Arizona Supreme Court seemed equally inclined to reject subrogation on the basis that a mortgagor in a "subject" to situation is simply not entitled to subrogation under traditional substantive rules.

This latter position seems incorrect both technically and in terms of fairness. First, it is true that when the mortgagor pays the mortgage debt in a "subject" to transaction, he is, in a sense, paying *his* debt. Indeed, it is also true that he is not a personal surety in the same sense that he would be if the grantee had assumed. Nevertheless, as one noted decision has aptly put it, "when the grantee merely takes subject to the mortgage, while it is true that the grantee assumes no personal liability whatever, nevertheless the security in his hands is liable for the payment of the mortgage debt, which liability as between the grantee and the mortgagee is primary. Therefore, to the extent of the value of such security properly applicable to the mortgage debt, the original mortgagor and the grantee subject to the mortgage stand in a relation one to another, which, while not a true suretyship, is nevertheless equitably analogous thereto and subject to the operation of the same principles."[10] Second, the Best Fertilizer approach can lead to inequitable results. Indeed, in the actual case, E–2 obtained an unexpected windfall in being promoted to senior lien status. Moreover, "subject" to grantees could be the more likely dubious beneficiaries of the decision. When a "subject" to grantee acquires mortgaged land, while he is not personally liable, it is the expectation of the parties that the grantee will pay off the debt. To be sure, at the time of sale by the mortgagor to the grantee, the mortgage debt is probably subtracted from the sale price in determining the amount of the grantee's cash payment to the mortgagor. Suppose then that the grantee fails to pay off the mortgage and, threatened with a probable personal judgment against him in favor of the mortgagee, the mortgagor reluctantly pays the mortgage debt. What our surprised mortgagor discovers is that, under the Best Fertilizer reasoning, instead of being an assignee of a mortgage, he has just bestowed on the grantee a title free of the mortgage. Thus we are faced with the anomalous result that while

---

8. See Osborne, Mortgages § 271 (2d Ed.1970).

9. See Clark, Suretyship in the Uniform Commercial Code, 46 Tex.L.Rev. 453, 454 (1968). Indeed, the mortgagor is probably protected by suretyship principles when the mortgagee enters into extension agreements with subsequent grantees. See § 5.19, infra.

10. Zastrow v. Knight, 56 S.D. 554, 560, 229 N.W. 925, 930 (1930).

normally one acquires land free and clear of a mortgage by paying it off, here the grantee can achieve that result by failing to do so.

Although it has been stated that subrogation by payment of the mortgage debt is the sole remedy available to the mortgagor against the non-assuming grantee, two others are possible. First, the mortgagor may be aided in those jurisdictions with "one action" rules or statutes. Under the one action concept, there can be only one action for the enforcement of a mortgage-secured obligation, that action being a foreclosure proceeding in which a deficiency judgment may be obtained.[11] To the extent that such a concept is applicable to a "subject" to situation, the mortgagor would be able to compel the mortgagee to foreclose first before going against the mortgagor personally. In any event, the personal liability would then be limited to the deficiency, if any, resulting from the foreclosure sale.

Another related and remote possibility is the invocation of the suretyship doctrine of Pain v. Packard [12] in those few jurisdictions in which it may be followed.[13] This would enable the mortgagor after maturity of the debt to demand of the mortgagee that he institute an action of foreclosure so that, to the extent of its value, it would be used to pay the debt. The mortgagor, then, would not have to do so. Failure to comply would result in a discharge to the extent of the loss thereafter sustained. There is considerable doubt as to whether the doctrine applies to a suretyship relation arising subsequent to the mortgage by virtue of the transfer of the property.[14] Nevertheless there is some authority applying it to the case of a non-assuming grantee.[15]

WESTLAW REFERENCES

digest(subrogat*** surety! /p mortgage* /p debt default*** paid pay!)

§ 5.10 Rights of Transferor—Assuming Grantee

As against an assuming grantee, the mortgagor has the same rights in respect to reaching the property in his hands as in the case of a nonassuming grantee. In addition, however, he has personal rights against the transferee. One of these is to pay the debt and then sue for

---

11. See § 8.2, infra.

12. 13 Johns. 174 (N.Y.1816).

13. See Friedman, Discharge of Mortgage Debts, 52 Yale L.J. 771, 796 (1943).

14. See Friedman, supra note 13, 796. Fish v. Glover, 154 Ill. 86, 39 N.E. 1081 (1894), rejects the doctrine in the case of mortgages on the ground it applies only to conventional suretyship.

15. Gottschalk v. Jungmann, 78 App. Div. 171, 79 N.Y.S. 551 (N.Y.1903); 3 Col.L. Rev. 199 (1903); National Savings Bank of

City of Albany v. Fermac Corp., 241 App. Div. 204, 271 N.Y.S. 836 (1934) affirmed 266 N.Y. 443, 195 N.E. 145; Osborne v. Heyward, 40 App.Div. 78, 57 N.Y.S. 542 (N.Y.1899); see cases in Union Trust Co. v. Rogers, 261 App.Div. 882, 25 N.Y.S.2d 120 (N.Y.1941). But see Marshall v. Davies, 78 N.Y. 414 (1879). The Fermac case, supra, was affirmed solely on the ground that the mortgagor had made a tender. National Savings Bank v. Fermac Corp., 266 N.Y. 443, 195 N.E. 145 (1934).

reimbursement. Moreover, this right accrues as soon as the mortgagor makes any payment on the mortgage debt, whether the accelerated debt or simply the arrearages.[1] It is self-evident that this right exists under any theory of the nature of the contract of assumption.[2] Furthermore, it could rest upon a quasi-contractual basis, at least in those jurisdictions in which the assumption gives to the mortgagee a personal right against the assuming grantee.[3] In such a case the grantor would be benefiting the grantee by discharging the latter's obligation to pay. The grantor would be privileged to make the payment because he remained liable; the grantee is unjustly enriched because he had the primary duty of payment.

A few jurisdictions have limited the right of the mortgagor to the foregoing relief, holding that the grantor may not sue until he has paid the debt.[4] However, the weight of authority is that the assumption agreement calls for the payment of the debt when it falls due and consequently it is broken when it is not paid.[5] The objection to the majority rule is that "a grantee might be subjected to two judgments for the same debt; one in favor of the grantor, and the other in favor of the mortgagee. One answer to this is that he has brought this upon himself by not carrying out his agreement. Had he paid the mortgage debt (which is in reality the balance of the purchase price) when it became due, as he agreed, he would not have been sued. And, if sued by the grantor, payment then of the mortgage would be a perfect defense."[6] Further, if the transferor-plaintiff does collect the debt he

§ 5.10

1. See, e.g., Brice v. Griffen, 269 Md. 558, 307 A.2d 660 (1973).

2. Taintor v. Hemmingway, 18 Hun 458 (N.Y.1879), affirmed 83 N.Y. 610 (1880); Comstock v. Drohan, 71 N.Y. 9 (1877); Evans v. Sperry, 12 F.2d 438 (D.C.Ill.1926). See 21 A.L.R. 504, 520 (1922); 97 A.L.R. 1076, 1079 (1935); 76 A.L.R. 1191, 1196 (1932) for collections of cases.

3. Graham v. Burnbaugh, 44 Cal.App. 482, 186 P. 798 (1919); Harvey v. Lowry, 204 Ind. 93, 183 N.E. 309 (1932), semble; Poe v. Dixon, 60 Ohio St. 124, 54 N.E. 86, 71 Am.St.Rep. 713 (1899); see Glenn, Morts. § 260. In some cases the right of reimbursement is regarded as merely a surety's relational right of reimbursement against his principal. See Hildrith v. Walker, 187 S.W. 608, 610 (Mo.App.1916); Poe v. Dixon, supra, the relational right being looked upon as justified by reason of the conference of a benefit by the surety; John Deere Plow Co. of Moline v. Tuinstra, 47 S.D. 555, 200 N.W. 61 (1924).

4. See Gustafson v. Koehler, 177 Minn. 115, 224 N.W. 699 (1929) 21 A.L.R. 504, 514 (1922); 76 A.L.R. 1192, 1195 (1932); 97

A.L.R. 1076, 1078 (1935). This result is reached on different grounds. E.g., in Sloan v. Klein, 230 Pa. 132, 79 A. 403 (1911), and in Tritten's Estate, 238 Pa. 555, 86 A. 461 (1913), it was so decided partly on the ground that the agreement of assumption, properly interpreted, was merely one of "indemnity," i.e., reimbursement. Other cases arrive at the same result for the reason that the right is not contractual but a surety's relational right to compensation against his principal.

5. White v. Schader, 185 Cal. 606, 198 P. 19, 21 A.L.R. 499 (1921); Locke v. Homer, 131 Mass. 93, 41 Am.Rep. 199 (1881); Gustafson v. Koehler, 177 Minn. 115, 224 N.W. 699 (1929) commented on, 13 Minn.L. Rev. 737 (1929); Kirk v. Welch, 212 Minn. 300, 3 N.W.2d 426 (1942); Sanderson v. Turner, 73 Okl. 105, 174 P. 763, 2 A.L.R. 347 (1918).

6. Gustafson v. Koehler, 177 Minn. 115, 118, 224 N.W. 699, 700 (1929). The danger of double payment would not exist in jurisdictions denying to the holder of the mortgage debt a direct right against the assuming grantee. See 38 Harv.L.Rev. 502, 506 (1925).

can be compelled to hold it as trustee for the payment of the mortgage debt.[7]

In addition to the courses previously discussed the mortgagor has open to him a suit in equity to compel an assuming grantee to exonerate him by paying the debt to the mortgagee.[8] In theory this is a completely satisfactory remedy but in practice it is not. The reason is that before the mortgage debt can be paid off by judicial process the amount of the debt then due must be ascertained. To do this requires an accounting to which the mortgagee must be a party. Further if there are several successive grantees all are necessary parties, in addition to the mortgagee. The absence from the state of either the mortgagee or an assuming grantee will make the remedy useless.

The right of a mortgagor to compel the payment of the debt assumed by his grantee extends to a grantee or successive grantees of the first grantee who in their turn assume payment.[9] The fact that a grantee who has assumed the payment of a mortgage has subsequently sold the land to another is no defense to an action by the grantor for a breach of his contract of assumption.[10]

What rights, if any, does a mortgagor have against a subsequent grantee who in buying from a non-assuming grantee assumes the payment of the mortgage? If the mortgagor has paid off the debt he should be entitled to be subrogated to any rights its holder had not only against the land but against the later assuming grantee.[11] To the extent that he has discharged any personal obligation of such a person or freed his land from the lien of the mortgage he has conferred a benefit upon that person for which he should be able to collect.[12] If the

---

7. Gustafson v. Koehler, note 98, supra. See Parke, B., in Loosemore v. Radford, 9 M. & W. 657 (1842). See also Heins v. Byers, 174 Minn. 350, 219 N.W. 287 (1928). For various suggested ways of relieving the grantee from risk of further payment see Williston, Contracts, Rev. ed., 1936, § 392; Wilson v. Stilwell, 9 Ohio St. 467, 75 Am. Dec. 477 (1859); Locke v. Homer, 131 Mass. 93, 108, 41 Am.Rep. 199 (1881); 38 Harv.L. Rev. 502, 505 (1925); 13 Minn. 737 (1929); Campbell, Cases on Mortgages, 2d ed., 435 n. 3; Williston, Contracts, Rev. ed., § 392; Restatement, Contracts, §§ 141(1), 136(1)c.

8. Marsh v. Pike, 10 Paige 595 (N.Y. 1844); Mowry v. Mowry, 137 Mich. 277, 100 N.W. 388 (1904), semble; see 41 Mich. L.Rev. 975 (1943); Williston, Contracts, Rev. ed., § 392, n. 3; Restatement, Contracts, § 138.

9. Robson v. O'Toole, 60 Cal.App. 710, 214 P. 278 (1923); Comstock v. Drohan, 71 N.Y. 9 (1877). See 21 A.L.R. 504, 507 (1922); 76 A.L.R. 1191, 1194 (1932); 97 A.L.R. 1076, 1077 (1935). Williston, Contracts, Rev. ed., § 386. The problem of the

rights of a mortgagor against an assuming grantee after a break in the chain is analyzed in Maxwell and Meyers, The Mortgagor's Rights Against Remote Assuming Grantees, 29 Tex.L.Rev. 869, 880 (1952). See also Storke and Sears, Transfer of Mortgaged Property, 38 Corn.L.Q. 185, 198 (1953).

10. Kollen v. Sooy, 172 Mich. 214, 137 N.W. 808 (1912); Reed v. Paul, 131 Mass. 129 (1881); Kirker v. Wylie, 207 Pa. 511, 56 A. 1074 (1904). The same is true of quasi-contractual liability. Reilly v. Lucraft, 34 Idaho 41, 198 P. 674 (1921), deficiency judgment already paid by grantor. See Williston, Contracts, Rev. ed., § 386. But see Penn.Act of June 12, 1878, P.L. 205 (21 P.S. 655, 656).

11. As to the rights of a mortgagee against one who assumes the mortgage after a break in the chain of assumptions, see § 5.15, infra.

12. Harvey v. Lowrey, 204 Ind. 93, 183 N.E. 309 (1932) discussed, 42 Yale L.J. 798

mortgagor has not paid it is doubtful whether he has any rights against such an assuming grantee.[13] It is true that the third party beneficiary doctrine has been held to permit a mortgagee to recover against an assuming grantee after a break in the chain of assumptions.[14] But to extend a similar right to a remote grantor whose immediate grantee did not personally assume the debt is a step beyond this and one which courts seem unlikely to take in the absence of special circumstances indicating that such grantor should be regarded as within the class of third persons who can sue as beneficiaries of a contract to which they are not parties.[15] A non-assuming grantee who in turn sells to one who assumes the payment of the debt has no interest in having the debt paid. He never became personally bound for the debt and he no longer owns land he might lose if the debt is not discharged. Technically he has a contract right against his grantee on which he might sue. Since he suffers no injury his damages should be nominal. As against grantees subsequent to the first one who also assume the mortgage whether or not the non-assuming grantor himself can recover depends upon whether in the particular jurisdiction the rule permitting third party beneficiaries to sue will be extended to such a person.[16]

WESTLAW REFERENCES

equit! reimburse! /p assum! /8 mortgage /p debt default***
   paid pay!

(later subsequent 3 buyer grantee purchaser) "third party beneficiary"
   /p assum! /8 mortgage

§ 5.11 Mortgagee vs. Assuming Grantee—In General

Where there has been a transfer by the mortgagor to an assuming grantee, the mortgagee continues to have his original right against the mortgagor and his security interest in the land follows it into the hands of the transferee.[1] The mortgagor, as has been seen, acquires personal rights against the grantee upon this undertaking. The question remains whether only the mortgagor can enforce the promise to assume the mortgage, or whether the mortgagee acquires a right to do so.

All American jurisdictions confer on the mortgagee, in some manner, the right to enforce the promise of an assuming grantee. There is, however, diversity of view both as to the substantive basis of the right

(1933), is to the contrary, but seems incorrect on this point.

13. Harvey v. Lowrey, supra note 12, holds that he does not have; Carter v. Holohan, 92 N.Y. 498 (1883), accord. Semble, McGinty v. Dennehy, 2 S.W.2d 546 (Tex.Civ.App.1927), noted 7 Tex.L.Rev. 482 (1929). The court put the decision on the ground that the defendant's assumption had not been accepted by the mortgagee.

14. See § 5.15, infra. There is a division of authority on the point.

15. See 42 Yale L.J. 798 (1933), commenting on Harvey v. Lowrey, n. 12 supra.

16. At least one decision has allowed recovery. Calder v. Richardson, 11 F.Supp. 498 (D.C.Fla.1935), commented on, 49 Harv.L.Rev. 652 (1936). Recovery should be limited, where allowed, to any actual damage the non-assuming grantor may be exposed to. Id.

§ 5.11

1. See § 5.1, supra.

and the procedural method of enforcing it.[2] Since each view creates its own logical corollaries,[3] it is essential, for an intelligent consideration of a large number of mortgage problems, that these various theories be explored.

In general, there are two bases of recovery by the mortgagee against an assuming grantee: (1) by virtue of a direct and independent right of the mortgagee; (2) by virtue of enforcing the promise of the assuming grantee derivatively, i.e., through the right against him of the mortgagor or other transferor. Different reasons are assigned in different states for adopting one or the other of these approaches. Frequently identical results are reached regardless of purported theory. Not only do the theory and rules governing a given rationale vary from state to state, but they have changed in the process of development in the same state.[4] Further, in single jurisdictions there has been a shift from one basis to another and sometimes more than one has been recognized simultaneously.[5] The result of such changes is that many of the decisions are outdated. Hence, any precise classification of jurisdictions is difficult, would be transient and not particularly helpful. Nevertheless, an analysis of the theories themselves is important to understanding fundamental mortgage law concepts and, moreover, provides a useful foundation for the consideration of related problems dealt with later in this chapter.

 WESTLAW REFERENCES
derivative** right /s mortgage /p assum! /8 mortgage

2. Union Mutual Life Insurance Co. v. Hanford, 143 U.S. 187, 189, 12 S.Ct. 437, 438, 36 L.Ed. 118 (1891), "Few things have been the subject of more difference of opinion and conflict of decision than the nature and extent of the right of a mortgagee of real estate against a subsequent grantee who by the terms of the conveyance to him agrees to assume and pay the mortgage." Some courts either fail or refuse to adopt a precise rationale. See e.g., LaGrange Federal Savings and Loan Association v. Rock River Corp., 97 Ill.App.3d 712, 53 Ill.Dec. 112, 423 N.E.2d 496 (Ill.App.1981).

3. See Berick, Personal Liability for Deficiency in Mortgage Foreclosures, 8 U. of Cin.L.Rev. 103 (1934); 19 Va.L.Rev. 624 (1933); 25 Va.L.Rev. 993, 995 (1939).

4. E.g., for the evolution in Virginia, see 25 Va.L.Rev. 993 (1939); Warm, Rights and Liabilities of Mortgagee, Mortgagor, Grantee, 10 Temple L.Q. 116, 130 n. 41 (1936). See 84 U. of Pa.L.Rev. 909 (1936) for the development in Pennsylvania. See also 88 U.Pa.L.Rev. 611, 612 (1940), giving as examples the experience in Minnesota and Rhode Island. For a consideration of the problems in Massachusetts see Note, 8 Suffolk L.Rev. 130 (1973).

5. This seems to be the situation in New York, with some resulting uncertainty as to which rule is to be applied. Seaver v. Ransom, 224 N.Y. 233, 120 N.E. 639, 2 A.L.R. 1187 (1918). See Friedman, Personal Liability on Mortgage Debts in New York, 50 Yale L.J. 224, 231–236, 236 n. 90 (1940); 88 U. of Pa.L.Rev. 611, 612 (1940); see also 25 Va.L.Rev. 993, 996 (1939), for the law in Virginia. In California by statute, West's Ann.Cal.Civ.Code § 1559, a third party beneficiary may sue the promisor directly. See note, 1938, 26 Cal.L.Rev. 627. A mortgagee may sue an assuming grantee of the mortgagor under this statutory provision. Bank of Alameda County v. Hering, 134 Cal.App. 570, 25 P.2d 1004 (1933); see Alvord v. Spring Valley Gold Co., 106 Cal. 547, 40 P. 27 (1895). Yet he also is able to reach such an assuming grantee from his mortgagor, not under the statute, but on the theory of "equitable subrogation." Hopkins v. Warner, 109 Cal. 133, 41 P. 868 (1895).

§ 5.12 Mortgagee vs. Assuming Grantee—Third Party Beneficiary

The first and most important view is that the mortgagee is allowed to sue the assuming grantee simply as a third party beneficiary of a contract.[1] The great weight of authority accepts this view[2] but this fact does not free it from difficulty. The right of recovery depends upon theories and rules of general contract law which are still in a period of growth, not only varying from state to state but within a given jurisdiction.[3] Among the more important points on which there

§ 5.12

1. "Where the performance of a promise in a contract will benefit a person other than the promisee, that person is classified as a * * * beneficiary." Aetna Life Insurance Co. v. Maxwell, 89 F.2d 988, 993 (4th Cir.1937). Beneficiaries who may recover are of two kinds, donee beneficiaries and creditor beneficiaries. Id. A person is classified as a creditor beneficiary when "the performance of the promise will satisfy an actual or supposed or asserted duty of the promisee to the beneficiary." Restatement, Contracts, § 133(1)b. In jurisdictions accepting the third party beneficiary rationale the mortgagee as a general proposition normally recovers as a creditor beneficiary. The Restatement Second has dropped the use of the "donee" and "creditor" beneficiary designations because they carried "overtones of obsolete doctrinal difficulties". Instead, the terms "intended" beneficiary and "incidental" beneficiary are used to distinguish those beneficiaries who have rights from those who do not. See Restatement of Contracts, Second, § 133 and Introductory Note thereto. While the older terminology is dropped, the "donee-creditor" distinction is recognised as a factual rather than conceptual distinction. See Calamari and Perillo, Contracts 607 (2d Ed.1977).

2. See Williston, Contracts, § 383 n. 11 (Jaeger Ed. 1959), listing 36 jurisdictions that appear to give relief to the mortgagee on some version of a third party beneficiary theory. See elaborate compilation of authorities in 21 A.L.R. 439, 454 (1922); 47 A.L.R. 339, 341 (1927). For analysis of the concept, see Williston, Contracts for the Benefit of a Third Person, 15 Harv.L.Rev. 767 (1902), and Corbin, Contracts for the Benefit of Third Persons, 27 Yale L.J. 1008 (1918). See also Whittier, Contract Beneficiaries, 32 Yale L.J. 790 (1923); Hening, History of the Beneficiary's Action in Assumpsit, 1909, 3 Select Essays in Anglo-American Legal History; Finlay, Contracts for the Benefit of Third Persons, 1939; 26

Va.L.Rev. 778 (1940). For other discussions, dealing primarily with the assuming grantee of a mortgagor, see Friedman, Personal Liability on Mortgage Debts in New York, 50 Yale L.J. 224 (1940); Mechem, Assumption of Mortgages, 18 Cent.L.J. 23 (1884); Tucker, Personal Liability of One Assuming Payment of a Deed of Trust, 4 Va.L.Rev. 464 (1917); Glassie, The Assuming Vendee, 9 Va.L.Rev. 196 (1923); Hand, Purchase of Incumbered Land—Rights and Liabilities of Parties, 48 Cent.L.J. 489 (1899); Warm, Some Aspects of the Rights and Liabilities of Mortgagee, Mortgagor, and Grantee, 10 Temple L.Q. 116 (1936); Berick, Personal Liability for Deficiency in Mortgage Foreclosures, 8 U. of Cin.L.Rev. 103 (1934); notes, 25 Va.L.Rev. 993 (Virginia law) (1939); 13 St. John's L.Rev. 215 (1938); 11 Cal.L.Rev. 139 (1923); 11 Cal.L. Rev. 429 (1923); 26 Cal.L.Rev. 627 (1938); 10 Col.L.Rev. 765 (1910); Note, The Third Party Beneficiary Concept: A Proposal, 57 Col.L.Rev. 406 (1957); 4 Cornell L.Q. 53 (1919); 9 Cornell L.Q. 213 (1924); 84 U. of Pa.L.Rev. 909 (1936); 17 Va.L.Rev. 844 (1931); 19 Va.L.Rev. 624 (1933); 39 Yale L.J. 746 (1930). See also 21 A.L.R. 439 (1922); 47 A.L.R. 339 (1927). As to the right of a mortgagee as creditor beneficiary in Pennsylvania under the statute in that state, see 10 U. of Pitt.L.Rev. 419 (1949).

3. "The history of the third party beneficiary doctrine since Lawrence v. Fox has been a checkered one of sorties and retreats." Friedman, supra note 14, 233. 88 U.Pa.L.Rev. 611, 612 (1940); In Berick, Personal Liability for Deficiency in Mortgage Foreclosure, 8 U. of Cin.L.Rev. 103, 112 (1934), the beneficiary cases are grouped into three classes. 1. Those permitting the third person to sue only if the promise was made for his sole and exclusive benefit. 2. Those requiring as prerequisites: (a) a clear intent to benefit the third person, and (b) an obligation owing by the promisee to the third person. These limitations were laid down by the New York courts "because of early efforts to

is divergence are whether the promisee must be liable to the mortgagee;[4] when the right vests indefeasibly in him;[5] how far it may be affected by defenses between (a) the assuming grantee and his promisee and (b) the promisee and the mortgagee;[6] the effect of subsequent agreements between the promisor and promisee on the rights of the mortgagee,[7] and the consequences as to a mortgagee's other rights of binding extensions of time or releases by him to an assuming grantee.[8] Where the third party beneficiary doctrine is accepted as the foundation of the mortgagee's right, it is clearly an independent one enforceable by an action at law.[9]

 WESTLAW REFERENCES
"third party beneficiary" /p assum! /8 mortgage*

§ 5.13   Mortgagee vs. Assuming Grantee—"Suretyship" Subrogation

A second group of cases, applying a "suretyship" theory, invoke the doctrine of equitable subrogation. As used here, it means that the mortgagee-creditor is enabled to reach a right in the hands of his debtor, the mortgagor, against a third party, the assuming grantee, on the theory that the mortgagor-debtor has become a surety-debtor.[1] In

find a justification for the doctrine." See other discussions of the New York cases in notes, 4 Cornell L.Q. 53 (1919); 27 Yale L.J. 1008, 1027 (1918); Friedman, op. cit. supra, this note. Those which do not concern themselves with justifying the rule but accept it as well established, and require only an intent to benefit, with the one limitation that incidental or indirect benefit to the third person is insufficient to confer rights upon him. See Aetna Life Insurance Co. v. Maxwell, 89 F.2d 988, 993 (4th Cir.1937). See also Restatement, Contracts, §§ 133–136, 147.

4. See § 5.16, infra.

5. See § 5.19, infra.

6. See § 5.18, infra.

7. See Restatement, Contracts, §§ 142, 143; Restatement, Second, Contracts, § 142.

8. See §§ 5.20–5.21, infra.

9. "The promise creates a duty which the promisor must perform, and this duty, if not performed, may be made the basis of an action by the beneficiary against the promisor." Aetna Life Insurance Co. v. Maxwell, 89 F.2d 988, 993 (4th Cir.1937). See Williston, Contracts, Rev. ed., §§ 357, 383; Restatement, Contracts, §§ 136(1)a; 135, 141(1).

§ 5.13

1. See Williston, Contracts for the Benefit of a Third Person, 15 Harv.L.Rev. 767, 789 (1902). See also Arant, Suretyship, 370 et seq. But see Warm, Rights and Liabilities of Mortgagee, Mortgagor, Grantee, 10 Temple L.Q. 116, 129 (1936). This "suretyship" theory of solution has been accepted in a good many jurisdictions: Hopkins v. Warner, 109 Cal. 133, 136, 41 P. 868 (1895); Crawford v. Edwards, 33 Mich. 354 (1876); Klapworth v. Dressler, 13 N.J. Eq. 62, 78 Am.Dec. 69 (1860); Crowell v. Hospital of St. Barnabas, 27 N.J.Eq. 650, 655 (1876); Willard v. Worsham, 76 Va. 392 (1882); Keller v. Ashford, 133 U.S. 610, 623, 10 S.Ct. 494, 497, 33 L.Ed. 667 (1890). See Warm, Rights and Liabilities of Mortgagee, Mortgagor, Grantee, 10 Temple L.Q. 116, 128 (1936); Friedman, Personal Liability on Mortgage Debts in New York, 50 Yale L.J. 224, 230 (1940); Glassie, The Assuming Vendee, 9 Va.L.Rev. 196, 199 (1923); notes, 17 Va.L.Rev. 844, 847 (1931); 19 Va.L.Rev. 624, 625 (1933); 10 Col.L.Rev. 765, 767 (1910); 4 U. of Chi.L.Rev. 469, 476 (1937); 25 Ill.L.Rev. 721, 723 (1931); 26 Cal.L.Rev. 627 (1938); 25 Va.L.Rev. 993, 996 (1939); 21 A.L.R. 439, 451 (1922); 47 A.L.R. 339, 341 (1927). It has been adversely criticized. See Corbin, Contracts for Benefit of Third Persons, 1918, 27 Yale L.J. 1008, 1015. The grantee has deposited

order for the principle to apply a "suretyship" situation must exist. A suretyship situation requires a triangle with the person at each foot of the triangle being bound to the creditor at the apex by their respective contracts.[2] Where there is only one person owing a single obligation to another person no suretyship situation can exist. For a person's duty to be that of a surety, in addition to his obligation to the creditor, there must be a separate one, the principal, for whose performance it stands surety. In a mortgage, to begin with, there is a personal obligation running between the mortgagor and the mortgagee. There is also existing between the mortgagee and the land in the hands of the mortgagor, a relationship normally referred to as a security interest in the property. When the land is transferred by the mortgagor to a grantee, as between the continuing personal duty of the mortgagor to the mortgagee and the continuing relationship between the mortgagee and the land now in the hands of another, the situation may be treated with some certainty as one of suretyship. In such a case the mortgagee has two rights, one against the land, the other against the mortgagor. Which one is surety and which is principal depends upon the terms of the transfer.[3] If the mortgagor received the full value of the land and agreed to pay the debt he would be principal and the land would be surety. And *vice versa* if the transferee paid only the value of the redemption interest and took "subject" to the mortgage or assumed it.[4]

When the mortgagor transfers to an assuming grantee, the suretyship situation just described will exist as between the mortgagor, the land and the mortgagee.[5] But the suretyship situation to which the cases purport to apply the principle is a different and additional one in which the assuming grantee personally, not the land, is the principal. If the assumption creates a new direct right in the mortgagee against the assuming grantee, a suretyship situation results in which the new right is the principal obligation and the old right against the mortgagor becomes that of a surety. However, unless the mortgagee does acquire such a separate right against the assuming grantee in addition to his continuing personal right against the mortgagor no suretyship relation in the ordinary sense can exist.[6] If the assuming grantee is not personally a principal, i.e., obligated directly to the mortgagee, his promise to the mortgagor to pay the debt cannot be regarded as the collateral security given by him, as principal, to the mortgagor, as his

with the grantor nothing except a promise to protect him against the enforcement of the mortgage debt. To treat this as security given to him is at variance with the ordinary understanding of the term. See Arant, Suretyship, 370 et seq.

2. See Glenn, Mortgages, § 268; 4 U. of Chi.L.Rev. 469, 476 (1937).

3. See §§ 5.1–5.3, supra.

4. Id.

5. See § 5.10, supra.

6. 4 U. of Chi.L.Rev. 469, 476 (1937). But see Friedman, Discharge of Mortgage Debts, 52 Yale L.J. 771, 796 (1943), "True, the conventional suretyship triangle is not present but similar logic might once have been urged against the creation of constructive and resulting trusts. * * * Furthermore, the right of subrogation, and the penalty for its impairment, appears in situations other than that of conventional suretyship."

surety, for indemnity against liability to the mortgagee. It follows that, if the situation is really one of suretyship, the courts actually are recognizing that the contract of assumption creates a new right in the mortgagee against the assuming grantee—a result in substance no different from that which recognizes openly that it does so under the doctrine that the beneficiary of a contract may enforce it.[7] In spite of this, the theory on which the process of enforcement goes is that the mortgagee is enforcing his right against the mortgagor-surety and reaching the assuming grantee through the right which the mortgagor as surety has against him. Consequently the mortgagee's right on this theory must be classed as a derivative one.[8] A logical consequence is that, if the promisee-grantor is not bound to pay the debt he is not a surety, the doctrine is inapplicable, and the mortgagee cannot reach the assuming grantee.

 WESTLAW REFERENCES
derivative** subrogat*** surety! /p assum! /8 mortgage

§ 5.14 Mortgagee vs. Assuming Grantee—Miscellaneous Theories

Several additional bases that have been utilized to justify permitting the mortgagee to recover against an assuming grantee. While these approaches have not commanded a substantial acceptance, they, nevertheless, merit some consideration.

The Equitable Assets Theory

The equitable assets theory was initially advanced by Professor Williston.[1] Under this approach, instead of looking at the assuming

---

7. "For the mortgagor to be a surety, it is necessary that the mortgagee have an independent right against the grantee. Yet for the mortgagee to get this 'direct' right by the above analogy [i.e., that of suretyship subrogation of the mortgagee to the rights of the mortgagor,] it was necessary to assume that the mortgagor was a surety; thus assuming the conclusion." 4 U. of Chi.L.Rev. 469, 476 (1937). "The doctrine of subrogation has no doubt been very beneficial in spite of fiction and artificiality; but in this instance it has been used to confer new security and new rights upon a creditor, as a gift out of a clear sky. In suretyship it is used only as against one who is already legally indebted in order to secure the fulfillment of that legal duty. A doctrine whose purpose was the enforcement of a previously recognized duty cannot properly be given as the sole reason for creating an entirely new duty." Corbin, Contracts for the Benefit of Third Persons, 27 Yale L.J. 1008, 1015 (1918). "The ex-

tension of the subrogation theory to cover this case, where the promisor was not indebted to the third party by reason of any operative fact other than his promise to the promisee, is merely a cumbrous intellectual expedient for holding that a contract between two parties can create an enforceable right in a third." Corbin, supra, at 1016, n. 32.

8. See cases, note 1, supra. See also Binns v. Baumgartner, 105 N.J.Eq. 58, 60, 146 A. 879 (1929), "The equity on which his relief depends is the right of the mortgagor against his vendee, to which right the mortgagee is permitted to succeed, by substituting himself in the place of the mortgagor." Duvall-Percival Trust Co. v. Jenkins, 16 F.2d 223, 226 (10th Cir.1926).

§ 5.14

1. Williston, Contracts for the Benefit of a Third Person, 15 Harv.L.Rev. 766, 767 (1902).

grantee's promise to the grantor-promisee as indemnity security in the latter's hands as surety, given to him by the principal obligor, it is regarded as an asset of the mortgagee's only debtor, the mortgagor, of a sort which can be reached only by the aid of equity.[2]

The theory has certain distinct merits. On the one hand it avoids both the difficulty of giving reasons why a person who is not privy to a contract may nevertheless maintain an action on it against the promisor and the practical objection to permitting it that the promisor may be exposed to possible double liability on one promise. On the other hand, it escapes the fictitious, or apparently contradictory, aspects of the "suretyship" solution which seems to create, or at least recognize the existence of, a primary personal obligation of the assuming grantee running to the mortgagee and yet holds that the only way to realize on that obligation is by reaching, in equity, security in the form of a promise to indemnify given by the grantee-promisor as principal to his grantor-promisee as surety.[3]

Nevertheless certain aspects of the theory have been criticized. For one thing, the asset is a peculiar sort of one in that, unlike other assets, it is available only to one particular creditor, the mortgagee. This is because the promisor cannot be required to do anything other than what he promised. This feature has caused one critic to assert that "[t]o apply the 'equitable asset' theory is merely to recognize the third party beneficiary's right under another and mis-descriptive name."[4] This is not, of course, entirely true, for the right on this theory is purely derivative, a fact that has important consequences.[5] Another possible criticism of the doctrine is that, by offering a good, if not perfect solution of the problem, it tends to retard the complete triumph of the third party beneficiary direct right rule.

2. "Obviously a promise to pay a debt due a third person cannot be taken on an execution against the debtor, nor is it the subject of garnishment; for the promisor, if he is willing to perform his promise, cannot be compelled to do anything else, and as the promise is not to pay the promisee, the promisor cannot be charged as garnishee or trustee for him. The aid of equity is, therefore, necessary in order to compel the application of such property to the creditor's claim, and acting as it does by personal decree, equity can readily give the required relief." Williston, supra note 11. The theory was initially adopted in Massachusetts. See Forbes v. Thorpe, 209 Mass. 570, 582, 95 N.E. 955, 959 (1911), for the first recognition. It was also acknowledged as existing in Gillis v. Bonelli-Adams Co., 284 Mass. 176, 187 N.E. 535 (1933); Bloch v. Budish, 279 Mass. 102, 180 N.E. 729 (1932) discussed 1933, 19 Va.L.Rev. 624, 628. However, there is some basis for concluding that Massachusetts today follows the equitable subrogation theory. See Note, 8 Suffolk L.Rev. 130, 145 n. 73 (1973).

3. See § 5.13, supra.

4. Corbin, Contracts for the Benefit of Third Persons, 27 Yale L.J. 1008, 1021 (1918). "By differentiating this particular creditor from other creditors and this particular 'asset' from other assets we are merely recognizing that he has obtained a special right in personam as against the promisor, a right that is created by a contract to which he was not a party. He gains this special right because the contracting parties intended that he should have it, or at least that the performance should go direct to him." Idem. But see Friedman, Personal Liability on Mortgage Debts, 50 Yale L.J. 224, 230 (1940).

5. See § 5.17 infra.

Statutory Bases

In a few jurisdictions, statutes specifically confer on the mortgagee a right against the assuming grantee.[6] It is not entirely clear whether, assuming the mortgagee may bring his action by virtue of a statute, the right he is enforcing is a direct one or a derivative one. It should depend upon whether the statute is interpreted to be merely procedural or whether it creates substantive rights.[7] If the latter, the right so created would seem to be direct. If the former, the substantive law apart from statute would determine.

Some courts have utilized statutes or court rules that provide that actions shall be brought in the name of the real party in interest as a method of giving the mortgagee the right to sue the assuming grantee.[8] This approach seems to beg at least two questions. The prior question is, of course, whether he is the real party in interest. And that goes back to the question of substantive law as to whether the promise of the assuming grantee creates any right against him in favor of the mortgagee.[9]

Plurality of Actions Theory

Another small group of cases assert that the mortgagee is permitted to reach the assuming grantee to avoid plurality of actions and harassment of the mortgagor.[10] Here again, no new rationale of the substantive right itself is advanced. Rather the existence of the procedural relief is predicated upon the existence of a substantive right by the mortgagee against the mortgagor which in turn makes operative a right over by the mortgagor against his assuming grantee. In other words the right of the mortgagee here, as in the "suretyship" or equitable assets rationales, is derivative.

 WESTLAW REFERENCES
"equitable asset" "plurality of actions" (statut*** /6 mortgagee) /p
assum! /8 mortgage*

---

6. E.g., Conn.Gen.Stat.Ann. § 52–75; Schneider v. Ferrigno, 110 Conn. 86, 147 A. 303 (1929).

7. See Warm, Rights and Liabilities of Mortgagee, Mortgagor, Grantee, 10 Temple L.Q. 130, n. 42 (1936), criticizing Schneider v. Ferrigno, supra note 6.

8. Marianna Lime Products Co. v. McKay, 109 Fla. 275, 147 So. 264 (1933); Cooper v. Bane, 110 Neb. 74, 193 N.W. 97 (1923); see Ellis v. Harrison, 104 Mo. 270, 277, 16 S.W. 198 (1891).

9. See Corbin, Contracts for the Benefit of Third Persons, 27 Yale L.J. 1008, 1029

(1918); Williston, Contracts, Rev. ed., § 366.

10. Y.M.C.A. v. Crofts, 34 Or. 106, 114, 55 P. 439, 441, 75 Am.St.Rep. 568 (1898); Osborne v. Cabell, 77 Va. 462, 467 (1883). While New Jersey apparently earlier followed this theory, it is clear that now a mortgagee in that state has a direct right of action against the assuming grantee based on N.J.Stat.Ann. 2A:15–2. See Cunningham and Tischler, Transfer of the Real Estate Mortgagor's Interest, 27 Rutgers L.Rev. 24, 42–43 (1973).

§ 5.15 Successive Purchasers

Frequently there is a series of sales of the mortgaged property with each grantee in turn agreeing with his immediate grantor to assume the mortgage. In such a case all of them become liable to the mortgage creditor who may successfully invoke as to each one in succession whichever doctrine enabled him to reach the first grantee of the mortgagor.[1] The same reasoning which justifies holding the first grantee by virtue of his promise to the mortgagee's debtor applies to charge the second grantee by reason of his promise to the first grantee and so on down to the last grantee. If the mortgagee reached the first grantee derivatively through the right of the mortgagor against him he can reach the second one derivatively through the right of the first grantee since the mortgagor, whose right he is using could have done so. If his right is a direct one as creditor beneficiary of the contract between his original debtor, the mortgagor, and the first grantee, so too his right will be a direct one against the second grantee as creditor beneficiary of the assumption contract between his new obligor, the first grantee, and the second grantee. Moreover all who have thus assumed the mortgage are liable regardless of having in turn parted with land to subsequent grantees and even though the later transferees assumed the mortgage.[2] Each one's own valid contract, which is the source of his liability, is not affected by his selling the premises. His protection, in case he is forced to pay, lies in his rights against his own and subsequent grantees and the land.[3]

Where one of the successive transferees takes title without promising his vendor to assume the mortgage he incurs no personal responsibility to anyone for the payment of the debt. If such a purchaser in turn sells to a grantee who promises him to pay the debt, the question arises whether the second purchaser, thus bound to his vendor, is liable also to the mortgage creditor. On this point there is diversity of decision.[4] His liability depends upon the rationale under which the mortgagee is allowed to hold an assuming grantee in the particular jurisdiction and the rules governing liability under the rationale followed in that jurisdiction.

Insofar as the mortgagee's rights against an assuming grantee are derivative, i.e., rest upon the theory that he is allowed to apply the rights of his own debtor through subrogation or as an equitable asset

---

§ 5.15

1. Robson v. O'Toole, 45 Cal.App. 63, 187 P. 110 (1919); Carnahan v. Tousey, 93 Ind. 561 (1883); Corning v. Burton, 102 Mich. 86, 62 N.W. 1040 (1894); Hurst v. Merrifield, 144 Or. 78, 23 P.2d 124 (1933).

2. See § 5.12, supra.

3. See §§ 5.9–5.10, supra.

4. See Calamari and Perillo, Contracts, § 17.4 (2d Ed. 1977). See cases cited in succeeding footnotes. Also see notes, 11 Cal.L.Rev. 139 (1923); 88 U. of Pa.L.Rev. 611 (1940); 6 U. of Cin.L.Rev. 361 (1932); 8 U. of Cin.L.Rev. 103, 125 (1934); 9 Cornell L.Q. 213 (1924); 16 Minn.L.Rev. 114 (1931); 13 Va.L.Rev. 500 (1927); 17 Va.L.Rev. 844 (1931); 39 Yale L.J. 746 (1930); Restatement, Contracts, §§ 133, 144, Illustration 2; Williston, Contracts, Rev.Ed., § 386A. See also 12 A.L.R. 1528 (1921); L.R.A.1916D, 154.

the mortgagee cannot compel payment by any transferee who takes after the break in the chain of assumptions. The assuming vendees in such a case have promised a vendor against whom the mortgage creditor has no right and, consequently, to whose claim against the assuming vendee he can lay no claim. The same would be true of those cases which permit the mortgagee to proceed against the assuming grantee to prevent plurality of actions, for in order to have plurality of actions there must first be a right of action by the mortgage creditor against the promisee-grantor. Hence the rule in all these cases is that the mortgagee's right stops with the last grantee who assumed in direct succession.[5]

In those jurisdictions which give the mortgagee a direct right as third party beneficiary of a contract there is a conflict in the decisions as to whether recovery should be allowed. The mortgagee is usually regarded as a creditor beneficiary. Since he actually has no right against the promisee-grantor, those cases that insist that an obligation to pay must exist in order for a creditor beneficiary to have rights against the assuming grantee would deny recovery to him as such.[6] Courts also deny recovery on the ground that there is no intent to benefit the mortgagee.[7] A broader test, adopted by the Restatement of Contracts, First, classifies a person as a creditor beneficiary when the "performance of the promise will satisfy an actual or supposed or asserted duty of the promisee to the beneficiary."[8] If the stipulation was inserted intentionally, it most likely was to guard against a supposed or possible liability of the promisee which did not in fact exist.[9] If so, it would fall under this test of a creditor beneficiary and it is possible to justify a good many decisions allowing recovery on this ground although the opinions in them do not explicitly adopt it.[10]

Some courts deny the mortgagee recovery as a creditor beneficiary and also as a donee beneficiary.[11] There are other courts that appar-

5. Ward v. De Oca, 120 Cal. 102, 52 P. 130 (1898); Morris v. Mix, 4 Kan.App. 654, 46 P. 58 (1896); Colorado Savings Bank v. Bales, 101 Kan. 100, 165 P. 843 (1917); Norwood v. De Hart, 30 N.J.Eq. 412 (1879); Eakin v. Shultz, 61 N.J.Eq. 156, 47 A. 274 (1900); Osborne v. Cabell, 77 Va. 462 (1883); see South Carolina Insurance Co. v. Kohn, 108 S.C. 475, 480, 95 S.E. 65 (1917). See also Berick, Deficiency in Mortgage Foreclosures, 8 U. of Cin.L.Rev. 103, 108 (1934). Dail v. Campbell, 191 Cal.App. 416, 12 Cal.Rptr. 739 (1961), is in accord as to the remote grantee who assumed a purchase price mortgage where an intermediate grantee had not assumed the mortgage.

6. Vrooman v. Turner, 69 N.Y. 280 (1877), Walsh & Simpson, Cases Security Transactions, 312; Wager v. Link, 134 N.Y. 122, 31 N.E. 213 (1892); see Hinckley Estate Co. v. Gurry, 56 Idaho 38, 48 P.2d 1111 (1935); De Leon v. Rhines, 64 App.

D.C. 73, 75, 74 F.2d 477, 479 (1934). See also 9 Cornell L.Q. 213 (1923); 39 Yale L.J. 746 (1930).

7. Case v. Egan, 57 Cal.App. 453, 207 P. 388 (1922); Y.M.C.A. v. Crofts, 34 Or. 106, 55 P. 439, 75 Am.St.Rep. 568 (1898); Fry v. Ausman, 29 S.D. 30, 135 N.W. 708, 39 L.R.A.,N.S., 150, Ann.Cas.1914C 842 (1912). See also cases in preceding note.

8. § 133(1)b.

9. See Williston, Contracts, (3d Ed.), § 386A; 39 Yale L.J. 746 (1930); 9 Cornell L.Q. 213 (1923).

10. Scott v. Wharton, 226 Ala. 601, 148 So. 308 (1933).

11. The cases in notes 47, 48, supra, may rest upon this ground. See 39 Yale L.J. 746 (1930); 9 Cornell L.Q. 213 (1923); 88 U.Pa.L.Rev. 611, 613 (1940).

ently recognize a right to recover as a donee beneficiary.[12] Some of them reason that since the non-assuming grantor is not personally liable to the mortgagee and is no longer owner of the premises he has no interest in the performance of the assumption promise. The only object of exacting such a stipulation is to confer a gratuitous benefit or right upon the mortgagee.[13] In others, the courts seem to assume the donative intent, treating it as a question of the power of the promisee to create such a right in the mortgagee. The reasoning on this is that, since the contract is enforceable by the promisee, he can direct that the performance go to whomsoever he wishes and the promisor cannot object.[14]

The Restatement of Contracts, Second, has abandoned the use of the terms "creditor" and "donee" beneficiary, those beneficiaries that had rights under the original Restatement. Instead, these terms are subsumed under the label of "intended" beneficiaries.[15] Under the Restatement, Second, rights are conferred on "intended" beneficiaries, but not on "incidental" beneficiaries.[16] A person is included as an intended beneficiary if "recognition of a right to performance in the beneficiary is appropriate to effectuate the intention of the parties and * * * the circumstances indicate that the promisee intends to give the beneficiary the benefit of the promised performance." [17] Thus, in the mortgage context, so long as the non-assuming transferor has the requisite intent to benefit the mortgagee, the mortgagee would have a direct right against the assuming grantee.[18] The Georgia Supreme Court, in endorsing the position of the Restatement, Second, stated its position succinctly: "A person should do that which he or she promises to do, and generally where that promise is supported by consideration, the courts will enforce it unless it is contrary to law or public policy.

---

12. Schneider v. Ferrigno, 110 Conn. 86, 147 A. 303 (1929) intent to confer right of action sufficient to make mortgagee a donee beneficiary; South Carolina Insurance Co. v. Kohn, 108 S.C. 475, 480, 95 S.E. 95 (1917). See 25 Ill.L.Rev. 723 (1931). Also cases in following footnotes.

13. Casselman's Administratrix v. Gordon & Lightfoot, 118 Va. 553, 88 S.E. 58 (1916); see 25 Va.L.Rev. 993, 997 (1939).

14. Dean v. Walker, 107 Ill. 540, 47 Am. Rep. 467 (1883); Marble Savings Bank v. Mesarvey, 101 Iowa 285, 70 N.W. 198 (1897); Clement v. Willett, 105 Minn. 267, 117 N.W. 491, 17 L.R.A.,N.S., 1094 (1908); 127 Am.St.Rep. 562, 15 Ann.Cas. 1053; Crone v. Stinde, 156 Mo. 262, 55 S.W. 863 (1900); Hare v. Murphy, 45 Neb. 809, 64 N.W. 211, 29 L.R.A. 851 (1895); Brewer v. Maurer, 38 Ohio St. 543, 43 Am.Rep. 436 (1882); Mullin v. Claremont Realty Co., 39 Ohio App. 103, 177 N.E. 226 (1930); Walser

v. Farmers' Trust Co., 126 Ohio St. 367, 185 N.E. 535 (1933); Merriman v. Moore, 90 Pa. 78, 7 W.N.C. 425 (1879); Title Guaranty etc. Co. v. Bushnell, 143 Tenn. 681, 228 S.W. 699, 12 A.L.R. 1512 (1921); Corkrell v. Poe, 100 Wash. 625, 171 P. 522, 12 A.L.R. 1524 (1918); Enos v. Sanger, 96 Wis. 150, 70 N.W. 1069, 37 L.R.A. 862, 65 Am. St.Rep. 38 (1897); Prudential Insurance Co. of America v. Clybourn Realty Co., 214 Wis. 409, 253 N.W. 397 (1934); Duvall-Percival Trust Co. v. Jenkins, 16 F.2d 223 (10th Cir.1926).

15. Restatement, Second, Contracts, § 133.

16. Restatement, Second, Contracts, § 133 Introductory Note.

17. Restatement, Second, Contracts, § 133.

18. See Restatement, Second, Contracts, § 144, Illus. 3.

No law or public policy has been . . . found which would invalidate the remote grantee's promise".[19]

WESTLAW REFERENCES

remote subsequent successive /5 buyer grantee purchaser /p
assum! /8 mortgage*

§ 5.16 Assumption by Second Mortgagee

When a mortgagor, instead of selling the property to a purchaser who assumes the mortgage, gives a second mortgage to one who agrees to pay off the first mortgage, the first mortgagee cannot enforce the assumption agreement against the second mortgagee, at least absent separate consideration flowing from the first mortgagee to the second.[1]

The above rule of law may be significant in connection with the commonly used "wrap-around" mortgage. This transaction entails "a second mortgage securing a promissory note, the face amount of which is the sum of the existing first mortgage liability plus the cash or equity advanced by the lender. The wrap-around borrower must make payments on the first mortgage debt to the wrap-around lender, who, as required by the wrap-around agreement, must in turn make payments on the first mortgage debt to the third party, the first mortgagee. If the wrap-around mortgagee should fail to perform his obligation to pay off the first mortgage, the wrap-around agreement normally gives the non-defaulting mortgagor the right to pay the interest and principal owing on the first mortgage, reducing his wrap-around obligation pro tanto." [2] While these transactions often entail purchase-money financing, a refinancing situation is more illustrative for our purposes. Suppose a mortgagor owns land worth $200,000 subject to a first mortgage of $90,000 carrying a 9% interest rate. Mortgagor wishes to obtain an additional $75,000 by further encumbering his equity in the land. A second mortgage lender may offer a wrap-around mortgage for $165,000 ($90,000 + $75,000) at a 12% interest rate. If this arrangement is accepted, the wrap-around mortgagee will promise to pay off the first mortgage with funds received from mortgagor's payments on the wrap-around mortgage.

To the extent that the wrap-around mortgagee formally assumes the first mortgage debt, the first mortgagee cannot enforce such an assumption against the wrap-around mortgagee. This is true because the first mortgagee normally will not have parted with any consideration in such a transaction. As a practical matter, however, this problem may not always be significant because the wrap-around mort-

---

19. Somers v. Avant, 244 Ga. 460, 462, 261 S.E.2d 334, 336 (1979).

§ 5.16

1. Garnsey v. Rogers, 47 N.Y. 233, 7 Am.R. 440 (1872); Walsh & Simpson, Cases Security Transactions, 316; Savings Bank of Southern California v. Thornton, 112 Cal. 255, 44 P. 466 (1896); Downs v. Ziegler, 13 Ariz.App. 387, 477 P.2d 261 (1971).

2. Comment, The Wrap-Around Mortgage: A Critical Inquiry, 21 U.C.L.A.L.Rev. 1529, 1529–1530 (1974).

gagee in any event very often does not unconditionally assume the first mortgage debt. The obligation on the part of the wrap-around mortgagee to pay the first mortgage is often conditioned on the receipt from the mortgagor of the debt service amount.[3]

If, however, the second mortgagee, whether a wrap-around mortgagee or not, actually formally assumes the first mortgage, it does not seem unreasonable to allow the first mortgagee to enforce that assumption. Indeed, most of the case law to the contrary was decided at a time when courts were not overly sympathetic to mortgagee recovery from assuming grantees. It is true, of course, that the usual assuming grantee-purchaser receives real estate and the assumption is part of the purchase price. Moreover, such is not the case with respect to the assuming second mortgagee. On the other hand, mortgagees in general would rarely assume a first mortgage by mistake. The decision, for example, to enter into a wrap-around transaction is presumably based on financially advantageous reasons. Moreover, the mortgagor in such a situation may desire additional assurance that the appropriate part of his payment to the wrap-around mortgagee will be applied to the first mortgage debt. The assumption of that first mortgage debt may very well provide the mortgagor with that added assurance. Consequently, whether a jurisdiction normally uses a third party beneficiary theory or some derivative theory to find assuming grantees liable to a mortgagee, there seems ample basis to utilize similar reasoning in the second mortgagee assumption situation.

Even under traditional case law, there may be clear situations where a first mortgagee will be able to enforce an assumption against a second mortgagee. These will involve situations where consideration for the assumption flows from the first mortgagee to the second. For example, suppose that a first mortgage goes into default and that the second mortgagee approachs the first mortgagee and offers to assume the first mortgage debt if the first mortgagee forbears for one year in foreclosing.[4] Acceptance of this arrangement by the first mortgagee clearly confers a benefit on the second mortgagee. A year's time could very well mean that the mortgagor will be able to reinstate the defaulted first mortgage. If this does occur, the second mortgagee will have avoided having his mortgage wiped out a first mortgage foreclosure sale.

 WESTLAW REFERENCES
second wrap-around 1 mortgage /p assum! /8 mortgage*

§ 5.17   Grantee's Defenses Against Mortgagee

Whether the mortgagee can enforce the mortgage or the mortgage debt against a transferee of the mortgagor to a different extent than he

3. Gunning, The Wrap-Around Mortgage * * * Friend or U.F.O.?, 2 Real Estate Rev. Summer, 1972 at 35.

4. See Kozan v. Levin, 50 A.D.2d 663, 374 N.Y.S.2d 829 (1975).

could against the mortgagor had there been no transfer properly depends upon the terms of the transfer and the intention of the transferor.[1] If the transferee promises to take subject to or to assume a specific mortgage, the amount of which has been deducted from the agreed on purchase price of the property, he becomes bound by contract to have the land in his hands subjected to payment of the full amount of the debt so agreed upon and, where he assumes its payment, to pay it. It is immaterial whether his promisee is actually indebted to that amount by an enforceable obligation.[2] By so including it and making its payment binding on the land, or the land and the transferee personally, he has shown that he intends the obligation to be valid so far as his transferee is concerned, and thus negatives any intention to confer a benefit upon him to the extent that the debt may be invalid or unenforceable. To permit the transferee under such circumstances to defeat the mortgagee on the ground that the mortgagor was not liable in whole or in part would unjustly enrich the transferee by enabling him to get the property for an amount less than he had agreed to pay for it, contrary to the intention of the transferor.[3] Where the grantee has assumed or taken subject to a specific mortgage most of the cases refuse to permit him to set up usury[4] or other defenses[5] which would

§ 5.17

1. See 141 A.L.R. 1184 (1942).

2. "If one assumes to pay a definite amount of the indebtedness of another, it is none of his concern whether the debt thus assumed is greater or less than the actual indebtedness." Oglesby v. South Georgia Grocery Co., 18 Ga.App. 401, 402, 89 S.E. 436 (1917).

3. Where, for example, usury that could not be collected from the mortgagor formed part of the consideration for the purchase, it "would be permitting a fraud to allow the grantee to plead usury. If the mortgagor chooses to affirm his contract, and sets apart, out of the purchase price for the complete title, an amount sufficient to pay it, whether with an express agreement of the grantee to make such payment, or with an option to either pay or suffer foreclosure, the grantee cannot question the amount. If the usury has become a part of the consideration in the agreement between the mortgagor and his grantee, it is an affirmance of the debt by the mortgagor; and when the grantee contracts with a view to the payment of the incumbrance, equity demands that he shall pay it, or lose the property." Crawford v. Nimmons, 180 Ill. 143, 54 N.E. 209 (1899); Davis v. Davis, 19 Cal.App. 797, 127 P. 1051 (1912); Trusdell v. Dowden, 47 N.J. Eq. 396, 20 A. 972 (1890); United States Bond Co. v. Keahey, 53 Okl. 176, 155 P. 557, L.R.A.1917C (1916), 829, accord.

4. Crawford v. Nimmons, 180 Ill. 143, 54 N.E. 209 (1899); Pinnell v. Boyd, 33 N.J. Eq. 190 (1880), reversed 33 N.J.Eq. 600; Central Holding Co. v. Bushman, 238 Mich. 261, 213 N.W. 120 (1927). See 8 L.R.A.,N.S., 814 (1907); 48 L.R.A.,N.S., 840 (1914); L.R.A. 1917C, 832. See also notes, 67 U.S.L.Rev. 163 (1933); 14 Tex.L.Rev. 559 (1936); 13 Tex.L.Rev. 375 (1935).

5. Kansas Savings & Loan Association v. Rich Eckel Construction Co., 223 Kan. 493, 576 P.2d 212, 223 (1978) (waiver of statutory redemption rights); Michigan Wineries, Inc. v. Johnson, 68 Mich.App. 310, 242 N.W.2d 568 (1976), affirmed 402 Mich. 306, 262 N.W.2d 651 (1978); Ortega et al. v. Gennitti, 93 N.M. 135, 597 P.2d 745 (1979); Pacific First Federal Savings & Loan Association v. Lindberg, 64 Or.App. 140, 667 P.2d 535 (1983) (unconscionability). Freeman v. Auld, 44 N.Y. 50 (1870), failure of consideration; Davis v. Davis, 19 Cal.App. 797, 127 P. 1051 (1912) (statute of limitations); see Bogart v. Geo. K. Porter Co., 193 Cal. 197, 223 P. 959, 31 A.L.R. 1045 (1924), statute of limitations; Bennett v. Bates, 94 N.Y. 354, 370 (1884), invalidity of mortgage; Exchange Tr. Co. v. Ireton, 88 Okl. 262, 213 P. 309 (1923), forgery in creation of mortgage debt; see Roberts, The Defense of Jus Tertii in Mortgage Cases, 16 Bost.Univ.L.Rev. 644 (1936) for a survey of a large variety of defenses; Cunningham and Tischler, Transfer of the Real Estate Mortgagor's Interest, 27 Rutgers L.Rev. 24, 54–55 (1973).

have been available to the mortgagor. A good many of the cases do so, however, on the ground either that the transferee is estopped [6] to deny the validity or extent of the mortgage or that the defense is personal to the mortgagor.[7] Neither doctrine is properly applicable. The amount of the debt is not a term of the mortgage to which estoppel by deed applies and no showing of reliance by the mortgagee upon the terms of the promise, a requirement of estoppel generally, is insisted upon. If the defense were really personal to the mortgagor it should be so in all cases. Yet in cases where the terms of the contract indicate that the transferee is binding himself only to be subject to or to pay the amount of the debt actually due or legally enforceable,[8] no objection is raised to his setting up defenses which have been at other times denied as personal to the mortgagor. The same is true if the conveyance is by way of gift.[9] In neither case would the grantee be getting any greater benefit than was intended by being allowed to cut down the mortgagee's recovery out of the land to the amount he could have collected had there been no transfer.

Where the grantee has not withheld any part of the purchase price, the grantee should be permitted to set up defenses to a foreclosure action which are available to the mortgagor.[10] And the same is true *a fortiori* if it is established that the full value of the land was paid with an agreement for the mortgagor to discharge the mortgage. It would be extraordinary to construe such a contract as intended to preclude the mortgagor from using his defenses if he wished to. The grantee is interested only in having the land free and clear of any incumbrance, not in having a portion of the money he has paid being earmarked for the full face of the mortgage debt to go to the mortgagee regardless of his right to it as against the mortgagor. Consequently, the grantee who is in the position of a surety with respect to the mortgagor should be entitled to have the mortgagor exonerate him only to the extent of the valid obligation of the mortgagor. So, too, if he paid the mortgagee, as he may, his right of reimbursement, whether enforced directly or by

6. Ortega et al. v. Gennitti, 93 N.M. 135, 597 P.2d 745 (1979); Key West Wharf & Coal Co. v. Porter, 63 Fla. 448, 58 So. 599 (1912); Freeman v. Auld, 44 N.Y. 50, Campbell (1870), Cases on Mortgages, 2d ed., 427; see Bogart v. Geo. K. Porter Co., 193 Cal. 197, 223 P. 959, 31 A.L.R. 1045 (1924). See note, 141 A.L.R. 1184 (1942).

7. Central Holding Co. v. Bushman, 238 Mich. 261, 213 N.W. 120 (1927); Higbee v. Aetna Building & Loan Association, 26 Okl. 327, 109 P. 236, Ann.Cas.1912B, 223 (1910); see Hartley v. Harrison, 24 N.Y. 170, 172 (1861). See 24 Minn.L.Rev. 124 (1940); 87 U. of Pa.L.Rev. 881 (1939).

8. National Mutual Building & Loan Association v. Retzman, 69 Neb. 667, 96 N.W. 204 (1903); Washington National Building & Loan Association v. Andrews,

95 Md. 696, 53 A. 573 (1902); National Loan & Insurance Co. of Detroit v. Stone, 46 S.W. 67 (Tex.Civ.App.1898); Loder v. Hatfield, 71 N.Y. 92 (1877). A general assumption of all liens or debts would be given this interpretation. Purdy v. Coar, 109 N.Y. 448, 17 N.E. 352, 4 Am.St.Rep. 491 (1888); Crowe v. Malba Land Co., 76 Misc. 676, 135 N.Y.S. 454 (1912). See 67 U.S.L.Rev. 164 (1933).

9. First National Bank v. Drew, 226 Ill. 622, 80 N.E. 1082, 10 L.R.A.,N.S., 857, 117 Am.St.Rep. 271 (1907).

10. Grove v. Great Northern Loan Co., 17 N.D. 352, 116 N.W. 345, 138 Am.St.Rep. 707 (1908); see Ford v. Washington National Building & Loan Investment Association, 10 Idaho 30, 76 P. 1010, 109 Am.St. Rep. 192 (1904).

virtue of subrogation, should be no greater. Since this is so, he should be entitled to discharge the debt by paying only what the mortgagor actually owed or, if the mortgagee sues to collect by foreclosure, limit the foreclosure recovery to the same amount.

A second mortgagee who takes his mortgage subject to a prior one should be permitted, in a foreclosure action by the first mortgagee, to set up defenses available to his mortgagor.[11] There is, however a diversity of view among the cases on the point. Those that deny the privilege do so on the ground that the defense is personal to the borrower and those in privity with him.[12] The cases allowing him to set up the defenses are clearly preferable.[13] The junior mortgagee has an interest in having the senior mortgage discharged at the least possible cost. Although he would be increasing the value of his security by thus cutting down the amount of the prior lien he would not be unjustly enriched by such a result. He has the right to collect the amount of his debt and will not get more than that in any event. Further, to deny such a right would confer an unwarranted benefit on the prior mortgagee at the expense of the junior encumbrancer. The junior mortgagee may pay off the senior mortgage to protect his own interest and then be subrogated to the senior mortgagee's rights against the mortgagor. The mortgagor could then limit recovery against him on the right to which he is subrogated to the amount that the senior mortgagee could have collected.[14]

A grantee of the mortgagor who assumes or takes subject to a specific mortgage is permitted to set up as against the mortgagee any defenses he could use against his transferor.[15] This clearly is correct where the mortgagee's rights are derived through the mortgagor.[16] But it is equally true where the rights are direct ones as a third party beneficiary.[17] The beneficiary of a contract should take his rights subject to any defects in them as against the promisee who created them in his behalf.

11. As to the right of a subsequent mortgagee to raise the question of usury in a prior mortgage transaction, see notes, 87 U. of Pa.L.Rev. 881 (1939); 24 Minn.L.Rev. 124 (1939); 30 Col.L.Rev. 902 (1930).

12. Union National Bank v. International Bank, 123 Ill. 510, 14 N.E. 859 (1888); Pritchett v. Mitchell, 17 Kan. 355, 22 Am.Rep. 287 (1876); Richardson v. Baker, 52 Vt. 617 (1872); Ready v. Huebner, 46 Wis. 692, 1 N.W. 344, 32 Am.Rep. 749 (1879). See 24 Minn.L.Rev. 124 (1940); 87 U. of Pa.L.Rev. 881 (1939).

13. Evans v. Faircloth-Byrd Mercantile Co., 165 Ala. 176, 51 So. 785, 21 Ann.Cas. 1164 (1910); Pinnix v. Maryland Casualty Co., 214 N.C. 760, 200 S.E. 874, 121 A.L.R. 871 (1939). See 24 Minn.L.Rev. 124 (1940); 87 U. of Pa.L.Rev. 881 (1939).

14. 87 U. of Pa.L.Rev. 881 (1939).

15. Dunning v. Leavitt, 85 N.Y. 30, 39 Am.Rep. 617 (1881). On the right of an assuming grantee to set up, as against the mortgagee, defenses which he has against his grantor, see notes 12 N.Car.L.Rev. 383 (1934); 22 Va.L.Rev. 355 (1936); 36 Mich.L. Rev. 847 (1938).

16. Dunning v. Leavitt, note 78, supra; Waddell v. Roanoke Mutual Building & Loan Association, 165 Va. 229, 181 S.E. 288, 100 A.L.R. 906 (1935), noted, 22 Va.L. Rev. 355 (1936).

17. Fulmer v. Goldfarb, 171 Tenn. 218, 101 S.W.2d 1108 (1937), discussed, 36 Mich. L.Rev. 847 (1938).

WESTLAW REFERENCES

denial deny*** estop! personal /s defense /p buyer grantee
     purchaser transferee /p mortgagee
266k274

§ 5.18   Subsequent Discharge or Modification of Rights Between Grantor and Grantee

There is great diversity of authority as to the extent to which an assumption may be ended or modified by a transaction between a grantor and an assuming grantee.[1] For the most part this variance stems from the differences in theory upon which the right of the mortgagee depends.[2] If the security of the land is sufficient to pay the debt, the question is of no practical importance to the mortgagee, for no agreement between the mortgagor or later transferors and grantees can affect his mortgage on the land.[3]

Where the mortgagee's right is held to be derivative, i.e., merely a right to avail himself of the benefit of the contract right of the transferor,[4] that there can be no rescission or alteration after action has been brought by the mortgagee.[5] Indeed this is the rule without dissent no matter what rationale is followed.[6] But short of bringing an action does the mortgagee have power to prevent the parties wiping out or changing this contract? Most courts permit discharge or variation of the contract by the promisee at any time before suit by the mortgagee [7] with two limitations: 1. The mortgagee must not have materially changed his position in reliance on the assumption before he knows of

---

§ 5.18

1. For discussions and collections of authorities see Page, The Power of the Contracting Parties to Alter a Contract for Rendering Performance to a Third Person, 12 Wis.L.Rev. 141, 181 (1937); notes, 7 Boston U.L.Rev. 316 (1927); 13 Cornell L.Q. 123 (1927); 10 Col.L.Rev. 765 (1910); 24 Ill.L.Rev. 828 (1930); 9 Minn.L.Rev. 295 (1925); 8 U. of Cin.L.Rev. 103, 109, 122 (1934). See also 21 A.L.R. 439, 462 (1922); 41 A.L.R. 317 (1926); 47 A.L.R. 340, 342 (1927); 100 A.L.R. 911 (1936).

2. See §§ 5.11–5.15, supra.

3. See § 5.1, supra.

4. See §§ 5.13–5.15, supra.

5. Wallace v. Hammonds, 170 Ark. 952, 281 S.W. 902 (1926); Field v. Thistle, 58 N.J.Eq. 339, 43 A. 1072 (1899), affirmed 60 N.J.Eq. 444, 46 A. 1099 (1900); Carnahan v. Tousey, 93 Ind. 561 (1883). See Restatement, Contracts, § 143. See also Morstain v. Kircher, 190 Minn. 78, 250 N.W. 727

(1933) discussed in note, 47 Harv.L.Rev. 1065 (1934), accord.

6. Gifford v. Corrigan, 117 N.Y. 257, 22 N.E. 756, 6 L.R.A. 610, 15 Am.St.Rep. 508 (1889); New York Life Insurance Co. v. Aitkin, 125 N.Y. 660, 26 N.E. 732 (1891); Whiting v. Gearty, 14 Hun 498 (N.Y.1878). See Friedman, Personal Liability on Mortgage Debts, 50 Yale L.Jour. 224, 238 (1940); note 13 Cornell L.Q. 123 (1928). This is on the theory that an acceptance makes the mortgagee's direct right indefeasible and the institution of an action is conclusive evidence of an acceptance. See also West's Ann.Cal.Civ.Code § 1559; Orloff v. Metropolitan Trust Co., 38 Cal.App.2d 688, 102 P.2d 562 (1940).

7. Biddel v. Brizzolara, 64 Cal. 354, 30 P. 609 (1883); Crowell v. Currier, 27 N.J. Eq. 152 (1876) affirmed 27 N.J.Eq. 650; see note, 12 A.L.R. 1528, 1529 (1921). But cf. Willard v. Worsham, 76 Va. 392 (1882); McCown v. Nicks, 171 Ark. 260, 284 S.W. 739, 47 A.L.R. 332 (1926).

the discharge or variation.[8] 2. The promisee's action is not in fraud of creditors.[9]

The general rule and first limitation are sound. The mortgagee has admittedly picked up an unexpected windfall in being able to reach the assuming grantee and there is no policy in favor of helping him at the expense of free dealing between the grantee and grantor. If, however, the mortgagee can show material change of position in reliance on the promise, familiar principles would justify preventing the destruction or alteration of the asset.[10] The second limitation, except as to the amount the mortgage debt exceeds the value of the security, is on less firm ground. It has been criticized as invoking in favor of a secured creditor the doctrine of conveyances in fraud of creditors, which should be restricted to unsecured creditors.[11] If the promisee did not assume the mortgage, he should under a derivative theory be able to release the grantee at any time, even after an action to foreclose is commenced. Since the mortgagee's right to reach the assuming grantee depends upon his having an enforceable claim against the promisee-transferor, he has no ground to object to a release or alteration of the grantee's promise when that claim does not exist.[12]

In jurisdictions that accept the third party beneficiary direct right rationale, the problem would seem to be one of what the basis for according the right is and, consequently, one of when it vests in the mortgagee. A few such courts hold that the mortgagee's right becomes indefeasibly vested immediately upon the assumption.[13] If the argument is that the relationship established is purely contractual, the contract being the offer, acceptance and consideration between the promisor and promisee,[14] such a conclusion would be logical.[15] That contract is complete on the making of the promise of assumption. The weight of authority, however, requires acceptance or adoption by the

---

8. See note 5, supra.

9. See Youngs v. Trustees, 31 N.J.Eq. 290, 298–302 (1879). What would constitute fraud of creditors would depend upon the law of fraudulent conveyances in the particular jurisdiction. If the promisee is solvent, has no actual intent to defraud creditors, or, even if insolvent, gives the discharge bona fide for valuable consideration, it would not be in fraud of creditors. See Williston, Contracts, (3d Ed.1959), § 397.

10. See Gifford v. Corrigan, 105 N.Y. 223, 229, 11 N.E. 498 (1887), "to permit a change * * * while the creditor is relying upon it, would be grossly inequitable."

11. See Glenn, Mortgages, §§ 271, 5.1; Restatement, Security, § 140.

12. There are some decisions that apparently consider that "acceptance" by the mortgagee is necessary and sufficient. E.g., Hubard & Appleby v. Thacker, 132

Va. 33, 53, 110 S.E. 263, 21 A.L.R. 423 (1922). Such a requirement seems insupportable, except upon the dubious ground that "from that moment, certainly in equity, even more than at law, the mortgagee must be assumed to have acted or to have omitted to act in reliance upon it." Since the right is an unanticipated bonus, it would seem preferable to require that the mortgagee establish affirmatively that he had actually relied upon it before giving him an indefeasible right to it.

13. Bay v. Williams, 112 Ill. 91, 1 N.E. 340, 54 Am.Rep. 209 (1884); Starbird v. Cranston, 24 Colo. 20, 48 P.2d 652 (1897).

14. Corbin, Contracts for the Benefit of Third Persons, 27 Yale L.J. 1008, 1020 (1918).

15. See 10 Col.L.Rev. 765, 766 (1910); 13 Cornell L.Q. 123, 126 (1927). Friedman, Personal Liability on Mortgage Debts, 50 Yale L.J. 224, 239 (1940).

mortgagee before deeming the right vested.[16] There is divergence as to what will satisfy these requirements. Thus it has been held that acceptance will be presumed and therefore on this ground the right arises at the time the contract is made subject only to disaffirmance by the mortgagee.[17] On the other hand, there is authority that notice must be given by the mortgagee to the promisor.[18] Others seem to make the test of acceptance or adoption synonymous with material change of position that will make it inequitable to deprive the mortgagee of the right.[19] These last would seem perfectly sound. If the mortgagee's right is regarded as a contract right arising by conduct between the promisor and the beneficiary, the necessity of an "acceptance" is supportable. But if the analogy on which the right is given is to a trust or an insurance policy without right to change the beneficiary an opposite result would follow.[20] In any event it has been suggested "that no fetish should be made of the mortgagee's 'acceptance,' particularly in those communities where it is the general practice to let mortgages run past due if taxes and interest are paid." [21]

Many courts following the direct right theory have permitted recovery in spite of non-liability of the promisee-grantor to the mortgagee, but it is not altogether clear in all cases whether he does so as a donee or as a creditor beneficiary.[22] If he is classed as the former it does not necessarily follow that the rule generally followed in such cases [23] as to the indefeasibility of the beneficiary's right should apply to the mortgagee. The rule was established in cases in which there are present social considerations which do not exist in mortgage cases.[24] This is especially important because of the extremely dubious basis in fact of a donative intent on the part of either the promisee or promisor.[25] If he is regarded as a creditor beneficiary there seems no substan-

16. Gifford v. Corrigan, 117 N.Y. 257, 262, 22 N.E. 756, 757, 6 L.R.A. 610, 15 Am. St.Rep. 508 (1889); Smith v. Kibbe, 104 Kan. 159, 163, 178 P. 427, 429, 5 A.L.R. 483 (1919); New York Life Insurance Co. v. Aitkin, 125 N.Y. 660, 675, 26 N.E. 732 (1891); and Hill v. Hoeldtke, 104 Tex. 594, 142 S.W. 871, 40 L.R.A.,N.S., 672 (1912). That the assumption may be revoked any time before the mortgagee brings suit, knowledge or any acceptance or adoption not being shown, Ellis v. Kristoferson, 129 Misc. 443, 222 N.Y.S. 370 (1927), see Wheat v. Rice, 97 N.Y. 296, 302 (1884); 9 Minn.L. Rev. 295 (1925); 47 Harv.L.Rev. 1066, 1067 (1934).

17. Rogers v. Gosnell, 58 Mo. 589 (1875).

18. Berkshire Life Insurance Co. v. Hutchings, 100 Ind. 496 (1884); see Carnahan v. Tousey, 93 Ind. 561, 562, 564 (1883).

19. Morstain v. Kircher, 190 Minn. 78, 250 N.W. 727 (1933).

20. See Friedman, op. cit. supra note 95.

21. Idem, citing Union Trust Co. v. Kaplan, 249 App.Div. 280, 284, 292 N.Y.S. 152, 159 (1936), judicial knowledge of custom.

22. See § 5.15, supra.

23. See Williston, Contracts, § 396 (3d Ed.1959).

24. See Note 13 Corn.L.Q. 123, 128 (1927); Friedman Personal Liability on Mortgage Debts, 50 Yale L.J. 224, 240. It should be noted that the mortgagee, unlike the usual donee beneficiary, already has rights against the mortgagor, even if not the promisee-grantor, and the land. And he differs from most creditor beneficiaries in his security right in the land in the hands of the transferee-promisor in addition to his claim against the mortgagor or other transferor.

25. See § 5.15, supra.

tial reason for treating him, so far as this point is concerned, as in a different position than one to whom the promisee-grantor is liable.

 WESTLAW REFERENCES

alter*** alteration change* rescind rescission /p contract! /p
     mortgagee /p grantor mortgagor seller transferor
266k272

§ 5.19   Extension, Release and Other Modification—Suretyship and the Mortgagor

In spite of certain conceptual difficulties in those states following a derivative theory of the right of a mortgagee against an assuming grantee,[1] courts generally agree today that a suretyship relationship is created by a conveyance from a mortgagor to an assuming grantee. The mortgagor is looked upon as a surety while the land and the assuming grantee are regarded as principals.[2] Further, accepting the suretyship concept, they also follow suretyship rules in defining the rights of the mortgagor-transferor with respect to such matters as subrogation and reimbursement.[3] In addition, they tend for the most part to follow uncritically those rules of suretyship which give a defense to the surety, in whole or in part, as a consequence of extension agreements or releases given by the creditor to the principal debtor.[4]

Extensions of Time

Suretyship rules of discharge are invoked in cases where mortgagees give binding extensions of time to grantees of the mortgagor. Transactions in which the grantee assumes the mortgage have to be differentiated from those in which he merely takes subject to it. In the former, by the great weight of authority, if the mortgagee with knowledge of the conveyance and assumption,[5] gives time to an assuming

§ 5.19

1. See §§ 5.13–5.14, supra.

2. See §§ 5.11–5.14, supra.

3. See §§ 5.9–5.10, supra.

4. Restatement, Security, § 83, Comment on Clause (c). See note, 4 U. of Chi. L.Rev. 469 (1937) for a thorough exposition of the rationales, criticisms, and limitations of the suretyship rule that a binding extension of time to a principal by a creditor without the consent of the surety will release the latter, followed by a critical discussion of its application, by analogy, to mortgage cases. See also Cardozo, Nature of the Judicial Process, 152; Glassie, The Assuming Vendee, 9 Va.L.Rev. 196, 203 (1923); note, 15 Iowa L.Rev. 79 (1929) (discussing the Iowa view which gives the mortgagor no defense); note, 79 U. of Pa.L. Rev. 1151 (1931) (effect of mortgagee's ignorance of the grantee's assumption); 41 A.L.R. 277 (1926); 43 A.L.R. 89 (1926); 72 A.L.R. 389 (1931); 81 A.L.R. 1016 (1932); 112 A.L.R. 1324; Friedman, Discharge of Mortgage Debts, 52 Yale L.J. 771, 796 (1943). Warm, Rights and Liabilities of Mortgagee, Mortgagor, Grantee, 10 Temple L.Q. 116, 136 (1936).

5. Since usually assumption terms will be in the conveyance, of which a mortgagee should be on notice, this requirement normally will be fulfilled in mortgage assumption cases. But see Blumenthal v. Serota, 129 Me. 187, 151 A. 138 (1930). Even if the grantee's deed is silent, it would be an extraordinary case in which the mortgagee has known enough about the grantee to give him an extension of time and yet be able to establish that he was unaware of the existence of the assumption agreement. See Murray v. Marshall, 94 N.Y. 611 (1884), "the fact that he dealt with the grantee for an extension of the mortgage

grantee by a binding agreement with him, the mortgagor is completely discharged regardless of any showing of injury.[6] The same is true as to any intermediate grantees.[7] Moreover, while a reservation of rights against the mortgagor contained in the mortgage itself may sometimes operate to prevent an extension from effecting a discharge of the mortgagor,[8] such clauses will be strictly construed against the mortgagee.[9] In addition, the inclusion of a similar reservation in the extension agreement generally will not so operate.[10] On the other hand, the mortgagor must establish that a binding extension of time was granted to the assuming grantee—the fact, for example, that the mortgagee merely delayed foreclosure as a temporary expedient or "indulgence"

shows that he knew of the conveyance, and that it left the land bound in the hands of the grantee. Knowing this he is chargeable with knowledge of the mortgagor's equitable rights, and meddled with them at his peril." But in some cases the mortgagor is held not to be discharged unless the mortgagee had knowledge that the relationship of principal and surety existed between the grantee and mortgagor. Pratt v. Conway, 148 Mo. 291, 49 S.W. 1028, 71 Am.St.Rep. 602 (1899), in which the agreement of assumption was not contained in the deed of conveyance; Wolfe v. Murphy, 47 App.D.C. 296 (1918), in which the mortgagee was not charged with knowledge although the agreement of assumption was in the deed of conveyance and it was recorded. That the mortgagor is not discharged if the mortgagee did not know of the assumption at the time of the execution of the extension agreement, De Lotto v. Zipper, 116 N.J.Eq. 344, 173 A. 588 (1934), affirmed 120 N.J.Eq. 339, 185 A. 54 (1936). See 79 U. of Pa.L.Rev. 1151 (1931); 41 A.L.R. 277, 302 (1926); 72 A.L.R. 389, 397 (1931); 81 A.L.R. 1016, 1023 (1932); 112 A.L.R. 1324, 1340 (1938).

6. Cunningham and Tischler, Transfer of the Real Estate Mortgagor's Interest, 27 Rutgers L.Rev. 24, 59 (1973); Calvo v. Davies, 73 N.Y. 211, 29 Am.Rep. 130 (1878); Union Mutual Life Insurance Co. v. Hanford, 143 U.S. 187, 12 S.Ct. 437, 36 L.Ed. 118 (1892). See 41 A.L.R. 277 (1926); 72 A.L.R. 389 (1931); 81 A.L.R. 1016 (1932); 112 A.L.R. 1324 (1938).

7. Phoenix Trust Co. v. Garner, 227 Mo. App. 929, 59 S.W.2d 779 (1933); Meldola v. Furlong, 142 Misc. 562, 255 N.Y.S. 48 (1932). Whether an extension to a grantee who assumes but whose grantor had not will discharge the mortgage completely depends on the local law as to whether such an assumption creates a personal liability. See § 5.15, supra. In DeLeon v. Rhines, 64 U.S.App.D.C. 73, 74 F.2d 477 (1934), an

extension to the last grantee whose predecessors had not assumed gave no discharge. Even though the grantee incurred no personal liability the case should be governed by the rule of conveyances subject to the mortgage.

8. Bailey v. Inman, 105 Fla. 1, 140 So. 783 (1932); Continental National Bank & Trust Co. v. Reynolds, 286 Ill.App. 290, 3 N.E.2d 319 (1936); Kent v. Rhomberg, 288 Ill.App. 328, 6 N.E.2d 271 (1937); Mutual Life Insurance Co. v. Rothschild, 160 N.Y.S. 164 (1916), affirmed 226 N.Y. 599, 123 N.E. 880 (1918); Kohn v. Beggi, 147 Misc. 701, 264 N.Y.S. 274 (1933).

9. First Federal Savings & Loan Association of Gary v. Arena, 406 N.E.2d 1279 (Ind.App.1980); Friedman, Discharge of Personal Liability on Mortgage Debts in New York, 52 Yale L.J. 771, 788 (1943).

10. Calvo v. Davies, 73 N.Y. 211, 29 Am.Rep. 130 (1878), holding that such an agreement is only conditional on the consent to it of the surety; Metzger v. Nova Realty Co., 160 App.Div. 394, 145 N.Y.S. 549 (1915), affirmed 214 N.Y. 26, 107 N.E. 1027; Maier v. Thorman, 234 S.W. 239 (Tex.Civ.App.1921); see 4 A.L.R. 277, 304 (1926); 72 A.L.R. 387, 398 (1931); 81 A.L.R. 1016, 1025 (1932); 112 A.L.R. 1325, 1342 (1938): Such a reservation does not give a grantee an unconditional extension but possibly a mere substitution of creditors. The effect is to leave the mortgagor an unconditional right to pay and enforce subrogation and therefore is without effect on either the rights or liabilities of the mortgagor. This result in mortgage cases is justified. See Glenn, Morts., § 276, "Here [in mortgage transfer cases] an extension may seriously alter the mortgagor's position, inasmuch as meanwhile the assuming grantee is in possession. * * * and so the rule cannot apply that, in other situations, will sanction 'reservation of recourse' in connection with extensions."

may not establish the existence of an extension agreement.[11] More-over, there are a few cases that hold that an extension does not discharge the mortgagor, the theory being that the mortgagee is not bound by the suretyship relation between the mortgagor and the transferee but may treat both as principals severally liable unless he assents to the arrangement.[12]

Two major justifications have been advanced for the general rule of discharge outlined above. First, it is argued that any time extension increases the risk to the surety. The theory is that "the surety calculated and undertook the probability of debtor default on the original term, but did not undertake the supposedly greater probability of default over a longer period."[13] Second, a related rationale is that an extension of time impairs the surety's rights by depriving him of his right of subrogation to the creditor's cause of action against the principal debtor.[14]

The general rule of discharge has been subjected to substantial criticism. Some have noted, for example, that no empirical evidence exists to show that extensions of time in fact increase the risk of non-payment by the principal debtor.[15] Indeed, in some instances it could be argued that an extension may enable a hard-pressed principal-debtor-grantee to rehabilitate his precarious financial situation, thus actually decreasing the likelihood of mortgagor-surety liability. In those jurisdictions using subrogation to the mortgagor's rights or other derivative notions on which to found the mortgagee's ability to proceed against the assuming grantee personally, impairment of the power to be subrogated to the mortgagee's rights is manifestly an untenable basis for granting a discharge beyond the value of the mortgaged property. "The only right the mortgagee has is to enforce the obligation of the grantee to the mortgagor, and no action of the mortgagee can deprive the mortgagor of this right. He does not need to be subrogated to the right; he has it without subrogation."[16] In jurisdic-

---

11. See Osborn v. Aetna Life and Casualty Co., 308 So.2d 355 (La.App.1975), writ refused 312 So.2d 340 (Sup.1975). The waiver of an acceleration clause is not an extension of time to a grantee so as to release the mortgagor, see notes, 7 N.Y. Univ.L.Q.Rev. 214 (1929); 31 Col.L.Rev. 328 (1931). See Friedman, Discharge of Mortgage Debts, 52 Yale L.J. 771, 782–787 (1943) for other agreements between mortgagee and grantees of the mortgagor that will discharge the mortgagor. But see, Germania Life Insurance Co. v. Casey, 98 App.Div. 88, 90 N.Y.S. 418 (1904), (mortgagor was completely discharged by the acceptance by the mortgagee from the assuming grantee of a payment of the interest for six months one day before it was due, thus extending the time of payment of the mortgage debt by one day.)

12. Bailey v. Inman, 105 Fla. 1, 140 So. 783 (1932); Blank v. Michael, 208 Iowa 402, 226 N.W. 12 (1929). See 81 U. of Pa.L. Rev. 641 (1933); 15 Iowa L.Rev. 79 (1929); 13 N.Car.L.Rev. 337 (1935); 41 A.L.R. 277, 285 (1926); 72 A.L.R. 383, 389 (1931); 112 A.L.R. 1324, 1331 (1938).

13. White and Summers, Uniform Commercial Code, 523 (2nd Ed. 1980).

14. Id.

15. Id.

16. Williston, Contracts, § 386 (3d Ed. 1959). Restatement, Contracts, § 146, accord. Wolfe v. Murphy, 47 U.S.App.D.C. 296 (1918); see Keller v. Ashford, 133 U.S. 610, 625, 10 S.Ct. 494, 33 L.Ed. 667 (1890). Courts which do not allow the mortgagee to sue the grantee at all, it may be assumed, would not release the mortgagor

tions where the mortgagee's right is recognized as direct, discharge of the mortgagor to an amount above the value of the mortgaged property has been attacked. It is argued that no possibility of injury exists beyond the value of the property since the extension does not affect his rights other than that of subrogation and they give him in every respect a practical equivalent of it. Any discharge as to this is purely technical.[17] In addition it is urged that, because the mortgagor does not assume his obligation gratuitously, having received a loan or other value and having usually been the principal debtor for some time, he resembles one of the more protected type of sureties commonly described as compensated.[18] Such sureties are not discharged by mere extension of time; they must show injury.[19]

The cases dealing with the effect on the liability of the original mortgagor of an extension given by a mortgagee to a subject-to grantee are not unanimous.[20] It has been held that the rights of the mortgagee against the mortgagor are not in any manner affected thereby.[21] It has also been held that, under such circumstances, the mortgagor is released entirely.[22] Another rule of discharge is the amount which, due to the extension, the value of the property has depreciated below the

when there has been an extension of time to the grantee.

17. See Williston, Contracts, Rev. ed., § 386; cf. 15 Iowa L.Rev. 79 (1929).

18. See Stevens, Extension Agreements in the "Subject-to" Mortgage Situation, 15 U. of Cin.L.Rev. 58, 73 (1941) "the 'mortgagor-surety' in such cases is not just compensated but has actually received the *quid pro quo.*" See also 4 U. of Chi.L.Rev. 469, 478 (1937); 42 Harv.L.Rev. 712 (1929); Tiffany, Real Prop., 3d ed., § 445, n. 54. But cf. 29 Harv.L.Rev. 314, 317 (1916).

19. See Arant, Suretyship, § 299.

20. See Stevens, Extension Agreements in the "Subject-to" Mortgage Situation, 15 U. of Cin.L.Rev. 58, 70 (1941) for a critical analysis of the several rules. See also Campbell, Cases on Mortgages, 2d ed., 442, n. 4. As to the effect of an extension agreement on the rights of junior mortgagees, see Meislin, Extension Agreements and the Rights of Junior Mortgagees, 42 Va.L.Rev. 939 (1956).

21. Chilton v. Brooks, 72 Md. 554, 20 A. 125 (1890); DeLeon v. Rhines, 64 U.S.App. D.C. 73, 74 F.2d 477 (1934); Pfeifer v. W.B. Worthen Co., 189 Ark. 469, 74 S.W.2d 220 (1934), accord. See notes, 15 Iowa L.Rev. 79 (1929); 13 N.Car.L.Rev. 337 (1935). In Maryland and in the federal courts it is held, however, that an extension granted to an assuming grantee will discharge the mortgagor. George v. Andrews, 60 Md. 26,

45 Am.Rep. 706 (1882); Asbell v. Marshall Building & Loan Association, 156 Md. 106, 143 A. 715 (1928); Keller v. Ashford, 133 U.S. 610, 10 S.Ct. 494, 33 L.Ed. 667 (1890). The distinction has been explained as follows: "The argument is that an extension can have no effect unless there is privity between the three parties—mortgagee, mortgagor and grantee; and privity there cannot be unless all three are under contract, which is not the case unless the grantee assumes." Glenn, Morts., § 1201. The distinction is fallacious. The requirement of "privity" is artificial. Even if insisted upon, it can be argued that it is satisfied. "The theorem * * * starts with the land as common security, and this brings the parties into privity; the assumption is merely additional collateral, and naturally the privity remains which always was in effect." Glenn, Mortgages, § 278.

22. Braun v. Crew, 183 Cal. 728, 192 P. 531 (1920), discussed in notes, 5 Minn.L. Rev. 150 (1921); 19 Mich.L.Rev. 351 (1921); 10 Not.D.Law. 83, 84 (1934). A provision in the California Civil Code influenced the decision. See also 41 A.L.R. 277, 292 (1926); 112 A.L.R. 1324, 1334 (1938). A later decision in California rejects this rule where the mortgage secures a negotiable note. Mortgage Guarantee Co. v. Chotiner, 8 Cal.2d 110, 64 P.2d 138, 108 A.L.R. 1080 (1936).

mortgage debt.[23] The weight of authority, however, is that, under such circumstances, the mortgagor is released to the extent of the value of the security properly applicable to the mortgage debt in the hands of the grantee at the time the extension is granted.[24]

The right of subrogation of a surety to his creditor's rights gives him nothing of substantial value if the creditor has no security or other priority rights and if he himself has rights over against the principal debtor. The personal right of the creditor against the principal debtor is no better than his own personal rights. But if the creditor has security which the surety might reach by subrogation at the maturity of the debt, it is obvious that his risk has been increased by an extension which prevents him or the mortgagee from realizing on it until later.[25] Thus the cases that deny any discharge would seem to be wrong. But the maximum injury would be the value of the land at the time of the injury and therefore a complete release, unless the land exceeded the amount of the debt, would seem to be unjustified. The burden of proof to establish the elements of the defense in these cases is upon the mortgagor.[26] If it were a difficult and onerous task to establish the actual amount of injury suffered by the extension, the majority rule could be accepted without objection. However, it would seem practicable to prove the extent to which the property has depreciated below the mortgage debt during the extension. Further, whether this rule or discharge to the full value of the land at the date of extension is adopted, a presumption that the land was equal in value to the debt at the time the extension was granted seems justified as founded on normal practice and business common sense.[27]

23. North End Savings Bank v. Snow, 197 Mass. 339, 83 N.E. 1099, 125 Am.St. Rep. 368 (1908). This may be the New York rule. See Syracuse Trust Co. v. First Trust & Deposit Co., 141 Misc. 603, 252 N.Y.S. 850 (1931) commented on in 9 N.Y. Univ.L.Q.Rev. 502 (1932); Feigenbaum v. Hizsnay, 187 App.Div. 126, 175 N.Y.S. 223 (1919).

24. Murray v. Marshall, 94 N.Y. 611 (1884); Spencer v. Spencer, 95 N.Y. 353 (1884); Zastrow v. Knight, 56 S.D. 554, 229 N.W. 925, 72 A.L.R. 379 (1930). See notes, 22 Va.L.Rev. 964 (1936) (discussing Commercial Casualty Insurance Co. v. Roman, 269 N.Y. 451, 199 N.E. 658 (1936) in which the mortgagor was held for a deficiency equal to the amount that the mortgage debt exceeded the value of the land at the time of the extension); 4 U. of Chi.L.Rev. 469, 478 (1937); 10 Not.D.Law. 83 (1934); 5 Br.Rul.Cas. 633 (1916). See also 41 A.L.R. 277, 292 (1926); 72 A.L.R. 389, 394 (1931); 81 A.L.R. 1016, 1021 (1932); 112 A.L.R. 1324, 1331 (1938). As was stated before, this amount was urged as the proper measure in both assumption and non-assump-tion cases. Williston, Contracts, § 386 (3rd Ed. 1959). But see Glassie, The Assuming Vendee, 9 Va.L.Rev. 196, 205, n. 36 (1923). "With submission, this [discharge equal to value of land at time of extension] does not help in a practical sense. For it introduces the most gaseous of all questions of fact—the value of land at some time other than that of a sale." See also Stevens, Extension Agreements in the "Subject-to" Mortgage Situation, 15 U. of Cin.L.Rev. 58, 74 (1941).

25. See Zastrow v. Knight, 56 S.D. 554, 564, 229 N.W. 925, 930, 72 A.L.R. 379 (1930).

26. Meldola v. Furlong, 142 Misc. 562, 255 N.Y.S. 48 (1932); Commercial Casualty Insurance Co. v. Roman, 269 N.Y. 451, 199 N.E. 658 (1936), amended 270 N.Y. 563, 200 N.E. 319; Mutual Benefit Life Insurance Co. v. Lindley, 97 Ind.App. 575, 183 N.E. 127 (1933), commented on in, 33 Col.L.Rev. 368 (1933), 81 U. of Pa.L.Rev. 641 (1933).

27. Mutual Benefit Life Insurance Co. v. Lindley, 97 Ind.App. 575, 183 N.E. 127 (1932), noted 33 Col.L.Rev. 368 (1933) and,

Releases of Obligation or Security

Release by the mortgagee of the personal obligation of an assuming grantee operates, in jurisdictions following suretyship ideas, to discharge the mortgagor completely.[28] Even if the mortgagor and assuming grantee were regarded as co-principals, the same result would follow from the general rule that the release of one joint and several debtor discharges the others.[29]

The effect of the release of the mortgaged property in the hands of an assuming grantee or one who took it subject to the mortgage is not so clear cut. The general rule of suretyship law is that when a secured creditor surrenders to the debtor, negligently loses, or damages the security it discharges a surety to the extent of the value so lost.[30] This same reasoning has been applied to releases of the mortgaged property, completely or in part, in the hands of grantees who assumed or took subject to the mortgage.[31] Other courts, however, refusing to inquire

81 U. of Pa.L.Rev. 641 (1933). "In fact, one cannot imagine a stronger presumption. Whoever heard of a man deliberately lending upon inadequate security, in the absence of a special reason." Glenn, Mortgages, § 277.

28. Gilliam v. McLemore, 141 Miss. 253, 106 So. 99, 43 A.L.R. 79 (1925); Merriam v. Miles, 54 Neb. 566, 74 N.W. 861, 69 Am.St.Rep. 731 (1898); Insley v. Webb, 122 Wash. 98, 209 P. 1093, 41 A.L.R. 274 (1922). The release from a deficiency judgment of a purchaser who assumed the mortgage discharges the mortgagor. Wagoner v. Brady, 221 App.Div. 405, 223 N.Y.S. 99 (1927), discussed in note, 41 Harv.L.Rev. 261 (1927); note, 93 Cent.L.J. 183 (1921). Getting a deficiency judgment against the mortgagor alone which, under a local statute, barred obtaining a similar judgment against the assuming grantee, is ground for setting aside the judgment. Tousey v. Barber, 132 Misc. 861, 231 N.Y.S. 133 (1928), discussed in note, 42 Harv.L.Rev. 583 (1929). See 41 A.L.R. 277, 311 (1926); 72 A.L.R. 389, 398, 399 (1931); 81 A.L.R. 1016, 1025 (1932); 112 A.L.R. 1324, 1343 (1938). See also, Arant, Suretyship, § 49. It might be expected that jurisdictions following the derivative theory of the mortgagee's personal rights against an assuming grantee would not discharge a mortgagor by reason of a purported release by the mortgagee of his rights against such a grantee since he would not have anything to release. See 88 U. of Pa.L.Rev. 611, 615 (1940). But there are cases to the contrary. Herd v. Tuohy, 133 Cal. 55, 65 P. 139 (1901); Codman v. Deland, 231 Mass. 344, 121 N.E. 14 (1918); Reeves v. Cordes, 108 N.J.Eq. 469, 155 A. 547 (1931).

29. See Williston, Contracts, § 334 (3d Ed. 1959).

30. Security, Restatement, § 132. See Arant, Suretyship, §§ 62, 63.

31. Woodward v. Brown, 119 Cal. 283, 51 P. 2, 63 Am.St.Rep. 108 (1897), modified 119 Cal. 283, 51 P. 542, 63 Am.St.Rep. 108; Mann v. Bugbee, 113 N.J.Eq. 434, 167 A. 202 (1933); see 41 A.L.R. 277, 306 (1926); 72 A.L.R. 389 (1931); 81 A.L.R. 1016, 1025 (1932); 112 A.L.R. 1324, 1343 (1938). Similarly, a mortgagee who fails to record his mortgage and thus permits a grantee of the mortgagor to sell the full title to the property to a bona fide purchaser cannot enforce the mortgage debt against the mortgagor. Hampe v. Manke, 28 S.D. 501, 134 N.W. 60 (1912). However, a mortgagee has been held to have a right to a deficiency judgment against the mortgagor in spite of his knowledge of the commission of waste by the mortgagor's grantee. Damiano v. Bergen County Land Co., 118 N.J.Eq. 535, 180 A. 489 (1935), commented on in 36 Col.Rev. 328 (1936). But the mortgagor was discharged in Lynn Five Cents Bank v. Portnoy, 306 Mass. 436, 28 N.E.2d 418 (1940), where the mortgagee consented to the guarantee making wasteful changes in the premises. An increase in the amount of the mortgage debt by an agreement between the mortgagee and the mortgagor's grantee discharges the mortgagor to the extent of the increase. Union Bank of Brooklyn v. Rubenstein, 78 Misc. 461, 138 N.Y.S. 644 (1912), commented on in note, 13 Col.L.Rev. 238 (1913).

into the extent of the injury caused by the giving up of security, give a complete discharge to the mortgagor even where there has been a release of only part of the mortgaged property.[32]　One New York decision [33] exemplifies this latter approach.　There a mortgagee authorized a subsequent purchaser from an assuming grantee to demolish a building and, in addition, gave a release of the mortgage lien to the assuming grantee as to that part of the mortgaged land that the grantee had not sold.　Later the mortgagee foreclosed and sought a deficiency judgment against the original mortgagors.　The court held that in view of the fact that the mortgagors had not consented to the building destruction and lien release, they were completely discharged as to the mortgage debt.

Increase in Mortgage Interest Rate

During the period of rising interest rates of the past two decades and the advent of the due-on-sale clause, which affords a mortgagee the right to accelerate the mortgage debt if the property is transferred without the mortgagee's consent,[34] it has become increasingly common for the mortgagee to condition consent on the grantee's willingness to pay a higher mortgage interest rate.　This practice has created problems for careless mortgagees because courts are increasingly applying the suretyship principles considered earlier in this section as a basis for holding that such interest rate adjustments, without the consent of the original mortgagor, releases him or her from personal liability on the mortgage debt.[35]　As one court explained, "this should come as no surprise since the mortgagor occupies the position of a surety, and the law of suretyship provides that a surety is entitled to stand on the strict letter of the contract upon which he is liable, and where he does not consent to a variation * * * it is fatal * * *.　Therefore, an agreement between the principals for a higher interest rate than called for in the original contract will, if made without the surety's consent release him from all liability." [36]

---

32. The release of the mortgaged property in the hands of an assuming grantee on the grantee's paying the full market value of the land to the mortgagee was held to give a complete defense to the mortgagor in Farmers' & Merchants' State Bank v. Tasche, 53 S.D. 603, 222 N.W. 139 (1928), criticized in note, 42 Harv.L.Rev. 712 (1929); Elsey v. People's Bank, 166 Ky. 386, 179 S.W. 392 (1915), noted, 1916, 16 Col.L.Rev. 165; In re Hunter's Estate, 257 Pa. 32, 101 A. 79 (1917), mortgagee takes risk that unreleased portion is of sufficient value to secure his debt; Albright v. Aliday, 37 S.W. 646 (Tex.Civ.App.1896), part only released; Brown v. Turner, 202 N.C. 227, 162 S.E. 608 (1932), discussed in note, 11 N.Car.L.Rev. 96 (1932) release of

part of the mortgaged premises; Restatement, Contracts, § 146, accord.　See Glenn, Mortgages, § 281, approving this result.

33. Lundquist v. Nelson, 57 A.D.2d 1045, 395 N.Y.S.2d 568 (1977).

34. See §§ 5.21–5.26 infra.

35. See First Federal Savings & Loan Association of Gary v. Arena, ___ Ind.App. ___, 406 N.E.2d 1279 (1980); Oellerich v. First Federal Savings & Loan Association, 552 F.2d 1109 (5th Cir.1977) (interpreting Georgia law).

36. First Federal Savings & Loan Association of Gary v. Arena, ___ Ind.App. ___, 406 N.E.2d 1279, 1284–1285 (1980).

Mortgagees, however, have the means to avoid such results. First, they can include in the original mortgage a reservation of the right to make interest rate modifications as to subsequent grantees. Such reservations, however, may not be a complete panacea because they are likely to be construed strictly against the mortgagee.[37] Better, the mortgagee should obtain the written consent to the interest rate increase from the mortgagor at the time of the proposed transfer. Such consent will usually be forthcoming because the mortgagor in such a situation will typically be eager to facilitate the sale of his or her real estate.

Suppose that instead of releasing a subsequent grantee, the mortgagee releases the original mortgagor of personal liability on the mortgage debt. A recent Washington case, MGIC Financial Corp. v. H.A. Briggs Co.,[38] is interesting in this regard. In that case mortgagor was liable on a $1.42 million dollar debt secured by a mortgage on several parcels of land. Later one of the parcels was conveyed to grantees for approximately $8,000. The latter took subject to the mortgage. When the mortgagor later got into financial difficulty, the mortgagor and the mortgagee entered into an agreement under which the mortgagor gave a deed in lieu of foreclosure covering all parcels then owned by the mortgagor and the latter was released from all personal liability on the mortgage debt. After the mortgagee then sought to foreclose on the grantees' parcel, the Court of Appeals of Washington ultimately held that the prior release of the mortgagor operated to free the grantees' parcel from the mortgage. According to the court, this result was justified by the "spirit" of the suretyship rules that release an original mortgagor-surety when a mortgagee releases an assuming grantee-principal of personal liability. "When the mortgagee released the mortgagor from personal liability * * *, it released the principal debtor from liability on a deficiency judgment without the consent of the surety. Equity requires that the surety [the grantees], likewise be released from the burden of having to forfeit their land to satisfy a debt for which the principal debtor already has been released."[39] The mortgagee argued that the release of the mortgagor's personal obligation created an insufficient prejudice to the grantees because "they could not have paid off the debt in the first place and * * * even if they had paid the debt, they would have been subrogated to nothing more than the dubious right to seek a personal judgment against a bankrupt [mortgagor]."[40] According to the court, however, no "minimum requirement of legal detriment" need be shown. "It is sufficient that there was a release, without which the grantees could have paid off the note and been subrogated to whatever rights [mortgagee] had against [the mortgagor] in federal bankruptcy court."[41]

37. See id.; Friedman, Discharge of Personal Liability on Mortgage Debts in New York, 52 Yale L.J. 771, 788 (1943).

38. 24 Wn.App. 1, 600 P.2d 573 (1979).

39. Id. at 24 Wn.App. 3, 600 P.2d 577.

40. Id.

41. Id.

The result in *Briggs* is probably justifiable, at least if the grantees $8,000 payment represents the full purchase price of their parcel. Whenever a grantee pays the full price without making an arrangement for the release of the parcel from the blanket mortgage, it is usually because the grantees were unsophisticated and unrepresented by competent counsel. Thus, in *Briggs* the court probably concluded that as against a large institutional mortgagee, it would be unfair to make the grantees foreclosure sale losers.

However, the court's suretyship analysis seems flawed. The problem with using the "spirit" of the grantee release cases is that in a subject-to transfer, the mortgagor typically is deemed to be a surety and the land, the principal.[42] Consequently, to characterize the grantee as a surety is logically difficult.

The *Briggs* result, however, is perhaps justifiable on two other theories. If, in fact, the mortgagor received the full value of the grantees' parcel, it could be argued that the mortgagor, implicitly, if not specifically, agreed to undertake the removal of the mortgage lien from it. Under such circumstances, it would further be argued, the mortgagor became a principal and the land the surety.[43] Finally, it seems logical, under such reasoning, to conclude that the release of the mortgagor-principal should free the land from the burden of the mortgage.

Alternatively, a marshalling principle may be applicable. Under the inverse order of alienation concept, where a grantee acquires his or her parcel on terms which impose on the mortgagor the primary obligation of paying the blanket mortgage debt, the land in the hands of the grantee, although still liable, stands merely in the position of surety.[44] Under such circumstances, the grantee has a right to have the remaining property in the hands of the mortgagor exonerate the grantee's parcel.[45] Since the mortgagee in *Briggs* took a deed in lieu of foreclosure as to the other parcels covered by the blanket mortgage it could be argued that, in so doing, it thwarted the grantees' marshalling right to have the value of the mortgagor's retained land tested by a foreclosure sale. Such a sale might well have disclosed that the retained land (covered by the deed in lieu) was indeed sufficiently valuable to pay the full balance on the debt. Since this right was denied to the grantees, it is arguably only fair to compensate them by releasing their parcel from the mortgage.

 WESTLAW REFERENCES
266k283(3)

Extensions of Time
additional extend*** extension extra /4 agreement binding time /p
   buyer grantee purchaser transferee /p mortgagee

42. See § 5.3 supra.   **44.** See § 10.10 infra.

43. See § 5.13 supra.   **45.** Id.

```
additional extend*** extension extra  /4  agreement binding time  /p
    (damage*  /5  establish! proof prove) depreciat*** valu!  /p
    mortgag**
```

Releases of Obligation or Security

```
synopsis, digest(releas***  /s  mortgag** obligation security  /p
    buyer grantee purchaser transferee)
```

Increase in Mortgage Interest Rate

```
releas*** surety!  /p  higher increas*** rais***  /s  "interest rate"
    /p  mortgag**
releas***  /s  grantor mortgagor seller transferor  /p  marshall***
266k283(2)
```

---

§ 5.20 Effect of the Uniform Commercial Code on Suretyship Defenses

Where the mortgage secures a negotiable instrument, the impact of an extension or release granted by a mortgagee is governed by Section 3–606 of the Uniform Commercial Code (UCC). Under the Negotiable Instruments Law, the UCC's predecessor, the weight of authority held that the usual suretyship defenses were unavailable to the mortgagor.[1] On the other hand, under the UCC those suretyship defenses are probably available[2] and, for the most part, the rules governing the discharge of the mortgagor are probably identical to those considered in the preceding section. Section 3–606(1) provides:

"The holder discharges any party to the instrument to the extent that without such party's consent the holder

(a) without express reservation of rights releases or agrees not to sue any person against whom the party has to the knowledge of the holder a right of recourse or agrees to suspend the right to enforce against such person the instrument or collateral or otherwise discharges such person, except that failure or delay in effecting any required presentment, protest or notice of dishonor with respect to any such person does not discharge any party as to whom presentment, protest or notice of dishonor is effective or unnecessary; or

(b) unjustifiably impairs any collateral for the instrument given by or on behalf of the party or any person against whom he has a right of recourse."

§ 5.20

1. Mortgage Guaranty Co. v. Chotiner, 8 Cal.2d 110, 64 P.2d 138, 108 A.L.R. 1080 (1936), commented on, 10 So.Cal.L.Rev. 511 (1937); Continental Mutual Savings Bank v. Elliott, 166 Wash. 283, 6 P.2d 638, 81 A.L.R. 1005 (1932), commented on in, 19 Va.L.Rev. 618 (1933); 2 Idaho L.J. 143 (1932); 17 Minn.L.Rev. 220 (1933); Peter v. Finzer, 116 Neb. 380, 217 N.W. 612, 65 A.L.R. 1418 (1928) noted in 42 Harv.L.Rev. 136 (1928); 6 Neb.L.Bull. 417 (1928); 26 Mich.L.Rev. 929 (1928); 12 Minn.L.Rev. 668 (1928); Washer v. Tontar, 128 Ohio St. 111, 190 N.E. 231 (1934).

2. White and Summers, Uniform Commercial Code, § 13–14 (2nd Ed. 1980). Clark, Suretyship in the Uniform Commercial Code, 46 Tex.L.Rev. 453, 457 (1968).

In focusing on the key language of the above provision, note that absent the surety's consent, if the holder "releases or agrees not to sue * * * or agrees to suspend the right to enforce * * * the instrument or collateral * * * or otherwise discharges * * *" the principal debtor, the surety is discharged. Note also that a discharge may be asserted even though the principal debtor is not a party to the instrument.[3] Thus, although the matter is not free from doubt, Section 3–606 probably authorizes most of the suretyship defenses that we considered in the preceding section, including extension of time for payment by the principal debtor, release of the principal debtor from liability and release of the security interest.[4] Moreover, the language "any person against whom the party has to the knowledge of the holder a right of recourse" seems "clearly broad enough to include not only 'personal' principal debtors such as assuming grantees, but also 'real' principal debtors such as grantees who expressly take subject to the mortgage without assuming it."[5]

The UCC and the suretyship concepts considered in the preceding section differ, however, in one important respect. While an express reservation of rights against the mortgagor included in the original mortgage may operate to prevent discharge of the mortgagor,[6] we saw that a similar reservation in the extension or modification agreement normally will not prevent discharge.[7] On the other hand, where the UCC is applicable, while the blanket mortgage reservation clause is probably ineffective to prevent discharge, the mortgagee can reserve his rights against the mortgagor-surety by adding an "express reservation" of those rights to the extension agreement or agreement releasing the grantee.[8] It should be noted, however, that the mortgagee is not

3. White and Summer, supra Note 3 at 524. Comment 1 to Section 3–606 states: "The suretyship defences here provided are not limited to parties who are 'secondarily liable' but are available to any party who is in the position of a surety, having a right of recourse either on the instrument or dehors it, * * *."

4. There has been confusion under Section 3–606 as to which persons may assert suretyship defenses. While the literal language encompasses "any party to the instrument", there is case authority that only accommodation parties and not makers or co-makers may assert suretyship defenses. See Main Bank of Chicago v. Baker, 86 Ill.2d 188, 56 Ill.Dec. 14, 427 N.E.2d 94 (1981); Wohlhuter v. St. Charles Lumber & Fuel Co., 62 Ill.2d 16, 388 N.E.2d 179 (1975). Cf. Commerce Union Bank v. Davis, 581 S.W.2d 142 (Tenn.App.1979). An accommodation party is "one who signs the instrument in any capacity for the purpose of lending his name to another party to it." U.C.C. § 3–415. Since most mortgagors initially are principally liable on the mort-

gage debt and only become sureties after the transfer of the mortgaged land, a narrow definition of the word "party" to include only accommodation parties would prevent most mortgagors from asserting suretyship defenses. Nevertheless, as Professors White and Summers have pointed out, "if the draftsmen intended 3–606 to apply only to accommodation parties, they did not say so." White and Summers, Uniform Commercial Code 524, n.125 (2d Ed. 1980). Moreover, there is both case law and significant scholarly commentary to support the use of suretyship defenses by mortgagors under Section 3–606. See Philco Finance Co. v. Patton, 248 Or. 310, 432 P.2d 686 (1967); Cunningham and Tischler, Transfer of the Real Estate Mortgagor's Interest, 27 Rutgers L.Rev. 24, 68 (1973).

5. Cunningham and Tischler, supra note 4 at 68–69.

6. See § 5.19 supra.

7. Id.

8. See Stanley v. Ames, 378 Mass. 364, 391 N.E.2d 908, 910 (1979); White and

authorized by the UCC to reserve his rights to avoid discharge when he authorizes the impairment of collateral (security).[9]

 WESTLAW REFERENCES
u.c.c. "uniform commercial" 3–606 /p grantor mortgagor seller transferor surety!

B. RESTRICTIONS ON TRANSFER BY THE MORTGAGOR

§ 5.21 The Due-on Clauses—Introduction

The law of real property usually develops in an evolutionary fashion. Change is often measured in terms of decades and centuries rather than in months and years. Yet economic turmoil can accelerate this process. Just as the Great Depression of the 1930s spurred the enactment of mortgage moratoria and antideficiency legislation,[1] so too has the inflationary economic climate of the 1970s and early 1980s engendered new mortgage law.

The major focus of this latter period has been on the due-on-sale clause, a mortgage provision that affords the mortgagee the right to accelerate the mortgage debt and to foreclose if the mortgaged real estate is transferred without the mortgagee's consent.[2] While the clause is sometimes used to protect mortgagees against transfers that endanger mortgage security or increase the risk of default, its major purpose is to enable mortgagees to recall lower-than-market interest rate loans during periods of rising interest rates.[3] Because its use in this context pits lenders against borrowers and real estate buyers, the clause has become a major economic, political, and legal issue. It has been confronted and evaluated by most state supreme courts,[4] many legislatures,[5] certain federal regulatory agencies,[6] the United States Supreme Court,[7] and ultimately Congress.[8] It has also been the subject of a great deal of scholarly commentary.[9]

Summers, supra note 2 § 13–15; Cunningham and Tischler, supra note 4 at 69.

9. White and Summers, supra note 2 at 525–527.

§ 5.21

1. See G. Osborne, Mortgages § 333 (2d ed. 1970).

2. A typical due-on-sale clause provides: "If all or any part of the Property or an interest therein is sold or transferred by Borrower without Lender's prior written consent, ∗ ∗ ∗ Lender may, at Lender's option, declare all the sums secured by this mortgage to be due and payable." Federal National Mortgage Association/Federal Home Loan Mortgage Corporation Mortgage, Clause 17 (one to four family) [hereinafter cited as FNMA/FHLMC Mortgage].

3. See Volkmer, The Application of Restraints on Alienation Doctrine to Real Property Security Interests, 58 Iowa L.Rev. 747, 769 (1973). The clause usually does not mention interest rate increases per se, but the lender will frequently use the threat of acceleration as leverage to exact from the transferee an agreement to pay a higher interest rate.

4. See § 5.22 infra.

5. See § 5.23 infra.

6. See § 5.24 infra.

7. See § 5.24 infra.

8. See § 5.25 infra.

9. See Gorinson & Manishin, Garn-St. Germain: A Harbinger of Change, 40 Wash. & Lee L.Rev. 1313 (1983); Nelson &

Given recent economic conditions, this close scrutiny is hardly surprising. Due to high interest rates and the limited availability of home financing, large numbers of potential home buyers have been excluded from the housing market.[10] For many purchasers, the assumption of an existing lower-than-market interest mortgage has represented one of the few practical financing alternatives. The financial climate has also made it much more difficult for owners to sell. Many sellers have been forced either to reduce significantly the price of their properties to enable buyers to qualify for institutional high-interest financing, or to suffer an effective price reduction by financing part of the purchase price themselves at lower-than-market interest rates. Thus, for those sellers with lower-than-market interest rate mortgages on their properties, assumability of the mortgage may be the key to obtaining a higher asking price for the property.[11]

Whitman, Congressional Preemption of Mortgage Due-on-Sale Law: An Analysis of the Garn-St. Germain Act, 35 Hast.L.J. 241 (1983); Comment, Section 341 of the Garn-St. Germain Depository Institutions Act of 1982: An End to the Due-on-Sale Controversy?, 14 Tol.L.Rev. 1427 (1983); Note, The Due-On-Sale Controversy: Beneficial Effects of the Garn-St. Germain Depository Institution Act of 1982, 1984 Duke L.J. 121 (1984); Ashley, Use of "Due-On" Clauses to Gain Collateral Benefits: A Common Sense Defense, 10 Tulsa L.J. 590 (1975); Bonanno, Due on Sale and Prepayment Clauses in Real Estate Financing in California in Times of Fluctuating Interest Rates—Legal Issues and Alternatives, 6 U.S.F.L.Rev. 267 (1972); Hetland, Real Property and Real Property Security: The Well-Being of the Law, 53 Calif.L.Rev. 151 (1965); Maxwell, The Due-On-Sale Clause: Restraints on Abenation and Adhesion Theory in California, 28 U.C.L.A.L.Rev. 197 (1982); Segreti, The Borrower as Servant of the Lender: Enforcement of Mortgage Due-on-Sale Clauses, 51 U.Cin.L.Rev. 779 (1982); Volkmer, The Application of the Restraints on Alienation Doctrine to Real Property Security Interests, 58 Iowa L.Rev. 747 (1973); Comment, The Future of the Due-On-Sale Clause in Alabama, 33 Ala.L. Rev. 83 (1981); Comment, Mortgages—A Catalogue and Critique on the Role of Equity in the Enforcement of Modern-Day "Due-on-Sale" Clauses, 26 Ark.L.Rev. 485 (1973); Comment, Applying the Brakes to Accelera Clauses: Controlling Their Misuse in Real Property Secured Transactions, 9 Cal.W.L.Rev. 514 (1973); Comment, Beyond Tucker v. Lassen: The Future of the Due-on-Sale Clause in California, 27 Hastings L.J. 475 (1975); Comment, South Dakota's Approach to the Due-on-Sale Clause: An Analysis of Automatic Enforcement, 27 S.D.L.Rev. 261 (1982); Comment, Judicial Treatment of the Due-on-Sale Clause: The Case for Adopting Standards of Reasonableness and Unconscionability, 27 Stan.L. Rev. 1109 (1975); Note, Property—The Demise of the Due-on-Sale Clause, 64 Calif.L. Rev. 573 (1976); Note, Mortgages—Due-on-Sale Clause: Restraint on Alienation—Enforceability, 28 Case W.Res.L.Rev. 493 (1978); Note, Due on Sale and Due on Encumbrance Clauses in California, 7 Loy. L.A.L.Rev. 306 (1974); Note, Deeds of Trust—Restraints Against Alienation-Due-on Clause is an Unreasonable Restraint on Alienation Absent a Showing of Protection of Mortgagee's Legitimate Interests, 47 Miss.L.J. 331 (1976); Note, Mortgages—Use of Due on Sale Clause by a Lender is Not a Restraint on Alienation in North Carolina, 55 N.C.L.Rev. 310 (1977); Note, The Due-on-Sale Clause: Enforcement Standards, 60 Neb.L.Rev. 594 (1981); Note, Due-on-Sale Clauses: Separating Social Interests From Individual Interests, 35 Vand. L.Rev. 357 (1982).

10. See, e.g., The Great Housing Collapse, Newsweek, Mar. 29, 1982, at 61–62.

11. See, Williams v. First Federal Savings & Loan Association, 651 F.2d 910 (4th Cir.1981), where the court suggested that real estate that would sell for $100,000, assuming the buyer obtained new 30-year, fixed rate first mortgage financing at 15% per annum, would sell for $115,000 if the buyer were able to assume an existing $50,000 fixed rate mortgage at 10% with a remaining term of 27 years. Id. at 915 n.8. For further consideration of the seller's situation, see Note, Separating Interests, supra note 9, at 376. See also Sirmans, Sirmans & Smith, The Effect of Assumption Financing on Residential Property Values, 16 Fed. Home Loan Bank Board J.,

On the other hand, the economic stake of institutional lenders in upholding due-on-sale clauses is also great. During the past several years many institutional lenders, especially savings and loan associations, have experienced severe economic difficulty. Because they hold portfolios that include large numbers of fixed rate, lower-yielding mortgage loans, they have been hard pressed to pay the higher short-term rates demanded by depositors.[12] Many savings and loan associations and similar institutions have failed, and others remain in precarious financial positions.[13] Because the due-on-sale clause provides one means of eliminating lower-interest mortgage loans from institutional portfolios, and does so without resort to expensive federal "bailout" or other subsidy schemes, its enforceability has been deemed important for the economic health of the thrift industry.[14]

Other policy arguments have been utilized to buttress due-on-sale enforceability. First, one arguably should focus on the reasonable expectations of the mortgagor at the time a mortgage loan is first made. Usually, at least in the residential setting, the borrower is concerned most with his immediate cost, i.e., the interest rate and how much his monthly payment is going to be. Normally, he will not be concerned with his mortgage as a method for facilitating a future sale of his home. In other words, perhaps it is simply unwise to conceive of a method utilized to *acquire* a home as also a device to *facilitate its sale.* Second, the enforcement of due-on-sale clauses tends to reduce the discrimination that otherwise exists in favor of those buyers who are fortunate enough to find a low interest loan to assume against those who are forced to obtain new mortgage financing. Indeed, because existing low interest loans have been paid down to some extent, and because of

Aug. 1983, at 22 (suggesting that home sellers capture only about 35% of the value of their assumable below-market-rate loans).

12. This problem has been with the thrift industry at least since the first major post-war interest rate upswing in 1966. See, e.g., Staff of Senate Comm. on Banking, Housing and Urban Affairs, 92d Cong., 1st Sess., Federal National Mortgage Association Public Meeting on Conventional Mortgage Forms 203–04 (Comm. Print 1971) (statement of the Executive Vice President of the California Savings and Loan League); see also infra notes 13–14.

13. The Federal Savings and Loan Insurance Corporation, which bears the responsibility for salvaging or liquidating failed savings and loan associations carrying deposit insurance, placed 14 associations in receivership during 1982. All but one of these insolvencies were resolved by mergers with other associations (the remaining one was liquidated). In all, there were 210 "supervisory mergers" of finan-

cially troubled associations during 1982. Of those, 44 required financial assistance from the FSLIC to compensate for the weakness of one of the merger partners. These statistics are higher than for any previous year. See Federal Home Loan Bank Board Annual Report 1982, 16 Fed. Home Loan Bank Board J., Apr. 1983, at 13–20.

14. "[T]he [savings and loan associations'] practice of borrowing short and lending long, * * * combined with rising interest rates, has increased the cost of funds to these institutions and reduced their income. Exercising due-on-sale clauses enables savings and loan associations to alleviate this problem by replacing long-term, low yield loans with loans at the prevailing interest rates and thereby to avoid increasing interest rates across the board." Fidelity Federal Savings & Loan Association v. de la Cuesta, 458 U.S. 141, 168, 102 S.Ct. 3014, 3030, 73 L.Ed.2d 664 (1982).

inflation in the value of real estate, those who are able to assume an existing loan generally will be those who can come up with a significant amount of cash, whereas those who are not so fortunate in this regard will be forced to obtain new financing at higher market interest rates. Thus, to the extent that due-on-sale clauses are not enforced, an inordinate interest rate advantage may be afforded to higher net worth buyers over those who are less fortunate.[15]

Due-on-Encumbrance Restrictions

Mortgages may restrict mortgagor transfers by means other than a due-on-sale clause.[16] For example, a mortgage may contain a clause authorizing the mortgagee to accelerate the debt if the mortgagor "further encumbers" the mortgaged real estate. Such language is usually referred to as a "due-on-encumbrance" provision.[17] While due-on-encumbrance language is often included as part of a due-on-sale clause,[18] it is not uncommon for a mortgage to contain a separate due-on-encumbrance clause.[19] Unlike the due-on-sale situation, in which the mortgagee's desire to increase the interest rate predominates, due-on-encumbrance language is utilized mainly to protect against impairment of mortgage security by a debtor who incurs a junior mortgage debt and thus reduces his or her economic stake in the mortgaged real estate.[20] However, the due-on-encumbrance clause probably is used much less frequently than its due-on-sale counterpart.[21]

15. See Cassidy, Monte Carlo Simulation Estimates of the Expected Value of the Due-on-Sale Clause in Home Mortgages, 2 Housing Fin. Rev. 33 (1983), estimating that prohibition of due-on-sale enforcement would result in mortgage interest rates 0.3% to 0.8% higher than without the prohibition.

16. For an unusual illustration, see Investors Savings & Loan Association v. Ganz, 174 N.J.Super. 356, 361, 416 A.2d 918, 921–22 (1980) (upholding a clause giving the mortgagee the right to accelerate if the property ceased to be owner-occupied).

17. See Volkmer, supra note 9, at 769.

18. For an example of this approach, consider the following clause: "Should trustor (mortgagor) sell, convey, transfer, dispose of, *or further encumber* said property, or any part thereof, or any interest therein, or agree so to do, without the written consent of the Beneficiary (mortgagee) being first obtained, then Beneficiary shall have the right at his option, to declare all sums secured hereby forthwith due and payable." Comment, Judicial Treatment, supra note 9, at 1110 n.5 (emphasis added).

19. See, e.g., Chilivis v. Tumlin Woods Realty Associates, Inc., 250 Ga. 179, 179, 297 S.E.2d 4, 4 (1982) ("If Grantor further encumbers the premises by any mortgages, loans or security deeds securing loans made to Grantor without notice to and prior written permission from Grantee (mortgagee), such will constitute an event of default.").

20. See Volkmer, supra note 9, at 769–70.

21. The mortgage form specified for use by lenders who sell mortgages to the Federal National Mortgage Association (FNMA) and the Federal Home Loan Mortgage Corporation (FHLMC) on the secondary market specifically excludes any restriction on further encumbrances: "If all or any part of the Property or an interest therein is sold or transferred by Borrower without Lender's prior written consent, excluding (a) the creation of a lien or encumbrance subordinate to this Mortgage * * * Lender may, at Lender's option, declare all the sums secured by this mortgage to be due and payable." FNMA/FHLMC Mortgage, supra note 2, Clause 17 (one to four family).

Increased-Interest-on-Transfer Clauses

Another provision closely related to the due-on-sale clause authorizes the mortgagee to increase or adjust the mortgage interest rate in the event of a transfer by the mortgagor. We refer to this as an "increased-interest-on transfer" clause.[22] This type of clause fulfills the same economic function as the due-on-sale clause in that it enables the mortgagee to use a transfer by the mortgagor as the basis for increasing the interest yield on the mortgage. However, unlike a due-on-sale clause, it does not confer on the mortgagee an absolute right to accelerate the mortgage debt upon a transfer; hence it gives no direct protection against transfer to an uncreditworthy buyer. Only if the transferee fails to pay the increased mortgage payments will there be grounds for declaration of a default and acceleration of the debt.

Installment Land Contract Prohibitions on Transfer

Transfer restrictions may also appear in installment land contracts, which are probably the most commonly used mortgage substitute.[23] Known in many areas of the country as a "contract for deed" or "long term land contract," the installment land contract performs the same economic function as a purchase-money mortgage: it provides seller financing of all or part of the unpaid real estate purchase price.[24] Vendors often find the installment land contract attractive because of its forfeiture clause—language specifying that "time is of the essence" and that upon vendee default in payment or other contract obligations the vendor has the option to terminate the contract, retake possession of the premises, and retain all prior payments as liquidated damages.[25] However, in many jurisdictions legislatures and courts have placed restrictions on the forfeiture remedy, especially when the vendee has acquired substantial equity in the property.[26] Other jurisdictions have gone so far as to treat the installment land contract as a mortgage, thus affording the vendee the traditional substantive and procedural rights

22. A recent example of an "increased interest on transfer clause" provides: "the Mortgagees hereby agree that the Mortgagors may assign this Purchase Money Mortgage, but the rate of interest, at the time of assignment, shall be adjusted upward to correspond with the prevailing interest rate of banks, savings and loan associations, and other mortgage lenders in the community." O'Connell v. Dockendorff, 415 So.2d 35, 36 (Fla.App.1982). See also Miller v. Pacific First Federal Savings & Loan Association, 86 Wn.2d 401, 402, 545 P.2d 546, 547 (1976).

23. See, Randall v. Riel, 123 N.H. 757, 465 A.2d 505, 507 (1983) (citing Nelson & Whitman, The Installment Land Contract—A National Viewpoint, 1977 B.Y. U.L.Rev. 541).

24. See § 3.26 supra; Nelson & Whitman, The Installment Land Contract—A National Viewpoint, 1977 B.Y.U.L.Rev. 541, 541.

25. Id. at 542. See also Jenkins v. Wise, 58 Hawaii 592, 596, 574 P.2d 1337, 1341 (1978); Sebastian v. Floyd, 585 S.W.2d 381, 382 (Ky.App.1979); Comment, Forfeiture: The Anomaly of the Land Sale Contract, 41 Albany L.Rev. 71, 72 (1977).

26. See, e.g., Arizona Rev.Stat. §§ 33, 741–742; Iowa Code Ann. §§ 656.1–.6; Minn.Stat.Ann. § 559.21. See also §§ 3.28, 3.29 supra.

of a mortgagor, including the right to a public sale after a judicial foreclosure proceeding.[27]

Installment land contracts frequently include a provision that prohibits assignment by the vendee without the vendor's permission.[28] Violation of such a provision constitutes a default and might result in vendor termination of the contract and loss of the purchaser's equity. In this respect the provision differs from a due-on-sale clause, under which an unapproved transfer will at most trigger an acceleration of the mortgage debt and, if the accelerated debt is unpaid, a public foreclosure sale of the mortgaged real estate.[29]

Events Triggering Acceleration

A common question is what kind of event will trigger acceleration of a debt under a due-on-sale or other transfer restriction clause. While some early clauses used a "sale" alone as the triggering event, most of the recent forms employ broader language, often modeled after the mortgage form specified for use by lenders who sell mortgages to the Federal National Mortgage Association (FNMA) and the Federal Home Loan Mortgage Corporation (FHLMC). This language refers to a transfer of any part of the property or any interest in it.[30] Under such language, in principle at least, even a short-term lease [31] or a grant of an easement or other limited interest in the land would suffice to trigger the lender's right to accelerate.

Perhaps the most significant question is whether a sale by installment land contract permits acceleration. The answer depends on the exact wording of the clause in question,[32] but under broad language like

27. See, e.g., Skendzel v. Marshall, 261 Ind. 226, 301 N.E.2d 641 (1973), certiorari denied 415 U.S. 921, 94 S.Ct. 1421, 39 L.Ed. 2d 476 (1974), appeal after remand 264 Ind. 77, 339 N.E.2d 57 (1975); Sebastian v. Floyd, 585 S.W.2d 381 (Ky.App.1979); Bean v. Walker, 95 A.D.2d 70, 464 N.Y.S.2d 895 (1983); 16 Okla.Stat. § 11a. See § 3.29 supra.

28. See Volkmer, supra note 9, at 753 n.34.

29. In the context of the traditional restraint-on-alienation analysis considered later in this chapter, see infra § 5.22, the "no-transfer" provision probably represents a forfeiture type of direct restraint.

30. See supra note 2 for the text of the due-on-sale clause found in the FNMA/ FHLMC Mortgage.

31. But see FNMA/FHLMC Mortgage, supra note 2 (expressly exempting leases for less than three years which include no option to purchase).

32. In Tucker v. Lassen Savings & Loan Association, 12 Cal.3d 629, 116 Cal.Rptr.

633, 526 P.2d 1169 (1974), for example, a sale by installment contract under a clause as broad as that of the FNMA/FHLMC was held not to trigger acceleration. Id. at 638–39, 526 P.2d at 1174, 116 Cal.Rptr. at 639–40. The court felt enforcing the clause would constitute an unreasonable restraint on alienation where the vendor retained legal title under the contract and the vendor's legitimate interest was not threatened. Id. at 637, 116 Cal.Rptr. at 639, 526 P.2d at 1174. This distinction between installment and "outright" sales was subsequently discarded by the California Supreme Court in Wellenkamp v. Bank of America, 21 Cal.3d 943, 950, 148 Cal. Rptr. 379, 383, 582 P.2d 970, 974 (1978). See Income Realty & Mortgage, Inc. v. Columbia Savings & Loan Association, 661 P.2d 257, 260 (Colo.1983) (rejecting any distinction between installment and "outright" sales on policy grounds). It is doubtful that today any court would follow the distinction.

that of the FNMA/FHLMC clause the courts have nearly uniformly permitted acceleration.[33]

Congress, responding to the financial distress of many institutional lenders [34] after a decade of judicial, legislative, and regulatory turmoil at both the state and federal levels, attempted to resolve the controversy concerning due-on-sale clauses and related issues by enacting section 341 of the Garn-St. Germain Depository Institutions Act of 1982 (the Act).[35] While the Act generally favors due-on enforcement, it is complex and has created problems of its own. The following sections not only explore the Act in detail, but also focus on those aspects of earlier due-on law that either are fundamental to an understanding of the Act or are unaffected by it.

 WESTLAW REFERENCES
di due-on-sale clause
text (due-on-sale)

Due-on-Encumbrance Restrictions
"due on encumbrance"

Increased-Interest on Transfer Clauses
due "increased interest" /3 transfer /s clause

Installment Land Contract Prohibitions on Transfer
contract /3 deed (instalment installment long-term +1 land) /p
     assign! transfer! /s permi! prohibit!

---

33. See Income Realty & Mortgage, Inc. v. Columbia Savings & Loan Association, 661 P.2d 257, 259–60 (Colo.1983); Rustic Hills Shopping Plaza, Inc. v. Columbia Savings and Loan Association, 661 P.2d 254 (Colo.1983); Freedom Savings and Loan Association v. La Monte, 448 So.2d 51 (Fla. App.1984); Pioneer Federal Savings and Loan Association v. Reeder, 453 So.2d 126 (Fla.App.1984), decision approved and quashed in part ___ So.2d ___ (1985); Tucker Federal Savings & Loan Association v. Alford, 169 Ga.App. 38, 311 S.E.2d 229 (1983); Capitol Federal Savings & Loan Association v. Glenwood Manor, Inc., 235 Kan. 935, 686 P.2d 853 (1984); Century Federal Savings & Loan Association v. Van Glahn, 144 N.J.Super. 48, 50, 55, 364 A.2d 558, 563 (1976); In re Foreclosure of a Deed of Trust Given by Bill M. Taylor, 60 N.C.App. 134, 135, 298 S.E.2d 163, 165–66 (1982); Smith v. Frontier Federal Savings & Loan Association, 649 P.2d 536, 538 (Okl. 1982); New Home Federal Savings and Loan Association v. Trunk, 482 A.2d 625 (Pa.Super.1984); Lipps v. First American Service Corp., 223 Va. 131, 140, 286 S.E.2d 215, 216–17, 220 (1982); Mutual Federal Savings & Loan Association v. Wisconsin Wire Works, 58 Wis.2d 99, 101, 110, 205 N.W.2d 762, 769 (1973), appeal after remand 71 Wis.2d 531, 239 N.W.2d 20 (1976). But see Fidelity Federal Savings & Loan

Association v. Grieme, 112 Ill.App.3d 1014, 1019, 68 Ill.Dec. 558, 561, 446 N.E.2d 292, 295 (1983) (entering into agreement for deed held insufficient to trigger clause allowing lender to accelerate upon "change of ownership"); Peoples Federal Savings and Loan Association of East Chicago, Indiana v. Willsey, ___ Ind.App. ___, 466 N.E.2d 470 (1984) (transfer by contract for deed not a sale or conveyance for purposes of due-on-sale clause); First Federal Savings & Loan Association of Alexandria v. Botello, 725 F.2d 350 (5th Cir.1984) (contract for deed transaction not a "sale" or "transfer" for due-on-sale clause purposes under Louisiana law). Compare: Century Savings Association v. C. Michael Franke & Co., 9 Kan.App.2d 776, 689 P.2d 915 (1984) (contract for deed transfer deemed "transfer of title" for due-on-sale purposes).

34. See The Depository Institutions Amendments of 1982: Hearings on S. 2879, H.R. 4603, and H.R. 6267 Before the Subcomm. on Financial Institutions Supervision, Regulation and Insurance of the House Comm. on Banking, Finance and Urban Affairs, 97th Cong., 2d Sess. (1982) (containing the statements of representatives of savings and loan associations and banks); see also supra notes 13–14.

35. Pub.L. No. 97–320, 96 Stat. 1505 (codified at 12 U.S.C.A. § 1701j–3).

Events Triggering Acceleration

activat*** engage* trigger***   /s   accelerate*** due-on-sale   /p
    clause mortgage

---

§ 5.22   Due-on Clauses—Pre-Garn-St. Germain Act State Judicial and Legislative Response

Due-on-Sale Clauses

Due-on-sale clauses have come under judicial attack as unreasonable restraints on alienation.[1] Traditionally, a direct restraint on alienation has been viewed by many courts as invalid per se unless the restraint falls within certain limited exceptions.[2] Under a minority approach, a direct restraint is void unless the policy underlying its purpose outweighs the degree of restraint imposed on the property interest.[3] Indirect restraints, on the other hand, are generally deemed valid if they are reasonable.[4] An indirect restraint is one that arises "when an attempt is made to accomplish some purpose other than the restraint on alienability, but with the incidental result that . . . [it] would restrain practical alienability."[5] Thus, a mortgage that provides for forfeiture of the mortgaged real estate to the mortgagee upon an impermissible transfer probably constitutes a direct restraint.[6] To the extent that the mortgagee is able to enforce, through specific performance or injunctive relief, a mortgagor's promise not to convey without the mortgagee's consent, a promissory and presumably direct restraint exists.[7]

Under this analysis it is unclear whether the due-on-sale clause constitutes a direct or an indirect restraint on alienation. On the one hand, it can be argued that it constitutes an indirect restraint: enforcement of the clause will result in a foreclosure sale rather than a forfeiture of the mortgaged real estate to the mortgagee, and the due-on-sale mortgagee does not have an enforceable right to prevent the mortgagor from transferring the property.[8] Moreover, while the practical effect of the clause may be to discourage the mortgagor from selling the mortgaged real estate, its primary purpose is to confer an economic benefit, not to restrain alienability.[9]

§ 5.22

1. See infra notes 2–26 & accompanying text.

2. See cases cited in Note, Unreasonable Restraint, § 5.21, supra note 9, at 335–36.

3. Id.

4. L. Simes & A. Smith, The Law of Future Interests § 1112, at 5 (2d ed. 1956).

5. Id.

6. Volkmer, § 5.21 supra note 9, at 748.

7. Id.

8. R. Bernhardt, California Mortgage and Deed of Trust Practice 47–48 (1979); 1 H. Miller & M. Starr, Current Law of California Real Estate 179 (Supp.1982).

9. See § 5.21, supra note 3.

On the other hand, at least one commentator has concluded that a due-on-sale clause is so "closely akin" to a promissory restraint as to "justify designating it as a direct restraint." [10]

Although written as an acceleration clause, the due-on-sale clause directly and fundamentally burdens a mortgagor's ability to alienate as surely and directly as a classical promissory restraint. As such, the due-on-sale clause is truly a direct restraint insofar as the category of direct restraints can be articulated. [11]

The vast majority of courts has been unconcerned about classifying the clause into traditional "restraint" categories. No court has held that a due-on-sale clause is per se unlawful as a restraint on alienation. Indeed, some courts have suggested that it is not a restraint on alienation at all. [12] While many courts probably view the clause as an indirect restraint on alienation, all courts recognize that there are circumstances in which enforcement of the clause is reasonable and thus permissible. [13] Some courts, however, are more sympathetic to enforcement than others, and two broad judicial approaches to the clause have emerged.

Under the predominant judicial approach, the clause is deemed per se reasonable unless the borrower can show that the lender engaged in unconscionable conduct. [14] The courts employing this approach have recognized the desirability of protecting the mortgagee from the vagar-

10. Volkmer, § 5.21 supra note 9, at 773–74. But see First Federal Savings & Loan Association of Toledo v. Perry's Landing, Inc., 11 Ohio App.3d 135, 463 N.E.2d 636 (1984) (due-on-sale clause not promissory restraint).

11. Id.

12. See, e.g., Martin v. Peoples Mutual Savings & Loan Association, 319 N.W.2d 220, 228 (Iowa 1982); Capital Federal Savings & Loan Association v. Glenwood Manor, Inc., 235 Kan. 935, 686 P.2d 853 (1984); Occidental Savings & Loan Association v. Venco, 206 Neb. 469, 471, 293 N.W.2d 843, 846 (1980); Sonny Arnold, Inc. v. Sentry Savings Association, 633 S.W.2d 811, 815 (Tex.1982).

13. See, e.g., State ex rel. Bingaman v. Valley Savings & Loan Association, 97 N.M. 8, 12, 636 P.2d 279, 289 (1981); Continental Federal Savings & Loan Association v. Fetter, 564 P.2d 1013, 1018–19 (Okla. 1977).

14. See, e.g., Tierce v. APS Co., 382 So. 2d 485, 487 (Ala.1979); Income Realty & Mortgage Inc. v. Columbia Savings & Loan Association, 661 P.2d 257, 265 (Colo.1983); Olean v. Treglia, 190 Conn. 756, 765, 463 A.2d 242, 248 (1983); Baker v. Loves Park Savings & Loan Association, 61 Ill.2d 119,

125, 333 N.E.2d 1, 5 (1975); Martin v. Peoples Mutual Savings & Loan Association, 319 N.W.2d 220, 228–29 (Iowa 1982); Dunham v. Ware Savings Bank, 384 Mass. 63, 68, 423 N.E.2d 998, 1001 (Mass.1981); Occidental Savings & Loan Association v. Venco Partnership, 206 Neb. 469, 482, 293 N.W.2d 843, 848 (1980); First National Bank of Vicksburg v. Caruthers, 443 So.2d 861 (Miss.1984) (overruling Sanders v. Hicks, 317 So.2d 61 (Miss.1975); Stenger v. Great Southern Savings and Loan Association, 677 S.W.2d 376 (Mo.App.1984); First Commercial Title Insurance Co. v. Holmes, 92 Nev. 363, 365, 550 P.2d 1271, 1272 (1976); Mills v. Nashua Federal Savings & Loan Association, 121 N.H. 722, 725, 433 A.2d 1312, 1315–16 (1981); Crockett v. First Federal Savings & Loan Association, 289 N.C. 620, 630–31, 224 S.E.2d 580, 587 (1976); Gunther v. White, 489 S.W.2d 529, 530 (Tenn.1973); Sonny Arnold, Inc. v. Sentry Savings Association, 633 S.W.2d 811, 815 (Tex.1982); Slusky v. Coley, 668 S.W.2d 930 (Tex.Civ.App.1984); United Virginia Bank v. Best, 223 Va. 112, 114–15, 286 S.E.2d 221, 223 (1982), certiorari denied 459 U.S. 879, 103 S.Ct. 175, 74 L.Ed.2d 144 (1982); Magney v. Lincoln Mutual Savings Bank, 34 Wn.App. 45, 659 P.2d 537, 541 (1983).

ies of the interest rate market.[15] The mortgagee need not establish that a proposed transfer would impair security; the validity of the due-on-sale clause is not normally judged by the facts of an individual case.[16] Under one variant of this approach, such facts are relevant only to the extent that the mortgagor attempts to meet the burden of proving that enforcement is unconscionable or inequitable in his or her case.[17] An increase in the market interest rate is not usually thought sufficient to meet this burden, and due-on-sale clauses in such jurisdictions are usually enforced.[18]

Under the minority approach, enforcement of due-on-sale clauses must be reasonable in individual cases, necessitating a case-by-case determination.[19] Under this approach, the mortgagee's desire to increase interest rates is not considered a sufficient reason to justify the clause. The mortgagee has the burden to establish reasonableness, and normally must establish that the transfer would result in security impairment or an increased risk of default.[20] As a practical matter, lenders have rarely sought due-on-sale enforcement in jurisdictions that follow this approach.

Some of the courts that apply the majority approach display a concern that the borrower be fairly warned that the clause can be employed to exact a higher interest rate upon transfer, and insist that language explicitly stating that possibility be included in the documents.[21] There may well be a valid need for such a warning; the FNMA/FHLMC clause, for example, is extraordinarily technical and difficult for a lay reader to follow, and its implication that a higher

15. See, e.g., Income Realty & Mortgage, Inc. v. Columbia Savings & Loan Association, 661 P.2d 257, 261 (Colo.1983).

16. See, e.g., Baker v. Loves Park Savings & Loan Association, 61 Ill.2d 119, 124, 333 N.E.2d 1, 5 (1975).

17. See, e.g., Tierce v. APS Co., 328 So. 2d 485 (Ala.1979).

18. Id. at 487.

19. See, e.g., Baltimore Life Insurance Co. v. Harn, 15 Ariz.App. 78, 81, 486 P.2d 190, 193 (1971); Tucker v. Pulaski Federal Savings & Loan Association, 252 Ark. 849, 855, 481 S.W.2d 725, 728 (1972); Abrego v. United Peoples Federal Savings and Loan Association, 281 Ark. 308, 664 S.W.2d 858 (1984), appeal after remand ___ Ark. ___, 688 S.W.2d 724 (1985); Wellenkamp v. Bank of America, 21 Cal.3d 943, 953, 148 Cal.Rptr. 379, 385–86, 582 P.2d 970, 976–77 (1978); Nichols v. Ann Arbor Federal Savings & Loan Association, 73 Mich.App. 163, 168, 173, 250 N.W.2d 804, 808 (1977) (does not decide if a rate increase would have been reasonable if the clause had mentioned rate increases); State ex rel. Bingaman v. Valley Savings & Loan Association, 97 N.M. 8, 12, 636 P.2d 279, 283 (1981) (judicial extension of statute to loans made before statute's effective date); Consolidated Capital Properties, II, Inc. v. National Bank of North America, 420 So.2d 618, 622 (Fla.App.1982); Magney v. Lincoln Mutual Savings Bank, 34 Wn.App. 45, 659 P.2d 537, 541 (1983). Cf. O'Boskey v. First Federal Savings & Loan Association of Boise, 106 Idaho 339, 678 P.2d 1112 (1984) (impairment of security must be shown where due-on-sale clause title referred to protecting security); North Point Patio Offices Venture v. United Benefit Life Insurance Co., 672 S.W.2d 35 (Tex.App.1984), error refused n.r.e. (use of due-on-sale clause to "coerce" transfer fee deemed unreasonable).

20. Wellenkamp v. Bank of America, 21 Cal.3d 943, 952, 148 Cal.Rptr. 379, 385, 582 P.2d 970, 976 (1978).

21. See First Southern Federal Savings & Loan Association v. Britton, 345 So.2d 300, 304 (Ala.Civ.App.1977), overruled by Tierce v. APS Co., 382 So.2d 485 (Ala.1979); Silver v. Rochester Savings Bank, 73 A.D.2d 81, 86, 424 N.Y.S.2d 945, 947 (1980).

interest rate may result from a transfer is oblique at best.[22] One court has been even more punctilious, requiring that the clause be inserted in the promissory note and not merely in the mortgage.[23]

As noted above, majority or "automatic enforcement" jurisdictions often state that due-on-sale clauses are unenforceable when the mortgagor can establish that enforcement would be "unconscionable" or "inequitable." [24] While it is difficult to articulate precisely when enforcement will be so categorized, it is probable that most courts will be unwilling to enforce the clauses in "non-substantive" or "non-sale" transfers. For example, one court has indicated that enforcement should be denied in situations such as transfers to a spouse who becomes a co-owner, transfers to a spouse incidental to a marriage dissolution proceeding or settlement, and transfers to an inter vivos trust of which the mortgagor is a beneficiary.[25] This principle is recognized in the FNMA/FHLMC form due-on-sale clause, which specifically exempts transfers "by devise, descent or by operation of law upon the death of a joint tenant." [26]

Yet due-on-sale clauses should not be automatically unenforceable in all "non-substantive" or "non-sale" settings. For example, if a mortgagor transfers realty as a gift to a donee-charity that is barely solvent, the possession and ownership by the charity is likely to reduce the value of the property or reduce the probability of payment of the debt. In this situation it would hardly seem "unconscionable" or "inequitable" to enforce a due-on-sale clause.

Due-on-Encumbrance Clauses

The validity of due-on-encumbrance clauses has rarely been litigated. As we noted earlier,[27] such clauses are used primarily as a means of protecting against security impairment that may occur when junior mortgage indebtedness reduces the mortgagor's economic stake in the

---

22. The FNMA/FHLMC Mortgage, Clause 17 is thoroughly critiqued in Squires, A Comprehensible Due-on-Sale Clause, 27 Prac. Law 67 (1981).

23. See 2140 Lincoln Park West v. American National Bank & Trust Co., 88 Ill.App.3d 660, 664, 43 Ill.Dec. 857, 860, 410 N.E.2d 990, 993 (1980) (requirement justified on ground that rule of law requires mortgage and trust deed to be interpreted separately). It is not clear that this sort of technicality serves any purpose, and it may simply reflect the hostility of the court to enforcement of the clause.

24. See supra, text accompanying notes 14–17.

25. Mills v. Nashua Federal Savings & Loan Association, 121 N.H. 722, 433 A.2d 1312, 1316 (1981). See also Powell v. Phoenix Federal Savings & Loan Association, 434 So.2d 247, 253 (Ala.1983) (suggesting that enforcement of a due-on-sale clause may be "unconscionable" where the mortgagor sells part of the mortgaged real estate, but retains title to and continues to live on the other part); Home Savings Bank v. Baer Properties, Limited, 92 A.D.2d 98, 101, 460 N.Y.S.2d 833, 835–36 (1983) (mortgagee attempt to invoke due-on-sale clause upon transfer of property from a corporation to its sole shareholder held unconscionable and unenforceable). On the other hand, the sale to a third party of all the shares of a mortgagor-corporation has been deemed sufficient to trigger due-on-sale enforcement. See United States v. Med O Farm, Inc., 701 F.2d 88 (9th Cir.1983).

26. FNMA/FHLMC Mortgage, Clause 17 (one to four family).

27. See § 5.21, text accompanying note 20.

mortgaged real estate. Interest market motivation, if it exists in the due-on-encumbrance situation, is clearly less significant than in the due-on-sale setting.[28] Thus it is not surprising that the few reported due-on-encumbrance decisions permitted enforcement of the clause only when "reasonably necessary to protect the lender's security."[29]

Increased-Interest-on-Transfer Clauses

Increased-interest-on-transfer clauses are much less common than due-on-sale clauses and there is relatively little case law concerning their validity. Interestingly, the few courts that have confronted such clauses have upheld them,[30] even though these same jurisdictions restrict due-on-sale enforcement to situations in which the mortgagee can prove impairment of security.[31] One of these courts justified the difference in treatment between the two types of clauses by saying that an increased-interest-on-transfer provision, unlike a due-on-sale clause, "simply raises the interest rate should the mortgagor assign his rights and benefits under the mortgage to a subsequent purchaser."[32] From a policy viewpoint this distinction makes little sense, as the primary goal of both types of clauses is higher interest rates. Legally there is some difference, in that an unconsented transfer under an increased-interest clause does not automatically constitute a default; acceleration and foreclosure ensue only if the transferee refuses to make mortgage payments based on the increased interest rate.[33] Increased-interest clauses should find an even more favorable enforcement environment in states that automatically enforce due-on-sale clauses in the absence of unconscionability. Because increased-interest clauses are technically less burdensome on alienation than are due-on-sale clauses, logically they should be enforced at least to the same extent as their due-on-sale counterparts.

No-Transfer Provisions in Installment Land Contracts

While there was some early support for enforcement of "no-transfer" provisions in installment land contracts,[34] contemporary courts are

28. See Volkmer, § 5.21, note 9, at 770.

29. La Sala v. American Savings & Loan Association, 5 Cal.3d 864, 881, 97 Cal. Rptr. 849, 860, 489 P.2d 1113, 1124 (1971). See also Chilivis v. Tumlin Woods Realty Association, Inc., 250 Ga. 179, 184, 297 S.E.2d 4, 8 (1982) (suggesting a "reasonableness—impairment of security" standard).

30. See, e.g., O'Connell v. Dockendorff, 415 So.2d 35, 36–37 (Fla.App.1982); Miller v. Pacific First Federal Savings & Loan Association, 86 Wn.2d 401, 406–07, 545 P.2d 546, 549 (1976).

31. See First Federal Savings & Loan Association v. Lockwood, 385 So.2d 156, 159 (Fla.App.1980); Bellingham First Fed-eral Savings & Loan Association v. Garri-son, 87 Wn.2d 437, 441, 553 P.2d 1090, 1092 (1976).

32. O'Connell v. Dockendorff, 415 So.2d 35, 36 (Fla.App.1982).

33. However, even with a due-on-sale clause, foreclosure cannot automatically follow the transfer. The loan principal must first be accelerated; the default is the failure to pay the accelerated amount upon demand. See Miller v. Cote, 127 Cal. App.3d 888, 179 Cal.Rptr. 753 (1982).

34. See L. Simes & A. Smith, supra note 4, § 1164; Goddard, Non-Assignment Provisions in Land Contracts, 31 Mich.L. Rev. 1, 9-11 (1932); Grismore, Effect of a much less sympathetic. This attitude is reflected in two ways. First, "no-transfer" language is often construed narrowly against the vendor.[35] Second, in contrast to the majority approach to due-on-sale clause enforcement, courts often eschew an "automatic enforcement" approach; the "no-transfer" language is enforced only when it is established that the transfer will impair the vendor's security.[36] Moreover, even when a vendor demonstrates such an impairment, it is likely that a court will avoid the imposition of forfeiture by permitting the transferee to pay off the contract balance, or by ordering that the real estate be foreclosed by public sale.[37]

State Legislation

Several states have imposed legislative limitations on due-on-sale clauses.[38] While the details of these statutes vary considerably, they commonly prohibit due-on-sale enforcement in residential mortgages unless the mortgagee can establish that a transfer would impair mortgage security.[39] Most of the statutes permit the mortgagee to condition transfer of the property upon payment of a limited "assumption fee" or upon an increase in the mortgage interest rate by a modest amount,

Restriction on Assignment in a Contract, 31 Mich.L.Rev. 299, 316–17 (1933).

35. See, e.g., Conner v. First National Bank & Trust Co., 108 Ill.App.3d 534, 537, 64 Ill.Dec. 193, 196, 439 N.E.2d 122, 125 (1982) (transfer by trustee holding the vendee's contract interest to a successor trustee held not to constitute a "conveyance or assignment" for purposes of no-transfer clause); Murray First Thrift & Loan Co. v. Stevenson, 534 P.2d 909, 911 (Utah 1975) (transfer by vendee to a lender as security for a loan held not within meaning of a no-transfer clause).

36. See Lemon v. Nicolai, 33 Mich.App. 646, 649, 190 N.W.2d 549, 550 (1971); Pellerito v. Weber, 22 Mich.App. 242, 244–45, 177 N.W.2d 236, 237–38 (1970); Terry v. Born, 24 Wn.App. 652, 655, 604 P.2d 504, 506 (1979).

37. See Handzel v. Bassi, 343 Ill.App. 281, 289, 99 N.E.2d 23, 26 (1951) (assignee permitted to perform fully rather than undergo forfeiture); Murray First Thrift & Loan Co. v. Stevenson, 534 P.2d 909, 912 (Utah 1975) (assignee allowed to pay off balance); Coraci v. Noack, 61 Wisc.2d 183, 190, 212 N.W.2d 164, 167 (1973) (assignee granted right to redemption). In Terry v. Born, 24 Wn.App. 652, 604 P.2d 504 (1979), for example, the court held that the vendor should have been required to establish that enforcement of the contract provision was necessary to protect his security. Id. at 655, 604 P.2d at 506. The court also emphasized that even if, on remand, the trial

court found the requisite impairment of security, it should give serious consideration to permitting vendee to prepay the contract balance as an alternative to forfeiture.

38. See Ariz.Rev.Stat. § 33–806.01; Colo.Rev.Stat. 38–30–165; O.C.G.A. § 44–14–5; Iowa Code Ann. § 535.8; N.M.Stat. Ann.1981, §§ 48–7–11 to –14; Minn.Stat. Ann. § 47.20; Utah Code Ann.1981, 57–15–1 to –10.

A few additional states have statutes of only minor or procedural importance, and are not discussed in the text. See West's Ann.Cal.Civ.Code § 2924.5 (requiring that due-on-sale clause in loan secured by one to four unit dwelling be placed in both the promissory note and deed of trust to be enforceable); N.Y.—McKinney's Real Prop. Law § 254–a (if due-on-sale clause is triggered, mortgagee may not collect any prepayment penalty); 41 Pa.Stat. § 403(6) (prior to foreclosure, lender must notify debtor of debtor's right, if any, to transfer the property to another subject to the security interest); S.D.Comp. Laws 44–8–28 (due-on-sale clause enforceable only if notice by statutory language is given in the mortgage in capital letters or underlined). See also La.Stat.Ann.-R.S. 6.837 (building and loan associations expressly authorized to enforce due-on-sale clauses).

39. See, e.g., Colo.Rev.Stat. 38–30–165(a); Iowa Code Ann. § 535.8; N.M.Stat. Ann.1979, § 48–7–13.

usually no more than one percent.[40] Some of the statutes impose similar restrictions on increased-interest-on-transfer provisions.[41] In addition, at least one state, Iowa, confers generous post-foreclosure redemption rights when real estate is foreclosed incident to enforcement of a due-on-sale clause.[42]

A few other states legislatively prohibit due-on-sale enforcement in "non-substantive" and certain non-sale transfers.[43] In California, for example, acceleration is prohibited in residential mortgages when there is a transfer to a spouse resulting from the death of the mortgagor, to a spouse who becomes a co-owner, to a spouse incident to a marriage dissolution, or to an inter vivos trust of which the mortgagor is a beneficiary.[44] In addition, some statutes deny enforcement of due-on-encumbrance clauses in a variety of residential housing settings.[45]

 WESTLAW REFERENCES

Due-On-Sale Clauses

aliena! /s due-on-sale /s restrain*** restrict***

due-on-sale /80 ("case by case" "per se" /s reasonable! unreasonable!) inequitable unconscionable

Due-On-Encumbrance Clauses

due-on-encumbrance /80 inequitable reasonable! unconscionable unreasonable!

Increased-Interest-on-Transfer Clauses

"increased interest" /10 transfer /95 inequitable reasonable! unconscionable unreasonable!

---

40. See, e.g., Ariz.Rev.Stat. § 33–806.01(c) (½ of 1% maximum rate increase); Colo.Rev.Stat. 38–30–165(b)–(c) (1% maximum rate increase, ½% maximum fee); O.C.G.A. § 44–14–5 (1% maximum rate increase, ½% to 1% maximum fee, depending on whether borrower is released and whether rate is raised); Iowa Code Ann. § 535.8 (1% maximum fee); N.M.Stat.Ann.1981, § 48–7–14 (½% maximum fee); Utah Code Ann.1981, 57–15–8.5 (1% maximum rate increase at time of assumption, further 1% increase 5 years later, but rate may never exceed 1% below weighted average yield at most recent FHLMC weekly auction; 1% maximum fee).

41. See, e.g., O.C.G.A. § 44–14–5 (1% maximum rate increase per annum); Utah Code Ann.1981, 57–15–2, –4 (assumption fee limited to 1% of outstanding indebtedness).

42. See Iowa Code Ann. § 535.8(2)(e). While normally an Iowa mortgagor has only a one year post-sale redemption right, id. § 628.3, when foreclosure of a mortgage on real property results from the enforcement of a due-on-sale clause, the mortga-

gor may redeem the real property at any time within three years from the day of sale, id. § 535.8(2)(e). In the meantime, the mortgagor is entitled to possession of the property and for the first thirty months after the sale, the right of redemption is exclusive. Id. The time for redemption by creditors is extended to thirty-three months in any case in which the mortgagor's period for redemption is extended. Id. This statute represents a significant burden on lenders.

This type of redemption should not be confused with "equitable redemption," available in every state, which allows the mortgagor and junior lienors to pay off a mortgage in default at any time until a valid foreclosure sale has occurred. See § 7.1 infra.

43. See, e.g., West's Ann.Cal.Civ.Code § 2924.6.

44. Id.

45. See, e.g., id. § 2949 (single family, owner-occupied dwellings); Va.Code 1979, § 6.1–2.5 (one to four family residential dwellings).

§ 5.23 Due-on Clauses—Pre-Garn-St. Germain Act Federal Regulation

In 1976 the Federal Home Loan Bank Board (the Board), the federal agency that regulates federally-chartered and federally-insured savings and loan associations, became concerned about the increasing controversy over whether federally-chartered associations had the authority to enforce due-on-sale clauses. The Board issued a regulation effective July 31, 1976 (the 1976 Regulation) which provided that a federal association

> continues to have the power to include * * * a provision in its loan instrument whereby the association may, at its option, declare immediately due and payable sums secured by the association's security instrument if all or any part of the real property securing the loan is sold or transferred by the borrower without the association's prior written consent.[1]

Except as provided in paragraph (g) of the regulation, the Board authorized federal associations to exercise the due-on-sale option and provided that all rights and remedies of the association and borrower "shall be exclusively governed by the terms of the loan contract."[2] Paragraph (g) prohibited due-on-sale enforcement in certain "nonsubstantive" transfers of mortgagor-occupied homes resulting from junior liens, purchase-money security interests in household appliances, transfers by devise, descent, or operation of law upon the death of a joint tenant, and leaseholds for less than three years with no option to purchase.[3] In the preamble to the 1976 Regulation the Board also expressed its intent that the due-on-sale practices of federal associations be governed exclusively by federal law, and emphasized that federal associations "shall not be bound by or subject to any conflicting state law which imposes different * * * due-on-sale requirements."[4]

A similar regulation was promulgated in 1978 by the National Credit Union Administration (NCUA) to apply to due-on-sale clauses in federal credit union mortgages.[5] The NCUA regulation went beyond the 1976 Board Regulation by specifically requiring federal credit

§ 5.23

1. 12 C.F.R. § 545.8–3(f) (1983).

2. Id.

3. Id. § 545.8–3(g). This language tracks the FNMA/FHLMC Mortgage, Clause 17 (one to four family).

4. 41 Fed.Reg. 18,286, 18,287.

5. See 12 CFR 701.21–6(d).

unions to utilize due-on-sale clauses as well as preempting state restrictions on due-on-sale clause enforcement.[6]

While lower federal courts concluded that the 1976 Board Regulation foreclosed the application of state due-on-sale law to federal associations,[7] a few state courts reached contrary results.[8] Ultimately, this conflict was resolved by the United States Supreme Court in Fidelity First Federal Savings & Loan Association v. de la Cuesta,[9] a case that addressed the effect of the 1976 Regulation on California law. California generally limited due-on-sale enforcement to situations in which impairment of mortgage security was established.[10] In *de la Cuesta*, the Supreme Court held that: 1) the Board intended to preempt state law;[11] 2) the 1976 Regulation in fact conflicted with California law, despite the fact that it merely authorized, and did not require, federal associations to utilize due-on-sale clauses;[12] 3) the Board acted within its statutory authority under section 5(a) of the Home Owner's Loan Act,[13] which authorized the Board to promulgate rules for the operation and regulation of federal associations;[14] and 4) although the 1976 Regulation's merits might be debatable, it was a reasonable, and therefore a valid, exercise of the Board's authority.[15]

The *de la Cuesta* Court did not address the enforceability of due-on-sale clauses included in the mortgage loans made by federal associations before the effective date of the 1976 Board Regulation.[16] The Board had issued an earlier regulation[17] that one federal court held sufficient to preempt contrary state due-on-sale law as to pre-1976

6. Id.

7. See, e.g., Dantus v. First Federal Savings & Loan Association, 467 F.Supp. 1139, 1141 (C.D.Ill.1979), appeal dismissed 638 F.2d 1221 (7th Cir.1980); Glendale Federal Savings & Loan Association v. Fox, 459 F.Supp. 903, 907 (C.D.Cal.1978).

8. See, e.g., Panko v. Pan American Federal Savings & Loan Association, 119 Cal.App.3d 916, 924, 174 Cal.Rptr. 240, 245 (1981), vacated 458 U.S. 1117, 102 S.Ct. 3503, 73 L.Ed.2d 1380 (1982); see also First Federal Savings & Loan Association v. Lockwood, 385 So.2d 156, 160 (Fla.App. 1980) (Board Regulation, while "not invalid," does not prohibit a state court from applying traditional equitable principles to deny acceleration "absent any allegation or proof of impairment of security"); Holiday Acres No. 3 v. Midwest Federal Savings & Loan Association, 308 N.W.2d 471, 477–78 (Minn.1981).

9. 458 U.S. 141, 102 S.Ct. 3014, 73 L.Ed. 2d 664 (1982). For a critical analysis of *de la Cuesta*, see Segreti, supra § 5.21 note 9, at 803–06.

10. See Wellenkamp v. Bank of America, 21 Cal.3d 943, 953, 148 Cal.Rptr. 379, 385–86, 582 P.2d 970, 976–77 (1978).

11. Fidelity First Federal Savings & Loan Association v. de la Cuesta, 458 U.S. at 154, 159, 102 S.Ct. at 3014, 3024.

12. Id. at 154, 102 S.Ct. at 3024.

13. 12 U.S.C.A. § 1464(a).

14. Fidelity First Federal Savings & Loan Association v. de la Cuesta, 458 U.S. at 159–61, 102 S.Ct. at 3025.

15. Id. at 170, 102 S.Ct. at 3026–3027.

16. Id. at 170–71, 102 S.Ct. at 3031. One court avoided the retroactivity issue as to a July 23, 1976 transfer by holding that the effective date of the 1976 Regulation was June 8, 1976 rather than July 31, 1976. See First Federal Savings and Loan Association of Winter Haven v. Quigley, 445 So.2d 1052 (Fla.App.1984), petition for review denied 453 So.2d 45 (1984), certiorari denied ___ U.S. ___, 105 S.Ct. 513, 83 L.Ed.2d 403 (1984).

17. 12 CFR 545.8–3(a) (originally promulgated July 3, 1979). The regulation stated only that loan instruments "shall * * * provide for full protection to the Federal association." Id.

Regulation loans.[18]　Also, the 1976 Regulation specified that a federal association *"continues"* to have the power to include due-on-sale clauses in their mortgages.[19]　Although this language may have represented bureaucratic timidity in dealing with the retroactivity issue, it can be argued that it signified the Board's view that it had already preempted state law before 1976.　The Supreme Court in *de la Cuesta,* however, expressly avoided reaching the retroactivity question.[20]　While *de la Cuesta* confirmed the validity of the Board's response to the needs of federally-chartered savings associations with respect to due-on-sale clauses, it did nothing for other types of lenders.　Therefore, these lenders sought a uniform national solution: congressional preemption of state laws restricting the enforcement of due-on-sale clauses.

WESTLAW REFERENCES
date(after 1975) & board "federal home loan" f.h.l.b.b. /p due-on-sale /s federal I association "credit union" savings

§ 5.24 Due-on Clauses—The Garn-St. Germain Act

The enactment of section 341 of the Garn-St. Germain Depository Institutions Act of 1982 (Act)[1] signaled the dawn of a new era for due-on-sale clause enforcement.　The Act broadly preempts state laws that restrict the enforcement of due-on-sale clauses, thereby making such clauses generally enforceable.

Yet Congress responded to effective lobbying by the real estate brokerage industry and related interests[2] by softening the impact of the Act in most states that previously restricted due-on-sale enforcement.　To accomplish this, Congress created complex exceptions to the preemption based on so-called "window periods,"[3] and conferred authority on states with window periods to enact legislation to avoid the impact of the Act on certain mortgage loans.[4]　In so doing, Congress

---

18.　Conference of Federal Savings & Loan Associations v. Stein, 495 F.Supp. 12 (E.D.Cal.1979).　Note that this decision was rendered prior to *de la Cuesta.*　Contra: Haven Federal Savings and Loan Association v. Carl, 456 So.2d 1290 (Fla.App.1984).

19.　12 CFR 545.8–3(f).　See supra text accompanying note 1.

20.　Two of the deeds of trust in *de la Cuesta* were executed prior to both the *Wellenkamp* decision in 1978 and the effective date of the Board Regulation in 1976.　The debtors argued that the Board Regulation could not be applied so as to destroy the debtors' rights.　However, the Supreme Court avoided this question because it concluded that California law in effect at the date the two deeds of trust were executed was consistent with the Board Regulation.　See Fidelity Federal Savings & Loan Association v. de la Cuesta, 458 U.S. 141, 170 n.

24, 102 S.Ct. 3014, 3031 n.24, 73 L.Ed.2d 664 (1982).

§ 5.24

1.　12 U.S.C.A. § 1701j–3.

2.　See generally Savings and Loan Aid Package Boosts Powers of Banks, Thrifts, 40 Cong.Q. 2423 (1982); Mortgage Assumption Plan Approved, 40 Cong.Q. 2126 (1982); Senate Passes Comprehensive Financial Institutions Bill, 10 Hous. & Dev. Rptr. (BNA) 356 (1982); The Washington Front, Cal.Real Est., Nov. 1982, at 2; U.S. Law on Home-Mortgage Assumptions Will Create Legal Limbos in Some States, Wall St.J., Oct. 4, 1982, at 10, col. 1.

3.　12 U.S.C.A. § 1701j–3(c)(1).　See infra text accompanying notes 75–99.

4.　12 U.S.C.A. § 1701j–3(c)(1).　See infra notes 1–7 & accompanying text.

created a host of important and difficult interpretation problems. Congress delegated to the Board the authority to issue regulations interpreting the Act,[5] and in April, 1983, the Board issued a final regulation entitled "Preemption of State Due-on-Sale Laws" (Regulation).[6] The following material analyzes the more important provisions of the Act and Regulation, their scope, and the complex problems of interpretation they have engendered.

Lenders Covered

The Act covers any "person or government agency making a real property loan." [7] According to the Regulation, the foregoing definition includes,

> without limitation, individuals, Federal associations, state-chartered savings and loan associations, national banks, state-chartered banks and state-chartered mutual savings banks, Federal credit unions, state-chartered credit unions, mortgage banks, insurance companies and finance companies which make real property loans, manufactured-home retailers who extend credit, agencies of the Federal government, [and] any lender approved by the Secretary of Housing and Urban Development for participation in any mortgage insurance program under the National Housing Act.[8]

The Board emphasized that the foregoing list is "intended to be representative and not exclusive." [9] Consequently, every mortgagee, wheth-

---

5. 12 U.S.C.A. § 1701j–3(e)(1). The Board is required to consult with the National Credit Union Administration and the Comptroller of the Currency before issuing regulations.

6. 48 Fed.Reg. 21,554 (codified at 12 CFR 591).

7. 12 U.S.C.A. § 1701j–3(a)(2). Also included is "any assignee or transferee, in whole or in part, of such a person or agency."

8. 48 Fed.Reg. 21,561 (codified at 12 CFR 591.2(g)).

9. 48 Fed.Reg. 21,555 (definitions section of the Regulation). In one case, Lucas v. Jones, 148 Cal.App.3d 1008, 1012 n.6, 196 Cal.Rptr. 437, 440 n.6 (1983), certiorari denied ___ U.S. ___, 105 S.Ct. 87, 83 L.Ed. 2d 34 (1984), the California Court of Appeal held that the Regulation is inapplicable to individuals making private loans. This conclusion is obviously wrong: the Regulation refers to coverage of "individuals," see supra text accompanying note 108, and the Act refers to "a person * * * making a real property loan," 12 U.S.C.A. § 1701j–3(a)(2). The *Lucas*

court's mistaken interpretation is based on language in the Preamble to the Regulation, as published in the Federal Register, that describes "Small entities to which the rule will apply." 48 Fed.Reg. 21,560. While this description mentions only financial institutions and government and corporate entities, it clearly is not intended to limit the coverage of the Regulation to such entities. Rather, the language was inserted in the Preamble merely to comply with the Regulatory Flexibility Act, 5 U.S.C.A. § 604(a)(3), which requires an agency publishing a final rule to describe "alternatives * * * designed to minimize any significant economic impact of the rule on small entities." The Act defines "small entity" to include businesses, nonprofit enterprises, and local government jurisdictions. Id. § 601(6). Since individuals are not included in this definition, they were not explicitly mentioned by the Board in the portion of the Preamble described above. See Casa Grande, Inc. v. Minnesota Mutual Life Insurance Company, 596 F.Supp. 1385 (S.D.Miss. 1984) (Act applicable to private lender).

er a natural person, business entity, or government agency, is covered by the Act.

Although Congress clearly has the power under the commerce clause of the United States Constitution [10] to regulate institutional lenders insofar as their activities affect interstate commerce,[11] an argument could be made that Congress lacks the power to regulate due-on-sale clauses in purely intrastate mortgage transactions between private, non-institutional parties. Congress is authorized to regulate intrastate activity so long as it rationally concludes that the activity affects interstate commerce or commerce in more than one state.[12] At first glance, it seems difficult to conclude that an isolated, intrastate, non-institutional mortgage transaction meets this test.[13] However, under the prevailing commerce clause interpretation the impact on commerce of a single transaction is largely irrelevant.[14] Indeed, the Court has suggested that federal courts lack the power to make an independent determination as to the interstate ramifications of each litigant's behavior: "Where the *class of activities* is regulated and that *class* is within the reach of federal power, the courts have no power 'to excise, as trivial, individual instances' of the class." [15]

Application of this reasoning leads to the conclusion that Congress has ample power under the commerce clause to reach purely local and private mortgage transactions. Perhaps Congress believed that making due-on-sale clauses enforceable in non-institutional mortgage settings would encourage private seller financing at a time when institutional financing was both expensive and difficult to obtain. In any event,

10. U.S.Const. Art. I, § 8, cl. 3.

11. See McInnis v. Cooper Communities, Inc., 271 Ark. 503, 611 S.W.2d 767 (1981); J. Nowak, R. Rotunda & J. Young, Constitutional Law 165–67 (2d ed. 1983).

12. See, e.g., Perez v. United States, 402 U.S. 146, 151–54, 91 S.Ct. 1357, 1360–61, 28 L.Ed.2d 686 (1971); Katzenbach v. Mc-Clung, 379 U.S. 294, 301–05, 85 S.Ct. 377, 382–84, 13 L.Ed.2d 290 (1964); Heart of Atlanta Motel, Inc. v. United States, 379 U.S. 241, 248, 255, 85 S.Ct. 348, 353, 356, 13 L.Ed.2d 258 (1964); Wickard v. Filburn, 317 U.S. 111, 125, 63 S.Ct. 82, 89, 87 L.Ed. 122 (1942). See generally, McLain v. Real Estate Board of New Orleans, 444 U.S. 232, 241, 100 S.Ct. 502, 508, 62 L.Ed.2d 441 (1979), on remand 614 F.2d 535 (5th Cir. 1980); J. Nowak, R. Rotunda & J. Young, supra note 111, at 161–70.

13. Suppose, for example, that after the effective date of the Act, ME sold an unimproved lake lot located in State X to MR and that ME took back a note and mortgage for part of the purchase price. Both ME and MR were residents of State X. The mortgage contained a due-on-sale clause. A year later MR sold and con-

veyed the lot to Grantee, a wealthy resident of State X, without permission of ME. ME then accelerated the mortgage debt and commenced a judicial foreclosure proceeding. If under the case law of State X, a due-on-sale clause is enforceable only if the transfer impairs mortgage security, a requirement which ME cannot satisfy, ME cannot accelerate the loan. If the Act applies, however, the due-on-sale clause is automatically enforceable. The issue is whether Congress has sufficient commerce clause authority to reach this type of isolated, intrastate non-institutional transaction.

14. See Wickard v. Filburn, 317 U.S. 111, 63 S.Ct. 82, 87 L.Ed. 122 (1942) (cumulative effect of "trivial" local activities can have substantial impact on interstate commerce); see also Perez v. United States, 402 U.S. 146, 91 S.Ct. 1357, 28 L.Ed.2d 686 (1971); Katzenbach v. McClung, 379 U.S. 294, 85 S.Ct. 377, 13 L.Ed.2d 290 (1964).

15. Perez v. United States, 402 U.S. 146, 154, 91 S.Ct. 1357, 1361, 28 L.Ed.2d 686 (1971) (quoting Maryland v. Wirtz, 392 U.S. 183, 193, 88 S.Ct. 2017, 2022, 20 L.Ed. 2d 1020 (1968)) (emphasis in original).

while a due-on-sale clause included in an isolated private mortgage transaction probably cannot be said to affect interstate commerce, it was not irrational for Congress to conclude that the cumulative impact of many such transactions on the national mortgage market is significant.

Loans Covered

The Act covers every "loan, mortgage, advance, or credit sale secured by a lien on real property, the stock allocated to a dwelling unit in a cooperative housing corporation, or a residential manufactured home, whether real or personal property." [16] Although the Act makes no reference to mortgages on leasehold interests, the Regulation provides that a loan is secured by a lien on real property if it is made on the "security of any instrument * * * which makes * * * a leasehold or subleasehold * * * specific security for payment of the obligation secured by the instrument." [17]

As Professor Richard Powell aptly observed, "[w]hen a statute affecting 'real property' is in preparation, careful consideration should be addressed to the policy question of its applicability to the interests of lessees, and * * * unambiguous language should be inserted in the statute to define its intended inclusion, or exclusion, of such interests." [18] It is unfortunate that Congress neglected to follow this useful advice. Since Congress failed specifically to place leasehold mortgages within the coverage of the Act, it could be argued that the Board lacked authority to do so in the Regulation. Under this reasoning, a leasehold mortgage cannot be a "lien on real property" because the leasehold is personal property or a "chattel real." [19] The phrase "real or personal" property, as utilized in the Act,[20] refers only to liens on residential manufactured homes, and thus cannot be used to buttress a conclusion that the Act covers all leasehold mortgages.

It seems probable, however, that the foregoing argument will fail. To be sure, courts continue to characterize leaseholds as personal property for some purposes [21] and, as Professor Powell noted, this is a "field of judgment and of pragmatic utility, where disagreement is not unlikely." [22] Nevertheless, the courts have treated leasehold mortgages

16. 12 U.S.C.A. § 1701j–3(a)(3).

17. 48 Fed.Reg. 21,561 (codified at 12 CFR 591.2(h)).

18. 2 R. Powell, Real Property 190–91 (1982).

19. See 1 American Law of Property § 3.12 (1952); Restatement of Property § 8 comment c (1936).

20. See supra text accompanying note 16.

21. See, e.g., Stagecrafters' Club, Inc. v. District of Columbia Division of American

Legion, 110 F.Supp. 481 (D.D.C.1953) (leasehold deemed personalty and thus subject to execution sale for federal taxes owed by lessee); Shaeffer v. Baeringer, 345 Pa. 32, 29 A.2d 697 (1943) (lessee held not a person having an "interest in land" under a statute requiring all such persons to join in a judicial application to compel a mortgagee to assign his mortgage after payment).

22. 2 R. Powell, supra note 18, at 189. See also Moynihan, Introduction to the Law of Real Property 64 (1962).

as mortgages on real estate in a variety of contexts.[23] Most contemporary mortgages on leasehold interests arise in commercial real estate settings where the mortgagor is often an experienced and sophisticated real estate developer.[24] It seems unlikely that Congress intended due-on-sale clauses to be enforceable against residential fee owner mortgagors, who generally have a relatively weak bargaining position as against their mortgagees, while states remain free to restrict enforcement of such clauses for the benefit of commercial mortgagor-lessees who frequently have relatively strong negotiating strength vis-a-vis their mortgage lenders.

Types of Mortgage Transfer Restrictions Covered

The Act preempts state law only with respect to due-on-sale clauses that "authoriz[e] a lender, at its option, to declare due and payable sums secured by the lender's security instrument if all or any part of the property, or an interest therein, securing the real property loan is sold or transferred without the lender's prior written consent." [25] The Regulation adopts this statutory definition virtually unchanged.[26]

Presumably the Act is inapplicable to an increased-interest-on-transfer clause because that type of clause confers on the lender only the right to modify or increase the interest rate upon a sale or transfer and not the "option to declare [the debt] due and payable." [27] Consequently, every state is probably free to make increased-interest-on-transfer provisions unenforceable. This result is bizarre, for such clauses have an economic effect similar to that of the due-on-sale clauses.[28] Nevertheless, the practical effect of excluding increased-interest-on-transfer provisions from the scope of the Act is unlikely to be substantial. Mortgagees can simply include due-on-sale language in any mortgages executed after the Act's effective date. As to pre-Act loans, few state courts are likely to exercise their freedom. In states

---

23. See, e.g., Harbel Oil Co. v. Steele, 83 Ariz. 181, 184–86, 318 P.2d 359, 361 (1957) (assignment of lease as security for a loan and sublease back to lessee deemed to be a real property mortgage which could only be foreclosed by judicial action); Fidelity Trust Co. v. Wayne County, 244 Mich. 182, 188, 221 N.W. 111, 112 (1928) (statute imposing tax on real estate mortgages held applicable to a mortgage on a term for years); Abraham v. Fioramonte, 158 Ohio St. 213, 222–25, 107 N.E.2d 321, 326–27 (1952) (leasehold could not be made subject of chattel mortgage, but must be mortgaged in accordance with formalities associated with real estate mortgages).

24. See generally G. Nelson & D. Whitman, Real Estate Transfer, Finance and Development 1062–75 (2d ed. 1981); Committee on Leases, Ground Leases and Their Financing, 4 Real Prop.Prob. & Tr.J. 437, 438 (1969).

25. 12 U.S.C.A. § 1701j–3(a)(1).

26. 48 Fed.Reg. 21,561 (codified at 12 CFR 591.2(b)). The only substantive difference in the Regulation's due-on-sale definition is the insertion of the word "immediately" prior to the words "due and payable."

27. Acceleration can occur only if the transferee defaults in paying the increased mortgage payments. See also O'Connell v. Dockendorff, 415 So.2d 35 (Fla.Ct.App. 1982) (increased interest on transfer provision is not a due-on-sale clause for purposes of state case law that limits due-on-sale enforcement to impairment of security situations).

28. See supra § 5.21, note 24, and § 5.22, notes 30–33 and accompanying text.

that follow an automatic enforcement approach to the due-on-sale clause,[29] courts are unlikely to restrict enforcement of an increased-interest-on-transfer provision, as it is the less burdensome of the two clauses. Even in states that impose substantial restrictions on due-on-sale clause enforcement, courts that have addressed the issue have been less hostile toward enforcement of increased-interest-on-transfer clauses.[30] Courts in these latter states are thus not likely to take advantage of this "loophole" in the Act's preemptive effect.

One could draft mortgage language that would fall outside the Act's definition of a due-on-sale clause. For example, a provision for *automatic* acceleration upon transfer seems to be outside the definition, which speaks of the lender's "option" to accelerate. Similarly, a clause that merely makes an unapproved transfer by the mortgagor a default, but says nothing about acceleration, may fall outside the Act. However, this argument is weakened if the mortgage or note also contains a standard acceleration-for-default clause that the courts could read together with the no-transfer clause to find the equivalent of a due-on-sale clause. These illustrations should have little practical importance, since in post-Act mortgages well-advised lenders will simply refrain from using such uncommon and idiosyncratic language. An occasional pre-Act document may raise this sort of problem, but the number of documents with such non-standard clauses is small. In any event, only clauses in states that restrict due-on-sale enforcement potentially pose a problem. In overall economic terms, then, the Act's narrow definition of a due-on-sale clause is likely to be of little importance.

Coverage of Installment Land Contracts

While the Act itself does not specifically mention installment land contracts, its preemption does apply to any "loan, mortgage, advance, or credit sale secured by a lien on real property." [31] Does an installment contract vendor retain a "lien on real property," as well as legal title? The Regulation answers affirmatively,[32] and is probably correct.[33] While a few courts have had conceptual difficulty with the notion that one can have legal title to land and a lien on it simultaneously,[34] there is substantial authority that the installment land contract vendor retains a "vendor's lien" for the unpaid purchase price.[35] More-

---

29. See supra § 5.22, notes 14–18 and accompanying text.

30. See supra § 5.22, notes 30–31 and accompanying text.

31. 12 U.S.C.A. § 1701j–3(a)(3).

32. 48 Fed.Reg. 21,561 (codified at 12 CFR 591.2(h)) (" 'loan secured by a lien on real property' means a loan on the security on any instrument (whether a mortgage, deed of trust, or *land contract*) which makes the interest in real property (whether in fee or on a leasehold or subleasehold) specific security for the payment of the

obligation secured by the instrument") (emphasis added).

33. See Karim v. Werner, 333 N.W.2d 877, 878 n. 1 (Minn.1983) (noting the possible application of the Act, but concluding that the due-on-sale clause was valid under state law).

34. See, e.g., Allen v. Wilson, 178 Cal. 674, 174 P. 661 (1918).

35. See, e.g., Forty-Four Hundred East Broadway Co. v. 4400 E. Broadway, 135 Ariz. 265, 267, 660 P.2d 866 (App.1983); Bean v. Walker, 95 A.D.2d 70, 73, 464 over, courts are increasingly equating installment land contracts with mortgages, and requiring foreclosure as the vendor's primary remedy. In such cases the vendor is surely foreclosing a "lien." [36] Finally, while the analytical underpinnings for their decisions are not always clear, numerous courts routinely afford the vendor the option to foreclose an installment land contract as a mortgage.[37] This practice constitutes a persuasive argument that the contract vendor is also a "lienor."

The conclusion that the Act's preemption applies to installment land contracts does not mean that a violation of a contract prohibition on transfer will necessarily result in a forfeiture of the vendee's interest. When no-transfer provisions are upheld, it is likely that foreclosure of the contract will instead be ordered, and then only after the vendee has been afforded the opportunity to pay off the contract balance.[38] The Act does not appear to change this. Literally, it only validates "due-on-sale" clauses—those that authorize the acceleration of the debt when the real estate is transferred without the lender's consent.[39] A prohibition on transfer that purports to go beyond simple acceleration, and defines the remedies (such as forfeiture) to be imposed on the vendee, is unaffected by the Act and is thus still subject to pre-Act state law. It is highly improbable that a state court would enforce forfeiture, with its harsh consequences, simply because a transfer was made without the vendor's consent. A more likely judicial response would be to permit foreclosure of the contract as a mortgage. Such an approach would not be inconsistent with the policy inherent in the Act.

Time of Transfer

The Act applies to all mortgage *loans,* whether consummated before or after October 15, 1982, the effective date of the Act. However, a *transfer* is covered only if it is made after the Act's effective date.[40] Although the Act itself does not state this, this conclusion is supported by the well-settled rule that a statute has only prospective effect unless Congress evinces a clear intent that it have retroactive effect.[41] Con-

---

N.Y.S.2d 895, 897 (1983); Braunstein v. Trottier, 54 Or.App. 687, 690, 635 P.2d 1379, 1381 (1981), review denied 292 Or. 568, 644 P.2d 1129 (1982); 3 American Law of Property § 11.73 (1952); Comment, supra note 26, at 89.

36. See supra § 5.21, note 31 and accompanying text.

37. See, e.g., Land Associates, Inc. v. Becker, 294 Or. 308, 314, 656 P.2d 927, 931 (1982); Note, Forfeiture and the Iowa Installment Land Contract, 46 Iowa L.Rev. 786, 795–96 (1961); § 3.32 supra.

38. See supra § 5.22, note 37 and accompanying text.

39. 12 U.S.C.A. § 1701j–3(a)(1).

40. See Home Savings Bank v. Baer Properties, Limited, 92 A.D.2d 98, 101, 460

N.Y.S.2d 833, 835–36 (1983); Pioneer Federal Savings and Loan Association v. Reeder, 453 So.2d 126 (Fla.App.1984), decision approved and quashed in part ___ So.2d ___ (1985); Weiman v. McHaffie, 448 So.2d 1127 (Fla.App.1984), decision approved and quashed in part ___ So.2d ___ (1985); Morris v. Woodside, 101 Wn.2d 812, 682 P.2d 905 (1984); Kiefer v. Fortune Federal Savings and Loan Association, 453 So. 2d 430 (Fla.App.1984); North Community Bank v. Northwest National Bank of Chicago, 126 Ill.App.3d 581, 82 Ill.Dec. 21, 467 N.E.2d 1094 (1984). The Regulations seem to agree with respect to window period loans. See 12 CFR 591.4(c)(2).

41. United States v. Security Industrial Bank, 459 U.S. 70, 103 S.Ct. 407, 413, 74 L.Ed.2d 235 (1982), appeal dismissed as gress indicated no such intent regarding the Act. Note, however, that federally-chartered savings and loan associations have the authority to enforce due-on-sale clauses as to many pre-Act transfers by virtue of the 1976 Regulation upheld in the *de la Cuesta* case.[42] The Act itself recognizes this authority.[43]

The application of the Act can be illustrated as follows. Suppose that on March 1, 1982, MR transferred mortgaged real estate located in State X to Grantee in violation of a due-on-sale clause contained in the mortgage executed in 1980. During early 1983, ME (a state-chartered lender) accelerated the debt and commenced judicial foreclosure proceedings. Because the transfer took place before October 15, 1982, the Act is inapplicable and the State X court is free to apply state law to such pre-Act transfers.

While the Act is inapplicable to pre-Act transfers, it is retroactive in the sense that it governs mortgage loans executed prior to the Act's effective date. Thus, if in the previous example the property had been mortgaged in 1980, but the transfer had taken place on December 20, 1982, the Act would have applied, and the due-on-sale clause would have been enforceable.

Is this type of retroactivity unconstitutional? While the contract clause[44] of the United States Constitution limits only state power to impair the obligation of contracts, certain restrictions on federal power to enact retroactive legislation are implicit in the due process clause of the fifth amendment.[45] In applying the due process clause to legislation that has retroactive effects, the Supreme Court has often focused on whether the legislation defeats the reasonable expectations of the parties.[46] However, even when this is the case, retroactive legislation will be sustained if it is rationally related to a valid governmental purpose.[47]

The Act clearly satisfies this constitutional standard. First, it applies only to mortgages that contain due-on-sale clauses. Consequently, the Act is relevant only when the parties have specifically agreed that the debt could be accelerated in the event of an unapproved transfer. Under these circumstances a mortgagor can hardly argue that enforcement of the agreement is a total surprise. In a sense, therefore, the Act enhances rather than impairs the obligations created by the contract. Second, although certain mortgagors in states that previously restricted due-on-sale enforcement may argue that they executed their mortgages under the assumption that such clauses were

moot 459 U.S. 1081, 103 S.Ct. 562, 74 L.Ed. 2d 927 (1982).

42. See supra § 5.23, notes 1–20 and accompanying text.

43. See 12 U.S.C.A. § 1701j–3(c)(2)(C); see also 48 Fed.Reg. 21,562 (codified at 12 CFR 591.3).

44. U.S. Const. Art. I, § 10, cl. 1.

45. U.S. Const. Amend. V. See J. Nowack, R. Rotunda & J. Young, supra note 11, at 471–72.

46. J. Nowack, R. Rotunda & J. Young, supra note 11, at 474–75.

47. See, e.g., Usery v. Turner Elkhorn Mining Co., 428 U.S. 1, 19, 96 S.Ct. 2882, 2894, 49 L.Ed.2d 752 (1976).

usually unenforceable and that the Act upset their reasonable expectations, such mortgagors are protected by the "window period" concept, examined in detail later in this Article.[48] Finally, even without the window period provisions, the retroactive effect of the Act is rationally related to a valid governmental purpose. The Act reflects a legitimate congressional concern about the economic distress of the savings and loan industry.[49] Enforcing due-on-sale clauses as to future transfers under pre-Act mortgages surely is one rational means of alleviating that financial distress.[50]

Transfers in Which Due-on-Sale Enforcement is Prohibited

The Act expressly enumerates several types of transfers that may not be used as the basis for due-on-sale acceleration. The list is similar, but not identical, to the analogous provisions of the FNMA/FHLMC mortgage form and the 1976 FHLBB regulations.[51] It includes:

(1) the creation of a lien or other encumbrance subordinate to the lender's security instrument which does not relate to a transfer of rights of occupancy in the property;

(2) the creation of a purchase money security interest for household appliances;

(3) a transfer by devise, descent, or operation of law on the death of a joint tenant or tenant by the entirety;

(4) the granting of a leasehold interest of three years or less not containing an option to purchase;

(5) a transfer to a relative resulting from the death of a borrower;

(6) a transfer where the spouse or children of the borrower become an owner of the property;

(7) a transfer resulting from a decree of a dissolution of marriage, legal separation agreement, or from an incidental property settlement agreement, by which the spouse of the borrower becomes an owner of the property;

(8) a transfer into an inter vivos trust in which the borrower is and remains a beneficiary and which does not relate to a transfer of rights of occupancy in the property; or

(9) any other transfer or disposition described in regulations prescribed by the Federal Home Loan Bank Board.[52]

When a transfer of one of these types is involved, the Act is preemptive: acceleration under a due-on-sale clause is prohibited even if permitted by state law. However, the above transfers are insulated from acceler-

---

48. See infra text accompanying notes.

49. See supra § 5.21, notes 12–14 & accompanying text.

50. See supra § 5.21 note 14 & accompanying text.

51. See § 5.23 note 3 & accompanying text.

52. 12 U.S.C.A. § 1701j–3(d).

ation only if the mortgaged real estate contains "less than five dwelling units." [53] The latter language was added to the Act on November 30, 1983. In its original form, the Act contained no such qualification. Thus, prior to the amendment, there was substantial concern that the above exceptions would prevent due-on enforcement in a variety of purely commercial and non-residential settings. For example, in item (1) above, the Act prohibits due-on-sale enforcement upon the creation of a junior lien if no transfer of occupancy is involved.[54] Suppose a first mortgage on a shopping center contains a prohibition on further encumbrances without the mortgagee's consent. If the mortgagor borrows money for a non-business purpose and gives the lender a junior mortgage on the center, the Act appears to prohibit acceleration. This is true even if the first mortgagee can establish that the junior lien will increase the risk of mortgagor default or will impair the security of its mortgage. This result doubtless came as an unpleasant surprise to countless mortgage lenders who had relied on the due-on-encumbrance concept in a variety of commercial lending contexts.

The Board had sought to avoid such a result by limiting the application of the statutory list to mortgage loans made "on the security of a home occupied * * * by the borrower." [55] Even though such a limitation was absent from the Act itself, the Board argued in its preamble to the Regulation that "this approach is most consistent with the Congressional purpose of restricting due-on-sale exercise to protect consumers." [56] While it is true that courts sometimes defer to an interpretation of a statute by the agency charged with its administration,[57] there is also a strong tradition that the "plain meaning" of an unambiguous statute should be respected.[58] In short, there was substantial doubt as to the validity of the Board's attempt to limit the impact of the Act's exceptions.[59] In any event, because of the 1983 amendment by Congress, this issue remains important only for transfers that were consumated after the date of the Act, but prior to the amendment.

53. Pub.L. 98–181, Tit. IV, § 473, Nov. 30, 1983 codified as 12 U.S.C.A. § 1701j–3(d).

54. 12 U.S.C.A. § 1701j–3(d)(1). If the creation of such a junior lien cannot trigger enforcement of a due-on-sale clause in a senior mortgage, should a transfer incident to foreclosure of the junior lien do so? See Matter of Foreclosure of Ruepp, 71 N.C.App. 146, 321 S.E.2d 517 (1984) (foreclosure of junior mortgage held not to trigger due-on-sale clause in senior mortgage where the clause expressly authorized the creation of junior liens).

55. 48 Fed.Reg. 21,562 (codified at 12 CFR 591.5(b)).

56. Id. at 21,559.

57. Federal Deposit Insurance Corp. v. Sumner Financial Corp., 451 F.2d 898, 902 (5th Cir.1972).

58. See e.g., United States v. American Trucking Associations, 310 U.S. 534, 60 S.Ct. 1059, 84 L.Ed. 1345 (1940); Caminetti v. United States, 242 U.S. 470, 37 S.Ct. 192, 61 L.Ed. 442 (1917). See generally H. Read, J. MacDonald, J. Fordham & W. Pierce, Materials on Legislation 790–815 (1973).

59. See Nelson and Whitman, Congressional Preemption of Mortgage Due-on-Sale Law: Analysis of the Garn-St. Germain Act, 35 Hast.L.J. 241, 270–271 (1983).

Although limiting the further encumbrance exception to loans made on the security of less than five dwelling units may be justifiable,[60] the case for restricting the other exceptions to such loans is less appealing. The Report of the Senate Committee on Banking, Housing and Urban Affairs (Senate Committee Report) for example, emphasized that it would be unfair for lenders to enforce due-on-sale clauses under certain circumstances, such as "involuntary transfers resulting from the death of a borrower, transfers which rearrange ownership rights within a family, or transfers resulting from a separation or dissolution of a marriage."[61] If it is unfair to enforce a due-on-sale clause when a marriage dissolution necessitates a title transfer of a family home, is it less unfair to invoke the clause when the real estate is the family grocery store? If an owner of a family home should be able to transfer it to an inter vivos trust of which she is the beneficiary, why should her transfer of raw land held for speculation be treated any differently?

Perhaps Congress would have been wiser to impose the "less than five dwelling unit" limitation only under the further encumbrance exception. Such an approach would have accommodated the Senate Committee's specific concern for the owner-occupant in the further encumbrance situation, while at the same time deferring in the main to the language of the Act. In the further encumbrance situation, lenders have a legitimate concern that further liens may reduce the mortgagor's economic stake in the real estate to the point of security impairment.[62] It is true, of course, that certain of the other "non-substantive" or "non-sale" transfers can occasionally threaten mortgage security.[63] Yet we believe concerns about security impairment, in general, are normally less justified in most "nonsubstantive" or "non-sale" transfers than in the further encumbrance setting.[64]

The Regulation modifies the Act's exceptions to due-on-sale enforcement in other respects. For example, the Regulation adds to the further encumbrance exception by making it clear that a transfer by installment land contract does not constitute "[t]he creation of a lien or other encumbrance subordinate to the lender's security instrument."[65] This addition is probably unnecessary because installment land contract transfers almost always entail the transfer of occupancy rights while, in order for the exception to apply, the Act states that the creation of the lien or encumbrance must "not relate to a transfer of

---

60. See infra text accompanying notes 62–64.

61. Report of Sen. Comm. on Banking, Housing and Urban Affairs on S. 2879, S.Rep. No. 536, 97th Cong., 2d Sess. (1982) at 24 (hereinafter cited as Senate Committee Report).

62. See § 5.21 supra notes 19–21 and accompanying text.

63. For example, the building that houses a family grocery business may, be-

cause of the death of the original mortgagor, wind up in the hands of an inexperienced and unreliable spouse or child whose actions may result in security impairment.

64. See § 5.21 supra, notes 19, 21 and accompanying text.

65. 48 Fed.Reg. 21,562 (codified at 12 CFR 591.5(b)(1)(i)).

rights of occupancy in the property." [66]   In any event, the Board's interpretation of the exception is correct. The Act's "further encumbrance" exception is aimed at protecting mortgagors who have no intent to sell or transfer ownership, but want to create non-purchase money junior liens on their real estate for a variety of business or personal reasons.[67]

The Regulation, unlike the Act, in either its original or amended form, specifies that for certain non-substantive transfers to escape due-on-sale enforcement, the transferee must be a person "who occupies or will occupy the property." [68]   This requirement is applicable to any transfer resulting from the death of the borrower, and to transfers to a spouse or child or those incident to marriage dissolution.[69]   For example, if a parent gives his home to a daughter, and the daughter then occupies it herself, under the Regulation no acceleration may take place. However, if the daughter chooses to rent it out, the due-on-sale clause is enforceable. There appears to be no direct support in the legislative history for the Board's addition of this "transferee occupancy" requirement, and its validity is dubious at best.

Finally, while the Act prohibits due-on-sale enforcement when there is "a transfer into an inter vivos trust in which the borrower is and remains a beneficiary" [70] and retains the right of occupancy, the Regulation conditions this exception on the borrower providing the lender with "reasonable means acceptable to the lender" by which the lender will be "assured of timely notice of any subsequent transfer of the beneficial interest or change in occupancy." [71]   Lenders had told the Board that under certain devices, such as the Illinois land trust,[72] the beneficiary is free to direct the sale of the beneficial interest without any public record or notice to the lender.[73]   The Regulation seems consistent with congressional intent on this issue as it simply aids the mortgagee in making future determinations as to whether a "real" or "substantive" transfer has occurred that would justify invoking the due-on-sale clause.

The Exemption for Window Period Loans

As a result of pressure from the real estate brokerage industry [74] and a desire to protect the reasonable expectations of borrowers who believed that they had acquired "assumable" loans for purposes of

---

66. 12 U.S.C.A. § 1701j–3(d)(1).

67. See Senate Committee Report, supra note 60, at 24. At least one case supports this conclusion. See Smith v. Frontier Federal Savings & Loan Association, 649 P.2d 536 (Okl.1982).

68. 48 Fed.Reg. 21,563 (codified at 12 CFR 591.5(b)(1)(v)).

69. Id.

70. 12 U.S.C.A. § 1701j–3(d)(8).

71. 48 Fed.Reg. 21,563 (codified at 12 CFR 591.5(b)(1)(vi)).

72. Under such a trust, the trustee (typically a financial institution) holds "bare" legal title, but has no management duties. See Flaherty, Illinois Land Trusts and the Due-on-Sale Clause, 65 Ill.B.J. 376 (1977).

73. 48 Fed.Reg. 21,559.

74. See supra note 2.

future resale,[75] Congress provided partial relief from the Act's preemption. Thus, in some states the Act's effect is deferred and state law continues to govern enforcement of certain due-on-sale clauses. This was accomplished through creation of "window periods," which give rise to the postponement of the Act's preemptions.[76] The concept of window periods is complex, and is not clearly defined in the Act or susceptible to easy explanation. On the other hand, as the following material indicates, the problems created by the window period are relatively short-lived.

A state may be a window period state if it restricted enforcement of due-on-sale clauses before the Act. The window period in such a state began when the state first restricted enforcement of due-on-sale clauses, and ended when the state ended such restrictions, or upon passage of the Act. Certain loans in a state that had a window period remained assumable for three years if they would have been assumable under state law prior to the passage of the Act. This three-year deferral period began on October 15, 1982, (the effective date of the Act), and lasted until October 15, 1985.[77] Only states that "prohibited the exercise of due-on-sale clauses" [78] before the effective date of the Act qualify for window period treatment and the three year extension. To qualify, a state must have prohibited exercise of the due-on-sale clause by a statute, its constitution, or a decision of its highest court (or if no such decision, a decision by the state's next highest appellate court whose decisions apply statewide).[79]

However, not all loans in states qualifying for window period treatment were assumable for this three year period. Only loans that were "made or assumed" between the date of the state's prohibition of enforcement of the due-on-sale clause and October 15, 1982, are governed by state law and thus remained assumable.[80] The Regulation defines "assumed" to include transfers under which a grantee takes "subject to" the mortgage but does not agree to be personally liable for the mortgage debt.[81]

The window period concept can be best understood through factual examples. Suppose State X enacted a statute on July 1, 1979, limiting due-on-sale enforcement in mortgages on single family dwellings to situations in which the mortgagee can establish impairment of mortgage security. MR purchased his house on September 1, 1981, and simultaneously executed a mortgage on it that contained a due-on-sale clause. If MR sold his house on April 1, 1984, to Grantee, the mortgage

---

75. See Senate Committee Report, supra note 61, at 22.

76. 12 U.S.C.A. § 1701j–3(c)(1) (1982). States may also extend this window period protection indefinitely. See infra notes 100–106 & accompanying text. The term "window period" appears in Senate Committee Report, supra note 61 at 22, rather than in the Act.

77. 12 U.S.C.A. § 1701j–3(c)(1).

78. Id.

79. Id.

80. Id.

81. 48 Fed.Reg. 21,561 (codified at 12 CFR 591.2(a)).

was assumable by Grantee unless the mortgagee could establish that the transfer impaired mortgage security. This would also be true if MR had assumed an existing mortgage on September 1, 1981, rather than obtaining a new loan, since the assumption would have occurred after July 1, 1979, the effective date of the state statute. Finally, the transferees of Grantee, if any, were able to assume the mortgage so long as the transfer took place prior to October 15, 1985, and the mortgagee was not able to establish that such a transfer would impair mortgage security.

Although the Board was requested to identify the states that qualify for window period treatment, it declined to do so [82] on the ground that Congress intended window period determinations to be left to "state interpretation and state judicial decision." [83] Only states that have "prohibited the exercise of due-on-sale clauses" [84] qualify for window period treatment. This language is susceptible to several possible interpretations. If it is taken to refer to total and absolute prohibitions, no window periods would be created anywhere, as no state bars the enforcement of due-on-clauses under all circumstances.[85] Such a reading would mean that no post-Act transfers would be exempt from the Act's preemption, even though the transfers took place in a state that substantially restricts due-on-sale enforcement. This result would obviously be contrary to congressional intent. In reliance on language in the Senate Committee Report,[86] the Regulation takes a more moderate view, providing that a state qualifies for window period treatment when it has "adopted a law * * * prohibiting the *unrestricted* exercise of due-on-sale clauses upon *outright transfers* of property." [87]

82. Id. at 21,555.

83. Id.

84. 12 U.S.C.A. § 1701j–3(c)(1).

85. See supra § 5.22, note 13 and accompanying text.

86. See Senate Committee Report, supra note 61 at 22 (citing Fidelity Federal Savings & Loan Association v. de la Cuesta, 458 U.S. 141, 170 n.24, 102 S.Ct. 3014, 3031, 73 L.Ed.2d 664 (1982)).

87. 48 Fed.Reg. 21,562 (to be codified at 12 CFR 591.2(p)(2)(i)–(ii)) (emphasis added). The Board expressly refused to identify specific window period states. See id. at 21,555. However, the two major federally-sponsored purchasers of mortgage loans on the secondary market have attempted to identify such states. The FNMA listed Arizona, California, Colorado, Georgia, Iowa, Michigan, Minnesota, New Mexico, Utah, and Washington as "window period" states. See FNMA Press Release, Feb. 22, 1983. See Perry v. Island Savings and Loan Association, 101 Wn.2d 795, 684 P.2d 1281 (1984) (Washington has window period for loans by non-federally chartered lender from August 19, 1976 to October 15, 1982).

The FHLMC designated the same states as having window periods. The only variation is the date of commencement of the Arizona period, with the FNMA listing of Mar. 13, 1978 (the date of Patton v. First Federal Savings & Loan Association, 118 Ariz. 473, 578 P.2d 152 (1978)), and the FHLMC listing of July 8, 1971 (the date of Baltimore Life Insurance Co. v. Harn, 15 Ariz.App. 78, 486 P.2d 190 (1971)). See Freddie Mac Issues Guidelines for Due-on-Sale Enforcement, 11 Hous. & Dev.Rep. (BNA) 26 (1983). In Scappaticci v. Southwest Savings & Loan Association, 135 Ariz. 456, 662 P.2d 131 (1983), the Arizona Supreme Court resolved the issue by using *Harn* for deeds of trust as well as mortgages. For a detailed consideration of the Arizona situation, see Nelson and Whitman, supra note 59 at 286–294.

The Comptroller of the Currency has issued a regulation that includes a state-by-state list of window periods. See 48 Fed. Reg. 21,561–63. This list agrees with that

The Regulation identifies two specific types of state restrictions (whether legislative or judicial) that will trigger a window period. These are restrictions on mortgagee's rights to exercise due-on-sale clauses when 1) the security or probability of repayment is impaired, or 2) the lender is required to permit a transfer of the property without

of the FHLMC, except that it adds Arkansas.

Several states not listed by FNMA or FHLMC may have window periods. The Arkansas Supreme Court adopted a rule requiring lenders to show impairment of security in Tucker v. Pulaski Federal Savings & Loan Association, 252 Ark. 849, 481 S.W.2d 725 (1972). Subsequent cases have held that *Tucker's* restrictions on due-on-sale clause enforcement have been preempted by federal regulation as to savings and loan associations. See First Federal Savings & Loan Association v. Myrick, 533 F.Supp. 1041, 1045–46 (W.D.Ark.1982); Schulte v. Benton Savings & Loan Association, 279 Ark. 275, 651 S.W.2d 71 (1983); Independence Federal Savings & Loan Association v. Davis, 278 Ark. 387, 646 S.W.2d 336 (1983). However, *Tucker* still appears to be good Arkansas law except for federal and state savings associations, and it is unclear why Arkansas was omitted from the FNMA and FHLMC lists.

California has a complex window period situation. See Nelson and Whitman, supra note 59 at 275–286.

The Florida district courts of appeals have consistently required a showing of impairment of security for due-on-sale enforcement. See Consolidated Capital Properties, II, Inc. v. National Bank of North America, 420 So.2d 618, 622–23 (Fla. App.1982), petition for review dismissed 429 So.2d 7 (1983); Woodcrest Apartments, Limited v. IPA Realty Partners, 397 So.2d 364, 366 (Fla.App.1981); First Federal Savings & Loan Association v. Lockwood, 385 So.2d 156, 159–60 (Fla.App.1980); see also Turner, Due-on-Sale Clause: Forcing the Issue, 56 Fla.B.J. 360 (1982). There is Florida Court of Appeal authority that Florida is a window period state. See First Federal Savings & Loan Association v. Siegel, 456 So.2d 579, 581 (Fla.App.1984). Florida may have been omitted from the FNMA and FHLMC lists on the supposition that the decisions of the Florida Courts of Appeals are not decisions which apply Statewide, whatever that phrase from the Act may mean. See 12 U.S.C.A. § 1701j–3(c) (1), see also Nelson and Whitman supra note 59 at 291–294.

A probable window period in Mississippi has been "repealed" by that state's supreme court. In Sanders v. Hicks, 317 So. 2d 61 (Miss.1975), the court refused to enforce a mortgage clause which prohibited the mortgagor from transferring or encumbering the property. Id. at 64. While the language was not literally a due-on-sale clause, the court cited with approval several cases restricting due-on-sale enforcement. Id. It held that the no-transfer clause would be enforceable only upon a showing of increased risk to the mortgagee's security. Nevertheless, in First National Bank of Vicksburg v. Caruthers, 443 So.2d 861 (Miss.1984), the Mississippi Supreme Court expressly overruled *Sanders* and held that Mississippi thus had no window period. This approach seems dubious at best. Whatever the ability of the court to limit the impact of *Sanders* by interpreting it narrowly, or even to overrule it, the court cannot retroactively eliminate the window period impact of its own earlier decision. See Nelson and Whitman, supra, note 59 at 288. Surely reasonable mortgagors could have relied on *Sanders* as placing significant limits on the enforcement of due-on-sale clauses. See also Casa Grande Inc. v. Minnesota Mutual Life Insurance Company, 596 F.Supp. 1385 (S.D.Miss. 1984) (Mississippi has no window period).

For the view that Illinois is not a window period state, see North Community Bank v. Northwest National Bank of Chicago, 126 Ill.App.3d 581, 82 Ill.Dec. 21, 467 N.E.2d 1094 (1984).

The Louisiana situation is even more ambiguous. Rayford v. Louisiana Savings Association, 380 So.2d 1232 (La.App.1980) refused to enforce a due-on-sale clause, id. at 1234, but the case's impact for window period purposes is unclear because of the presence of several unusual factors: an intermediate appellate court was involved, see Nelson and Whitman supra note 59 at 291–294, the lender actually did not seek acceleration but rather an "assumption fee"; the proposed sale was from one co-owner to another; and a Louisiana statute, La.Stat.Ann.–R.S. 6:837, appeared to authorize savings and loan associations (but not other lenders) to exercise due-on-sale clauses. See Breaux, Due-on-Sale Litigation, 30 La.B.J. 18 (1982).

raising the interest rate to the current market level.[88] Thus, the Regulation asserts that different or less restrictive state law limitations on enforcement of due-on-sale clauses will not trigger a window period. For example, even state courts in "automatic enforcement" jurisdictions will not usually enforce due-on-sale clauses when to do so would be "unconscionable" or "inequitable." [89] Almost all courts will refuse to enforce the clauses in non-substantive transfers such as a transfer to a spouse who becomes a co-owner, a transfer incident to a marriage dissolution, or a transfer by operation of law upon the death of a joint tenant.[90] Yet such judicial restrictions probably will not trigger a window period under the Regulation. The Board, in its preamble, offers the illustration of a state statute that imposes a more onerous foreclosure procedure than the standard procedure used when the default results from the exercise of a due-on-sale clause.[91] This type of restriction, according to the Regulation, will not create a window period, and the state statute itself will be preempted by the Act.[92]

It is doubtful that the Board acted within its power in limiting window periods to states with the two enumerated types of restrictions. When "non-substantive" or "non-sale" transfers, such as spousal, marriage dissolution, and death transfers are involved, the question has little practical importance. This is because federal law and state law are likely to have much the same effect.[93] But the Iowa statute, which grants a longer post-sale redemption period when foreclosure results from due-on-sale enforcement,[94] presents a more serious problem. If Congress intended to preserve the reasonable expectations of mortgagors until 1985, it seems improper for the Board to deny them the benefit of the long redemption period provided by the state statute. In its desire to aid lenders, the Board may have neglected congressional intent.

The Regulation also expressly provides that a state with a window period cannot modify its law to extend the protection from due-on-sale enforcement to loans that were not of a type protected during the window period.[95] Thus, in our prior example,[96] suppose that on March 1, 1984 (after the effective date of the Act), the state legislature amended its 1979 statute to include mortgages on duplexes within the restriction on due-on-sale enforcement. Suppose further that MR purchased a duplex that he resold to Grantee in 1985. Mortgagee would be entitled to accelerate the mortgage debt incident to the transfer to Grantee, even though no security impairment was shown, because

88. 48 Fed.Reg. 21,562 (codified at 12 CFR 591.2(p)(3)).

89. See supra § 5.22, notes 24–26 and accompanying text.

90. Id.

91. Iowa has such a statute. Iowa Code Ann. § 535.8(2)(e).

92. See 48 Fed.Reg. 21,556 (preamble).

93. See supra § 5.22, notes 24–26 and accompanying text.

94. See supra § 5.22, note 42.

95. 48 Fed.Reg. 21,561 (codified at 12 CFR 591.2(p)(1)) (a window period loan must have been "made or assumed during a window-period created by state law and *subject to* that law") (emphasis added).

96. See supra text following note 81.

during the window period state law only affected enforcement of due-on-sale clauses contained in mortgages on single family dwellings. Although the Act itself does not limit its protection in this way, this result seems sensible in light of the Act's purpose of protecting the reasonable expectations of those who purchased property in reliance on state law.[97]

Establishing if and when the window period began and what loans it encompassed has hardly been an easy task. Assuming that a state has a window period, one solution to the problem would simply be to identify its commencement date and include all loans, whatever their nature, within its coverage. The Board apparently has chosen this approach.[98] While such an approach has the virtue of simplicity and ease of application, it may have sacrificed common sense for administrative convenience. Even this simplicity may be illusory because Board's approach is likely to be attacked as contrary to Congressional intent. A better, if more complex, way to determine if a particular mortgage qualifies as a window period loan is to focus on whether the mortgagor or grantee could *reasonably have believed,* based on the then current state law and the nature of the transaction, that she was acquiring an assumable mortgage. If so, window period protection should be available. Admittedly, this "reasonable reliance" approach may result in separate window periods for different types of mortgage transactions, and will inevitably entail a close analysis of state law. Nevertheless, it is probably most consistent with congressional intent to protect those who consummated transactions in reliance on state law.[99]

State Extension of Window Period Protection

If a state has a window period, it was permitted, prior to October 15, 1985, to enact legislation "otherwise regulat[ing]" window period loans originated by lenders other than certain federally-chartered institutions.[1] Thus, the legislature in such a state conceivably could insulate window period loans from the Act's preemption indefinitely. While this means that such a state could effectively extend preexisting

---

97. Id.

98. See Nelson and Whitman, supra note 59, at 282–283, 298.

99. Because of the self-limiting nature of the window period concept, we have chosen not to consider it in detail in this volume. For a more extensive analysis with a special emphasis on California, Arizona and Florida, see Nelson and Whitman, supra note 59 at 278–296.

1. See 12 U.S.C.A. § 1701j–3(c)(1)(A). The Senate Committee noted that the three year period * * * provides State Legislatures * * * with the opportunity to review the impact Due-On-Sale restrictions have imposed * * * on lenders * * * and to formulate an alternative

approach to window period loans if they so desire. For example * * * a State might repeal existing Due-On-Sale restrictions. A State might also lengthen the time that State Due-On-Sale restrictions would apply to window period loans * * *.

Senate Committee Report, supra note 159, at 23. The Arizona legislature has exercised this power, extending the grace period for window-period loans to October 15, 1987. 1983 Ariz.Legis.Serv. ch. 321 (West). New Mexico extended its window period indefinitely, but permitted mortgagees to raise the interest rate on window period loans to a "blended" rate. See N.M.S.A. 48–7–15 to 48–7–24 (1983).

state law with regard to some loans, it had to recognize the power of mortgagees to use due-on-sale clauses as a tool to ensure that proposed transferees meet customary credit standards.[2] Thus, in no circumstances could a state absolutely prohibit enforcement of the clause. Since virtually all state judicial decisions and statutes have recognized the validity of the clause for the limited purpose of insuring the credit worthiness of proposed transferees,[3] the Act is not likely to present a serious conflict with state law in this respect. Finally, it should be emphasized that states without window periods could not restrict enforcement of due-on-sale clauses.

The exact nature of this authority to "otherwise regulate" certain window period loans is not clear. Suppose that in 1980 the Supreme Court of State X held that a due-on-sale clause could not be enforced with respect to loans on single family dwellings unless the mortgagee could establish that the transfer would impair security or create an increased risk of default. State X thus has a window period for mortgage loans that were made or assumed on such dwellings after the 1980 judicial decision. A mortgagor or his transferee was free to transfer, subject only to state law restrictions, until October 15, 1985.

Suppose further that during 1984 State X enacted legislation with a clear intent to insulate such window period loans from the Act's preemption. Assume that the legislation extended this protection to pre-Act mortgage loans on duplexes made or assumed after the 1980 judicial decision. The time extension is valid, but according to the preamble to the Regulation, the duplex provision is invalid because a state could not "expand the type of loan to which the window period applies."[4] This seems a justifiable restriction on state legislative action. If, as was noted earlier,[5] a state legislature cannot expand the type of loan protected from the Act's preemption during the 1982–1985 grace period, it surely should be unable to do so for the life of the loan.

The Board's interpretation on this point is entirely reasonable. Unfortunately, the drafting of the relevant portion of the Act was extremely inept. While the Act provides that state legislatures "may otherwise regulate such contracts,"[6] it is unclear whether "such contracts" refers to all real property loans except those originated by federally-chartered lenders, or only to window period loans. The latter construction is more consistent with the Act's overall objective of protecting reasonable reliance, and the Board's view should be upheld.

On the other hand, it appears that legislatures in window period states had the power to modify the *content* of existing state law so long as they did not attempt to extend it to non-window period loans. In the example above, the legislature could have theoretically affected due-on-

---

2. 12 U.S.C.A. § 1701j–3(c)(2)(A).

3. See supra § 5.22, notes 13, 19–20, 39 and accompanying text.

4. 48 Fed.Reg. 21,558.

5. See supra text accompanying notes 95–97.

6. 12 U.S.C.A. § 1701j–3(c)(2)(A).

sale enforcement for window period loans by adopting specific credit standards, either more or less severe than those in the hypothetical 1980 judicial decision, which a prospective grantee would then be required to meet. As we noted, however, the legislature could not take away the power of lenders to apply "customary credit standards."[7] In light of this limitation, the practical ability of legislatures to change credit standards was unidirectional: they could only impose standards stiffer than "customary" standards.

Special Rules Under the Act for Certain Federally-Chartered Lenders

As noted earlier, federally-chartered savings and loan associations had the pre-Act power to enforce due-on-sale clauses by virtue of the 1976 Bank Board regulation upheld in *de la Cuesta*.[8] The Act, with minor modifications, simply continued that power.[9] Moreover, while prior to the Act some doubt existed as to the enforceability of due-on-sale clauses in pre-1976 regulation mortgage loans, the Act's preemption definitely applies to such clauses, which are now clearly enforceable.[10] Neither the window period concept nor a window period state's ability to "otherwise regulate" window period loans is applicable to such federal associations.[11] Thus, so far as any post-Act transfer is concerned, federal associations are entirely free of state due-on-sale law.

With respect to national banks and federal credit unions, window period loans originated by these lenders were subject to state law until October 15, 1985,[12] unless the Comptroller of the Currency (Comptroller) or the National Credit Union Administration (NCUA) acted prior to that date otherwise to regulate these loans.[13] Thus, the Comptroller or the NCUA had the power to either extend or contract the time period in which these loans were subject to state law. The NCUA acted, effective November 18, 1982, to render immediately enforceable due-on-sale clauses in transfers made on or after that date.[14] In effect, the NCUA's rules preempted state law, regardless of the reasonable expectations of the consumers in states that would otherwise have had assumable window period loans.

The Comptroller's rule, effective December 8, 1983, was similar to the NCUA rule but more lenient to owners of one to four family homes who obtained or assumed loans during a window period. Until April 15, 1984, such loans could be assumed to the extent allowed by state law, except that the lender could increase the interest rate to a "blended" level that was the average of the original contract rate and the current average contract interest rate on existing homes, as pub-

7. See supra text accompanying note 101.

8. See § 5.23 supra, notes 9–20 and accompanying text.

9. 12 U.S.C.A. § 1701j–3(c)(2)(C).

10. 12 U.S.C.A. § 1701j–3(b)(1), (c)(2)(C).

11. Id. § 1701j–3(c)(2)(C).

12. Id. § 1701j–3(c)(1)(B).

13. Id.

14. 47 Fed.Reg. 54,425 (codified at 12 CFR 701.21–6(d)(2)(i)).

lished by the Board. For other types of loans, the full federal preemption was effective immediately.[15]

Mortgagee's Duty to Respond Under the Act

When a mortgagor and a proposed transferee seek mortgagee approval for a transfer of a window period loan, the Regulation requires the mortgagee to respond in writing with its decision within thirty days after receipt of a completed credit application and supporting information.[16] If the mortgagee decides to disapprove a proposed transfer, its decision must be accompanied by a statement of the reasons supporting the disapproval.[17] Failure to respond in this way prohibits a mortgagee from enforcing a due-on-sale clause as to the proposed transfer.[18] The foregoing requirements are apparently inapplicable to non-window period loans and to all loans originated by federally-chartered savings and loan associations.[19] Perhaps this exclusion was based on a Board belief that since the due-on-sale clauses in such loans are usually enforceable, the mortgagor and his or her transferee should be deemed to assume that permission to transfer will be denied. Thus, the Board could have concluded that the imposition of a formal response requirement on the mortgagee under such circumstances would not be justifiable.

This limitation of the response requirement to window period loans whose due-on-sale clauses are likely to be unenforceable is unfortunate. To be sure, the probability of obtaining permission to transfer may be significantly lower in circumstances involving a non-window period loan. On the other hand, there may well be instances when a mortgagee will permit a transfer with no interest rate change, notwithstand-

---

15. 48 Fed.Reg. 51,283 (codified at 12 CFR 30.1). The Comptroller took the unprecedented step of expressly designating, for purposes of his regulation, the window period for each state. See supra note 87.

The Comptroller's use of "blended" rates is supported by the Act, which specifically encourages the use of such rates. 12 U.S. C.A. § 1701j–3(b)(3). The Board, believing this provision to be merely persuasive and not mandatory, did not include a similar provision in the Regulation. See 48 Fed. Reg. 21,561–63 (codified at 12 CFR 591.1–.6).

16. Id. at 21,562 (codified at 12 CFR 591.4(d)(3)).

17. Id.

18. Id.

19. The language of 12 CFR 592.4(d)(3) does not specifically exempt non-window period loans and all loans originated by federally-chartered savings and loan associations from the formal mortgagee response requirement. But when it is read in context with other parts of 12 CFR 591.4, an inference that the Board intend-

ed such an exclusion is strongly warranted. For example, the section itself is entitled "Loans originated by lenders other than Federal associations." Moreover, 12 CFR 591.4(d)(2), which immediately precedes the formal response requirement, deals specifically with the circumstances under which a transfer of a *window period loan* may be denied when the transferee does not meet the mortgagee's customary credit standards. In this context it is unlikely that the Board could have intended to apply 12 CFR 591.4(d)(3) to non-window period loans or to those loans originated by federally-chartered lenders. Moreover, in view of the Board's apparent intention to impose the response requirement only in situations where due-on-sale enforcement is restricted, it is unlikely that mortgagee response is required even as to window period loans once the grace period for such loans expires. The expiration date will be either October 15, 1985 or such later date specified by state legislation extending the period of protection for window period loans. See text at notes 1–7 supra.

ing the enforceability of the due-on-sale clause. This could occur, for example, if the current market rate does not differ markedly from the mortgage rate. It is common for lenders to approve transfers on the condition that the interest rate be raised to a "blended" level somewhere between the original and current market rates. The Senate Report and the Act itself specifically encourage this practice.[20] In any event, it hardly seems equitable to leave the parties to a proposed transfer in a state of uncertainty for an unduly long period. This is especially true where, as here, the response requirement appears to impose a relatively insignificant burden on the mortgagee.

In certain relatively rare situations, a mortgagee may by judicial decision be held estopped to assert, or to have waived, its rights under an otherwise enforceable due-on-sale clause.[21] Suppose a mortgagor requests permission to transfer and receives no reply from the mortgagee. Nonetheless, the proposed transfer is consummated. If the mortgagee delays acceleration of the mortgage debt for a significant period of time, a court may be convinced that any subsequent attempt to enforce the clause as to that transfer is barred by waiver or estoppel principles. The probability of this result will be increased if the transferee has made significant improvements to the mortgaged real estate or has entered into substantial commercial relationships with respect to that real estate, prior to a belated attempt by the mortgagee to accelerate the mortgage debt. Unfortunately, the judicial application of waiver or estoppel concepts in this setting is uncertain at best. Ideally, the Board should simply broaden the lender-response requirement to encompass loans that contain enforceable due-on-sale clauses.

The Board's authority to take this step is debatable. The Act contains nothing about lender response. It merely states that lenders of window period loans may insist that transferees meet customary credit standards.[22] The Board apparently reasoned from this provision that it had authority to standardize the procedure by which the meeting of applicable credit standards would be determined and communicated. This conclusion seems unexceptionable. Of course, the

---

20. See 12 U.S.C.A. § 1701j–3(b)(3); Senate Committee Report, supra note 61, at 21.

21. The cases frequently focus on whether the lender has delayed an unreasonable time after the transfer before accelerating. See, e.g., Malouff v. Midland Federal Savings & Loan Association, 181 Colo. 294, 304, 509 P.2d 1240, 1245–46 (1973) (one-month delay is reasonable, but one year would not be); First National Bank v. Brown, 90 Ill.App.3d 215, 219, 45 Ill.Dec. 496, 500, 412 N.E.2d 1078, 1082 (1980) (18-month delay gave rise to estoppel where mortgagee had notice and mortgagor detrimentally relied). Rubin v. Los Angeles Federal Savings & Loan Association, 159 Cal.App.3d 292, 205 Cal.Rptr. 455 (1984) (one year delay constitutes waiver). Cf. Bakker v. Empire Savings, Buildings & Loan Association, 634 P.2d 1021, 1022 (Colo.App.1981), appeal dismissed 653 P.2d 385 (1982) (no waiver despite lender's acceptance of payments after notice of transfer); Dunham v. Ware Savings Bank, 384 Mass. 63, 67, 423 N.E.2d 998, 1000 (1981) (three month delay, no waiver or estoppel); Stenger v. Great Southern Savings and Loan Association, 677 S.W.2d 376 (Mo.App. 1984) (insufficient evidence to establish waiver or estoppel.)

22. 12 U.S.C.A. § 1701j–3(c)(2)(A).

Board's plenary power to regulate federally chartered associations [23] would permit it to apply this rule to such lenders with respect to all loans originated by them. A harder case would arise if the Board attempted to make non-federally chartered lenders comply with the response rule for non-window period loans. On the one hand, the Act provides that the power of such lenders to enforce their due-on-sale clauses "shall be exclusively governed by the terms of the loan contract, and all rights and remedies of the lender and the borrower shall be fixed and governed by the contract." [24] This language may prevent the Board from interposing even mere procedural requirements if they are not mentioned in the loan contract.

On the other hand, the Act gives the Board authority "to issue rules and regulations and to publish interpretations governing the implementation of this section." [25] The grammatical structure of this sentence seems to suggest that issuing rules and publishing interpretations are separate activities, and this in turn may indicate that rules can be issued that go beyond mere interpretations of the Act. Under this view, a rule giving non-window period borrowers a right to a timely response to their requests for loan assumption approval might well be within the Board's powers. At least, such a rule is well within the general subject matter of the Act, something that cannot be so easily said about the Board's rule on prepayment penalties.

Further support for this position is found in the Act's language, appearing at the end of the list of "non-substantive transfers" discussed earlier in this section,[26] that prohibits due-on-sale enforcement upon "any other transfer or disposition described in regulations prescribed by the Federal Home Loan Bank Board." [27] The Senate Committee Report indicates that the Board was given this authority "to provide protections for consumers by prohibiting the enforcement of due-on-sale clauses where such enforcement would be inequitable." [28] Since it is probably inequitable for a lender to accelerate after failing to give a timely response to the borrower's request for approval to transfer title, this language seems to fit the present situation rather nicely. It seems very likely that if the Board issued a broad rule requiring all lenders to respond to such requests within a reasonable time, the courts would uphold it.

Release of The Original Mortgagor Under the Act

When a mortgagee waives its right to accelerate under a due-on-sale clause (typically after a higher interest rate or "assumption fee" is agreed upon) and the transferee assumes (rather than merely takes

23. See Fidelity Federal Savings & Loan Association v. de la Cuesta, 458 U.S. 141, 160, 102 S.Ct. 3014, 3024, 73 L.Ed.2d 664 (1982).

24. 12 U.S.C.A. § 1701j–3(b)(2).

25. Id. § 1701j–3(e)(1).

26. See supra text accompanying notes 51–52.

27. 12 U.S.C.A. § 1701j–3(d)(9).

28. Senate Committee Report, supra note 61, at 25.

"subject to" [29]) the existing mortgage, the Regulation requires that the mortgagee release the original mortgagor from personal liability on the mortgage debt.[30] For several years this requirement has been part of Board regulations applicable to federally-chartered savings and loan associations.[31] The mortgage form specified for use by lenders who sell mortgages to the FNMA and the FHLMC on the secondary market also imposes such a requirement on mortgagees.[32] There is no policy ground for objecting to the Board's requirement, but there is also no justification for it in the Act. Hence the Board's authority to impose the requirement on lenders other than federally-chartered savings associations must rest on the rather thin reed of its general power to issue rules.[33]

 WESTLAW REFERENCES

citation(12 +3 1701j–3)

Lenders Covered

date(after 1981) & (garn +3 germain) (section 12 3 1701j–3 341) /p cover*** (property /3 loan)

Loans Covered

date(after 1981) & (garn +3 germain) (section 12 +3 1701j–3 341) /p loan /s lease! mortgage property

Types of Mortgage Transfer Restrictions Covered

date(after 1981) & (garn +3 germain) (section 12 +3 1701j–3 341) /p "increased interest"

Coverage of Installment Land Contracts

date(after 1981) & (garn +3 germain) (section 12 +3 1701j–3 341) /p contract /3 deed (installment long-term +1 land)

Time of Transfer

date(after 1981) & (garn +3 germain) (section 12 +3 1701j–3 341) /s applicable apply*** effect*** retroactive

Transfers in Which Due-On-Sale Enforcement is Prohibited

date(after 1981) & (garn +3 germain) (section 12 +3 1701j–3 341) /p enforce! exempt! prohibit! /12 dispos! due-on-sale

The Exemption for Window Period Loans

date(after 1981) & (garn +3 germain) (section 12 +3 1701j–3 341) /p "three year" "window period"

State Extension of Window Period Protection

date(after 1981) & (garn +3 germain) (section 12 +3 1701j–3 341) /p otherwise state /5 regulat!

29. A grantee who "assumes" an existing mortgage becomes personally liable for the payment of the mortgage debt. A grantee who merely takes "subject to" the mortgage implicitly agrees that if the debt is not paid the mortgagee may look to the mortgaged real estate for satisfaction of the debt, but the grantee does not become personally liable on that debt. See, e.g., Del Rio Loan, Inc. v. Haument, 110 Ariz. 7, 9, 514 P.2d 1003, 1005 (1973); Elluckson v. Dull, 34 Colo.App. 25, 28, 521 P.2d 1282, 1284 (1974); Brice v. Griffin, 269 Md. 558, 561, 307 A.2d 660, 661 (1973); Nutz v. Sheperd, 490 S.W.2d 366, 372 (Mo.App. 1973).

30. 48 Fed.Reg. 21,563 (codified at 12 CFR 591.5(b)(3)).

31. 12 CFR § 545.8–3(g).

32. FNMA/FHLMC Mortgage, Clause 17 (one to four family).

33. See supra text accompanying note 25.

*Special Rules Under the Act for Certain Federally-Chartered Lend-
ers*

date(after 1981) & (garn +3 germain) (section 12 +3 1701j–3
    341) /p federal +1 association "credit union" savings

Mortgagee's Duty to Respond Under the Act

date(after 1981) & (garn +3 germain) (section 12 +3 1701j–3
    341) /p lender mortgagee timely /s answer*** approv***
    respond*** response

Release of the Original Mortgagor Under the Act

date(after 1981) & (garn +3 germain) (section 12 +3 1701j–3
    341) /p releas*** /s grantor mortgagor seller

§ 5.25 The Due-on Clauses—Concealment of Transfers

In jurisdictions where due-on-sale clauses have been automatically enforceable or where there has been some doubt as to their enforceability, parties to real estate transactions may be tempted to avoid the consequences of the due-on-sale clause by concealing the transfer from the mortgagee. Because the Act will increase the number of enforceable due-on-sale clauses, these concealment attempts will probably increase. For example, to decrease the risk of discovery, the parties may arrange to have the transferee make the mortgage payments to the mortgagor-transferor or to a third party, who in turn will make the payment to the mortgagee in the mortgagor's name. Usually the parties continue to use the payment book originally issued to the mortgagor-transferor.

For a variety of reasons these concealment strategies often fail. Some mortgagees, for example, may closely monitor the public records for evidence of new real estate recordings affecting their mortgaged properties. Ownership changes may also become apparent from the annual real estate tax statements that the mortgagee receives in its capacity as an escrow agent for real estate taxes and insurance. Similar information can be obtained when a new casualty insurance policy is issued and the mortgagee's copy reveals the new owner. Moreover, mortgagees can keep abreast of transfers through a program of regular inspection of the real estate on which they hold mortgages.

Transferees may attempt to reduce the chances of discovery by not recording the transfer. This approach not only frustrates mortgagee discovery of the transfer from an examination of the public records, but also usually prevents the revelation of a new owner incident to the issuance of new tax statements. In addition, the parties may also keep the casualty insurance policy in force in the mortgagor's name, but utilize a side agreement that purports to assign the beneficial interest in the policy to the transferee.

Even assuming that the foregoing tactics succeed in preventing mortgagee discovery of a transfer, the failure to record can create substantial problems for transferees in some states. If the transferee takes possession, in most jurisdictions that constitutes constructive notice of the transferee's interest and should protect the transferee against mortgages or other interests that are created by or arise against the mortgagor-transferor.[1] In such situations, possession is the functional equivalent of recording.[2] A few jurisdictions, however, require actual notice; possession alone does not qualify as constructive notice.[3] Even when possession constitutes constructive notice, "establishing the existence of that possession could require litigation, while the fact of a recorded document would not."[4] Failure to record is unacceptably risky, in our view.

If the mortgagee ultimately discovers the transfer, as will often happen, does it have a remedy against the parties to the concealment beyond a belated acceleration of the mortgage debt? The answer will depend in part on whether the parties have a duty to notify the mortgagee of the transfer. One court suggested that no such duty is implicit in the due-on-sale clause itself.[5] This conclusion is by no means inescapable. A court could conceivably impose a duty of good faith on the mortgagor that would be violated by concealment attempts. Moreover, some mortgagees have begun to include express mortgage language that requires the mortgagor-transferor to notify the mortgagee in the event of a transfer. When such language is utilized, the mortgagee may have a cause of action even when a window period loan is involved. Even though the due-on-sale clause in such a loan will often prove to be unenforceable, the mortgagee has a valid interest in discovering the identity of the transferee so as to be able to assess his or her creditworthiness or the impact of the transfer on mortgage security.

Suppose there is a duty to notify the lender, or at least a duty of good faith that would be violated by active concealment efforts. What damages might the lender recover for breach? If the mortgagee had been informed at the time of the transfer and had accelerated, and if the funds could have then been re-lent at a higher rate, the mortgagee has lost this interest income. In reality, most lenders are willing to forego acceleration under due-on-sale clauses in a rising-interest market if the transferee agrees to begin paying an interest rate that is higher than that provided in the original contract but nearer to the current

§ 5.25

1. See G. Nelson & D. Whitman, supra § 5.24 note 24 at 194–195.

2. See McCannon v. Marston, 679 F.2d 13, 16 (3d Cir.1982); Grand Island Hotel Corp. v. Second Island Development Co., 191 Neb. 98, 214 N.W.2d 253, 257 (1974).

3. See, e.g., Drey v. Doyle, 99 Mo. 459, 469, 12 S.W. 287, 289 (1889); M.G.L.A. c. 183, § 4; Comment, Possession as Notice Under Missouri Recording Act, 16 Mo.L. Rev. 142 (1951).

4. § 3.33 supra at note 7. A bankruptcy decision involving concealment of a transfer to avoid due-on-sale enforcement illustrates another hazard of failure to record. There the deed to an assuming grantee together with a second purchase-money deed of trust by the grantees to the seller were not recorded for a significant time period. When recording of the deed of trust finally did occur, it was within 90 days of grantees' bankruptcy. Thus the deed of trust was deemed a voidable preference under § 547 of the Bankruptcy Code. See In re Strom, 46 B.R. 144 (Bkrtcy.E.D.N.C. 1985).

5. Medovoi v. American Savings & Loan Association, 89 Cal.App.3d 244, 152 Cal.Rptr. 572 (1979) (depublished).

market rate. In a concealment case the mortgagee might show damages by proving the interest rate that it customarily demanded on transferred properties at the time the concealed transfer occurred. It is doubtful that punitive damages could be recovered even for bad faith on the mortgagor's part.[6] It would appear that only the original mortgagor can be liable for compensatory damages; the transferee who has taken subject to a mortgage has no contractual relationship with the lender, and it is hard to see any other basis for liability.

Concealment can raise serious legal problems between the mortgagor and the transferee. If the lender subsequently discovers the transfer and accelerates, the transferee may well sue his seller for damages. The suit could claim, for example, a breach of an implied warranty or covenant that the loan would not be called due. We have found no case authority for such an action, but it is not inconceivable. This implied covenant notion is, in a sense, the exact opposite of the traditional implied covenant of marketable title,[7] for here a continuing encumbrance is desired by the buyer and bargained for by the parties. The buyer would argue that acceleration by the lender breaches this term and understanding of the sales agreement. The buyer's damages would represent the excess interest (and possibly settlement and related costs) that the buyer would incur in the future upon refinancing the property after acceleration. Moreover, if the buyer is unable to qualify for new financing and foreclosure ensues, the seller may be liable for damages incident to the buyer's loss of his or her equity in the mortgaged real estate. Conceivably the seller could be faced with two suits: one by the lender for lost interest up to the date of actual acceleration, and one by the buyer for increased interest payments or loss of the property thereafter. In any transaction in which the lender is not fully informed, the seller is well-advised to include in the sale contract language by which the transferee acknowledges the risk of future acceleration and agrees to hold the seller harmless in the event acceleration occurs.[8]

Should a lawyer be troubled by the ethical implications of counseling a client to conceal a transfer, or of arranging the details of the transaction? At most, the concealment is a breach of contract, and the Model Code of Professional Responsibility apparently does not prohibit advising a client to breach a contract, although Disciplinary Rule 7–102(A)(7) provides that a lawyer shall not "counsel or assist his client in conduct that the lawyer knows to be illegal or fraudulent." [9] Of course, "illegal" is a slippery word, and could conceivably include contract

---

6. Punitive damages are not generally available for contract breaches unless a tort has also been committed. See Restatement (Second) of Contracts § 355 (1981); 5 A. Corbin, Contracts § 1077 (1960).

7. See 6A R. Powell, supra § 5.24 note 18, at ¶ 925(2); 3 American Law of Property, supra note § 5.24 note 19, § 11.47.

8. See Liss, Drafting Around the Mortgage "Due on Sale" Clause in the Installment Sale of Real Estate, 62 Chi.B.Rec. 312 (1981) (suggesting various other protective clauses).

9. Model Code of Professional Responsibility EC 7–5 (1980) states the same principles in even more general terms.

breaches. But the opinions of the American Bar Association's Committee on Ethics and Professional Responsibility consistently treat this rule as referring only to criminal conduct or something very close to it.[10] The rule has never been regarded as applying to breaches of contract.

The lawyer who counsels concealment in the face of an enforceable due-on-sale clause may be (and we think usually is) guilty of giving poor advice, but it does not appear to be an ethical violation under the Code. We are uncomfortable with this conclusion. The Code does not adequately deal with the issue, and perhaps reflects the larger societal indecision regarding the morality of breaching contracts.[11]

 WESTLAW REFERENCES

grantor mortgagor seller /p conceal! denial hid*** /s transfer sale /s mortgage property

§ 5.26 Due-on Clauses—Conclusion

Congressional preemption of due-on-sale law has not proved to be an unmixed blessing. The Act too frequently evidences the fact that it was drafted and passed in haste.[1] Moreover, while the Regulation corrects many of the Act's problems, in some instances it exacerbates them. The principal deficiency of the Act, however, is its treatment of the window period concept. Congress apparently wanted to protect, for at least a three-year period, those borrowers who reasonably relied upon favorable state law. This objective is praiseworthy, but the technique Congress selected to accomplish it is fraught with pitfalls. To make legal rights turn on when and how a state rule of law was adopted by a state court ignores the vagaries and complexities of

---

10. See ABA Comm. on Ethics and Professional Responsibility, Informal Op. 1314 (1975) (perjury by client); ABA Comm. on Ethics and Professional Responsibility, Formal Op. 335 (1974) (securities fraud); ABA Comm. on Professional Ethics and Grievances, Formal Op. 281 (1952) (representation of a criminal syndicate).

11. Liss, supra note 8, appears to see no ethical problems in concealment. Id. at 312.

§ 5.26

1. On September 24, 1982, the Senate took the House version of the bill, H.R. 6267, and deleted everything in it except for the title and the statement of intent, replaced the text with S. 2879, and sent it back to joint conference. See generally 128 Cong.Rec. S12,221–63 (daily ed. Sept. 24, 1982). On September 30, Representative St. Germain won from the rules committee a closed rule waiving certain procedural requirements—essentially those prohibiting consideration of the bill without debate. The text of the bill was distributed to the House members on the morning of October 1, 1982. At approximately 9:30 p.m. on the last night of the second session (October 1, 1982) the bill was put on the floor for a vote, despite the fact that most of the members had not yet seen the legislation. Intense controversy ensued: "[T]here is total disagreement as to what is in this bill. Very likely it perpetuates high interest rates—but we don't know, because we don't know what is in this bill. We ought to vote down this rule until we can take a good look at this legislation, none of us knows what it does." 128 Cong.Rec. H8429 (daily ed. Oct. 1, 1982) (statement of Rep. Perkins). Even one of the senior members of the banking committee—Representative Gonzalez—asked to postpone voting on the bill because he had not been able to study it. 128 Cong.Rec. H8434–35 (daily ed. Oct. 1, 1982) (statement of Rep. Gonzalez).

judicial lawmaking. Perhaps Congress would have been far wiser to have simply enacted a list of window period states and corresponding dates. Thankfully, however, because of the Act's sunset provision, this problem will be short-lived, at least for those states that do not choose to enact legislation extending window period protection.

On balance, we believe the Act reflects sound public policy. A uniform national policy enforcing due-on-sale clauses was long overdue. The arguments that have been raised against enforceability of due-on-sale clauses as interest rate adjustment tools do not appear to us to be logical. As the mortgage finance market has evolved, the arguments seem even less persuasive, even if one ignores the grave economic crisis that depository financial institutions have weathered.[2] In an era when short-term balloon mortgages and adjustable rate loans have become common, the latter with rate adjustments perhaps every six months or every year,[3] we believe it does not make sense to regard enforcement of the due-on-sale clause as unconscionable. From the borrower's viewpoint, a fixed-rate long-term mortgage with a due-on-sale clause is usually much more humane and agreeable than a short-term rollover loan or a frequently-adjusted variable interest mortgage. With the former, the borrower is at least assured that the rate will be stable so long as he or she owns the property. When one considers the general decline in the use of prepayment penalties in the past few years, the fixed-rate loan with a due-on-sale clause often gives the borrower the best of all available worlds—protection against rising rates, and at the same time, freedom to refinance if rates fall—so long as the property is not transferred. Of course, the contract is not as advantageous as it would be if continued restrictions on enforcement of due-on-sale clauses made the loan transferrable at its existing contract rate. However, compared to the alternative kinds of contracts that have become popular without so much as a whimper of protest from the courts, it is very attractive.

The restraint on alienation argument has always been, in our opinion, a weak one. Those who have pressed it have usually managed to avoid direct discussion of its major premise: that mortgage lenders somehow have an obligation to finance not only the ownership of their immediate borrowers, but of the transferees of those borrowers as well.

---

2. The impact of decisions restricting due-on-sale enforcement on the well-being of financial institutions has been substantial. One economist has estimated that the effect of the *Wellenkamp* decision, in calendar year 1981 was to transfer between $58 million and $170 million from California state-chartered savings and loan associations to borrowers. Ozanne, The Financial Stakes in Due-on-Sale: The Case of California's State Chartered Savings and Loans 2 (unpublished paper prepared for the Federal Home Loan Bank Board, July 1982).

Another study estimated that *Wellenkamp* reduced the market value of the mortgage portfolios of California-chartered associations by an amount equal to about 45% of the associations' net worth. See Dietrich, Langetieg, Dale-Johnson & Campbell, The Economic Effects of Due-on-Sale Clause Invalidation, 2 Housing Fin.Rev. 19 (1983).

3. See § 11.4 infra.

If one accepts this premise, then it is true that the due-on-sale clause is a practical restraint on alienation. On the other hand, if lenders have no such duty then their insistence on being paid off when the borrower sells the property, or on extending the loan only at a higher interest rate, cannot be thought to restrain the sale, any more than would the refusal of some other lending institution to finance the new owner's purchase. Again, the analogy to more recently popularized forms of mortgage financing is telling. Does the lender who takes only a one-year or three-year note have a duty to extend it merely because the property that secures it is sold? Does the lender who contracts for an adjustable interest rate have a duty to refrain from adjusting it upward because that action may make it more difficult for the borrower to sell the property? If these lenders do not have the sorts of duties outlined, as they quite obviously do not, why should a fixed-rate long-term lender have any analogous duty? Viewed in this light, the notion that the due-on-sale clause is a restraint on alienation does not withstand analysis.

 WESTLAW REFERENCES
[no queries]

C. TRANSFER BY THE MORTGAGEE

§ 5.27 Introduction—Nature of the Mortgagee's Interest

The mortgagee of real property has two things: the personal obligation owed by the mortgagor, and the interest in the realty securing that obligation. This twofold character of the rights of the mortgagee must be kept in mind when transfers by the mortgagee are considered. For a transfer to be complete both the obligation and the security interest must pass to the same person.[1]

The practical context in which these issues arise is the trading of mortgages as investments on the "secondary mortgage market." When a lender, having originated a mortgage loan, sells it to another investor, a secondary market transaction is said to occur, and the transfer by the original mortgagee is loosely termed an "assignment." Three federally-sponsored agencies, the Federal National Mortgage Association (FNMA), the Federal Home Loan Mortgage Corporation (FHLMC), and the Government National Mortgage Association (GNMA), are actively involved in purchasing assignments of mortgages, primarily on residential properties, from local lenders throughout the nation. Their opera-

---

§ 5.27

1. Subrogation can act as an equitable assignment of a mortgage; see §§ 10.1–10.8, infra. This chapter is concerned only with voluntary assignments. In such an assignment, the assignee gets all of the assignor's rights, such as the right to foreclose by power of sale, which are generally available under state law; see Strike v. Trans-West Discount Corp., 92 Cal.App.3d 735, 155 Cal.Rptr. 132 (1979), appeal dismissed 444 U.S. 948, 100 S.Ct. 417, 62 L.Ed. 2d 317 (1979). Note that the mortgagor's consent is unnecessary to a valid assignment; see United States v. 1300 Lafayette East, 455 F.Supp. 988 (E.D.Mich.1978).

tions are described elsewhere in this book.[2] In addition, mortgage assignment transactions among private lending institutions are very common, and provide a means of moving mortgage capital from one area of the nation to another. The existence of a smoothly-working national market in mortgages is an important element of national housing policy.[3] Hence, the matters discussed in these sections are of intense practical significance.

While a wide variety of types of obligations may be secured by mortgages,[4] by far the most common is the obligation to repay a debt of money. The debt is usually evidenced by a promissory note executed by the borrower-mortgagor. Whatever the nature of the obligation, the law applicable to it will determine the method or methods by which it may be transferred. In general the law of contracts applies, but in the special case of promissory notes the Uniform Commercial Code governs transfers. The obligation is correctly regarded as the principal thing being transferred, with the interest in the land attached to it in an extremely important, but subsidiary, capacity.[5] This notion is of fundamental importance. It means that the security is inseparable from the obligation, and that whoever can establish his claim to the obligation gets with it the security interest in the land, provided it is still in existence.[6]

In lien theory jurisdictions, any attempt by the mortgagee to transfer the interest in the land while expressly reserving the obligation simply does not work; the realty transfer is held to be a nullity.[7]

2. The activities and authority of these agencies are discussed at § 11.3, infra.

3. See The Report of the President's Commission on Housing 111–21 (1982); Miles, Housing Finance: Development and Evolution in Mortgage Markets, in House Comm. on Banking, Finance and Urban Affairs, 98th Cong., 1st Sess., Housing—A Reader 45 (Comm.Print 1983); Grebler, The "New System" of Residential Mortgage Finance, Mortgage Banker, Feb. 1972, at 4.

4. On the necessity and nature of the obligation, see §§ 2.1–2.2, supra.

5. The classic statement is Carpenter v. Longan, 83 U.S. (16 Wall.) 271, 21 L.Ed. 313 (1872): "All the authorities agree that the debt is the principal thing and the mortgage an accessory." See First National Bank v. Larson, 17 B.R. 957, 965 (Bkrtcy.N.J.1982); Goetz v. Selsor, 628 S.W.2d 404 (Mo.App.1982); Bautista and Kennedy, The Imputed Negotiability of Security Interests Under the Code, 38 Ind. L.J. 574 (1963); Note, Transfer of the Mortgagee's Interest in Florida, 14 U.Fla.L.Rev. 98 (1961); Britton, Assignment of Mortgages Securing Negotiable Notes, 10 Ill.L. Rev. 337 (1915).

6. Margiewicz v. Terco Properties, 441 So.2d 1124 (Fla.App.1983); Moore v. Lewis, 51 Ill.App.3d 388, 9 Ill.Dec. 337, 366 N.E.2d 594 (1977); Domarad v. Fisher & Burke, Inc., 270 Cal.App.2d 543, 76 Cal.Rptr. 529 (1969); Kernohan v. Manss, 53 Ohio St. 118, 41 N.E. 258, 29 L.R.A. 317 (1895). See West's Ann.Cal.Civil Code, § 2936: "The assignment of a debt secured by a mortgage carries with it the security."

The assignment is held to include a warranty that the mortgage is a valid obligation against the real estate; see General Electric Credit Corp. v. Air Flow Industries, Inc., 432 So.2d 607 (Fla.App.1983).

7. In re Caperonis' Estate, 95 Misc.2d 690, 408 N.Y.S.2d 231 (1978); Commercial Products Corp. v. Briegel, 101 Ill.App.2d 156, 242 N.E.2d 317 (1968); Bryan v. Easton Tire Co., 262 Ark. 731, 561 S.W.2d 79 (1978); Domarad v. Fisher & Burke, Inc., note 6, supra. There is even some authority, probably erroneous, that an attempted transfer of the security interest alone extinguishes it; see Teas v. Republic National Bank, 460 S.W.2d 233 (Tex.Civ.App. 1970).

"Among the 'gems' and 'free offerings' of the late Professor Chester Smith of the

In title jurisdictions, it is technically possible for the mortgagee to transfer his land interest and keep the obligation.[8] This may happen, for example, if the mortgagee dies and his land (including the security interest represented by the mortgage) descends to his heir, while the promissory note passes to his personal representative.[9] But whoever takes the realty interest in this fashion cannot assert it in any way; for example, he cannot foreclose if the obligation is in default.[10] Moreover, the holder of the obligation can go into equity and compel a transfer of the security to him. In fact, he may accomplish this by a bill to foreclose the mortgage;[11] if the holder of the realty interest is named as a party, the court will impress a constructive trust on his interest and foreclose it in behalf of the noteholder.

The benefit of the security goes to the one who owns the debt, even if he did not realize when he bought it that it was secured.[12] To hold otherwise would give a windfall to the mortgagor, since no one but the holder of the debt could assert the security. Of course, the rule stated gives a windfall, in a sense, to the assignee of the debt, but it has the advantage of consistency and predictability. The debtholder would be able to execute a judgment upon the land in any event,[13] so the real significance of his ability to foreclose the mortgage is its priority against subsequent lienors or encumbrancers. They will have had notice of the mortgage from the chain of title, and so cannot complain.

 WESTLAW REFERENCES
prelim(federal national +2 "home loan" mortgage +2 association corporation % farm)

§ 5.28 Methods of Transfer

The methods of transferring an obligation and the mortgage which secures it depend on the nature of the obligation. To a great extent the Uniform Commercial Code specifies these methods, at least when the obligation in question is a promise to pay money. The Code's treatment of this subject is complex, and we can cover it here in only a

---

University of Arizona College of Law was the following analogy. The note is the cow and the mortgage the tail. The cow can survive without a tail, but the tail cannot survive without the cow." Best Fertilizers of Arizona, Inc. v. Burns, 117 Ariz. 178, 571 P.2d 675 (App.1977).

8. Second National Bank v. Dyer, 121 Conn. 263, 184 A. 386 (1936); Stewart v. Crosby, 50 Me. 130 (1863).

9. Demarest v. Wynkoop, 3 Johns Ch. (N.Y.) 129, 8 Am.Dec. 467 (1897).

10. Only the owner of the debt can foreclose; Swinton v. Cuffman, 139 Ark. 121, 213 S.W. 409 (1919); Stribling v. Splint Coal Co., 31 W.Va. 82, 5 S.E. 321 (1888).

11. Lawrence v. Knap, 1 Root (Conn.) 248, 1 Am.Dec. 42 (1791); Pettus v. Gault, 81 Conn. 415, 71 A. 509 (1908); Kinna v. Smith, 3 N.J.Eq. 14 (1834); Rembert v. Ellis, 193 Ga. 60, 17 S.E.2d 165, 137 A.L.R. 479 (1941).

12. Mankato First National Bank v. Pope, 85 Minn. 433, 89 N.W. 318 (1902); Betz v. Heebner, 1 Pen. & W. (Pa.) 280 (1830).

13. It is possible that the mortgagor would file a homestead declaration on the property and thereby defeat the debt-holder's execution, but there can hardly be a public policy favoring such a result if the mortgage had been given at a time when no homestead was on file.

sparse way; the reader should refer to works on the Code itself for more detail.[1]

Under the Code a note may either be negotiable or nonnegotiable, depending on factors which we will discuss later. If the note is nonnegotiable, it can be transferred only by assignment, and not by negotiation.[2] The assignment may be carried out in any of several ways: by indorsement on the note by the original payee-mortgagee, by the use of a separate document which the payee-mortgagee executes, stating that his rights under the note are transferred to the assignee, and if the amount is small, even by an oral statement to the assignee that he is effecting a transfer.[3] To assign a nonnegotiable note, it is not necessary that possession of the note itself be given to the transferee.[4]

On the other hand, if a negotiable note is involved, and if the transferee wants to have the special and desirable status of a holder in due course,[5] the mode of transfer (which is termed "negotiation" in this situation) is much more narrowly constrained. The note must be indorsed by the payee-mortgagee, and it must be physically transferred into the hands of the new holder.[6] The use of a separate document of

---

§ 5.28

1. See, e.g., Anderson, Uniform Commercial Code § 3–101 et seq. (1971); White & Summers, Uniform Commercial Code (2d ed. 1980), at chs. 13–14; Weber & Speidel, Commercial Paper (Nutshell Series 3d ed. 1982); Annot., 23 A.L.R.3d 932 (1969). It is clear that the UCC applies to the note, notwithstanding that it is secured by a mortgage; see First Valley Bank v. First Savings & Loan Association, —— Ind.App. ——, 412 N.E.2d 1237 (1980); Best Fertilizers of Arizona, Inc. v. Burns, 116 Ariz. 492, 570 P.2d 179 (1977).

2. The basis for the statement in the text is a bit convoluted. UCC § 3–202(1) provides that "Negotiation is the transfer of an instrument in such form that the transferee becomes a holder." § 3–102(1) (e) in turn defines "instrument" as it is used in Article 3 to mean a negotiable instrument. See White & Summers, Uniform Commercial Code (2d ed. 1980), at § 14.4.

3. If the assignment is not evidenced by a writing, it is not enforceable "beyond five thousand dollars in amount or value." U.C.C. § 1–206. It might be argued that all assignments of notes secured by realty mortgages must be in writing, since the assignment of the note automatically conveys an interest in land simultaneously, and therefore should comport with the real estate statute of frauds. A similar argument can be raised with regard to the necessity of delivery, which is ordinarily a prerequisite to an effective conveyance of

an interest in realty. Here as in other areas the dual nature of the debt and security creates a conflict, but by far the most common resolution, at least in equity, is to disregard the real estate requirements of writing and delivery if the debt itself is properly transferred and if no rights of third parties are prejudiced. Hebrew Home for Orphans & Aged v. Freund, 208 Misc. 658, 144 N.Y.S.2d 608 (1955); Thatcher v. Merriam, 121 Utah 191, 240 P.2d 266 (1952); Braidwood v. Harmon, 31 Mich.App. 49, 187 N.W.2d 559 (1971) (valid gift by delivery of note and mortgage without writing); Hall v. O'Brien, 218 N.Y. 50, 112 N.E. 569 (1916); Note, 36 Ky.L.J. 121 (1947).

4. Margiewicz v. Terco Properties, 441 So.2d 1124 (Fla.App.1983) (no indorsement of note required; separate assignment is sufficient); Felin Association v. Rogers, 38 A.D.2d 6, 326 N.Y.S.2d 413 (1971); Davin v. Isman, 228 N.Y. 1, 126 N.E. 257 (1920).

5. The advantages of HDC status are discussed at § 5.31, infra.

6. U.C.C. § 3–202(1); Security Pacific National Bank v. Chess, 58 Cal.App.3d 555, 129 Cal.Rptr. 852 (1976). A holder must have possession of the note; U.C.C. § 1–201(20). No indorsement is required if the note was originally payable to bearer, but this is very uncommon in mortgage transactions; normally a mortgage note will be payable to the mortgagee, so his indorsement is necessary for negotiation. See Second National Bank v. G.M.T. Properties, Inc., 364 So.2d 59 (Fla.App.1978).

assignment is not necessarily objectionable, but it cannot substitute for the indorsement and delivery of the note. If the transferee is willing to forego holder in due course status, or if for other reasons he is ineligible for that status, then the methods discussed in the preceding paragraph as applicable to nonnegotiable notes may be used with negotiable notes as well.

Unfortunately, many of the cases do not distinguish between negotiable and nonnegotiable notes, and they often make statements about assignment which clearly could not be correct as representing attempts to negotiate the note to a holder in due course.[7] This is true, for example, of the two other modes of transfer discussed later in this section: a deed of the land and a written mortgage assignment. These acts may become the basis of an assignment of the obligation, but they surely cannot, by themselves, amount to a negotiation. The difference lies in the rights which the transferee will have, and it can be of great significance.[8]

Finally, observe carefully that, as between the parties to a transfer, the assignment or negotiation of the note itself is all that must be done. It is unnecessary to have any separate document purporting to transfer or assign the security interest in the real estate, for it will follow the obligation automatically.[9] Written assignments of mortgages are nonetheless very common, and perhaps the most frequent method of transfer consists of executing a document of assignment of the mortgage and also indorsing the note to the transferee. As against certain third parties, to be discussed later, the execution and even recording of a written assignment may be wise and desirable steps,[10] but they are not essential as between the mortgagee and his transferee.

Conveyance of the Land

Suppose the mortgagee executes to his transferee what purports to be a deed to the land.[11] In title jurisdictions, as we have already noted, it is technically possible to separate the security interest from the obligation it secures, although to do so is an idle act, since one who holds the security without the obligation cannot assert it. But the

---

7. See, e.g., Phillips v. Latham, 523 S.W.2d 19 (Tex.Civ.App.1975), ref. n.r.e., appeal after remand 551 S.W.2d 103 (1977); Peterson v. John J. Reilly, Inc., 110 N.H. 1, 259 A.2d 393 (1969).

8. See §§ 5.31, 5.32, infra.

9. Domarad v. Fisher & Burke, Inc., 270 Cal.App.2d 543, 76 Cal.Rptr. 529 (1969); Miller v. Frederick's Brewing Co., 405 Ill. 591, 92 N.E.2d 108 (1950); Jones v. Titus, 208 Mich. 392, 175 N.E. 257 (1919); cases cited § 5.27 note 11, supra. If the mortgagee does transfer the realty interest by some written conveyance, equity will impress a trust upon it in favor of the assign-ee of the obligation. See Powell, Real Property, ¶ 455 at note 9 (1966).

10. See § 5.34, supra.

11. An interesting problem arises if the original mortgage is in the form of an absolute deed, and if the mortgagee-grantee executes a further absolute deed to a bona fide purchaser. Since the chain of title to the purchaser appears to be perfect, he will take the fee and divest the original grantor-mortgagor. This is a fundamental and serious risk to one who gives an absolute deed to secure an obligation. Mooney v. Byrne, 163 N.Y. 86, 57 N.E. 163 (1900); see §§ 3.3 et seq., supra.

question with which we are now concerned is this: can the deed of the land be construed as transferring both the security and the obligation? The cases are divided, with some holding affirmatively.[12] Others take the view that the deed is a nullity,[13] or that it transfers a naked legal title to the land which equity will restore to the owner of the obligation.[14] The test should be intent, and it is hard to imagine a situation in which the mortgagee intends either of the two latter results; in most cases he obviously wants to transfer both the obligation and the realty interest, and this should be presumed in the absence of rather clear contrary evidence.

In lien states it is often even more difficult to establish that a deed by the mortgagee acts as a transfer of the note and the security interest; the courts tend to hold it a nullity,[15] or in some cases to recognize it as an effective transfer of the obligation only if the intent to accomplish this is affirmatively shown.[16] There is really no basis for distinguishing between the lien and title theories in this context, and in either type of jurisdiction the natural presumption should be that a full transfer has been accomplished.

Where a purchaser buys at a void foreclosure sale and is given a conveyance in terms of the land, both the mortgage debt and the security are treated as having passed to him even though this was not the intent because it was supposed that full title to the property was

---

12. Welsh v. Phillips, 54 Ala. 309, 25 Am.Rep. 679 (1875), warranty deed; Ruggles v. Barton, 79 Mass. (13 Gray) 506 (1859); Hinds v. Ballou, 44 N.H. 619 (1863), quitclaim. Even a release has been held to be sufficient. Welch v. Priest, 90 Mass. (8 Allen) 165 (1864).

13. "A conveyance of the land does not transfer the debt, because, so long as the mortgage is considered as an incident to the debt it cannot pass without a transfer of the principal." Smith v. Smith, 15 N.H. 55, 65 (1844). See Farnsworth v. Kimball, 112 Me. 238, 243, 91 A. 954, 956 (1914); Devlin v. Collier, 53 N.J.L. 422, 22 A. 201 (1891); Delano v. Bennett, 90 Ill. 533 (1878). For a general discussion of the effect of a conveyance of the mortgaged premises by the mortgagee, see Rollison, Priorities in the Law of Mortgages, 9 Notre Dame Law. 50 (1933).

14. Farrell v. Lewis, 56 Conn. 280, 14 A. 931 (1887); Island Pond National Bank v. Lacroix, 104 Vt. 282, 158 A. 684 (1932). Where the mortgagee has previously disposed of the debt to another this is the only operation the conveyance can have. Wolcott v. Winchester, 81 Mass. (15 Gray) 461 (1860); see Ruggles v. Barton, 79 Mass. (13 Gray) 506 (1859).

See Note, Effect of Assignment Without Assigning the Debt—Formalities Necessary to Transfer the Mortgagee's Title to the Mortgaged Property, 36 N.C.L.Rev. 225 (1958), discussing Gregg v. Williamson, 246 N.C. 356, 98 S.E.2d 481 (1957).

15. "A transfer of the mortgage without the debt is a nullity, and no interest is acquired by it. The security cannot be separated from the debt and exist independently of it. This is the necessary legal conclusion, and recognized as the rule by a long course of judicial decisions." Merritt v. Bartholick, 36 N.Y. 44 (1867); Peters v. Jamestown Bridge Co., 5 Cal. 334, 63 Am. Dec. 134 (1855); Carter v. Bennett, 4 Fla. 283, 347 (1852); Merritt v. Bartholick, 36 N.Y. 44 (1867); Johnson v. Cornett, 29 Ind. 59 (1867); Swan v. Yaple, 35 Iowa 248 (1872); see Devlin v. Collier, 53 N.J.L. 422, 427, 22 A. 201, 203 (1891). Cf. Gottlieb v. City of New York, 128 App.Div. 148, 112 N.Y.S. 545 (1908); Hawley v. Levee, 66 Misc. 280, 123 N.Y.S. 4 (1910).

16. Noble v. Watkins, 48 Or. 518, 87 P. 771 (1906); Greve v. Coffin, 14 Minn. 345, Gil. 263, 269 (1869); Blessett v. Turcotte, 20 N.D. 151, 127 N.W. 505 (1910); McCammant v. Roberts, 87 Tex. 241, 27 S.W. 86 (1894).

being transferred.[17] Moreover, if the purchaser of the property at the void foreclosure sale then conveys it, his deed will operate at least as an equitable assignment of both the mortgage title and the mortgage debt.[18] The last two cases do not depend upon a contractual assignment of the mortgage debt; the result comes by operation of law through the doctrine of equitable subrogation.[19]

Assignment of the "Mortgage"

As we have already noted, it is common for an assigning mortgagee to execute an instrument, usually termed an "assignment", and deliver it to his transferee. If the transferee expects to record this document, as he usually does, it should be in appropriate form to satisfy the local recording act; this generally means that it must identify the parties and the original mortgage, describe the land, and bear an acknowledged signature of the mortgagee.

If the "assignment" also mentions that the debt is being transferred,[20] or if there is a separate indorsement and delivery of the note, the transfer is unquestionably complete. If neither of these is present, however, can the "assignment" of the mortgage alone be deemed to include the obligation as well? While some cases hold the transfer to fail entirely on these facts,[21] and others impose the burden of showing an intent to transfer the debt on the assignee,[22] the preferable rule is to presume that intent in the absence of contrary proof.[23] This approach is more compelling with an "assignment" by the mortgagee than with an absolute deed, since the phrase "assign the mortgage" is so commonly employed among those in the banking and real estate industries to refer to a complete transfer of both the debt and the realty interest.

17. Muir v. Berkshire, 52 Ind. 149 (1875); Dutcher v. Hobby, 86 Ga. 198, 12 S.E. 356, 10 L.R.A. 472, 22 Am.St.Rep. 444 (1890).

18. Cooper v. Harvey, 21 S.D. 471, 113 N.W. 717 (1907); Lawrence v. Murphy, 45 Utah 572, 147 P. 903 (1915); Lamprey v. Nudd, 29 N.H. 299 (1854).

19. See Rollison, Priorities in the Law of Mortgages, 9 Notre Dame Law. 50, 66 (1933).

20. Geffen v. Paletz, 312 Mass. 48, 43 N.E.2d 133 (1942).

21. In re Hurricane Resort Co., 30 B.R. 258 (Bkrtcy.Fla.1983) (pledge of mortgage alone is a nullity); Domarad v. Fisher & Burke, Inc., 270 Cal.App.2d 543, 76 Cal. Rptr. 529 (1969) (dictum); Hamilton v. Browning, 94 Ind. 242, semble (1883); Pope & Slocum v. Jacobus, 10 Iowa 262 (1859); Miller v. Berry, 19 S.D. 625, 104 N.W. 311 (1905); see Merritt v. Bartholick, 36 N.Y. 44 (1867). See Note, Transfer of the Mortgagee's Interest in Florida, 14 U. of Fla.L. Rev. 98 (1961).

22. See Lawson v. Estate of Slaybaugh, 619 S.W.2d 910 (Mo.App.1981); Fletcher v. Carpenter, 37 Mich. 412 (1877).

23. In Sobel v. Mutual Development, Inc., 313 So.2d 77 (Fla.App.1975), the court refused to find that an assignment of the mortgage included the note, but observed that such a result might follow if the assignee brought an action for reformation. See Buell v. Underwood, 65 Ala. 285 (1880); Seabury v. Henley, 174 Ala. 116, 56 So. 530 (1911); Andrews v. Townshend, 56 Super. 140, 16 St.R. 876, 1 N.Y.S. 421 (1888); id., 16 N.Y.St.Rep. 876; Loveridge v. Shurtz, 111 Mich. 618, 70 N.W. 132 (1897), semble; Foster v. Johnson, 39 Minn. 378, 40 N.W. 255 (1888), semble. See, also, Rollison, Priorities in the Law of Mortgages, 9 Notre Dame Law. 50, 86 (1933); Note, Effect of Assignment Without Assigning the Debt— Formalities Necessary to Transfer the Mortgagee's Title to the Mortgaged Property, 36 N.C.L.Rev. 225 (1958) discussing Gregg v. Williamson, 246 N.C. 356, 48 S.E. 2d 481 (1957).

A final reminder: while a deed or an assignment by the mortgagee can and generally should be deemed to act as a transfer of the note as well, neither of these techniques will result in a negotiation; even if the note is negotiable, the transferee who takes by these means alone will not be a holder in due course. The importance of this status is discussed in the next section.

Assignments for Security Purposes

Mortgage lenders, particularly mortgage bankers, often seek credit from commercial banks and pledge as security mortgages which they have originated and hold in portfolio. For example, a mortgage banker may deliver to his bank a package of numerous notes and mortgages on a temporary basis in return for a short-term loan or a line of credit. When the mortgage banker has arranged a sale of the same loans to a permanent investor, he will retrieve them from the bank, either replacing them with others or retiring the bank's debt which they secured. The practice is known as "mortgage warehousing." A similar procedure is sometimes used when the mortgage banker has made a construction loan; he may deposit the loan documents with his bank as security for credit advanced to him during the construction period, and will recover and cancel the documents when the project is completed and the permanent or "take-out" loan is made by another lender.[24]

In order to save time and expense, pledges of notes and mortgages of this type are often handled in a very informal way, without either the execution of written assignments or the indorsement of the notes. Sometimes even the physical delivery of the documents to the bank is omitted, with the bank appointing the mortgagee its "custodian" over the papers. Seldom is any assignment to the bank recorded, even if one is executed.

Pledges of notes secured by mortgages occur in other contexts as well. One common example is the homeowner who sells his house, taking a purchase money note and mortgage for part of the price. He may later need to borrow funds from a bank for unrelated purposes, and may pledge the financing documents from the house sale as security. Similarly, a financial institution which holds mortgage loans in portfolio may from time to time pledge them as security for the repayment of advances of funds made to it by other institutions, such as the Federal Home Loan Banks.[25]

As we have seen above, it is entirely clear that Article 3 of the Uniform Commercial Code governs negotiation of promissory notes,

---

24. See First National Bank v. Larson, 17 B.R. 957 (Bkrtcy.N.J.1982); R. Kratovil & R. Werner, Modern Mortgage Law & Practice § 32.11 (2d ed. 1981); Krasnowiecki, Miller & Ziff, The Kennedy Mortgage Co. Bankruptcy Case: New Light Shed on the Position of Mortgage Warehousing Banks, 56 Am.Bankr.L.J. 325 (1982); Goodwin, Mortgage Warehousing— A Misnomer, 104 U.Pa.L.Rev. 494 (1956).

See § 5.35 regarding partial assignments and participations, which may also be given for security purposes.

25. See the discussion of the Federal Home Loan Bank system at § 11.3 infra.

even when they are secured by mortgages. In contrast, UCC Article 9, which concerns transactions secured by chattels or other personal property, does not usually affect real estate mortgages. Section 9–104(j) provides that Article 9 does not apply "to the creation or transfer of an interest in or lien on real estate * * *."

However, when the real estate lien and its associated obligation are themselves being employed as security for a separate debt, it may be argued that the documents (the note and mortgage) are personal property rather than real estate, and that their pledge is covered by Article 9. The language quoted above from Section 9–104(j) might be read to negate this argument, since a pledge of a note and mortgage obviously involves, in part, a "transfer of a * * * lien on real estate." However, this reading of Section 9–104(j) is contradicted by Section 9–102(3), which states that application of Article 9 is "not affected by the fact that the obligation [being pledged] is itself secured by a transaction or interest to which this Article does not apply."

Indeed, the drafters of the Code appear to have intended precisely that pledges of mortgage notes be governed by Article 9, as indicated by their Official Comment to Section 9–102:

> The owner of Blackacre borrows $10,000 from his neighbor, and secures his note by a mortgage on Blackacre. This Article is not applicable to the creation of the real estate mortgage. * * * However, when the mortgagee pledges the note to secure his own obligation to X, *this Article applies to the security interest thus created, which is a security interest in an instrument* even though the instrument is secured by a real estate mortgage. This Article leaves to other law the question of the effect on rights under the mortgage of delivery or non-delivery of the mortgage or of recording or non-recording of an assignment of the mortgagee's interest. See Section 9–104(j).[26]

The Comment is clear on one crucial point, but ambiguous on another. The clarity exists with respect to the pledgee's rights in the note. While a mere written assignment will suffice to *create* a security

---

26. Emphasis added. In the original version of the UCC, the Official Comment to § 9–102 simply stated, in the factual illustration above, that Article 9 applied "to the security interest thus created in the note and mortgage." It made no reference to the note's character as an "instrument." As a result the Comment caused concern among some creditors' counsel that the note might be considered a "general intangible," a pledge of which is perfectable only by the filing of a financing statement, rather than an "instrument," a pledge of which is perfectable by possession. This issue is raised in G. Gilmore, Security Interests in Personal Property § 10.1 (1965), at 311. Clarification of the point was at least one objective of the revision of the Comment in 1966. See Note, Security Interests in Notes and Mortgages: Determining the Applicable Law, 79 Colum.L.Rev. 1414, 1425 nn. 65–69.

Another change wrought by the 1966 amendment was the omission of the statement, made in the original Official Comment, that Article 9 applied to "the security interest thus created in *the note and mortgage*" (emphasis added.) The 1966 amendment quoted in the text above seems to refer only to the security interest in *the note*, leaving unclear the application of Article 9 to the mortgage.

interest in the note as between the pledgor and pledgee,[27] the pledgee must follow Article 9's procedures if she is to *perfect* her rights as against other claimants to the note, such as the pledgor's trustee in bankruptcy or subsequent good faith purchasers or assignees of the pledgor. Transfer of possession of the note to the pledgee is the only method of accomplishing this perfection.[28] This is plainly true if the note is negotiable, and very likely so even if it is non-negotiable.[29] Arrangements in which the note is left with the mortgagee-pledgor or his employee, designated the pledgee's "custodian," "collection agent," or the like are of very dubious efficacy.[30] Moreover, it is clear that the most formal written assignment, even if recorded in the local real estate records, will not perfect the pledge if the note is not delivered.[31] The same is true of the filing of a financing statement under Article 9. Only a transfer of possession will suffice.

The ambiguity in the Official Comment, and in the Code itself, lies in its treatment of the mortgage. Obviously the pledgee wants rights in both the note and the mortgage; it is pretty cold comfort to be left with an unsecured debt against the original mortgagor. But the Code is silent as to whether the pledgee must take some further action to perfect her rights in the mortgage, or whether perfection as to the note (by delivery) will automatically carry the mortgage along. One reading of the Official Comment above is that the matter must be resolved by non-Code law rather than by interpretation of the Code. Alternatively, one may argue that the Comment merely intends that rights *under the mortgage*—that is, rights to enforce and foreclose the mortgage—must be determined by non-Code rules—namely the state law of mortgages. Perfection of the pledgee's claim *to the mortgage,* under this view, is merely a matter that the Code does not clearly address, but which

---

27. U.C.C. § 9–203(1)(a), which makes the security interest *unenforceable* unless the secured party has either possession of the collateral or a signed security agreement.

28. U.C.C. § 9–304(1); Greiner v. Wilke, 625 F.2d 281, 283 (9th Cir.1980); Armstrong v. Isbell, 27 B.R. 926 (Bkrtcy.Wis. 1983); Nazar v. Southern, 32 B.R. 761 (Bkrtcy.Kan.1983); Johnstone v. Mills, 22 B.R. 753 (Bkrtcy.Wash.1982). Under certain limited circumstances, perfection of a security interest in an instrument may be accomplished without possession for brief periods; see U.C.C. § 9–304(4), (5); § 9–306(3).

29. U.C.C. § 9–105(g) defines "instrument" to include only a paper "of a type which is in ordinary course of business transferred by delivery with any necessary indorsement or assignment." It is very likely that even non-negotiable mortgage notes would be included in this definition; see In re Columbia Pacific Mortgage, Inc., 22 B.R. 753 (Bkrtcy.Wash.1982).

It might be argued that a negotiable note, when secured by a mortgage, forms a package which is not an "instrument" since it is ordinarily transferred only with both an indorsement of the note and an assignment of the mortgage. See Rucker v. State Exchange Bank, 355 So.2d 171 (Fla.App.1978), which seems to assume this characterization of mortgage notes. But this conclusion seems directly contradicted by the Official Comment to § 9–102. See note 26 supra; Greiner v. Wilke, 625 F.2d 281 (9th Cir.1980).

30. See Starr v. Bruce Farley Corp., 612 F.2d 1197 (9th Cir.1980).

31. Starr v. Bruce Farley Corp., 612 F.2d 1197 (9th Cir.1980); Armstrong v. Isbell, 27 B.R. 926 (Bkrtcy.Wis.1983).

might well be decided on the basis of the Code's framework and policies.[32]

Some commentators have taken the view that the pledgee's rights to the mortgage are a non-Code issue, and hence must be perfected under state recording act principles.[33] A few cases have agreed.[34] But for numerous reasons the better view is that the mortgage simply follows the note, and that a perfected claim to the note is equally perfected as to the mortgage. One can rationalize this approach either by arguing that the Code implicitly adopts it, or by asserting that it is the natural result of the common law doctrine that the mortgage automatically accompanies the note.[35]

Whichever rationale is employed, this result fits comfortably with the normal mortgage assignment concepts discussed in the previous section.[36] It is simple to follow, and avoids the necessity of multiple precautions, such as recordation of a mortgage assignment or filing of a financing statement, to protect the pledgee against competing creditors. Finally, it precludes any risk that the security interest in the note will end up in the hands of a different creditor than the security interest in the mortgage [37]—a ridiculous situation, since as we have seen, one who has the mortgage but not the obligation it secures has, in essence, a nullity.[38]

32. See Note, supra note 26, at 1426–27. The last sentence of the Comment, as quoted in the text above, seems inherently defective and confusing; it is hard to see what possible effect the delivery of the mortgage or the recording of an assignment can have on "rights under the mortgage," if this phrase means rights of enforcement and foreclosure.

33. See, e.g., G. Gilmore, Security Interests in Personal Property § 10.1 (1965), at 311; Comment, An Article Nine Scope Problem—Mortgages, Leases, and Rents as Collateral, 47 U.Colo.L.Rev. 449, 456–57 (1976). Some have gone so far as to suggest that neither the note nor the mortgage is governed by Article 9; see Coogan, Kripke & Weiss, The Outer Fringes of Article 9: Subordination Agreements, Security Interests in Money and Deposits, Negative Pledge Clauses, and Participation Agreements, 79 Harv.L.Rev. 229, 270 (1965).

34. Peoples Bank of Polk County v. McDonald, 31 B.R. 597 (E.D.Tenn.1983), reversing 27 B.R. 701 (Bkrtcy.Tenn.1983); Rucker v. State Exchange Bank, 355 So.2d 171 (Fla.App.1978). See also In re Bristol Associates, Inc., 505 F.2d 1056 (3d Cir.1974) (collateral assignment of real estate lease held outside Article 9). Although the Rucker case "holds" that the mortgage as-

signment is outside the scope of Article 9, it is not square authority on the matter of perfection of security interests in mortgages discussed in the text, since it pitted the pledgee, not against a competing creditor of the pledgor-mortgagee, but rather against the grantee of the real estate, who attempted to pay off the mortgage to the original mortgagee. See the discussion at § 5.34 notes 2–6, 25, infra.

35. See Krasnowiecki, Miller & Ziff, The Kennedy Mortgage Co. Bankruptcy Case: New Light Shed on the Position of Warehousing Banks, 56 Am.Bkrptcy L.J. 325, 332 n. 22 (1982), for an explicit discussion of the two rationales.

36. See § 5.27 supra at notes 5–6.

37. Such a risk is quite conceivable if Article 9 governs rights to the note while state mortgage and recording law governs rights to the mortgage. This could occur, for example, if the mortgagee-pledgor gives a recorded assignment of the mortgage to the pledgee but does not deliver possession of the note, and the pledgor is subsequently declared bankrupt. See Note, supra note 26, at 1422. The trustee in bankruptcy is entitled to the status of a lien creditor of the bankrupt; see 11 U.S.C.A. § 110(c).

38. See § 5.27 supra at note 10.

This approach has been endorsed by most of the commentators [39] and the recent cases.[40] It is fairly safe to predict that it will stand the test of time. However, a conservative pledgee's lawyer will not be satisfied merely to accept delivery of the note, but if practical will want to record a mortgage assignment as well. There are good reasons for doing so, but they involve protection against subsequent takers of the real estate, not subsequent creditors or trustees in bankruptcy of the mortgagee.[41] These reasons are discussed in a later section.[42]

 WESTLAW REFERENCES

negotia! non-negotiable   /p   mortgage   /s   assign! transfer!

Conveyance of Land

mortgagee   /s   convey! deed transfer   /s   land property security   /p
    intend intent! "legal title" null!

Assignment of the "Mortgage"

mortgagee   /s   assign! deed transfer   /s   debt mortgage note
    obligation   /p   fail*** intend intent! null!

266k224

39. See Collier, Real Estate Transactions and the Bankruptcy Code ¶ 4.05[1] (1984); Bowmar, Real Estate Interests as Security Under the UCC: The Scope of Article Nine, 12 U.C.C.L.J. 99, 121 (1979); Krasnowiecki et al., supra note 35; Note, supra note 26.

40. Greiner v. Wilke, 625 F.2d 281, 284 (9th Cir.1980) (deed of trust follows note under California law); Starr v. Bruce Farley Corp., 612 F.2d 1197 (9th Cir.1980) (appearing to require delivery of both note and deed of trust); First National Bank v. Larson, 17 B.R. 957, 965 (Bkrtcy.N.J.1982) (mortgage follows note under New Jersey law); Landmark Land Co., Inc. v. Sprague, 529 F.Supp. 971, 976–77 (S.D.N.Y.1981), reversed on other grounds 701 F.2d 1065 (2d Cir.1983) (Art. 9 governs both note and mortgage). Contra, see Peoples Bank v. McDonald, 743 F.2d 413 (6th Cir. 1984) (note governed by Art. 9 and must be perfected by delivery; security interest in deed of trust governed by recording act).

A number of cases have held mortgages and mortgage notes to be personal property in contexts other than the perfection issue discussed in the text. See, e.g., E.I.C., Inc. v. M & O Enterprises, 156 Cal.Rptr. 275 (Cal.App.1979) (depublished) (pledge of note and mortgage is considered personal property for purposes of antideficiency statute); Black v. Sullivan, 48 Cal.App.3d 557, 122 Cal.Rptr. 119 (1975) (assignees of note and deed of trust given for security purposes not bound by California law requiring beneficiary of a deed of trust to give a statement of balance due on demand); Bank of California v. Leone, 37

Cal.App.3d 444, 112 Cal.Rptr. 394 (1974) ("one-action" rule is inapplicable to the pledgee of an assignment for security purposes of a note and deed of trust; the pledgee may seek a personal judgment without first attempting to realize on the security); E. Landau Industries v. 385 McClean Corp., 5 U.C.C.Rep.Serv. 1279 (N.Y. Sup.Ct.1969) (pledgee of bond secured by mortgage must use Art. 9 procedures to realize on security); Riebe v. Budget Financial Corp., 264 Cal.App.2d 576, 70 Cal. Rptr. 654 (1968) (pledge of note and deed of trust held proper although made to personal property broker who, by law, could not accept real estate security.) See Stewart, Trust Deed Collateral Loans and the California Commercial Code, 2 West.St.L.Rev. 57 (1974).

41. See First National Bank v. Larson, supra note 40, at 965 n. 5.

42. See § 5.34, infra. Note that if the pledgee's rights are governed by the U.C.C., she may proceed, upon the pledgor's default, to collect and sue on the mortgage debt (U.C.C. § 9–502), retain the pledged note and mortgage as her own property (U.C.C. § 9–505), or dispose of them in a commercially reasonably manner (U.C.C. § 9–504). The pledgee could presumably foreclose on the mortgage, if the underlying debtor is in default, without further ado; see Tamiami Abstract & Title Co. v. Berman, 324 So.2d 137 (Fla.App. 1975), certiorari denied 336 So.2d 604 (1976); State Realty Co. v. MacNeil Brothers Co., 334 Mass. 294, 135 N.E.2d 291 (1956).

Assignments for Security Purposes

mortgage /s assign! convey! deed transfer /p (article +3 3 9)
perfect*** "security interest" "uniform commercial" u.c.c.

§ 5.29 Negotiability and Negotiation

We have already indicated that holder in due course status may be exceedingly useful to the transferee of a note secured by a mortgage. The reason why this is so is elaborated in a later section, but in essence it is that the HDC takes free of many defenses to which the note would be subject in the hands of the original payee, including such important defenses as failure of consideration, payment, and even certain types of fraud. In this section we explore the prerequisites to achieving HDC status. They are essentially two: the note itself must be in the proper form, that is, *negotiable;* and the process by which it is transferred must be appropriate, that is, a *negotiation.* Works on the UCC or commercial paper discuss these two concepts at length,[1] and we will provide only a brief outline of them here, with special reference to the unique bearing which mortgage security may have on them.

Negotiability

The Code spells out the requirements of negotiability as follows:

Any writing to be a negotiable instrument within this Article must

(a) be signed by the maker * * *; and

(b) contain an unconditional promise * * * to pay a sum certain in money and no other promise, order, obligation or power given by the maker * * * except as authorized by this Article; and

(c) be payable on demand or at a definite time; and

(d) be payable to order or to bearer.[2]

Mortgage notes are ordinarily signed by the maker, and so requirement (a) poses no particular problem. Requirement (b) obviously means that promises to maintain the property, to insure, to refrain from waste, and the like must not be included in the note; they are typically put in the mortgage itself instead. Moreover, the note must not incorporate the mortgage by reference, with two exceptions: it may refer to the mortgage for rights as to prepayment or acceleration.[3] Any further incorporation will make the note nonnegotiable.[4] There is, however, no objection to a statement in the note that it is secured by a mortgage.[5] These rules may seem unduly technical. They arise out of

§ 5.29

1. See, e.g. White & Summers, Uniform Commercial Code (2d ed. 1980), at ch. 14; Annot., 23 A.L.R.3d 932 (1969).

2. U.C.C. § 3–104(1).

3. U.C.C. § 3–105(1)(c).

4. Johnstone v. Mills, 22 B.R. 753 (Bkrtcy.Wash.1982); Holly Hill Acres, Limited v. Charter Bank of Gainesville, 314 So. 2d 209 (Fla.App.1975).

5. U.C.C. § 3–105(1)(c) and comments 3 and 8.

the idea that the holder of a negotiable instrument should be able to ascertain all of its essential terms from its face.[6] In the mortgage context this makes little sense; no intelligent transferee would take the note without inspecting both it and the mortgage which secures it, and it is hard to see any policy rationale forbidding incorporation, or even placing the documents on the same piece of paper. Still, the law is clear and easy enough to observe, with loss of negotiability the price of a violation.

Requirement (d) is extremely significant: the note must be payable to bearer or to order. Bearer notes are rare in mortgage transactions; the note is ordinarily made payable to the mortgagee. To be negotiable, some "order" language must be included, such as "I promise to pay to the order of John Mortgagee" or "I promise to pay to John Mortgagee or order." "Order" is a magical term in this context. In effect, it warns the mortgagor that he is signing a negotiable instrument, with the potential liabilities which that implies. Perhaps many mortgagors have no idea what this means, but the rule is there, all the same. The official comment indicates that the courts should take this terminology requirement strictly, and that doubtful cases should be resolved against negotiability.[7]

Negotiation

Once we have determined that the note is in proper form and thus negotiable, we must scrutinize the process by which it is transferred. We have already seen that the transfer must be by indorsement (if the note is in "order" rather than "bearer" form) and that possession of it must be delivered to the transferee.[8] In addition, the transferee, to be a HDC must take it for value, in good faith, and without notice that it is overdue, has been dishonored, or is subject to any defense or claim to it on the part of any person.[9] For our purposes value is not a difficult issue; an executory promise to give value does not count, but giving a negotiable instrument does.[10] Taking the transfer in satisfaction of a pre-existing claim is also value.[11]

The tests of good faith and lack of notice are more complicated. In general they are treated by the courts as much the same thing: if one has notice he cannot take in good faith, and vice versa. One possible

6. U.C.C. § 3–105 at comment 8.

7. U.C.C. § 3–104 at comment 5.

8. U.C.C. § 3–202(1); see § 5.28, supra at notes 5–6; Bailey v. Mills, 257 Ala. 239, 58 So.2d 446 (1952) (endorsement on separate piece of paper, clipped to note, insufficient for negotiation); Borgonovo v. Henderson, 182 Cal.App.2d 220, 6 Cal.Rptr. 236 (1960) (unauthorized delivery of note by escrowee to assignee does not result in negotiation).

9. U.C.C. § 3–302(1). See Georgia Railroad Bank v. Doolittle, 272 S.C. 249, 252 S.E.2d 556 (1979) (no evidence that assignee bank was HDC, but contract of sale, which expressly gave it same rights as HDC, was valid.)

10. U.C.C. § 3–303(a), (c).

11. U.C.C. § 3–303(b). Value does not mean the face amount of the note, and a purchase at a discount does not alone impair the assignee's HDC status; Gribble v. Mauerhan, 188 Cal.App.2d 221, 10 Cal. Rptr. 296 (1961).

distinction has been suggested. Knowledge by the assignee of a pervasive pattern of fraud or misdealing by the assignor might not give him notice of a defect in a particular transaction, but might still make it impossible for him to take in good faith.[12]

The Code defines notice as including both actual knowledge and facts and circumstances which indicate that the assignee "has reason to know."[13] There is an element of objectivity in this test; it suggests that one cannot be wilfully ignorant of information of which an ordinary person would have become aware.[14] While the application of this idea can be quite unpredictable, some cases are easy. The notice may appear on the face of the documents. For example, a note's stated maturity date may show that it is overdue;[15] its stated interest rate may be obviously usurious; it may have erasures, blanks, or visible evidence of forgery or modification.[16] The same problems may be apparent upon an inspection of the mortgage which accompanies the note; if it is actually delivered to the assignee, he will be held to knowledge of its contents, including discrepancies of the type mentioned.[17]

Another type of notice may come from sources outside the documents. If the mortgagor-maker telephones or visits the assignee prior to the assignment and says "Don't buy that note. I signed it under duress" (or fraud, or without consideration, or what have you), the assignee must at least investigate or he will imperil his HDC status. Even information from third parties, if appearing to be reasonably reliable, will have the same effect.[18] Moreover, the information may be about the assignor's objectionable or fraudulent business practices in transactions of this type generally, rather than about the particular transaction in question.[19] This view may seem extreme, but there is little doubt that the courts are moving, if cautiously, in this direction.

12. See Financial Credit Corp. v. Williams, 246 Md. 575, 229 A.2d 712 (1967); White & Summers, Uniform Commercial Code § 14–6 (2d ed. 1980).

13. U.C.C. § 1–201(25).

14. See Woodard v. Bruce, 47 Tenn. App. 525, 339 S.W.2d 143 (1960); cf. New Jersey Manufacturing & Investment Corp. v. Calvetti, 68 N.J.Super. 18, 171 A.2d 321 (1961).

15. Cast Stone Co. v. McGowan, 102 N.E.2d 615 (Ohio App.1951); see also Stewart v. Thornton, 116 Ariz. 107, 568 P.2d 414 (1977) (note assigned within 48-hour recission period under federal law; assignee held subject to maker's recission.)

16. See U.C.C. § 3–304(1); Goetz v. Selsor, 628 S.W.2d 404 (Mo.App.1982).

17. First National Bank v. North Adams Hoosac Savings Bank, 7 Mass.App.Ct. 790, 391 N.E.2d 689 (1979) (accompanying documents referred to claim of a prior assignee); United States Finance Co. v. Jones, 285 Ala. 105, 229 So.2d 495 (1969) (notice of completion dated simultaneously with promissory note, suggesting that work by assignor on maker's house would not actually be completed); HIMC Investment Co. v. Siciliano, 103 N.J.Super. 27, 246 A.2d 502 (1968) (accompanying documents disclosed payment of commission in violation of N.J. Secondary Mortgage Loan Act.)

18. Financial Credit Corp. v. Williams, note 12, supra (newspaper stories of widespread fraud by assignor.)

19. Id. Local Acceptance Co. v. Kinkade, 361 S.W.2d 830 (Mo.1962); United States Finance Co. v. Jones, 285 Ala. 105, 229 So.2d 495 (1969); Slaughter v. Jefferson Federal Savings & Loan Association, 361 F.Supp. 590 (D.D.C.1975), 538 F.2d 397 (D.C.Cir.1976).

The maker's case for piercing the HDC veil is strengthened on such facts if it can be shown that the paper was sold to the assignee at an unusually large discount, since that suggests that he recognized the risk of losing his HDC protection.[20]

Finally, the courts are beginning to recognize quite widely the "close-connectedness" promulgated by the Arkansas Supreme Court in 1940 in Commercial Credit Corp. v. Childs.[21] If the business relationships between assignor and assignee are suspiciously close, notice may be imputed or good faith denied on that basis alone, without any direct showing of knowledge on the part of the assignee. White and Summers suggest the following factors as influential in establishing "close-connectedness",[22] although clearly not all five are simultaneously necessary.

(1) The assignee drafts or provides the forms used by the assignor.

(2) The assignee establishes or approves the assignor's procedures, such as the interest rate, credit standards, or appraisers.

(3) The assignee independently checks the debtor's credit or has other direct contact with the debtor.

(4) The assignee customarily takes all or a substantial part of the assignor's paper.[23]

(5) The assignee and assignor have common or affiliated ownership or management.[24]

Other factors, not always mentioned in the opinions of the courts, also seem to play a role. The HDC doctrine is more likely to be rejected if the debtor is a consumer rather than a business-person,[25] if the debtor has been shamefully and egregiously treated by the assignor,[26] and if

---

20. Stewart v. Thornton, 116 Ariz. 107, 568 P.2d 414 (1977); Financial Credit Corp. v. Williams, 246 Md. 575, 229 A.2d 712 (1967); United States Finance Co. v. Jones, 285 Ala. 105, 229 So.2d 495 (1969).

21. 199 Ark. 1073, 137 S.W.2d 260 (1940). The doctrine was given renewed life by Unico v. Owen, 50 N.J. 101, 232 A.2d 405 (1967). The case involved a seller of recordings and record players which took notes from its customers, and then assigned them to a finance company. The assignee was formed for the purpose of taking paper from the particular assignor, and largely controlled the assignor's business. The assignee established all credit guidelines for the assignor and supervised its business and records closely. See 4 UCC Rep.Serv. 542, 551–52 (1967).

22. White & Summers, Uniform Commercial Code (1972), at § 14–8; the factors have been revised slightly in the text to focus on transactions secured by mortgages.

23. Financial Credit Corp. v. Williams, supra note 20; United States Finance Co. v. Jones, supra note 20.

24. Home Security Corp. v. Gentry, 235 So.2d 249 (Miss.1970); see also Goetz v. Selsor, 628 S.W.2d 404 (Mo.App.1982); Western Savings & Loan Association v. Diamond Lazy K Guest Ranch, Inc., 18 Ariz.App. 256, 501 P.2d 432 (1972).

25. Most of the cases involve contests between consumers (as makers) and finance companies (as holders); but see Kaw Valley State Bank v. Riddle, 219 Kan. 550, 549 P.2d 927 (1976), applying the close-connectedness doctrine even though the maker was a businessman and the holder a bank.

26. See Jones v. Approved Bancredit Corp., 256 A.2d 739 (Del.1969).

the assignee bought the paper at a deep discount. The results of the cases are not wholly consistent, but there is little doubt that the HDC doctrine is easier to overcome now than a few years ago.[27]

 WESTLAW REFERENCES

"uniform commercial" u.c.c. 3–202 /p negotiation +s instrument +s holder

di holder in due course

Negotiability

"uniform commercial" u.c.c. 3–104 3–105 /p negotia! /s mortgage

Negotiation

"holder in due course" h.d.c. /s "good faith" notice notif! valu! /p mortgage

§ 5.30 Statutory and Regulatory Limitations on the Holder In Due Course Doctrine

A few scattered states have reversed or modified the holder in due course doctrine by individualized statutes; their details vary and space will not permit a complete discussion of them.[1] This section will concentrate instead on three enactments having nationwide importance which in some circumstances alter the normal provisions of the UCC giving HDC status to holders of negotiable notes. The first is the Uniform Consumer Credit Code, adopted by 12 jurisdictions at this writing.[2] The second is the Federal Trade Commission's "Holder In Due Course Rule", which has nationwide application. The third is the

27. The finding is by no means automatic, and the maker is often expected to produce some evidence of notice, lack of good faith, or close-connectedness; see Ritz v. Karstenson, 39 Ill.App.3d 877, 350 N.E.2d 870 (1976); Jeminson v. Montgomery Real Estate & Co., 47 Mich.App. 731, 210 N.W.2d 14 (1973); Slaughter v. Jefferson Federal Savings & Loan Association, 538 F.2d 397 (D.C.Cir. 1976), all rejecting the "close-connectedness" doctrine for lack of evidence. While the Code indicates that once the maker has shown that he has a defense, the holder has the burden of establishing that he is a HDC, the cases do not always follow this allocation of proof strictly. See, e.g., Austin v. Atlas Subsidiaries of Mississippi, Inc., 223 So.2d 297 (Miss.1969); cf. Kreutz v. Wolff, 560 S.W.2d 271 (Mo.App.1977).

§ 5.30

1. See, e.g., Md. Code, Commercial Law, § 12–507; Mass.Gen.Laws Ann. c. 225D, § 25A; 9 Vt.Stat.Ann. § 2455; West's RCWA 63.14.020. See Randolph National Bank v. Vail, 131 Vt. 390, 308 A.2d 588 (1973); White & Summers, Uniform Commercial Code § 14–8 n. 52 (2d ed. 1980).

2. The UCCC was originally promulgated in 1968, and that version has been adopted by eight jurisdictions at this writing: Colorado, Guam, Indiana, Oklahoma, South Carolina, Utah, Wisconsin, and Wyoming. A new version was released in 1974 and has been adopted by four states: Idaho, Iowa, Kansas, and Maine. All references in the text are to the 1974 version. Both versions contain the basic prohibition on the use of negotiable instruments in consumer transactions, but the 1968 version does not contain the provisions, discussed in the text at note 8 infra, making direct lenders subject to claims and defenses of consumers if the lender is closely related to seller.

The details of differences between the two versions vary, as do the actual enactments of the states. Space does not permit an elaborate discussion of these variations. See Uniform Consumer Credit Code, Official 1974 Text with Comments, 7 Unif.L. Ann. 158, 164–66 (1977 supp.); Comment, The Uniform Consumer Credit Code and Real Estate Financing—A Square Peg in a Round Hole, 28 U.Kan.L.Rev. 601, 615–16 (1980).

Uniform Land Transactions Act, recently promulgated by the National Conference of Commissioners on Uniform State Laws and not yet adopted in any state. In all three of these contexts we will concentrate on the impact on mortgage transactions of the rule under discussion.

Uniform Consumer Credit Code

Before we examine the operational aspect of the UCCC, it is first necessary to outline the two major fact situations in which it applies. As the discussion of the negotiability concept in the preceding section shows, many litigated cases have arisen because a home improvement contractor or other vendor of goods or housing has taken from his customer a negotiable note secured by a mortgage on the customer's home. The vendor then negotiates the note to a finance company or institution. When the customer discovers that the vendor will not perform as promised, or finds that the papers he has signed constitute a note and mortgage even though he did not so understand them when he signed, the stage is set for a battle over the assignee's HDC status. For present purposes, we emphasize that the original note and mortgage run to the vendor as payee-mortgagee. We might term this "vendor financing"; in the language of the UCCC, it is a *consumer credit sale*.[3]

Compare the following alternative method of arranging the transaction. The customer is introduced to the financial institution before the documents are signed. The institution gives a loan to the customer, who immediately pays that money to the vendor. The customer also gives a note and mortgage directly to the lender. The vendor, having been fully paid, nonetheless performs his contract inadequately. The transaction might be referred to as "third-party financing" to distinguish it from the "vendor financing" of the preceding paragraph; the UCCC calls it a *consumer loan*.[4]

The economic effect of these two transactions may be virtually identical, but in legal contemplation they are quite different. In the consumer credit sale, the lender's HDC status is critical to his ability to collect the debt despite the vendor's default. By contrast, the lender in the consumer loan situation appears to have no need at all of the HDC doctrine. Defenses which the customer could raise against the vendor cannot be raised against him, not because he holds in due course, but because he does not hold paper which originally ran to the vendor; the debtor-lender transaction is, at least on its face, entirely separate from the debtor-vendor one. Of course, the lender might later assign the note and mortgage to another financial institution, and it might well be a HDC, but even there HDC status would be relevant only to ward off defenses arising out of the debtor-lender aspect of the transaction.

In the recent past the more disreputable vendors have usually employed the consumer credit sale method of financing, while those of

3. U.C.C.C. § 1.301(12).

4. U.C.C.C. § 1.301(15).

greater honesty have generally used the consumer loan approach. Yet it is clear that either type of transaction can have the same bleak result for the debtor: half-finished or defective workmanship accompanied by an absolute and secured obligation to pay the full price. It is to the credit of the drafters of the UCCC that they recognized that either situation can be unfairly disastrous to consumers, and that they took steps to address each.[5]

In the consumer credit sale situation, the UCCC's basic approach is an attack on the HDC doctrine. It provides bluntly that the vendor "may not take a negotiable instrument other than a check * * * as evidence of the obligation of the consumer."[6] In addition, if the vendor violates this provision by taking a negotiable instrument from the consumer, any assignee of the paper is subject to all claims and defenses which the consumer could have raised against the vendor arising out of the sale;[7] the HDC doctrine is abrogated. The underlying assumption of the UCCC seems to be that any lender who buys consumer paper from a vendor should be expected to superintend the vendor's behavior, or omit to do so at its peril. Note that no "close-connectedness" need be shown; in a sense, the Code conclusively presumes the connection from the very fact of assignment of the paper.

In the consumer loan situation the matter is more complicated. In some consumer loan cases the lender and the vendor are actually completely unconnected; for example, the customer may have selected each in an entirely separate shopping effort, and the lender may have no knowledge whatever of the vendor's business operations. The drafters of the 1974 version of the UCCC wished to subject the lender to claims and defenses arising out of the vendor-debtor transaction if it could be shown that some relationship existed between the lender and vendor which would justify lender liability. They listed the objectionable relationships as follows:

   (a) the lender knows that the seller * * * arranged for the extension of credit by the lender for a commission, brokerage, or referral fee;

   (b) the lender is a person related to the seller * * *, unless the relationship is remote or is not a factor in the transaction;

   (c) the seller * * * guarantees the loan or otherwise assumes the risk of loss by the lender upon the loan;

---

5. See comments to 1974 Official Text, supra note 2, at 165–66; Note, Consumer Defenses and Financers as Holders in Due Course, 4 Conn.L.Rev. 83 (1971); Note, Consumer Notes and Rights of Assignee, 56 Minn.L.Rev. 510 (1972).

6. U.C.C.C. § 3.307. See Stevens v. Rock Springs National Bank, 577 P.2d 1374 (Wyo.1978); Wenning v. Jim Walter Homes, Inc., 606 F.2d 784 (7th Cir.1979).

7. U.C.C.C. § 3.404(1); See Circle v. Jim Walter Homes, Inc., 535 F.2d 583 (10th Cir. 1976). Under the 1968 version of the U.C. C.C., the assignee loses HDC status only if she has notice that the instrument was issued in violation of the U.C.C.C.; see U.C. C.C. § 2.403 (1968 vers.)

(d) the lender directly supplies the seller * * * with the contract document used by the consumer to evidence the loan, and the seller * * * has knowledge of the credit terms and participates in preparation of the document;

(e) the loan is conditioned upon the consumer's purchase * * * of the property or services from the particular seller * * *, but the lender's payment of proceeds of the loan to the seller * * * does not in itself establish that the loan was so conditioned; or

(f) the lender, before he makes the consumer loan, has knowledge or, from his course of dealing with the particular seller * * * or his records, notice of substantial complaints by other buyers * * * of the particular seller's * * * failure or refusal to perform his contracts with them and of the particular seller's * * * failure to remedy his defaults within a reasonable time after notice to him of the complaints.[8]

Where one or more of these features is present, the lender is subject to both defenses and affirmative claims growing out of the transaction. The factors listed are reminiscent of the "close-connectedness" doctrine developed by the courts in some HDC cases, and discussed in the preceding section, but the context is different, for here the lender is not a HDC at all, but the payee-mortgagee under a purportedly separate transaction. The effect of the list is to place the lender in the position of a non-HDC assignee. Indeed, his position may be even worse, for the Code says he is "subject to all *claims* * * * arising from that sale,"[9] although only to the extent of the amount owing to the lender when he receives notice of the claim. Suppose a home improvement contractor has properly completed the work, but in the process has damaged some other part of the house. Can this affirmative claim be asserted against the third party lender if his relationship with the contractor fits the list above? Ordinarily even an assignee of a note, whether an HDC or not, is not affirmatively liable for obligations of the assignor not contained in the note;[10] perhaps liability might be extended for obligations set out in the accompanying mortgage, such as a promise to pay interest on a tax impound account or to permit fire insurance proceeds to be used for restoration of the property.[11] But the UCCC, if taken at face value,

8. U.C.C.C. § 3.405(1). The 1968 version does not include this provision. See Stevens v. Rock Springs National Bank, supra note 6.

9. U.C.C.C. § 3.405(1), (2).

10. Black v. Sullivan, 48 Cal.App.3d 557, 122 Cal.Rptr. 119 (1975); Williams Construction Co. v. Standard-Pacific Corp., 254 Cal.App.2d 442, 61 Cal.Rptr. 912 (1967). See official comment, Unif. Land Trans. Act § 1–313.

11. A rule imposing affirmative liability on the Department of Housing and Urban Development when it has taken an assignment of an FHA-insured mortgage has been applied on a showing that HUD provided all documentation and closely supervised the making of the original mortgage; see Trans-Bay Engineers & Builders, Inc. v. Lynn, 551 F.2d 370 (D.C.Cir.1975); Lindy v. Lynn, 395 F.Supp. 769 (E.D.Pa. 1974) affirmed 515 F.2d 507 (3d Cir.1975); F.W. Eversley & Co. v. East New York goes much further; it seems to make the lender the vendor's alter ego for purposes of all liabilities "arising from that sale." The same potential liabilities, incidentally, face an assignee in a transaction of the consumer credit sale type under the Code. He too is subject to "all claims and defenses of the consumer." [12] Perhaps the courts will interpret "claim" or "arising out of" more restrictively; [13] if they do not, the Code has accomplished a rather remarkable extension of the vendor's liability to those who finance his work.

The application of the UCCC to mortgage transactions is limited sharply by the definitions contained in the code. Obviously refinancings and other loans not related to a sale are not covered. In addition the Code will apply only if the debtor is an individual rather than an organization [14] and the debt or sale is primarily for a personal, family, household, or agricultural purpose. [15] The original creditor must be regularly engaged in transactions of the kind involved. [16] If the sale is of goods or services (such as home improvements) rather than an interest in land, the Code applies only if the amount financed does not exceed a dollar amount which is readjusted biennially in accordance with changes in the Consumer Price Index, [17] and is $45,000 at this writing. [18] Finally, the Code is inapplicable if the debt is secured by a mortgage and the interest rate is 12 percent or lower. [19] Only since the 1980's have interest rates on first mortgage loans in the United States generally exceeded 12 percent. Thus, the UCCC's principal mortgage law application is in second mortgage transactions which finance the sale of goods or home improvements. The protections given to consumers cannot be waived, [20] and hence are likely to be highly effective in litigated cases. Whether they will bring about widespread changes in the home improvement industry, as the draftsmen hoped, remains to be seen.

Non-Profit HDFC, Inc., 409 F.Supp. 791 (S.D.N.Y.1976). These cases also relieve the original mortgagee of further liability when the assignment has been completed.

12. U.C.C.C. § 3.404; again, liability is limited to the amount owing to the assignee at the time he has notice of the claim.

13. The official comment says cryptically, "Suggestions that * * * lenders should be responsible for * * * product liability that might arise out of the transaction are rejected as neither feasible nor reasonable." Official Comment, supra note 2, at 166. Precisely what is meant by "product liability" we are not told, and there seems to be no warrant in the Code itself for excluding product liability claims.

14. U.C.C.C. § 1.301(12)(a)(ii), (15)(a)(i).

15. U.C.C.C. § 1.301(12)(a)(iii), (15)(a)(ii). See Brown v. Loveland, 678 P.2d 292 (Utah 1984); Anderson v. Foothill Industrial

Bank, 674 P.2d 232 (Wyo.1984); Hall v. Owen County State Bank, 175 Ind.App. 150, 370 N.E.2d 918 (1977).

16. U.C.C.C. § 1.301(12)(a)(i), (15)(a).

17. U.C.C.C. § 1.301(12)(a)(v), (15)(a)(iv).

18. U.C.C.C. § 1.106; the dollar amounts are changed on July 1 of even numbered years; they change only in multiples of ten percent and only if the Consumer Price Index (1967 = 100) changes by at least ten percent.

19. U.C.C.A. § 1.301(12)(b)(ii), (15)(b)(ii), and official comments thereto. See Circle v. Jim Walter Homes, Inc., 654 F.2d 688 (10th Cir.1981).

20. "An agreement may not limit or waive the claims or defenses of a consumer under this section." U.C.C.C. § 3.404(4); § 3.405(4).

Federal Trade Commission Rule

Many of the concepts of the UCCC were borrowed by the Federal Trade Commission in 1975 when it adopted a "trade regulation rule" entitled "Preservation of Consumers' Claims and Defenses." [21] The rule simply makes it an unfair trade practice for a seller of goods or services to finance his sale without including in the "consumer credit contract"—a note or other evidence of debt—language which makes the lender subject to the consumer's claims and defenses. The rule spells out the exact language which must be used.[22] Recovery is limited to the amounts the debtor has paid under the contract,[23] as contrasted with the UCCC which permits recovery up to the amount owing to the lender.[24]

Both consumer loans and consumer credit sales, in the UCCC's parlance, are covered by the FTC rule. If third-party lender financing is the mode employed (as the FTC rule terms it, a "purchase money loan"), there is a type of "close-connectedness" criterion which must be satisfied, but it is much simpler and looser than the UCCC's. The lender is brought within the rule's ambit if the seller of the goods or services refers consumers to the lender or is affiliated with the creditor by common control, contract, or business arrangement.[25] Another interesting difference between the UCCC and the FTC rule is that the latter does not apply to sales of interests in real estate, irrespective of

---

21. 16 CFR 433.1–.2; 40 Fed.Reg. 53506 (Nov. 18, 1975). See also Guidelines on Trade Regulation Rule Concerning Preservation of Consumers' Claims and Defenses, 41 Fed.Reg. 20022 (May 14, 1976), discussing the background of the rule in detail; White & Summers, Uniform Commercial Code § 14–8 & Appendix A (2d ed.1980); Banks, The FTC Holder in Due Course Rule: A Rule Without a Private Remedy, 44 Mont.L.Rev. 113 (1983); Lawrence & Minan, The Effect of Abrogating the Holder-In-Due-Course Doctrine on the Commercialization of Innovative Consumer Products, 64 B.U.L.Rev. 325 (1984); Note, The New FTC Trade Regulation Rule on Holder in Due Course, 13 Houston L.Rev. 789 (1976). See generally Report of the National Commission of Consumer Finance, Consumer Credit in the United States (1972).

22. The language must appear in at least ten point bold-face type and reads as follows: "NOTICE. ANY HOLDER OF THIS CONSUMER CREDIT CONTRACT IS SUBJECT TO ALL CLAIMS AND DEFENSES WHICH THE DEBTOR COULD ASSERT AGAINST THE SELLER OF GOODS OR SERVICES OBTAINED WITH THE PROCEEDS HEREOF. RECOVERY HEREUNDER BY THE DEBTOR SHALL NOT EXCEED AMOUNTS PAID BY THE DEBTOR HEREUNDER."

The quoted language applies to consumer loans by third-party lenders; the text applicable to vendor paper which is assigned to a lender is similar.

23. See text quoted in note 22, supra. State law may, however, allow a larger recovery; see Saporita v. Delco Corp., 104 Misc.2d 527, 428 N.Y.S.2d 581 (1980); Hempstead Bank v. Babcock, 115 Misc.2d 97, 453 N.Y.S.2d 557 (1982).

24. The questions raised in the text at notes 9–13 supra, regarding the scope of possible claims seem equally applicable, and equally unanswered, here.

25. 16 CFR 433.1(d); a "business arrangement" is further defined as "any understanding, procedure, course of dealing, or arrangement, formal or informal, between a creditor and a seller, in connection with the sale of goods or services to consumers or the financing thereof." This language appears to be broad enough to cover virtually every purchase-money loan in which the lender knows what the use of the funds will be; a more refined definition, like that of U.C.C.C. § 3.405(1), would be preferable.

the amount or interest rate.[26] It does, however, apply to sales of goods or services even if a mortgage on real estate is taken to secure payment of the purchase price.

In most other respects the coverage of the FTC rule and the UCCC are similar. The FTC rule applies only to natural persons who buy goods or services for personal, family, or household use.[27] The lender must be engaged in financing such transactions in the ordinary course of business.[28] By virtue of a reference to the Truth-in-Lending Act and its accompanying Regulation Z, the FTC rule covers only purchases involving an expenditure of $25,000 or less.[29]

Uniform Land Transactions Act

Promulgated in 1975 and extensively amended in 1977, the Uniform Land Transactions Act has not been adopted by any legislature at this writing. Nonetheless, the ULTA provides an interesting treatment of the holder-in-due-course doctrine which may form the basis for future state legislation. Unlike the UCCC and the FTC rule, the ULTA does not attempt to deal with the third party lender who provides purchase money financing to a vendor's customers and who is also closely related to the vendor; it deals only with direct assignment, as by a vendor to the lender. This seems an unfortunate omission, since as we have noted either form of transaction can give rise to the same abuses.

The ULTA's basic position is that, absent a waiver, the debtor may assert against the assignee all claims and defenses which arise before the debtor receives notice of the assignment.[30] The language of the act imposes no specific limit on affirmative claims, but since it provides that the assignee's "rights * * * are subject to" such claims, the courts would probably not permit recoveries against the assignee in excess of the total debt, or perhaps the unpaid balance. The act does not limit claims to those growing out of the same transaction in which the debt was incurred, but this may be largely irrelevant if a limitation on the amount of claims is imposed as suggested above; in effect a "claim" would be viewed as a setoff or counterclaim to the assignee's foreclosure action or suit on the debt, and the act's only effect might be to permit the introduction of otherwise non-germane counterclaims in the lender's action.[31]

---

26. 16 CFR 433.1(c).

27. 16 CFR 433.1(b).

28. 16 CFR 433.1(c).

29. 16 CFR 433.1(d), (e).

30. U.L.T.A. § 3–206(a). The provision is copied essentially verbatim from U.C.C. § 9–318.

31. The official comment to U.L.T.A. § 1–313 states "Some recent acts have subjected the assignee to 'all claims and defenses' of a consumer-obligor. This Act, however, speaks only to defenses." The statement is obviously erroneous, since § 3–206 explicitly refers to claims as well as defenses. The same comment also raises, but does not answer, the question whether a consumer can recover payments already made to an assignee; in light of the "claims" language of § 3–206, an affirmative answer seems probable. Compare Bank of Wyandotte v. Woodrow, 394 F.Supp. 550 (W.D.Mo.1975).

The ULTA's protection of debtors from actions by assignees is broader than that of the UCCC and the FTC rule, since it is not on its face confined to consumer debt or to junior mortgages. However the ULTA, unlike the other enactments mentioned, permits the debtor to waive his ULTA protections to an extent which will place the assignee in the same position as a holder in due course.[32] No waiver is permitted in cases in which an owner-occupant of a home [33] gives a mortgage and note to a vendor who is in the business of selling real estate, or gives a junior mortgage on his home.[34] Waivers are allowed in first mortgages, a policy designed to protect the secondary mortgage market and attract investors to home mortgages; [35] presumably waiver clauses will be included in all first mortgages in jurisdictions which adopt the ULTA. The secondary market in junior mortgages is more limited, and is not considered essential to national housing policy. The net result is that the coverage of the ULTA in protecting debtors from the HDC doctrine is roughly equivalent to that of the UCCC and the FTC rule.

 WESTLAW REFERENCES

mortgage /p "holder in due course" h.d.c. /s rule statut! /6 alter! change* exact! modif!

Uniform Consumer Credit Code

mortgage /p "consumer credit sale" "uniform consumer" u.c.c.c. /63 "holder in due course" h.d.c.

mortgage /p "consumer loan" "uniform consumer" u.c.c.c. /p lender mortgagee payee

Federal Trade Commission Rule

citation(16 +3 433)

(16 +3 433) "preservation of consumer claim" "purchase money loan" /54 mortgage "trade commission" f.t.c.

Uniform Land Transactions Act

"uniform land transaction" u.l.t.a. /p mortgage

§ 5.31   Rights of Holders in Due Course

If the assignee of a note secured by a mortgage is a holder in due course, he is free of most of the defenses which the maker of the note might attempt to assert against collection or foreclosure. The UCC

---

32. U.L.T.A. § 1–314. In effect, this means that an effective waiver clause will still leave the assignee subject to so-called "real" defenses, but not to "personal" defenses; see § 5.31, infra.

33. The act's term is "protected party", which includes an occupying owner or purchaser of a building containing four or fewer dwelling units on not more than three acres.

34. U.L.T.A. § 1–313.

35. Official Comment, U.L.T.A. § 1–313. Whether HDC protection is really necessary to attract investors to the home mortgage market is questionable, but there is, as the comment points out, little evidence of widespread abuses by first mortgage originators. Thus the presence or absence of HDC status probably makes little difference to either debtors or assignees.

lists certain defenses against which even HDC status does not immunize the assignee; they are traditionally termed "real" defenses:

(a) infancy, to the extent that it is a defense to a simple contract; and

(b) such other incapacity, or duress, or illegality of the transaction, as renders the obligation of the party a nullity; and

(c) such misrepresentation as has induced the party to sign the instrument with neither knowledge nor reasonable opportunity to obtain knowledge of its character or its essential terms; and

(d) discharge in insolvency proceedings; and

(e) any other discharge of which the holder has notice when he takes the instrument.[1]

This definition of the real defenses is largely straightforward. Incapacity, duress, and illegality may make a note void or voidable, depending on the jurisdiction and the circumstances. The Code leaves the void-voidable distinction to other state law,[2] but only facts which would make the note void can be asserted against a HDC; indeed, that is the very definition of a void instrument.

The sort of misrepresentation, described in subparagraph (c) above, which will survive negotiation to an HDC, is roughly equivalent to "fraud in the factum," but the Code attempts a more detailed definition. The official comment suggests that in judging whether the maker had a "reasonable opportunity to obtain knowledge", his age, sex, education, intelligence, business experience, linguistic ability, relationship with the payee, and the urgency of the transaction should all be considered, as should the availability of some other person, perhaps a friend or relative, who might have been able to advise him.[3] It is clear that mere "fraud in the inducement", based on false statements about the underlying performance of the payee-mortgagee rather than about the documents being signed, will not be considered a real defense.[4]

The Code defines "personal defenses"—that is, those cut off by negotiation to an HDC—by exclusion from the list quoted above. Such defenses include fraud in the inducement and some types of incapacity,

§ 5.31

1. U.C.C. § 3–305(2).

2. See U.C.C. § 1–103.

3. U.C.C. § 3–305, official comment 7. See Colburn v. Mid-State Homes, Inc., 289 Ala. 255, 266 So.2d 865 (1972); Gallegos v. Gulf Coast Investment Corp., 483 S.W.2d 944 (Tex.Civ.App.1972), set aside 491 S.W.2d 659 (Sup.1973). Hidalgo v. Surety Savings & Loan Association, 502 S.W.2d 220 (Tex.Civ.App.1971); Cranesville Block Co. v. Pentagon Construction Co., 51 App. Div.2d 610, 378 N.Y.S.2d 127 (1976); cf.

Venable v. Payne, 138 Ga.App. 237, 225 S.E.2d 716 (1976); Leedy v. Ellsworth Construction Co., 9 Ohio App.2d 1, 222 N.E.2d 653 (1966); Burchett v. Allied Concord Financial Corp., 74 N.M. 575, 396 P.2d 186 (1964).

4. See Federal National Mortgage Association v. Gregory, 426 F.Supp. 282 (E.D. Wisc.1977); Citizens National Bank v. Brazil, 141 Ga.App. 388, 233 S.E.2d 482 (1977); Myers v. Bank of Prattville, 341 So.2d 726 (Ala.1977); Austin v. Atlas Subsidiaries of Mississippi, 223 So.2d 297 (Miss.1969).

duress, and illegality, as mentioned. They also include lack of consideration (which would make the note unenforceable under normal contract theory),[5] partial or total failure of consideration (e.g., the failure of the mortgagee-creditor to make the loan of money which the note is supposed to evidence an obligation to repay),[6] accord and satisfaction, waiver,[7] and any sort of setoff or counterclaim[8] which the debtor-mortgagor might raise against the original mortgagee.[9] Payment of the debt by the mortgagor is also regarded as a personal defense; its implications are so important that it is discussed in a separate section, infra.[10]

When a negotiable note is secured by a mortgage, the majority of states considering the question have held that the HDC benefits available with respect to the note apply to the mortgage as well.[11] Thus, a HDC may foreclose the mortgage despite fraud in the inducement,

5. Mozingo v. North Carolina National Bank, 31 N.C.App. 157, 229 S.E.2d 57 (1976), certiorari denied 291 N.C. 771, 232 S.E.2d 204 (1977); Manufacturers & Traders Trust Co. v. Murphy, 369 F.Supp. 11 (W.D.Pa.1974).

6. Mecham v. United Bank of Arizona, 107 Ariz. 437, 489 P.2d 247 (1971); Hidalgo v. Surety Savings & Loan Association, 462 S.W.2d 540 (Tex.Civ.App.1971), appeal after remand 481 S.W.2d 208 (Civ.App.1972), reversed 487 S.W.2d 702 (Sup.1972) appeal after remand 502 S.W.2d 220 (Tex.Cir. 1973); Holt v. Queen City Loan & Investment Co., 377 S.W.2d 393 (Mo.1964).

7. See, e.g., Stern v. Itkin Brothers, Inc., 87 Misc.2d 538, 385 N.Y.S.2d 753 (1975), in which the mortgagor and mortgagee executed a side agreement that only the mortgage, and not the note, would be sued upon in the event of default. Such an arrangement is sometimes referred to loosely as a "non-recourse mortgage", and may be desirable for tax reasons when the mortgagor is a limited partnership. The court held that the agreement would be binding against a non-HDC holder, but would not be valid against a HDC.

8. Gramatan Co. v. D'Amico, 50 Misc.2d 233, 269 N.Y.S.2d 871 (1966).

9. Even usury is frequently no defense against an HDC, unless the usurious rate of interest is apparent on the face of the note; Szczotka v. Idelson, 228 Cal.App.2d 399, 39 Cal.Rptr. 466 (1964); cf. Davenport v. Unicapital Corp., 267 S.C. 691, 230 S.E.2d 905 (1976).

10. See § 5.33, infra.

11. Carpenter v. Longan, 83 U.S. (16 Wall.) 271, 21 L.Ed. 313 (1872), the leading case; American Savings Bank & Trust Co. v. Helgesen, 64 Wash. 54, 116 P. 837, Ann. Cas.1913A, 390 (1911). See Restatement, Security, § 34; Gramatan Co. v. D'Amico, 50 Misc.2d 233, 269 N.Y.S.2d 871 (1966). Courts have held that the same is true even though there has not been an assignment or delivery of the mortgage. Hawley v. Bibb, 69 Ala. 52 (1881); see Morgan v. Farmington Coal & Coke Co., 97 W.Va. 83, 94, 124 S.E. 591, 596 (1924). And it has been held to be unnecessary for the mortgagor to be a party to the note. Gabbert v. Schwartz, 69 Ind. 450 (1880).

The same rule is applied when the security is a deed of trust; see Gribble v. Mauerham, 188 Cal.App.2d 221, 10 Cal. Rptr. 296 (1961); Goetz v. Selsor, 628 S.W.2d 404 (Mo.App.1982); Mayes v. Robinson, 93 Mo. 114, 122, 5 S.W. 611, 613 (1887); Borgess Investment Co. v. Vette, 142 Mo. 560, 573, 44 S.W. 754, 757, 64 Am. St.Rep. 567 (1898); Webb v. Hoselton, 4 Neb. 308, 19 Am.Rep. 638 (1876); Buehler v. McCormick, 169 Ill. 269, 48 N.E. 287 (1897).

In Carolina Housing and Mortgage Corp. v. Reynolds, 230 S.C. 491, 96 S.E.2d 485 (1957), criticized in Karesh, Security Transactions, in Survey of South Carolina Law, 10 S.C.L.Q. 114, 117 (1957), an assignee for value before maturity of a negotiable note, without actual knowledge of the defense of failure of consideration by the maker, took free of the defense on the note, but, since the mortgage was defectively executed on its face the lower court held, and the holding was not appealed, that he could not enforce the mortgage. See also Note, Transfer of the Mortgagee's Interest in Florida, 14 U. of Fla.L.Rev. 98, 100 (1961); Bautista & Kennedy, The Imputed Negotiability of Security Interests Under the Code, 38 Ind.L.J. 574 (1963).

failure of consideration, or other personal defenses. This rule has been criticized as an unwarranted extension of the rights of holders of commercial paper,[12] but it is firmly entrenched and seems entirely justified. To the extent that secondary mortgage market investors regard the HDC doctrine as a significant attraction,[13] for example, it is clear that they do so only because the mortgage remedies are a part of it.

Some limitations exist on this "negotiable mortgage" concept. Obviously the mortgage cannot be asserted by the HDC if by its very terms it is unavailable, even though the note contains no reference to the mortgage's restrictions or conditions. In addition, since the mortgage is a conveyance of or a lien on realty, it is subject to the normal operation of the recording acts and the doctrine of constructive notice. Thus, an adverse conveyance in the record chain of title of a mortgage will be effective even though there has been an assignment of the mortgage to a HDC. To illustrate, if a land owner executes two mortgages, the first is recorded, and the second is subsequently assigned to a HDC, the holder will nonetheless be subordinate to the recorded first mortgage.[14] The result may be explained by saying that the holder has a duty to search the records, and hence cannot claim to lack notice of the prior mortgage.

A final advantage of HDC status should be mentioned: a HDC may further assign the note and mortgage, even to one with notice of defects, and yet the assignee will take free of those defects. If this were not so, the entire HDC concept would be endangered, for the HDC might find himself with an instrument good in his hands only, but unmarketable as a consequence of widespread notice of its defects.[15] One exception is made to this "shelter" idea. If the HDC reassigns the instrument to a previous holder who was not a HDC, that assignee is subject to the maker-mortgagor's defenses.[16]

 WESTLAW REFERENCES
mortgage /p "holder in due course" h.d.c. /s defense duress
      fraud! illegal*** infancy right

§ 5.32 Rights of Assignees Who Are Not Holders in Due Course

This section is concerned with the rights of non-HDC holders of negotiable notes, and of assignees of non-negotiable notes. Before we

12. The leading critical case is Baily v. Smith, 14 Ohio St. 396 (1863). Ironically, Ohio has subsequently adopted the majority view; see Dennis v. Rotter, 43 Ohio App. 330, 183 N.E. 188 (1932). Only Minnesota still appears to adhere to the minority rule; see note, 32 Ill.L.Rev. 120 (1937); 127 A.L.R. 190 (1940).

13. See § 5.30, supra, at note 35.

14. Johnson v. Masterson, 193 S.W. 201 (Tex.Civ.App.1917), error refused.

15. U.C.C. § 3–201(1) and official comment 3; Brock v. Adams, 79 N.M. 17, 439 P.2d 234 (1968).

16. See Coplan Pipe and Supply Co. v. Ben-Frieda Corp., 256 So.2d 218 (Fla.App. 1972).

can deal with these rights, it is necessary to introduce some basic terminology. Two types of fact situations present themselves. The first is the case in which the maker of the note (who is also the mortgagor of the mortgage which secures it) has some defense which can be raised against its enforcement.[1] Such a defense is sometimes termed a "patent equity." The term is a bit archaic and perhaps not very descriptive, but its meaning can be easily grasped. The assignee of a note who realizes that he will or may lack HDC protection is well-advised to inquire of the maker-mortgagor before accepting the assignment.[2] Such an assignee will commonly request that the maker sign an "estoppel certificate", averring that the note is valid and that the maker has no defenses. Such a certificate is generally effective,[3] and if broadly drafted provides even better protection for the assignee than would the HDC doctrine, since it insulates him from both real and personal defenses.[4] By making such an inquiry and obtaining such a

§ 5.32

1. The defense may be either real or personal; in this context the distinction is unimportant. See § 5.31, supra, at notes 1, 5–9. Claims of the original mortgagee or others in the chain of assignments are also considered "patent" on the same rationale discussed in the text; Stevenson Brewing Co. v. Iba, 155 N.Y. 224, 49 N.E. 677 (1898).

2. Long ago it was stated that though "in fact it does happen that assignments of mortgages are taken without calling upon the mortgagor;" to do so is regarded as "extremely unfit and very rash, and a very indifferent security" and "no conveyancer of established reputation would recommend" it "without making the mortgagor a party and being satisfied that the money was really due." Matthew v. Wallwyn, 4 Ves. 118, 127 (1798). These statements are still true today as applied to mortgages securing non-negotiable notes. Some mortgage forms include language obligating the mortgagor to give an estoppel statement upon request.

3. Harrison v. Galilee Baptist Church, 427 Pa. 247, 234 A.2d 314 (1967). Not only the immediate assignee for whom the certificate is given, but subsequent assignees from him as well, may rely upon the certificate. See generally Griffiths v. Sears, 112 Pa. 523, 4 A. 492 (1886); Nixon v. Haslett, 74 N.J.Eq. 789, 70 A. 987 (1908), affirmed 75 N.J.Eq. 302, 78 A. 1134 (1911); 23 L.R.A.,N.S., 177 (1910). See Smyth v. Munroe, 84 N.Y. 354 (1881) on the establishment of reliance by the assignee on the certificate. Weyh v. Boylan, 85 N.Y. 394, 39 Am.Rep. 669 (1881), second assignee

may prevail even though first assignee had notice of the defense of usury.

Estoppel may also arise from oral statements by the mortgagor, or even from his conduct, but the courts are reluctant to imply an estoppel from evidence that is less than clearcut; see Bush v. Cushman, 27 N.J.Eq. 131 (1876), mortgagor affirmatively persuaded the assignee to take the assignment; see Melendy v. Keen, 89 Ill. 395 (1878); Rothschild v. Title Guaranty & Trust Co., 204 N.Y. 458, 97 N.E. 879, 41 L.R.A.,N.S., 740 (1912), semble; Pomeroy, Equity Juris., 5th ed., § 704.

Language in the original mortgage itself is unlikely to be considered an effective estoppel. For example, a recitation in the mortgage that the full loan has been disbursed will not prevent the mortgagor from showing later that it was not; the reason is that too commonly future advances mortgages recite the full consideration as though it had been disbursed in its entirety, when in fact it has not. See § 12.7, infra.

Finally, an estoppel certificate may be ineffective if the assignee has actual knowledge of the mortgagor's defenses despite the certificate's contrary statement; Hammelburger v. Foursome Inn Corp., 54 N.Y.2d 580, 446 N.Y.S.2d 917, 431 N.E.2d 278 (1981); Fidelity Trust Co. v. Gardiner, 191 Pa.Super. 17, 155 A.2d 405 (1959).

4. For an more extensive discussion of estoppel against the mortgagor, see Osborne, Mortgages § 228 (2d ed. 1970); Hammelburger v. Foursome Inn Corp., 54 N.Y.2d 580, 446 N.Y.S.2d 917, 431 N.E.2d 278 (1981).

statement, the prospective assignee can easily discover the maker's defenses, if any; that is, he can make them "patent."

By contrast, "latent equities" are those which cannot be discovered in this manner. They consist of claims to the instrument, or claims which will defeat it, which are asserted by third parties—persons other than the maker. Two general classes of these claims may be considered. First, there are persons whose rights are prior in time and title to the maker's. The maker, for example, may have obtained the mortgaged land by fraud or other device which makes the conveyance to him subject to being set aside.[5] He may have obtained it without payment of consideration under circumstances which would cause a court to subject it to a constructive trust in his hands.[6] It may even be subject to an express but unrecorded trust of which the maker-mortgagor was the trustee.[7] It may have been conveyed to the maker in fraud on the rights of the previous owner's creditors.[8]

Latent equities may also exist in persons whose interests are derived from the maker of the note and mortgage. The most obvious example is the execution of a previous assignment of the note and mortgage by the mortgagee; that is, he purports to assign the same note and mortgage twice.[9] Similarly, a building contractor may do work on the land in question prior to the assignment of the note and mortgage, and his work may give rise to a mechanic's lien which relates back to the time the work was commenced.[10]

In all of these cases the equities are "latent" because an inquiry of the maker will not necessarily disclose their existence, and because the maker's estoppel statement will not cut them off.[11] From the prospective assignee's viewpoint they are hidden.[12] In some of these cases, the recording acts may come into play. For example, in the two-assignment case mentioned in the preceding paragraph, some jurisdictions hold that the first assignment is subject to the recording acts, and if unrecorded is cut off by the second assignment to a bona fide purchas-

5. Humble v. Curtis, 160 Ill. 193, 43 N.E. 749 (1895); Simpson v. Del Hoyo, 94 N.Y. 189 (1883).

6. Capital Investors Co. v. Executors of Estate of Morrison, 484 F.2d 1157 (4th Cir. 1973).

7. Mott v. Clark, 9 Pa.St. 399, 1 Am.L.J. 379, 49 Am.Dec. 566 (1848).

8. Moffett v. Parker, 71 Minn. 139, 73 N.W. 850, 70 Am.St.Rep. 319 (1898); Danbury v. Robinson, 14 N.J.Eq. 213, 82 Am. Dec. 244 (1862); McMurtry v. Bowers, 91 N.J.Eq. 317, 109 A. 361 (1920).

9. The problem can arise, of course, only if the first mortgage note is not delivered to the first assignee, but an effective assignment without delivery is entirely possible as between the parties if the assignee is willing to forego HDC status; see

§ 5.28, supra, at notes 2–6; Guaranty Mortgage & Insurance Co. v. Harris, 193 So.2d 1 (Fla.1966) in which the first assignment was a pledge evidenced only by a notation on the books of the assignor corporation.

10. Wilson Brothers v. Cooey, 251 Md. 350, 247 A.2d 395 (1968).

11. "He may inquire of all the persons in the chain of title, but their admissions will not affect a party in possession of an equitable right derived from them." Bush v. Lathrop, 22 N.Y. 535 (1860).

12. See Bautista & Kennedy, The Imputed Negotiability of Security Interests Under the Code, 38 Ind.L.J. 574 (1963); Note, Latent Equities, 20 U.Chi.L.Rev. 692 (1952).

er.[13] Conceivably the same result would be reached with regard to the maker who got the land as trustee under an unrecorded express trust.[14] But clearly many cases remain—the constructive trust, for example— which are not subject to the recording acts of any jurisdiction.

The question, then, is to what extent an assignee who is not a HDC is subject to the maker's defenses (that is, patent equities), and to the claims of third parties (that is, latent equities). Note that we have said "claims" in referring to third parties; this is not meant to imply that they will necessarily assert their rights by becoming plaintiffs in suits, but merely that they have some affirmative rights to assert; they are not merely using their "equities" to defend against the note and mortgage, since they are not the normal objects of a suit on the note or an action to foreclose the mortgage.

Patent Equities

With regard to the defenses of the maker-mortgagor, the law is clear and simple; the non-HDC assignee is fully subject to them, just as the original mortgagee would be. If the note is negotiable but the holder has notice or fails to pay value, or if the note is nonnegotiable merely because it omits "bearer" or "order" language,[15] the UCC applies. It specifically provides that the assignee is subject to "all defenses of any party which would be available in an action on a simple contract." [16] If the note is non-negotiable for other reasons, such as incorporation of the mortgage by reference or language which makes the obligation conditional, the UCC does not control but the common law rule is the same. The assignee is subject to all patent equities [17] when he attempts to enforce either the note or the mortgage.

13. See Johnson v. Sowell, 80 N.M. 677, 459 P.2d 839 (1969); cf. Neal v. Bradley, 238 Ark. 714, 384 S.W.2d 238 (1964).

14. See Bogert, Trusts and Trustees §§ 881, 893 (1962).

15. Under U.C.C. § 3–805, a note which is nonnegotiable because of these particular omissions is covered by U.C.C. Art. 3, except that a holder of such a note cannot be a HDC. See Locke v. Aetna Acceptance Corp., 309 So.2d 43 (Fla.App.1975); Jones v. United Savings & Loan Association, 515 S.W.2d 869 (Mo.App.1974); D. Nelson & Sons, Inc. v. General American Development Corp., 6 Ill.App.3d 6, 284 N.E.2d 478 (1972).

16. U.C.C. § 3–306(b); see § 5.31, supra, at notes 1–10; Reynolds v. Ramos, 188 Conn. 316, 449 A.2d 182 (1982); Lapis Enterprises, Inc. v. International Blimpie Corp., 84 App.Div.2d 286, 445 N.Y.S.2d 574 (1981).

17. Inland Real Estate Corp. v. Oak Park Trust & Sav. Bank, 127 Ill.App.3d 535, 82 Ill.Dec. 670, 469 N.E.2d 204 (1983); Lincoln First Bank v. Bankers Trust Co., 23 B.R. 410 (Bkrtcy.N.Y.1982), reversed on other grounds 32 B.R. 742 (S.D.N.Y.1983) (apparently decided without reference to U.C.C. § 3–306(b); Sosebee v. Atha, 140 Ga. App. 555, 231 S.E.2d 381 (1976); Bittner v. McGrath, 186 Pa.Super. 477, 142 A.2d 323 (1958); Fidelity Trust Co. v. Gardiner, 191 Pa.Super. 17, 155 A.2d 405 (1959). "The rule is conceded that the assignee of the mortgage takes subject to the equities between the original parties, and has no greater rights than the original mortgagee." Rapps v. Gottlieb, 142 N.Y. 164, 36 N.E. 1052 (1894); Davis v. Bechstein, 69 N.Y. 440, 25 Am.Rep. 218 (1877). See also Karesh, Security Transactions, in Survey of South Carolina Law, 10 S.C.L.Q. 114, 120 (1957), discussing Carolina Housing & Mortgage Corp. v. Orange Hill A.M.E. Church, 230 S.C. 498, 97 S.E.2d 28 (1957).

Latent Equities

When latent equities are asserted by third parties, it is essential to determine whether the UCC governs the transaction. As indicated above, it applies either if the note is negotiable (and the assignee's conduct has deprived him of HDC status), or if it is nonnegotiable because not payable to "order" or "bearer." [18] If the Code does apply, its relevant language states that the assignee is subject to "all valid claims to [the instrument] on the part of any person." [19] This language is startlingly broad, and may well be read to include all latent equities. This conclusion is strengthened by the official comment, which states that the quoted phrase "includes not only claims of legal title, but all liens, equities, or other claims of right against the instrument or its proceeds." [20]

Precisely this view of the Code was taken in Capital Investors Co. v. Executors of Estate of Morrison.[21] Morrison, who owned certain real estate, deeded it to a business associate in an apparent attempt to deprive his wife of any interest in it upon his death.[22] The grantee, without Morrison's authority, retransferred the property and took back a purchase-money mortgage which he then assigned to a person who allegedly had no notice of Morrison's interest. The assignee was not, however, a HDC, since the notes were past due and the assignee had notice that they were in default. The court applied the UCC literally and held that the assignee would be subject to the claim of Morrison's executor that the original grant by Morrison was subject to a constructive trust in favor of his estate. The court cannot be faulted for following the Code,[23] but in terms of general policy the result is hard to accept; plainly the assignee is being held subject to rights which no reasonable investigation by him would have disclosed.

In cases in which the instrument is not negotiable for reasons other than omission of "bearer" or "order" language, the UCC has no applica-

---

18. See note 15, supra.

19. U.C.C. § 3–306(a).

20. U.C.C. § 3–306, Official Comment 2.

21. 484 F.2d 1157 (4th Cir.1973).

22. Further background on Mr. Morrison's dealings appears in Capital Investors Co. v. Devers, 360 F.2d 462 (4th Cir.1966), certiorari denied 385 U.S. 934, 87 S.Ct. 294, 17 L.Ed.2d 214 (1966), rehearing denied 385 U.S. 1021, 87 S.Ct. 702, 17 L.Ed.2d 560 (1967), appeal after remand 387 F.2d 591 (4th Cir.1968).

23. The court's opinion may be criticized in the following respect. It persistently speaks of a claim of constructive trust by Morrison's estate on the notes or their proceeds; perhaps more aptly the constructive trust should have been imposed on the real estate which Morrison had transferred in fraud on his wife's

rights. Moreover, the UCC refers only to the holder of the "instrument" as taking subject to all claims of other persons (§ 3–306(a)). It makes no reference whatever to the mortgage or land. It might thus have been held that the assignee of the mortgage was, under the common law principles discussed at note 26 infra, free of the latent equity in the mortgage, and that no latent equity properly existed in the note; the assignee would thus prevail. If it is conceded that estate's constructive trust claim is properly asserted against the note, and is supported by the UCC, the assignee might still argue that the realty interest is, under non-Code principles, free of the trust. However, that argument would leave the assignee with a mortgage and no note for it to secure, an essentially meaningless position.

tion and the common law of contracts controls.[24] Should an assignee of such a note, if he pays value and has no notice [25] of the latent equities, take free of them? The cases are badly split, but it is probable that a slight majority take an affirmative view.[26] The Restatement of Contracts Second concludes that the assignee should prevail, at least if the latent equities are in the nature of an express or constructive trust, an equitable lien, or a right of avoidance in a third party.[27] Some case law supports the same result in the "two assignments of the same mortgage" case mentioned earlier.[28]

This contrast between Code and non-Code results is exceedingly difficult to justify in policy terms. If the note is non-negotiable because it omits "bearer" or "order", the assignee will lose; if it is non-negotiable because it is conditional or incorporates the mortgage by reference, the assignee will probably win, assuming he pays value and has no notice of the latent equity. Since these cases all involve two innocent parties one of which must lose, there seem to be no powerful

24. See notes 15–16, supra.

25. If the assignee has actual notice, or constructive notice from previously recorded documents, of the third party's claim, he should of course take subject to it; the same is true if the third party is in possession of the property. Seymour v. McKinstry, 106 N.Y. 230, 12 N.E. 348, 14 N.E. 94 (1887). But see American Metropolitan Mortgage, Inc. v. Maricone, 423 So.2d 396 (Fla.App.1982) (possession is not notice, where possessor has placed record title in another.) See Cunningham, Stoebuck & Whitman, Property § 11.10 (1984) at n. 33.

An equitable vendor's lien, the vendor remaining in possession after conveyance, has been held to prevail over a bona fide assignee for value of the mortgage given by the vendee to one who had knowledge of the vendor's claim. The mortgage had been recorded but the continued possession of the vendor put the assignee upon notice of his interest. See Fisk v. Potter, 2 Keyes, N.Y., 64 (1865); cf. Bloomer v. Henderson, 8 Mich. 395, 77 Am.Dec. 453 (1860).

26. The leading case is Simpson v. Del Hoyo, 94 N.Y. 189 (1883). See also American Metropolitan Mortgage, Inc. v. Maricone, 423 So.2d 396 (Fla.App.1982); Baker v. F & F Investment Co., 489 F.2d 829 (7th Cir.1973) (where the point was argued but not decided); Robertson v. United States Livestock Co., 164 Iowa 230, 145 N.W. 535 (1914); Bloomer v. Henderson, 8 Mich. 395, 77 Am.Dec. 453 (1860); Moffett v. Parker, 71 Minn. 139, 73 N.W. 850, 70 Am.St.Rep. 319 (1898); McMurtry v. Bowers, 91 N.J. Eq. 317, 109 A. 361 (1920). A good many of the cases preferring the assignee have oth-

er or additional explanations. Thus Congregational Church Building Society v. Scandinavian Free Church of Tacoma, 24 Wash. 433, 64 P. 750 (1901), could rest upon the ground that the latent equity in the land was unrecorded and therefore defeated by the operation of the recording acts; it was also in a jurisdiction rejecting the doctrine giving supremacy to latent equities in choses in action. Mott v. Clark, 9 Pa.St. 399, 1 Am.L.J. 379, 49 Am.Dec. 566 (1848) similarly relies upon the nonrecordation of the latent equitable interest in the land to defeat its owner on the ground of laches.

New York has long held BFP assignees subject to latent equities; see Lincoln First Bank v. Bankers Trust Co., 23 B.R. 410 (Bkrtcy.N.Y.1982), reversed on other grounds 32 B.R. 742 (S.D.N.Y.1983).

See generally Note, Latent Equities, 20 U.Chi.L.Rev. 692 (1952); Osborne, Mortgages § 230 (2nd Ed.1970); 2 Glenn, Mortgages §§ 324, 324.1 (1943). If the note is usurious, it is often held that latent equities will prevail; see United States v. Desert Gold Mining Co., 282 F.Supp. 614 (D.Ariz.1968), reversed 433 F.2d 713 (9th Cir.1970), appeal after remand 448 F.2d 1230 (9th Cir.1971).

27. Restatement, Second, Contracts § 343 (1981); the first Restatement, Contracts § 174 took the same position.

28. Guaranty Mortgage & Insurance Co. v. Harris, 193 So.2d 1 (Fla.1966); Wilson Brothers v. Cooey, 251 Md. 350, 247 A.2d 395 (1968).

arguments for either result, but it is anomalous to make consequences turn on such minor fact variations.[29]

At least where notes secured by mortgages are involved, the Restatement position has more to commend it than does the UCC. To subject a mortgage assignee to latent equities is particularly odd in light of the fact that the original mortgagee himself (if a bona fide purchaser) is free of those same equities under well-settled law.[30] Thus the UCC, as interpreted in the Morrison case discussed above, goes well beyond merely placing the assignee in the shoes of the mortgagee; it places him in much worse shoes! Perhaps the UCC drafters did not have mortgages in mind, but it now seems clear that an appropriate amendment to the UCC would place all non-HDC assignees of mortgage notes in the same status, and would give them priority over latent equities if they took for value without notice.

WESTLAW REFERENCES

mortgag** /p assignee /s estoppel +1 certificate statement /p defense right

Patent Equities

mortgage /p assignee /p maker mortgagor /s defense right

Latent Equities

mortgage note /p assignee /p (latent secret +1 equity) derivative earl*** prior third /5 claim party

mortgage note /p assignee purchaser /p "uniform commercial" u.c.c. /s derivative earl*** prior third valid*** /5 claim party

§ 5.33　Payment to Assignor as a Defense

After a mortgage has been assigned by the mortgagee, to whom should the mortgagor make further payments? If the assignee gives the mortgagor reasonable notice that the assignment has occurred, it is clear that further payments made to the original mortgagee do not count against the assignee, and may not be raised by the mortgagor as a defense to foreclosure or an action on the debt by the assignee.[1] This result is unsurprising and entirely acceptable. The bulk of this section, however, deals with the more difficult case in which the assignee gives the mortgagor no notice that he now owns the debt and mortgage, and in which the mortgagor innocently continues paying the original mortgagee.

---

29. The drafters of the Restatement apparently intended to observe this distinction, however; § 343 Comment (c) states "The rule of this Section is negated with respect to negotiable instruments * * * which are transferred but not duly negotiated by Uniform Commercial Code § 3–306 * * *."

30. See Osborne, Mortgages §§ 180, 184–85 (2d ed. 1970); 2 Glenn, Mortgages § 324.1 (1943); International State Bank v.

Bray, 87 N.M. 350, 533 P.2d 583 (1975). This is the rule in both lien and title theory states; see Haynsworth v. Bischoff, 6 S.C. 159, 166 (1874); Durfee, Lien Theory of the Mortgage, 11 Mich.L.Rev. 495 (1913).

§ 5.33

1. Wood v. Gulf States Capital Corp., 217 So.2d 257, 269 (Miss.1968); Kaufman v. Bernstein, 100 So.2d 801 (Fla.1958).

Negotiable Instruments

If the obligation is represented by a negotiable note and the assignee is a HDC, the UCC provides that the assignee takes it free from "all defenses of any party to the instrument with whom the holder has not dealt",[2] except for real defenses.[3] Payment is clearly a personal defense, and that is apparently the end of the matter: payment to anyone except the holder or his agent does not count.[4] The reasoning behind this result is that the maker of a negotiable note is entitled to demand production of the note before making any payment, and to demand its surrender when making the final payment. Since the maker can protect himself against a secret assignment by this means, he fails to do so at his peril.[5] The fact that no mortgage assignment has been recorded, or that the payment is made to the apparent record holder, is immaterial.[6]

The risk is said to be absolute. If the mortgagor asks for the note, but instead is given a plausible but false explanation for its nonproduction, his payment will still be no defense to the true holder's later claim.[7] A grantee of the original mortgagor is also bound by the same rule, for even though he may not be personally liable on the note and hence may not have the right to demand its surrender upon a final payment, he can still insist upon inspecting it before any payment, installment or final.[8]

The rule stated has great potential for mischief and unfairness, since it produces far different results than most lay mortgagors would expect. Fortunately, its relevance in the world of modern mortgage assignments is fairly limited. While secondary market assignments of mortgages are very common, it is quite generally the practice for the

2. U.C.C. § 3–305(2).

3. See § 5.31, supra at note 1.

4. Culbertson State Bank v. Dahl, __ Mont. __, 617 P.2d 1295 (1980); Groover v. Peters, 231 Ga. 531, 202 S.E.2d 413 (1973); Carter v. South Texas Lumber Co., 422 S.W.2d 951 (Tex.Civ.App.1967); American Security & Trust Co. v. John J. Juliano, Inc., 203 Va. 827, 127 S.E.2d 348 (1962); Silver Spring Title Co. v. Chadwick, 213 Md. 178, 131 A.2d 489 (1957). The leading case is Assets Realization Co. v. Clark, 205 N.Y. 105, 98 N.E. 457 (1912), affirming 137 A.D. 881, 123 N.Y.S. 1105 (1909).

A few states follow an intermediate rule in which the note and mortgage are viewed separately; if the note is assigned but no assignment of the mortgage has been recorded, payment to the mortgagee will discharge the mortgage, but personal liability on the note will remain. See Ark.Stat. § 51–1016, discussed in Neal v. Bradley, 238 Ark. 714, 384 S.W.2d 238 (1964); Bartholf v. Bensley, 234 Ill. 336, 84 N.E. 928 (1908); Johnson v. Howe, 176 Minn. 287, 223 N.W. 148 (1929), discussed in Note, 13 Minn.L.Rev. 622 (1929).

5. Pre-U.C.C. law was the same. See Tilton v. Boland, 147 Or. 28, 31 P.2d 657 (1934); Smith v. Jarman, 61 Utah 125, 211 P. 962 (1922); Garrett v. Fernauld, 63 Fla. 434, 57 So. 671 (1912); see Annots., 89 A.L.R. 171 (1934); 104 A.L.R. 1301 (1936).

6. City Bank v. Plank, 141 Wisc. 653, 124 N.W. 1000 (1910); Eggert v. Beyer, 43 Neb. 711, 62 N.W. 57 (1895); Smith v. Jarman, note 5, supra.

7. Kellogg v. Smith, 26 N.Y. 18 (1862); cf. Clinton Loan Association v. Merritt, 112 N.C. 243, 17 S.E. 296 (1893).

8. Bautz v. Adams, 131 Wis. 152, 111 N.W. 69, 120 Am.St.Rep. 1030 (1907); Shoemaker v. Minkler, 202 Iowa 942, 211 N.W. 563 (1926). See Ross, Double Hazard of a Note and Mortgage, 16 Minn.L.Rev. 123, 125 (1931).

assignee to designate the original mortgagee as his agent for purposes of "servicing" the loan—that is, receiving the payments from the mortgagor.[9] If such an agency relationship exists, it is largely irrelevant whether the mortgagor has notice of the assignment or not; he will be fully credited with the payments made to the agent.[10] If the assignee terminates the agency relationship without notifying the debtor, the agent should surely be deemed to have continuing power to receive payments under an apparent authority or inherent authority principle,[11] and this should follow even if the debtor did not realize that the mortgagor was acting as an agent rather than for its own account.

The problems with the rule arise mainly in transactions among natural persons rather than institutions, and are particularly acute with mortgages calling for a single final payment rather than installments. In such cases an assignment may well be made without notice to the mortgagor and without any appointment of the mortgagee as an agent.[12] These situations represent only a small fraction of all mortgages given, but they are sufficiently troublesome that a change in the law is needed, as discussed below.

Nonnegotiable Notes

If the assignee is not a HDC or the note is nonnegotiable, the UCC [13] and the applicable common law subject the assignee to all the mortgagor's defenses, including payment if made before the mortgagor was given notice of the assignment.[14] Even here, there is some authority that, if a final payment is being made, it is so customary and natural for the debtor to demand surrender of the physical note that his failure to do so is negligence, and hence that his payment will give him no defense against the assignee.[15] It is difficult to see how this result can

---

9. See § 11.1, infra, for a more complete description of servicing.

10. Northside Building & Investment Co. v. Finance Co. of Georgia, 119 Ga.App. 131, 166 S.E.2d 608 (1969); American Security & Trust Co. v. John J. Juliano, Inc., 203 Va. 827, 127 S.E.2d 348 (1962); California Title Insurance & Trust Co. v. Kuchenbeiser, 20 Cal.App. 11, 127 P. 1039 (1912).

11. See Seavey, Agency §§ 50–51 (1964).

12. E.g., Groover v. Peters, 231 Ga. 531, 202 S.E.2d 413 (1973).

13. The UCC applies if the note is negotiable and the holder lacks HDC status, or if the note is nonnegotiable because it lacks "order" or "bearer" language; U.C.C. §§ 3–306, 3–805; see § 5.32, supra at note 15. If the note is nonnegotiable for other reasons the common law applies.

14. First National Bank v. Larson, 17 B.R. 957 (Bkrtcy.N.J.1982) (dictum); Felin Associates, Inc. v. Rogers, 38 A.D.2d 6, 326 N.Y.S.2d 413 (1971); Kansas City Mortgage Co. v. Crowell, 239 So.2d 130 (Fla.App.

1970); Olshan Lumber Co. v. Bullard, 395 S.W.2d 670 (Tex.Civ.App.1965) (in the two preceding cases the note was presumably non-negotiable, although the opinions are not explicit on the point); Northside Building & Investment Co. v. Finance Co. of Georgia, supra note 10; Hand v. Kemp, 207 Ala. 309, 92 So. 897 (1922); O'Maley v. Pugliese, 272 Pa. 356, 116 A. 308 (1922), 42 Harv.L.Rev. 1082 (1929). The question is one of contract law; see Restatement, Second, Contracts § 338 (1981); Note, Mortgages: Effect of Failure to Record a Mortgage Assignment in Florida, 7 U.Fla.L.Rev. 93 (1954).

15. Johnstone v. Mills, 22 B.R. 753 (Bkrtcy.Wash.1982); Assets Realization Co. v. Clark, 205 N.Y. 105, 98 N.E. 457 (1912), affirming 137 A.D. 881, 123 N.Y.S. 1105 (1909): "[When a final payment is made], the evidence of the debt naturally and ordinarily is produced and delivered, and therefore the failure to do this in the absence of sufficient explanation constitutes notice which makes the payment or trans-follow under the UCC,[16] but it may still be the law with notes which are nonnegotiable due to reasons other than omission of "order" or "bearer" language.[17] To the extent that it is the law, it is tempered in one respect; if the mortgagor demands to see the note and is given a reasonable explanation for the mortgagee's inability to produce it, he may safely make his payment.[18]

Since notice is essential to protect fully the rights of the assignee of a nonnegotiable note, to whom should he give notice when a conveyance of the mortgaged land has occurred? If the assignment occurs and notice is given to the mortgagor before he deeds away his land, that should certainly be sufficient.[19] On the other hand, if the land has been conveyed first, and if the assignee knows or can readily learn from the assignor the identity of the new owner, it seems reasonable to require the assignee to give notice directly to him. The assignee probably should not be required to search the title in order to learn whether the title has been conveyed, but the increasingly widespread use of due-on-sale clauses[20] means that the original mortgagee will usually know of the land conveyance and can easily inform the assignee of the new owner's identity. The wise assignee of a nonnegotiable note will wish to contact the grantee of the title in any event to obtain an estoppel certificate from him.

If the assignee has recorded his assignment, he might argue that the presence of the document in the public records gives constructive notice to the mortgagor or to grantees from the mortgagor. A few cases[21] and statutes[22] expressly provide that recordation of the assignment will have this effect, but at least as against the mortgagor himself

action unavailing as against a prior assignment although unrecorded."

While the practice as described may have been prevalent in New York in 1912, it is certainly not so in the latter half of the Twentieth Century. Today the note is often unavailable when the final payment is made. The payment is generally transmitted by an attorney or title company by mail and the mortgagee is trusted and expected to mark the note "paid" and mail it to the mortgagor within a reasonable time after receipt of the payment. Certainly no inference of notice should be drawn from failure to deliver the note immediately upon the tender of the final payment.

See also Baxter v. Redevco, Inc., 279 Or. 117, 566 P.2d 501 (1977).

16. U.C.C. § 3–306 provides without exception that the non-HDC holder is subject to "all defenses of any party which would be available in an action on a simple contract."

17. See § 5.31, supra at note 1.

18. See Rodgers v. Seattle-First Nat'l Bank, 40 Wash.App. 127, 697 P.2d 1009 (1985); Brown v. Blydenburgh, 7 N.Y. 141, 146, 57 Am.Dec. 506 (1852); Clinton Loan

Association v. Merritt, 112 N.C. 243, 17 S.E. 296 (1893).

19. To expect the assignee to keep track of all future sales of the property and to keep the grantees informed of his assignment is unrealistic. Recording the assignment easily accomplishes the same purpose; see text at note 25, infra.

20. See §§ 5.21–5.26, supra.

21. The cases usually derive from over-enthusiastic interpretations of recording statutes which provide that recordation is "notice to all the world." See, e.g. Rucker v. State Exchange Bank, 355 So.2d 171 (Fla.App.1978), discussed at note 25 infra; Ross v. Johnson, 171 Wash. 658, 19 P.2d 101 (1933); Dotto v. Ciamboli, 8 N.J.Misc. 37, 148 A. 197 (1929), affirmed 107 N.J.Eq. 596, 154 A. 631 (1931); Bale v. Wright, 120 Okl. 174, 252 P. 56 (1926). See Annot., 89 A.L.R. 171, 196 (1934). Recordation, in practical terms, can only be notice to takers of *subsequent* interests; the mortgagor has a *prior* interest. See generally Cunningham, Stoebuck & Whitman, Property § 11.10 n. 58 (1984).

22. See note 22 on page 396.

this idea seems totally out of touch with reality, for it implies that the mortgagor will take the trouble to examine the title to his own property before making each payment.[23] This is hardly ever done, and it makes no sense to penalize the mortgagor for failure to do it. The great majority of cases do not do so.[24] As against a grantee from the mortgagor, on the other hand, imputing notice of a previously recorded assignment does make sense, for he will have had occasion to examine the title as part of the purchase transaction, and thus will have had ample opportunity and reason to learn of the assignment.[25]

A few jurisdictions have enacted statutes which appear to be aimed at aiding an innocent mortgagor on a negotiable note who pays his original mortgagee. In Kansas and New Mexico the legislatures have expressly provided that if the assignment is unrecorded, the mortgagor may pay the assignor with impunity;[26] the former Maryland statute

22. N.J.Stat.Ann. 46:18–4 is the most direct illustration, for it expressly provides that recordation of an assignment is notice to all persons; this was held to include mortgagors in Dotto v. Ciamboli, 8 N.J. Misc. 37, 148 A. 197 (1930), affirmed 107 N.J.Eq. 596, 154 A. 631 (1931). See also United States v. Goldberg, 362 F.2d 575 (3d Cir.1966), certiorari denied 386 U.S. 919, 87 S.Ct. 881, 17 L.Ed.2d 790 (1967). The Maryland statute, which formerly provided in substance that ownership of a mortgage shall be conclusively presumed vested in the person having record title to it, was construed to give mortgagors constructive notice of assignments in Sennett v. Taylor, 157 Md. 107, 145 A. 358 (1929); this result has now been reversed by legislation described at note 27 infra. The Kansas statute, K.S.A. 67–321, –322, was similarly construed in Walmer v. Redinger, 116 Kan. 580, 227 P. 329 (1924); see text at notes 26–30, infra.

23. "[I]t would be an intolerable hardship if, every time he may wish to make a payment and obtain a credit on his debt, he should be compelled to visit the recorder's office to ascertain whether or not his mortgage had been assigned." Foster v. Carson, 159 Pa. 477, 28 A. 356 (1894); see also Giorgi v. Pioneer Title Insurance Co., 85 Nev. 319, 454 P.2d 104 (1969). See Md. Code, § 7–103, official comment.

24. In some states statutes expressly provide that recordation gives no constructive notice to the mortgagor; see, e.g., Blumenthal v. Jassoy, 29 Minn. 177, 12 N.W. 517 (1882). Ward & Stewart, Mortgage Assignment and Payment Statutes, 8 J.Bar. Ass'n Kan. 488, 495 (1940), lists 10 states with such statutes; Cal., Id., Kan., Mich., Minn., Mont., N.Y., Neb., Wisc., and Wyo. In other states the result follows

from recording act language which states that only "subsequent purchasers and creditors" have constructive notice. See Annot., 89 A.L.R. 171, 197 (1934).

25. First National Bank v. Larson, 17 B.R. 957, 965 n. 5 (1982) (dictum); Rucker v. State Exchange Bank, 355 So.2d 171 (Fla.App.1978); Gilcrist v. Wright, 167 Neb. 767, 94 N.W.2d 476 (1959); Assets Realization Co. v. Clark, 205 N.Y. 105, 98 N.E. 457, 41 L.R.A.,N.S., 462 (1912); Cornish v. Woolverton, 32 Mont. 456, 81 P. 4, 108 Am.St.Rep. 598 (1905); Viele v. Judson, 82 N.Y. 32 (1880). See Robbins v. Larson, 69 Minn. 436, 72 N.W. 456, 65 Am. St.Rep. 572 (1897); Mutual Life Insurance Co. v. Talbot, 113 Ind. 373, 14 N.E. 586 (1887).

With the exception of New York (N.Y.— McKinney's Real Prop.Law § 324), the statutes discussed at note 24, supra, exempting mortgagors from constructive notice of assignments, are inapplicable to grantees of the mortgaged land who take after the assignment is recorded.

The *Rucker* case, supra, misapplies this theory, for the mortgage assignment there was not recorded until *after* the grantee had bought the land, and thus should not have been held constructive notice to the grantee. The court's alternative holding, that the grantee's payment was ineffective against the assignee because the grantee failed to demand production of the note, is correct under the principles discussed at notes 2–6, supra. See § 5.28 note 34, supra.

26. Kan.Stat.Ann. 58–2321 to 58–2322; N.M.Stat.Ann., §§ 48–7–2 and 48–7–3; see Seed, Mortgage "Payment" Statutes in Kansas and New Mexico, 3 Kan.L.Rev. 87 (1954).

was interpreted similarly.[27] In the case of a negotiable note such statutes provide a theoretical benefit to mortgagors, but it does not amount to much in practical terms, since examination of the records before making payment, particularly on an installment mortgage, is far more effort than most mortgagors can be expected to go to.[28] Moreover, in Kansas the statute has been interpreted by the courts as a sword for the assignee; in the case of nonnegotiable instruments it is held that recordation of the assignment gives constructive notice to the mortgagor whether he actually examines the records or not.[29] This is, as noted above, an unrealistic and undesirable viewpoint.[30]

Policy Considerations

The rule that innocent payment to the assignor of a negotiable mortgage note is ineffective is seriously out of touch with modern practices and should be revised. It ignores several changes which have occurred in the mortgage market in the last few decades. First, it assumes that the note can readily be produced by the mortgagee upon the mortgagor's request if it has not been assigned or if the mortgagee is the holder's agent. The expansion of financial institutions, the advent of increased branching in many states, and the widespread assignment of mortgages with the mortgagor designated as servicer, all make this assumption wholly unrealistic. The note usually resides in a vault, often many miles from the location at which the mortgagor makes his payments. Moreover, mortgage payments today are very often made by mailed check or by automatic deduction from the mortgagor's checking account; these convenient procedures would be frustrated if the mortgagor really needed to inspect the note before each payment. In truth, a modern mortgagor who demanded to see his note before each payment would probably be viewed as if he had just arrived from Mars.

A further change of significance is the advent of computerized recordkeeping of mortgage payments. In earlier times it was customary to record each payment on a ledger printed on the reverse side of the note itself; thus, production of the note was natural and caused no inconvenience. This practice has almost entirely disappeared in favor of separate, usually computer-based, accounting of mortgagors' payments. The modern practice is more accurate and saves expense for all parties concerned, but the savings would be negated to the extent that production of the physical note were required.

27. Nussear v. Hazard, 148 Md. 345, 129 A. 506 (1925). As amended in 1972, however, the Maryland statute provides a far more pro-mortgagor rule: whether the assignment is recorded or not, payment to the assignor is good until the mortgagor is given actual notice of the assignment. Md. Code, Real Property, § 7–103(b).

28. But see Pletcher v. Albrecht, 186 Kan. 273, 350 P.2d 58 (1960), where the mortgagor *did* examine the records before each payment!

29. Walmer v. Redinger, 116 Kan. 580, 227 P. 329 (1924).

30. See Seed, Mortgage "Payment" Statutes in Kansas and New Mexico, 3 Kan.L.Rev. 87, 95–96 (1954).

The law should be changed to make payment to the assignor binding until notice of the assignment has been given. The Uniform Commercial Code takes this position with respect to notes secured by chattel paper in Article 9,[31] and its policy is equally sound with respect to real estate security. So do the Uniform Land Transactions Act [32] and the Uniform Consumer Credit Code, in the limited mortgage situations to which they apply.[33] Payment as a defense is qualitatively different from other defenses which a mortgagor might raise against a HDC, for it is the one defense which the holder can prevent from arising for the small cost of a form letter and a stamp.[34] A change is needed with respect to both negotiable paper and final payments on nonnegotiable paper; no distinctions between the two types of payments or the two types of notes can be justified. The present law is too far out of touch with the practices and expectations of the participants in mortgage transactions.

An amendment to the UCC would not be necessary to accomplish this suggested change.[35] Several courts have held that when an installment note secured by a mortgage is assigned and the assignor continues to collect the payments and remit them to the mortgage, this course of dealing constitutes the assignor the "secret agent" of the assignee, and payment to the assignor is good though he subsequently defaults in passing it through to the assignee. This interpretation is apparently followed even if there was never any formal agency relationship created.[36] There is no reason the concept should not be extended to single-

---

31. U.C.C. § 9–318(3). Under the Code it is not enough that the debtor has notice that an assignment has occurred; he must be notified specifically that he is to begin making payments to the assignee.

32. U.L.T.A. § 3–206(c).

33. U.C.C.C. § 2–412 (1968 vers.); § 3–204 (1974 vers.); Young v. Hawks, 624 P.2d 235 (Wyo.1981). On the application of the U.C.C.C., see § 5.30 notes 3–4, 14–19, supra.

34. The ease with which this may be done is illustrated by the requirement of the Federal National Mortgage Association (FNMA), applicable to single-family conventional home loans which it purchases, that the originating mortgagee send the mortgagor a letter which reads in part as follows:

> We are pleased to inform you as the owner of the property located at [address] that the mortgage on your property has been purchased by the Federal National Mortgage Association (FNMA). This transaction will in no way affect the amount or method of payment of your monthly mortgage payment; you should continue to submit your payment on or before the first day of each month to the address to which you are currently making your payments.

FNMA Conventional Selling Contract Supplement Sec. 301(F).

It is presumably FNMA's practice to send a letter of its own to the mortgagor in the event the originating mortgagee's servicing contract with FNMA is cancelled. If the servicing were reassigned or taken over directly by FNMA (an unlikely event) without such notification, it is almost impossible to believe that a court would deny the mortgagor credit for further payments innocently made to the original mortgagee.

35. This is not to suggest that amendment is a bad idea. Maryland did so in effect in 1972, enacting a statute which explicitly makes payment to the mortgagee good until actual notice of the assignment is given to the mortgagor. Md.Code, § 7–103(b); the official comment to this statute nicely explains the "intolerable burden" which the prior law imposed on mortgagors.

36. Rodgers v. Seattle-First Nat'l Bank, 40 Wash.App. 127, 697 P.2d 1009 (1985); Holsclaw v. Catalina Savings & Loan Association, 13 Ariz.App. 362, 476 P.2d 883 (1971); Northside Building & Investment payment notes as well. Moreover, an agency could well be inferred even if the mortgagee-assignor defaulted at the outset in remitting the payments to the assignee. This theory can be made equally applicable to negotiable and nonnegotiable notes. The agency relationship is too typical, too widely expected, and too consistent with business practices to be denied by the assignee who has not taken the trouble to send an appropriate notice to negate it. Absent such a notice, it should be presumed.

 WESTLAW REFERENCES

mortgage note /p assignee /s notice notif! /7 mortgagor

Negotiable Instruments

"holder in due course" h.d.c. (negotiabl! promissory /4 instrument note) /p agen** assignee /p maker mortgagor /s paid pay! & mortgage

Nonnegotiable Notes

non-negotiab! /4 instrument note /p agen** assignee /p maker mortgagor /s paid pay! & mortgage
instrument note /p agen** assignee /p record! /s mortgage

Policy Considerations
(no queries)

§ 5.34 Impact of Recording Acts

This section is concerned with whether the assignee of a note secured by a mortgage ought to record an assignment of the mortgage, and with the risks to which he may become subject if he does not record. These risks may arise in a variety of fact situations, and each will be discussed in turn. From the viewpoint of counsel for permanent secondary market mortgage investors, however, the proper advice is quite clear: unless there is some overriding need for secrecy, recordation should always be recommended. The cost and trouble in doing so are trivial, and the risks eliminated by recording are certainly substantial. This is indeed the position taken by most responsible mortgage assignees.[1]

Co. v. Finance Co. of America, 119 Ga.App. 131, 166 S.E.2d 608 (1969); Hoiden v. Kohout, 12 Ill.App.2d 161, 138 N.E.2d 852 (1956); Walmer v. Redinger, 116 Kan. 580, 227 P. 329 (1924); Erickson v. Kendall, 112 Wash. 26, 191 P. 842 (1920); Weigell v. Gregg, 161 Wis. 413, 154 N.W. 645 (1915). It must be conceded that these cases do not quite go so far as the text suggests the law should go, since they all involve established patterns or practices of collection by the assignor for the assignee, even though the mortgagor was unaware of the assignment. There are also several cases in which the courts have refused to find an agency on rather appealing facts; see, e.g., American Security and Trust Co. v. John J.

Juliano, Inc., 203 Va. 827, 127 S.E.2d 348 (1962); Silver Spring Title Co. v. Chadwick, 213 Md. 178, 131 A.2d 489 (1957); Ulen v. Knecttle, 50 Wyo. 94, 58 P.2d 446, 111 A.L.R. 565 (1936); Tilton v. Boland, 147 Or. 28, 31 P.2d 657 (1934).

§ 5.34

1. See, e.g., Government Nat'l Mortg. Ass'n Sellers Guide § 603 (1983); Federal Home Loan Mortgage Corporation, Sellers' Guide Conventional Mortgages § 1211(b) (1984). The latter provides that "The assignment must be duly recorded if recordation is either • necessary under applicable law to perfect a first lien security interest in the mortgaged premises in favor of

One further introductory comment may be helpful. Those who purchase interests in real estate are accustomed to recording. Those who purchase interests in promissory notes generally are not; this is particularly true of negotiable notes, as to which possession of the original note is the essential indicium of ownership. A note secured by a mortgage has one foot in each of these camps,[2] and the law has had considerable difficulty reconciling the expectations associated with the two documents. In general, its approach has been to require recording only when the natural expectations of those dealing with the real estate interest would be seriously frustrated if the recording acts were not applied.[3]

We turn now to a consideration of the classic fact patterns in which recordation or its absence becomes an issue.

As Between Assignor and Assignee

It is clearly unnecessary in the great majority of states for the assignee to record in order to have a completed assignment as against the assignor.[4] This result is not surprising, for it would be reached under the usual rules pertaining to either instruments or real property. The typical recording act makes unrecorded conveyances ineffective only as against "subsequent purchasers and creditors for value and without notice [who record first]", with the bracketed phrase being added in "notice-race" jurisdictions.[5] As between the original parties to the transfer, recordation is almost never required.[6]

Effect of Recordation on Payment to the Mortgagee

The preceding section[7] has discussed the effect of recordation on the efficacy of payments made by the mortgagor or his grantees to the mortgagee. The applicable rules will be only briefly summarized here. If the note is negotiable and the holder is in due course, a payment made to anyone else (except the holder's agent) is ineffective. This is true whether the assignment has been recorded or not. If the note is nonnegotiable or the assignee is not a HDC, payments made to the

Freddie Mac or its designee, or • commonly required by private institutional mortgage investors in the area where the mortgaged premises are located."

2. See § 5.27, supra.

3. See generally Osborne, Mortgages § 234 (2d Ed.1970).

4. United States v. Goldberg, 362 F.2d 575 (3d Cir.1966), certiorari denied 386 U.S. 919, 87 S.Ct. 881, 17 L.Ed.2d 790 (1967); Wilson v. Pacific Coast Title Insurance Co., 106 Cal.App.2d 599, 235 P.2d 431 (1951). Similarly, recording is unnecessary for the assignee to perfect its rights as against the original mortgagor; see Rowe v. Small Business Administration, ___ Ind. App. ___, 446 N.E.2d 991 (1983).

5. See Cunningham, Stoebuck & Whitman, Property § 11.9 (1984); Powell, Real Property ¶ 895, ¶ 914 (Rohan ed. 1968).

6. One apparent exception is Md.Ann. Code Real Property § 3–101, which provides that conveyances must be recorded to be valid. However, a conveyance supported by consideration will be given effect as a contract to convey; see Nickel v. Brown, 75 Md. 172, 23 A. 736 (1892). Thus, the only conveyances ultimately made void by non-recordation in Maryland are gifts.

7. § 5.33, supra, at notes 21–30.

mortgagee are good until the mortgagor receives notice of the assignment, but the recording of the assignment gives him no constructive notice. In sum, as between mortgagor and assignee, recording is irrelevant.

If the original mortgagor transfers the land, however, and if the assignment of the mortgage is already on record when this occurs, the assignment will give constructive notice to the grantee of the land. This is unimportant if the assignment is to a HDC, but if it is not, the constructive notice will oblige the transferee to make any further payments to the assignee or fail to do so at his peril. In effect, recordation saves the non-HDC assignee the trouble of giving personal notice to those who might subsequently buy the land. This does not mean, however, that a transferee of the land can safely rely exclusively on the record. If the note is negotiable, he must seek it out and pay its holder or his agent even though the records show no assignment. As was suggested in the preceding section, this burden ought to be confined to negotiable notes, and even there it is not supported by sound policy.

Wrongful Satisfaction by the Original Mortgagee

Suppose a mortgage securing a negotiable note is assigned to a HDC who does not record the assignment. Then the original mortgagor and mortgagee engage in a bit of skullduggery. The mortgagor induces the mortgagee (quite wrongfully) to execute and record the customary form of discharge or satisfaction of the mortgage.[8] Having now ostensibly cleared his title, the mortgagor sells the land to a bona fide purchaser for full value who supposes that the mortgage has been properly discharged.

This case presents a fundamental conflict between the UCC, which protects a HDC in his ownership of the note (and by usual extension, the mortgage also), and the innocent land buyer who has relied on the public records. The cases resolve the conflict in favor of the BFP of the land, and he takes free of the mortgage.[9] Obviously the opposite result would seriously jeopardize the usefulness of the entire recording system. In addition, the HDC could easily have prevented the problem from arising by recording his assignment. The original mortgagor, who

---

8. If the note has been negotiated, this ploy will be impossible or at least difficult in the few states, like Missouri, which require the note to be presented to the recorder for cancellation before the mortgage can be satisfied of record. See Vernon's Ann.Mo.Stat. § 443.060(1).

9. Fannin Investment & Development Co. v. Neuhaus, 427 S.W.2d 82 (Tex.Civ. App.1968); Kansas City Mortgage Co. v. Crowell, 239 So.2d 130 (Fla.App.1970); Brenner v. Neu, 28 Ill.App.2d 219, 170 N.E.2d 897 (1960); Henniges v. Paschke, 9 N.D. 489, 84 N.W. 350, 81 Am.St.Rep. 588

(1900); Merrill v. Hurley, 6 S.D. 592, 62 N.W. 958, 55 Am.St.Rep. 859 (1895).

Merrill v. Luce, 6 S.D. 354, 61 N.W. 43, 55 Am.St.Rep. 844 (1894); Marling v. Nommensen, 127 Wis. 363, 368, 106 N.W. 844, 845 (1906), upon an estoppel theory. Cf. Northup v. Reese, 68 Fla. 451, 67 So. 136, L.R.A.1915F, 554 (1914); Note, 5 U.Chi.L. Rev. 151 (1937); 16 Minn.L.Rev. 126 n. 19 (1932). The same principle applies if the BFP takes a mortgage rather than a deed; he will have priority over the previous mortgage.

was far from innocent and who was personally liable on the note, remains so, but the debt is no longer secured by the mortgage.[10]

A similar scheme may be devised by a non-assuming grantee of mortgaged land. If he approaches the mortgagee (who has already assigned) and gets and records a wrongful satisfaction from him, it seems equally clear that further grantees may rely on the record of that satisfaction. But who is personally liable on the note is not so clear. It seems quite unjust to permit the assignee of the note to hold the original mortgagor liable, for the price he received when he sold the land was undoubtedly discounted by the then-outstanding balance on the mortgage, and in addition he cannot claim an equitable subrogation of the assignee's rights in the mortgage;[11] it, after all, is satisfied and no longer binds the land. While there is no obvious legal theory on which the assignee of the mortgage can recover from the wrongdoing non-assuming grantee on the note, he can be held liable on a fraud theory. If recovery from him is impossible, perhaps the assignee of the mortgage should go without further relief as a penalty for his own carelessness in failing to record his assignment.

To return to our first example, in which the mortgagor is the procurer of the fraudulent release, some courts are a bit more troubled if the release is given as a part of the very transaction in which the innocent grantee buys the land. Perhaps the result should be reversed, and the land continue to be subject to the mortgage, if the grantee himself paid off the mortgagee without determining that the mortgagee still possessed the note.[12] On the other hand, if the ostensible discharge is obtained by the mortgagor-grantor, or by an escrow or title company acting in the transaction as the mortgagor's agent, the grantee can hardly be blamed and should take free of the mortgage.[13]

---

10. Note that it is most improbable that the grantee will have assumed personal liability on the debt, for the land is represented to him as being debt-free.

11. See § 10.2, infra.

12. Windle v. Bonebrake, 23 F. 165 (C.C.Kan.1885); Note, 5 U. of Chi.L.Rev. 151 (1937); Metropolitan Life Insurance Co. v. Guy, 223 Ala. 285, 135 So. 434 (1931); Heintz v. Kebba, 5 Neb.Unoff. 289, 98 N.W. 431 (1904), seems to be in this category. See 16 Minn.L.Rev. 127, n. 21 (1932), for a collection of cases; Federal Land Bank v. Corinth Bank & Trust Co., 214 Ala. 146, 107 So. 88 (1926). Cf. Beckman v. Ward, 174 Wash. 326, 24 P.2d 1091 (1933), in which the court conceded that the grantee had been negligent in failing to demand the note, but allowed him to take free of the mortgage on the ground that the assignee's failure to record had been more negligent.

13. Bacon v. Van Schoonhoven, 87 N.Y. 446 (1882). Chittick v. Thompson Hill Development Corp., 230 App.Div. 410, 245 N.Y.S. 71 (1930), affirmed 259 N.Y. 223, 181 N.E. 458 (1932), after reasonable excuse for non-production of documents had been given; Swasey v. Emerson, 168 Mass. 118, 46 N.E. 426, 60 Am.St.Rep. 368 (1897), (apparently); Heintz v. Klebba, 5 Neb.Unoff. 289, 98 N.W. 431 (1904), contra; Vann v. Marbury, 100 Ala. 438, 14 So. 273, 23 L.R.A. 325, 46 Am.St.Rep. 70 (1893); Lewis v. Kirk, 28 Kan. 497, 42 Am.Rep. 173 (1882); Marling v. Jones, 138 Wis. 82, 119 N.W. 931, 131 Am.St.Rep. 996 (1909); City Bank of Portage v. Plank, 141 Wis. 653, 124 N.W. 1000, 135 Am.St.Rep. 62, 18 Ann. Cas. 869 (1910); see 29 Col.L.Rev. 61, 63 (1929); Foss v. Dullam, 111 Minn. 220, 126 N.W. 820 (1910).

Finally, note that if the grantee can rely on the records as against a holder in due course of a negotiable note, *a fortiori* he can do so as against a non-HDC. Here there is no competing UCC policy against which the operation of the recording acts must be weighed.

Other Wrongful Acts by Mortgagee

The failure of the assignee of a mortgage to record it places the mortgagee in a position to do a variety of wrongful acts which the law makes binding as against the assignee. Instead of giving a release of the mortgage as discussed above, the mortgagee might obtain from the mortgagor by fraud a renewal note and mortgage, and might then assign them to a bona fide purchaser. Such a purchaser has been held to have priority over the original assignee.[14] Alternatively, the mortgagee might proceed to foreclose the mortgage (assuming it is in default), thereby passing title to a bona fide purchaser at the sale or buying in the property himself and later selling it to a bona fide purchaser; again, such a purchaser should take free of the mortgage even though the mortgagee had no right to foreclose it.[15] Another possibility is that the government will institute an eminent domain action against the property, naming only the mortgagor and mortgagee as defendants, with the assignee omitted because his name does not appear in the public records. If the condemnation award is paid to the named parties, the land will be taken by the government free of the mortgage and the assignee will have no claim against the government for any further money.[16]

Finally, suppose the mortgagee, pretending to continue to hold the note and mortgage after he has assigned them, induces the defaulting mortgagor to give him a deed in lieu of foreclosure. On the face of the record, all interests in the property have now merged in the same person—the mortgagee—and he proceeds to sell the land to a bona fide purchaser. Can such a purchaser take title relieved of the unrecorded assignee's interest? The cases are divided,[17] but the answer plainly

14. Central Trust Co. v. Stepanek, 138 Iowa 131, 115 N.W. 891 (1908); Jackson v. Stickney, 107 U.S. 478, 2 S.Ct. 814, 27 L.Ed. 529 (1882) (secured debt negotiable and in hands of holder in due course); Merrill v. Hurley, 6 S.D. 592, 62 N.W. 958, 55 Am.St.Rep. 859 (1895) (same facts as in preceding case)—accord. See also Havighorst v. Bowen, 214 Ill. 90, 73 N.E. 402 (1905); Torrey v. Deavitt, 53 Vt. 331 (1881). See Note, 16 Minn.L.Rev. 123, 127 (1932).

15. Huitink v. Thompson, 95 Minn. 392, 104 N.W. 237, 111 Am.St.Rep. 476, 5 Ann. Cas. 338 (1905). The mortgagor, in such a case, will have a remedy against the mortgagee who foreclosed wrongfully. See 18 N.Car.L.Rev. 61, 65 (1939). See generally 89 A.L.R. 170, 182–83 (1934).

16. First National Bank v. Paris, 358 Ill. 378, 193 N.E. 207 (1934).

17. Cases favoring the bona fide purchaser include Gregory v. Savage, 32 Conn. 250 (1864); McCormick v. Bauer, 122 Ill. 573, 13 N.E. 852 (1887), in effect overruling Edgerton v. Young, 43 Ill. 464 (1867); Artz v. Yeager, 30 Ind.App. 677, 66 N.E. 917 (1903); Jenks v. Shaw, 99 Iowa 604, 48 N.W. 900, 61 Am.St.Rep. 256 (1906); Ames v. Miller, 65 Neb. 204, 91 N.W. 250 (1902); see Lands, To Use of Security Savings & Trust Co. v. Robacker, 313 Pa. 271, 273, 169 A. 891, 892 (1933).

Cases allowing the unrecorded assignment to survive include Thauer v. Smith, 213 Wis. 91, 250 N.W. 842 (1933), commented on in 82 U. of Pa.L.Rev. 547 (1934); 29 Ill.L.Rev. 121 (1934); 9 Wis.L.Rev. 408

should be yes. The purchaser, after all, cannot make any more effective inquiry of anyone. The mortgagee has already lied to him, and may further claim that the mortgage note was destroyed after the alleged merger occurred; such a statement is not implausible. Inquiry of the mortgagor is probably useless, for he is likely to be as ignorant of the assignment as the purchaser. There is really no reason to distinguish this case from the one in which the mortgagee gives a wrongful release of the mortgage. Here, his deed to the purchaser is tantamount to a release. The merger in him seems perfect [18] and it should be so held to protect the reliability of the recording system.[19]

In all of these cases in which the mortgagee has employed his power to mislead others because the assignment was unrecorded, the question arises whether the debt, now unsecured, is still enforceable as before. There is little authority,[20] but the answer would seem to be that it can be asserted only against one primarily liable on it, and even then perhaps, only if the debtor has not made an apparent payment of the debt, as by means of a foreclosure or deed in lieu. Here the distinction between assignees who are HDC's and those who are not again becomes relevant. As against the HDC, the foreclosure or deed in lieu would presumably be an ineffective form of payment, for the debtor would be bound to discover who held his note. But if the assignee were not a HDC, and if the debtor had no actual notice of the assignment, the foreclosure or deed in lieu should be held to satisfy the debt.[21]

Wrongful Acts by Trustee under Deed of Trust

Certain of the wrongful acts in which a mortgagee might engage, as discussed above, might also be perpetrated by the trustee if a deed of trust were employed rather than a mortgage as the security device. In particular, a trustee might, without the assignee's assent, collude with the debtor to release the deed of trust, or he might foreclose wrongfully, and in either case title might then pass to a bona fide purchaser. If the

---

(1934); 10 Wis.L.Rev. 292 (1935); Merchants' Trust Co. v. Davis, 49 Idaho 494, 290 P. 383 (1930); Purdy v. Huntington, 42 N.Y. 334, 1 Am.Rep. 532 (1869); Curtis v. Moore, 152 N.Y. 159, 46 N.E. 168, 57 Am. St.Rep. 506 (1897), decided not only on the ground of constructive notice arising from non-production of the instruments, but also on the ground that the recording act did not require an assignment to be recorded to be effective against subsequent purchasers of the fee, a curious belief in view of Bacon v. Van Schoonhoven, 87 N.Y. 446 (1882); Zorn v. Van Buskirk, 111 Okl. 211, 239 P. 151 (1925), emphasizing the absence of a recorded release; Howard v. Shaw, 10 Wash. 151, 38 P. 746 (1894), on the ground that assignments were not covered by the recording acts then in force.

18. An exception may be made if a title examination by the purchaser disclosed the existence of junior liens, since their presence may suggest that no merger occurred upon the transfer of the equity of redemption to the mortgagee; see generally § 6.15, infra.

19. See 9 Wisc.L.Rev. 408 (1934); 29 Ill. L.Rev. 121 (1934); 82 U.Pa.L.Rev. 547 (1934).

20. See Ross, The Double Hazard of a Note and Mortgage, 16 Minn.L.Rev. 123 (1932); Brown and Dougherty, Assignment of Realty Mortgages in Oregon, 17 Or.L. Rev. 83 (1938).

21. See § 5.33, supra.

note had been assigned to a new holder who had recorded no assignment, these acts of the trustee would quite clearly deprive him of his security in the real estate, much as would similar acts of a mortgagee as we have already seen.

But the use of the deed of trust introduces a striking new dimension to our analysis: such acts of the trustee are equally devastating to the assignee even if the assignment is recorded! Recording does not improve the assignee's position.[22] The reason for this result lies in the nature of the deed of trust. In most jurisdictions, it is the normal role of the trustee to do two things: to reconvey when the debtor pays off the debt, and to foreclose if he defaults. The trustee has a fiduciary duty to perform these functions properly, and he was originally selected by the parties (practically speaking, by the lender in most instances) because of their confidence that he would carry them out. When the original creditor assigns the note, there is ordinarily no change of trustees. Rather, the assignee is generally satisfied to have the original trustee continue in his role.

Innocent third parties who deal with the land are entitled to assume that the trustee, whether he is acting to reconvey the property or to foreclose, is performing in accordance with the instructions and wishes of the current holder of the note. They have no duty to contact the holder personally to make certain that the trustee is acting within those instructions. Hence an assignment of the beneficiary's interest, even if recorded, is not of any great interest to third parties, for the assignment will merely indicate to whom the trustee owes his duty, and not whether he is acting within it. As a practical matter, recordation of the assignment is irrelevant so far as the rights of innocent purchasers relying on a reconveyance or foreclosure of the security are concerned. In other contexts, such as that of successive assignments to be discussed below, however, recordation of the assignment of a deed of trust may be of great importance.

Successive Assignments by the Mortgagee: Nonnegotiable Note

We come now to the most complex area of application of the recording acts to mortgage assignments. When a mortgagee, concededly acting unethically, executes two successive assignments of the same mortgage to two different assignees, which will prevail? In the very

---

22. Mann v. Jummel, 183 Ill. 523, 56 N.E. 161 (1900); Lennartz v. Quilty, 191 Ill. 174, 60 N.E. 913, 85 Am.St.Rep. 260 (1901); Vogel v. Troy, 232 Ill. 481, 83 N.E. 960 (1908) discussed in 3 Ill.L.Rev. 97 (1908); Marsh v. Stover, 363 Ill. 490, 2 N.E.2d 559 (1936); Williams v. Jackson, 107 U.S. 478, 2 S.Ct. 814, 27 L.Ed. 529 (1882). See Greeley, Note, 26 Ill.L.Rev. 688 (1931); Leesman, Note, 31 Ill.L.Rev. 352 (1936). See also W.Va.Rev.Code, c. 38, Art. 12, § 2 (1931), discussed by Carlin, Release of As-

signed Liens, 44 W.Va.L.Q. 175, 191 (1938), extending the power of a trustee under a trust deed mortgage to execute a valid release regardless of authority in the deed of trust.

On the rights of a mortgagor not in default against a bona fide purchaser after a wrongful sale under the power of sale by the trustee in a trust deed mortgage, see note, 18 N.Car.L.Rev. 61 (1939).

few jurisdictions in which the recording acts do not apply to mortgage assignments,[23] and assuming that the secured note is nonnegotiable (or that it has not in fact been negotiated to either assignee as a HDC), the common law of contracts will apply. According to the Restatement,[24] the fundamental rule is "first in time, first in right." [25] However, a number of exceptions exist. If the second assignee lacks knowledge of the first and pays value, he will prevail over the first if he receives payment or satisfaction, gets a judgment against the maker of the note, or enters into a novation with the maker. Perhaps most important, a second assignee who is a BFP will prevail if he obtains "possession of a writing of a type customarily accepted as a symbol or as evidence of the right assigned." [26] Almost certainly the note itself, even though non-negotiable, would be considered such a writing, and if the mortgagee gives possession of the note to the second assignee rather than the first, the second will prevail.

In most jurisdictions, the foregoing is merely academic, for the recording acts do apply to mortgage assignments.[27] They, like other conveyances, are generally made void if unrecorded, as against subsequent purchasers [28] for value and without notice; in some jurisdictions, the subsequent purchaser must also himself record first. Again assuming that the note in question is nonnegotiable, the application of the recording acts generally works as follows. If the first assignee records immediately, he will be fully protected against subsequent assignees, and this is so whether or not he obtained possession of the note.[29] If the first assignee does not record, however, the second assignee will prevail, at least if he *does* get possession of the note.[30] (In race-notice

23. Neal v. Bradley, 238 Ark. 714, 384 S.W.2d 238 (1964), construing Ark.Stat. § 51–1016, the recording act, as inapplicable to assignments of mortgage notes.

24. Restatement, Second, Contracts, § 342 (1981). The English rule of Dearle v. Hall, 3 Russ., Ch. 1 (1823), which gives priority to the first assignee who gives notice to the obligor, has been fairly widely adopted in the United States. However, it is rejected by the Restatement, and does not apply to interests in land in any event. See Glenn, Assignment of Choses in Action, 20 Va.L.Rev. 621, 652 (1934).

25. See Neal v. Bradley, note 23 supra.

26. Restatement, Second, Contracts, § 342(b)(iv) (1981).

27. See Annot., 89 A.L.R. 170 (1934).

28. The second assignee is generally considered a "purchaser" for purposes of the recording act; Price v. Northern Bond & Mortgage Co., 161 Wash. 690, 297 P. 786 (1931).

29. Crane v. Turner, 67 N.Y. 437 (1876); Stein v. Sullivan, 31 N.J.Eq. 409 (1879), even where the bond and mortgage were

obtained from the first assignee and sold to the second; Mott v. Newark German Hospital, 55 N.J.Eq. 722, 37 A. 757 (1897); Murphy v. Barnard, 162 Mass. 72, 38 N.E. 29, 44 Am.St.Rep. 340 (1894), negotiable note involved, redelivered to mortgagee after recorded assignment and then sold to a second assignee; Strong v. Jackson, 123 Mass. 60, 25 Am.St.Rep. 19 (1877).

30. In re Vermont Fiberglass, Inc., 44 B.R. 505 (Bkrtcy.Vt. 1984), motion denied 45 B.R. 603 (Bkrtcy.D.Vt. 1984) (unclear whether note was negotiable); Nazar v. Southern, 32 B.R. 761 (Bkrtcy.Kan.1983) (unclear whether note was negotiable); In re Columbia Pacific Mortgage, Inc., 20 B.R. 259 (Bkrtcy.Wash.1981) (dictum); Second National Bank v. Dyer, 121 Conn. 263, 184 A. 386, 104 A.L.R. 1295 (1936); Price v. Northern Bond & Mortgage Co., 161 Wash. 690, 297 P. 786 (1931) (second assignee prevailed although he did not demand possession of note); Morrow v. Stanley, 119 Md. 590, 87 A. 484 (1913), decided after amendment of earlier statute made title to the debt secured by a mortgage conclusively presumed to be in the person holding jurisdictions, he will of course also need to record his own assignment in order to prevail.) On the other hand, if the first assignee fails to record but takes possession of the note, the mortgagee's failure to tender it to the second assignee has been held to give him notice that a prior assignment has occurred, and thus to rob him of his BPF status under the recording acts.[31] Whether this much importance should be attached to physical possession of a nonnegotiable note as against the normal operation of the recording acts may be debatable. But here we are dealing with relatively sophisticated business persons in most instances, and there is no doubt that most investors in mortgages consider possession of even a nonnegotiable note to be a highly significant indicator of ownership. Hence the assignor's failure to produce the note would indeed tip off most investors that something is wrong with the deal being offered.

Successive Assignments by the Mortgagee: Negotiable Note

Where the mortgage debt is in the form of a negotiable instrument there is greater diversity of opinion as to the effect both of recordation and non-recordation of mortgage assignments. Where the first assignee not only records his assignment but gets and keeps possession of the mortgage documents there would be no question that he would be protected against a later assignee. The controversy arises where, although the first assignment has been recorded, the negotiable note and mortgage have been left in the possession of the mortgagee, redelivered to him, or obtained by him from the assignee wrongfully through fraudulent representations or otherwise, and are then sold to one who, aside from any effect of the recording acts upon the situation, would be a holder in due course entitled to the note and mortgage as against the prior assignee.

On this question there are three views.[32] One is that a promissory note, by virtue of being secured by a real estate mortgage, does not lose its character as commercial paper and imparts its negotiable character to the mortgage, thus bringing them both within the purview of statutes dealing with commercial paper. The result is that recording

record title to the mortgage; Blunt v. Norris, 123 Mass. 55, 25 Am.Rep. 14 (1877); see 89 A.L.R. 171, 177 (1934); 104 A.L.R. 1303 (1936).

31. Syracuse Bank v. Merrick, 182 N.Y. 387, 75 N.E. 232 (1905); cf. Price v. Northern Bond & Mortgage Co., 161 Wash. 690, 297 P. 786 (1931). If the recording act is worded strongly enough, it may be totally controlling, and may make possession of the note in the first assignee irrelevant if he does not record. The Florida statute may be read to have this effect; see West's Fla.Stat.Ann. § 701.02, discussed in Note, Transfer of the Mortgagee's Interest in Florida, 14 U.Fla.L.Rev. 98 (1961).

32. For discussions of the problem, see Krasnowiecki, Miller & Ziff, The Kennedy Mortgage Co. Bankruptcy Case: New Light Shed on the Position of Mortgage Warehousing Banks, 56 Am.Bkrtcy.L.J. 325, 337–39 (1982); Notes, 8 Minn.L.Rev. 347 (1924); 22 Cal.L.Rev. 677, 681, 684 (1934); 10 Jour.B.A.Kan. 282, 284 (1942); Ross, Double Hazard of a Note and Mortgage, 16 Minn.L.Rev. 130 (1932); Brown and Daugherty, Assignment of Realty Mortgages, 17 Or.L.Rev. 83, 91–93 (1938). See semble, Note, 78 U. of Pa.L.Rev. 108 (1929); 16 Tex.L.Rev. 534, 535 (1938).

the prior assignment has no effect upon the later transferee of the note and mortgage security. Any constructive notice from the recordation is insufficient to prevent him being a holder in due course of the note, since actual notice is necessary for that; this appears to be the position of the Uniform Commercial Code.[33] And the same is true as to the mortgage which is regarded as accompanying the note as an inseparable incident of it.[34]

A second view, at the opposite extreme from the first, is that the later indorsee of the note takes no title to the note since his vendor in fact had none, and the prior recorded assignment was notice to him of the infirmity so as to preclude him from being a holder in due course.[35] Courts taking this view find it necessary to distinguish between unsecured notes, as to which it is clear that no title examination is necessary to become a HDC, and secured notes, as to which it is supposed that the existence of the mortgage should lead the assignee to search the title.[36]

The third view is that the transferee of the note is a holder in due course as to it; but since the element of negotiability is lacking in mortgages, he takes the mortgage with notice of the prior, recorded assignment and cannot foreclose in the collection of the note.[37] Apart from its holding as to the note, this last solution has little to commend it. It infringes upon the basic principle that the assignment of a debt secured by a mortgage carries with it the right to the security.[38] Further, while giving the indorsee of the note the right to collect the debt, the prior holder's recorded interest as assignee of the mortgage is

33. Although no case is yet decided under the Uniform Commercial Code § 3–302 as to whether a previously-recorded mortgage assignment will deprive a holder of HDC status by giving him constructive notice, the Code provides that "The filing or recording of a document does not of itself constitute notice within the provisions of this Article to a person who would otherwise be a holder in due course." U.C.C. § 3–304(5). In National Surety Fire & Casualty Co. v. Mazzara, 289 Ala. 542, 268 So. 2d 814 (1972), the existence of a recorded deed was held not to constitute constructive notice to a mortgagee, to whom an insurance company's draft for fire insurance proceeds was endorsed, that the grantee under the deed might have a claim to the proceeds.

34. Foster v. Augustana College & Theological Seminary, 92 Okl. 96, 218 P. 335, 37 A.L.R. 854 (1923); United States National Bank v. Holton, 99 Or. 419, 195 P. 823 (1921); Ross v. Title Guarantee & Trust Co., 136 Cal.App. 393, 29 P.2d 236 (1934), discussed 22 Cal.L.Rev. 677, 681, 684 (1934); 23 Cal.L.Rev. 108 (1934); Security Mortgage Co. v. Delfs, 47 Cal.App.

599, 191 P. 53 (1920), semble; prior assignment recorded first but not until after the second assignment. See 37 A.L.R. 860 (1925); 127 A.L.R. 201 (1940).

35. Murphy v. Barnard, 162 Mass. 72, 38 N.E. 29, 44 Am.St.Rep. 340 (1894); Strong v. Jackson, 123 Mass. 60, 25 Am.St. Rep. 19 (1877).

36. This supposition can lead to anomalous results. If the assignee does not know that the note is secured by a mortgage, he automatically gets the security anyway. But if he does not realize that it is secured, it can hardly serve to warn him to search the title. See § 5.27, supra.

37. Taylor v. American National Bank, 64 Fla. 525, 60 So. 783 (1912); Wood v. Sparks, 59 S.W.2d 361 (Tex.Com.App.1933), rehearing denied 63 S.W.2d 1109 (1933), discussed in note, 10 Tex.L.Rev. 201 (1932); note, 16 Tex.L.Rev. 534, 537 (1938)—accord. See Note, Transfer of the Mortgagee's Interest in Florida, 14 U.Fla.L.Rev. 98 (1961), recommending this view under the Florida mortgage assignment recording statute.

38. See § 5.27, supra.

valueless because he has no right to collect the debt which is essential to its utilization. "Thus, either the mortgage lien is extinguished because there is no one entitled to enforce the security, and the maker of the note gets a windfall in having the premises freed of the lien of the mortgage or deed of trust; or the holder of the prior recorded right to the mortgage, through a power to assign the mortgage to the indorsee of the note, is in a position to use pressure to obtain from the indorsee the practical value of the security." [39]

As between the other two views, the first one seems preferable,[40] and may well be required by the U.C.C.[41] Assignees of mortgages are engaged, dominantly, in buying a debt claim, and therefore the rules applying to that particular form of debt should govern its sale. If it is in the form of a negotiable instrument, just as its negotiability is not affected by the fact that it is secured by a mortgage, neither should it be subject to the hazard of the assignee's having to investigate real property records in order to be sure that he will be a holder in due course. And this is true even though, in good part, the value of the claim is high because it is secured, and even though title to the security may be investigated in determining whether to buy. If he does not wish to investigate he should not be under compulsion to do so on penalty of not getting the main thing he was bargaining for, the note. As was just pointed out, if he gets the note, he should get the mortgage with it.

Where the assignee of a mortgage securing a negotiable note fails to record his assignment but gets and keeps possession of the note he should, and by what is believed to be the better authority, does prevail over a subsequent purchaser of the mortgage from its record owner.[42] The reason is substantially the same one that should leave the purchaser of the secured negotiable note free to ignore prior recorded assignments of the mortgage, i.e., the principal thing that is being bought is the note itself, not its accessory, the mortgage. At least that is the controlling thought and should prevail in determining the rules governing the priorities of the parties who take successive assignments of it. Commercial policy in the free mobility of the debt is more important in a case of this sort than the land policy. It is true that the assignment transaction may be and is sometimes couched in terms which do not mention the debt as distinct from the security; and when this is the case the agreement nevertheless will carry at least an equitable right to the negotiable note or the bond as well as the security

---

39. Note, 22 Cal.L.Rev. 677, 695 (1934).

40. See 2 Glenn, Mortgages § 315.2 (1943).

41. See note 33, supra.

42. Syracuse Savings Bank v. Merrick, 182 N.Y. 387, 75 N.E. 232 (1905); Barringer v. Loder, 47 Or. 223, 81 P. 778 (1905) Richards Trust Co. v. Rhomberg, 19 S.D. 595, 104 N.W. 268 (1905); Miller Brewing Co. v. Manasse, 99 Wis. 99, 74 N.W. 535 (1898). Adler v. Newell, 109 Cal. 42, 41 P. 799 (1895) under a special recording statute making recordation of a mortgage assignment notice but not requiring recordation for validity as in the case of recording of conveyances. See Krasnowiecki, et al., note 32 supra.

interest in the property.[43] Nevertheless, whenever a purchaser is apprised, whether from recitals in the mortgage or otherwise, that the obligation he is about to buy is expressed in the written form of a negotiable instrument, the natural, and the only prudent, course is to ask for the document, for that is what he wants.[44] Indeed he normally wants both the note and the mortgage. So far as he is concerned they are indispensable documents. If they are not forthcoming, he has adequate warning that something may be amiss. He cannot rely upon the records in such a case any more than can one who goes to pay the debt.[45] And it follows that an assignee who gets and holds onto the negotiable note and mortgage, although he runs some risks if he does not record his mortgage,[46] should not run the hazard of losing to a subsequent assignee from his assignor.

In spite of the foregoing there are several cases in which the failure of a prior assignee who held the negotiable note and mortgage to record his mortgage resulted in a subsequent assignee prevailing. It is possible to account for some of the results on the basis of the language of the statute involved,[47] or special facts justifying reliance upon appearances created by the wrongful conduct of the mortgagee for which, it is true, the assignee was not responsible but which were made possible by the assignee's failure to do the simple act of recordation.[48]

 WESTLAW REFERENCES
di recordation
di recording acts

As Between Assignor and Assignee
(no queries)

Effect of Recordation on Payment to the Mortgagee
record! /p assign! /s mortgage note /p "holder in due course"
    h.d.c. mortgagee negotiab! non-negotiable

Wrongful Satisfaction by the Original Mortgagee
discharg*** releas*** satisfact*** /s mortgage /s record! /177
    note /p assign! "holder in due course" h.d.c.

Other Wrongful Acts By Mortgagee
condemn! deed "eminent domain" foreclos*** renew*** /s mortgage
    /s record! /177 note /p assign! "holder in due course"
    h.d.c.

43. See § 5.27, supra.

44. See Thauer v. Smith, 213 Wis. 91, 250 N.W. 842 (1933).

45. See § 5.33, supra.

46. The risks are those created by wrongful releases or other acts of his assignor. See notes 8–22, supra.

47. Morrow v. Stanley, 119 Md. 590, 87 A. 484 (1913), under a strongly worded statute making record ownership of the mortgage conclusive of ownership of the debt.

48. Blunt v. Norris, 123 Mass. 55, 25 Am.Rep. 14 (1877), a new, genuine note obtained by fraud by the mortgagee from the mortgagor and transferred together with an assignment of the mortgage; Second National Bank v. Dyer, 121 Conn. 263, 184 A. 386, 104 A.L.R. 1295 (1936), criticized in Note, 6 Pitt.L.Rev. 300 (1940), forged instruments transferred to the second assignee (cf. Morris v. Bacon, 123 Mass. 58, 25 Am.Rep. 17 (1877)).

Wrongful Acts by Trustee Under Deed of Trust
discharg*** releas*** satisfact*** /s "deed of trust" /s record!
     /177 note /p assign! "holder in due course" h.d.c.
condemn! "eminent domain" foreclos*** renew*** /s "deed of trust"
     /s record! /177 note /p assign! "holder in due course"
     h.d.c.

Successive Assignments By the Mortgagee: Nonnegotiable Note
additional alternat*** second successive two /3 assign! /p
     mortgage note /s "bona fide purchaser" b.f.p. non-negotiable
     record!

Successive Assignments By the Mortgage: Negotiable Note
additional alternat*** second successive two /3 assign! /p
     mortgage note /s "holder in due course" h.d.c. negotiab!

§ 5.35 Partial Assignments and Participations

A mortgage lender may frequently wish to assign partial interests
in a loan or a group of loans to one or more investors.[1] Such transactions occur in two common contexts. The first is the case of a very
large loan which may be beyond the financial resources of the originating or "lead" lender. The creation of "participation" interests by way
of partial assignments which can be sold to one or more other financial
institutions allows the lead lender to recoup some of its cash immediately, and at the same time spreads the risk of a possible default on the
underlying loan. Participations of this type are sometimes arranged on
both construction [2] and permanent loans.

The other context in which participations are frequently employed
involves the accumulation by the lead lender of a large group or
"package" of relatively small mortgage loans, usually on one-family
houses. Here the participation device is used as an alternative to
direct sale and assignment of the loans on the secondary mortgage
market. A large number of participation interests, perhaps hundreds
or thousands, may be created; each interest will represent a small
share in each of a large number of loans. The participations may be
sold to financial institutions or to individual investors. The Federal
Home Loan Mortgage Corporation (FHLMC), for example, has used this
type of participation sale very effectively in recent years.[3]

Generally at least two documents are involved in the sale of
participation interests of the latter type: a participation agreement and

§ 5.35

1. See generally Simpson, Loan Participations: Pitfalls for Participants, 31 Bus.
Law. 1977 (1976); Drake & Weems, Mortgage Loan Participations: The Trustee's
Attack, 52 Am.Bankr.L.J. 23 (1978).

2. See Essay, The Aftermath of Penn
Square Bank: Protecting Loan Participants from Setoffs, 18 Tulsa L.J. 261, 274
(1982), for a participation agreement form;
Arnold, Modern Real Estate and Mortgage

Forms 4–29 (1970), for a participation
agreement intended for use on a construction loan; Tockarshewsky, Loan Participations are Meaningful Commitments, 8 Real
Est.Rev. 61 (No. 3, Fall 1978).

3. See King & Andrukonis, Who Holds
PCs?, 1 Secondary Mortg. Markets 12 (Feb.
1984); Brinkerhoff, PC's Biggest Year: $5
Billion Worth Sold by The Mortgage Corporation, FHLBBJ, Dec.1977, at 19; see generally § 11.3, infra.

a participation certificate (PC). The first will set forth the parties' rights and duties in general,[4] while the second will state the particular share or percentage which the investor is receiving, and may also identify the loans which are included in the package. In the first type of participation, involving a single large loan, all of this information will usually be contained in a single agreement. Whatever the format, the documents should be drafted to state the parties' agreement on a number of important issues, including the following.[5] As among the participants, and as against the lead lender, who will have priority in the loan and foreclosure proceeds? Almost always the participants have equal priority; whether the lead lender will share their priority or be subordinate to them as to any retained interest in the loans is a matter for negotiation. The lead lender is generally given the right to retain the notes and other loan documents, to satisfy the mortgages as they are paid, and if the participation is on a package of home loans, to make the necessary decisions concerning acceleration, forbearance, appointment of receivers, foreclosure, redemption, collection of deficiencies, settlement with mortgage insurers, and the like. In the case of a large loan with only a few participants, they may arrange to vote or otherwise collaborate among themselves in the making of such decisions triggered by loan delinquency. The agreement will spell out the liability of the parties for foreclosure and property carrying and disposition costs. It will require the lead lender to remit the participants' shares of mortgage payments to them, and it may constitute him a trustee for the participants' benefit. Finally, the lead lender may or may not guarantee payment of the participants' shares of principal and interest.[6]

Priorities in the Absence of Agreement

The common law rules concerning priorities among participants, and as between the participants and the lead lender, are seldom of much practical importance today. This is because participation agreements nearly always deal with these matters fully and competently, as mentioned above. Hence only a brief outline of these priorities issues will be given here.

As among the participants, the great majority of courts today would unquestionably grant a pro-rata priority in the absence of agree-

---

4. See, e.g., Hibernia National Bank v. Federal Deposit Insurance Corp., 733 F.2d 1403 (10th Cir.1984); FHLMC Participation Sales Agreement Series 300 (covering sales of participation interests by FHLMC to investors); FHLMC Mortgage Participation Agreement 210 (covering sales to FHLMC of participations by originating mortgagees).

5. See sources cited notes 2, 4, supra for illustrative coverage of these points. There is no question that an express agreement regarding priority among the participants will control, and the same is presumably true of all other important issues in the management of the loans. See Conway v. Yadon, 132 Okl. 36, 269 P. 309 (1928); Wilson v. Eigenbrodt, 30 Minn. 4, 13 N.W. 907 (1882); Walker v. Dement, 42 Ill. 272 (1866); Note, 25 Cal.L.Rev. 504 (1937).

6. FHLMC's guarantee of its PC's has been an important element in their marketability. See sources cited note 3, supra.

ment.[7] Some earlier cases took the view that the order in which the partial assignments were made controlled the priority of the interests they took;[8] others held that the interests of the participants, if represented by separate notes executed by the mortgagor (an unusual situation in modern times, when a single note is typically employed), were determined by the order of maturity of the notes.[9] A previous edition of this book quite effectively points out the impracticality and irrationality of these views,[10] and they are so unlikely to be advanced by any court today that it does not seem worthwhile to attempt to demolish them further. Quite clearly the rule of pro-rata distribution among the participants is most likely to comport with the intent of the parties.

With respect to priority in the mortgage repayments or foreclosure proceeds as between the lead lender and the participants, the matter is somewhat more open to question. Absent a guarantee of payment to the participants by the lead, the better view is that they have no special priority as against the interest retained by the lead.[11] Contrary cases are based on a number of dubious arguments: that the lead is, in effect, a trustee for the participants and should not be permitted to recover from the land at their expense;[12] that the inverse order of alienation

---

7. "It may be said, however, that by the great weight of authority the courts of this country * * * are agreed that as between assignees of notes bearing the same maturity date there is not, in the absence of contract, a preference or priority. Studebaker Brothers, Manufacturing Co. v. McCurgur, 20 Neb. 500, 30 N.W. 686 (1887); Adams v. Lear, 3 La.Ann. 144 (1848); Burhans v. Mitchell, 42 Mich. 417, 4 N.W. 178 (1880); Penzel v. Brookmire, 51 Ark. 105, 10 S.W. 15, 14 Am.St.Rep. 23 (1889); Smith v. Bowne, 60 Ga. 484; Campbell v. Johnston, 4 Dana, Ky., 177, 178 (1895); Dixon v. Clayville, 44 Md. 573 (1876); Wilson v. Eigenbrodt, 30 Minn. 4, 13 N.W. 907, 908 (1882); Bank of England v. Tarleton, 23 Miss. 173 (1856); Bridenbecker v. Lowell, 32 Barb., N.Y., 9 (1865); Andrews v. Hobgood, 1 Lea, Tenn., 693 (1887); Keyes v. Wood, 21 Vt. 331 (1849); First National Bank v. Andrews, 7 Wash. 261, 34 P. 913, 38 Am.St.Rep. 885 (1893)." Domeyer v. O'Connell, 364 Ill. 467, 4 N.E.2d 830, 108 A.L.R. 476 (1936); see Land Title Bank v. Schenck, 335 Pa. 419, 6 A.2d 878 (1939); Annot., 115 A.L.R. 40 (1938); see Note, 10 Tulane L.Rev. 303 (1936).

8. Cullum v. Erwin, 4 Ala. 452 (1842). This was the earlier rule in Virginia but after vigorous attack upon it by J.W.H. Pilson, 19 Va.L.Rev. 878 (1933), it was changed by statute. Va.Code, § 55–60–1. See also Miami Oil Co. v. Florida Discount Corp., 102 Fla. 209, 135 So. 845 (1931),

commented on in 6 U. of Cin.L.Rev. 247 (1932).

9. In Conway v. Yadon, 132 Okl. 36, 269 P. 309 (1928), the court said that it was "more or less consistently followed in Alabama, Florida, Illinois, Indiana, Iowa, Kansas, Ohio, New Hampshire, and Wisconsin." See Wilson v. Hayward, 6 Fla. 171 (1855). For modifications of the order of maturity rule where accepted, see Campbell, Cases on Mortgages, 2d ed., 586 n. 3.

10. See Osborne, Mortgages § 244 (2d Ed.1970).

11. Domeyer v. O'Connell, 364 Ill. 467, 4 N.E.2d 830, 108 A.L.R. 476 (1936). This case contains an elaborate discussion of the entire question together with a good collection of authorities. In large part its reasoning is followed in the text. For comments on it see Notes, 4 U. of Chi.L.Rev. 502 (1937); 2 John Marshall L.Q. 422 (1937); 31 Ill.L.Rev. 111 (1936). See 50 A.L.R. 543 (1927); 108 A.L.R. 485 (1937); 115 A.L.R. 40 (1938). Look also at Title Guarantee & Trust Co. v. Mortgage Commission, 273 N.Y. 415, 7 N.E.2d 841 (1937), discussed in Notes, 37 Col.L.Rev. 1010 (1937); 14 N.Y.Univ.L.Q.Rev. 259 (1937).

12. While there is authority for the statement that the lead lender is a fiduciary, see Capitol Sav. & Loan Ass'n v. First Financial Sav & Loan Ass'n, 364 N.W.2d 267 (Iowa 1984); Robbins v. Wilson Creek State Bank, 5 Wn.2d 584, 105 P.2d 1107 (1940), there is no reason to extend this rule, which applies to protect the grantee of a portion of a mortgaged parcel of land, should also apply here; [13] and that the partial assignment constitutes an implied promise by the lead lender to give the participants priority over himself.[14] None of these arguments has much persuasive power, and the better cases hold that the assignor and the participants share pro rata if they have not agreed to the contrary.

In cases in which the lead lender has guaranteed payment to the participants, the balance of the authorities clearly shifts to favor the latter, and they are usually held to have first claim on the mortgage payments or foreclosure proceeds as against the lead lender.[15] Such cases typically arise only when the mortgagee is insolvent and the claim to pro-rata priority is made by his trustee in bankruptcy or his unsecured creditors. The reasoning of the majority cases is that it is unfair for the mortgagee, who has obligated himself to see that the participants' claims are paid, to compete with them for the limited funds available.[16] A minority of cases take the position that the participants' claim based on the guarantee merely gives them an

idea so far as to deny the lead what is, under the apparent terms of the agreement, rightfully his; his trusteeship should extend only to the funds he is obligated to pay over to the participants.

13. See § 10.10, infra. The rule is intended to apply only where the grantee has paid full value for the land without deduction for the mortgage, and thus is entirely inapplicable in the present context.

14. Absent contract language, the supposition is far-fetched. Under ordinary contract law the assignor does not even warrant that the obligor will perform; Restatement, Second, Contracts, § 333(2) (1981).

15. If the lead lender makes an explicit guarantee of payment, see Matter of Lawyers Mortgage Co., 151 Misc. 744, 272 N.Y.S. 390 (1934); Matter of Lawyers Mortgage Co., 157 Misc. 813, 284 N.Y.S. 740 (1936); In re Title and Mortgage Co., 275 N.Y. 347, 9 N.E.2d 957, 115 A.L.R. 35 (1937); Pink v. Thomas, 282 N.Y. 10, 24 N.E.2d 724 (1939) commented on, 26 Va.L. Rev. 825 (1940); In re Lawyers Title and Guaranty Co., 287 N.Y. 264, 39 N.E. 233 (1942) commented on 55 Harv.L.Rev. 882 (1942); Ferris v. Prudence Realization Corp., 292 N.Y. 210, 54 N.E.2d 367 (1944), affirmed on certiorari, Prudence Realization Co. v. Ferris, 323 U.S. 650, 65 S.Ct. 539, 89 L.Ed. 528 (1945); commented on, 32 Va.L.Rev. 176 (1945); In re 1934 Realty Corp., 150 F.2d 477 (2d Cir.1945) commented on, 32 Va.L.Rev. 176 (1945); In re Phillippi, 329 Pa. 581, 198 A. 16 (1938); Cannon v. McDaniel & Jackson, 46 Tex. 303 (1876). For a discussion of problems aris-

ing in connection with guaranteed mortgages, see 34 Col.L.Rev. 663 (1934).

If the lead lender indorses particular negotiable notes of the mortgagor to particular participants, and the indorsements are unqualified, they constitute the indorser's contract that he will pay the instruments according to their tenor upon dishonor and any necessary notice of dishonor and protest; U.C.C. § 3–414. In this situation, see Anderson v. Sharp, 44 Ohio St. 260, 6 N.E. 900 (1886); Dixon v. Clayville, 44 Md. 573 (1876); Fourth National Bank's Appeal, 123 Pa. 473, 16 A. 779, 10 Am.St.Rep. 538 (1889); Louisville Title Co.'s Receiver v. Crab Orchard Banking Co., 249 Ky. 736, 61 S.W.2d 615 (1933); Fidelity Trust Co. v. Orr, 154 Tenn. 538, 289 S.W. 500 (1926); Reconstruction Finance Corp. v. Smith, 96 S.W.2d 824 (Tex.Civ.App.1936), noted, 15 Tex.L.Rev. 271 (1937); see 37 Col.L.Rev. 1010 (1937); 31 Ill.L.Rev. 1111, 1114 (1937); 77 U. of Pa.L.Rev. 266, 269 (1928).

Note, however, that in the usual case the note is singular, is not indorsed, and is not delivered to any of the assignees. Hence there is usually no guarantee by the lead lender in the absence of a specific agreement. See also Restatement, Second, Contracts, note 14 supra.

16. Reconstruction Finance Corp. v. Smith, 96 S.W.2d 824 (Tex.Civ.App.1936) noted, 15 Tex.L.Rev. 271 (1937); Pustejovsky, v. K.J.Z.T. Lodge, 124 Tex. 504, 79 S.W.2d 1084 (1935); In re Title and Mortgage Guaranty Co. of Sullivan County, 275 N.Y. 347, 9 N.E.2d 957, 115 A.L.R. 35 (1937) commented on 47 Yale L.Jour. 480 (1938).

unsecured right to the insolvent mortgagee's general assets, just as other unsecured creditors.[17] An intermediate view, taken by the United States Supreme Court, holds that the priority of the mortgagee depends on whether he retained his participation interests at the outset or acquired them from other participants in free market transactions (in which case he will have an equal priority with the other participants), or whether he repurchased his interests from participants pursuant to his guarantee (in which case he will have a subordinate priority).[18] There has been little development in the law in this area in several decades, and it is difficult to say whether the general rule subordinating the guaranteeing lead lender would still be followed today.

Third Party Attacks on Participations

In recent years concern has been growing that participations may be subject to successful attack by third parties who have some claim on the lead lender or his assets. This concern derives from the looseness and informality with which most modern participations are handled. Specifically, the mortgagor's note, the mortgage, and other individual loan documents are usually left in the lead lender's hands. There is generally no recordation of the participation agreement or certificates, and no filing of a financing statement under Article 9 of the UCC.[19]

It is quite clear that the participants in this sort of arrangement are not holders in due course of the mortgage note or notes, even if negotiable. Normally the notes are not indorsed to the participants,[20] and even if they were, physical delivery to the participants is impossible if each mortgage loan is represented by a single note,[21] as is the

17. Kelly v. Middlesex Title Guaranty & Trust Co., 115 N.J.Eq. 592, 171 A. 823 (1934) affirmed 116 N.J.Eq. 574, 174 A. 706; Prudence Realization Corp. v. Geist, 316 U.S. 89, 62 S.Ct. 978, 86 L.Ed. 1293 (1942). See also Hinds v. Mooers, 11 Iowa 211 (1860), rule of priority of maturity applied; Wilcox v. Allen, 36 Mich. 160, 172 (1877), pro rata rule applied.

18. Under such circumstances "if the surety were allowed to prove his own claim before the creditor is paid, he would to that extent diminish the creditor's dividends upon his claim, and thus defeat the purpose for which he had given the indemnity." * * * "For like reasons equity requires the surety who holds security of the insolvent principal to give the benefit of it to the creditor for whom he is surety until the debt is paid." Prudence Realization Corp. v. Geist, 316 U.S. 89, 96, 62 S.Ct. 978, 86 L.Ed. 1293 (1942). See also Prudence Realization Corp. v. Ferris, 323 U.S. 650, 657, 65 S.Ct. 539, 89 L.Ed. 528 (1944), concurring opinion of Stone, C.J.

19. See Essay, supra note 2, at nn. 20–22; Drake & Weems, Mortgage Loan Participations: The Trustee's Attack, 52 Am. Bankr.L.J. 23 (1978); Simpson, Loan Participations: Pitfalls for Participants, 31 Bus.Law 1977 (1976); Coogan, Kripke & Weiss, The Outer Fringes of Article 9: Subordination Agreements, Security Interests in Money and Deposits, Negative Pledge Clauses and Participation Agreements, 79 Harv.L.Rev. 229 (1965).

20. Negotiation of order paper can be accomplished only by indorsement and delivery. U.C.C. § 3–202(1). The indorsement must be written on the notes themselves or on a paper firmly affixed to each note. U.C.C. § 3–202(2). The payee's signature on a separate piece of paper cannot constitute an indorsement. Tallahassee Bank & Trust Co. v. Raines, 125 Ga.App. 263, 187 S.E.2d 320 (1972).

21. A holder of an instrument must receive physical possession of it. U.C.C. § 1–201(20); Official Comment, U.C.C. § 3–804; Rex Smith Propane, Inc. v. National Bank typical procedure. Indeed, the Code appears to make indorsement of fractional interests in a note to holders in due course impossible.[22]

The continuing presence of the note or notes in the lead lender's hands gives him the power to misdeal with them in several ways. For example, he may reassign them, either as additional participation interests or in toto.[23] He may pledge them to another creditor to secure other debts he owes.[24] He may receive payment from the mortgagors, and may effectively cancel the notes and satisfy the mortgages,[25] even if he fails to pass the participants' shares of the payments through to them. He may cancel the notes and record releases or satisfactions of the mortgages even without payment, and thereby allow bona fide purchasers of the land to take free of the mortgages.[26]

The participants normally have confidence that the lead lender will do none of these things, and they usually take no precautions to prevent them. But the failure of several major commercial banks during the 1970's suggests that such confidence may sometimes be misplaced.[27] The participants might insist that the notes be stamped or marked with a notation that they are subject to the interests of the participants;[28] this action would be effective to prevent most of the types of misdealing mentioned in the previous paragraph,[29] but it would also seriously complicate the giving of valid satisfactions to mortgagors who repaid their loans, since it would presumably require the consent of all of the participants to a cancellation of the notes. This approach may make sense in a case in which there are only a few participants on a single large loan, but it is probably impractical with a package of small loans sold to a large number of participants. In the latter situation the participants must take the risk of misdealing by the lead.

of Commerce, 372 F.Supp. 499 (N.D.Tex. 1974).

22. U.C.C. § 3–202(3), Official Comment 4 states: Any indorsement which purports to convey to any party less than the entire amount of the instrument is not effective for negotiation. This is true of * * * "Pay A one-half", or "Pay A two-thirds and B one-third", * * * and neither A nor B becomes a holder.

23. U.C.C. § 3–301: "The holder of an instrument whether or not he is the owner may transfer or negotiate it * * *." The original payee may be a holder; U.C.C. § 3–302. See In re Columbia Pacific Mortgage, Inc., 20 B.R. 259, 264 (Bkrtcy.Wash. 1981) (dictum).

24. See § 5.28, supra, at notes 24–32.

25. U.C.C. § 3–301: "The holder of an instrument, whether or not he is the owner may * * * discharge it or enforce payment in his own name.

26. This is always a possibility, whether the assignment is unitary or in the form of

participations, if it is not recorded; see § 5.34, supra, at notes 8–13.

27. Banks which failed or were merged with other banks under FDIC supervision included Eatontown National Bank of New Jersey (1970), U.S. National Bank of San Diego (1973), Franklin National Bank of Chattanooga (1974), Security National Bank of New York (1975), American Bank and Trust of New York (1976), and Penn Square Bank of Oklahoma City (1982). See Skillern, Federal Deposit Insurance Corporation and the Failed Bank: The Past Decade (Part I), 99 Banking L.J. 233 (1982); Hibernia National Bank v. FDIC, supra note 4; Note, 62 Tex.L.Rev. 1115 (1984).

28. Such a notation would presumably give notice to any later taker of the instrument and preclude his becoming a HDC. See U.C.C. § 9–308 and Official Comment 3.

29. It would not of course, prevent a wrongful recording of a satisfaction or release by the mortgagee; see § 5.34, supra, at notes 8–13.

A better approach, although somewhat cumbersome, is to require the lead lender to deliver the note and mortgage (with indorsement and a recorded assignment) to an independent institutional trustee who will continue to hold them for the life of the loan.[30] If the trustee is well chosen, the risk of any misdealing of the types described above is virtually eliminated.

Even in the absence of specific improper conduct by the lead lender, it is possible in the event of his insolvency that his general creditors or his trustee in bankruptcy may attack the very essence of the participation transaction, claiming that it is not an effective transfer of ownership in the notes, and thus that they remain part of the insolvent lead lender's estate.[31]

To a great extent such an argument is blunted by Section 541(d) of the Bankruptcy Code,[32] which seems to have been adopted to resolve precisely this question.[33] It provides that the property of the bankrupt's estate does not include equitable interests in mortgages which the bankrupt debtor has sold but in which he retains legal title for purposes of servicing. Since the participants in a mortgage loan cannot be holders, the legal title to the note and mortgage may well be regarded as remaining in the hands of the lead lender; but Section 541(d) makes it clear that only the fractional share (if any) which the lead lender has *not* sold to participants will become an asset of the estate in the hands of the trustee in bankruptcy.[34]

Notwithstanding Section 541(d), however, a trustee might argue that the participation "sales" are not sales at all, but instead are merely loans by the participants to the lead lender, with the interests

---

30. This is essentially the approach taken by the GNMA mortgage-backed securities program; the notes and mortgages are held by a "custodian". See Government National Mortgage Association, Mortgage Backed Securities Guide § 8–3 (1980); Krasnowiecki, Miller & Ziff, The Kennedy Mortgage Co. Bankruptcy Case: New Light Shed on the Position of Mortgage Warehousing Banks, 56 Am.Bankr.L.J. 325, 341 nn. 60–64 (1982).

31. This argument was apparently first made in 1976 in In re Hamilton Mortgage Corp., No. BK–1–76–264 (E.D.Tenn., So. Div., unreported). The case was settled. See Drake & Weems, Mortgage Loan Participations: The Trustee's Attack, 52 Am. Bankr.L.J. 23, 43–54 (1978); but see Mac-Donald, Loan Participations as Enforceable Property Rights in Bankruptcy—A Reply to the Trustee's Attack, 53 Am.Bankr.L.J. 35 (1979).

See also Franklin v. Commissioner, 683 F.2d 125 (5th Cir.1982), at 128 n. 9; Hutch-ins, What Exactly is a Loan Participation?, 9 Rut.Cam.L.Rev. 447 (1978).

32. 11 U.S.C.A. § 541(d).

33. The legislative history indicates that Congress' concern was to insulate the secondary mortgage market from attacks by bankruptcy trustees; see 124 Cong.Rec. S 17,413 (daily ed. Oct. 6, 1978). The text of the section speaks both of "a mortgage secured by real property" and "an interest in such a mortgage;" the latter phrase seems plainly to contemplate participation interests. See Collier, Bankruptcy ¶ 541.24.

The language of § 541(d) seems absolute, and will apparently protect the participating lenders even if the lead lender has represented the mortgage notes to its creditors as being its exclusive property.

34. In re Columbia Pacific Mortgage, Inc., 20 B.R. 259 (Bkrtcy.Wash.1981).

in the mortgage notes serving as security for repayment.[35] These security interests are, of necessity, unperfected, since perfection could be accomplished only by a transfer of possession to the participants, which is practically impossible.[36] The trustee in bankruptcy, acting under the "strong-arm" powers granted by Section 544(a)(1) of the Bankruptcy Code, could arguably assume the role of a judgment lien creditor and thus take priority over these unperfected security interests.[37]

With a properly-drafted participation agreement, this argument has little substance. Ordinarily, the parties' agreement that a sale, not a loan, is intended, should control. However, the parties may add features which rebut the sale characterization. For example, if the participation agreement includes a guarantee by the lead lender of payment of the underlying obligation, or a repurchase provision which obliges the lead lender to buy back the participation interest in the event of default, the courts may conclude that the participants do not have the normal risks of ownership, and thus that the transaction is in reality a loan with the underlying mortgage and note serving as security for its repayment.[38]

Another possible argument for the trustee is that the participants have received only assignments of the proceeds from the ultimate mortgage loan payments or foreclosures, and not property interests in the notes themselves. In a technical sense, it is true that the participants cannot be holders of the notes, and hence probably cannot enforce them directly.[39] But it is apparent that the participants have acquired

35. See Drake & Weems, supra note 31, at 43–54; Note, 62 Texas L.Rev. 1115, 1120–1133 (1984).

36. See § 5.27 supra at notes 27–31. Note that a transfer to an independent trustee or custodian, as described in the text at note 30 supra, would solve this problem.

37. U.C.C. § 9–301(1)(b) provides that an unperfected security interest is subordinate to the claim of a judicial lien creditor. U.C.C. § 9–301(3) defines lien creditors to include a trustee in bankruptcy, and the Bankruptcy Code, 11 U.S.C.A. § 544(a)(1), gives the trustee in bankruptcy the rights of a lien creditor.

It is debatable whether the rights of the participants should be regarded as real property, and hence as subject to the trustee's power under 11 U.S.C.A. § 544(a)(3) to act as a bona fide purchaser of real property under state recording acts; see § 5.34 supra at notes 23–47, and especially note 30. In most cases the point is moot, since the participation agreement will make it clear that a sale, not a security interest, is involved, and 11 U.S.C.A. § 541(d) will

clearly exempt the participants from the necessity of complying with the recording acts; see In re Columbia Pacific Mortgage, Inc., 20 B.R. 259, 263–64 (Bkrtcy.Wash. 1981). Concern on the point can be entirely alleviated by delivery of the note and mortgage to an independent trustee or custodian; see text at note 30 supra.

38. The presence of a guarantee and a repurchase right were factors in the court's conclusion that a loan, not a participation, existed in Castle Rock Industrial Bank v. S.O.A.W. Enterprises, Inc., 32 B.R. 279 (Bkrtcy.Tex.1983). However, such factors are not necessarily dispositive; see Stratford Financial Corp. v. Finex Corp., 367 F.2d 569 (2d Cir.1966), upholding a participation as a trust despite the lead lender's guaranty of payment.

39. U.C.C. §§ 3–301, 3–603. There is some possibility that the participants could enforce the notes, by analogy to cases which allow pledgors of notes to enforce them under certain conditions notwithstanding their lack of possession; see 43 A.L.R.3d 824 (1972).

an ownership interest in the underlying obligations which the notes represent. Only the lead lender can directly enforce the notes, but when it does so, surely a court of equity will recognize the participants' equitable ownership rights and require the lead lender to account to them for their shares of ownership in the obligation.

In many participation agreements this equitable right is explicitly recognized by language constituting the lead lender a trustee or agent of the participants.[40] Inclusion of such language is wise,[41] but even if it is absent a court should have no difficulty imposing a remedial constructive trust on the lead lender, requiring it to account to the participants. Whether this is "legal" ownership may be debatable, but surely it is "equitable" ownership of the kind referred to in Section 541(d) of the Bankruptcy Code. The parties seem quite obviously to have something more than a mere assignment of the right to proceeds in mind, and there is no reason for the courts to refuse to recognize it in bankruptcy.

Careful drafting of the participation agreement can strengthen it against these attacks. The agreement should clearly spell out that a transfer of ownership of the notes and mortgages is intended.[42] It should negate the concept of a loan from the participants to the lead lender. The lead lender should agree to (and should in fact) segregate the notes and mortgages in question from its portfolio of loans held for its own account, and should refrain from interchanging loans between the two portfolios.[43] The agreement should include no provision for a guarantee of payment by the lead lender or a repurchase obligation. It should identify the lead as either an agent or a trustee for the participants, and stipulate its powers and duties in terms which are consistent with the agency or trust theory utilized.[44] The interest yield to the participants should be computed as the equivalent or composite of the interest yields on the underlying mortgage loans, less an appropriate fee to the lead lender as compensation for its duties in servicing the loans.[45] If these precautions are followed, the chances of the courts sustaining the participation in bankruptcy should be excellent.

 WESTLAW REFERENCES
di participation loan

40. See, e.g., the participation agreement reproduced in 18 Tulsa L.J. 261, 274 (1982).

41. See In re Columbia Pacific Mortgage, Inc., 20 B.R. 259, 262–63 (Bkrtcy. Wash.1981), upholding language of express trust; Coffey v. Lawman, 99 F.2d 245 (6th Cir.1938).

42. See, e.g., FHLMC Participation Sales Agreement 300, at (1): "The terms and conditions of this Agreement shall govern the transfer, sale and assignment of . . ." the participation interests.

43. See In re Alda Commercial Corp., 327 F.Supp. 1315 (S.D.N.Y.1971).

44. See, e.g., FHLMC Participation Sales Agreement 300 at (6): "FHLMC shall act as the representative of Holders in the control, management and servicing of the Mortgages or property acquired in realization or liquidation."

45. This was another fatal flaw in the participation agreement successfully attacked in Castle Rock Industrial Bank v. S.O.A.W. Enterprises, Inc., supra note 38.

Priorities in the Absence of Agreement

"lead lender" partial** participa! /9 assign! /p mortgage note /p
equal** priority "pro rata" share

Third Party Attacks on Participations

mortgage note /s assign! /9 "lead lender" partial** participa! /p
cancel! pledge reassign! releas*** satisfact***

§§ 5.36–6.0 are reserved for supplementary material.

Chapter 6

DISCHARGE OF THE MORTGAGE

Table of Sections

A. PAYMENT

§ 6.1 Prepayment—General Considerations

Contrary to what is probably pervasive popular belief, absent a specific provision in the note or mortgage so providing, there is no common law right to pay off a mortgage debt prior to its maturity. This rule is derived from the classic case of Brown v. Cole,[1] where the court stated that if mortgagors "were allowed to pay off their mortgage money at any time after the execution of the mortgage, it might be attended with extreme inconvenience to mortgagees, who generally advance their money as an investment." Consequently, the mortgagee has a right to refuse an early tender of principal and interest and courts will not compel premature discharge of the mortgage.[2] On the other hand, a growing number of jurisdictions, either by statute [3] or judicial decision,[4] have abrogated the common law rule in a variety of contexts. For example, under the approach adopted by the Supreme Court of Pennsylvania, "where a mortgage note is silent as to the right of prepayment, there arises a presumption that the debt may be prepaid." [5]

In any event, most mortgagees permit prepayment, but exact a fee or "prepayment penalty" for the "privilege" of prepaying the loan. The prepayment penalty occasionally takes the form of the *non-option* type, where the loan agreement omits any mention of prepayment; when the mortgagor wishes to prepay the mortgagee is then in a position to determine the amount of the penalty.[6] However, the *non-option* situation could sometimes result in the mortgagor being unable to collect a prepayment penalty because a few states prohibit the imposition of such a penalty unless it is specifically provided for in the loan agreement.[7] The common practice, however, is to utilize the *option* type where the penalty is actually spelled out in the loan agreement. A "typical" prepayment clause will often read as follows:

> "Privilege is reserved to make additional payments on the principal of this indebtedness at any time without penalty, except that as to any such payments made which exceed twenty percent (20%) of the original principal amount of this loan during any successive twelve (12) month period beginning with the date of this promissory note, the undersigned agree to pay, as consideration for the acceptance of such prepayment,

---

§ 6.1

1. 14 L.J. (N.S.) Ch. 167, Chancery, 1845.

2. See Comment, Secured Real Estate Loan Prepayment and the Prepayment Penalty, 51 Cal.L.Rev. 923, 924 (1963); Smiddy v. Grafton, 163 Cal. 16, 124 P. 433 (1912); Carpenter v. Winn, 566 P.2d 370 (Colo.App.1977); Bowen v. Julius, 141 Ind. 310, 40 N.E. 700 (1895); Moore v. Kime, 43 Neb. 517, 61 N.W. 736 (1895); Dugan v. Grzybowski, 165 Conn. 173, 332 A.2d 97 (1973); Henderson v. Guest, 197 Okla. 443, 172 P.2d 605 (1946). Peter Fuller Enterprises Inc. v. Manchester Savings Bank, 102 N.H. 117, 152 A.2d 179 (1959).

3. See e.g., West's Fla.Stat.Ann. § 697.06; N.Y.—McKinney's Banking Law § 393(2); N.Y.—McKinney's Gen.Obl.Law § 5–501(3)(b).

4. See e.g., Mahoney v. Furches, 503 Pa. 60, 468 A.2d 458 (1983).

5. Id. at 461.

6. Comment, supra note 2 at 924. See, e.g., Feldman v. Kings Highway Savings Bank, 278 App.Div. 589, 102 N.Y.S.2d 306 (195–), affirmed mem. 303 N.Y. 675, 102 N.E.2d 835 (1951).

7. See, e.g., Beth-June, Inc. v. Wil-Avon Merchandise Mart, Inc., 211 Pa.Super. 5, 233 A.2d 620 (1967); Burks v. Verschuur, 35 Colo.App. 121, 532 P.2d 757 (1975).

six (6) months advance interest on that part of the aggregate amount of all prepayments in excess of such twenty percent (20%). The privilege of paying amounts not in excess of said twenty percent (20%) of the original principal sum without consideration shall be noncumulative, if not exercised." [8]

Importantly, some of these clauses, in addition, specify that the prepayment charge "shall be due and payable whether said prepayment is voluntary or involuntary, including any prepayment effected by the exercise of any acceleration clause provided for herein." [9] While the penalty will in rare instances be as low as one or two months' interest, the most common maximum is six months or one hundred and eighty days' interest. This is because of a Federal Home Loan Bank Board (FHLBB) regulation, applicable to all federally chartered savings and loan associations, which limits the prepayment penalty for payment of the entire principal balance to a maximum of six months' interest.[10] This regulation also requires penalty-free prepayment of up to 20% of the balance of the mortgage debt in any twelve month period.[11]

The prepayment penalty is utilized by mortgagees for at least two reasons. The traditional justification for such provisions is that the mortgagee's fixed cost of making a loan are not recaptured entirely at the inception of the loan, but are amortized over the life of the loan.[12] Thus, the collection of a prepayment penalty should, in theory, make it possible for the mortgagee to recapture those costs. It has been argued, however, that the closing costs and other charges collected by the mortgagee at the inception date of the loan more than compensate for such fixed costs.[13] Such clauses are also used as an economic complement to the due on sale clause.[14] While the due on sale clause enables a mortgagee to force early payment of lower than market interest rate loans, the prepayment penalty is used to discourage refinancing by the mortgagor when market interest rates fall below the rate on the mortgagor's existing mortgage. The prepayment clause tends to "lock in" loans made at higher than current market interest rates. As such, it is another imperfect method for achieving a higher longterm return on the mortgagee's loan portfolio. It should be pointed out, however, that the use of the two clauses together does *not* result in an approximation of the functional equivalent of variable interest rates. When variable interest rates are utilized, interest rates on long term mortgages will rise or fall in conjunction with some index that is tied or at least related to market interest rates.[15] On the other hand, when the

---

8. Lazzareschi Investment Co. v. San Francisco Federal Savings and Loan Association, 22 Cal.App.3d 303, 305, 99 Cal. Rptr. 417, 419 (1971).

9. Id. at 305, 99 Cal.Rptr. at 419.

10. 12 CFR 545.6–12(b).

11. Id.

12. Bonanno, Due on Sale and Prepayment Clauses in Real Estate Financing in California in Times of Fluctuating Interest Rates—Legal Issues and Alternatives, 6 San.Fran.L.Rev. 267, 295 (1972).

13. Id. at 295.

14. See § 5.21 supra.

15. See § 11.4 infra.

two clauses are used successfully together, the mortgagee uses due on sale clauses to reloan money at higher rates, but the prepayment penalty is used to keep the mortgagee's portfolio interest return from dropping. In essence, the mortgagee seeks to achieve the effect of variable rates only when market interest rates are going up. When such rates are dropping, the prepayment penalty insulates the mortgagee in part from the economic effect of that downturn, an effect that would not be achieved by variable interest rates.

 WESTLAW REFERENCES

prepay! /s clause penalty charge premium /p mortgag**

di pre-payment penalty

due-on-sale /p pre-pay! /s clause penalty premium charge

---

§ 6.2 Prepayment Clauses—Judicial Treatment

While mortgagors have sometimes attacked prepayment charges on a usury theory, this attack has been uniformly rejected.[1] The usury argument in theory arises when the sum of the actual interest paid plus the prepayment amount exceed the maximum lawful interest rate calculated to the date of prepayment.[2] In the *non-option* type situation, it is generally held that the prepayment penalty is not interest, but rather represents value given by the mortgagor for a new agreement to terminate the original loan agreement.[3] In the *option* situation, where prepayment is expressly provided for in the loan agreement, courts stress that the mortgagor controls both the timing and the imposition of the prepayment charge.[4] As one Texas court put it, the "charge . . . was not for the use of money, but for the privilege of repaying the loan before maturity. [Mortgagor] could have paid the note under the terms set out and avoided any prepayment penalty. Instead, he chose to prepay the note long before maturity. The [mortgagee] accepted . . . the prepayment, but charged him for the privilege. This charge is not interest."[5] Indeed, courts have determined that the loan is not rendered usurious where the total interest plus the prepayment amount

§ 6.2

1. See, e.g., Williams v. Fasler, 110 Cal. App.3d 7, 167 Cal.Rptr. 545 (1980); McCarty v. Mellinkoff, 118 Cal.App. 11, 4 P.2d 595 (1931); Dezell v. King, 91 So.2d 624 (Fla.App.1956); Hanson v. Acceptance Finance Co., 270 S.W.2d 143 (Mo.App.1954); Marley v. Consolidated Mortgage Co., 102 R.I. 200, 229 A.2d 608 (1968); Bell Bakeries, Inc. v. Jefferson Standard Life Insurance Co., 245 N.C. 408, 96 S.E.2d 408 (1957); Annot., 75 A.L.R.2d 1265 (1961).

2. Comment, Secured Real Estate Loan Prepayment and the Prepayment Penalty, 51 Cal.L.Rev. 923, 926.

3. See, e.g., Abbot v. Stevens, 133 Cal. App.2d 242, 284 P.2d 159 (1955); Webb v.

Southern Trust Co., 227 Ky. 79, 11 S.W.2d 988 (1928); Luchesi v. Capitol Loan & Finance Co., 83 R.I. 151, 113 A.2d 725 (1955); Annot., 75 A.L.R.2d 1265, 1267 (1961). But see Lyons v. National Savings Bank of City of Albany, 200 Misc. 652, 110 N.Y.S.2d 564 (1951), reversed 280 A.D. 339, 113 N.Y.S.2d 695 (1952).

4. Comment, Secured Real Estate Loan Prepayment and the Prepayment Penalty, 51 Cal.L.Rev. 923, 926 (1963).

5. Boyd v. Life Insurance Co. of the Southwest, 546 S.W.2d 132 (Tex.Civ.App. 1977), error refused.

does not exceed the lawful maximum interest computed from the date of the loan to its final maturity date specified in the loan agreement.[6]

Other avenues of judicial attack have also thus far been unsuccessful. For example, in Lazzareschi Investment Co. v. San Francisco Savings & Loan Association,[7] a California appellate decision, the court upheld the standard six month prepayment penalty provision against the allegation that the prepayment charge constituted an invalid penalty because the damages imposed did not bear a reasonable relationship to the injury caused by the prepayment. There, a purchaser of commercial real estate at a judicial sale sought to refinance an existing 7¾% loan on the premises. The mortgagee insisted on collection of the prepayment charge even though the mortgagee had the ability to reloan the money at a higher interest rate. While the appellate court recognized that the mortgagee could reloan the money at a higher rate, it also noted that if the interest rates fell, many mortgagees would refinance. Under the circumstances, the court concluded that the clause used here was reasonable, in part, because it complied with the regulation of the Federal Home Loan Bank Board (FHLBB) governing prepayment penalties in the residential loan setting. The court looked to the FHLBB regulation as a guide even though this case involved a non-residential transaction. Thus, the impression left by the court was that this particular mortgagee could have charged a higher penalty had it so chosen because a residential transaction was not involved in the case. Finally, the court concluded that the prepayment charge did not constitute an invalid restraint on alienation because the restraint was not absolute and was considered to be reasonable under the circumstances.

Lazzareschi has proved to be an important bellwether for subsequent prepayment litigation. One California appellate court, in Meyers v. Home Savings & Loan Association [8] upheld a prepayment provision similar to that in *Lazzareschi* against the argument that the prepayment charge constituted invalid liquidated damages under section 1670 of the California Civil Code.[9] The court noted that the purpose of the provision was to give the mortgagor the option to prepay and that the clause did not penalize for the "breach of an obligation" as contemplated by section 1670. "No breach is involved in the prepayment transac-

6. See, e.g., Eldred v. Hart, 87 Ark. 534, 113 S.W. 213 (1908); Redmond v. Ninth Federal Savings & Loan Association, 147 N.Y.S.2d 702 (1955); Annot., 75 A.L.R.2d 1265, 1268 (1961).

7. 22 Cal.App.3d 303, 99 Cal.Rptr. 417 (1971).

8. 38 Cal.App.3d 544, 113 Cal.Rptr. 358 (1974).

9. West's Ann.Cal.Civil Code § 1670 provides: "Every contract by which the amount of damages to be paid, or other compensation to be made, for a breach of an obligation, is determined in anticipation thereof, is to that extent void, except as expressly provided in the next section."

West's Ann.Cal.Civil Code § 1671 provides: "The parties to a contract may agree therein on an amount which shall be presumed to be the amount of damage sustained by a breach thereof, when, from the nature of the case, it would be impracticable or extremely difficult to fix the actual damage."

tion, only the exercise of the option given to the debtor for an alternative method of paying the debt." [10]

Moreover, a more recent California decision, confronted with a *Lazzareschi* type prepayment clause, found that "the lender has a justifiable interest in imposing the penalty to cover his costs due to potential lag time and administrative processing prior to making a new loan." [11] Thus, the court concluded that "the restraint on alienation caused by the assessment of the prepayment penalty is reasonably related to protecting the legitimate interests of the lender."[12] Indeed, the Oregon Supreme Court has held that a complete prohibition of prepayment for an 11 year period was not an unreasonable restraint on alienation.[13]

Moreover, courts have upheld prepayment charges more onerous than the *Lazzareschi* six months' interest amount. For example, a Florida appellate court relied on *Lazzareschi* in upholding a twelve months' interest charge under a clause similar to the one in *Lazzareschi*.[14] Williams v. Fasler,[15] a California appellate court decision, upheld a prepayment charge of 50% of the amount prepaid. In that case, the mortgagee-seller included the provision to avoid the negative tax consequences under the then existing federal income tax law that could have resulted if more than 30% of the total purchase price had been paid during the year of sale. The court held the charge valid and not a penalty because it was deemed to be "reasonably related to the mortgagee's anticipated risk of incurring increased tax liability upon the occurrence of the prepayment." [16]

On the other hand, it would be imprudent to suggest that a 50% prepayment charge is valid beyond the confines of the *Williams* case unless the same federal income tax or similar considerations make it reasonable. It should be emphasized that *Lazzareschi* and its progeny upheld six months' and even twelve months' charges because such provisions were commonly utilized and, in slightly different contexts, authorized by federal regulatory agencies or legislation. In other words, such courts largely took an objective approach and did not pay significant attention to the facts of the cases before them. On the other hand, when the charge is as substantial as it was in *Williams*, it probably will be upheld only when it is deemed to be reasonable under

---

10. Meyers v. Home Savings and Loan Association, 38 Cal.App.3d 544, 546, 113 Cal.Rptr. 358, 359–60 (1974). See Aronoff v. Western Federal Savings and Loan Association, 28 Colo.App. 151, 470 P.2d 889 (1970), where the court upheld a prepayment penalty against the argument that enforcement of a prepayment penalty against a subsequent grantee who wished to prepay was "inequitable."

11. Sacramento Savings & Loan Association v. Superior Court, 137 Cal.App.3d 142, 186 Cal.Rptr. 823 (1982).

12. Id. at 146, 186 Cal.Rptr. at 826.

13. Hartford Life Insurance Co. v. Randall, 283 Or. 297, 583 P.2d 1126 (1978).

14. Century Federal Savings & Loan Association v. Madovsky, 353 So.2d 868 (Fla.App.1978).

15. 110 Cal.App.3d 7, 167 Cal.Rptr. 545 (1980).

16. Id. at 13, 167 Cal.Rptr. at 549.

the facts and circumstances of the individual case. This approach thus is necessarily subjective.

WESTLAW REFERENCES
digest,synopsis(pre-pay! /s penalty)
restraint /3 alienation /p pre-pay!

§ 6.3   Prepayment Clauses—Involuntary Prepayment

The breach of the loan agreement that triggers a prepayment charge may be the result of an involuntary as well as a voluntary act of the mortgagor. Most of the time the prepayment penalty does indeed result from the mortgagor's desire to refinance at a lower rate, but it can also arise from a mortgagor's default in the payment of the loan and subsequent acceleration by the mortgagee. For example, once a mortgagor defaults and the mortgagee accelerates and initiates foreclosure proceedings, should the mortgage debt, for purposes of the mortgagor's right to redeem or for purposes of calculating the amount of a possible sale surplus or deficiency, include the amount of the prepayment penalty? If we consider that one of the purposes of such clauses is to enable the mortgagee to recoup fixed loan costs over the life of the loan, then the exaction of the charge is perhaps justified. If the primary purpose of the clause, however, is to discourage mortgagor refinancing at lower interest rates, then the requirement of the penalty cannot be justified, at least when the mortgagor's default is not intentional. In any event, several cases have refused to permit the collection of a prepayment charge where the default consisted of an apparent honest inability to pay.[1] The theory of such cases is that when default in payment occurs and there is an acceleration, no prepayment, as such, can take place. At that stage the mortgagor cannot opt to prepay, but only to exercise his equity of redemption by redeeming from the mortgage.[2] As one court reasoned, the "lender loses its right to a prepayment charge when it elects to accelerate the debt. This is so

---

§ 6.3

1. In re LHD Realty Corp., 726 F.2d 327 (7th Cir.1984); George H. Nutman, Inc. v. Aetna Business Credit, Inc., 115 Misc.2d 168, 453 N.Y.S.2d 586 (1982); Kilpatrick v. Germania Life Insurance Co., 183 N.Y. 163, 75 N.E. 1124 (1905). Cf. Berenato v. Bell Savings & Loan Association, 276 Pa. Super. 599, 419 A.2d 620 (1980) (prepayment charge collectible where mortgagor's sale of real estate was made necessary by adverse business conditions). See also, West Portland Development Co. v. Ward Cook, Inc., 246 Or. 67, 424 P.2d 212 (1967) (prepayment charge collectible where loan was paid off after lender rescinded a prior acceleration). For an analysis of *West Portland*, see Nelson & Whitman, Real Estate Finance Law 376 (2nd Ed.1979).

2. See Kilpatrick v. Germania Life Insurance Co., 183 N.Y. 163, 75 N.E. 1124 (1905); where the New York Court of Appeals held that once there had been a default and the mortgage brings a suit to foreclose, it was improper for the mortgagee to include a prepayment penalty in calculating the amount mortgagor needed to pay to redeem from the mortgagee. The court reasoned that since the payment of the mortgage debt was under the threat of foreclosure the payment of the prepayment penalty was not "voluntary" and therefore not a valid prepayment. "Under these circumstances the compulsion was illegal, unjust, and oppressive, and the [mortgagor], having submitted under protest, had the right to recover [the prepayment amount]." Id. at 167, 75 N.E. at 1125. See also, Bell Bakeries, Inc. v. Jefferson Standard Life because acceleration, by definition, advances the maturity date of the debt so that payment thereafter is not prepayment but instead is payment made after maturity." [3]

Suppose, however, the mortgagee utilizes prepayment clause language that requires a prepayment penalty whether such payment was "voluntary or involuntary, including any prepayment effected by the exercise of any acceleration clause provided for herein." [4] Here the argument that the mortgagor has not chosen to prepay presumably will not prevent calculating the amount of the penalty as part of the mortgage debt because the parties have agreed to its inclusion. On the other hand, where prepayment is involuntary should such language be considered an invalid penalty imposed "for a breach of an obligation" under section 1670 of the California Civil Code? [5] One California commentator has stated: "Perhaps the answer is that the [mortgagee] may so recover when his note and deed of trust say he can. But since this is not an otherwise recoverable item, the clause appears to impose a penalty on the [mortgagor] unrelated to any compensable loss incurred by the [mortgagee]." [6] Nevertheless, if the penalty amount falls within the range imposed by most of the mortgage lending community and, thus, cannot be attacked as exorbitant or inequitable, does not such a clause serve the arguably valid purpose of compensating the mortgagee for the fixed costs of a mortgage loan that normally are amortized over the life of such loan?

Finally, it is conceivable that a mortgagor could intentionally default and trigger a foreclosure proceeding in order to avoid payment of the prepayment charge. His plan would be to exercise his equitable right to redeem prior to foreclosure by paying an accelerated mortgage debt that would not include a prepayment penalty. Although there is no case law considering this problem, the equities here clearly favor enforcement of the clause against the mortgagor. Assuming the prepayment clause is otherwise valid, the mortgagor would be voluntarily using default as a means of avoiding the application of a valid loan agreement provision. Unlike the situation where a mortgagor defaults in the payment of the loan without the prepayment penalty clause in mind, here the mortgagor *chooses default as his means of prepayment.* As one court has stated, "should such intentional defaults become a problem, . . . we believe courts could deal with the difficulty by denying the acceleration exception in appropriate cases." [7]

Insurance Co., 245 N.C. 408, 418, 96 S.E.2d 408, 417 (1957), where court permitted collection of prepayment penalty after a waiver by mortgagee of past defaults, but stated: "[h]ad defendant * * * declared a default and demanded payment, it would only have been entitled to collect the debt and interest accrued thereon to the date of payment."

3. In re LHD Realty Corp., 726 F.2d 327, 330–331 (7th Cir.1984).

4. See § 6.1, note 9 supra.

5. See § 6.2, note 9 supra.

6. Bernhardt in Hetland, California Real Estate Secured Transactions, 200 (1970).

7. In re LHD Realty Corp., 726 F.2d 327, 331 (7th Cir.1984).

Should the lender be able to collect a prepayment penalty when there has been an involuntary disposition of the mortgage security followed by a mortgagee's election to have the proceeds of that disposition apply to pay off the mortgage debt? Suppose, for example, that the mortgage premises have been destroyed by fire and that the mortgagee elects to have the proceeds used to pay off the debt, an option that the mortgagee has under many common mortgage forms. In mortgagor's favor, it can be argued that the prepayment is not voluntary on his part and that, indeed, normally the prepayment is not *by* him, but by the insurance carrier. The mortgagee, on the other hand, can argue that absent the collection of the prepayment penalty, it would not fully recover its fixed cost of making the loan. The closest decided case is Chestnut Corp. v. Bankers Bond & Mortgage Co.[8] There the Pennsylvania Supreme Court held that the mortgagee could not collect an additional 2% prepayment penalty, where the payment of the mortgage had been triggered by the application of fire insurance proceeds to pay off the debt. The court recognized the above arguments on behalf of both of the parties, but noted that "in such a situation both parties suffer, but the owner [mortgagor] suffers most."[9] The above case is not always helpful, however, because, unlike in *Chestnut,* many mortgagees, as we have noted, specifically provide for collection of a prepayment penalty in the event of all involuntary prepayment. Yet it can be argued that while the prepayment is involuntary on the mortgagor's part, it may be voluntary on the part of the mortgagee in the sense that commonly used mortgage forms often give the mortgagee the option to reduce the debt or repair the premises. Thus, it can be argued that "it is the [mortgagee] who is compelling the [mortgagor] to prepay the loan and simultaneously asserting a charge for the [mortgagor's] exercise of his 'privilege' to prepay."[10]

A more common problem seems to be whether prepayment that results from a condemnation of the security permits the mortgagee to exact a prepayment penalty. Where the language of the mortgage does not specifically authorize prepayment penalties for involuntary prepayment, the case law thus far uniformly holds that the mortgagee has no right to collect a prepayment penalty either against the mortgagor or the condemning authority.[11] These cases found persuasive the mortgagor's argument in *Chestnut* that there was no voluntary prepayment on the part of the mortgagor and that the latter was not exercising a "right" or "privilege" of prepayment within the language of the prepayment clause. Suppose, however, as discussed in the fire insurance situation in the preceding paragraph, that the prepayment clause

8. 395 Pa. 153, 149 A.2d 48 (1959).

9. Id. at 157, 149 A.2d at 50.

10. Bernhardt in Hetland, California Real Estate Secured Transactions, 197 (1970).

11. See DeKalb County v. United Family Life Insurance Co., 235 Ga. 417, 219 S.E.2d 707 (1975), on remand 136 Ga.App. 822, 222 S.E.2d 644 (1975); Associated Schools, Inc. v. Dade County, 209 So.2d 489 (Fla.App.1968); Silverman v. State, 48 A.D.2d 413, 370 N.Y.S.2d 234 (1975); Jala Corp. v. Berkeley Savings & Loan Association, 104 N.J.Super. 394, 250 A.2d 150 (1969).

specifically authorizes collection of the penalty in involuntary situations. By partial analogy to the insurance proceeds situation, it can be argued that the mortgagee, nevertheless, should be allowed no prepayment penalty. The mortgagee always has the option in almost all mortgage forms to apply the condemnation award to the debt or to allow the mortgagor to take the award. Thus, in a sense, it is the *mortgagee* who is compelling the mortgagor to prepay and also demanding the payment of a prepayment penalty. On the other hand, a persuasive argument can be made that the insurance and condemnation situations are not analogous. While it can be said that a mortgagee's right in the insurance setting to pay the debt or to rebuild the premises is a "true option," it is much more difficult to conclude that the condemnation mortgagee's ability to pay the debt or give the proceeds to the mortgagor is similarly such a "true option." In the former situation, the mortgagee gets either the debt paid or the security intact whereas in the latter situation, the "choice" is between payment of the debt or loss of a security. Thus, in this latter situation where the loan agreement specifically provides for a prepayment penalty in involuntary situations, and where, as always, the mortgagee can argue that prepayment means less than full recovery of the fixed costs of making the loan, a court is possibly justified in following the loan agreement language.

 WESTLAW REFERENCES
accelerat! /p pre-pay! /s penalty clause charge premium

§ 6.4 Prepayment Clauses—Legislative and Other Nonjudicial Regulation

State legislation regulating prepayment penalties is increasing and varies considerably in substance. The one pervasive element in all such legislation is that it is limited to loans secured by residential real estate, the latter being defined variously by such terminology as: "single family dwellings," "owner-occupied single family dwellings," "one to four family dwellings," or "an owner-occupied one to six family residence." In any event, the legislation thus far has not attempted to regulate prepayment penalties in the context of the larger non-residential loan transactions.

Within the confines of the above qualifications, the legislation ranges from flat prohibitions on prepayment penalties to relatively mild codification of existing practices. For example, at one extreme is the Pennsylvania statute [1] which simply prohibits all prepayment penalties in residential mortgage obligations entered into after the effective date of the statute. New Jersey has similar legislation.[2] Illinois achieves the same practical effect by prohibiting prepayment penalties

§ 6.4   2. N.J.Stat.Ann. 46:10B–1, 10B–3.

1. 41 Pa.Stat. § 405.

in all residential mortgages carrying an interest rate in excess of 8%.[3] Since few, if any, such loans in today's market will have interest rates of 8% or lower, the legislation amounts to a flat prohibition on prepayment penalties in residential transactions. Missouri, on the other hand, prohibits the imposition of all prepayment penalties in residential real estate loans after five years from the date of the execution of the loan.[4] Michigan cuts off such penalties after three years for single family dwellings, but limits such charges within three years to 1% of the amount of any prepayment.[5] In New York, any mortgage loan made by a savings and loan association may be prepaid. However, the loan agreement may provide for a period during which prepayment may not be made without penalty. Where the mortgage loan is an owner-occupied one to six family residence, the penalties may be imposed only during the first year of the loan and may not exceed interest for a period of three months on the principal so prepaid, or interest for the remaining months in the first year, whichever is the lesser amount.[6] Similar New York legislation exists for mortgage loans made by mortgagees other than savings and loan associations.[7] Mississippi permits prepayment penalties as to single family dwellings under the following conditions: if prepayment is made during the first year of the loan, the prepayment charge is 5% of the mortgage amount; thereafter, the charge drops by 1% annually until after five years no penalty may be collected.[8]

The California legislation is perhaps the least stringent on the mortgagee.[9] Prepayment charges may be assessed with respect to mortgages on residential real estate of four units or less within the first five years. Within such period, 20% of the unpaid balance may be prepaid free of penalty within a twelve month period. However, the maximum charge on a prepayment in excess of the 20% amount is six months' interest. This legislation is similar to the regulation issued by the Federal Home Loan Bank Board (FHLBB) which governs all feder-

3. Ill.—S.H.A. ch. 17, § 6404(2)(a).

4. V.A.M.S. § 408.036. See also, V.A. M.S. § 408.234 (creates the right to prepay certain second mortgage loans, but is unclear as to whether prepayment charges are permitted.).

5. Mich.Comp.L.Ann. § 438.31c. Kansas prohibits any prepayment penalty in excess of 1.5% of the prepayment. Kan. Stat.Ann. 17–5512.

6. New York—McKinney's Banking Law § 393(2). See also R.I.Gen.Laws (1974), § 34–23–5.

7. New York—McKinney's Gen.Obl. Law § 5–501(3)(b). As to first mortgages on mortgagor-occupied dwellings of three or fewer families, Massachusetts permits up to three months' interest prepayment penalty for the first three years of the mortgage loan if the mortgagor refinances; prepayments for other reasons may be made with a maximum penalty of the lesser of three months' interest or the balance of the first year's interest. Apparently, after the first year of the loan prepayment for reasons other than to refinance may be made without penalty. Mass.Gen. L.Ann. c. 183, § 56.

8. Miss.Code (1974) § 75–17–1(11).

9. West's Ann.Cal.Civil Code § 2954.- 9(b). See also West's Ann.Cal.Bus. & Prof. Code § 10242.6 (same as to loans negotiated by real estate licensees, except that a 7 year period is used).

ally chartered savings and loan associations and, thus, to some extent, tends to codify existing practices.

The Mississippi type legislation appears to be the most satisfactory in taking into account the valid interests of both mortgagor and mortgagee. First, by permitting the imposition of a flexible prepayment penalty during the early years of the loan based on the age of the loan, it recognizes the mortgagee's interest in preventing the mortgagor from refinancing at lower rates and, in part, the mortgagee's interest in recouping some of the fixed cost that may otherwise accrue if prepayment is permitted with no penalty at all. On the other hand, by setting a fixed and relatively early time after which no penalty may be imposed, the legislation recognizes the fact that residential real estate is typically sold long before the maturity of the mortgage loan which financed its purchase and that prepayment of the loan is often merely incidental to the sale rather than a scheme to refinance because of falling interest rates. While one may argue whether the five year date, after which no penalty may be imposed, is appropriate, the concept underlying the statute is a desirable one. Many of the other statutes lack the sophistication of this approach. The flat prohibition of the Pennsylvania statute, for example, recognizes no legitimate mortgagee interest in utilizing a prepayment penalty. Moreover, the New York prohibition of prepayment penalties after one year is probably also too harsh on the mortgagee. On the other hand, the California six month interest penalty authorized for complete prepayment during the first five years is relatively severe on the mortgagor.

Some of the foregoing states that have general regulation of prepayment penalties in the residential setting, and a few states that do not, specifically regulate a variety of prepayment situations that do not arise from voluntary refinancing by the mortgagor. For example, both New York and Virginia prohibit the enforcement of a prepayment penalty, if the prepayment is triggered by the mortgagee's enforcement of a due on sale clause.[10] In addition, a few states prohibit the collection of a prepayment penalty where such penalty would be caused by the exercise of the eminent domain power.[11]

The Uniform Consumer Credit Code (UCCC), which is in effect in eleven states, prohibits the imposition of prepayment penalties, with some qualifications, on real estate loans for personal, family, household or agricultural purpose whose interest rates exceed 12% per annum. This legislation does not affect lending to commercial entities and,

10. See New York—McKinney's Real Prop.Law § 254–a; Va.Code 1975, § 6.1–330.33. The New York statute was upheld against a constitutional challenge in Rogers v. Williamsburgh Sav. Bank, 79 Misc.2d 852, 361 N.Y.S.2d 531 (1974).

11. Mass.Gen.Laws Ann. c. 183, § 57; West's Ann.Cal.Code of Civil Pro. § 1246.2;

Arizona requires reimbursement to the owner "to the extent [the acquiring agency] deems fair and reasonable * * * expenses [owner] necessarily incurred for * * * [p]enalty costs for prepayment of any preexisting recorded mortgage entered into in good faith encumbering such real property." Ariz.Rev.Stat. § 11–965.

because of the above interest rate provision, a significant amount of first mortgage residential lending.[12]

Finally, regulations issued by federal or quasi-federal agencies regulate or limit, to some extent, the imposition of prepayment penalties. Federal Reserve Regulation Z, enforcing the Federal Truth in Lending Act, requires virtually all mortgage lenders who loan money in the ordinary course of business to disclose to the mortgagor the terms, conditions and method of computation of any prepayment penalty imposed by the mortgagee.[13] As previously noted, a regulation of the Federal Home Loan Bank Board (FHLBB), which regulation governs all federally chartered savings and loan associations, limits those associations from imposing more than a six month interest penalty and permits penalty-free earlier prepayment of 20% of the loan balance in any twelve month period.[14] Since a good deal of residential lending is carried out by federally chartered savings and loan associations, the FHLBB regulation tends to set minimum national standards for prepayment penalties. On the other hand, to the extent that state legislation places heavier restrictions on the collection of prepayment charges, it is preempted by the FHLBB regulation.[15] The standard note form approved by the Federal Home Loan Mortgage Corporation (FHLMC) and the Federal National Mortgage Corporation (FNMA) both quasi-federal entities, permits prepayment without penalty.[16] This form has a significant impact on national standards because the above two entities require its use as a condition precedent to their purchase of mortgage loans on the secondary market. This is significant because many lending institutions sell their mortgages on this market. Moreover, prepayment penalties in mortgage loans guaranteed by the Veterans Administration and insured by the Federal Housing Administration are prohibited and the loans may be prepaid at any time.[17] Finally, prepayment without penalty is permitted under a variety of adjustable rate mortgages insured by or otherwise regulated by governmental or quasi-governmental agencies.[18]

12. U.C.C.C. § 2.509 (1974); the UCCC originally was promulgated in 1968 and, after intervening drafts, the 1974 UCCC was promulgated. The UCCC, in one of the foregoing versions, is in effect with a variety of modifications in at least eleven states including Oklahoma, Utah, Colorado, Idaho, Indiana, Wyoming, Kansas, Iowa, Maine, South Carolina and Wisconsin.

13. 12 CFR 226.8(b)(6).

14. See § 6.1, note 10 supra.

15. See Toolan v. Trevose Federal Savings & Loan Association, 501 Pa. 477, 462 A.2d 224 (1983).

16. The current FNMA–FHLMC form has been in use since January 1, 1980.

The prior form limits prepayment penalties to the first five years of the loan and permits imposition of a penalty in the first five only where the mortgagor prepays as a result of refinancing. FNMA currently does not enforce prepayment penalties in any mortgage it holds, while FHLMC continues to do so on its pre-1980 loans. See FNMA Conventional Home Mortgage Selling Contract Supplement § 301.05; FHLMC Servicers' Guide § 4.113.

17. See 38 CFR 36.4310; 24 CFR 203.22(b).

18. See § 11.4 infra.

§ 6.5 Prepayment Penalties—Collection Incident to Due-on-Sale Enforcement

Mortgagees sometimes attempt to collect prepayment penalties incident to due-on-sale clause enforcement. State law consistently has been unsympathetic to this type of "double dipping." As we have seen,[1] a few state statutes prohibit the enforcement of a prepayment penalty is triggered by the mortgagee's enforcement of a due-on-sale clause. Several courts have reached the same result without the benefit of a statute.[2] These cases reason that once a mortgagor has exercised the due-on-sale clause and accelerated the mortgage debt, payment by the mortgagor is then legally due and by definition cannot be a "prepayment."[3]

Moreover, a Federal Home Loan Bank Board regulation, promulgated in 1983, prohibits all lenders, whether federally chartered or not, from collecting prepayment penalties resulting from acceleration under due-on-sale clauses contained in loans secured by a home "occupied or to be occupied by the borrower."[4] This regulation is an outgrowth of the Garn-St. Germain Depository Institutions Act of 1982 (the "Act"), which, as we explored in detail earlier in this volume,[5] makes most due-on-sale clauses enforcible.

Interestingly, the Act contains no language giving the Board authority to extend the prepayment penalty prohibition to non-federally chartered lenders. The Board relied on a statement in the legislative history that referred to the need for uniform, homogeneous mortgage documents in the operation of an efficient secondary mortgage market.[6] While it is hard to quarrel with this goal, it is also hard to see how this rather ambiguous and insubstantial statement can authorize Board action that changes a type of mortgage clause never mentioned in the Act. Lenders are likely to attack the amended Regulation as *ultra vires,* and they may well succeed.

The regulation nevertheless is sound from a policy perspective. As the Board has pointed out, "[w]hile the ability to impose a prepayment

---

§ 6.5

1. See § 6.3 supra, note 10 and accompanying text.

2. See e.g., Tan v. California Federal Savings & Loan Association, 140 Cal.App. 3d 800, 809, 189 Cal.Rptr. 775, 782 (1983); Slevin Container Corp. v. Provident Federal Savings & Loan Association, 98 Ill.App. 3d 646, 648, 54 Ill.Dec. 189, 191, 424 N.E.2d 939, 941 (1981); American Federal Savings & Loan Association v. Mid-America Service Corp., 329 N.W.2d 124, 125–26 (S.D.1983).

3. Id.

4. 12 CFR 591.59(b)(2). For further consideration of the background of this regulation see Nelson and Whitman, Congressional Preemption of Mortgage Due-on-Sale Law: An Analysis of the Garn-St. Germain Act, 35 Hast.L.J. 241, 299–301 (1983).

5. See §§ 5.22–.26 supra.

6. Report of Sen.Comm. on Banking, Housing and Urban Affairs on S. 2879, S.Rep. No. 536, 97th Cong., 2d Sess. (1983) at 21.

or equivalent fee upon due-on-sale acceleration may be of some economic benefit to the lender, it is in no sense essential to effective use of the due-on-sale clause for the purpose of raising portfolio yields to current market rates." [7] Moreover, neither of the two reasons normally used to justify prepayment penalty provisions justify their use incident to due-on-sale enforcement. First, collection of the penalty is not, in this context, needed to "lock in" a loan that earns a higher than market interest rate. Except in the relatively rare situation in which the due-on-sale clause is invoked to prevent impairment of security, it is used when current market interest rates exceed the rate being paid by the mortgagor-transferor and any rational mortgagee would be only too delighted to accept a prepayment. Further, while any prepayment of the loan principal without collection of the penalty may frustrate the mortgagee's ability to recover fully the fixed cost of making the loan, such an argument is hardly persuasive when, in the due-on-sale context, it is the mortgagee rather than the mortgagor who is insisting on prepayment.

The foregoing regulation has not resolved all due-on-sale clause—prepayment problems. The Board has been troubled by whether borrowers should be required to pay prepayment charges when prepayment results from a threatened or anticipated, rather than an actual, due-on-sale acceleration. According to the Board, some lenders have increasingly attempted to collect such charges in the latter setting in order "to improve their weakened financial condition." [8] Accordingly, the Board has issued a proposed regulation which would not only prohibit collection of a prepayment charge incident to actual acceleration, but also if the lender "fails to consent within a reasonable time to the written request of a qualified purchaser * * * to assume the loan in accordance with its terms, and thereafter the borrower sells or transfers the security property to such purchaser and prepays the loan in full." [9]

 WESTLAW REFERENCES
due-on-sale /p pre-pay!
"garn-st. germain"

§ 6.6 Acceptance of Payment—Effect

It has long been established that payment [1] of the mortgage debt on "law day" will extinguish the mortgagee's security interest in the property and restore full legal ownership to the mortgagor without the necessity of a reconveyance, release or any other instrument being

7. 48 Fed.Reg. 21,560 (1983).

8. 49 Fed.Reg. 32,081 (1984).

9. 49 Fed.Reg. 32,083 (1984).

§ 6.6

1. Payment is here used in a broad and generic sense to include not only the doing of the very act the mortgage was given to secure, whether that act be payment of money or rendering some other performance, but also any other act the operative effect of which is to satisfy the mortgage obligation.

executed by the mortgagee.[2] And the same effect is given to payment which is accepted before the law day.[3]

In some respects it is outmoded to speak in terms of payment or tender on or after "law day." It is true that until the late 1930's many, if not most, mortgages called for the payment of all or substantially all of the payment of principal on a certain date. In the cases where this type of mortgage is still utilized, it can be said that there is a law day in the common law sense. However, with the advent of the evenly amortized long term installment mortgage in housing and other real estate financing transactions, the concept of the law day in the traditional sense is significantly less important.[4] Indeed, in a certain sense, the usual installment mortgage has a monthly law day and failure to pay on that monthly date can trigger a range of consequences from the imposition of a late payment charge[5] to the acceleration of the entire mortgage debt.[6] Once an acceleration has taken place perhaps the date of acceleration can be termed a "law day."

Moreover, when we talk today of payment or tender *after* law day, we very often have in mind payment or tender after an acceleration has occurred, but prior to a valid foreclosure. We will consider the consequences of acceleration in substantial detail in the following chapter.[7] In any event, we should view payment or tender after law day or after the "maturity date" of the obligation in the context of this and the foregoing paragraph. If we do, much of the case law in this area and the analysis in this and the succeeding section will be of continuing significance.

In title and intermediate jurisdictions payment after maturity does not by itself operate to revest title in the mortgagor because the concept of the title theory is that only prompt performance of the condition does that.[8] However, once the mortgagor pays, the mortgagee becomes a holder of the bare legal title in trust[9] for the mortgagor who can

---

2. In title states this is because the condition on which the conveyance was made is performed. "If the money is paid on the very day appointed for the payment of it, the condition is said to be performed, and the mortgagor, as in any other case where the grantee of land on condition performs the condition, may enter on the land and hold it, as of his former estate." Hargrave & Butler's Note to Coke upon Littleton, § 332. Munson v. Munson, 30 Conn. 425, 437 (1862), accord. In lien states since the mortgage lien is regarded as security only for the performance of an obligation, if the obligation is performed or satisfied in any way, the lien is automatically extinguished. Decker v. Decker, 64 Neb. 239, 89 N.W. 795 (1902); Bogert v. Bliss, 148 N.Y. 194, 42 N.E. 582, 51 Am.St. Rep. 684 (1896); Cumps v. Kiyo, 104 Wis. 656, 80 N.W. 937 (1899).

3. Holman v. Bailey, 44 Mass. (3 Metc.) 55 (1841); Cumps v. Kiyo, 104 Wis. 656, 80 N.W. 937 (1899), lien state, mortgage by deed absolute.

4. See § 1.1, supra.

5. See § 6.8, infra.

6. See § 7.6, infra.

7. See §§ 7.6–7.8, infra.

8. Phelps v. Sage, 2 Day 151 (Conn. 1805); Smith v. Vincent, 15 Conn. 1, 14, 38 Am.Dec. 52 (1842); Cross v. Robinson, 21 Conn. 379, 387 (1851). See Moore v. Norman, 43 Minn. 428, 45 N.W. 857, 9 L.R.A. 55, 19 Am.St.Rep. 247 (1890); Farmers Fire Insurance & Loan Co. v. Edwards, 26 Wend. 541 (N.Y.1841).

9. Palmer v. Uhl, 112 Conn. 125, 128, 151 A. 355, 356 (1930); Burroughs v. Garner. 43 Md.App. 302, 405 A.2d 301 (1979);

require a reconveyance on application to a court of equity.[10] Some courts have departed from the logic of the title concept to permit the mortgagor to recover possession from the mortgagee in an action at law[11] and to deny a similar recovery by the mortgagee from the mortgagor after the debt has been paid.[12] Statutes also have altered the rule as to revesting of title on late payment.[13]

In lien theory states, payment of the mortgage debt, whether made on, before, or after default, extinguishes the mortgage lien at law as well as in equity.[14] This flows from the view that a lien is security only for the performance of an act and if the act has been performed, nothing remains for the lien to secure, and it is therefore extinguished.[15]

However, even though payment may extinguish a mortgage, it usually has been recorded and thus it becomes necessary to have it discharged of record. This the mortgagor may compel the mortgagee to do by whatever means is required by the state where the real estate is located.[16] In some states, the mortgagor has a common law right to recover damages for mortgagee failure to cancel of record a satisfied mortgage.[17] For example, a mortgagor may have a common law breach of contract action based on explicit or, perhaps, implicit mortgage

Desiderio v. Iadonisi, 115 Conn. 652, 655, 163 A. 254, 255, 88 A.L.R. 1349 (1932); Cooper v. Cooper, 256 Ill. 160, 99 N.E. 871 (1912). See Stewart v. Crosby, 50 Me. 130, 134 (1863), approved in Hooper v. Bail, 133 Me. 412, 415, 179 A. 404, 405 (1935).

10. Kelly v. Martin, 107 Ala. 479, 18 So. 132 (1894); Town of Clinton v. Town of Westbrook, 38 Conn. 9 (1871); Parsons v. Welles, 17 Mass. 419 (1821); Stewart v. Crosby, 50 Me. 130 (1863); Gardner v. Buckeye Savings & Loan Co., 108 W.Va. 673, 152 S.E. 530, 78 A.L.R. 1 (1930) accord. And see Holman v. Bailey, 44 Mass. (3 Metc.) 55 (1841).

11. E.g., Perkins' Lessee v. Dibble, 10 Ohio, 433, 434, 440, 36 Am.Dec. 97 (1841).

12. See Stewart v. Crosby, 50 Me. 130, 134 (1863); Baker v. Gavitt, 128 Mass. 93 (1880). Cf., Pollock v. Maison, 41 Ill. 516 (1866).

13. See, e.g., Code of Ala., Tit. 47 § 181. "Alabama nominally classifies itself as a 'title' state, * * * Hence, the necessity for our defeasance statute." Lloyd's of London v. Fidelity Securities Corp., 39 Ala. App. 596, 105 So.2d 729, 733 (1958).

14. McMillan v. Richards, 9 Cal. 365, 70 Am.Dec. 655 (1858); Hendricks v. Hess, 112 Minn. 252, 127 N.W. 995 (1910); Tobin v. Tobin, 139 Wis. 494, 121 N.W. 144 (1909); Decker v. Decker, 64 Neb. 239, 89 N.W. 795 (1902); Wakefield v. Day, 41 Minn. 344, 43 N.W. 71 (1889); Nilson v. Sarment, 153 Cal. 524, 530, 96 P. 315, 317, 126 Am.St.Rep. 91 (1908).

15. "The debt, in the eye of the law, thus becomes the principal, and the landed security merely appurtenant and secondary; * * * Acceptance of payment of the amount due on a mortgage, at any time before foreclosure, has always been held to discharge the incumbrance on the land * * *" Kortright v. Cady, 21 N.Y. 343, 347, 78 Am.Dec. 145 (1860). See Caruthers v. Humphrey, 12 Mich. 270 (1864), accord.

16. See 78 A.L.R. 24, 101 (1932). A tender conditioned upon the execution of a release, etc., is a proper tender. Harding v. Home Investment & Savings Co., 49 Idaho 64, 286 P. 920 (1930) rehearing denied, 49 Idaho 75, 297 P. 1101 (1931); Wallowa Lake Amusement Co. v. Hamilton, 70 Or. 433, 142 P. 321 (1914).

17. Tenneco Oil Co. v. Clevenger, 363 So.2d 316 (Ala.App.1978); Skorpios Properties, Limited v. Waage, 172 Conn. 152, 374 A.2d 165 (1976); Mickie v. McGehee, 27 Tex. 134 (1881); Knox v. Farmers State Bank of Merkel, 7 S.W.2d 918 (Tex.Civ. App.1928), commented on in 7 Tex.L.Rev. 323 (1929). Contra: Hasquet v. Big West Oil Co., 29 F.2d 78 (C.C.A.Mont.1928).

language obligating the mortgagee to deliver a prompt release.[18] More-over, in a large number of states, statutes afford the mortgagor a cause of action and impose penalties on a mortgagee who refuses to give a release, satisfaction, reconveyance or whatever is necessary to establish a clear record title.[19] In addition, there is case law that the statutory remedy is not exclusive and to the extent that common law remedies exist, they represent a valid alternative for the mortgagor.[20] This issue becomes significant where the mortgagor suffers substantial damages because of the mortgagee's recalcitrance and the statutory remedy, as is sometimes the case, provides for nominal damages only.[21]

 WESTLAW REFERENCES
"law day" /p pay! paid tender
266k298

§ 6.7 Tender on or After Maturity

Proper tender [1] on the law day, though not accepted, discharges the mortgage in title and lien states [2] but it does not affect the obligation secured [3] except to stop the accumulation of interest and prevent the

---

18. See e.g., Skorpios Properties, Limited v. Waage, 172 Conn. 152, 374 A.2d 165 (1976); Dugan v. Grzybowski, 165 Conn. 173, 332 A.2d 97 (1973).

19. See, e.g., Ala.Code (1975), § 35–10–30; Conn.Gen.Stat.Ann. § 49–8; O.C.G.A. § 44–14–3; 27 Vt.Stat.Ann. § 464; Mass. Gen.Laws Ann. c. 183, § 55; Reissue Neb. Rev.Stat.1943, § 76–255; Mitchell v. Oliver, 254 Ga. 112, 327 S.E.2d 216 (1985); Mr. U Inc. v. Mobil Oil Corp., 197 Neb. 612, 249 N.W.2d 909 (1977).

20. See Tenneco Oil Co. v. Clevenger, 363 So.2d 316 (Ala.App.1978); Skorpios Properties, Limited v. Waage, 172 Conn. 152, 374 A.2d 165 (1976). But see Taylor v. Taylor, 5 Mass.App.Ct. 844, 363 N.E.2d 1342 (1977) (statute constitutes sole remedy).

21. See e.g., Ala.Code 1975, § 35–10–30 ($200); Conn.Gen.Stat.Ann. § 49–8 ($1,000).

§ 6.7

1. What constitutes a proper tender is, for the most part, a matter of general law not peculiar to mortgages. For a recent definition, however, consider the following: "A tender is more than a mere offer to pay. It is an offer to perform coupled with the present ability of immediate performance, so were it not for the refusal of cooperation by the party to whom the tender is made, the condition or obligation would be immediately satisfied. A tender is the offer of a sum of money in satisfaction of a debt and is made by producing and showing the amount to the creditor and expressing verbally a willingness to pay it." Mr. U Inc. v. Mobil Oil Corp., 197 Neb. 612, 617, 249 N.W.2d 909, 912 (1977). See also, Owens v. Idaho First National Bank, 103 Idaho 465, 649 P.2d 1221 (App.1982) (mere spoken offer to pay insufficient; rather "actual present physical offer" required). Harpe v. Stone, 212 Ga. 341, 92 S.E.2d 522 (1956), noted by Loiseaux, Security Transactions, in Annual Survey of Georgia Law, June 1, 1955—June 1, 1956, 8 Mercer L.Rev. 144, 149 (1956), held that where the amount due on a debt is in dispute, the mortgagor must tender at least the amount admittedly due, even if the creditor is demanding more than that amount.

2. Mr. U Inc. v. Mobil Oil Corp., 197 Neb. 612, 249 N.W.2d 909 (1977); Security State Bank v. Waterloo Lodge, 85 Neb. 255, 122 N.W. 992 (1909); Depon v. Shawye, 263 Mass. 206, 161 N.E. 243 (1928); see Security State Bank v. Waterloo Lodge, 85 Neb. 255, 122 N.W. 992 (1909); West's Ann.Cal. Civ.Code §§ 1504, 2909. See also 93 A.L.R. 12, 25, 31 (1934). If the mortgagee waives payment at maturity it is not certain that a tender at a later date, in reliance on the waiver, will extinguish the mortgage although it will stop interest and costs on the debt. Wood v. Babb, 16 S.C. 427 (1882).

3. See Williston, Contracts, 3d Ed.1959, § 1817; Co.Lit. 209a, 209b; Bacon's Abridgment, title Tender (f); Dixon v. Clark, 5 C.B. 365, 377 (1848).

debtor from being liable for costs, at least if the tender is kept good.[4] Although it is commonly said that such a tender constitutes performance of the condition,[5] this obviously is not so. A more accurate statement would be that, the performance of the condition having been prevented by the mortgagee's refusal to accept payment, it will be excused.

Where tender is made after maturity, in states following the title theory of mortgages it does not extinguish the mortgage lien if the mortgagee refuses to accept it.[6] The courts in these states reason logically, if technically, that a mortgage is an absolute conveyance defeasible by performance of a condition subsequent in the manner and at the time stipulated for in the defeasance, i.e., the law day. In case of nonperformance the mortgagee's estate becomes absolute, and it cannot thereafter be divested even by a full payment of the mortgage debt. It follows as an obvious consequence that mere tender should not be given greater effect than actual payment. The mortgagor's only remedy, except insofar as she may have relief by statute, is in equity by a bill to redeem.[7] In a few states professing to accept the title theory a tender after maturity suspends the mortgagee's right to exercise a power of sale if the mortgage contains one, a result substantially impairing the mortgagee's security.[8]

In lien jurisdictions the weight of authority is that an unaccepted tender made after default discharges the mortgage lien.[9] There are,

---

4. Lutton v. Rodd, 2 Cas.Ch. 206 (1675), "the plaintiff ought to make oath that the money was kept, and no profit made of it"; Bank of New South Wales v. O'Connor, 14 Ann.Cas. 273 (1889); see Gyles v. Hall, 2 P.Wms. 378 (1726); Crain v. McGoon, 86 Ill. 431, 29 Am.Rep. 37 (1877). See also Note, Comparison of California Mortgages, Trust Deeds and Land Sale Contracts, 7 U.C.L.A.L.Rev. 83 (1960).

5. E.g., "Tender of the mortgage debt on the day named is performance of the condition, and, by force of the terms of the condition, determines the estate of the mortgagee, and the condition being complied with, the land reverts to the mortgagor by the simple operation of the condition." Shields v. Lozear, 34 N.J.L. 496, 504, 3 Am.St.Rep. 256 (1869).

6. Shields v. Lozear, 34 N.J.L. 496 (1869), is the leading case. Davis v. Ashburn, 224 Ala. 572, 574, 141 So. 226, 227 (1932); Stockton v. Dundee Manufacturing Co., 22 N.J.Eq. 56 (1871); Sandler v. Green, 287 Mass. 404, 407, 192 N.E. 39, 41 (1934); Maynard v. Hunt, 22 Mass. (5 Pick.) 240 (1827), accord. See 94 A.L.R. 25–30 (1934).

7. For clear statements of the rationale of tender after the law day in title jurisdic-

tions, see Moore v. Norman, 43 Minn. 428, 45 N.W. 857, 9 L.R.A. 55, 19 Am.St.Rep. 247 (1890); Shields v. Lozear, note 73, supra; Farmers' Fire Insurance & Loan Co. v. Edwards, 26 Wend. 541 (N.Y.1841). See also 93 A.L.R. 12, 15, 25 (1934).

8. Garrett v. Cobb, 202 Ala. 241, 80 So. 79 (1918); Greer v. Turner, 36 Ark. 17 (1880); Wingert v. Brewer, 116 Md. 518, 82 A. 157 (1911); Tonkel v. Shields, 125 Miss. 461, 87 So. 646 (1921). See Wickhem, Tender in Security Transactions, 27 Iowa L.Rev. 579, 593 (1942); 1934, 93 A.L.R. 12, 30. Contra: Cranston v. Crane, 97 Mass. 459, 93 Am.Dec. 106 (1867); Debnam v. Watkins, 178 N.C. 238, 100 S.E. 336 (1919).

9. Kortright v. Cady, 21 N.Y. 343 (1860), is the leading case. Caruthers v. Humphrey, 12 Mich. 270 (1864), accord. See 93 A.L.R. 31 (1934). Bowman v. Poole, 212 Ga. 261, 91 S.E.2d 770 (1956), noted by Loiseaux, Security Transactions, in Annual Survey of Georgia Law June 1, 1955—June 1, 1956, 8 Mercer L.Rev. 144, 150 (1956), held that a proper tender by a second mortgagee, which was refused, discharged the first mortgage and invalidated the deed executed by the first mortgagee to himself under a foreclosure sale.

however, several lien jurisdictions that hold such a tender does not affect it.[10] And in some states the rule is not settled.[11]

Reasons given for the majority rule begin with the nature of the mortgage in lien states as contrasted with title states. Unlike a title theory mortgage, the lien mortgage technically remains the same after default as on or before the due day. Failure to perform at maturity does not vest indefeasibly any legal or other interest in the mortgagee as it does in title states. In contrast to a common law mortgage, payment after the law day extinguishes the mortgage just as does payment on the law day. This being so, there is no ground for not giving the same effect to tender made after default as is given to tender on the due day. If it is fair to deprive the mortgagee of his security when he refuses to accept a performance on the law day, it is equally fair to do so when he refuses a performance which would have that effect at a later time. The foregoing reasoning, while logical, does not get to the merits of the rule anymore than does the rule to the opposite effect in title jurisdictions. Each is based on its own conceptual view of the mortgage.

As a practical matter, the major problem with failing to discharge the mortgage on tender boils down to a question of hardship. The hardship problem consists of two factors: (1) the marketability of the mortgagor's property is impaired by the cloud upon it of the continuing lien and (2) she remains exposed to the danger of foreclosure. As to the first, the answer is that almost invariably a mortgage is recorded and, as such, it constitutes as much of a practical cloud on marketability as does the existence of the lien itself. Moreover, no jurisdiction, even though holding that the substantive lien is gone, will give the mortgagor affirmative relief without payment to the mortgagee or into court in a proceeding which is equivalent to an action to redeem.[12] The mortgagor is always at liberty to bring such an action. Further, not only is the ordinary action in equity available for this purpose, but many states have enacted statutes giving summary relief so as to minimize hardship that might result from the slower equity action.

---

10. E.g., Keese v. Parnell, 134 S.C. 207, 132 S.E. 620 (1925); but cf. Peoples National Bank of Greenville v. Upchurch, 183 S.C. 147, 153, 190 S.E. 515, 518 (1937), holding mortgage lien discharged if mortgagor pays money into court. See 93 A.L.R. 12, 38–45 (1934).

11. E.g., Perre v. Castro, 14 Cal. 519, 76 Am.Dec. 444 (1860), and Himmelmann v. Fitzpatrick, 50 Cal. 650 (1875), hold that the mortgage is not discharged. Wiemeyer v. Southern Trust & Commerce Bank, 107 Cal.App. 165, 173, 290 P. 70, 73 (1930), holds that it is. And see Walker v. Houston, 215 Cal. 742, 746, 12 P.2d 952, 87 A.L.R. 937 (1932). See 3 Cal.L.Rev. 336 (1915). See also 93 A.L.R. 12, 46–49 (1934).

12. Tender cannot be made the basis of an action to cancel a mortgage or for other affirmative relief in equity. Cowles v. Marble, 37 Mich. 158 (1877); Tuthill v. Morris, 81 N.Y. 94 (1880); Nelson v. Loder, 132 N.Y. 288, 30 N.E. 369 (1892); McClellan v. Coffin, 93 Ind. 456 (1883); Murray v. O'Brien, 56 Wash. 361, 105 P. 840, 28 L.R.A.,N.S., 998 (1910). See 10 Col.L.Rev. 252 (1910); 93 A.L.R. 12, 53 (1934); L.R.A.1918C, 186. See also the analogous situation as to the mortgagee in possession in lien states, § 4.26, supra. Cf. also § 6.9, infra.

These provide for a short form petition which will result in an order for cancellation of debt and mortgage on the mortgagor paying the money into court.[13] These statutes are in addition to the statutes mentioned earlier giving to the mortgagor a right to damages against a mortgagee who refuses to execute a release, etc., on payment.[14] The availability of such remedies which enable the mortgagor to end any possibility of foreclosure by the mortgagee answers the second objection. Additionally, if the foreclosure is by court action she always can end it by paying into court the amount of the debt.

The strongest argument in favor of the majority rule was advanced by a leading case as follows: "It is not perceived how the mortgagee is to be embarrassed, or his security impaired by the adoption of this rule. * * * If the mortgagor does not tender the full amount due, the lien of the mortgage is not extinguished. The mortgagee runs no risk in accepting the tender. If it is the full amount due, his mortgage lien is extinguished. * * * His acceptance of the money tendered, if inadequate and less than the amount actually due, only extinguishes the lien pro tanto, and the mortgage remains intact for the residue." [15]

In general this provides a sufficient answer to the claim that the rule is unfair in contrast to the rule of discharge by tender on the law day because at that time the mortgagee would "have anticipated payment and * * * have prepared himself to state the account accurately" [16] whereas at a later time he might not be ready with an exact computation of the amount due at that particular moment.[17] However, this is not the only question. The real question is whether, even if the mortgagee will not be harmed by taking whatever payment is offered, the penalty for his failure to do so should be the drastic one of losing his substantive rights in the security.

Courts in which the majority rule is thoroughly established nevertheless have placed far-reaching restrictions upon the doctrine. The most important of these has already been mentioned. It is the generally held rule that if the mortgagor is seeking affirmative relief, e.g., to remove the cloud of the mortgage on his title or to restrain the exercise of a power of sale, he must "do equity" by paying the principal and, at least, the interest and costs accruing up to the time of tender.[18] In addition, the mortgagee's refusal must be absolute and not in good faith; [19] the proof of a proper tender must be very clear and satisfacto-

13. E.g., New York Real Prop. Actions and Proceedings Law § 1921; McKinney's Consol.Laws of N.Y.Book. 49½.

14. See note 11, § 6.5 supra.

15. Kortright v. Cady, 21 N.Y. 343, 354 (1860).

16. Crain v. McGoon, 86 Ill. 431, 434, 29 Am.Rep. 37 (1877).

17. See Hudson Brothers Commission Co. v. Glencoe Sand & Gravel Co., 140 Mo.

103, 41 S.W. 450, 62 Am.St.Rep. 722 (1897); Crain v. McGoon, note 83, supra.

18. Note 12, supra.

19. Myer v. Hart, 40 Mich. 517, 29 Am. Rep. 553 (1879); see Lanier v. Mandeville Mills, 183 Ga. 716, 720, 189 S.E. 532, 535 (1937). Cf. Easton v. Littooy, 91 Wash. 648, 654, 158 P. 531, 533 (1916). See 93 A.L.R. 12, 67 (1934).

ry;[20] and the tender must be unconditional, although on this last point there is a dispute.[21] Furthermore only the mortgagor or an assuming grantee can take advantage of the rule; a non-assuming grantee, cannot.[22] Also, unless the tender is kept good, the mortgagor must pay interest accruing thereafter.[23]

Moreover, in some states for a tender to discharge a mortgage when it is refused it must be kept good.[24] There is some authority that seems to limit this requirement to a tender after the law day [25] but some cases apply it to a tender on the law day.[26] It has been argued that such a requirement is in effect a negation of the rule that tender will operate to discharge a mortgage because until "some action has been brought arising out of the debt or the mortgage and it is shown that the tender has been kept good and the money has been paid into court" [27] the lien cannot be regarded as discharged. The obvious answer is that the same could be said of the requirement of a tender. Until the fact has been established by an action, it cannot be said with certainty that it has discharged the mortgage even if tender was all that the law requires. Of greater validity is the observation that if this is made a requirement, so far as the mortgagor is concerned, the rule operates substantially the same as title states principle which holds that the mortgage persists in spite of a tender after default until ended by an action to redeem in which she must tender payment. There is one difference which the statement does not take into account. The

20. See Engle v. Hall, 45 Mich. 57, 58, 7 N.W. 239 (1880); Hayward v. Chase, 181 Mich. 614, 618, 148 N.W. 214, 215–216 (1914).

21. There is some authority that a tender on condition that the mortgagee give a release or a receipt in full is effective to discharge the mortgage. E.g., Wallowa Lake Amusement Co. v. Hamilton, 70 Or. 433, 142 P. 321 (1914). See 93 A.L.R. 12, 74 (1934).

22. Harris v. Jex, 66 Barb. 232 (N.Y.1873), affirmed 55 N.Y. 421, 14 Am.R. 285. See L.R.A., 1918C, 186. As to the place of tender and party to whom it should be made, see Weyand v. Park Terrace Co., 202 N.Y. 231, 95 N.E. 723, 36 L.R.A.,N.S., 308, Ann.Cas.1912D, 1010 (1911); Hopkins Manufacturing Co. v. Ketterer, 237 Pa. 285, 85 A. 421, Ann.Cas. 1914B, 558 (1912). Bowman v. Poole, 212 Ga. 261, 91 S.E.2d 770 (1956), noted by Loiseaux, Security Transactions, in Annual Survey of Georgia Law, June 1, 1955—June 1, 1956, 8 Mercer L.Rev. 144, 150 (1956), held that a second mortgagee by a proper tender which was refused could discharge a first mortgage.

23. Nelson v. Loder, 132 N.Y. 288, 30 N.E. 369 (1892). See 93 A.L.R. 12, 53 (1934); 39 Yale L.J. 434, 435 (1930).

24. Crain v. McGoon, 86 Ill. 431, 29 Am. Rep. 37 (1877); "In order that the tender may extinguish the mortgage lien, it must be kept up, * * * which is practically much the same thing as a bill in equity by the mortgagor or those holding under him to redeem." Knollenberg v. Nixon, 171 Mo. 445, 455, 72 S.W. 41, 44, 94 Am.St.Rep. 790 (1902). See Williston, Contracts, Rev. Ed., § 1816; 12 A.L.R. 938 (1921); 93 A.L.R. 12, 50 (1934). Cf., Nelson v. Loder, 132 N.Y. 288, 30 N.E. 369 (1892), tender must be kept good to prevent liability for subsequently accruing interest.

25. E.g., Crain v. McGoon, 86 Ill. 431, 29 Am.Rep. 37 (1877). See Wickhem, Tender in Security Transactions, 27 Iowa L.Rev. 579, 594 (1942); 93 A.L.R. 12, 52 (1934).

26. E.g., see White v. Eddy, 202 Ala. 672, 81 So. 628 (1919). But see, Mitchell v. Roberts, 17 F. 776, 5 McCrary 425 (C.C.A. Ark.1883); Balme v. Wambaugh, 16 Minn. 116, Gil. 106 (1870). See also Storke and Sears, Discharge of Security Transactions, 26 Rocky Mt.L.Rev. 115, 123 (1954).

27. 93 A.L.R. 12, 50 (1934).

tender and payment into court will operate to end all power of the mortgagee to foreclose the mortgage without the mortgagor taking any additional affirmative ction. Under the other rule the mortgagor must actively bring an action to redeem or to clear her title. The difference is not, however, substantial. If the mortgagor has to put up her money she will want to go ahead and finish the business which will necessitate bringing suit. Moreover, even though the act of tendering followed by payment into court may have destroyed a mortgagee's rights, judicial action is frequently necessary to prevent the attempted exercise of invalid claims by persons who nevertheless persist in asserting them.

WESTLAW REFERENCES

di tender

tender /p default! /p discharg! /p mortgag!

374k11

cloud /p mortgag! /p discharg!

266k301

mortgag** /p refus! accept! /s tender % chattel

266k401(5)

---

§ 6.8   Late Payment Charges—Introduction

A common practice in installment type mortgages is for mortgagees to require the payment of "late payment charges" or "delinquency payments" on the failure of the mortgagor to tender timely payment of a mortgage loan installment.[1] The amount of these charges varies but they are often computed in terms of a fixed percentage either of the principal amount owing or of the late installment. Sometimes the charge is simply a fixed dollar amount, but more commonly it is stated in terms of the lesser or greater of a percentage or a fixed dollar amount. Typically, for example, a late charge might be stated as "2% of the late installment or $5 whichever is the greater." Less common today, would be a charge of "additional interest at the rate of 2% per annum on the unpaid balance of this note from the date unpaid interest started to accrue until the close of the business day upon which payment curing the default is received."[2]

WESTLAW REFERENCES

late delinquen! /5 payment charge /p mortgag**

---

§ 6.8

1. See Comment, Late-Payment Charges: Meeting the Requirements of Liquidated Damages, 27 Stan.L.Rev. 1133, 1133 n. 1 (1975).

2. Garrett v. Coast and Southern Federal Savings & Loan Association, 9 Cal.3d 731, 108 Cal.Rptr. 845, 848, 511 P.2d 1197, 1199 (1973). A 1969 survey of late payment charges among California savings and loan associations indicated that a majority of the associations (113) charged between 1% and 10% of the monthly installment as the late payment charge, 21 charged 1% of the unpaid principal balance, and 11 charged a flat fee, usually $5. Id. at 738 n. 6, 108 Cal.Rptr. at 853, 511 P.2d at 1204.

§ 6.9 Late Payment Charges—Judicial Interpretation

There traditionally have been two judicial approaches taken toward late payment charges; they are somewhat contradictory in language, if not in theory. Some courts have taken the position that these provisions should be viewed as attempts to provide for liquidated damages and the question in those cases is whether the charge constitutes valid liquidated damages or an invalid penalty.[1] In some of these cases, the court found no invalid "penalty" because the charge was determined to be "increased interest" or an "alternative method of performance."[2] On the other hand, late payment charges are sometimes conceptualized as agreements for additional interest and thus are subjected to analysis under usury principles.[3] In so doing, language difficulties arise. For example, some courts, in upholding late charges against the usury attack, have taken the view that such charges are in the nature of "penalties" for delinquency or non-performance and therefore not usurious.[4] According to the reasoning of these cases, the term "penalty" presumably has a lawful connotation and therefore should not be interpreted as being an "invalid penalty" instead of valid "liquidated damages."

The only major case to confront the above inconsistencies is Clermont v. Secured Investment Corp.,[5] a California appellate decision. There plaintiffs, in a class action, challenged the imposition of a late payment charge of 1% of the original amount of the loan or $45, whichever was smaller. The plaintiffs contended that while there were cases holding that such charges were not interest and thus not usurious, and while there were other cases holding that such charges were not valid liquidated damages within sections 1670–71 of the Civil Code,[6] such charges had to be either interest or liquidated damages. Thus, plaintiffs argued, such clauses had to be invalid either as usurious or as

---

§ 6.9

1. See Clermont v. Secured Investment Corp., 25 Cal.App.3d 766, 102 Cal.Rptr. 340 (2nd Dist.1972); Garrett v. Coast and Southern Federal Savings & Loan Association, 9 Cal.3d 731, 108 Cal.Rptr. 845, 511 P.2d 1197 (1973).

2. See e.g., Walsh v. Glendale Federal Savings & Loan Association, 1 Cal.App.3d 578, 81 Cal.Rptr. 804 (2nd Dist.1969); O'Conner v. Richmond Savings & Loan Association, 262 Cal.App.2d 523, 68 Cal.Rptr. 882 (1st Dist.1968).

3. See Annot., 63 A.L.R.3d 50, 61 (1975); Randall v. Home Loan & Investment Co., 244 Wis. 623, 12 N.W.2d 915 (1944).

4. See, e.g., Hayes v. First National Bank, 507 S.W.2d 701 (Ark.1974); First American Title Insurance & Trust Co. v. Cook, 12 Cal.App.3d 592, 90 Cal.Rptr. 645 (1970).

5. 25 Cal.App.3d 766, 102 Cal.Rptr. 340 (2nd Dist.1972).

6. West's Ann.Cal.Civ.Code § 1670 provides:

"Every contract by which the amount of damage to be paid, or other compensation to be made, for breach of an obligation, is determined in anticipation thereof, is to that extent void, except as expressly provided in the next section."

West's Ann.Cal.Civ.Code § 1671 provides:

"The parties to a contract may agree therein upon an amount which shall be presumed to be the amount of damage sustained by a breach thereof when, from the nature of the case, it would be impracticable or extremely difficult to fix the actual damage."

invalid penalties. The court concurred in recognizing the inconsistency of the prior cases and held that the charge constituted a liquidated damages provision. The court noted that this was a contractually established fee, based strictly on the size of the loan and charged in every instance of tardiness, regardless of the length. "We fail to see how this fixed fee can be characterized as anything but an attempt to provide for liquidated damages."[7] The court then acknowledged that its reasoning was in "apparent conflict" with the California usury line of cases but it noted that these were decided before passage of the usury law or involved exempt lenders. "While the late charge here * * * must constitute either damages or interest, it may not * * * constitute both."[8] Having determined that the clause was a liquidated damages provision, the court believed it was unnecessary to look at the usury allegation and remanded the case for a determination of the liquidated damages issue.

The leading late payment case, Garrett v. Coast & Southern Federal Savings & Loan Association,[9] accepted the *Clermont* characterization of the late charge. There a class action challenged a late payment fee of 2% per annum assessed against the principal balance. The California Supreme Court rejected the mortgagee's argument that to the extent that the late payment provision required the payment of additional interest, it merely gave the mortgagor the option of an alternative performance of the obligation. The court determined that the only reasonable interpretation of the provision was that the parties had agreed on a basic interest rate that would govern the transaction, and that, recognizing that the mortgagors might fail to make prompt payment, the parties agreed, in addition, that mortgagors were to pay an extra amount as damages for their breach. Since the late payment charge was assessed only after a default, it was invalid unless it qualified as liquidated damages. The court further determined that the parties "made no 'reasonable endeavor * * * to estimate a fair average compensation for any loss that might be sustained' by the delinquency in the payment of the installment."[10] The purpose of such charges, the court concluded, is twofold: (1) to compensate the mortgagee for his administrative expenses and the cost of money wrongfully withheld and (2) to encourage the mortgagor to make timely installment payments.[11] According to the court, if the charge imposed on the mortgagor exceeds substantially the mortgagee's damages, the charge represents an invalid attempt to impose a penalty. While the court recognized that a valid late payment charge can be fixed in advance if the mortgagee can show the damages to be "extremely difficult" or "impracticable" to fix for purposes of sections 1670–71 of the Civil Code,

7. 25 Cal.App.3d at 768, 102 Cal.Rptr. at 342.

8. Id.

9. 9 Cal.3d 731, 108 Cal.Rptr. 845, 511 P.2d 1197 (1973).

10. Id. at 739, 511 P.2d at 1206, 108 Cal. Rptr. at 854.

11. Id.

it held that a *charge measured against the unpaid principal balance* was punitive and invalid.[12]

In cases from other jurisdictions, the usury approach has had mixed results. For example, where contract purchasers of a mobile home asserted as a defense to a replevin action that a late charge, equal to the lesser of $5 or 5% of any late payment, rendered the transaction usurious, the Arkansas Supreme Court held that such charges were free from usury because the purchaser had it in his power to avoid the penalty by paying the debt.[13] On the other hand, the Supreme Judicial Court of Massachusetts held that a note secured by a junior mortgage on real estate was usurious because it treated as interest a late payment charge of 5% of an unpaid installment if it was not paid within five days of its due date and 15% if not paid within ten days of that date.[14] The court rejected the Arkansas approach that "late charges * * * do not have to pass muster under usury statutes because the [mortgagor] can avoid them by discharging the debt in a timely manner. This argument assumes that persons who do not make timely payments are financially able to do so, but voluntarily choose not to."[15] The Wisconsin Supreme Court, in Randall v. Home Loan Investment Co.,[16] utilized a different usury theory in sustaining a late payment charge. In this case, one of the few non-California late payment decisions involving real estate, the late charge was 1% of the monthly installment. If this charge had been considered as interest, the total interest rate would have been usurious. The court sustained the late payment charge by applying the concept that a provision for an interest rate higher after maturity than would be permissible prior thereto, does not render a loan usurious. Applying this notion to the usual installment mortgage, however, seems questionable because, although late charges are routinely collected after a default in a monthly installment, there usually is not an acceleration resulting in the "maturity" of the entire debt. On the other hand, in Louisiana, a series of recent cases in the chattel security area, have held late charges invalid on a usury theory.[17] For example, one of these decisions has stated it to be "settled law in Louisiana that late charges or bonus payments for extension of an indebtedness are tantamount to interest payments and are usurious if they exceed the legal maximum."[18]

Although, nationwide, there are relatively few decisions regarding late payment charges, certain observations are, nevertheless, justified.

12. Id.

13. Hayes v. First National Bank, 507 S.W.2d 701 (Ark.1974).

14. Begelfer v. Najarian, 381 Mass. 177, 409 N.E.2d 167 (1980).

15. Id. at 172.

16. 244 Wis. 623, 12 N.W.2d 915 (1944).

17. See Gordon Finance Co. v. Chambliss, 236 So.2d 533 (La.App.1970), certiorari denied 256 La. 869, 239 So.2d 364 (1970); Thrift Funds of Baton Rouge, Inc. v. Jones, 274 So.2d 150 (La.1973), certiorari denied 414 U.S. 820, 94 S.Ct. 115, 38 L.Ed.2d 53 (1973).

18. Consolidated Loans, Inc. v. Smith, 190 So.2d 522, 527 (La.App.1966), application denied 249 La. 753, 190 So.2d 913 (1966).

First, while the California "liquidated damages-penalty" approach is based on specific California statutes, a similar common law approach should be applicable to challenge late charges there or elsewhere. For example, Professor Corbin has stated the general common law rule that to sustain "the payment of a definite sum as a liquidation of damages, it is necessary that at the time the contract is made it must appear that the injury that will be caused by breach will be difficult of estimation." [19] Second, the usury argument will be difficult to sustain, in part because the often harsh penalties imposed on usurious transactions, such as total loss of interest or, sometimes, principal, make courts reticent to take a broad view of the usury approach.[20]

Finally, some generalizations are appropriate as to which type of late payment clauses are most likely to be sustained. Late charges that are a substantial fixed lump sum or are calculated as a percentage of the principal balance of the loan will, at best, be suspect, because they bear no rational connection to the mortgagee's actual damages caused by late payment.[21] In the average residential mortgage transaction, the administrative costs caused by a late payment are relatively small and the same for all loans. "The components of servicing a late payment consist of the employee and computer time involved in adjusting the borrower's file to reflect the default and charge, plus the material cost of computer card, envelope, stamp and notice form." [22] One commentator has estimated such administrative cost at less than $5 per late payment, an amount that will rise to some extent with inflation.[23] The mortgagee also deserves to be reimbursed for the interest that would have been earned on the installment had it been paid promptly.[24] To the extent that a mortgagee relies on the above two factors in establishing that its late charge approximates its actual loss, the less inclined a court will be to invalidate it, whatever the legal theory utilized in attacking it.

 WESTLAW REFERENCES

late delinquen! /5 payment charge /p penalty /p mortgag**
    loan

late delinquen! /5 payment charge /p usur! /p mortgag**

---

19. 5 A. Corbin, Corbin on Contracts § 1060 (1964).

20. See Comment, Secured Real Estate Loan Prepayment and the Prepayment Penalty, 51 Cal.L.Rev. 923, 927–28 (1963).

21. Compare Sybron Corp. v. Clark Hospital Supply Corp., 76 Cal.App.3d 896, 143 Cal.Rptr. 306 (1978) ($100,000 lump sum late payment invalidated) with Fox v. Federated Department Stores, Inc., 156 Cal.

Rptr. 893, 94 Cal.App.3d 867 (1979) (late payment of 1½% of installment due upheld).

22. Comment, Late-Payment Charges: Meeting the Requirements of Liquidated Damages, 27 Stan.L.Rev. 1133, 1141 (1975).

23. Id. at 1141.

24. Id. at 1141.

§ 6.10 Late Payment Charges—Legislative and Other Regulatory Impact

An increasing number of state legislatures are regulating late payment charges. To some extent, the *Garrett* philosophy is reflected in this legislation because one common feature to such legislation is that any percentage utilized in determining a valid late payment charge is calculated on the amount of the late installment, rather than on the principal balance of the loan.

The Uniform Consumer Credit Code (UCCC), which is in effect in at least eleven states, limits, as to real estate installment loans for personal, family, household or agricultural purposes whose interest rates exceed 12% per annum, the imposition of late charges to the lesser of $5 or 5% of the late installment.[1] There is a ten-day grace period and only one penalty may be assessed for each late installment. Any payment tendered by the mortgagor must be applied to the most recent payment due. This legislation does not affect lending to commercial entities and, because of the above interest rate provision, most first mortgage residential lending.

A few states regulate late payment penalties with specific legislation. New York limits late payment penalties with respect to mortgages on owner-occupied one to six family dwellings to a maximum of 2% of the past due installment and requires a fifteen day grace period after an installment due date before penalty may be assessed. Any late charge must be separately charged and collected and not subtracted from any regular payment.[2] In California, as to loans secured by mortgages on single family, owner-occupied dwellings, the maximum late charge is 6% of each delinquent installment or $5, whichever is the greater, and it may be imposed only after a ten day grace period. Any payment tendered by the mortgagor must be applied to the most recent installment due.[3] Massachusetts limits late penalties on first mortgages on owner-occupied dwellings of four or less households to 3% of the late installment; no penalty may be assessed within fifteen days from the due date.[4]

§ 6.10

1. U.C.C.C. § 2.502. The UCCC originally was promulgated in 1968 and, after intervening drafts, the 1974 UCCC was promulgated. The UCCC, in one of the foregoing versions, with a variety of modification, in Oklahoma, Utah, Colorado, Idaho, Indiana, Wyoming, Kansas, Iowa, Maine, South Carolina and Wisconsin. The Uniform Land Transaction Act (ULTA) limits late charges in loans on owner-occupied residences to the greater of $5 or 5% of the late installment, but apparently allows the parties to contract differently. See U.L.T.A. § 3–404. The ULTA is not yet law in any jurisdiction.

2. New York—McKinney's Real Prop. Law § 254–b. See DiMitri v. Tutunjian, 103 Misc.2d 977, 427 N.Y.S.2d 362 (1980) (mortgagor entitled to recover difference between actual late charges imposed and statutory maximum).

3. West's Ann.Cal.Civil Code § 2954.4. See also West's Ann.Cal.Bus. and Prof. Code § 10242.5 (as to loans negotiated by real estate licensees). Oregon has similar legislation. See Ch. 427, Laws 1977 (Eff. Jan. 1, 1978).

4. Mass.Gen.Laws Ann. c. 183, § 59.

A Federal Home Loan Bank Board (FHLBB) regulation, which is applicable to all federally chartered thrift institutions, authorizes the imposition of late charges, but prohibits, as to all loans on owner-occupied dwellings, prepayment penalties in excess of 5% of the amount of the late installment and their assessment during a fifteen day grace period.[5] Moreover, it should be emphasized that the regulation "preempts application of any state law concerning the imposition, assessment or collection of late charges" to federally-chartered thrift institutions.[6] Consider the implications of this federal preemption for California lenders. Unlike the California statute, the FHLBB regulation provides that "an installment payment made by the borrower shall be applied to the *longest* outstanding installment due."[7] Both the California statute and the FHLBB regulation permit only one late charge for each delinquent installment. Thus, if several installments are in default and the mortgagor makes one regular payment, in California the payment would be applied to the most recent installment due. No penalty could be assessed as to that payment. Under the FHLBB regulation however, if our mortgagor makes the same payment, it will be applied to cover the "longest" outstanding installment due and thus a new penalty will be assessed as to the most recent installment due. Because of the federal preemption, however, the tardy mortgagor of a federally chartered thrift institution will, in this context, be less fortunate than mortgagors of numerous other California lenders.

The official policies of the two quasi-federal institutions that purchase first mortgage loans on the secondary market to some extent work at cross purposes. The Federal National Mortgage Association (FNMA) policy as to non-federally insured or guaranteed (conventional) mortgages states that the "note shall provide that the borrower *shall* pay a late charge in the amount of 4%, or such lesser amount as permitted by the laws of the jurisdiction, computed on the monthly installment of principal and interest when such installment is not received on or before the fifteenth day after the installment due date."[8] On the other hand, the Federal Home Loan Mortgage Corporation (FHLMC) *permits, but does not require,* the collection of late charges after a fifteen day grace period in an amount no greater than 5% of the late installment of principal and interest.[9] Thus, FNMA requires a late payment charge while the FHLMC simply authorizes it. Since many lending institutions sell loans on the secondary market, and since these institutions, for purposes of maximum flexibility, will probably want to be able to sell their loans to either of these quasi-federal agencies, the practical effect of these agencies' policies will be that the

---

5. 12 CFR 545.8–3(d), (e).

6. Colins v. Union Federal Savings & Loan Association, ___ Nev. ___, 662 P.2d 610, 614 (1983).

7. 12 CFR 545.8–3(e)(2) (emphasis added).

8. FNMA Conventional Selling Contract Supplement, § 304 (emphasis added).

9. FHLMC Servicer's Guide § 3.103 (March 21, 1977).

lending institutions will opt to *require* a late payment penalty.[10] Thus FNMA, in effect, may be setting some type of national norm that requires late payment penalties as to nonfederally insured or guaranteed (conventional) first mortgage loans.

Prepayment penalties on federally insured or guaranteed loans are limited by federal regulation. With respect to loans insured by the Federal Housing Administration (FHA), late payment charges are limited to 4% of each installment that is more than fifteen days late.[11] The maximum late charge for loans guaranteed by the Veterans Administration (VA) is 4% of any installment that is delinquent more than fifteen days.[12]

 WESTLAW REFERENCES

(federal /4 bank /2 board) f.h.l.b.b. /p late delinquen! /s charge payment

B. STATUTES OF LIMITATION

§ 6.11 Relationship of Obligation and Mortgage

The effect of lapse of time upon mortgages is complicated by the separate existence of the mortgage from the debt that it secures and the availability of separate remedies for the enforcement of each which, in most states, may be pursued independently.[1] The mortgage debt may take several forms. It may be a simple oral or written debt, it may be in the form of a negotiable promissory note or bond, or it may be a covenant under seal either in the deed or apart from it. Quite commonly statutes of limitations provide longer or shorter periods of time depending upon the character of the obligation. In this connection, where a mortgage executed to secure a note also contains a covenant in which the mortgagor agrees to pay the loan, even though a shorter statute of limitations has run on the note the mortgagee may still enforce the covenant.[2] The rule illustrates and emphasizes the separate existence of remedies and the rule that barring one has no necessary effect upon another.

---

10. See § 11.3 infra. Interestingly, the note form prescribed by both FNMA and FHLMC contains a late payment clause. The penalty is stated in terms of a percentage of the late installment but the actual percentage amount is left blank. Thus, both agencies, in effect, tend to encourage late payment penalties because mortgagees are not likely to omit the penalty language from the note form.

11. 24 CFR 203.25.

12. 38 CFR 36.4212(c).

§ 6.11

1. See §§ 2.1–2.2, supra and Chapter 7, infra.

2. Dinniny v. Gavin, 4 App.Div. 298, 39 N.Y.S. 485 (1896), affirmed 159 N.Y. 556, 54 N.E. 1090 (1899); Empire Trust Co. v. Heinze, 242 N.Y. 475, 152 N.E. 266 (1926). See also Harris v. Mills, 28 Ill. 44, 81 Am. Dec. 259 (1862). The mortgagee may foreclose and get a deficiency judgment on the covenant. Holcomb v. Webley, 185 Va. 150, 37 S.E.2d 762 (1946), commented on, 32 Va.L.Rev. 1043 (1946); Guardian Depositors Corp. of Detroit v. Savage, 287 Mich. 193, 283 N.W. 26, 124 A.L.R. 635 (1938), discussed in notes, 87 U. of Pa.L.Rev. 741 (1939); 37 Mich.L.Rev. 1340 (1939).

The title and lien theories also play an important role because the effect of the running of the statute of limitations upon a chose in action is quite different from that upon rights in real and personal property.[3] Again the mortgagee has different remedies to enforce its right in the land. It may bring an action at law to recover possession in title states; it may use a bill in equity to foreclose; or it may foreclose by exercising a power of sale contained in the mortgage.[4] The effect of the passage of time upon each one of these is a separate and distinct problem. The barring of the right to recover possession of the land is governed by statutes of limitations and doctrines quite distinct from those covering the debt obligation.[5] The former have led to a requirement by a few title theory courts that, in order to bar a mortgagee's right to possession of the mortgaged property in title states there had to be some act by the mortgagor in the nature of a disseizin.[6] The concept behind the reasoning goes back to the early idea in the common law classical form mortgage that the mortgagor in possession was a tenant of some sort of the mortgagee.[7] The rule seems unfortunate. The time should begin to run on any remedy the mortgagee has to recover possession from the time it may exercise it without injecting notions of disseizin or adverse possession.

The foreclosure action, being equitable, originally was not governed by statutes of limitation, which applied only to actions at law, but rather by the doctrine of laches, a concept that is sometimes referred to as an equitable statute of limitations. Under the laches principle a party who is guilty of unreasonable delay in bringing an action will be denied equitable relief.[8] While what constitutes unreasonable delay is often unclear, it is frequently characterized as the passage of time coupled with prejudice to the defendant.[9] Although it is sometimes stated that statutes of limitation bar only legal relief only unless otherwise expressly provided and that only laches operates to bar equitable relief,[10] many states have made their statutes of limitation applicable to equity suits, either by express statutory language or by judicial construction.[11] Nevertheless, laches remains an important defense because unreasonable delay can constitute a bar to equitable relief even though the statutory period has not expired. For example, in an interesting Florida case, judicial foreclosure was barred by laches

3. See, e.g., Chapin v. Freeland, 142 Mass. 383, 8 N.E. 128, 56 Am.Rep. 701 (1886).

4. See Chapter 7, infra.

5. Chapin v. Freeland, note 3, supra.

6. See note, 25 Ill.L.Rev. 563 (1931).

7. See § 4.1, supra.

8. See generally, Leavell, Love and Nelson, Equitable Remedies and Restitution 156–159, 387–389 (3rd Ed.1980).

9. See e.g., Lusk v. Krejci, 187 Cal.App. 2d 553, 9 Cal.Rptr. 703 (1960); Shell v. Strong, 151 F.2d 909 (10th Cir.1945).

10. See DeFuniak, Handbook of Modern Equity § 24 (1956); Blankenship v. Boyle, 329 F.Supp. 1089 (D.D.C.1971), stay denied 447 F.2d 1280 (D.C.Cir.1971), opinion supplemented 337 F.Supp. 296 (1972).

11. See e.g., Ludwig v. Scott, 65 S.W.2d 1034 (Mo.App.1933); Leavell, Love and Nelson, Equitable Remedies and Restitution, 387 (3rd. Ed.1980).

notwithstanding the fact that seven years remained to run under a twenty year foreclosure statute of limitations.[12]

Title theory states appear to hold that the running of the statute of limitations upon the mortgage debt has no effect upon the existence of or remedies upon the mortgage.[13] Having title, the mortgagee may take possession peaceably or maintain an action of ejectment or writ of entry.[14] This is true even though not only action on the debt has been barred but an action to foreclose as well, provided the statute of limitations on the remedy of ejectment has not run.[15] Or he may maintain an action to foreclose.[16] The reasoning usually is that the statute of limitations bars merely the remedy on the debt, not the right. And it does not purport to affect any other independent remedy on the mortgage or the mortgage itself. The debt remaining, the mortgage continues to secure it and is not extinguished indirectly upon any theory that a destruction of the obligation secured necessarily destroys the mortgage securing it.[17]

Lien states are in conflict. The majority probably follows the reasoning of the courts in title states. There are independent rights and remedies on the debt and the mortgage lien. Barring of a remedy upon the debt does not affect the debt itself, nor does it have any operative effect upon either the lien or the remedy to enforce it. Consequently the mortgagee can foreclose its lien judicially [18] or by exercising a power of sale contained in the mortgage.[19] Moreover, the

---

12. Ratner v. Miami Beach First National Bank, 368 So.2d 1326 (Fla.App.1979), certiorari denied 381 So.2d 769 (1980); cf. Phinney v. Levine, 117 N.H. 968, 381 A.2d 735 (1977).

13. See 161 A.L.R. 886, 887 (1946); Phinney v. Levine, 359 A.2d 636 (N.H.1976); Note, The Statute of Limitations as a Defense to Foreclosure in Illinois, U. of Ill.L.Forum 469 (1957).

14. Bradfield v. Hale, 67 Ohio St. 316, 65 N.E. 1008 (1902); Taylor v. Quinn, 68 Ohio App. 164, 39 N.E.2d 627 (1941), noted 91 U. of Pa.L.Rev. 85 (1942); Thayer v. Mann, 36 Mass. (19 Pick.) 535 (1837), writ of entry.

15. Bradfield v. Hale, supra note 43; Taylor v. Quinn, supra note 14.

16. Belknap v. Gleason, 11 Conn. 160, 27 Am.Dec. 721 (1836); Elkins v. Edwards, 8 Ga. 325 (1850) and see Ga.Code of § 67–101 (1933); Norton v. Palmer, 142 Mass. 433, 8 N.E. 346 (1886). See 161 A.L.R. 886, 887 (1946). The rule is otherwise in Illinois, an intermediate state. Harris v. Mills, 28 Ill. 44, 81 Am.Dec. 259 (1862); Markus v. Chicago Title etc. Co., 373 Ill. 557, 27 N.E.2d 436, 128 A.L.R. 567 (1940). So too, in Arkansas. Johnson v. Lowman, 193 Ark. 8, 97 S.W.2d 86 (1936).

17. See §§ 2.1–2.2 supra, on the dependence of a mortgage upon the existence of an obligation to secure. See also, 11 Cal.L. Rev. 429 (1923); 8 U. of Cin.L.Rev. 121, 123 (1934).

18. "The right to foreclose a mortgage lien on property given to secure a debt which has not been discharged exists independently of the right to bring an action for money damages on the note and that, under common law, the holder of a note and mortgage may proceed either at law to recover on the bond or in equity to foreclose the mortgage. Indeed, the right to foreclose survives when an action on the debt is barred." Cracco v. Cox, 66 A.D.2d 447, 414 N.Y.S.2d 404 (1979); See Lundberg v. Northwestern National Bank of Minneapolis, 299 Minn. 46, 216 N.W.2d 121 (1974); Hulbert v. Clark, 128 N.Y. 295, 28 N.E. 638, 14 L.R.A. 59 (1891); Mich. Ins. Co. of Detroit v. Brown, 11 Mich. 265 (1863); Slingerland v. Sherer, 46 Minn. 422, 49 N.W. 237 (1891).

19. House v. Carr, 185 N.Y. 453, 78 N.E. 171, 6 L.R.A.,N.S., 510, 7 Ann.Cas. 185 (1906); Menzel v. Hinton, 132 N.C. 660, 44 S.E. 385, 95 Am.St.Rep. 647, nullified by N.C.C.S. § 2589 (1903); Grant v. Burr, 54 Cal. 298 (1880), trust deed mortgage. Cf. Faxon v. All Persons, etc., 166 Cal. 707, 137

same result has even been reached in a jurisdiction in which the running of the statute on the debt is regarded as extinguishing it, not merely barring the remedy to enforce it.[20] A number of lien states, however, hold that when the remedy on the obligation is barred so to is the remedy on the mortgage. The reason usually given is that the mortgage is merely an incident of the debt and should not be enforceable if the debt is not.[21] This minority rule has been applied to deeds absolute intended as mortgages.[22] In some jurisdictions statutes bar a remedy on the mortgage whenever an action on the debt is barred.[23] Under this approach, however, if the remedy on the debt is revived the mortgage also will again become enforceable.[24] A different type of statute provides that "a lien is extinguished by the lapse of time within which an action can be brought upon the principal obligation."[25] Under this type of statute a mortgage is destroyed by the running of the statute so that it cannot be revived by any act of the mortgagor although the debt can be.[26]

Nevertheless, it should be stressed that generalizations in this area are hazardous and often mortgage limitations questions will turn completely on the peculiarities of local law. New Hampshire is an interesting case in point. Under its statute, "actions upon notes secured by mortgage on real estate may be brought as long as the plaintiff is entitled to bring an action upon the mortgage."[27] Thus, "the period for enforcing the mortgage does not depend on the limitation period for the note. Rather, the statute extends the time during which an action may be brought on the note."[28] For example, even though the cause of

P. 919, L.R.A.1916B, 1209 (1913); Emory v. Keighan, 88 Ill. 482 (1878).

20. First National Bank of Madison v. Kolbeck, 247 Wis. 462, 19 N.W.2d 908, 161 A.L.R. 882 (1945).

21. Allen v. Shepherd, 162 Ky. 756, 173 S.W. 135 (1915); see Prewitt v. Wortham, 79 Ky. 287, 288, 2 Ky.Law Rep. 282 (1881); 32 Ky.L.Rev. 78 (1943); Duty v. Graham, 12 Tex. 427, 62 Am.Dec. 534 (1943). See also note 41, 42, supra. And see 161 A.L.R. 886, 890 (1946). Tennant v. Hulet, 65 Ind.App. 24, 116 N.E. 748 (1917), reached the same result but is superseded by Yarlott v. Brown, 192 Ind. 648, 138 N.E. 17 (1923). Cf., 22 Col.L.Rev. 451 (1922). See 29 Col.L.Rev. 210 (1941), on the methods of pleading the statute of limitations as a bar.

22. Kern Valley Bank v. Koehn, 157 Cal. 237, 107 P. 111 (1910); Pratt v. Pratt, 121 Wash. 298, 209 P. 535, 28 A.L.R. 548 (1922), discussed in notes, 8 Cornell L.Q. 172 (1923); 71 U. of Pa.L.Rev. 284 (1923); 32 Yale L.J. 611 (1923). See also 11 L.R.A.,N.S., 825 (1908).

23. See, e.g., Vernon's Ann.Mo.Stat. § 516.150.

24. Schmucker v. Sibert, 18 Kan. 104, 26 Am.Rep. 765 (1877); Schifferstein v. Allison, 123 Ill. 662, 15 N.E. 275 (1888). Cf., Clinton County v. Cox, 37 Iowa 570 (1873), extension.

25. West's Ann.Cal.Civ.Code § 2911.

26. Wells v. Harter, 56 Cal. 342 (1880); Sanford v. Bergin, 156 Cal. 43, 103 P. 333 (1909); San Jose Safe Deposit Bank of Savings v. Bank of Madera, 144 Cal. 574, 78 P. 5 (1904). The destruction of the mortgage by the running of the statute of limitations also destroys any power of sale in the mortgage so that equity, at the request of the mortgagor, will restrain an attempted exercise of it without requiring the mortgagor to tender payment to the mortgagee. Goldwater v. Hibernia Savings & Loan Society, 19 Cal.App. 511, 126 P. 861 (1912), rehearing denied 19 Cal.App. 511, 126 P. 863. And the mortgagor can quiet title against a purchaser under the sale without paying his debt. Faxon v. All Persons, etc., 166 Cal. 707, 137 P. 919, L.R.A., 1916B, 1209 (1913).

27. N.H.Rev.Stat.Ann. 508:6.

28. Phinney v. Levine, 116 N.H. 379, 381, 359 A.2d 636 (1976).

action on the obligation secured by a mortgage is six years, because the limitation period for mortgage foreclosure is twenty years, an action on the obligation also has the benefit of the longer period.[29] On the other hand, the New Hampshire statute also operates as a two-edged sword. For example, where the New Hampshire Supreme Court determined that laches barred a foreclosure action long before the foreclosure statute had run, it held that any further action on the underlying debt likewise was prohibited.[30]

The deed of trust requires separate consideration in connection with the statute of limitations. Although the distinction between a mortgage in such a form and a regular mortgage is becoming increasingly less significant, it has not been totally destroyed. One of the most important persisting notions is that it, like other trusts, continues until the performance of the trust purpose, viz., the payment of the debt for which the trust was created.[31] One result is that there is no time limit on it [32] except as specifically provided by statute.[33] Barring of the remedy on the debt has no effect upon the trustee's power to sell the property and pay the debt with the proceeds.[34] Moreover, this has often been true under statutes extinguishing the "lien of a mortgage" when the remedy on the debt is barred. Courts reason that a trust deed mortgage is not a "lien" within the meaning of such statutory language.[35]

The deed of trust that is undischarged of record has especially been a problem in California. This is because it "continues to remain an encumbrance on real property until the trustee satisfies it by a reconveyance pursuant to directions of the creditor. The underlying debt may or may not have been discharged." [36] Consequently, the Marketable Record Title Act was enacted in 1982.[37] The legislation removes as

---

29. Id. See N.H.Rev.Stat.Ann. 508:2.

30. Phinney v. Levine, 117 N.H. 968, 381 A.2d 735 (1977).

31. See Cunningham v. Williams, 178 Va. 542, 17 S.E.2d 355 (1941); Basye, Clearing Land Titles, § 73 (2d Ed. 1970).

32. A common expression is "that the statute of limitations never runs against the power of sale in a deed of trust." Bank of Italy National Trust & Savings Association v. Bentley, 217 Cal. 644 20 P.2d 940 (1933). See note, 27 Cal.L.Rev. 66, 67. See also Note, Comparison of California Mortgages, Trust Deeds and Land Sale Contracts, 7 U.C.L.A.L.Rev. 83, 85 (1960).

33. There are now a good many statutes declaring that a deed of trust may not be foreclosed after the time that a mortgage, if it rather than a deed of trust had been given to secure the debt, could be foreclosed by action or after the debt it secures is barred by the statute. See e.g., Vernon's Ann.Mo.Stat. § 516.150.

34. See 58 W.Va.L.Q. 417 (1956), commenting on Kuhn v. Shreeve, 141 W.Va. 170, 89 S.E.2d 685 (1955).

35. Grant v. Burr, 54 Cal. 298 (1880); Travelli v. Bowman, 150 Cal. 587, 89 P. 347 (1907); Sacramento Bank v. Murphy, 158 Cal. 390, 115 P. 232 (1910). Cf. Hurley v. Estes, 6 Neb. 386 (1877). Illogically, however, the danger exists that an action to foreclose a trust deed mortgage, brought and prosecuted to judgment after the statute has run on the debt, may, if the debtor or even a grantee pleads the statute, result in the security interest being extinguished. Flack v. Boland, 11 Cal.2d 103, 77 P.2d 1090 (1938).

36. Basye, Clearing Land Titles 38 (1983 Supp.)

37. West's Ann.Cal.Civ.Code §§ 882.020—882.040.

apparent liens all old mortgages and deeds of trust "with respect to which the final maturity date or the date fixed for payment of the debt or performance of the obligation ascertainable from the record is more than 10 years." [38] Where such date cannot be determined from the record or no date is fixed, the lien is terminated 60 years after the recording date of the instrument creating it. Expiration of the lien not only renders it unenforcible, it also acts as the equivalent of a regularly recorded satisfaction. According to Professor Basye, the legislation should "go far in removing the effect of ancient * * * deeds of trust from continuing as clogs upon real estate in California." [39]

Even in lien jurisdictions there is case law that a mortgagor may not maintain an action to cancel a mortgage or to quiet title based on the running of the statute of limitations, unless payment of the debt is tendered to the mortgagee.[40] This approach is based on the equitable maxim that those "who seek equity, must do equity," a corollary of which is that the mortgagor should perform his moral obligation to pay as a condition precedent to equitable relief. Whatever the merits of such an approach, the majority of states appear to have reversed it by statute.[41]

Interestingly, prior to statutes of limitations as to debts, a common law presumption existed that a debt was presumed to have been paid if twenty years passed without recognition of its existence by the debtor.[42] The rule was also extended to include mortgages where the mortgagor had been in possession for the full twenty year period.[43] This presumption, for the most part, "has been superceded by statutes of limitations, and the rule is further submerged by statutes that destroy the efficacy of a judgment after the lapse of a certain period." [44] The presumption, nevertheless, is applicable in a few jurisdictions for the purpose of compelling the cancellation of a mortgage after a twenty year lapse.[45]

---

38. Basye, supra note 36 at 38.

39. Id. at 38.

40. Aguilar v. Bocci, 39 Cal.App.3d 475, 114 Cal.Rptr. 91 (1974); Tracy v. Wheeler, 15 N.D. 248, 107 N.W. 68 (1906). Cf. Gibson v. Johnson, 73 Kan. 261, 84 P. 982 (1906); Mitchell v. Bickford, 192 Mass. 244, 78 N.E. 453 (1906). See notes, 15 Col.L. Rev. 720 (1915); 22 Col.L.Rev. 451 (1922) (also discussing the question whether a grantee of the mortgagor may have such relief). See 164 A.L.R. 1387 (1946). But cf., 7 Wash. & Lee L.Rev. 220 (1950).

41. See Bayse, Clearing Land Titles, § 75 and n. 4 (2d Ed. 1970) and 1983 Supp. § 75 n. 4.

42. Id. at § 71; See 1 A.L.R. 781 (1919), for an extensive collection of cases on the presumption of payment generally; Wigmore, Evidence, 2d ed. § 2517.

43. Basye, supra note 37 at § 71.

44. Glenn, Mortgages, § 56 at p. 373 (1943).

45. Kuhn v. Shreeve, 141 W.Va. 170, 89 S.E.2d 685 (1955), commented on in 58 W.Va.L.Q. 417 (1956). Proof that no payment of principal or interest has been received by the mortgagee during more than twenty years after maturity, does not rebut the presumption of payment. Osborne Estate, 382 Pa. 306, 115 A.2d 201 (1955). See Note, Admissibility and weight of admissions and acknowledgments to rebut presumption of payment from lapse of time, 48 A.L.R.2d 868 (1956). See also Plowman, in Mortgages and Security Transactions, in 1956–1957 Survey of Pennsylvania Law, 19 U. of Pitt.L.Rev. 292, 294 (1958) noting Oaks Fire Co. v. Herbert, 389 Pa. 357, 132 A.2d 193 (1957); see, Secured Transactions, in 1957–1958 Survey of Pennsylvania Law, 20 U. of Pitt.L.Rev. 371 (1958), noting Sandman v. Old Delancy Building & Loan

In the absence of proof sufficient to rebut the presumption, the mortgagor "is entitled to have the cloud of the mortgage removed since the underlying issue is whether there has been payment of the mortgage, not whether the statute of limitations has barred the remedy on it." [46]

 WESTLAW REFERENCES
"statute of limitation" /p mortgag** /p remedy
241k167(2)
di laches
digest,synopsis(mortgag** /p laches)
foreclos! /p mortgag** /p debt /s bar barr***
"marketable record title act"

§ 6.12 Effect of Acts of Mortgagor Upon Junior Interests

Any act of a mortgagor which extends the statute of limitations as to the mortgage obligation also extends it as to the mortgage provided the property remains unencumbered by junior liens.[1] Where third parties have acquired junior interests in the property as grantees or lienors, however, the cases exhibit both confusion and disagreement.[2] Certain propositions nevertheless are clear. For one thing, the courts generally agree that when such persons acquire their rights after the mortgagor has done an act sufficient to extend the period of the statute as to the mortgage debt, it likewise extends the statute as to the mortgage both against the mortgagor and the third parties.[3] The same is true of an act which revives a debt which had been barred.[4] Again, if the statute has run before the junior interest is acquired, the mortgagor cannot revive the mortgage as against the third party who may have acquired it on the faith of the bar,[5] even though her act may revive the debt and mortgage as to herself.[6] Further, in the great majority of

Association, 184 Pa.Super. 470, 135 A.2d 819 (1957).

46. Basye, supra note 37 at p. 217.

§ 6.12

1. Colton v. Depew, 60 N.J.Eq. 454, 46 A. 728, 83 Am.St.Rep. 650 (1900); Hansen v. Branner, 52 N.D. 892, 204 N.W. 856, 41 A.L.R. 814 (1925). See 41 A.L.R. 822 (1926); Niehaus v. Niehaus, 2 Ill.App.2d 434, 120 N.E.2d 66 (1954), noted, 33 Chi. Kent L.Rev. 82 (1954).

2. For discussions of the problem and collections of cases on it, see notes 49 Harv. L.Rev. 639 (1936); 27 Cal.L.Rev. 66 (1938); 32 Ill.L.Rev. 750 (1938); 9 Col.L.Rev. 718 (1909); 9 Minn.L.Rev. 166 (1924). See also 28 L.R.A.,N.S., 169 (1910); 26 L.R.A.,N.S. 898 (1910); 38 A.L.R. 833 (1925); 41 A.L.R. 822, 827, 828 (1926); 101 A.L.R. 337 (1936). Note, 51 Col.L.Rev. 1031 (1951).

3. See Storke and Sears, Discharge of Security Transactions, 26 Rocky Mt.L.Rev. 115, 131 (1954).

4. Clark v. Grant, 26 Okl. 398, 109 P. 234, 28 L.R.A.,N.S., 519, Ann.Cas.1912B, 505 (1910). Contra, by statute, Musser v. First National Bank, 165 Miss. 873, 147 So. 783 (1933).

5. Schmucker v. Sibert, 18 Kan. 104, 26 Am.Rep. 765 (1877); Cason v. Chambers, 62 Tex. 305 (1884); De Voe v. Rundle, 33 Wash. 604, 74 P. 836 (1903); see Kerndt v. Porterfield, 56 Iowa, 412, 9 N.W. 322 (1881). See also 28 L.R.A.,N.S., 169, 170 (1910); 41 A.L.R. 822, 828 (1926); 101 A.L.R. 330, 343 (1936). Note, 32 Ill.L.Rev. 750, 751, n. 6 (1938).

6. Brandenstein v. Johnson, 140 Cal. 29, 73 P. 744 (1903); Colonial & U.S. Mortgage Co. v. Flemington, 14 N.D. 181, 103 N.W. 929, 116 Am.St.Rep. 670 (1905); Cason v. Chambers, 62 Tex. 305 (1884). See 9 Col.L.Rev. 718, 719 (1909).

cases, the courts do not differentiate between the effect upon the statute of the mortgagor's absence from the state and affirmative acts such as part payments of principal or interest or an acknowledgment of the indebtedness.[7] Beyond this harmony ceases.

Where a junior interest in the mortgaged property is acquired before the statute of limitations has run and before the mortgagor has done any act which extends the statute, there are two broad lines of authorities. A minority of courts hold that the mortgagor cannot extend or revive the mortgage as to such third parties.[8] The chief argument in favor of this approach is that it is unfair to allow the mortgagor, after she has conveyed away title or a security interest in the property to another, to increase the burden on the transferred junior interest.[9] As applied to a grantee, the point has merit, and a few courts limit the doctrine to such a case.[10] A junior lienor, though, holds through the mortgagor and should be bound by the latter's conduct so far as it affects the first mortgage debt and mortgage.[11] Often, however, it is impossible to tell whether a court will distinguish between cases in which the mortgagor has divested of all property interest by a conveyance and those in which she has merely subjected the property to another lien.[12] Some cases clearly indicate no such line of demarcation is drawn.[13] Nor is any distinction drawn between subsequent mortgage liens and any other valid lien (by judgment, attachment, etc.).[14] Additional arguments supporting the rule are that it enables one taking a junior interest in the mortgaged property to know exactly the extent of the lien and that there is no hardship on the mortgagee because it does not affect its right to foreclose during the normal period of the statute.[15]

Most minority courts hold that the mortgagee must be given notice of the intervention of the rights of the grantee or the latter will be bound by the acts of the mortgagor. However, they generally fail to

7. See Wood v. Goodfellow, 43 Cal. 185, 188 (1872). See also 49 Harv.L.Rev. 639, n. 2 (1936). As to the basis for extension because of the mortgagor's absence, see 46 Harv.L.Rev. 703 (1933).

8. Storke and Sears, Discharge of Security Transactions, 26 Rocky Mt.L.Rev. 115, 134 (1954).

9. See Lord v. Morris, 18 Cal. 482, 490 (1861); Wood v. Goodfellow, 43 Cal. 185, 189 (1872); Zoll v. Carnahan, 83 Mo. 35, 43–44 (1884); Consolidated National Bank v. Van Slyke, 27 Ariz. 501, 234 P. 553, 38 A.L.R. 825 (1925). See also 47 Harv.L.Rev. 639, 641 (1936); 27 Cal.L.Rev. 66, 71 (1938).

10. E.g., Hess v. State Bank, 130 Wash. 147, 226 P. 257, 38 A.L.R. 829 (1924), discussed in notes, 9 Minn.L.Rev. 166 (1925); 49 Harv.L.Rev. 639, 642 (1936); 27 Cal.L.

Rev. 66, 71 (1938), in which the court draws this distinction; George v. Butler, 26 Wash. 456, 67 P. 263, 57 L.R.A. 396, 90 Am.St.Rep. 756 (1901). Cf. Smith v. Bush, 173 Okl. 172, 44 P.2d 921, 101 A.L.R. 330 (1935). See 27 Cal.L.Rev. 66, 71; 1925, 38 A.L.R. 833 (1938).

11. Hess v. State Bank, note 10, supra.

12. See, e.g., 27 Cal.L.Rev. 69, 70, n. 24 (1938). See also 32 Ill.L.Rev. 750, 752 (1938).

13. E.g., see Lord v. Morris, 18 Cal. 482, 490 (1861).

14. Brandenstein v. Johnson, 140 Cal. 29, 73 P. 744 (1903); Watt v. Wright, 66 Cal. 202, 5 P. 91 (1884); De Voe v. Rundle, 33 Wash. 604, 74 P. 836 (1903).

15. See 9 Col.L.Rev. 718, 719 (1909).

distinguish between "actual or constructive" notice to the mortgagee [16] and hold that recordation of a subsequent change in the status of the mortgaged property acts as constructive notice.[17] Moreover, occasionally, it is stated flatly that, regardless of notice of any sort to the mortgagee, the mortgagor cannot affect the running of the statute in favor of subsequently acquired interests.[18]

The majority view [19] is that any conduct that keeps the debt enforceable as to the mortgagor also keeps the mortgage alive as to grantees and junior lienors.[20] These courts argue, technically, that the mortgage is a mere incident of the debt and therefore anything that keeps the debt alive should likewise keep the mortgage alive.[21] If the remedy on the debt is now available, it is argued, so should be the remedy on the mortgage. In criticism of this line of reasoning it should be emphasized that the remedy on the mortgage was available even though the remedy on the debt was barred. Moreover, the remedy on the mortgage might be barred independently of the barring of the remedy on the debt. And if this is so, it is questionable whether the extension or revival of the remedy on the debt should have any effect upon the remedy on the mortgage.

In addition, the majority urge that any purchaser of a junior interest with notice of the paramount mortgage, actual or constructive, must be regarded as taking subject to the mortgage and all of its incidents including the possibility of extension of the debt by conduct of the mortgagor.[22] Further, the mortgagee should be free to deal with the mortgagor, without having the burden of discovering and taking

---

16. See, e.g., Boucofski v. Jacobsen, 36 Utah, 165, 177, 104 P. 117, 121, 26 L.R.A.,N.S., 898 (1909).

17. E.g., Filipini v. Trobock, 134 Cal. 444, 66 P. 587 (1901).

18. See Benedict v. Griffith, 92 Ark. 195, 199, 122 S.W. 479, 480 (1909); Cook v. Union Trust Co., 106 Ky. 803, 809, 51 S.W. 600, 601–2, 45 L.R.A. 212 (1899).

19. See notes 2, 6 supra.

20. Consolidated National Bank v. Van Slyke, 27 Ariz. 501, 234 P. 553, 38 A.L.R. 825 (1925); Smith v. Bush, 173 Okl. 172, 44 P.2d 921, 101 A.L.R. 330 (1935); Hess v. State Bank, 130 Wash. 147, 226 P. 257, 38 A.L.R. 829 (1924), as to junior mortgagee. In many of the decisions in which the junior interest was acquired before the mortgagor's conduct extending the time or reviving the debt occurred and also before the statute had run, the courts are not concerned with whether the mortgagor's act occurred before or after the statute had run. See 101 A.L.R. 330, 342 (1936). In some cases, however, the fact that the tolling occurred after the bar was complete was important in preventing recovery by

the mortgagee. Cook v. Prindle, 97 Iowa 464, 66 N.W. 781, 59 Am.St.Rep. 424 (1896). See 101 A.L.R. 337, 343 (1936). Johnson v. Johnson, 81 Mo. 331 (1884), contra. Similarly, the fact that such tolling was made before the bar was complete has been a decisive factor in a few decisions refusing to permit the junior encumbrancer to plead the statute. Kaiser v. Idleman, 57 Or. 224, 108 P. 193, 28 L.R.A.,N.S., 169 (1910). See 32 Ill.L.Rev. 750, 752; 1925, 9 Minn.L.Rev. 166 (1938).

21. Schmucker v. Sibert, 18 Kan. 104, 26 Am.Rep. 765 (1877); Johnson v. Johnson, 81 Mo. 331 (1884); Smith v. Bush, 173 Okl. 172, 44 P.2d 921, 101 A.L.R. 330 (1935); see Clift v. Williams, 105 Ky. 559, 565, 49 S.W. 328, 329 (1899), rehearing denied 105 Ky. 559, 51 S.W. 821 (1899). But see Colonial & U.S. Mortgage Co. v. Northwest Thresher Co., 14 N.D. 147, 103 N.W. 915, 70 L.R.A. 814, 116 Am.St.Rep. 670, 8 Ann.Cas. 1160 (1905), criticizing the incident theory as applied to the statute of limitations.

22. See 49 Harv.L.Rev. 639, 643 (1936); 9 Col.L.Rev. 718, 719 (1909).

into account, until foreclosure, persons who might have acquired a junior interest in the property in the interim. Such a rule imposes no hardship on a transferee since it merely continues a claim on the land which was taken into account when she acquired her interest.[23]

 WESTLAW REFERENCES
extend! extension /5 statute /p mortgag**
di constructive notice

§ 6.13 Effect of Acts of Grantees or Junior Interests on Mortgagor

Turning around the question in the preceding section, can a grantee or junior lienor of mortgaged property extend the period of the statute of limitations as to the mortgagor by a new promise, acknowledgment of, or payment on the debt? In general, in order for such an act to interrupt or revive the running of the statute of limitations it must be made by the obligor or someone legally authorized to act for him.[1] On this test neither an assuming grantee nor one who takes subject to the mortgage should be able to affect the running of the statute as to the mortgagor. Their obligations are separate and independent and create no power to affect the remedies against their grantor. While many courts take this view both as to assuming and subject-to grantees,[2] some courts, however, have held that any payments by assuming grantee are made with the implied authority of the mortgagor and for the benefit of both. Hence these courts hold that interest payments toll the statute on the debt as well as the mortgage and so extend the running of the statute against the mortgagor.[3]

Although a grantee should not be able to bind the mortgagor by any acts that have the effect of extending or reviving the statute of

---

23. See Kerndt v. Porterfield, 56 Iowa 412, 415, 9 N.W. 322, 323 (1881). See also 27 Cal.L.Rev. 66, 71 (1938).

§ 6.13

1. Woodcock v. Putnam, 101 Minn. 1, 111 N.W. 639 (1907); cf. Brooklyn Bank v. Barnaby, 197 N.Y. 210, 90 N.E. 834, 27 L.R.A.,N.S., 843 (1910), reargument denied, 198 N.Y. 522, 92 N.E. 1079 (1910); Vaughan v. Mansfield, 229 Mass. 352, 118 N.E. 652 (1918). But cf., Innocenti v. Guisti, 71 R.I. 274, 43 A.2d 700, 165 A.L.R. 1394 (1945), criticized in 24 Tex.L.Rev. 390 (1946).

2. As to assuming grantees, see Old Alms-House Farm of New Haven v. Smith, 52 Conn. 434 (1884); Trent v. Johnson, 185 Ark. 288, 47 S.W.2d 12, 80 A.L.R. 1431 (1932); Provident Institute for Saving in Town of Boston v. Merrill, 311 Mass. 168, 40 N.E.2d 280 (1942); Regan v. Williams 185 Mo. 620, 84 S.W. 959, 105 Am.St.Rep.

600 (1904); Frost v. Johnson, 140 Ohio St. 315, 43 N.E.2d 277, 142 A.L.R. 609 (1942); Cottrell v. Shepherd, 86 Wis. 649, 57 N.W. 983, 39 Am.St.Rep. 919 (1894). See 18 A.L.R. 1027, 1033 (1922); 142 A.L.R. 615, 621 (1943). See also 17 Minn.L.Rev. 97 (1932). As to subject-to grantees, see Home Life Insurance Co. v. Elwell, 111 Mich. 689, 70 N.W. 334 (1897); Fitzgerald v. Flanagan, 155 Iowa 217, 135 N.W. 738, Ann.Cas.1914C, 1104 (1912), noted, 26 Harv.L.Rev. 89 (1912); Turner v. Powell, 85 Mont. 241, 278 P. 512 (1929); Winter v. Kram, 3 A.D.2d 175, 159 N.Y.S.2d 417 (2d Dept.1957), approved in Mortgages, in 1957 Survey of New York Law, 32 N.Y.U.L.Rev. 1426 (1957).

3. Biddle v. Pugh, 59 N.J.Eq. 480, 45 A. 626 (1900); Ramsey v. Hutchinson, 117 N.J.L. 222, 187 A. 650 (1936); Guardian Depositors Corp. v. Wagner, 287 Mich. 202, 283 N.W. 29 (1938).

limitations, she clearly should be able to and can bind herself or the property acquired.[4] If she is an assuming grantee her act will affect her personal liability as well as the time within which the mortgage can be enforced against the property.[5] Indeed, the very act of assuming or of taking subject to the mortgage is one which starts a new period of limitations as to rights against the grantee.[6] A grantee who merely takes subject to the mortgage extends the statute only as to the mortgage on the land.[7]

Whatever the theory that enables the mortgagee to reach an assuming grantee, the latter's liability [8] rests upon an agreement separate and independent from that of the mortgagor.[9] It arises at the time she enters into the contract of assumption and not before. If at that time the debt of the mortgagor was not yet due, no cause of action would arise until maturity although her obligation became binding at the time of the agreement.[10] In such a case the statute of limitations would begin to run on the grantee's obligation at the same time as on the right of the mortgagee against the mortgagor, viz., at time of default at maturity.[11] This is not because there is only one obligation on which both are bound, but because the maturity date of each separate obligation is the same. If the assumption is after maturity, or even after the statute has run on the mortgagor's obligation, the grantee's obligation arises at that time and becomes enforceable at once because her promise is to pay a debt which is then owing. The statute, therefore, starts to run at once.[12]

Where a grantee merely takes subject to the mortgage the agreement confines her liability to the land she bought as a source of payment.[13] Apart from this more restricted coverage, the foregoing also applies to her.[14] Although the mortgagee's original mortgage rights in the land follow it into the hands of the grantee,[15] the latter's

4. Daniels v. Johnson, 129 Cal. 415, 61 P. 1107, 79 Am.St.Rep. 123 (1900); 11 Cal. L.Rev. 429, 431, 432 (1923). See also Fourth National Bank in Wichita v. Hill, 181 Kan. 683, 314 P.2d 312 (1957).

5. Daniels v. Johnson, 129 Cal. 415, 61 P. 1107, 79 Am.St.Rep. 123 (1900); Schmucker v. Sibert, 18 Kan. 104, 112 (1877).

6. Hendricks v. Brooks, 80 Kan. 1, 101 P. 622, 133 Am.St.Rep. 186 (1909); Bement v. Ohio Valley Banking Co., 99 Ky. 109, 35 S.W. 139, 59 Am.St.Rep. 445 (1896). See 142 A.L.R. 615, 616 (1943).

7. Curtis v. Holee, 184 Cal. 726, 195 P. 395, 18 A.L.R. 1024 (1921); Fitzgerald v. Flanagan, 155 Iowa 217, 135 N.W. 738, Ann.Cas.1914C, 1104 (1912). See 142 A.L.R. 615, 619 (1943).

8. See §§ 5.11–5.15, supra.

9. Schmucker v. Sibert, 18 Kan. 104 (1877); Hendricks v. Brooks, 80 Kan. 1, 101 P. 622 (1909). See note 96, supra.

10. Carnahan v. Lloyd, 4 Kan.App. 605, 46 P. 323 (1896); Bogart v. Geo. K. Porter Co., 193 Cal. 197, 223 P. 959, 31 A.L.R. 1045 (1924).

11. See 11 Cal.L.Rev. 429, 431 (1923).

12. See 11 Cal.L.Rev. 429, 432. In a state like California where the running of the statute on the debt extinguishes the mortgage, a contract of assumption made after the statute is run, although it will be effective as to the debt will not revive the mortgage. Cf., Weinberger v. Weidner, 134 Cal. 599, 66 P. 869 (1901).

13. Curtis v. Holee, 184 Cal. 726, 195 P. 395, 18 A.L.R. 1024 (1921).

14. See Schmucker v. Sibert, 18 Kan. 104, 112 (1877).

15. See § 5.1, supra.

agreement that it shall be subject to the mortgage is a new promise with respect to the land which has an effect upon the period for enforcing the mortgage on the land similar to that of an assumption upon the debt period.[16]

 WESTLAW REFERENCES
266k318

§ 6.14 Statutory Trends

Every state has experienced the problem of a substantial number of old, recorded mortgages that have never been released of record. As Professor Basye has aptly pointed out, "in the normal course of events most mortgages were paid, but there was a tendency to overlook the necessity of recording a formal discharge. Of those that were not paid some became barred by the passage of time or were abandoned, but others were regarded by the parties themselves as subsisting obligations because of partial payments on them or extension agreements. Passing decades, however, left numerous mortgages unsatisfied of record to become a serious impediment to the transfer of land."[1] This problem was also heightened by the existence of separate periods of limitations for the debt and mortgage and the independence of either in many cases of powers of sale, especially in deeds of trust. As a result, a variety of statutory approaches have been utilized to deal with this problem.

One such approach, as we have examined earlier, has been to enact statutes making the period of the statute the same as to both the debt and the lien so that the elapse of the same amount of time would bar both simultaneously. Some of these statutes simply bar the enforcement of a mortgage after the mortgage debt has become barred.[2] Others extinguish the mortgage lien after "the lapse of time within which an action can be brought upon the principal obligation."[3] In addition there has been a tendency to shorten the longer periods applicable in the older statutes to foreclosure actions.[4] However, doctrines of tolling statutes of limitations, or of reviving barred obligations together with the mortgages securing them constitute hazards to title completely outside of the record and unaffected by such changes. Further equitable doctrines limit the employment of statutes of limitations and presumptions of payment to use as a shield and prevent them

16. Curtis v. Holee, 184 Cal. 726, 195 P. 395, 18 A.L.R. 1024 (1921); Fitzgerald v. Flanagan, 155 Iowa 217, 135 N.W. 738, Ann.Cas.1914C, 1104; see Schmucker v. Sibert, 18 Kan. 104, 112 (1877); cf., Daniels v. Johnson, 129 Cal. 412, 61 P. 1107, 79 Am.St.Rep. 123 (1900).

§ 6.14

1. Basye, Clearing Land Titles, 215 (2d Ed.1970).

2. See, e.g., Vernon's Ann.Mo.Stat. § 516.150. N.M.Stat.Ann.1978, § 37–1–20.

3. West's Ann.Civ.Code § 2911. See Colo.Rev.Stat. 38–40–112; Miss.Code 1972, §§ 15–1–21, 15–1–3; Mont.Code Ann. 71–3–122.

4. See e.g., New York—McKinney's Civ. Pract.Law and Rules § 213(4) (6 years); Vernon's Ann.Tex.Civ.Stat. art. 5520 (4 years).

from being employed as an affirmative basis for clearing title. These added to the difficulties of perfecting a marketable title.

To remedy these defects many states have adopted additional legislation to enable a title examiner to rely entirely on the record in determining whether an unreleased mortgage is still legally alive. While the details of this type of legislation vary, it generally provides that a mortgage shall no longer be a lien and that foreclosure is prohibited after the expiration of a certain number of years from the maturity of the mortgage debt as shown by the record or from the date to which payment thereof has been extended by agreement or other written notice recorded before that period.[5] The Florida legislation, as amended in 1974, is illustrative. It both terminates the lien and bars all actions to enforce or foreclose with respect to mortgages and other encumbrances after the expiration of five years from the final maturity of the mortgage debt as evidenced by the record or, if the final maturity date is not indicated in the record, twenty years from the date of the mortgage itself, unless an extension agreement is recorded prior to the expiration of such period.[6] If such a recording takes place the period is extended for a like period of five or twenty years.[7] "Under this type of statute nothing in the way of disability or any other fact not of record is permitted to toll or extend the operation of the statute * * *. By this means a favorable appraisal of title in this respect has finally become a reality in some states."[8]

Other states have adopted statutes which apply ordinary statutes of limitation to the original mortgagor, but provide for a termination of the mortgage lien after the expiration of a fixed period of time as to subsequent purchasers or encumbrancers for value.[9] The purpose of this type of legislation is "to permit such purchasers and encumbrancers in appraising the title, to ignore mortgages whose maturity, as it appears of record, exceeds the statutory period. According to many of these statutes provision is made for extending the mortgage lien by recording an extension agreement or an affidavit of notice as to the amount remaining unpaid on the mortgage debt, or by rerecording the mortgage itself."[10] The effect of this recording will not in itself keep the mortgage lien alive, but rather its purpose is to provide notice to subsequent purchasers or encumbrancers for value "who could otherwise ignore the existence of outstanding mortgages which have ceased to have life as against such purchasers or encumbrancers."[11] This type

---

5. Basye supra note 1 at 222. See, e.g., Minn.Stat.Ann. § 582.14; West's A.I.C. 32–8–4–1, 32–8–4–2.

6. West's Fla.Stat.Ann. § 95.281. See Basye, supra note 1 § 87 (1983 Supp.). For an interpretation of the Florida legislation, see Conner v. Coggins, 349 So.2d 780 (Fla. App.1977).

7. Id.

8. Basye, supra note 1 at 223.

9. Basye, supra note 13 at 223 lists the following states as having this type of legislation: Alabama, Alaska, Arkansas, Kentucky, Louisiana, Michigan, Mississippi, Montana, North Carolina, Ohio, Oregon, South Dakota and Texas.

10. Id. at 223.

11. Id. at 223.

of statute has not eliminated title problems because the validity of the mortgage lien depends on matters that are not of record such as the state of mind of the purchaser or encumbrancer with respect to unreleased mortgages or whether the purchaser or encumbrancer qualifies as one for value.[12]

Marketable Title Acts in effect in over a dozen states also enable a title examiner to ignore certain old unreleased mortgages of record.[13] For example, the Michigan Act expressly states that its purpose is to allow "persons dealing with the record title owner to rely on the record title covering a period of not more than 40 years prior to the date of such dealing and to that end to extinguish all claims that affect the interest thus dealt with, the existence of which claims arises out of or depends upon any act, transaction, event or omission antedating such 40 year period, unless within such 40 year period a notice of claim * * * shall have been duly filed for record."[14] While the 40 year period is common, 30[15] or 50[16] year periods are also found in such legislation. Under such legislation, a mortgage recorded more than 40 years earlier would be barred notwithstanding its maturity date, unless the holder had filed a notice of claim within the 40 year period.[17]

 WESTLAW REFERENCES
95.281(3) & court(fl)
marketable /3 title /2 act

C. MERGER

§ 6.15 Merger—General Considerations

The concept of merger is one of the most complex and confusing areas of the law of mortgages. The basic doctrine itself can be stated in a few sentences and is deceptively simple. The theory is that when a mortgagee's interest and a fee title coincide and meet in the same person, the lesser estate, the mortgage, merges into the greater, the fee, and is extinguished.[1] Courts also state that "whether a merger has occurred depends on the intent of the parties, especially the one in whom the interests unite. If merger is against that party's best interest, it will not be deemed intended by the parties."[2]

12. Note, 38 Harv.L.Rev. 651, 653 (1925); Basye, supra note 1 at 223.

13. See, e.g., West's Ann.Cal.Civ.Code §§ 882.020–882.040; Iowa Code Ann. § 614.29–§ 614.38; West's A.I.C. 32–1–5–1 to 32–1–5–10; Kan.Stat.Ann. 58–3401–3412; Note, Kansas Marketable Title Act, 13 Wash.L.J. 33 (1974).

14. Mich.Comp.Laws Ann. § 565.101–109.

15. See, e.g., N.C.Gen.Stat. §§ 47B–1 to 47B–9, noted in 10 Wake Forest L.Rev. 312 (1974).

16. See, e.g., West's A.I.C. 32–1–5–1 to 32–1–5–10.

17. Basye, supra note 1 at 248–249.

§ 6.15

1. See, e.g., Alden Hotel Co. v. Kanin, 88 Misc.2d 546, 387 N.Y.S.2d 948 (1976); Aladdin Heating v. Trustees of Central States, 93 Nev. 257, 563 P.2d 82 (1977).

2. Aladdin Heating v. Trustees of Central States, 93 Nev. 257, 563 P.2d 82, 85 (1977).

Once having stated the basic doctrine, our confusion begins. This is often because the merger doctrine can be utilized either as a defense to the mortgage debt or as an argument that the mortgage no longer exists. For example, suppose that in lieu of a foreclosure proceeding, a mortgagor agrees to convey the mortgaged estate to the mortgagee.[3] Does the merger of the two estates in the mortgagee extinguish the mortgage debt so that the mortgagee will be unable to pursue the mortgagor personally? On the other hand, the same facts may result in a merger problem with the focus on the *mortgage* and not the debt. Suppose that our mortgagee was a first mortgagee and that, through inadvertence, he took a deed in lieu of foreclosure without first checking to see if junior liens existed on the real estate. If such a junior lienor did exist and now claims to be a senior lienor, will our former first mortgagee be able to keep his mortgage alive and foreclose it to wipe out the junior, or has merger destroyed it?

It should be pointed out that the merger concept is more often a debt problem when the controversy is between the person who holds the debt, mortgage and title and the person who has the duty of paying the debt. On the other hand, merger arguments more commonly focus on the continued existence of the *mortgage* when the controversy is between the person who is the holder of the debt, mortgage and title and the person who represents an intervening lienor or other third party claimant. While these generalizations, like all generalizations, do not represent universal truth, the two fact patterns underlying them provide a helpful framework and basis for attempting to understand the merger concept.

 WESTLAW REFERENCES
di merger
266k295

§ 6.16 Merger—Between the Parties to the Mortgage

The problem of merger as between the holder of the debt, mortgage and title and the person who is liable for the payment of the debt may arise in at least five settings: (1) The mortgagee may acquire the title (redemption interest) from the mortgagor. (2) The mortgagee may acquire the title from a grantee of the mortgagor. (3) The holder of more than one mortgage may acquire title on the foreclosure of one of those mortgages. (4) The mortgagee may transfer the debt and mortgage to the mortgagor. (5) The mortgagee may transfer the debt and mortgage to a grantee of the mortgagor.

Acquisition From Mortgagor by Mortgagee

Where the mortgage creditor acquires the redemption interest from the mortgagor, whether the acquisition will permit enforcement of the

---

3. See § 6.18, infra.

debt and mortgage according to the intention of acquisitor, or will preclude such enforcement regardless of intention, will depend upon the terms of the transfer. If it was a gift conveyance by the mortgagor it is obvious that the debt claim of the mortgage creditor would be unaffected and whether there would be a merger of the interests in the land would depend, as previously noted, upon the intent of the mortgage creditor. On the other hand, as, for example, in the deed in lieu of foreclosure situation,[1] if the conveyance is made and accepted as payment of the mortgage debt no question of merger is possible. The debt is discharged by payment, or perhaps more accurately, by substituted performance or accord and satisfaction; but not by merger.[2] The creditor now has full title to the property with no debt in existence for it to secure. If the mortgage debt is extinguished, the mortgage itself is never kept alive. Consequently there is automatic merger of the two interests in the property and no intent on the part of the creditor can keep them separate.

What should be the effect if the conveyance from the mortgagor to the mortgagee is accompanied by an assumption of the mortgage? If the mortgagee were permitted to recover from the mortgagor, the latter could turn around and sue to get back the same amount. To prevent this circuity of action a court of equity would give a complete defense to the mortgagor to any action on the debt. If there has been an assumption there is complete merger because there is complete circuity. No intent or self-interest on the part of the mortgage creditor could prevent this termination of the claim against the mortgagor and, with it, any mortgage interest in the property securing it.[3]

More commonly, the conveyance to the mortgagee will be subject to the mortgage either because the deed expressly so states or because of its silence. If the agreement is that it is to be accepted in satisfaction of the mortgage debt it will, of course, so operate.[4] If this is not the agreement there may be, technically, no extinguishment of the mortgage debt.[5] If there is an express agreement that it shall not operate to extinguish the mortgage, the agreement will be given effect.[6] Nevertheless, such a conveyance makes the land in the hands of the mortgage creditor the principal and the personal obligation of the mortgagor, up

§ 6.16

1. See § 6.15, supra, § 6.18, infra.

2. Dennis v. McEntyre Mercantile Co., 187 Ala. 314, 65 So. 774 (1914); McCabe v. Farnsworth, 27 Mich. 52 (1873); see, 95 A.L.R. 89, 95 (1935). If the conveyance is accepted at or before maturity it operates by way of substituted performance; if after maturity, by accord and satisfaction.

3. Forthman v. Deters, 206 Ill. 159, 69 N.E. 97, 99 Am.St.Rep. 145 (1903); Kneeland v. Moore, 138 Mass. 198 (1884); First State Bank v. Arneson, 109 Wash. 346, 186 P. 889 (1920); see 95 A.L.R. 89, 94 (1935).

But see § 6.15, as to whether the mortgage may be kept alive as to third parties.

4. See supra, this section. See also Tiffany, Real Prop., 3d ed., § 1479.

5. Murphy v. Zuigaro, 72 Pa.Super.Ct. 511 (1924); Sheehan Building & Loan Association v. Scanlon, 310 Pa. 6, 164 A. 722 (1933).

6. See Arthurs Travel Center, Inc. v. Alten, 268 Pa.Super. 330, 408 A.2d 490 (1979); Morton v. Rifai, 339 So.2d 707 (Fla. App.1976); Sheehan Building & Loan Association v. Scanlon, 310 Pa. 6, 164 A. 722 (1933).

to the value of the land, surety only.[7] Consequently, up to the value of the land, the mortgagor has a defense to any enforcement of the debt against him regardless of whether it is technically alive by agreement.[8] And usually the courts treat the situation as one of merger with the debt discharged, if the land equals the debt in value.[9] However, if there was no agreement that the conveyance should be a discharge and the value of the land was less than the debt, the mortgage creditor can maintain an action for the excess of the debt over the land.[10] In such a case there is merger of the debt only up to the value of the land because there is circuity only to this extent.

Acquisition by Mortgagee from Grantee of Mortgagor

The same principles govern where the redemption is obtained by the mortgage creditor from a grantee of the mortgagor, but the application of them becomes somewhat more complicated. First the terms on which the grantee held the property from the grantor and their legal results must be determined. Then the terms of acquisition by the creditor from the grantee must be ascertained. The grantee may have bought from the mortgagor paying full value with an agreement that the mortgagor was to pay the mortgage and then made a gift conveyance to the mortgage creditor. The result then would be the same as a gift conveyance directly from the mortgagor to the mortgagee. On the other hand, conveyances in satisfaction of the mortgage debt, or with the mortgage creditor assuming or taking the property subject to the mortgage debt, will operate as would similar direct transactions between the mortgagor and mortgage creditor.[11] If the grantee has taken subject to the mortgage debt the mortgage creditor will also take it in the same way with an automatic merger, at least to the extent of the value of the land.[12] If the grantee has assumed the debt, again the land also would be principal and, if it is acquired by the mortgage creditor, bars the debt up to its value.[13] If, in addition, the mortgage creditor, in

7. See §§ 5.3–5.4, supra.

8. E.g., Eagan v. Engeman, 125 App. Div. 743, 110 N.Y.S. 366 (1908).

9. Cock v. Bailey, 146 Pa. 328, 23 A. 370 (1892); see 8 U. of Cin.L.Rev. 212, 213 (1935); 95 A.L.R. 89, 93 (1935).

10. "'The purchase of the equity of redemption by the mortgagee at a sale by the mortgagor's assignee in insolvency, or on execution is not at law a satisfaction of the mortgage debt, and the mortgagee is not estopped from claiming that the property is of less value than the amount of the debt.'" Clark v. Jackson, 64 N.H. 388, 391, 11 A. 59 (1887); Findlay v. Hosmer, 2 Conn. 350 (1817); Marston v. Marston, 45 Me. 412 (1858); Spencer v. Harford's Executors, 4 Wend. 381 (N.Y.1830). Cf. Miller

v. Little, 37 N.D. 612, 164 N.W. 19 (1917); Ex parte Powell, 68 S.C. 324, 47 S.E. 440 (1904). See 8 U. of Cin.L.Rev. 213 (1935); 15 Harv.L.Rev. 740 (1902); 95 A.L.R. 89, 94 (1935). But see Glassie, The Assuming Vendee, 9 Va.L.Rev. 196, 205, n. 36, quoted § 250, n. 35 (1923), supra.

11. E.g., Dickason v. Williams, 129 Mass. 182, 37 Am.Rep. 316 (1880); National Investment Co. v. Nordin, 50 Minn. 336, 52 N.W. 899 (1892), assuming grantees of mortgagor conveyed to mortgagee subject to the mortgage and thus extinguished it.

12. Lilly v. Palmer, 51 Ill. 331 (1869), see 95 A.L.R. 89, 95 (1935).

13. Russell v. Pistor, 7 N.Y. 171, 57 Am. Dec. 509 (1852); cases notes 45–46, supra.

its turn, assumes the payment of the debt it will operate to preclude enforcement of any of the debt.

Two Mortgages in Same Hands—Purchase at Foreclosure Sale by Mortgagee

Where the mortgage creditor holds not only a first mortgage but a second as well, how does its purchase on foreclosure sale of one of the mortgages affects its rights under the other one? The general rule is that the purchase by the holder of a junior mortgage at a foreclosure sale of the senior mortgage, does not extinguish the debt secured by the junior mortgage.[14] Moreover, the same is true even though the foreclosed first mortgage also was owned by the purchasing second mortgagee.[15] However, if the holder of both a junior and senior mortgage forecloses the junior and buys at the foreclosure sale it is generally held that, in the absence of an agreement to the contrary,[16] the mortgagor's personal liability for the debt secured by the first mortgage is extinguished.[17] The reason given is that upon a foreclosure sale under a junior mortgage the purchase is subject to the payment of the prior lien with the result that "the mortgagor has an equitable right to have the land pay the mortgage before his personal liability is called upon"[18] and the purchaser, if he owns or acquires the mortgage, will not be permitted to enforce it against the mortgagor personally. The second mortgagee purchaser is presumed to have made allowance for the prior lien in making its bid.

The above result and analysis are logical and fair only if one assumes that the land was worth at least an amount equal to the sum of the two mortgage debts. Thus, for example, if the first mortgage debt is $40,000, the second mortgage debt is $20,000 and the fair market value of the land free and clear of liens is at least $60,000, and the mortgagee purchases for $20,000 (fair market value less $40,000) it makes sense to apply merger to destroy the senior debt. In such a case, the mortgagee would be unjustly enriched if he were permitted to

14. Ferry v. Fisk, 54 Cal.App. 763, 202 P. 964 (1921). Cf. Miller v. Little, 37 N.D. 612, 164 N.W. 19 (1917).

15. Blackwood v. Sakwinski, 221 Mich. 464, 191 N.W. 207, 29 A.L.R. 1314 (1922); Sautter v. Frick, 229 App.Div. 345, 242 N.Y.S. 369 (1930), affirmed 256 N.Y. 535, 177 N.E. 129 (1931) reversing, 133 Misc. 517, 232 N.Y.S. 529 (1929). Cf. Fischer v. Spierling, 93 N.J.L. 167, 107 A. 420 (1919). See 29 A.L.R. 1318 (1924); 95 A.L.R. 89, 103 (1935). After foreclosure and sale under a first mortgage, a conveyance by the first mortgagee, who bought it in, to the mortgagor will not revive the second mortgage on the land in his hands. See 12 N.Y. U.L.Q.Rev. 319 (1935).

16. Continental Title & Trust Co. v. Devlin, 209 Pa. 380, 58 A. 843 (1904); Tos-

ton v. Utah Mortgage Loan Co., 115 F.2d 560 (C.C.A.Idaho 1940); Van Woerden v. Union Improvement Co., 156 Wash. 555, 287 P. 870 (1930).

17. Belleville Savings Bank v. Reis, 136 Ill. 242, 26 N.E. 646 (1891); Maulding v. Sims, 213 Ill.App. 473 (1919); McDonald v. Magirl, 97 Iowa 677, 66 N.W. 904 (1896); Wright v. Anderson, 62 S.D. 444, 253 N.W. 484, 95 A.L.R. 81 (1934); see 95 A.L.R. 89, 104 (1935). It will not merge the first mortgage, however, as against intervening liens. Citizens State Bank v. Peterson, 114 Neb. 809, 210 N.W. 278 (1926); see Wright v. Anderson, 62 S.D. 444, 450, 253 N.W. 484, 487, 95 A.L.R. 81, 86 (1934).

18. See Wright v. Anderson, 62 S.D. 444, 450, 253 N.W. 484, 487, 95 A.L.R. 81, 86 (1934).

become the owner of land worth at least an amount equal to the sum of the two mortgage debts and also allowed to collect on the senior debt. But where the land is not worth at least the sum of the two debts, to apply the merger doctrine to destroy completely the senior debt short-changes the mortgagee. For example, suppose the fair market value of the land free and clear of liens is $20,000 and the two mortgages are in the same amounts described above. If the mortgagee purchases for $20,000 at the foreclosure of the second mortgage he obtains land that is worth $20,000. To allow him to recover the other $40,000 from the mortgagor personally would not result in unjust enrichment and should not be barred by the merger doctrine.

Where both mortgages are in default, a mortgagee should nevertheless be able to avoid the above merger predicament. For example, if judicial foreclosure is utilized, the court could order both mortgages foreclosed simultaneously. If the mortgagee purchased at that sale and the sale price was for less than the combined mortgage debt, there is no reason why the mortgagee should not be able to obtain a deficiency decree for that difference. The merger concept would simply be inapplicable. This approach will probably not work, however, with power of sale foreclosure. Although a court clearly can approve such a procedure, it is doubtful that the person holding a power of sale would have similar authority, if for no other reason than that power of sale legislation does not ordinarily provide for the foreclosure of more than one mortgage at a time.

Acquisition From Mortgagee by Mortgagor

When the mortgage creditor transfers the debt claim and mortgage securing it to the mortgagor the inevitable result as between them is to extinguish both the debt and, along with it, the mortgage.[19] The same person cannot be both debtor and creditor.[20] This would be true regardless of whether the transfer was by way of gift or for value. In the latter case, especially if the value given was the amount of the mortgage debt, the transaction is likely to be intended to extinguish the debt by payment or an accord and satisfaction. If so, its demise should not be considered as resulting from the doctrine of merger.[21]

Acquisition From Mortgagee by Grantee of Mortgagor

A similar situation occurs where the mortgagor has conveyed to a grantee who assumes the mortgage and the mortgage creditor then assigns the debt and mortgage to him. As the principal debtor in such

19. Hussey v. Hill, 120 N.C. 312, 26 S.E. 919, 58 Am.St.Rep. 789 (1897); Hill v. Hall, 4 Rob. 416 (La.1843).

20. "The fundamental principle is that a man cannot be both debtor and creditor with respect to the same debt at the same time and when a situation arises where the hand that is obligated to pay the debt is the same hand that is entitled to receive it, the debt is extinguished and forever gone." Wright v. Anderson, 62 S.D. 444, 253 N.W. 484, 95 A.L.R. 81 (1934).

21. See Tiffany, Real Prop., 3d Ed., § 1482.

a case, his acquisition of the claim not only extinguishes it as to him [22] but also as to the mortgagor who stands in the position of a surety.[23] This would be true whether the transfer was a gift or whether value was paid. In the latter case the debt may be regarded as extinguished by payment, substituted performance or accord and satisfaction rather than by merger. If the mortgagor was bound by agreement with the grantee to pay off the debt, an assignment of the debt and mortgage to the grantee would not prevent the enforcement of it against the principal debtor, the mortgagor.[24] Whether there would be merger as to the land would here again depend upon the intent or interest of the holder of it.

If the grantee had merely taken subject to the mortgage the only one personally liable is the mortgagor. Where such a grantee takes an assignment of the mortgage, as a general rule the debt secured by the mortgage is held to be extinguished and personal liability on it cannot be enforced.[25] Up to the value of the land there would seem no question as to the result. The mortgagor is surety only and the land principal with the result that, to prevent circuity the mortgagor could defeat any recovery up to that amount, and this is true regardless of whether the mortgage is acquired for value or as a gift. Where the debt exceeds the value of the land a question may arise as to the right of such a grantee-assignee to recover a deficiency. If the grantee paid the amount of the debt for the assignment, the mortgagor should be able to insist that it constituted payment of the debt rather than purchase of it. The reason is that, although the grantee incurred no personal obligation to pay off the mortgage, nonetheless when he bought the land subject to it, the bargain included as a part of the price the amount of the mortgage debt. As a consequence, even though the mortgagor could not compel him to pay and the mortgage creditor has no right against him personally, yet it is so far his duty to discharge the debt that if he does so he should have no recourse against the mortgagor for reimbursement.[26] It would seem, therefore, that regardless of the value of the land, when a grantee subject to the mortgage buys in the mortgage, he cannot enforce any right on it against the mortgagor.

It has been suggested, however, that if the mortgage creditor assigned the debt and mortgage to such a grantee by way of gift or for less than the amount of the debt it could be enforced by him as to any

---

22. Russell v. Pistor, 7 N.Y. 171, 57 Am. Dec. 509 (1852); Barnett & Jackson v. McMillan, 176 Ala. 430, 58 So. 400 (1912); Fouche v. Delk, 83 Iowa 297, 48 N.W. 1078 (1891); Lydon v. Campbell, 204 Mass. 580, 91 N.E. 151, 134 Am.St.Rep. 702 (1910). See 95 A.L.R. 89, 111 (1935); 46 A.L.R. 329 (1927).

23. See §§ 5.17–5.18, supra.

24. Barnett & Jackson v. McMillan, 176 Ala. 430, 58 So. 400 (1912), as to the second mortgage.

25. Baxter v. Redevco, Inc., 279 Or. 117, 566 P.2d 501 (1977) (quoting text); Lilly v. Palmer, 51 Ill. 331 (1869); Atherton v. Toney, 43 Ind. 211 (1873); Price v. Rea, 92 Iowa 12, 60 N.W. 208 (1894); Wonderly v. Giessler, 118 Mo.App. 708, 93 S.W. 1130 (1906); see 95 A.L.R. 89, 107 (1935).

26. Baxter v. Redevco, Inc., 279 Or. 117, 566 P.2d 501 (1977) (quoting text).

excess of the debt over the value of the land.[27]   An argument can be made in favor of such a result as follows: The mortgage creditor could have enforced the mortgage debt to the amount of its excess over the value of the land against the mortgagor without the latter having any recourse against the grantee who took subject to the mortgage. If it did so, after collecting it, the mortgagee could make a gift of those proceeds to anyone it wishes, including the grantee, free of any claim of the mortgagor to it. It would seem to follow that the mortgagee has equal ability to make a gift of the right to collect the deficiency. Thus it might have given it to third person or to the mortgagor. If, instead, the donee is the mortgagor's grantee subject to the mortgage, it seems logical to say that the mortgagor cannot object to grantee's enforcement of it.

 WESTLAW REFERENCES

Acquisition from Mortgagor by Mortgagee
266k295 /p merge*

Acquisition by Mortgagee from Grantee of Mortgagor
mortgagee /s grantee /s mortgagor /p merge*

Two Mortgages in Same Hands—Purchase at Foreclosure Sale by Mortgagee
first senior /2 mortgag** /p second junior /2 mortgag** /p
    foreclos! /p merge* extinguish!
266k295(5)
di power of sale

Acquisition from Mortgagee by Mortgagor
"accord and satisfaction" /p mortgagor /p mortgagee

Acquisition from Mortgagee by Grantee of Mortgagor
assum! /2 grantee /s mortgagor

§ 6.17 Merger—Intervening Interests

Merger problems also can occur when a senior lienor acquires title from the mortgagor or his grantee. Here the problem usually is that a junior lienor claims that acquisition of title by the senior has resulted in the destruction of the senior lien so that it can no longer be foreclosed against the junior. If merger has occurred, the junior lien is thus promoted to a higher status. This merger argument is most commonly found in the deed in lieu of foreclosure situation discussed earlier.[1] However, it can arise in other contexts. For example, junior lienors have attempted to utilize merger to destroy a senior mortgage where the senior mortgagee acquired the mortgagor's interest at a bankruptcy sale.[2]

It should be emphasized, however, that whether there is merger as between the mortgage creditor and the mortgagor or a grantee of the

---

27. See Tiffany, Real Property, § 1432.

§ 6.17

1. See § 6.15, supra and § 6.17, infra.

2. See Lampert Yards, Inc. v. Thompson-Wetterling Construction & Realty, Inc., 302 Minn. 83, 223 N.W.2d 418 (1974).

mortgagor is not decisive as to whether it also occurs as between the mortgage creditor and holders of junior incumbrances [3] or other interests.[4] When the question arises in the latter situation courts repeat the general merger concept that merger is a question of intention and that intention will be presumed, in the absence of express manifestation, in accordance with the interests of the party in whom all interests in the debt and mortgaged property are united.[5] This statement, while it has certain merits, is an inadequate exposition of the principles governing the decisions. A more satisfactory explanation of the results of the cases requires an analysis of the proper role of actual intention and the basis for "presuming" an intention in accordance with interest.

In the first place, in certain cases both intent and self interest will be immaterial. If the mortgage creditor in acquiring the land assumes not merely the first mortgage but also the payment of the junior incumbrance no expression of intent to keep the mortgage alive, or self interest in doing so, will avail as against the junior incumbrancer.[6] A plea of circuity of action by the later mortgagee will effectively preclude enforcement of the earlier mortgage in the hands of such a creditor. The same would be true up to the value of the land if the property were acquired subject to the later mortgage.

It is also clear that if the mortgage creditor knew of the intervening interest and nevertheless clearly indicated an intention that its prior mortgage should be discharged there will be merger and the junior encumbrance will be elevated to priority regardless of its best interests being to the contrary.[7]

Normally, however, courts reject the merger argument and hold that the first mortgage will be preserved or reinstated as against the intervening interest. In some cases the mortgage creditor clearly indicated its intention to keep the first mortgage in existence as against such interests and the courts rest the result upon that ground.[8] For example, one court noted that having the deed run to a nominee of the mortgagee, rather than to the mortgagee itself indicated such an intent

3. See 39 L.R.A.,N.S., 834 (1909); 95 A.L.R. 628 (1935), for collections of cases. See also Note, The Rights of a Junior Lienholder in Wisconsin, 42 Marq.L.Rev. 89, 94 (1959).

4. See 46 A.L.R. 322 (1927).

5. See, e.g., Aladdin Heating v. Trustees of Central States, 93 Nev. 257, 563 P.2d 82 (1977); McCraney v. Morris, 170 S.C. 250, 170 S.E. 276, 95 A.L.R. 622 (1933); note, 95 A.L.R. 628, 629 (1935).

6. Ernst v. McChesney, 186 Ill. 617, 58 N.E. 399 (1900); Kneeland v. Moore, 138 Mass. 198 (1884); Drew v. Anderson, Clayton & Co., 120 Okl. 250, 252 P. 64 (1927), noted, 27 Col.L.Rev. 609; Bolln v. La Prele Live Stock Co., 27 Wyo. 335, 196 P. 748 (1921); Brown v. Stead, 5 Sim. 535 (1832).

7. Townsend v. Provident Realty Co., 110 App.Div. 226, 96 N.Y.S. 1091 (1905); Beacham v. Gurney, 91 Iowa 621, 60 N.W. 187 (1894); Errett v. Wheeler, 109 Minn. 157, 123 N.W. 414, 26 L.R.A.,N.S., 816 (1909); Stantons v. Thompson, 49 N.H. 272 (1870).

8. See Bay Minette Production Credit Association v. Federal Land Bank, 442 So. 2d 47 (Ala.1983); Fidelity Savings Association of Kansas v. Witt, 8 Kan.App.2d 640, 665 P.2d 1108 (1983); Citizens Security Bank of Bixby v. Courtney, 572 P.2d 1302 (Okl.App.1977); Gibbs v. Johnson, 104 Mich. 120, 62 N.W. 145 (1895). See 95 A.L.R. 628, 649, 650 (1935).

to keep the mortgage alive.[9] On the other hand, in numerous cases in which there is no evidence of intention to keep the prior mortgage alive, other than that it would be to the interest of the mortgage creditor to do so, courts have found no merger.[10] But the courts go beyond this and hold, in spite of an undisputed intent on the part of the mortgage creditor to discharge the first mortgage, that it nevertheless may use it for foreclosure purposes against junior interests.[11] This is the almost uniform result where the mortgage creditor was ignorant of the intervening lien.[12] Although there is some authority that its negligence in not discovering the existence of the later interest [13] or in mistakenly relying on its not being enforced [14] will prevent it using it against the subsequent claimant, other and better authority holds to the contrary.[15]

Indeed, the rule may be stated broadly that, except for the two cases stated at the outset of this section, merger will not operate to permit a later incumbrance to be elevated to a position of priority over the first mortgage regardless of its fate as between the parties to that first mortgage.[16] Actual intent, where it exists, is an adequate basis for the result. The mortgage creditor has a legitimate interest to protect

---

9. See Alden Hotel Co. v. Kanin, 88 Misc.2d 546, 387 N.Y.S.2d 948 (1976).

10. See Aladdin Heating Co. v. Trustees of Central States, 93 Nev. 257, 563 P.2d 82 (1977); Lampert Yards, Inc. v. Thompson-Wetterling Constr. & Realty, Inc., 302 Minn. 83, 223 N.W.2d 418 (1974). See 18 Col.L.Rev. 280 (1918). See also cases in following footnotes.

11. Brooks v. Rice, 56 Cal. 428 (1880), conveyance by mortgagor to mortgagee in satisfaction of the mortgage held not to operate as a merger against an intervening mortgage; Richardson v. Hockenhull, 85 Ill. 124 (1877); Moffet v. Farwell, 222 Ill. 543, 78 N.E. 925 (1906); Sullivan v. Saunders, 66 W.Va. 350, 66 S.E. 497, 42 L.R.A.,N.S., 1010, 19 Ann.Cas. 480 (1909); Fitch v. Applegate, 24 Wash. 25, 64 P. 147 (1901); See 39 L.R.A.,N.S., 834 (1912); 95 A.L.R. 628, 643 (1935).

"On this point, I am of the opinion that upon such a state of facts, showing a title intervening between the mortgage and quitclaim deed, it is to be presumed, as a matter of law, that the parties did not intend to extinguish the mortgage. * * *" Stantons v. Thompson, 49 N.H. 272, 276 (1870). See also Wilson v. Vanstone, 112 Mo. 315, 20 S.W. 612 (1892); Grellet v. Heilshorn, 4 Nev. 526 (1869). See note, 18 Col.L.Rev. 280 (1918); note, 12 N.Y.Univ.L.Q.Rev. 317 (1934).

12. Silliman v. Gammage, 55 Tex. 365 (1881); Seiberling v. Tipton, 113 Mo. 373,

21 S.W. 4 (1893); Howard v. Clark and Teachout, 71 Vt. 424, 45 A. 1042, 76 Am.St. Rep. 782 (1899); see Woodhurst v. Cramer, 29 Wash. 40, 48, 69 P. 501, 503 (1902); 95 A.L.R. 628, 643 (1935); 40 W.Va.L.Q. 280 (1934); Frazee v. Inslee, 2 N.J.Eq. 239 (1839), contra. *A fortiori,* the same would be true where the discharge of the prior lien was obtained by fraud. See 95 A.L.R. 628, 647 (1935).

13. See Fort Dodge Building & Loan Association v. Scott, 86 Iowa 431, 434, 53 N.W. 283, 284 (1892), semble. And see Rice v. Winters, 45 Neb. 517, 63 N.W. 830 (1895); Bohn Sash & Door Co. v. Case, 42 Neb. 281, 60 N.W. 576 (1894).

14. Woodside v. Lippold, 113 Ga. 877, 39 S.E. 400, 84 Am.St.Rep. 267 (1901); cf. Beacham v. Gurney, 91 Iowa, 621, 60 N.W. 187 (1894); Errett v. Wheeler, 109 Minn. 157, 123 N.W. 414, 26 L.R.A.,N.S., 816 (1909); Frazee v. Inslee, 2 N.J.Eq. 239 (1839); Gainey v. Anderson, 87 S.C. 47, 68 S.E. 888, 31 L.R.A.,N.S., 323 (1910). See 27 L.R.A.,N.S., 816 (1910). See also note, 27 Col.L.Rev. 609 (1927).

15. McCraney v. Morris, 170 S.C. 250, 170 S.E. 276, 95 A.L.R. 622 (1933); Home Owners Loan Corp. v. Collins, 120 N.J.Eq. 266, 184 A. 621 (1936) semble; see 27 Col.L. Rev. 609 (1927).

16. See 95 A.L.R. 628, 629 (1935).

itself against the elevation of the later interest. By bringing a foreclosure action in which they were joined as parties defendant the property could have been sold free and clear of their interests and the mortgagee could have bought it in that state. Acquisition of the redemption in any other way should not prejudice its position with respect to such junior interests if the mortgagee did not intend to do so and was not under a duty to do acts which would have that result. The owner of the junior interest, under such circumstances, cannot object to being kept or returned to a subordinate position because he never bargained for an advancement that would result by destruction of the first mortgage. But more generally the decisions may be justified on grounds of unjust enrichment. By the destruction of the prior mortgage, the later lien or interest is elevated to a priority for which its owner paid nothing and hence is, as to him, a pure windfall at the expense of the prior mortgagee. If the owner of the prior mortgage knew of the later interest and intended nevertheless to discharge or otherwise wipe out the first mortgage, there is, of course, no injustice in permitting the later claimant to take advantage of his unmerited advancement. Where the first mortgagee knew of the second and intended to prevent him getting this benefit it would be unconscionable to permit the second to have it. The same seems true of a case where a mortgagee gave up its mortgage in the mistaken belief that a junior lien would not be enforced. So, too, if it did not know of the junior interest and so didn't know that the result of its action would be to confer an advantage on the second. That the ignorance or mistake was due to negligence should make no difference. The only consequence of the negligence is to confer a benefit upon the later lienors or other claimants which, if taken away, would leave them in no worse position than they were before the occurrence. Since it does not put them at any disadvantage or cause them any loss, it should not prevent the first mortgagee from being restored to its position by reinstating its mortgage.[17] Indeed, whether the courts clearly analyse the problem in this way or not, it represents the best rationale for their reiterated statements that in the absence of express intention on the part of the mortgagee its intention will be presumed in accordance with its interests.

WESTLAW REFERENCES

intervening /4 interest /p mortgag**
bankrupt** /p mortgagee /s acquir! acquisition! /p merge*
intent! /p merge* /p first senior /p second junior /s
       mortgage

---

17. See McCraney v. Morris, 170 S.C. 250, 260, 170 S.E. 276, 280, 95 A.L.R. 622, 627 (1933).

D. THE DEED IN LIEU OF FORECLOSURE

§ 6.18 Reasons for Use

As we noted earlier, the rule against contemporaneous clogging of the equity of redemption is generally inapplicable to transactions *subsequent* to the original mortgage transaction.[1] Thus most courts, in theory at least, permit the mortgagee to purchase the mortgagor's equity of redemption; however, such transactions are subjected to careful review to ensure that the transaction is free from fraud, is based on an adequate consideration, and that it is, in fact, actually subsequent to the mortgage and not contemporaneous with it.[2]

Relying on the foregoing subsequent transaction exception, a mortgagee will commonly take a deed from the mortgagor in satisfaction of the mortgage debt. We noted this practice briefly in our preceding sections dealing with merger.[3] The mortgagee engages in this practice, ordinarily, to avoid the further expense of a foreclosure action in which, even though he gets it, a deficiency judgment will often be worthless.[4] The mortgagor on his part is quite frequently glad to give the deed in order to avoid, in states not having anti-deficiency legislation, a possible personal judgment against him which might cause him trouble in the future even though at present it was uncollectable. Also, some mortgagees are actuated either by a genuine desire to aid the mortgagor, an aversion to the publicity and trouble of a court action, or both.

 WESTLAW REFERENCES
mortgagee /s purchas! acquir! buy bought /s mortgagor /p "equity of redemption"
266k297

§ 6.19 Potential Pitfalls for the Mortgagee

Whatever its seeming simplicity, the deed in lieu of foreclosure can create substantial problems for the mortgagee and is often, from its perspective, a dangerous device. These problems can entail potential clouds on title and possible difficulties with intervening lienors and other interests. The following materials examine some of these problem areas.

First, we have already noted that courts carefully examine subsequent transactions for evidence of fraud and the adequacy of consideration. Such a transaction "is subject to close scrutiny in an effort to determine whether it was voluntarily entered into on the part of the mortgagor under conditions free of undue influence, oppression, unfairness or unconscientious advantage. Further the burden of proving the

§ 6.18

1. See § 3.3, supra.

2. Id.

3. See §§ 6.15, 6.16, supra.

4. See Note, 36 Mich.L.Rev. 111 (1937).

fairness rests on the mortgagee."[1] There is in this scrutiny the underlying notion that the mortgagor and mortgagee do not share equal bargaining strength. Thus it is possible, "especially if the consideration paid is disproportionately less than the value of the equity or if none is paid where the equity has value, that the whole transaction will be construed as unfair and unconscionable."[2] Moreover, if the deed is not by the mortgagor but by a non-assuming grantee of the mortgagor, a release of the debt, since there was no personal liability, would be no consideration for the conveyance to the mortgagee and subject it to being set aside. Where the transaction is subject to being set aside on such grounds, the mortgagor or his grantee will be permitted to redeem.[3]

Second, there is always the possibility that a court will construe the deed in lieu transaction itself as simply another mortgage transaction. As earlier material has explained, grantor-mortgagors are often successful in establishing by clear and convincing evidence that an absolute deed in favor of a grantee-mortgagee was actually intended as a mortgage.[4] Although a mortgagee will, of course, contest the mortgagor's view of the deed in lieu transaction, mortgagors do occasionally succeed in persuading courts to conceptualize it as a mortgage cast in the form of an absolute deed.[5] If the mortgagor is successful, he will be treated as a mortgagor under two mortgages—under the original mortgage which was not eliminated by the deed in lieu and under the deed in lieu treated as a second mortgage.

Moreover, the possibility exists that because of insolvency of the mortgagor or an actual intent on his part to defraud his creditors the conveyance may be subject to avoidance at the suit of creditors outside of bankruptcy or under the bankruptcy laws should the mortgagor go or be forced into bankruptcy.[6]

Finally, the deed in lieu transaction raises the related problems of the intervening lienor and the merger doctrine. If, subsequent to the original mortgage, the mortgagor has voluntarily or involuntarily created other liens, the deed in lieu to the mortgagee will not operate to cut off such intervening liens.[7] Foreclosure will still be necessary to eliminate such interests. Moreover, to make matters worse, the junior lienor may well utilize the merger doctrine to assert that since, as a result of the deed in lieu, the mortgage and the redemption interest are

---

§ 6.19

1. Robar v. Ellingson, 301 N.W.2d 653, 657–658 (N.D.1981) (insufficient threshold evidence of oppression or unfairness to trigger mortgagee's burden of proof).

2. Note, 31 Mo.L.Rev. 312, 314–315 (1966).

3. Id. at 315.

4. See §§ 3.4–3.9, supra.

5. The classic case is Peugh v. Davis, 96 U.S. 332, 24 L.Ed. 775 (1877). See also,

Noelker v. Wehmeyer, 392 S.W.2d 409 (Mo. App.1965). But see Kerr Land & Livestock, Inc. v. Glaus, 107 Idaho 767, 692 P.2d 1199 (App.1984) (insufficient evidence that deed in lieu constituted a mortgage); Robar v. Ellingson, 301 N.W.2d 653 (N.D.1981) (mortgagor failed to meet burden of establishing that what purported to be a deed in lieu constituted a mortgage).

6. See § 8.12 infra.

7. See Note, 31 Mo.L.Rev. 312, 314 (1966).

now held by the first mortgagee, the first mortgage has been destroyed.[8] Thus, the junior lienor will argue that his lien has been promoted in priority. While this merger argument, as we noted earlier, will seldom succeed,[9] it is nevertheless often asserted[10] and, for that reason alone, worth avoiding. The problems discussed in this paragraph can be avoided only by a thorough title search by the mortgagee prior to taking the deed in lieu to determine whether such intervening interests exist. If such liens or interests are discovered, the only prudent alternative for the mortgagee is to foreclose. However, even if the result of the title search is negative, that result will do nothing to obviate the other problems inherent in the deed in lieu transaction that were considered in earlier paragraphs of this section.

The practice of taking a deed in lieu of foreclosure is probably understandable in states where a judicial proceeding is the only authorized foreclosure method. In such a situation, the problems and risks discussed above may sometimes be outweighed by the costs and delay inherent in judicial foreclosure. However, where valid power of sale foreclosure statutes exist, foreclosure is relatively quick and inexpensive[11] and compelling reasons for such foreclosure alternatives as the deed in lieu simply do not exist.

 WESTLAW REFERENCES
mortgage /s deed /p unfair! undue overreach! /p intent! intend!
peugh /p mortgag**
merge* /p deed /s lieu
merge* /p foreclos! /p deed /p extinguish!

---

8. See § 6.17, supra.

9. Id.

10. See e.g., Bay Minette Production Credit Association v. Federal Land Bank, 442 So.2d 47 (Ala.1983); Gourley v. Wollam, 348 So.2d 1218 (Fla.App.1977); Fidelity Savings Association of Kansas v. Witt, 8 Kan.App.2d 640, 665 P.2d 1108 (1983); Citizens Security Bank of Bixby v. Courtney, 572 P.2d 1302 (Okl.App.1977); Lampert Yards, Inc. v. Thompson-Wetterling Construction & Realty, Inc., 302 Minn. 83, 223 N.W.2d 418 (Minn.1974); Aladdin Heating Corp. v. Trustees of Central States, 93 Nev. 257, 563 P.2d 82 (1977).

11. See § 7.19 infra.

§§ 6.20–7.0 are reserved for supplementary material.

Chapter 7

FORECLOSURE

Table of Sections

A. REDEMPTION FROM THE MORTGAGE

§ 7.1 Redemption From the Mortgage and Statutory Redemption—Definitions

Because the concept of redemption is so basic to the law of mortgages and is especially intertwined with the procedural and substantive rules governing foreclosure, it is important at this point to reexamine the concept in some detail. In this connection, it is also necessary to reemphasize the two significantly different types of redemption. The first type is variously referred to as the "equity of redemption", the "equity of tardy redemption" or as "redemption from the mortgage." The second type is referred to as "statutory redemption."

When courts utilize the terminology of the first type of redemption, they are referring to the mortgagor's right after default in every jurisdiction, title, lien or intermediate, to perform his obligation under the mortgage and have the title to his property restored free and clear of the mortgage.[1] The important words to emphasize here are "after default." While there is, as we have seen earlier, no right to prepay a mortgage debt absent mortgage language so specifying, the mortgagor nevertheless has the right to pay or otherwise perform his obligations after default under the mortgage at any time until a valid foreclosure sale. Indeed, it is this right, as we saw in earlier sections, that courts jealously protect against attempts at contemporaneous clogs and other devices aimed at defeating or restricting the right.[2]

---

§ 7.1

1. See e.g., In re Crawford, 2 B.R. 589 (Bkrtcy.Ill.1980); Mendez v. Rosenbaum, 62 Or.App. 825, 662 P.2d 751 (1983).

Cf. West's Ann.Cal.Civ.Code § 2903, "Every person, having an interest in property subject to a lien, has a right to redeem it from the lien, at any time after the claim is due, and before his right of redemption is foreclosed * * *."

2. See e.g., Mollerup v. Storage Systems, International, 569 P.2d 1122 (Utah 1977); Downey State Bank v. Major-Blakeney, 578 P.2d 1286 (Utah 1978); In re Crawford, 2 B.R. 589 (Bkrtcy.Ill.1980). See § 3.1, supra.

Statutory redemption, on the other hand, is, as the name implies, a creature of legislative grace.[3] In about half the states, the mortgagor, his successors in interest and, in many instances, junior lienors are permitted for a specific period after a valid foreclosure sale to redeem "from the sale" by paying to the foreclosure sale purchaser the foreclosure sale price plus, in some instances, certain additional amounts.[4] It is a helpful oversimplification to look upon "redemption from the mortgage" in its variety of terminology as a right that exists after default until there has been a valid foreclosure.[5] Statutory redemption rights, on the other hand, ripen only *after* there has been such a valid foreclosure.[6] Detailed analysis of statutory redemption as a matter of logic thus will be deferred until after we have considered the intricacies of foreclosure.[7] On the other hand, proper understanding of the procedure and substance of foreclosure necessitates further exploration of the first category of redemption at this point.

 WESTLAW REFERENCES
digest(equity /3 redemption)
digest("statutory redemption")

§ 7.2 Who May Redeem

Aside from the mortgagor, numerous other persons have the right to redeem from the mortgage. "Any person who may have acquired any interest in the premises, legal or equitable, by operation of law or otherwise, in privity of title with the mortgagor, may redeem, and protect such interest in the land. * * * But it must be an interest in the land, and it must be derived in some way, mediate or immediate from or through, or in the right of the mortgagor; so as, in effect, to constitute a part of the mortgagor's original equity of redemption. Otherwise it cannot be affected by the mortgage, and needs no redemption." [1] To put it more succinctly, "the law favors redemption by anyone who has an interest in the mortgaged premises who would be a loser by foreclosure." [2] Among those who qualify, in addition to the mortgagor,[3] are purchasers of the equity from the mortgagor,[4] contract

3. See § 8.4, infra; Dominex, Inc. v. Key, 456 So.2d 1047 (Ala.1984).

4. See Wayne Savings & Loan Co. v. Young, 49 Ohio App.2d 35, 358 N.E.2d 1380, 3 O.O.3d 107 (1976).

5. Id. See also, Dominex, Inc. v. Key, 456 So.2d 1047 (Ala.1984).

6. Trauner v. Lowrey, 369 So.2d 531 (Ala.1979); Land Associates v. Becker, 294 Or. 308, 656 P.2d 927 (1982).

7. See §§ 8.4–8.7, infra.

§ 7.2

1. Christiancy, J., in Smith v. Austin, 9 Mich. 465, 474 (1862). See also, Dawson v. Overmyer, 141 Ind. 438, 431, 40 N.E. 1065 (1895), "A person can only redeem when he has an interest to protect, and where, without such redemption, he would be a loser."

2. John Stepp, Inc. v. First Federal Savings & Loan Association of Miami, 379 So. 2d 384 (Fla.App.1980).

3. See Smith v. Varney, 309 A.2d 229 (Me.1973).

4. Purcell v. Gann, 113 Ark. 332, 168 S.W. 1102 (1914); Loomis v. Knox, 60 Conn. 343, 22 A. 771 (1891); Dunlap v. Wilson, 32 Ill. 517 (1863); Watts v. Symes, 16 Sim. 640 (1849).

vendees of the mortgagor [5] an heir or devisee,[6] or any other person who succeeds to the mortgagor's interest in the mortgaged property, e.g., a purchaser at an execution or judicial sale.[7] Likewise an owner of a limited interest such as a tenant for life or lessee,[8] a remainderman or reversioner,[9] one who has dower even though it be inchoate only,[10] or the holder of an easement.[11] Similarly, joint tenants and the like may redeem.[12] So too, many persons who have become owners of fractional portions of land that are covered by the same underlying mortgage.[13] Junior lienors, whether by reason of a judgment or execution or because of a later mortgagee are also entitled to redemption.[14]

It should be emphasized that the equitable right to redeem afforded junior lienholders is not the same as that possessed by the mortgagor and his successors in interest. As one court stressed, the "phrase 'right of redemption' has a two-fold meaning. When it is used with respect to a mortgagor, it refers to his right, prior to being foreclosed from that right, to satisfy the mortgage indebtedness which encumbers his property. When the phrase is used with reference to a junior mortgagee, it refers to his right to satisfy a prior mortgage by payment of the debt it secures and thereby become equitably subrogated to all rights of the prior mortgagee. [It] applies to the rights of senior mortgagees and not to the underlying real property. This right does not confer greater rights upon the junior mortgagee exercising the right of redemption than were held by the senior mortgagee."[15] Stated another way, the

5. Polish National Alliance of Brooklyn, U.S.A. v. White Eagle Hall, Co., Inc., 98 A.D.2d 400, 470 N.Y.S.2d 642 (1982).

6. Hunter v. Dennis, 112 Ill. 568 (1884); Zaegel v. Kuster, 51 Wis. 31, 7 N.W. 781 (1881); Chew v. Hyman, 7 F. 7 (C.C.Ill. 1881); Lewis v. Nangle, 2 Ves.Sr. 431 (1752).

7. Dalton v. Brown, 130 Ark. 200, 197 S.W. 32 (1917); Jackson v. Weaver, 138 Ind. 539, 38 N.E. 166 (1894); Millett v. Blake, 81 Me. 531, 18 A. 293, 10 Am.St. Rep. 275 (1889); Hayward v. Cain, 110 Mass. 273 (1872); Isam Mitchell & Co., Inc. v. Norwach, 26 Mass. 33 (1927).

8. G.B. Seely's Son, Inc. v. Fulton-Edison, Inc., 52 A.D.2d 575, 382 N.Y.S.2d 516 (1976); Big Apple Supermarkets, Inc. v. Corkdale Realty, Inc., 61 Misc.2d 483, 305 N.Y.S.2d 531 (1969).

9. Thielen v. Strong, 184 Minn. 333, 238 N.W. 678 (1931); see Coote, Mortgages 9th ed., p. 723.

10. Mackenna v. Fidelity Trust Co., 184 N.Y. 411, 77 N.E. 721, 3 L.R.A., N.S. 1068 (1906).

11. Dundee Naval Stores Co. v. McDowell, 65 Fla. 15, 61 So. 108, Ann.Cas.1915A, 387 (1913); Bacon v. Bowdoin, 39 Mass. (22 Pick.) 401, 405 (1839).

12. McQueen v. Whetstone, 127 Ala. 417, 30 So. 548 (1900); Titsworth v. Stout, 49 Ill. 78, 95 Am.Dec. 577 (1868); Merritt v. Hosmer, 77 Mass. (11 Gray) 276 (1858); Hubbard v. Ascutney Mill Dam Co., 20 Vt. 402, 50 Am.Dec. 41 (1848).

13. Howser v. Cruikshank, 122 Ala. 256, 25 So. 206, 82 Am.St.Rep. 76 (1899); Douglass v. Bishop, 27 Iowa 214 (1869).

14. See e.g., Shipp Corp., Inc. v. Charpilloz, 414 So.2d 1122 (Fla.App.1982); Glendale Federal Savings & Loan Association v. Guadagnino, 434 So.2d 54 (Fla.App. 1983); See Lyon v. Sandford, 5 Conn. 544 (1825) (judgment creditor); Schuck v. Gerlach, 101 Ill. 338 (1882) (judgment creditor); Hasselman v. McKernan, 50 Ind. 441 (1875) (junior mortgagee); Wright v. Howell, 35 Iowa 288 (1872) (judgment creditor); Long v. Richards, 170 Mass. 120, 48 N.E. 1083, 64 Am.St.Rep. 281 (1898) (junior mortgagee). Cf. Kirkham & Woods v. Dupont, 14 Cal. 559 (1860); Bigelow v. Willson, 18 Mass. (1 Pick.) 485 (1823); Cardwell v. Virginia State Ins. Co., 186 Ala. 261, 65 So. 80 (1914).

15. Shipp Corp., Inc. v. Charpilloz, 414 So.2d 1122, 1123 (Fla.App.1982); see Land Associates v. Becker, 294 Or. 308, 656 P.2d 927 (1982).

mortgagor's equitable redemption right is to pay off the mortgage in default and redeem *the land.* The junior lienor's right in redeeming is to purchase the senior mortgage. While this distinction is usually not crucial, it nevertheless can become important, as we shall see later in this chapter, in assessing the rights of junior lienholders who were not made parties to a judicial foreclosure and in related contexts.[16]

It should also be emphasized that as among several persons who may be entitled to redeem, the one whose interest is superior has priority, e.g., a second mortgagee comes ahead of a third mortgagee.[17] Further, "where there are successive mortgages, any subsequent mortgagee may redeem a prior mortgage and every redeeming party is liable to be redeemed in his turn by those below him, and these latter are all liable to be redeemed by the mortgagor."[18]

As indicated above, only those with an interest in the property that will be prejudiced by foreclosure can redeem. Consequently a mortgagor who has conveyed away or otherwise lost all interest in the property cannot redeem.[19] The same is true of persons who, although they once had an interest giving them a right to redeem, have lost it, e.g., a junior lienor which has been discharged.[20] The principle also excludes interests superior to the mortgage from which redemption is sought, e.g., a lien for taxes, a senior mortgage,[21] or the owner of a dower interest not subject to the mortgage.[22] Such interests cannot be affected by foreclosure and therefore give no right to redemption.

 WESTLAW REFERENCES
"junior lienholder" heir devisee lessee (tenant /3 life joint) remainder*** reversion** /s redemption redeem***

§ 7.3   Amount to be Paid

The mortgagee is entitled to payment in full and to retain its lien on every part of the land until the debt is completely paid.[1] Therefore, in order to redeem, anyone seeking to do so must pay the entire amount

16. See § 7.15 infra.

17. Wiley v. Ewing, 47 Ala. 418 (1872); Loomis v. Knox, 60 Conn. 343, 22 A. 771 (1891); Moore v. Beasom, 44 N.H. 215 (1862); Wimpfheimer v. Prudential Insurance Co., 56 N.J.Eq. 585, 39 A. 916 (1898).

18. Snell's Equity, 18th ed., 290.

19. Smith v. Varney, 309 A.2d 229 (Me. 1973); Cardwell v. Virginia State Insurance Co., 186 Ala. 261, 65 So. 80 (1914); Phillips v. Leavitt, 54 Me. 405 (1867); Ingersoll v. Sawyer, 19 Mass. (2 Pick.) 276 (1824).

20. Colwell v. Warner, 36 Conn. 224 (1869); Thomas v. Stewart, 117 Ind. 50, 18 N.E. 505, 1 L.R.A. 715 (1888); McHenry v. Cooper, 27 Iowa 137 (1869).

21. See Dawson v. Overmyer, 141 Ind. 438, 441, 40 N.E. 1065, 1066 (1895), "The prior or senior lienholder has no right to redeem from the junior, because it does not protect any interest he has." See also Harwood v. Underwood, 28 Mich. 427 (1874).

22. Opdyke v. Bartles, 11 N.J.Eq. 133 (1856); Huston v. Seeley, 27 Iowa 183 (1869). Cf., Smith v. Austin, 9 Mich. 465 (1862), no interest shown.

§ 7.3

1. See Graham v. Linden, 50 N.Y. 547, 550 (1872); Sun First National Bank of Orlando v. R.G.C., 348 So.2d 620 (Fla.App. 1977).

to which the mortgagee is entitled even though the redeeming party owns only a fractional part of the property [2] or a limited interest in it as in some of the cases mentioned above.[3] This amount is the mortgage debt, or so much of it as may be due, plus interest to the time of redemption, costs and such additional items as the mortgagee may be entitled to add onto his debt, e.g., taxes paid.[4] Nor can the owner of only a partial interest compel the owners of the rest of the property subject to the mortgage to contribute their shares of the obligation at the time of payment. He must advance the whole amount and recover from them later, being granted subrogation to the mortgage lien against them for that purpose as an effective remedy.[5]

The mortgagee may, of course, consent to a partial redemption.[6] Moreover, it sometimes may *insist* upon only a partial redemption, the right of election as to full redemption or redemption only to the extent of the redeeming party's interest in the property resting with the mortgage creditor.[7] Where the mortgagee has become owner of the

---

2. E.g., Douglass v. Bishop, 27 Iowa 217 (1869); Street v. Beal, 16 Iowa, 68, 85 Am. Dec. 504 (1861); but cf., Coffin v. Parker, 127 N.Y. 117, 27 N.E. 814, 3 St.R. 143 (1891). See note 13, § 7.2 supra.

3. E.g., Springer Corp. v. Kirkeby-Natus, 80 N.M. 206, 453 P.2d 376 (1969) (junior mortgagee); McGough v. Sweetser, 97 Ala. 361, 12 So. 162, 19 L.R.A. 470 (1893); Gibson v. Crehore, 22 Mass. (5 Pick.) 146 (1827) (dower); a junior mortgage: Smith v. Simpson, 129 Ark. 275, 195 S.W. 1067 (1917); see Titley v. Davis, 2 Eq.Cas.Abr. 604 (1739); and note 19, supra. But cf., Green v. Dixon, 9 Wis. 485, 489 (1859); and see 25 Ill.L.Rev. 720 (1931). Or an owner of a part interest in the right of redemption: Merritt v. Hosmer, 77 Mass. (11 Gray) 276 (1858).

4. In the United States a mortgagor, in order to redeem, generally does not have to pay debts other than that for which the mortgage is given as security. Mackenna v. Fidelity Trust Co., 184 N.Y. 411, 77 N.E. 721, 3 L.R.A., N.S. (1906), 12 Am.St.Rep. 620, 6 Ann.Cas. 471 (1968). See Mahoney v. Bostwick, 96 Cal. 53, 30 P. 1020, 31 Am. St.Rep. 175 (1892). Cf. Brown v. Coriell, 50 N.J.Eq. 753, 26 A. 915, 21 L.R.A. 321, 35 Am.St.Rep. 789 (1893).

5. See Chapter 10, infra.

6. Union Mutual Life Insurance Co. v. Kirchoff, 133 Ill. 368, 27 N.E. 91 (1890); Kerse v. Miller, 169 Mass. 44, 47 N.E. 504 (1896). See Quinn Plumbing Co. v. New Miami Shores Corp., 100 Fla. 413, 129 So. 690, 73 A.L.R. 600 (1930).

7. E.g., where the mortgagee has become owner of the redemption interest apart from that share of it belonging to the plaintiff. In such a case, if the plaintiff were required to pay the entire mortgage debt he would at once acquire a right of reimbursement against the mortgagee as owner of the other share of the redemption interest for the amount that share should contribute to the redemption and be subrogated to the mortgage in order to collect it. As a short cut, the rule stated in the text applies. Robinson v. Fife, 3 Ohio St. 551 (1854); Simonton v. Gray, 34 Me. 50 (1852); Gibson v. Crehore, 22 Mass. (5 Pick.) 146 (1827). See Quinn Plumbing Co. v. New Miami Shores Corp., 100 Fla. 413, 129 So. 690, 73 A.L.R. 600 (1930). Cf. Barr v. Van Alstine, 120 Ind. 590, 22 N.E. 965 (1889). But cf. West's Ann.Cal.Code Civ.Proc. § 347.

The same principle has permitted the mortgage creditor a choice between requiring full redemption or releasing from the mortgage the part belonging to the party seeking to redeem or paying its value. Boqut v. Coburn, 27 Barb. 230 (N.Y.1858); Wilson v. Tarter, 22 Or. 504, 30 P. 499 (1892). Cf. Mackenna v. Fidelity Trust Co., 184 N.Y. 411, 77 N.E. 721, 3 L.R.A., N.S., 1068, 12 Am.St.Rep. 620, 6 Ann.Cas. 471 (1906).

Cooper v. Peak, 258 Ala. 167, 61 So.2d 62 (1952), certiorari denied 345 U.S. 957, 73 S.Ct. 939, 97 L.Ed. 1377 (1953), rehearing denied 346 U.S. 842, 74 S.Ct. 14, 98 L.Ed. 362 (1953), commented on in 52 Mich.L. Rev. 312 (1953) followed the general rule permitting the mortgagee to insist upon a partial redemption.

interest in that part or undivided share of the mortgaged property which is primarily or proportionately bound to discharge the mortgage, the rule that the owner of the other part or undivided interest must pay the whole debt is inapplicable. He may have redemption by paying only the amount that his interest in the property would have to contribute.[8]

When subdividing is contemplated at the time of the mortgage a section may be inserted in the mortgage providing for it. Some courts have held that the partial release privilege under such a clause is personal to the mortgagor.[9] Others hold that it runs with the land.[10] The latter result is better "since the provision for partial release is made specifically with a view to the sale or further incumbrance of part of the property; and a rule limiting the privilege to the mortgagor will either diminish considerably the sale value of the property, or result merely in the release money changing hands twice."[11]

 WESTLAW REFERENCES
partial** /2 redeem*** redemption release /p mortgage

§ 7.4   The Procedure of Redemption

A person who desires to assert a right of redemption must do so by bringing a bill in equity.[1] In it, first of all, she must set forth the mortgage. Then she must state the facts which show that she is one entitled to redeem.[2] Although there is some authority saying that prior to bringing the bill, she must have tendered full performance and so aver in her bill,[3] this is not necessary.[4] Nor is it essential that she

---

8. Bradley v. George, 84 Mass. (2 Allen) 392 (1861); Tillinghast v. Fry, 1 R.I. 53 (1841).

9. Gilman v. Forgione, 129 Me. 66, 149 A. 620 (1930), unless words "or his assigns" are included; Rugg v. Record, 255 Mass. 247, 151 N.E. 95 (1926); Cf. Dimeo v. Ellenstein, 106 N.J.Eq. 298, 150 A. 675 (1930). As to the time within which partial release may be exercised when the covenant for it has no express limitation, see 24 Iowa L.Rev. 176 (1938). Also look at Rosenberg v. General Realty Service, Inc., 231 App. Div. 259, 247 N.Y.S. 461 (1931), commented on in 31 Col.L.Rev. 894 (1931); and 3 Pittsburgh L.Rev. 71 (1936).

10. Gammel v. Goode, 103 Iowa 301, 72 N.W. 531 (1897); Vawter v. Crafts, 41 Minn. 14, 42 N.W. 483 (1889); Rosenberg v. General Realty Service Co., 231 App.Div. 259, 274 N.Y.S. 461 (1931); Kerschensteiner v. Northern Michigan Land Co., 244 Mich. 403, 221 N.W. 322 (1928).

11. 31 Col.L.Rev. 894, 895 (1931). See also Storke and Sears, Transfer of Mort-

gaged Property, 38 Corn.L.Q. 185, 211 (1953).

§ 7.4

1. See Hubbell v. Sibley, 50 N.Y. 468 (1872). See Coote, Mortgages, 9th ed., pp. 745–765.

2. See Smith v. Austin, 9 Mich. 465, 474 (1862); Dawson v. Overmyer, 141 Ind. 438, 40 N.E. 1065 (1895). Coote, op. cit. supra note 1, p. 715 et seq. See also § 8.5, infra.

3. E.g., Lumsden v. Manson, 96 Me. 357, 52 A. 783 (1902); cf. Toole v. Weirick, 39 Mont. 359, 102 P. 590, 133 Am.St.Rep. 576 (1909).

4. Daubenspeck v. Platt, 22 Cal. 330, 334 (1863); Aust v. Rosenbaum, 74 Miss. 893, 21 So. 555 (1897); Casserly v. Witherbee, 119 N.Y. 522, 23 N.E. 1000 (1890); Nye v. Swan, 49 Minn. 431, 52 N.W. 39 (1892); Gerhardt v. Ellis, 134 Wis. 191, 114 N.W. 495 (1908); Beach v. Cooke, 28 N.Y. 508, 86 Am.Dec. 260 (1864). But see Higman v. Humes, 133 Ala. 617, 32 So. 574 (1901); Kopper v. Dyer, 59 Vt. 477, 489, 9 make tender or payment into court at the time of initiating the action.[5] It is sufficient that she assert that she stands ready and willing to pay the sum.[6] Her prayer then is that, upon such payment, the mortgage creditor shall discharge the mortgage and do any other acts necessary to restore completely the mortgagor's full interest in the property. It frequently is the case that the amount due is uncertain and can only be ascertained by an accounting, in which case the bill will ask for one.[7]

Assuming that all of these allegations are established the court will then enter a decree for redemption "on terms." [8] That is, it will provide that the mortgagor may redeem by paying the amount found due plus costs,[9] and fixes a date in the future on or before which the specified payment must be made.[10] The time allowed is discretionary, but it will usually be in the three to 12 month range.[11] It is further decreed that if the proper payment is made within the time specified the defendant shall discharge the mortgage, give over possession and do whatever else is necessary for a complete redemption. If the mortgagor fails to redeem within the specified time, the bill is dismissed and the mortgagor stands foreclosed.[12] Thus a bill to redeem may turn into a foreclosure and, although this is anticipating a later topic, the reverse also is true. If the mortgagee seeks to foreclose, its bill is granted "on terms", the court again fixing an early day in the future within which the mortgagor may redeem and decreeing that, in default of such redemption, the mortgage be foreclosed.[13]

A. 4, 59 Am.Rep. 742 (1887); Hudkins v. Crim, 72 W.Va. 418, 427, 78 S.E. 1043 (1911).

5. Casserly v. Witherbee, 119 N.Y. 522, 23 N.E. 1000 (1890).

6. Perry v. Carr, 41 N.H. 371 (1860); Casserly v. Witherbee, 119 N.Y. 522, 23 N.E. 1000 (1890); Kopper v. Dyer, 59 Vt. 477, 9 A. 4, 59 Am.Dec. 742 (1887); Powell v. Woodbury, 85 Vt. 504, 83 A. 541, Ann. Cas.1914D, 606 (1915).

7. See Daubenspeck v. Platt, note 4, supra. Look at Frost v. Beekman, 1 Johns. Ch. 288 (N.Y.1814).

8. See Coote, Mortgages, 9th Ed. 759.

9. Ryer v. Morrison, 21 R.I. 127, 42 A. 509 (1899). See Daubenspeck v. Platt, note 4 supra.

10. Collins v. Gregg, 109 Iowa 506, 80 N.W. 562 (1899); Dennett v. Codman, 158 Mass. 371, 33 N.E. 574 (1893); Turner v. Turner, 3 Munf. 66 (Va.1812). See also Durfee and Doddridge, Redemption for Foreclosure Sale—The Uniform Act, 23 Mich.L.Rev. 825, 826 (1925).

11. See Perine v. Dunn, 4 Johns.Ch. 140, 141 (N.Y.1819) (6 months); Clark v. Reyburn, 75 U.S. (8 Wall.) 318, 322, 324, 19 L.Ed. 354 (1869) (6 months); Perine v.

Dunn, supra, note 11. Murphy v. New Hampshire Sav. Bank, 63 N.H. 362 (1885) (one year); Taylor v. Dillenburg, 168 Ill. 235, 48 N.E. 41 (1897), (thirty days too short, ninety days allowed); Lindsey v. Delano, 78 Iowa 350, 43 N.W. 218 (1889) (nine months).

12. Flanders v. Hall, 159 Mass. 95, 34 N.E. 178 (1893); Perine v. Dunn, 4 Johns. Ch. 140 (N.Y.1819); Bolles v. Duff, 43 N.Y. 469 (1871); Smith v. Bailey, 10 Vt. 163 (1838); Martin v. Ratcliff, 101 Mo. 254, 13 S.W. 1051, 20 Am.St.Rep. 605 (1890); Sloane v. Lucas, 37 Wash. 348, 79 P. 949 (1905). Cf. Carpenter v. Plagge, 192 Ill. 82, 99, 61 N.E. 530 (1901); Stevens v. Miner, 110 Mass. 57 (1872); Cline v. Robbins, 112 Cal. 581, 44 P. 1023 (1896); Hollingsworth v. Campbell, 28 Minn. 18, 8 N.W. 873 (1881); see Turner v. Turner, 3 Munf. 66 (Va.1812); Inman v. Wearing, 3 De G. & Sm. 729 (1850). Meigs v. McFarlan, 72 Mich. 194, 40 N.W. 246 (1888); Fosdick v. Van Husan, 21 Mich. 567 (1870); Ingram v. Smith, 41 N.C. 97 (1849); Turner v. Turner, 3 Munf. 66 (Va., 1812). Cf. Odell v. Montross, 68 N.Y. 499 (1877).

13. "This is not a caprice of the chancellor, but is a natural consequence of the fact that either bill brought all the parties

WESTLAW REFERENCES
bill /2 equity /p redeem*** redemption
ready /s willing /s pay! /s redeem*** redemption

§ 7.5   Limitations on the Right to Redeem

Foreclosure is the usual method by which a right of redemption is ended. However it may be lost in other ways. Its exercise may be barred by estoppel in cases where its owner by conduct or words has induced some one to purchase or make expenditures upon the property in reliance upon representations that no right of redemption exists.[1] And it may be barred by such lapse of time as makes operative an applicable statute of limitations or a doctrine apart from statute the effect of which is to end the right to relief. As a general rule neither sort of bar will arise if the mortgagor is in possession.[2]

Laches may also bar the action to redeem. Prior to the enactment of statutes of limitations applying to actions in equity, laches alone affected the time within which such an action could be brought.[3] Laches continues as a general equitable doctrine applicable to actions to redeem from a mortgage.[4] In applying it, a court is bound by no inflexible rules and, looking at the particular circumstances of each case, may deny relief even though the elapsed period is less than that allowed under an analogous statute of limitations or may grant it even though it is longer.[5] To invoke it, the very staleness of the claim itself may persuade the court that it would be unjust to enforce it, but usually material changes in condition, such as altered value of the

---

before the court and sought a solution of the mortgage relation, which is essentially a relation of suspense, looking toward further adjustments. That redemption has, in either case, the right of way over foreclosure, is a necessary consequence of the doctrine of redemption." Durfee and Doddridge, 23 Mich.L.Rev. 825, 827, n. 4 (1925).

§ 7.5

1. Purcell v. Thornton, 128 Minn. 255, 150 N.W. 899 (1915); Ferguson v. Boyd, 169 Ind. 537, 81 N.E. 71 (1907); Munro v. Barton, 98 Me. 250, 56 A. 844 (1903); Kelly v. Hurt, 61 Mo. 463 (1875); Houston v. National Mutual Building & Loan Association, 80 Miss. 31, 31 So. 540, 92 Am.St.Rep. 565 (1902); Ross v. Leavitt, 70 N.H. 602, 50 A. 110 (1900)—accord. Cf. Mellish v. Robertson, 25 Vt. 603 (1853).

2. Miner v. Beekman, 50 N.Y. 337 (1872); Sumner v. Sumner, 217 App.Div. 163, 164, 216 N.Y.S. 389, 390 (1926); Knowlton v. Walker, 13 Wis. 264, 274 (1860); Waldo v. Rice, 14 Wis. 286 (1861). Cf. Bradley v. Norris, 63 Minn. 156, 167, 65 N.W. 357, 359 (1895).

3. See Leavell, Love and Nelson, Equitable Remedies and Restitution 387 (3d Ed. 1973).

4. For cases dealing with the matter of laches, see Brost v. L.A.N.D. Inc., 37 Wn. App. 372, 680 P.2d 453 (1984); Caudle v. First Federal Savings & Loan Association of Sylacauga, 295 Ala. 274, 327 So.2d 911 (1976); Lucas v. Skinner, 194 Ala. 492, 70 So. 88 (1915); Askew v. Sanders, 84 Ala. 356, 4 So. 167 (1888); Walker v. Warner, 179 Ill. 16, 53 N.E. 594, 70 Am.St.Rep. 85 (1899); Deadman v. Yantis, 230 Ill. 243, 82 N.E. 592, 120 Am.St.Rep. 291 (1907); Chace v. Morse, 189 Mass. 559, 76 N.E. 142 (1905); Hoffman v. Harrington, 33 Mich. 392 (1876); Walker v. Schultz, 175 Mich. 280, 141 N.W. 543 (1913); Cassem v. Heustis, 201 Ill. 208, 66 N.E. 283, 94 Am.St.Rep. 160 (1903); Mahaffy v. Faris, 144 Iowa, 220, 122 N.W. 934, 24 L.R.A., N.S., 840 (1909); Tukey v. Reinholdt, Iowa, 130 N.W. 727 (1911).

5. E.g., Askew v. Sanders, 84 Ala. 356, 4 So. 167 (1888); Chace v. Morse, 189 Mass. 559, 76 N.E. 142 (1905); see Kelley v. Boettcher, 85 F. 55, 62, 29 C.C.A. 14 (1898).

property, the state of the evidence or other circumstances must be shown in addition.

More generally, courts have barred the right to redeem when the mortgagee is in possession by holding that the action must be brought within the time fixed by an analogous statute of limitations. Statutes of limitations on actions at law to recover land or those fixing the time within which an action to foreclose may be brought are the ones usually chosen for this purpose.[6] But the character of the possession by the mortgagee required during the period in order for the mortgagor's claim to be ended has proved more troublesome.[7] On this, the cases divide into two main categories. In one, the mortgagee's possession must be actively adverse in the sense that it cannot be considered as being under the mortgage but is in pursuance of acts repudiating the existence of the mortgage relationship and in hostility to any claim to redeem by the other party,[8] and these facts are brought to the latter's actual notice.[9] The burden of proving both the fact of actual hostile holding and notice to the mortgagor are on the mortgagee.[10] In states where the mortgagee has no right to possession, such possession may be initiated when it is taken without the consent of the mortgagor.[11] Where the mortgagee is in possession as a mortgagee, other unequivocal acts of repudiation of the mortgage relation are essential.[12]

6. See Roberts v. Littlefield, 48 Me. 61, 63 (1860). See also Jarvis v. Woodruff, 22 Conn. 548 (1853). Clark v. Hannafeldt, 79 Neb. 566, 113 N.W. 135 (1907) accord. Bradley v. Norris, 63 Minn. 156, 65 N.W. 357 (1895), "The limitation upon the right to redeem, adopted by this court by analogy, is the statutory limitation on foreclosure by action."

7. See 20 Va.L.Rev. 464 (1934); 70 U. of Pa.L.Rev. 239 (1922); note, 52 Can.L.J. 414 (1916); note, 53 Can.L.J. 401 (1917); Pugh, Some Peculiarities of the Ohio Law of Mortgages, 4 U. of Cin.L.Rev. 297, 316 (1930). See also 23 L.R.A., N.S., 754 (1910); 7 A.L.R.2d 1131 (1949); note, 30 N.C.L.Rev. 310 (1952).

8. Munro v. Barton, 98 Me. 250, 254, 56 A. 844, 846 (1903); Arrington v. Liscom, 34 Cal. 365, 94 Am.Dec. 722 (1868); see Grattan v. Wiggin, 23 Cal. 16, 34 (1863); Becker v. McCrea, 193 N.Y. 423, 86 N.E. 463, 23 L.R.A., N.S., 754 (1908), under statute; Ham v. Flowers, 214 S.C. 212, 51 S.E.2d 753, 7 A.L.R.2d 1124 (1949). See 1949, 7 A.L.R.2d 1131, 1133 (1954); Knight v. Hilton, 224 S.C. 452, 79 S.E.2d 871, noted by Karesh, Survey of South Carolina Law: Security Transactions, 7 S.C.L.Q. 171 (1954).

9. Hurlburt v. Chrisman, 100 Or. 188, 197 P. 261 (1921); cf. Cohn v. Cohn, 7 Cal. 2d 1, 59 P.2d 969 (1936). See 7 A.L.R.2d 1131, 1141 (1949).

10. See 7 A.L.R.2d 1131, 1134 (1949).

11. Frady v. Ivester, 129 S.C. 536, 125 S.E. 134 (1924). See 7 A.L.R.2d 1131, 1137 (1949).

12. E.g., Cory v. Santa Ynez Land & Improvement Co., 151 Cal. 778, 91 P. 647 (1907). See 7 A.L.R.2d 1131, 1139 (1949).

Strictly speaking, in title states, since the mortgagee in possession already has legal title as well as possession it would seem to be technically inaccurate to describe his freeing the land of the mortgagor's right of redemption as acquiring title by adverse possession. What he has done, of course, is to bar the mortgagor's equity of redemption. Brown v. Berry, 89 N.J.Eq. 230, 108 A. 51 (1918).

In lien states, however, since the mortgagee has only a lien and the mortgagor has title, it is quite correct to talk in terms of acquiring title by adverse possession. However, in both cases the substantial question should be, and is, what sort of possession by the mortgagee is necessary to end the mortgagor's right to redeem, regardless of the technical nature of his interest in the property. Cf. § 16, supra.

The other line of authorities find the possession of the mortgagee for the required period to be sufficient to bar redemption, even though it be rightfully acquired under the mortgage and continued without active repudiation, provided that the mortgagee during that time has made no acknowledgment of the right to redeem.[13] The party seeking to redeem after the end of the period has the burden of showing such an acknowledgment.[14]

Some courts hold that the right to foreclose and the right to redeem are reciprocal, and when one is barred, the other is also.[15] The mutuality idea is valid to the extent that " 'it shall not be competent for one party alone to consider it a mortgage.' "[16] Thus, if the mortgagee, through possession has been freed from an action to redeem by the mortgagor, and then, in order to clear up his title, brings an action to foreclose, this treatment of the mortgage as a subsisting relationship as to the mortgagee involves the consequence that it will be treated also as a mortgage in respect to the mortgagor.[17] If, however, a mortgagee or foreclosure sale purchaser has thus barred the mortgagor's redemption interest, he is not precluded from clearing his title except at peril of bringing to life the mortgagor's right. He may do so by an action designed for that purpose based, not upon a theory that the mortgage still exists, but upon the idea that the mortgage is gone and the plaintiff is now complete owner.[18]

However the doctrine never required that the rights of the parties should be completely parallel. Certainly that is true as to the time within which the respective rights may be enforced, "for it is every day's practice, that one party may not be able to foreclose when the other may redeem."[19] Moreover, it would be objectionable to hold that they must be, because then "a person might one day be a mortgagee, having, in most jurisdictions, a lien merely on the premises, and the next day be their absolute owner,"[20] a result flowing from mere failure to enforce his rights. Additionally "it would give to one claimant the benefit of disabilities to which his opponent is subject."[21]

13. Dexter v. Arnold, 3 Sumner 152, F.Cas. No. 3,859 (C.C.R.I.1837). See, 7 A.L.R.2d 1131, 1142 (1949).

14. See 7 A.L.R.2d 1131, 1134 (1949).

15. Fitch v. Miller, 200 Ill. 170, 183, 65 N.E. 650, 655 (1902); Locke v. Caldwell, 91 Ill. 417, 420 (1879); (but compare comment in Walker v. Warner, 179 Ill. 16, 27, 53 N.E. 594, 598, 70 Am.Dec. 85) (1899); Cunningham v. Hawkins, 24 Cal. 403, 85 Am. Dec. 73 (1864); Crawford v. Taylor, 42 Iowa 260, 263 (1875); Adams v. Holden, 111 Iowa 54, 60, 82 N.W. 468, 470 (1900); (but cf. Tukey v. Reinholdt, 130 N.W. 727) (Iowa 1911); Leland v. Morrison, 92 S.C. 501, 75 S.E. 889, Ann.Cas.1914B, 349 (1913); Gould v. McKillip, 55 Wyo. 251, 99 P.2d 67, 129 A.L.R. 1427 (1940). But cf. Bradley v. Norris, 63 Minn. 156, 165, 65 N.W. 357, 358 (1895).

16. Bradley v. Norris, 63 Minn. 156, 165, 65 N.W. 357, 358 (1895).

17. Calkins v. Isbell, 20 N.Y. 147 (1859), affirming Calkins v. Calkins, 3 Barb. 305 (N.Y.1848).

18. Arrington v. Liscom, 34 Cal. 365, 94 Am.Dec. 722 (1868); Chapin v. Wright, 41 N.J.Eq. 438, 5 A. 574 (1886).

19. Bradley v. Norris, 63 Minn. 156, 165, 65 N.W. 357, 358 (1895).

20. Tiffany, Real.Prop., 3d ed., § 1501, citing Bradley v. Norris, 63 Minn. 156, 65 N.W. 357 (1895).

21. Ibid.

The rule may correctly apply to redemption by a junior mortgagee; his right of redemption from the senior mortgage, in lien states at least, is dependent upon his right to foreclose his own mortgage and hence, when it is barred he also loses his right to redeem.[22] It has also been suggested that the statement means merely that, in fixing the equitable limitation upon suits to redeem, instead of adopting the statutory period for bringing ejectment, a court will follow the time rule governing the bringing of an action to foreclose as more nearly analogous.[23]

 WESTLAW REFERENCES
statute action   /2   limitation   /s   redeem*** redemption

B. ACCRUAL OF THE RIGHT TO FORECLOSURE

§ 7.6 Acceleration Clauses—In General

Most installment payment mortgages today contain acceleration clauses. These clauses empower the mortgagee in the event of a default by the mortgagor to declare the whole amount of the mortgage debt due and payable. Moreover, the general concept of acceleration clauses is universally accepted.[1] Indeed, in the absence of such provisions, mortgagees would be forced to utilize cumbersome and impractical procedures for foreclosing for each installment as it comes due, procedures that we will examine later in this chapter.[2] It is important to recognize that acceleration is permitted not only for failure to pay the debt promptly, but also for such other defaults as the failure to pay taxes,[3] maintain insurance[4] or for the commission of waste.[5]

22. Gower v. Winchester, 33 Iowa 303 (1871); Krutz v. Gardner, 25 Wash. 396, 65 P. 771 (1901).

23. Parsons v. Noggle, 23 Minn. 328 (1877). See Bradley v. Norris, 63 Minn. 156, 166, 65 N.W. 357, 359 (1895). Some states have enacted statutes applying specifically to actions to redeem. See e.g., West's Ann.Cal.Code Civ.Proc. § 346 (5 years); N.Y.—McKinney's Civ.Prac.Law and Rules § 212(c) (ten years). While these statutes set a definite time limit they do not necessarily dispose of the question of what kind of possession by the mortgagee is necessary for the period to run. See Peshine v. Ord, 119 Cal. 311, 51 P. 536, 63 Am.St.Rep. 131 (1897); Cory v. Santa Ynez Land and Improvement Co., 151 Cal. 778, 91 P. 647 (1907); Cohn v. Cohn, 1936, 7 Cal.2d 1, 59 P.2d 969 (1936); Sumner v. Sumner, 217 App.Div. 163, 164, 216 N.Y.S. 389, 390 (1926).

§ 7.6

1. E.g., David v. Sun Federal Savings & Loan Association, 461 So.2d 93 (Fla.1984);

Saunders v. Stradley, 25 Md.App. 85, 333 A.2d 604 (1975); Campbell v. Werner, 232 So.2d 252 (Fla.App.1970); Poydan, Inc. v. Agia Kiriaki, 130 N.J.Super. 141, 325 A.2d 838 (1974); United States Savings Bank of Newark, New Jersey v. Continental Arms, Inc., 338 A.2d 579 (Del.Super.1975).

2. See § 7.8, infra.

3. See Jeffery v. Seven Seventeen Corp., 461 A.2d 1009 (Del.1983); Chapa v. Herbster, 653 S.W.2d 594 (Tex.App.1983); Saunders v. Stradley, 25 Md.App. 85, 333 A.2d 604 (1975); First National Bank of Atlanta v. Blum, 141 Ga.App. 485, 233 S.E.2d 835 (1977); Ford v. Waxman, 50 A.D.2d 585, 375 N.Y.S.2d 145 (1975); Eisen v. Kostakos, 116 N.J.Super. 358, 282 A.2d 421 (1971).

4. Cf. Strong v. Merchants Mutual Insurance Co., 2 Mass.App. 142, 309 N.E.2d 510 (1974), modified 366 Mass. 751, 322 N.E.2d 765 (1975).

5. United States v. Angel, 362 F.Supp. 445 (E.D.Pa.1973).

It is important to emphasize, however, that most acceleration clauses are "optional" as opposed to "automatic" in the sense that they are triggered only after a default by the mortgagor *and* a decision by the mortgagee to accelerate.[6] When or if acceleration actually occurs can have crucial consequences for the tardy mortgagor who seeks to reinstate the mortgage by tendering arrearages. While such a tender prior to acceleration will defeat foreclosure,[7] once a valid acceleration takes place, only tender of the accelerated amount will do so.[8] Indeed, post-acceleration acceptance of arrearages by the mortgagee will serve only to reduce the mortgage debt and not impair the validity of the foreclosure itself.[9] What constitutes a valid acceleration, however, is somewhat less clear. Texas, for example, requires, at least where there is no mortgagor waiver, both notice of an intent to accelerate and, in addition, separate notice of acceleration itself.[10] "Notice of intent to accelerate is necessary in order to provide the debtor an opportunity to cure his default prior to harsh consequences of acceleration and foreclosure. Proper notice that the debt has been accelerated * * * cuts off the debtor's right to cure his default and gives notice that the entire debt is due and payable." [11] Most courts, however, are less specific and simply require that the mortgagee "perform some affirmative, overt act evidencing his intention to take advantage of the acceleration provision." [12] For example, under this approach, a letter to the mortgagor

---

6. See Rosenthal, The Role of Courts of Equity in Preventing Acceleration Predicated Upon a Mortgagor's Inadvertent Default, 22 Syr.L.Rev. 897, 899 n. 8 (1971).

7. See e.g., First Federal Savings and Loan Association v. Stone, ___ Ind.App. ___, 467 N.E.2d 1226 (1984); Jeferne, Inc. v. Capanegro, 89 A.D.2d 577, 452 N.Y.S.2d 236 (1982); Redmond v. Merrill Lynch Relocation Management, Inc., 163 Ga.App. 346, 294 S.E.2d 575 (1982); Dunfee v. Waite, ___ Ind.App. ___, 439 N.E.2d 664 (1982); Trinity County Bank v. Haas, 151 Cal. 553, 91 P. 385 (1907); Van Vlissingen v. Lenz, 171 Ill. 162, 49 N.E. 422 (1897); Cresco Realty Co. v. Clark, 1908, 128 App. Div. 144, 112 N.Y.S. 550 (1908); Bisno v. Sax, 175 Cal.App.2d 714, 346 P.2d 814 (1960).

8. See e.g., City Savings Bank of Bridgeport v. Dessoff, 3 Conn.App. 644, 491 A.2d 424 (1985); Bank of Honolulu v. Anderson, 3 Hawaii App. 545, 654 P.2d 1370 (1982); Bell Federal Savings & Loan Association of Bellevue v. Laura Lanes, Inc., 291 Pa. Super. 395, 435 A.2d 1285 (1981); Dime Savings Bank of New York v. Dooley, 84 A.D.2d 804, 444 N.Y.S.2d 148 (1981); La Plant v. Beechley, 182 Iowa 452, 165 N.W. 1019 (1918); Robinson v. Miller, 317 Ill. 501, 148 N.E. 319 (1925); Odell v. Hoyt, 73 N.Y. 343 (1878), See, 53 A.L.R. 525 (1928); 41 A.L.R. 732 (1926); 19 A.L.R. 284 (1925);

5 A.L.R. 437 (1920). See Mortgages in 1957 Survey of New York Law, 32 N.Y. U.L.Rev. 1426 (1957), noting Mayer v. Myers, 155 N.Y.S.2d 129 (S.Ct.1956) and Clark-Robinson Corp. v. Jet Enterprises, Inc., 159 N.Y.S.2d 214 (S.Ct.1957).

9. Id.

10. See Ogden v. Gibraltar Savings Association, 640 S.W.2d 232 (Tex.1982); Tamplen v. Bryeans, 640 S.W.2d 421 (Tex.App. 1982), error refused n.r.e. But see Cortez v. Brownsville National Bank, 664 S.W.2d 805 (Tex.App.1984) (provision in note deemed to waive notice).

11. Ogden v. Gibraltar Savings Association, 640 S.W.2d 232, 234 (Tex.1982).

12. Spires v. Lawless, 493 S.W.2d 65, 73 (Mo.App.1973). See First Federal Savings and Loan Association v. Stone, ___ Ind. App. ___, 467 N.E.2d 1226 (1984); Jeferne, Inc. v. Capanegro, 89 A.D.2d 577, 452 N.Y.S.2d 236 (1982); Miller v. Jones, 635 S.W.2d 360 (Mo.App.1982); Lowry v. Northwestern Savings & Loan Association, 542 S.W.2d 546 (Mo.App.1976); United States Savings Bank of Newark, New Jersey v. Continental Arms, Inc., 338 A.2d 579 (Del.Super.1975); Cf. Allendale Furniture Co. v. Carolina Commercial Bank, ___ S.C. ___, 325 S.E.2d 530 (1985) (affirmative act not required where note provided for acceleration "without further notice").

stating that acceleration has occurred has been deemed sufficient.[13] Moreover, often the commencement of a judicial foreclosure proceeding constitutes adequate evidence of an election to accelerate.[14] In the power of sale context, courts have held that letters to the mortgagor threatening foreclosure unless arrearages are promptly paid coupled with oral expressions to the mortgagor of an intention to foreclose supply the requisite evidence of such an election.[15] Normally, however, prudent mortgagees will follow the Texas approach by mailing to the mortgagor a notice of intent to accelerate unless the default is cured. Moreover, in the event the default is not corrected, such mortgagees will mail a second notice to inform the mortgagor that acceleration has in fact occurred and that foreclosure proceedings will be commenced.

Acceleration of the entire mortgage debt may be triggered, as pointed out above, not only by failure to pay installments of principal or interest, but also by such defaults as failure to pay taxes or insurance premiums.[16] Once acceleration has occurred because of non-debt related defaults, it arguably cannot be avoided simply by paying the overdue taxes or by reinstating the insurance, but only by tendering prior to foreclosure the full accelerated mortgage debt.[17]

WESTLAW REFERENCES

synopsis,digest(accelerat*** ±1 clause provision section /p mortgage)

fail*** default*** commi***** /s tax** insurance waste /s accelerat*** /p mortgage

---

13. Butter v. Melrose Savings Bank, 13 Mass.App.Ct. 1086, 435 N.E.2d 1057 (1982).

14. United States Savings Bank of Newark, New Jersey v. Continental Arms, Inc., 338 A.2d 579 (Del.Super.1975); Pizer v. Herzig, 120 App.Div. 102, 105 N.Y.S. 38 (1907); Swearingen v. Lahner, 93 Iowa 147, 61 N.W. 431, 26 L.R.A. 765, 57 Am.St.Rep. 261 (1894). As to what will constitute, for this purpose, the commencement of a foreclosure action, see Trowbridge v. Malex Realty Corp., 111 Misc. 211, 183 N.Y.S. 53 (1920), reversed on other grounds 198 App. Div. 656, 191 N.Y.S. 97 (1922). See also Walsh v. Henel, 226 App.Div. 198, 235 N.Y.S. 34 (1929) noted 7 N.Y.Univ.L.Q.Rev. 214 (1929). See further Updike, Mortgages, in 1954 Annual Survey of American Law, 30 N.Y.U.L.Rev. 805, 812 (1955) noting Jacobson v. McClanahan, 43 Wn.2d 751, 264 P.2d 253 (1953). But see, Basse v. Gallegger, 7 Wis. 442, 76 Am.Dec. 225 (1858). Look at Albertina Realty Co. v. Rosbro Realty Corp., 258 N.Y. 472, 180 N.E. 176 (1932), affirmed 233 App.Div. 737, 250 N.Y.S. 841 (1931), and comment on it

in Walsh & Simpson, Cases Security Transactions, 482, Note (2).

15. Lowrey v. Northwestern Savings & Loan Association, 542 S.W.2d 546 (Mo.App. 1976). "It is only necessary that the mortgagee show an unmistakable intention to exercise the option, and this may be done by taking steps for foreclosure, filing foreclosure suit, sale pursuant to the mortgage, or advertisement of the property for sale pursuant to the terms of the mortgage." 2 Jones, Mortgages, § 1512 (8th Ed.).

16. See notes 3 and 4 supra.

17. See, e.g., Jeffery v. Seven Seventeen Corp., 461 A.2d 1009 (Del.1983); Saunders v. Stradley, 25 Md.App. 85, 333 A.2d 604 (1975); Lotterer v. Leon, 138 Md. 318, 113 A. 887 (1921). But compare Eisen v. Kostakos, 116 N.J.Super. 358, 282 A.2d 421 (1971); Spires v. Lawless, 493 S.W.2d 65, 72 (Mo.App.1973). Cf. Eberly v. Balducci, 61 Md.App. 80, 484 A.2d 1043 (1984) (payment of taxes prior to commencement of foreclosure action defeats acceleration, payment after does not).

§ 7.7   Limitations on Acceleration

Once a valid acceleration has occurred, in theory the mortgagor's only recourse normally is to redeem by paying the accelerated debt prior to foreclosure. However, a variety of concepts derived from case law and legislation operate in varying degrees to defeat or at least ameliorate the harsh consequences of acceleration.

Acceleration is sometimes defeated by waiver, estoppel or related considerations. As we noted in the prior section, tender or payment before election destroys the right to accelerate.[1] Normally, however, a mere failure to foreclose on the first default in payment does not operate as a waiver of the option to foreclose because of later defaults.[2] On the other hand, there are numerous cases in which mortgagors have been relieved for defaults in payment of principal or interest because courts have detected a *consistent* prior pattern of acceptance of late payments by the mortgagee.[3] Other courts, however, have refused to find waiver in similar circumstances.[4] Indeed, some such courts look upon such repeated defaults and mortgagee forbearance as factors to be held against the mortgagor.[5]

Even assuming there is no prior pattern of forbearance, a mortgagee may sometimes be estopped to accelerate and foreclose based on a single transaction. For example, a mortgagee may give an oral assurance to the mortgagor that foreclosure will be delayed for a certain period of time to enable the mortgagor to consummate an unforced sale of the real estate. To the extent that the mortgagor relies to her detriment and absent withdrawal of the extension by reasonable notice to the mortgagor, the latter may have a valid defense to foreclosure.[6]

Absent the foregoing defenses under what circumstances, if any, will a court relieve a mortgagor from the consequences of an acceleration in cases involving extreme hardship to the mortgagor? The general rule is that an acceleration clause works neither a forfeiture nor a penalty but is simply a matter of contract determining when the

§ 7.7

1. See note 7, § 7.6 supra.

2. Dunn v. Barry, 35 Cal.App. 325, 169 P. 910 (1917); Bower v. Stein, 101 C.C.A. 299, 177 F. 673 (1910).

3. See e.g., La Boutique of Beauty Academy, Inc. v. Meloy, 436 So.2d 396 (Fla.App. 1983); Smith v. Landy, 402 So.2d 441 (Fla. App.1981); Edwards v. Smith, 322 S.W.2d 770 (Mo.1959); Short v. A.H. Still Investment Co., 206 Va. 959, 147 S.E.2d 99 (1966); Annot., 97 A.L.R.2d 997 (1964); Cf. Massachusetts Mutual Life Insurance Co. v. Transgrow Realty Corp., 101 A.D.2d 770, 475 N.Y.S.2d 418 (1984).

4. See e.g., Moseley v. Lathan, 448 So. 2d 341 (Ala.1984); Scarfo v. Peever, 405 So. 2d 1064 (Fla.App.1981); North Star Apartments v. Goppert Bank & Trust Co., 657 S.W.2d 253 (Mo.App.1983); Mariash v. Bastianich, 88 A.D.2d 829, 452 N.Y.S.2d 190 (1982); Stroop v. Southern Life Insurance Co., 660 S.W.2d 46 (Tenn.App.1983); Westlund v. Melson, 7 Ark.App. 268, 647 S.W.2d 488 (1983); Federal National Mortgage Association v. Walter, 363 P.2d 293 (Okl.1961); Campbell v. West, 86 Cal. 197, 24 P. 1000 (1890).

5. See, e.g., Har Rich Realty Corp. v. American Consumer Industries, Inc., 351 F.2d 785 (D.C.Cir.1965).

6. See e.g., Naussau Trust Co. v. Montrose Concrete Products Corp., 56 N.Y.S.2d 175, 451 N.Y.S.2d 663, 436 N.E.2d 1265 (1982), reargument denied 57 N.Y.2d 674, 454 N.Y.S.2d 1032, 439 N.E.2d 1247 (1982).

debt is payable.[7] Consequently, courts often state that a mortgagor will not be relieved against its enforcement for a default occurring by his negligence, mistake or by accident in the absence of fraud, bad faith or other conduct on the part of the mortgagee rendering it unconscionable for him to avail himself of it.[8] Indeed, as one court has pointed out, "mere improvidence or neglect or poverty or illness is not sufficient basis for relief in equity from foreclosure under a mortgage acceleration clause. A mortgagee may be ungenerous, perhaps even uncharitable, but generosity and charity are voluntary attributes and cannot be enforced by the Court." [9] On the other hand, there is a growing number of decisions that a mortgagor will be protected from defaults that are the result of an accident or a mistake while acting in good faith, or unusual circumstances beyond his control.[10] For example, in one recent decision,[11] a court "deaccelerated" a mortgage debt where, unknown to the mortgagor, whose payment record was previously "unblemished", the latter's bookkeeper embezzled the funds that he should have been using to make the monthly mortgage payments. The court also was influenced by the fact that the co-mortgagor was an ex-spouse who had relied on her ex-husband to make the payments and who was, in the eyes of the court, totally "blameless." [12] Another Florida decision is further indicative of this judicial trend.[13] There

---

7. Graf v. Hope Building Corp., 254 N.Y. 1, 171 N.E. 884, 70 A.L.R. 984 (1930). The case, because of an important dissenting opinion by Cardozo, J., was widely discussed. See notes: 40 Yale L.J. 141 (1930); 30 Col.L.Rev. 1064 (1930); 17 Va.L.Rev. 80 (1930); 16 Cornell L.Q. 106 (1930); 10 Boston U.L.Rev. 558 (1930); 29 Mich.L.Rev. 380 (1930); 8 N.Y.Univ.L.Q.Rev. 331 (1930); 79 U. of Pa.L.Rev. 229 (1930); 6 Wis.L.Rev. 45 (1930); 70 A.L.R. 993 (1931). See David v. Sun Federal Savings & Loan Association, 429 So.2d 1277 (Fla.App.1983), judgment affirmed 461 So.2d 93 (1984); Poydan, Inc. v. Agia Kiriaki, Inc., 130 N.J. Super. 141, 325 A.2d 838 (1974); Verna v. O'Brien, 78 Misc.2d 288, 356 N.Y.S.2d 929 (1974); Collins v. Nagel, 200 Iowa 562, 203 N.W. 702 (1925). See further Updike, Mortgages, in 1954 Annual Survey of American Law, 30 N.Y.U.L.Rev. 812 (1955), noting Law v. Edgecliff Realty Co., 133 N.Y.S.2d 418 (S.Ct.1954), and August Tobler, Inc. v. Goolsby, 67 So.2d 537 (Fla. 1953). And see A–Z Servicenter v. Segall, 334 Mass. 672, 138 N.E.2d 266, 269 (1956) citing text.

8. See cases in previous footnote.

9. Verna v. O'Brien, 78 Misc.2d 288, 292, 356 N.Y.S.2d 929, 932 (1974).

10. See e.g., Savarese v. Schoner, 464 So.2d 695 (Fla.App.1985); Rice v. Campisi, 446 So.2d 1120 (Fla.App.1984), petition for review denied 456 So.2d 1182 (1984); Community Federal Savings & Loan Association of the Palm Beaches v. Orman, 446 So. 2d 1129 (Fla.App.1984); Dimatteo v. North Tonawanda Auto Wash Inc., 101 A.D.2d 692, 476 N.Y.S.2d 40 (1984); Fairmont Associates v. Fairmont Estates, 99 A.D.2d 895, 472 N.Y.S.2d 208 (1984), appeal denied 62 N.Y.2d 602, 465 N.E.2d 375 (1984); Karas v. Wasserman, 91 A.D.2d 812, 458 N.Y.S.2d 280 (1982); Rockaway Park Series Corp. v. Hollis Automotive Corp., 206 Misc. 955, 135 N.Y.S.2d 588 (1954), affirmed 285 App.Div. 1140, 142 N.Y.S.2d 364, commented on by Million, Property Law, in 1955 Survey of New York Law, 30 N.Y.U.L.Rev. 1065, 1074 (1955); Bisno v. Sax, 175 Cal.App.2d 714, 346 P.2d 814 (1960); Federal Home Loan Mortgage Corp. v. Taylor, 318 So.2d 203 (Fla.App. 1975); Middlemist v. Mosier, 151 Colo. 113, 377 P.2d 110 (1963). See J.N.A. Realty Corp. v. Cross Bay Chelsea, Inc., 42 N.Y.2d 392, 397 N.Y.S.2d 958, 366 N.E.2d 1313 (1977) (expressing displeasure with, but not overruling Graf: dictum).

11. Community Federal Savings & Loan Association of the Palm Beaches v. Orman, 446 So.2d 1129 (Fla.App.1984).

12. Id. at 1131.

13. Federal Home Loan Mortgage Corp. v. Taylor, 318 So.2d 203 (Fla.App.1975).

after three years of regular payments, there was one lapse of a month and 20 days in making a payment. That was followed by a three month lapse, but immediately thereafter the mortgagor paid three installments with late charges. The mortgagee accepted these payments. However, a payment made on September 10, 1973 did not include the installment that fell due on September 1. This latter installment was paid prior to October 4, but the mortgagee refused to accept it because the October 1 installment was not included. In upholding relief from acceleration, the court noted the general delays in mail delivery caused by the fact that the mortgagor was a serviceman stationed overseas. "It is to be noticed here that the mortgagors were not in the Phillipines by mere choice but due to a military assignment. Though the personal hardship arising from the daughter's need of stateside hospitalization is not a circumstance to excuse payment of a debt when due, the distance between the mortgagor and mortgagee's agent because of military obligations of the mortgagor is not to be ignored as a factor impairing the ability of the parties to communicate demands and responses thereto. The total evidence indicates a good faith effort on the part of the mortgagor to meet the mortgagee's conditions of bringing the account current." [14]

"Arrearages" legislation permitting the mortgagor to defeat acceleration by curing the default that existed prior to the acceleration is becoming increasingly common.[15] Under the Pennsylvania statute, for example, a residential mortgagor may until one hour prior to the foreclosure sale "avoid acceleration" by paying or tendering "all sums which would have been due at the time of payment or tender in the absence of default and the exercise of an acceleration clause." [16] Moreover, when the acceleration is triggered by such defaults as failure to pay taxes or insurance premiums, it may be defeated by the mortgagor simply by performing the defaulted obligation that caused the acceleration.[17] Other states, moreover, confer the benefits of such legislation on *all* as opposed to just residential mortgagors.[18] This is true, for example, in Illinois, where a mortgagor may reinstate a delinquent mortgage by payment of arrearages, costs and mortgagee's reasonable attorney's fees within 90 days of the foreclosure summons, but prior to the final foreclosure order.

It could be argued that the above statutes are subject to abuse because some mortgagors may default repeatedly, knowing that they can defeat acceleration simply by paying the arrearages. However, many of the statutes, to some extent at least, discourage this behavior

14. Id. at 208. Accord: Savarese v. Schoner, 464 So.2d 695 (Fla.App.1985).

15. See, e.g., West's Ann.Cal.Civ.Code, § 2924c; Colo.Rev.Stat. 38–39–118(1)(a); Ill.Rev.Stat. Ch. 95, § 57; Minn.Stat.Ann. § 580.30, V.A.Mo.Stat. § 408.555(4) (certain junior mortgages only). 41 Pa.S. § 404; Utah Code Ann.1953, 57–1–31. For an interesting interpretation problem in the Minnesota statute, see Davis v. Davis, 293 Minn. 44, 196 N.W.2d 473 (1972).

16. 41 P.S. § 404(b)(1).

17. 41 P.S. § 404(b)(2).

18. E.g., Minn.Stat.Ann. § 580.30; Utah Code Ann.1953, 57–1–31.

by requiring the reinstating mortgagor to pay attorney's fees and other expenses such as the cost of foreclosure publication requirements.[19] Moreover, some statutes limit the number of mortgage reinstatements permitted within specified time periods.[20] Thus there are probably enough economic and other deterrents to discourage the average home mortgagor from intentionally abusing such statutes. However, many commercial mortgagors may very well be willing repeatedly to accept the relatively mild economic penalties of such statutes as the cost of defeating acceleration, especially where multi-million dollar mortgages are involved. Thus the approach of the Pennsylvania statute limiting reinstatement rights to residential mortgagors may be a desirable ingredient of arrearages legislation.

Mortgagors have sometimes sought to defeat acceleration by relying on section 1–208 of the Uniform Commercial Code which states that a "term providing that one party or his successor in interest may accelerate payment or performance * * * 'at will' or 'when he deems himself insecure' or in words of similar import shall be construed to mean that he shall have power to do so only if he in good faith believes that the prospect of payment or performance is impaired." Two observations are initially appropriate with respect to the foregoing statute. First, it focuses on the state of mind or actions of the mortgagee rather than on the hardship that acceleration imposes on the mortgagor. Second, to the extent that a mortgage note permits the mortgagee to accelerate "at will" or when it deems itself "insecure" the good faith requirement is applicable.[21] On the other hand, most mortgage notes either do not contain such "at will" or "insecurity" language or, in any event, actual acceleration results from specific mortgagor defaults such as failure to pay the debt, real estate taxes or to maintain insurance coverage. Interestingly, some courts have applied the good faith requirement of section 1–208 in the latter as well as the former context.[22] As one court stated, "it seems to recognize that acceleration is a harsh remedy which should be allowed only if there is some reasonable justification for doing so such as a good faith belief that the prospect of payment is impaired."[23] Moreover, some of these decisions

---

19. E.g., Ill.Rev.Stat. ch. 95, § 57 (1979); Minn.Stat.Ann. § 580.30; West's Ann.Cal. Civ.Code, § 2924c.

20. See 41 P.S. § 404. (3 reinstatements in one year); Ill.Rev.Stat. ch. 95, § 57 (1979). The Illinois statute permits only one reinstatement in a five year period. This limitation was upheld against an argument that it represented an unconstitutional infringement on the inherent equitable powers of the court. See First Federal Savings & Loan Association of Chicago v. Walker, 91 Ill.2d 218, 62 Ill.Dec. 956, 437 N.E.2d 644 (1982).

21. See e.g., McKay v. Farmers & Stockmens Bank of Clayton, 92 N.M. 181,

585 P.2d 325 (1978), certiorari denied 92 N.M. 79, 582 P.2d 1292 (1978); Clayton v. Crossroads Equipment Co., 655 P.2d 1125 (Utah 1982). As to what constitutes "good faith" see Comment, Acceleration Clauses in Sales and Secured Transactions: The Debtor's Burden under Section 1–208 of the U.C.C., 11 B.C.Ind. & Com.L.Rev. 531, 539 (1970).

22. See e.g., State Bank of Lehi v. Woolsey, 565 P.2d 413 (Utah 1977); Williamson v. Wanless, 545 P.2d 1145 (Utah 1976); Brown v. Avemco Investment Corp., 603 F.2d 1367 (9th Cir.1979).

23. Williamson v. Wanless, 545 P.2d 1145, 1149 (Utah 1976).

have applied such an approach even where the note itself apparently lacked "at will" or "insecurity" language.[24] More courts, however, correctly focus on the literal language of section 1–208 and hold that it cannot be utilized to defeat an acceleration based on specific mortgagor defaults.[25] Moreover, there is scholarly support for the latter approach.[26]

The Federal Housing Administration (FHA) and the Veterans Administration (VA) have both promulgated guidelines to be followed in the foreclosure of loans which they have insured or guaranteed.[27] The guidelines extend the time which must elapse between default and foreclosure, require the mortgagee to permit reinstatement by payment of arrearages, and set up counselling procedures which are to be followed before foreclosure. Whether these guidelines are legally binding on mortgagees, so that failure to follow them will constitute grounds for enjoining a foreclosure, setting aside a sale, or awarding damages to the mortgagor, has been the subject of considerable litigation. While the earlier cases were divided,[28] it is now the clear weight

---

24. See e.g., Williamson v. Wanless, 545 P.2d 1145 (Utah 1976); Brown v. Avemco Investment Corp., 603 F.2d 1367 (9th Cir. 1979).

25. See e.g., Bowen v. Danna, 276 Ark. 528, 637 S.W.2d 560 (1982); Matter of Sutton Investments, Inc., 46 N.C.App. 654, 266 S.E.2d 686 (1980); Don Anderson Enterprises, Inc. v. Entertainment Enterprises Inc., 589 S.W.2d 70 (Mo.App.1979). See also, Note, 36 Ark.L.Rev. 643 (1983). Notwithstanding *Bowen*, Arkansas has applied the section 1–208 good faith requirement to an acceleration based on a violation of a due-on-sale clause. "[In *Bowen*] we held the good faith requirement is applicable to clauses which place exclusive control in the creditor. However, should the acceleration clause provide for default upon occurrence of an event exclusively within the control of the debtor, such as failure to maintain insurance coverage, then the creditor cannot bring about the occurrence of that specific event and there is no need for the protection of the good faith requirement of [1–208]. The sale [in violation of a due-on-sale clause] by the debtor in the case at bar was the occurrence of an event exclusively within the control of the debtor, and yet, the creditor is subject to the requirements of [1–208]. The reason for this exception is that [a prior Arkansas due-on-sale case] has become a rule of property. This rule of property exists for all due-on-sale clauses except those in favor of savings and loan associations which were executed on or after July 31, 1976." Abrego v. United Federal Savings & Loan

Association, 281 Ark. 308, 664 S.W.2d 858, 862–863 (1984).

26. "Section 1–208 is not concerned with default type acceleration clauses." Comment, Acceleration Clauses in Sales and Secured Transactions: The Debtor's Burden under Section 1–208 of the U.C.C., 11 B.C.Ind. & Com.L.Rev. 531, 539 (1970). The Comment to U.C.C. § 1–208 hardly suggests that the good faith requirement should be read broadly:

> The increased use of acceleration clauses either in the case of sales on credit or in time paper or in security transactions has led to some confusion in the cases as to the effect to be given to a clause which seemingly grants the power of an acceleration at the whim and caprice of one party. This Section is intended to make clear that despite language which can be so construed and which further might be held to make the agreement void as against public policy or to make the contract illusory or too indefinite for enforcement, the clause means that the option is to be exercised only in the good faith belief that the prospect of payment or performance is impaired.

U.C.C. § 1–208 Official Comment.

27. See e.g., HUD Handbook, 4330.1 (formerly 4191.02); VA Lenders Handbook, 26–7, Section F(1)(b) (1977). Concerning FHA and VA mortgage insurance operations generally, see § 11.2 infra.

28. Compare Federal National Mortgage Association v. Ricks, 83 Misc.2d 814, 372 N.Y.S.2d 485 (1975) and Cross v. Federof authority that the guidelines are only advisory and not a legal condition precedent to foreclosure.[29]

More recently, the FHA servicing guidelines, including provisions dealing with forbearance and counseling, have been promulgated as regulations.[30] Judicial response to this change has been mixed. There is case law that failure to comply with the forbearance and counseling provisions may be raised by the mortgagor as an affirmative defense to judicial foreclosure.[31] On the other hand, one court has held that the "Regulations and procedures in the [FHA] Handbook are discretionary, not mandatory, and are not a legal prerequisite to foreclosure * * *. A private cause of action may not be implied against a mortgagee for violation of the [FHA] regulations and the procedures outlined in the [FHA] Handbook."[32] In any event, a court may well consider them in reaching a decision as to whether foreclosure would be inequitable or unconscionable, and may, in the exercise of its inherent equitable powers, refuse to order foreclosure if the lender has violated the guideline or regulations in an egregious fashion.[33]

Where an apartment project mortgage has been insured by HUD under the National Housing Act and HUD subsequently acquires the mortgage, acceleration and foreclosure may be limited by the principles of United States v. Winthrop Towers.[34] In that case the United States Court of Appeals for the Seventh Circuit held that HUD's decision to foreclose, while in large measure discretionary, "may be reviewed to determine whether it is consistent with national housing objectives."[35] The court held the review should be based on whether HUD's action was "arbitrary, capricious, an abuse of discretion or otherwise not in

al National Mortgage Association, 359 So. 2d 464 (Fla.App.1978) with Brown v. Lynn, 385 F.Supp. 986 (N.D.Ill.1974), Brown v. Lynn, 392 F.Supp. 559 (N.D.Ill.1975), and Roberts v. Cameron-Brown Co., 556 F.2d 356 (5th Cir.1977), rehearing denied 559 F.2d 1217 (5th Cir.1977).

29. See e.g., Rank v. Nimmo, 677 F.2d 692 (9th Cir.1982), certiorari denied 459 U.S. 907, 103 S.Ct. 210, 74 L.Ed.2d 168 (1982); Simpson v. Cleland, 640 F.2d 1354 (D.C.Cir.1981); Gatter v. Nimmo, 672 F.2d 343 (3d Cir.1982).

30. See 24 CFR 203.500, 604, 606; Bankers Life Co. v. Denton, 120 Ill.App.3d 576, 76 Ill.Dec. 64, 458 N.E.2d 203 (1983). In 1980 the VA promulgated several regulations governing forbearance and partial payment. See 38 CFR 4275(f), 4315(b), 4600(c)(15). The former two provisions also state: "a failure by the holder to comply with the provisions of this paragraph may result in a partial or total loss of guaranty or insurance * * *, but such failure shall not constitute a defense to any legal action to terminate the loan." 38 CFR 4275(f)(3), 4315(b)(3).

31. See Bankers Life Co. v. Denton, 120 Ill.App.3d 576, 76 Ill.Dec. 64, 458 N.E.2d 203 (1983).

32. Heritage Bank, N.A. v. Ruh, 191 N.J.Super. 53, 61, 465 A.2d 547, 564 (1983).

33. Compare Federal National Mortgage Association v. Ricks, 83 Misc.2d 814, 372 N.Y.S.2d 485 (1975) (lender's conduct unconscionable; mortgagee's motion to dismiss denied) and Cross v. Federal National Mortgage Association, 359 So.2d 464 (Fla. App.1978) (deviation from guidelines may constitute equitable defense to foreclosure) with Government National Mortgage Association v. Screen, 85 Misc.2d 86, 379 N.Y.S.2d 327 (1976) (lender's conduct reasonable; foreclosure ordered) and Heritage Bank, N.A. v. Ruh, 191 N.J.Super. 53, 465 A.2d 547 (1983) (lender's conduct not unconscionable; foreclosure permitted).

34. 628 F.2d 1028 (7th Cir.1980), on remand 542 F.Supp. 1042 (D.Ill.1982).

35. Id. at 1035.

accordance with law." [36] In doing so, the court referred approvingly to two earlier federal district court decisions that suggested limits on HUD's discretion in its foreclosure decisions. In one case a foreclosure was enjoined because HUD seemed to be violating its own self-imposed moratorium on foreclosure.[37] In the other, a trial court had denied summary judgment for HUD where the mortgagor had alleged that HUD had failed, in violation of its own regulations, to consider modification, recasting or refinancing of the mortgage.[38] Nevertheless, the *Winthrop Towers* court emphasized that HUD's discretion was very broad when foreclosing on a large commercial mortgagor. According to the court, "if agency discretion could be calculated on a scale of 1 to 9, where 1 represents the narrowest and most constrained discretion, then HUD's discretion in foreclosing a mortgage granted, for example, by a large commercial developer would be somewhere in the area of 7 or 8." [39]

Use of the *Winthrop Towers* principle has largely proved fruitless. For example, one court held that an assertion by a mortgagor that the mortgaged premises had a high occupancy rate and provided safe and sanitary housing was insufficient to call into question HUD's decision to foreclose.[40] Also unavailing was a mortgagor foreclosure defense that HUD had refused to approve a proposed sale of the mortgaged property.[41] Still another decision refused to block foreclosure when the mortgagor allegation was HUD violation of a "proposed work-out agreement." [42] In sum, in the absence of a clear violation by HUD of its own policies or a specific agreement with the mortgagor, *Winthrop Towers* will be a slim reed on which to rely.

Finally, it should be emphasized that the Federal National Mortgage Association—Federal Home Loan Mortgage Corporation (FNMA—FHLMC) mortgage—deed of trust form contains substantial limitations on the acceleration process. Not only does it require detailed mailed notice and a thirty-day grace period as a condition precedent to acceleration, it also affords the mortgagor the right to defeat acceleration until five days prior to foreclosure by the payment of arrearages and mortgagee's reasonable costs and attorney's fees.[43] These provisions may be omitted from the FNMA—FHLMC form only when state law is more protective of the mortgagor with respect to pre-acceleration requirements and the ability to defeat acceleration once it has occurred.

---

36. Id. at 1036, quoting from 5 U.S.C.A. § 706(2)(A).

37. Kent Farm Co. v. Hills, 417 F.Supp. 297 (D.D.C.1976).

38. United States v. American National Bank and Trust Co. of Chicago, 443 F.Supp. 167 (N.D.Ill.1977).

39. Id. note 34 at 1035. Accord: United States v. Beacon Terrace Mutual Homes, Inc., 594 F.Supp. 53 (D.Md.1984); United States v. American National Bank

and Trust Company of Chicago, 595 F.Supp. 324 (N.D.Ill.1983).

40. United States v. Golden Acres, Inc., 520 F.Supp. 1073 (D.Del.1981).

41. United States v. OCCI Co., 580 F.Supp. 645 (E.D.Wis.1984), order affirmed 758 F.2d 1160 (7th Cir.1985).

42. United States v. Victory Highway Village, Inc., 662 F.2d 488 (8th Cir.1981).

43. See FNMA–FHLMC Deed of Trust (1 to 4 family) §§ 18–19.

Because most institutional lenders wish to retain the option of selling their home mortgages to these two secondary market entities, they will be likely to use the FNMA—FHLMC form. Thus vast numbers of mortgagors in states that have not enacted legislation regulating acceleration, or whose legislation or case law is less restrictive than the requirements of the form, will nevertheless have substantial protection against abuse of the acceleration process.

Agricultural mortgagors have found protection against acceleration and foreclosure by the Farmers Home Administration (FmHA) under Section 1981(a) of the Agricultural Credit Act of 1978.[44] Under the foregoing provision, the Secretary of Agriculture "may permit, at the request of the borrower, the deferral of principal and interest on any outstanding loan made, insured, or held by the Secretary * * * and may forego foreclosure of any such loan, for such period as the Secretary deems necessary upon a showing by the borrower that due to circumstances beyond the borrower's control, the borrower is temporarily unable to continue making payments of such principal and interest when due without unduly impairing the standard of living of the borrower."[45]

Section 1981(a) became the focal point of national controversy during the severe agricultural recession of the early and mid-1980's. The Secretary took the position that the section itself imposed no procedural or substantive limitations of loan acceleration and foreclosure and that the decision whether to hear individual requests under it or to implement it all was solely within his discretion. Numerous federal courts rejected these contentions and held that the FmHA is obligated to afford a mortgagor pre-acceleration notice that "he may apply for a moratorium on payment of his loan and that he be given an opportunity to demonstrate that he is eligible for it * * *"[46] Under this reasoning, the words "may permit" in Section 1981(a) refer to the discretion of the Secretary to grant a deferral *after* a showing by the mortgagor and does not mean that he has the authority to determine whether to enforce the section at all.[47] Rather, the Secretary was obligated to promulgate regulations under it establishing a procedure and substantive standards for deferrals and related relief.[48]

44. 7 U.S.C.A. § 1981(a).

45. Id.

46. Shick v. Farmers Home Administration of United States Department of Agriculture, 748 F.2d 35, 40 (1st Cir.1984). See Matzke v. Block, 732 F.2d 799 (10th Cir.1984) (affirming on this issue 564 F.Supp. 1157 (D.Kan.1983)); Allison v. Block, 723 F.2d 631 (8th Cir.1983) (affirming 556 F.Supp. 400 (W.D.Mo.1982)); United States v. Hamrick, 713 F.2d 69 (4th Cir.1983) (per curiam); Gamradt v. Block,

581 F.Supp. 122 (D.Minn.1983); Coleman v. Block, 580 F.Supp. 194 (D.N.D.1984) and 562 F.Supp. 1353 (D.N.D.1983); Jacoby v. Schuman, 568 F.Supp. 843 (E.D.Mo.1983); Curry v. Block, 738 F.2d 1556 (11th Cir. 1984). See generally, Note, 60 N.Dak.L. Rev. 555 (1984).

47. See Matzke v. Block, 732 F.2d 799 (10th Cir.1984).

48. Id; Allison v. Block, 723 F.2d 631 (8th Cir.1983); Jacoby v. Schuman, 568 F.Supp. 843 (E.D.Mo.1983).

In response to this judicial mandate, the Secretary proposed regulations in 1984 implementing Section 1981(a).[49]   These regulations require a series of notices to inform mortgagors of "any proposed action FmHA will intend to take on their loan accounts and give the borrowers the opportunity to be considered for servicing alternatives before such action is taken.   Alternatives will include rescheduling, reamortization, deferral of payments and having loans rewritten at [lower] interest rates."[50]   The regulations authorize such relief for a variety of natural and economic reasons beyond the mortgagor's control.[51]   However, "a reduction of income does not by itself mean that a borrower is entitled to deferral.   A reduction in income due to inadequate or poor financial management decisions, such as untimely marketing practices, is not an acceptable reason for a deferral since the borrower had control over the situation."[52]   The maximum period of deferral is five years.[53]

 WESTLAW REFERENCES
waiv** estopp** /s accelerat*** /p mortgage

§ 7.8   The Absence of An Acceleration Clause—Effect on Foreclosure

As one court has noted "security agreements without acceleration clauses are no longer common in modern real estate dealings *   *   *"[1]   Nevertheless, such situations do occasionally arise, and when they do, mortgagor default poses substantial foreclosure problems.   The mortgagee is faced with two undesirable foreclosure alternatives.   First, the mortgagee presumably could wait, in some instances for many years, for all of the installments to come due and then foreclose for the total accrued debt.   The second alternative is to foreclose based on a default in the payment of one or more installments.

When the mortgagee must follow the second alternative, there are several possible methods for handling the foreclosure.   Some courts take the view that the security is indivisible and that a foreclosure action must be of the entire security regardless of whether the default being sued for is of a portion or all of the debt.[2]   The result of this harsh doctrine is that if a mortgagee forecloses for an installment or interest he will be barred later from foreclosing for the balance or any

---

49. 49 Fed.Reg. 47007 (1984).

50. 49 Fed.Reg. 47008.

51. 49 Fed.Reg. 47008.

52. 49 Fed.Reg. 47020.

53. 49 Fed.Reg. 47007.

§ 7.8

1. Adkinson v. Nyberg, 344 So.2d 614, 615 (Fla.App.1977).

2. Curtis v. Cutler, 76 F. 16, 22 C.C.A. 16, 37 L.R.A. 737 (1896), abrogated by Gen.

Stat.Minn., Mason, § 9610 (1927).   See Prideaux v. Des Moines Joint Stock Bank, 34 F.2d 308 (D.C.Minn.1929), appeal dismissed 282 U.S. 800, 51 S.Ct. 40, 75 L.Ed. 720 (1930); Rains v. Mann, 68 Ill. 264 (1873); Cf., Wells v. Ordway, 108 Iowa 86, 78 N.W. 806, 75 Am.St.Rep. 209 (1899); Mascarel v. Raffour, 51 Cal. 242 (1876), foreclosing on only one parcel.   But cf., Widman v. Hammack, 110 Wash. 77, 187 P. 1091, 42 A.L.R. 468 (1920).

other portion of his obligation. But most courts, either by decision or under statutes, arrive at more equitable solutions. Thus, if it is possible to divide the property into parcels without injury to the whole a sale will be decreed of only so much of the premises as will be sufficient to satisfy the amount due, and the unsold portion of the property will remain encumbered by a lien for the balance of the debt as it comes due.[3] Where the property is not susceptible to piecemeal sale without injury to the whole, it may be sold as an entirety free and clear of the entire mortgage debt.[4] The surplus over the amount necessary to satisfy the partial default is then handled in various ways.[5] Even absent a statute, it has been held that the court will direct its application to the liquidation of the balance of the debt, with a fair and equitable rebate of interest on it.[6] Moreover, the same practice is authorized by statute in some jurisdictions.[7] Others direct that the surplus be held in trust to meet the unmatured portion of the debt.[8] Another proper alternative that would avoid the surplus problem would be to sell the premises at a foreclosure sale subject to the continued lien of the balance of the debt.[9] This is conceptually the same as treating

---

3. Blazey v. Delius, 74 Ill. 299 (1874); Griffin v. Reis, 68 Ind. 9 (1879); Caufman v. Sayre, 2 B.Mon. 202 (Ky.1841). See Reno v. Black, 59 F. 917 (C.C.Mo.1894); 37 L.R.A. 737, 743 (1905). See also Minn.Stat. Ann., § 580.09, "Where a mortgage is given to secure the payment of money by instalments—each instalment, either for principal or interest may be taken and deemed to be a separate and independent mortgage, and such mortgage for each instalment may be foreclosed in the same manner as if a separate mortgage was given for each subsequent instalment"; West's Ann.Cal.Code Civ.Proc., § 728, "If the debt for which the mortgage, lien, or incumbrance is held is not all due, so soon as sufficient of the property has been sold to pay the amount due, with costs, the sale must cease; and afterwards, as often as more comes due, for principal or interest, the court may, on motion, order more to be sold."

4. A mortgagee foreclosed his mortgage upon the mortgagor's partial default. Held, the premises, when sold under the decree, passed to the purchaser discharged from the mortgage lien. Poweshiek County v. Dennison, 36 Iowa, 244, 14 Am.Rep. 521 (1873); Buford v. Smith, 7 Mo. 489 (1842); Reno v. Black, note 8, supra. But see Borden v. McNamara, 20 N.D. 225, 127 N.W. 104, Ann.Cas.1912C, 841, 846 (1910); Edgar v. Beck, 96 Mich. 419, 56 N.W. 15 (1893).

5. For cases dealing with the disposition of surplus arising from a sale under foreclosure for partial default, see Hatcher

v. Chancey, 71 Ga. 689 (1883); Peyton v. Ayres, 2 Md.Ch. 64 (1849); Fowler v. Johnson, 26 Minn. 338, 3 N.W. 986, 6 N.W. 486 (1880); Cox v. Wheeler, 7 Paige 248 (N.Y. 1838); Schreiber v. Carey, 48 Wis. 208, 4 N.W. 124 (1879).

6. E.g., Black v. Reno, note 8, supra; 37 L.R.A. 737 (1905).

7. N.J.Stat.Ann., 2A:50–33 (1952), payment with rebate for interest, if mortgagee willing to receive it; Cal.Code Civ.Proc., § 728, rebate of interest where such rebate is proper; N.Y.—McKinney's RPAP § 1351(c), payment with rebate for interest, or investment; Wis.Stat.Ann. 278.07– 08, payment with rebate for interest, or investment.

8. Official Code Ga.Ann., § 44–14–191. And see New York and Wisconsin statutes—in preceding note.

9. See e.g., Adkinson v. Nyberg, 344 So. 2d 614 (Fla.App.1977); Wordinger v. Wirt, 112 Fla. 822, 151 So. 47 (1933); Light v. Federal Land Bank, 177 Ark. 846, 7 S.W.2d 975 (1928); Miami Mortgage & Guaranty Co. v. Drawdy, 99 Fla. 1092, 1097, 127 So. 323, 325 (1930); Hughes v. Frisbie, 81 Ill. 188, 193 (1876); Chicago Title & Trust Co. v. Prendergast, 335 Ill. 646, 167 N.E. 769 (1929); Fremont Joint Stock Bank v. Foster, 215 Iowa 1209, 247 N.W. 815 (1933); McCurdy v. Clark, 27 Mich. 445 (1873); Cary v. Metropolitan Life Insurance Co., 141 Or. 388, 17 P.2d 1111 (1933); McDougal v. Downey, 45 Cal. 165 (1872); Burroughs v. Ellis, 76 Iowa 649, 38 N.W. 141 (1888). See, generally, Leesman, The Efthe sale as a second mortgage foreclosure sale with the purchaser buying the premises subject to a first mortgage in the amount of the balance of the debt.

WESTLAW REFERENCES
digest (mortgage) & default*** foreclos*** /p indivisible (entire** /3 security)

C. STRICT FORECLOSURE

§ 7.9 The Nature of Strict Foreclosure

As mentioned earlier, there are two major methods of mortgage foreclosure in use in the United States and each is accompanied by a foreclosure sale. The most pervasive method is judicial foreclosure in equity. While this type of foreclosure is available in every state, in many states it is the only type permitted. In about half the states, the prevailing method is non-judicial foreclosure under a "power of sale." This power of sale is sometimes vested in the mortgagee, but more often in some public official such as a sheriff. If a deed of trust is used, the power of sale is in the trustee. These two methods of foreclosure will receive most of our attention in this chapter.

Another type of foreclosure, limited in use, is strict foreclosure. Unlike the above predominant methods, strict foreclosure entails no foreclosure sale. When it is used, strict foreclosure usually is judicial. However, the defaulting mortgagor is given a period of time by the court to pay the mortgage debt. Failure to do so within the prescribed time will result in title to the mortgaged real estate vesting in the mortgagee without sale. The following section focuses on the use of this foreclosure device in the United States.

WESTLAW REFERENCES
di foreclosure

§ 7.10 Use of Strict Foreclosure

In most states strict foreclosure of a mortgagor's interest by a mortgagee is not permitted. However, it is still used in Connecticut[1]

fect of Foreclosure of Part Only of a Mortgage Debt, 31 Ill.L.Rev. 1056 (1937); note, 1930, 30 Col.L.Rev. 893. See also, 37 L.R.A. 737 (1897). In New York, by an amendment in 1927, Laws of 1927, c. 683, N.Y.—McKinney's RPAP § 1351(c) was changed to permit this as an alternative practice. In the face of the statute it was held improper to decree a sale for the defaulted portion of a debt with a continuing lien for the unmatured balance. Bank of America National Association v. Dames, 135 Misc. 391, 239 N.Y.S. 558, 30 Col.L.

Rev. 893 (1930). A later case, however, held the other way, giving effect to the clear language of the act. Prudence Co. v. Sussman, 143 Misc. 686, 258 N.Y.S. 241 (1932).

§ 7.10

1. See Conn.Gen.Stat.Ann. § 49–15 (1975); Abacus Mortgage Insurance Co. v. Whitewood Hills Development Corp., 2 Conn.App. 460, 479 A.2d 1231 (1984); Maresca v. Allen, 181 Conn. 521, 436 A.2d 14 (1980).

even though a statute in that state provides for foreclosure sale on written notice by any party, the granting of which is discretionary with the court.[2] Moreover, while a strong showing by the mortgagor or junior lienholders that the mortgaged real estate is worth more than the mortgage debt may sometimes convince a court to order foreclosure by sale, it rarely will be found to have abused its discretion in refusing to do so.[3] Strict foreclosure is also the predominant remedy in Vermont.[4] However, foreclosure by sale may be ordered if the mortgage authorizes such foreclosure and the plaintiff or any defendant requests it.[5]

The constitutionality of Vermont's strict foreclosure practice was upheld by the United States Court of Appeals for the Second Circuit in *Dieffenbach v. Attorney General of Vermont*.[6] The primary assertion in that case was that strict foreclosure violated the due process and equal protection clauses of United States Constitution because, while the mortgagee can obtain a deficiency judgment against the mortgagor in the event the value of the mortgaged real estate is less than the mortgage debt, the mortgagor has no claim to a surplus is the mortgagee resells the property at a profit. In rejecting that claim, the court emphasized that strict foreclosure was rationally related to a legitimate state interest. According to the court, "One possible purpose of strict is to make it easier for banks or other creditors to lend by giving them a speculative interest in the property, for the bank realizes that it may retain the excess if the property's value happens to exceed the debt. Another purpose might be to compensate the bank for its expense * * * in a foreclosure suit and subsequent sale. A third possibility is that, in an implicit quid pro quo, the legislature has granted the banks this speculative interest in return for requiring the banks to lend money at lower interest rates, and to permit prepayment without penalty."[7] The court also rejected a second argument, based on the equal protection, that Vermont strict foreclosure impermissively burdens only those mortgagors whose property is worth more than the mortgage debt. The court reasoned that the "legislature may reasonably have concluded that strict foreclosure laws equitably distribute the commercial costs of mortgages because every mortgagor * * * is

---

2. Conn.Gen.Stat.Ann. § 49–24. See Hartford Federal Savings and Loan Ass'n v. Tucker, 196 Conn. 172, 491 A.2d 1084 (1985); Bradford Realty Corp. v. Beetz, 108 Conn. 26, 31, 142 A. 395, 397 (1928); North End Bank & Trust Co. v. Mandell, 113 Conn. 241, 245; 155 A. 80, 81 (1931).

3. See Hartford Federal Savings and Loan Ass'n v. Tucker, 196 Conn. 172, 491 A.2d 1084 (1985); Abacus Mortgage Insurance Co. v. Whitewood Hills Development Corp., 2 Conn.App. 460, 479 A.2d 1231 (1984); Constitution Bank & Trust Co. v. Robinson, 179 Conn. 232, 425 A.2d 1268 (1979). See also cases in preceding footnote.

4. See 12 Vt.Stat.Ann. § 4528; Vt.R. Civ.P., Rule 80.1(a)–(1); Stowe Center, Inc. v. Burlington Savings Bank, 141 Vt. 634, 451 A.2d 1114 (1982); Comment, The Relation of the Equitable Doctrine of Subrogation to Vermont's Strict Foreclosure Laws, 7 Vt.L.Rev. 71, 77–82 (1982).

5. See 12 Vt.Stat.Ann. § 4531a; Vt.R. Civ.P., Rule 80.1(h). Moreover, foreclosure by sale is required when the United States has a lien or other interest in the mortgaged real estate. See 12 Vt.Stat.Ann. § 4531.

6. 604 F.2d 187 (2d Cir.1979).

7. Id. at 196.

equally subject to the risk that his property's value will exceed the portion of his debt that he is unable to pay. The state's failure to 'insure' against the unequal actual incidence of this risk by permitting banks to absorb the risk in their interest rates does not amount to a violation of equal protection." [8]

Illinois also apparently uses strict foreclosure, but only under very limited circumstances.[9] Decisions in that state specify three requirements for its employment: the property must not be worth more than the mortgage debt plus interest and costs; the mortgagee must be willing to take the property in full satisfaction of the debt; and the mortgagor must be insolvent.[10]

Two related foreclosure methods authorized, but at most only sporadically used in some of the New England States are *Entry Without Process* and *Actions at Law for a Writ of Entry or Possession.*[11] Under the former method, a mortgagee after a default may take possession of the premises without legal help. Then, after the expiration of a time period varying from one to three years, the mortgagor's equity of redemption is forever barred. The entry must be peaceable; however possession by the mortgagee may be constructive. In other words, in theory the mortgagor can become the tenant of the mortgagee. In the *Action at Law for a Writ of Entry,* the mortgagee goes into court and alleges that the mortgage is in default. There is an accounting for what is due and owing and then a judgment for possession of the premises. Then the mortgagee goes into possession and if possession is maintained for a one to three year period, depending on the jurisdiction, the mortgagor's equity of redemption is barred. Both of these methods result in strict foreclosure.

Except in those few states where strict foreclosure is authorized in normal foreclosure proceedings, the use of the remedy is limited to

8. Id. at 197.

9. See Great Lakes Mortgage Corp. v. Collymore, 14 Ill.App.3d 68, 302 N.E.2d 248 (1973); Carpenter v. Plagge, 192 Ill. 82, 99, 61 N.E. 530, 536 (1901); Johnson v. Donnell, 15 Ill. 97, 99 (1853); Carpenter v. Plagge, 192 Ill. 82, 61 N.E. 530 (1901); Barnes v. Ward, 190 Ill.App. 392, 395, 398, 399 (1914). Griesbaum v. Baum, 18 Ill. App. 614 (1886); Miller v. Davis, 5 Ill.App. 474 (1879); Rabbit v. First National Bank, 237 Ill.App. 289 (1925). For the requirements of strict foreclosure in Illinois, see Prather, Foreclosure of the Security Interest, U. of Ill.L.Forum, 420, 446 (1957). See also Brodkey, Current Changes in Illinois Real Property Law, 10 DePaul L.Rev. 566, 580 (1960).

10. Id.

11. As to both types of foreclosure, see Mass.Gen.Laws Ann. c. 244 §§ 1–10; N.H. Rev.Stat.Ann. 479:19; R.I.Gen.Laws 1956, 34–23–3; Me.Rev.Stat.Ann. c. 14 § 6201.

In Maine strict foreclosure may be accomplished by advertisement of service of notice of default and intention to foreclose followed by the passage of one year's time. Me.Rev.Stat.Ann. c. 14 §§ 6203, 6204. This statute arguably may not constitutionally be used by any entity that would constitute the state or federal government under the 14th and 5th amendments of U.S. Constitution. See Ricker v. United States, 417 F.Supp. 133 (D.Me.1976). Alternatively, Maine mortgagees, without taking possession, may foreclose simply by serving notice on the mortgagor. The mortgagor may redeem the property within one year after service of the notice. Me. Rev.Stat.Ann. c. 14 §§ 6203(2), 6204. For a consideration of the constitutionality of both methods, see Comment, The Constitutionality of Maine's Real Estate Mortgage Foreclosure Statutes, 32 Maine L.Rev. 147 (1980); Fitzgerald v. Cleland, 498 F.Supp. 341 (D.Me.1980), affirmed in part, vacated in part 650 F.2d 360 (1st Cir.1981).

special situations. For example, some states authorize its use in actions to have absolute deeds declared to be mortgages.[12] Moreover, as we have seen elsewhere, its equivalent is sometimes used in statutory actions to cancel installment land contracts.[13]

The most common special situation where strict foreclosure is utilized is where a mortgagee has foreclosed by sale but has failed to join some party who has an interest in the property subject to the mortgage. The mortgagee, or a third person, may purchase at the foreclosure sale and thus unite in himself all interest in the property[14] save that of the unjoined party which is of course, unaffected by the action.[15] Where the prior foreclosure is defective because the mortgagor or owner of the property was not joined, strict foreclosure generally is not allowed.[16] In such a case the legal title, at least in lien theory states, in whole or in part remains outstanding in the unjoined party; the mortgagee or third party purchaser, who succeeds in such a case only to the interest of the mortgagee and joined parties, is still only a mortgagee and must foreclose by sale in order to protect the title holder.[17] Where the legal title has passed to the purchaser on foreclo-

12. See, e.g., Hermann v. Churchill, 235 Or. 327, 385 P.2d 190 (1963), commented on in Note, 43 Or.L.Rev. 350 (1964), the court held that strict foreclosure may be decreed in a suit to have a deed absolute declared a mortgage, in spite of a statute providing for foreclosure of "all liens" by a foreclosure sale. The court said the statute did not apply to an action to redeem. See also Lenske v. Steinberg, 415 F.2d 711 (9th Cir. 1969) (strict foreclosure allowed where mortgagor in possession for two years had made no payments and value of land did not exceed the debt).

13. See § 3.28, supra.

14. E.g., Miles v. Stehle, 22 Neb. 740, 36 N.W. 142 (1888); Sears, Roebuck & Co. v. Camp, 124 N.J.Eq. 403, 1 A.2d 425, 118 A.L.R. 762 (1938); noted, 23 Minn.L.Rev. 388 (1939). See 118 A.L.R. 769 (1939); 88 U. of Pa.L.Rev. 994 (1949). The same situation occurs where the mortgagee buys in the premises on an execution sale under a judgment against the mortgagor. Benedict v. Mortimer, 8 A. 515 (N.J.Eq.1887); Eldridge v. Eldridge, 14 N.J.Ch. 195 (1862).

15. In the absence of statute, this is generally true even though the foreclosing mortgagee has no knowledge or notice of the subordinate interest of another person in the mortgaged property. See Haines v. Beach, 3 Johns.Ch. 459, 461 (N.Y.1818); § 7.5, supra; Campbell, Cases on Mortgages, 2d ed., 273 n. 1. However, under recording acts, in accordance with their policy, if a purchaser on foreclosure sale has no actual notice of the existence of

such an interest, and is not charged with constructive notice because its holder has failed to record, the latter will be bound by the foreclosure to the same extent as if he had been joined as a party. Sibell v. Weeks, 65 N.J.Eq. 714, 55 A. 244 (1903); Rogers v. Houston, 94 Tex. 403, 60 S.W. 869 (1901); Walker v. Schreiber, 47 Iowa 529 (1877), actual notice; Hoppin v. Doty, 22 Wis. 621 (1868), actual notice. See 88 U. of Pa.L.Rev. 994, 997 (1940). And if the unjoined party held only an equitable interest, it could be cut off by the foreclosure sale purchaser under the doctrine of bona fide purchase if the buyer had no notice of its existence and paid value bona fide.

16. Georgia Casualty Co. v. O'Donnell, 109 Fla. 290, 147 So. 267 (1933); Gamut v. Gregg, 37 Iowa 573 (1873); United States Savings Bank v. Schnitzer, 118 N.J.Eq. 584, 180 A. 624 (1935); Surety Building & Loan Association v. Risack, 118 N.J.Eq. 425, 179 A. 680, 22 Va.L.Rev. 227 (1935); Mickelson v. Anderson, 81 Utah 444, 19 P.2d 1033 (1933). See 118 A.L.R. 769, 779 (1939).

17. "Conceivably the interest of the omitted party, though he be not a mere encumbrancer, may be so insignificant, remote, or contingent, or be so affected by his inequitable conduct, as to render the requirement of a second foreclosure sale unnecessary, impractical, or unjust." 118 A.L.R. 769 (1939). Kansas courts have held that, in their discretion, they may permit strict foreclosure against a mortgagor or other owner to even a "mortgagee in possession." Bankers' Mortgage Co. of To-

sure sale, but is still subject to a redemptive right in some person whose interest is subordinate to the mortgage and who was not joined as a party to the foreclosure action strict foreclosure may be ordered.[18] We will examine further when it may be utilized against such omitted interests, chiefly junior lienors, in a subsequent section that explores all of the available remedies in the omitted party situation.[19]

 WESTLAW REFERENCES
synopsis,digest("strict foreclosure")

D. JUDICIAL FORECLOSURE

§ 7.11   Judicial Foreclosure—General Characteristics

Judicial foreclosure by sale in a court action in equity is the predominant method of foreclosure in the United States. It is the exclusive or generally used method of foreclosure in at least half of the states.[1] Moreover, it is available in every jurisdiction, either by virtue of express statutory enactment or as an incident to the inherent

---

peka v. O'Donovan, 137 Kan. 309, 312, 20 P.2d 809, 811 (1933); Sutor v. First National Bank, 146 Kan. 52, 69 P.2d 315 (1937).

18. See 88 U. of Pa.L.Rev. 994, 1006 (1940); 25 Va.L.Rev. 947, 951; 118 A.L.R. 769, 770 (1939); Campbell, Cases Mortgages, 248 n. 4. Examples of such interests include: a junior mortgage, Leslie v. Smith, 58 S.D. 14, 234 N.W. 669 (1931); Quinn Plumbing Co. v. New Miami Shores Corp., 100 Fla. 413, 129 So. 690, 73 A.L.R. 600 (1930); Evans v. Atkins, 75 Iowa 448, 39 N.W. 702 (1888); Miles v. Stehle, 22 Neb. 740, 36 N.W. 142 (1888); Shepard v. Barrett, 84 N.J.Eq. 408, 93 A. 852 (1915); Sears, Roebuck & Co. v. Camp, 124 N.J.Eq. 403, 1 A.2d 425, 118 A.L.R. 762 (1938); a judgment lien, Koerner v. Willamette Iron Works, 36 Or. 90, 58 P. 863 (1899); Lockard v. Hendrickson, N.J.Ch., 25 A. 512 (1892); a lease, Mesiavech v. Newman, 120 N.J.Eq. 192, 184 A. 538 (1936); an easement, Hinners v. Birkevaag, 113 N.J.Eq. 413, 167 A. 209 (1933); but cf. Monese v. Struve, 155 Or. 68, 62 P.2d 822 (1936) noted, 50 Harv.L.Rev. 990 (1937); and dower, Northwestern Trust Co. v. Ryan, 115 Minn. 143, 132 N.W. 202 (1911); Loeb v. Tinkler, 124 Ind. 331, 24 N.E. 235 (1890); Eldridge v. Eldridge, 14 N.J.Eq. 195 (1862); Ross v. Boardman, 22 Hun. 527 (N.Y.1880); see 118 A.L.R. 769, 782 (1939).

19. See § 7.15 infra.

§ 7.11

1. As of 1968 judicial foreclosure was the exclusive or generally used foreclosure

method in Arizona, Arkansas, Connecticut, Delaware, Florida, Illinois, Indiana, Iowa, Kansas, Kentucky, Louisiana, Montana, Nebraska, New Jersey, New Mexico, New York, North Dakota, Ohio, Oklahoma, Pennsylvania, South Carolina, Utah (mortgages only), Vermont and Wisconsin. See Comment, Cost and Time Factors in Foreclosure of Mortgages, 3 Real Prop.Prob. & Tr.J. 413, 414 (1968). In two of these states, Connecticut and Vermont, the foreclosure is judicial, but it is strict foreclosure. See § 7.10, supra. In Pennsylvania it was by scire facias; however, 21 Pa.Stat. § 791 which authorized scire facias was suspended in 1950 by Rule of Civ.Pro. 1460. As a practical matter, Pennsylvania seems to be a judicial foreclosure state. See 3 Real Prop.Prob. & Tr.J. at 427. Delaware utilizes scire facias. Upon default, the mortgagee may obtain a writ of scire facias directing the mortgagor to appear and show cause why the property should not be seized and sold in satisfaction of the debt. If the mortgagor fails to appear, the court is empowered to enter a judgment by default and direct that the mortgagee is entitled to execution by levari facias. See Monroe Park v. Metropolitan Life Insurance Co., 457 A.2d 734 (Del.1983); Pennamco v. Nardo Management Co., Inc., 435 A.2d 726 (Del.Super.1981); Gelof v. First National Bank of Frankford, 373 A.2d 206 (Del.1977). For a further consideration of scire facias, see Osborne, Mortgages, § 316 (2d Ed.1970).

jurisdiction of courts of equity.[2] Even in jurisdictions where power of sale foreclosure is dominant, judicial foreclosure is required in certain special situations. For example, it will be necessary where the mortgage fails to create a power of sale. This situation will arise where the mortgage form omits any reference to a power of sale. It can also occur where one is seeking to foreclose an absolute deed as a mortgage because, by its very nature, the absolute deed will not contain a power of sale.[3] Finally judicial foreclosure will be required where there is a serious lien priority dispute. In such a situation a judicial determination of lien priority will be enable potential foreclosure sale purchasers to know the state of the title they will be bidding on and thus judicial foreclosure will be encouraged. On the other hand, if power of sale foreclosure were used, the uncertainty as to lien priority would discourage bidding and create title problems for the ultimate sale purchaser.

In spite of being the most pervasive method of foreclosure in America today, it has serious disadvantages. It is complicated, costly, and time-consuming.[4] A typical action in equity to foreclose and sell involves a long series of steps: a preliminary title search to determine all parties in interest; filing of the foreclosure bill of complaint and lis pendens notice; service of process; a hearing, usually by a master in chancery who then reports to the court; the decree or judgment; notice of sale; actual sale and issuance of certificate of sale; report of the sale; proceedings for determination of the right to any surplus; possible redemptions from foreclosure sale; and the entry of a decree for a deficiency.[5] The following sections focus on some of the more important aspects and problems of judicial foreclosure.

 WESTLAW REFERENCES
date(after 1967) & foreclos*** /5 judicial** /p mortgag**

§ 7.12 Parties Defendant and the "Necessary-Proper" Party Distinction

Persons are made parties defendant in a foreclosure action for one of two purposes: one is to give the court jurisdiction to make a valid order to sell the person's interest in the mortgaged property at the

---

2. Chancellor Kent in Mills v. Dennis, 3 Johns.Ch. 367 (N.Y.1818), sustained the power, and nine years later, in a basic decision, it was recognized as both an inherent part of equity jurisdiction and also authorized by statute. Lansing v. Goelet, 9 Cowen, 346 (N.Y.1827). See Belloc v. Rogers, 9 Cal. 123 (1858); Sprague, History of Chancery and Advertisement Foreclosures in Michigan, 5 Detroit L.Rev. 63, 64ff (1935).

3. See § 3.8, supra.

4. See Comment, Cost and Time Factors in Foreclosure of Mortgages, 3 Real Prop.

Prob. & Tr.J. 413 (1968); McElhone & Cramer, Loan Foreclosure Costs Affected by Varied State Regulations, 36 Mortgage Banker 41 (1975); Comment, Power of Sale After Fuentes, 40 U.Chi.L.Rev. 206, 210–211 (1972); Carey, et al., Studies in Foreclosures in Cook County: Foreclosure Methods and Redemption, 27 Ill.L.Rev. 595, 596–609 (1933); Bridewell, The Effects of Defective Mortgage Laws on Home Financing, 5 Law & Contemp.Probs. 545, 549ff (1938), especially Table I, p. 555.

5. Carey, et al. and Bridewell, supra note 4.

foreclosure sale; the other is to obtain a decree against him on the mortgage obligation. Strictly speaking, foreclosure is only concerned with the first objective. However, in jurisdictions where a decree for a deficiency may be had in the same equitable action after the property has been sold in the foreclosure suit,[1] it is a customary feature of the proceeding, even though the nature of that part of the action and decree is fundamentally different from the foreclosure sale portion of it.

In dealing with the question of who should or may be made parties defendant in a foreclosure action, it is common to draw a distinction between "necessary" and "proper" parties.[2] There is, however, no generally agreed-on meaning for either term.[3] The terminology is useful, however, if it is used in the context of the basic purposes of the foreclosure proceeding. Two such purposes are often articulated. First, it is said that foreclosure should, if successful, terminate the rights of all interested parties who have a right to redeem from or are "subject to" the mortgage being foreclosed.[4] To state this proposition however is to beg the question "why"? The answer is found in the more fundamental and descriptive purpose of foreclosure, which is to give the foreclosure sale purchaser essentially the same title to the land as that possessed by the mortgagor when the foreclosed mortgage was executed.[5] In this sense, then, a party is "necessary" if failure to join him will not accomplish the purposes for foreclosure described above. For example, if a first mortgage is judicially foreclosed and a second mortgagee is not made a party, the foreclosure will not affect or terminate the rights of the junior mortgagee. The latter's mortgage will remain on the land. The sale purchaser will receive a title fundamentally different from the one the mortgagor had when the foreclosed mortgage was executed. It should be emphasized, however, that the failure to join such a necessary party does not render the entire foreclosure proceeding invalid; rather it is deemed to be ineffective only as to those necessary parties who were not joined.[6]

§ 7.12

1. E.g., West's Ann.Cal.Code, Civ.Proc., § 726.

2. E.g., Iowa County Board of Supervisors v. Mineral Point Railroad Co., 24 Wis. 93 (1869). See Terrell v. Allison, 88 U.S. (21 Wall.) 289, 22 L.Ed. 634 (1874); Gage v. Perry, 93 Ill. 176 (1879).

3. "The question as to who may or may not be necessary or proper parties * * * constitutes of itself a title in the law of equity jurisprudence, upon which great learning has been expended, without the ascertainment of any rule of general or universal application." Iowa County Board of Supervisors v. Mineral Point Railroad Co., 24 Wis. 93 (1869). See note, 88 U. of Pa.L.Rev. 994, 996 (1940), bringing out that the tests differ according to the stage at which the question is raised, this being

especially true as between the period before and after sale.

4. See § 7.2, supra.

5. See, e.g., Valentine v. Portland Timber and Land Holding Co., 15 Wn.App. 124, 547 P.2d 912 (1976); San Francisco v. Lawton, 18 Cal. 465 (1861). See also, Dye v. Lewis, 67 Misc.2d 426, 324 N.Y.S.2d 172 (1971).

6. E.g., Baldi v. Chicago Title & Trust Co., 113 Ill.App.3d 29, 68 Ill.Dec. 808, 446 N.E.2d 1205 (1983); Polish National Alliance of Brooklyn, U.S.A. v. White Eagle Hall Co., Inc., 98 A.D.2d 400, 470 N.Y.S.2d 642, 646 (1983); Citibank N.A. v. Oxford Properties & Finance, Limited, 688 F.2d 1259 (9th Cir.1982); Iowa County Board of Supervisors v. Mineral Point Railroad Co., 24 Wis. 93 (1869); Spokane Savings & Loan Society v. Liliopoulos, 160 Wash. 71, 294 P.

A "proper" party, on the other hand, is one whose presence in the suit is convenient and desirable, and who, if joined, will be bound by the proceedings, but whose absence will not defeat the purposes of foreclosure outlined in the preceding paragraph. It is often said that only those who are subject to the mortgage being foreclosed can properly be joined without their consent.[7] A senior lienor is not a necessary party because it is not subject to or subordinate to the mortgage being foreclosed. To omit it from a foreclosure suit brought by a junior lienor will not defeat the purposes of foreclosure because the senior lien existed on the land as of the time the mortgage being foreclosed was executed. Nevertheless, there are occasions when it is desirable to make the senior lienor a party, at least for limited purposes. For example, in order that a foreclosure purchase subject to the senior lien be intelligently made and bring a maximum amount, it is important that the senior lienor be made a party for the purpose of making clear and definite the nature and extent of the prior lien.[8] The extent to which such senior interests may be joined and for what purposes will be explored later in this chapter.[9]

A comprehensive catalogue of all the various classes of persons who would qualify under the foregoing principles as necessary defendants in an action to foreclose a mortgage by sale is so formidable [10] that only a few of the more important instances can serve as examples.[11]

First is the one who has title to the property subject to the mortgage or any part of it. The mortgagor so long as he retains the property falls under this category and must be joined.[12] But the mortgagor frequently sells the property and in that case the purchaser of the entire property or any part of it must be made a party.[13] If the mortgagor has parted with all of the property he is no longer a necessary party for foreclosure purposes.[14] Since he is the obligor, and

---

561 (1930). See 88 U. of Pa.L.Rev. 994 (1940); Hagan v. Gardner, 283 F.2d 643 (9th Cir.1960).

7. See § 7.14, infra.

8. See Dye v. Lewis, 67 Misc.2d 426, 324 N.Y.S.2d 172 (1971); § 7.14, infra.

9. See § 7.14, infra.

10. E.g., in Wiltsie, Mortgage Foreclosure, 5th ed., § 329, are listed 51 different classes of persons who, either normally or under certain circumstances or in certain states, may be joined as defendants. 103 pages are devoted to covering parties who are such by having an interest in the property subject to the mortgage. Chs. XX, XXI. An additional 15 pages is devoted to prior lienors and adverse claimants, Ch. XXIII. And another 20 pages to parties who are made defendants because personally liable. Ch. XXIV.

11. Section 7.2, supra, contains a discussion of those who have a right to re-

deem from the mortgage. By definition, those who have a right to redeem are generally necessary parties.

12. See Polish National Alliance of Brooklyn, U.S.A. v. White Eagle Hall Co., Inc., 98 A.D.2d 400, 470 N.Y.S.2d 642 (1983); Goodenow v. Ewer, 16 Cal. 461, 76 Am.Dec. 540 (1860).

13. Peoples Savings Bank of New York v. D & P Realty Corp., 96 A.D.2d 899, 466 N.Y.S.2d 70 (1983); Terrell v. Allison, 88 U.S. (21 Wall.) 289, 22 L.Ed. 634 (1874); Walker v. Warner, 179 Ill. 16, 53 N.E. 594, 70 Am.St.Rep. 85 (1899); Fowler v. Lilly, 122 Ind. 297, 23 N.E. 767 (1889); Winslow v. Clark, 47 N.Y. 261 (1872). See Slingluff, The Mortgagee's Right in the Event of a Deficiency, 1 Md.L.Rev. 128 (1937).

14. Smith v. Varney, 309 A.2d 229 (Me. 1973); Thompson v. Menfee, 218 Ala. 332, 118 So. 587 (1928); Brockway v. McClun, 243 Ill. 196, 90 N.E. 374 (1909); Fitzgerald normally remains such, he is usually joined in order that a personal decree may be entered against him in case of a deficiency. A transferee who in turn has disposed of the property is likewise unnecessary for foreclosure.[15] If he has assumed the mortgage debt he may be joined so as to get a deficiency decree against him as in the similar case of a mortgagor who has divested himself of all interest in the property.[16] Where the mortgagor has sold the real estate on an installment land contract, the vendee becomes a necessary party.[17] On the death of a mortgagor or person in whom the present ownership of the property subject to the mortgage is vested, the persons in whom the title then vests, the heirs or devisees, must be joined in the foreclosure.[18] Where a dower interest is made subject to a mortgage the wife or widow is an essential party to foreclosure.[19] Where there are future interests created in the property subject to the mortgage, there are many statements that holders of contingent interests need not be made parties to a foreclosure action, that it is sufficient to join the first person in being who has a vested estate of inheritance.[20] However, if contingent remaindermen are living and available, they should be joined.[21] Although the general rule is that both trustees and beneficiaries should be made parties,[22] there are important exceptions.[23] One of these, "as well established as the rule itself, * * * is, that whenev-

v. Flanagan, 155 Iowa 217, 135 N.W. 738, Ann.Cas.1914C, 1104 (1912); Delacroix v. Stanley, 113 N.J.Eq. 121, 165 A. 882 (1933); McNeal v. Moberly, 150 Okl. 253, 1 P.2d 707 (1931).

15. Howell v. Baker, 106 N.J.Eq. 434, 151 A. 117 (1930); James v. Brainard-Jackson Co., 64 Wash. 175, 116 P. 633 (1911).

16. Scarry v. Eldridge, 63 Ind. 44 (1878); Vrooman v. Turner, 69 N.Y. 280, 25 Am.R. 195 (1877). See § 8.1, infra; §§ 5.11–5.16, supra.

17. See Polish National Alliance of Brooklyn, U.S.A. v. White Eagle Hall Co., Inc., 98 A.D.2d 400, 470 N.Y.S.2d 642 (1983); Brost v. L.A.N.D., Inc., 37 Wn.App. 372, 680 P.2d 453 (1984).

18. White v. Rittenmyer, 30 Iowa 268 (1870); Abbott v. Godfroy's Heirs, 1 Mich. 178 (1849); Chadbourn v. Johnston, 119 N.C. 282, 25 S.E. 705 (1896); Chew v. Hyman, 7 F. 7 (C.C.Ill.1881). Cf., Reedy v. Camfield, 159 Ill. 254, 42 N.E. 833 (1896). Statutes sometimes provide that the personal representative rather than the heir or devisee shall be made a party. See Tierney v. Spiva, 97 Mo. 98, 10 S.W. 433 (1888); Kelsey v. Welch, 8 S.D. 255, 66 N.W. 390 (1896). For a holding that the personal representative is a necessary party, apparently in absence of statute, see Citizens Bank, Dumright v. Satcher, 521 P.2d 819 (Okl.1974).

19. Bigoness v. Hibbard, 267 Ill. 301, 108 N.E. 294 (1915), commented on in, 10 Ill.L.Rev. 137 (1915); McArthur v. Franklin, 15 Ohio St. 485, 16 Ohio St. 193 (1865).

20. See Jones, Mortgages, 8th ed., § 1401; Wiltsie, Mortgage Foreclosure, 5th ed., § 362. See also Hanna, Cas. Security, 3d ed., 1019, note, citing, Shackley v. Homer, 87 Neb. 146, 127 N.W. 145, L.R.A.1915C, 993 (1910); McCampbell v. Mason, 151 Ill. 500, 38 N.E. 672 (1894); see Clarke v. Cordis, 86 Mass. (4 Allen) 466, 478 (1862); Powell v. Wright, 7 Beav. 444 (1844).

21. See Hess v. Hess, 233 N.Y. 164, 135 N.E. 231 (1922); N.Y.—McKinney's Real Prop. Actions & Proc.Law, § 1311 and N.Y.—McKinney's Estates Powers & Trusts Law, § 6–5.1; Mass.Gen.Laws Ann. c. 244, § 13.

22. Clark v. Reyburn, 75 U.S. (8 Wall.) 318, 19 L.Ed. 354 (1868). See Iowa County Board of Supervisors v. Mineral Point Railroad Co., 24 Wis. 93 (1869); White v. Macqueen, 360 Ill. 236, 195 N.E. 832, 93 A.L.R. 1115 (1935); Williamson v. Field's Executors & Devisees, 2 Sandf.Ch. 533 (N.Y.1845). First National Bank v. Leslie, 106 N.J.Eq. 564, 151 A. 501 (1930).

23. See Wiltsie, Mortgage Foreclosure, 5th ed., § 360.

er the parties in interest are, or from the nature of the case, may be, so numerous that it would be difficult or impractical to bring them all before the court, and their rights are such as may be fairly and fully represented and tried without joining them, the application of the rule may be dispensed with." [24]

In addition to the foregoing, all persons who have an interest in the mortgaged premises acquired by or through the owner of the property subject to the mortgage subsequent to its execution must be made defendants.[25] Under this classification fall junior mortgagees, mechanics lienors and holders of other subordinate liens.[26] The owner of an easement or restrictive covenant falls within the same reasoning.[27]

Lessees present special problems in foreclosure proceedings. It is well settled that a lease prior to a mortgage is unaffected by a foreclosure. The purchaser at the sale obtains the mortgagor's interest and becomes the lessee's landlord.[28] Since the lease is unaffected by the foreclosure, the lessee is not a "necessary" party in a judicial foreclosure proceeding. On the other hand, where the mortgage is prior to the lease and the lessee is joined, the foreclosure extinguishes the lease.[29] "There is no privity of either estate or contract between the mortgagee and the lessee of the mortgagor to bind either, and the foreclosure of the mortgage avoids the lease and releases the lessee from any obligation. * * * Whenever the estate which the landlord had at the time of making the lease is defeated or determined, the lease is extinguished with it." [30]

Suppose, however, that the junior lessee is not joined. Under the majority rule the lessee's interest remains unaffected by the foreclosure.[31] But what does this mean as a practical matter for the lessee

24. Iowa County Board of Supervisors v. Mineral Point Railroad Co., 24 Wis. 93 (1869). See State ex rel. Ashley v. Circuit Court, 219 Wis. 38, 47, 261 N.W. 737, 741 (1935). See also 20 L.R.A. 535 (1893); 1908, 16 L.R.A.,N.S., 1006 (1908); 35 L.R.A.,N.S., 196 (1912).

25. See, e.g., Yarbrough v. John Deere Industrial Equipment Co., 526 S.W.2d 188 (Tex.Civ.App.1975).

26. E.g., Yarbrough v. John Deere Industrial Equipment Co., 526 S.W.2d 188 (Tex.Civ.App.1974); Polish National Alliance of Brooklyn, U.S.A. v. White Eagle Hall Co., Inc., 98 A.D.2d 400, 470 N.Y.S.2d 642 (1983); Baldwin-Bellmore Federal Savings & Loan Association v. Stellato, 55 Misc.2d 1043, 287 N.Y.S.2d 516 (1968); Motor Equipment Co. v. Winters, 146 Kan. 127, 69 P.2d 23 (1937) (junior mortgage); Lenexa State Bank & Trust Co. v. Dixon, 221 Kan. 238, 559 P.2d 776 (1977).

27. Rector of Christ Protestant Episcopal Church v. Mack, 93 N.Y. 488, 45 Am.R.

260 (1883); Krich v. Zemel, 99 N.J.L. 191, 122 A. 739 (1897).

28. Annot. 14 A.L.R. 664, 678.

29. Annot. 109 A.L.R. 447, 451.

30. Roosevelt Hotel Corp. v. Williams, 227 Mo.App. 1063, 56 S.W.2d 801, 802 (1933).

31. Metropolitan Life Insurance Co. v. Childs, 230 N.Y. 285, 130 N.E. 295, 14 A.L.R. 658 (1921), reargument denied 231 N.Y. 551, 132 N.E. 885 (1921); Krochta v. Green, 121 Misc.2d 471, 467 N.Y.S.2d 995 (Cty.Ct.1983); Dundee Naval Stores Co. v. McDowell, 65 Fla. 15, 61 So. 108, Ann.Cas. 1915A, 387 (1913). See 17 Wash.L.Rev. 37, 43 (1942); 21 Minn.L.Rev. 610 (1937); 8 Wash.L.Rev. 184 (1934). See also 14 A.L.R. 664, 672 (1921); L.R.A.1915C, 190, 204. There is some divergence of opinion as to the effect of nonjoinder. The New York rule is that the purchaser on foreclosure sale takes the property subject to the lease just as though he were a purchaser of the reversion. Metropolitan Life Insurance and the mortgagee? In theory one compelling upshot of the majority rule is that the mortgagee, at its option, may have the property sold subject to the lease or free and clear of it. The mortgagee exercises this option by joining or not joining the lessee in the foreclosure action.[32] If the lessee is not joined her lease is unaffected by the foreclosure sale and the purchaser may enforce the lease as the transferee of the reversion.[33] If she is joined, the purchaser takes the property title as it existed at the time the mortgage was entered into, i.e., free of the subsequent lease, and may therefore evict the lessee.

To permit the above option results in conferring a bonus on the mortgagee who violates the normal foreclosure maxim encouraging the joinder of all junior interests. Indeed, a mortgagee, operating on the usually sound assumption that he will be the foreclosure sale purchaser, could very well intentionally omit a junior lessee in order to preserve a lease that is substantially more pro-landlord than would be possible if negotiated under current market conditions. Perhaps a preferable approach would be to give the unjoined junior lessee the option of being bound by the lease or of treating it as terminated. Such an approach would tend to encourage pre-foreclosure settlement of lease problems between the lessee and the mortgagee-probable purchaser and would discourage manipulation of traditional foreclosure concepts. There is some case law support for it.[34]

 WESTLAW REFERENCES
necessary /3 proper /s party /p foreclos*** /p mortgag**

Co. v. Childs, supra. See 17 Wash.L.Rev. 37, 44 et seq. (1942). Other states leave the status of an unjoined lessee somewhat in doubt. See 21 Minn.L.Rev. 611 (1937). A minority of cases seem to hold that a junior lease is extinguished, whether or not joined. See Dolese v. Bellows-Claude Neon Co., 261 Mich. 57, 245 N.W. 569 (1932) discussed in note, 32 Mich.L.Rev. 119 (1933); McDermott v. Burke, 16 Cal. 580 (1860). See 14 A.L.R. 664, 668 (1921).

32. See notes, 14 A.L.R. 664 (1921); Ann.Cas.1915A, 397; 42 Harv.L.Rev. 280 (1928); 13 Col.L.Rev. 553 (1913), 21 Minn.L. Rev. 610 (1937); 1942, 42 Wash.L.Rev. 37. See generally, Hyde, The Real Estate Lease as a Credit Instrument, 20 Bus.Law, 359, 389 (1965).

33. See Metropolitan Life Insurance Co. v. Childs Co., 230 N.Y. 285, 130 N.E. 295, 14 A.L.R. 658 (1921) reargument denied 231 N.Y. 551, 132 N.E. 885 (1921), "If * * * he [the tenant] is not a party to the action, his rights are not affected. There

is never an eviction. Until the sale he must pay his landlord. Afterwards the purchaser. As to the latter there is no necessity of attornment." The foreclosure sale "was a grant of what interest the mortgagor had in the property at the time the mortgage was given, less the leased estate—the grant of what was left after the leased estate was subtracted. It is precisely the same so far as the estate granted was concerned as if the lease had been prior to the mortgage."

34. See Dolese v. Bellows-Claude Neon Co., 261 Mich. 57, 245 N.W. 569 (1932), where the court held that a mortgage foreclosure purchaser could not recover rent from the lessee even though the lessee was junior and not joined in the foreclosure action. See also, New York Life Insurance Co. v. Simplex Products Corp., 135 Ohio St. 501, 21 N.E.2d 585, 14 O.O. 396 (1939); Davis v. Boyajian, Inc., 11 Ohio Misc. 97, 229 N.E.2d 116, 40 O.O.2d 344 (1967).

§ 7.13 Joinder—Effect of Recording Acts and Lis Pendens

The general rule is that lack of knowledge or notice of the subordinate interest of another person in the mortgaged land does not excuse a foreclosing mortgagee from making such person a party to his suit. If it fails to do so, the subordinate interest, regardless of whether it be legal or equitable and one of ownership or lien, is not subject to the decree.[1] There are, however, limitations upon the operation of this rule. A foreclosure sale purchaser who acquires the legal title for which he pays value without notice of the unjoined interest qualifies as a *bona fide* purchaser and thus will take free of such an interest if it is equitable only.[2] Similarly, under the familiar type of statute avoiding unrecorded conveyances as against subsequent purchasers, a foreclosure sale purchaser who buys without knowledge or notice of an outstanding but unrecorded interest may take free and clear of it just as effectively as though its holder had been joined in the foreclosure action.[3] Moreover, while there is authority to the contrary,[4] there is recent case law for the proposition that the foreclosing mortgagee can qualify as a bona fide purchaser under such statutes.[5] Other statutes, either explicitly or as interpreted, go beyond this and have the effect of concluding an unjoined party whose interest was not recorded as effectively as though he had been made a party to the suit.[6] Under the most extreme of these, this is true even though the mortgagee at the

§ 7.13

1. First National Bank v. Leslie, 106 N.J.Eq. 564, 151 A. 501 (1930), commented on, Campbell, Cases Mortgages, 2d ed. 274 n. 3; Pancoast v. Geishaker, 58 N.J.Eq. 537, 43 A. 883 (1899); White v. Melchert, 208 Iowa 1404, 1407, 227 N.W. 347, 348, 73 A.L.R. 595 (1929); Nelson v. First National Bank, 199 Iowa 804, 202 N.W. 847 (1925); Holliger v. Bates, 43 Ohio St. 437, 2 N.E. 841 (1885); Mesiavich v. Newman, 120 N.J. Eq. 192, 184 A. 538 (1936).

2. See First National Bank of Union City v. Leslie, 106 N.J.Eq. 654, 151 A. 501 (1930); Pancoast v. Geishaker, 58 N.J.Eq. 537, 43 A. 883 (1899). See §§ 6.5, 6.9, supra. *"Bona fide suit* in which the legal title is brought before the court is analogous to *bona fide purchase* of legal title, and it may well be asked why the suitor is not equally protected. * * * Yet we know of no case which has extended the equitable doctrine of bona fide purchase to the case of the suitor." Durfee and Fleming, Res Judicata and Recording Acts, 28 Mich.L.Rev. 811, 814, n. 6 (1930).

3. Valentine v. Portland Timber and Land Holding Co., 15 Wn.App. 124, 547 P.2d 912 (1976); Pinney v. The Merchants' National Bank, 71 Ohio St. 173, 72 N.E. 884 (1904); Duff v. Randall, 116 Cal. 226,

48 P. 66, 58 Am.St.Rep. 158 (1897); Shippen v. Kimball, 47 Kans. 173, 27 P. 813 (1891); Ehle v. Brown, 31 Wis. 405 (1872). Possession under some circumstances may give notice. See Ehle v. Brown, 31 Wis. 405, 413 (1872); Hodson v. Treat, 7 Wis. 263 (1858); Noyes v. Hall, 97 U.S. (7 Otto) 34, 24 L.Ed. 909 (1877). See 89 A.L.R. 171, 182 (1934).

4. See Durfee and Fleming, Res Judicata and Recording Acts, 28 Mich.L.Rev. 811, 819 (1926).

5. "Public policy reasons dictate that the recording statute should protect the foreclosing mortgagee as well as the purchaser at a foreclosure sale against unrecorded and unknown interests." Valentine v. Portland Timber and Land Holding Co., 15 Wn.App. 124, 129, 547 P.2d 912, 916 (1976).

6. See Durfee and Fleming, Res Judicata and Recording Acts: Does a Judgment Conclude Non-Parties of Whose Interests the Plaintiff Has No Notice? 28 Mich.L. Rev. 811 (1930). See also Campbell, Cases Mortgages, 2d ed., 277, n. 3; note, 25 Cal.L. Rev. 480 (1937); note 88 U. of Pa.L.Rev. 994, 997 (1940). See Curtis, The Commission and the Law of Real Property, 40 Cornell L.Q. 755 (1955).

time he began his foreclosure action had actual knowledge of the unrecorded interest.[7] It seems highly desirable to protect both the foreclosing mortgagee as well as a foreclosure purchaser against interests that are acquired but remain unrecorded prior to the beginning of a foreclosure action. That protection should extend at least far enough to cut off all such interests of which there was no actual notice before suit, or actual knowledge during the pendency of the litigation.[8]

While the bona fide purchase rule and the recording statutes aid the foreclosing mortgagee, his interests are, in addition, substantially served by the lis·pendens doctrine. That doctrine concerns persons who acquire an interest in real estate which is subject to litigation. If the property is specifically described and within the court's jurisdiction, it is taken subject to the final determination in the action;[9] it is immaterial that the person acquiring it is not named as a party or that he has no actual knowledge of either the suit or the claim under litigation.[10] Some cases erroneously fail to differentiate the doctrine from that of actual notice of the plaintiff's rights,[11] which would bind a taker of the property regardless of pendency of litigation, the principle of privity of title which applies to alienees after judgment against a grantor,[12] and the rule that property in custody of the court cannot be alienated in derogation of the court's later order.[13] Courts frequently speak of the doctrine as resting upon constructive notice,[14] but its true basis is public policy, the necessity of having such a rule in order to give effect to the judgments of courts. Without such a rule, it would be possible to defeat

---

7. West's Ann.Cal.Code Civ.Proc., § 726, "No person holding a conveyance from or under the mortgagor of the property mortgaged, or having a lien thereon, which conveyance or lien does not appear of record in the proper office at the time of the commencement of the action need be made a party to such action, and the judgment therein rendered, and the proceedings therein had, are as conclusive against the party holding such unrecorded conveyance or lien as if he had been a party to the action." Hager v. Astorg, 145 Cal. 548, 79 P. 68, 104 Am.St.Rep. 68 (1904); Collingwood v. Brown, 106 N.C. 362, 10 S.E. 868 (1890); cf. Holman v. Toten, 54 Cal.App.2d 309, 128 P.2d 808 (1942).

8. See Valentine, supra note 5, quoting text with approval.

9. Land Associates, Inc. v. Becker, 294 Or. 308, 656 P.2d 927 (1982).

10. See 47 Harv.L.Rev. 1023, 1024 (1934); 25 Cal.L.Rev. 480 (1937).

11. E.g., not observing the distinction between lis pendens and actual notice: Fogg v. Providence Lumber Co., 15 R.I. 15, 23 A. 31 (1885); Dent v. Pickens, 59 W.Va. 274, 53 S.E. 154 (1906). On the other

hand, observing the difference: Dillard & Coffin Co. v. Smith, 105 Tenn. 372, 59 S.W. 1010 (1900); People's Bank of Wilkesbarre v. Columbia Collieries Co., 75 W.Va. 309, 84 S.E. 914 (1914). See also Overland Park Savings & Loan Association v. Braden, 6 Kan.App.2d 876, 636 P.2d 797 (1981). Cf. Jorgensen v. Endicott Trust Co., 100 A.D. 2d 647, 473 N.Y.S.2d 275, 277 (1984).

12. Gale v. Tuolumne County Water Co., 169 Cal. 46, 145 P. 532 (1914); Hungate v. Hetzer, 83 Kan. 265, 111 P. 183 (1910); Comanche Ice & Fuel Co. v. Binder & Hillery, 70 Okl. 28, 172 P. 629 (1917).

13. E.g., where the property has been attached, sequestered or is in the hands of a receiver. Merchants' National Bank of Omaha v. McDonald, 63 Neb. 363, 88 N.W. 492 (1901) rehearing denied 63 Neb. 363, 89 N.W. 770; Sherburne v. Strawn, 52 Kan. 39, 34 P. 405 (1883); Young v. Clapp, 147 Ill. 176, 32 N.E. 187 (1892), affirmed 147 Ill. 176, 35 N.E. 372 (1893).

14. E.g., "A *lis pendens* duly prosecuted is notice to a purchaser so as to effect and bind his interest." Jackson ex dem. Hendricks v. Andrews, 7 Wend. 152, 156, 22 Am.Dec. 574 (N.Y.1831).

the judgment by a conveyance to some stranger, and the plaintiff would be forced to commence a new action against him.[15]

The hardship of the judicial doctrine of lis pendens upon innocent purchasers of property who, as a practical matter, could not discover pending litigation affecting the property they bought, led to the enactment generally in the United States of statutes compelling litigants to file notice of the pendency of their suits in order for third parties to be bound by the doctrine.[16] Since few of the statutes [17] include the entire field of the judicial doctrine, and since the judicial doctrine is unaffected except to the extent that the statutes apply, there are many situations in which it still operates [18]—a fact that might prove a pitfall to the unwary purchaser who relied solely upon an investigation of the records of notice.[19]

Even as to situations covered by the statutes there are problems as to their effect. Clearly the recorded notice of lis pendens will bind all subsequent mortgagees and grantees of the property, but what is its effect upon prior unrecorded mortgages and other conveyances? There seems no doubt that if a foreclosing party has actual knowledge of the unrecorded mortgage at the time of filing his notice, the mortgagee will not be bound by the foreclosure proceeding unless made a party to the action.[20] Where he learns of the unrecorded mortgage after recording notice and before judgment at least one jurisdiction [21] imposes upon him the affirmative duty of joining the holder of the mortgage, but several others merely permit the latter to intervene and, if he fails to do so, he is bound by the judgment.[22]

  WESTLAW REFERENCES

joind** joined unjoin** /p "bona fide purchaser" (lis action /3 penden**) "recording act" /p mortgage

---

15. See Newman v. Chapman, 23 Va. 93, 102, 14 Am.Dec. 766 (1823); Jarrett v. Holland, 213 N.C. 428, 196 S.E. 314 (1938); Brown v. Cohn, 95 Wis. 90, 69 N.W. 71, 60 Am.St.Rep. 83 (1896). "This necessity [of the rule] is so obvious, that there was no occasion to resort to the presumption that the purchaser really had or by inquiry might have had, notice of the pendency of the suit, to justify the existence of the rule. In fact, it applied in cases in which there was a physical impossibility that the purchaser could know, with any possible diligence on his part, of the existence of the suit, * * *." Newman v. Chapman, supra, at 102.

16. E.g., West's Ann.Cal.Code Civ.Proc. § 409; N.Y.—McKinney's CPLR 6501; Hawaii Rev.Stat. § 634–51. See Harada v. Ellis, ___ Hawaii App. ___, 667 P.2d 834 (1983).

17. Only three statutes embrace all of lis pendens. West's Fla.S.A. § 48.23;

Mich.C.L.A. § 565.25; Va.Code 1950, §§ 8.01–268, 8.01–269.

18. Land Associates, Inc. v. Becker, 294 Or. 308, 656 P.2d 927 (1982).

19. See 20 Iowa L.Rev. 476, 480–483 (1934).

20. See Munger v. T.J. Beard & Brothers, 79 Neb. 764, 113 N.W. 214, 126 Am.St. Rep. 688 (1907); Lamont v. Cheshire, 65 N.Y. 30 (1875).

21. Chaudoin v. Claypool, 174 Wash. 608, 25 P.2d 1036 (1933), note, 8 Wash.L. Rev. 197 (1934).

22. Bristol Lumber Co. v. Dery, 114 Conn. 88, 157 A. 640 (1931); Polish National Alliance, U.S.A. v. White Eagle Hall, Co., Inc., 98 A.D.2d 400, 470 N.Y.S.2d 642 (1983); Ayrault v. Murphy, 54 N.Y. 203 (1873). N.Y.—McKinney's C.P.L.R. 6501.

§ 7.14 Senior Lienors and Adverse Interests

The general rule is that the holder of a paramount lien cannot be made a party to a foreclosure action without his consent.[1] The reasons are both logical and practical in nature. Ultimately the purpose is to place the foreclosure sale purchaser in the position of the mortgagor when the foreclosed mortgage was executed.[2] Thus, the proper object of a foreclosure action is to sell the property given as security by the mortgagor and in doing so cut off the rights of redemption in that property of the mortgagor and everyone claiming under him. A junior mortgagee's security is the property subject to prior encumbrances. That, therefore, is all that can be sold when he forecloses his lien, and only rights of redemption based upon it can be cut off by the sale.[3] Since a senior mortgagee's interest cannot be affected by an action to foreclose a junior lien, it follows that an attempt to join him as a party to such an action can be defeated through timely objection. Such is the logic of the rule. To it is added the practical reason that the prior mortgagee should be able to choose his own time for selling and not be forced to realize in a market that in his judgment is unfavorable.[4] The argument is especially strong when the junior's foreclosure action is brought before the senior lien has matured, and it has force even if it is due.

There are, however, qualifications. One of them is suggested by the rule as stated. There is no reason why, if the first mortgagee is willing to be a party to the action, he should not be.[5] Consequently if he becomes a party on his own motion he will be bound by the decree.[6]

§ 7.14

1. Hudnit v. Nash, 16 N.J.Eq. 550, 560 (1862); Krause v. Hartung, 108 N.J.Eq. 507, 155 A. 621 (1931); Osage Oil & Refining Co. v. Muber Oil Co., 43 F.2d 306, 308 (10th Cir.1930); Jerome v. McCarter, 94 U.S. (4 Otto) 734, 24 L.Ed. 136 (1876); Cf. Scott & Wimbrow v. Calwell, 31 Md.App. 1, 354 A.2d 463 (1976).

2. See § 7.12, supra.

3. Fendley v. Smith, 217 Ala. 166, 115 So. 103 (1928); Armand's Engineering, Inc. v. Town and Country Club Inc., 113 R.I. 515, 324 A.2d 334 (1974).

4. "Lands which today are a slender security for money which may have been loaned by way of mortgage become amply sufficient tomorrow. But if the plaintiff's [subsequent lienor] theory be correct, the mortgagee, as against a subsequent incumbrancer by way of mortgage, cannot exercise his own judgment as to whether he will retain his lien until the security becomes good. * * * The rights of the parties could not thus be reversed, except with the express consent of the prior incumbrancer." McReynolds v. Munns, 41 N.Y. (2 Keyes) 214 (N.Y.1865). See Campbell, Cases Mortgages, 2d ed., 261 n. 5a, for additional authorities.

5. "But prior lienors may consent to become parties to such an action, or may be made such, where the object is to ascertain the extent of their claims, and to have the premises sold subject thereto, or absolutely to create a fund out of which the several incumbrances shall be paid in their order; but such purpose or object should clearly appear from the complaint." Foster v. Johnson, 44 Minn. 290, 292, 46 N.W. 350 (1890). Cf. Gargan v. Grimes, 47 Iowa 180 (1877); Champlin v. Foster, 7 B.Mon., Ky., 104 (1846); Cochran v. Goodell, 131 Mass. 464 (1881); Roll v. Smalley, 6 N.J. Eq. 464 (1847); Western Insurance Co. v. Eagle Fire Insurance Co., 1 Paige, N.Y., 284 (1828); Vanderkemp v. Shelton, 11 Paige, N.Y., 28 (1844).

6. See Kraus v. Hartung, 111 N.J.Eq. 531, 533, 162 A. 724, 725 (1932); 89 U. of Pa.L.Rev. 373, 379 (1941). Cf. Palmer v. Guaranty Trust Co., 111 F.2d 115 (2d Cir. 1940). But cf., McReynolds v. Munn, 41

Furthermore, if he is joined in an action in which the plaintiff alleges that the defendant's lien is a prior one and asks that the property be sold free of it, his failure to appear and object operates as consent and bars his mortgage.[7]   In such a case the property is sold free of both liens, but the respective priorities persist as to the proceeds.

The possibility of joinder, however, goes beyond active consent or acquiescence of a prior lienor. The junior mortgagee is seeking a sale, and in order to have one in which possible buyers will participate and pay a proper price for the property, the nature and extent of prior liens should be determined so that a prospective purchaser may know with certainty for what he is paying his money. Consequently, even though the senior lien is not yet due, the foreclosing junior mortgagee may join its owner for the purpose of such determination.[8]   Moreover, there is authority that the question of priority of encumbrances, i.e., whether another lien is prior or subsequent to the one being foreclosed, may be litigated in a foreclosure action.[9]   Where a paramount mortgage debt is due and payable, or will be before decree and sale, such prior mortgagee may be joined and the property sold under what amounts to a joint foreclosure of both mortgages, the proceeds being used to pay off the mortgagees in the order of their priority.[10]   This deprives an earlier mortgagee of the privilege of exercising his own judgment as to when he will foreclose and sell his security.[11]   It is justified as being, in effect, the enforcement of the junior mortgagee's right to redeem in order to protect his own security; and to do so without the necessity of advancing out of his own funds the amount necessary to do so, a requirement which often makes the right, as a practical matter, illusory.[12]   And

N.Y. (2 Keyes) 214 (1865). See note 5, supra.

7. Jacobie v. Wickle, 144 N.Y. 237, 39 N.E. 66 (1894).

8. Missouri K. & T. Trust Co. v. Richardson, 57 Neb. 617, 78 N.W. 273 (1899); see Foster v. Johnson, 44 Minn. 290, 292, 46 N.W. 350, 351 (1890); Jerome v. McCarter, 94 U.S. (4 Otto) 734, 736, 24 L.Ed. 136 (1876). But see Kraus v. Hartung, 111 N.J.Eq. 531, 533, 162 A. 724, 725 (1932).

9. Iowa County Board of Supervisors v. Mineral Point Railroad Co., 24 Wis. 93 (1869); see Whipple v. Edelstein, 148 Misc. 681, 684, 266 N.Y.S. 127, 131 (1933); cf. Ruyter v. Wickes, 22 N.Y.S. 200, 4 N.Y.S. 743 (S.Ct.1889), affirmed 121 N.Y. 498, 24 N.E. 791, 31 St.R. 387 (1890). Contra, Krause v. Hartung, 1931, 108 N.J.Eq. 507, 155 A. 621 (1931), second mortgage expressly subject to first mortgage. And cf. Dawson v. Danbury Bank, 15 Mich. 489 (1867); Strobe v. Downer, 13 Wis. 11, 80 Am.Dec. 709 (1860).

10. Hagan v. Walker, 55 U.S. (14 How.) 29, 37, 14 L.Ed. 312 (1852); Masters v.

Templeton, 92 Ind. 447 (1883); see Emigrant, etc., Savings Bank v. Goldman, 75 N.Y. 127, 132 (1878).

11. See note 4, supra. See also Threefoot v. Hillman, 130 Ala. 244, 30 So. 513, 89 Am.St.Rep. 39 (1906); Waters v. Bossel, 58 Miss. 602 (1881); cf., Bigelow v. Cassedy, 26 N.J.Eq. 557 (1875).

12. See Hefner v. Northwestern Life Insurance Co., 123 U.S. 747, 754, 8 S.Ct. 337, 31 L.Ed. 309 (1887), "the bill in such a case being in effect both a bill to foreclose the second mortgage and a bill to redeem from the first mortgage." See also Peabody v. Roberts, 47 Barb. 91 (N.Y.1866), "And in Norton v. Warner (3 Edw.Ch. 106) it was held that there is no objection to a second mortgagee's filing a bill for a foreclosure and sale to pay off all the incumbrances according to their respective priorities, * * *. It is very important for the promotion of the interests of junior mortgagees that this right should be carefully maintained; for where they do not possess the pecuniary ability of redeeming the senior mortgage, it is the only means af-

there are other instances where the interests of the mortgagor and encumbrancers require that a prior mortgagee be joined and the property be sold free and clear of both junior and senior liens.[13]

The holder of a claim in the property adverse to the title of the mortgagor is usually bracketed with senior lienors as one who is not a necessary or proper party to a foreclosure action.[14] If his claim is a valid one, his interest cannot be sold in the foreclosure because it is not under the mortgage sued upon. Whether it is valid should not be determined incidentally in an action whose purpose is not to decide such an issue but merely to sell property that secures the plaintiff's claim. Such is, at least, the argument and prevailing view. Yet if the claimant appears and litigates the question of his title he is bound by the decree, the court having power to decide the question if the claimant acquiesces.[15] And the same is true if he is properly joined and defaults in a case in which the foreclosing mortgagee sets forth facts from which he claims that the defendant's title is subordinate to his mortgage.[16] Furthermore, it has been urged that there is no good reason why the claimant should ever object to having the validity of his claim passed upon, whereas to exclude the question "has the unfortunate result of requiring a sale of a very uncertain quantity largely defeating the purpose of the change from strict foreclosure to that of sale." [17]

 WESTLAW REFERENCES
senior junior ± 1 lien! mortgag** /p foreclos***

---

forded them through which the security can be applied to the payment of the debt it secures."

13. E.g., where the first mortgage extended only to a small part of the property covered by the second mortgage, a sale under foreclosure of the latter could not be made advantageously if a purchase had to take subject to a partial mortgage. Shepherd v. Pepper, 133 U.S. 626, 10 S.Ct. 438, 33 L.Ed. 706 (1890).

14. Gage v. Perry, 93 Ill. 176 (1879); San Francisco v. Lawton, 18 Cal. 465 (1861); Dial v. Reynolds, 96 U.S. 340, 24 L.Ed. 644 (1877); Toucey v. New York Life Insurance Co., 314 U.S. 118, 62 S.Ct. 139, 86 L.Ed. 100, 137 A.L.R. 967, 137 footnote 8 (1941); Wells v. American Mortgage Co., 109 Ala. 430, 20 So. 136 (1895); Corning v. Smith, 6 N.Y. 82 (1851)—accord. Provident Loan Trust Co. v. Marks, 59 Kan. 230, 52 P. 449, 68 Am.St.Rep. 349 (1898), contra. See also Masters v. Templeton, 92 Ind. 447 (1884); Bradley v. Parkhurst, 20 Kan. 462 (1878); note, 7 Cent.L.J. 473 (1878); note, 21 Cent.L.J. 223 (1885).

15. See Beronio v. Ventura County Lumber Co., 129 Cal. 232, 61 P. 958, 79 Am.St.Rep. 118 (1900); Goebel v. Iffla, 111 N.Y. 170, 18 N.E. 649 (1888).

16. " * * * We think that * * * a default ought to be construed, as an admission that, at the time he [the holder of a paramount title] failed to appear as required, he had no interest in the property in question, and hence as conclusive of any prior claim of interest or title adverse to the plaintiff." Barton v. Anderson, 104 Ind. 578, 581, 4 N.E. 420 (1886). It has been held that a purchaser at a tax sale held subsequent to the giving of a mortgage is a proper party to a foreclosure of the mortgage, and the validity of such purchaser's title may be settled in the foreclosure action. Hefner v. North Western Mutual Life Insurance Co., 123 U.S. 747, 754, 8 S.Ct. 337, 31 L.Ed. 309 (1887). See also Upjohn v. Moore, 45 Wyo. 96, 16 P.2d 40, 85 A.L.R. 1063 (1932), commented on in, 33 Col.L.Rev. 543 (1933). But cf., Erie County Savings Bank v. Shuster, 187 N.Y. 111, 79 N.E. 843 (1907).

17. Durfee, Cases Mortgages, 296 n.

§ 7.15 Omitted Parties

When any party having the right to redeem is omitted from a foreclosure action, her interest is not terminated by that action.[1] So far as she is concerned the foreclosure is void and her rights of redemption are the same as before the foreclosure. The purchaser at the foreclosure sale succeeds to the rights of the mortgagee even though the sale is void as to an omitted party,[2] and he also succeeds to the rights of all owners of interests in the property subject to the mortgage who were joined in the foreclosure.[3] If the omitted party is owner of the entire redemption interest, the foreclosure sale is entirely void as to her interest, but the purchaser stands as assignee of the mortgage [4] and subject to an accounting as such.[5] As an omitted owner, she may then redeem the land by paying the mortgage debt to the foreclosure sale purchaser.[6] When she redeems, she redeems the title to *the land,* and in so doing, he cuts off any further interest of the foreclosure sale purchaser in the land. Unlike where the party omitted is a junior lienor, a situation we will examine in detail next, the foreclosure sale purchaser has no right to redeem or pay off the owner-mortgagor.

Where the omitted party is a junior lienor, the situation becomes more complicated. He too has a certain type of equitable redemption right and when he is omitted from a foreclosure proceeding, he does not

§ 7.15

1. Springer Corp. v. Kirkeby-Natus, 80 N.M. 206, 453 P.2d 376 (1969); Quinn Plumbing Co. v. New Miami Shores Corp., 100 Fla. 413, 129 So. 690, 73 A.L.R. 600 (1930); Decker v. Patton, 120 Ill. 464, 11 N.E. 897 (1887); Holmes v. Bybee, 34 Ind. 262 (1870); Arnold v. Haberstock, 213 Ind. 98, 10 N.E.2d 591 (1937) rehearing denied 213 Ind. 98, 10 N.E.2d 682 (1937); Peabody v. Roberts, 47 Barb. 91 (N.Y.1866); Mackenna v. Fidelity Trust Co., 184 N.Y. 411, 77 N.E. 721, 3 L.R.A.,N.S., 1668, 12 Am.St. Rep. 620, 6 Ann.Cas. 471 (1906); Monese v. Struve, 155 Or. 68, 62 P.2d 822 (1936); Milmo National Bank v. Rich, 16 Tex.Civ. App. 363, 40 S.W. 1032 (1897); Godfrey v. Chadwell, 2 Vern. 601 (1707). See Haines v. Beach, 3 Johns.Ch. 459 (1818). See Note, Rights of Junior Lienholders in Wisconsin, 43 Marq.L.Rev. 89, 96 (1959).

2. Robinson v. Ryan, 25 N.Y. 320 (1862); Quinn Plumbing Co. v. New Miami, etc. Corp., 100 Fla. 413, 129 So. 690, 73 A.L.R. 600 (1930). In spite of some authority in New York to the effect that the purchaser on foreclosure sale acquires the mortgagee's interest in the mortgage and the debt as well even though the price he paid was less than the amount of the debt, e.g., Brainard v. Cooper, 10 N.Y. 356, 359 (1852), the correct rule is, or should be, that the purchaser is entitled "to be subro-

gated to the place and rights of the mortgagee *pro tanto,* for the amount so paid to the mortgagee upon the mortgage debt. * * * The residue of the mortgage debt was * * * due to the holder of the bond mentioned in the mortgage." Childs v. Childs, 10 Ohio St. 339, 346, 75 Am.Dec. 512 (1859). Accord: Givins v. Carroll, 40 S.Ct. 413, 18 S.E. 1030, 42 Am.St.Rep. 889 (1894). See Wells v. Lincoln Co., 80 Mo. 424 (1883). Cf., Collins v. Riggs, 81 U.S. (14 Wall.) 491, 493, 20 L.Ed. 723 (1871). See also 73 A.L.R. 612, 630, 633, 635 (1931); Ann.Cas.1917D, 576.

3. Christ Protestant Episcopal Church v. Mack, 93 N.Y. 488, 45 Ab.R. 260 (1883); Smith v. Shay, 62 Iowa 119, 17 N.W. 444 (1883); Ferguson v. Cloon, 89 Kan. 202, 131 P. 144, Ann.Cas.1914D, 281 (1913); Renard v. Brown, 7 Neb. 449 (1878); Dorff v. Bornstein, 277 N.Y. 236, 14 N.E.2d 51 (1938), motion granted 278 N.Y. 566, 16 N.E.2d 105 (1938); Murphy v. Farwell, 9 Wis. 102. See 1931, 73 A.L.R. 612, 644 (1859). See Chapter 10 infra.

4. Robinson v. Ryan, 25 N.Y. 320 (1862).

5. See §§ 4.27–4.34 supra. See also Updike, Mortgages in 1953 Annual Survey of American Law, 29 N.Y.U.L.Rev. 829, 935 (1954).

6. See § 7.3, supra.

lose his lien and is generally unaffected by the foreclosure.[7] However, why would it be unfair to terminate his lien even though he was not a party? After all, there has been a judicial sale, and in the great majority of cases, the high bid probably does not exceed the amount of the senior mortgage. Where this is so, is it not proof enough that the property's value was insufficient to cover the amount owing to the junior as well, and therefore that the junior must and should go away empty-handed?

The answer to this is that, while a sale has been held, it is not a sale in which the junior was a participant. He had no opportunity to bid for the property himself, nor to attempt to stir up other bidders in order to maximize the price paid for the property.[8] It is well known that in most judicial sales the bidding is scarcely spirited. Often the foreclosing senior lienor will be the only bidder. Of course, it is possible that even if the junior had been a party and present at the sale, no amount of effort on his part would have resulted in a higher bid. But this is a fact which cannot be established by speculation. What seems to be needed is a procedure which will duplicate, insofar as possible, the right of which the junior was deprived by his omission from the foreclosure proceeding—the right to have the value of the property tested at a judicial sale *in which he is a participant,* so that he has full opportunity to maximize the price paid by the highest bidder.[9]

How can this result be achieved? There are two principal remedies which the courts have granted to omitted junior lienors: foreclosure[10] and redemption.[11] The first remedy is foreclosure by the junior of his own lien, with a resulting judicial sale. Such a sale will be subject to the first mortgage,[12] which is, in effect, revived for this purpose. Indeed, the courts sometimes say that, as to the junior lienor, the original foreclosure sale has never taken place.[13] Both the mortgagor's

7. Citibank, N.A. v. Oxford Properties & Finance Limited, 688 F.2d 1259 (9th Cir. 1982). Akeley v. Miller, 264 So.2d 473 (Fla.App.1972); Lenexa State Bank & Trust Co. v. Dixon, 221 Kan. 238, 559 P.2d 776 (1977); Springer Corp. v. Kirkeby-Natus, 80 N.M. 206, 453 P.2d 376 (1969).

8. Polish National Alliance of Brooklyn, U.S.A. v. White Eagle Hall Co., Inc., 98 A.D.2d 400, 470 N.Y.S.2d 642 (1983).

9. See Note, 88 U.Pa.L.Rev. 994, 998–999 (1940).

10. See, e.g., Lenexa State Bank & Trust Co. v. Dixon, 221 Kan. 238, 559 P.2d 776 (1977); Catterlin v. Armstrong, 101 Ind. 258, 263 (1884); see Peabody v. Roberts, 47 Barb. 91, 99 (N.Y.1866). See 88 U. of Pa.L.Rev. 994, 998 (1940); Cronin v. Hazeltine, 85 Mass. (3 Allen) 324 (1862); Vanderkemp v. Shelton, 11 Paige 28 (N.Y.1844); Peabody v. Roberts, 47 Barb. 91 (N.Y.1866) Cf. McGraw v. Premium Fi-

nance Co. of Missouri, 7 Kan.App.2d 32, 637 P.2d 472 (1981) (both foreclosure and redemption available to junior, but redemption preferred).

11. See, e.g., More v. United States, 505 F.Supp. 612 (N.D.Fla.1980); Sims v. Smith, 502 F.Supp. 609 (N.D.Fla.1980); Baldi v. Chicago Title & Trust Co., 113 Ill.App.3d 29, 68 Ill.Dec. 808, 446 N.E.2d 1205 (1983); McGraw v. Premium Finance Co. of Missouri, 7 Kan.App.2d 32, 637 P.2d 472 (1981); Akeley v. Miller, 264 So.2d 473 (Fla.App.1972); Springer Corp. v. Kirkeby-Natus, 80 N.M. 206, 453 P.2d 376 (1969).

12. Cronin v. Hazeltine, 85 Mass. (3 Allen) 324 (1862); Vanderkemp v. Shelton, 11 Paige 28 (N.Y.1844); Peabody v. Roberts, 47 Barb. 91 (N.Y.1866).

13. Catterlin v. Armstrong, 101 Ind. 258, 263 (1884); see Peabody v. Roberts, 47 Barb. 91, 99 (N.Y.1866). See 88 U. of Pa.L.

and mortgagee's rights have become vested in the buyer at the original sale. If the junior subsequently forecloses his lien, the judicial sale held at his instance will convey the original mortgagor's interest to the buyer at the second sale; but the original mortgagee's interest (revived for this purpose) will remain in the hands of the buyer at the original sale.

It is of course possible that there will be no bidders for the property under these conditions. This will normally be so if the property's value is lower than the amount owing on the senior lien. But even if there are no bidders, the junior lienor has had an opportunity to prove that the property has excess value above the balance owing on the senior lien, and it is this right to which he is entitled and of which he was previously deprived.

Note that the amount of the "revived" first lien is the balance which was previously owing on it prior to the first foreclosure sale. This may be more or less than the amount the purchaser at the first sale bid when he took the property. If it is more, the original purchaser obtains a windfall (assuming that the buyer at the second sale ultimately pays off the senior lien); but this is not surprising, since if the property is more valuable than the price paid by the original sale purchaser, he could have simply sold it for that higher price and gained a similar windfall. On the other hand, if the purchaser at the original sale paid more than the amount of the senior lien, the second foreclosure sale will deprive him of his title to the property, and replace it with a lien for a smaller amount than his original investment. This could be a serious detriment to the original purchaser, and might in general act to discourage buyers at foreclosure sales from bidding more than the amount of the lien being foreclosed. It could be argued that this detriment is a reasonable penalty to impose on the purchaser, who should have discovered the fact that the junior lienor had been omitted before he bid at the first foreclosure sale. This argument proceeds from the theory that in all cases the existence of the junior lien is discoverable by a foreclosure sale bidder from a careful search of the public records. Thus, if the bidder makes no search or searches negligently, he has only himself to blame. This argument appears sound if the junior lienor is the holder of a *mortgage,* since it will be rendered nugatory by the recording act unless it has in fact been recorded, or unless the bidder has other notice of its existence. But it is less valid if the junior lien is a mechanics lien which is unrecorded at the time of the senior foreclosure sale, but which is later recorded and which, by statute, relates back to an earlier time when the mechanic performed work on the property.[14]

Rev. 994, 998 (1940). And see Durfee, Cases on Security, 221 (1951).

14. See, e.g., Lenexa State Bank & Trust Co. v. Dixon, 221 Kan. 238, 559 P.2d 776 (1977).

The other principal remedy available to the omitted junior is redemption.[15] By this we mean that the junior may tender to the buyer at the senior foreclosure sale the balance which was owed on the senior lien at the time of foreclosure, and by so doing in effect compel an assignment of a "revived" senior lien to the junior lienor. The junior thus becomes the holder of two liens, a senior and a junior, and he may foreclose either or both of them. Note that unlike where an omitted owner redeems, the term "redemption" here does not refer to the vesting of *title* to the property in the junior, but merely to his power to compel an assignment to him of the senior lien.[16] Sometimes it is said that, by tendering payment of the balance owing on the senior lien, he becomes subrogated to the senior mortgagee's rights—rights which have now, by the first sale, been vested in the sale purchaser.[17]

Note that redemption requires that the omitted junior come up with a substantial amount of money, and that he is not in a position to use the property itself as security for the obtaining of that capital from some other lender. For this reason, redemption by an omitted junior lienor is probably not very common. Nevertheless, there is language in a few cases that suggests that redemption is the junior lienor's sole remedy.[18] Such a result seems difficult to justify. It is hardly fair or logical to say, on the one hand, that the prior foreclosure proceeding in which the junior lienor was not a party "is not binding on him" [19] and, on the other, to use it as the basis for destroying his right to foreclose.

There is yet a third remedy available to the omitted junior lienor, although it is rarely useable in practice. Some jurisdictions hold that, if the foreclosure sale of the senior lien has produced a surplus, and if that surplus is still identifiable in the hands of the original mortgagor or of some lienor who is subordinate even to the omitted junior, the junior can assert a lien on the surplus funds.[20] Obviously, cases in which these circumstances exist will be very rare indeed.

Let us now turn to the methods which the buyer at the senior sale can employ to protect his interests in cases in which an omitted junior exercises one of the two principal remedies (foreclosure or redemption) described above. There seem to be three such techniques available to

15. More v. United States, 505 F.Supp. 612 (N.D.Fla.1980); Baldi v. Chicago Title & Trust Co., 113 Ill.App.3d 29, 68 Ill.Dec. 808, 446 N.E.2d 1205 (1983); Note, 88 U.Pa.L.Rev. 994, 1000 (1940).

16. "The owner of a junior encumbrance redeems not the premises, strictly speaking, but the senior encumbrance; and then he is entitled not to a conveyance of the premises, but to an assignment of the security." Pardee v. Van Anken, 3 Barb. 534 (N.Y.1848).

17. See § 7.2, supra.

18. More v. United States, 505 F.Supp. 612 (N.D.Fla.1980); Sims v. Smith, 502 F.Supp. 609 (N.D.Fla.1980); Baldi v. Chicago Title & Trust Co., 113 Ill.App.3d 29, 68 Ill.Dec. 808, 446 N.E.2d 1205 (1983). Cf. McGraw v. Premium Finance Co. of Missouri, 7 Kan.App.2d 32, 637 P.2d 472 (1981) (redemption preferred remedy).

19. Baldi, supra note 18 at 1207.

20. See, e.g., Caito v. United California Bank, 20 Cal.3d 694, 144 Cal.Rptr. 751, 576 P.2d 466 (1978); Soles v. Sheppard, 99 Ill. 616 (1881).

the original sale purchaser: redemption, re-foreclosure, and in some states, strict foreclosure. Let us look first at redemption. If the omitted junior has not taken any further action, it is obvious that the senior sale purchaser may simply pay off the junior lien and thereby clear his title. This is because, as we noted earlier, the senior foreclosure purchaser succeeds not only to the rights of the mortgagee, but to the rights of the foreclosed mortgagor as well. Since the mortgagor would have had the right to pay off the junior lien, the senior foreclosure purchaser will have the same right.[21] Whether this is an attractive alternative to the senior purchaser obviously depends on how large the junior lien is, but the right to do so is always available to him up until the moment the junior lienor forecloses his own lien. If the senior buyer doubts that the property is worth the additional investment, perhaps he is well-advised to allow the junior to proceed to foreclosure, since the senior buyer will still have a first mortgage on the property in the amount of the original senior lien.

Even if the junior lienor redeems the senior debt from the original sale purchaser, the position of the parties is not really changed significantly. The senior buyer can simply pay off the senior lien in the junior's hands, using the very dollars which the junior paid the buyer when *he* redeemed. The redemption by the senior foreclosure purchaser will have priority simply because he stands in the shoes of the foreclosed mortgagor. Once an owner exercises redemption rights in equity against a lienor, the lienor no longer has a further interest in the land. His only right is to be paid off. As Professor Glenn has pointed out, the junior lienor "can be met at the gate by the purchaser at the sale * * *. In other words, the purchaser at the sale can dispose of the junior mortgagee by redeeming the land from his lien." [22] Thus the transaction is, in effect, a wash, and if the senior buyer is willing to add enough money out of his own pocket, he can also pay off the junior lien at the same time. The result of all this is that redemption by an omitted junior lienor is always an act that the senior sale purchaser can easily nullify if he wishes to do so. If the senior buyer does not wish to take the next step and pay off the junior lien as well, the omitted junior lienor still has the power to compel a test of the property's value in his own foreclosure sale.

An alternative route which the senior sale purchaser may take is to re-foreclose the first mortgage.[23] This time, we may be sure that he will not omit the junior lienor. He takes this action while standing in the shoes of the original mortgagee. The junior will have full opportu-

---

21. See text at notes 6–7, supra.

22. Glenn, Mortgages, § 86.5 (1943); See Portland Mortgage Co. v. Creditors Protective Association, 199 Or. 432, 262 P.2d 918 (1953); Murphy v. Farwell, 9 Wis. 102 (1859).

23. Deming National Bank v. Walraven, 133 Ariz. 378, 651 P.2d 1203 (App.1982);

Jorgensen v. Endicott Trust Co., 100 A.D.2d 647, 473 N.Y.S.2d 275 (1984); Mortgage Commission Realty Corp. v. Columbia Heights Garage Corp., 169 Misc. 618, 7 N.Y.S.2d 740 (1938). See note, 88 U. of Pa. L.Rev. 994, 1006 (1940). See 73 A.L.R. 612, 633 (1931).

nity to participate in the sale, and will thus have the right denied to him when the original foreclosure sale was held. The proceeds of the sale will be used to pay off both liens in the order of their priority, with any additional surplus going to the re-foreclosing party.

There are two objections to this procedure from the viewpoint of the original sale purchaser. One is that he stands the risk of losing his title to the property if he is outbid at the second sale. Moreover, if this occurs, and if the successful bid at the second sale does not produce a surplus above the total of both liens, the original sale purchaser stands to lose any amount he bid at the first sale in excess of the balance owing on the senior lien. He may have a right to go back against the original mortgagor for the loss, but we may well imagine that in most cases such a right is not worth much.

The third method available to the senior sale purchaser, when he discovers an omitted junior lienor, is sometimes called strict foreclosure. It is not available in all jurisdictions. In substance it amounts to a judicial decree that the junior lien be cancelled unless the junior pays off the senior debt within a court-determined period.[24]

There is authority that in order to have strict foreclosure against such omitted junior interests the plaintiff must establish both that he bought in good faith without knowledge of the outstanding interest and that its holder knew of the sale and permitted the plaintiff to buy without disclosing his own interest.[25] And it is quite clear that if the holder of the junior interest is intentionally omitted from the foreclosure action, the mortgagee cannot later have strict foreclosure to cut off his redemption right.[26] Other cases follow a flexible rule that there must be equitable grounds for relief and, in general, require that the omission must be through inadvertence or mistake untinged with bad faith.[27] In addition, the courts look at the amount the property sold for at the prior foreclosure sale or the value of the property.[28] If the premises are worth no more than the encumbrances prior to the one

24. See § 7.9, supra.

25. Moulton v. Cornish, 138 N.Y. 133, 33 N.E. 842, 20 L.R.A. 370 (1893). See note, 88 U. of Pa.L.Rev. 994, 1007 (1940).

26. Indiana Investment Co. v. Evens, 121 N.J.Eq. 72, 187 A. 158 (1936), denying even a later foreclosure by sale, criticised on this point in 17 Chi-Kent L.Rev. 148 (1938); Moulton v. Cornish, note 26, supra; see 118 A.L.R. 769, 775 (1939). See also Surety Building & Loan Association v. Risack, 118 N.J.Eq. 425, 427, 179 A. 680, 681 (1935), party originally joined but not served.

27. See Sears, Roebuck & Co. v. Camp, 124 N.J.Eq. 403, 407, 1 A.2d 425, 428, 118 A.L.R. 762 (1938), constructive notice insuf-

ficient to prevent strict foreclosure even though search was careless; Mesiavich v. Newman, 120 N.J.Eq. 192, 184 A. 538 (1936); Koerner v. Willamette Iron Works, 36 Or. 90, 58 P. 863 (1899), strict foreclosure against a junior lienor although no showing of "good faith." See also note, 88 U. of Pa.L.Rev. 994, 1007 (1940); 118 A.L.R. 769, 774 (1939). "Knowledge of and acquiescence" in the foreclosure by the omitted party is not essential. See Campbell, Cases on Mortgages, 2d ed. 249 n. 4. But cf. Denton v. Ontario County National Bank, 150 N.Y. 126, 44 N.E. 781 (1896).

28. See note, 88 U. of Pa.L.Rev. 994, 1007 (1940).

sought to be foreclosed, it is persuasive that strict foreclosure should be granted.[29]

Until this point, we have assumed that an omitted party, whether owner or junior lienor, if he redeems, is acting under his equitable right to redeem from the mortgage rather than pursuant to statutory redemption.[30] In general, the two rights would not seem to exist simultaneously. The equitable right accrues at mortgage maturity and ends only by a valid foreclosure. On the other hand, statutory redemption begins when a valid foreclosure takes place and ends at the expiration of the requisite statutory period. Thus, since no foreclosure has taken place as to the omitted owner, it is generally assumed that only the equitable right of redemption is available to him.[31]

As to the omitted junior lienor, however, matters are somewhat more complicated. Moreover, there are several reasons why the choice of redemption methods might be especially attractive to him. While statutory redemption will be covered in detail later,[32] several features of that type of redemption need to be briefly considered here. For example a junior lienor who redeems under a statutory right of redemption normally gets fee title to the property (rather than merely an assignment of a revived first lien). Moreover, to exercise statutory redemption rights, one must usually pay the price paid at the original foreclosure sale, rather than the balance which was owed on the first lien. One additional point: the statutes sometimes give the original mortgagor a priority right to redeem, with others (presumably including omitted junior lienors) having the right if the mortgagor does not exercise it within a given period of time.

Some have maintained that the omitted junior lienor has the choice of proceeding under either form of redemption.[33] The reasoning, in part, is that whenever the mortgagor has been validly foreclosed, statutory redemption is triggered [34] and, since junior lienors normally have rights under such statutes, "unless it were to be held that the statutes applied only to those subsequent lienors whose liens were cut off by foreclosure, it would seem that the omitted lienor also possesses the statutory right." [35] On the other hand, Professor Glenn has stated that the junior lienor "cannot resort to statutory redemption, because he is not within the terms of the statute. The latter comes into effect

29. Mesiavich v. Newman, 120 N.J.Eq. 192, 184 A. 538 (1936); Miles v. Stehle, 22 Neb. 740, 36 N.W. 142 (1888); see 25 Va.L. Rev. 947, 953 (1939). But contra, see Denton v. Ontario County National Bank, 150 N.Y. 126, 44 N.E. 781 (1896). Of course if the foreclosure sale produced an excess over the amount of the mortgage debt, a mortgagee-purchaser cannot have strict foreclosure to eliminate junior liens. Pettingill v. Hubbell, 53 N.J.Eq. 584, 32 A. 76 (1895).

30. See § 7.1, supra.

31. Note, 88 U.Pa.L.Rev. 994, 1003 (1940); See Herrmann v. Churchill, 235 Or. 327, 385 P.2d 190 (1963).

32. See §§ 8.4–8.7, supra.

33. Note, 88 U.Pa.L.Rev. 994, 1003 (1940); Cf. Century Enterprises, Inc. v. Butler, 526 P.2d 1350 (Colo.App.1974).

34. Land Associates, Inc. v. Becker, 294 Or. 308, 656 P.2d 927 (1982).

35. Note, supra note 33 at 1003.

at and with foreclosure * * * but the statute envisages those only whom the foreclosure has barred. It follows that one who has never been foreclosed cannot resort to statutory redemption. His remedy remains where it always was, regardless of whether the particular state has provided for statutory redemption. The remedy is redemption in equity after the ancient mode." [36] Moreover, subsequent case authority directly confronting the question has supported the latter view.[37]

WESTLAW REFERENCES

redeem redemption foreclos*** (sale sold sell*** /4 real ±1
     estate property) /s omit*** omission /s party lienor owner

§ 7.16   Conduct of the Sale

The method of conducting a foreclosure sale is now largely regulated by statute and is, therefore, mostly a matter of local law which must be consulted in each jurisdiction. Such legislation ordinarily provides for a public sale under the direction of either the sheriff or an officer of the court appointed for that purpose.[1] In the absence of statutory provision, a court of equity has ample power to order a master to make a judicial sale. The decree in such cases will commonly contain provisions specifying the giving of notice, the time, place, manner and terms of conducting the sale, and other matters that are generally covered by statutory regulation.[2]

Although under statutory provision, or by provision of a chancery decree, the sale is to be conducted by the sheriff as in sales under execution,[3] it usually differs from such sales in important respects. The most fundamental is that "the whole business is * * * under the guidance and superintendence of the court [of chancery] itself." [4] One

---

36. Glenn, Mortgages, § 238 (1943).

37. See, e.g., Portland Mortgage Co. v. Creditors Protective Association, 199 Or. 432, 262 P.2d 918 (1953). But cf. Century Enterprises, Inc. v. Butler, 526 P.2d 1350 (Colo.App.1974).

§ 7.16

1. Typical statutes are West's Ann.Cal. Code Civ.Proc., §§ 726, 729, incorporating by reference provisions governing the conduct of a sale under execution by a sheriff but authorizing court to appoint a commissioner or elisor to do the job; Official Code Ga.Ann. § 44–14–187, "sold in the manner and under the same regulations which govern sheriff's sales under execution"; Minn. Stats.Ann., § 581.03. See State ex rel. Elliott v. Holliday, 35 Neb. 327, 53 N.W. 142 (1892). As to the practice in federal courts, see Blossom v. Milwaukee & C.R. Co., 70 U.S. (3 Wall.) 196, 18 L.Ed. 43 (1865), "by the marshal of the district where the decree was entered, or by the master ap-

pointed by the court, as directed in the decree."

2. See Leesman, Some Considerations Involving the Decretal Parts of the Decree of Sale in a Foreclosure Proceeding, 6 J.Marshall L.Q. 314 (1941).

3. See provisions in statutes, note 1, supra.

4. Blossom v. Milwaukee & Chicago Railroad Co., 70 U.S. (3 Wall.) 196, 18 L.Ed. 43 (1865). "The whole proceeding, from the beginning to the final confirmation of the reported sale, and the passing of title to the vendee and the money to the persons entitled to it, was under the supervision and control of the court." Penn's Administrator v. Tolleson, 20 Ark. 652, 661 (1859). Look at Jones v. Williams, 155 N.C. 179, 71 S.E. 222, 36 L.R.A.,N.S., 426 (1911). National Reserve Life Insurance Co. v. Kemp, 184 Kan. 648, 339 P.2d 368 (1959).

consequence of the sale being a judicial one under direction of the court is that the sale is equally for the benefit of all lienholders whose rights have been adjudicated by it.[5] Moreover, foreclosure courts more than occasionally order the sale of property based on the principle of the inverse order of alienation.[6] For example, where a mortgage covers several lots, some of which the mortgagor has already sold, the foreclosure court will order the lots retained by the mortgagor sold first before subjecting the already conveyed lots to sale.[7] In addition, the foreclosure decree may, under some circumstances, as we will note later, fix a minimum or "upset" price under which the property may not be sold at the sale.[8]

The fact that the foreclosure sale is judicial also has a bearing upon when title passes under the sale. In a sheriff's sale it usually passes when the successful bidder completes his purchase, there being no need for court approval of either the sale or the sheriff's deed.[9] A foreclosure sale, however, requires confirmation by the court. Even in states where the foreclosure takes place by way of execution, confirmation may be required by statute [10] or the court may reserve power to confirm the sale when made.[11] Moreover, the court has power to set aside a sale under certain circumstances and order a new one.[12]

Certain problems connected with the sale frequently are litigated within the context of the judicial foreclosure action. These often include problems associated with notice of the sale, sale by parcel or in bulk, and adequacy of the foreclosure sale price. Moreover, these problems will have their greatest impact in a cumulative sense. While one of these problems may not always be sufficient to set aside a sale, the more of them that are present in one fact situation, the greater the likelihood that a new sale will be ordered.

5. Welsh v. Lawler, 73 N.J.Eq. 371, 68 A. 218, 133 Am.St.Rep. 737 (1907). Look also at Laub v. Warren Guarantee etc., Co., 54 Ohio App. 457, 8 N.E.2d 258 (1936). Brant v. Lincoln National Life Insurance Co. of Fort Wayne, 209 Ind. 268, 198 N.E. 785 (1935).

6. See § 10.10, infra.

7. Season, Inc. v. Atwell, 86 N.M. 751, 527 P.2d 792 (1974).

8. See § 7.16, infra.

9. Coulter v. Blieden, 104 F.2d 29 (8th Cir.1939), certiorari denied 308 U.S. 583, 60 S.Ct. 106, 84 L.Ed. 488 (1939); Glenn v. Hollums, 80 F.2d 555 (5th Cir.1936); Shreiner v. Farmers Trust Co., 91 F.2d 606 (3d Cir.1937), certiorari denied 58 S.Ct. 36, 302 U.S. 686, 82 L.Ed. 530 (1937); State

Bank of Hardinsburg v. Brown, 317 U.S. 135, 63 S.Ct. 128, 87 L.Ed. 140 (1942), rehearing denied 317 U.S. 712, 63 S.Ct. 432, 87 L.Ed. 567 (1943); Leviston v. Swan, 33 Cal. 480 (1867); Pollard v. Harlow, 138 Cal. 390, 71 P. 648 (1903); Bateman v. Kellogg, 59 Cal.App. 464, 472, 474, 211 P. 46 (1922).

10. E.g., Minn.Stat.Ann. § 581.08.

11. E.g., Laub v. Warren Guarantee, etc. Co., 54 Ohio App. 457, 8 N.E.2d 258 (1936).

12. Von Senden v. O'Brien, 61 App.D.C. 137, 58 F.2d 689 (1932); Bank of American National Trust & Savings Association v. Reidy Lumber Co., 15 Cal.2d 243, 101 P.2d 77 (1940); Ellis v. Powell, 117 S.W.2d 225 (Mo.1938); Kloepping v. Stellmacher, 21 N.J.Eq. 328 (1871).

Notice Problems

The purpose of notice is to inform the public as to the date, place, nature and condition of the property to be sold and terms of the sale.[13] Questions as to the sufficiency and definiteness of notice to accomplish these purposes sometimes are of importance.[14]

For example, where there is a conflict between the foreclosure decree and the notice of foreclosure sale as to whether part of the land is to be sold subject to a prior lien, enough uncertainty among bidders is created to justify setting aside a sale.[15] Sales also are subject to being set aside where there is a substantial discrepancy between the time of sale specified in the notice of sale and the actual time of sale.[16] On the other hand, there is authority that once a mortgagor receives adequate notice of the commencement of the foreclosure action and then defaults, notice of further proceedings, including the sale itself is unnecessary.[17]

Sales by Parcel or In Bulk

Where the mortgage being foreclosed covers more than one parcel of land, the problem arises as to whether the court should order the land sold in parcels or in bulk. Frequently this problem is regulated by statute and typically such legislation creates a presumption in favor of sale by parcel.[18] Nevertheless, such presumptions have been overridden where the mortgage itself authorized sale in bulk.[19] In the absence of legislation, the court usually will direct the sale in the manner and mode that is likely to secure the highest price.[20] Here again, there normally will be a preference for parcel sales.[21] Moreover, where the sale of one parcel is likely to satisfy the mortgage debt, the decree

---

13. See Leesman, supra note 2.

14. See notes, 2 Minn.L.Rev. 157 (1918); 5 Minn.L.Rev. 325 (1921); 9 Tex.L.Rev. 454 (1931). See also 120 A.L.R. 660 (1939).

15. See, e.g., Bates v. Schuelke, 191 Neb. 498, 215 N.W.2d 874 (1974).

16. Ohio Realty Investment Corp. v. Southern Bank of West Palm Beach, 300 So.2d 679 (Fla.1974).

17. Vanjani v. Federal Land Bank of Louisville, ___ Ind.App. ___, 451 N.E.2d 667 (1983).

18. See Security Savings Bank of Cedar Rapids v. King, 198 Iowa 1151, 199 N.W. 166 (1924); Metropolitan Life Insurance Co. v. Foote, 95 Mich.App. 399, 290 N.W.2d 158 (1980); Clark v. Kraker, 51 Minn. 444, 53 N.W. 706 (1892); Thomas v. Thomas, 44 Mont. 102, 119 P. 283, Ann.Cas.1913B, 616 (1911); Miller v. Trudgeon, 16 Okl. 337, 86 P. 523, 8 Ann.Cas. 739 (1905); Person v. Leathers, 67 Miss. 548, 7 So. 391 (1890).

See West's Ann.Cal.Code Civ.Proc. § 726; Mich.C.L.Ann. § 27A.3165; Wis.Stat.Ann. § 278.06, provides that "the court before rendering judgment shall ascertain by reference or otherwise the situation of mortgaged premises and whether they can be sold in parcels without injury to the interests of the parties; and if it shall appear that they can be so sold the judgment shall direct a sale in parcels * * *." For an interpretation of that statute, see Citizens Bank of Sheboygan v. Rose, 59 Wis.2d 385, 208 N.W.2d 110 (1973).

19. See e.g., Metropolitan Life Insurance Co. v. Foote, 95 Mich.App. 399, 290 N.W.2d 158 (1980).

20. See Semmes Nurseries, Inc. v. McDade, 288 Ala. 523, 263 So.2d 127 (1972); Wiltsie, Mortgage Foreclosure, § 683 (5th Ed.), 61 A.L.R.2d 505, 558.

21. Id.

should direct the sale of such parcel only.[22] On the other hand, some situations may favor the sale in bulk. For example, there is considerable authority that where more than one parcel comprises a farm or other enterprise or where subdivision is impractical, a sale in bulk is permitted.[23]

Adequacy of the Sale Price

To some extent, legislation in many states is aimed at encouraging an adequate foreclosure sale price. This is one of the purposes of statutory redemption and a major function of anti-deficiency legislation. Both types of legislation will be considered later in this volume.[24] Absent legislation, however, the rule is well-settled, at least in normal times, that a court will not refuse to confirm a sale or set it aside unless the price obtained was "grossly inadequate" [25] or the inadequacy was "so gross as to shock the conscience or raise a presumption of fraud or unfairness." [26] Thus, in the absence of other irregularities, courts have, for example, upheld foreclosure sale prices of a third [27] or half [28] the fair market value of the property. On the other hand, courts have set aside as "inequitably less than the real value of the property" a sale price of approximately one-seventh of the fair market value.[29] Moreover, where the disparity is substantial, courts will seize upon any other irregularity or misconduct to provide the additional basis for setting aside the sale. For example, where the purchaser bid in $5,000 for property appraised at $73,000, the court set aside the sale and focused on two factors: the foreclosure sale purchaser had persuaded the sheriff to dispense with reading the sale notice at the sale and the mortgagee

---

22. See Dozier v. Farrior, 187 Ala. 181, 65 So. 364 (1914); Blazey v. Delius, 74 Ill. 299 (1874); Hughes v. Riggs, 84 Md. 502, 36 A. 269 (1897); Miller v. Kendrick, 15 A. 259 (N.J.1888); Guarantee Trust & Safe Deposit Co. v. Jenkins, 40 N.J.Eq. 451, 2 A. 13 (1885). See also Leesman, supra note 39; note, 25 Cal.L.Rev. 469 (1937); L.R.A.1917B, 517. Cf. also 15 S.Cal.L.Rev. 19 (1941).

23. See e.g., Cox v. Townsend, 20 Mich. App. 12, 282 N.W.2d 223 (1979); 61 A.L.R.2d 505, 574, § 17.

24. See §§ 8.4–8.7, 8.1–8.3, infra.

25. Venda-a-Matic, Inc. v. Frankford Trust Co., 296 Pa.Super. 492, 442 A.2d 1158 (1982).

26. George v. Cone, 77 Ark. 216, 91 S.W. 557. Shipp Corp., Inc. v. Charpilloz, 414 So.2d 1122 (Fla.App.1982); See Connecticut Mutual Life Insurance Co. v. Carter, 446 F.2d 136 (5th Cir.1971), certiorari denied 404 U.S. 857, 92 S.Ct. 104, 30 L.Ed. 2d 78 (1971), certiorari denied 404 U.S. 1000, 92 S.Ct. 563, 30 L.Ed.2d 553 (1971);

Wiesel v. Ashcraft, 26 Ariz.App. 490, 549 P.2d 585 (1976); Speers Sand & Clay Works, Inc., v. American Trust Co., 52 F.2d 831 (4th Cir.1931), certiorari denied 286 U.S. 548, 52 S.Ct. 500, 76 L.Ed. 1284 (1952); Raleigh & Charleston Railroad Co. v. Baltimore National Bank, 41 F.Supp. 599 (D.S.C.1941); Detroit Trust Co. v. Hart, 277 Mich. 561, 269 N.W. 598 (1936); Graffam v. Burgess, 117 U.S. 180, 6 S.Ct. 686, 29 L.Ed. 839 (1886). See also Durfee and Doddridge, Redemption from Foreclosure Sale—The Uniform Act, 23 Mich.L.Rev. 833 (1925); Vaughan, Reform of Mortgage Foreclosure Procedure, 88 U. of Pa.L.Rev. 957, 963 (1940).

27. Shipp Corp., Inc. v. Charpilloz, 414 So.2d 1122 (Fla.App.1982).

28. See, e.g., Guerra v. Mutual Federal Savings and Loan Association, 194 So.2d 15 (Fla.App.1967).

29. Southern Realty & Utilities Corp. v. Belmont Mortgage Corp., 186 So.2d 24 (Fla. 1966).

who arrived a few minutes late had been willing to submit a bid of over $55,000.[30]

Moreover, it is also important to emphasize that in some jurisdictions the vestigial remains of judicial doctrines developed during the depression of the 1930's still linger on. The economic hardship was of unprecedented magnitude. Among the factors affecting real property mortgages were a disastrous decline in cash income from lands, a precipitous drop in land values, the prevailing practice in the majority of cases of lending, not on a long term amortization basis, but on short term mortgages which were periodically refunded, and the collapse of thousands of banks and other lending institutions which necessitated liquidation of mortgages held by them and made refinancing impossible. While the legislatures responded with a variety of statutory approaches,[31] courts became more receptive to the notion that they had inherent power, without the aid of legislation, to develop methods to protect the parties when there was an almost complete lack of a market for real estate. Probably the best known of these methods is that enunciated in Suring State Bank v. Giese.[32] That decision authorized the foreclosure court to do the following: (1) refuse to confirm the sale where the bid is substantially inadequate; (2) in ordering a sale or a resale, in the court's discretion and after a proper hearing, fix a minimum upset price at which the land must be bid in if the sale is to be confirmed; and (3) in cases where no upset price has been fixed, establish the value of property at a hearing and require that its fair value be credited upon the foreclosure judgment as a condition to confirmation. Other courts endorsed similar controls to avoid sacrifice prices.[33] While the Suring approach has been restricted by later decisions,[34] it would be a mistake to believe that it has been abandoned.

---

30. Johnson v. Jefferson Standard Life Insurance Co., 5 Ariz.App. 587, 429 P.2d 474 (1967). The leading American case refusing confirmation because of inadequacy of price (property worth seven times the amount bid) is Ballentyne v. Smith, 205 U.S. 285, 27 S.Ct. 527, 51 L.Ed. 803 (1907). See note, 26 Mich.L.Rev. 87 (1927).

31. See §§ 8.1–8.3, infra.

32. Suring State Bank v. Giese, 210 Wis. 489, 246 N.W. 556, 85 A.L.R. 1477 (1933), commented on in, 33 Col.L.Rev. 744 (1933); 42 Yale L.J. 960 (1933); 81 U. of Pa.L.Rev. 883 (1933); 27 Ill.L.Rev. 950 (1933); 17 Minn.L.Rev. 821 (1933); 8 Wis.L. Rev. 286 (1933); 21 Cal.L.Rev. 522 (1933); 18 St. Louis L.Rev. 265 (1933); 17 Marq.L. Rev. 154 (1933); 85 A.L.R. 1480 (1933). See also Perlman, Mortgage Deficiency Judgments During an Economic Depression, 20 Va.L.Rev. 771, 806 et seq. (1934); 47 Harv.L.Rev. 299, 307 (1934).

33. Among such cases are Federal Title and Mortgage Guaranty Co. v. Lowenstein,

113 N.J.Eq. 200, 166 A. 538 (1933), commented on, 19 Cornell L.Q. 316 (1934); California Joint Stock Land Bank v. Gore, 153 Or. 267, 55 P.2d 1118 (1936), noted 15 Or.L. Rev. 385 (1936), order of resale proper, but fixing upset price is not; Michigan Trust Co. v. Cody, 264 Mich. 258, 249 N.W. 844 (1933); see Michigan Trust Co. v. Dutmers, 265 Mich. 651, 252 N.W. 478 (1934); Monaghan v. May, 242 App.Div. 64, 273 N.Y.S. 475 (1934). In Home Owners' Loan Corp. v. Wood, 164 Misc. 215, 298 N.Y.S. 427 (1937) noted, 51 Harv.L.Rev. 749 (1938).

34. For example, for limitations on the Suring case, look at Kremer v. Rule, 216 Wis. 331, 257 N.W. 166 (1934); Weimer v. Uthus, 217 Wis. 56, 258 N.W. 358 (1935); Buel v. Austin, 219 Wis. 397, 263 N.W. 82 (1935); Drach v. Hornig, 221 Wis. 575, 267 N.W. 291 (1936); Wahl v. H.W. & S.M. Tullgren, 222 Wis. 306, 267 N.W. 278 (1936); and in New Jersey, the Lowenstein case has been restricted. Young v. Weber,

Indeed, its principles are to some extent preserved by statute.[35] Interestingly, the Wisconsin Supreme Court recently appeared to reaffirm the Suring options.[36] Were the inflation of the past few decades to give way suddenly to severe recession or worse, then those or similar options stand available for use.

 WESTLAW REFERENCES
foreclos*** /p public** /10 sale sold auction** /50 sheriff (officer official /3 court) judicial**

§ 7.17 Position of Purchaser

A bid at a foreclosure sale is only an offer to buy which is accepted and becomes binding upon the bidder when the officer in charge of the sale strikes it off to him.[1] An accepted bidder, it is usually said, "acquires no independent rights until the sale be confirmed by the court, and * * * the court may exercise a discretion in either confirming or rejecting the sale."[2] What this means is that the purchaser has no contract right to have the sale confirmed, and until it is confirmed, the sale agreement is not enforceable by him. Whether it will be is to be determined according to whether the terms of the sale conform to certain requirements to be determined by the court in its discretion.[3] The discretion, however, is a judicial, not an arbitrary one, and must be exercised in accordance with legal rules governing it. Consequently, the purchaser may insist that "confirmation must follow unless there exists some reason recognized by law as warranting a refusal to confirm,"[4] and, in this sense, he does have a vested right at once. And, for the purpose of encouraging bidding, it is highly important that a bidder should have this degree of certainty of confirmation.[5]

Once the purchaser's bid is accepted, "he submits himself to the jurisdiction of the court and becomes a party to the cause in which the

117 N.J.Eq. 242, 175 A. 273 (1934) see Fidelity Union Trust Co. v. Pasternack, 122 N.J.Eq. 180, 181, 192 A. 837, 838 (1937), affirmed 123 N.J.Eq. 181, 196 A. 469 (1938). See 24 Va.L.Rev. 44, 46–47 (1937); 33 Ill.L.Rev. 299, 310–314 (1938).

35. See, e.g., West's Rev.Code Wash. Ann. 61.12.060, which provides that the court, "in ordering the sale, may, in its discretion, take judicial notice of economic conditions, and after a proper hearing, fix a minimum or upset price to which the mortgaged property must be bid or sold before confirmation of the sale. The court may, upon application for confirmation of a sale, if it has not theretofore fixed an upset price, conduct a hearing, establish the value of the property, and, as a condition to confirmation, require that the fair value of the property be credited upon the foreclosure judgment." See National Bank of Washington v. Equity Investors, 86 Wn.

2d 545, 546 P.2d 440 (1976) for an example of the upset price mechanism.

36. See First Wisconsin National Bank of Oshkosh v. KSW Investments, Inc., 71 Wis.2d 359, 238 N.W.2d 123 (1976).

§ 7.17

1. Blossom v. Milwaukee & Chicago Railroad Co., 70 U.S. (3 Wall.) 196, 18 L.Ed. 43 (1865).

2. George v. Cone, 77 Ark. 216, 91 S.W. 557, 113 Am.St.Rep. 143, 7 Ann.Cas. 171 (1905).

3. George v. Cone, note 2, supra; Blossom v. Milwaukee, etc., Ry., note 70, supra; Kable v. Mitchell, 9 W.Va. 492 (1876).

4. Allen v. Martin, 61 Miss. 78 (1883).

5. See Morrisse v. Inglis, 46 N.J.Eq. 306, 19 A. 16 (1890), quoted with approval in George v. Cone, note 71, supra; Stump v. Martin, 72 Ky. 285, 292 (1873).

sale has been decreed, and he may be compelled to stand by the offer he has made."[6] The court, after confirmation, may compel the purchaser to take title and pay the bid price, or it may order a resale and hold the purchaser liable for any loss that may result.[7] In this respect the purchaser's contract obligations are governed by substantially the same rules that apply to a vendee in the ordinary contract for the sale of land.[8] Consequently he is entitled to a marketable title and has a reasonable time within which to make an examination and raise the question as to defects which he discovers.[9] These are of two types: (a) defects in the title the mortgagor possessed at the execution of the mortgage; and (b) those that are the result of flaws in the foreclosure action.[10] There is authority that the doctrine of *caveat emptor* applies to sales in foreclosure action. However, even courts which accept the doctrine as a general proposition may refuse to apply it to irregularities in the foreclosure proceedings, such as the failure to join the mortgagor or his successors or a party holding a subsequent interest under the mortgagor, which result in the estate directed to be sold not passing, or passing subject to defects due to the irregularity.[11] As to the first type of defect some courts proceed upon the theory that there is no warranty of title by anyone to a purchaser on a judicial foreclosure sale, that what is offered for sale is the interest of the mortgagor, whatever it may be, subject to all defects and that the buyer purchases this at his peril.[12] Coupled with this is the doctrine that the chancellor, if a defect of this sort is discovered and objected to before the sale is completed, will grant relief but that he will not act after the buyer has accepted the deed.[13] The objection to this view is that a would-be purchaser at a

6. Allen v. Martin, supra note 4; Dills v. Jasper, 33 Ill. 262, 272 (1864); Traveller's Insurance Co. v. Thompson, 140 Neb. 109, 299 N.W. 329 (1941).

7. Camden v. Mayhew, 129 U.S. 73, 9 S.Ct. 246, 32 L.Ed. 608 (1888); Fienhold v. Babcock, 275 Ill. 282, 113 N.E. 962 (1916). See Thomas v. San Diego College Co., 111 Cal. 358, 366, 43 P. 965 (1896).

8. "The Court, however, treats a contract made with one of its officers as being made with the court itself, and will deal with the contractee upon equitable principles,—the same principles, indeed, which govern in all cases of specific performance." Boorum v. Tucker, 51 N.J.Eq. 135, 26 A. 456 (1893), 52 N.J.Eq. 587, 33 A. 50 (1895).

9. E.g., Jorgenson v. Endicott Trust Co., 100 A.D.2d 647, 473 N.Y.S.2d 275 (1984); Timmermann v. Cohn, 204 N.Y. 614, 97 N.E. 589 (1912); Raleigh & Charleston Railroad Co. v. Baltimore National Bank, 41 F.Supp. 599 (D.S.C.1941).

10. See Boggs v. Fowler, 16 Cal. 559, 564, 76 Am.Dec. 561 (1860). For New York legislation establishing procedure by which

a purchaser in a defective foreclosure may perfect his title, see Curtiss, The Commission and the Law of Real Property, 40 Cornell L.Q. 735, 739 (1955).

11. Jorgenson v. Endicott Trust Co., 100 A.D.2d 647, 473 N.Y.S.2d 275 (1984); Boggs v. Fowler, 16 Cal. 559, 564, 76 Am.Dec. 561 (1860). See 73 A.L.R. 612, 620 (1931). If a foreclosure sale is irregular, but not void, or caused by the fraud of any of the parties thereto, objection to the irregularity must be made at or prior to confirmation. Watson v. Tromble, 33 Neb. 450, 50 N.W. 331, 29 Am.St.Rep. 492 (1891); Clement v. Ireland, 138 N.C. 136, 50 S.E. 570 (1905); Allison v. Allison, 88 Va. 328, 13 S.E. 549 (1891); Strand v. Griffith, 63 Wash. 334, 115 P. 512 (1911); Core v. Strickler, 24 W.Va. 689 (1884).

12. Farmers' Bank of Kentucky v. Peter, 13 Bush 591, 594 (Ky.1878); Brown v. Gilmor's Executors, 8 Md. 322 (1855), accord. Cf. Lawrence v. Cornell, 4 Johns.Ch. 542 (N.Y.1820). See Boggs v. Fowler, note 80, supra.

13. See notes 11, 12, supra.

foreclosure sale must either make an intensive title search before bidding on property he has no assurance of acquiring or else forego bidding except at a figure that would take into account the potential title defects. Usually the first course is impracticable, and the second is sure to dampen bidding and result in sacrificing the property at a price below that normally attendant upon a forced sale.[14] The better practice, therefore, is to purport to sell a clear title except as to paramount interests in the property which are definitely stated in the pleadings and notices of sale.[15]

When all the steps of the foreclosure sale, including confirmation, have been completed, the purchaser is invested with title, this being accomplished under the usual practice by a deed executed and delivered to him by the master or other officer under order of the court. The title so acquired, as has been seen in different connections previously, is the "entire interest and estate of mortgagor and mortgagee as it existed at the date of the mortgage." [16] This statement, of course, is subject to the qualifications as to defects in joinder of parties [17] and, of course, the immediately preceding discussion.

 WESTLAW REFERENCES
[no queries]

§ 7.18　Judicial Foreclosure—Defects and Title Stability

As we will note later in this chapter,[1] power of sale foreclosure is subject to attacks on numerous grounds including, among others, chilled bidding, defective notice of sale, failure to comply with statutory requirements, selling in gross rather than by parcel or vice versa, conflicts of interest problems where trustees or mortgagees sell the property, selling at the wrong time or place, and constitutional attacks on procedural due process notice and hearing grounds. Of course, because judicial foreclosure affords all interested parties the right to notice and an opportunity to be heard, constitutional attacks are not normally a problem. Some of the other defects listed above, however,

14. See Walsh, Mortgages, 310.

15. See Walsh & Simpson, Cases Security Trans., 503 Note (3).

16. Rector of Christ Protestant Episcopal Church v. Mack, 93 N.Y. 488, 45 Am.R. 260 (1883); Gem Valley Ranches, Inc. v. Small, 92 Idaho 232, 440 P.2d 352 (1968); Valley National Bank of Arizona v. Avco Development Co., 14 Ariz.App. 56, 480 P.2d 771 (1971). See also Champion v. Hinkle, 45 N.J.Eq. 162, 16 A. 701 (1888); Coomes v. Frey, 141 Ky. 740, 133 S.W. 758 (1911). A mortgagee may be estopped from setting up a reversionary interest of record unless, at the foreclosure sale, he specifies that the property is to be sold subject to it. Ferguson v. Cloon, 89 Kan. 202, 131 P. 144, Ann. Cas.1914D, 281 (1913). Cf. Young v. Brand, 15 Neb. 601, 19 N.W. 494 (1884). See additionally Survey of Illinois Law, 34 Chi.-Ken L.Rev. 81 (1954–1955), commenting on Kling v. Ghilarducci, 3 Ill.2d 454, 121 N.E.2d 752, 46 A.L.R.2d 1189 (1954).

17. See § 7.15, supra.

§ 7.18

1. See §§ 7.19–7.30, infra.

can as we have seen,[2] arise in the judicial, as well as the power of sale context.

Nevertheless, judicial foreclosure is significantly less vulnerable than is power of sale foreclosure to such attacks and, as a result, produces a more stable title. There are at least three reasons for this. First, because judicial foreclosure is under court supervision, that very fact will prevent many of the above defects from arising. After all, in the power of sale setting, the mortgagee or the trustee normally controls the steps through foreclosure. Judicial foreclosure, on the other hand, entails judicial second guessing prior to and after the sale. Not only are fewer defects likely to arise when a disinterested party is, in theory, doublechecking the process, but the mere presence of the judge may discourage the more overt and intentional defects that may otherwise occur. Second, because judicial foreclosure is an adversary proceeding, the other parties aid the court in calling its attention to potential defects, a second type of check on the mortgagee not found in power of sale foreclosure. Finally, even if defects do go uncorrected, the normal concepts of judicial finality provide the ultimate insulation from attack for a judicial foreclosure decree.[3] If a party in a judicial foreclosure who feels aggrieved by the trial court's action allows the time period for filing objections with the trial court or for appeal to expire, his chances for a successful collateral attack on the foreclosure proceeding are extremely slim. Indeed, in one recent case where a mortgagor did just that, the reaction of the court is illustrative: "Clearly she knew or should have known the manner in which her real estate was advertised, offered, and sold by the time the period for filing objections expired. Judicial sales must have finality and judgment debtors may not assert untimely challenges on the basis of irregularities which were readily ascertainable before the close of the statutory period for filing objections."[4] Moreover, if there is an appeal, the ultimate foreclosure judgment will have even more finality. Indeed, one of the few defects that will not so easily be cured by the passage of time is the omitted party problem we considered in a preceding section.[5] An omitted junior lienor, as a necessary party not bound by the judicial foreclosure, can, of course, collaterally attack the validity of that foreclosure even after the time periods for direct review have expired. In any event, with power of sale foreclosure, the security of judicial finality is simply absent. While the passage of time inevitably will

2. See § 7.16, supra.

3. Shuput v. Lauer, 109 Wis.2d 164, 325 N.W.2d 321 (1982). See also Zeballos v. Zeballos, 104 A.D.2d 1033, 481 N.Y.S.2d 11 (1984).

4. Virgin Islands National Bank v. Tyson, 506 F.2d 802, 805 (3d Cir.1974), certiorari denied 421 U.S. 976, 95 S.Ct. 1976, 44 L.Ed.2d 467 (1975). See Gray v. Bankers Trust Co. of Albany, N.A., 82 A.D.2d 168, 442 N.Y.S.2d 610 (1981), appeal denied 58 N.Y.2d 604, 459 N.Y.S.2d 1026, 445 N.E.2d 654 (1983); Milwaukee Western Bank v. Cedars of Cedar Rapids, Inc., 170 N.W.2d 670 (Iowa 1969).

5. See § 7.15, supra.

help a defective title derived from a power of sale foreclosure, it is largely by means of variable and unreliable concepts such as statutes of limitations, laches and related notions.

 WESTLAW REFERENCES
foreclos*** /p title /5 stab!

E. POWER OF SALE FORECLOSURE

§ 7.19 General Considerations

The other main foreclosure method, permitted in about twenty-five states, is power of sale foreclosure.[1] After varying types and degrees of notice, the property is sold at a public sale, either by a public official, such as a sheriff, by some other third party, or by the mortgagee.

In some states utilizing the power of sale method, the deed of trust is the most commonly used mortgage instrument. The mortgagor-trustor conveys the real estate to a trustee who holds the property in trust for the mortgagee-beneficiary until full payment of the mortgage debt. In the event of foreclosure, the power of sale is exercised by the trustee, who holds a public sale of the mortgaged property; the sale is usually not judicially supervised.

As previously indicated, the notice requirements under power of sale foreclosure vary, but are usually less rigorous than those associated with judicial foreclosure. Notice, as used here, may be simply notice of foreclosure or notice of default or a combination of the two. While some states require that notice by mail or personal service be provided for any person having a record interest in the real estate junior to the mortgage being foreclosed,[2] many do not. A few states require only notice of publication.[3] This publication sometimes takes the form of newspaper advertisement and sometimes consists only of public posting. Other states, in addition to published notice, require notice either by mail or personal service to the mortgagor and the owner of the mortgaged real estate, but not to junior lienors and others holding an

---

§ 7.19

1. One recent article identifies almost 30 jurisdictions in which power of sale foreclosure exists. These include Alabama, Alaska, Arizona, California, Colorado, District of Columbia, Georgia, Guam, Hawaii, Idaho, Maine, Maryland, Massachusetts, Michigan, Minnesota, Mississippi, Missouri, Nevada, New Hampshire, North Carolina, Oregon, Rhode Island, South Dakota, Tennessee, Texas, Utah, Washington, West Virginia, and Wyoming. Jones and Ivens, Power of Sale Foreclosure in Tennessee: A Section 1983 Trap, 51 Tenn.L.Rev. 279, 293–294 (1984). The authors also identify Illinois as a power of sale jurisdiction. In

this they seem to be mistaken. See Ill.—S.H.A. ch. 110, ¶ 15–101 which states: "No real estate within this state may be sold by virtue of any power of sale contained in any mortgage, trust deed or other conveyance in the nature of a mortgage ∗ ∗ ∗."

2. See, e.g., Alaska Stat. 34.20.070; Ariz.Rev.Stat. § 35–809(B); Colo.Rev.Stat. 38–37–113(2), (3); Idaho Code § 45–1506; West's Rev.Code Wash.Ann. § 61.24.040; Mont.Rev.Codes Ann. § 93–6005.

3. See, e.g., Official Code Ga.Ann. §§ 9–13–141, 44–14–162, 44–14–162.2, 44–14–162.3 (nonresidential mortgages); Miss. Code 1972, § 89–1–55.

interest subordinate to the mortgage being foreclosed.[4] A few states attempt to protect those interested parties who are neither mortgagors nor owners by requiring that the notice of foreclosure be mailed to any person who has previously recorded a request for such notice.[5] In any event, whatever the notice requirements of the foregoing statutes, federal legislation makes power of sale foreclosure ineffective against a junior federal tax lien unless written notice is provided to the United States at least 25 days prior to the sale by registered or certified mail or by personal service.[6] Finally, almost no power of sale foreclosure statutes provide for an opportunity for a hearing prior to the foreclosure sale.[7]

The Uniform Land Transactions Act (ULTA)[8] authorizes power of sale foreclosure under methods not unlike many of those used in state statutes. After default, a minimum of five weeks must expire before the mortgagee officially notifies the mortgagor of his intent to foreclose.[9] After this official notice, there is an additional minimum three week grace period, after which the mortgagee must inform the mortgagor which default remedy he intends to use.[10] If the mortgagee chooses power of sale foreclosure, there is a requirement of mailed notice to the debtor and to all other parties whose interests would be cut off by foreclosure.[11] If a mortgagor qualifies as a "protected party", basically a person who is an owner-occupant of a residence, certain notice requirements and other protections are somewhat more substantial.[12]

The Multifamily Mortgage Foreclosure Act of 1981 (the "Act") authorizes a nonjudicial power of sale foreclosure for federally insured and certain other mortgages on property other than one-to-four-family dwellings held by the Secretary of Housing and Urban Development.[13] Such foreclosure may be utilized even though the mortgage was execut-

---

4. See, e.g., D.C.Code § 45–615; V.T. C.A., Prop.Code § 51.002 (mailed notice to each "debtor" only). Compare Minn.Stat. Ann. § 580.03 (personal service on person in possession only). For an example of who is a person in possession, see Varco-Purden Buildings v. Becker & Sons Construction, Inc., 361 N.W.2d 457 (Minn.App. 1985).

5. See, e.g., V.A.Mo.S. § 443.325. Some states combine required mailed notice to all parties having record interest in the real estate together with mailed notice to any other person who has previously recorded a request for it. See, e.g., Ariz.Rev. Stat. § 33–809; West's Ann.Cal.Civ.Code, § 2924(b).

6. See 26 U.S.C.A. § 7425(b) and (c); Southern Bank of Lauderdale County v. Internal Revenue Service, 586 F.Supp. 12 (N.D.Ala.1984).

7. North Carolina uses power of sale foreclosure, but provides for a hearing be-

fore a clerk of court. See N.C.Gen.Stat. § 45–21.16. In Colorado, the public trustee must obtain a court order authorizing the trustee's sale. See Colo.Rev.Stat. 38–37–140; Cru.Pro.Rule 120.

8. The Uniform Land Transactions' Act was approved by the National Conference of Commissioners on Uniform State Laws in August, 1975 and recommended for enactment in all of the states. It was amended substantially in 1977, although these amendments for the most part did not effect the foreclosure sections. No state thus far has adopted the ULTA in whole or in part.

9. U.L.T.A. § 3–505.

10. U.L.T.A. § 3–508.

11. U.L.T.A. § 3–508(a).

12. See U.L.T.A. §§ 3–505, 3–507.

13. 12 U.S.C.A. §§ 3701–3717. For legislative history of the Act, see 1981 U.S. Code, Cong. and Adm.News, 560–562.

ed prior to the effective date of the Act and, apparently, whether or not it actually contains a power of sale.[14] After a default occurs and the decision to foreclose is made, the Secretary designates a Commissioner to conduct the foreclosure and sale.[15] The foreclosure is initiated by service of a Notice of Default and Foreclosure Sale containing information concerning the property being foreclosed, the date and place of sale and related information.[16] This notice must be published once a week for three consecutive weeks and posted on the property for at least seven days prior to the sale.[17] In addition, it must be sent by certified mail, return receipt requested, at least twenty-one days before the date of foreclosure sale to the original mortgagor, to those liable on the mortgage debt and to the "owner" of the property and, at least ten days before the sale, to all persons having liens thereon.[18] The sale date must be at least thirty days "after the due date of the earliest unpaid installment or the occurrence of a nonmonetary default." [19] Unless one takes a broad view of who is an "owner" under the statute, neither the Act nor the Regulations promulgated thereunder require that mailed notice be provided to holders of leases, easements and similar interests junior to the mortgage being foreclosed. Finally, though the Act itself makes no provision for a hearing, the Regulations specify that "HUD will provide to the mortgagor [and current owner] an opportunity informally to present reasons why the mortgage should not be foreclosed. Such opportunity may be provided before or after the designation of the foreclosure commissioner but before service of the notice of default and foreclosure." [20]

The underlying theory of power of sale foreclosure is simple. It is that by complying with the above type statutory requirements, the mortgagee accomplishes the same purposes achieved by judicial foreclosure without the substantial additional burdens that the latter type of foreclosure entails. Those purposes are to terminate all interests junior to the mortgage being foreclosed and to provide the sale purchaser with a title identical to that of the mortgagor as of the time the mortgage being foreclosed was executed.[21] Moreover, where it is in common use, power of sale foreclosure has provided an effective foreclosure remedy with a cost in time and money substantially lower than that of its judicial foreclosure counterpart.[22]

14. 24 CFR 27.2(b). HUD, however, is not precluded from using state law. See 24 CFR 27.2(a).

15. 12 U.S.C.A. § 3704; 24 CFR 27.10.

16. 12 U.S.C.A. § 3706; 24 CFR 27.15.

17. 12 U.S.C.A. § 3708; 24 CFR 27.15(c).

18. 12 U.S.C.A. § 3708(1); 24 CFR 27.15(c).

19. 12 U.S.C.A. § 3710(a).

20. 24 CFR 27.5(b).

21. See e.g., Alaska Stat. 34.20.090(a) which provides: "The sale and conveyance transfers all title and interest which the party executing the deed of trust had in the property sold at the time of its execution, together with all title and interest he may have acquired before the sale * * *." See § 7.12 supra.

22. See McElhone & Cramer, Loan Foreclosure Costs Affected By Varied State Regulations, 36 Mortgage Banker 41 (1975).

Notwithstanding the fact that power of sale foreclosure generally works and that it is more efficient and less costly than judicial foreclosure, the titles it produces have been somewhat less stable than those resulting from judicial foreclosure. As we noted earlier, there are at least three reasons for this.[23] First, the court supervision involved in judicial foreclosure will prevent many defects from arising. Second, because judicial foreclosure is an adversary proceeding, the presence of other parties who will bring possible defects to the court's attention constitutes added protection against a faulty end product. Finally, the concept of judicial finality provides substantial insulation against subsequent collateral attack even on technically defective judicial foreclosure proceedings. None of these protections are inherent in power of sale foreclosure. Moreover, as we will examine in detail later in this chapter, power of sale foreclosure has been subjected recently to the further uncertainty of constitutional attack because of its alleged notice and hearing deficiencies.[24]

 WESTLAW REFERENCES
power-of-sale /3 foreclos***

§ 7.20 Defective Power of Sale Foreclosure—The "Void-Voidable" Distinction

While we examine in detail in the next section a variety of defects that provide grounds for setting aside power of sale foreclosures, it is important initially to consider those defects from a broader perspective. Generally, defects in the exercise of a power of sale can be categorized in at least three ways. Some defects are so substantial as to render the sale void. In this situation no title, legal or equitable, passes to the sale purchaser or subsequent grantees, except perhaps by adverse possession.[1] Such a result typically occurs where, notwithstanding mortgagee compliance with the prescribed foreclosure procedure, there was no right to exercise the power of sale.[2] A forged mortgage, for example, would fall into this category. The most common example, however, of a defect that would render a sale void is where the power of sale is exercised when there has been no default in the mortgage obligation.[3]

---

23. See § 7.18, supra.

24. See §§ 7.23–7.30, infra.

§ 7.20

1. Henke v. First Southern Properties, Inc., 586 S.W.2d 617 (Tex.Civ.App.1979), error refused n.r.e.; Dingus, Mortgages—Redemption After Foreclosure Sale in Missouri, 25 Mo.L.Rev. 261, 277 (1960); Tiffany, Real Property, § 1552 (3d Ed. 1939). But cf. Phillips v. Latham, 523 S.W.2d 19 (Tex. Civ.App.1975), refused n.r.e., appeal after remand 551 S.W.2d 103 (Tex.Civ.App.1977).

2. Graham v. Oliver, 659 S.W.2d 601, 603 (Mo.App.1983). But see Bottomly v.

Kabachnick, 13 Mass.App.Ct. 480, 434 N.E.2d 667 (1982), review denied 440 N.E.2d 1176 (1982) (sale void even though default existed where notice failed to identify the holder of the mortgage).

3. See, e.g., Bradford v. Thompson, 470 S.W.2d 663 (Tex.1971), certiorari denied 405 U.S. 955, 92 S.Ct. 1174, 31 L.Ed. 232 (1972). "The power of sale is ordinarily conditioned upon a failure to pay the debt at a time named, and consequently a sale before that time would, it seems, ordinarily be invalid for any purpose, even in favor of an innocent purchaser from the purchaser at the sale." Tiffany, Real Property,

So too will a sale be characterized as void where the person foreclosing did not own the note [4] or where a trustee under a deed of trust forecloses without being authorized by the noteholder to do so.[5] Moreover, the failure to follow certain fundamental procedural requirements may render a sale void. For example, the omission of part of the mortgaged real estate from the notice of sale has been held to render the sale of omitted land void.[6]

Most defects that we will examine in the next section render the foreclosure *voidable* and not void. This means that bare legal title passes to the sale purchaser, subject to the rights of redemption of those injured by the defective foreclosure. Typically such a defect is "an irregularity in the execution of a foreclosure sale" and must be "substantial or result in a probable unfairness." [7] A common example of a voidable sale in many jurisdictions is the purchase by a trustee under a deed of trust at his own sale.[8] Further examples include the publication of the notice of sale for slightly fewer than the statutorily prescribed number of times [9] or the sale at the east door instead of the west front door of the county courthouse.[10] However, where the defect only renders the sale voidable, the rights of redemption can be cut off if the land falls into the hands of a bona fide purchaser for value.[11] Where this occurs, an action for damages against the foreclosing mortgagee or trustee may be the only remaining remedy.

Finally, some defects are treated as so inconsequential as to render the sale neither void nor voidable. Such defects commonly involve minor discrepancies in the notice of sale. For example, where the first of four published notices of sale omitted the place of sale, the court held that since there was "substantial compliance" with the requirements specified by the deed of trust and since the parties were not affected in a "material way", the sale was valid.[12] Similarly, a sale was deemed valid where the notice of sale was sent by regular rather than by the statutorily required certified or registered mail and the mortgagor had actual notice of the sale for more than the statutory period prior to the sale.[13]

§ 1552 at 637 (3d Ed. 1939). See also Wellman v. Travelers Insurance Company, 689 P.2d 1151 (Colo.App.1984) (sale void where debt deemed previously satisfied).

4. See Graham v. Oliver, 659 S.W.2d 601 (Mo.App.1983); Cobe v. Lovan, 193 Mo. 235, 92 S.W. 93 (1906).

5. Graham v. Oliver, 659 S.W.2d 601 (Mo.App.1983); Lustenberger v. Hutchinson, 343 Mo. 51, 119 S.W.2d 921 (1938).

6. Graham v. Oliver, 659 S.W.2d 601 (Mo.App.1983).

7. Id. at 604.

8. See, e.g., Whitlow v. Mountain Trust Bank, 215 Va. 149, 207 S.E.2d 837 (1974); Dingus, Mortgages—Redemption After

Foreclosure Sale in Missouri, 25 Mo.L.Rev. 261, 276–282 (1960).

9. See e.g., Kennon v. Camp, 353 S.W.2d 693 (Mo.1962).

10. See Wakefield v. Dinger, 234 Mo. App. 407, 135 S.W.2d 17 (1939).

11. See, e.g., Jackson v. Klein, 320 S.W.2d 553 (Mo.1959); Dingus, supra note 8 at 277, 280.

12. Bailey v. Pioneer Federal Savings and Loan Association, 210 Va. 558, 172 S.E.2d 730 (1970).

13. Macon-Atlanta State Bank v. Gall, 666 S.W.2d 934 (Mo.App.1984). For a complete catalogue of defects deemed "insubstantial", see Graham v. Oliver, 659

Assuming that the defective sale is only voidable, who should be treated as a bona fide purchaser? It would seem that a mortgagee-purchaser would rarely, if ever, qualify as a bona fide purchaser. Indeed, it is normally the mortgagee or his attorney who manages the power of sale foreclosure proceeding and who would be responsible for defects that arise. Moreover, even where a deed of trust is involved, while the trustee presumably is in charge of the proceedings, it is not unlikely that, for purposes of determining BFP status, he will be treated as an agent of the mortgagee. If the sale purchaser has paid value and is unrelated to the mortgagee, it would seem that he should take free of voidable defects if: (a) he has no actual knowledge of the defects; (b) he is not on reasonable notice from recorded instruments; and (c) the defects are not such that a person attending the sale exercising reasonable care would have been aware of the defect.[14] Where a subsequent grantee is involved, BFP status would seem slightly easier to achieve. If that grantee did not attend the sale, he should be treated as a bona fide purchaser unless he had actual notice of the defect or was on reasonable notice from the recorded documents. Where, however, the sale purchaser or some later purchaser is a BFP, but he conveys to a person such as the original mortgagee who would not otherwise qualify for such status, what should be the result? Most jurisdictions would probably refuse to confer BFP status on the mortgagee (or any intervening purchaser with notice of the defect), since such persons could not reacquire the property in good faith.[15]

 WESTLAW REFERENCES
power-of-sale /p void**** defect***

---

§ 7.21 Defective Power of Sale Foreclosure—Specific Problems

In this section we focus on commonly raised grounds for setting aside a power of sale foreclosure. As we will note, some irregularities are considered so prejudicial that the presence of one of them alone may be sufficient to invalidate a foreclosure. Other deficiencies, however, may only be significant if they are found in conjunction with other defects. In any event, it is almost a truism that the chances for reversal of a sale are always strengthened by the cumulative impact of several irregularities in one foreclosure proceeding.

S.W.2d 601, 604 (Mo.App.1983). See also, Burrill v. First National Bank of Shawnee Mission, N.A., 668 S.W.2d 116 (Mo.App. 1984).

14. Swindell v. Overton, 310 N.C. 707, 314 S.E.2d 512 (1984) (quoting text with approval).

15. See McDaniel v. Sprick, 297 Mo. 424, 249 S.W. 611 (1923). See also, 3 Pomeroy, Equity Jurisprudence 55–57 (5th Ed. 1941) (support by analogy to recording act cases).

Inadequacy of the Sale Price

All jurisdictions adhere to the recognized rule that mere inadequacy of the foreclosure sale price will not invalidate a sale, absent fraud, unfairness or other irregularity.[1] Stating the rule in a slightly different manner, courts sometimes say that inadequacy of the sale price is an insufficient ground unless it is so gross as to shock the conscience of the court, warranting an inference of fraud or imposition.[2]

Absent the presence of such additional circumstances, it is extremely difficult to get a sale set aside on mere price inadequacy. While some courts have found that sales for one-seventh[3] and one-sixtieth[4] of fair market value "shock the conscience," one commentator has noted with respect to his jurisdiction that "such sales have been upheld where the price paid for the property was only one-half, one-third, one-fourth, one-fifth, or even one-twentieth of its reasonable value."[5] On the other hand, where other factors are present, such as chilled bidding, unusual hour of sale or any other indicia of unfairness, courts do set sales aside.[6] For example, in a case where the mortgaged real estate sold for 3% of the fair market value, the court set aside the sale because of the additional factor that the mortgagee had informed the mortgagor of the incorrect sale date.[7] Moreover, one further factor needs to be stressed. Where sales *are* overturned, whatever the nature of the additional factors, price inadequacy is the key factor because, after all, had the price been adequate, no prejudice would have existed.

Finally, it should be noted that inadequacy of the sale price looms larger on its own when it is the mortgagee who is seeking to validate it for purposes of seeking a deficiency judgment. In other words, courts scrutinize the sale price much more closely where the mortgagee is

§ 7.21

1. Robert R. Wisdom Oil Company v. Gatewood, 682 S.W.2d 882 (Mo.App.1984); Mueller v. Simmons, 634 S.W.2d 533 (Mo. App.1982); Ogden v. Gibralter Savings Association, 620 S.W.2d 926 (Tex.Civ.App. 1981), judgment reversed on other grounds 640 S.W.2d 232 (1982); Phillips v. Atlantic Bank & Trust Co., 168 Ga.App. 590, 309 S.E.2d 813 (1983); Lippold v. White, 181 Md. 562, 31 A.2d 170 (1943); Gilbert v. Lusk, 123 Ind.App. 167, 106 N.E.2d 204 (1952); Handy v. Rogers, 143 Colo. 1, 351 P.2d 819 (1960); Kouros v. Sewell, 225 Ga. 487, 169 S.E.2d 816 (1969); Tiffiny, Real Property, § 1550 (3rd Ed. 1939).

2. See e.g., Cedrone v. Warwick Federal Savings and Loan Association, ___ R.I. ___, 459 A.2d 944 (1983); Rife v. Woolfolk, ___ W.Va. ___, 289 S.E.2d 220 (1982) (burden sustained); Anderson v. Anderson, 107 R.I. 202, 266 A.2d 56 (1970) (burden sustained); Pugh v. Richmond, 58 Tenn.App. 62, 425 S.W.2d 789 (1968); Dingus, Mortgages—Redemption After Foreclosure Sale in Missouri, 25 Mo.L.Rev. 261, 262–263 (1960). But see Holt v. Citizens Central Bank, 688 S.W.2d 414 (Tenn.1985) (sale upheld even where price "shockingly inadequate").

3. Rife v. Woolfolk, ___ W.Va. ___, 289 S.E.2d 220 (1982).

4. Gottlieb v. McArdle, 580 F.Supp. 1523 (E.D.Mich.1984).

5. Dingus, supra note 2 at 263–264.

6. See e.g., Whitman v. Transtate Title Company, 165 Cal.App.3d 312, 211 Cal. Rptr. 582 (1985); Jinkins v. Chambers, 622 S.W.2d 614 (Tex.App.1981); Blades v. Ossenfort, 481 S.W.2d 531 (Mo.App.1972). Watson v. United American Bank in Knoxville, 588 S.W.2d 877 (Tenn.App.1979).

7. Kouros v. Sewell, 225 Ga. 487, 169 S.E.2d 816 (1969); See also Matter of Strawberry Commons Apartment Owners Association, 356 N.W.2d 401 (Minn.App. 1984).

seeking a deficiency judgment plus retention of the land.[8] This is especially the case where statutes require confirmation of the price in power of sale foreclosures as a condition precedent to a deficiency judgment.[9]

It should also be stressed that bankruptcy courts may be able to set aside foreclosure sales in certain settings where the price obtained was substantially less than the fair market value of the real estate. There is controversial case authority that to the extent that the sale price was less than 70 percent of the "reasonably equivalent value" of the real estate, the mortgagor was insolvent at the time of the sale and the bankruptcy took place within a year of the sale, it can be set aside as a fraudulent conveyance. This issue is considered in detail later in this volume.[10]

Time of Sale

The time of the sale can create at least two common problems. First, the sale is sometimes held at a different day or hour than specified by the notice of foreclosure. Second, even though the sale is held at the time indicated by the notice, it may not be held at the usual hour for such sales in the particular community involved. The danger, in either event, is that possible bidders will not attend the sale and, thus, that the highest possible price for the property will not be obtained.

In the first situation, the impact of the defect on the sale will obviously depend on how serious the discrepancy is between the advertised date and the actual date of sale. Where the discrepancy is substantial, that alone may be enough to set aside the sale. For example, where a sale was advertised for the first Tuesday of August, but not held until the first Tuesday of September, the court found that the defect not only was sufficient to invalidate the sale, but also to hold it to be void.[11] On the other hand, a few minutes discrepancy between the advertised time and the actual sale time will be considered insubstantial.[12] Obviously, most cases will fall in between these two extremes and whether the sale will be set aside will depend on whether the error prejudiced the parties and whether additional circumstances also weigh in favor of sale invalidation.

Where the sale is held at the time or within the times advertised, but at an unusual time, the cases vary substantially and generalizations are hazardous. However, most require, as an additional factor, inadequacy of the sale price as a condition precedent to setting aside

8. See Danvers Savings Bank v. Hammer, 122 N.H. 1, 440 A.2d 435 (1982) (citing text with approval); Davis v. Sheffield, 123 Ga.App. 228, 180 S.E.2d 263 (1971).

9. See, e.g., Official Code Ga.Ann. §§ 44–14–161 to 44–14–162. See also, Davie v. Sheffield, 123 Ga.App. 228, 180 S.E.2d 263 (1971); Adams v. Gwinnett Commercial Bank, 238 Ga. 722, 235 S.E.2d 476 (1977).

10. See § 8.16 infra.

11. Hood Oil Co. v. Moss, 134 Ga.App. 477, 214 S.E.2d 726 (1975).

12. Silver Spring Development Corp. v. Guertler, 257 Md. 291, 262 A.2d 749 (1970).

the sale.[13] Moreover, some courts hold that if a statute specifies the range of sale hours, e.g., "between 10 o'clock A.M. and 4 o'clock P.M.," there is no need to delineate the time of sale more specifically and a sale at any time within the statutory range is acceptable.[14] Indeed, some courts have held that sale on a national holiday is permissible unless expressly prohibited by statute.[15] On the other hand, other courts have held that, absent statutory regulation, sale at an unusual hour coupled with price inadequacy will be sufficient to set aside a sale.[16]

Suppose that the foreclosure sale takes place, as advertised, on a date that satisfies statutory requirements and at a usual hour of the day in the community. The problem, however, is that it takes place a few days earlier than the date specified in the mortgage. One recent decision held that a two day discrepancy under such circumstances was insufficient to invalidate a sale.[17] Here the argument for setting aside the sale is less than compelling. Unlike in the prior two settings, there is little danger that potential third party bidders will either be led astray or otherwise discouraged from attending the sale. Only in the relatively remote likelihood that an especially scrupulous title examination by a potential third party discloses the discrepancy between the mortgage language and the advertisement will the possibility of acquiring a defective foreclosure title arguably deter his or her participation in the sale.

Place of Sale

Normally, statutes require that land be foreclosed in the county where it is located.[18] Thus, for example, where a deed of trust covered noncontiguous parcels of land in two counties, a trustee's sale in one county of both parcels was probably void as to the parcel in the other county.[19] Absent such a statutory requirement, however, some courts indicate that the parties may contract in the mortgage instrument for foreclosure in other than the situs county.[20]

Suppose, however, that the parties do agree in the mortgage instrument on a particular place of sale and that provision is violated by the mortgagee or trustee. There is authority that under those

13. See Dingus, Mortgages—Redemption After Foreclosure Sale in Missouri, 25 Mo.L.Rev. 261, 266 (1960).

14. Bering v. Republic Bank of San Antonio, 581 S.W.2d 806 (Tex.Civ.App. 1979), error refused n.r.e.; Mabry v. Abbott, 471 S.W.2d 442 (Tex.Civ.App.1971).

15. See Koehler v. Pioneer American Insurance Co., 425 S.W.2d 889 (Tex.Civ. App.1968). But see National Life Insurance Co. v. Silverman, 454 F.2d 899, 915 (D.C.Ct.App.1971).

16. See, e.g., Hanson v. Neal, 215 Mo. 256, 114 S.W. 1073 (1908).

17. Bullock v. Bishop, 435 So.2d 24 (Ala.1983).

18. See, e.g., Minn.Stat.Ann. § 580.06; Vernon's Ann.Mo.Stat. § 443.310; Utah Code Ann.1953, § 57-1-25.

19. See Dingus, Mortgages—Redemption From Foreclosure Sale in Missouri, 25 Mo.L.Rev. 261, 284 (1960); Metropolitan Life Insurance Co. v. Coleman, 99 S.W.2d 479 (Mo.App.1936).

20. See, e.g., Pugh v. Richmond, 425 S.W.2d 789 (Tenn.App.1968).

circumstances the sale is at least voidable.[21] However, the chances of voidability appear to be enhanced when the place specified in the published notice of sale coincides with that called for in the mortgage instrument.[22]

Indeed, where, as in the preceding sentence, the place of sale described in the published notice varies from the actual place of sale, a stronger case for voidability can be made than when the variance is simply between the actual place and the place specified in the mortgage instrument. In the latter situation, after all, only the mortgagor or perhaps a third party who conducted an extremely thorough title examination, who is likely to be affected. In the former case, however, it is third party potential bidders who most likely would be deterred from attending the sale. Outside pressure to raise the sale price would thus be missing. However, all cases do not necessarily follow this reasoning. For example, in one recent case the published notice specified that the sale was to take place at the "Clark County Courthouse in North Las Vegas". In fact, the courthouse is in Las Vegas and the sale took place there. The court indicated that, absent proof that bidders went to the wrong place, the sale should not be set aside.[23] Perhaps the real question should have been, however, how many third party bidders might have attended had the notice stated the correct place of sale.

Sale By Parcels or in Bulk

Mortgaged real estate often is capable of being divided into parcels for purposes of foreclosure sale as an alternative to selling it in bulk. This will especially be the case where the land consists of lots in a subdivision or where a large tract of undivided land is readily capable of subdivision. Where a mortgage covers such land, the question becomes which method of sale the mortgagee or trustee should utilize. Substantial authority requires that the party exercising the power of sale adopt the mode of sale that will be most beneficial to the mortgagor.[24] Normally this creates a presumption in favor of selling in

21. See Dingus, supra note 19 at 284; Schanawerk v. Hobrecht, 117 Mo. 22, 22 S.W. 949 (1893). Cf. Mueller v. Simmons, 634 S.W.2d 533 (Mo.App.1982) (sale upheld even though mortgage specified, Hannibal, Monroe County, a place that did not exist, instead of Hannibal, Marion County).

22. See, e.g., Stewart v. Brown, 112 Mo. 171, 20 S.W. 451 (1892).

23. Hankins v. Administrator of Veterans Affairs, 555 P.2d 483 (Nev.1976).

24. See, e.g., J.H. Morris v. Indian Hills, Inc., 282 Ala. 443, 212 So.2d 831 (1968); Thompson, Real Property, § 5182 (1977 Supp.); Dingus, Mortgages—Redemption After Foreclosure Sale in Missouri, 25 Mo.L.Rev. 261, 270 (1960). "Where property is susceptible of division, and it will bring more by being divided and sold in separate parcels or lots than by being sold in a body, or where by a sale of a part of the premises a sufficient amount can be realized to pay off the secured debt, then it is the duty of the trustee to make the division and sell a portion accordingly, and if he fails in this the sale will be held invalid on application of the party aggrieved. There are instances in which the whole of a piece of property will sell for more than it would by being separated, and in all such cases the trustee must exercise a sound discretion." Tatum v. Holliday, 59 Mo. 422, 428 (1875). See also Hill v. Farmers & Mechanics' Bank, 97 U.S. (7 Otto) 450, 24 L.Ed. 1051 (1878);

parcels because "a sale in parcels or lots opens a field to a greater number of bidders, is conducive to a better price, tends to prohibit odious speculation upon the distress of the debtor, and enables him to redeem some of the property without being compelled to redeem it all." [25] Moreover, a few courts seem to require that only as many parcels as are necessary to pay the mortgage debt be sold, even though selling all of the parcels separately would have yielded more money than one sale in bulk.[26] Sales that are set aside are usually held to be voidable.[27] On the other hand, there is significant, but probably minority, authority that, absent specific direction in the mortgage instrument, the method of sale is discretionary and that sales in bulk will ordinarily be upheld.[28] Moreover, several cases hold that mortgage language authorizing sale "either as a whole or in separate parcels" negates the presumption in favor of sale by parcels and, absent other defects in the sale process, is effective in validating a sale in bulk.[29]

A condition precedent, in any event, is that the mortgagor establish that the method of sale utilized caused injury.[30] Normally, this will entail establishing that the property would have brought more money had another method of sale been used. On the other hand, this need not always be the case. Suppose the mortgagor is claiming that the sale should be set aside because, even though a sale in bulk brought more money than would a sale of all of the parcels individually, the sale of only a few of the parcels would have satisfied the mortgage debt. Here the mortgagor should presumably be able to show injury simply by establishing the latter fact, even though he may not have suffered monetary injury because the method of sale actually used may have served his best financial, though not other, interests.

There is considerable statutory regulation of this problem. For example, one typical statute provides that "if the mortgaged premises consist of separate and distinct farms or tracts, they shall be sold separately, and no more farms or tracts shall be sold than are necessary to satisfy the amount due on such mortgage." [31] Some statutes simply

Loveland v. Clark, 11 Colo. 265, 18 P. 544 (1888); Singleton v. Scott, 11 Iowa 589 (1859); Patterson v. Miller, 52 Md. 388 (1879); Terry v. Fitzgerald, 32 Grat. 843; L.R.A.1917B, 526 (Va.1879).

25. J.H. Morris v. Indian Hills, Inc., 282 Ala. 443, 453, 212 So.2d 831, 843 (1968); See Conway v. Andrews, 286 Ala. 28, 236 So.2d 687 (Ala.1970).

26. See, e.g., Moore v. Hamilton, 151 W.Va. 784, 155 S.E.2d 877 (1967). "If it is sold in parts, no more of the property shall be sold than is necessary to satisfy the lien and the costs and expenses of the proceedings." So.Dak.Compiled Laws, 21–54–9.

27. See Dingus, note 24 at 268; J.H. Morris v. Indian Hills, Inc., 282 Ala. 443, 212 So.2d 831 (1968).

28. See Thompson, supra note 24, § 5182 at 17; 61 A.L.R.2d 505, 515–527; Classic Enterprises, Inc. v. Continental Mortgage Investors, 135 Ga.App. 105, 217 S.E.2d 411 (1975). Cf. Federal Land Bank of Columbia v. Wood, ___ S.C.App. ___, 327 S.E.2d 360 (1985).

29. McHugh v. Church, 583 P.2d 210 (Alaska 1978); Ames v. Pardue, 389 So.2d 927 (Ala.1980); Bellah v. First National Bank of Hereford, 474 S.W.2d 785 (Tex.Civ. App.1971), error refused n.r.e.

30. See Bellah v. First National Bank of Hereford, 474 S.W.2d 785 (Tex.Civ.App. 1971); Dingus, supra note 24 at 269–70.

31. Minn.Stat.Ann. § 580.08. See, e.g., No.Dak.Cent.Code 35–22–09.

appear to give the party exercising the power of sale discretion as to the method of sale.[32] A few states take the rather unique approach of giving the mortgagor the option of determining the method of sale. For example, the Utah statute provides that the mortgagor may, if present at the sale, "direct the order in which the (mortgaged) property shall be sold when such property consists of several known lots of parcels which can be sold to advantage separately and the trustee shall follow such directions." [33] A variation on this type of legislation allows the junior lienors in order of priority to make the choice in the event the mortgagor does not exercise his rights.[34] This type of legislation would seem to bar the mortgagor, and, in some situations, junior lienors from getting the sale set aside based on the method of sale actually used. This, in turn, would tend to increase the stability of power of sale titles obtained under such statutes.

There are nevertheless potential problems with this latter type of legislation. Normally, of course, it has to be presumed that the mortgagor will exercise the choice most beneficial to his interests. Suppose, however, that for purely spiteful reasons, a judgment-proof mortgagor chooses the method that results either in a deficiency for the foreclosing mortgagee or little or no surplus for the junior lienors. Perhaps a court later would hold that such a choice would be impermissible because it might determine that the parcels could not be "sold to advantage separately" within the meaning of the statute. In any event, such mortgagor activity would be aberrational and thus not a substantial problem under such statutes.

As a practical matter, where a statute does not specifically direct the method of sale, it probably makes sense for the mortgagee or trustee to advertise and conduct the sale both by parcel and by bulk. The property ultimately should be sold to the highest bidder under the particular method most beneficial to the parties.[35] Some courts have looked with approval on this approach.[36] Moreover, where possible, it is a good idea for the party selling to obtain the mortgagor's agreement in advance as to the method of sale. For example, if the mortgagor so specifies in advance, the mortgagee or trustee should sell only so much as is necessary to satisfy the debt, even though a sale in bulk or of all the parcels individually would bring more money for the mortgagor. Ideally, junior lienors should also be consulted. Many times, of course, agreement as to the method of sale will not be possible. However, a good faith effort by the selling party to obtain advance agreement will reduce the likelihood that a court would upset a sale because of the sale method ultimately utilized.

32. E.g., Or.Rev.Stat. 86.755.

33. Utah Code Ann.1953, 51–1–27. See, also, Ariz.Rev.Stat. § 33–810.

34. E.g., So.Dak.Compiled Laws 21–54–9.

35. See Dingus, supra note 24 at 271.

36. See Lazarus v. Caesar, 157 Mo. 199, 57 S.W. 751 (1900).

A related, yet distinct problem is presented where multiple mortgages, each on a separate parcel are foreclosed simultaneously. It should be stressed that mortgagee or trustee discretion as to the mode of sale may be more circumscribed and much of the foregoing analysis less relevant under such circumstances. Suppose, for example, that mortgagor gave mortgagee two promissory notes, the first secured by a mortgage on Blackacre, and the second by a mortgage on Whiteacre. Suppose further that both notes went into default and that they were foreclosed simultaneously. At the foreclosure sale both parcels were sold *en masse* without the consent of the mortgagor and others having junior interests in the parcels. Such a sale is defective and voidable.[37] As the Supreme Court of North Carolina emphasized, in confronting a similar problem, "had the two tracts of land been sold separately, the [mortgagor] might have recouped an amount on one tract sufficient to repay the debt on the second, thus saving at least one of the two pieces of property * * *. Arguments having to do with the discretion of the trustee to sell land as a whole or in parcels have no place here, but are properly considered where the land in question is conveyed in a single mortgage instrument."[38]

Chilled Bidding

Where the mortgagee or trustee engages in irregular conduct that suppresses bidding, the result is often known as "chilled bidding" and is a ground for setting aside a sale.[39] There can be at least two types of chilled bidding.[40] The first occurs where there is collusion involving the mortgagee or trustee and potential purchasers to hold down the bidding or where the mortgagee or trustee by other actions seek to accomplish the same result. The second type encompasses inadvertent and unintentional acts by the trustee or mortgagee that suppress bidding.

The first type of chilled bidding can be involved in a myriad of fact situations, and it arguably can render a sale void rather than merely voidable.[41] A mortgagee or trustee could, for example, get third parties to agree not to bid at a foreclosure sale either by paying them off or on the understanding that if the mortgagee purchases, the third parties will share in the resale profits. Or the mortgagee or trustee may discourage bidding by intentionally misrepresenting the state of the title or the physical condition of the mortgaged premises.[42]

---

37. Swindell v. Overton, 310 N.C. 707, 314 S.E.2d 512 (1984).

38. Id. at 517.

39. Dingus, supra note 24 at 274. See also, Biddle v. National Old Line Insurance Co., 513 S.W.2d 135 (Tex.Civ.App.1974), refused n.r.e.; Sullivan v. Federal Farm Mortgage Corp., 62 Ga.App. 402, 8 S.E.2d 126 (1940); Aultman & Taylor Co. v. Meade, 121 Ky. 241, 89 S.W. 137, 123 Am.

St.Rep. 193 (1905); Fenton v. Torrey, 133 Mass. 138 (1882).

40. Dingus, Id. at 274–275.

41. Id.

42. For similar fact situations, see McDaniel v. Sprick, 297 Mo. 424, 249 S.W. 611 (1920); Hanson v. Neal, 215 Mo. 256, 114 S.W. 1073 (1908).

A more difficult problem is raised when there is collusion among third parties alone. This could involve an agreement among several third parties that they will discourage others from attending the sale and that they will only bid the property up to a specified price. They might further agree that if one of them actually purchases at the sale, he will, upon resale, split the profits with the others. If, of course, the trustee or mortgagee has advance knowledge of this agreement, the sale should be postponed. On the other hand, if there is no such knowledge and the mortgagee purchases the property in spite of the third party agreement, it would seem unfair to set aside the sale against the mortgagee even though the collusion among the third parties may have meant that the mortgagee was able to purchase for a lower price. However, if one of the third parties is successful bidder, it would seem that the mortgagor should be able to get the sale set aside against the third party purchaser. The collusion, after all, probably kept the price down and setting aside the sale would foster a public policy that encourages open and honest bidding.

Chilled bidding problems can arise as the result of inadvertent or unintentional erroneous statements by the mortgagee or trustee at the foreclosure sale or in the foreclosure advertisement. A common example is the statement that the mortgaged premises are being sold subject to a senior lien.[43] This, of course, could result in a lower sale price than if the bidders were certain the land was free and clear of senior liens. Similarly, it has been argued, albeit unsuccessfully, that an overstatement of the mortgage debt in the advertisement constituted chilled bidding because it made it appear that a higher bid would be required to purchase the property and satisfy the mortgage indebtedness than was actually the case.[44]

Conversely, it is sometimes argued that *failure* to mention in the advertisement the existence of a prior lien constitutes chilled bidding. For example, while specifically overruling a prior case that had held that such a failure resulted per se in chilled bidding, the Georgia Supreme Court recognized that actionable chilled bidding can arise under such circumstances: "While we agree that the better practice is to include such information, we also conclude that the issue of whether or not the failure to do so is chilling is for the jury. The failure to recite the existence of a prior [mortgage] could be chilling if, for example, assumption were possible and it would be of advantage to prospective purchasers to assume such a mortgage."[45]

It should be emphasized, however, that truthful statements that suppress bidding do not constitute chilled bidding. For example, in one

43. See, e.g., Hoffman v. McCracken, 168 Mo. 337, 67 S.W. 868 (1902). But see Tifton Corp. v. Decatur Federal Savings & Loan Association, 136 Ga.App. 710, 222 S.E.2d 115 (1975) (notice of foreclosure and recorded documents held not to suggest property was subject to a first lien).

44. Nicholas McPickolus Realty Corp. v. Jamaica Plain Cooperative Bank, 16 Mass.App.Ct. 964, 452 N.E.2d 285 (1983).

45. Smith v. Citizens & Southern Financial Corp., 245 Ga. 850, 268 S.E.2d 157, 159–160 (1980), overruling Sims v. Etheridge 169 Ga. 400, 150 S.E. 647 (1929).

case a mortgagor unsuccessfully claimed that bidding was chilled because the trustee stated at the sale that an undivided interest was being sold.[46] The problem was that the statement was correct. Similarly, the truthful announcement at a foreclosure sale that a notice of lis pendens had been filed on the mortgaged property has been held not to create chilled bidding.[47] In any event, unintentionally chilled bidding probably renders the sale voidable and not void.[48]

The chilled bidding concept normally requires that the mortgagor actually establish that the bidding was suppressed; this is often done by showing inadequacy of the sale price. This clearly makes sense where the chilled bidding claim is based on mere inadvertent mortgagee or trustee action.[49] However, where the chilled bidding is of the first type, it would seem that public policy, even in the absence of clearly established injury, dictates a presumption in favor of setting aside the sale as a deterrent to such intentional or collusive behavior.

Mortgagee Purchase under Mortgage with Power of Sale

Where a mortgage contains a power of sale in favor of the mortgagee, the mortgagee normally may not purchase at a sale carried out pursuant to that power.[50] As one leading decision stated, "a mortgagee may not purchase at his own sale; if he does so, he does not acquire an absolute estate. The sale does not alter the relation of mortgagor and mortgagee existing between the parties. * * * Such sale is voidable at the election of the mortgagor."[51] Moreover, the prohibition also applies where the purchase by the mortgagee is made indirectly through a third party.[52] A few states however, by statute[53] reject the foregoing approach and permit mortgagee purchase at his own sale. Moreover, a few cases contain dicta to the same effect.[54]

46. Cleveland v. Cleveland, 235 Ga. 361, 219 S.E.2d 715 (1975).

47. Boyce v. Hughes, 241 Ga. 357, 245 S.E.2d 308 (1978).

48. Dingus, supra note 24 at 275–276.

49. Id.

50. Mills v. Mutual Building & Loan Association, 216 N.C. 664, 6 S.E.2d 549 (1940); Jackson v. Blankenship, 213 Ala. 607, 105 So. 684 (1925); Imboden v. Hunter, 23 Ark. 622, 79 Am.Dec. 116 (1861); Dyer v. Shurtleff, 112 Mass. 165, 17 Am. Rep. 77 (1873); Martin v. McNeely, 101 N.C. 634, 8 S.E. 231 (1888); Blockley v. Fowler, 21 Cal. 326, 82 Am.Dec. 747 (1863). See 27 Va.L.Rev. 926, 931 (1941); Dingus, Mortgages—Redemption After Foreclosure Sale in Missouri, 25 Mo.L.Rev. 261, 282–283 (1960).

51. Mills v. Mutual Building & Loan Association, 216 N.C. 644, 668, 6 S.E.2d 549, 552 (1940).

52. See Dingus, supra note 50 at 283; Byrne v. Carson, 70 Mo.App. 126 (1897).

53. See Mass.Gen.Laws ch. 183 § 25; Danvers Savings Bank v. Hammer, 122 N.H. 1, 440 A.2d 435 (1982) (interpreting Massachusetts law), cf. Cambridge Savings Bank v. Cronin, 289 Mass. 379, 194 N.E. 289 (1935) (mortgagee may not purchase absent statutory authorization).

54. See Southern Trust & Mortgage Co. v. Daniel, 143 Tex. 321, 184 S.W.2d 465 (1943) ("the rule is well-settled in this state that a mortgagee with a power to sell may purchase at his own sale made at public auction * * *."); Skeen v. Glenn Justice Mortgage, Inc., 526 S.W.2d 252 (Tex.Civ. App.1975); Brown v. Eckhardt, 23 Tenn. App. 217, 129 S.W.2d 1122 (1939). Since the foregoing cases all involved deeds of trust, they are questionable authority for the proposition that a mortgagee may purchase himself under a mortgage with a power of sale.

Some jurisdictions that use the mortgage with power of sale have solved the foregoing problems by legislation that specifies that the power of sale be exercised by a public official, usually the sheriff, and that specifically authorizes the mortgagee to purchase.[55] The practical effect of such legislation is to create a financing device that is functionally the equivalent of a deed of trust with a power of sale in a public trustee, a device that is used in a few jurisdictions.[56]

Trustee Purchase at Foreclosure Sale and Related Problems

It is stated so frequently as to be a truism that a trustee in a deed of trust is a fiduciary for both the mortgagor and mortgagee and must act impartially between them.[57] As one leading decision has stated, "the trustee for sale is bound by his office to bring the estate to a sale under every possible advantage to the debtor as well as to the creditor, and he is bound to use not only good faith but also every requisite degree of diligence in conducting the sale and to attend equally to the interest of debtor and creditor alike, apprising both of the intention of selling, that each may take the means to procure an advantageous sale."[58] Yet because he represents two parties whose interests are often antithetical, he is not treated as a traditional trustee for all purposes. Indeed, as one California court stated, "the trustee of a trust deed is not a trustee in the strict sense of the word. The role of such a trustee is more nearly that of a common agent of the parties to the instrument."[59] Thus, courts have held that a trustee has no duty to make an affirmative investigation to determine whether the debt is in default[60] or to ascertain whether the mortgage debt should be offset by the debtor's unliquidated claim against the creditor.[61] Nor does he have a duty to disclose to the debtor alternatives to foreclosure such as private sale or refinancing.[62] Moreover, while there is authority to the contrary,[63] there is case law that in the absence of fraud or misconduct

---

55. See Minn.Stat.Ann. §§ 580.06, 580.11; Wyo.Stat.1957, § 34–74; Mich. Comp.Laws Ann. § 600.3216.

56. See, e.g., Colo.Rev.Stat. §§ 38–37–101 through 38–37–139.

57. See e.g., McHugh v. Church, 583 P.2d 210 (Alaska 1978); Blodgett v. Martsch, 590 P.2d 298 (Utah 1978); Spires v. Edgar, 513 S.W.2d 372 (Mo.1974); Whitlow v. Mountain Trust Bank, 215 Va. 149, 207 S.E.2d 837 (1974); Cox v. Helenius, 103 Wn.2d 383, 693 P.2d 683 (1985); White v. Macqueen, 360 Ill. 236, 195 N.E. 832, 98 A.L.R. 1115 (1935). See Spruill v. Ballard, 61 App.D.C. 112, 58 F.2d 517 (1932); 90 A.L.R.2d 501, 505–506.

58. Mills v. Mutual Building & Loan Association, 216 N.C. 664, 670, 6 S.E.2d 549, 554 (1940).

59. Lancaster Security Investment Corp. v. Kessler, 159 Cal.App.2d 649, 656, 324 P.2d 634, 638 (1958).

Compare I.E. Associates v. Safeco Title Insurance Co., 158 Cal.App.3d 52, 204 Cal. Rptr. 340 (1984), where the court characterized duties as "an amalgam of the terms of the deed of trust, the applicable statutory law, and ordinary agency principles." Id. at 344.

60. Spires v. Edgar, 513 S.W.2d 372 (Mo.1974).

61. Villers v. Wilson, ___ W.Va. ___, 304 S.E.2d 16 (1983).

62. Perry v. Virginia Mortgage & Investment Co., Inc., 412 A.2d 1194 (D.C.App. 1980).

63. Spruill v. Ballard, n. 57, supra; Morgan v. Glendy, 92 Va. 86, 22 S.E. 854 (1895); Spencer v. Lee, 19 W.Va. 179 (1881).

a foreclosure by a trustee under a power of sale is not invalidated because the trustee owns an interest in the mortgage debt.[64] In addition, so long as the trustee is not employed by or otherwise associated with the beneficiary (the holder of the note and deed of trust), it is both permissible and a standard practice for the beneficiary to purchase at the foreclosure sale.[65] Indeed, one of the possible advantages of the deed of trust over the mortgage with power of sale is that in the former situation the beneficiary is able to purchase at the sale.[66]

Yet it is equally clear that a trustee, at least without the express consent of the trustor (the debtor) or his successor, may not purchase the premises himself at his own foreclosure sale.[67] As one court has noted, "when a trustee buys at his own sale, a constructive fraud exists; the transaction is voidable; and when attacked, the sale must be set aside."[68] In such a situation, the fact that the trustee otherwise acted fairly and with good motives is not controlling.[69] The prohibition applies equally when the purchase is made indirectly through a family member.[70] Moreover courts will set aside a purchase by the trustee from a foreclosure sale purchaser that occurs immediately after the foreclosure sale.[71]

More complex problems arise when, as is common, the beneficiary purchases at a trustee's sale and the trustee is an employee or part owner of the beneficiary. While for some courts this may result in closer scrutiny of the sale, it usually does not operate to invalidate it.[72] On the other hand, more skeptical courts analyze the problem in at least two ways. First, where the connection between the trustee and the beneficiary is substantial, courts treat the situation as an indirect purchase by the trustee and thus voidable.[73] For example, in one recent case the court took this approach where the trustee owned 13% of the stock and was vice president of the beneficiary, a closely held corporation.[74] As a second method of analyzing such situations, a few courts have determined that, as a practical matter, the "instrument—in form a deed of trust—executed to the chief executive officer of a

---

64. Jackson v. Klein, 320 S.W.2d 553 (Mo.1959); Dingus, Mortgages—Redemption After Foreclosure Sale in Missouri, 25 Mo.L.Rev. 261, 281 (1960).

65. Dingus, supra note 60 at 282. See, e.g., Utah Code Ann.1953, 57–1–27.

66. See text at notes 50–56, supra.

67. See Whitlow v. Mountain Trust Bank, 215 Va. 149, 207 S.E.2d 837 (1974); Mills v. Mutual Building & Loan Association, 216 N.C. 664, 6 S.E.2d 549 (1940); Dingus, supra note 60 at 276; 90 A.L.R.2d 501, 567. But see Fuqua v. Burrell, 474 S.W.2d 333 (Tex.Civ.App.1971).

68. Whitlow v. Mountain Trust Bank, 215 Va. 149, 151, 207 S.E.2d 837, 840 (1974).

69. Id.

70. See Lee v. Lee, 236 Miss. 260, 109 So.2d 870 (1959).

71. Smith v. Haley, 314 S.W.2d 909 (Mo.1958).

72. Perry v. Virginia Mortgage & Investment Co., Inc., 412 A.2d 1194 (D.C.App. 1980).

73. See Whitlow v. Mountain Trust Bank, 215 Va. 149, 207 S.E.2d 837 (1974); Southern Trust and Mortgage Co. v. Daniel, 143 Tex. 321, 184 S.W.2d 465 (1944).

74. Whitlow v. Mountain Trust Bank, 215 Va. 149, 207 S.E.2d 837 (1974).

corporation is, in effect, a mortgage, and the law relating to foreclosure of mortgage deeds rather than the law relating to trust deeds is applicable." [75] The sale thus becomes voidable because the beneficiary is treated as if he purchased pursuant to his own power of sale.

The problems presented by the foregoing paragraph are not insurmountable. At least one state by statute seems to authorize a bank or savings and loan association to be both a trustee and beneficiary under the same deed of trust.[76] Since another statute states that "any person, including the beneficiary, may bid at the sale",[77] it would seem to authorize such an institution to purchase at a foreclosure sale from itself in its capacity as trustee. In the many states without such legislative authorization, it is a common practice for trustees to be employed by, part-owner of, or be otherwise associated with the beneficiary. This is often done largely for convenience and probably is harmless in most instances because the vast majority of deeds of trust are never foreclosed. As to those deeds of trust that do reach the foreclosure stage, beneficiaries obviously want to be able to purchase at the foreclosure sale. A simple expedient at that stage would be for the beneficiary to have the related trustee resign and to replace him with an independent trustee. This can be accomplished by making sure that the deed of trust specifically authorizes replacement of the trustee or, in most states, by relying on statutory authorization for such replacement.[78]

Whatever the trustee's fiduciary duty to the debtor, his or her obligations vis a vis third party foreclosure sale bidders is less ambiguous. Generally, such persons may not assert the debtor's objections to the conduct of the sale.[79] As to title or physical defects in the real estate, many courts apply a *caveat emptor* approach.[80] As one court stated, "to the bidders he owes no duty except to refrain from doing anything to hamper them in their search for information or to prevent the discovery of defects by inspection. He is under no duty to make representations or to answer questions; but if questions are asked and he undertakes to answer, then such answers must be full and accurate—nothing must then be concealed." [81] On the other hand, some jurisdictions have modified this approach somewhat by imposing on the trustee the duty to disclose material facts within his knowledge that would not otherwise "be readily observable upon reasonable inspection

---

75. Mills v. Mutual Building & Loan Association, 216 N.C. 664, 6 S.E.2d 549 (1940).

76. Utah Code Ann.1953, 57–1–21.

77. Utah Code Ann.1953, 57–1–27.

78. See, e.g., Vernon's Ann.Mo.Stat. § 443.340.

79. See Block v. Tobin, 45 Cal.App.3d 214, 119 Cal.Rptr. 288 (1975); Monolith Portland Cement Co. v. Tendler, 206 Cal. App.2d 800, 24 Cal.Rptr. 38 (1962). Third

parties may, however, under some circumstances, be able to recover against the trustee for fraud or deceit. See § 7.22 infra.

80. See e.g., Feldman v. Rucker, 201 Va. 11, 109 S.E.2d 379 (1959); Ivrey v. Karr, 182 Md. 463, 34 A.2d 847 (1943); Adams v. Boyd, 332 Mo. 484, 58 S.W.2d 704 (1933); Buckman v. Bragaw, 192 N.C. 152, 134 S.E. 422 (1926).

81. Feldman v. Rucker, 201 Va. 11, 18, 109 S.E.2d 379, 385–386 (1959).

by the purchaser." [82] The advantage of this modified approach to purchasers may be more apparent than real. Many, if not most, title defects are capable of being uncovered by a reasonably careful examination of the chain of title. Moreover, as to physical defects in the mortgaged premises, most trustees rarely visit the property, let alone become aware of its condition.

Statutory Presumptions

Some states have statutes that provide that recitals of statutory compliance contained in a trustee's deed executed upon foreclosure create, in general, prima facie evidence of compliance with statutory requirements "relating to the exercise of the power of sale and sale of the property described therein, including recitals concerning any mailing, personal delivery and publication of the notice of default, any mailing and publication and posting of notice of sale, and the conduct of the sale." [83] As to bona fide purchasers and encumbrancers, some of these statutes also provide that the recitals create conclusive evidence of compliance.[84] A variation on the above statute provides that the trustee's deed *itself* provides the same evidence of compliance.[85]

The above legislation seems to have significant impact in two respects. First, it creates a general rebuttable presumption that the statutory sale requirements have been satisfied and that the sale is valid.[86] This would be available to a foreclosure title holder whether a bona fide purchaser or not. To that extent, the effect of such statutes is to add slightly more stability to foreclosure titles and thus is desirable. Second, and more important, it would seem that any defect in the foreclosure proceeding which is contradicted by a recital in the trustee's deed renders the sale merely voidable and not void. As we noted earlier, if a defect renders a sale void, the sale passes no title even to a bona fide purchaser and thus the defect can be raised against such a purchaser.[87] If, on the other hand, the defect renders a sale voidable, the sale cannot be set aside against a BFP.[88] Under these statutes, the recitals themselves constitute conclusive evidence in favor of BFP's, and hence any sale would be voidable at most. Does this mean that defects which normally render a sale void, such as a forged deed of trust or the absence of a default, could not be raised against a BFP? At least

---

82. See e.g., McPherson v. Purdue, 21 Wn.App. 450, 585 P.2d 830 (1978).

83. Utah Code Ann.1953, 57–1–28. See, e.g., Colo.Rev.Stat. 38–39–115; Ore.Rev. Stat. 86.780; So.Dak.Compiled Laws 21–48–23.

84. Utah Code Ann.1953, 57–1–28; West's Ann.Cal.Civ.Code, § 2924; Ore.Rev. Stat. 86.780.

85. Ariz.Rev.Stat. § 33–811.

86. See, e.g., Wolfe v. Lipsy, 209 Cal.App.3d 633, 209 Cal.Rptr. 801 (1985); Triano v. First American Title Insurance Co. of Arizona, 131 Ariz. 581, 643 P.2d 26 (App.1982); New England Loan & Trust Co. v. Brown, 157 Mo. 116, 57 S.W. 760 (1900). See generally, Basye, Clearing Land Titles, § 43 (2d Ed. 1970).

87. See § 7.20, supra.

88. Id.

two state statutes seem specifically to go this far.[89] However, the statute quoted above and those similar to it probably do not. Rather these statutes seem to cover defects that arise in connection with the mechanics of exercising the power of sale and not those that relate to whether there was a substantive basis to foreclose in the first place. In any event, it would seem unfair to allow a BFP to prevail over a mortgagor who was not in default or, indeed, over a person who never executed a mortgage to begin with.

 WESTLAW REFERENCES

foreclos*** /p inadequa** /s price /p mortgage (real +1 estate property)

foreclos*** /p locat*** place county /s sale sold sell*** /s property "real estate" realty /p descri! publi! notice*

foreclos*** /p parcel bulk lot /7 sale sold sell*** /s property "real estate" realty

chill*** /3 bid****

§ 7.22   Defective Power of Sale Foreclosure—Remedies

As we have noted, there are numerous grounds which can render a power of sale foreclosure either void or voidable. Moreover, these defective sales give grounds for relief not only to mortgagors, but also to any other party who is junior to the mortgage being foreclosed. The nature and scope of the remedy will depend on several variables. Among these are whether the defect is discovered before or after sale, the nature of the defect, and, importantly, if the sale has already been completed, whether the sale purchaser or any subsequent grantee is a bona fide purchaser.

Injunction Against Sale

Where the defective power of sale foreclosure has not yet been consummated, the most common remedy for the mortgagor or other injured party is an injunction suit against it.[1] In theory this relief should be available for any defects that would be serious enough to set aside an already completed sale. However, because the sale will not yet have taken place, and because many of the defects we examined in the preceding section could not yet have occurred, very often the basis for the injunction suit will be substantive defenses to the obligation itself and related matters. For example, injunctive relief will be

---

89. See Rev.Code Mont.1947, § 52–410; Nev.Rev.Stat. 107.030(8). See also, Uniform Land Transactions Act (ULTA) § 3–511 (1975).

§ 7.22

1. See, e.g., Greater Houston Bank v. Conte, 641 S.W.2d 407 (Tex.App.1982); Bekins Bar V Ranch v. Huth, 664 P.2d 455 (Utah 1983); Erickson v. Rocco, 433 S.W.2d 746 (Tex.Civ.App.1968); National Life Insurance Co. v. Cady, 227 Ga. 475, 181 S.E.2d 382 (1971); Nelson, Constitutional Problems with Power of Sale Foreclosure: A Judicial Dilemna, 43 Mo.L.Rev. 25, 32 (1978); Tiffany, Real Property, § 1549 (3d Ed.1939). The remedy is available to a junior lienor, see F & H Investment Co. v. Sackman-Gilliland Corp., 232 N.W.2d 769 (Minn.1975).

available where the claim is that the debt has already been paid or tendered,[2] or that, for a variety of reasons, the mortgage is not in default or there is no underlying obligation to support the mortgage.[3] Other grounds have included defective advertisement of the sale[4] attempting to sell property not covered by the mortgage[5] and that the acceleration of the mortgage debt was invalid.[6] Moreover, in a more modern context, relief has been granted on the ground that the mortgage debt should have been paid for a disabled mortgagor by disability insurance that originally had been required by and purchased through the mortgagee.[7]

Often the mortgagor or junior lienor will seek both temporary and permanent relief against the sale. Where temporary relief is sought the petitioner often must post an injunction bond to protect the mortgagee against injury arising from the improper issuance of the temporary injunction.[8] Moreover, the court must balance the relative hardships to determine whether temporary relief is appropriate.[9] While the ultimate merits of the controversy affect this process, the focus is on the relative hardship imposed on the parties by granting or refusing temporary relief.[10] On the other hand, as one court noted, "in order for one to be entitled to a temporary injunction, it is not necessary that he sustain the burden of proving that he will ultimately prevail in the dispute. It is sufficient that he show a probable right and a probable injury."[11] In theory, a decision on the actual merits is not reached until the hearing on the permanent injunction. The second alternative for the petitioner is to request a permanent injunction alone. This avoids the expense of an injunction bond. On the other hand, it also means that in principle the mortgagee is free to go ahead with the power of sale foreclosure, since he will not be subject to an injunctive decree as of the time of sale. However, with the cloud of the pending permanent injunction suit hovering over the power of sale foreclosure, many mortgagees may very well postpone the sale.

2. See Miller v. Deering, 209 Ga. 377, 72 S.E.2d 722 (1952).

3. National Life Insurance Co. v. Cady, 227 Ga. 475, 181 S.E.2d 382 (1971); Moore v. Parkerson, 255 N.C. 342, 121 S.E.2d 533 (1965); Jones v. Garcia, 538 S.W.2d 492 (Tex.Civ.App.1976).

4. See, e.g., Walker v. Boggess, 41 W.Va. 588, 23 S.E. 550 (1895).

5. Preiss v. Campbell, 59 Ala. 635 (1877).

6. Greater Houston Bank v. Conte, 641 S.W.2d 407 (Tex.App.1982).

7. Exchange Bank of Milledgeville v. Hill, 236 Ga. 445, 224 S.E.2d 23 (1976).

8. See Hummell v. Republic Federal Savings & Loan, 133 Cal.App.3d 49, 183 Cal.Rptr. 708 (4th Dist.1982); Broad & Locust Associates v. Locust-Broad Realty Co., 318 Pa.Super. 38, 464 A.2d 506 (1983); Dobbs, Should Security Be Required As a Pre-Condition to Provisional Injunctive Relief? 52 N.C.L.Rev. 1091, 1099 (1974).

9. Leavell, Love & Nelson, Equitable Remedies and Restitution, 25–32 (3rd Ed. 1980).

10. Id.

11. Erickson v. Rocco, 433 S.W.2d 746, 749 (Tex.Civ.App.1968): See also Hutchison v. Bristol Court Properties, Limited, 508 S.W.2d 486 (Tex.Civ.App.1974).

Some courts require that a mortgagor seeking any type of injunctive relief tender to the court the amount due on the mortgage.[12] Where that amount is in dispute, these courts will at least require that the mortgagor tender what he concedes is due.[13] The theory behind this tender requirement is the concept that one who seeks equitable relief must do equity.[14] Whatever the underlying historical or equitable basis, the tender requirement is objectionable. This is especially so if the mortgagor is seeking temporary as well as permanent injunctive relief because, in that situation, he will be required to post an injunction bond that protects the mortgagee financially against the wrongful issuance of the temporary injunction. Even if only permanent injunctive relief is sought, the mortgagee is free to go ahead and foreclose and take his chances on the ultimate outcome of the suit. Since the mortgagee will be the likely purchaser at the sale, if the injunction suit proves to have been unwarranted, he will then have clear title to the land. While the mortgagee may have been unable to resell the land during this period because of the cloud of the injunction suit, the mortgagor will also possibly have suffered injury. This is so because, had the foreclosure sale not been clouded more bidding may have resulted and there may have been a surplus for the mortgagor. It is reasonable to conclude that the equities as between the parties are equally balanced, even in the absence of a tender by the mortgagor.

There is a further reason that tender should not be required. The mortgagor is, by hypothesis, in default, and is probably in serious financial straits. The fundamental concept of foreclosure is that, despite his economic condition he is entitled to an orderly liquidation of the security in a manner consistent with law. It is plainly a violation of this concept to enjoin a wrongful foreclosure only if he can tender the balance owing on the debt; if he could do so, it is likely that no foreclosure would have been necessary. Of course, if the debtor wishes to redeem by tendering, that is his right, but he should not be compelled to exercise it in order to prevent an illegal foreclosure sale.

Apparently a few courts also require that a junior lienor tender the amount of the senior debt admittedly owing as a precondition to injunctive relief.[15] This seems equally objectionable as the requirement imposed by some courts on the mortgagor, if for different reasons. Unlike the normal mortgagor, the junior lienor has a right to redeem a senior lien in default, but he normally has no obligation to do so. Moreover, the junior lienor has an additional important right to foreclose his lien. It seems anomalous to require him to pay off a senior

12. See Ginther-Davis Center, Limited v. Houston National Bank, 600 S.W.2d 856 (Tex.Civ.App.1980); see also Tiffany, Real Property, § 1549 (3d Ed. 1939) for a list of cases. See also, Durfee, Cases on Security, 278 (1951); 93 A.L.R. 12, 30–31; Thompson, Real Property § 5179 (1957). Cf. Grella v. Berry, 647 S.W.2d 15 (Tex.App.1982).

13. Tiffany, Id. See Glines v. Theo R. Appel Realty Co., 201 Mo.App. 596, 213 S.W. 498 (1919).

14. Id.

15. See Thompson, Real Property, § 5179 (1957).

mortgage that he claims is being improperly foreclosed in order to preserve his own right to foreclose.

Suits to Set Aside the Sale

After a defective power of sale foreclosure has been consummated, the universal remedy available to mortgagors and junior lienors is a suit in equity to set aside the sale.[16] It is available to a mortgagor whether in or out of possession of the mortgaged real estate. One deterrent to this remedy in a few states is the requirement that the mortgage debt be tendered as a condition precedent to such equitable relief.[17] As in the injunction situation, the requirement is rationalized by the maxim that doing equity is a pre-condition to obtaining equitable relief.[18] In any event, even if such a tender requirement is imposed, it surely is subject to the limitation that tender be made only of the amount admittedly due.[19] Moreover, it would seem even more difficult to justify the requirement where the grounds for challenging the validity of the sale are the absence of default or the invalidity of the mortgage.[20]

In any event, as in the injunctive setting, the tender requirement is a questionable roadblock to equitable relief.[21] As in that situation, the mortgagor, albeit in default, has a right to an orderly and, more important, a legally correct disposition of his security. It is not only unfair to condition this right on the payment of the debt, it is also illogical, since if he pays the mortgage debt the right to be foreclosed lawfully will have been destroyed. Moreover, the junior lienor, who, as we noted earlier, has a right, but no obligation, to redeem the senior lien also has the additional right to foreclose his lien. More important, he, like the mortgagor, has a right to expect that the senior lienor will follow legally acceptable procedures in dealing with the mortgage security. He should not be compelled to pay an alleged wrongdoer in order to assert those rights. While both the mortgagor and junior lienor may, if successful, choose to redeem, they should have the option simply of forcing reinstatement of the mortgage. The mortgagee could

16. The frequency with which this remedy is utilized is attested to by the fact that Volume 25, Part I of the West Ninth Decennial Digest (1976–1981) contains over 100 cases involving suits to set aside. So to does Volume 30 of the Eighth Decennial Digest (1966–1976).

17. See e.g., Arnolds Management Corp. v. Eischen, 158 Cal.App.3d 575, 205 Cal. Rptr. 15 (1984); Berry v. Government Nat. Mortgage Association, 231 Ga. 503, 202 S.E.2d 450 (1973); Massey v. National Homeowners Sales Service Corp. of Atlanta, 225 Ga. 93, 165 S.E.2d 854 (1969); Pachter v. Woodman, 534 S.W.2d 940 (Tex. Civ.App.1976), reversed, seemingly, on other grounds 547 S.W.2d 954 (Tex.1977); See

also, Dingus, supra, note 94 at 293. Cf., Phillips v. Latham, 523 S.W.2d 19 (Tex.Civ. App.1975), refused n.r.e., appeal after remand 551 S.W.2d 103 (Tex.Civ.App.1977); Blades v. Ossenfort, 481 S.W.2d 531 (Mo. App.1972). But see Leslie, Inc. v. Solomon, 141 Ga.App. 673, 234 S.E.2d 104 (1977) (tender unnecessary where mortgagor alleged total failure of consideration).

18. See note 92, supra.

19. See text at note 91, supra.

20. See Massey v. National Homeowners Sales Service Corp. of Atlanta, 225 Ga. 93, 165 S.E.2d 854 (1969).

21. See text at notes 90–93, supra.

then pursue his remedies again, although this time, one would hope, in a legally correct manner.

Even though a mortgagor should not be required to tender simply to set aside a defective sale, he still may be forced to do so if he wishes to regain possession of the mortgaged real estate. For example, in a title or intermediate jurisdiction, the mortgagee in possession cannot be removed simply by setting an invalid foreclosure sale aside. This is because he has a right to possession, at least after a default by the mortgagor, until the mortgage debt is satisfied.[22] This may also be the case in those lien jurisdictions that confer valid mortgagee-in-possession status on mortgagees who take possession after a void or voidable foreclosure sale.[23]

The ability to bring a suit to set aside a foreclosure sale and to redeem can be cut off by certain events. When this occurs, the mortgagor or junior lienor will be left with a damages action for wrongful foreclosure against the foreclosing mortgagee or trustee. This can arise, for example, where the defect in the foreclosure sale rendered it voidable and not void and a bona fide purchaser has obtained title to the land.[24] Moreover, even where the defect rendered the sale void, adverse possession by the sale purchaser or his subsequent grantee may defeat any attempt to reach the title. The latter situation may be further complicated by the fact that unless the adverse possession statutory period is relatively short,[25] the applicable statute of limitations will probably also have run on the damages action. Finally, one case [26] illustrates how even though a relatively long statute of limitations can run on one's ability to reach the foreclosed title, a damages action may nevertheless still be available. In that case the mortgagors sued the foreclosing mortgagee and his subsequent grantee to recover title on the theory that the deed of trust had been foreclosed without being in default. A ten year statute of limitations precluded any contradiction of the recital of default contained in the trustee's deed. The court held that although the statute barred any attempt to regain the title, a damages action was available against the foreclosing mortgagee because no statute of limitations had been raised against that cause of action. Interestingly, absent the ten-year statute of limitations, the action to set aside probably would have been available because the defect alleged was the absence of a default, which, if proved, would have rendered the sale void.[27] Thus, the mortgagors could have reached the title even if it had been in the hands of a BFP.

22. See §§ 4.1, 4.3, supra.

23. See § 4.24, supra.

24. See e.g., Danvers Savings Bank v. Hammer, 122 N.H. 1, 440 A.2d 435 (1982); § 7.20, supra.

25. In a few states, however, the statute of limitations for adverse possession may be relatively short. See, e.g., Ariz.Rev. Stat. § 12–523 where under some circumstances the period of limitations can be three years.

26. Calverley v. Gunstream, 497 S.W.2d 110 (Tex.Civ.App.1973), refused n.r.e.

27. See § 7.20, supra.

Damages

Suppose that for one of the reasons suggested in the foregoing paragraph, a mortgagor brings an action for damages for wrongful foreclosure against a foreclosing mortgagee or trustee. Whether they are recoverable may depend, in some jurisdictions, on the nature of the foreclosure defect. According to this view, if the mortgagee had a "right to foreclose", but the execution of the foreclosure was defective, no damages are recoverable.[28] Thus, for example, if the mortgage was not in default, a cause of action for damages would be appropriate, but not if the claim was defective notice of foreclosure or some other defect in the sale process. In the latter situation, the mortgagor would be left with the equitable remedy to set aside the sale, assuming that such a remedy is still available.[29] On the other hand, there is contrary authority,[30] and even courts that purport to follow the "right to foreclose-defect in the sale process" approach are clearly troubled by it.[31] Moreover, other courts seek to avoid the problem by taking a broad view of those defects that go to right of the mortgagee to foreclose.[32] In any event, the distinction is both illogical and unfair. As we noted earlier in a slightly different context, a mortgagor, albeit in default, has a right to an orderly and substantially correct disposition of her security.[33]

The emphasis should be on whether the defect, substantive or procedural, could have prejudiced the mortgagor. If a defect could arguably have deterred third party bidding, or impaired the mortgagor's ability to protect her rights, then an action for damages should lie. Only those defects which in no event could have affected the fairness of the foreclosure process should preclude an action for damages. The Texas Supreme Court recently appeared to follow this reasoning in holding that the failure to record a notice of a substitute trustee, where the mortgagor in default had actual knowledge of the substitution, could not have prejudiced him and that therefore an action for damages was inappropriate.[34]

The basic measure of damages in an action for wrongful foreclosure is the difference between the market value of the real estate and the aggregate amount of liens thereon as of the date of the defective sale.[35]

28. See Moore v. Moore, 544 S.W.2d 279 (Mo.App.1976); Peterson v. Kansas City Life Insurance Co., 339 Mo. 700, 98 S.W.2d 770 (1936); Annot. 108 A.L.R. 592, 594.

29. Peterson v. Kansas City Life Insurance Co., 339 Mo. 700, 98 S.W.2d 770 (1936).

30. See Annot., 108 A.L.R. 592.

31. See Spires v. Lawless, 493 S.W.2d 65, 71–72 (Mo.App.1973).

32. See e.g., Burnett v. Manufacturer's Hanover Trust Co., 593 S.W.2d 755 (Tex. Civ.App.1979), error refused n.r.e.

33. See text at notes 14–15 supra.

34. University Savings Association v. Springwoods Shopping Center, 644 S.W.2d 705 (Tex.1982).

35. See Danvers Savings Bank v. Hammer, 122 N.H. 1, 440 A.2d 435 (1982); Munger v. Moore, 11 Cal.App.3d 1, 89 Cal.Rptr. 323 (1970); Adkison v. Hannah, 475 S.W.2d 39, 43 (Mo.1972). Cf. Burnett v. Manufacturer's Hanover Trust Co., 593 S.W.2d 755, 756 (Tex.Civ.App.1979), error refused n.r.e. See generally, 97 A.L.R. 1059.

Other courts, using slightly different terminology to state the same rule, refer to the measure of damages as the value of the mortgagor's equity in the property at the time of the foreclosure sale.[36] There can be situations where this rule undercompensates the mortgagor. Suppose, for example, that there are three mortgages on Blackacre, a first for $10,000, a second for $5,000 and a third for $3,000. Suppose further the second is wrongfully foreclosed and the property is purchased at the sale for $5,000, the amount of the mortgage debt. The fair market value of Blackacre at the time of sale was $20,000. By subtracting the aggregate amount of liens from $20,000, the mortgagor's recovery would be $2,000, her equity in the real estate. However, if she is personally liable on the third mortgage debt, she is still worse off than if there had been no wrongful foreclosure because the third mortgagee, who can no longer look to Blackacre to satisfy the $3,000 debt, will now be more likely to attempt to recover it from the mortgagor's other assets. Perhaps a better approach in such a situation would be to subtract from the fair market value only the amount of the senior lien and the mortgage that was wrongfully foreclosed. Under such an approach, the mortgagor would recover $5,000. This recovery will, however, not overcompensate the mortgagor because, after paying off the third mortgage, she will retain $2,000, the amount of her equity that was lost because of the wrongful foreclosure.

Moreover, it could be argued that the mortgagor should have the option, at least where the mortgagee was the foreclosure purchaser or a subsequent grantee, of valuing the land either as of the date of sale or the date of the damages action. To apply the normal rule, in view of the substantial inflation of the past two decades, would permit the foreclosing mortgagee, a wrongdoer, to gain the benefit of the appreciation of land value between the sale date and the damages action. In the rather unlikely event that the land goes down in value, the mortgagor would have been unable to protect himself by selling the land that was then in the hands of the wrongdoer. Where the damage action is against the trustee, it probably makes sense to value the land as of the sale date, at least where the trustee has not benefitted from being an owner of the land.

Where the junior lienor is bringing the damages action for wrongful foreclosure, the measure of damages is the difference between the market value of the real estate and the aggregate value of the senior liens thereon as of the date of foreclosure.[37] However, in no event may the junior lienor recover more than the value of his lien.[38]

36. See, e.g., Guay v. Brotherhood Building Association, 87 N.H. 216, 177 A. 409 (1935). The damages would presumably be further reduced by any sale surplus which had been paid to the mortgagor.

37. See Munger v. Moore, 11 Cal.App. 3d 1, 89 Cal.Rptr. 323, n. 6 (1970); Howe v.

City Title Insurance Co., 255 Cal.App.2d 85, 63 Cal.Rptr. 119 (1967). Stephans v. Herman, 225 Cal.App.2d 671, 37 Cal.Rptr. 746 (1964).

38. Id.

Suppose that a defect renders the foreclosure sale void or, alternatively, that it is only voidable but the purchaser or grantee was not a bona fide purchaser. Should the mortgagor's only remedy be a suit to set aside the sale or should he, alternatively, have the option to bring a suit for damages for wrongful foreclosure? Some courts take the view that "to recover damages at law it is necessary to show that the land went to an innocent holder so that the plaintiff's interest in it was lost." [39] In other words, under this view, the damages remedy is available only when the suit to set aside is not. Most courts, however, allow the mortgagor to pursue the damages remedy whether or not the land is still available to him.[40] Damages are allowed on "the theory that the wrong committed somewhat resembles that of a conversion of personal property. Conversion of personal property is a tort growing out of the unlawful interference with possession giving the owner a cause of action against the wrongdoer even though the title to the property did not pass." [41] Even if the defective foreclosure sale was void, and not merely voidable, the mortgagor may "elect to let the sale stand and recover at law for damages" because he will then be "forever barred from attacking the trustee's deed." [42] The majority view seems preferable because the mere right to set aside the sale, without the damages alternative, in some instances fails to give adequate protection to the mortgagor. For example, if the real estate goes down in value after the defective foreclosure, "a right simply to set aside the sale does not restore to the debtor what he has lost." [43] After all, had the wrongful foreclosure not taken place, the mortgagor could possibly have sold the property to prevent further loss from a drop in market value.

Damage recoveries may not always be limited to the measure of damages or the theories discussed above. Occasionally, for example, damages may be recoverable ancillary or incidental either to an action to set aside a defective sale or to an action to recover damages for the loss of the mortgagor's equity. This should be the case where the mortgagor has lost possession because of a wrongful foreclosure and has been forced to pay higher rental costs for comparable housing. While the case law is sparse and inconclusive,[44] he may also be able to recover for mental distress and suffering associated with wrongfully being deprived of his house or other property. Where the conduct of the

39. Bowen v. Bankers Life Co., 185 Minn. 35, 239 N.W. 774 (1935). Cf. Gonzales v. Gem Properties, Inc., 37 Cal.App.3d 1029, 112 Cal.Rptr. 884 (1974).

40. See, e.g., Rogers v. Barnes, 169 Mass. 179, 47 N.E. 602 (1897); Stansberry v. McDowell, 186 S.W. 757 (Mo.App.1916); Chandler v. Cleveland Savings and Loan Association, 24 N.C.App. 455, 211 S.E.2d 484 (1975); Owens v. Grimes, 539 S.W.2d 387 (Tex.Civ.App.1976) refused n.r.e.; National Life Insurance Co. v. Silverman, 454 F.2d 899 (D.C.Cir.1971). Cf. Parker v. Sheldon, 47 N.C.App. 493, 267 S.E.2d 403

(1980), review denied 301 N.C. 236, 283 S.E.2d 133 (1980). See generally, 97 A.L.R. 1059.

41. Owens v. Grimes, 539 S.W.2d 387, 390 (Tex.Civ.App.1976).

42. Id. at 390.

43. National Life Insurance Co. v. Silverman, 454 F.2d 899, 918 (D.C.Cir. 1971).

44. See Phillips v. Latham, 523 S.W.2d 19 (Tex.Civ.App.1975). Compare Jarchow v. Transamerica Title Insurance Co., 48 Cal.App.3d 917, 122 Cal.Rptr. 470 (1975).

mortgagee or trustee is wilful or wanton, punitive damages may be recoverable.[45] Moreover, there is some authority for damages recovery by parties other than the mortgagor or junior lienors. One California Court of Appeals decision is interesting in this regard.[46] There prospective third party bidders sued the beneficiary under a deed of trust and certain employees of the corporate trustee for damages for deceit based on allegations that the beneficiary and other defendants conspired to make sure that the beneficiary purchased and mortgaged property at the trustee's sale without competition. It was alleged that after an advertisement of sale was published, the sale was repeatedly postponed and that at the time of the actual sale, a private trustee was substituted for the corporate trustee, and the land was secretly sold for below fair market value. While the court held that the prospective bidders could not recover anticipated profits for resale of the land or maintain an action to enforce the trustee's fiduciary duty to the trustor, it determined that the allegations stated a cause of action for deceit and that recovery was permissible for time and effort expended in reliance on defendants' misrepresentations. Moreover, punitive damages were held to be recoverable.

 WESTLAW REFERENCES

(defect*** /5 power) injunct*** enjoin*** /s sale sold sell*** /p
     foreclos*** /p property "real estate" realty

---

§ 7.23 Constitutionality of Power of Sale Foreclosure— Introduction

In an earlier section we described in some detail the varying notice requirements of power of sale statutes and noted that rarely does such legislation provide an opportunity for a hearing prior to foreclosure sale. Recent constitutional litigation has focused on whether these notice requirements and the absence of a pre-foreclosure hearing violate the procedural due process requirements of the 14th amendment to the United States Constitution.[1] The following material analyzes these questions in some detail.

45. See Alaska Statebank v. Fairco, 674 P.2d 288 (Alaska 1983); Gilbert v. Cherry, 136 Ga.App. 417, 221 S.E.2d 472 (1975); Block v. Tobin, 45 Cal.App.3d 214, 119 Cal. Rptr. 288 (1975). National Mortgage Co. v. Williams, 357 So.2d 934 (Miss.1978); Cf. Gonzales v. Gem Properties Inc., 37 Cal. App.3d 1029, 112 Cal.Rptr. 884 (1974).

46. Block v. Tobin, 45 Cal.App.3d 214, 119 Cal.Rptr. 288 (1975).

§ 7.23

1. See Jones and Ivens, Power of Sale Foreclosure in Tennessee: A Section 1983 Trap, 51 Tenn.L.Rev. 279 (1984); Comment, The Constitutionality of Maine's Real Estate Mortgage Foreclosure Statutes, 32 Maine L.Rev. 147 (1980); Leen, Galbraith & Gant, Due Process and Deeds of Trust—Strange Bedfellows, 48 Wash.L.Rev. 763 (1973); Nelson, Deed of Trust Foreclosure Under Power of Sale—Constitutional Problems—Legislative Alternatives, 28 J.Mo.B. 428 (1972); Pedowitz, Current Developments in Summary Foreclosure, 9 Real Prop., Prob. & Tr.J. 421 (1974); Comment, The Constitutionality of California Trustees Sale, 61 Calif.L.Rev. 1282 (1973); Comment, Power of Sale Foreclosure After Fuentes, 40 U.Chi.L.Rev. 206, 217–20 (1972); Comment, Due Process Problems of Mississippi Power of Sale Foreclosure, 47 Miss.L.J. 67 (1976); Comment, Notice Requirements of the Nonjudicial Foreclosure

WESTLAW REFERENCES

(14 14th /1 amendment) "due process" constitutional*** /p
notice* hearing /p foreclos*** /p realty (real +1 estate
property)

§ 7.24 Constitutional Problems—Notice

Until recently, it had been assumed that where a mortgagor gave a power of sale in a mortgage or deed of trust, the specific level of notice required was merely a contractual or statutory consideration, not a constitutional problem. Indeed, in Scott v. Paisley [1] the United States Supreme Court stated in dictum in 1927:

> Plainly the right of one who purchases property subject to a security deed, with a statutory power of sale which must be read into the deed, is no greater than that of one who purchases property subject to a mortgage or trust deed, with a contractual power of sale. The validity of such a contractual power of sale is unquestionable. In Bell Mining Co. v. Butte Bank, 156 U.S. 470, 477, this court said: " 'There is nothing in the law of mortgages, nor in the law that covers what are sometimes designated as trust deeds in the nature of mortgages, which prevents the conferring by the grantor or mortgagor in such instrument of the power to sell the premises described therein upon default in payment of the debt secured by it, and if the sale is conducted in accordance with the terms of the power, the title to the premises granted by way of security passes to the purchaser upon its consummation by a conveyance.' In the absence of a specific provision to that effect, the holder of a mortgage or trust deed with power of sale, is not required to give notice of the exercise of the power to a subsequent purchaser or incumbrancer; and the validity of the sale is not affected by the fact that such notice is not given." [2]

Such reasoning, of course, took into account neither the impact of Mullane v. Central Hanover Bank & Trust Co. [3] nor its recent progeny, Mennonite Board of Missions v. Adams, [4] on power of sale foreclosure. That case involved the sufficiency of notice to beneficiaries of a judicial settlement of accounts by a trustee of a common trust fund established under New York banking law. The only notice given the beneficiaries of the proceeding was publication in a local newspaper in strict compliance with the statutory requirements. The Supreme Court held that the type of notice used must be "reasonably calculated * * * to

---

Sale, 51 N.C.L.Rev. 1110 (1973). Note, Power of Sale Foreclosure in Tennessee, 8 Mem.St.L.Rev. 871 (1978).

§ 7.24

1. 271 U.S. 632, 46 S.Ct. 591, 70 L.Ed. 1123 (1927).

2. Id. at 635, 46 S.Ct. at 592.

3. 339 U.S. 306, 70 S.Ct. 652, 94 L.Ed. 865 (1950).

4. 462 U.S. 791, 103 S.Ct. 2706, 77 L.Ed. 2d 180 (1983). For a thorough analysis, see Note, 49 Mo.L.Rev. 385 (1984).

apprise interested parties ＊ ＊ ＊."[5] The Court also noted that "[w]here the names and post office addresses of those affected by a proceeding are at hand, the reasons disappear for resort to means less likely than the mails to apprise them of its pendency."[6] In *Mennonite* the Supreme Court relied on *Mullane* in holding that notice by publication and posting to a mortgagee of property being sold for nonpayment of real estate taxes violated the notice requirements of the due process clause of the 14th Amendment. The Court emphasized that "when the mortgagee is identified in a mortgage that is publicly recorded, constructive notice by publication must be supplemented by notice mailed to the mortgagee's last known available address, or by personal service. But unless the mortgage is not reasonably identifiable, constructive notice alone does not satisfy the mandate of *Mullane*."[7]

Assuming that the requisite state action required by the 14th Amendment is present, and absent a valid waiver by the affected parties of constitutional notice rights, it is difficult to escape the conclusion that the notice provisions of many state power of sale statutes are unconstitutional. Certainly those that require only notice to owners by publication and posting must fail to pass constitutional muster. Indeed, several lower federal courts have so concluded.[8] In *Ricker v. United States*[9] the Farmers Home Administration (FmHA), under a Maine nonjudicial foreclosure statute,[10] foreclosed a mortgage securing a direct loan that it had made to the mortgagors. After the proceedings were completed and the FmHA conveyed the land to a subsequent purchaser, the mortgagors sued in federal court to nullify the sale, in part on the theory that the Maine statute's notice requirements did not satisfy the requirements of the due process clause of the fifth amendment. The notice required by statute, and that actually provided, was published notice for three successive weeks. The mortgagors did not see the notices but heard about the proceedings through rumors and other second-hand sources. The court held that the published notice "plainly failed to meet" the *Mullane* standards and emphasized that published notice will not suffice constitutionally where a party's name and address are known or are very easily ascertained.[11] Similarly, in Turner v. Blackburn[12] a three-judge federal court invali-

---

5. Mullane supra note 3 at 314, 70 S.Ct. at 657.

6. Id. at 318. See also, Schroeder v. City of New York, 371 U.S. 208, 83 S.Ct. 279, 9 L.Ed.2d 255 (1962) (advertisement insufficient in condemnation); Walker v. City of Hutchinson, 352 U.S. 112, 77 S.Ct. 200, 1 L.Ed.2d 178 (1956) (advertisement insufficient in condemnation).

7. Mennonite Board of Missions v. Adams, 462 U.S. 791, 103 S.Ct. 2706, 2711, 77 L.Ed.2d 180 (1983).

8. See Rau v. Cavenaugh, 500 F.Supp. 204 (D.S.D.1980); Ricker v. United States, 417 F.Supp. 133 (D.Me.1976); Roberts v. Cameron–Brown Co., 410 F.Supp. 988 (S.D. Ga.1975); Turner v. Blackburn, 389 F.Supp. 1250 (W.D.N.C.1975). See also Law v. United States, 366 F.Supp. 1233 (N.D.Ga.1973). Cf., Matter of Strawberry Commons Apartment Owners Association 1, 356 N.W.2d 401 (Minn.App.1984). Contra: Federal Deposit Insurance Corp. v. Morrison, 747 F.2d 610 (11th Cir.1984).

9. 417 F.Supp. 133 (D.Me.1976).

10. 14 Me.Rev.Stat. §§ 6203–6204.

11. 417 F.Supp. at 138.

12. 389 F.Supp. 1250 (W.D.N.C.1975).

dated a North Carolina power of sale statute that provided for notice only by newspaper publication and posting. The court stated: "To propose to a homeowner that he trek to the courthouse or spend 20 cents to examine fine-print legal notices, *daily* for the duration of a twenty-year mortgage, as his sole protection against summary eviction, seems to us to offer him nothing of value." [13] Finally, in Federal Deposit Insurance Corporation v. Morrison,[14] a federal district court invalidated a power of sale foreclosure conducted under Alabama legislation that afforded a mortgagor notice by publication only. The court emphasized that if notice by publication is constitutionally deficient with respect to a mortgagee, as in *Mennonite*, it "a fortiori" is as to a mortgagor. According to the court, "under *Mennonite* the notice published * * * simply was not 'such as one desirous of actually informing the [mortgagor] might reasonably adopt to accomplish it.' " [15] This thoughtful opinion was, however, reversed by the Eleventh Circuit on the bizarre ground that foreclosure "did not deprive [the mortgagor] of his equity of redemption, but only terminated it," and hence that no taking had occurred.[16]

Statutes that fail to provide for notice by mail or personal service to junior lienors are probably also defective. While courts have yet to deal with this issue, the message of *Mennonite* seems unmistakable. If notice by publication or posting is insufficient for mortgagees whose liens face destruction by the foreclosure of a real estate tax lien, so to it must be for those whose liens are jeopardized by senior mortgage foreclosure. It could, of course, be argued that such parties tend to be sophisticated commercial lenders able to keep themselves informed of the status of the senior mortgage. However, as the *Mennonite* decision stressed, "a mortgage need not involve a complex commercial transaction among knowledgeable parties, and it may well be the least sophisticated creditor whose security interest is threatened by a tax sale." [17] Indeed, many lienors are persons who have financed part of the sale price of their homes by taking purchase money junior mortgages. In the last analysis, however, the relative sophistication of the parties is probably irrelevant. To use the language of the Supreme Court in this regard, "personal service or mailed notice is required even though sophisticated creditors have means at their disposal to discover whether property taxes have not been paid and whether tax sale proceedings are therefore likely to be initiated. * * * [A] party's ability to take steps to safeguard its interests does not relieve the State of its constitutional obligation." [18]

13. Id. at 1258 (emphasis in original).

14. 568 F.Supp. 1240 (N.D.Ala.1983), order reversed 747 F.2d 610 (11th Cir.1984).

15. Id. at 1244.

16. Federal Deposit Insurance Corporation v. Morrison, 747 F.2d 610 (11th Cir. 1984).

17. Mennonite Board of Missions v. Adams, 462 U.S. 791, 103 S.Ct. 2706, 2714, 77 L.Ed.2d 180 (1983).

18. Id. at 103 S.Ct. 2714.

The foregoing considerations may also doom those statutes that provide for notice by mail or personal service both for the mortgagor and the owner, but for others only if they previously have recorded a request to receive it. Proponents of such legislation would, of course, argue that the relative sophistication of junior lienors as a *class* at least should be recognized in this context; after all, such parties can assure themselves of a constitutional form of notice merely by requesting it. On the other hand, it is also inescapable that under such legislation an interest party could be wiped out without being provided an notice "reasonably calculated to provide actual notice." More important, however, the *Mennonite* majority not only "fashioned its rule from the view of the least sophisticated creditor[s]",[19] it also clearly refused to dilute 14th Amendment notice protections for their more sophisticated and powerful counterparts. Probably the only notice provisions that are clearly constitutional are those that closely approximate the notice provided to interested parties under judicial foreclosure: at least notice by mail to all parties who have a record interest in the foreclosed property junior to the mortgage being foreclosed. In the last analysis perhaps a finding of constitutionality is justified only as to this latter type of notice provision; whatever the arguments in favor of more limited notice, the cost and time involved in searching the title for those who have a record interest subsequent to the mortgage being foreclosed are minor.

The question remains to what extent a foreclosing mortgagee may remedy the problem of a constitutionally defective notice provision by providing more extensive notice to interested parties than the statute requires. Logically, if such notice was provided to all interested parties, no person would have standing to challenge the foreclosure and the statute because no one would have suffered injury.[20] Several decisions either hold or suggest that constitutional notice requirements were satisfied where the mortgagee supplied greater notice to the mortgagor than the power of sale statute required.[21] Moreover, the court in Ricker v. United States [22] emphasized the fact that the mortgagee did not attempt to notify the mortgagor other than by complying with the statutory requirement. The court implied that had the mortgagee made an effort to give actual notice, the foreclosure would not have been constitutionally defective on notice grounds.

19. Note, 49 Mo.L.Rev. 385, 393 (1984).

20. See Warth v. Seldin, 422 U.S. 490, 95 S.Ct. 2197, 45 L.Ed.2d 343 (1975); C. Wright A. Miller & E. Cooper, Federal Practice and Procedure § 3531 (1975).

21. See e.g., Laughlin v. Walters, 718 F.2d 513 (1st Cir.1983); United States v. Ford, 551 F.Supp. 1101 (N.D.Miss.1982); Fitzgerald v. Cleland, 498 F.Supp. 341 (D.Me.1980), affirmed in part, vacated in part 650 F.2d 360 (1st Cir.1981); United States v. White, 429 F.Supp. 1245 (N.D. Miss.1977). Cf. Lehner v. United States, 685 F.2d 1187 (9th Cir.1982), certiorari denied 460 U.S. 1039, 103 S.Ct. 1431, 75 L.Ed. 2d 790 (1983). Cf. Johnson v. United States Department of Agriculture, 734 F.2d 774, 782 (11th Cir.1984).

22. 417 F.Supp. 133 (D.Me.1976), order supplemented 434 F.Supp. 1251 (D.Me. 1976).

Notwithstanding those cases, because of the United States Supreme Court's decision in Wuchter v. Pizzutti,[23] there is still doubt that a foreclosing mortgagee has the ability to conduct a constitutional power of sale foreclosure by supplying necessary notice not required by the applicable statute. In *Wuchter* the Supreme Court held that a nonresident motorist service of process statute that required only service on the secretary of state violated the fourteenth amendment due process clause even though the secretary of state in that case actually mailed notice to the nonresident defendant. According to the Court, such service, "[n]ot having been directed by the statute * * * cannot, therefore, supply constitutional validity to the statute or the service under it." [24] Such reasoning seems unsound because no one was injured as a result of the statutory notice provision. Indeed, the Restatement of Judgments, Second, suggests that the supplying of actual notice should, notwithstanding the deficiency of the statutory language, satisfy due process requirements.[25] Nevertheless, *Wuchter* should make mortgagees cautious as to their ability to resurrect invalid foreclosure statutes through their own resources. However, such resurrection attempts certainly can do no harm and, as the power of sale notice decisions referred to in the foregoing paragraph suggest, they may actually help to insulate the foreclosures, if not the underlying statutes, from constitutional challenge.

 WESTLAW REFERENCES
mullane ricker mennonite wuchter /p notice /p foreclos***

§ 7.25 Constitutional Problems—Hearing

Independently of the constitutionality of notice provisions, power of sale statutes frequently have been attacked on the ground that the due process clause of the fourteenth amendment requires the opportunity for a hearing before a person may be deprived of a significant property interest. This attack is centered on Sniadach v. Family Finance Corp.[1] and Fuentes v. Shevin.[2] In *Sniadach* the Supreme Court held that, except in exceptional circumstances, prejudgment garnishment without provision for a judicial hearing prior to the garnishment violated the due process clause of the fourteenth amendment. In *Fuentes*, a 4–3 decision, the Court struck down certain state replevin statutes because they did not provide for an opportunity to be heard before chattels were

23. 276 U.S. 13, 48 S.Ct. 259, 72 L.Ed. 446 (1928).

24. Id. at 24, 48 S.Ct. at 270, 72 L.Ed. at 457.

25. Restatement (Second) of Judgments § 2, comment d (1980). For further consideration of whether *Wuchter* retains it full vitality, see Jones and Ivens, Power of Sale Foreclosure in Tennessee: A Section 1983 Trap, 51 Tenn.L.Rev. 279, 316–317 (1984).

Cf. Fitzgerald v. Cleland, 498 F.Supp. 341, 350 n. 10 (D.Me.1980), affirmed in part, vacated in part 650 F.2d 360 (1st Cir.1981).

§ 7.25

1. 395 U.S. 337, 89 S.Ct. 1820, 23 L.Ed. 2d 349 (1969).

2. 407 U.S. 67, 92 S.Ct. 1983, 32 L.Ed.2d 556 (1972), rehearing denied 409 U.S. 902, 93 S.Ct. 177, 34 L.Ed.2d 165 (1972).

taken from the possessor, even on a temporary basis, pending a trial on the merits. At least three principles were established in *Fuentes*:

1. Procedural due process requires notice and an opportunity for a hearing before the state authorizes its agents, on the application of another, to seize property in the possession of a third person. A bond requirement is not a sufficient substitute for a hearing.

2. The debtors, who had already made substantial payments under installment contracts, had a sufficient property interest to invoke fourteenth amendment protection even though they lacked full title to the goods.

3. The hearing requirement is applicable whether or not the items to be seized are "necessities."

Based on *Fuentes,* a strong argument may be made that power of sale foreclosure statutes which do not provide the opportunity for a hearing prior to the foreclosure sale violate the due process hearing requirement of the fourteenth amendment. If *Fuentes* requires some type of hearing before chattel security may be seized even temporarily, surely it may be argued that the due process clause does not permit the *permanent* taking of real estate security by passage of title with no opportunity for a hearing *at all.* Several courts that have reached the hearing issue directly have utilized *Fuentes* to invalidate power of sale provisions.[3] In Turner v. Blackburn,[4] which invalidated the North Carolina power of sale statute, the three-judge federal court held, based on *Fuentes,* that a hearing prior to foreclosure and sale is essential. At a minimum, due process "requires the trustee to make an initial showing before the clerk or similar neutral official that the mortgagor is in default under the obligation; the mortgagor must of course be afforded the opportunity to rebut and defend the charges."[5] In Ricker v. United States[6] the government argued that in the context of a Maine nonjudicial mortgage foreclosure the opportunity to be heard would be "mere surplusage" because the issues were "open and shut": the existence of an overdue debt and a valid mortgage. The federal district court rejected this argument on two grounds. First, the simplicity of issues does not necessarily obviate the constitutional necessity for a hearing. Second, in the case at hand the mortgagors had also challenged the validity of the government's decision to foreclose on the theory that the mortgage notes lacked consideration. The court con-

3. See Ricker v. United States, 417 F.Supp. 133 (D.Me.1976); Turner v. Blackburn, 389 F.Supp. 1250 (W.D.N.C.1975); Garner v. Tri-State Development Co., 382 F.Supp. 377 (E.D.Mich.1974); Northrip v. Federal National Mortgage Association, 372 F.Supp. 594 (E.D.Mich.1974), reversed on other grounds 527 F.2d 23 (6th Cir. 1975); Valley Development at Vail v. Warder, 557 P.2d 1180 (Colo.1976). Cf. Johnson v. United States Department of Agriculture, 734 F.2d 774 (11th Cir.1984) (substantial probability *Fuentes* violated). Contra, Guidarelli v. Lazaretti, 233 N.W.2d 890 (Minn.1975).

4. 389 F.Supp. 1250 (W.D.N.C.1975).

5. Id. at 1259.

6. 417 F.Supp. 133 (D.Me.1976).

cluded that, at a minimum, fifth amendment due process requires "a hearing at which [mortgagors] could challenge both the legal right of the [mortgagee] to foreclose and the propriety of the decision to do so." [7]

Some temporary concern existed that a subsequent Supreme Court decision had deprived *Fuentes* of its strength. In Mitchell v. W. T. Grant Co.[8] the Supreme Court upheld the constitutionality of a Louisiana sequestration statute which required the secured creditor to come before a judge who, based on a verified complaint delineating the specific facts supporting the claim, could then issue a writ of sequestration. There was no right to a hearing prior to the seizure of the chattel, but the procedure did provide for an immediate right to a hearing thereafter and dissolution of the writ if the plaintiff failed to establish adequate grounds for its issuance. In a dissenting opinion, Justice Stewart concluded that *Mitchell,* in effect, had overruled the *Fuentes* decision.[9] However, the subsequent decision in North Georgia Finishing, Inc. v. Di-Chem, Inc.[10] made it clear that Justice Stewart's prediction of *Fuentes'* demise was premature. The Court struck down a Georgia prejudgment garnishment statute that did not provide for a hearing prior to the imposition of the garnishment remedy. The Court distinguished *Mitchell* by noting that, unlike the Louisiana procedure, the garnishment writ was issued by a clerk, not a judge, upon an affidavit stating only conclusory and non-specific supporting grounds for the garnishment.[11] Moreover, the Court noted that, unlike *Mitchell,* there was no opportunity under the Georgia statute for an early post-seizure hearing to demonstrate at least probable cause for the garnishment.[12]

The significance of the foregoing for the power of sale foreclosure hearing problem is two-fold. First, the *North Georgia* decision sets to rest the argument that *Fuentes* has been overruled and therefore has no effect on power of sale real estate foreclosure. Second, in view of the fact that *Fuentes* is still good law, the impact of the *Mitchell* case really does not weaken the lower federal court cases considered earlier that invalidate the power of sale statutes on *Fuentes* hearing grounds.[13] The Louisiana statute was upheld in *Mitchell* in large measure because the statute guaranteed the right to an early post-seizure hearing. Power of sale foreclosure statutes, on the other hand, usually make no provision for a hearing at *any* time, *before or after* the *final* deprivation of the mortgagor's real estate. Thus some type of hearing prior to the foreclosure sale is probably required. Indeed, in Garner v. Tri-State Development Co.,[14] a post-*Mitchell* but pre-*North Georgia* case, the federal trial court held that the Michigan power of sale statute violated

---

7. Id. at 139.

8. 416 U.S. 600, 94 S.Ct. 1895, 40 L.Ed. 2d 406 (1974).

9. Id. at 629–36, 94 S.Ct. at 1910–14.

10. 419 U.S. 601, 95 S.Ct. 719, 42 L.Ed. 2d 751 (1975).

11. Id. at 606–07, 95 S.Ct. at 722–23.

12. Id.

13. See text accompanying notes 1–5 supra.

14. 382 F.Supp. 377 (E.D.Mich.1974).

the fourteenth amendment due process clause because no opportunity for a hearing was provided *at all*. The *Garner* court focused on the fact that in *Mitchell* a judge issued the writ of sequestration and, more importantly, that there was a right to a hearing immediately after the seizure. Thus, the court concluded: "Evaluated by these criteria the foreclosure by advertisement method now before the court fails to meet due process requirements. The procedure used has no provision for a hearing before or immediately after the seizure." [15]

It has been argued that there is in fact an opportunity for a hearing under most power of sale statutes because a mortgagor has the right, based on either common law or statute,[16] to bring suit to enjoin the foreclosure sale. In many jurisdictions this is a common practice and is a primary vehicle for developing the law of mortgages in the power of sale context.[17] While several courts have found this argument persuasive,[18] others have rejected it.[19] To equate the foregoing procedure with the constitutional right to a hearing required by *Fuentes* seems questionable for several reasons. First, what *Fuentes* seems to be saying is that the opportunity for a hearing must be an integral part of any statutory procedure that can be used to deprive a person of a property interest. The mortgagor's ability to bring a separate injunction suit normally exists independently of any power of sale statute. To maintain that the ability to bring such an injunction suit satisfies the constitutional hearing requirement would be analogous to contending that a 42 U.S.C. section 1983 injunction suit filed by a tenured college professor to prevent his termination would be a constitutionally permissible substitute for a hearing requirement as an integral part of the college's termination procedure.[20] One court has aptly characterized the injunction suit as a form of "self-help" that does not meet the requirements of either *Fuentes* or *Mitchell*.[21] Second, where the remedy sought is a temporary injunction, the mortgagor often must post an injunction bond.[22] Such a requirement seems to condition unfairly the mortgagor's right to a hearing on his ability to pay. It is true, of course, that a mortgagor could avoid the bond requirement in many jurisdictions by simply bringing an action for a permanent injunction.

15. Id. at 380. Accord, Roberts v. Cameron-Brown Co., 410 F.Supp. 988 (S.D.Ga. 1975).

16. See e.g., West's Rev.Code Wash. Ann. 61.24.130.

17. See § 7.22 supra; Nelson, Deed of Trust Foreclosure Under Power of Sale—Constitutional Problems—Legislative Alternatives, 28 J.Mo.Bar 428, 432 (1972).

18. See Laughlin v. Walters, 718 F.2d 513 (1st Cir.1983); Fitzgerald v. Cleland, 650 F.2d 360 (1st Cir.1981); Young v. Ridley, 309 F.Supp. 1308 (D.D.C.1970).

19. See, e.g., Turner v. Blackburn, 389 F.Supp. 1250 (W.D.N.C.1975); Northrip v. Federal National Mortgage Association, 372 F.Supp. 594 (E.D.Mich.1974), reversed on other grounds 527 F.2d 23 (6th Cir. 1975).

20. See Perry v. Sindermann, 408 U.S. 593, 92 S.Ct. 2694, 33 L.Ed.2d 570 (1972).

21. Garner v. Tri-State Development Co., 382 F.Supp. 377, 380 (E.D.Mich.1974).

22. D. Dobbs, Remedies § 2.10 (1973); Dobbs, Should Security Be Required As A Pre-Condition To Provisional Injunctive Relief?, 52 N.C.L.Rev. 1091 (1974); Leavell, Love and Nelson, Equitable Remedies and Restitution 44–57 (3rd Ed.1980).

However, although such an action deters many mortgagees from proceeding with the sale, it does not guarantee such a result. Third, for the mortgagor to bring a separate injunction suit inevitably will require the services of a lawyer. On the other hand, even an impecunious mortgagor at least would be able to answer a summons and appear to state his case without counsel at a hearing required as part of a statutory procedure.

The hearing probably need not be judicial.[23] For example, as the *Turner* court indicated, a hearing before a "clerk or a similar neutral official" will suffice.[24] Moreover, in United States v. Ford,[25] a federal district court held that a federal agency administrative hearing procedure can be used to supplement state power of sale legislation that itself fails to satisfy due process hearing requirements. In that case, the administrative hearing was the Farmers Home Administration (FmHA) "Appeal Procedure," the current version of which affords an administrative hearing and review to any "applicant for FmHA assistance or an FmHA borrower or grantee." [26]

Intra-agency hearing procedures, however, vary drastically. For example, in the FmHA situation, detailed regulations govern the hearing officer, the nature of the hearing and appeal procedure.[27] In stark contrast, HUD regulations issued pursuant to the Multifamily Foreclosure Act of 1981 treat the hearing issue almost as an afterthought. Such regulations state simply that "HUD will provide to the mortgagor [and current owner] an opportunity informally to present reasons why the mortgage should be foreclosed." [28] Interestingly, the FmHA hearing officer typically will be a higher ranking administrative official in that agency.[29] Some question may be raised as to whether such a person is suitably "neutral". Indeed, the United States Court of Appeals for the Eleventh Circuit,[30] in reversing a trial court refusal to issue preliminary injunctive relief against FmHA power of sale foreclosure in Alabama, stated: "A fair hearing requires an impartial arbiter. We have serious reservations about the neutrality of the hearing officers. The regulations establish that the hearing officer is a nearby district director. On its face, the regulation appears less than neutral. The nearby director will be evaluating a decision to foreclose made by a peer and already approved by his boss, the state director. The Supreme Court [31] has stated that hearing officers are presumed to be unbiased

23. See United States v. Ford, 551 F.Supp. 1101 (N.D.Miss.1982); Fitzgerald v. Cleland, 498 F.Supp. 341, 346 (D.Me. 1980), affirmed in part, vacated in part 650 F.2d 360 (1st Cir.1981); Turner v. Blackburn, 389 F.Supp. 1250 (W.D.N.C.1975).

24. Turner v. Blackburn, 389 F.Supp. 1250, 1259 (W.D.N.C.1975).

25. 551 F.Supp. 1101 (N.D.Miss.1982).

26. 7 CFR § 1900.51–.60.

27. 7 CFR 1900.56–.60.

28. 24 CFR 27.5(b).

29. See 7 CFR 1900, Exhibit D to Subpart B.

30. Johnson v. United States Department of Agriculture, 734 F.2d 774 (11th Cir.1984).

31. Schweiker v. McClure, 456 U.S. 188, 195, 102 S.Ct. 1665, 1669, 72 L.Ed.2d 1 (1982).

until a conflict of interest or other specific reason for disqualification is shown. It is plaintiff's burden of proof to show a conflict of interest in the hearing officers. On the surface, the plaintiffs have shown a substantial likelihood that a conflict may exist that would impinge the hearing officer's impartiality." [32]

Both the FmHA and HUD procedures, however, may be constitutionally deficient for a more basic reason. Neither procedure affords hearing rights to junior lienors or, for that matter, to other holders of subordinate interests who are not mortgagors or owners. If our earlier analysis of the notice rights of junior interests has any meaning,[33] it seems unlikely that the property interests of such parties are significant enough to require adequate notice of foreclosure, but not of such importance as to create a right to a hearing as well.

WESTLAW REFERENCES
sniadach fuentes turner ricker mitchell "georgia finishing" di-chem
garner /p hearing /p foreclos*** & (14 14th /1
amendment) "due process"

§ 7.26 Constitutional Problems—Waiver

Even if a power of sale foreclosure statute is constitutionally deficient as to notice and hearing, such rights, in theory at least, are capable of being waived. In this connection, several cases are important. A few weeks prior to *Fuentes,* the United States Supreme Court in D. H. Overmyer v. Frick Co.[1] and Swarb v. Lennox[2] rejected a fourteenth amendment due process argument and sustained the constitutionality of certain state statutes authorizing summary entry of judgment based on confession of judgment clauses contained in promissory notes. These cases stand for the proposition that "under [the] appropriate circumstances, a cognovit debtor may be held effectively and legally to have waived those rights he would possess if the document he signed had contained no cognovit provision."[3] In *Fuentes* itself, the Court recognized that waiver was possible, but rejected it in that case. The *Fuentes* contract provided that "in the event of default of any payment or payments, Seller at its option may take back the merchandise."[4] Other contracts provided that the seller "may retake" or "repossess" the merchandise in the event of a "default in any payment."[5] These "waivers" were ineffectual for several reasons: the contracts did not provide specifically for a waiver of constitutional rights nor did they specify how or through what process "the seller could take back the goods"; there was a lack of awareness by the

32. Johnson, supra note 30 at 782–783.

33. See § 7.24 supra.

§ 7.26

1. 405 U.S. 174, 92 S.Ct. 775, 31 L.Ed.2d 124 (1972).

2. 405 U.S. 191, 92 S.Ct. 767, 31 L.Ed.2d 138 (1972), rehearing denied 405 U.S. 1049, 92 S.Ct. 1303, 31 L.Ed.2d 592 (1972).

3. Id. at 200, 92 S.Ct. at 772.

4. 407 U.S. at 94, 92 S.Ct. at 2001.

5. Id.

parties of the significance of the waiver; and there was no bargaining over contractual terms between parties who were equal in bargaining position.[6]

Two pre-*Fuentes* cases determined that the presence of a power of sale in the mortgage or deed of trust constituted the mortgagor's waiver of notice and hearing rights,[7] but subsequent decisions have rejected such an approach.[8] In Turner v. Blackburn, for example, the court emphasized that there was a presumption against waiver. In rejecting waiver, the *Turner* court pointed out that there was no waiver of specific constitutional rights, that the purported waiver language was in fine print, and that there was no evidence that the mortgagor was made aware of the significance of that language. Other courts have stressed that merely consenting to foreclosure pursuant to state law is not a sufficient substitute for a delineation of the specific constitutional rights waived.[9] Moreover, in Ricker v. United States,[10] the court noted that even if the waiver of specific rights had been spelled out, the government-mortgagee did not show that the mortgagors "were actually aware or made aware of the fine print now relied on as a waiver of constitutional rights." [11] The court also emphasized that when the mortgage was executed the mortgagors were elderly, ill-educated, and without the services of an attorney.[12] Finally, one court, in Rau v. Cavenaugh,[13] focused not only on the mortgagors' probable inability to comprehend a waiver of constitutional rights, but it also emphasized bargaining inequality: [T]here was no equality of bargaining position between the parties. All of the terms and conditions of the transaction were dictated by [mortgagee]. Consequently, this transaction has assumed the color of a contract of adhesion. * * * [W]e must conclude that [mortgagor] did not effectively waiver her constitutional rights to due process.[14]

The foregoing illustrates that the waiver concept will not be a practical solution to the constitutional problems of power of sale foreclosure.[15] If a valid waiver depended only upon ensuring that the

---

6. Id. at 95–96, 92 S.Ct. at 2002.

7. See Young v. Ridley, 309 F.Supp. 1308 (D.D.C.1970); Huggins v. Dement, 13 N.C.App. 673, 187 S.E.2d 412, appeal dismissed 281 N.C. 314, 188 S.E.2d 898 (1972) certiorari denied 409 U.S. 1071, 93 S.Ct. 677, 34 L.Ed.2d 659 (1972).

8. Rau v. Cavenaugh, 500 F.Supp. 204 (D.S.D.1980); United States v. White, 429 F.Supp. 1245 (N.D.Miss.1977); Ricker v. United States, 417 F.Supp. 133 (D.Me. 1976); Turner v. Blackburn, 389 F.Supp. 1250 (W.D.N.C.1975); Garner v. Tri-State Development Co., 382 F.Supp. 377 (E.D. Mich.1974); Law v. United States, 366 F.Supp. 1233 (N.D.Ga.1973).

9. 389 F.Supp. 1250 (W.D.N.C.1975).

Ricker v. United States, 417 F.Supp. 133 (D.Me.1976); Northrip v. Federal National Mortgage Association, 372 F.Supp. 594 (E.D.Mich.1974), reversed on other grounds 527 F.2d 23 (6th Cir.1975).

10. 417 F.Supp. 133 (D.Me.1976).

11. Id. at 139.

12. Id. at 139–40. See United States v. White, 429 F.Supp. 1245 (N.D.Miss.1977).

13. 500 F.Supp. 204 (D.S.D.1980).

14. Id. at 208. See also, Johnson v. United States Department of Agriculture, 734 F.2d 774, 783–784 (11th Cir.1984).

15. Jones and Ivens, Power of Sale Foreclosure in Tennessee: A Section 1983 Trap, 51 Tenn.L.Rev. 279, 315–316 (1984).

waived rights are specified and the mortgagor is aware that he is waiving those rights, a carefully drafted document probably would suffice. For example, the mortgagee could have a mortgagor execute a separate recordable document in bold type that clearly specifies a waiver of constitutional rights to notice and hearing and that further contains a statement by the mortgagor that the waiver has been fully explained to him. Although even this type of document could engender later disputes as to whether the mortgagor *actually* understood the significance of the waiver, most title examiners probably would be willing to rely on such a document in approving a title derived from a power of sale foreclosure. If, on the other hand, as *Fuentes* and other cases suggest, a valid waiver depends on such factors as equality of bargaining position and similar considerations, an impossible burden is placed on the title examiner.[16] How can an examiner, evaluating a five-year-old mortgage foreclosure, determine from the record that there was equality of bargaining position? Is there ever equality of bargaining position? Would a recorded statement contemporaneous with the original mortgage certifying that such equality existed suffice? For title examiners who by nature rely primarily on the record, the waiver concept becomes an almost impossible burden and, to the extent that titles thereby become unmarketable, waiver must be considered an impractical concept.

Even assuming that title examiners could be convinced that a foolproof waiver could be developed to bind a mortgagor, it is doubtful that such a waiver would also be effective against holders of subordinate interests in the mortgaged real estate. If, in fact, there is a presumption against waiver and if a party must be made aware of what rights are being waived, how can waiver be accomplished with respect to subsequent grantees of the real estate or junior mortgagees? They, after all, are not parties to the original mortgage transaction, yet they often have a significant financial stake in the mortgaged real estate. It could be argued that such parties stake their interests on notice of the record and that they therefore implicitly consent to the terms of previously recorded documents.[17] However, it is doubtful that constitutional rights can be waived in such a manner. Moreover, whatever the likelihood that subsequent grantees and junior mortgagees will search the record prior to taking their interests in the mortgaged real estate, it is less likely that either judgment creditors or mechanics lienors will make such a search. It would, indeed, be stretching the waiver concept to conclude that these latter parties could have waived notice and hearing rights. Accordingly, since the waiver concept may well prove unworkable as a practical matter with respect to *some* parties, it probably cannot be relied upon at all.

16. Nelson, Deed of Trust Foreclosure Under Power of Sale—Constitutional Problems—Legislative Alternatives, 28 J.Mo. Bar 428 (1972).

17. Id. at 431.

WESTLAW REFERENCES
(14 14th /1 amendment) "due process" constitutional*** /p notice hearing /p foreclos*** /p waive*

§ 7.27 Constitutional Problems—State Action

The fourteenth amendment requires sufficient notice and an opportunity for a hearing; it is, however, fundamental that state action must be found before the amendment is applicable. Unless sufficient state action is found in connection with power of sale foreclosure, a court will not reach the notice or hearing issues, no matter how deficient a statute may be in those respects. Interestingly, some of the early power of sale fourteenth amendment cases resolved the constitutional issues without a consideration of state action.[1] However, the issue has become increasingly important, and the trend of the case law is clearly against finding state action.[2] This trend is significant because, as a practical matter, it means that power of sale statutes continue to provide an effective foreclosure method for nongovernmental mortgagees even where the statutes are noticeably deficient in the notice and hearing area.

At least five theories have been advanced to find state action in the power of sale foreclosures.[3] These are the "direct" state action theory, the "encouragement" theory, the governmental function theory, the judicial enforcement theory, and the "pervasiveness" theory.

Under the first theory, state action exists when state officials act directly to enforce rights arising from a state statute. *Fuentes* illustrates this theory. State action was found, albeit without analysis, because the replevin statute provided for the writ to be issued by a clerk of court and the service of the writ and seizure of the property to be carried out by the sheriff. This theory was used in the mortgage

---

§ 7.27

1. See Young v. Ridley, 309 F.Supp. 1308 (D.D.C.1970); Huggins v. Dement, 13 N.C.App. 673, 187 S.E.2d 412, appeal dismissed 281 N.C. 314, 188 S.E.2d 898 (1972), certiorari denied 409 U.S. 1071, 93 S.Ct. 677, 34 L.Ed.2d 659 (1972).

2. See Charmicor, Inc. v. Deaner, 572 F.2d 694 (C.A.Nev.1978); Northrip v. Federal National Mortgage Association, 527 F.2d 23 (6th Cir.1975); Barrera v. Security Building & Investment Corp., 519 F.2d 1166 (5th Cir.1975); Bryant v. Jefferson Federal Savings & Loan Association, 509 F.2d 511 (D.C.Cir.1974); Kenly v. Miracle Properties, 412 F.Supp. 1072 (D.Ariz.1976); Lawson v. Smith, 402 F.Supp. 851 (N.D.Cal. 1975); Y Aleman Corp. v. Chase Manhattan Bank, 414 F.Supp. 93 (D.Guam 1975); Global Industries, Inc. v. Harris, 376 F.Supp. 1379 (N.D.Ga.1974); Federal National Mortgage Association v. Howlett, 521 S.W.2d 428 (Mo. En Banc), appeal dismissed 423 U.S. 909, 96 S.Ct. 471, 46 L.Ed. 2d 400 (1975); Wright v. Associates Financial Services Co. of Oregon, Inc., 59 Or.App. 688, 651 P.2d 1368 (1982), review denied 294 Or. 391, 656 P.2d 945 (1983), certiorari denied ___ U.S. ___, 104 S.Ct. 117, 78 L.Ed. 2d 116 (1983); Kennebec Inc. v. Bank of the West, 88 Wn.2d 718, 565 P.2d 812 (1977); Dennison v. Jack, ___ W.Va. ___, 304 S.E.2d 300 (1983); Contra, Turner v. Blackburn, 389 F.Supp. 1250 (W.D.N.C. 1975).

3. See Barklage, Constitutional Law— Mortgages—Extra-Judicial Mortgage Foreclosure Not State Action, 41 Mo.L.Rev. 278 (1976); Jones and Ivens, Power of Sale Foreclosure in Tennessee: A Section 1983 Trap. 51 Tenn.L.Rev. 279, 298–300 (1984).

context in Turner v. Blackburn.[4] Under the North Carolina power of sale statute, certain relatively unusual powers were conferred on the clerk of court. For example, within thirty days after the receipt of the sale proceeds, the person holding the power of sale had to file a final report with the clerk. The clerk then audited and approved the final report and filed it. The filing of the report and the lapse of a ten-day period was a precondition to the trustee's power to convey to the highest bidder at the foreclosure sale. During the ten-day period the clerk had the authority to reject or accept an upset bid. This was held to constitute direct participation by a state official and thus state action for purposes of the fourteenth amendment. On the other hand, the Missouri Supreme Court rejected this argument in Federal National Mortgage Association v. Howlett [5] because the intervention of public officials was limited primarily to ministerial functions performed by the recorder of deeds.[6] While the direct state action theory was useful in *Blackburn,* its impact in the power of sale area is limited because most power of sale statutes do not inject state officials into the process to the same extent as did North Carolina. In many jurisdictions a power of sale foreclosure will normally be consummated without the knowledge, much less the participation, of any public official other than perhaps the recorder of deeds.[7]

The "encouragement" theory asserts that state action may be found when state statutes tend to "encourage" objectionable, but otherwise private, activity.[8] The case most representative of this concept is Reitman v. Mulkey,[9] where state action was premised on the adoption of a constitutional amendment that protected a person's right to refuse to sell or rent his property to anyone for any reason. The United States Supreme Court, in a 5–4 vote, concurred in the finding of the California Supreme Court that the sole purpose of the amendment was to invalidate state anti-discrimination statutes, to prohibit their future enactment and to create a constitutional right to discriminate.[10] Thus the state became at least a "partner" in racial discrimination in violation of the fourteenth amendment.

It can be argued that the existence of state power of sale foreclosure statutes encourages this method of foreclosure and therefore is state action for purposes of the fourteenth amendment. However, most courts have rejected this argument,[11] advancing at least three reasons

4. 389 F.Supp. 1250 (W.D.N.C.1975).

5. 521 S.W.2d 428 (Mo. En Banc 1975).

6. See Northrip v. Federal National Mortgage Association, 527 F.2d 23 (6th Cir. 1975); Barrera v. Security Building & Investment Corp., 519 F.2d 1166 (5th Cir. 1975). But see Garner v. Tri-State Development Co., 382 F.Supp. 377 (E.D.Mich. 1974).

7. See, e.g., V.A.M.S. § 443.320–.330, V.T.C.A., Prop.Code § 51.002.

8. See Comment, Power of Sale Foreclosure After Fuentes, 40 U.Chi.L.Rev. 206, 217–18 (1972).

9. 387 U.S. 369, 87 S.Ct. 1627, 18 L.Ed. 2d 830 (1967).

10. Mulkey v. Reitman, 64 Cal.2d 529, 413 P.2d 825, 50 Cal.Rptr. 881 (1966).

11. See Northrip v. Federal National Mortgage Association, 527 F.2d 23 (6th Cir. 1975); Barrera v. Security Building & Investment Corp., 519 F.2d 1166 (C.A.Tex. 1975); Bryant v. Jefferson Federal Savings for doing so. First, *Reitman* involved racial discrimination and there is some indication that such cases will receive "special scrutiny" for state action purposes.[12] Second, power of sale statutes do not encourage nonjudicial foreclosure because the method existed prior to its authorization by the legislature.[13] Third, the extension of the "encouragement" theory to power of sale foreclosure would subject a vast range of private conduct to fourteenth amendment coverage, since statutes regulate so many forms of private activity and to some extent encourage such activity.[14]

The governmental function theory would find state action when a private person performs a function that is essentially governmental in nature.[15] Perhaps the classic example of this theory is found in Marsh v. Alabama,[16] where a "company town" was held to the same first amendment standards as a municipal corporation.[17] On the other hand, the Supreme Court recently has refused to expand this concept to such arguably quasi-municipal functions as covered mall shopping centers.[18] It could be argued that power of sale statutes have delegated the traditional governmental function of judicial foreclosure to private parties.[19] The Court of Appeals for the Fifth Circuit rejected this argument in confronting the Texas deed of trust power of sale statute in Barrera v. Security Building and Investment Corp.[20] The court found that there was no state action based on a governmental function theory because foreclosure of the mortgagor's equity of redemption had never been the exclusive prerogative of the state. The court noted that

& Loan Association, 509 F.2d 511 (D.C.Cir. 1974); Federal National Mortgage Association v. Howlett, 521 S.W.2d 428 (Mo. En Banc 1975).

12. See Northrip v. Federal National Mortgage Association, 527 F.2d 23 (6th Cir. 1975). See also Comment, supra note 8 at 217–18.

13. See Northrip v. Federal National Mortgage Association, 527 F.2d 23 (6th Cir. 1975); Barrera v. Security Building & Investment, 519 F.2d 1166 (5th Cir.1975); Federal National Mortgage Association v. Howlett, 521 S.W.2d 428 (Mo. En Banc 1975).

14. See Federal National Mortgage Association v. Howlett, 521 S.W.2d 428 (Mo. En Banc 1975); Comment, supra note 79, at 217–18. Many power of sale cases have utilized decisions under section 9–503 of the Uniform Commercial Code, which permits "self-help" repossession of secured chattels. These cases have found no state action under U.C.C. § 9–503 and, inter alia, have rejected the "encouragement" theory. See Gibbs v. Titelman, 502 F.2d 1107 (3d Cir.1974); Turner v. Impala Motors, 503 F.2d 607 (6th Cir.1974); Shirley v. State National Bank, 493 F.2d 739 (2d Cir.

1974); Adams v. Southern California First National Bank, 492 F.2d 324 (9th Cir.1973); Bichel Optical Laboratories Inc. v. Marquette National Bank, 487 F.2d 906 (8th Cir.1973).

15. See Barklage, supra note 3, at 280.

16. 326 U.S. 501, 66 S.Ct. 276, 90 L.Ed. 265 (1946).

17. See Evans v. Newton, 382 U.S. 296, 86 S.Ct. 486, 15 L.Ed.2d 373 (1966), on remand 221 Ga. 870, 148 S.E.2d 329 (1966) (private trustees' management of park on segregated basis was determined to be a governmental function); Terry v. Adams, 345 U.S. 461, 73 S.Ct. 809, 97 L.Ed. 1152 (1953) rehearing denied 345 U.S. 1003, 73 S.Ct. 1128, 97 L.Ed. 1408 (1953) (pre-primary elections with no apparent state involvement held subject to the fifteenth amendment).

18. See Lloyd Corp. v. Tanner, 407 U.S. 551, 92 S.Ct. 2219, 33 L.Ed.2d 131 (1972), conformed to 463 F.2d 1095 (1972).

19. See Muller, Deed of Trust Foreclosure: The Need for Reform * * * Fair Play and the Constitution Revisited, 29 J.Mo.B. 222, 229 (1973).

20. 519 F.2d 1166 (5th Cir.1975).

extrajudicial foreclosure dated back to 1774. Thus, the trustee exercising a power of sale was not deemed to be performing a governmental function.[21]

Each of the foregoing state action theories was raised, but found inapplicable by the United States Supreme Court in Flagg Brothers, Inc. v. Brooks.[22] In that case the plaintiff challenged section 7–210 of the New York Uniform Commercial Code as being unconstitutional under the procedural due process and equal protection requirements of the 14th amendment. Section 7–210 provides for the private sale of goods by a warehouseman to enforce the warehouseman's lien on goods entrusted to him for storage. The Supreme Court, in a 5–4 decision, refused to find the requisite state action for purposes of the 14th amendment. First, it apparently rejected the "direct" state action theory because no public officials were involved in the sale. Thus, the *Fuentes* line of cases was distinguished. Second, the Court held that the mere enactment of section 7–210 was not within the "encouragement" theory because a state's mere acquiescence in a private action does not convert such action to that of the state. Finally, the governmental function concept was held inapplicable because the statute did not delegate to a private party an exclusive prerogative of the government. The Court noted other private remedies were available for dispute resolution between debtors and creditors. The Brooks case tends to buttress an argument that no state action exists in the power of sale foreclosure setting. First, as we have pointed out earlier, most power of sale statutes do not utilize a public official in any significant manner. At least this is true in most deed of trust power of sale situations. Moreover, it can be argued that power of sale legislation is mere acquiesence by the state in private action, and, as in *Brooks*, therefore not enough state involvement for state action purposes. Lastly, a power of sale statute, like the warehouseman's lien provision, arguably does not delegate an exclusive sovereign prerogative to private parties because, in theory at least, settlement of disputes between mortgagees and mortgagors also "is not traditionally an exclusive public function." [23] Such disputes are often resolved privately without recourse to power of sale legislation.[24]

Under the judicial enforcement theory state action exists when state courts enforce the rights of private parties. The origin of this theory is Shelley v. Kraemer,[25] in which the Supreme Court held that specific judicial enforcement of a racially restrictive covenant constituted state action and was violative of the fourteenth amendment equal

21. See Roberts v. Cameron-Brown Co., 556 F.2d 356 (5th Cir.1977); Northrip v. Federal National Manufacturing Association, 527 F.2d 23 (6th Cir.1975); Federal National Mortgage Association v. Howlett, 521 S.W.2d 428 (Mo. En Banc 1975).

22. 436 U.S. 149, 98 S.Ct. 1729, 56 L.Ed. 2d 185 (1978).

23. Id. at 156, 98 S.Ct. at 1733.

24. See § 6.17, supra.

25. 334 U.S. 1, 68 S.Ct. 836, 92 L.Ed. 1161 (1948).

protection clause. If *Shelley* were extended to power of sale foreclosure, it could be argued that judicial enforcement of power of sale mortgages would constitute state action. Where such foreclosures ultimately entail intervention by a court, either in the form of a sheriff ejecting a holdover mortgagor or in a subsequent quiet title suit based on the foreclosure, judicial recognition of the mortgage agreement arguably could be considered state action. However, most power of sale foreclosures are accomplished with no subsequent judicial second-guessing, making the *Shelley* concept inapplicable. The Supreme Court has refused to apply the *Shelley* concept outside of the racial covenant area and to some extent has restricted its scope.[26] The Missouri Supreme Court in *Howlett* refused to apply the *Shelley* theory to power of sale deed of trust foreclosure. It noted that title passed by virtue of the trustee's deed and without judicial intervention; courts were used only when mortgagors did not surrender possession. In such a situation, the court noted, possession is obtained by an unlawful detainer action in which the Missouri courts are not permitted to inquire into the merits of title. Thus, courts are not involved in the process by which title passes.[27] This reasoning is problematic. If a mortgagor brings a subsequent suit in equity to set aside a power of sale foreclosure, a court would be called upon to enforce the private agreement, and the logic of *Shelley* would be inescapable. Perhaps the better approach is simply to say that the *Shelley* concept should not be extended beyond the racial covenant area; otherwise judicial enforcement of every private agreement could be brought within the state action ambit.[28]

Finally, state action is sometimes found under a "pervasiveness" theory. Under this concept state action exists when statutory regulation pervasively governs otherwise private conduct. This theory, however, was rejected by the Supreme Court in Jackson v. Metropolitan Edison Co.,[29] where an attempt was made to find state action in a public utility termination of services. According to the Court,

> [the] mere fact that a business is subject to State regulation does not by itself convert its action into that of the State for purposes of the Fourteenth Amendment. Nor does the fact

---

26. The other Supreme Court decision to apply *Shelley* was Barrows v. Jackson, 346 U.S. 249, 73 S.Ct. 1031, 97 L.Ed. 1586 (1953), rehearing denied 346 U.S. 841, 74 S.Ct. 19, 98 L.Ed. 361 (1953), a case involving a suit for damages for breach of a racial covenant. The Court avoided *Shelley* in Lombard v. Louisiana, 373 U.S. 267, 83 S.Ct. 1122, 10 L.Ed.2d 338 (1963), a sit-in case involving racial segregation in public accommodations. More recently the Court rejected the application of the *Shelley* concept in Evans v. Abney, 396 U.S. 435, 90 S.Ct. 628, 24 L.Ed.2d 634 (1970), where a state court ruled that a trustor's intention to provide a park for whites only could not be carried out and that therefore the prop-erty reverted to his heirs. The Supreme Court held that the state court ruling did not constitute state action under the fourteenth amendment.

27. See Federal National Mortgage Association v. Howlett, 521 S.W.2d 428, 437 (Mo. En Banc 1975).

28. See Global Industries, Inc. v. Harris, 376 F.Supp. 1379, 1383 (N.D.Ga.1974).

29. 419 U.S. 345, 95 S.Ct. 449, 42 L.Ed. 2d 477 (1974). See also, Moose Lodge No. 107 v. Irvis, 407 U.S. 163, 92 S.Ct. 1965, 32 L.Ed.2d 627 (1972) (state licensing and regulation of a private club not sufficient to find state action).

that the regulation is extensive and detailed, as in the case of most public utilities, do so * * *. [T]he inquiry must be whether there is a sufficiently close nexus between the state and the challenged action of the regulated entity so that the action of the latter may be fairly treated as that of the State itself.[30]

The *Barrera* court rejected the application of this theory to the Texas power of sale statutes. It found the nexus between state and private activity required by *Jackson* to be absent and determined that in its absence state regulation alone is not sufficient to establish state action.[31]

The foregoing illustrates that it will be difficult to establish the state action required by the fourteenth amendment in most power of sale contexts. By finding no state action, many courts avoid the myriad of complex constitutional issues considered earlier. These include: the form of notice which is required; whether all parties, including junior lienors, should be entitled to notice; and the type of hearing which is required, judicial or otherwise. By avoiding these difficult issues such courts apparently defer to legislatures which are perhaps better equipped to deal with them.[32]

Nevertheless it would be imprudent to suggest that no state action problems remain with power of sale foreclosure. While most state power of sale foreclosures take place without the knowledge or participation of any public official other than perhaps the recorder of deeds, this is not universally the case. In some states the sheriff conducts the foreclosure sale.[33] Moreover, in some deed of trust jurisdictions, statutes authorize the appointment of the sheriff as trustee where the named trustee refuses or is unable to act.[34] Some have argued that the role of the sheriff in conducting the sale is merely ministerial and thus not significant enough official involvement to create state action.[35] However, it is important in this connection to emphasize the Supreme Court's recent statement in *Lugar v. Edmundson Oil Co., Inc.*[36] in describing the state action in the *Fuentes-Mitchell* line of cases: "* * * in each case the Court entertained and adjudicated the defendant debtor's claim that the procedure under which the private creditor secured the disputed property violated federal constitutional standards of due process. Necessary to that conclusion is the holding that private

---

30. 419 U.S. at 350–51, 95 S.Ct. at 453.

31. Barrera v. Security Building & Investment Corp., 519 F.2d 1166, 1171–72 (5th Cir.1975).

32. See Barrera v. Security Building & Investment Corp., 519 F.2d 1166, 1174 (5th Cir.1975).

33. See e.g., Minn.Stat.Ann. § 580.06.

34. See e.g., V.A.M.S. § 443.330.

35. See Comment, The Constitutionality of Maine's Real Estate Foreclosure Stat-

utes, 32 Maine L.Rev. 147, 158 (1980). See also, Northrip v. Federal National Mortgage Association, 527 F.2d 23 (6th Cir.1975) (sheriff's conduct of foreclosure sale not state action because deemed "incidental, and not essential" to use of a private remedy "entered into privately by the mortgagee and mortgagor.")

36. 457 U.S. 922, 102 S.Ct. 2744, 73 L.Ed.2d 482 (1982).

use of the challenged state procedures *with the help* of state officials constitutes state action for purposes of the Fourteenth Amendment." [37] Thus, it would seem that where a sheriff or public official actually conducts the sale, however one might otherwise choose to characterize that action, there is a strong argument that the private mortgagee is acting "with the help" of a state official and that state action thus is present.

 WESTLAW REFERENCES
(14 14th /1 amendment) "due process" constitutional*** /p "state action" /p foreclos***

§ 7.28 Constitutional Problems—Federal Action

Where power of sale constitutional litigation involves a direct instrumentality of the state or federal government as the mortgagee, courts cannot avoid the constitutional issues of notice and hearing. Even though a court would find that a particular state power of sale statute lacks the requisite state action when a private party is the mortgagee, the presence of the government as a mortgagee provides the "governmental action" necessary to reach the constitutional issues. If the foreclosing mortgagee is a direct instrumentality of the state, the fourteenth amendment state action requirement is readily satisfied. If the foreclosing mortgagee is a direct federal instrumentality, then the requisite "federal action" exists, and a court will apply fifth amendment due process standards to test the constitutionality of the foreclosure.[1]

It is a relatively common practice for a direct instrumentality of the federal government to be a foreclosing mortgagee under local power of sale statutes. This situation will arise, for example, where direct loans made by the Veterans Administration (VA) or the Farmers Home Administration (FmHA) under various government programs are foreclosed.[2] It also could occur where the Federal Housing Administration (FHA) opts to take an assignment of an FHA insured mortgage that is in default and then forecloses.[3]

Normally one would assume that federally-owned corporations utilizing power of sale foreclosure will be treated as the federal government for Fifth Amendment purposes. There is at least one federal

---

37. Id. at 933, 102 S.Ct. at 2752.

§ 7.28

1. See e.g., Johnson v. United States Department of Agriculture, 734 F.2d 774 (11th Cir.1984); Federal Deposit Insurance Corp. v. Morrison, 568 F.Supp. 1240 (N.D. Ala.1983), order reversed on other grounds 747 F.2d 610 (11th Cir.1984); Matzke v. Block, 564 F.Supp. 1157 (D.Kan.1983), affirmed in part, reversed in part 732 F.2d 799 (10th Cir.1984); Rau v. Cavenaugh, 500 F.Supp. 204 (D.S.D.1980); United States v. Ford, 551 F.Supp. 1101 (N.D.Miss.1982); Ricker v. United States, 417 F.Supp. 133 (D.Me.1976), order supplemented 434 F.Supp. 1251 (D.Me.1976).

2. See G. Nelson & D. Whitman, Cases and Materials on Real Estate Transfer, Finance and Development, 710–723 (2nd Ed. 1981).

3. Id. at 721.

district court decision to that effect with respect to the Federal Deposit Insurance Corporation,[4] an agency that, as a result of taking over the assets of failed banking institutions, frequently finds itself foreclosing mortgages. The Government National Mortgage Association (GNMA) presumably, should be similarly treated. After all, it is a corporation wholly-owned by the United States government that purchases federally-insured or guaranteed mortgages on the secondary market.[5] However, the United States Court of Appeals for the Eighth Circuit, in Warren v. Government National Mortgage Association,[6] held that GNMA as a foreclosing mortgagee under Missouri power of sale legislation should not be considered the federal government for purposes of the Fifth Amendment. While the reasoning is unclear, the court could be saying simply that GNMA, because of its unique role as a corporation dealing on the secondary mortgage market, acts, for the most part, like a private corporation and therefore should not be treated as a direct federal instrumentality. Indeed this view was adopted by a concurring judge.[7] On the other hand, the opinion can easily be read more broadly for the proposition that even a direct instrumentality of the United States can foreclose without "federal action" being triggered so long as the agency simply follows state power of sale statutes and "neither mandate[s] nor approve[s] the method of foreclosure to be followed in the event of default."[8] Finally, perhaps the court was suggesting that even the United States can act in a proprietary or commercial, as opposed to governmental, fashion and that foreclosure of mortgages can be classified as proprietary or commercial activity. If either of these latter interpretations is accurate and either were to be accepted by other circuits, then even FmHA, the VA and HUD could be deemed nongovernmental and insulated from the requirements of Fifth Amendment due process. Such a view would surely come as a surprise to the numerous federal courts that routinely either expressly find or assume the presence of federal action in federal agency cases.[9] As one recent commentary stressed, "to the extent that [*Warren*] purports to state that in some circumstances a government mortgagee acting as a private entity is not a state actor, [it] is wrong and contrary to the strong trend in the other circuits."[10]

Difficult federal action questions arise when the mortgagee is one of numerous other federally chartered corporations where the relationship to the federal government is more ambiguous. Such entities include, for example, the Federal Land Bank, Federal National Mortgage Association (FNMA) and the Federal Home Loan Mortgage Corpo-

---

4. Federal Deposit Insurance Corp. v. Morrison, 568 F.Supp. 1240 (N.D.Ala.1983), order reversed on other grounds 747 F.2d 610 (11th Cir.1984).

5. See § 11.3 infra.

6. 611 F.2d 1229 (8th Cir.1980), cert. denied 449 U.S. 847, 101 S.Ct. 133, 66 L.Ed. 2d 57 (1980).

7. Id. at 1235.

8. Id. at 1234.

9. See cases cited in note 1, infra.

10. Jones and Ivens, Power of Sale Foreclosure in Tennessee: A Section 1983 Trap, 51 Tenn.L.Rev. 279, 302 (1984).

ration (FHLMC). The Land Bank, while federally chartered, is now cooperatively owned by the farmers it serves.[11] Consequently, it is not surprising to find case authority that it is not the federal government for purposes of the Fifth Amendment.[12] FNMA and FHLMC share certain common traits. Both entities are quasi-federal and purchase large quantities of mortgage loans on the secondary market.[13] They commonly foreclose mortgages under power of sale statutes with respect to those mortgage loans they have purchased and which subsequently go into default. Are these entities the "federal government" for purposes of the fifth amendment due process clause? Courts thus far have concluded that FNMA is not.[14] Until 1968, FNMA was wholly owned and administered by the federal government. In 1968 Congress changed its status to a federally-sponsored private corporation whose purpose was to provide a secondary market for residential mortgages.[15] The stock is completely privately owned, but the President of the United States appoints five of the fifteen members of the Board of Directors.[16] The federal government regulates FNMA in many respects, such as establishing debt limits, approving the sale of stock, and requiring that a certain portion of its mortgage purchases be related to furthering the development of low and middle income housing.[17] In Northrip v. Federal National Mortgage Association,[18] the Court of Appeals for the Sixth Circuit found that FNMA, while evidencing "significant" federal involvement, should not be treated as the federal government for fifth amendment purposes when it forecloses mortgages. The court thought that Jackson v. Metropolitan Edison Co.,[19] which found no state action involved in a public utility's termination of customer service, represented an analogous case. According to the court in *Northrip,* "here as in *Jackson* there is not a 'sufficiently close nexus' between the state and the challenged act of foreclosure."[20]

The FHLMC poses a somewhat more difficult federal action problem. It was created in 1970 by Congress to strengthen the secondary market in federally insured and conventional mortgages. Its stock is wholly owned by the twelve Federal Home Loan Banks.[21] The Board of Directors is composed of the three members of the Federal Home Loan Bank Board, the members of which are appointed by the President of the United States.[22] FHLMC probably should be treated as the federal government for purposes of the fifth amendment. While Congress

11. DeLaigle v. Federal Land Bank of Columbia, 568 F.Supp. 1432 (S.D.Ga.1983).

12. Id.

13. See § 11.3 infra.

14. See Northrip v. Federal National Mortgage Association, 527 F.2d 23 (6th Cir. 1975); Federal National Mortgage Association v. Scott, 548 S.W.2d 545 (Mo. En Banc 1977).

15. 12 U.S.C.A. § 1716.

16. 12 U.S.C.A. § 1723a(b).

17. 12 U.S.C.A. § 1723a(h).

18. 527 F.2d 23 (6th Cir. 1975).

19. 419 U.S. 345, 95 S.Ct. 449, 42 L.Ed. 2d 477 (1974).

20. 527 F.2d 23, 32 (6th Cir. 1975).

21. 12 U.S.C.A. § 1453(a).

22. 12 U.S.C.A. § 1452(a).

clearly intended to make FNMA a private corporation,[23] FHLMC is more substantially tied to the federal government. There is, for example, no private market for FHLMC shares as is the case with respect to FNMA. Moreover, because the directors are Presidentially appointed, FHLMC's day-to-day operations are inevitably more significantly intertwined with the federal government than those of FNMA.

Even where the federal government is not the mortgagee, it has been argued that federal action may exist where the mortgage being foreclosed was initiated pursuant to a federally subsidized and regulated program. *Roberts v. Cameron-Brown Co.*[24] illustrates this type of situation. The mortgage being foreclosed under a Georgia power of sale statute was initiated under section 235 of the National Housing Act and subsequently sold to FNMA, the foreclosing mortgagee.[25] The section 235 program was designed to encourage homeownership by low income groups; to accomplish this goal, the federal government makes mortgage assistance payments to the mortgagee on the mortgagor's behalf.[26] The economic effect of the program is to reduce the cost of the mortgage to the equivalent of a mortgage with a one percent per annum interest rate.[27] Private mortgagees who take part in the section 235 program are extensively controlled by federal statutes and regulations.[28] In *Roberts* the federal district court concluded that even though no state action existed for purposes of the fourteenth amendment, the combination of federal subsidy to the mortgagor and substantial federal regulation of the mortgage transaction resulted in federal action for purposes of the due process clause of the fifth amendment. In an ambiguous opinion, the Fifth Circuit reversed and determined that the federal government's involvement was insufficient to sustain a finding of federal action.[29] Even though the presence of FNMA as the foreclosing party was not emphasized in the district court's reasoning, the court of appeals stressed the fact that FNMA is not a federal instrumentality. Although the Fifth Circuit rejected the pervasive federal regulation and participation argument, its opinion failed to confront the significance of the financial subsidy provided by the section 235 program.

Similarly, there is case law that the foreclosure by a private lender of a VA guaranteed mortgage is not subject to Fifth Amendment restrictions, even though the lender is extensively regulated by the VA and the veteran receives some federal subsidy.[30] Moreover, a recent

23. See Northrip v. Federal National Mortgage Association, 527 F.2d 23, 32 (6th Cir. 1975).

24. 410 F.Supp. 988 (S.D.Ga.1975).

25. 12 U.S.C.A. § 1715z(a).

26. See G. Nelson & D. Whitman, supra note 2 at 752.

27. Id.

28. See, e.g., 12 U.S.C.A. § 1715z(b); 24 CFR § 235; U.S. Dept. of Hous. & Urban Dev., Handbook No. 4155.1, Mortgage Credit Analysis (July 25, 1972).

29. 556 F.2d 356 (5th Cir.1977).

30. See Rank v. Nimmo, 677 F.2d 692 (9th Cir.1982), certiorari denied 459 U.S. 907, 103 S.Ct. 210, 74 L.Ed.2d 168 (1982); Fitzgerald v. Cleland, 498 F.Supp. 341 (D.Me.1980), affirmed in part, reversed in part 650 F.2d 360 (1st Cir.1981).

decision by the United States Court of Appeals for the Fifth Circuit in a related non-mortgage context may be of some significance to foregoing mortgage subsidy type situations.[31] In that case, the court relied on *Roberts* in finding no federal action where tenants whose rents were subsidized by the federal government under the Section 8 housing program challenged the constitutionality of the use by their private landlord of state unlawful detainer legislation. Such cases illustrate some reluctance to find federal action despite significant federal regulation and subsidy.

WESTLAW REFERENCES

synopsis,digest((5 5th /1 amendment) ''due process''
    constitutional***) & foreclos*** /p ''federal action'' /p (real
    + property estate) realty mortgage

§ 7.29 Constitutional Problems—Title Difficulties

In the event a court surmounts the state action problem and determines that a particular power of sale statute is unconstitutional, the question arises whether a sale held under such a statute will be classified as void or merely voidable. If the sale is rendered void, no title passes in law or equity. Thus the sale purchaser, whether the mortgagee or a third party, cannot obtain title of any kind and no title would pass to subsequent purchasers.[1] On the other hand, if the constitutional sale is only voidable, the right to set aside the foreclosure and regain the land will be cut off as against any purchaser for value without notice.[2] Few cases have considered this problem. Ricker v. United States,[3] in holding that a nonjudicial foreclosure under a Maine statute violated the notice and hearing requirements of the fifth amendment due process clause, avoided classifying the foreclosure as either void or voidable; instead, the court determined that the subsequent purchasers from the federal government were not bona fide, since the original mortgagors stayed in possession and since recorded documents established that the foreclosure was nonjudicial. "Under Maine law a purchaser at a foreclosure sale cannot claim protection as a bona fide purchaser where, as here, it appears from documents and facts known at the time of purchase that there may be a substantial defect in the seller's claim of title."[4] The court may be correct in its assertion that the mortgagors' continued possession gave subsequent purchasers notice of their claim, thus depriving them of bona fide purchaser status. However, the mere presence in the public records of a document

31. Miller v. Hartwood Apartments, Limited, 689 F.2d 1239 (5th Cir.1982). Cf. Jeffries v. Georgia Residential Finance Authority, 678 F.2d 919 (11th Cir.1982), certiorari denied 459 U.S. 971, 103 S.Ct. 302, 74 L.Ed.2d 283 (1982) (participation of GFRA in termination and eviction procedures under Section 8 constituted state action even though landlord is private.).

§ 7.29

1. See § 7.20 supra.

2. Id. See also, Dingus, Mortgages—Redemption After Foreclosure Sale in Missouri, 25 Mo.L.Rev. 261 (1960).

3. 417 F.Supp. 133 (D.Me.1976).

4. Id. at 140. See § 7.20, supra.

indicating that nonjudicial foreclosure had been employed is hardly tantamount to notice of a defect in the title. At present the law is far from clear on the constitutional issues; if the United States Supreme Court, or a majority of lower federal decisions, firmly establish that foreclosures without notice and hearing are unconstitutional, then it will be fair to say that purchasers who trace their titles through foreclosures conducted thereafter lack bona fides. That time is not here yet. The Ricker court's holding would make it virtually impossible for any person to claim BFP status and hence would in effect make all such foreclosures void; that view is simply unreasonable at this stage of the law's development.

For the countless thousands of people in the United States who may "own" land whose title was derived from a foreclosure sale under an arguably unconstitutional power of sale statute, the above problems are hardly theoretical. Unless they have been in possession for the applicable period to establish adverse possession, they may not own their land. As a practical matter, if a court is to invalidate a state power of sale statute, it virtually will be compelled to make the decision prospective only. At least one federal district court has so held.[5] Although it has been the traditional rule that newly announced constitutional doctrines are given retroactive effect, the Supreme Court has been loath to do so when there are important overriding societal considerations.[6] Given the substantial reliance on the power of sale foreclosure method in this country, a retroactive application of unconstitutionality could cloud countless titles and result in enormous volumes of costly litigation. This is especially true in inflationary periods when rising land values will encourage potential claimants to upset past foreclosure sales. In fact, the spectre of retroactivity doubtless encourages courts to find other methods, such as the lack of state action, to avoid reaching the constitutional questions involved in power of sale foreclosure. Whatever standards the United States Supreme Court has applied to the retroactivity question in the past in the criminal and other areas, the practical necessities would seem to dictate prospective application of unconstitutionality in the power of sale situation.

 WESTLAW REFERENCES
[no queries]

---

5. Ricker v. United States, 434 F.Supp. 1251 (D.Me.1976).

6. See G. Gunther, Constitutional Law 546 (9th Ed.1975); Court, the Great Writ, and the Due Process of Time and Law, 79 Harv.L.Rev. 56 (1965); Schwartz, Retroactivity, Reliability, and Due Process: A Reply to Professor Mishkin, 33 U.Chi.L.Rev. 719 (1966); Wellington Common Law Rules and Constitutional Double Standards, 83 Yale L.J. 221 (1973).

§ 7.30 Constitutional Problems—Conclusion

Assuming fourteenth amendment state action exists, many state power of sale statutes are deficient on notice grounds, and nearly all fail to satisfy the constitutional hearing requirement. As we have seen, waiver of the rights to notice and hearing, as a practical matter, simply will not work.[1] While many courts have avoided the constitutional problems by utilizing the "no state action" approach, this is a doubtful long-range solution to the problem.

The reason the "no state action" approach can probably be only a temporary expedient is because of a two-tier private-governmental foreclosure situation that to some extent currently exists. It is true that if courts continue to follow the "no state action" approach, private mortgagees can continue to utilize current power of sale foreclosure statutes. Moreover, it may be that the Supreme Court will agree that such state statutes lack the requisite fourteenth amendment state action. However, as the majority of federal decisions[2] graphically illustrate, mortgagees that are federal agencies for purposes of the fifth amendment due process clause will not be able to utilize such foreclosure statutes because such foreclosures will be unconstitutional. These federal mortgagees, as noted earlier, may include such quasi-federal agencies as the Federal Home Loan Mortgage Corporation (FHLMC) as well as direct federal instrumentalities. State agencies which hold mortgages, such as state housing finance agencies, may also be subject to analogous fourteenth amendment standards.

In theory, of course, the federal government may be satisfied with judicial foreclosure by federal agencies even though private mortgagees continue to use power of sale statutes. However, this is not the likely result, if for no other reason than judicial foreclosure is both more time-consuming and costly than its power of sale counterpart.[3] One possible solution, as we noted earlier, is the use of intra-agency hearing procedures to supplement otherwise constitutionally deficient state power of sale legislation.[4] This approach, however, is problematical for at least two reasons. First, it will probably be difficult to establish any substantial regulatory uniformity among the numerous federal agencies that would use such procedures. In addition, because state power of sale legislation varies considerably, drafting supplementary regulations that "fit" such legislation may well prove difficult. In any event, the Multifamily Foreclosure Act of 1981 is at best marginally helpful because of its limited scope and probable constitutional deficiencies.[5]

§ 7.30

1. See § 7.26.

2. See e.g., Rau v. Cavenaugh, 500 F.Supp. 204 (D.S.D.1980); Ricker v. United States, 417 F.Supp. 133 (D.Me.1976), order supplemented 434 F.Supp. 1251 (D.Me. 1976). Contra: Federal Deposit Insurance Corporation v. Morrison, 747 F.2d 610 (11th Cir.1984).

3. See McElhone & Cramer, Loan Foreclosure Costs Affected By Varied State Regulations, 36 Mortgage Banker 41 (1975).

4. See § 7.25 supra.

5. See §§ 7.19, 7.25 supra.

It is quite possible to fashion a workable foreclosure system that is efficient, fair and constitutional. First, as has been noted earlier, if a statute requires notice by mail to all parties of record subordinate to the mortgage being foreclosed, the constitutional notice requirement can be satisfied. Such notice could be mailed to each subordinate party at the address provided in the recorded document that evidences such party's interest in the real estate. Moreover, it is possible for the legislation to provide for a hearing and still retain a power of sale feature. For example, the statute could require that a two-part postcard be mailed to all the subordinate parties described above. The postcard would apprise them, in simple nontechnical language, of the foreclosure proceeding, and inform them that if a hearing is desired the second half of the postcard should be returned by mail to the court. If any card is returned, a judicial or, alternatively, an administrative hearing would be scheduled. However, if no cards are returned the power of sale contained in the mortgage instrument would be exercised without a hearing. The latter result would, in fact, be likely; even judicial foreclosure actions culminate with a high percentage of default judgments. Finally, in order to achieve the highest possible sale price and, thus, to be fair to both mortgagor and junior lienholders alike, the currently pervasive public auction system should be discarded. Rather the mortgaged real estate where possible should be sold in much the same fashion as in normal non-forced sale settings. The details of such a sale system are considered elsewhere in this volume.[6]

Moreover, whatever configuration such ideal legislation might ultimately take, perhaps it should be enacted by Congress rather than by state legislatures. It may even be desirable for such legislation to encompass the foreclosure of all mortgages and security devices, whether federally-insured or otherwise federally-connected or not. While a 1970's attempt at broad federal foreclosure legislation proved unsuccessful,[7] economic forces for change are now much more powerful. Mortgages not only are more and more traded on a national basis much like other investment securities, mortgage financing has an enormous and ever increasing impact on the national economy. Moreover, the Commerce Clause of the Constitution undoubtedly provides ample power to Congress for such legislation.[8]

Political considerations may well represent the largest obstacle to such a federal legislative solution. Federalism concerns and the notion that real property law is inherently local could well prove to be the undoing of such a federal approach to foreclosure. In that event, uniformity perhaps could be achieved by state adoption of uniform foreclosure legislation in much the same fashion as state acceptance of the Uniform Commercial Code created substantial national uniformity in the law of banking and chattel security.

6. See § 8.8 infra.

7. See S.2057, 93rd Cong., 2nd Sess. § 401 et seq. (1973); G. Nelson & D. Whit-

man, Cases & Materials on Real Estate Finance & Development 517–520 (1976).

8. See § 5.24 supra.

WESTLAW REFERENCES
[no queries]

F. DISPOSITION OF SURPLUS

§ 7.31 Surplus—General Rules

Where the foreclosure sale produces a surplus, the rules governing who participates in the surplus and the priority of that participation are generally clear. The major underlying principle is that the surplus represents the remnant of the equity of redemption and security wiped out by the foreclosure. Consequently, the surplus stands in the place of the foreclosed real estate and the liens and interests that previously attached to that real estate now attach to the surplus.[1] They are entitled to be paid out of the surplus in the order of priority they enjoyed prior to foreclosure.[2] The claim of the foreclosed mortgagor or the owner of the equity of redemption normally is junior to those of all valid liens wiped out by the foreclosure.[3]

Statutes often regulate the distribution of surplus, especially in the power of sale setting. Some simply codify the principles described above.[4] Others seem on their face to give the surplus to the mortgagor and make no reference to the rights of junior lienors.[5] However, these latter statutes have generally been interpreted to give junior lienors rights in the surplus and the priority over mortgagors generally described in the preceding paragraph.[6] A few statutes make no mention of priorities, but simply authorize the mortgagee or trustee to pay the surplus to the clerk of court.[7]

§ 7.31

1. Roosevelt Savings Bank v. Goldberg, 118 Misc.2d 220, 459 N.Y.S.2d 988 (1983); Mall v. Johnson, 97 Misc.2d 889, 412 N.Y.S.2d 773 (1979); First Federal Savings & Loan Association v. Brown, 78 A.D.2d 119, 434 N.Y.S.2d 306 (1980), appeal after remand 86 A.D.2d 963, 448 N.Y.S.2d 302 (1982); Third National Bank in Nashville, 688 S.W.2d 446 (Tenn.1985); Tobler v. Frey Auctioneers, Inc., 462 F.Supp. 788 (S.D.Ga. 1978), judgment affirmed 620 F.2d 508 (5th Cir.1980); Western Savings Fund Society of Philadelphia v. Goodman, 103 N.J. Super. 307, 247 A.2d 151 (1968); Security Trust Co. of Rochester v. Miller, 72 Misc.2d 269, 338 N.Y.S.2d 1015 (1972); Sadow v. Poskin Realty Corp., 63 Misc.2d 499, 312 N.Y.S.2d 901 (1970).

2. Id. In addition, see Republic National Life Insurance Co. v. Lorraine Realty Corp., 279 N.W.2d 349 (Minn.1979); Builders Supply Co. of Hattiesburg v. Pine Belt Savings & Loan Association, 369 So.2d 743 (Miss.1979); Banks-Miller Supply Co. v. Smallridge, 154 W.Va. 360, 175 S.E.2d 446 (1970).

3. See, e.g., Sens v. Slavia, Inc., 304 So. 2d 438 (Fla.1974); Note, Rights in the Proceeds of a Foreclosure Sale—The Court Helps Those Who Help Themselves, 51 N.C.L.Rev. 1100 (1973); Imperial—Yuma Production Credit Association v. Nussbaumer, 22 Ariz.App. 485, 528 P.2d 871 (1974).

4. See, e.g., Ariz.Rev.Stat. § 33–727: "If there are other liens on the property sold, or other payments secured by the same mortgage, they shall be paid in their order * * *." See Or.Rev.Stat. 87–765.

5. See, e.g., Minn.Stat.Ann. § 580.10; Ind.Code 1971, 34–1–53–10; West's Rev. Code Wash.Ann. 61.12.150.

6. See, e.g., Brown v. Crookston Agriculture Association, 34 Minn. 545, 26 N.W. 907 (1886); Fuller v. Langum, 37 Minn. 74, 33 N.W. 122 (1887); White v. Shirk, 20 Ind. App. 589, 51 N.E. 126 (1898).

7. See, e.g., Utah Code Ann.1953, 57–1–29.

One important corollary of the above rules needing closer analysis is that only those whose interests were cut off by the foreclosure sale have a right to share in the surplus.[8] The party that comes to mind first as qualifying is the foreclosed owner of the equity of redemption. But some courts have included certain subordinate parties who shared in that ownership interest, such as, for example, a foreclosed easement owner.[9] If such easement owners qualify, so, too, should a subordinate lessee to the extent that the fair market value of his destroyed leasehold interest exceeds his obligations under the lease. Another obvious group cut off by the foreclosure sale are junior lienors. In order to qualify for lienor status, it must be established that the claim was reduced to a lien prior to the foreclosure sale.[10] Thus, mere general creditors or those holding contract claims unrelated to the land have no claim to the surplus.[11] Moreover, senior lienors have no right to share in the surplus.[12] In one case, for example, where the foreclosed mortgagor was insolvent, two senior mortgagees attempted to utilize the surplus created by the foreclosure of a third mortgage to pay down part of the senior mortgage debt. The court held that since the senior liens were unaffected by the foreclosure they had no right to the surplus.[13]

Where land sale contracts are destroyed by a foreclosure of a prior mortgage given by the vendor, special problems arise if the foreclosure sale results in a surplus. It is not uncommon for vendees to make substantial payments under such contracts either in ignorance of a prior mortgage on the land or in reliance on the vendor's promise to satisfy it by the time the contract is fully paid. However, it too commonly happens that the mortgage is foreclosed and the contract vendee is wiped out.[14] In the event of a foreclosure surplus, should the vendee share in it? If so, with what priority? A Maryland case

---

8. Sadow v. Poskin Realty Corp., 63 Misc.2d 499, 312 N.Y.S.2d 901 (1970).

9. Anderman v. 1395 E. 52nd Street Realty Corp., 60 Misc.2d 437, 303 N.Y.S.2d 474 (1969).

10. Pindus v. Newmat Leasing Corp., 71 A.D.2d 948, 420 N.Y.S.2d 10 (1979); Sadow v. Poskin Realty Corp., 63 Misc.2d 499, 312 N.Y.S.2d 901 (1970). The lien of a judgment docketed after the delivery of the deed of a referee in foreclosure but before the confirmation of the foreclosure sale in New York shares in surplus moneys pro rata with other similar liens without priorities. Id.

11. Pindus v. Newmat Leasing Corp., 71 A.D.2d 948, 420 N.Y.S.2d 10 (1979); Balance Limited, Inc. v. Short, 35 Md.App. 10, 368 A.2d 1116 (1977); Sens v. Slavia, Inc., 304 So.2d 438 (Fla.1974); Sadow v. Poskin Realty Corp., 63 Misc.2d 499, 312 N.Y.S.2d 901 (1970) (tenant security deposits not a lien on surplus nor is electric utility bill of

the mortgagor). Northwestern Mutual Life Insurance Co. v. Nebraska Land Co., 192 Neb. 588, 223 N.W.2d 425 (1974).

12. See United States v. Sage, 566 F.2d 1114 (9th Cir.1977); Walsky v. Fairmont Arms, Inc., 27 A.D.2d 671, 276 N.Y.S.2d 931 (1967); Armands Engineering Inc. v. Town and Country Club, Inc., 113 R.I. 515, 324 A.2d 334 (1974). But see Jefferson Federal Savings & Loan Association v. Berks Title Insurance Co., 472 A.2d 893, 894 (D.C.App.1984) for the questionable statement that "if there is a senior encumbrance or lien on the property, such as the federal estate tax lien in this case, the trustee must satisfy that lien before applying the sale proceeds to the obligation secured by the deed of trust."

13. Armands Engineering Inc. v. Town and Country Club, Inc., 113 R.I. 515, 324 A.2d 334 (1974).

14. See § 3, supra.

involving a somewhat similar situation is interesting in this regard.[15] In that case a contract for the sale of land was apparently wiped out by the foreclosure of a mortgage that had arisen through the vendor. Under Maryland law a contract vendee obtains a lien on the land to the extent of the payments made under the contract in the event the contract, through the fault of the vendor, is not consummated.[16] The court determined that this equitable lien of the vendee came into existence at least as of the date the vendee filed a lien claim in the foreclosure proceeding. As a result, the vendee was permitted to share in the foreclosure surplus and his claim was deemed to be prior to that of another creditor who obtained a judgment two days thereafter.[17]

An alternative, and perhaps better, method of analyzing the vendee's interest is also available. The vendee, like the subordinate easement holder, can be viewed as owning part of the equity of redemption rather than as a lienor. Indeed, under the doctrine of equitable conversion the vendee is regarded in equity as *the* owner of the land for many purposes.[18] It may sometimes be advantageous for the foreclosed vendee to stake his claim to a foreclosure surplus in his equitable role as owner rather than as an equitable lienor. This would be true if a court were to hold that the equitable lien arises only on the vendor's default rather than as of the date of the land contract. In that event the vendee's claim to any foreclosure surplus may be rendered subordinate to post-contract liens arising through the vendor. Under the "ownership" approach, however, it is clear that the vendee's priority would date from the execution of the contract so as to take precedence over such intervening vendor-caused liens. At least this would be true if the vendee promptly recorded his contract or took equivalent steps to establish constructive notice of its existence.[19] If the vendee's equitable lien is viewed as arising as of the date of the contract rather than later, the theory utilized by the foreclosed vendee to reach the surplus becomes less significant.

 WESTLAW REFERENCES
surplus /p foreclos***

§ 7.32 Surplus—Some Special Problems

Suppose that for some reason a senior lien has been foreclosed and a surplus was produced, but a junior lien exists that is not in default. Should that junior lienor be entitled to payment from the surplus?

15. Gribble v. Stearman & Kaplan, Inc., 249 Md. 289, 239 A.2d 573 (1968).

16. The rule is the same in many states. See Cunningham, Stoebuck & Whitman, Property § 10.8 (1984).

17. For an interesting recent Maryland decision that refused to allow a vendee's claim to a foreclosure surplus to exceed the amount of his contract payments, see Stahl v. Roulhac, 50 Md.App. 382, 438 A.2d 1366 (1982).

18. See Leavell, Love & Nelson, Equitable Remedies and Restitution, 356–362 (3rd Ed.1980).

19. See §§ 3.33–3.34, supra.

Some courts have said yes.[1] In re Castilian Apartments [2] is an interesting contrary case in this regard. In that case a senior mortgage was foreclosed and produced a substantial surplus. The junior mortgage was not in default and contained no acceleration clause that would have made it due and payable whenever the senior mortgage went into default. Moreover, because the junior debt had previously been determined to be usurious, under North Carolina law all right to receive interest on it was forfeited. As a result, the North Carolina Supreme Court approved a lower court determination that the surplus should not be paid to the junior lienor and that it instead should be invested in a certificate of deposit for junior lienor's benefit but with interest to be paid to the debtor.

The foregoing situation is relatively uncommon for several reasons. First, when a foreclosure sale results in a surplus, the debts of junior lien claimants normally will be in default. This will be true automatically with respect to junior judgment lienors. Moreover, if the mortgagor has allowed senior debt to go into default, the chances are strong that the junior debt is in default as well.[3] Second, even if the mortgagor has not otherwise defaulted on senior debt, many junior mortgages provide as a ground for acceleration that any default or foreclosure with respect to a senior encumbrance will give the junior mortgagee the option to accelerate the junior debt. Acceleration for such a reason is generally upheld.[4] Finally, a few states appear to give junior lienors that are not in default the right to be paid from a foreclosure surplus.[5]

Although, as we have seen in the preceding section, the foreclosing mortgagee or trustee is guided by relatively clear substantive law governing the rights of those cut off by a foreclosure sale to share in any surplus, certain practical problems nevertheless sometimes remain. If, of course, the foreclosure is judicial, all interested parties normally are before the court and the court will make a determination as to entitlement to surplus.[6] Also, even in the power of sale setting, there very often will be no problems in identifying those entitled to the surplus and their relative priorities. However, there is always the possibility that the foreclosing mortgagee or trustee will be confronted by conflicting claims as to surplus. In this connection suppose that one of two junior liens claiming rights to the surplus had a lien on only part of the foreclosed real estate. Should the lienor that is prior in time, but whose lien only covered part of the real estate be entitled to all of the

---

§ 7.32

1. See, e.g., Fagan v. Peoples Savings & Loan Association, 55 Minn. 437, 57 N.W. 142 (1893); Moss v. Robertson, 56 Neb. 774, 77 N.W. 403 (1898).

2. 281 N.C. 709, 190 S.E.2d 161 (1972). See Note, Rights in the Proceeds of a Foreclosure Sale—The Court Helps Those Who Help Themselves, 51 N.C.L.Rev. 1100, 1101 (1973).

3. See Note, supra note 2 at 1102.

4. See, e.g., Crescent Beach Co. v. Conzleman, 321 So.2d 437 (Fla.App.1975).

5. See, e.g., Ariz.Rev.Stat. § 33–727.

6. See, e.g., N.Y.—McKinney's Real Prop.Actions & Proc. §§ 1441–1445.

remaining surplus if there is not enough to cover both liens?[7] Suppose a foreclosure sale yields a surplus, but it is insufficient to satisfy the claims of both second and third mortgagees. If the second mortgage debt is more than adequately secured by other property of the mortgagor, should the third mortgagee whose debt is not otherwise secured have a superior claim to the surplus?[8] Payment of the surplus in such situations without judicial guidance would be risky at best. Or suppose a foreclosing trustee, in a state where the power of sale statute does not require notice to junior lienors for foreclosure purposes, fails to conduct a title search and pays out the surplus. If, in fact, another junior lien existed, there is authority for holding the trustee personally liable to the junior lienor.[9] A few statutes, as we have noted in the preceding section, attempt to deal with these problems by authorizing the payment of surplus to the court.[10] In any event, where there is any doubt, the prudent person holding the surplus will seek judicial guidance instead of proceeding at her own risk.

A few courts have asserted that one who accepts a foreclosure surplus elects to ratify the sale and thus may not "treat the sale as a nullity and have it set aside, or sue the trustee for wrongfully conducting the sale." [11] Unless one adheres to the view that any rule that discourages litigation is automatically sound, the foregoing statement seems at best overbroad and at worst unfair. Suppose, for example, that a power of sale foreclosure of a $20,000 mortgage yields a $24,000 sale price. Suppose further that no other liens exist and that the mortgagor accepts the $4,000 surplus. Assume that the sale was not void and that no bona fide purchaser is now the titleholder of the land. The mortgagor, believing that the land was worth considerably more than $24,000, sues to set aside the sale, alleging chilled bidding and a variety of other foreclosure defects. If the mortgagor ultimately prevails, the land will be resold and could yield a foreclosure price either higher or lower than the earlier sale price. If the second sale yields another surplus, the fact that the mortgagor accepted the $4,000 surely does not prejudice the mortgagee, who automatically gets its debt satisfied out of the second sale proceeds. On the other hand, suppose the second sale yields less than the first and produces a deficiency. Under such circumstances, to have allowed mortgagor to

7. See Banks-Miller Supply Co. v. Smallridge, 175 S.E.2d 446 (W.Va.1970). For examples of how courts have resolved similar problems that a trustee would have resolved at his peril, see General Builders Supply Co. v. Arlington Co-op Bank, 359 Mass. 691, 271 N.E.2d 342 (1971); Gribble v. Stearman & Kaplan, Inc., 249 Md. 289, 239 A.2d 573 (1968).

8. See United States v. Century Federal Savings & Loan Association, 418 So.2d 1195 (Fla.App.1982).

9. See, e.g., W.A.H. Church, Inc. v. Holmes, 46 F.2d 608 (D.C.Cir.1931).

10. See, e.g., N.C.Gen.Stat. § 45–21.32; Utah Code Ann. 1953, § 57–1–29. North Dakota legislation instructs the person conducting the sale under a power of sale to wait thirty days after the sale and if no claimants show up he is directed to pay the surplus to the mortgagor.

11. Leonard v. Pell, 56 N.C.App. 405, 407, 289 S.E.2d 140, 142 (1982). See Flake v. High Point Perpetual Building and Loan Association, 204 N.C. 650, 169 S.E. 223 (1933).

retain the prior surplus could prejudice the mortgagee who now would have to attempt to collect a deficiency judgment from a mortgagor who may be insolvent and who may have disposed of that surplus. A fair approach to this potential problem, which would protect the mortgagee, would simply be to require the mortgagor to tender the $4,000 to the court to be held as part of the mortgage res pending the outcome of the suit to set aside. Such an approach would meet the legitimate concern of the mortgagee without burdening the mortgagor with the harsh consequences of the election of remedies concept.

Suppose, however, that the mortgagor decides instead to sue the mortgagee and the trustee for damages for wrongful foreclosure. This remedy may be pursued either because the land is held by a bona fide purchaser or because the jurisdiction affords the mortgagor the option of seeking to set aside the sale or damages.[12] In this setting no legitimate interest of the defendants would be protected by applying the election of remedies principle or by requiring tender by the mortgagor. Because the first sale is not affected by the damages action, the mortgagee's debt remains fully satisfied. Moreover, only if the mortgagor succeeds in establishing that the foreclosure was wrongful and that the market value of the real estate at the time of the foreclosure exceeded the mortgage debt by more than the amount of the surplus,[13] will the mortgagee or trustee be liable for damages, (at least assuming that there is no basis for recovering punitive damages from them).[14]

 WESTLAW REFERENCES
surplus /p foreclos*** /p ratif! null*** "set aside"

---

12. See § 7.22 supra.   14. Id.

13. Id.

§§ 7.33–8.0 are reserved for supplementary material.

Chapter 8

STATUTORY IMPACTS ON FORECLOSURE

Table of Sections

A. REGULATION OF DEFICIENCY JUDGMENTS

§ 8.1 Deficiency Judgments—In General

Generally, the mortgagee has two basic methods of collecting the mortgage debt. The mortgagee may sue and obtain a judgment at law upon the personal obligation and enforce it by levy upon any property of the debtor.[1] Or he may foreclose upon the property. Usually these options may be pursued concurrently or consecutively.[2] In some states, however, while the mortgagee may utilize either of the above options, once he elects one type of action, the prosecution of the other is subject to being dismissed or at least stayed.[3]

Regardless of the method of foreclosure, the mortgagee in most states can obtain a judgment for a deficiency. Where foreclosure is by sale under judicial decree in a court action, the usual method in America and the one under chief consideration here, the amount realized on sale is often an automatic determination of the amount to be applied upon the debt and mortgage creditor, is entitled to recover the balance.[4] Today this ordinarily may be obtained by a deficiency decree given by the equity court in the foreclosure action itself. If there is a power of sale foreclosure the sale price determines the amount to be credited on the debt and the mortgagee can then sue for the balance in an action at law. In those few instances where a mortgagee may obtain strict foreclosure, either by equitable action or by cutting off the mortgagor's rights through taking and holding possession, he can obtain a deficiency judgment for the difference between the value of the land as appraised, normally by the verdict of a jury in the action for the deficiency, and the amount of the debt plus interest and costs.[5] And such a judgment does not reopen the foreclosure so as to give the mortgagor another chance to redeem.

There are a variety of procedural prerequisites to obtaining deficiency judgments.[6] Many states impose strict notice require-

§ 8.1

1. See e.g., Stein v. Nellen Development Corp., 123 Misc.2d 268, 473 N.Y.S.2d 331 (1984); Copp v. Sands Point Marina, Inc., 17 N.Y.2d 291, 270 N.Y.S.2d 599, 217 N.E.2d 654 (1966).

2. See Gottschamer v. August, Thompson, Sherr, Clark & Shafer, P.C., 438 So.2d 408 (Fla.App.1983); Siuslaw Valley Bank, Inc. v. Christopher H. Canfield Associates, Oregon, Limited, 64 Or.App. 198, 667 P.2d 1035 (1983); Berg v. Liberty Federal Savings and Loan Association, 428 A.2d 347, 349 (Del.1981); Belote v. McLaughlin, 673 S.W.2d 27 (Mo.En.Banc.1984); Foothills Holding Corp. v. Tulsa Rig, Reel & Manufacturing Co., 155 Colo. 232, 393 P.2d 749 (1964); Rossiter v. Merriman, 80 Kan. 739, 104 P. 858, 24 L.R.A.,N.S., 1095 (1909); Jewett v. Hamlin, 68 Me. 172 (1878); Bateman v. Grand Rapids & I. R. Co., 96 Mich. 441, 56 N.W. 28 (1893); Gibson v. Green's Administrator, 89 Va. 524, 16 S.E. 661, 37 Am.St.Rep. 888 (1893).

3. See 3 Powell, Real Property, 616 (1977). There are some state statutes that provide that if separate actions are brought upon the debt and to foreclose, the mortgagee must elect which he desires to pursue and the other will be dismissed. See Ariz.Rev.Stat. § 33–722; Iowa Code Ann. § 654.4. Of course, the mortgagee's options will be more substantially limited in those jurisdictions following a "one action" type rule. See the following section.

4. Although the point was considered by Chancellor Kent in Dunkley v. Van Buren, N.Y. 3 Johns.Ch. 330 (1818), and not definitely decided until Lansing v. Goelet, 9 Cow. 346 (N.Y.1827) no case held that a foreclosure sale discharged the personal obligation beyond the amount it produced at the sale. In accord is McKnight v. United States, C.A.9th, 259 F.2d 540 (1958). However, this rule has been substantially altered in those states that have enacted anti-deficiency legislation. See § 8.3, infra.

5. See Tefft, The Myth of Strict Foreclosure, 4 U. of Chi.L.Rev. 575, 594 (1937). See § 7.9, supra.

6. See generally, Comment, The Role of State Deficiency Judgment Law in FHA Insured Mortgage Transactions, 56 Minn.L. Rev. 463, 465–466 (1972).

ments [7] and statutory time limits.[8] The consequences to the mortgagee in failing to comply with such requirements can be harsh. For example, in some states, if the mortgagee fails to seek the deficiency judgment within the specified time period, the foreclosure sale proceeds are deemed to have fully satisfied the mortgage debt.[9]

Moreover, deficiency judgments are subject to certain judicially imposed limitations, at least in the power of sale foreclosure context. For example, in computing the deficiency, some courts will "scrutinize the sale price very closely to assure that the mortgagee acted with strict impartiality." [10] Other cases suggest that a deficiency judgment may be denied where there are sufficient grounds to set aside the sale itself.[11] Price inadequacy may be relevant factor in such a setting if other factors point to an invalid sale.[12] Such circumstances, as we noted in an earlier chapter,[13] may include chilled bidding by the mortgagee or trustee, an unusual hour or unauthorized place of sale, or trustee self-dealing, but these circumstances are usually difficult for the mortgagor to establish.

While the application of the latter standard may be appropriate in a suit to set aside a foreclosure sale, using it to determine the availability of a deficiency judgment is unsound. When a foreclosure sale is set aside, the court may upset third party expectations.[14] A third party may have acquired title to the foreclosed real estate by purchase at the sale or by conveyance from the mortgagee-purchaser. Such a third party may have substantially relied to his detriment on the validity of his purchase. Thus, a strong presumption against setting aside the foreclosure sale is sensible. Moreover, it probably is justified in such a

---

7. See, e.g., Me.Rev.Stat.Ann. § 6203–E (mortgagee required to give at least 21 days notice of his intention to seek a deficiency judgment); Purdon's 12 Penn.Stat. § 2621.3 (notice to mortgagor required ten days before hearing).

8. Statutes often require that the deficiency judgment be sought within a certain period after foreclosure. See, e.g., Nev. Rev.Stat. 40.455 (three months); N.J.Stat. Ann. 2A:50–2 (three months); NDCC 32–19–06 (ninety days) 42 Pa.C.S.A. § 8103. See Valley Trust Company of Palmyra v. Lapitsky, ___ Pa.Super. ___, 488 A.2d 608 (1985); United States v. Merrick Sponsor Corp., 421 F.2d 1076 (C.A.N.Y.1970). Moreover some states limit the time for completion of execution on a deficiency judgment. See, e.g., NDCC 32–19–06 (two years); Ohio Rev.Code § 2329.08 (two years for certain residential and farm property).

9. See N.Y.—McKinney's Real Prop.Actions & Proc.Law § 1371(3); Amsterdam Savings Bank v. Amsterdam Pharmaceutical Development Corporation, 106 A.D.2d 797, 484 N.Y.S.2d 217 (1984); 12 Okl.Stat. Ann. § 686.

10. Danvers Savings Bank v. Hammer, 122 N.H. 1, 440 A.2d 435, 437 (1982) (interpreting Massachusetts law).

11. Regional Investment Co. v. Willis, 572 S.W.2d 191 (Mo.App.1978); Carondelet Savings & Loan Association v. Boyer, 595 S.W.2d 744 (Mo.App.1980); Drannek Realty Co. v. Nathan Frank, Inc., 346 Mo. 187, 139 S.W.2d 926 (1940). Moreover, if a sale is deemed invalid, but the property has been sold to a third party, the mortgagor will be given credit in an action for a deficiency for the reasonable market value of the foreclosed real estate. See In re Estate of Stalcup, 627 S.W.2d 364 (Tenn. App.1981) (interpreting Texas law); Crow v. Heath, 516 S.W.2d 225 (Tex.Civ.App. 1974).

12. See § 7.21 supra. Cf. Fairhaven Savings Bank v. Callahan, 391 Mass. 1011, 462 N.E.2d 112 (1984).

13. See § 7.21 supra.

14. See § 7.20 supra.

setting to deny a mortgagor's claim for relief based solely on price inadequacy. On the other hand, the interests of third parties are not prejudiced in a deficiency proceeding. Because such a proceeding is an in personam action against a mortgagor for money, a deficiency judgment will not divest title from a foreclosure purchaser. Consequently, it seems inappropriate to use in a deficiency context a rule that was developed to make divestiture of title relatively difficult.

Nevertheless, courts have used the foregoing standard to deny deficiency judgments where the fact setting was especially compelling. One Missouri appellate decision, Regional Investment Co. v. Willis,[15] is interesting in this regard. In that case, the mortgagee foreclosed on a deed of trust and purchased the land at the foreclosure sale for approximately $21,000, which was over $6,000 less than the mortgage debt. The mortgagee then sued for a deficiency judgment. The mortgagor alleged that prior to the foreclosure sale, the mortgagee had contracted to sell the lot for $29,000, an amount greater than the mortgage debt. The trial court granted summary judgment for the mortgagee. The court of appeals reversed and stated:

> If the trier of fact found that * * * [the mortgagee] bid the sum of $21,083.94 on * * * [the mortgaged lot] after binding itself to a contract by which it would receive $29,000 immediately after the foreclosure sale, and if the bid was made for the purpose of creating a deficiency, then a sufficient factual basis could be established on which to deny * * * [the mortgagee] recovery for such deficiency. The basis of such a denial would be the legal conclusion that the sale was rendered fundamentally unfair to * * * [the mortgagor] and as such, the trustee's sale price could not be the basis by which to measure a deficiency.[16]

The *Willis* court's reasoning purports to require that a deficiency defense be based on the unfairness of the sale, rather than on the inadequacy of the foreclosure sale price. Indeed, the court suggested that if the mortgagee went to the sale with the property already sold and with the intent to bid less than the mortgage debt, the sale itself would be fundamentally unfair. Logic, however, hardly compels such an automatic result because the trustee, not the mortgagee, conducts the sale. If the trustee is not closely connected to the mortgagee, there is no reason to assume, absent other evidence of trustee misconduct, that the sale is unfair. Absent improper advertising, attempted chilled bidding, or similar traditional bases for upsetting a foreclosure sale,[17] third parties, in theory, have an opportunity to bid. If the property is worth more than the amount the mortgagee had planned on bidding, third party bidding could destroy the mortgagee's scheme in a *Willis*-type situation. In short, the true focus of the *Willis* court probably was

15. 572 S.W.2d 191 (Mo.App.1978).   **17.** See § 7.21 supra.

16. Id. at 193.

not on the fairness of the sale. Rather, the probable basis for the decision was the unfairness in allowing the mortgagee to recover more than the mortgage debt. The court must have been concerned more with the unjust enrichment of the mortgagee than with the fairness of the sale.

 WESTLAW REFERENCES
di deficiency judgment
topic(266) /p deficiency /s judgment /p foreclos!
digest,synopsis(deficiency /s judgment /s notice /p mortgag**)

§ 8.2 The "One Action" Rule

Deficiency judgment questions are often closely related to the "one action" rule in effect in several states. This rule means, in general, that in the event of a default, the mortgagee's sole remedy is a foreclosure action and that any deficiency claim must be sought in that proceeding.[1] The purpose of this rule is two-fold. One is to protect the mortgagor against multiplicity of actions when the separate actions, though theoretically distinct, are so closely connected that normally they can and should be decided in one suit.[2] The other is to compel a creditor who has taken a mortgage on land to exhaust his security before attempting to reach any unmortgaged property to satisfy his claim.[3] The mortgagee, under these provisions, cannot disregard his security even if he wishes to do so, and sue upon the note or debt.[4] Nor may the requirement of the statute be waived by the mortgagor through a provision in the mortgage.[5] On the other hand, the rule does

§ 8.2

1. West's Ann.Cal.Code Civ.Proc. § 726 (a) provides in relevant part: "There can be but one form of action for the recovery of any debt for the enforcement of any right secured by mortgage upon real property, which action must be in accordance with the provisions of this chapter. In the action the court may, by its judgment, direct the sale of the encumbered property." Four other states, Montana, Nevada, Utah, and Idaho, have a "one action" statute patterned after the California statute. Mont. Code Ann. 71–1–222; Nev.Rev.Stat. 40.430; Utah Code Ann. 1969, 78–37–1; Idaho Code § 6–101. See also Note, Anti-Deficiency Judgment Legislation in California, 3 U.C.L.A.L.Rev. 192 (1956). New Jersey has a one action statute, but it is applicable mainly to residential mortgages. See N.J.Stat.Ann. 2A:50–2; Central Penn. National Bank v. Stonebridge Limited, 185 N.J.Super. 289, 448 A.2d 498 (1982).

2. Utah Mortgage and Loan Co. v. Black, 618 P.2d 43 (Utah 1980); Toby v. Oregon Pacific Railroad Co., 98 Cal. 490, 33 P. 550 (1893); Felton v. West, 102 Cal. 266, 36 P. 676 (1894).

3. Bank of Italy v. Bentley, 217 Cal. 644, 20 P.2d 940 (1933), noted, 20 Cal.L. Rev. 318 (1932); 5 So.Cal.L.Rev. 227 (1932); 6 ibid. 7 (1932); 8 ibid. 35 (1934). But see 31 Cal.L.Rev. 429, 431 (1943).

4. Woodruff v. California Republic Bank, 75 Cal.App.3d 108, 141 Cal.Rptr. 915 (1977); Barbieri v. Ramelli, 84 Cal. 154, 23 P. 1086 (1890); Crescent Lumber Co. v. Larson, 166 Cal. 168, 135 P. 502 (1913); Eastern Idaho Production Credit Association v. Placerton, Inc., 100 Idaho 863, 606 P.2d 967 (1980); Clark v. Paddock, 24 Idaho 142, 132 P. 795 (1913), 46 L.R.A.,N.S., 475; Coburn v. Bartholomew, 50 Utah 566, 167 P. 1156 (1922); Cf., Barth v. Ely, 85 Mont. 310, 278 P. 1002 (1929). See note, 25 Cal.L.Rev. 469, 476 (1937).

5. Winklemen v. Sides, 31 Cal.App.2d 387, 88 P.2d 147 (1939), Sup.Ct. hearing den., commented on 27 Cal.L.Rev. 752 (1939). Cf., California Bank v. Stimson, 89 Cal.App. 552, 201 P.2d 39 (1949), commented on, 22 So.Cal.L.Rev. 502 (1949). In 1937

not apply where the security has become valueless.[6] However, some courts take a narrow view of this exception. In Utah,[7] for example, the mortgagee will not be permitted to prove that the total amount of senior liens equals or exceeds the value of the mortgaged real estate. "[I]t is not enough to speculate that the security is valueless, or might become valueless if foreclosed by the senior lienholder. Rather, the security must be, in fact, exhausted and a deficiency established to a certainty in order for the exception to apply. * * * [T]he mortgagee [must] show the security has been foreclosed and sold or otherwise lost by no fault of [the mortgagee] prior to commencement of the action on the note." [8]

Procedurally, a mortgagor may use the rule both defensively and as a sanction. If the mortgagor successfully raises the rule as an affirmative defence, the mortgagee will be required to exhaust the security before obtaining a deficiency judgment.[9] On the other hand, suppose the mortgagor does not raise the rule in the personal action. As the California Supreme Court has stated, the mortgagor "may still invoke it as a sanction against the mortgagee on the basis that the latter by not foreclosing on the security in the action brought to enforce the debt, has made an election of remedies and waived the security." [10]

Some of the states that have "one action" legislation not only apply it to deeds of trust as well as mortgages,[11] but also to power of sale as well as to judicial foreclosure.[12] This means that either judicial foreclo-

such a waiver was explicitly prohibited by code amendment. West's Ann.Cal.Civ. Code § 2953.

6. Hibernia Savings & Loan Society v. Thornton, 109 Cal. 427, 42 P. 447, 50 Am. St.Rep. 52 (1895). See Barbieri v. Ramelli, 84 Cal. 154, 23 P. 1086 (1890); note, 25 Cal. L.Rev. 469, 473 (1937). See also 108 A.L.R. 397 (1937).

7. Lockhart Co. v. Equitable Realty, Inc., 657 P.2d 1333 (Utah 1983).

8. Id. at 1336.

9. Salter v. Ulrich, 22 Cal.2d 263, 138 P.2d 7 (1943); Walker v. Community Bank, 10 Cal.3d 729, 111 Cal.Rptr. 897, 518 P.2d 329 (1974).

10. Walker, supra note 9 at 518 P.2d 334. Interestingly, North Dakota has interpreted its anti-deficiency legislation in such a manner as to create a modified "one action" rule. In that state a mortgagee can either "(1) foreclose without asking for a deficiency judgment, or (2) foreclose, asking for a deficiency judgment in a separate action after the sale of the property, and obtain a judgment for only the difference between the mortgage debt plus costs and the fair value determined by a jury against [the mortgagor] or (3) sue on the note without foreclosure but with recovery limited

to the difference between the amount due on the note plus costs and the fair value of the property determined by a jury." First State Bank of Cooperstown v. Ihringer, 217 N.W.2d 857, 869 (N.D.1974). NDCC 32–19–06 and 32–19–07. Under this interpretation the mortgagee cannot accomplish what he could under the common law, that is, to recover the full debt in a personal action against the mortgagor.

11. See Bank of Italy v. Bentley, 217 Cal. 644, 20 P.2d 940 (1933), certiorari denied 290 U.S. 659, 54 S.Ct. 74, 78 L.Ed. 571 (1933); McMillan v. United Mortgage Co., 82 Nev. 117, 412 P.2d 604 (1966), appeal after remand 84 Nev. 99, 437 P.2d 878 (1968); Nevada Land & Mortgage Co. v. Hidden Wells Ranch, Inc., 83 Nev. 501, 435 P.2d 198 (1967).

12. See Bank of Italy v. Bentley, 217 Cal. 644, 20 P.2d 940 (1933), certiorari denied 290 U.S. 659, 54 S.Ct. 74, 78 L.Ed. 571 (1933); Walker v. Community Bank, 10 Cal.3d 729, 111 Cal.Rptr. 897, 518 P.2d 329 (1974) (where mortgagee sues on the obligation, he thereby "waives his right to foreclose on the security or to sell the security under a power of sale."); Nevada Land & Mortgage Co. v. Hidden Wells Ranch, Inc., 83 Nev. 501, 435 P.2d 198 (1967) (mortgagee may select either judicial foreclosure

sure or the exercise of the power of sale will be a condition precedent to a subsequent action for a deficiency.[13] Where power of sale foreclosure is the predominant method of foreclosure, it is thus perhaps more accurate to refer to the "one action" rule as the "security first" principle.

One action or security first legislation is hardly an unmixed blessing. Even though it generally may be desirable that the mortgagee foreclose on the encumbered real estate before proceeding against other assets of the mortgagor, most mortgagees probably follow such a course of action anyway, at least when the mortgaged real estate was intended to be the primary security for the loan transaction. Many mortgagees, however, rely primarily on the debtor's personal net worth rather than on real estate security. Indeed, the mortgage is often a minor part of the loan transaction. In such a setting, it seems unfair to require the lender to foreclose on the real estate before proceeding against the debtor personally.

 WESTLAW REFERENCES
deficiency /s judgment /p "one action"

§ 8.3 Anti-deficiency Legislation

The great depression of the 1930's, as might be expected, produced a substantial amount of varied state legislation to provide relief for mortgagors. Perhaps best-known were the various mortgage moratoria statutes, most of which have lapsed or have been repealed. This legislation differed substantially from state to state.[1] Some statutes gave courts authority to grant foreclosure postponements on petition of mortgagors in individual cases. Other statutes often extended the period of statutory redemption beyond the usual period or stretched out

or power of sale foreclosure under a deed of trust and then bring an action on the mortgage note for a deficiency judgment.) See also Second Baptist Church v. First National Bank, 89 Nev. 217, 510 P.2d 630 (1973).

13. See notes 11 and 12, supra.

§ 8.3

1. The mortgage moratoria legislation spawned by the 1930's depression is explored in detail in Osborne, Mortgages, § 331 (2d ed. 1970). A few states enacted mortgagor relief legislation in response to the recession of the early 1980's. Connecticut and Minnesota legislation authorize a six-month foreclosure postponement for unemployed homeowners and, in the case of Minnesota, in certain agricultural settings as well. See 1983, Conn.Pub. Act No. 83–547; Minn.Stat.Ann. § 583.07. Pennsylvania legislation, on the other hand, provides for state financial assistance in making mortgage payments to homeown-

ers who suffer financial hardship beyond their control. Such assistance can continue for a maximum period of three years, during which foreclosure would be barred. The mortgagor is obligated to repay the state for any assistance advanced with 9% interest. See 35 Pa.Stat. § 1680.401(c) et seq. See generally, Sclar, Mortgage Foreclosure Relief—Connecticut and Minnesota Act to Protect the Unemployed, 12 Real Est.L.J. 366 (1984). There is a similar financial assistance program for FHA insured loans. See 12 U.S.C.A. § 1715u. In response to the economic dislocation of the 1974–75 recession, Congress enacted the Emergency Homeowners Relief Act of 1975, which authorizes temporary mortgage assistance to homeowners unable who because of unemployment or underemployment are unable to make mortgage payments. The program has as of yet not been funded. See 12 U.S.C.A. §§ 2701–2712.

the periods of time in a foreclosure action. While this type of legislation was subjected to substantial constitutional attack, most of it was upheld. The United States Supreme Court, for example, specifically upheld the Minnesota Moratoria legislation against the attack that it unconstitutionally impaired the obligations of contracts under the Contract Clause of the United States Constitution.[2]

However, the great variety of anti-deficiency legislation of the 1930's probably represents the most significant and enduring legislative impact of mortgage law arising out of the great depression. As we noted in an earlier section,[3] a mortgagee traditionally has been able to obtain a deficiency judgment calculated by subtracting the foreclosure sale price from the mortgage debt. This has usually been the case whether the foreclosure is judicial or by power of sale. Normally, a forced sale, even under stable economic conditions, will not bring a price that will reflect the reasonable market value of the property if it were sold outside of the foreclosure context. In times of depression, moreover, mortgaged property often sells for nominal amounts. The result is that the mortgagee can purchase at the sale for less than the mortgage debt, resell the property at fair market value and, in addition, attempt to realize on a deficiency judgment determined by the difference between the mortgage debt and the foreclosure sale price.

The anti-deficiency legislation of the 1930's represented a new approach to this problem. Instead of focusing on measures aimed at insuring an adequate sale price for the property,[4] the price obtained though the foreclosure sale was often abandoned as a test for the deficiency. The methods employed and the coverage of statutes enacted to cut down the amount of deficiency judgments have been diverse.[5] If the foreclosure is by court action, the court, depending

---

2. See Home Building & Loan Association v. Blaisdell, 290 U.S. 398, 54 S.Ct. 231, 78 L.Ed. 413 (1934).

3. See § 8.1, supra.

4. See § 7.16, supra.

5. See generally, Washburn, The Judicial and Legislative Response to Price Inadequacy in Mortgage Foreclosure Sales, 53 S.Cal.L.Rev. 843 (1980); Nelson, Deficiency Judgments After Real Estate Foreclosures in Missouri: Some Modest Proposals, 47 Mo.L.Rev. 151 (1982); Comment, The Role of State Deficiency Judgment Law in FHA Insured Mortgage Transactions, 56 Minn.L.Rev. 463, 466–68 (1972); Perlman, Mortgage Deficiency Judgments During an Economic Depression, 20 Va.L. Rev. 771 (1934); Poteat, State Legislative Relief for the Mortgage Debtor During the Depression, 5 Law and Contemp.Probs. 517, 539 (1938); Vaughan, Reform of Mortgage Foreclosure Procedure—Possibilities Suggested by Honeyman v. Jacobs, 88 U. of Pa.L.Rev. 957 (1940); Warm, A Study of

Some of the Problems Concerning Foreclosure Sales and Deficiency Judgments, 6 Brooklyn L.Rev. 167 (1936); Skilton, Government and the Mortgage Debtor, Ch. VII; Skilton, Government and the Mortgage Debtor, 1946, 95 U. of Pa.L.Rev. 119, 127. Although earlier decisions sometimes invalidated anti-deficiency statutes on constitutional grounds, later decisions upheld them. Moreover there is little question as to their validity when applied prospectively. See Osborne, Mortgages, § 336 (2d ed. 1970).

Several states have anti-deficiency legislation. See, e.g., West's Ann.Calif.Code Civ.Proc. § 726(b); Idaho Code § 6–108; Nev.Rev.Stat. 40.451 et seq.; N.Y.—McKinney's Real Prop. Actions & Proc. Law § 1371; N.C.Gen.Stat. § 45–21–36; 12 Okl. Stat.Ann. § 686; 12 Purdon's Penn.Stat. § 2621.1; S.C.Code 1962, §§ 29–3–660–29–3–760; So.Dak. Compiled Laws 21–47–16, 21–48–15, 21–49–27; West's Rev.Code Wash.Ann. 61.12.060; Utah Code Ann.

upon the terms of the particular statute, either on the demand of a party, or its own motion, or automatically upon application by the plaintiff for a deficiency, must ascertain the "fair value"[6] of the property and give a decree for the difference between it and the debt.[7] If foreclosure is by sale out of court under a trust deed or power of sale, then similarly the value is to be ascertained in an action at law on the debt with a judgment for the difference only.[8] The "fair value" is sometimes determined by the court,[9] sometimes by a jury[10] and, occasionally, by appraisers.[11]

Fair value legislation has not been free from criticism. Such legislation clearly protects the mortgagor, and may be desirable in the common situation in which the mortgagee purchases at the foreclosure sale, since he ultimately may realize the amount of the debt or more by the resale of the property. When a third party purchases, however, fair value statutes "tend to protect the mortgagor at the expense of the nonpurchasing mortgagee, who receives the sale price rather than the market value for credit against the debt."[12] Indeed, a few states address this concern by limiting the fair value concept to situations where the mortgagee is the sale purchaser.[13]

Florida deficiency legislation is both unique and ambiguous.[14] Under its language, where a deficiency judgment is sought, "the amount bid at the sale may be considered by the court as one of the factors in determining a deficiency under the usual equitable principles."[15] This language[16] has created substantial difficulty for Florida appellate

---

1953, 57–1–32; NDCC 32–19–04, 32–19–06, 32–19–07; Official Code Georgia Ann. § 44–14–161(a).

6. The statutes use a variety of terms to define the "value" of the property for purposes of a deficiency judgment, including "fair value", "true value," "true market value," "reasonable value," "appraised value," "actual value," and "market value." See statutes in preceding footnote. See also, Baumgarten v. Bubolz, 104 Wis.2d 210, 311 N.W.2d 230 (App.1982). Although indefinite, these terms are intended to convey some amount that is not necessarily the same as the foreclosure sale price. See Comment, 47 Mich.L.Rev. 254, 249 (1948). Some courts hold that "fair value" means "intrinsic value". See Rainer Mortgage v. Silverwood Limited, 163 Cal.App.3d 359, 209 Cal.Rptr. 294 (1985).

7. See, e.g., West's Ann.Calif.Code Civ. Proc. § 726(b); N.Y.—McKinney's Real Prop. Actions & Proc.Law § 1371; So.Dak. Compiled Laws 21–47–16.

8. See, e.g., So.Dak. Compiled Laws 21–48–15, 21–49–27; Utah Code Ann. 1953, 57–1–32. For a recent interpretation of the Utah legislation, see Bullington v. Mize, 25 Utah 2d 173, 478 P.2d 500 (1970).

9. See, e.g., West's Ann.Calif.Code Civ. Proc. § 726; N.Y.—McKinney's Real Prop. Actions & Proc.Law § 1371.

10. See, e.g., NDCC 32–19–04, 32–19–06, 32–19–07. For an analysis of this statute, see First State Bank of Cooperstown v. Ihringer, 217 N.W.2d 857 (N.D.1974). See, also, § 8.2, supra.

11. In South Carolina, the value is to be determined by appraisers. See S.C.Code §§ 29–3–660—29–3–760.

12. Washburn, supra note 5 at 940.

13. Me.Rev.Stat.Ann. § 6324. See Kennebec Savings Bank v. Chandler, 447 A.2d 824 (Maine 1982).

14. See West's Fla.Stat.Ann. § 45.031(7).

15. Id.

16. The statutory language was in response to R.K. Cooper Construction Co. v. Fulton, 216 So.2d 11 (Fla.1968), a Florida Supreme Court decision which held:

"The value of the property as established by the sale is conclusive insofar as consideration to support title to the property in the purchaser, but the statutory automatic approval cannot bind the trial courts. While one court has taken the position that "if the value of the foreclosed property exceeds the debt, the chancellor is authorized in denying a deficiency," [17] other decisions emphasize that the granting of a deficiency judgment based on the foreclosure sale price "is the rule rather than the exception" unless fraud or other inequitable conduct infects the sale process.[18] Even these latter cases suggest that a deficiency judgment may be denied or reduced where the foreclosure sale price is "shockingly inadequate" or "unconscionable." [19] Moreover, there is some evidence that Florida trial courts allow mortgagors to introduce evidence of the fair market value of foreclosed real estate and that those courts use their determination of value, rather than the foreclosure sale price, to calculate the amount of the deficiency judgment.[20] Consequently, while it would be inaccurate to assert that Florida is a "fair value" jurisdiction, it would also be misleading to suggest that Florida trial courts have no flexibility in determining whether to use the foreclosure sale price or the market value of the foreclosed real estate as the crucial factor in deficiency judgment proceedings.

Some statutes flatly prohibit a deficiency judgment where the foreclosure has been by power of sale.[21] In California, for example, this prohibition was enacted because of the absence of statutory redemption under power of sale foreclosure. As one commentator pointed out, "by exercising the power [of sale] instead of foreclosing judicially, the creditor could obtain a deficiency judgment as well as the enhanced proceeds of a redemption-free sale. This procedure allowed the creditor to bid in the property himself at an unfairly low price—or offer that opportunity to someone else—secure in the knowledge that any defi-

---

court when a suit at law is filed to enforce collection of the remaining amount due on the note. A shockingly inadequate sale price in the foreclosure proceeding can be asserted as an equitable defense and the trial judge has the discretion and duty to inquire into the reasonable and fair market value of the property sold, the adequacy of the sale price, and the relationship, if any, between the foreclosing mortgagee and the purchaser at the sale, before entering a judgment on the note." Id. at 612.

17. Hamilton Investment Trust v. Escambia Developers, Inc., 352 So.2d 883, 884 (Fla.App.1977). Cf., Fara Manufacturing Co. Inc. v. First Federal Savings and Loan Association of Miami, 366 So.2d 164 (Fla. App.1979).

18. Federal Deposit Insurance Corp. v. Circle Bar Ranch, Inc., 450 So.2d 921 (Fla. App.1984); Lloyd v. Cannon, 399 So.2d 1095, 1096 (Fla.App.1981), review denied 408 So.2d 1092 (1981); Flagship State Bank of Jacksonville v. Drew Equipment Co., 392 So.2d 609, 613 (Fla.App.1981); S/D Enter-

prises, Inc. v. Chase Manhattan Bank, 374 So.2d 1121 (Fla.App.1979).

19. Id. See Wilson v. Adams & Fusselle, Inc., 467 So.2d 345 (Fla.App.1985).

20. See e.g., Coppola v. Housing Investment Corp. of Florida, 400 So.2d 112 (Fla. App.1981).

21. See e.g., Alaska Stat. 34.20.100; Hull v. Alaska Federal Savings & Loan Association, 658 P.2d 122 (Alaska 1983); Suber v. Alaska State Bond Committee, 414 P.2d 546 (Alaska 1966); West's Ann. Calif.Code Civ.Proc. § 580(d); Prunty v. Bank of America, 37 Cal.App.3d 430, 112 Cal.Rptr. 370 n. 7 (1974); Minn.Stat.Ann. § 580.23(1); Victory Highway Village, Inc. v. Weaver, 480 F.Supp. 71 (D.Minn.1979); American National Bank v. Blaeser, 326 N.W.2d 163 (Minn.1982); Norwest Bank Hastings, National Association v. Franzmeier, 355 N.W.2d 431 (Minn.App. 1984); West's Rev.Code Wash.Ann. 61.24.010, 61.24.040, 61.24.100; Helbling Brothers Inc. v. Turner, 14 Wn.App. 494, 542 P.2d 1257 (1975).

ciency would be recoverable in a personal judgment against the [mortgagor]. The absence of a redemption right rendered the [mortgagor] vulnerable to an unrealistically low sales price and prevented * * * him * * * from protecting [himself] by redeeming for the property's true worth. The creditor had an opportunity for a 'double recovery' on the debt." [22]

Some states also prohibit deficiency judgments where the foreclosed mortgage is a purchase money mortgage.[23] While some of these states limit the purchase money concept to transactions in which a vendor takes a mortgage,[24] others also include a variety of third party lenders within the statutory prohibition.[25] A few of them interpret their legislation as barring not only a deficiency judgment, but all mortgagor personal liability as well.[26] In other words, in such jurisdictions, the mortgagee is not permitted to waive the security and sue only on the note.[27]

The Uniform Land Transactions Act (ULTA), promulgated by National Conference of Commissioners on Uniform State Laws in 1975, but as of this writing not adopted by any state, permits deficiency judgments in general, but prohibits them as to purchase money mortgages given by mortgagor-occupants of residential real estate.[28] Purchase money mortgages include both the third party as well as the vendor variety.[29]

Like other anti-deficiency legislation, purchase money statutes have raised their share of problems. An important purpose of such legislation, at least in the residential context, is to protect the mortgagor against the double misfortune of both losing his home in a foreclosure proceeding and incurring a deficiency judgment.[30] Although these statutes "discourage land sales that are unsound because the land is

22. Comment, Exonerating the Surety: Implications of California Anti-deficiency Scheme, 57 Cal.L.Rev. 218, 232 (1969).

23. See West's Ann.Calif.Code Civ.Proc. § 580(b); Ariz.Rev.Stat. § 33–729(A); N.C. Gen.Stat. § 45–21.38; Rev.Code Mont. § 93–6008; Ore.Rev.Stat. 88.070; So.Dak. Compiled Laws 44–8–20—44–8–25.

24. See N.C.Gen.Stat. § 45–21–38; Childers v. Parkers, Inc., 274 N.C. 256, 162 S.E.2d 481 (1968) (statute inapplicable to non-vendor purchase money mortgagees); Currie and Lieberman, Purchase-Money Mortgages and State Lines: A Study in Conflicts of Laws Method, 1960 Duke L.J. 1 (1960). See So.Dak. Compiled Laws 44–8–25.

25. See West's Ann.Calif.Code Civ.Proc. § 580(b); Ariz.Rev.Stat. § 33–729(A).

26. Ross Realty Co. v. First Citizens Bank & Trust Co., 296 N.C. 366, 250 S.E.2d 271 (1979). On the other hand, deficiency judgments are not barred in North Carolina in situations where the mortgagee has previously released a purchase money deed of trust pursuant to agreement or where such a deed of trust has been destroyed by foreclosure of a senior lien. See Barnaby v. Boardman, 70 N.C.App. 299, 318 S.E.2d 907 (1984), review allowed 212 N.C. 621, 323 S.E.2d 921 (1984), reversed __ N.C. __, __ S.E.2d __ (1985) (release); Blanton v. Sisk, 70 N.C.App. 70, 318 S.E.2d 560 (1984) (foreclosure of senior lien).

27. Id.

28. U.L.T.A. § 3–510(b) (1975).

29. Id. at Comment 2.

30. Washburn, supra note 5, at 916.

overvalued," [31] they also may discourage vendor financing of residential sales today, when such financing is often crucial to the transaction. Because high interest rates and tight money often prevent many purchasers from obtaining conventional financing, more vendors must finance all or part of the sale of their residences. To deny such vendor-mortgagees deficiency judgments in the event of a foreclosure may deter the use of socially useful financing. Moreover, it is also undesirable to deny a deficiency judgment to a third party purchase money mortgagee. Indeed, it is especially anomalous to penalize the person or institution who enabled the mortgagor to obtain the real estate in the first place.

If a waiver of the benefit of the anti-deficiency statutes is permitted their effectiveness as a protection to mortgagors may be eroded. [32] There is legislative recognition of such danger in some states in statutes enacted to prevent it. [33] And similar awareness is found in some court decisions. [34] However, a distinction between a waiver entered into at the time the mortgage is given and one subsequent in time has been drawn, the former being bad and the latter good. [35] This corresponds to the similar distinction broadly drawn by the courts when the question is one of protecting the mortgagor's right of redemption. [36]

In some states limitations on the amount of a deficiency have been coupled with restrictions on the bringing of an action on the debt alone under which unmortgaged assets can be reached. This is true, of course, in states already having the "one action" rule. [37] But other states have enacted legislation somewhat toward the same end, notably New York. [38] There an action on the note and an action to foreclose

---

31. Bargioni v. Hill, 59 Cal.2d 121, 123, 28 Cal.Rptr. 321, 322, 378 P.2d 593, 594 (1963).

32. See Skilton, Government and the Mortgage Debtor, 125.

33. E.g., 12 Pa.Stat. § 2621.10; West's Ann.Cal.Civ.Code § 2953.

West's Ann.Cal.Civ.Code § 2953 vitiates "any express agreement made or entered into at the time of or in connection with the making or renewing of any loan secured by a deed of trust, mortgage or other instrument creating a lien on real property, whereby the borrower agrees to waive the rights, or privileges conferred upon him by sections 2924, 2924b, 2924c of the Civil Code or by sections 580a or 726 of the Code of Civil Procedure." Even though sections 580b and 580d are not covered by the above statute, they may not be waived at the time the loan is made. See Freedland v. Greco, 45 Cal.2d 462, 289 P.2d 463 (1955); Valinda Builders v. Bissner, 230 Cal.App.2d 106, 40 Cal.Rptr. 735 (1964); Hetland, Secured Real Estate Transactions, 220 (1974).

34. Salter v. Ulrich, 22 Cal.2d 263, 266, 138 P.2d 7, 146 A.L.R. 1344 (1943); Morello v. Metzenbaum, 25 Cal.2d 494, 154 P.2d 670 (1944); Cf., Winklemen v. Sides, 31 Cal.App.2d 387, 88 P.2d 147 (1939); Cf. also California Bank v. Stimson, 89 Cal.App.2d 552, 201 P.2d 39 (1949); commented on 22 So.Cal.L.Rev. 502 (1949). See Notes, 27 Cal.L.Rev. 752 (1939); 31 Cal.L.Rev. 429, 434 (1943); Cf., 31 Cal.L.Rev. 429 (1943).

35. West's Ann.Cal.Civ.Code § 2953; Salter v. Ulrich, 22 Cal.2d 263, 266, 138 P.2d 7, 146 A.L.R. 1344 (1943); Morello v. Metzenbaum, 25 Cal.2d 494, 499, 154 P.2d 670 (1944). See Russell v. Roberts, 39 Cal. App.3d 390, 114 Cal.Rptr. 305 (1974). But in Pennsylvania a waiver or release is void regardless of whether before, after, or at the time the mortgage is given. 12 Pa. Stat. § 2621.10.

36. See § 3.1, supra.

37. See § 8.2, supra.

38. N.Y.—McKinney's Real Property Actions and Proc.Law § 1301. See Friedman, Personal Liability on Mortgage Debts in New York, 51 Yale L.J. 382, 387 (1942).

cannot be pursued concurrently.[39] If the mortgagee sues upon the debt, he cannot later foreclose until execution has been returned wholly or partially unsatisfied.[40] Conversely, while a foreclosure action is pending or after final decree he cannot bring an action on the debt alone without permission of the court in which the foreclosure action was brought.[41] While such legislation does not compel the mortgagee to foreclose first, it does, like the "one action" rule, protect the mortgagor from the burden of defending simultaneously closely related multiple actions where only one proceeding may be necessary to satisfy the mortgagee's claim.

Guarantors of the mortgage debt frequently attempt to invoke the protection of anti-deficiency legislation. While the case law is substantial,[42] generalization in this area is hazardous for a variety of reasons. First, most of the cases involve questions of legislative intent and, in many instances, that intent is hardly apparent. Often cases will turn on the specific and sometimes unique language of a particular statute. Finally, all anti-deficiency legislation does not serve identical policy objectives and, consequently, courts may interpret certain types of statutes more broadly than others.

Notwithstanding these difficulties, certain observations are appropriate. There clearly is a judicial predisposition to deny guarantors the protection of anti-deficiency legislation.[43] Courts typically reason that the liability of a guarantor is based on a separate and distinct contract of guaranty and not imposed by the note or the mortgage securing it.[44] Moreover, some courts stress that where the statute does not clearly encompass guarantors, they will be reluctant to extend statutory protection to them.[45] Guarantors are, however, sometimes successful. For example, where a statute specifically applied to persons "directly or indirectly or contingently liable", courts have protected guarantors under it.[46] Moreover, courts are sometimes responsive to "substance over form" arguments. Thus, anti-deficiency protection has been extended to persons who formally played the role of guarantor, but who were in substance the principal obligors of mortgage debt incurred by

39. See Stein v. Nellen Development Corp., 123 Misc.2d 268, 473 N.Y.S.2d 331 (1984); Stein v. Blatte, 118 Misc.2d 633, 461 N.Y.S.2d 189 (1983); D'Agostino v. Wheel Inn, Inc., 65 Misc.2d 227, 317 N.Y.S. 2d 472 (1970); Citibank (Mid-Hudson), N.A. v. Rohdie, 82 Misc.2d 372, 368 N.Y.S.2d 109 (1975).

40. N.Y—McKinney's Real Property Actions and Proc.Law § 1301(1).

41. Id. at § 1301(3). See cases in note 39, supra.

42. See generally Annot., 49 A.L.R.3d 554 (1973).

43. See, e.g., Mariners Savings and Loan Association v. Neil, 22 Cal.App.3d 232, 99 Cal.Rptr. 238 (1972); Thomas v.

Valley Bank of Nevada, 97 Nev. 320, 629 P.2d 1205 (1981); Mandan Security Bank v. Heinsohn, 320 N.W.2d 494 (N.D.1982); Bank of Kirkwood Plaza v. Mueller, 294 N.W.2d 640 (N.D.1980); Victory Highway Village, Inc. v. Weaver, 480 F.Supp. 71 (D.Minn.1979).

44. See, e.g., Thomas v. Valley Bank of Nevada, 97 Nev. 320, 629 P.2d 1205 (1981); Mandan Security Bank v. Heinsohn, 320 N.W.2d 494 (N.D.1982).

45. See, e.g., Bank of Kirkwood Plaza v. Mueller, 294 N.W.2d 640 (1980).

46. See Klinke v. Samuels, 264 N.Y. 144, 190 N.E. 324 (1934); Kramer v. Relgov Realty Co., 268 N.Y. 592, 198 N.E. 420 (1935).

"dummy" or straw party mortgagors.[47] A somewhat similar approach has been utilized in less obvious situations. Some courts have held, for example, that where an individual partner guarantees the debt of the partnership, she can assert anti-deficiency protection because, given the nature of the partnership entity, the guarantor is "nothing more than the principal obligor under another name." [48] Other courts, however, have been unwilling to extend such protection to partner-guarantors.[49]

The California Anti-deficiency Scheme

Perhaps more than any jurisdiction, California has a complex and pervasive anti-deficiency legislative scheme. First, under its "one action" rule contained in section 726(a) of the Code of Civil Procedure (CCP), the mortgagee's sole judicial remedy is a foreclosure action and any deficiency judgment must be sought in that action.[50] Moreover, the section 726(a) bar, as noted in an earlier section,[51] can be used both defensively and as a sanction. The mortgagor may raise it in any proceeding on the debt in order to force the mortgagee to foreclose. However, if the mortgagor does not raise the section 726(a) defense in the debt proceeding, he nevertheless will be permitted to utilize it in any subsequent foreclosure proceeding to prevent the mortgagee from reaching the real estate security.[52]

This sanction has been rigorously imposed. For example, resort to real estate foreclosure has been barred where the creditor first proceeded against chattel security without simultaneously seeking foreclosure of the real estate.[53] Moreover, where a bank filed no formal action against a mortgagor, but simply set off against accrued interest on the mortgagor's delinquent loan the balance in his bank account, it was held to have violated section 726(a) and thus to have waived its right to foreclose on the mortgagor's real estate.[54] Finally, the Ninth Circuit Court of Appeals held that even where a creditor proceeded properly by one action and included all security, real and personal, but failed after

---

47. See, e.g., In re Wilton-Maxfield Management Co., 117 F.2d 913 (9th Cir. 1941); Valinda Builders, Inc. v. Bissner, 230 Cal.App.2d 106, 40 Cal.Rptr. 735 (1964).

48. See Union Bank v. Dorn, 254 Cal. App.2d 157, 61 Cal.Rptr. 893 (1967); Riddle v. Lushing, 203 Cal.App.2d 831, 21 Cal. Rptr. 902 (1962).

49. See Mandan Security Bank v. Heinsohn, 320 N.W.2d 494 (N.D.1982).

50. See § 8.2, note 1 supra.

51. See § 8.2 supra.

52. See § 8.2, notes 9 and 10, supra. Numerous related problems arise under the "one action" rule when there are mul-tiple security devices and multiple debts or combinations thereof. Problems also are created when debt is secured by both chattel and real property security. See Hetland, Secured Real Estate Transactions, §§ 9.14, 9.6 (Calif.Cont.Ed.Bar 1974); Walker v. Community Bank, 10 Cal.3d 729, 111 Cal.Rptr. 897, 518 P.2d 329 (1974). Further complications can arise with piecemeal foreclosure of multiple security devices. See Hetland, supra, at § 9.16.

53. Walker v. Community Bank, 10 Cal. 3d 729, 111 Cal.Rptr. 897, 518 P.2d 329 (1974).

54. Bank of America National Trust and Savings Association v. Daily, 152 Cal. App 3d 767, 199 Cal.Rptr. 557 (1984).

the foreclosure sale of the real estate to seek a "fair value" hearing, it forfeited its security interest in the personalty.[55]

If the mortgage or deed of trust contains a power of sale, the mortgagee may foreclose nonjudicially. If he elects to do so, however, section 580d of the CCP prohibits any deficiency judgment at all.[56] Assuming that the mortgagee chooses instead to foreclose judicially, he nevertheless will be prevented from obtaining a deficiency judgment if he is a purchase money mortgagee of the type that we will consider in succeeding paragraphs. Finally, assuming that our mortgagee both forecloses judicially and has no purchase money mortgage problem, the amount of the deficiency will be governed by section 726(b), which imposes a "fair value" limitation of the type considered earlier in this section.[57]

The prohibition on deficiency judgments for purchase money mortgagees has presented special and complex problems. Under section 580b of the CCP, purchase money lenders include all vendors who take back real estate security and those third party lenders who take a mortgage or deed of trust to secure all or part of the purchase price of purchaser-occupied dwellings of less than five families.[58] The twin purposes of section 580b, according to earlier case law, were "to discourage land sales that are unsound because the land is overvalued and, in the event of a depression in land values to prevent the aggravation of the downturn that would result if defaulting purchasers lost the land and were further burdened with personal liability." [59]

The soundness of the overvaluation rationale is highly dubious. Professor Hetland has argued that section 580b actually *encourages*

---

55. In re Kristal, 37 B.R. 659 (Bkrtcy. App. 9th Cir.1984), affirmed 758 F.2d 454 (9th Cir.1985). Accord: In re Rivers, 39 B.R. 608 (Bkrtcy.Cal.1984) (same rule but second item of security was real estate).

56. Section 580d provides in pertinent part: "No judgment shall be rendered for any deficiency upon a note secured by a deed of trust or mortgage upon real property hereafter executed in any case in which real property has been sold by the mortgagee or trustee under power of sale contained in such a mortgage or deed of trust * * *."

57. See West's Ann.Cal.Civ.Code § 726(b); Rainer Mortgage v. Sherwood Limited, 163 Cal.App.3d 359, 209 Cal.Rptr. 294 (1985).

58. West's Ann.Cal.Civ.Code § 580b, provides:

"No deficiency judgment shall lie in any event after any sale of real property for failure of the purchaser to complete his contract of sale, or under a deed of trust, or mortgage, given to the vendor to

secure payment of the balance of the purchase price of real property, or under a deed of trust, or mortgage, on a dwelling for not more than four families given to a lender to secure repayment of a loan which was in fact used to pay all or part of the purchase price of such dwelling occupied, entirely or in part, by the purchaser."

Section 580b has even been interpreted to bar a post-foreclosure fraud action by mortgagee against mortgagor where alleged fraud arose out of the mortgage transaction. See First Federal Savings and Loan Association v. Lehman, 159 Cal. App.3d 537, 205 Cal.Rptr. 600 (1984).

On the other hand, section 580b does not bar a deficiency judgment where a purchase money mortgage was released, its note was extinguished, and a new note was executed secured by a non-purchase money mortgage. See Goodyear v. Mack, 159 Cal. App.3d 654, 205 Cal.Rptr. 702 (1984).

59. Bargioni v. Hill, 59 Cal.2d 121, 28 Cal.Rptr. 321, 378 P.2d 593 (1963).

overvaluation, since "The seller will sell for as high a price as he can, even though he is to be undersecured, CCP § 580b notwithstanding. If he cannot get additional security and chooses not to take a separate unsecured note, the seller certainly has nothing to lose by taking a purchase-money trust deed that includes the part of the price that is in excess of the property's value or that exceeds the price he could obtain elsewhere. Because of CCP § 580b, he can look only to the property for satisfaction in case of default, regardless of what price he can obtain. A valueless encumbrance for the excess leaves the seller in no worse position than if he had not had it." [60]

In Brown v. Jensen,[61] the California Supreme Court held that section 580b barred a junior purchase money lender, the vendor, from recovering a personal judgment from the vendee-borrower even though his security had been lost through foreclosure by the senior purchase money deed of trust. The court reached this result notwithstanding the fact that for purposes of section 726a, the "one action" rule, it was well settled that if the security has become valueless through no fault of the mortgagor or trustor, the secured creditor may then proceed directly against the mortgagor or trustor.[62] To reach its result, the court held that the section 726b analogy was inapplicable because the action was for a deficiency on a note secured by a purchase money trust deed, stating that "a deficiency is nothing more than the difference between the security and the debt" and therefore may consist of the whole debt.[63] The court said that the nature of the security transaction as a purchase money one is determined and fixed for all time at the time it is executed so that no deficiency judgment may be obtained regardless of whether the security becomes valueless. It also relied on the language of section 580b which states that in *no event* shall there be a deficiency judgment.

Institutional lenders infrequently can, or will, take a junior encumbrance. Consequently the vast majority of junior purchase money lenders are individual sellers. Furthermore, the enormous increase in recent years of the use of subordination agreements by sellers who are nonprofessionals in the real property business has resulted in the junior encumbrancer being a seller, frequently a farmer or rancher, who has subordinated his purchase money lien to the construction loan mortgage of the buyer, a real estate promotor or developer.[64] The application of Brown v. Jensen to this kind of a transaction results in a patent inequity. "Since the construction loan typically is several times larger than the seller's land loan, the subordinated seller rarely has any hope

---

60. Hetland, Secured Real Estate Transactions 212–13 (Calif.Cont.Ed.Bar 1974), quoted with approval in Budget Realty, Inc. v. Hunter, 157 Cal.App.3d 511, 204 Cal.Rptr. 48 (1984).

61. 41 Cal.2d 193, 259 P.2d 425 (1953), certiorari denied 347 U.S. 905, 74 S.Ct. 430, 98 L.Ed. 1064 (1954).

62. See § 8.2, supra.

63. Brown v. Jensen, supra at 195, 198, 259 P.2d at 426, 427.

64. See § 12.9, infra.

of reinstating the construction loan in the event of the developer's default. If doing so is a prerequisite to his protection, as it is under Brown v. Jensen, he is without remedy. There is nothing in section 580b that expressly precludes the junior from recovering a judgment against the developer for the amount owing after the construction lender takes the security; only Brown v. Jensen's strained construction of section 580b prevents it." [65]

That "strained interpretation" was rejected by the California Supreme Court in Spangler v. Memel,[66] a case involving the subordinated vendor referred to in the preceding paragraph. There a seller of land to a commercial developer took back a deed of trust which she subordinated to the lien of a construction lender. The construction lien was foreclosed and the vendor's junior lien was thus destroyed. Contrary to Brown v. Jensen, the court held that the sold out purchase money junior lienor was not subject to the deficiency prohibition of section 580b. Although the court emphasized the overvaluation function of section 580b, it "no longer looked at overvaluation from the viewpoint of the seller or lender who would presumably accommodate the buyer/borrower by making an unsound loan. Instead, the court viewed the purchase from the standpoint of the buyer/developer and concluded that the imposition of personal liability, rather than its prevention, would preclude overvaluation!" [67] Because the imposition of personal liability on the developer would reduce the inclination of developers to obtain subordinated financing, the likelihood of overvaluation in subordinated financing devices would be lessened.[68] The Spangler court made it clear, however, that it was not overruling Brown v. Jensen. Rather, section 580b still prevented a deficiency in favor of the sold out junior purchase money lienor in "standard", as opposed to "varietal" purchase money transactions.[69]

Moreover, *Spangler* cannot be interpreted to create a section 580b exception for all vendors who agree to subordinate their liens to construction financing. In Budget Realty, Inc. v. Hunter,[70] the Court of Appeals applied section 580b to deny a deficiency judgment to a foreclosed vendor-mortgagee who had agreed to subordinate his lien to up to $400,000 of construction financing. However, it was not the foreclosure of a construction loan that destroyed the vendor's lien. Rather, it was wiped out by the foreclosure of a deed of trust which vendor apparently had earlier placed on the property and to which the purchaser had taken subject. In fact, the construction financing contemplated by the agreement to subordinate never took place. Thus the

---

65. See Hetland, Real Property and Real Property Security: The Well Being of the Law, 53 Cal.L.Rev. 151, 161 (1965).

66. 7 Cal.3d 603, 102 Cal.Rptr. 807, 498 P.2d 1055 (1972). For an excellent consideration of this case, see Hetland, Secured Real Estate Transactions, § 9.24 (1974); Leipziger, Deficiency Judgments in Califor-

nia: The Supreme Court Tries Again, 22 U.C.L.A.L.Rev. 753 (1975).

67. Leipziger, supra note 66 at 766.

68. Id. at 768.

69. Hetland, supra note 66 at 210.

70. 157 Cal.App.3d 511, 204 Cal.Rptr. 48 (1984).

court reasoned that *Spangler* did not dictate an exception to the protection afforded purchasers by section 580b. In conclusion, it stated:

> "By examining the additional jeopardy the purchase money security is exposed to, we focus on the substance of the subordination transaction. If the simple presence of a subordination clause takes a transaction outside 580b protection, a seller could insert an agreement accepting subordination of his purchase money mortgage to a one dollar construction loan. To create absurd forms that effect waiver where the Legislature does not allow explicit waiver is undesirable. If the Legislature determines that commercial transactions should be outside 580b application, the Legislature could amend 580b to apply only to residential transactions. Explicit negotiations in commercial contexts might be desirable. However, imposition of personal liability should not turn on form." [71]

California courts seem intent on protecting the residential borrower in section 580b contexts. The Court of Appeal decision in Prunty v. Bank of America [72] illustrates this tendency. In that case the Pruntys borrowed money from the bank to build a single family dwelling on a lot they had acquired earlier. They gave the bank a note and deed of trust on the lot and used the proceeds to build the dwelling. After they moved in, the house and part of the lot were destroyed by a landslide. The Pruntys sought a declaratory judgment that section 580b barred a deficiency judgment in favor of the bank even though the loan proceeds had not been used to acquire the lot. The Court of Appeal held in favor of the Pruntys. It believed that the overvaluation purpose of section 580b was served by applying the statute in this case because it would tend to discourage unsound construction lending where the construction is overvalued.[73] Second, the depression "cushion" function of section 580b was enhanced because the court believed that no distinction should be drawn between devaluation caused by natural acts and that resulting from the economic cycle.[74] Moreover, the court also indicated that, in view of the control the bank exercised over the plans and construction of the Prunty residence, it was not unreasonable for the bank to bear the loss. The court appeared to follow the implications of *Spangler* "by affording section 580b protection to a residential borrower while applying the judicially created policies undergirding the purchase money anti-deficiency legislation to the facts of the case." [75]

It would be a mistake, however, to suggest that California courts have forsaken the commercial investor-purchaser for section 580b purposes. In Shepherd v. Robinson,[76] the Court of Appeal applied section 580b to deny a deficiency judgment to a vendor whose junior lien on an

---

71. Id. at 52.

72. 37 Cal.App.3d 430, 112 Cal.Rptr. 370 (1974). See Leipziger, supra note 65 at 784–785.

73. Hetland, supra note 66 at 215.

74. Id. at 215.

75. Id.

76. 128 Cal.App.3d 615, 180 Cal.Rptr. 342 (1981).

apartment complex had been destroyed by the foreclosure of a senior lien. The court identified as exceptions to 580b only construction financing situations such as *Spangler* and settings involving a "special relationship between the parties." [77]

One example of the "special relationship" type case is Nickerman v. Ryan,[78] a 1979 Court of Appeal decision. In that case the court limited the impact of section 580b on a mortgage transaction that was incident to a post-dissolution agreement adjusting the interests of an ex-wife and ex-husband in property held as tenants in common. The agreement provided for the conveyance of the ex-wife's interest in a motel and certain other real estate to the ex-husband. In return, ex-husband delivered to her a promissory note for $25,000 secured by a deed of trust on the motel and conveyed to her his interest in the former family home and certain other property. Later, foreclosure of a senior lien on the motel wiped out her junior deed of trust lien. She then sued him for a deficiency judgment on the note. The ex-husband asserted that section 580b barred such a judgment because the deed of trust was given to secure the "purchase" by him of her interest in the motel and other real estate. The trial court found that the "note and deed of trust were not given to [ex-wife] to secure payment of the balance of the purchase price of the [motel], but rather to equalize a division of community property after a decree of divorce".[79] In affirming this trial court finding, the Court of Appeal also determined that "the transaction * * * is such a variation on the standard purchase money mortgage or deed of trust transaction that it would not subserve the purposes of section 580b * * * to deny a deficiency judgment in this case." [80] According to the court, "it would be ironic to hold that the [ex-wife] who entered into the transaction to be free of the vicissitudes of the commercial enterprises, and so surrendered her joint right of control, should find that her fair share of the joint property was lost because of the sole management of the [ex-husband] who assumed the risks of the motel and apartment business." She is deserving of the same consideration given the vendor in Spangler v. Memel." [81]

Interestingly, the non-purchase money junior lienor whose lien is destroyed by a senior foreclosure is in a stronger position than his purchase money counterpart. Unlike the purchase money anti-deficiency provision, section 580d requires that there have been an actual sale by the mortgagee or trustee under the power, and excludes situations in which the security is exhausted in some other fashion.[82] There is a certain logic to this position. As noted earlier, California power of sale foreclosure legislation does not afford statutory redemption rights to those whose interests are destroyed by foreclosure.[83] As Professor

77. Id. at 625, 180 Cal.Rptr. at 346.

78. 93 Cal.App.3d 564, 155 Cal.Rptr. 830 (1979).

79. Id. at 572, 155 Cal.Rptr. at 834.

80. Id. at 568, 155 Cal.Rptr. at 831.

81. Id. at 575–576, 155 Cal.Rptr. at 836.

82. See Riesenfeld, California Legislation Curbing Deficiency Judgments, 48 Cal. L.Rev. 705, 722 (1960).

83. See text at notes 21–22, supra.

Hetland has pointed out, section 580d should "not bar a junior creditor * * * who has not himself had the nonjudicial sale which exhausted the security. A redemption statute substitute should bar no one other than a creditor whose lien is foreclosed; certainly it should not impair the remedy of one who himself would have the right to redeem." [84]

On the other hand, section 580d will probably apply where both junior and senior liens are owned by the same lender and power of sale foreclosure of the senior destroys the junior. A Court of Appeal decision has held that an action to enforce the junior debt in such a situation was barred by section 580d.[85] While the court's reasoning was not completely discernible, two themes clearly emerge. First, the opinion of the court indicated that the junior debt was really secured by the first deed of trust because the latter contained a "dragnet" clause that had the effect of making the first deed of trust security for the debtor's future obligations to the creditor.[86] Second, there is the perhaps more persuasive policy argument of the concurring opinion. That opinion noted that the central question was whether by making two loans on the same security, a lender was permitted, by power of sale foreclosure of the first deed of trust "(1) to obtain title to the real property security, and then (2) hold the borrower liable for a deficiency, * * * the security for which had been rendered valueless by the lender's own act. Such a practice would be contrary to the provisions of section 580d, and to the policy expressed thereby. It would permit the lender to frustrate the statute's purpose by obtaining the real property security at [a power of sale foreclosure] thus denying the borrower any right of redemption, and also obtaining a judgment for the remaining deficiency." [87] Indeed, to place a slightly different emphasis on Professor Hetland's analysis referred to earlier, the application of section 580d in such a situation bars a junior creditor whose *own* nonjudicial sale exhausted the security. Moreover, since a party presumably cannot under statutory redemption redeem from himself as sale purchaser, the bar of section 580d is not here impairing the remedy of "one who himself would have had the right to redeem." [88]

Another part of the California anti-deficiency scheme, section 580a of the Code of Civil Procedure,[89] has recently taken on new significance.

---

84. Hetland, Deficiency Judgment Legislation in California—A New Judicial Approach, 51 Cal.L.Rev. 1, 31 (1963).

85. Union Bank v. Wendland, 54 Cal. App.3d 393, 126 Cal.Rptr. 549 (1976).

86. Id. at 401–407, 126 Cal.Rptr. at 556–558.

87. Id. at 409, 126 Cal.Rptr. at 561.

88. Hetland, supra note 81 at 31.

89. See West's Ann.Cal.Civ.Code § 580a, which provides in relevant part:

Whenever a money judgment is sought for the balance due upon an obligation for the payment of which a deed of trust or mortgage with power of sale upon real property or any interest therein was given as security, following the exercise of the power of sale in such deed of trust or mortgage, the plaintiff shall set forth in his complaint the entire amount of the indebtedness which was secured by said deed of trust or mortgage at the time of sale, the amount for which such real property or interest therein was sold and the fair market value thereof at the date of sale * * *. Before rendering any judgment the court shall find the fair market value of the real property, or

That section, like its section 726(b) judicial foreclosure counterpart, imposes a fair value limitation on actions for a deficiency judgment following power of sale foreclosure. Section 580a is usually irrelevant because, as we have seen earlier,[90] section 580d already bars a mortgagee foreclosing by power of sale from obtaining a deficiency judgment.

However, section 580a has always had some potential for debtor protection in those situations where a junior lien is wiped out by a power of sale foreclosure of a senior interest. Suppose, for example, that a senior lien of $30,000 is foreclosed by power of sale, thus eliminating a $15,000 junior lien. Suppose further that the fair market value of the land at the time of the senior sale was $50,000 and that the foreclosed junior lienor seeks a deficiency judgment against the debtor for $15,000. Arguably, it is unfair to allow the junior lienor to recover because he could have protected himself by taking part at the foreclosure sale. By so doing, he either could have obtained land that was worth enough to cover his debt or, if someone else was the ultimate purchaser, the junior's bidding could have insured that the sale yielded enough of a surplus so that his lien would have been satisfied out of the sale proceeds. As we noted earlier, section 580d would not bar our foreclosed junior lienor from obtaining a deficiency judgment because he was not the foreclosing party. However, if the fair value concept of section 580a is applicable to non-foreclosing parties as well as to foreclosing lienors, it could be used to deny deficiency relief to the foreclosed junior to the extent that the fair value of the property exceeded the senior debt. Since in our fact situation, the fair value of the land exceeded the senior debt by $20,000, there was sufficient value to cover the junior debt and the junior arguably should be denied any deficiency judgment against the debtor.

Such an interpretation of section 580a was rejected by the California Supreme Court in 1963 in Roseleaf Corp. v. Chierighino.[91] The *Roseleaf* court stated:

> The position of a junior lienor whose security is lost through a senior sale is different from that of a selling senior lienor. A selling senior can make certain that the security brings an amount equal to his claim against the debtor or the fair market value, whichever is less, simply by bidding in for that amount. He need not invest any additional funds. The junior lienor, however, is in no better position to protect himself than is the debtor. Either would have to invest additional funds to

interest therein sold, at the time of sale. The court may render judgment for not more than the amount by which the entire amount of the indebtedness due at the time of sale exceeded the fair market value of the real property or interest therein sold at the time of sale with interest thereon from the date of sale; provided, however, that in no event shall the amount of said judgment, exclusive

of interest after the date of sale, exceed the difference between the amount for which the property was sold and the entire amount of the indebtedness secured by said deed of trust or mortgage.

* * *

90. See note 56 supra.

91. 59 Cal.2d 35, 27 Cal.Rptr. 873, 378 P.2d 97 (1963).

redeem or buy in at the sale. Equitable considerations favor placing this burden on the debtor, not only because it is his default that provokes the senior sale, but also because he has the benefit of his bargain with the junior lienor who, unlike the selling senior, might otherwise end up with nothing.[92]

However, in Bank of Hemet v. United States,[93] the United States Court of Appeals for the Ninth Circuit rejected this interpretation of section 580a and, in so doing, drew a distinction between the foreclosed junior who purchases at the senior sale and one who does not. In the former setting, the one confronting the court, "only to the extent the combined debts exceed the fair market value of the property should a deficiency judgment be permitted. In addition, in no event should the deficiency judgment exceed the amount by which the combined debts are greater than the amount for which the property sold."[94] This conclusion required the court to interpret "the entire amount of the indebtedness due at the time of the sale" to include the amount of both senior and junior debt. This gloss was, according to the court, "consistent with the general purpose of section 580a, *viz.*, to protect against buying in the property at a deflated price, obtaining a deficiency judgment, and achieving a recovery in excess of the debt by reselling the property at a profit."[95]

Whether the California courts adopt the *Bank of Hemit* view of section 580a remains to be seen. However, at least one commentator believes they should. "California's anti-deficiency rules * * * are best viewed, not as a completed system of regulation, but only as a framework for that system. It is left to the courts to build from that framework, a coherent scheme of debtor protection. Seen in this light, *Roseleaf's* reading of section 580a, which in terms applies only to deficiency judgments obtained by the foreclosing beneficiary, was an unnecessarily literal one. The *Bank of Hemit* court correctly perceived that fair value provisions such as section 580a are intended to prevent *any* creditor from reaping a windfall at the debtor's expense by combining a deficiency judgment with a bargain purchase of the property."[96]

 WESTLAW REFERENCES

anti-deficiency /p mortgag**
"fair value" /p foreclos! /p deficiency
"power of sale" /p foreclos! /p deficiency
"purchase money mortgage" /p foreclos! /p deficiency
guarantor /p anti-deficiency
anti-deficiency /p 580a 580b & court(ca)
266k559(2) /p deficiency

---

92. Id. at 41, 378 P.2d at 100, 27 Cal. Rptr. at 876.

93. 643 F.2d 661 (9th Cir.1981).

94. Id. at 669.

95. Id. at 669.

96. Comment, California Fair Value Limitations Applied to Non-Foreclosing Junior Lienholder, 12 Golden Gate L.Rev. 317, 322–323 (1982).

B. STATUTORY REDEMPTION

§ 8.4 General Characteristics

When a valid foreclosure has taken place, the equitable right of redemption or the "right to redeem from the mortgage" ends.[1] However, more than half the states authorize a statutory right of redemption which provides an additional time period for mortgagors, their successors in interest, and, in many instances, junior lienors, to pay a certain sum of money, usually the foreclosure sale price, to redeem the title to the property.[2] To some extent we have already considered the impact of such legislation in the context of the omitted lienor situation.[3] The statutory time periods vary greatly from state to state, being as short as six months in a few states [4] and as long as two years in others.[5] Most statutes specify a twelve month period. In the vast majority of states, the mortgagor will have the right to possession during the statutory period,[6] although in one or two states both statutory redemption itself, as well as the right to possession, is conditioned on the posting of a bond by the mortgagor.[7] In most states statutory redemption is available in both judicial and power of sale type foreclosure, although in several it is unavailable in the power of sale setting [8] and in one other it

§ 8.4

1. See § 7.1 supra.

2. See Code of Ala.Code 1975, §§ 6–5–230, 231, 232; Alaska Stats. 09.45.190, 09.35.250; Ariz.Rev.Stat. § 12–1282; Ark. Stats. § 30–440; West's Ann.Calif.Civ.Code §§ 729.010–729.090, 726(e); Colo.Rev.Stat. 118–9–2; Ill.—S.H.A. ¶ 12–127 et seq.; Kan.Stat.Ann. 60–2414; Ky.Rev.Stat. 426.220; 14 Me.Rev.Stat.Ann. § 6204; Mich.Comp.Laws Ann. § 600.3140; Minn. Stat.Ann. §§ 580.23, 580.24; Iowa Code Ann. §§ 628.28, 628.3; Vernon's Ann.Mo. Stat. § 443.410; Rev.Code Mont.1947, § 93–5836(2); N.Mex.1953 Comp. § 24–2–19; N.Dak.Cent.Code 32–19–18; Ore.Rev. Stat. 23.560; So.Dak.Comp.Laws 21–52–1; Tenn.Code Ann. §§ 66–8–101, 102; Utah Rules Civ.Proc., Rule 69(f)(3); West's Rev. Code Wash.Ann. 6.24.140; Wyoming Stat. § 1–480. For further classification the foregoing statutes, see Bauer, Statutory Redemption Reconsidered: The Operation of Iowa's Redemption Statute in Two Counties Between 1881 and 1980, 70 Iowa L.Rev. 343, 345 n. 11 (1984). See generally, Durfee & Doddridge, Redemption from Foreclosure Sale—The Uniform Mortgage Act, 23 Mich.L.Rev. 825 (1925); Blum, Iowa Statutory Redemption After Mortgage Foreclosure, 35 Iowa L.Rev. 72 (1949); Madsen, Equitable Considerations of Mortgage Foreclosure and Redemption in Utah: A Need for Remedial Legislation, 1976

Utah L.Rev. 327 (1976); Bridewell, The Effects of Defective Mortgage Laws on Home Financing, 5 Law & Contemp.Prob. 544 (1938).

3. See § 7.15, supra.

4. See, e.g., Colo.Rev.Stat. 1963, 118–9–2; Minn.Stat.Ann. § 580.23.

5. See Tenn.Code Ann. §§ 66–8–101, 66–8–102.

6. Ropfogel v. Enegren, 7 Kan.App.2d 644, 646 P.2d 1138 (1982); Cross Companies, Inc. v. Citizens Mortgage Investment Trust, 305 Minn. 111, 232 N.W.2d 114 (1975).

7. See Vernon's Ann.Mo.Stat. § 443.410. Moreover, redemption rights are applicable only if the mortgagee purchases at the sale. For a detailed consideration of the Missouri system, see Devenney, Statutory Redemption Following Power of Sale Foreclosure in Missouri, 47 Mo.L.Rev. 309 (1982).

8. See e.g., Ariz.Rev.Stat. § 12–1281; Idaho Code § 1–508; Utah Code Ann. 57–1–28; West's Rev.Code Wash.Ann. 61–24.050. In California this is so clear in the case of powers of sale in a trust deed mortgage that citation of primary authority is superfluous. See Kidd, Trust Deeds and Mortgages in California, 3 Cal.L.Rev. 381, 387 (1916); Cormack and Irsfeld, Jr., Mortgages and Trust Deeds in California, 26

is available *only* with that method of foreclosure.[9] Finally, in a few states, statutory redemption is unavailable when a deficiency judgment is either waived or otherwise prohibited.[10]

Federal law has a substantial impact on statutory redemption in a variety of contexts. For example, courts sometimes apply a "federal common law" rule to hold state statutory redemption inapplicable to foreclosures by federal mortgagees, a matter we consider in greater detail elsewhere in this volume.[11] In general, the United States, as a foreclosed junior lienor has "one year from the date of sale within which to redeem."[12] However, as to federal tax liens, the redemption period is the longer of 120 days or the state redemption period, if any.[13] The basic redemption amount is the foreclosure sale price.[14] To the extent that state legislation is less protective of the interests of junior lienors, it is preempted by the federal statutes.[15] For example, the United States Supreme Court has held that state redemption legislation that gives the mortgagor the exclusive right to redeem for one year after the foreclosure sale could not constitutionally be applied to restrict the federal government's statutory redemption rights during that period.[16]

Yet the approach of the Multifamily Foreclosure Act of 1981 is strikingly different.[17] That legislation authorizes power of sale foreclosure for federally-insured mortgages on one-to-four-family dwellings held by the Secretary of Housing and Urban Development and provides that, as to any foreclosure under it, "there shall be no [post-sale] right of redemption, or right of possession based upon a right of redemption in the mortgagor or others."[18] How Congress could have concluded that the federal government should have the benefit of statutory redemption, but not be subject to its burdens, at first glance seems puzzling. In fact, however, while the 1981 legislation was strongly motivated by a Congressional desire to create a uniform and expeditious federal foreclosure remedy,[19] there is no evidence to suggest that Congress was aware of the double standard it was creating. Otherwise, one would be tempted to conclude that Congress was unwilling to subscribe to the old adage that "what is sauce for the goose should be sauce for the gander."

Cal.L.Rev. 206, 216 (1938). See Note, Comparison of Mortgages, Trust Deeds and Land Sale Contracts, 7 U.C.L.A.L.Rev. 83, 88, 90 (1960).

9. Vernon's Ann.Mo.Rev.Stat. § 443.-410.

10. See West's Ann.Cal.Civ.Code §§ 726(e), 729.010. Cf. Iowa Code Ann. § 628.28 (period of redemption shortened where deficiency is waived).

11. See § 11.6 infra.

12. 28 U.S.C.A. § 2410.

13. 26 U.S.C.A. § 7425; 28 U.S.C.A. § 2410(c).

14. 28 U.S.C.A. § 2410(d).

15. See United States v. John Hancock Mutual Life Insurance Co., 364 U.S. 301, 81 S.Ct. 1, 5 L.Ed.2d 1 (1960).

16. Id.

17. See 12 U.S.C.A. §§ 3701–3717.

18. 12 U.S.C.A. § 3713(d).

19. 12 U.S.C.A. § 3701(a).

Statutory redemption has engendered both substantial criticism and praise. It has been argued that because a mortgagor knows that he can regain the land even after the foreclosure sale, he will be less responsible in making his mortgage payments.[20] In addition, the availability of statutory redemption means that the foreclosure sale purchaser acquires a defeasible title and this uncertainty may discourage outside bidding. Moreover, the mortgagor may regard the eventual loss of the property as inevitable and the ability in most jurisdictions to retain possession during the statutory period may simply encourage him to milk the property as much as possible prior to surrendering it to the purchaser.[21] On the other hand, such legislation may serve several valid purposes. These include "protecting persons who purchased the property subject to the mortgage, allowing time for the mortgagor to refinance and save his property, permitting additional use of the property by the hard-pressed mortgagor, and probably most important, encouraging those who do bid at the sale to bid in a fair price. By allowing junior lienors to redeem, the statutes permit them to protect the security they would otherwise lose." [22]

Although the various state statutes on redemption, in addition to the differences mentioned above, have widely varying phraseology and differ in a multitude of details, nevertheless there are certain main features that are common to all. These are (1) a specification of persons who may redeem, the owner of the equity of redemption being universally included, and usually, but not always,[23] junior lienors and some others; (2) a specification of the sum which must be paid to redeem, the basic factor in which is the sale price to which is added interest and, in differing detail, usually other items; (3) a fixing of a time limit for redemption, which, in addition to the variations mentioned above often provides different periods for different classes of persons; and (4) provisions as to order and effect of redemption.[24]

 WESTLAW REFERENCES
di right of redemption
statut! /5 redemption /p deficiency
digest(statut! /5 redemption)

§ 8.5 Who May Redeem—Nature of Interest

Statutes providing for redemption from foreclosure sale usually divide those who may exercise the right into two groups: first, the mortgagor, including by variously worded language, his successors in

---

20. Comment, The Statutory Right of Redemption in California, 52 Calif.L.Rev. 846, 848 (1964).

21. Id.

22. Id. at 848.

23. See e.g., West's Ann.Cal.Civ.Code § 729.020 (only persons entitled to redeem

are "the judgment debtor or the judgment debtor's successor in interest.") Cf. Iowa Code Ann. 628.28.

24. See Durfee and Doddridge, Redemption from Foreclosure Sale—The Uniform Act, 23 Mich.L.Rev. 825, 835 (1925).

interest in the whole or in any part of the premises, not including lienors;[1] and second, junior lienors whether by judgment or otherwise.[2] Depending on the exact language of the statute, a variety of persons, other than the mortgagor, have qualified for the right to redeem in the first group. These have included the spouses of the mortgagor,[3] life tenants[4] and vendees under an installment land contract.[5] Although under some statutes a mortgagee is permitted to redeem from the sale ordered upon the foreclosure of his mortgage,[6] probably most jurisdictions hold that he cannot do so.[7] The latter is clearly preferable, the former diminishing to an important degree the pressure on the foreclosing creditor to bid more than the minimum necessary to obtain the property.[8] Although there is some divergence of opinion and reasoning in interpreting the language of different statutory provisions, both pre-foreclosure sale transferees[9] and post-foreclosure sale transferees[10] of the mortgagor have been included among those in the first group as ones who may exercise the right of redemption. The mortgagor's statutory right of redemption is usually regarded as alienable.[11] However, it probably cannot be levied on by the mortgagee on an execution under a deficiency judgment in the foreclosure action which resulted in the sale of the property.[12]

Jurisdictions vary considerably on the validity of a waiver of statutory redemption rights. In some states, a valid waiver of such

---

§ 8.5

1. E.g., Ariz.Rev.Stat. § 12–1281 ("the judgment debtor or his successor in interest in the whole or any part of the property"); Minn.Stat.Ann. § 580.23, ("the mortgagor, his personal representatives, or assigns")

2. E.g., Ariz.Rev.Stat. § 12–1281 ("a creditor having a lien by judgment or mortgage on the property sold"); Minn. Stat.Ann. § 580.24; ("creditor having a lien, legal or equitable").

3. Martin v. Sprague, 29 Minn. 53, 11 N.W. 143 (1882).

4. Thielen v. Strong, 184 Minn. 333, 238 N.W. 678 (1931).

5. Forty-Four Hundred East Broadway Co. v. 4400 East Broadway, 135 Ariz. 265, 660 P.2d 866 (App.1983); Pine v. Pittman, 211 Kan. 380, 506 P.2d 1184 (1973).

6. See e.g., Crowder v. Scott State Bank, 365 Ill. 88, 5 N.E.2d 387, 108 A.L.R. 990 (1936); Strause v. Dutch, 250 Ill. 326, 95 N.E. 286, 35 L.R.A.,N.S., 413 (1911).

7. Hervey v. Krost, 116 Ind. 268, 19 N.E. 125 (1888); San Jose Water Co. v. Lyndon, 124 Cal. 518, 57 P. 481 (1899). See 35 L.R.A.,N.S., 413 (1912); 108 A.L.R. 993 (1937).

8. See Durfee and Doddridge, Redemption from Foreclosure Sale, 23 Mich.L.Rev. 825, 845, n. 59 (1925); 5 U. of Chi.L.Rev. 624, 629 (1937).

9. E.g., Pollard v. Harlow, 138 Cal. 390, 71 P. 648 (1903); Warner Brothers Co. v. Freud, 138 Cal. 651, 655, 72 P. 345 (1903); White v. Costigan, 134 Cal. 33, 66 P. 78 (1901); Willis v. Miller, 23 Or. 352, 31 P. 827 (1893); Cooper v. Maurer, 122 Iowa 321, 98 N.W. 124 (1904).

10. Big Sespe Oil Co. v. Cockran, 276 F. 216, 264 (C.C.A.Cal.1921); Phillips v. Hagart, 113 Cal. 552, 45 P. 843, 54 Am.St. Rep. 369 (1896); Kaston v. Storey, 47 Or. 150, 80 P. 217, 114 Am.St.Rep. 912 (1905).

11. See Southwest State Bank v. Quinn, 198 Kan. 359, 424 P.2d 620 (1967). See cases in preceding footnote. But cf., Mixon v. Burelson, 203 Ala. 84, 82 So. 98 (1919); Smith v. Shaver, 112 Kan. 790, 212 P. 666 (1923); 29 L.R.A.,N.S., 508 (1911).

12. See Kan.Stat.Ann. 60–2414(k); Wheeler and Durfee, Evasion of Moratoria by Prosecution of Personal Remedies, 33 Mich.L.Rev. 1196, 1202 (1935). There seems no reason why execution should not be levied under the deficiency judgment after redemption from the sale. Id. 1205.

rights may be made at any time,[13] while in others, courts have held that waiver agreements are unenforcible, whether entered into contemporaneous with the execution of the mortgage or thereafter.[14] These latter courts reason that to enforce such agreements not only defeats legislative intent, but also violates the public policy underpinnings of statutory redemption.[15] In a few jurisdictions, the validity of a waiver attempt seems to turn on when the agreement was consummated.[16] If it is contained in the mortgage or is executed contemporaneous with it, it probably will be invalid just as any similar attempt to clog the mortgagor's equity of redemption would be unenforcible. On the other hand, just as a mortgagor may, based on new consideration, consummate a valid subsequent transaction with the mortgagee if it is free from fraud, oppression and unconscionability, without running afoul of the clogging doctrine, so too should the mortgagor be able to enter into an enforcible subsequent agreement to waive his or her statutory redemption rights.[17] In a few states, a waiver of such rights is expressly authorized by statute and will be valid whether it takes place at the time of mortgage execution or thereafter.[18] Finally, some state statutes permit waiver by corporate mortgagors.[19] Indeed, there is case authority upholding waiver of statutory redemption rights where an individual mortgagor was incorporated simply for the purpose of buttressing a waiver attempt.[20]

 WESTLAW REFERENCES
waive! /s statut! right /5 redemption /p mortgag**

---

§ 8.6 Effect of Redemption—By Mortgagor or Successor

Redemption by the mortgagor or his successor is a universal feature of statutory redemption. Statutes usually give them a priority in redemption over lienors for a certain period of time.[1] In several states concurrent periods of redemption are provided for both mortgagors and lienors, with the latter subject to a redemption by the former if they should act first.[2] A redemption by the mortgagor is final.[3]

---

13. See e.g., Cook v. McFarland, 78 Iowa 528, 43 N.W. 519 (1889); King v. King, 215 Ill. 100, 74 N.E. 89 (1905). In Iowa, waiver of statutory rights occurs if appeal is taken from judgment of foreclosure. See I.C.A. §§ 628.3, 628.4; Farmers Trust and Savings Bank v. Manning, 359 N.W.2d 461 (Iowa 1985).

14. See e.g., Elson Development Co. v. Arizona Savings & Loan Association, 99 Ariz. 217, 407 P.2d 930 (1965); Mace v. Norwood, 155 Kan. 302, 124 P.2d 497 (1942).

15. Id.

16. See Russo v. Wolbers, 116 Mich. App. 327, 323 N.W.2d 385 (1982).

17. Id.

18. See e.g., Tenn.Code Ann. § 64–801; Ball, Waiver of the Right to Redeem Real Property Conveyed as Security in Tennessee, 1 Memphis St.L.Rev. 53, 59 (1970).

19. See e.g., Ill.—S.H.A. ch. 110, ¶ 12–125; Kan.Stat.Ann. 60–2410(d), 60–2414(a).

20. See Palcar Real Estate Co. v. Commissioner, 131 F.2d 210 (8th Cir.1942). Cf. Jenkins v. Moyse, 254 N.Y. 319, 172 N.E. 521, 74 A.L.R. 205 (1930).

§ 8.6

1. See e.g., Ariz.Rev.Stat. § 12–1282; Minn.Stat.Ann. §§ 80.23, 580.23, 580.24.

2. See e.g., Utah Rule of Civ.Proc., Rule 69(f); Ill.—S.H.A. ch. 110, ¶¶ 12–122, 12–

While a redemption by the mortgagor is "final", problems nevertheless can arise where two parties claim to be redeeming as "mortgagor." A Kansas case is illustrative.[4] There both the assignee of a vendee under an installment land contract and the assignee of the vendor were claiming preemptive redemption rights after a foreclosure sale under a mortgage that antedated the land contract. While under the Kansas statute the "defendant owner" had a superior right to redeem vis à vis lienors, so too did the "holder of the legal title". In view of the fact that the original vendee and his assignee had been in possession of the real estate for over seven years and that the vendor's assignee had only a nominal investment in the real estate, the Kansas Supreme Court determined that the vendee's assignee, as the equitable owner of the real estate, had the superior redemption right and therefore the right to possession during the redemption period.

Irrespective of the particular vagaries of the Kansas redemption statute, the holding is sensible both on theoretical and practical grounds in its implications for redemption statutes generally. Under the theory of equitable conversion, vendees under such land contracts are considered to be owners in equity of the real estate while the vendor's legal title is sometimes viewed as personalty.[5] Moreover, as a practical matter, a vendee under an installment land contract is the functional equivalent of a mortgagor and the vendor, in reality, is like a purchase money mortgagee.[6] Indeed, when there is a superior mortgage on the fee title, the vendor can more accurately be characterized as a second mortgagee. Thus, after a superior mortgage on the fee has been foreclosed, it makes sense, in the statutory redemption setting, to treat the vendee as the mortgagor and the vendor as a junior lienor. As a result, the vendee should normally have a preemptive redemption right over the vendor. Indeed, such reasoning has been utilized to sustain the vendee's right to redeem over that of his vendor even though the vendee was in default under the contract.[7]

It is usually difficult for a mortgagor to obtain a judicial extension of the statutory redemption period. Normally such an extension is possible only where fraud, accident, mistake or waiver are established.[8] In one case, for example, the mortgagor tendered payment to the purchaser's attorney one day before the statutory period expired. Eight days later the payment was returned with the explanation that it

---

128, 12–132. See also, Note, 5 U.Chi.L. Rev. 624, 630 (1937).

3. See e.g., Ill.—S.H.A. ch. 110, ¶¶ 12–122, 12–137; Utah Rule of Civ.Proc., Rule 69(f)(5).

4. Pine v. Pittman, 211 Kan. 380, 506 P.2d 1184 (1973).

5. Forty-Four Hundred East Broadway Co. v. 4400 East Broadway, 135 Ariz. 265, 660 P.2d 866 (App.1983); Leavell, Love and Nelson, Equitable Remedies and Restitution, 356–365 (3rd Ed. 1980).

6. See § 3.26 supra.

7. Forty-Four Hundred East Broadway Co. v. 4400 East Broadway, 135 Ariz. 265, 660 P.2d 866 (App.1983).

8. Johnson v. Smith, 675 P.2d 307 (Colo. 1984); United States v. Loosley, 551 P.2d 506 (Utah 1976); Phoenix Mutual Life Insurance Co. v. Legris, 30 Ill.App.3d 678, 334 N.E.2d 399 (1975).

had been tendered to the wrong person and with other technical objections. The court determined that under the circumstances the technical defects had been waived and that redemption would be permitted.[9] Moreover, an extension has been sustained where the mortgagor relied on a trustee's erroneous advice that the redemption period was six months rather than 75 days.[10] Other courts have indicated that late redemption will be permitted where substantial irregularities cause a sale that results in a gross sacrifice of the mortgagor's property.[11] But it should be emphasized that such judicial extensions represent exceptional cases. Indeed, relief has been denied where a foreclosure court erroneously fixed the beginning of the redemption period.[12] Moreover, courts have refused to extend the time for redemption simply because the mortgagee impermissibly had been in possession during the redemption period.[13]

When a mortgagor or his transferee redeems, the effect is to "nullify" the foreclosure sale.[14] However, no court treats the sale as avoided for all purposes.[15] On the other hand, all courts probably would agree that the sale is avoided, at least for the purpose of ending the title of the purchaser; that the redeeming owner is restored to the title he had before foreclosure sale; and that he does not become a transferee of the title of the purchaser as does a lienor who redeems.[16] The important question, however, is whether nullification of the foreclosure sale will be carried to the extent that it will revive previously existing liens insofar as they have not been satisfied by the proceeds of the foreclosure sale.

Courts take a variety of approaches to this question. Some seem to hold that all junior liens existing prior to the sale are revived.[17] Others

9. United States v. Loosley, 551 P.2d 506 (Utah 1976); See also, Skach v. Sykora, 6 Ill.2d 215, 127 N.E.2d 453 (1955).

10. Arnold v. Gebhardt, 43 Colo.App. 387, 604 P.2d 1192 (1979).

11. See Moreland v. Marwich, Limited, 665 P.2d 613 (Colo.1983); Arnold v. Gebhardt, 43 Colo.App. 387, 604 P.2d 1192 (1979); Mollerup v. Storage Systems International, 569 P.2d 1122 (Utah 1977).

12. Phoenix Mutual Life Insurance Co. v. Legris, 30 Ill.App.3d 678, 334 N.E.2d 399 (1975).

13. See Cross Companies, Inc. v. Citizens Mortgage Investment Trust, 305 Minn. 111, 232 N.W.2d 114 (1975); Milwaukee Western Bank v. Cedars of Cedar Rapids, Inc., 170 N.W.2d 670 (Iowa 1969).

14. Most statutes so provide explicitly by clauses in which, although the language is not identical, the purport is the same. See e.g., Ill.—S.H.A. ch. 110, ¶ 12–122; Utah Rule of Civ.Proc., Rule 69(f)(5). Even when the statute has no such express stip-

ulation, courts have reached the same conclusion. E.g., Allen v. McGaughey, 31 Ark. 252, 260 (1876); Fields v. Danenhower, 65 Ark. 392, 46 S.W. 938, 43 L.R.A. 519 (1898). See Storke and Sears, Colorado Security Law, 1952, 1954–59, for Colorado law on redemption by the "owner" or "any person who might be liable on a deficiency."

15. See 9 Cornell L.Q. 208, 209 (1924). To do so would involve holding that the mortgage lien was restored to its original amount and require repayment by the mortgagee of any proceeds he might have received from the sale. See Durfee & Doddridge, Redemption from Foreclosure Sale—The Uniform Act, 23 Mich.L.Rev. 825, 850 (1925).

16. See Durfee, supra note 15.

17. See e.g., Mihoover v. Walker, 63 Colo. 22, 164 P. 504 (1917); Feldman v. M.J. Associates, 117 Mich.App. 770, 324 N.W.2d 496 (1982). See also Call v. Thunderbird Mortgage Co., 58 Cal.2d 542, 25 Cal.Rptr. 265, 375 P.2d 169 (1962) (pre-1983 include even the lien of the mortgage under which the property was sold to the extent of the unpaid deficiency.[18] Finally, some hold that while redemption will revive the general lien acquired by the personal decree in the foreclosure proceeding to the extent of any deficiency, it will not reinstate the specific mortgage lien.[19] While the distinction between these two approaches may seem at best highly theoretical, it has proved important in some cases. For example, in one case adopting the latter approach, if the revived judgment was a mortgage lien, the redeemed real estate, for purposes of a particular state statute, was not protected against execution by virtue of a homestead declaration; but if the judgment became a general one because of the foreclosure and redemption, the real estate did obtain such protection.[20]

The opposite approach is represented by recent California legislation which provides that "[l]iens extinguished by the sale * * * do not reattach to the property after redemption and the property that was subject to the extinguished lien may not be applied to the satisfaction of the claim or judgment under which the lien was created." [21] According to its legislative history, the foregoing statute "changes the prior rule [22] that liens subordinate to that under which the sale was held reattach upon redemption by the judgment debtor or a successor in interest. The prior rule [23] that upon redemption by the judgment debtor the judgment lien under which the property was sold reattaches for the amount of the deficiency is also not continued. * * * This encourages the judgment creditor and subordinate lienholders to protect their interests by looking to the property sold. * * * [This legislation] makes it clear that once a lien is extinguished a lien may not be created on the same property to enforce the same claim or judgment. Hence, for example, a judgment creditor whose judgment lien is extinguished may not again record the judgment to create a lien on the same property, nor may the judgment creditor obtain an execution lien by levy of a writ of execution on the property." [24] As one commentator has noted, this legislation "may have put a higher premium on a policy

California law). Cf. Skousen v. L.J. Development Co., Inc., 134 Ariz. 289, 655 P.2d 1341 (App.1982).

18. Although the cases holding that redemption revives the original lien under which the property was sold, except to the extent that the purchase price on the sale discharged it, are those involving judgment liens, no distinctions between them and mortgage liens can be upheld. New York is, perhaps, the leading jurisdiction for the doctrine. See note, 9 Cornell L.Q. 208 (1924); 67 Am.St.Rep. 510 (1899). See also Wheeler and Durfee, Evasion of Mortgage Moratoria by Prosecution of Personal Remedies, 33 Mich.L.Rev. 1196, 1205 (1935). See Lindsey v. Meyer, 125 Cal.App.3d 536, 178 Cal.Rptr. 1 (1981) (pre-1983 California law).

19. See e.g., Damascus Milk Co. v. Morriss, 1 Wn.App. 501, 463 P.2d 212 (1969).

20. Damascus Milk Co. v. Morriss, 1 Wn.App. 501, 463 P.2d 212 (1969).

21. West's Ann.Cal.Civ.Code § 729.-080(e).

22. See Call v. Thunderbird Mortgage Co., 58 Cal.2d 542, 25 Cal.Rptr. 265, 375 P.2d 169 (1962).

23. See Moore v. Hall, 250 Cal.App.2d 25, 58 Cal.Rptr. 70 (1967).

24. Cal.Legislative Committee Comment, § 729.080(e) (1982). See 15 Cal.L. Rev.Comm.Reports 2001.

giving the lienor only one chance to satisfy a lien from the encumbered property, than on a rule that the property should be applied to satisfy all liens against it." [25]

A variety of other approaches exist. Some states differentiate between the effect of a redemption by the debtor-mortgagor and one by his transferee, the latter taking free of previously existing liens regardless of whether they might revive as against the former on redemption by him.[26] The distinction has been criticised as violating the fundamental rule that a successor in interest, unless he be a bona fide purchaser for value without notice, "simply occupies the shoes of his predecessor." [27] However, the rule may be a most effective factor in forcing a foreclosing mortgagee to bid up for the property.[28] Some authority distinguishes between the restoration on redemption of the lien under which the property was sold and liens inferior to it, restoring the latter but not the former.[29]

 WESTLAW REFERENCES
priority /p mortgag** /p statut! right /5 redemption

25. Dyer, Judicial Foreclosure After the Revised Enforcements of Judgments Act, 6 CEB Real Prop.Law.Rep. 53, 57 (1983). Iowa traditionally has followed a similar approach. See Blum, Iowa Statutory Redemption After Mortgage Foreclosure, 35 Iowa L.Rev. 72, 75 (1949); Tirrill v. Miller, 206 Iowa 426, 218 N.W. 303 (1928), prior judgment against mortgagor; Danforth v. Lindsey, 178 Iowa 834, 160 N.W. 318 (1916), deficiency judgment; see Cadd v. Shell, 219 Iowa 728, 734, 259 N.W. 590, 593 (1935); cf. Paulsen v. Jensen, 209 Iowa 453, 228 N.W. 357 (1929). See also Cooper v. Maurer, 122 Iowa 321, 98 N.W. 124 (1904). The above Iowa cases were before the 1934 amendment in that state. That enactment, however, changed the existing rule only as to redemption by the debtor-mortgagor.

26. See Madsen, Equitable Considerations of Mortgage Foreclosure and Redemption In Utah: A Need for Remedial Legislation, 1976 Utah L.Rev. 327, 335 (1976); Simpson v. Castle, 52 Cal. 644 (1878); Sigler v. Phares, 105 Kan. 116, 181 P. 628, 5 A.L.R. 141 (1919), junior liens cut off as to grantee. See also 47 L.R.A.,N.S., 1048, 1050 (1913), as to liability for a deficiency on indebtedness for which it was originally sold; 128 A.L.R. 796 (1940); 5 A.L.R. 145 (1920), as to subordinate liens. See Call v. Jeremiah, 246 Or. 568, 425 P.2d 502 (1967) (junior mortgages cut off by redemption by grantee—alternative holding).

27. Flanders v. Aumack, 32 Or. 19, 25, 51 P. 447, 449, 67 Am.St.Rep. 504 (1897). While the criticism is valid insofar as it concerns liens existing, even though suspended against the property in the hands of the mortgagor before the transfer, the distinction would seem sound enough as to the lien of a judgment obtained against the mortgagor after the transfer and accruing for the first time, if at all, not before that date. Would it be a fraudulent conveyance to permit an insolvent debtor to transfer his redemption right to one who, on redemption, takes the property free and clear of the debtor's creditors? The question would be even more acute if the debtor claimed exemption of the consideration received for the transfer. See note, 5 U. of Chi.L.Rev. 625 (1928). And look at Kerr v. Miller, 259 Ill. 516, 102 N.E. 1050 (1913), commented on in 9 Ill.L.Rev. 60 (1914). But see Glenn, Mortgages, § 234.

28. See 5 U. of Chi.L.Rev. 624, 633 (1938).

29. See Rist v. Anderson, 70 S.D. 579, 19 N.W.2d 833, 161 A.L.R. 197 (1945). See also 5 A.L.R. 145, 149 (1920). But contrast Sigler v. Phares, 105 Kan. 116, 181 P. 628, 5 A.L.R. 141 (1919). "Confining the inquiry to the restoration of liens, it is possible to distinguish between senior liens and junior liens, restoring the latter but not the former, and, with respect to each class, a further distinction is suggested,—as to senior liens, a distinction between mortgage liens and judgment liens, the latter being restored but the former not; as to junior liens, a diversity between a passive lienor and one who, as defendant in a suit to foreclose the senior lien, files a cross bill and obtains a decree enforcing his lien, the latter being classed with the senior lienor." Durfee and Doddridge, § 8.5, supra, note 8.

di equitable conversion
extend! extension   /s   statut! right   /5   redemption

§ 8.7   Effect of Redemption—By Lienors

Holders of liens junior to that under which the property is foreclosed are empowered to redeem,[1] although their right to do so is usually postponed to a time after that during which the right is exclusively reserved to the mortgagor and his successors in interest.[2] Where there are several junior lienors, although the provisions on the subject are not uniform, they usually are given the privilege of redemption at certain periods of time in accordance with their priority.[3] The Minnesota statute [4] exemplifies such a system. After the foreclosure sale, the mortgagor or his successor generally has a six month period (in certain situations 12 months) to redeem by payment of the foreclosure sale price plus a statutory rate of interest to the sale purchaser. The mortgagor's right to redeem is preemptive—in other words, if the mortgagor redeems there can be no further redemption. If, however, the mortgagor fails to redeem within the specified period, then junior lienholders each have a five day period, in order of their pre-foreclosure priority, to redeem by paying the sale purchaser the foreclosure price (including interest), plus the amount of the lien of any lienor who has redeemed in a previous five day period.

The foregoing statute is best understood in the context of a specific fact situation. Suppose that a senior mortgage was foreclosed and the purchaser at the sale paid $30,000 for the mortgaged real estate that now has a fair market value of $55,000. At the time of the sale, E–2 had a second mortgage with a balance of $10,000. E–3 had a third mortgage with a balance of $12,000 and J had a $5,000 judgment lien on the property junior to all of the other liens. Under the Minnesota scheme, mortgagor has the right for six months to redeem from Purchaser by paying $30,000 plus interest. If mortgagor redeems, redemption ends. If mortgagor fails to act during that period, then E–2 has a 5 day period to redeem by paying the same amount to Purchaser as mortgagor would have paid. If E–2 redeems, then E–3 has 5 days to redeem from E–2 by paying E–2 an amount equal to the sales price plus the amount of E–2's lien including interest or approximately $40,000. ($30,000 + $10,000). Finally, J can then redeem by paying E–3 approximately $52,000 ($30,000 + $10,000 + $12,000). Thus, for J it is a risky redemption. If the land is worth $55,000 and he or she must pay $52,000 for it, $3,000 of the $5,000 judgment can be satisfied out of the value of the land. On the other hand, J may correctly conclude that putting up $52,000 to recoup part of a $5,000 loss may not be

---

§ 8.7

1. See § 8.5 supra.

2. See § 8.6 supra.

3. See e.g., Minn.Stat.Ann. §§ 580.23, 580.24, 581.10; Ill.—S.H.A. ch. 110, ¶ 12–136.

4. Minn.Stat.Ann. §§ 580.23, 580.24, 581.10.

worth it. Note that if any junior lienor allows the five day period to run without redemption, the next junior lienor in redeeming can subtract the amount of that prior lien in calculating the redemption amount. Thus if E–2 fails to redeem, E–3 can redeem by paying Purchaser $30,000 plus interest. J then could redeem by paying E–3 $42,000.

Under most statutes the effect of redemption by a junior lienor is to transfer to him the rights of the purchaser on foreclosure sale which, if there is not a redemption from him by someone else, will ripen into the same title that the purchaser would have got if no one redeemed.[5] This solution has several advantages. It is fair to the owner;[6] it makes any further proceeding to enforce the rights so acquired unnecessary; and it is in accord with the policy of the statute in that, by providing an incentive to redeem, it increases probability of redemption and, therefore, puts pressure on the foreclosing mortgagee to bid up the price.[7]

In some states, notably Illinois, the effect of redemption is not to transfer the title of the purchaser to the redeeming junior lienor, but merely to avoid it as in the case of a redeeming mortgagor. At the same time the junior lien, which may be considered to be suspended, is revived and to it is added the amount which had to be paid in order to redeem. The junior lienor then has to bring further proceedings to enforce his original mortgage augmented by the sum he has paid out in order to redeem.[8]

The effect of redemption by a junior lienor upon the mortgage debt has received varying answers. In jurisdictions where the effect of redemption is merely to continue or revive the subordinate lien, adding to it the amount paid to redeem, the original indebtedness remains unaffected.[9] In Minnesota, however, the court likened the effect of the statute in this respect to a strict foreclosure. Then, proceeding upon the theory that the policy underlying the legislation, i.e., "to have the property of the debtor applied as it will go—as far as creditors will voluntarily apply it—in satisfaction of the debts of the mortgagor," would be furthered by such a construction, it held that redemption extinguished the debt to the extent that the value of the land exceeded

---

5. E.g., Minn.Stat.Ann. § 580.27; Eldridge v. Wright, 55 Cal. 531 (1880). See 135 A.L.R. 196, 198 (1941).

6. The owner, being given a prior or subsequent opportunity to redeem, or both, cannot complain. See § 8.1, supra.

7. Durfee and Doddridge, § 8.6 supra, note 15 at 847.

8. Ogle v. Koerner, 140 Ill. 170, 29 N.E. 563 (1892). See 5 U. of Chi.L.Rev. 624, 630 (1937); Durfee and Doddridge, § 8.6 supra, note 15 at 846; 135 A.L.R. 196, 206 (1941). In Illinois priority of redemption rights of creditors rank in the order of their judgments or decrees. Ill.—S.H.A. ch. 110,

¶ 12–136. And a judgment or decree under which the property is sold is treated the same for this purpose as any other, such a creditor being permitted to redeem from his own enforcement sale. Crowder v. Scott State Bank, 365 Ill. 88, 5 N.E.2d 387, 108 A.L.R. 990 (1932). As to whether a purchaser at a foreclosure sale can prevent "statutory redemption" by a junior lien holder by tendering payment of the debt which the lien secures, see Note, Effect of Satisfying a Junior Lien on Statutory Right of Redemption, 15 Wyo.L.J. 223 (1961).

9. See note 8, supra.

the redemption payment.[10] The argument in favor of no satisfaction is the incentive to redemption thus offered to a junior lienor, which in turn spurs bidding by the foreclosing mortgagee.[11] This last may offset the apparent injustice to the mortgagor of not having the real value of the property directly applied to the satisfaction of his mortgage debt by the junior lienor. The uncertain amount by which the redeeming junior encumbrancer's debt will be reduced is left to future litigation, which in itself is a deterrent to taking the action, is a strong objection to the rule, minimizing as it does the policy of the statute.

The Iowa approach to this problem seems more desirable. It provides that, on redemption, the junior lienor may file a statement of the amount which he is willing to credit on his debt and if he does so, that amount only is credited. If he does not file such a statement, the whole debt is satisfied. And the land in his hands, whichever course he follows, is subject to re-redemption upon paying what he paid to redeem plus the amount credited on his debt.[12] This eliminates any litigation over the value of the property which would discourage redemption, permits the redemptioner to fix the amount he will credit on his debt, and safeguards against an undervaluation on this point by permitting redemption against him.[13]

 WESTLAW REFERENCES
junior successor /s lien** /p redeem! redemption

§ 8.8 Reforming the Foreclosure Process

The foreclosure sale process, whether judicial or under a power of sale, is hardly designed to bring a fair price for mortgaged real estate. Frequently, the mortgagee is not only the foreclosure sale purchaser, but the only bidder attending the sale. There are several reasons for this phenomenon. First, because the mortgagee can bid up to the amount of the mortgage debt without putting up new cash, he has a distinct bidding advantage over a third party bidder, who will have out-of-pocket expense from the first dollar bid. Second, while foreclosure statutes require notice by publication to potential third party bidders, the notice, especially in urban areas, is published in legal newspapers of

---

10. Sprague v. Martin, 29 Minn. 226, 13 N.W. 34 (1882). The decision was approved or followed in Northland Pine Co. v. Northern Insulating Co., 145 Minn. 395, 177 N.W. 635 (1920); Crown Iron Works Co. v. Melin, 159 Minn. 198, 198 N.W. 462 (1924); Work v. Braun, 19 S.D. 437, 103 N.W. 764 (1909), affirmed 23 S.D. 582, 122 N.W. 608 (1909). Miller v. Little, 37 N.D. 612, 164 N.W. 19 (1918), commented on in, 16 Mich.L.Rev. 204 (1918), reached a result similar to that in Sprague v. Martin, supra, by invoking the doctrine of merger. Look at Moore v. Penney, 141 Minn. 454, 170 N.W. 599, 3 A.L.R. 161 (1919). See

Durfee and Doddridge, § 8.6 supra, note 15, at 847.

11. Durfee and Doddridge, § 8.6 supra, note 15 at 848. See 5 U. of Chi.L.Rev. 624, 628 (1937).

12. Iowa Code Ann. §§ 628.13, 628.17, 628.19. See Durfee and Doddridge, § 8.6 supra, note 15 at 849, 861. Blum, op. cit. supra note 44. See also Code of Alabama 1975, §§ 6–5–233, 6–5–239. Kan.Stat.Ann. 60–2414.

13. See Durfee and Doddridge, § 8.6 supra, note 15.

limited circulation. Moreover, because the publication is technical in nature, a potential third party purchaser has little idea what real estate is being sold. Third, many potential third party purchasers are reluctant to buy land at a foreclosure sale because of the difficulty of ascertaining if a purchaser will receive good and marketable title. Fourth, when a mortgagee forecloses on improved real estate, potential bidders often find it difficult to inspect the premises prior to sale. While it may be in the self-interest of the mortgagor to allow third party inspection of the premises, mortgagors who are about to lose their real estate through a foreclosure sale understandably are reluctant to cooperate.

Traditional legislative attempts to remedy the abuses of the foreclosure sale process have proved inadequate at best. For example, while anti-deficiency legislation limits the mortgagee who acquires real estate at a bargain price at a foreclosure sale from using a deficiency to compound the mortgagor's plight, it does nothing to encourage bidding above the amount of the mortgage debt. Moreover, the advantages of statutory redemption may be more illusory than real. Because it uses the foreclosure sale price as the redemption amount and affords redemption rights to a wide variety of lien creditors as well as the mortgagor, it arguably encourages those who take part at the sale to bid higher as a means of protecting their prospective purchase from loss by redemption. However, as we have seen earlier,[1] it is equally likely that the defeasible nature of the purchaser's title coupled with the fact that the mortgagor often retains possession during the redemption period may actually serve to suppress rather than enhance bidding and, hence, may depress the ultimate foreclosure price.

A more fundamental reform of the foreclosure sale system is necessary. Not only should the goal be fewer deficiency judgments, but more frequent and larger surpluses which benefit junior lienholders as well as mortgagors. Such a legislative approach should incorporate at least two components. First, the sale should be conducted by customary commercial methods used in the sale of real estate in a nonforeclosure setting, including the use of real estate brokers and normal commercial descriptive and pictorial advertising. Second, the person who conducts the sale should be a truly independent public official and should be given a strong incentive to achieve the highest possible foreclosure price. He should have substantial experience and expertise in real estate matters. While the title for this person is not particularly important, the one who now conducts foreclosure sales is often called a "trustee", and that title is probably as appropriate as any other.[2] To implement this latter concept, legislation should specify a

---

§ 8.8

1. See § 8.4 supra.

2. Colorado currently uses a public trustee system. See Colo.Rev.Stat. 38–37–101 to –139. The governor appoints the trustee in first and second class counties. In smaller counties, the county treasurer is the public trustee. Id. 38–37–102. Under the author's proposal, the local county court or the governor should appoint the

reasonable time, e.g., ninety days, during which the trustee could sell the property by usual commercial means. The method of compensating the trustee should encourage him to obtain the highest possible sale price. For example, if the sale price does not exceed the mortgage debt, the trustee's fee should be relatively low, perhaps a fixed amount. If the foreclosure sale price exceeds the mortgage debt, the trustee should receive a percentage of the excess that increases as the excess increases.[3] The trustee should be permitted to employ brokers, pay for advertising, and incur other normal expenses of sale. He would be subject to ordinary fiduciary duties of good faith and fair dealing.

Under the scheme outlined above, a prospective purchaser would deal with the trustee in much the same way as he would deal with a seller of real estate in a normal sale context, using the customary earnest money contract and title examination procedures. If the trustee could not sell the property during the statutory time period, a regular public auction foreclosure sale of the real estate would be conducted. On the other hand, if the trustee and a potential purchaser agree on sale terms, the trustee would be required to notify the mortgagor and junior lienholders of the proposed sale price. If neither the mortgagor nor any junior lienholders object within a short time (say, seven days), the transaction between the trustee and the purchaser would be consummated. If, however, the mortgagor or a junior lienholder objects to the sale, the trustee would be required to hold a public auction. This procedure would estop the mortgagor or junior lienholders from subsequently attacking a sale between the trustee and a purchaser. If the real estate sells for less than the mortgage debt,

public trustee to ensure adequate expertise and experience; he should not be elected.

3. The methods of compensation could vary widely within this broad framework. One possible method would operate as follows. When mortgaged real estate is sold for the amount of the debt or less, the trustee's fee would be $200. For up to the first $20,000 by which the sale price exceeds the debt, the trustee also would receive 1% of the excess. For the next $20,000, the trustee would receive 1.25%. The percentages could then increase by .25 with each $20,000 increment. For example, if the total price negotiated by the trustee is $230,000 and the mortgage debt is $150,000, the fee would be calculated as follows:

$ 200—Flat fee for $150,000 (the amount of the debt)
     200—1% of the first $20,000 in excess of the mortgage debt
     250—1.25% of the second $20,000
     300—1.5% of the third $20,000
     350—1.75% of the fourth $20,000
$1,300—Total trustee's fee

To avoid inordinately high trustee's fees in cases of expensive real estate, such a system could limit the trustee's total compensation to 3% of the total foreclosure sale price.

An alternative method of compensating the trustee would be to tie the fee to the amount by which the sale price exceeds a certain percentage of the appraised value of the real estate. This percentage could be 70% or higher. Under such a system, the trustee could collect more than the minimum or fixed fee only when the sale price exceeds 70% of the appraised value of the property. This would prevent windfall trustee's fees when the mortgage debt is especially low compared to the value of the foreclosed property.

The Colorado public trustee is compensated by a fixed salary, which would not provide an economic incentive for the trustee to obtain the highest possible price for the foreclosed real estate. See id. 38–37–105. Accordingly, that feature of the Colorado system should not be adopted.

whether by negotiated sale or at auction, the mortgagee could seek a deficiency judgment. The amount of the deficiency would be the difference between the sale price and the mortgage debt and would not be subject to other antideficiency limitations.[4]

Such a system would have weaknesses. It would be more time-consuming and costly than current power of sale foreclosure practice. Mortgagors, notwithstanding their self-interest in obtaining the highest possible price for the mortgaged real estate, may discourage physical inspection of improved real estate. Moreover, in economically depressed periods, the proposed system probably would not yield a higher price than would result under the current practice. Nevertheless, under most economic conditions, it should result in foreclosure sale prices that more closely approximate the fair market value of the foreclosed real estate. Such higher prices not only would compensate for the increased costs of the system but also might provide a surplus that would benefit the mortgagor and junior lienholders.[5] In addition, higher prices should substantially reduce the incidence of deficiency proceedings. Even in the worst case, the proposed system would not result in prices below those obtained under current practices.

Several additional observations are appropriate. First, such a system would probably prove impractical in states with pervasive statutory redemption schemes. As noted earlier,[6] the prospect of receiving a defeasible title probably discourages third party interest and bidding. Second, because the proposed system focuses on the mechanics of the sale rather than on the foreclosure proceeding itself, it can be utilized with judicial as well as power of sale foreclosure. As we emphasized earlier, however, because we believe that power of sale foreclosure can be constitutional as well as efficient,[7] a power of sale approach is probably preferable. Moreover, such a system need not be unfair to residential mortgagors and others thought to need special protection. The time period *prior* to the sale could, for example, be longer for such parties than for commercial mortgagors. Finally, as we

---

4. This proposal is similar in some respects to Uniform Land Transactions Act § 3–508, which was promulgated by the National Conference of Commissioners on Uniform State Laws, but has not been adopted by any state. According to id. § 3–508(a), in power of sale foreclosures, the

> sale may be made at public sale or by private negotiation, by one or more contracts, as a unit or in parcels, at any time and place, and on any terms including sale on credit, but every aspect of the sale, including the method, advertising, time, place, and terms, must be reasonable.

Unlike the author's proposal, however, the uniform act "does not require that the sale be conducted by a disinterested third party such as a trustee." Id. § 3–508, Comment 1. Thus, the mortgagee could conduct the sale under the uniform act. Commentators have criticized the uniform act's assumption that the mortgagee's interest is always to maximize the foreclosure price. See Kuklin, The Uniform Land Transactions Act: Article 3, 11 Real Prop., Prob. & Tr.J. 12 (1976); Washburn, The Judicial and Legislative Response to Price Inadequacy in Mortgage Foreclosure Sales, 53 S.Cal.L.Rev. 843, 938 (1980).

5. Normally, junior lienholders have priority over the mortgagor with respect to any foreclosure surplus. See § 7.31 supra.

6. See § 8.4 supra.

7. See § 7.30 supra.

also noted elsewhere in this volume,[8] we are emboldened to suggest that such a system come from Congress rather than the state legislatures. Because the mortgage market is pervasively national in scope and its impact on the national economy increasingly significant, the traditional state by state approach to real estate foreclosure is a luxury of federalism we can ill continue to afford.

WESTLAW REFERENCES
266k330 266k360 /p trustee
digest,synopsis(statut! /p trustee /p foreclos! /s sale sell!)

C. THE SOLDIERS' AND SAILORS' CIVIL RELIEF ACT

§ 8.9 General Considerations

The Soldiers' and Sailors' Civil Relief Act of 1940,[1] as amended, ("SSCRA") can substantially affect the options of the real estate mortgagee in proceeding against a mortgagor who is in the military service. However, it is important to emphasize that the Act is primarily significant in its impact on secured real estate transactions entered into *prior* to entry by the debtor into the military service.

The purpose of the SSCRA is to provide "for the temporary suspension of legal proceedings and transactions which may prejudice the civil rights of persons" [2] in the military. While it does not extinguish any rights or obligations of debtors or creditors, certain legal proceedings, actions and transactions may be suspended and remedies altered to assure that certain property relationships remain unimpaired during military service.[3] Although the Act is complex and affects a myriad of debtor-creditor relationships, we will limit our consideration to some of its more important consequences for the real estate mortgagee.

The SSCRA is intended to protect primarily persons on active duty in military service and defines such persons as enlisted persons and officers of the Army, Navy, Marine Corps, Coast Guard, and officers of the Public Health Service detailed for duty with the military service.[4] "Active duty" means full-time service in one of the above branches, including "training or education * * * preliminary to induction" and time absent from duty due to sickness, wounds, leave, or other lawful cause.[5] Army and Air National Guard members are protected only while performing full-time duty for which they are entitled to pay.[6]

8. Id.

§ 8.9

1. 50 U.S.C.A.App. §§ 501–48, 560–90. See generally, 40 A.L.R.2d 462.

2. 50 U.S.C.A.App. § 511(1).

3. Bagley, The Soldiers' and Sailors' Civil Relief Act—A Survey, 45 Mil.L.Rev. 1

(1969); Goldman, Collection of Debts Incurred by Military Personnel: The Creditor's View, 10 Tulsa L.J. 537, 541 (1970).

4. 50 U.S.C.A.App. § 511.

5. Id. Goldman, supra note 3, at 544.

6. Bagley, supra note 3, at 3.

Section 591, a Vietnam era amendment, extends powers of attorney executed by servicepersons missing in action if a spouse, parent, or other relative was named as attorney in fact.[7] Members of reserve units and retired military personnel not on active duty are not covered.[8] Deserters are not protected, but a serviceperson who is absent without leave may still be entitled to relief, depending on the facts of each case.[9]

Protection sometimes encompasses a civilian whose liability is connected with the serviceperson's obligation, such as a co-defendant, guarantor, or co-signer.[10] Moreover, a dependent may be granted protection if his ability to pay an obligation is materially affected by military service of the person upon whom he depends.[11] A typical case is where an individual had formerly given a parent contributions which were used to make mortgage payments. After showing that a decreased income during active duty impaired the ability to make contributions, resulting in the parent's inability to make mortgage payments, the parent could be extended the same benefits the serviceperson would receive were he liable.[12]

In addition to the "stay" sections discussed hereafter, several general relief provisions are significant for real estate mortgagees. For example, section 525 automatically tolls all statutes of limitations during the period of service that would otherwise run against a serviceperson.[13] The broad, self-executing language of this section in theory tolls not only properly denominated statutes of limitations, but any period limited by law, specifically including periods relating to redemption of real property sold or forfeited to enforce any obligation, tax, or assessment.[14] For example, section 525 has been held to extend the time for redemption under state statutory redemption legislation by a period equal to the mortgagor's period of service.[15] Title defects are not curable by adverse possession.[16] Moreover, it also applies to re-

---

7. 50 U.S.C.A.App. § 591(a)(1)–(3); Goldman, supra note 3, at 563.

8. Bagley, supra note 3, at 2; Goldman, supra note 3, at 544.

9. Bagley, supra note 3 at 3; Shayne v. Burke, 158 Fla. 61, 27 So.2d 751 (1946), states that the Act should be liberally construed in AWOL cases. See also Mantz v. Mantz, 69 N.E.2d 637 (Ohio Ct.App.1946), where five years of confinement by court martial was held to remove SSCRA protection.

10. 50 U.S.C.A.App. § 513; Bagley, supra note 3, at 1744.

11. 50 U.S.C.A.App. § 536; Bagley, supra note 3, at 3. See Nassau Savings & Loan Association v. Ormond, 179 Misc. 447, 39 N.Y.S.2d 92 (1942).

12. 50 U.S.C.A.App. §§ 531, 532; Bagley, supra note 3, at 3–4.

13. 50 U.S.C.A.App. § 525. See e.g., King v. First National Bank of Fairbanks, 647 P.2d 596 (Alaska 1982); Bickford v. United States, 228 Ct.Cl. 321, 656 F.2d 636 (1982).

14. Id., specifies tolling of any period "limited by any law, regulation or order". Wilkin v. Shell Oil Co., 197 F.2d 42 (10th Cir.1952); Lester v. United States, 487 F.Supp. 1033 (D.C.Tex.1980).

15. See Illinois National Bank v. Gwinn, 390 Ill. 345, 61 N.E.2d 249 (1945); Peace v. Bullock, 252 Ala. 155, 40 So.2d 82 (1949); Wilkin v. Shell Oil Co., 197 F.2d 42 (10th Cir.1952). See §§ 8.4–8.7, supra.

16. Comment, 24 Mo.L.Rev. 101, 106 (1959).

demption periods after real estate tax sales. Thus, in one case, an acknowledged career officer was allowed to redeem land fourteen years after a sale for delinquent taxes.[17] Several recent cases, however, have held in the tax sale redemption setting that section 525 does not protect "career" servicepersons.[18] If the same reasoning is applied to the statutory redemption area, career serviceperson-mortgagors will also no longer be protected.

In addition, the Act theoretically can also affect mortgage interest rates. Section 526 limits interest to six percent during military service on obligations incurred before entering service, even though a higher rate was originally agreed upon.[19] Interest, which includes all carrying, service, and other charges, is automatically reduced unless the mortgagee proves that military service has no material effect on the ability to pay more than six percent.[20] Thus, for example, if a mortgagor executes a 11% mortgage note and then joins the military, the burden in effect falls on the mortgagee to justify the higher rate of interest. This burden should not be difficult to sustain in view of the fact that normal contemporary interest rates substantially exceed the six percent rate.

WESTLAW REFERENCES

"soldiers and sailors" /p 525

redeem! redemption /p "soldiers and sailors"

---

§ 8.10   The "Stay" Provisions

The major judicial power granted by the SSCRA is to order stays which suspend enforcement of civil obligations. In discussing provisions affecting land-secured obligations, individual sections are considered specifically, but when applying the SSCRA to actual problems it is important to view the sections of the Act as complementary to each other rather than in isolation. It is important to note that application of one section does not necessarily bar relief based on others. For example, use of section 590, a stay provision for obligations in general, is not necessarily excluded by the application of other stay sections addressed specifically to mortgages or installment land contracts. Likewise, where possible, stay sections should be considered in conjunction with general relief provisions such as those tolling statutes of limitations.

17. Hedrick v. Bigby, 228 Ark. 40, 305 S.W.2d 674 (1957).

18. See Pannell v. Continental Can Co. Inc., 554 F.2d 216 (5th Cir.1977); King v. Zagorski, 207 So.2d 61 (Fla.App.1968); Bai-

ley v. Barranca, 83 N.M. 90, 488 P.2d 725 (1971).

19. 50 U.S.C.A.App. § 526 (1970); Bagley, supra note 59, at 18.

20. Goldman, supra note 3, at 551.

Civil Obligations and Taxes

Section 590 may be the most important stay provision.[1] Under this section, during military service or within six months thereafter, a serviceperson-debtor may ask the court to suspend enforcement of (1) any civil obligation which arose prior to military service, or (2) any tax or assessment due either prior to or during military service.[2] However, the debtor must first prove that military service materially affects his ability to pay the obligation.[3]

Several factors distinguish section 590 from other stay sections:[4] (1) While most obligations must have been incurred prior to service, the section is applicable to taxes that may have occurred prior to or during service. (2) Only the serviceperson may request relief. He usually takes the initiative by going to court, but this section may be raised defensively. (3) The court has no power to grant relief on its own motion; the desired relief must be affirmatively requested. However, the court is not bound by such request and may grant less or conditional relief. (4) The serviceperson has the burden of proving material effect on his ability to pay the obligation. (5) Relief may be requested although no judicial proceeding is pending and even if no default has occurred. (6) The relief granted may extend after the period of service, making section 590 especially effective for ultimate resolution of problems rather than mere postponement. (7) Judicial discretion to impose "such other terms as may be just" allows the court to suspend enforcement of the entire obligation or to condition suspension on terms such as partial payment by the serviceperson.

As noted above, section 590 also helps the serviceperson to adjust financially *after* service. Because immediate payment of the principal and interest accumulated during the stay can sometimes be difficult at the termination of service, additional time may be provided to allow the orderly liquidation of such arrearages. Post-service extensions equal to the time spent in service may be granted for any obligation. However, land-secured obligations may get extensions equal to the time spent in service plus the time yet to run on the obligation as of the date of discharge (or date of application for relief, if made after discharge).[5] For example, suppose that an individual had twelve years of installments remaining on a home mortgage at the time he entered the Army for a term of four years. A stay of principal and interest payments could be granted during the service period, during which time nothing would be paid. After discharge from service, the mortgagor would have twelve years to pay the four year arrearages. This is calculated by

---

§ 8.10

1. Goldman, Collection of Debts Incurred by Military Personnel: The Creditor's View, 10 Tulsa L.J. 537, 554 (1970).

2. 50 U.S.C.A.App. § 590. Bagley, The Soldiers' and Sailors' Civil Relief Act—A Survey, 45 Mil.L.Rev. 1, 6 (1969).

3. Bagley, supra note 2, at 6; Goldman, supra note 1, at 555.

4. See Bagley, supra note 2, at 7; Goldman, supra note 1, at 555.

5. 50 U.S.C.A.App. § 590(1)(a)–(b); Bagley, supra note 2, at 8.

adding four years, the time equal to the service period, to the eight years remaining on the mortgage as of the discharge date.[6] This example illustrates the maximum extension, but the court has discretion to grant more modest relief. It should be emphasized that relief by stay and extension applies only to arrearages and not to payments falling due after discharge.[7] After ending service, the mortgagor must make normal payments with respect to the eight years yet to run as of the discharge date while also paying the arrearages within the twelve year extension period.[8] Interestingly, under the above example, the former serviceperson obtains a longer period to pay the arrearages than to pay the balance of the original obligation. On the other hand, arrearages must be paid in equal installments. The mortgagor cannot wait and pay a lump sum at the end of the extension.[9] As noted earlier, other conditions may also be imposed, such as granting additional interest on the arrearage during the post-service extension.[10]

Installment Land Contracts

Section 531 governs stays on installment land contracts.[11] If the serviceperson defaults on payments or breaches any other term of such a contract during military service it is a crime for the seller to exercise any right or option such as termination of the contract, rescission, or repossession of the land, except by judicial action.[12] However, the contract must have been made and a deposit or installment paid prior to entering service.[13] If the seller files such a judicial action, the court may condition its order on repayment of all or part of the deposit and prior installments.[14] If military service materially affected the serviceperson's ability to comply with the terms of payment, the court may order a stay, either absolute or conditioned on partial payment by the serviceperson. The court in its discretion may even order sale of the property and division of the proceeds.[15]

It is important to emphasize here that section 531 stays differ from section 590 stays in several aspects: (1) Section 531 requires that a stay be granted upon request by the defendant unless the court is of the opinion that ability to comply with the contract was not materially affected by military service. The court also may grant a stay on its own motion if such material effect is found.[16] (2) Violation of section 531 is a crime.[17] (3) Section 590 puts the burden of proving material

---

6. But note that for personal property, even though more expensive and requiring a 20 year security instrument, such as an airplane, the maximum extension would still be only four years. Goldman, supra note 1, at 556.

7. Bagley, supra note 2, at 9.

8. Id.

9. Id.

10. Id.

11. 50 U.S.C.A.App. § 531.

12. Goldman, supra note 1 at 552; 50 U.S.C.A.App. § 531(2).

13. See Ryan v. Bloom, 120 Mont. 443, 186 P.2d 879 (1947).

14. Goldman, supra note 1, at 552.

15. Bagley, supra note 2, at 10.

16. Id.

17. 50 U.S.C.A.App. § 531(2) makes violation a misdemeanor punishable by a $1000 fine, a year in jail, or both.

effect on the serviceman, but section 531 makes no such express provision.[18]

Mortgages and Deeds of Trust

Section 532 governs obligations secured by mortgages and deeds of trust. It is similar in language and effect to section 531.[19] After default in payment or other breach, the mortgagee cannot sell, foreclose, or seize the mortgaged property during the term of service or three months thereafter except by court order or pursuant to a valid waiver by the serviceperson.[20] This prohibition on the mortgagee applies only if the mortgagor both owned the land and executed the underlying mortgage obligation prior to military service.[21] In states where power of sale mortgages or deeds of trust are widely used to avoid the expense and delay of judicial foreclosure,[22] section 532 not only defeats this purpose, but makes foreclosure in violation of this provision a crime.[23] In addition, foreclosure without court action is probably void, making it impossible for anyone, including a bona fide purchaser for value, to obtain good title.[24]

Once a judicial foreclosure proceeding has begun, as in the installment land contract situation, it is subject to being stayed. As a condition precedent, section 532 requires that: (1) The serviceperson owned the property both prior to entering service and at the time relief is sought; (2) the obligation secured by the mortgage, deed of trust, or other similar instrument arose prior to military service; (3) breach of the obligation occurred prior to or during military service; and (4) the proceeding which the serviceperson seeks to stay was commenced during military service. As in section 531, the court must grant the stay upon request, absent a finding that military service had no material effect on ability to pay. The court also has discretion to grant a stay on its own motion upon finding material effect.[25]

Judicial Proceedings and Execution of Judgments

Two other SSCRA sections with potential effect on land-secured obligations differ from other stays because they apply to obligations

---

18. Bagley, supra note 2, at 11.

19. 50 U.S.C.A.App. § 532; Bagley, supra note 2, at 11, notes that section 532 mentions nothing about the necessity of a pre-service payment or deposit as does section 531.

20. Goldman supra note 1 at 553.

21. See Brown v. Gerber, 495 P.2d 1160 (Colo.App.1972).

22. See § 7.19, supra.

23. Supra note 20. For an example of how one state has attempted to comply with the SSCRA and retain power of sale for use against servicemen, see Colo.R.C.P. 120.

24. Goldman, supra note 1, at 553, n. 100, notes that a bona fide purchaser for value may obtain good title under some circumstances, at least where the serviceman's interest is unrecorded and the purchaser's duty to ascertain possible military service of any mortgagors has been satisfied. See also 24 Mo.L.Rev. supra note 72 at 105, discussing Godwin v. Gerling, 362 Mo. 19, 30, 239 S.W. 352, 359 (1951) (en banc), where section 525 relief was denied to a serviceman with an unacknowledged, unrecorded deed. But cf. § 7.20, supra.

25. Bagley, supra note 2, at 12.

arising either prior to or during military service. Section 521 allows a stay to be granted at any stage of a judicial proceeding if the ability of the serviceperson to participate, as either plaintiff or defendant, is materially affected by military service. Moreover, the burden is on the party opposing the postponement to establish the absence of such material effect.[26] Section 523 provides that in any action resulting in a judgment or order against the serviceperson, a stay of execution may be granted if military service has materially affected ability to comply with the judgment.[27] Under both sections, absent a finding of no material effect, the court must grant the requested stay.[28] The court may also grant the stay on its own motion. Both sections apply to actions commenced during military service or within 60 days thereafter. However, section 523 applies also to actions commenced prior to service so long as the resulting judgment or order is unsatisfied during service or within 60 days thereafter.[29]

 WESTLAW REFERENCES

Civil Obligations and Taxes
("soldiers and sailors"　/p　590) (usca　+10　590)

Installment Land Contracts
("soldiers and sailors"　/p　530) (usca　+10　531)

Mortgages and Deed of Trust
mortgage (deed　/3　trust)　/p　foreclos!　/p　"soldiers and sailors"

Judicial Proceedings and Execution of Judgments
material**　/5　affect!　/p　"soldiers and sailors"

§ 8.11　Default Judgments

Section 520 provides servicepersons certain protections against default judgments. These protections will, of course, extend to judicial foreclosure actions. Section 520 requires default plaintiffs to file an affidavit indicating whether the defendant is in military service.[1] Although the statute requires such an affidavit in every action where default occurs, failure to file one is not a jurisdictional defect and civilian parties such as co-defendants cannot object to noncompliance.[2] Unless the affidavit shows that the defendant is not in service, the default judgment will not be entered until after an attorney is appointed to represent the defendant. The attorney may take steps, such

26. See 50 U.S.C.A.App. § 521; Coburn v. Coburn, 412 So.2d 947 (Fla.App.1982). Mortgagees, however, are occasionally successful in satisfying that burden. See Gainey v. Gainey, 279 S.C. 68, 301 S.E.2d 763 (1983) (affirming trial court finding of no material effect on ability of mortgagor-serviceman to defend against judicial foreclosure).

27. 50 U.S.C.A.App. § 523; Bagley, supra note 2, at 12–13; Goldman, supra note 1, at 549.

28. See e.g., Boothe v. Henrietta Egleston Hospital for Children, Inc., 168 Ga. App. 352, 308 S.E.2d 844 (1983); Mays v. Tharpe & Brooks, Inc., 143 Ga.App. 815, 240 S.E.2d 159 (1977).

29. See note 27 supra.

§ 8.11

1. 50 U.S.C.A.App. § 560.

2. Bagley, The Soldiers' and Sailors' Civil Relief Act—A Survey, 45 Mil.L.Rev. 1, 15 (1969).

as making an investigation, that are clearly in the defendant's interest, but he has no power to waive any rights or otherwise bind the absentee serviceperson.[3]

A default judgment may be set aside even after full statutory compliance as to the affidavit and appointment of an attorney. The serviceperson must make application to set aside the judgment and reopen the case within 90 days after ending military service and he must establish that (1) military service prejudiced his defense, and (2) a meritorious defense exists for at least some part of the action.[4] It should be noted that any appearance by the serviceperson or his attorney, even a special appearance to contest jurisdiction or assert rights under SSCRA, waives section 520 protection.[5]

Interestingly, section 520 specifies that any right or title acquired by a bona fide purchaser for value under the default judgment shall not be impaired if the judgment is set aside.[6] This provision limits the effectiveness of section 520 for the mortgagor or vendee attempting to recover possession of land, whether or not the default was intentional. However, if the purchaser is not a bona fide purchaser for value, the judgment can be vacated and the title of the purchaser invalidated.[7]

 WESTLAW REFERENCES
default! /p 520 /p "soldiers and sailors"

D. BANKRUPTCY

§ 8.12 General Considerations

In theory, mortgagees should be unconcerned when insolvency forces mortgagors to file bankruptcy. Indeed, protection from such occurrences is the very reason for creation of mortgage security interests. In reality, however, mortgagees' rights, contractual and statutory, are often substantially affected by federal bankruptcy law, as many learn when they are forced into bankruptcy court to defend their security interests from the trustee's attack.[1] Familiar state laws, requiring minimal time and effort to foreclose, are often neutralized by federal bankruptcy provisions which may freeze property for years.

---

3. Bagley, supra note 2, at 15–16.

4. Id. at 16. Taurus Leasing Corp. v. Chalaire, 400 So.2d 303 (La.App.1981), writ denied 406 So.2d 604 (1981) (insufficient proof of meritorious defense).

5. Id.

6. Goldman, Collection of Debts Incurred by Military Personnel: A Creditor's View, 10 Tulsa L.J. 537, 548 (1970); Taurus Leasing Corp. v. Chalaire, 400 So.2d 303 (La.App.1981), writ denied 406 So.2d 604 (1981) (default not set aside, in part because BFP now owner of real estate).

7. Id. See Flagg v. Sun Investment & Loan Corp., 373 P.2d 226 (Okl.1962), where a foreclosure and sheriff's sale were set aside because the serviceman had filed a "caveat" after default and before the sale, giving the purchasers (who were also the plaintiffs in the original foreclosure action) notice of his military status.

§ 8.12

1. See § 8.13 infra.

The Bankruptcy Code (the "Code") provides for three types of bankruptcy proceedings: Chapter 7 [2] ("straight bankruptcy"), Chapter 11,[3] and Chapter 13.[4] Straight bankruptcy entails the liquidation of the debtor's non-exempt assets to satisfy his or her creditors according to the priority and amount of their claims. Such a proceeding ultimately discharges the debtor of most pre-bankruptcy debts. It is the most common type of bankruptcy proceeding. Relief may be sought by the debtor ("voluntary") or by creditors ("involuntary"). Chapter 11 proceedings, on the other hand, provide for the reorganization of corporate and other business debtors.[5] Rehabilitation, not liquidation, is the purpose of such proceedings. Reorganization plans can result in extension of debts and broad judicial control over both secured and unsecured creditors. Finally, Chapter 13 is to some extent a Chapter 11 equivalent for individuals. Such proceedings are aimed at the rehabilitation of the debtor by extension and reduction of both unsecured and certain secured claims. Such a proceeding may be used by an individual who owes less than $100,000 in unsecured debt and $350,000 in secured debt.[6]

The most immediate impact of debtor bankruptcy on the real estate mortgagee is the automatic stay. Under section 362(a) of the Code, all foreclosure proceedings, whether judicial or power of sale, are automatically stayed by the filing of any of the three types of bankruptcy proceedings.[7] The stay is applicable whether or not the foreclosure was initiated prior to the bankruptcy petition.[8] Moreover, in Chapter 13 proceedings the stay is also applicable to foreclosure and other proceedings against third persons who have guaranteed the bankrupt's consumer debt or put up property to secure it.[9] The only significant exception from the stay is for foreclosure "actions" brought by the Secretary of HUD on federally insured mortgages on property consisting of five or more living units.[10] The impact of the stay on the real estate mortgagee can be substantial. For example, a mortgagee can be in the middle of a complex judicial foreclosure in state court, and the filing of a bankruptcy petition can bring the action to an absolute halt. Not only will any foreclosure consummated in violation of the stay be ineffective, the mortgagee risks being punished for contempt as well.[11]

---

2. See 11 U.S.C.A. §§ 701–766.

3. See 11 U.S.C.A. §§ 1101–1174.

4. See 11 U.S.C.A. §§ 1301–1330.

5. Individuals can use Chapter 11, although the typical case is a business case. See 11 U.S.C.A. § 109(d).

6. See 11 U.S.C.A. § 109(e).

7. See 11 U.S.C.A. § 362(a)(4); Whelan, Lenders' Rights in Bankruptcy Stays, Mortgage Banker, Oct. 1984, 57; Nimmer, Real Estate Creditors and the Automatic Stay: A Study in Behavioral Economics, 1983 Ariz.St.L.J. 281; Nimmer, Secured Creditors and the Automatic Stay: Variable Bargain Models of Fairness, 68 Minn.L. Rev. 1 (1983).

8. See 11 U.S.C.A. § 362(a).

9. See 11 U.S.C.A. § 1301.

10. See 11 U.S.C.A. § 362(b)(8).

11. See Collier on Bankruptcy ¶ 362.11 (15th Ed. 1984).

WESTLAW REFERENCES
foreclos! /p stay** /p bankrupt**
topic(51) /p mortgagee
di bankrupt

§ 8.13 Straight Bankruptcy

As we noted in the preceding section, the filing of a petition in straight bankruptcy stays any pending or planned foreclosure proceeding. However, assuming the mortgage is valid, the trustee has a legitimate interest in the mortgaged real estate only if the mortgagor-debtor has "equity" in that real estate—the amount by which the value of the property exceeds the total amount of mortgage debt against it. If a mortgagee seeks relief from the stay and such equity does not exist, the trustee should abandon the real estate to the mortgagee who then can proceed to foreclose.[1] If equity is found to exist, the real estate will be sold by the bankruptcy court, either (1) subject to the existing mortgages and other liens, or (2) free and clear of them.[2] If the latter course is chosen, those liens will be transferred to the sale proceeds and satisfied in order of their priority.[3] Suppose, for example, that E–1 has a valid first mortgage on Blackacre with a $60,000 balance and that E–2 has a valid second mortgage on it with a $15,000 balance. If the trustee determines that Blackacre is worth less than $75,000, she will release it and either lienor will be free to foreclose under state law. If, however, Blackacre proves to be worth more than $75,000, she will either sell it subject to the foregoing mortgages or free and clear of them. If she chooses the latter course, the two mortgages will attach to the sale proceeds and be satisfied in order of their priority.

Because the trustee represents the interests of the bankrupt's unsecured creditors, her primary goal is to enlarge the asset pool available to satisfy their claims. Since each mortgage invalidated usually serves that purpose, she will be especially watchful for opportunities to attack vulnerable security interests. The Code affords her an impressive arsenal of weapons in this regard. Perhaps most basic is section 558, which gives the trustee "the benefit of any defense available to the debtor" against the mortgagee even if the debtor waives it after the commencement of bankruptcy.[4] Thus, for example, to the extent that a debtor would be able to invalidate a mortgage based on fraud, usury, incapacity or other grounds, so too will the trustee. Also important is section 544(a)(3) which affords the trustee, irrespective of

§ 8.13

1. See 11 U.S.C.A. § 554; In re Thayer, 38 B.R. 412 (Bkrtcy.Vt.1984). See Whelan, Lender's Rights in Bankruptcy Stays, Mortgage Banker, Oct. 1984, 58. In re Victor Builders, Inc., 418 F.2d 880 (C.A.Cal. 1969); In re Polumbo, 271 F.Supp. 640, 643 (W.D.Va.1967); In the Matter of Ira Haupt & Co., 398 F.2d 607 (C.A.N.Y.1968).

2. See 11 U.S.C.A. § 363(f); Collier on Bankruptcy ¶ 363.07 (15th Ed. 1984).

3. Collier, supra note 2 at ¶ 363.07.

4. See 11 U.S.C.A. § 558; In re Hayes, 39 B.R. 1 (Bkrtcy.Ill.1983).

knowledge on her part, the status of a bona fide purchaser of real property from the debtor who has perfected under state law.[5] Such status can be utilized whether such a purchaser actually exists or not.[6] Consequently, the trustee will always be able to defeat any mortgage of the debtor that is unrecorded as of the commencement of bankruptcy. Because she is deemed to have perfected under state law, the type of state recording act (e.g., whether race-notice, notice or pure race)[7] and its requirements become irrelevant.

While section 544(a)(3) permits the trustee to defeat any prior unrecorded mortgage, situations may arise where it is to her advantage to be able to assert its priority. Suppose, for example, that after a mortgage on Blackacre is executed, but never recorded, a second mortgage is recorded by another creditor who, under the applicable state recording act, qualifies as a bona fide purchaser against that unrecorded mortgage. The debtor-mortgagor then files a bankruptcy petition. While section 544(a)(3), as noted earlier, allows the trustee to avoid the unrecorded mortgage, it does not prevent the second mortgage, which is admittedly valid, from being promoted in priority. However, section 551 of the Code then comes to the rescue.[8] Under the latter provision, a trustee who avoids a senior lien becomes subrogated to the rights of the senior lienor up to the amount of the senior debt. For example, suppose the unrecorded mortgage has a balance of $10,000 and the recorded second mortgage a balance of $20,000. If the real estate is sold by the bankruptcy court for $25,000, the trustee, as subrogee, will have a right to $10,000 and the second mortgagee will receive $15,000.

Certain mortgages may be vulnerable to a fraudulent conveyance attack. Under section 548 of the Code,[9] transfers made by the debtor within one year of bankruptcy may be set aside by the trustee if they were made with the intent to hinder, delay or defraud any creditor to which the debtor was or became indebted.[10] Thus, for example, suppose a debtor, in order to conceal his substantial equity in Blackacre, grants mortgagee a mortgage on it within a year of filing a bankruptcy petition. The trustee will be able to set aside the mortgage. Moreover, as we explore in detail in a subsequent section,[11] the constructive fraud provision of section 548 has increasingly become the basis for setting aside certain pre-bankruptcy foreclosure sales of the debtor's real estate that yield less than its "reasonably equivalent value." The trustee may have a further fraudulent conveyance weapon. To the extent that state fraudulent conveyance law confers on unsecured creditors broader powers to avoid debtor mortgages than are afforded by its section 548

---

5. See 11 U.S.C.A. § 544(a)(3); Jackson, Avoiding Powers in Bankruptcy, 36 Stan.L. Rev. 725, 732–742 (1984). Collier, supra note 2 at ¶ 544.02; In re Duffy-Irvine Associates, 39 B.R. 525 (Bkrtcy.Pa.1984).

6. 11 U.S.C.A. § 544(a)(3).

7. See generally, Cunningham, Stoebuck and Whitman, Property § 11.9 (1984).

8. 11 U.S.C.A. § 551.

9. 11 U.S.C.A. § 548.

10. 11 U.S.C.A. § 548(a)(1). See Jackson, supra note 5 at 777–786.

11. See § 8.15 infra.

counterpart, section 544(b) of the Code empowers the trustee to take advantage of that state law, a matter which we explore further in a subsequent section of this chapter.[12]

Finally, many mortgages given within 90 days of the mortgagor's bankruptcy will be voidable by the trustee as a preference under section 547 of the Act.[13] A significant policy embodied in the bankruptcy law is that similarly situated creditors be treated equally. However, once a debtor becomes financially unstable, creditors commonly violate that policy by seeking to gain advantage vis á vis their creditor brethren. Often this entails acquiring real estate mortgages from the debtor to secure pre-existing debt. To the extent that such mortgages are granted by an insolvent mortgagor within 90 days of bankruptcy and they would otherwise enable the creditor to realize more on its claim than it would in a straight bankruptcy liquidation, they constitute voidable preferences.[14] Moreover, there is a presumption of debtor insolvency during this 90 day period.[15] Moreover, if the creditor is an "insider",[16] the preference period is one year rather than 90 days.[17]

Another preference problem arises because of a bankruptcy policy against secret and unrecorded liens. Even though a mortgage is valid between the parties at the time of its execution, for bankruptcy purposes the transfer is deemed to occur on the date the mortgage is recorded if recordation occurs more than ten days after the mortgage is received.[18] Since the transfer under such circumstances occurs as of the date of recording, it will be treated as a transfer for an antecedent debt even though present value was given when the mortgage became effective between the parties. For example, suppose that on January 15 mortgagor, who is insolvent, borrows $10,000 from creditor and the latter takes back a mortgage on Blackacre as security. On February 10 creditor records the mortgage. On March 15, mortgagor files a bankruptcy petition. Even though the $10,000 loan would otherwise represent new value,[19] because of the tardy recording, the transfer will be deemed to be for an antecedent debt within 90 days of bankruptcy. Accordingly, the mortgage can be set aside as a voidable preference.

While the foregoing trustee's powers are numerous and important, it would be a mistake to overemphasize their danger for the real estate mortgagee. Most straight bankruptcy proceedings are consummated relatively rapidly, and normally the mortgage security and lien priority will be preserved. It is true that in some instances, a trustee may delay

12. 11 U.S.C.A. § 544(b). See e.g., In re Penn Packing Co., 42 B.R. 502 (Bkrtcy.Pa. 1984); § 8.16 infra. See generally, Note, Good Faith and Fraudulent Conveyances, 97 Harv.L.Rev. 495 (1983).

13. See 11 U.S.C.A. § 547; Jackson, supra note 5 at 756–777; Ross, The Impact of Section 547 of the Bankruptcy Code Upon Secured and Unsecured Creditors, 69 Minn.L.Rev. 39 (1984).

14. Id.

15. 11 U.S.C.A. § 547(f).

16. 11 U.S.C.A. § 101(28).

17. 11 U.S.C.A. § 547(b)(4)(B).

18. 11 U.S.C.A. §§ 547(e)(1)(A), 547(e) (2). See Collier, supra note 2 at ¶ 547.44.

19. 11 U.S.C.A. § 547(a)(2).

temporarily the disposition of income-producing real estate in an attempt to accumulate some of those rents for the benefit of unsecured creditors. This problem is examined in a later section.[20] By and large, however, the most significant impact of a straight bankruptcy on the mortgagee will be the loss of part of all of its deficiency judgment and that should pose no problem to the prudent mortgagee who made sure initially that the debt was well-secured.

 WESTLAW REFERENCES

11 + 7 558 /p trustee

11 + 7 548 /p bankrupt**

bankrupt** /p secret unrecord** /s lien /p mortgag**

§ 8.14   The Chapter 11 Reorganization

Because the purpose of a Chapter 11 proceeding is the rehabilitation rather than the liquidation of the debtor, the debtor typically continues to operate the estate as a "debtor-in-possession."[1] Parties in interest (usually creditors) may obtain the appointment of a trustee only for cause "including fraud, dishonesty, incompetence, or gross mismanagement" on the part of the debtor[2] or where appointment is otherwise in such parties' "best interests."[3] The appointment of a trustee is considered "an extraordinary remedy"[4] and there is thus a strong presumption in favor of the debtor remaining in possession, at least through the plan formulation period.[5] Moreover, the debtor-in-possession is entitled to exercise the avoidance powers of a Chapter 7 trustee.[6]

From the moment the mortgagor files a Chapter 11 petition, the mortgagee is stayed from foreclosing.[7] Usually the stay will remain in effect at least while a reorganization plan is being formulated and often during its execution. However, under section 362 of the Code, the bankruptcy court may "terminat[e], annul, modify or condition such stay (1) for cause, including the lack of adequate protection of an interest in property of such [mortgagee]; or (2) with respect to a stay of an act against property, if—(A) the [mortgagor] does not have an equity in such property; and (B) such property is not necessary to an effective reorganization."[8]

The first ground for relief has provided some difficulty for the bankruptcy courts. Some courts, for example, suggest that "adequate

---

20. See § 8.17 infra.

§ 8.14

1. See Collier on Bankruptcy, ¶ 1104.01 (15th Ed. 1984); 11 U.S.C.A. § 1107.

2. 11 U.S.C.A. § 1104(a)(1).

3. 11 U.S.C.A. § 1104(a)(2); Collier on Bankruptcy, ¶ 1104.01(d) (15th Ed. 1984).

4. Collier on Bankruptcy, ¶ 1104.01(b) (15th Ed. 1984).

5. Id.

6. 11 U.S.C.A. § 1107. See In re Hartman Paving, Inc., 745 F.2d 307 (4th Cir. 1984).

7. See 11 U.S.C.A. § 362(a).

8. See 11 U.S.C.A. § 362(d).

protection" exists if there is an "equity cushion" in the mortgaged real estate.[9] Others stress that the foregoing language is designed to protect against post-filing decline in the value of the real estate.[10] In a few instances, mortgagor failure to pay real estate taxes or to keep the mortgaged premises insured have been deemed to cause a lack of adequate protection.[11] When such adequate protection is lacking, section 361 sets out three permissible ways to provide it.[12] As summarized by Professor Kennedy, "first, the trustee may be required to make periodic cash payments to the [mortgagee] in an amount sufficient to compensate for the decrease in the value of the [mortgagee's] interest resulting from the stay. Second, the [mortgagee] may be provided with an alternative or additional lien equal in value to the decrease in the value of the [mortgagee's] interest resulting from the stay. Finally, any other relief may be granted that will give the [mortgagee] realization of the 'indubitable equivalent' of its interest in property." [13] The latter alternative is a "catch-all" concept that awaits case by case development. Nevertheless, as one commentator has stressed, "[g]iving a creditor which holds security of the highest quality with an ample cushion alternative security of dubious value or of a value barely that of the debt would not meet 'indubitable equivalent' standard." [14]

The second ground for stay relief is more commonly relied upon by mortgagees. Under this approach two requirements must be satisfied. First, the mortgagor must lack equity in the mortgaged real estate and second, that real estate must not be necessary to an "effective reorganization." [15] The meaning of the term "equity" has proved especially troublesome for the bankruptcy courts. Under the predominate approach, "equity" refers to "the difference between the value of the property and all encumbrances against it." [16] A sizeable minority of

9. See e.g., In re Jamaica House, 31 B.R. 192 (Bkrtcy.Vt.1983); In re Tucker, 5 B.R. 180 (Bkrtcy.N.Y.1980); In re Penn York Manufacturing, Inc., 14 B.R. 51 (Bkrtcy.Pa.1981); Hagendorfer v. Marlette, 42 B.R. 17 (S.D.Ala.1984).

10. See e.g., In re Development, Inc., 36 B.R. 998 (Bkrtcy.Hawaii 1984); In re Riviera Inn of Wallingford, Inc., 7 B.R. 725 (Bkrtcy.Conn.1980); In re Gaim Development Corp., 9 B.R. 17 (Bkrtcy.Fla.1981); In re Palmer River Realty, Inc., 26 B.R. 138 (Bkrtcy.R.I.1983); In re BBT, 11 B.R. 224 (Bkrtcy.Nev.1981); La Jolla Mortgage Fund v. Rancho El Cajon Associates, 18 B.R. 283 (Bkrtcy.Cal.1982).

11. In re Jenkins, 36 B.R. 788 (Bkrtcy. Fla.1984); In re Jamaica House, Inc., 31 B.R. 192 (Bkrtcy.Vt.1983); In re Ausherman, 34 B.R. 393 (Bkrtcy.Ill.1983).

12. 11 U.S.C.A. § 361.

13. Kennedy, Automatic Stays Under the New Bankruptcy Law, 12 U.Mich.J.L. Ref. 3.43–44 (1979). See In re Develop-

ment, Inc., 36 B.R. 998 (Bkrtcy.Hawaii 1984).

14. Collier on Bankruptcy, ¶ 361.01[4] (15th Ed.1984).

15. See 11 U.S.C.A. § 362(d)(2).

16. See e.g., Stewart v. Gurley, 745 F.2d 1194 (9th Cir.1984); In re Faires, 34 B.R. 549 (Bkrtcy.Wash.1983); In re Development, Inc., 36 B.R. 998 (Bkrtcy.Hawaii 1984); In re Trina-Dee, Inc., 26 B.R. 152 (Bkrtcy.Pa.1983); In re Koopmans, 22 B.R. 395 (Bkrtcy.Utah 1982); In re Crescent Beach Inn, Inc., 22 B.R. 161 (Bkrtcy.Me. 1982); La Jolla Mortgage Fund v. Rancho El Cajon Associates, 18 B.R. 283 (Bkrtcy. Cal.1982); In re Saint Peter's School, 16 B.R. 404 (Bkrtcy.N.Y.1982); First Connecticut Small Business Investment Co. v. Ruark, 7 B.R. 46 (Bkrtcy.Conn.1980); In re Dallasta, 7 B.R. 883 (Bkrtcy.Pa.1980); Note, "Automatic Stay under the 1978 Bankruptcy Code: An Equitable Roadblock to Secured Creditor Relief," 17 San Diego L.Rev. 1113, 1123 (1980). Whelan, Lend-

decisions, however, take the position that the term "means the difference between the value of the property and the lien which is the subject of the [request for stay relief], along with any liens senior thereto." [17] Under this view, it makes no difference how many junior encumbrances are outstanding against the subject property so long as the [mortgagor] has a substantial and meaningful equity cushion over and above the senior encumbrances." [18] Because it enhances the likelihood that equity will exist and that relief from the stay will thus be denied, the minority view is especially appealing to junior lienholders. By keeping the stay in effect they postpone the day of reckoning when they must either satisfy the senior indebtedness or suffer foreclosure of their liens.[19]

If the court finds that equity exists, it must then determine whether the mortgaged real estate is "necessary to an effective reorganization." [20] As one court has stressed, it is "not enough for a debtor to argue that the automatic stay should continue because it needs the secured property in order to propose a reorganization. If this were the test all property held by debtors could be regarded as necessary for the debtor's reorganization. The key work is 'effective'." [21] The mere fact that the real estate is essential to the survival of the mortgagor's business is insufficient.[22] Rather, the mortgagor is required to demonstrate that there is "a reasonable likelihood of a successful reorganization within a reasonable period of time." [23]

On the surface it would seem that a mortgagee should invariably prefer the "adequate protection" route to stay relief over the "no equity—necessary to an effective reorganization" approach. For example, suppose the mortgagee can establish that an "equity cushion" no longer exists in the mortgaged real estate. If such a showing is enough to show inadequate protection, why should the mortgagee run the risk that mortgagor will be able to establish that the real estate is necessary to an effective reorganization? Perhaps the answer lies in the fact that

ers' Rights in Bankruptcy Stays, Mortgage Banker, Oct. 1984, 57, 58.

17. In re Faires, 34 B.R. 549 (Bkrtcy. Wash.1983). See e.g., In re Cote, 27 B.R. 510 (Bkrtcy.Or.1983); In re Palmer River Realty, Inc., 26 B.R. 138 (Bkrtcy.R.I.1983); Matter of Certified Mortgage Corp., 25 B.R. 662 (Bkrtcy.Fla.1982); Matter of Spring Garden Foliage, Inc., 15 B.R. 140 (Bkrtcy. Fla.1981); In re Wolford Enterprises, Inc., 11 B.R. 571 (Bkrtcy.Va.1981).

18. Matter of Spring Garden Foliage, Inc., 15 B.R. 140, 143 (Bkrtcy.Fla.1981).

19. "There may be many instances when the holder of a lien inferior to the lien of a plaintiff does not want relief from the stay afforded to the plaintiff. In a foreclosure a junior lienholder is faced with the possibility that unless it purchases the interests of those holders of superior liens it will lose any recovery upon its lien. The junior lienholder may prefer to negotiate with the debtor for different payment terms or a reduction in the amount due to it."

In re Cote, 27 B.R. 510, 513 (Bkrtcy.Or. 1983).

20. 11 U.S.C.A. § 362(d)(2)(B).

21. In re Clark Technical Associates, Limited, 9 B.R. 738, 740 (Bkrtcy.Conn. 1981).

22. In re Development, Inc., 36 B.R. 998 (Bkrtcy.Hawaii 1984); In re Mikole Developers, Inc., 14 B.R. 524 (Bkrtcy.Pa.1981).

23. In re Development, Inc., 36 B.R. 998 (Bkrtcy.Hawaii 1984); In re Sundale Associates, Limited, 11 B.R. 978 (Bkrtcy.Fla. 1981). In re Smith, 42 B.R. 276 (Bkrtcy.Pa. 1984).

if the court finds both a lack of equity and that the property is unnecessary to an effective reorganization, it will invariably dissolve the stay because, by definition, there is no reason for the court to retain control over it. On the other hand, a finding of inadequate protection alone may simply result in a decree ordering additional protection for the mortgagee or some modification, rather than dissolution, of the stay.[24]

The Reorganization Plan

Once the Chapter 11 petition is filed, the debtor has the exclusive right for 120 days to submit a reorganization plan.[25] That period may be extended for "cause." [26] If the debtor files a plan within the specified period, no other party can file a plan during the first 180 days of the case.[27] If he fails to file a plan, the other parties may file anytime after the expiration of the 120 day period.[28] Also, other parties can file at any time after a trustee has been appointed.[29] While the Code specifies in elaborate detail the contents of the plan,[30] two elements are especially important. First, the plan must classify creditor claims and, second, it must describe in detail its treatment of each creditor class. Claims generally are categorized as secured or unsecured.[31] Further distinctions are drawn based on the character or priority of the claims. For example, while two separate debts secured by one mortgage on Blackacre may be placed in one class, a junior mortgage on the same real estate arguably will not be included in it.[32] A detailed description of class treatment is required to place creditors on notice of the plan's prejudicial impact on them. For example, the plan will often restructure existing debt to provide for reduced payments over an extended period of time. Moreover, it may provide for an actual reduction in the amount of both secured and unsecured claims.[33]

After the plan is filed, a period for soliciting creditor acceptance begins.[34] Each creditor must receive a copy of the plan or a plan summary and a judicially approved disclosure statement.[35] Thereafter, the debtor solicits creditor approval for the plan. In general, each class must either accept the plan or not be "impaired" by it.[36] If a class is unimpaired, it is deemed to have accepted the plan.[37]

24. See e.g., In re Jenkins, 36 B.R. 788 (Bkrtcy.Fla.1984); In re Jamaica House, Inc., 31 B.R. 192 (Bkrtcy.Vt.1983). For further analysis of the two approaches, see In re Augustus Court Associates, 46 B.R. 619 (Bkrtcy.Pa.1985).

25. 11 U.S.C.A. § 1121(b).

26. 11 U.S.C.A. § 1121(d).

27. 11 U.S.C.A. § 1121(c)(2), (3).

28. Id.

29. 11 U.S.C.A. § 1121(c)(1).

30. See 11 U.S.C.A. § 1123.

31. See Comment, Real Estate Reorganizations: The New Bankruptcy Code v. Chapter XII, 1980 Ill.L.F. 251, 254 (1980).

32. Id. A plan can only put a claim into a particular class if it is "substantially similar" to other claims in the same class. See 11 U.S.C.A. § 1122(a).

33. Id.

34. Id. at 255.

35. Id.

36. 11 U.S.C.A. § 1129(a)(8).

37. 11 U.S.C.A. § 1126(f).

In general, in order for a class to qualify as "unimpaired", the plan may not alter the legal equitable or contractual rights of any claim in the class.[38] Importantly, under section 1124(2), a claim is not impaired even though the plan cures a "default that occurred before * * * the commencement of the case * * * and reinstates the maturity of [the] claim * . * * as such maturity existed before such default." [39] According to the legislative history of the foregoing section, a "claim * * * is unimpaired by curing the effect of a default and reinstating the original term of an obligation when maturity was brought on or accelerated by the default. The intervention of bankruptcy and the defaults represent a temporary crisis which the plan of reorganization is intended to clear away. The holder of a claim * * * who under the plan is restored to his original position, when others receive less or get nothing at all, is fortunate indeed and has no cause to complain." [40]

While the foregoing section clearly sanctions deacceleration where a Chapter 11 petition is filed before the mortgagee invokes a state foreclosure procedure, courts disagree about the effect of a petition filed thereafter. Some hold that a foreclosure judgment cuts off the mortgagor's deacceleration rights,[41] while others take the position that "it is the foreclosure sale rather than the entry of judgment which cuts off" those rights.[42] This issue ultimately should be resolved by focusing on when, under state law, the mortgagor's equity of redemption is cut off. So long as such a termination has not yet occurred, deacceleration should be permitted. Such an approach was utilized by the United States Court of Appeals for the Seventh Circuit [43] in a case where a Chapter 11 petition intervened after the mortgagee had obtained a judicial order of foreclosure, but before that order had been reduced to judgment. The court emphasized that the result would have been the same even had the judgment been obtained and it quoted approvingly from a Seventh Circuit decision in an analogous Chapter 13 setting that " 'pursuant to Wisconsin law, a judgment of foreclosure does little more than determine that the mortgagor is in default, the amount of principal and interest due and unpaid, the amount due to the plaintiff mortgagee for taxes, etc. The judgment does not destroy the lien of the mortgage but rather judicially determines the amount thereof. Accordingly, the mortgagee's failure to obtain a judgment of foreclosure on its accelerated loan is of no consequence here.' "[44] Indeed, deacceleration

38. 11 U.S.C.A. § 1124.

39. 11 U.S.C.A. § 1124(2).

40. S.Rep. No. 989, 95th Cong., 2d Sess. 120.

41. See e.g., Matter of Celeste Court Apartments, Inc., 47 B.R. 470 (D.Del.1985); In re Monroe Park, 18 B.R. 790 (Bkrtcy. Del.1982); In re St. Peter's School, 16 B.R. 404 (Bkrtcy.N.Y.1982); In re Garner, 13 B.R. 799 (Bkrtcy.N.Y.1981).

42. In re Orlando Tennis World Development Co., Inc., 34 B.R. 558, 560 (Bkrtcy. Fla.1983); In re Hewitt, 16 B.R. 973 (Bkrtcy.Alaska 1982).

43. In Matter of Madison Hotel Associates, 749 F.2d 410 (7th Cir.1984).

44. Id. at 422 (quoting from In re Clark, 738 F.2d 869 (7th Cir.1984). See § 8.15 infra at notes 34–43.

will probably be permitted *after* the foreclosure sale in those states that afford the mortgagor statutory "post-sale" redemption rights.[44a]

Suppose, however, it is determined that a class is impaired. It is deemed to accept the plan when a majority in number and two-thirds in total amount of the claims approve the plan.[45] Moreover, each member of an impaired class must, in any event, either accept the plan or "receive or retain * * * on account of the plan property of a value that is not less than the amount that such holder would so receive or retain if the debtor were liquidated" in straight bankruptcy.[46] In addition, at least one class of impaired claims must accept the plan.[47] Finally, the plan must satisfy a "feasibility test."[48] Under section 1129(a)(11) of the Code, the bankruptcy court must determine that confirmation "is not likely to be followed by the liquidation, or the need for further financial reorganization, of the debtor * * * under the plan, unless such liquidation or reorganization is proposed in the plan."[49] Under this standard, the court must examine "the adequacy of the capital structure; the business's earning power; economic conditions; management's ability; the probability of the present management's continuation; and any other factors related to the successful performance of the plan."[50] The court must satisfy itself that a reasonable expectation of success exists.[51]

The Cram-Down Concept

Suppose that an impaired class fails to approve the plan. In that event, the debtor may invoke the "cram-down" power of the Act to gain confirmation of the plan over the objection of such a class.[52] However, "cram-down" is permitted only if the plan does not discriminate unfairly, and is "fair and equitable, with respect to each class of claims * * * that is impaired under, and has not accepted, the plan."[53] The unfair discrimination concept applies "only to the dissenting class and not to the plan in its entirety."[54] While there is little case law on this issue, there is authority, for example, that unfair discrimination exists when

44a. See In re Hewitt, 16 B.R. 973, 977 (Bkrtcy.Alaska 1982). There is substantial authority in the Chapter 13 context. See § 8.15 infra at notes 34–43.

45. 11 U.S.C.A. § 1126(c).

46. 11 U.S.C.A. § 1129(a)(7)(A)(ii); Broude, Cramdown and Chapter 11 of the Bankruptcy Code: The Settlement Imperative, 39 Bus.Lawyer 441, 448 (1984).

47. 11 U.S.C.A. § 1129(a)(10).

48. Broude, supra note 46 at 448.

49. 11 U.S.C.A. § 1129(a)(11).

50. In re Polytherm Industries, Inc., 33 B.R. 823, 831 (Bkrtcy.Wis.1983) See In re White, 41 B.R. 227 (Bkrtcy.Tenn.1984); Matter of Huckabee Auto Co., 33 B.R. 141, 145 n. 2 (Bkrtcy.Ga.1981); In re Merri-

mack Valley Oil Co., Inc., 32 B.R. 485, 488 (Bkrtcy.Mass.1983).

51. See In re White, 41 Bankr. 227 (Bkrtcy.Tenn.1984); Matter of Huckabee Auto Co., 33 B.R. 141 (Bkrtcy.Ga.1981).

52. See Broude, supra note 46 at 450–451; Comment, supra note 29 at 256–258. See generally, Coogan, Confirmation of a Plan Under the Bankruptcy Code, 32 Case W.Res.L.Rev. 301 (1982); Pachulski, the Cram Down and Valuation Under Chapter 11 of the Bankruptcy Code, 58 N.C.L.Rev. 925 (1980); Klee, All You Ever Wanted to Know About Cram Down Under the Bankruptcy Code, 53 Am.Bankr.L.J. 133 (1979).

53. 11 U.S.C.A. § 1129(b); Broude, supra note 38 at 450–451.

54. Broude, supra note 46 at 451.

trade debt claims are treated separately from the unsecured claims of otherwise secured creditors.[55]

To be "fair and equitable" in the dissenting real estate mortgagee creditor context, section 1129(b)(2)(A) requires that one of three approaches be followed.[56] Under the first, the debtor can continue to operate the real estate subject to the mortgage, but the mortgagee must receive present or deferred cash payments equal to the amount of the mortgage debt and having a value that is not less than the value of the mortgaged real estate.[57] This approach "allows the [mortgagee] to recover the face amount of the debt, because he can elect to have his entire claim treated as secured even if in fact it is undersecured. Moreover, the debtor must pay for any deferment or debt extension at current interest rates. * * * "[58] Under the second alternative, the real estate will be sold, but the mortgage lien will transfer to the sale proceeds.[59] This option will be unappealing to a debtor whose major asset is a single piece of rental real estate.[60] The final approach allows a court to confirm a plan that provides for the mortgagee to realize the "indubitable equivalent" of its claim.[61] As one commentator has noted, "[m]ore has been written on indubitable equivalence with less effect than on almost any other area of bankruptcy law."[62] Moreover, as one bankruptcy court noted, "there seems to be little controlling precedential definition of indubitable equivalent."[63] Legislative history suggests that the concept was intended to encompass abandonment of the security to the mortgagee or the granting of a lien on substitute security.[64]

Constitutional arguments have sometimes been asserted against stays and reorganization plans that mortgagees and other secured creditors have believed unduly threatened their security.[65] The two main constitutional theories advanced are that such proceedings constitute a "taking" without just compensation under the 5th Amendment and that they unconstitutionally impair the obligations of contracts. For example, the Court of Appeals for the Third Circuit has indicated that when reorganization plans go beyond mere postponement of the secured creditor's rights so as to constitute an erosion of the security, a taking may occur.[66] However, even if a reorganization plan did go so far as to constitute a taking, the Supreme Court has indicated that the

---

55. Id.

56. 11 U.S.C.A. § 1129(b)(2)(A).

57. 11 U.S.C.A. § 1129(b)(2)(A)(i).

58. Comment, supra note 29 at 273.

59. 11 U.S.C.A. § 1129(b)(2)(A)(ii).

60. Comment, supra note 29 at 273.

61. 11 U.S.C.A. § 1129(b)(2)(A)(iii).

62. Broude, supra note 46 at 452.

63. Matter of Gemini at Dadeland, Limited, 36 B.R. 129, 130 (Bkrtcy.Fla.1983).

64. Broude, supra note 46 at 452.

65. See generally, Comment, Adequate Protection and the Automatic Stay Under the Bankruptcy Code: Easing Restraints on Debtor Reorganization, 131 U.Pa.L.Rev. 423, 440–455 (1982).

66. In re Penn Central Transportation Co., 494 F.2d 270 (3d Cir.1974), certiorari denied 419 U.S. 883, 95 S.Ct. 147, 42 L.Ed. 2d 122 (1974). For a thorough consideration of this case and the constitutional claims, see Countryman, Real Estate Liens in Business Rehabilitation Cases, 50 Am. Bankr.L.J. 303, 334–339 (1976).

Court of Claims, and not the Bankruptcy Court, is the proper forum to raise that constitutional issue.[67] The impairment of contracts argument has generally failed, either because courts did not believe that postponement constituted an impairment [68] or because secured creditors were on notice of the bankruptcy reorganization powers when they took their security.[69] A third constitutional argument has been that the automatic stay violates 5th Amendment procedural due process rights of the secured creditor in that the stay becomes effective without notice or an opportunity to be heard. This argument has been rejected on the theory that the bankruptcy proceeding provide for prompt notice and hearing after the stay becomes effective.[70]

 WESTLAW REFERENCES

di chapter 11 corporate reorganization

"chapter 11" /p mortgag**

"effective reorganization" /p mortgag** lien (real /3 estate property)

11 + 7 362(d) /p reorganiz!

The Reorganization Plan

reorganiz! /5 plan /p "chapter 11" /p 1121 1123

51k641

impair** unimpair** /p 11 + 7 1129

default! /p 11 + 7 1124 /p impair** unimpair**

the Cram-Down Concept

"cram-down" /p "chapter 11"

fair /4 equitable /p cram-down

"due process" (5 5th /3 amendment) /p "chapter 11"

§ 8.15 The Chapter 13 "Wage Earner" Plan

The Chapter 13 plan to some extent is to the salaried person or wage earner what Chapter 11 is to the corporate or other commercial entity. Such a proceeding may be utilized by an individual who has a regular income and owes secured debt not in excess of $350,000 and unsecured debt not exceeding $100,000.[1] The plan must be completed within three years of confirmation unless the bankruptcy court approves a longer period not to exceed five years.[2] The Chapter 13 trustee may exercise the same avoidance powers that are available to his or her straight bankruptcy counterpart.[3] However, the trustee

---

67. Regional Rail Reorganization Act Cases, 419 U.S. 102, 95 S.Ct. 335, 42 L.Ed. 2d 320 (1974); See Countryman, supra note 58 at 338.

68. See Chicago, Rock Island & Pacific Railway v. Fleming, 157 F.2d 241, 247 (7th Cir.1946), certiorari denied 329 U.S. 780, 67 S.Ct. 201, 91 L.Ed. 669 (1946).

69. In re Prima, 88 F.2d 785, 788–789 (7th Cir.1937). For an example of a plan that one authority deems unconstitutional,

see In re Yale Express System, Inc., 384 F.2d 990 (2d Cir.1967).

70. See Fidelity Mortgage Investors v. Camelia Builders, Inc., 550 F.2d 47 (2d Cir. 1977).

§ 8.15

1. 11 U.S.C.A. § 109(e).

2. 11 U.S.C.A. § 1322(c).

3. 11 U.S.C.A. § 1302(b).

usually is passive and the debtor typically remains in possession of the estate.[4] Even though the Act confers no general avoidance powers on the debtor, bankruptcy courts frequently authorize the debtor to exercise such powers.[5] The legislative history of Chapter 13 provides a valuable insight into its purpose and operation:

> "The purpose of chapter 13 is to enable an individual, under court supervision and protection, to develop and perform under a plan for the repayment of his debts over an extended period. In some cases, the plan will call for full repayment. In others, it may offer creditors a percentage of their claims in full settlement. During the repayment period, creditors may not harass the debtor or seek to collect their debts. They must receive payments only under the plan. This protection relieves the debtor from indirect and direct pressures from creditors, and enables him to support himself and his dependents while repaying his creditors at the same time.

> "The benefit to the debtor of developing a plan of repayment under chapter 13, rather than opting for liquidation under chapter 7, is that it permits the debtor to protect his assets. In a liquidation case, the debtor must surrender his nonexempt assets for liquidation and sale by the trustee. Under chapter 13, the debtor may retain his property by agreeing to repay his creditors. Chapter 13 also protects a debtor's credit standing far better than a straight bankruptcy, because he is viewed by the credit industry as a better risk. In addition, it satisfies many debtors' desire to avoid the stigma attached to straight bankruptcy and to retain the pride attendant on being able to meet one's obligations. The benefit to creditors is self-evident: their losses will be significantly less than if their debtors opt for straight bankruptcy."[6]

When the debtor has completed the plan, all unsecured debts are discharged except alimony and child support obligations and those debts where the last payment is to be made after the expiration of the plan.[7] While the plan can regulate or sometimes modify the repayment of installments and arrearages on real estate mortgage debts (with the possible exception of mortgages on the debtor's principal residence) until the expiration of the plan, it cannot affect those

4. 11 U.S.C.A. § 1306(b): Henning, An Analysis of *Durrett* and its Impact on Real and Personal Property Foreclosures: Some Proposed Modifications, 63 N.C.L.Rev. 501, 526 n. 154 (1984).

5. See e.g., In re Willis, 48 B.R. 295 (S.D.Tex.1985); In re Dudley, 38 B.R. 666 (Bkrtcy.Pa.1984); In re Wheeler, 34 B.R. 818 (Bkrtcy.Ala.1983); Matter of Lozano, 42 B.R. 966 (D.Puerto Rico 1984); In re Worcester, 28 B.R. 910 (Bkrtcy.Cal.1983);

In re Cowart, 43 B.R. 110 (Bkrtcy.Fla.1984); Henning, supra note 4 at 526, n. 154.

6. H.R.Rep. No. 595, 95th Cong., Ist Sess. 118 (1977), U.S.Code Cong. & Admin. News, p. 6079.

7. 11 U.S.C.A. § 1328; See Comment, Home Foreclosures Under Chapter 13 of The Bankruptcy Reform Act, 30 U.C.L.A.L. Rev. 637, 643–646 (1983).

mortgage payments coming due after its expiration date.[8] Thereafter, the debtor is required to make future payments as if no plan had existed.

Real estate mortgagees in a Chapter 13 proceeding are subject to the general stay provisions contained in section 362 of the Code.[9] In addition, there is a special stay provision protecting third parties who have guaranteed the bankrupt's debt or put up property to secure it.[10] Section 1301 provides that "a creditor may not act, or commence or continue any civil action, to collect all or any part of a consumer debt of the debtor from any individual that is liable on such debt with the debtor, or that secured such debt unless such individual became liable on or secured such debt in the ordinary course of such individual's business."[11] A "consumer debt" is one "incurred by an individual primarily for a personal, family or household purpose."[12] Thus, while the stay imposed by section 362 bars a mortgagee from foreclosing against the property of the mortgagor, section 1301 stays a mortgagee who holds "consumer debt" from foreclosing against the real estate of third parties that has been used as security for the mortgagor's non-business related debt.

De-acceleration of Home Mortgage

Often the only or, in any event, the most significant real estate mortgagee in a Chapter 13 proceeding is the holder of a mortgage on the debtor's home.[13] While section 1322(b)(2) provides that the plan may, under certain circumstances, "modify the rights of holders of secured claims",[14] it prohibits such modification as to any holder of a "claim secured only by a security interest in real property that is the debtor's principal residence."[15] As one court has noted, this latter exception "was in response to perceptions, or to suggestions advanced in the legislative hearings * * * that home-mortgagor lenders, performing a valuable social service through their loans, needed special protection against modification."[16] Yet section 1322(b) also contains important cross-current provisions. Section 1322(b)(3) provides for the "curing or waiving of any default."[17] Moreover section 1322(b)(5) specifies that "notwithstanding [section 1322(b)(2)]" the plan may "provide for the curing of any default within a reasonable time and maintenance of payments while the case is pending on any * * *

8. 11 U.S.C.A. § 1328(a)(1).

9. 11 U.S.C.A. § 362.

10. 11 U.S.C.A. § 1301.

11. 11 U.S.C.A. § 1301(a)(1).

12. 11 U.S.C.A. § 101(7).

13. See e.g., Comment, Home Foreclosures Under Chapter 13 of The Bankruptcy Reform Act, 30 U.C.L.A.L.Rev. 637, 646 (1983).

14. 11 U.S.C.A. § 1322(b)(2).

15. Id.

16. Grubbs v. Houston First American Savings Association, 730 F.2d 236, 246 (5th Cir.1984).

17. 11 U.S.C.A. § 1322(b)(3).

secured claim on which the last payment is due after the date on which the final payment under the plan is due." [18]

Attempts to reconcile the foregoing provisions have proved extremely difficult when debtors attempt to utilize the "cure" language to defeat a mortgage acceleration that has occurred prior to a Chapter 13 filing. Mortgagees argue that to permit "de-acceleration" under such circumstances would amount to an impermissible modification under section 1322(b)(2). Under this reasoning section 1322(b)(3) is read literally to be inapplicable to a home mortgage debt.[19] Consequently, a default on such a mortgage is curable, if at all, under section 1322(b)(5) and then *only* if "the last payment is due *after* the date on which the final payment under the plan is due." [20] As one federal Court of Appeals remarked, "if so read,—and if the term 'on which the last payment is due' is given its state law meaning as to an accelerated debt that thereby becomes fully 'due' * * * it would thus bar—whenever the home mortgage debt had been accelerated prior to a debtor's petition—any Chapter 13 relief by which the debtor could save his home by paying past-due amounts on his home-mortgage through periodic payments under the term of his Chapter 13 plan." [21] Indeed, several bankruptcy court decisions take such a restrictive approach to the right to cure.[22]

The foregoing approach was rejected in In re Taddeo,[23] a leading decision by the United States Court of Appeals for the Second Circuit. In that case, the debtors were permitted, pursuant to their Chapter 13 plan, to defeat a pre-petition mortgage acceleration by payment of arrearages and to reinstate the mortgage's original amortization schedule. Not only did the court hold that the "concept of 'cure' in section 1322(b)(5) contains the power to de-accelerate",[24] but also that "the ban on 'modification' in section 1322(b)(2) does not limit the [debtors'] exercise of their curative powers under either section 1322(b)(3) or (b) (5)." [25] Consequently, the debtors were permitted to cure their default under (b)(3) and thereafter maintain their payments pursuant to (b)(5). In butressing its conclusion, the Second Circuit not only rejected the argument that (b)(3) was inapplicable to home mortgages,[26] it emphasized:

> "First, we think that the power to cure must comprehend the power to "de-accelerate." This follows from the concept of "curing a default." A default is an event in the debtor-creditor

18. 11 U.S.C.A. § 1322(b)(5).

19. Grubbs v. Houston First American Savings Association, 730 F.2d 236, 240, n. 8 (5th Cir.1984).

20. Id.

21. Id. at 241.

22. See e.g., In re Williams, 11 B.R. 504 (Bkrtcy.Tex.1981); In re Lapaglia, 8 B.R. 937 (Bkrtcy.N.Y.1981); In re Britton, 35 B.R. 373 (Bkrtcy.Ind.1982); In re

Soderlund, 18 B.R. 12 (Bkrtcy.Ohio 1981); Matter of Allen, 17 B.R. 119 (Bkrtcy.Ohio 1981), reversed 42 B.R. 360 (D.Ohio 1984).

23. 685 F.2d 24 (2d Cir.1982). For an excellent analysis of *Taddeo,* see Zaretsky, Some Limits on Mortgagees' Rights in Chapter 13, 50 Brooklyn L.Rev. 433 (1984).

24. Id. at 28.

25. Id. at 28.

26. Id. at 27.

relationship which triggers certain consequences—here, acceleration. Curing a default commonly means taking care of the triggering event and returning to pre-default conditions. The consequences are thus nullified. This is the concept of "cure" used throughout the Bankruptcy Code.

* * *

"Secondly, we believe that the power to "cure any default" granted in § 1322(b)(3) and (b)(5) is not limited by the ban against "modifying" home mortgages in § 1322(b)(2) because we do not read "curing defaults" under (b)(3) or "curing defaults and maintaining payments" under (b)(5) to be *modifications* of claims." [27]

Moreover, *Taddeo* rejected the contention that state law governs the effect of acceleration and the debtor's ability to cure a default.[28] Rather, it concluded that, by enacting section 1322(b), Congress intended to permit cure in bankruptcy proceedings. The court did "not believe that Congress labored for five years over this controversial question only to remit consumer debtors—intended to be primary beneficiaries of the new Code—to the harsher mercies of state law." [29]

Taddeo is supported by important policy considerations. As the *Taddeo* court itself stressed, "conditioning a debtor's right to cure on its having filed a Chapter 13 petition prior to acceleration would prompt unseemly and wasteful races to the courthouse. Worse, there would be races in which mortgagees possess an unwarranted and likely insurmountable advantage: wage earners seldom will possess the sophistication in bankruptcy matters that financial institutions do, and often will not have retained counsel in time to do much good." [30] Moreover, even assuming a relatively high level of debtor sophistication, an anti-*Taddeo* approach may well encourage premature bankruptcy petitions rather than debtor attempts to resolve their financial problems by negotiation, mediation or other extrajudicial means.[31] In addition, a "refusal to permit de-acceleration * * * would probably * * * encourage mortgagees to declare defaults and accelerate earlier to avoid the necessity of dealing with a Chapter 13 debtor." [32] At a practical level, to the extent that a rejection of *Taddeo* results in foreclosure and forces the debtor to find other shelter, many Chapter 13 plans may well be jeopardized. More important, because the family residence is frequently the debtor's major asset and Chapter 13 is often utilized to protect it, and anti-*Taddeo* approach could substantially discourage Chapter 13 usage, a result which Congress, given its preference for debtor rehabilitation over liquidation, could hardly have intended.

27. Id. at 26, 27.

28. Id. at 28.

29. Id. at 25.

30. Id. at 27.

31. Zaretsky, supra, note 23 at 443.

32. Id. at 443.

Subsequent decisions by the federal Courts of Appeal and most bankruptcy courts have endorsed the *Taddeo* rationale.[33] So too has substantial scholarly commentary.[34] This does not mean that *Taddeo* affords an open-ended right to deaccelerate all home mortgage loans in default irrespective of their terms. Suppose, for example, that the total principal balance of a home mortgage debt becomes due, not as the result of acceleration based on mortgagor failure to make timely installment payments, but rather because the terms of the loan called for a final "balloon" payment which mortgagor failed to pay. It is unlikely that such a mortgagor will be able to use *Taddeo* and its progeny to deaccelerate the balloon in order to pay it off on an installment basis. Indeed, the United States Court of Appeals for the Ninth Circuit held in this connection that to permit "deacceleration" under such circumstances would constitute an impermissible "modification" under section 1322(b)(2).[34.5] According to the court, "[w]hen a debt has been accelerated, 'cure' results in the reinstatement of the original payment terms of the debt. But when, as here, a debt has already matured, 'cure' * * * cannot aid the debtor, since reinstatement of the original terms of the debt will merely make the debt immediately due and payable."[34.10] While the foregoing approach clearly burdens many homeowners who, because of "creative financing" techniques agree to balloon payments and find themselves unable to refinance them, it clearly is correct. It is one thing to deaccelerate a loan where the parties contemplated that it would be fully amortized by installment payments and quite another to do so where the balloon payment was an essential and bargained for element of the transaction.

However, substantial differences remain as to when in the foreclosure process the *Taddeo* de-acceleration right should be cut off. Several cases suggest that de-acceleration should not be permitted after a foreclosure judgment has been entered.[35] Such decisions reflect a

---

33. See Matter of Clark, 738 F.2d 869 (7th Cir.1984); Grubbs v. Houston First American Savings Association, 730 F.2d 236 (5th Cir.1984); In re Fisher, 35 B.R. 678 (Bkrtcy.Ohio 1983); Matter of Christian, 35 B.R. 229 (Bkrtcy.Ga.1983); In re Frey, 34 B.R. 607 (Bkrtcy.Pa.1983); In re Rippe, 14 B.R. 367 (Bkrtcy.Fla.1981), In re Davis, 15 B.R. 22 (Bkrtcy.Kan.1981), In re Davis, 16 B.R. 473 (D.Kan.1981), In re Hardin, 16 B.R. 810 (Bkrtcy.Tex.1982), In re Smith, 19 B.R. 592, 593 (Bkrtcy.Ga.1982), In re Gooden, 21 B.R. 456 (Bkrtcy.Ga.1982), In re Kokkinis, 22 B.R. 353 (Bkrtcy.Ill. 1982), In re Young, 22 B.R. 620 (Bkrtcy.Ill. 1982), In re Evans, 22 B.R. 980 (Bkrtcy.Cal. 1982), judgment affirmed 30 B.R. 530 (1983), In re Briggs, 25 B.R. 317 (D.N.D.1982), In re Acevedo, 26 B.R. 994 (D.N.Y.1982).

34. Zaretsky, supra note 23; Comment, supra note 7; Sable, A Chapter 13 Debtor's Right to Cure Default Under Section 1322(b): A Problem of Interpretation, 57 Am.Bankr.L.J. 127, 139–40 (1983); Comment, Home Foreclosures Under Chapter 13 of the Bankruptcy Reform Act, 30 U.C. L.A.L.Rev. 637, 658–665 (1983); Comment, Chapter 13 Bankruptcy: When May a Mortgage Debtor Cure the Accelerated Mortgage Debt Using Section 1322(b)(5)?, 8 U.Dayton L.Rev. 109, 121–25 (1982); Note, 52 U.Cin.L.Rev. 196, 206–07 (1983).

34.5 In re Seidel, 752 F.2d 1382 (9th Cir.1985).

34.10 Id. at 1386.

35. In re White, 22 B.R. 542 (Bkrtcy. Del.1982); In re Anderson, 16 B.R. 697 (Bkrtcy.Ohio 1982); In re Jenkins, 14 B.R. 748 (Bkrtcy.Ill.1981); In re Land, 14 B.R. 132 (Bkrtcy.Ohio 1981); In re Davis, 15 B.R. 22 (Bkrtcy.Kan.1981), affirmed, 16 B.R. 473 (D.Kan.1981); In re Wilson, 11

concern for protecting the finality of state court judgments and the avoidance of undue mortgage market uncertainty. Other cases, on the other hand, have permitted post-judgment acceleration.[36] The latter approach seems preferable. As one commentator has aptly pointed out, "the foreclosure judgment merely confirms what the parties already knew: the entire debt is due at once and the mortgagee may sell the property. But the debtor still has the property and the mortgagee does not yet have its payment. Although the mortgagee will have spent time and incurred some expense to obtain the judgment and will therefore have a greater interest in foreclosure, these are not sufficient reasons to deny a right to de-accelerate, particularly when the debtor's home is involved and the expense incurred by the mortgagee may be recoverable from the debtor under the mortgage agreement." [37]

To what extent should *Taddeo* de-acceleration be permitted after the foreclosure sale? The answer in large measure should depend on how "final" the foreclosure sale is under state law. For example, when the sale divests the mortgagor of all interest in the real estate, "there would seem to no basis for reversing the effect of the sale and permitting the debtor to restore the original payment schedule. Actual conveyance of the property to a purchaser who has no reason to expect to lose the property ought to end the debtor's interest once and for all." [38] On the other hand, about half the states have post-sale redemption statutes, under which the mortgagor and, in many cases, junior lienholders, have the right to redeem the foreclosed real estate for a specified period of time by paying the foreclosure sale purchaser the sale price.[39] Thus, the interest in finality is less compelling in a *Taddeo* sense because the foreclosure title is already defeasible. Indeed, several courts have applied the *Taddeo* concept in such situations.[40]

It may, however, be unwise to apply *Taddeo* in such contexts without drawing a further distinction between the mortgagee and a third party as foreclosure sale purchasers. When a mortgagor redeems under statutory redemption, as the foregoing indicates, she typically pays the foreclosure purchaser the foreclosure sale price in a lump sum.

B.R. 986 (Bkrtcy.N.Y.1981); In re Pearson, 10 B.R. 189 (Bkrtcy.N.Y.1981).

36. In re Glenn, 760 F.2d 1428 (6th Cir. 1985); Matter of Clark, 738 F.2d 869 (7th Cir.1984); In re Tuchman, 29 B.R. 39 (Bkrtcy.N.Y.1983); In re McCann, 27 B.R. 678 (Bkrtcy.Ohio 1982); In re McSorley, 24 B.R. 795 (Bkrtcy.N.J.1982); In re Hubbard, 23 B.R. 671 (Bkrtcy.Ohio 1982); In re Acevedo, 26 B.R. 994 (D.N.Y.1982); In re Young, 22 B.R. 620 (Bkrtcy.Ill.1982); In re Taylor, 21 B.R. 179 (Bkrtcy.Mo.1982); In re Smith, 19 B.R. 592 (Bkrtcy.Ga.1982);

37. Zaretsky, supra note 23 at 447.

38. Id. at 448. Accord: In re Smith, 43 B.R. 313 (Bkrtcy.Ill.1984); In re Wallace,

31 B.R. 64 (Bkrtcy.Md.1983); In re Cretella, 42 B.R. 526 (Bkrtcy.N.Y.1984), stay denied 47 B.R. 382 (D.N.Y.1984). Contra: In re Glenn, 760 F.2d 142 (6th Cir. 1985).

39. See § 8.4 supra.

40. See In re Ivory, 32 B.R. 788 (Bkrtcy. Or.1983); In re Chambers, 27 B.R. 687 (Bkrtcy.Fla.1983); Tinley Park Bank v. Phelps (In re Kokkinis), 22 B.R. 353 (Bkrtcy.Ill.1982); In re Taylor, 21 B.R. 179 (Bkrtcy.Mo.1982); In re Gooden, 21 B.R. 456 (Bkrtcy.Ga.1982); In re Thompson, 17 B.R. 748 (Bkrtcy.Mich.1982).

On the other hand, in post-sale de-acceleration, the goal of the mortgagor is simply to satisfy mortgage arrearages and to restore the original amortization schedule. If the mortgagee is the foreclosure sale purchaser, "the problem of de-accelerating the debt may not be significantly different after foreclosure than before. The mortgagee will have incurred some additional expense but that would presumably be added to the mortgage balance." [41] Indeed, in many statutory redemption states the mortgagor retains the right to possession during the statutory period and, in those jurisdictions, de-acceleration will have no effect on possession.[42] On the other hand, when a third party purchases at the foreclosure sale, he relies on the fact that if the property is redeemed, he will receive a refund of the purchase price in a lump sum. Consequently, it seems especially inequitable to force him to accept redemption by installment under a Chapter 13 plan. While even statutory redemption, as one commentator has stressed, "probably already reduces the prices paid at foreclosure sales because the purchaser undertakes the risk that he will subsequently be deprived of the property, [a] decision to permit such deprivation with a refund in installments under a reinstated mortgage would be likely to destroy the foreclosure sale concept." [43]

Relief from a Chapter 13 Stay

As we noted earlier, section 362(d) of the Act authorizes relief from the stay "(1) for cause, including the lack of adequate protection of an interest in property of [the mortgagor]; or (2) * * * if (A) the [mortgagor] does not have an equity in such property; and (B) such property is not necessary to an effective reorganization." [44] However, there has been substantial disagreement about whether (d)(2) as well as (d)(1) is applicable in Chapter 13 proceedings.[45] There is significant case law that it is and that a mortgagee is entitled to stay relief under either subsection.[46] Indeed, section 103 of the Act expressly states that Chapter 3, which includes section 362, is applicable to Chapter 13.[47] On the other hand, there is case authority to the contrary [48] and a supporting textual argument as well. Since section 362(d)(2) refers to a "reorganization", it has been asserted that it is applicable only to Chapter 11, which is entitled "Reorganization", and not to Chapter 13 because the latter chapter is entitled "Adjustment of Debts of an

---

41. Zaretsky, supra note 23 at 448.

42. See §§ 8.4–8.6 supra.

43. Zaretsky, supra note 23 at 450.

44. See 11 U.S.C.A. § 362(d); § 8.14 supra.

45. See Comment, supra note 7 at 646–647, 660–661.

46. See, e.g., In re Crouse, 9 B.R. 400 (Bkrtcy.Tex.1981); First Connecticut Small Business Investment Co. v. Ruark, 7 B.R.

46 (Bkrtcy.Conn.1980); In Matter of Zellmer, 6 B.R. 497, 3 CBC 2d 42 (Bkrtcy. Ill.1980).

47. See 11 U.S.C.A. § 103.

48. See e.g., In re Rhoades, 34 B.R. 168 (Bkrtcy.Vt.1983); In Matter of Feimster, 3 B.R. 11, 1 CBC 2d 956 (Bkrtcy.Ga.1979); see also, In re Sulzer, 2 B.R. 630, 1 CBC 2d 451 (Bkrtcy.N.Y.1980); In re Youngs, 7 B.R. 69, 3 CBC 2d 250 (Bkrtcy.Mass.1980).

Individual with Regular Income." [49] Moreover, a convincing policy argument may be made for the latter position.[50] According to one recent bankruptcy decision,

"If the subsection applies, a debtor who has no equity in property which is not necessary to consummate a Chapter 13 plan may be, through lift-stay actions, exposed to involuntary dispossession of such property. The purpose, however, of Chapter 13 is to enable individual debtors with regular incomes to develop and perform a plan for the repayment of debts over an extended period of time. The emphasis is on providing individuals with regular incomes an alternative to liquidation. Hence, it is the ability of the individual debtors to furnish the creditor with the value of his claim, in the form of property or from current earnings, which is the key to the protection of the creditor under a Chapter 13 plan. Whether the [property] being retained by the debtor is necessary to the subsistence or rehabilitation of the Chapter 13 debtor, or whether the debtor has any equity in [it] are not factors of concern applicable or relevant to Chapter 13 proceedings." [51]

In any event, stay relief after the confirmation of a Chapter 13 plan becomes much more problematical. However the foregoing section 362 question is ultimately resolved, once the plan becomes effective, bankruptcy courts will be reluctant to risk its failure by permitting foreclosure of the debtor's residence. Indeed, case law suggests that only significant debtor default under the plan will justify a dissolution of the stay.[52]

 WESTLAW REFERENCES
di chapter 13 Wage Earner's Plan
"consumer debt" /p 11 + 7 1301 101(7)

De-acceleration of Home Mortgage
accelerat! de-accelerat! /p cur* * * /p 11 + 7 1322
taddeo /p "chapter 13"
foreclos! /p de-accelerat! accelerat! /p "chapter 13"

Relief from a Chapter 13 Stay
relief /p automatic /s stay /p 11 + 7 362(d) /p "chapter 13"

§ 8.16 Setting Aside Pre-Bankruptcy Foreclosures

Traditionally, foreclosure sale purchasers have had relatively little to fear from subsequent mortgagor bankruptcy. Unless it could be established that the foreclosure violated state law or that the mortgage itself was avoidable, foreclosures were relatively secure from bankrupt-

49. Comment, supra note 7 at 648.

50. See In re Rhoades, 34 B.R. 168, 171 (Bkrtcy.Vt.1983); Comment, supra note 7 at 661.

51. In re Rhoades, 34 B.R. 168, 171 (Bkrtcy.Vt.1983).

52. See e.g., In re Pizzullo, 33 B.R. 740 (Bkrtcy.Pa.1983); In re Evans, 22 B.R. 980 (Bkrtcy.Cal.1982), affirmed 30 B.R. 530 (1983).

cy attack. To be sure, in jurisdictions that utilize statutory redemption,[1] a trustee in bankruptcy has the right to exercise the mortgagor-debtor's redemption rights.[2] However, the bankruptcy court probably does not have general equitable authority to stay the running of the redemption period.[3] Moreover, under the weight of authority, the automatic stay does not operate to toll the running of such periods.[4] The trustee may, however, pursuant to section 108(b) of the Bankruptcy Code redeem within the later of the expiration of the redemption period or 60 days after the filing of the bankruptcy petition.[5]

However troublesome the foregoing redemption rights may be for mortgagees and other foreclosure purchasers, they do not threaten the validity of pre-bankruptcy foreclosure sales. Recent developments, however, have eroded much of the traditional protection afforded such foreclosures. We have already explored in the preceding section how the *Taddeo* concept may be used in certain Chapter 13 contexts to deaccelerate previously foreclosed mortgage debts.[6] In addition, an increasing number of courts are utilizing the fraudulent conveyance provisions of the Bankruptcy Code to set aside pre-bankruptcy foreclosures. Moreover, to a much more limited extent, such foreclosures have been subjected to successful attack as voidable preferences. These latter two developments are explored in detail in this section.

1. *The Foreclosure Sale as a Fraudulent Conveyance*
   a. The *Durrett* problem

Under section 548(a) of the Bankruptcy Act not only may a trustee set aside a transfer by a debtor within a year of bankruptcy that was intended to defraud, hinder or delay present or future creditors, she may also avoid such a transfer, irrespective of debtor intent, if the

§ 8.16

1. See §§ 8.4–8.7 supra.

2. See In re Rice, 42 B.R. 838 (Bkrtcy. S.D.1984); authorities cited in notes 3–5 infra this section.

3. See Johnson v. First National Bank of Montevideo, Minnesota, 719 F.2d 270 (8th Cir.1983), certiorari denied ___ U.S. ___, 104 S.Ct. 1015, 79 L.Ed.2d 245 (1984); In re Martinson, 731 F.2d 543 (8th Cir. 1984). In re Martinson, 26 B.R. 648 (D.N.D.1983); In re Owens, 27 B.R. 946 (Bkrtcy.Mich.1983); In re Lally, 38 B.R. 622 (Bkrtcy.Iowa 1984).

4. See Johnson v. First National Bank of Montevideo, Minnesota, 719 F.2d 270 (8th Cir.1983), certiorari denied ___ U.S. ___, 104 S.Ct. 1015, 79 L.Ed.2d 245 (1984); Bank of Commonwealth v. Bevan, 13 B.R. 989 (D.Mich.1981); In re Owens, 27 B.R. 946 (Bkrtcy.Mich.1983); In re Cucumber Creek Development, Inc., 33 B.R. 820 (D.Colo.1983). Contra: In re Shea Realty, Inc., 21 B.R. 790 (Bkrtcy.Vt.1982); In re Smith, 43 B.R. 313 (Bkrtcy.Ill.1984).

5. See In re Owens, 27 B.R. 946 (Bkrtcy. Mich.1983); In re Cucumber Creek Development, Inc., 33 B.R. 820 (D.Colo.1983). Section 108(b) provides as follows:

(b) Except as provided in subsection (a) of this section, if applicable law, an order entered in a proceeding, or an agreement fixes a period within which the debtor or an individual protected under section 1301 of this title may file any pleading, demand, notice, or proof of claim or loss, cure a default, or perform any other similar act, and such period has not expired before the date of the filing of the petition, the trustee may only file, cure, or perform, as the case may be, before the later of—

(1) the end of such period, including any suspension of such period occurring on or after the commencement of the case; and

(2) 60 days after the order for relief.

11 U.S.C.A. § 108(b).

6. See § 8.15 supra.

debtor "received less than a reasonably equivalent value in exchange for such transfer * * * and was insolvent on the date that such transfer was made." [7] Durrett v. Washington National Insurance Co.,[8] a 1980 decision of the United States Court of Appeals for the Fifth Circuit under the predecessor to section 548(a), marked the first time that a court used the fraudulent conveyance concept to invalidate a non-collusive foreclosure sale that was otherwise valid under state law.[9] In that case, a trustee under a Texas deed of trust sold the mortgaged real estate having a fair market value of $200,000 to a third party purchaser for $115,400. Nine days later Durrett, the mortgagor, filed a petition for reorganization under the predecessor to Chapter 11 and, in his capacity as debtor-in-possession, sought to set aside the foreclosure as a fraudulent conveyance. The district court held that the foreclosure sale constituted a transfer by the debtor, but denied Durrett's request on the ground that the sale produced "a fair equivalent" of the value of the real estate. On appeal, the court of appeals agreed that a transfer had taken place, but reversed the district court on the consideration issue. The court acknowledged that two transfers had taken place—the first, when the deed of trust was executed eight years earlier and which was no longer vulnerable, and a second, when the foreclosure sale took place. The latter qualified as a transfer because, under Texas law, it passed to the purchaser the debtor-mortgagor's right to possession. Moreover, it clearly fell within the statutory period. As to the consideration issue, the court suggested that a foreclosure price of less than 70% of the property's fair market value failed to meet the "fair equivalency" test under the then existing statute.

Durrett has been followed in numerous section 548(a) cases, including a decision by the United States Court of Appeals for the Eighth Circuit.[10] It has been applied to judicial foreclosures,[11] strict foreclosures [12] and in a variety of power of sale and other non-judicial con-

---

7. 11 U.S.C.A. §§ 548(a)(2)(A), 548(a)(2)(B)(i). A debtor is "insolvent if its debts are greater than its assets, at a fair valuation, exclusive of property exempted or transferred with actual fraudulent intent." In re Wheeler, 34 B.R. 818, 822 (Bkrtcy. Ala.1983); 11 U.S.C.A. § 101(29).

8. 621 F.2d 201 (5th Cir.1980).

9. Several pre-*Durrett* cases concluded that a noncollusive foreclosure sale that yields less than fair market value was not a fraudulent conveyance. See Merriam v. Wimpfheimer, 25 F.Supp. 405 (S.D.N.Y. 1938); Pierce v. Pierce, 16 Cal.App. 375, 117 P. 580 (1911).

10. In re Hulm, 738 F.2d 323 (8th Cir. 1984), certiorari denied ___ U.S. ___, 105 S.Ct. 398, 83 L.Ed.2d 331 (1984), on remand ___ B.R. ___ (Bkrtcy.N.D.1984); see cases

in notes 11–13, infra this section. Contra: In re Madrid, 725 F.2d 1197 (9th Cir.1984), certiorari denied ___ U.S. ___, 105 S.Ct. 125, 83 L.Ed.2d 66 (1984); Matter of Winshall Settlor's Trust, 758 F.2d 1136 (6th Cir.1985).

11. See In re Hulm, 738 F.2d 323 (8th Cir.1984), certiorari denied ___ U.S. ___, 105 S.Ct. 398, 83 L.Ed.2d 331 (1984), on remand ___ B.R. ___ (Bkrtcy.N.D.1984); In re Dudley, 38 B.R. 666 (Bkrtcy.Pa.1984); In re Jones, 20 B.R. 988 (Bkrtcy.Pa.1982).

12. See In re Carr, 34 B.R. 653 (Bkrtcy. Conn.1983), affirmed 40 B.R. 1007 (D.Conn. 1984); In re Berge, 33 B.R. 642 (Bkrtcy. Wis.1983), motion denied in part, granted in part 37 B.R. 705 (1983); In re Perdido Bay Country Club Estates, Inc., 23 B.R. 36 (Bkrtcy.Fla.1982) (applying Vermont law).

texts.[13] The decisions involve reorganizations under Chapters 11 [14] and 13 [15] as well as liquidations under Chapter 7.[16] Moreover, the "70% rule of thumb" is being increasingly institutionalized.[17]

    b.   Cases Rejecting *Durrett*

    Two significant cases, each using a different rationale, reject the *Durrett* approach. The first, In re Alsop,[18] involved a power of sale foreclosure under a deed of trust that occurred two days prior to the filing of a Chapter 11 petition. The debtor-in-possession sought to avoid the foreclosure as a fraudulent transfer. The Bankruptcy Court for the District of Alaska rejected *Durrett* by applying a "relation back" analysis. While the *Alsop* court conceded that a transfer occurred at the time of the foreclosure sale, it stressed that section 548(d)(1) of the Act also needed to be considered.[19] Under this latter provision, a transfer is deemed to take place when "such transfer becomes so far perfected that a bona fide purchaser from the debtor against whom such transfer could have been perfected cannot acquire an interest in the property transferred that is superior to the interest in such property of the transferee." [20] In applying the foregoing section the *Alsop* court concluded that "since under Alaska law no purchaser from [mortgagors] subsequent to [mortgagors'] execution of the deed of trust and its recordation on November 8, 1978, could have acquired an interest superior to that of the transferee at the foreclosure sale, pursuant to the provisions of § 548(d)(1) the transfer was made as of November 8, 1978. Since this date is outside the one year period established by § 548(a), the foreclosure sale is not avoidable as a fraudulent transfer." [21]

    Alsop seems to misinterpret section 548(d)(1). As noted earlier, a separate transfer occurs at the time of the execution of the deed of trust and, later, at the time of the foreclosure sale.[22] The purpose of section 548(d)(1) in each context is to encourage prompt recording of the transfer instrument rather than to cause a separate and distinct

---

13. See In re Willis, 48 B.R. 295 (S.D.Tex.1985); In re Wheeler, 34 B.R. 818 (Bkrtcy.Ala.1983); In re Smith, 24 B.R. 19 (Bkrtcy.N.C.1982); In re Richardson, 23 B.R. 434 (Bkrtcy.Utah 1982); In re Thompson, 18 B.R. 67 (Bkrtcy.Tenn.1982); Matter of Marshall, 15 B.R. 738 (Bkrtcy.N.C.1981). However, the "transfer" will probably be deemed to take place at the time of the sale and not at the end of any statutory redemption period. See In re Kangas, 46 B.R. 102 (Bkrtcy.Minn.1985).

14. See e.g., In re Frank, 39 B.R. 166 (Bkrtcy.N.Y.1984); In re Berge, 33 B.R. 642 (Bkrtcy.Wis.1983), motion denied in part, granted in part 37 B.R. 705 (1983).

15. See e.g., In re Dudley, 38 B.R. 666 (Bkrtcy.Pa.1984); In re Wheeler, 34 B.R. 818 (Bkrtcy.Ala.1983); In re Worcester, 28 B.R. 910 (Bkrtcy.Cal.1983).

16. See e.g., In re Richard, 26 B.R. 560 (Bkrtcy.R.I.1983); In re Smith, 24 B.R. 19

(Bkrtcy.N.C.1982); In re Richardson, 23 B.R. 434 (Bkrtcy.Utah 1982).

17. See cases in notes 10–16 supra; In re Hulm, 45 B.R. 523 (Bkrtcy.N.D.1984). See generally, Davis and Standiford, Foreclosure Sale as Fraudulent Transfer Under the Bankruptcy Code: A Reasonable Approach to Reasonably Equivalent Value, 13 Real Estate L.J. 203 (1985).

18. 14 B.R. 982 (Bkrtcy.Alaska 1981), affirmed 22 B.R. 1017 (D.Alaska 1982).

19. 11 U.S.C.A. § 548(d)(1).

20. Id.

21. In re Alsop, 14 B.R. 982, 986 (Bkrtcy.Alaska 1981), affirmed 22 B.R. 1017 (D.Alaska 1982).

22. See text at note 9 infra. For the view that foreclosure is not a separate transfer, see Coppel & Kahn, Defanging Durrett: The Established Law of Transfer, 100 Banking L.J. 676 (1983).

transfer to relate back to an earlier one.[23] As Professor Henning has stressed:

> "Foreclosure of the deed of trust involves an involuntary conveyance of the debtor's remaining interest in the property except for a statutory right of redemption in those states that grant such a right. This involuntary conveyance constitutes a separate transfer. The most important rights affected by this second transfer are the right to possession and the debtor's equity in the property, neither of which were conveyed under the deed of trust. When a purchaser buys at the foreclosure sale, the deed of trust ordinarily will be considered discharged; if the purchaser fails to record the trustee's deed, however, he will not be protected against subsequent bona fide purchasers from the original debtor. Thus, recordation of the trustee's deed serves a different purpose than recordation of the original deed of trust because it protects a different set of rights. In this context, section 548(d)(1) refers to perfection of the interests acquired at the foreclosure sale, the second transfer, and not to perfection of the interests conveyed by the deed of trust, the first transfer. If the purchaser delays in perfecting his interest, the second transfer, like the first, can be brought forward into the avoidance period." [24]

According to Professor Henning, the "relation back" notion simply represents another way of "stating the general principle that the purchaser takes free of any interests that are subordinate to the foreclosing [mortgagee] * * * This principle, however, does not provide a satisfactory basis for fusing the two transfers for purposes of section 548(d)(1). [The latter section] should be applied strictly as a mechanism for bringing a transfer * * * forward into the avoidance period." [25]

The second major anti-*Durrett* case is In re Madrid,[26] a decision of the United States Court of Appeals for the Ninth Circuit. In that case, the bankruptcy court set aside a power of sale foreclosure in a Chapter 11 context that yielded 67% of the real estate's fair market value.[27] The Bankruptcy Appellate Panel, in reversing, did not deal with the transfer issue, but instead "constru[ed] the reasonably equivalent value requirement of § 548(a)(2) to mean the same as the consideration received at a noncollusive and regularly conducted foreclosure sale." [28] The court of appeals affirmed, but its reasoning differed from that used

---

23. See Henning, An Analysis of *Durrett* and Its Impact on Real and Personal Property Foreclosures: Some Proposed Modifications, 63 N.C.L.Rev. 257, 267–268 (1984).

24. Id. at 268–269.

25. Id. at 269–270. See also, Alden, Gross and Borowitz, Real Property Foreclosure as a Fraudulent Conveyance: Propos-als for Solving the *Durrett* Problem, 38 Bus.Law. 1605, 1609–1611 (1983).

26. 725 F.2d 1197 (9th Cir.1984), certiorari denied ___ U.S. ___, 105 S.Ct. 125, 83 L.Ed.2d 66 (1984).

27. In re Madrid, 10 B.R. 795 (Bkrtcy. Nev.1981).

28. In re Madrid, 21 B.R. 424, 427 (Bkrtcy.App. 9th Cir.1982).

by the bankruptcy appellate panel and *Alsop* as well. The court of appeals eschewed the "relation back" approach even though the deed of trust had been recorded more than a year before the filing of the Chapter 11 petition. Rather, the court concluded that section 548(a)(2) was simply not intended to apply to foreclosure sales under a valid lien. The latter section and its antecedents, according to the court, instead "provide authority for the proposition that conveyances are set aside when there is actual fraud or a situation indicative of fraud." [29]

The court of appeals reasoning in *Madrid* has been called into question by a provision of the Bankruptcy Amendments and Federal Judgeship Act of 1984 which amended the Bankruptcy Act's general definition of transfer to include "foreclosure of the debtor's equity of redemption." [30] Post-enactment senatorial statements indicate that the amendment "was not intended to have any effect one way or the other on the *Durrett* issue" or on *Madrid*. [31] On the other hand, Professor Henning has concluded that while "it is unclear whether [the amendment] signifies congressional approval of *Durrett*," it "probably overrules *Madrid*." [32] Whether one agrees with the latter assessment or not, the literal language of the amendment certainly emphasizes that a foreclosure sale can constitute a transfer and, at the very least, seriously undercuts the court of appeal's reasoning in *Madrid* that section 548(a) simply does not encompass foreclosures under valid liens.

c. Impact of *Durrett*

If *Durrett* ultimately prevails nationally, it in effect will create, de facto, in every state a one year statutory redemption system. [33] For those states that currently do not have a statutory redemption scheme, the impact of *Durrett* is dramatic. [34] However, its effect in most statutory redemption states will also be significant. This is because *Durrett* is broader in scope than state redemption statutes. First, the one year period is longer than under some state statutes. [35] Second, while state legislation typically confers redemption rights on mortgagors and, in some instances, on junior lienholders, [36] *Durrett* rights benefit unsecured creditors as well. Third, a party who redeems under statutory redemption usually must tender to the foreclosure purchaser the amount of the

---

29. In re Madrid, 725 F.2d 1197, 1200 (9th Cir.1984), certiorari denied ___ U.S. ___, 105 S.Ct. 125, 83 L.Ed.2d 66 (1984).

In a perplexing opinion, the United States Court of Appeals for the Sixth Circuit also rejected *Durrett* and appeared to base its reasoning on the "relation back" concept and, alternatively, on the notion that "reasonable equivalence" should be defined by when, under state law, a foreclosure can be set aside based on inadequacy of the sale price. See Matter of Winshall Settlor's Trust, 758 F.2d 1136 (6th Cir.1985).

30. See section 421(i) of the Bankruptcy Amendments and Federal Judgeship Act of 1984, Pub.L. No. 98–353, 98 Stat. 333, 368 (codified at 11 U.S.C.A. § 101(44)).

31. 130 Cong.Rec. S 13771–13772 (daily ed. Oct. 5, 1984).

32. Henning, supra note 23 at 271 n. 79.

33. Id. at 265.

34. Almost half of the states have no statutory redemption. See § 8.4 supra.

35. See § 8.4 supra.

36. See § 8.5 supra.

purchase price.[37] *Durrett,* on the other hand, imposes no such cost; rather, the purchaser ultimately will be reimbursed out of the proceeds of a bankruptcy resale.[38]

Under certain circumstances, *Durrett* can create uncertainty for more than a year. This can occur in those situations where a bankruptcy petition is, in fact, filed within a year of the foreclosure sale. Because a section 548 avoidance action "can be brought until the earlier of two years after the appointment of a trustee or the time the case is closed or dismissed, the period of uncertainty for the purchaser can exceed three years." [39] A Chapter 11 trustee, as noted in an earlier section,[40] may never be appointed and, under such circumstances, the debtor-in-possession in theory could pursue a *Durrett* action at any time during the reorganization proceeding.[41] Moreover, even in a Chapter 7 liquidation, there can be considerable delay in the appointment of a trustee.[42]

What is the impact on a foreclosure sale purchaser of a successful avoidance under *Durrett?* Any good faith purchaser for value obtains a lien on the real estate to the extent of value given.[43] This lien will also include the value of post-purchase improvements to the real estate.[44] Moreover, interest is probably recoverable at either the mortgage rate or a market rate.[45] It should be remembered that a Chapter 7 trustee will be seeking to enhance the value of the debtor's estate by attempting to squeeze excess value out of the recaptured real estate. Thus, she will resell the property either subject to the purchaser's lien or free and clear of it.[46] If the latter approach is utilized, the purchaser's lien will attach to the sale proceeds. In the event, however, the real estate cannot be sold for more than the lien, it should be abandoned to the purchaser.[47]

Proceedings under Chapters 11 and 13 pose special problems in the foregoing regard. While a Chapter 7 trustee will utilize *Durrett* to recover real estate for the purpose of prompt resale, recapture in the Chapter 11 or 13 context is typically sought to enhance the likelihood of a successful rehabilitation of the debtor. Consequently, in the latter setting the real estate could be tied up indefinitely as part of a reorganization plan. This probably does not impose an unfair burden on the mortgagee as a foreclosure purchaser. After all, so long as the

---

37. See § 8.4 supra.

38. Henning, supra note 23 at 276.

39. Id. at 509.

40. See § 8.14 supra.

41. Henning, supra note 23 at 265.

42. Id.

43. 11 U.S.C.A. § 548(c); Henning, supra note 23 at 279. Value means "property, or satisfaction or securing of a present or antecedent debt of the debtor." It has been suggested that in a noncollusive regularly conducted foreclosure, good faith will

not be a problem. See Henning, supra note 23 at 279, n. 134. But see Note, Nonjudicial Foreclosure under Deed of Trust May Be a Fraudulent Transfer of Bankrupt's Property, 47 Mo.L.Rev. 345, 351, n. 55 (1982).

44. 11 U.S.C.A. § 550(d)(1); Henning, supra note 23 at 279, n. 137.

45. Henning, supra note 23 at 280.

46. See § 8.13 supra.

47. Henning, supra note 23 at 280.

reorganization plan affords him adequate protection, "he is no worse off than he would have been if bankruptcy proceedings had been commenced before foreclosure was complete."[48] This is not the case, however, where the purchaser is a third party. In effect, a *Durrett* recapture forces such a purchaser to become an involuntary lender. Even if he ultimately recoups his investment, he could be substantially prejudiced by having his funds tied up for a substantial period of time. Under such circumstances, the bankruptcy court should perhaps exercise its equitable discretion by compelling the trustee or debtor-in-possession to obtain new financing for the purpose of "cashing out" the purchaser. In any event, if *Durrett* ultimately prevails, the Bankruptcy Act probably should be amended to permit recovery of property in reorganization contexts only where an immediate resale or refinancing is likely.[49]

d. An Evaluation of *Durrett*

The reaction to *Durrett* from the real estate bar and other real estate interests has been uniformly hostile.[50] This hostility reflects a variety of concerns. It has been argued that the long period of uncertainty about foreclosure title created by *Durrett* will "naturally inhibit a purchaser other than the mortgagee from purchasing at foreclosure."[51] Consequently, it is asserted, "by discouraging third-party buyers, [*Durrett*] may reduce sales prices and increase the likelihood of deficiency judgments. It will encourage secured creditors to foreclose on initial default in the hope that a quicker sale will lower the risk that the debtor will file for bankruptcy during the following year."[52]

Opposition to *Durrett* has been manifested in a variety of more tangible ways. Substantial effort has been devoted to seeking its repeal by Congress.[53] Indeed, concern about *Durrett* is reflected in the Uniform Fraudulent Transfer Act (UFTA), promulgated by the National

---

48. Id. at 283.

49. Id.

50. Groups that opposed *Durrett* include the American Land Title Association, the Mortgage Brokers Institute, the American Council of Life Insurance, the American College of Real Estate Lawyers, the California Bankers Association, and the California Bank Clearing House Association. See Alden, Gross & Borowitz, Real Property Foreclosure as a Fraudulent Conveyance: Proposals for Solving the *Durrett* Problem, 38 Bus.Law. 1605, 1607 n. 8 (1983).

51. Abramson v. Lakewood Bank & Trust Co., 647 F.2d 547, 549 (5th Cir.1981) (Clark, J., dissenting), rehearing denied 655 F.2d 1131 (5th Cir.1981), certiorari denied 454 U.S. 1164, 102 S.Ct. 1038, 71 L.Ed.2d 320 (1982).

52. Note, supra note 43 at 351. For a comprehensive criticism of *Durrett*, see Zinman, Houle and Weiss, Fraudulent Transfers According to Alden, Gross & Borowitz: A Tale of Two Circuits, 39 Bus. Law. 977 (1984).

53. See Summary of Action of the House of Delegates, 1983 A.B.A.Proc. 1, 31 (endorsing amendment to section 548); Gold, Proposed Amendment to Clarify Status of Property Bought in Foreclosure, N.Y.L.J., Nov. 17, 1982, at col. 1 (proposed amendment to section 548). An unsuccessful attempt was made in 1983 to amend section 548 to equate reasonably equivalent value with any amount paid at a good faith foreclosure. See S. 445, 98th Cong., Ist Sess. § 360, 129 Cong.Rec. 5972 (1983). A similar attempt in 1984 also failed.

Conference of Commissioners on Uniform State Laws in 1984.[54] Because of a fear that bankruptcy and state courts would interpret state law as incorporating *Durrett* principles,[55] the UFTA provides that "a person gives a reasonably equivalent value if the the person acquires an interest of the debtor in an asset pursuant to a regularly conducted, noncollusive foreclosure sale or execution of a power of sale * * * under a mortgage, deed of trust, or security agreement." [56] The foregoing language effectively insulates from a *Durrett*-type attack noncollusive foreclosures pursuant to any state procedure, judicial or otherwise, that entails a public sale.

While the merits of *Durrett* are debateable, on balance it was probably a desirable judicial development. To be sure, as we emphasized earlier in this volume, any post-sale period of title defeasibility discourages third party bidding and, for that reason, we are doubtful about the wisdom of statutory redemption systems.[57] Moreover, to some extent *Durrett* compounds such problems. This especially may be true in those states that currently do not have statutory redemption. Even in those that do, *Durrett*, as we have seen, may extend state redemption periods and, in other significant ways, make foreclosure sales easier to avoid. On the other hand, *Durrett's* benefits to unsecured creditors outweigh the foregoing concerns. As one commentator has stressed, "there is no reason to permit secured creditors to reap the benefit of assets that might have paid off unsecured creditors."[58] This reasoning is sound in reorganizations as well as liquidations. Moreover, while admittedly strong medicine, *Durrett* in a powerful way underscores the inadequacies of a foreclosure system that normally fails to produce an adequate price for foreclosed real estate.[59]

The foregoing, however, should not be interpreted as a wholesale endorsement of *Durrett* as a permanent part of the foreclosure landscape. Moreover, certain short-term modifications to *Durrett* are clearly in order. The burden on third party foreclosure purchasers where the subsequent bankruptcy proceeding is under, as we noted earlier in this section, Chapter 11 or 13 is clearly undesirable and should be modified judicially or by Congress. Moreover, Congress probably should reduce either the one year pre-bankruptcy avoidance period or the post-filing time requirement for trustee action, or both of them, so that the total period of title uncertainty is no longer than that associated with most statutory redemption schemes.[60]

54. See Uniform Fraudulent Transfer Act (1984).

55. Section 544(b) permits the trustee to avoid any transfer that could be avoided by an unsecured creditor under state or federal nonbankruptcy law. See 11 U.S.C.A. § 544(b); In re Penn Packing Co., 42 B.R. 502 (Bkrtcy.Pa.1984). Thus, the American Bar Association Section of Real Property, Probate and Trust Law urged the ULTA Drafting Committee to include anti-*Durrett* language.

56. U.L.T.A. § 3(b).

57. See § 8.8 supra.

58. Henning, supra note 23 at 276.

59. See § 8.8 supra.

60. For a thoughtful proposal, in this regard, see Henning, supra note 23 at 276.

The long term solution to the problems dealt with by *Durrett* lies in a major structural reform of state foreclosure practices. Earlier in this volume [61] we described in detail a foreclosure system that we believe will enhance the likelihood that fair market value will be obtained for foreclosed real estate. While the proposed system provides for a substantial pre-foreclosure time period to cure default, there would be no post-sale redemption. Such a system, we believe, would enhance the likelihood of foreclosure surpluses and reduce the number of deficiency judgments, a result that would benefit unsecured creditors as well as mortgagors and junior lienholders. Under such a system, *Durrett* and statutory redemption would be both unnecessary and self-defeating.

2. *The Foreclosure Sale as a Preference*

A pre-bankruptcy foreclosure may under certain circumstances be avoided as a preference, a theory that represents a potentially important alternative to *Durrett*. Under section 547 of the Code, the trustee may avoid a transaction if it was (1) a transfer of the debtor's property, (2) to or for the benefit of the creditor, (3) for or on account of an antecedent debt, (4) made while the debtor was insolvent (5) within 90 days of bankruptcy (one year in the case of insiders), and (6) which enables the creditor to realize more than he would receive in a Chapter 7 liquidation.[62] At least two bankruptcy courts have used the foregoing section as a foreclosure-avoidance tool.[63] In re Wheeler,[64] an Alabama bankruptcy decision, is illustrative of this development. In that case a mortgage executed eleven years earlier was foreclosed at a public sale at which the mortgagee purchased for $15,044, the amount of the debt and foreclosure expenses. Twenty-three days later the mortgagor-debtor filed a Chapter 13 petition and sought to set aside the foreclosure sale under both *Durrett* and section 547. The bankruptcy court found that the foreclosure sale price represented only 65% of the fair market value of the mortgaged real estate, which the court had determined to be $24,000. Since the 70% *Durrett* standard was not satisfied, the court held that the foreclosure sale was a fraudulent transfer. Alternatively, however, the court held that the foreclosure sale constituted a voidable preference under section 547. According to the court, each of the six preference criteria was satisfied. The court reasoned that the foreclosure sale effected a transfer of the debtor-mortgagor's property on account of an antecedent debt. It also found the debtor to be insolvent at the time of the foreclosure sale and determined that the timing of the sale and the Chapter 13 filing complied with the 90 day requirement. Moreover, the court concluded that:

> "It is clear that under a Chapter 7 liquidation, [the mortgagee], as a fully secured creditor, would be entitled to receive the full

61. See § 8.8 supra.

62. 11 U.S.C.A. § 547(b). See Collier on Bankruptcy ¶ 547.01 (15th Ed. 1984); In re Wheeler, 34 B.R. 818 (Bkrtcy.Ala.1983).

63. See In re Wheeler, 34 B.R. 818 (Bkrtcy.Ala.1983); Matter of Fountain, 32 B.R. 965 (Bkrtcy.Mo.1983).

64. 34 B.R. 818 (Bkrtcy.Ala.1983).

value of their $15,044 claim upon the disposition of the secured property. However, [mortgagee] would be entitled to no more than the amount of their claim. Yet, by reason of this foreclosure, [mortgagee] is receiving property with a market value several thousand dollars in excess of the amount of their claim. Thus, it becomes evident that the foreclosure sale did enable [mortgagee] to receive more than they would in a Chapter 7 liquidation." [65]

While *Durrett* and the section 547 approach espoused by *Wheeler* both serve a policy of avoiding mortgagee windfalls and protecting mortgagors and unsecured creditors, they differ significantly in their impact on the foreclosure process. For example, while section 547 may be asserted only against mortgagee purchasers, *Durrett* is available against third party purchasers as well. Moreover, while the *Durrett* avoidance period is one year, for section 547 it is 90 days. On the other hand, since the focus under the preference approach is on whether the mortgagee-purchaser received "more" than it would have under under a Chapter 7 liquidation, unlike *Durrett*, it might be used to recapture property where more than 70% of its fair market value was paid at the foreclosure sale.[66]

An argument can be made that the *Wheeler* analysis misreads the purpose of section 547.[67] This line of reasoning stresses that the latter section is applicable only to the extent that a creditor gets paid up to the full amount of her debt and not in those situations where she receives more than full payment. The excess, under this reasoning, is not a preference, but rather a fraudulent transfer voidable under either section 548 or, assuming state law is being utilized, section 544(b). In other words, if a creditor who is owed $1,000 would have received $300 in a Chapter 7 liquidation, and is paid $1,200 by the insolvent debtor within 90 days of bankruptcy, $700 is a preferential transfer while the $200 excess can only be a fraudulent transfer.

This argument is, however, unpersuasive. For one thing, it reaches the ironic conclusion that section 547 may be used to deal with the lesser of two wrongs—namely, the transfer that gives a creditor up to the full amount of her claim—but is unavailing to the extent the transfer gives her more than she is due. The more blameworthy creditor conduct must be dealt with, under this reasoning, only as a fraudulent conveyance. However unsatisfying such a conclusion may seem intuitively, it could nevertheless be defended if the language of section 547 either compelled such a result or was at least ambiguous. After all, Congress certainly has the prerogative to treat the problems of full payment and overpayment separately. The problem with this reasoning, however, is that the language of section 547 literally applies

---

65. Id. at 822.

66. See Henning, supra note 23 at 275, n. 110.

67. For further criticism of the preference approach in the foreclosure context, see Zinman, Houle and Weiss, supra note 52 at 985.

to the *Wheeler* type fact situation. Indeed, since *Wheeler* the 1984 amendment to the Code's general definition of "transfer" to include "foreclosure of the debtor's equity of redemption" actually reinforces the application of section 547 in such foreclosure contexts.[68] Moreover, even though *Durrett* and *Wheeler* both serve similar policy objectives, the impact of *Wheeler* on state foreclosure practice is, as we have seen, less extreme than that of *Durrett*. Thus, if one attributes to Congress an intent to deal with such problems in a manner least burdensome on state prerogatives, section 547 furthers that intent more than *Durrett*. In any event, it seems difficult to fault any court for refusing to read into the otherwise plain language of section 547 a meaning that would confer a windfall on a mortgagee at the expense of the debtor and his unsecured creditors.

So long as *Durrett* holds sway, the *Wheeler* preference approach will probably receive little attention. However, in those circuits where *Durrett* is not followed, the preference concept assumes greater importance. Indeed, this will especially be true if *Durrett* is either overruled or repealed by Congress.

 WESTLAW REFERENCES
11 + 7 108(b) /p redemption redeem!

1. The Foreclosure Sale as a Fraudulent Conveyance

a. The Durrett Problem
durrett /p fraud! /6 convey!

b. Cases Rejecting Durrett
alsop /p 548(d)
madrid /p "reasonably equivalent"

c. Impact of Durrett
11 + 7 548(c) /p value

d. An Evaluation of Durrett
durrett /8 oppos! reject! control!

2. The Foreclosure Sale as a Preference
avoid! /8 transfer /p 11 + 7 547 /p foreclos!

§ 8.17   Rents in Bankruptcy

As we noted earlier in this volume,[1] mortgagees frequently rely not only on real estate itself as security for the mortgage debt, but also on the rents and profits it produces. Sometimes access to rents is gained through the appointment of a receiver. Such receiverships typically are created after mortgagor default and incident to foreclosure.[2] Mortgagees also frequently find comfort in mortgage clauses or separate agreements by which the mortgagor assigns the rents and profits as

---

68. See text at note 30 supra, this section.

      § 8.17

1. See § 4.35 supra.

2. See §§ 4.33–4.35 supra.

additional security for the debt. Such assignment agreements, as we noted earlier, usually are not triggered until the mortgagee takes certain affirmative steps to activate them.[3] Typical of this approach is the Texas formulation that holds rent assignments ineffective until "the mortgagee obtains possession of the property, or impounds the rents, or secures the appointment of a receiver, or takes some other similar action." [4]

Once a mortgagor files a bankruptcy petition, an important question arises as between the trustee in bankruptcy, who represents the unsecured creditors, and the mortgagee as to whether the mortgagee has a valid security interest in rents collected from the mortgaged real estate during the pendency of the bankruptcy proceeding. This issue can be crucial for the mortgagee when the mortgage debt is not fully secured by the real estate. The ability to gain access to the rents under such circumstances could well determine the extent to which the mortgagee joins the ranks of the bankrupt's unsecured creditors.

Prior to 1979, the federal courts of appeal were divided as to what law governed entitlement to rents during this post-petition period. A majority of the circuits took the position that the mortgagee's rights should be governed by the state law which would have applied absent bankruptcy.[5] Thus the mortgagee was required to take those steps, either by leave of or through the bankruptcy court, as would have been necessary to activate its rights under state law. If, for example, a mortgagee was relying on a rents and profits clause, but state law required the appointment of receiver for its activation, the majority of federal decisions required that the bankruptcy court apply the same standard. A minority of federal circuits, however, utilized a federal rule of equity that afforded the mortgagee a security interest in the rents even if state law failed to recognize such an interest.[6]

The foregoing conflict was resolved in Butner v. United States,[7] in which the Supreme Court endorsed the majority view and held that state law governed in determining whether the mortgagee had a valid security interest in rents collected during bankruptcy. According to the Supreme Court, the bankruptcy court "should take whatever steps are necessary to ensure that the mortgagee is afforded * * * the same protection he would have under state law if no bankruptcy had ensued." [8]

3. See § 4.35 supra. See also Matter of Gotta, 47 B.R. 198 (Bkrtcy.Wis.1985).

4. Taylor v. Brennan, 621 S.W.2d 592, 594 (Tex.1981). See § 4.35 supra.

5. See In re Brose, 254 F. 664 (2d Cir. 1918); Tower Grove Bank & Trust Co. v. Weinstein, 119 F.2d 120 (8th Cir.1941); In re Hotel St. James Co., 65 F.2d 82 (9th Cir. 1933); In re American Fuel & Power Co., 151 F.2d 1242 (6th Cir.1945), affirmed 329 U.S. 156, 67 S.Ct. 237, 91 L.Ed. 162 (1946), rehearing denied 329 U.S. 833, 67 S.Ct. 497, 91 L.Ed. 706 (1947); See also Fidelity Bankers Life Insurance Co. v. Williams, 506 F.2d 1242 (4th Cir.1974).

6. See Bindseil v. Liberty Trust Co., 248 F. 112 (3d Cir.1917); In re Pittsburgh-Duquesne Development Co., 482 F.2d 243 (3d Cir.1973); In re Wakey, 50 F.2d 869 (7th Cir.1931).

7. 440 U.S. 48, 99 S.Ct. 914, 59 L.Ed.2d 136 (1979).

8. Id. at 56, 99 S.Ct. at 918.

Because *Butner* was decided under the Bankruptcy Act of 1898 and not under the Bankruptcy Code, some doubt has been raised as to its current validity. Under section 552(b) of the Code, "except as provided in section 363 * * * if the [mortgagor] and a [mortgagee] entered into a security agreement before [the filing of a bankruptcy petition] and if the security interest created by such security agreement extends to property of the [mortgagor] acquired before the [the filing] and to proceeds, product, offspring, rents or profits of such property, then such security interest extends to such * * * rents or profits acquired by the estate after [the filing] to the extent provided by such security agreement and by applicable non-bankruptcy law, except to the extent that the court, after notice and a hearing and based on the equities of the case, orders otherwise." [9] While the foregoing language "essentially codifies Congress' deference to state law in this area",[10] the exceptions could be viewed as affording a bankruptcy court the discretion in certain situations to alter the *Butner* state law mandate.[11]

This argument was rejected by the United States Court of Appeals for the Fifth Circuit in Matter of Village Properties, Limited.[12] Shortly after defaulting on a deed of trust containing an assignment of rents clause, mortgagor filed a Chapter 11 petition. Three months thereafter, the bankruptcy court granted mortgagee's request for relief from the automatic stay and a day later the deed of trust was foreclosed. Mortgagee was the purchaser. Because the value of the real estate was apparently less than the mortgage debt, mortgagee filed a claim for the amount of the deficiency and sought to satisfy this claim by asserting a security interest in the rents collected from the mortgaged real estate between the date of mortgagor default and the foreclosure sale. The bankruptcy court, relying on Texas law, denied the mortgagee's request and the district court affirmed. The Court of Appeals agreed with the two lower courts and held (1) that the mortgagee's rights under the rents clause were governed by Texas law and (2) that those courts correctly interpreted and applied that law.

First, the Court of Appeals acknowledged that section 552(b) permits a bankruptcy court, "based on the equities of the case," [13] to deviate from state law. However, it noted that the bankruptcy judge in this case had found no equitable reason for such a deviation. Moreover, the court stressed, the legislative history regarding the "equities of the case" exception indicates its purpose was "to cover cases where an expenditure of the estate's funds increases the value of the collater-

---

9. 11 U.S.C.A. § 552(b).

10. Note, Assignment of Rents Clauses Under California Law and in Bankruptcy; Strategy for the Secured Creditor, 31 Hast. L.J. 1433, 1440 (1980). For another excellent analysis of *Butner*, see Randolph The Mortgagee's Interest in Rents: Some Policy Considerations and Proposals, 29 Kan.L. Rev. 1 (1980).

11. Note supra note 10 at 1440.

12. 723 F.2d 441 (5th Cir.1984), certiorari denied ___ U.S. ___, 104 S.Ct. 2350, 80 L.Ed.2d 823 (1984).

13. Id. at 444.

al. [It] gives as an example the situation where raw materials are converted into inventory at the expense of the estate (which would thus deplete the fund available for general unsecured creditors)." [14]

Mortgagee also sought to use the section 363 exception to escape the application of Texas law. That section protects parties with an interest in cash collateral and forbids the trustee or the debtor-in-possession from using, selling or leasing such collateral unless each entity having an "interest" in it consents or the bankruptcy court so authorizes. [15] Under the definition then in effect, "cash collateral" meant "cash * * * or other cash equivalents in which the estate and an entity other than the estate have an interest." Mortgagee argued that rents are "cash collateral" and that its assignment created a lien or interest in them. Thus, mortgagee asserted, its interest in the rents could be protected by the bankruptcy court irrespective of state law. The debtor, however, argued that bankruptcy courts "must turn to state law to determine whether and at what time a mortgagee has an interest in the rents because it is only at that time that it becomes 'cash collateral' ". [16] The Court of Appeals agreed with this latter argument:

> "We reject [mortgagee's] unsubstantiated reasoning that Congress intended for section 363 to preempt state law which traditionally determines the property rights at dispute in this case. '[S]tate-created property rights, in a bankruptcy context, will not be destroyed by implication.' * * * (citing *Butner*). Moreover, the [legislative history] on which [mortgagee] relies, provides that rents received 'before or after the commencement of the case would be cash collateral *to the extent* that they are subject to a lien.' This language mirrors the provision in section 552(b), which provides that a security interest will exist 'to the extent provided by such security agreement and by applicable nonbankruptcy law . . . ' Thus if [mortgagee's] claim fails under section 552(b), 363 is to no avail." [17]

Consequently, the Court of Appeals concluded that "the *Butner* decision remains unscathed by the new Bankruptcy Code." [18] The court found further comfort in fact that numerous other decisions assumed the continued validity of *Butner*. [19]

14. 11 U.S.C.A. § 363.

15. Matter of Village Properties, Limited, 723 F.2d 441, 444 (5th Cir.1984), certiorari denied __ U.S. __, 104 S.Ct. 2350, 80 L.Ed.2d 823 (1984).

16. Id. at 445.

17. Id. at 445.

18. Id. at 445.

19. In re Jenkins, 13 B.R. 721, 723 (Bkrtcy.Colo.1981); reversed on other grounds 19 B.R. 105, 107 (D.Colo.1982); In re Oak Glen R-Vee, 8 B.R. 213, 216 n. 3 (Bkrtcy.Cal.1981); In re Gaslight Village, Inc., 6 B.R. 871, 874 (Bkrtcy.Conn.1980); In re Hellenschmidt, 5 B.R. 758, 760 (Bkrtcy. Colo.1980); In re Wheeler, 5 B.R. 600, 603 (Bkrtcy.Ga.1980); In the Matter of Jeffers, 3 B.R. 49, 56 (Bkrtcy.Ind.1980), see, e.g., In re Kuhn Construction Co., Inc., 11 B.R. 746 (Bkrtcy.Va.1981). See also, In re Southern Gardens, Inc., 39 B.R. 671, 672 (Bkrtcy.Ill. 1982).

Next, the Court of Appeals focused on whether the mortgagee had satisfied Texas requirements for perfection of an interest in the rents. It noted that the mortgagee had failed to "petition the bankruptcy court for the appointment of a receiver to collect rents for its benefit, for an order of sequestration or for any other order to impound rents." [20]   At least, it concluded the "or takes some other similar action" requirement of Texas case law "encompasses perfection of a mortgagee's interest by petitioning for sequestration or the like." [21]

Shortly after *Village Properties* was decided, Congress, as part of the Bankruptcy Amendments and Federal Judgeship Act of 1984, amended section 363(a) to provide that cash collateral "includes the proceeds, products, offspring, rents, or profits of property subject to a security interest as provided in section 552(b) * * * whether existing before or after the commencement of a [bankruptcy] case * * * " [22] Coming so close on the heels of *Village Properties,* it could be argued that Congress meant to make plain not only that rents can be cash collateral, but also that an assignment of such rents is enforcible by bankruptcy courts irrespective of state law. However, even assuming, as the *Village Properties* court was willing to do, that rents are "cash collateral", one is still confronted with the "have an interest" language of section 363(a), which was unaffected by the amendment. Nothing in the amendment suggests that the latter language is no longer to be governed by state law. Thus, it seems unlikely that Congress intended to alter the *Butner* state law mandate. At least, such a preference for state law should not, to use language endorsed by *Village Properties,* be deemed "destroyed by implication." [23]

Assuming the continued vitality of *Butner* and *Village Properties* certain practical observations are appropriate. First, to the extent that the mortgagee has gained access to the rents and profits prior to bankruptcy by taking lawful affirmative steps under state law, it will continue to be entitled to them during bankruptcy. Such pre-bankruptcy actions would include, for example, securing the appointment of a receiver or otherwise attaching or sequestering the rents and profits under state law.[24] Of course, if an assignment of rents clause is automatically effective under state law, such affirmative action would be unnecessary.[25] Second, where the mortgagee has not activated its security interest in the rents prior to bankruptcy, it may perfect its interest thereafter by taking those steps, either by leave of or through the bankruptcy court, as would have been necessary to trigger its rights under state law.[26] While sometimes this may require that the bank-

---

20. Matter of Village Properties, Limited, 723 F.2d 441, 446 (5th Cir.1984), certiorari denied ___ U.S. ___, 104 S.Ct. 2350, 80 L.Ed.2d 823 (1984).

21. Id. at 446.

22. 11 U.S.C.A. § 363(a).

23. Matter of Village Properties, Limited, 723 F.2d 441, 445 (5th Cir.1984), certio-

rari denied ___ U.S. ___, 104 S.Ct. 2350, 80 L.Ed.2d 823 (1984). See also Matter of Gotta, 47 B.R. 198 (Bkrtcy.Wis.1985).

24. See § 4.35 supra. See also Matter of Gotta, 47 B.R. 198 (Bkrtcy.Wis.1985).

25. Id.

26. Matter of Village Properties, Limited, 723 F.2d 441 (5th Cir.1984), certiorari ruptcy court actually appoint a receiver, there have been cases where bankruptcy courts, relying on state law, have found that the simple request for a receivership[27] or the mere demand on the trustee that rents be set aside will suffice.[28] Assuming the requisite steps are taken, the assignment clause will then become effective and subsequent rents should be applied to the satisfaction of the mortgage debt.

 WESTLAW REFERENCES

assign! /9 rent /s bankrupt**
butner /p rent /p bankrupt**
11 + 7 363(a) /p "cash collateral"

---

denied __ U.S. __, 104 S.Ct. 2350, 80 L.Ed.2d 823 (1984); In re Southern Gardens, Inc., 39 B.R. 671 (Bkrtcy.Ill.1982); In re Oak Glen R-Vee, 8 B.R. 213, 216 (Bkrtcy.Cal.1981); see also Groves v. Fresno Guarantee Savings & Loan Association, 373 F.2d 440, 442–43 (9th Cir.1967); Pol-lack v. Sampsell, 174 F.2d 415, 418–19 (9th Cir.1949).

27. See e.g., In re Flower City Nursing Home, Inc., 38 B.R. 642 (Bkrtcy.N.Y.1984).

28. In re Southern Gardens, Inc., 39 B.R. 671 (Bkrtcy.Ill.1982).

§§ 8.18–9.0 are reserved for supplementary material.

Chapter 9

SOME PRIORITY PROBLEMS

Table of Sections

§ 9.1 Purchase Money Mortgage Priority Concepts

The vendor of land may have security in the property for the payment of the purchase price in a variety of ways. She may frame the transaction in the form of an installment contract for the sale of the land, retaining the legal title in herself.[1] At the opposite extreme, she may have conveyed the property before receiving payment without any agreement for security, in which case she nevertheless may be given an equitable grantor's lien.[2] Or, in this second sort of transaction, she may expressly reserve to herself a security interest which will give to her a consensual equitable mortgage.[3] Usually however, she will convey title to the buyer, receive at the time part of the purchase money and receive back as part of the same transaction a mortgage upon the property to secure the balance of the purchase money. This last is the ordinary purchase money mortgage and it merits attention because of the special priority accorded it.

It is widely accepted that a purchase money mortgage, executed at the same time with the deed of purchase of land, or in pursuance of agreement as part of one continuous transaction, takes precedence over any other claim or lien attaching to the property through the vendee-

§ 9.1

1. See § 3.26, supra.

2. See Pomeroy, Equity Juris., § 1250, for a catalogue of the states accepting or rejecting the doctrine. See also, Patterson, Annual Survey of Georgia Law, 7 Mercer L.Rev. 151, 153 (1957).

3. Id.

mortgagor.[4] This is so even though the claim antedates the execution of the mortgage to the seller.[5] It will also have priority if it is in favor of a third person who advanced the purchase money paid to the vendor,[6] provided the money was loaned for this purpose only. In some states the priority of the purchase money mortgage is provided for by statute.[7] These apply, of course, to the mortgage executed to the grantor and there is a little authority construing them as limiting priority to such mortgages,[8] but the better view and authority extends them to the third party lender of the price.[9] Thus the purchase money mortgage will prevail over a claim of dower,[10] community property,[11] or homestead.[12]

One of the frequent and important instances of its superiority is over liens arising under judgments against the grantee-mortgagor under a judgment obtained and docketed or recorded before the purchase

4. Liberty Parts Warehouse, Inc. v. Marshall County Bank, __ Ind.App. __, 459 N.E.2d 738 (1984); Hursey v. Hursey, __ S.C. __, 326 S.E.2d 178 (1985); Commerce Savings Lincoln, Inc. v. Robinson, 213 Neb. 596, 331 N.W.2d 495 (1983); Nelson v. Stoker, 669 P.2d 390 (Utah 1983); Associates Discount Corp. v. Gomes, 338 So.2d 552 (Fla.App.1976); County of Pinellas v. Clearwater Federal Savings & Loan Association, 214 So.2d 525 (Fla.App.1968); Royal Bank of Canada v. Clarke, 373 F.Supp. 599 (D.Virgin Islands 1974); Stewart v. Smith, 36 Minn. 82, 30 N.W. 430 (1886).

5. See cases in note 4 supra; 29 Va.L. Rev. 491 (1943).

6. Sarmiento v. Stockton, Whatley, Davin & Co. 399 So.2d 1057 (Fla.App.1981); Hand Trading Co. v. Daniels, 126 Ga.App. 342, 190 S.E.2d 560 (1972); County of Pinellas v. Clearwater Federal Savings & Loan Association, 214 So.2d 525 (Fla.App. 1968); Huntingburg Production Credit v. Griese, __ Ind.App. __, 456 N.E.2d 448 (1983); Stewart v. Smith, 36 Minn. 82, 30 N.W. 430, 1 Am.St.Rep. 624 (1886); Protestant Episcopal Church of the Diocese of Ga. v. E.E. Lowe, 131 Ga. 666, 63 S.E. 136, 127 Am.St.Rep. 243 (1908); Laidley v. Aikin, 80 Iowa 112, 45 N.W. 384, 20 Am.St.Rep. 408 (1890); Hill v. Hill, 185 Kan. 389, 345 P.2d 1015 (1959); Commerce Savings, Lincoln, Inc. v. Robinson, 213 Neb. 596, 331 N.W.2d 495 (1983);

7. E.g., West's Ann.Cal.Civ.Code § 2898.

8. Heuisler v. Nickum, 38 Md. 270 (1873) and Stansell v. Roberts, 13 Ohio 148, 42 Am.Dec. 193 (1844), where the court relied upon the statutory definition of purchase money mortgages to give the judg-

ment priority. But see, Mutual Aid Building & Loan Co. v. Gashe, 56 Ohio St. 273, 46 N.E. 985 (1897); Ward v. Carey, 39 Ohio St. 361 (1883).

9. Hopler v. Cutler, 34 A. 746 (N.J.Ch. 1896); Bradley v. Bryan, 43 N.J.Eq. 396, 13 A. 806 (1887), semble; Home Owners Loan Corp. v. Humphrey, 148 Kan. 779, 85 P.2d 7 (1938); Kneen v. Halin, 6 Idaho 621, 59 P. 14 (1869); Jackson v. Austin, 15 Johns., N.Y., 477 (1818). See 36 Georgetown L.J. 676 (1948); Mercantile Collection Bureau v. Roach, 195 Cal.App.2d 355, 15 Cal.Rptr. 710 (1961).

10. Associates Discount Corp. v. Gomes, 338 So.2d 552 (Fla.App.1976); Stow v. Tift, 15 Johns. 458, 8 Am.Dec. 266 (N.Y.1818); Clark v. Munroe, 14 Mass. 351 (1817); Gilliam v. Moore, 4 Leigh (Va.) 30, 24 Am.Dec. 704 (1832); New York—McKinney's Real Prop.Law § 193. In all but two states, Georgia and Kentucky, the former by statute, this is the rule. See Note, 52 L.R.A.,N.S., 541 (1915).

11. Kneen v. Halin, 6 Idaho 621, 59 P. 14 (1899); Davidson v. Click, 31 N.M. 543, 249 P. 100, 47 A.L.R. 1016 (1926).

12. Associates Discount Corp. v. Gomes, 338 So.2d 552 (Fla.App.1976); Martin v. First National Bank of Opelika, 279 Ala. 303, 184 So.2d 815 (1966); Lassen v. Vance, 8 Cal. 271, 68 Am.Dec. 322 (1857); Foster Lumber Co. v. Harlan County Bank, 71 Kan. 158, 80 P. 49, 114 Am.St.Rep. 470, 6 Ann.Cas. 44 (1905); Powers v. Pense, 20 Wyo. 327, 123 P. 925, 40 L.R.A.,N.S., 785 (1912). But see Eyster v. Hathaway, 50 Ill. 521, 99 Am.Dec. 537 (1864), with which compare Jones v. Parker, 51 Wis. 218, 8 N.W. 124 (1881); 29 Va.L.Rev. 491, 495 (1943).

money mortgage is executed.[13]　It is given preference also over other mortgages which have been executed prior to or simultaneously with the purchase money mortgage and attach to the property when it is acquired by the mortgagor.　Thus it often wins over after-acquired property clauses in previously executed mortgages that would cover the subject matter of the purchase money mortgage.[14]　This should be so because such clauses operate only to create equitable mortgages and consequently cover only the property as it lies in the hands of the mortgagor.[15]　Even more clearly this is true if such a mortgage was taken with knowledge that the grantee-mortgagor did not yet have title.[16]

Several rationales have been advanced for this favoritism for the purchase money mortgagee.　The traditional and frequently stated explanation is that of transitory seizin.　The idea is that title shot into the grantee and out of him again into the purchase money mortgagee so fleetingly—*quasi uno flattu,* in one breath, as it were—that no other interest had time to fasten itself to it:　the grantee-mortgagor must be regarded as a mere conduit.[17]　Such a theory breaks down in lien states where the fee remains permanently in the grantee-mortgagor.　It also is inconsistent with the cases of quite common occurrence in which some considerable time elapses between the conveyance to the mortgagor and the execution of the mortgage.　If the reason were to be taken literally it would require the execution of the deed of purchase and the

13.　The cases are numerous.　See, e.g., Sarmiento v. Stockton, Whatley, Davin & Co., 399 So.2d 1057 (Fla.App.1981); Liberty Parts Warehouse, Inc. v. Marshall County Bank & Trust, __ Ind.App. __, 459 N.E.2d 738 (1984); Commerce Savings Lincoln, Inc. v. Robinson, 213 N.W.2d 596, 331 N.W.2d 495 (1983); Nelson v. Stoker, 669 P.2d 390 (Utah 1983); Associates Discount Corp. v. Gomes, 338 So.2d 552 (Fla.App. 1976); Hand Trading Co. v. Daniels, 126 Ga.App. 342, 190 S.E.2d 560 (1972); Scott, Carhart & Co. v. Warren, 21 Ga. 408 (1857); Stewart v. Smith, 36 Minn. 82, 30 N.W. 430, 1 Am.St.Rep. 624 (1886); Joseph v. Donovan, 118 Conn. 80, 171 A. 24 (1934); Holland Jones Co. v. Smith, 152 Va. 707, 148 S.E. 581 (1929).

14.　Associates Discount Corp. v. Gomes, 338 So.2d 552 (Fla.App.1976); United States v. New Orleans Railroad, 12 U.S. (12 Wall.) 362, 20 L.Ed. 434 (1870); Faulkner County Bank & Trust Co. v. Vail, 173 Ark. 406, 293 S.W. 40 (1927); see Chase National Bank v. Sweezy, 281 N.Y.S. 487 (1931), affirmed, 261 N.Y. 710, 185 N.E. 803 (1933); Pinellas v. Clearwater Savings & Loan Association, 214 So.2d 525 (Fla.App. 1968).　Louisiana and North Carolina hold the other way.　Equitable Securities Co. v. Talbert, 49 La.Ann. 1393, 22 So. 762 (1897)

Hickson Lumber Co. v. Gay Lumber Co. 150 N.C. 281, 63 S.E. 1048 (1909).

15.　See § 9.3, supra.

16.　Fecteau v. Fries, 253 Mich. 51, 234 N.W. 113 (1931), comment, 17 Iowa L.Rev. 99, Hanna, Cas.Security, 3d ed., 867 (1931); Hoffman v. Kleinjan, 54 S.D. 634, 224 N.W. 187 (1929), matter of notice in doubt.

17.　The principle is stated in Nash v. Preston, 3 Cro.Car. 190 (1631) and is found in Coke, Litt. § 31a who is cited as authority in early and leading American cases. Stow v. Tift, 15 Johns. 458, 8 Am.Dec. 266 (N.Y.1918); Scott, Carhart & Co. v. Warren, 21 Ga. 408 (1857).　Other important cases accepting the doctrine are Holbrook v. Finney, 4 Mass. 566, 3 Am.Dec. 243 (1808); Adams v. Hill, 29 N.H. 202 (1854); Wheatley's Heirs v. Calhoun, 39 Va. (12 Leigh) 264, 37 Am.Dec. 654 (1841); see Kent, Com., 5th ed., 173, 174.　The theory of transitory seizin is also used as an explanation of the priority of the mortgage to a third party lender of the purchase money. Protestant Episcopal Church of the Diocese of Ga. v. E.E. Lowe, 131 Ga. 666, 63 S.E. 136, 127 Am.St.Rep. 243 (1908); Marin v. Knox, 117 Minn. 428, 136 N.W. 15, 40 L.R.A.,N.S., 272 (1912).

execution of the mortgage to be practically simultaneous, something that is ordinarily not feasible and not required by the cases. As emphasized in a leading case, "An examination of the cases will show that the real test is not whether the deed and mortgage were in fact executed at the same instant, or even on the same day, but whether they were parts of one continuous transaction, and so intended to be, so that the two instruments should be given contemporaneous operation in order to promote the intent of the parties." [18] Again, if the theory has validity, it would seem it should apply to any case where the grantee mortgaged the property the instant he got the conveyance rather than confining it to mortgages for the purchase price in favor of the vendor or a third party lender. And, further, some theory other than transitory seizin would seem necessary to explain the priority of the vendor's purchase money mortgage over that of the third party lender of part of the purchase money insofar, at least, as the latter's priority is said to rest upon the same doctrine.[19] After all, in this latter context the title could just as readily shoot through the grantee-mortgagor as a conduit into the third party as to double back on its course and return to the vendor.

A better statement of the reason for the rule is that the title comes to the purchaser already charged with the encumbrance in favor of the grantor-mortgagor; that regardless of the form all that the transaction ever transfers is the redemption right.[20] While such a conclusion would square with the decisions where the purchase money mortgage goes to the vendor, it is more difficult to apply it to the mortgage going to a third party lender of the purchase price, although it has been advanced in such a case.[21] Furthermore, it would seem that the opposite conclusion could have been reached just as easily. Indeed, it would have been easier to do so, since in form there is a transfer of the full title without reservation, and the grantee then by a separate mortgage instrument creates the charge on it. So, unless the matter is

---

18. Mitchell, J., in Stewart v. Smith, 36 Minn. 82, 84, 30 N.W. 430, 431, 1 Am.St. Rep. 624 (1886). In Wheatley's Heirs v. Calhoun, 12 Leigh 264, 37 Am.Dec. 654 (Va.1841), a purchase money mortgage to the vendor, executed ten months after the conveyance, was held to have priority over the dower rights of the widow of the grantee. In Ray v. Adams, 4 Hun 332 (N.Y.1875), about a year elapsed after the vendee received title before he executed the previously agreed upon mortgage to secure E, who had loaned part of the purchase price; nevertheless E prevailed over a judgment obtained against the vendee before he obtained title. See, also, Demeter v. Wilcox, 115 Mo. 634, 22 S.W. 613, 37 Am.St.Rep. 422 (1893).

19. And there are cases stating that it does so rest. Moring v. Dickerson, 85 N.C.

466 (1881); Demeter v. Wilcox, 115 Mo. 634, 22 S.W. 613, 37 Am.St.Rep. 422 (1893).

20. See Huntingburg Production Credit v. Griese, ___ Ind.App. ___, 456 N.E.2d 448, 453 (1983); N.J. Building, Loan & Investment Co. v. Bachelor, 54 N.J.Eq. 600, 603, 35 A. 745, 747 (1896).

21. "One who executes a purchase-money mortgage is not regarded as obtaining the title and then placing an incumbrance on it. He is deemed to take the title charged with the incumbrance, which has priority over preexisting claims. And a mortgage given to a third person to obtain the money used in buying the property is entitled to the same preference." Warren Mortgage Co. v. Winters, 94 Kan. 615, 619, 146 P. 1012, 1013, Ann.Cas.1916C, 956 (1915).

considered more carefully, one is left unsatisfied as to why this one of two perfectly possible conclusions has been chosen. Further analysis, though, does give more illuminating answers. One is somewhat technical and legalistic, the other deals with the problem as a matter of intrinsic fairness based upon the just expectations on the part of the purchase money mortgagee. The first answer suggests that the purchase money mortgage always takes the place of an equitable interest in the property that precedes any lien or interest of any kind attaching to the purchaser's estate at the time of acquiring title.[22] Where there is a prior contract of sale this equitable interest consists of a specifically enforceable contract right to have the purchase money mortgage given on taking title and the equitable estate under the purchase contract is subject to this right. Where there is no prior contract the vendor retains on conveying title without receiving payment an equitable vendor's lien. When the purchase money mortgage is given it merely replaces and takes the priority of one or the other of these prior equities, and this is so whether it is given at once or subsequently, provided it is part of the same transaction. The third party lender of the purchase money is simply an extension of this. She is said to be in the position of an assignee of prior equitable rights of the vendor.[23]

The other answer justifies the doctrine on the fairness of protecting one who has parted with property on the faith of having a security interest in it until the money for which she was exchanging it is received as against persons who, for different reasons, have inferior claims.[24] Certainly the vendor should prevail over claimants of dower, curtesy, community property or homestead rights, for such persons would be acquiring a pure windfall for which they paid nothing and would be getting it out of the unpaid for property of the vendor.[25] As against judgment lien creditors she should win because they have not extended their credit in reliance on the right to be repaid out of *any* specific property, much less out of property previously owned by another and coming to the debtor unpaid for, with the seller of it relying upon that very property she has parted with for her payment. Furthermore, their judgments are obtained before their debtor receives the property to which it attaches on acquisition so they could not have relied upon it in getting their judgment lien. In such a case the general rule that such creditors' rights should rise no higher than their debtors' seems clearly appropriate.[26] As against other mortgagee claimants to the property, especially those who have made their loan

22. See Boorum v. Tucker, 51 N.J.Eq. 135, 26 A. 456 (1893), affirmed 52 N.J.Eq. 587, 33 A. 50 (1895); Davidson v. Click, 31 N.M. 543, 249 P. 100, 47 A.L.R. 1016 (1926); Walsh, Mortgages, 168.

23. Protestant Episcopal Church of the Diocese of Ga. v. E.E. Lowe Co., 131 Ga. 666, 63 S.E. 136, 127 Am.St.Rep. 243 (1908); Laidley v. Aikin, 80 Iowa 112, 45 N.W. 384, 20 Am.St.Rep. 408 (1890).

24. See Tiffany, Real Prop., 3d ed., § 1462.

25. See Davidson v. Click, 31 N.M. 543, 249 P. 100, 47 A.L.R. 1016 (1926).

26. See Nelson v. Stoker, 669 P.2d 390, 394 (Utah 1983) (quoting text with approval).

for the purpose of paying part of the purchase price, the question is closer; for these, unlike the others, have relied upon getting paid out of the same specific property and have parted with value on that reliance. Moreover, third party purchase money mortgagees, especially in residential transactions, often acquire a substantially greater economic stake in the mortgaged property than that retained by the vendor. Even so, the vendor has the edge because the property she is relying on for payment was previously hers up to the time of sale and mortgage back; there was never an instant when she relinquished a hold on it; and she would never have parted with it at all except upon the belief and faith that if her buyer defaulted she could either recapture the property or get paid out of it. And this is normally so even though she may know that her buyer is going to finance the deal in part by borrowing some of the purchase money from another and give him a mortgage on the property. Other mortgagees, on the other hand, even including lenders of purchase money, parted only with money in which they retained no interest whatsoever, and placed their reliance for repayment of their debts on getting a security interest in other property not only never previously owned by them but not even owned by the mortgagor at the time the money was loaned, even though they might not have known that fact. This difference in attitude toward the hazard of losing property previously owned and that of not getting an interest in property which had never before belonged to the claimant is an old and important one. Here it justifies preferring the vendor purchase money mortgagee over even the third party lender of the purchase money as well as the mortgagee under an after-acquired property clause. Much the same reasoning applies to the money-lending purchase money mortgagee to give it priority over all competing interests but the vendor. It relied upon getting security upon this very property and its money went into the payment of it. Without this advance of money, the mortgagor would never have received the property. It is this last feature that serves to give it priority over other mortgagees whose loans were not limited in their use to the acquisition of the property which was to be security for repayment. *A fortiori* it prevails over the other types of claimants.

 WESTLAW REFERENCES
266k158 (purchase /3 money /3 mortgage /p priority)

§ 9.2 Purchase Money Mortgages—Recording Act Problems

The priority of a purchase money mortgage is subject to being defeated by the operation of the recording acts. Under most recording acts a mortgagee is protected against a *prior* unrecorded mortgage if he took his mortgage without knowledge and, in some states, if he recorded it first.[1] If the subsequent mortgagee so qualifies, the fact that the prior mortgagee was for part of the purchase money is irrelevant. For example, suppose a vendor conveys title and takes back a mortgage, but does not record it. The mortgagor then gives a mortgage to a different mortgagee who takes and records his mortgage without knowledge of the earlier unrecorded mortgage. The subsequent mortgagee will have priority whether or not the subsequent mortgage is for part of the purchase money.[2] Moreover, an anomalous situation can arise where, because of the interplay of the purchase money doctrine and the recording acts, a negligent purchase money mortgagee can create a situation that results in his mortgage being superior to a prior judgment against the mortgagor but not to a subsequent mortgage. For example, suppose J has an outstanding judgment lien against P. L lends money to P to purchase Blackacre from V. V conveys Blackacre to P, which deed is recorded. At the same time P gives a mortgage for the purchase money to L. A few days later X lends money to P and takes and records a mortgage on Blackacre, X having no actual knowledge of L's mortgage; L then records his mortgage. In all probability, L's purchase money mortgage will be prior to J's lien because of the general priority rules governing purchase money mortgages, but junior to X's subsequent mortgage because of the operation of the recording act.[3]

It is common, especially in residential transactions, for purchase money mortgages to be given to both the vendor and to a third party institutional lender. Usually the third party lender finances the bulk of the transaction and the vendor lends a portion of the normally-required down payment. Notwithstanding this greater financial stake of the third party lender in the mortgaged property, the presumption rules regarding purchase-money mortgages produce a result the parties may not anticipate. As between a purchase money mortgage to a third

---

§ 9.2

1. The two major recording act types in use in the United States are: (1) those which "invalidate or subordinate an unrecorded conveyance as against the rights of a subsequent bona fide purchaser and (2) those which thus protect a subsequent bona fide purchaser provided his conveyance is the first to be recorded." Simes, Handbook for More Efficient Conveyancing, 18–19 (1961). The first type is referred to as a "notice" type statute and the second as a "notice-race" statute. A third type of statute, in effect in only a few states is the "pure race" statute. In this type of statute, priority of right is given to the purchaser who secures priority of record. In this situation, it "is a pure question of race to the records; the purchaser who first records, wins." Id. See also, Cunningham, Stoebuck & Whitman, The Law of Property § 11.9 (1984).

2. See, e.g., Royal Bank of Canada v. Clarke, 373 F.Supp. 599 (D.Virgin Islands 1974); Kemp v. Zions First National Bank, 24 Utah 2d 288, 470 P.2d 390 (1970); Jackson v. Reid, 30 Kan. 10, 1 P. 308 (1883). See generally, 26 A.L.R. 171, 173.

3. See, e.g., Thorpe v. Helmer, 275 Ill. 86, 113 N.E. 954 (1916) (intervening judgment lien); Trigg v. Vermillion, 113 Mo. 230, 20 S.W. 1047 (1892) (intervening mortgage). Cf. Commercial Bank v. Stafford, 149 Ga.App. 736, 256 S.E.2d 69 (1979) (purchase money mortgage senior to prior judgment lien against grantor, but, because of subordination agreement, junior to subsequent mortgage given by grantee). Cf. "So the last shall be first, and the first last." Holy Bible, King James Version, Matt., ch. 20, v. 16.

party lender and one to a vendor, the vendor's lien will be superior to that of the third party lender.[4] Most such institutional lenders either are required to, or at least desire to hold first mortgages.[5] The third party lender cannot, however, guarantee this priority status simply by making sure that its mortgage is recorded first, unless, of course, the land is in one of the few jurisdictions having a "race" recording act, under which merely being the first to record assures priority.[6] A couple of hypotheticals will illustrate why this is so. Suppose, for example, that vendor, purchaser and third party lender are each aware that the purchase price will be financed by two purchase money mortgages. Where two such mortgages are going to be utilized, it normally will be known by all of the parties because they will be referred to in the earnest money contract, a copy of which the third party lender routinely requires and examines before approving a loan. In this situation the third party lender cannot gain priority simply by recording first because it will have taken and recorded with knowledge of the vendor's mortgage.[7] While recording first will not, for the same reason, give the vendor priority, the general presumption in favor of vendor purchase money mortgagees probably will.[8] Moreover, even if the third party lender takes and records its mortgage prior to the execution of the vendor's mortgage and without knowledge of it, it cannot rely on the recording act to achieve priority because such legislation normally protects only those without notice who take *subsequent* to an unrecorded instrument.[9] While the vendor will, because of the recording by the third party lender, have at least constructive knowledge of its mortgage and thus will not be protected by the recording act, he nevertheless will again prevail because of the purchase money presumption in his favor. While some courts in the latter situation, at least if the vendor has actual knowledge of the third party mortgage, may be inclined to find an implied agreement on the part of the vendor to subordinate his mortgage to that of the third party lender, the implied agreement must be clearly established.[10]

How then can the third party lender be assured of priority over the vendor? The normal method is to have the vendor subordinate his lien to that of the third party lender.[11] This is usually done by including language in the vendor's mortgage specifically referring to the third party lender's mortgage and declaring its subordination to it. Normally, a vendor will agree to this for at least two reasons. First, he wants

---

4. See text § 9.1, at note 25, supra.

5. See § 11.1, infra.

6. See note 1, supra.

7. See e.g., Crystal Ice Co. of Columbia, Inc. v. First Colonial Corp., 273 S.C. 306, 257 S.E.2d 496 (1979).

8. See Schoch v. Birdsall, 48 Minn. 441, 51 N.W. 382 (1892). See also, Note, 40 Harv.L.Rev. 499 (1927); Fecteau v. Fries, 253 Mich. 51, 234 N.W. 113 (1931).

9. See note 1 supra.

10. Ex parte Johnson, 147 S.C. 259, 145 S.E. 113 (1928); Walter v. Kressman, 25 Wyo. 292, 169 P. 3 (1917); Truesdale v. Brennan, 153 Mo. 600, 55 S.W. 147, (1899); Boies v. Benham, 127 N.Y. 620, 28 N.E. 657, 14 L.R.A. 55 (1891).

11. See § 12.9, infra.

the third party mortgage transaction to be approved so that he can sell his property. Second, a vendor who takes a mortgage under such circumstances probably assumes, at the time of the initial transaction at least, that his will be a second mortgage.

Residential transactions also commonly involve two third party purchase money mortgagees, one institutional and one private. The private lender is very often a relative of the purchaser. Suppose, for example, the purchaser is able to supply only five percent of the purchase price himself. Then he arranges for an institutional loan for eighty per cent of the purchase price and a mortgage loan for the remaining fifteen percent from a relative. Both loans are secured by third party purchase money mortgages. Unlike the vendor-third party mortgagee situation discussed in the preceding paragraph, neither lender is benefitted by a legal presumption in his favor. The institutional lender, of course, for the same reasons indicated above, wants to ensure first mortgage status for its loans. Normally simply recording its mortgage first will not achieve this result. In the usual situation, because of questions on its loan application, the institutional lender will be aware of the other third party mortgage. Thus, when it takes its mortgage it will be on notice of the other mortgage. On the other side, of course, the relative's mortgage will likewise not have first mortgage status because at the time the mortgage to the relative is executed, the relative will obviously be aware of the institutional financing. In any event, a prior recording by the institutional lender will provide constructive notice to the relative. Thus neither mortgage will have the benefit of the recording act. If such a situation arises, a court could treat each as a coordinate first lien or alternatively, allow priority to be governed by common law principles and confer first mortgage status on the first mortgage to be delivered.[12]

If, in the above situation, neither the loan application nor other investigation by the institutional lender discloses the existence of another third party purchase money mortgage, the institutional lender will be in a stronger position. This at least will be true where a mortgage has in fact been executed in favor of the relative, but not yet recorded. In such a situation the institutional lender takes its mortgage without knowledge of a prior unrecorded mortgage and, by recording first, its mortgage will prevail. On the other hand, if the institutional mortgage is executed first, the recording act alone cannot be relied upon to confer first mortgage status on that mortgage because the institutional lender will not have taken it *subsequent* to an unrecorded mortgage.[13] Neither will the relative be able to rely on the recording act, because again he will either have actual notice of the institutional mortgage or be on constructive notice of a prior institutional recording.

12. See Cunningham, Stoebuck & Whitman, The Law of Property 773 (1984).

13. See text at note 9, supra.

When the institutional lender is aware of the existence of the mortgage to the relative, the safest course, as in the vendor-mortgagee situation, is to condition the institutional loan on the relative subordinating his mortgage in the manner described earlier.[14] Moreover, the relative will probably accede to this condition because he probably assumed in the first place that his would be a second mortgage. In any event, he will agree to subordinate if he really wants his relative to be able to obtain the institutional loan.

 WESTLAW REFERENCES

purchase /3 money /3 mortgage /p unrecorded record*** /p prior! interven***

§ 9.3 After-Acquired Property Clauses

Traditionally some mortgages have commonly included not only a description of the specific real estate being mortgaged, but also a clause purporting to mortgage all after acquired realty and personalty as well. The history of these clauses is long, complex and sometimes contradictory.[1] Moreover, there is no clear consensus as to their validity. Two commentators have summarized their current status as follows: "In * * * some * * * states, the after-acquired property clause is effective to create an equitable lien upon both real and personal property subsequently acquired by the mortgagor regardless of the character of the business in which the mortgagor is engaged, provided the new property bears a functional relation to the property originally mortgaged. In other states the after-acquired property clause is effective to create an equitable lien upon both realty and personalty if the mortgagor is a railroad or other public utility company, but is effective only with respect to realty if not within that class."[2] Other courts state that such clauses extend only to "other real estate or fixtures and attachments to the mortgaged real estate."[3] Still others limit their effectiveness as against third party creditors of the mortgagor. Under this view, "a general mortgage of after-acquired property will not

14. See text at note 11, supra. See § 12.9, infra.

§ 9.3

1. See Cohen and Gerber, The After-Acquired Property Clause, 87 U. of Pa.L. Rev. 635 (1939); Glenn Mortgages, § 409; Durfee, Cases on Security, 457–459 (1951); Francis, Mortgages of After-Acquired Property in Kentucky, 35 Ky.L.J. 320 (1947); Ethridge, The After-Acquired Property Doctrine and Its Application in Mississippi, 17 Miss.L.J. 153 (1945); After-Acquired Property Clauses—51 Tulane L.Rev. 314 (La.1941); Note, Mortgages—After-Acquired Property Clause in Mortgage Is Valid, 28 Rocky Mt.L.Rev. 432 (1956), commenting on United States v. Westmoreland Manganese Corp., 134 F.Supp. 898 (E.D.

Ark.1955); Note, After-Acquired Property and the Title Search, 24 Ford.L.Rev. 412 (1955), commenting on Fries v. Clearview Gardens Sixth Corp., 285 App.Div. 568, 139 N.Y.S.2d 573 (2d Dept.1955). See also, Arnold, After-Acquired Property as Mortgage Security in Maryland, 19 Md.L.Rev. 294 (1959). For a thorough examination of the problem of after-acquired property clauses in mortgages, see Cunningham and Tischler, Equitable Real Estate Mortgages, 17 Rutgers L.Rev. 679, 715–723 (1963).

2. Cunningham & Tischler, supra note 39 at 718.

3. Franklin v. Community Federal Savings & Loan Association, 629 F.2d 514, 516 (8th Cir.1980).

ordinarily be effective against creditors as to after-acquired property that is not an appurtenance to some existing property covered by the mortgage, or that is not made to have a definite and appropriate location, such as in a certain building, under the terms of the mortgage." [4] Finally, some jurisdictions seem to recognize the validity of such clauses with few, if any, of the qualifications mentioned above.[5] It should be noted that the equitable lien created by the clause arises only when the property is acquired and it is subject to any liens placed on it prior to the mortgagor's acquisition of it.[6] In addition, the lien of the clause will normally be subordinate to any purchase money mortgage given by the mortgagor to acquire the property.[7]

While several theories supporting the validity of after-acquired property clauses have been advanced,[8] the one most commonly adopted is the "specific performance" theory. Under this theory, the clause is treated as a promise to mortgage after-acquired property which will be specifically enforced when the mortgagor later acquires the property.[9] As one New Jersey case noted, "it is familiar learning, found in all cases, that a mortgage upon after-acquired property cannot rise higher than a contract to convey the title to that property when acquired, and a suit for its enforcement is, in effect, a suit for the specific performance of a contract." [10]

In considering the impact of after-acquired property clauses on real estate, it is important to distinguish between the mortgagor's placing of improvements on *Blackacre,* the land specifically described in the mortgage, and the subsequent acquisition by the mortgagor of *Whiteacre.* While an after-acquired property clause is necessary to reach Whitacre it is not with respect to the subsequent improvements on Blackacre. To the extent that such improvements are considered fixtures or, as Professor Glenn has pointed out, "if the mortgagor brings upon the premises a thing which by its very nature becomes a part of the land by virtue of the law of real property, the mortgagee may enjoy the resulting benefit without the need of an after-acquired property clause." [11] To state the foregoing, however, does not answer numerous and substantial priority questions, which would not be necessarily

4. In re Kansas City Journal-Post Co., 144 F.2d 808, 810 (8th Cir.1944), affirmed in part 144 F.2d 812 (8th Cir.1944), reversed 144 F.2d 819 (8th Cir.1944), certiorari dismissed 323 U.S. 807, 65 S.Ct. 559, 89 L.Ed. 644 (1945).

5. See Rose v. Lurton, 111 Fla. 424, 149 So. 557 (1933); American National Bank of Jacksonville v. International Harvester Credit Corp. 269 So.2d 726 (Fla.App.1972), modified in part 296 So.2d 32 (Sup.1974); Hickson Lumber Co. v. Gay Lumber Co., 150 N.C. 281, 63 S.E. 1048 (1909); Note, 28 Rocky Mtn. L.Rev. 432, 433 (1956).

6. Central Trust Co. of New York v. Kneeland, 138 U.S. 414, 423, 11 S.Ct. 357, 359, 34 L.Ed. 1014 (1891). See Cunningham and Tischler, Equitable Real Estate Mortgages, 17 Rutgers L.Rev. 679, 721 (1963).

7. See § 9.1, supra; Comment, Mortgages—After-Acquired Property Clause in Mortgage is Valid, 28 Rocky Mtn.L.Rev. 432, 433 (1956).

8. See 4 American Law of Property, § 1634.

9. See Cunningham & Tischler, supra note 6 at 718–719.

10. Daly v. New York & G.L.R. Co., 55 N.J.Eq. 595, 603, 38 A. 202, 205 (1897).

11. 3 Glenn, Mortgages, 1450 (1943).

altered or resolved even if an after-acquired property clause is used. Suppose, for example, a house is built on vacant land on which there is a preexisting mortgage. To say that the house becomes covered by that mortgage does not resolve the problem of what happens if the building contractor is not paid. The question then becomes one of priority between the mortgage and a possible mechanics lien, a problem we study in detail in a later section.[12] Or suppose that a furnace is installed in a house on which there is a pre-existing real estate mortgage. Again, to say that, as a fixture, the furnace is covered by the real estate mortgage, does not answer the difficult question of who has priority, as between the real estate mortgagee and the holder of a purchase money security interest in the furnace.[13]

The use of after-acquired property clauses to obtain a lien on the mortgagor's subsequently acquired Whiteacre is subject to a substantial and, perhaps, overriding difficulty because the nature of the recording acts. While the mortgagee's equitable lien is valid as to parties subsequently acquiring an interest in Whiteacre with notice of the after-acquired property clause, the problem, of course, is to determine what constitutes constructive notice under state recording acts. Suppose, for example, that R gives a mortgage on Blackacre to X containing an after-acquired property clause. R then acquires Whiteacre and later borrows money from Z and gives Z a mortgage on Whiteacre as security. If Whiteacre is not in the same county as Blackacre, unless a court is willing, as one has, to say that the recording of the Blackacre mortgage "is effectual notice against the world,"[14] it should not constitute constructive notice to Z because the records in each county relate only to land within that county.[15]

Suppose, however, that Blackacre and Whiteacre are in the same county. It is often said that a party does not obtain constructive notice of a recorded document that could not have been discovered by a reasonably diligent search or, as it is sometimes said, a document that is not in his chain of title.[16] The problem then is to determine what constitutes a reasonable search in the after-acquired property clause context. All jurisdictions presumably have grantor-grantee indexes in each county and, in theory, in examining title to Whiteacre, a person could examine every mortgage given at any time by all grantors in the chain of title or, at least, every mortgage that the proposed borrower may have executed previously. Such a search would seem to be unrealistically burdensome and unreasonable. As commentators have pointed out, "it is not customary to attempt to check the grantor index against any former owner *before* he acquired title or *after* he parted with it."[17] Moreover, the situation is not improved in those states that

12. See § 12.4, infra.

13. See §§ 9.5–9.7, infra.

14. Hickson Lumber Co. v. Gay Lumber Co., 150 N.C. 281, 63 S.E. 1048 (1909).

15. 3 Glenn, Mortgages, 1657 (1943).

16. Storke and Sears, The Perennial Problem of Security Priority and Recordation, 24 Rocky Mtn.L.Rev. 180, 194 (1952).

17. Id. at 194. See also, Cunningham & Tischler, supra note 6 at 721.

maintain an official tract index. Since the mortgage containing the after-acquired property clause will not contain a legal description of the subsequently acquired Whiteacre, it cannot show up in a tract index that deals with Whiteacre. Thus, Professor Glenn was surely correct when he stated that "the mortgage [containing the after-acquired property clause] is of record all right, but the difficulty is that it will not show up in the chain of title that relates to the new property." [18] Although there is some division of authority,[19] it seems difficult to visualize a court determining that the effort necessary to discover an after-acquired property clause is part of a reasonable title search.

Professor Glenn has suggested that where the mortgagor is a large corporation, subsequent parties ought to be on notice that the corporation probably has outstanding a general corporate mortgage containing an after-acquired property clause.[20] Presumably he is suggesting that the party examining title in such a situation be required to examine every document given by the corporate mortgagor, including even those given prior to its acquisition of title to the parcel in question, to determine whether such a clause exists.

The Uniform Land Transactions Act (ULTA), promulgated in 1975 by the National Conference of Commissioners on Uniform State Laws, but as of this writing not adopted by any state, expressly recognises the validity of an after-acquired real estate clause except in certain situations where the mortgagor is giving real estate security for residential real estate that he will or does occupy.[21] In the latter situation an after-acquired property clause will not attach to subsequently acquired real estate unless it is contiguous to the parcel described in the mortgage or unless the subsequently acquired property is itself described in the original mortgage.[22] While the explicit recognition of the validity of after-acquired property clauses is welcome, the ULTA can be criticized for not dealing with the problems of constructive notice discussed in the preceding paragraphs. Until those problems are resolved, the after-acquired property clauses will pose hazards not only for title examiners, but for the parties relying on the clauses as well.

The Uniform Commercial Code expressly recognises the validity of after-acquired property clauses in chattel security agreements.[23] However, such clauses are simply ineffective as to goods "used or bought for use primarily for personal, family or household purposes" unless the mortgagor acquires them within ten days after the mortgagee gives value.[24] Moreover, the lien of the clause will be subordinate to purchase money lenders who properly perfect security interests in the mortgagor's subsequently acquired inventory and other collateral.[25]

18. 3 Glenn, Mortgages, 1658 (1943).

19. See Glenn, supra note 18 at § 418.

20. Id. at § 418. See Cunningham & Tischler, supra note 6 at 721–722.

21. U.L.T.A. § 3–205(b) (1975).

22. Id.

23. U.C.C. § 9–204(1). See generally, Bailey, Secured Transactions in a Nutshell 72–75 (2nd Ed.1981).

24. U.C.C. §§ 9–204(2), 9–109(1).

25. U.C.C. §§ 9–312(3), 9–312(4).

How then should a real estate mortgagee proceed who is willing to accept the foregoing limitations, but otherwise wishes to have senior lien status as to a mortgagor's after-acquired personal property? Simply recording in the real estate records a real estate mortgage containing an after-acquired property clause that purports to reach personalty as well as realty will not suffice. This is so because unless a chattel security interest is perfected in accordance with the U.C.C. it generally will be subordinate to the interests of those who subsequently perfect a security interest in the after-acquired personalty.[26] The mortgagee could presumably perfect its interest in after-acquired chattels by filing the real estate mortgage containing the clause in the appropriate office for chattel security filings.[27] However, a conceptually cleaner and more reliable approach simply would be to treat the two types of security separately. Thus the mortgagee should record the real estate mortgage in the real estate records and, in accordance with the U.C.C.,[28] perfect separately a chattel security agreement containing an after-acquired property clause.

 WESTLAW REFERENCES
mortgage /p after-acquired /2 property

§ 9.4 Replacement and Modification of Senior Mortgages—Effect on Intervening Lienors

Replacement and modification of senior mortgages commonly occur.[1] For example, construction lenders who also provide permanent financing sometimes release the construction mortgage of record and immediately record a permanent mortgage even though the original mortgage indebtedness has not been satisfied.[2] Moreover, a senior mortgagee and the mortgagor frequently agree to certain modifications in the terms of the mortgage debt. These modifications often entail an extension of the term, a change in the interest rate, and, in some instances, an increase in the principal amount of the mortgage debt. Frequently, such modifications represent an attempt to deal with mortgagor financial distress. Some changes, however, are unrelated to such factors. For example, in lieu of acceleration under a due-on-sale clause, a mortgagee may consent to the transfer of the mortgaged real estate upon the transferee agreeing to an increased interest rate.[3] Sometimes the modifications will be reflected in a newly recorded "consolidation" mortgage; more frequently, they will be contained in a

---

26. U.C.C. § 9–312(5).

27. If the real estate mortgage is to be so used, it must comply with the formal requirements of U.C.C. § 9–203(1).

28. See U.C.C. § 402(1).

§ 9.4

1. See Kratovil and Werner, Mortgage Extensions and Modifications, 8 Creighton

L.Rev. 595 (1975); Meislin, Extension Agreements and the Rights of Junior Mortgagees, 42 Va.L.Rev. 939 (1956).

2. See e.g., Houston Lumber Co. v. Skaggs, 94 N.M. 546, 613 P.2d 416 (1980).

3. See §§ 5.21–5.26 supra.

new written agreement which may or may not be recorded. Each of the foregoing transactions and their variants can create priority disputes vis à vis intervening junior lienholders.

Replacement Mortgages

Generally, where a senior mortgagee discharges its mortgage of record and takes and records a replacement mortgage, it will not lose priority as against intervening lienors unless it intended a subordination of its mortgage or "paramount equities" are present.[4] Courts frequently deal with the intent issue by recognizing a presumption that the mortgagee intended a result that would be most beneficial to its security interest.[5] In any event, the prudent mortgagee should obviate the intent problem by spelling out carefully the parties' intent that the new mortgage retain the same priority as its predecessor.[6]

The "paramount equities" exception is grounded in notions of detrimental reliance.[7] A New Mexico Supreme Court decision [8] is instructive in this regard. In that case the mortgagee loaned mortgagor $37,000 for the construction of a home. When the construction was complete, the mortgagee released the construction mortgage and simultaneously recorded a permanent mortgage to take its place. Mechanics lienors, whose lien claims arose after the recording of the construction mortgage, but prior to the replacement transaction, asserted priority over the permanent mortgage. The New Mexico Supreme Court reversed a trial court judgment for the mechanics lienors. It stressed that the lien claimants "did not know the construction loan had been released and replaced by a permanent financing arrangement. The majority of the work had been completed prior to the change of financing. There is no showing that [they] detrimentally relied on the release in any way. Therefore, we fail to see how the paramount equities favor [them]." [9]

4. See e.g., Commerce Savings Lincoln, Inc. v. Robinson, 213 Neb. 596, 331 N.W.2d 495 (1983); Houston Lumber Co. v. Skaggs, 94 N.M. 546, 613 P.2d 416 (1980); Jackson & Scherer, Inc. v. Washburn, 209 Kan. 321, 496 P.2d 1358 (1972); Skaneateles Savings Bank v. Herold, 50 A.D.2d 85, 376 N.Y.S.2d 286 (1975), affirmed 40 N.Y.2d 999, 391 N.Y.S.2d 107, 359 N.E.2d 701 (1976); Financial Acceptance Corp. v. Garvey, 6 Mass.App.Ct. 610, 380 N.E.2d 1332 (1978); Piea Realty Co., Inc. v. Papuzynski, 342 Mass. 240, 172 N.E.2d 841 (1961); Guleserian v. Fields, 351 Mass. 238, 218 N.E.2d 397 (1966); Kellogg Brothers Lumber v. Mularkey, 214 Wis. 537, 252 N.W. 596 (1934); Kratovil and Werner, supra note 1 at 600–603; Annots. 98 A.L.R. 843 (1935); 33 A.L.R. 149 (1924).

5. See e.g., Hadley v. Schow, 146 Neb. 163, 18 N.W.2d 923 (1945); Kratovil and Werner, supra note 1 at 601–602.

6. See e.g., A & S Distributing Co. v. Nall-Tucker, Inc., 428 P.2d 254 (Okl.1967); Kratovil and Werner, supra note 1 at 602.

7. See e.g., Houston Lumber Co. v. Skaggs, 94 N.M. 546, 613 P.2d 416 (1980); Kellogg Brothers Lumber v. Mularkey, 214 Wis. 537, 252 N.W. 596 (1934).

8. Houston Lumber Co. v. Skaggs, 94 N.M. 546, 613 P.2d 416 (1980).

9. Id. at 548, 613 P.2d at 417. But see Carl M. Peterson Co. v. Zero Estates, 261 N.W.2d 346 (Minn.1977) (harm to intervening lienors shown).

Extensions of Time

Mortgagees frequently consent to an extension of the mortgage maturity date or to a rescheduling or "stretching out" of installment payments. Absent an increase in the principal amount of the mortgage debt or its interest rate, such modifications are generally held not to jeopardize the mortgagee's priority vis à vis intervening lienors.[10] Typically, courts assume that such transactions reduce the likelihood of foreclosure of the senior mortgage and that they therefore are helpful, rather than prejudicial, to the interests of junior lienors.[11]

Such reasoning, on balance, is probably sound. It is true that a time extension under certain circumstances may actually exacerbate the mortgagor's financial condition or contribute to further physical deterioration of the mortgaged premises and thus increase the risk to junior lienholders.[12] Such situations are, however, relatively rare. Moreover, most junior lienors are typically delighted to have a time extension of the senior debt forestall their own day of reckoning. It may also be argued that because extension agreements often cure existing senior mortgage defaults, they deprive junior lienholders of their equitable right to redeem from those mortgages.[13] Such a concern, however, is probably misplaced because junior lienholders are rarely willing to make the further financial investment in the mortgaged real estate that the exercise of such redemption rights entails.

Increases in Interest Rate and Principal Amount

Where the modification entails an increase in the senior mortgage interest rate or an increase in its principal amount, the junior lienor will gain priority over the earlier mortgage to the extent of the modification.[14] This result is premised on the assumption that such transactions prejudice the interests of such junior lienholders.[15] Sup-

---

10. See Crutchfield v. Johnson & Latimer, 243 Ala. 73, 8 So.2d 412 (1942); State Life Insurance Co. v. Freeman, 308 Ill.App. 127, 31 N.E.2d 375 (1941); Guleserian v. Fields, 351 Mass. 238, 218 N.E.2d 397 (1966) and cases cited therein. Skaneateles Savings Bank v. Herold, 50 A.D.2d 85, 376 N.Y.S.2d 286 (1975), affirmed 40 N.Y.2d 999, 391 N.Y.S.2d 107, 359 N.E.2d 701 (1976); Kratovil and Werner, supra note 1 at 607.

11. See Hastings v. Wise, 91 Mont. 430, 8 P.2d 636 (1932); Kratovil and Werner, supra note 1 at 609.

12. Kratovil and Werner, supra note 1 at 609.

13. See §§ 7.2, 7.15 supra.

14. See e.g., Skaneateles Savings Bank v. Herold, 50 A.D.2d 85, 376 N.Y.S.2d 286 (1975), affirmed 40 N.Y.2d 999, 391 N.Y.S.2d 107, 359 N.E.2d 701 (1976);

Barbano v. Central Hudson Steamboat Co., 47 F.2d 160 (2d Cir.1931); Mergener v. Fuhr, 189 Wis. 571, 208 N.W. 267 (1926); Prudential Insurance Co. v. Nuernberger, 135 Neb. 743, 284 N.W. 266 (1939); Werner v. Automobile Finance Co., 337 Pa. 433, 12 A.2d 31 (1940); Bank of Searcy v. Kroh, 195 Ark. 785, 114 S.W.2d 26 (1938); Kratovil and Werner, supra note 1 at 607, 610. Contra: Strong v. Stoneham Co-operative Bank, 2 Mass.App.Ct. 828, 310 N.E.2d 607 (1974); Commerce Savings Lincoln, Inc. v. Robinson, 213 Neb. 596, 331 N.W.2d 495 (1983).

15. Kratovil and Werner, supra note 1 at 610. Conversely, a decrease in the senior interest rate is not deemed to prejudice the interests of junior lienors. See Big Land Investment Corp. v. Lomas & Nettleton Corp., 657 P.2d 837 (Alaska 1983).

pose, for example, that a modification agreement results in an increase of the interest rate on $10,000 mortgage balance from 11% to 14%. If, as is likely, this increases the mortgage payments, this enhanced debt burden increases the risk of default and foreclosure as to both senior and junior mortgages. Moreover, the junior lienor's margin of protection in the real estate is reduced to the extent that the higher interest rate increases the amount of the senior debt. Similarly, if the principal balance of the senior debt is increased from $10,000 to $12,000, prejudice to the junior lienor is obvious. The mortgagor's higher total debt burden could increase the likelihood of default and foreclosure for all liens on the property, and the junior's margin of protection in the mortgaged real estate is reduced. Moreover, in both of the above modifications, if the junior lienor is forced to satisfy the senior mortgage in order to protect his or her position, the amount required for such a satisfaction will be more than could have been contemplated at the time the junior interest was acquired.

To what extent can a senior mortgagee obviate the foregoing priority problems by thoughtful drafting techniques? Suppose the mortgagee includes the following language in the senior mortgage: "All those claiming by, through or under the mortgagor consent to any extensions or increases in the interest rate or principal amount of the mortgage indebtedness agreed to by the mortgagee and the mortgagor, their successors and assigns." While some commentators doubt the enforcibility of such language,[16] at least one person has suggested that the right to increase the mortgage interest rate should be deemed an implicit provision of the senior mortgage: "Inferior mortgagees should be held to anticipate [that] * * * [modification] is liable to take place at increased rates of interest, rates which do not exceed the legal ceiling, where it exists, (and, where it does not, at or below upper limits reasonably capable of advance approximation)."[17] A less extreme argument would assert that a due-on-sale clause in the senior mortgage puts junior lienors on notice that the senior mortgage interest rate is subject to being increased, at least when the increase is incident to the mortgagee granting permission for a transfer.

The foregoing considerations are probably best evaluated by reference to an analogous context—the treatment of junior liens vis à vis optional future advances made pursuant to mortgage language authorizing them. While the latter subject is treated in detail elsewhere in this volume,[18] several observations are appropriate at this point. When optional future advances are authorized by the mortgage, they generally take priority over intervening liens and other interests unless the

---

16. "[M]any mortgages contain a clause which provides that the lender may increase the interest rate on the giving of any extension. The mere fact that this provision is included in the original mortgage as recorded will not be sufficient to secure the priority for that increased interest over those who take their interest prior to the extension." Id. at 610.

17. Meislin, supra note 1 at 955–956.

18. See § 12.7 infra.

mortgagee made the advances with notice of them.[19] Some courts hold that only actual knowledge of the intervening interests will defeat the priority of advances made by the senior mortgagee; others take the position that the constructive notice imparted by pre-advance recording by the junior interests will do so.[20] By analogy to the foregoing, it could be argued that subsequent interest rate or principal increases made pursuant to specific mortgage language authorizing them should be afforded priority over intervening lienors at least to the same extent that optional future advances made pursuant mortgage language will be superior to such intervening interests. Thus, senior mortgage interest rate and principal modifications would take priority where they occurred without mortgagee knowledge (however defined by local law) of the intervening claimants.[21]

A further refinement on the optional future advances analogy is desirable. Some optional future advances are made pursuant to mortgage language that, while it does not necessarily set a limit on the total amount of such advances, nevertheless at least makes it plain that such advances are contemplated.[22] Typically, a separate, unrecorded agreement spells out the terms and conditions of those advances. In any event, there is usually sufficient warning to intervening lienors to cause them to make further inquiry. However, optional advances made pursuant to "dragnet" clause are another matter. Such a clause is a mortgage provision which purports to make the real estate security for other, usually unspecified, debts which the mortgagor may already owe or may owe in the future to the mortgagee.[23] Because of their overbreadth and the fact they are seldom bargained for, courts often interpret such clauses narrowly against the mortgagee.[24] What, then, are the implications of the foregoing for "modification" clauses? To the extent that they make only a vague reference to potential interest rate or principal increases, they should be afforded the same judicial skepticism that is applied to dragnet clauses. On the other hand, if they accurately spell out the possible future modifications, they provide ample warning to intervening lienors and thus the latter should have no valid cause to complain. After all, such junior lienors would be no worse off under such circumstances than they currently are when the senior lien is an adjustable rate mortgage.[25] In both instances subsequent lienors are on notice that the senior debt can increase; they can adjust their lending decisions with respect to the mortgagor accordingly.

Suppose, however, that a specific modification clause is absent or that it proves to be ineffective. How then should the senior mortgagee who desires to make interest rate or principal modifications proceed?

19. Id.

20. Id.

21. Kratovil and Werner, supra note 1 at 611.

22. See § 12.7 infra.

23. Id.

24. Id.

25. See § 11.4 infra.

First, it should conduct a title search to determine if intervening liens exist. If they do not, the replacement mortgage or modification agreement should be recorded to protect against subsequent intervening interests. If the title search discloses intervening lienors, the latter may be willing to subordinate to the senior mortgage and, if so, an appropriate subordination agreement should be executed and recorded.[26] Where such lienors are unwilling to subordinate, the senior lienholder inevitably must assess whether the advantages of the modification outweigh the financial risk its reduced priority will create.

 WESTLAW REFERENCES

mortgage (financ*** /3 arrangement) /s permanent construct*** replac! /p prior*** /p mechanic junior interven*** /s lien!

mortgage /p (reschedule /s installment) refinance (exten! /5 time /s matur***)

mortgage /p increase /s interest principal /p reschedul*** exten! refinanc***

§ 9.5 Fixtures—Introduction

Conflicts in priority often arise between real estate mortgagees and claimants of chattel interests in goods attached to the real estate that are classified as "fixtures". What is classified as a fixture varies widely from state to state. Perhaps no more precise definition is available than this: "a fixture is a former chattel which, while retaining its separate physical identity, is so connected with the realty that a disinterested observer would consider it a part thereof."[1] Suppose that a real estate mortgage is executed and recorded, and the mortgagor purchases central air conditioning or a furnace or some other item that becomes a "fixture". If it becomes a fixture, under the normal rules of real property it becomes part of the real estate and therefore covered by the real estate mortgage.[2] However, to state that, as a fixture, the air conditioning or the furnace is covered by the real estate mortgage, does not answer the difficult question of who has priority, as between the real estate mortgagee and the holder of a purchase-money security interest in the air conditioning apparatus or the furnace. This type of problem and numerous variations thereon are considered in the following sections.

Fixture provisions in the Uniform Commercial Code have ameliorated the historically inconsistent treatment of fixture conflicts between chattel and real estate mortgagees.[3] However, the status of these mortgagees still varies depending on whether a particular juris-

---

26. See § 12.9 infra.

§ 9.5

1. 5 American Law of Property § 19.1 at 3–4 (1952).

2. See e.g., McIlroy Bank & Trust Fayetteville v. Federal Land Bank, 266 Ark. 481, 585 S.W.2d 947 (1979); Nelson and

Whitman, Real Estate Transfer, Finance and Development 642 (2nd Ed.1981).

3. See generally, Hawkland, The Proposed Amendments to Article 9 of the UCC—Part 3: Fixtures, 77 Com.L.J. 43 (1972); Berry, Priority Conflicts Between Fixture Secured Creditors and Real Estate diction has replaced the original 1962 fixture provisions with the amendatory 1972 version. While familiarity with both versions is still necessary, because the 1972 version has been enacted in over 40 jurisdictions, it is clearly the more important.[4] Rather than detail both versions, the following format will be used: (1) law prior to the UCC will be surveyed to establish the historical derivation of the code and the problems it was intended to remedy; (2) general aspects of both the 1962 and 1972 fixture provisions will be examined; and (3) specific priority problems will be analyzed, including major distinctions between the initial and revised codes where appropriate, to clarify the current status of fixture law.

 WESTLAW REFERENCES

mortgage /p prior*** /s fixture personalty (good /5 connect*** attach***)

u.c.c. code /p 9–313 /p fixture

§ 9.6 Fixtures—Pre-UCC Law

In theory, a few major doctrines summarize pre-UCC law. In reality, however, fixture conflicts were resolved on an ad-hoc case law basis regardless of the particular rule a state purportedly followed. Moreover, it is important to emphasize that these common law methods normally did not rely on recording statutes or concepts in resolving priority conflicts between chattel and real estate mortgagees. As a result, chaos often prevailed not only among the states, but also within the case law of each state.

One approach was represented by the Massachusetts Rule.[1] Under this rule there was a strong presumption that articles affixed to real estate became a part of that real estate. Moreover, once an item was classified as a fixture, in conflicts between the chattel and real estate mortgagees, the latter normally prevailed. The doctrine was originally based on the severely legalistic ground that the mortgagee got legal title and consequently acquired all additions which became a part of the realty, the mortgagor having no power "by any agreement made with a third person after execution of the mortgage, to give to such person the right to hold anything to be attached to the freehold, which as between mortgagor and mortgagee would become part of the real-

Claimants, 7 Memphis St.U.L.Rev. 209 (1977).

4. As of 1985, the 1972 version of § 9–313 governing fixtures has been adopted in Alaska, Alabama, Arizona, Arkansas, California, Colorado, Connecticut, District of Columbia, Florida, Georgia, Guam, Hawaii, Idaho, Illinois, Iowa, Kansas, Maine, Maryland, Massachusetts, Michigan, Minnesota, Mississippi, Montana, Nebraska, Nevada, New Hampshire, New Jersey, New York, North Carolina, North Dakota, Ohio, Okla-homa, Oregon, Pennsylvania, South Dakota, Texas, Utah, Virginia, Washington, West Virginia, Wisconsin and Wyoming. Because of its perceived shortcomings, the 1962 version of § 9–313 was simply omitted from the original adoption of the UCC in California and Iowa.

§ 9.6

1. Clary v. Owen, 81 Mass. (15 Gray) 522 (1860); Berry, supra § 9.5, note 3, at 210.

ty." [2] The purchase money chattel mortgagee was not simply relegated to a subordinate lienor's position. His security interest was instead rendered non-existent since the chattel was deemed likewise non-existent. The rule was harsh and, when strictly applied, often afforded mortgagees substantial windfalls. It was not surprising, therefore, to find courts avoiding the rule by going to extremes in declaring heavy and firmly affixed objects not to be fixtures at all.[3] Indeed Professor Gilmore suggested the Massachusetts rule perhaps did not exist at all or that the cases all "involve a factual variant which is not present in the majority cases or that accident rather than design has led some courts to accept a deviant formulation of a rule." [4]

The great weight of authority rejected the Massachusetts approach. Although the rationale for the results often varied, the majority approach was more pro-chattel mortgagor. When an attached article became a fixture, the majority approach favored the purchase money chattel mortgagee over the prior real estate mortgagee so long as removal of the chattel did not substantially injure the real estate.[5] When the real estate mortgage was subsequent to the purchase money chattel mortgage, the real estate mortgagee prevailed if he had no notice of the chattel mortgage and if he could reasonably have believed that the object in question was within the coverage of his mortgage.[6] Courts differed substantially, however, as to what constituted notice and while the majority approach seemed somewhat uniform, results varied from jurisdiction to jurisdiction.

2. Clary v. Owen, 81 Mass. (15 Gray) 522, 525 (1860). See Niles, The Intention Test in the Law of Fixtures, 12 N.Y.U.L. Q.R. 66, 73, 91 (1934).

3. Carpenter v. Walker, 140 Mass. 416, 5 N.E. 160 (1886), engine and boiler weighing 5600 pounds, and heavy planing and joining machinery fastened to the floor and connected with a central power shaft; Commercial Credit Corp. v. Gould, 275 Mass. 48, 175 N.E. 264 (1931), frigidaire system in apartment building, including compressor in basement with pipes to units in each apartment; Medford Trust Co. v. Priggen Steel Garage Co., 273 Mass. 349, 174 N.E. 126 (1930), sheet metal garages on cement pillars, one with cement floor; part of mortgage money even expressly advanced to pay for garages.

4. Gilmore, Security Interests in Personal Property, 759 (1965).

5. See Storke and Sears, The Perennial Problem of Security Priority and Recordation, 24 Colo.L.Rev. 180, 203–205 (1952).

6. "The exact question has often arisen in other states, and the overwhelming weight of authority is to the effect that the title of the seller of personal property of this character, which title is to be held by him until the price thereof is paid, and which is afterwards affixed to land of the vendee, so as to become part of the realty, is subject to the lien of a subsequent mortgagee in good faith without notice of the reserved title. This is fully shown in the elaborate note of Mr. Freeman to Fuller-Warren Co. v. Harter, 110 Wis. 80, 85 N.W. 698, 53 L.R.A. 603 (1901) in 84 Am.St.Rep. at pages 892 and 893, and also in the notes to Muir v. Jones, 23 Or. 332, 31 P. 646 (1893) in 19 L.R.A. 444, and Lawton, etc., Co. v. Ross-Kellar, etc., Co., 33 Okl. 59, 124 P. 43 (1912) in 49 L.R.A., N.S., at page 396, to which we refer for a list of the cases." Oakland Bank of Savings v. California Pressed Brick Co., 183 Cal. 295, 302, 191 P. 524, 527 (1920), commented on 8 Cal.L.Rev. 442 (1920); Alf Holding Corp. v. American Stove Co., 253 N.Y. 450, 171 N.E. 703 (1930), noted 5 St. John's L.Rev. 120, semble. See notes, 23 Geo.L.J. 563 (1935); 1 Idaho L.J. 199 (1931); 16 Iowa L.Rev. 116 (1926); 1927, 21 Ill.L.Rev. 517 (1927); 10 Minn.L.Rev. 348 (1930); 32 Harv.L.Rev. 732 (1919).

The Uniform Conditional Sales Act (UCSA) emerged from this case law as precursor of the UCC. Unlike its common law predecessors the UCSA utilized real property recording procedures to resolve fixture priority.[7] The UCSA left state law fixture definitions intact. Section 7 of the act divided chattels sold on conditional sale which have been affixed to realty so as to become a part thereof into two classes: those that could and those that could not be severed "wholly or in any portion without material injury to the freehold." If they fell into the first class, the reservation of title was void against subsequent purchasers, who included mortgagees of the land, unless the sales agreement, describing briefly the realty and stating that the goods were to be affixed to it, was recorded in the realty records before the purchase.[8] Without proper recordation, the reservation of title was void if the subsequent mortgagee took without notice and for value. As to prior mortgagees, the conditional vendor prevailed if the contract was properly recorded in the realty books prior to affixation of the chattel to the realty.[9] If the chattels fell into the second class, they could not be removed without the express consent of any person who had not assented to the title reservation, a category that included both prior and subsequent mortgagees of the land. Recordation by the conditional vendor was immaterial because in such cases the attempt to preserve title was itself ineffectual.

The UCSA was adopted by only a dozen states. Moreover, UCSA issues were rendered moot due to immediate, widespread acceptance of the UCC's initial fixture provisions in 1962.[10]

 WESTLAW REFERENCES

mortgage /p prior*** recorded recording filed filing /p fixture /p secur***

---

7. See Hawkland, supra § 9.5, note 3.

8. In his notes on this provision of the Uniform Act (2–A Uniform Laws, Annotated, § 64), George G. Bogert says: "The theory of the Act is that a conditional seller of a fixture should be given protection and allowed to retain title as security for the payment of the price of the fixture, but that in order to retain such title he should be required to give notice adapted as nearly as possible to reaching dealers in real property." * * *

9. American Laundry Machine Co. v. Larson, 217 Wis. 208, 257 N.W. 608 (1934). See 19 N.D.Law. 254 (1944). As to subsequent mortgages under the Massachusetts act, look at Security Co-operative Bank of Brockton v. Holland Furnace Co., 274 Mass. 389, 174 N.E. 721 (1931).

10. For thorough discussions of the fixture provisions in Article 9 of the Uniform Commercial Code, see Henning, The Impact of Revised Article 9 on Missouri's Fixture Financing Scheme, 48 Mo.L.Rev. 63 (1983); Coogan, Security Interests in Fixtures Under the Uniform Commercial Code, 75 Harv.L.Rev. 1319 (1962); Gilmore, Purchase Money Priority, 76 Harv.L.Rev. 1333 (1963); Shanker, Fixture Security Interests, 73 Yale L.Jour. 788 (1964); Shanker, A Further Critique of the Fixture Section of the Uniform Commercial Code, VI Boston College Industrial and Commercial L.Rev. 61 (1964); Kripke, Fixtures Under the Uniform Commercial Code, 64 Col. L.Rev. 44 (1964); Coogan & Clovis, The Uniform Commercial Code and Real Estate Law, 38 Ind.L.J. 535 (1963); Coogan, Public Notice and Chattel Security Law, 47 Iowa L.Rev. 289, 326 (1962); Hollander, Imperfections in the Perfection of Ohio Fixture Liens, 14 W.Res.L.Rev. 633 (1963); Project: California Chattel Security and Article Nine of the Uniform Commercial Code, 8 U.C.L.A.L.Rev. 812, 931–942 (1961).

§ 9.7 Fixtures Under the UCC

The purpose of both the 1962 original and 1972 amended UCC fixture provisions of the UCC was simply to specify the order of priorities, based on state law definitions of what is a fixture.[1] In theory, there was no intent to promulgate a uniform definition of fixtures which would encroach upon local realty laws.[2] Thus, much of the pre-UCC case law is still relevant.[3] Two reasons were asserted for perpetuating this local law: (1) the generalized nature of a uniform law was inadequate to meet the needs of diverse local circumstances; and (2) laws pertaining to traditionally unique real property were deeply entrenched; a wholesale attempt at displacement would simply have caused omission of the fixture provisions from states' enactments of the UCC.[4]

It should be noted that UCC provisions govern priorities only when a chattel security interest is involved.[5] However, the influence reasonably to be expected from virtual nationwide adoption would seem likely to affect case law concerning conflicts between real estate mortgagees and chattel claimants other than secured parties. To maximize understanding of the ensuing topics the 1972 draft of UCC 9–313 should be read carefully before proceeding further.[6] In addition, the following UCC terminology must be distinguished: (1) "attach": fulfillment of

§ 9.7

1. See e.g., White and Summers, Uniform Commercial Code 1054–1056 (2nd Ed. 1980); In re Shelton, 35 B.R. 505, 508–509 (Bkrtcy.E.D.Va.1983).

2. U.C.C. § 9–313(3) and Comment 3 (1972).

3. See e.g., Courtright Cattle Co. v. Dolsen Co., 94 Wn.2d 645, 619 P.2d 344 (1980); In re Shelton, 35 B.R. 505 (BkrtcyE.D.Va. 1983); In re Boden Mining Corp., 11 B.R. 562 (Bkrtcy.S.D.W.Va.1981); In re Avery, 7 B.R. 28 (Bkrtcy.D.S.C.1980); White and Summers, supra note 1 at 1055.

4. Indeed, Iowa and California choose to omit the 1962 version of § 9–313 anyway.

5. U.C.C. § 9–313 Comment 4 (1972).

6. Reading of both the 1962 and 1972 versions is strongly advised. The full text of the 1972 provision is set out herein:

§ 9–913. Priority of Security Interests in Fixtures

(1) In this section and in the provisions of Part 4 of this Article referring to fixture filing, unless the context otherwise requires

(a) goods are "fixtures" when they become so related to particular real estate that an interest in them arises under real estate law.

(b) a "fixture filing" is the filing in the office where a mortgage on the real estate would be filed or recorded of a financing statement covering goods which are or are to become fixtures and conforming to the requirements of subsection (5) of Section 9–402.

(c) a mortgage is a "construction mortgage" to the extent that it secures an obligation incurred for the construction of an improvement on land including the acquisition cost of the land, if the recorded writing so indicates.

(2) A security interest under this Article may be created in goods which are fixtures or may continue in goods which become fixtures, but no security interest exists under this Article in ordinary building materials incorporated into an improvement on land.

(3) This Article does not prevent creation of an encumbrance upon fixtures pursuant to real estate law.

(4) A perfected security interest in fixtures has priority over the conflicting interest of an encumbrancer or owner of the real estate where

(a) the security interest is a purchase money security interest, the interest of the encumbrancer or owner arises before the goods becomes fixtures, the security interest is perfected by a fixture filing requisites specified in UCC 9–203 for creation of an enforceable security interest in personalty enforcible against the debtor; (2) "affix": the physical act of joining or fastening personalty to land; (3) "perfect": unless noted otherwise, the act of filing in order to establish priority;[7] and (4) "fixture filing": a special perfection provision under the 1972 Code involving the filing of notice in the same office and by the same procedure used for recording real property interests.[8]

Although local law defining fixtures is still applicable,[9] the UCC has to some extent influenced these local fixture concepts by its apparent recognition of three classes of goods. Authorities uniformly accept this so-called "tri-partite" concept, which consists of the three following classes situated on a continuum: (1) incorporated building materials; (2) fixtures; and (3) purely personal property.[10]

before the goods become fixtures or within ten days thereafter, and the debtor has an interest of record in the real estate or is in possession of the real estate; or

(b) the security interest is perfected by a fixture filing before the interest of the encumbrancer or owner is of record, the security interest has priority over any conflicting interest of a predecessor in title of the encumbrancer or owner, and the debtor has an interest of record in the real estate or is in possession of the real estate; or

(c) the fixtures are readily removable factory or office machines or readily removable replacements of domestic appliances which are consumer goods, and before the goods become fixtures the security interest is perfected by any method permitted by this Article; or

(d) the conflicting interest is a lien on the real estate obtained by legal or equitable proceedings after the security interest was perfected by any method permitted by this Article.

(5) A security interest in fixtures, whether or not perfected, has priority over the conflicting interest of an encumbrancer or owner of the real estate where

(a) the encumbrancer or owner has consented in writing to the security interest or has disclaimed an interest in the goods as fixtures; or

(b) the debtor has a right to remove the goods as against the encumbrancer or owner. If the debtor's right terminates, the priority of the security interest continues for a reasonable time.

(6) Notwithstanding paragraph (a) of subsection (4) but otherwise subject to

subsections (4) and (5), a security interest in fixtures is subordinate to a construction mortgage recorded before the courts become fixtures if the goods become fixtures before the completion of the construction. To the extent that it is given to refinance a construction mortgage, a mortgage has this priority to the same extent as the construction mortgage.

(7) In cases not within the preceding subsections, a security interest in fixtures is subordinate to the conflicting interest of an encumbrancer or owner of the related real estate who is not the debtor.

(8) When the secured party has priority over all owners and encumbrancers of the real estate, he may, on default, subject to the provisions of Part 5, remove his collateral from the real estate but he must reimburse any encumbrancer or owner of the real estate who is not the debtor and who has not otherwise agreed for the cost of repair of any physical injury, but not for any diminution in value of the real estate caused by the absence of the goods removed or by any necessity of replacing them. A person entitled to reimbursement may refuse permission to remove until the secured party gives adequate security for the performance of this obligation.

7. U.C.C. § 9–303(1), § 9–302(1).

8. U.C.C. §§ 9–313(1)(b), 9–401, 9–402, 9–403.

9. See notes 1–4 supra and accompanying text.

10. U.C.C. § 9–313 Comment 3; Hawkland, § 9.5 supra, note 3 at 46. Adams, Security Interests in Fixtures Under Mississippi's Uniform Commercial Code, 47 Miss.L.J. 831, 836 (1976).

Under the UCC, no security interest exists in "ordinary building materials incorporated into an improvement on land" irrespective of whether local law classifies such materials as fixtures.[11] It should be emphasized that this prohibition does not affect rights of enforcement against the debtor personally as opposed to against the actual materials.[12] This provision derives from the Uniform Conditional Sales Act [13] and, as Professor Henning has noted, the policy underlying it is to prevent waste by prohibiting the dismantling of a completed structure.[14]

At the opposite extreme of the continuum is purely personal property. Upon first reading the UCC fixture scheme, one may form a common misconception that realty claimants can somehow prevail as to such property. Goods that are purely personal property do not become part of real estate mortgage, even though a chattel security interest is never perfected, merely because the goods are located on the mortgaged property.[15] For example, personalty such as stereo components or household furniture would not be subject to a real estate mortgage simply because they were situated inside a mortgaged home.

Fixtures, the dual-natured intermediate class, are thus the only items of concern under the UCC priority system. Rather than usurp local fixture definitions, the UCC draftsmen attempted to leave law untouched and focused instead on the concept of recordation as the method to regulate priorities.[16] In contrast to the common law, this system is based on filing and certain preferred status classes. It favors chattel mortgagees in most instances. This is predicated on the drafters' belief that fixture priority for real estate mortgages would generally be an undeserved windfall not contemplated in original mortgage agreements. Chattel mortgagees can usually assure priority by filing, thus undercutting the importance of preserving state law definitions which formerly tended to favor realty interests. Note that the act of fixture filing is not an admission or inference of fixture status.[17] Chattel security holders are encouraged to file according to both chattel and fixture rules, so the filing of notice in real estate records may be merely a precaution.

In order to accommodate real estate lending interests, one of the primary changes in the 1972 code was to increase the importance of fixture filing, as will be explained in greater detail below. Under the 1962 provisions, basic priority over prior real estate interests was given to unperfected chattel interests in most situations. Perfection by filing

---

11. U.C.C. § 9–313(2) and Comment 2.

12. Id.

13. See § 9.5 supra, notes 7–10 and accompanying text.

14. Henning, The Impact of Revised Article 9 on Missouri's Fixture Financing Scheme, 48 Mo.L.Rev. 63, 69–71 (1983).

15. U.C.C. § 9–313 Comment 4.

16. The Priority Rules of Article Nine, 62 Cornell L.Rev. 834, 920 (1977).

17. U.C.C. § 9–313 Comment 1.

under the 1962 version was necessary for priority as against most subsequent interests, including real estate mortgagees.[18]

Subsequent Real Estate Mortgages

As stated in the official comments, the basic rule of the 1972 code is identical to the usual conveyancing rule for real property: as between a subsequent mortgagee and a prior chattel security interest in fixtures, the first party to make a fixture filing or record his real estate mortgage attains priority.[19] Under this general tenet, a subsequent realty mortgagee cannot obtain priority over fixtures (with the exception of incorporated building materials) so long as the antecedent chattel claim was properly perfected by a fixture filing. Such notice of a fixture interest in the chain of title alerts subsequent purchasers and mortgagees. The fixture filing is an absolute requirement. Otherwise, this provision of the 1972 code will not operate to prefer chattel lienors over realty mortgagees. Thus, this basic priority rule favoring chattel financers requires the goods to (1) become fixtures, and (2) also be perfected by fixture filing, both occurring before the subsequent realty mortgage is recorded.[20] It is a pure race system.

In comparison, the 1962 code initially specifies that even unperfected chattel security interests are superior to subsequent real estate interests.[21] It then qualifies this priority, however, by a broad exception: if not perfected by filing, the priority is lost to subsequent good faith purchasers for value, including real estate mortgagees and lien creditors without knowledge of the unrecorded fixture security interest.[22]

Prior Real Estate Mortgagees

Even though a real estate mortgage precedes a chattel mortgagee's interest, the 1972 code nevertheless awards priority to the chattel claim if (1) it is a purchase money security interest, and (2) a fixture filing was made before or within ten days after the goods were affixed to the premises so as to become fixtures.[23] Several justifications were offered for this subordination of the realty mortgagee and these center on an historical preference for purchase money interests. Commentators note that the real estate mortgagee normally did not rely on the fixture as being part of his security in the original agreement. Moreover, the improvement often enhances the real estate value and, thereby, benefits the real estate mortgagee. To award the mortgagee priority over

---

18. U.C.C. § 9–313(4).

19. U.C.C. § 9–313, Comment 4(b); Corning Bank v. Bank of Rector, 265 Ark. 68, 576 S.W.2d 949 (1979).

20. In re Boden Mining Corp., 11 B.R. 562 (Bkrtcy.S.D.W.Va.1981).

21. Schroeder, Security Interests in Fixtures, 1975 Ariz.St.L.J. 319, 321 (1975).

22. Id. See U.C.C. § 1–201(33)(32); Courtright Cattle Co. v. Dolsen Co., 94 Wn. 2d 645, 619 P.2d 344 (1980). Cf., McCarthy v. Bank, 283 Pa.Super. 328, 423 A.2d 1280 (1980) (security interest unperfected, but realty purchaser had actual knowledge).

23. U.C.C. § 9–313(4)(a) and Comment 4(a): Schroeder, supra note 21 at 320–329.

the subsequently installed fixture would arguably give him an undeserved, unbargained-for windfall.[24]

However, suppose the chattel security interest arises after the goods become fixtures. Since no purchase money security interest is involved, the real estate mortgagee receives priority under both the 1962 and 1972 codes.[25] The debtor is not buying and affixing new goods to improve the freehold, but, rather, he is attempting to borrow against existing property on which the real estate mortgagee may have relied.[26]

In contrast to the 1972 requisite of fixture filing within a ten day grace period, the 1962 code specifies priority for purchase money security interests in fixtures even though the security interests were never perfected.[27] This rule, especially, was one that upset real estate lending proponents.[28] The 1972 code prefers chattel financers, only if they file within ten days after the fixtures in question are affixed to the realty.

Construction Mortgages

Construction mortgagees, for a variety of reasons, pay out the proceeds of their loans on an installment basis as the construction of the building progresses.[29] In an attempt to ensure that these subsequent advances relate back to the original date of the mortgage for priority purposes, construction mortgagees include "future advances" clauses in construction mortgages. Thus, construction mortgagees claim to give new value in the form of these future advances to a much greater extent than chattel mortgagees of fixtures installed during construction. Naturally, therefore, the construction mortgagees want to claim such fixtures as part of their security.

The 1962 code was unfavorable towards the interests of the construction lender. Under the 1962 version, "a creditor with a prior encumbrance of record on the real estate [will take priority] to the extent that he makes subsequent advances if * * * the subsequent advance under the prior encumbrance is made or contracted for without knowledge of the security interest and before it was perfected." [30] As a result of this provision, where a construction mortgagee advances money to the mortgagor-owner who then, instead of using the money to pay cash for certain articles needed for the building project, buys them

---

24. Id.

25. Schroeder, supra note 21 at 320–321. See McIlroy Bank & Trust Fayetteville v. Federal Land Bank of St. Louis, 266 Ark. 481, 585 S.W.2d 947 (1979). However, real estate mortgagees sometimes lose because of an inability to establish that the goods are fixtures. See e.g., In re Avery, 7 B.R. 28 (Bkrtcy.D.S.C.1980).

26. Schroeder, supra note 21 at 321. See McIlroy Bank & Trust Fayetteville v. Federal Land Bank of St. Louis, 266 Ark. 481, 585 S.W.2d 947 (1979).

27. Schroeder, supra note 21 at 320. See Funk, The Proposed Revision of Article 9 of the Uniform Commercial Code, 26 Bus. Law. 1465, 1471 (1972).

28. Funk, supra note 27 at 1471.

29. See §§ 12.7, 12.1, infra.

30. U.C.C. § 9–313(4)(c). See The Priority Rules of Article Nine, 62 Cornell L.Rev. 834, 924 (1977).

on credit subject to purchase money security interests, if the articles become fixtures, the chattel security will have priority over the construction mortgage even if it is not perfected.[31] The underlying premise is that the "construction mortgagee must protect himself by policing the debtor's use of advances or by withholding part of the loan to discharge the liens of unpaid suppliers." [32] Likewise, if the advance by the construction mortgagee is made *after* the articles have been installed as fixtures, the chattel mortgagee will have priority if he takes the precaution of filing or if the construction mortgagee has knowledge of his interest.[33] The theory here was to protect the construction mortgagee "from a danger against which he could not effectively guard—making an advance on the supposedly existing security of additions already made to the land when there are unknown and undiscoverable claims against those additions in favor of others." [34]

The 1972 code provides special protection for the construction mortgagee so long as the mortgage is recorded before the goods are affixed. As one commentator has noted, "as to any goods that become fixtures during the course of construction, the construction mortgagee enjoys priority to the extent of all advances made under the mortgage to finance the construction, including the cost of acquiring the land." [35] Such advances even prevail over purchase money security interests in such goods [36] and, moreover, it makes no difference whether the advances are "optional" or "obligatory." [37] The benefit of this priority is available to both assignees of the construction mortgage and to refinancing mortgagees.[38]

31. Adams, Security Interests in Fixtures Under Mississippi's Uniform Commercial Code, 47 Miss.L.J. 831, 852 (1976).

32. Id. at 852.

33. Id. at 852; U.C.C. § 9–313(4)(c).

34. Adams, supra note 31 at 853.

35. Id. at 908. In order to qualify as a construction mortgage, a mortgage must secure "an obligation incurred for the construction of an improvement on land." 1972 Official Text with Comments, § 9–313(1)(c).

36. See Funk, The Proposed Revision of Article 9 of the Uniform Commercial Code, 26 Bus.Law. 1465, 1472 (1972).

37. Comment 4(e), § 9–313 (1972).

38. Schroeder, Security Interests in Fixtures, 1975 Ariz.St.L.J. 319, 332 (1975).

To what extent does an after acquired property clause in the real estate mortgage strengthen the real estate mortgage vis a vis subsequent chattel security interests? While such clauses do generally give the real estate mortgagee a lien on the after acquired property of the mortgagor, fixtures installed on the mortgagor's real estate would in any event come within the coverage of the realty mortgage. See § 9.3, supra. Under the UCC the presence of the after acquired property clause probably does little to enhance the priority status of the real estate mortgagee. Under the 1962 code, a real estate mortgagee prevails only to the extent that he makes additional advances, even though the subsequent chattel mortgagee never perfects his fixture security interest. See U.C.C. § 9–313(4)(c); Berry, Priority Conflicts Between Fixture Secured Creditors and Real Estate Claimants, 7 Memphis St.L.J. 209, 230 (1977). Indeed, this would seem to mean that the presence of the after acquired property clause is irrelevant in its effect on priority. Berry, supra at 230–231. The same is also probably true under the 1972 code. Because of its emphasis on recording, the previously recorded realty mortgage will generally attain priority over a subsequently filed fixture interest whether or not an after acquired property clause is involved. Moreover, even if the real estate mortgage contains such a clause, in the case of a *purchase money* fixture interest (as the majority probably

Exceptions Favoring Fixture Financers

A real estate mortgagee with priority may consent to subordinate his claim to the security interest of the fixture financer.[39] Whether to avoid costly litigation, because he is fair-minded, or for other reasons as to which one might speculate, a mortgagee might give such consent if, for example, he had priority because a subsequent fixture financer did not file his purchaser money interest within the ten day grace period. Under the 1962 code, the situation might arise where the mortgagee or a subsequent bona fide purchaser of the real estate has priority over an unperfected antecedent fixture interest. Consenting to removal of an inconsequential fixture might be less troublesome than contending with the junior chattel lienor's claim if the real estate mortgagee foreclosed.

The 1972 Code adopts a dual perfection scheme under which a fixture filing in the real estate records gives the maximum protection possible but perfection by other methods is sometimes effective. For example, a security interest in fixtures has priority over a real estate mortgagee with respect to readily moveable office equipment and replacements for domestic appliances which are subject to chattel security interests perfected by any method permitted in the UCC.[40] This provision was included to alleviate the confusion in various jurisdictions as to whether these types of items are fixtures or pure personalty. Again, undermining the supposedly inviolate status of local laws, the UCC drafters decided the inherent chattel nature of office machines, stoves, refrigerators, and other similar domestic appliances warranted a guarantee of chattel priority in case conservative realty laws defined them as fixtures.

Perfection by fixture filing is not required under this exception due to the confusion over the fixture status of these items.[41] Moreover, since consumer goods in the debtor's hands, such as domestic appliances, are excused from any filing requirements where the chattel mortgagee has a purchase money security interest, the exemption was extended to this provision in the event a court would determine that such appliances are fixtures. Note, however, that the priority guarantee for chattel lienors applies only to replacement appliances. Thus, ordinary consumer purchases to replace worn out appliances do not require recording in the chain of title of underlying realty. In the official comments, the UCC drafters note that other relevant law, such as that governing construction mortgages, applies to original installations of domestic appliances.[42] The comments further state that appliances installed in commercial buildings, whether as originals or

are), the chattel claimant will be given priority, as explained earlier, if he fixture files within the requisite ten day period.

39. U.C.C. § 9–313(5)(a).

40. U.C.C. § 9–313(4)(c) and Comment 4(d).

41. Id.

42. Id.

replacements, are normally regarded as fixtures unless they are merely domestic appliances installed by a tenant.[43]

A second situation [44] in which the dual perfection system comes into play involves lien creditors, including a trustee in bankruptcy.[45] Since such creditors typically do not rely on the real estate records, a fixture filing is not necessary and perfection by any other method is effective against them. If the chattel mortgagee incorrectly assumes that goods will not become fixtures, he will be protected against non-reliance creditors if he takes the normal steps to perfect his interest even though he will be subordinated to recorded real estate mortgages because of his failure to make a fixture filing.

Finally, if fixtures are installed by a mortgagor's tenant, the UCC gives priority to the tenant/debtor's fixture claimant as against the realty mortgagee if the tenant has the right as against the mortgagor to remove the fixtures from the mortgaged property.[46] This priority continues for a reasonable time even after the tenant/debtor's right of removal terminates.[47]

Remedies

In the few instances where a real estate mortgagee is awarded priority under the UCC, the debtor, chattel mortgagee, or other claimant of a chattel interest is absolutely prohibited from removing the fixture from the real estate.[48] On the other hand, the chattel mortgage should be deemed subordinate to the realty mortgage, thus entitling the chattel lienor to payment from any surplus that may exist in the event of a foreclosure sale. However, some courts have erroneously extinguished the chattel security interest rather than designating it second in priority.[49] Alternatively, the chattel claim may always be enforced against the debtor personally rather than against the fixtures from a subordinate's status.

In contrast, where the chattel mortgage is granted priority, the holder of the interest has an absolute right to remove the fixture despite damage to the premises.[50] The UCC limits the fixture claimant's liability to the damage incurred in removal; he is not liable for any loss of value to the real estate resulting from removal of the fixture.[51]

43. Id.

44. U.C.C. § 9–313(4)(d). The term "lien creditor" is defined in U.C.C. § 9–301(3).

45. For an analysis of the interplay between U.C.C. § 9–313(4)(d) and the Bankruptcy Reform Act of 1978, see Henning, supra note 14, at 96–97. See also, White and Summers, supra note 1 at 1061.

46. U.C.C. § 9–313(5)(b); White & Summers, supra note 1 at 933–34; 62 Cornell L.Rev. at 926; Berry, supra note 38 at 237.

47. U.C.C. § 9–313(5)(b).

48. See Berry, supra note 38 at 232; Schroeder, supra note 21 at 322.

49. See In re Foskett, 7 U.C.C.Rep.Serv. 267 (W.D.Wis.1970).

50. U.C.C. § 9–313(8) and Comment 9; Hawkland § 9.5 supra, note 3 at 43, 44; Berry, supra note 38 at 232; Schroeder, supra note 21 at 322.

51. Id. Permission to remove may be conditioned on the secured party giving

WESTLAW REFERENCES

(u.c.c. code /p 9–313) (security /3 interest /s fixture personal**
　　good /p realty)

u.c.c. code /p 313 /p fixture

"adequate security" to cover expected damage. See U.C.C. § 9–313(8).

§§ 9.8–10.0 are reserved for supplementary material.

Chapter 10

SUBROGATION, CONTRIBUTION AND MARSHALING

Table of Sections

A. SUBROGATION AND CONTRIBUTION

A. SUBROGATION AND CONTRIBUTION

§ 10.1 General Principles

Subrogation is the substitution of another person in the place of a creditor whose claim he has satisfied so that the person subrogated (the subrogee) succeeds to all the rights, priorities, liens and securities of the creditor in relation to the debt.[1] It amounts to an assignment by

§ 10.1

1. See generally Restatement, Second, Restitution § 31 (Tent. Draft No. 2, 1984). See Stafford Metal Works, Inc. v. Cook Paint & Varnish Co., 418 F.Supp. 56 (D.C. Tex.1976); First National City Bank v. United States, 548 F.2d 928 (Ct.Cl.1977); Liberty Mutual Insurance Co. v. Davis, 52

operation of law of the original creditor's position to the subrogee. Subrogation is derived from Roman and civil law,[2] but there is some doubt as to how much those systems have influenced the Anglo-American development of the doctrine.[3] It is an equitable doctrine designed to prevent unjust enrichment and is closely related to the principles of suretyship and restitution.[4] Like the doctrine of constructive trust,[5] it is a device designed "to compel ultimate payment of a debt by one who in justice, equity and good conscience should pay it."[6] The facts and circumstances of each case determine whether the doctrine is applicable.[7]

The question of subrogation arises in mortgage law in three different types of situations: (1) When a person who is obligated as a surety for a mortgage debt pays that debt; (2) when a person pays a debt for which he is not liable for the purpose of protecting some interest of his own in the property; and (3) when a person makes a payment voluntarily or at the request of the principal obligor to pay off another mortgage or encumbrance on the property. Subrogation in the first two situations has been categorized as legal subrogation and is said to arise by operation of law.[8] Subrogation in the third example is called conventional subrogation and is sometimes said to arise from contract, the agreement between the subrogee and either the debtor or the creditor,[9]

Ohio Misc. 26, 6 O.O.3d 108, 368 N.E.2d 336, (1977). Rights of the original mortgagee against guarantors are included; U.S. Steel Homes Credit Corp. v. South Shore Development Corp., 277 Pa.Super. 308, 419 A.2d 785 (1980).

But see First Vermont Bank v. Kalomiris, 138 Vt. 481, 418 A.2d 43 (1980), noted 7 Vt.L.Rev. 71, 82 (1982), in which the court refused to give the subrogee (a junior mortgagee) the benefit of the decree of strict foreclosure which had been granted to the senior mortgagee; the subrogee was required to reforeclose.

2. United States v. Commonwealth of Pa., Department of Highways, 349 F.Supp. 1370 (E.D.Pa.1972); D.W. Jaquays & Co. v. First Security Bank, 101 Ariz. 301, 419 P.2d 85 (1966); 24 Va.L.Rev. 771 (1938).

3. Marasinghe, An Historical Introduction to the Doctrine of Subrogation: The Early History of the Doctrine, 10 Val.U.L. Rev. part 1 at 45, part 2 at 275 (1975–76); Jones, Roman Law Bases of Suretyship in Some Modern Civil Codes, 52 Tulane L.R. Rev. 129 (1977); Comment, 31 Mich.L.Rev. 826 (1933).

4. Rock River Lumber Corp. v. Universal Mortgage Corp. of Wisconsin, 82 Wis.2d 235, 262 N.W.2d 114 (1978); Reese v. AMF-Whitely, 420 F.Supp. 985 (D.Neb.1976); Garrity v. Rural Mutual Insurance Co., 77 Wis.2d 537, 253 N.W.2d 512 (1977).

5. Cole v. Morris, 409 S.W.2d 668 (Mo. 1966). "The doctrines of subrogation and constructive trust are analogous. The creditor is regarded as holding his claim against the principal debtor and his securities therefor in trust for the subrogee." New York Casualty Co. v. Sinclair Refining Co., 108 F.2d 65, 71 (10th Cir.1939). See First National Bank v. Huff, 441 So.2d 1317 (Miss.1983).

6. Skauge v. Mountain States Telephone & Telegraph Co., 172 Mont. 521, 565 P.2d 628 (1977).

7. Mellon Bank v. Barclays American/Business Credit, Inc., 527 F.Supp. 251 (W.D.Pa.1981); Cagle, Inc. v. Sammons, 198 Neb. 595, 254 N.W.2d 398 (1977); U.S. Fidelity and Guaranty Co. v. Maryland Casualty Co., 186 Kan. 637, 352 P.2d 70 (1960); Burgoon v. Lavezzo, 92 F.2d 726, 113 A.L.R. 944 (D.C.Cir.1937).

8. See Harrington v. Harrington, 427 A.2d 1314 (R.I.1981), at n. 3; Skauge v. Mountain States Telephone & Telegraph Co., 172 Mont. 521, 565 P.2d 628 (1977); Lawyers' Title Guaranty Fund v. Sanders, 571 P.2d 454 (Okl.1977).

9. Hoppe v. Phoenix Homes, Inc., 211 Neb. 419, 318 N.W.2d 878 (1982); Rock River Lumber Corp. v. Universal Mortgage Corp. of Wisconsin, 82 Wis.2d 235, 262 N.W.2d 114 (1978); Lentz v. Stoflet, 280 Mich. 446, 273 N.W. 763 (1937).

but there is serious doubt that its real basis is contractual.[10] An agreement between the debtor and the person claiming subrogation clearly does not in itself transfer the right of the creditor to such person.[11] And if there is really a contract between the subrogee and the creditor, the result may be an assignment or an agreement to assign enforceable in equity, of either a legal or an equitable chose in action—a perfectly valid idea, but not a part of the doctrine of subrogation.[12] In some cases equity will take into consideration the presence of an agreement in determining whether to allow subrogation,[13] and the extent of the right will be determined by the agreement.[14] But unless an assignment has been executed,[15] subrogation is always by operation of law.

"From our study we may draw the following conclusions: (1) That where a lender, in no way related to the property nor in any way required to protect an interest, advanced the money to pay off a lien, it could not be a case for legal subrogation, but must, if anything, come within the principles of conventional subrogation. (2) That in conventional subrogation there must be an agreement, express or implied, that the lender whose money pays off a lien will have the same status as the lien his money releases to the extent of the debt secured by that lien. (3) That equity applies the doctrine of subrogation in such cases, not in exacting a performance of the contract, but as a matter of doing justice under the circumstances; the so-called agreement only being of value showing such a situation where the doctrine should be applied in order to do justice and as evidence that the lender was not a volunteer." Martin v. Hickenlooper, 90 Utah 150, 179, 59 P.2d 1139, 1152, 107 A.L.R. 762 (1936), rehearing denied 90 Utah 185, 61 P.2d 307 (1936).

See Restatement, Second, Restitution § 31 comment c. (Tent. Draft No. 2, 1984).

10. "[S]ubrogation arises, not as a direct legal consequence of the contract of the parties, but rather as a matter of doing justice after a balancing of the equities, and * * * the agreement is merely a consideration—although an important consideration—in determining whether subrogation is appropriate." Rock River Lumber v. Universal Mortgage Corp. of Wis., 82 Wis.2d 235, 241, 262 N.W.2d 114, 117 (1978). "Even when there is an agreement to subrogate, the so-called right of subrogation is not one inherent in the contract, but arises in equity and can therefore be withheld or applied as in equity seems meet according to sound judicial discretion, which is another way of saying, according to the dictates of justice. The doctrine of subrogation has its roots in the soil of justice and equity, and not in contract." Martin v. Hickenlooper, 90 Utah 150, 161, 59 P.2d 1139, 1143, 107 A.L.R. 762 (1936), rehearing denied 90 Utah 185, 61 P.2d 307 (1936).

11. "Even where a definite agreement for subrogation is shown, therefore, subrogation will be denied where it would lead to an uncontemplated and inequitable result." Rock River Lumber Corp. v. Universal Mortgage, note 10 supra, at 117.

12. The difference between subrogation and assignments is illustrated by the question discussed, § 10.8, infra, as to whether one who is entitled to subrogation may compel an assignment.

13. "In the case of *conventional* subrogation, equity says: Where the lender of money did it with the intention and understanding that he was to be placed in the position of the creditor whose debt he paid, but without taking an assignment of the credit, equity, where no innocent parties will suffer or no right has intervened, will treat the matter as if an assignment had been executed." Martin v. Hickenlooper, 90 Utah 150, 157, 59 P.2d 1139, 1141, 107 A.L.R. 762 (1936) rehearing denied 90 Utah 185, 61 P.2d 307 (1936). See note 10, supra. Note, 21 Col.L.Rev. 470 (1971).

14. Millers Mutual Fire Insurance Co. of Tex. v. Farmers Elevator Mutual Insurance Co., 408 F.2d 776 (5th Cir.1969); Tennessee Farmers' Mutual Insurance Co. v. Rader, 219 Tenn. 384, 410 S.W.2d 171 (1966).

15. The assignment may be informal; see Tilden v. Beckmann, 203 Neb. 293, 278 N.W.2d 581 (1979). In such cases the line between conventional subrogation and assignment may be hard to distinguish.

WESTLAW REFERENCES
di legal subrogation
digest(mortgage /p subrogat***)

§ 10.2   Payment as Surety

Where a principal obligor and a surety are liable on a debt, if the surety pays the debt, he is clearly entitled to be subrogated to the rights of the creditor against the principal obligor.[1] Thus if a mortgagor sells the property to a grantee who assumes the mortgage, and the mortgagor must later pay off the mortgage, he is entitled to be subrogated to all rights of the mortgagee both against the assuming grantee personally and against the mortgaged property.[2] Similarly, if he sells the property subject to the mortgage and is forced to pay, he is subrogated to the creditor's security interest in the property now owned by the grantee—the property being regarded as the principal and the mortgagor the surety.[3] The suretyship relation can run the other way as well: Suppose the purchaser buys for the full value of the property, with the mortgagor being bound to pay off the mortgage. Should the purchaser be forced to pay, he is entitled to subrogation to the mortgagee's claim against the mortgagor.[4]

§ 10.2

1. Barnes v. Hampton, 198 Neb. 151, 252 N.W.2d 138 (1977); Langeveld v. L.R. Z.H., 74 N.J. 45, 376 A.2d 931 (1977). Note that the issuer of an irrevocable letter of credit is not a surety and is not subrogated to the mortgage rights of the letter's beneficiary; see Merchants Bank v. Economic Enterprises, Inc., 44 B.R. 230 (Bkrtcy.Conn. 1984).

2. First Vermont Bank v. Kalomiris, 138 Vt. 481, 418 A.2d 43 (1980); Konoff v. Lantini, 111 R.I. 691, 306 A.2d 176 (1973); French v. May, 484 S.W.2d 420 (Tex.Civ. App.1972); Malone v. United States, 326 F.Supp. 106 (N.D.Miss.1971) affirmed 455 F.2d 502 (5th Cir.1972); Toler v. Baldwin County Savings & Loan Association, 286 Ala. 320, 239 So.2d 751 (1970); Sanders v. Lackey, 59 Tenn.App. 207, 439 S.W.2d 610 (1968); Finance Co. of America v. Heller, 247 Md. 714, 234 A.2d 611 (1967). See also Edwards v. Columbia, S.C. Teachers Federal Credit Union, 276 S.C. 89, 275 S.E.2d 879 (1981) and Stanford v. Aulick, 124 Ariz. 487, 605 P.2d 465 (1979), where the one of the original mortgagors died, and her credit life insurance policy paid part of the loan.

3. "This relation between the mortgagor and his grantee does not deprive the obligee from enforcing the bond against the obligor. He is entitled to his debt, and has a right to avail himself of all his securities. Equity however requires that the obligor, on the payment of the debt out of his own funds, should be subrogated to the rights of the obligee, so that he can reimburse himself by a recourse to the mortgaged premises for that purpose. This cannot prejudice the creditor, and it is clearly equitable as between the debtor and the owner of the land." Johnson v. Zink, 51 N.Y. 333, 336–37 (1873); Howard v. Burns, 279 Ill. 256, 116 N.E. 703 (1917); Woodbury v. Swan, 58 N.H. 380 (1878); University State Bank v. Steeves, 85 Wash. 55, 147 P. 645, 2 A.L.R. 237 (1915), accord.

4. United States Steel Homes Credit Corp. v. South Shore Development Corp., 277 Pa.Super. 308, 419 A.2d 785 (1980); Simpson v. Ennis, 114 Ga. 202, 39 S.E. 853 (1901); Hazle v. Bondy, 173 Ill. 302, 50 N.E. 671 (1898); Wadsworth v. Lyon, 93 N.Y. 201, 45 Am.R. 190 (1883); Hudson v. Dismukes, 77 Va. 242 (1883). See Martynes & Associates v. Devonshire Square Apartments, 680 P.2d 246 (Colo.App.1984) and Cox v. Wooten Brothers Farms, Inc., 271 Ark. 735, 610 S.W.2d 278 (1981) for analogous situations.

The concept in the text is one possible explanation for MGIC Financial Corp. v. H.A. Briggs Co., 24 Wash.App. 1, 600 P.2d 573 (1979). See § 5.20 supra at note 6.

It is equally clear that a principal obligor who pays is not entitled to subrogation against a person acting as surety. Such a payment would be merely the performance of his own duty. So neither an assuming grantee [5] nor a mortgagor who had agreed to pay the mortgage to protect his grantee [6] would be entitled to subrogation upon paying the mortgage. A grantee subject to the mortgage who pays cannot have subrogation as against the mortgagor unless the amount of payment exceeds the value of the land, for up to that extent, clearly, he is paying on behalf of the principal, the land.[7] Whether he may have subrogation as to the excess of the debt he pays over the value of the land would seem to be governed by the same principles previously discussed in connection with merger.[8] It is believed he should not. The amount of the debt was included in the original purchase price of the land. Even though the agreement imposed no personal duty to pay, nevertheless the payment of the mortgage was a condition to his retention of the land and he should not be able, by paying it, to recover any portion of it from his vendor, the mortgagor, through the help of subrogation or otherwise. The fact that at the time the mortgage has to be paid the land is no longer equal in value to the amount of the debt would not justify him being able to recover from his seller, in the face of his original bargain, any excess paid over its then value.

Where the debt is in the form of a negotiable instrument, the UCC may arguably prevent subrogation in any case in which the ownership of the instrument passes into the hands of its maker; the Code (§ 3–601) indicates that when this occurs the debt no longer exists. However, the draftsmen of the Code almost certainly did not intend to affect subrogation rights by this provision, and it should not be so read.[9]

 WESTLAW REFERENCES

mortgage /p surety /p liable liability pay! /p subrogat***
guarant***

5. Dodds v. Spring, 174 Cal. 412, 163 P. 351 (1917); Drury v. Holden, 121 Ill. 130, 13 N.E. 547 (1887); Lydon v. Campbell, 204 Mass. 580, 91 N.E. 151, 134 Am.St.Rep. 702 (1910); cf. Lackawanna Trust & Safe Deposit Co. v. Gomeringer, 236 Pa. 179, 84 A. 757 (1912). See 15 Col.L.Rev. 171 (1915).

6. Wadsworth v. Williams, 100 Mass. 126 (1868); Byles v. Kellogg, 67 Mich. 318, 34 N.W. 671 (1887); Hooper v. Henry, 31 Minn. 264, 17 N.W. 476 (1883).

7. Drury v. Holden, 121 Ill. 130, 13 N.E. 547 (1887); Northwestern National Bank v. Stone, 97 Iowa 183, 66 N.W. 91 (1896); In re Wisner's Estate, 20 Mich. 442 (1870); Guernsey v. Kendall, 55 Vt. 201 (1880). Cf. Fortier v. Fortier, 200 So.2d 901 (La.App. 1967), writ refused 251 La. 59, 202 So.2d 661, (1967), appeal after remand 221 So.2d 653, (1969), application refused 254 La. 292, 223 So.2d 412 (Sup.1969); See 5 Hous.L. Rev. (1967) for catalogue of surety-principal relationships in all types of sales of encumbered property.

8. See § 6.14, supra.

9. In Best Fertilizers of Arizona, Inc. v. Burns, 116 Ariz. 492, 570 P.2d 179 (1977), subrogation was denied where the mortgagor-maker paid the holder of the note and took an assignment of it after an assuming grantee had defaulted. The court held that under the UCC all liability on the note was discharged when the maker reacquired the note and therefore the mortgage was released. See § 5.9 for summary of the case and authors' view that it was decided erroneously.

§ 10.3   Payment to Protect an Interest—Contribution

Another instance in which the right of subrogation is not questioned is where a person, although not personally bound to pay, is compelled to do so in order to protect some interest of his own.[1] This right may apply to a variety of interests in property subject to a mortgage.[2] Following are some examples:

1. A junior mortgagee may pay off a prior mortgage and be subrogated to all rights under it against the mortgagor.[3]

2. A wife who has joined in the mortgage, thus subjecting her dower interest to it, may pay off the entire mortgage but keep the mortgage alive through subrogation as against the other owners who have been benefitted by her payment.[4]

3. A remainderman may pay off the mortgage, where both the life interest and remainder were mortgaged, and be subrogated as against the life tenant.[5]

4. A creditor of the mortgagor who has levied an attachment or execution on the redemption interest may pay off the debt and have subrogation.

5. A cotenant of the mortgaged property whose cotenancy is subject to the mortgage is entitled to pay and be subrogated for the purpose of obtaining contribution from his fellow cotenant.[6]

§ 10.3

1. Martynes & Associates v. Devonshire Square Apartments, 680 P.2d 246 (Colo. App.1984); Harrington v. Harrington, ___ R.I. ___, 427 A.2d 1314 (1981) at n. 3; Cagle, Inc. v. Sammons, 198 Neb. 595, 254 N.W.2d 398 (1977); Cobb v. Osman, 83 Nev. 415, 433 P.2d 259 (1967). See cases cited § 10.2 note 4, supra.

2. See Hope, Officiousness, 15 Corn.L.Q. 25, 205, 239 (1930), for a survey of such interests. See also 93 A.L.R. 89 (1934) for a collection of authorities on the right to compel an assignment by one who has an interest to protect and pays.

In In re Keil's Estate, 51 Del. (1 Storey) 351, 145 A.2d 563, 76 A.L.R.2d 996 (1958), reargument denied 51 Del. (1 Storey) 351, 146 A.2d 398 (1958), discussed in 58 Mich. L.Rev. 137, 1959, 73 Harv.L.Rev. 425, the surviving mortgagor of entireties property given to secure a joint debt, the proceeds of which were used to improve the property, was held entitled to contribution against the estate of the deceased tenant.

See also Dolan v. Borregard, 466 So.2d 11 (Fla.App.1985) (senior mortgagee may pay off *junior* lien, in order to make the senior

mortgage more marketable, and will be subrogated.)

3. Rock River Lumber v. Universal Mortgage Corp. of Wisconsin, 82 Wis.2d 235, 262 N.W.2d 114 (1978); In the Matter of Forester, 529 F.2d 310 (9th Cir.1976).

4. Swaine v. Perine, N.Y., 5 Johns. Ch. 482, 9 Am.Dec. 318 (1821), Osborne, Cases Property Security, 2nd Ed., 546; cf. Gibson v. Crehore, 22 Mass. (5 Pick.) 146 (1827); Fitcher v. Griffiths, 216 Mass. 174, 103 N.E. 471 (1913); Harrington v. Harrington note 1 supra.

5. See Mosely v. Marshall, 22 N.Y. 545 (1860), life tenant; Wunderle v. Ellis, 212 Pa. 618, 62 A. 106 (1905), tenant for years pays; cf. also Federal Land Bank v. Newsom, 175 Miss. 114, 166 So. 346 (1936), discussed, 50 Harv.L.Rev. 534 (1937).

6. Aiello v. Aiello, 268 Md. 513, 302 A.2d 189 (1973); Taylor v. Jones, 285 Ala. 353, 232 So.2d 601 (1970); A.F.O., Inc. v. Brockett, 257 Cal.App.2d 40, 64 Cal.Rptr. 771 (1967); Eloff v. Reisch, 14 Wis.2d 519, 111 N.W.2d 578 (1961) holds that right of subrogation exists even where joint tenants are husband and wife. In Walters v. Walters, 1 Wash.App. 849, 466 P.2d 174

6. A lessee may pay off a mortgage debt to prevent foreclosure and may be subrogated to the rights of the holder of the lien.[7]

Since the payor, as well as the other parties holding interests in the property, benefits by the payment, he does not have a claim for the entire amount paid. He will be entitled to recover a ratable contribution from the other parties proportional to their shares of the value of the interest in the property from which the mortgage has been removed.[8] The problem of evaluation of the interest is not always easy although the right to contribution is well-recognized.[9]

 WESTLAW REFERENCES

mortgage /p subrogat*** /p pay! contribut*** /p junior second
wife husband spouse remainderman creditor cotenant lessee

§ 10.4 The Volunteer Rule

Courts repeatedly state that a volunteer is not entitled to subrogation.[1] A person who is obligated as a surety or who pays to protect his own interest is not a volunteer.[2] Even a moral obligation has been

(1970), subrogation was denied where one tenant in common was made primarily liable for obligations by divorce decree.

7. G.B. Seely's Son, Inc. v. Fulton-Edison, Inc., 52 A.D.2d 575, 382 N.Y.S.2d 516 (1976); Dominion Financial Corp. v. 275 Washington St. Corp., 64 Misc.2d 1044, 316 N.Y.S.2d 803 (1970).

8. "What rule should then govern the parties in adjusting the common burdens resting upon the property, in different parts of which they have respectively acquired an interest? We think the parties should contribute to the payment of the burden in proportion to the value of the property in which they are respectively interested." Tarbell v. Durant, 61 Vt. 516, 519, 17 A. 44, 45 (1889). See Carpenter v. Koons, 20 Pa. 222 (1852). Cf. McLaughlin v. Estate of Curtis, 27 Wis. 644 (1871).

9. E.g., the evaluation of a dower interest. See Swaine v. Perine, supra note 4. Similarly where the question arises between a life tenant and remainderman. "A tenant for life is bound to keep down the current interest, * * * but not to pay any part of the principal. Now if, for example, there is a tenant for life, and a remainderman in fee of an estate, subject to a mortgage which is due and must be paid at once to save foreclosure, and the remainderman, to save the estate, pays the mortgage, he is not obliged to take the share of the tenant for life in annual installments of interest to continue as long as he shall live. He is entitled, as equita-

ble assignee of the mortgagee, to immediate payment; and the sum which he thus has a right to claim is whatever the present worth of an annuity equal to the amount of the annual interest would be, computed for the number of years which the tenant will live." 2 Washburn, Real Prop., 6th Ed., § 1142. See also Todd's Executor v. First National Bank, 173 Ky. 60, 67, 190 S.W. 468 (1917); Damm v. Damm, 109 Mich. 619, 67 N.W. 984, 63 Am. St.Rep. 601 (1896); Tindall v. Peterson, 71 Neb. 160, 98 N.W. 688, 99 N.W. 659, 8 Ann. Cas. 721 (1904); Moore v. Simonson, 27 Or. 117, 39 P. 1105 (1895); Wilder's Executrix v. Wilder, 75 Vt. 178, 53 A. 1072 (1903); 3 Pomeroy, Eq.Jur., 4th Ed., § 1223. Cf. Leach v. Hall, 95 Iowa, 611, 619, 64 N.W. 790 (1895).

§ 10.4

1. Cox v. Wooten Brothers Farms, Inc., 271 Ark. 735, 610 S.W.2d 278 (1981); Lawyers Title Insurance Corp. v. Edmar Construction Co., 294 A.2d 865 (D.C.App.1972); Southwest Title & Trust Co. v. Norman Lumber Co., 441 P.2d 430 (Okl.1968); Zapata v. Torres, 464 S.W.2d 926 (Tex.Civ. App.1971).

2. Cagle, Inc. v. Sammons, 198 Neb. 595, 254 N.W.2d 398 (1977); Cobb v. Osman, 83 Nev. 415, 433 P.2d 259 (1967); First National City Bank v. United States 537 F.2d 426 (Ct.Cl.1976); Indemnity Insurance Co. v. Lane Contracting Corp., 227 F.Supp. 143 (D.Neb.1964).

considered sufficiently compelling to entitle the payor to subrogation,[3] but one who pays with no obligation but merely to preserve his goodwill will be held to be a volunteer.[4] Where the payment was made pursuant to an agreement or understanding with the debtor or creditor, the court may deny subrogation on the ground that the payor was a volunteer unless the particular agreement is one which falls within the limits of "conventional subrogation" as recognized in that jurisdiction.[5] It is therefore necessary to determine just which agreements will bring about subrogation. For example, it is sometimes held that the person paying the debt must have believed that he would receive the prior security.[6] If the payor was denied his security by fraud or was induced by fraud, he is not a volunteer.[7]

The limits as well as the rationale of the volunteer rule are a matter of dispute. It has been asserted that, whenever courts for any reason deny subrogation, they characterize the unsuccessful applicant as a volunteer.[8] Even when the rule is used with more discrimination it has sometimes been unclear whether subrogation was denied because the court found that the plaintiff did not intend any legal consequences to flow from his act, e.g., he intended a gift, or that his intervention was unsolicited and therefore officious.[9] A critical examination of the reasons [10] offered for using the rule to deny subrogation on payment of a creditor by a third person has revealed them to be so lacking in force

3. Springham v. Kordek, 55 Md.App. 449, 462 A.2d 567 (1983); Commercial Standard Insurance Co. v. American Employers Insurance Co., 209 F.2d 60 (6th Cir. 1954).

4. Lawyers Title Insurance Corp. v. Edmar Construction Co., 294 A.2d 865 (D.C.App.1972).

5. "[T]he facts or circumstances from which the agreement will be implied vary in the different courts, some requiring evidence from which an actual understanding between the parties may be inferred, while others hold that payment under such circumstances as show that the lender 'supposed' or 'intended' to get security of the same dignity as that released by his payment is sufficient; and some go as far as holding that such intention may be inferred from the mere fact that the money was advanced for the purpose of paying off another lien." Martin v. Hickenlooper, 90 Utah 150, 179, 59 P.2d 1139, 1152, 107 A.L.R. 762 (1936), rehearing denied 90 Utah 185, 61 P.2d 307 (1936).

6. Metropolitan Life Insurance Co. v. First Security Bank, 94 Idaho 489, 491 P.2d 1261 (1971), rehearing denied 94 Idaho 527, 492 P.2d 1400 (1972); Southwest Title & Trust Co. v. Norman Lumber Co., 441 P.2d 430 (Okl.1968).

7. Rees v. Craighead Investment Co., 251 Ark. 336, 472 S.W.2d 92 (1971); Bunge Corp. v. St. Louis Terminal Field Warehouse Co., 295 F.Supp. 1231 (N.D.Miss. 1969).

8. Pomeroy, Equity Juris., 4th ed., § 2348n.

"A good deal of the confusion concerning the volunteer rule has arisen because courts have carelessly termed the payor a volunteer in cases involving a situation where payment would ordinarily be considered not voluntary but subrogation is denied because of a superior intervening equity. It is submitted that these cases have misapplied the term and must be sharply distinguished." 32 Minn.L.Rev. 183, 185 (1948).

9. See 31 Mich.L.Rev. 826, 830 (1933).

10. The three basic reasons for not permitting subrogation on the ground that the person asking it is a volunteer are "(1) he is able to elect whether he is to pay or not, and knowing the facts he should protect himself by contract, (2) a debt paid without any agreement to keep it alive is extinguished, and (3) one cannot become a creditor of another against the other's will." 32 Minn.L.Rev. 183 (1948), citing Hope, Officiousness, 15 Corn.L.Q. 25 (1929), and note 24 Va.L.Rev. 771, 776 (1938).

as to make reasonable the suggestion that, in order for such a payment to be officious, it must be unnecessary and confer no benefit.[11] Because of the variety and unpredictability of its application [12] the voluntary payment test is of little value. Except in cases in which the payor clearly intended a gift, it should be discarded.

 WESTLAW REFERENCES
mortgage obligation debt /p subrogat*** /p volunteer

§ 10.5 Loans to Pay the Mortgage

The problem of the volunteer rule and subrogation in mortgage law has occurred most frequently in the case of lenders whose money is used to pay off a mortgage or other encumbrance. Where the payor already holds a lien junior to that of the creditor being paid off, the payment obviously protects the payor's own position and the courts have no difficulty giving subrogation.[1] In other cases whether subrogation will be given depends both on the terms of the arrangement and the attitude of the particular court toward subrogation.[2] Subrogation of the lender is based on the general principle that one who advances money upon a justifiable expectation of receiving security is entitled to the security.[3] When the question is one of the lender's rights as against the parties to the mortgage, the outcome depends on whether the lender relied only on the general credit of the mortgagor,[4] or whether the loan was made on the understanding that the lender was

---

11. Hope, Officiousness, 15 Cornell L.Q. 25, 205 (1929). A comment on this as a criterion stated, "Indeed, there would seem to be no great difference in principle in the case where a person theretofore unconnected with a transaction purchases a debt, which he can obviously do against the express will of the debtor, and where he pays the debt absent any intention to make a gift." 24 Va.L.Rev. 771, 776 (1938).

12. "All courts subscribe to the rule that subrogation will not be permitted a mere 'volunteer'. But there is no general agreement as to the personification of the word. A minority of courts is prone to call everyone a volunteer who was not in the position of a surety or who did not have some previous interest to protect in the subject matter in question. At the other extreme, the liberal view leads to the result that the only volunteer would be one who, without invitation from any other party and purely as a philanthropist, relieved another from an obligation." Note, 48 Yale L.J. 683, 686 (1939).

§ 10.5

1. First Vermont Bank v. Kalomiris, 138 Vt. 481, 418 A.2d 43 (1980), noted 7 Vt. L.Rev. 71, 82 (1982).

2. See Burgoon v. Lavezzo, 68 App.D.C. 20, 92 F.2d 726, 113 A.L.R. 944 (1937); Martin v. Hickenlooper, 90 Utah 150, 59 P.2d 1139, 107 A.L.R. 762 (1936), rehearing denied 90 Utah 185, 61 P.2d 307 (1936); Means v. United Fidelity Life Insurance Co., 550 S.W.2d 302 (Tex.Civ.App.1977), error refused n.r.e. Some cases require that the payoff be made at the debtor's instance; see Collateral Investment Co. v. Pilgrim, 421 So.2d 1274 (Ala.Civ.App.1982).

3. Leonard v. Brazosport Bank, 628 S.W.2d 216 (Tex.App.1982), error refused n.r.e.; Rock River Lumber Corp. v. Universal Mortgage Corp. of Wisconsin, 82 Wis.2d 235, 262 N.W.2d 114 (1978).

4. Southwest Title & Trust Co. v. Norman Lumber Co., 441 P.2d 430 (Okl.1968); Citizens State Bank v. Pittsburg County Broadcasting Co., 271 P.2d 725 (Okl.1954), commented on by Updike, Mortgages, in 1954 Annual Survey of American Law, 30 N.Y.U.L.Rev. 805, 809 (1955), followed this test in a chattel mortgage case.

to have the benefit of the existing mortgage or a mortgage having at least equal rank with that which was paid.[5]

Even if the lender pays off a prior encumbrance and receives a void or defective mortgage, he will be subrogated to the discharged encumbrance.[6] Subrogation has also been invoked where the loan which pays off the old mortgage is on the faith of a promise of a new mortgage which the owner refuses to execute,[7] or an oral agreement to convey title of the land to the lender.[8] Going beyond these are cases in which the money is loaned and used for the express purpose of paying off an encumbrance but the expectation of security does not relate to the particular property freed from the prior lien.[9] Finally, the most liberal cases allow subrogation simply where money is loaned and used for paying off an encumbrance.[10]

While lenders who have advanced money to pay the claims of laborers and suppliers on construction projects have sometimes been subrogated to their claims,[11] other cases have denied them subrogation

---

5. Hughes Co. v. Callahan, 181 Ark. 733, 27 S.W.2d 509 (1930); Home Owners Loan Corporation v. Collins, 120 N.J.Eq. 266, 184 A. 621 (1936); Federal Union Life Insurance Co. v. Deitsch, 127 Ohio St. 505, 189 N.E. 440 (1933); Martin v. Hickenlooper, 90 Utah 150, 59 P.2d 1139, 107 A.L.R. 762 (1936), rehearing denied 90 Utah 185, 61 P.2d 307 (1936); discussed in notes, 36 Mich.L.Rev. 151 (1937); 6 Fordham L.Rev. 138 (1937); 107 A.L.R. 785 (1937); Federal Land Bank of Baltimore v. Joynes, 179 Va. 394, 18 S.E.2d 917 (1942); Home Owners Loan Corporation of Washington, D.C. v. Dougherty, 226 Wis. 8, 275 N.W. 363 (1937). Cf. Boley v. Daniel, 72 Fla. 121, 72 So. 644, L.R.A.1917A, 734 (1916), denying recovery because lender did not stipulate for the original mortgage, only a "first lien." Where a lender advanced money to pay a valid encumbrance on a homestead, "under circumstances from which an understanding is to be implied that at least part of the advancement made is to be secured by a first lien on the land encumbered," he was subrogated to rights of prior encumbrancer which were superior to homestead rights and was allowed to foreclose the homestead. Means v. United Fidelity Life Insurance Co., 550 S.W.2d 302, 309 (Tex.Civ.App.1977).

In Davis v. Johnson, 241 Ga. 436, 246 S.E.2d 297 (1978), a bank made a new mortgage loan, the proceeds of which were used to pay off an old loan to it. It was held subrogated to its own rights!

6. Union Savings Bank of Patchogue v. Dudinee, 40 Misc.2d 155, 242 N.Y.S.2d 692 (1963); Means v. United Fidelity Life Insurance Co., note 4 supra.

7. Smith v. Sprague, 244 Mich. 577, 222 N.W. 207 (1928); Baker v. Baker, 2 S.Dak. 261, 49 N.W. 1064, 39 Am.St.Rep. 776 (1891); see 21 Cal.L.Rev. 471 (1921); 31 Mich.L.Rev. 826, 835 (1933).

8. Dobbs v. Bowling, 339 So.2d 985 (Miss.1976).

9. In Elmora & West End Building & Loan Association v. Dancy, 108 N.J.Eq. 542, 155 A. 796 (1931), commented on in 45 Harv.L.Rev. 390 (1931), M loaned the widow of his mortgagor, A, money, part of which was used to pay off the mortgage held by him, taking as security a mortgage on her dower interest in the property. M marked the mortgage "paid" and sent it to his solicitor for cancellation but it was never cancelled of record. Before the new debt was paid the widow died, thus extinguishing the security. M sued to foreclose on his original mortgage, and the land was sold. A's heirs petitioned to open the decree and set aside the sale. Held, that M was entitled to foreclose the original mortgage to the extent that the money borrowed from him was applied thereto.

10. Chrisman v. Daniel, 134 Neb. 326, 278 N.W. 565 (1938); see Martin v. Hickenlooper, 90 Utah, 150, 170, 178, 59 P.2d 1139, 1148, 1152, 107 A.L.R. 762 (1936), rehearing denied 90 Utah 185, 61 P.2d 307 (1936); 36 Mich.L.Rev. 151, 152 (1937).

11. Contractor who paid materialmen and laborers was subrogated to their claims under the material payment bond in Cagle, Inc. v. Sammons, 198 Neb. 595, 254 N.W.2d 398 (1977).

rights on the ground that the mechanics lien statutes were not intended to protect them.[12]

WESTLAW REFERENCES
subrogat*** /p mortgage* encumb! incumb! advance! /p prior*** junior senior second*** /p reliance rel*** benefit***

§ 10.6 Loans to Pay the Mortgage—Subrogation Against Intervening Interests

A more difficult question is whether the lender who has loaned money to pay off an encumbrance will be subrogated to the encumbrance when there are intervening junior liens on the property. Since the basis for subrogation in this context is the lender's justified expectation of receiving security, actual knowledge of the intervening lien will bar subrogation.[1] Where there is constructive notice, the courts are divided.[2] The better view is that constructive notice should be disregarded, since it is irrelevant to the question whether the lender actually expected to get priority of security in the property.[3]

Where the lender's ignorance is a result of his own negligence, many courts will consider that factor in balancing the equities between

12. "The object of the Legislature was to secure to a very meritorious but helpless class of persons the payment of the wages of their toil, and to that end to give them, personally, a paramount lien on the assets of the employer. It did not contemplate giving to creditors from whom the company might borrow money on its own credit with which to pay its workmen, such a lien or the assets for their reimbursement." Board of Educ. of City of Bayonne v. Kolman, 111 N.J.Super. 585, 270 A.2d 64 (1970) citing In re North River Construction Co., 38 N.J.Eq. 433, 437–438 (Ch. 1884), affirmed 40 N.J.Eq. 340 (E & A 1885).

§ 10.6

1. See Restatement, Second, Restitution § 31 comment f & Illustration 10 (Tent. Draft No. 2, 1984); 70 A.L.R. 1396, 1414 (1931). This may be the basis for denial of subrogation in Plymouth Fertilizer Co. v. Pitt-Greene Production Credit Association, 58 N.C.App. 207, 292 S.E.2d 732 (1982). But see Providence Institution for Savings v. Sims, 441 S.W.2d 516 (Tex.1969). "We hold that under these circumstances neither actual nor constructive knowledge of the intervening lien will defeat the right of subrogation to which the debtor agreed in the later deed of trust." Id. at 520.

2. Id.; Castelman Construction Co. v. Pennington, 222 Tenn. 82, 432 S.W.2d 669 (1968); Peterman-Donnelly Engineers &

Contractors Corp. v. First National Bank, 2 Ariz.App. 321, 408 P.2d 841 (1965). See Pipola v. Chicco, 274 F.2d 909 (2d Cir.1960), granting subrogation; Cheswick v. Weaver, 280 S.W.2d 942 (Tex.Civ.App.1955), subrogation denied; Carl H. Peterson Co. v. Zero Estates, 261 N.W.2d 346 (Minn.1977), subrogation denied even where the lender refinanced a prior mortgage held by himself.

3. Mutual Life Insurance Co. v. Grissett, 500 F.Supp. 159 (M.D.Ala.1980); Davis v. Johnson, 241 Ga. 436, 246 S.E.2d 297 (1978); Potter v. United States, 111 F.Supp. 585 (D.R.I.1953). Cf. Collateral Investment Co. v. Pilgrim, 421 So.2d 1274 (Ala.Civ.App.1982) (subrogee may not take priority over mechanics liens, where it had constructive notice from work in progress). Cf. Blaylock v. Dollar Inns of America, Inc., 548 S.W.2d 924 (1977), modified 576 S.W.2d 794 (Tex.1978) (subrogee given priority over intervening mechanics lien). See Comment, 20 So.Tex.L.J. 326, 330–32 (1979). See 48 Yale L.J. 683, 688 (1939); 21 Col.L.Rev. 471, 472, (1921) n. 18. But cf. 31 Mich.L.Rev. 826, 834 (1933).

See 21 Col.L.Rev. 471, (1921) "Constructive notice, which is intended to protect the rights of an equitable lienor, cannot be invoked to increase those rights by imputing to the new mortgagee a knowledge of facts and a consequent expectation which he did not in fact possess." Id. at 472 n. 18.

the lender and the parties holding intervening liens.[4] Some courts distinguish between negligence that is inexcusable and negligence that is only ordinary.[5] In connection with the negligence issue courts will consider whether the intervening lienors will be prejudiced by the subrogation.[6] One court held, for example, that intervening lienors would be prejudiced simply because subrogation would prevent their being able to enforce their liens.[7] However, most cases have held that the junior lienors are not prejudiced unless they have changed their position in reliance of extinguishment of the debt.[8] Where the junior lienor occupies the same position he occupied before the prior lien was paid and discharged, to deny subrogation and permit the lienor to advance would give him a windfall advantage at the expense of the justifiable expectation of the lender.[9] This would defeat the purpose of

4. Negligence on the part of one seeking subrogation is of some importance when the right is wholly dependent on equitable principles. Providence Institution for Savings v. Sims, 441 S.W.2d 516 (Tex.1969). Ordinary negligence of subrogee may be taken into consideration in ascertaining whether he be entitled to equitable relief of subrogation, but "[o]rdinary negligence alone will not be held as a complete bar to subrogation where in spite of such negligence the equities are still in favor of the subrogee." Castelman Construction Co. v. Pennington, 222 Tenn. 82, 432 S.W.2d 669, 677 (1968).

5. Castelman Construction Co. v. Pennington, 222 Tenn. 82, 432 S.W.2d 669 (1968). "[A]ccording to the modern view, indiligence in searching the record will not prevent equity from applying the doctrine unless it is culpable or unjustifiable negligence." Martin v. Hickenlooper, 90 Utah 150, 178, 59 P.2d 1139, 1152, 107 A.L.R. 762 (1936), rehearing denied 90 Utah 186, 61 P.2d 307 (1936). See also Banta v. Vreeland, 15 N.J.Eq. 103, 82 Am.Dec. 269 (1862).

6. See Federal Land Bank v. Joynes, 179 Va. 394, 18 S.E.2d 917 (1942), "the negligence should be chiefly of significance when there are subsequently intervening rights involved which would be prejudiced if subrogation were allowed."

"[I]n a case where the court feels the negligence so culpable that the junior lienor should advance to the senior position in preference to the payer, it will refuse to imply an agreement for subrogation of the payer; but where no harm is done and the payer's negligence only 'ordinary,' the courts are prone to find an implied agreement. * * * That is, in a case involving no change of position by the junior lienor in reliance on the

discharge of the original first lien, the courts will strain the concept of implied intent to the breaking point in order to prevent the junior lienor from claiming a windfall and advancing to the position of first encumbrancer, whereas their real reason for giving subrogation to the payer is that they feel he has superior equities on his side." Note, 36 Mich.L.Rev. 151, 153–154 (1937).

7. Carl H. Peterson Co. v. Zero Estates, 261 N.W.2d 346 (Minn.1977).

8. Rock River Lumber v. Universal Mortgage Corp. of Wisconsin, 82 Wis.2d 235, 262 N.W.2d 114 (1978); Credit Bureau Corp. v. Beckstead, 63 Wn.2d 183, 385 P.2d 864, 866 (1963): "The doctrine however will not be applied if it would work injustice to the rights of those having equal or superior equities; nor will it be enforced against a bona fide purchaser for value without notice or one who, in good faith, has changed his position in reliance upon the act which subsequently is claimed to have been a mistake."

9. Equity Savings & Loan Association v. Chicago Title Insurance Co., 190 N.J.Super. 340, 463 A.2d 398 (1983). Where intervening lienor remains with a lien prior to all claims except a mortgage given before he began work on the project, "Equity requires that appellee be afforded that security for which he obviously bargained." Peterman-Donnelly Engineer & Contractor Corp. v. First National Bank, 2 Ariz.App. 321, 408 P.2d 841, 846 (1965). "There is no reason for advancing [the junior lienor] to the position of a senior lienor, since all he ever contracted for was a junior encumbrance." 21 Col.L.Rev. 471, 472 (1921). "His advancement to first mortgagee on extinguishment of the prior lien is a purely fortuitous benefit, to which he has no equitable or legal right." Id. at n. 20.

subrogation, which is to prevent unjust enrichment and grant an equitable result between the parties.

The volunteer rule is not an obstacle where the lender paid at the request of the mortgagor. If he has advanced money with the understanding, or under circumstances which would give rise to an understanding, that the loan would be secured by a first lien on the property, he is not a mere volunteer and should be subrogated to the prior liens his advance was made to discharge.[10]

 WESTLAW REFERENCES

366k31   &   interven! junior mechanic senior prior***   /p   lien**

§ 10.7 Payments by Grantees—Subrogation Against Intervening Interests

Where a grantee of the mortgagor assumes the payment of a prior mortgage in actual ignorance of the existence of a later incumbrance, even though it might be of record, the question arises as to whether, on paying the earlier lien, he is entitled to be subrogated to it as against the later lienors.[1] A strong line of cases permits subrogation in such a case.[2] There are, however, a considerable number of authorities that refuse it.[3]

Those denying subrogation do so on several grounds. One is that the assuming grantee has become primarily liable for the debt and the general rule applies that one paying his own debt is not entitled to subrogation. Coupled with this is the idea that by assuming the mortgagor's debt he must be regarded as having stepped into his grantor's shoes and therefore the payment has the same effect as if it had been made by the grantor before he parted with the property.[4]

10. Blaylock v. Dollar Inns of America, Inc., 548 S.W.2d 924 (Tex.Civ.App.1977). See 48 Yale L.J. 683, 686; 1933, 31 Mich.L. Rev. 826, 830 (1939). The same is true of one who pays as part of the purchase price. Burgoon v. Lavezzo, 92 F.2d 726, 113 A.L.R. 944 (C.A.D.C.1937).

§ 10.7

1. See 113 A.L.R. 958 (1925); 87 U.Pa.L. Rev. 1012 (1939); 48 Yale L.J. 683 (1939). The same question is involved if the grantee, rather than assuming the senior debt, simply discharges it as part of the purchase transaction, provided he is unaware of the existence of intervening liens. See Burgoon v. Lavezzo, 92 F.2d 726 (D.C.Cir. 1937).

2. E.g., Johnson v. Tootle, 14 Utah 482, 47 P. 1033 (1897); Capitol National Bank v. Holmes, 43 Colo. 154, 95 P. 314, 16 L.R.A.,N.S., 470, 127 Am.St.Rep. 108 (1908); Young v. Morgan, 89 Ill. 199 (1878);

Smith v. Dinsmore, 119 Ill. 656, 4 N.E. 648 (1887), recorded junior incumbrance; Federal Land Bank v. Smith, 129 Md. 233, 151 A. 420 (1930); Dixon v. Morgan, 154 Tenn. 389, 285 S.W. 558 (1926).

Compare the discussion of merger in §§ 6.15, 6.17, supra.

3. Citizens' Mercantile Co. v. Easom, 158 Ga. 604, 123 S.E. 883, 37 A.L.R. 378 (1924) noted in 38 Harv.L.Rev. 266 (1924); Goodyear v. Goodyear, 72 Iowa 329, 33 N.W. 142 (1887); Kuhn v. National Bank, 74 Kan. 456, 87 P. 551, 118 Am.St.Rep. 332 (1906); Smith v. Feltner, 259 Ky. 833, 83 S.W.2d 506 (1935).

4. Kuhn v. National Bank, 74 Kan. 456, 87 P. 551, 118 Am.St.Rep. 332 (1906); Goodyear v. Goodyear, 72 Iowa 329, 33 N.W. 142 (1887); Poole v. Kelsey, 95 Ill. App. 233 (1900). See also a similar line of reasoning in 87 U. of Pa.L.Rev. 1012 (1939).

Where the grantee assumes any junior mortgages as well as a senior mortgage, as is the case when the assumption is of "all" encumbrances, no objection can be taken to this reasoning and the courts uniformly deny subrogation in such cases.[5] Since he has a duty to pay the junior liens he cannot complain if his payment and discharge of the earlier mortgage advances them in priority. If only the first mortgage is assumed and the grantee has actual knowledge of the junior liens at the time of assumption, it is arguable that the same result is justified,[6] although there are authorities to the contrary.[7] In such a case he pays under no mistake, and the view that it would not be unfair for the same consequences to follow payment by him as would flow from payment by the mortgagor, namely elevation of the junior lienors, is not an unreasonable one.

The same is not true when his assumption is of the first mortgage only and he pays and discharges it without knowledge of a junior lien. In such a case the grantee owes a duty to the mortgagor to pay off the first mortgage, but he has entered into no agreement with the second mortgagee to discharge it for his benefit. The only possible claim to heightened priority that the second lienor may urge is through the duty of the mortgagor to pay off prior mortgages for his benefit. But between the mortgagor and the grantee the mortgagor has a duty to pay off the second mortgage entirely, not to let it rise to a position of priority on the land now owned by the grantee. This being so, it would seem to follow clearly that the mortgagor could not claim that the grantee owed any duty to him, which could accrue derivatively to a second mortgagee, to pay off the first mortgage in order that the second mortgage, which he was bound to pay for the benefit of the grantee, might rise to a preferred position on the land. To permit the second mortgagee to rise to priority under these circumstances would give him an unwarranted enrichment at the expense of the grantee.[8]

---

5. E.g., Stastny v. Pease, 124 Iowa 587, 100 N.W. 482 (1904); Martin v. C. Aultman & Co., 80 Wis. 150, 49 N.W. 749 (1891); Morris v. Twichell, 63 N.D. 747, 249 N.W. 905 (1933), commented on in 19 Iowa L.Rev. 629 (1934), denied subrogation to a purchaser who assumed the first mortgage with knowledge of the second mortgage and who, when he paid the first mortgage, asked for and thought he had received an assignment instead of the cancellation which actually was executed. Although the purchaser did not expressly assume payment of the second mortgage the court stressed the fact that its amount had been deducted from the purchase price. The court said, "The rule is that when payment has been made by one primarily liable, it operates as an absolute satisfaction. * * * Neither by assignment nor by subrogation can he keep the mortgage alive as against other liens on the land."

6. In some of the cases in which the courts stress the grantee's assumption as the basis of the decision the grantee had actual notice of the intervening liens. E.g., Lackawanna Trust & Safe Deposit Co. v. Gomeringer, 236 Pa. 179, 84 A. 757 (1912); De Roberts v. Stiles, 24 Wash. 611, 64 P. 795 (1901); Willson v. Burton, 52 Vt. 394 (1880); Cady v. Barnes, 208 F. 361 (D.C. Ohio 1913), reversed 232 F. 318, 146 C.C.A. 366 (1913); cf. Kitchell v. Mudgett, 37 Mich. 81 (1877).

7. Joyce v. Dauntz, 55 Ohio St. 538, 45 N.E. 900 (1896); see Young v. Morgan, 89 Ill. 199, 202 (1878); cf. Stantons v. Thompson, 49 N.H. 272 (1870). See § 10.2, supra.

8. Tibbitts v. Terrill, 26 Colo.App. 64, 140 P. 936 (1914), commented on in 15 Col. L.Rev. 171 (1915), in which an assuming grantee was subrogated to the lien of the first mortgage which he paid, although he had actual knowledge of the recordation of

Cases sometimes arise in which the grantee had no actual knowledge of the intervening liens, but either failed to search the records or searched them negligently under circumstances in which a careful search would have disclosed the liens in question. By analogy to the discussion of loans to pay mortgages in the preceding section, negligence [9] or constructive notice [10] should be irrelevant. Here, as there, the issue is only whether the payor expected that his payment would free the property; [11] if he did, subrogation should be available to him. A contrary result would give the intervening lienors an unjustified and unearned windfall, advancing their priority for no good reason. Clearly this should be done only when the payor actually knew of them and failed to protect himself against them by obtaining an appropriate assignment of the senior debt.

The principles discussed above with respect to assuming grantees apply equally, and perhaps even more readily, to grantees who merely take subject to the senior mortgage.[12] On these facts it cannot even be argued that the grantee is paying off his own debt when he discharges the senior mortgage, since he has no personal obligation to do so. At the same time, both assuming and "subject to" grantees must be considered well outside the "volunteer" classification, since they clearly have a property interest to protect by payment.[13]

a lis pendens claim against the property at the time he bought it but bona fide, after legal advice, thought the claim invalid. The court made the point that to allow subrogation would work no hardship to the junior claimant. His security interest in the property when he acquired it was subject to this superior lien, and he should not reap the benefit of the other man's innocent mistake.

9. Lamoille County Savings Bank & Trust Co. v. Belden, 90 Vt. 535, 98 A. 1002 (1916); see Burgoon v. Lavezzo, 68 App. D.C. 20, 23, 92 F.2d 726, 729, 113 A.L.R. 944 (1937).

10. Ragan v. Standard Scale Co., 128 Ga. 544, 58 S.E. 31 (1907); Goodyear v. Goodyear, 72 Iowa 329, 33 N.W. 142 (1887); Kitchell v. Mudgett, 37 Mich. 81 (1877); see Stastny v. Pease, 124 Iowa 587, 591, 592, 100 N.W. 482, 483, 484 (1904). In Duke v. Kilpatrick, 231 Ala. 51, 163 So. 640 (1935), criticized in note, 14 N.Car.L.Rev. 295 (1936), subrogation for the purpose of obtaining contribution from his co-owner was denied to an assuming grantee who paid off the entire first mortgage on property which he had bought honestly thinking that he was getting full title when actually he was obtaining only a one-half interest in it. The fact of joint ownership of his grantor with another was on record and also appeared in the deed he received. Other courts allowing subrogation have ex-

pressly considered constructive notice as an obstacle and rejected it. E.g., see Prestridge v. Lazar, 132 Miss. 168, 177, 95 So. 837, 838 (1923); Burgoon v. Lavezzo, 68 App.D.C. 20, 24, 92 F.2d 726, 730, 113 A.L.R. 944 (1937). Look also at Smith v. Dinsmore, 119 Ill. 656, 4 N.E. 648 (1887); Neff v. Elder, 84 Ark. 277, 105 S.W. 260, 120 Am.St.Rep. 67 (1907). Compare Belcher v. Belcher, 161 Or. 340, 87 P.2d 762, 89 P.2d 893 (1939), noted 24 Minn.L.Rev. 121 (1939).

11. See § 10.6, supra.

12. Darrough v. Herbert Kraft Co. Bank, 125 Cal. 272, 57 P. 983 (1899), recorded junior encumbrance; Barnes v. Mott, 64 N.Y. 397, 21 Am.R. 625 (1876), recorded junior encumbrance; Ryer v. Gass, 130 Mass. 227 (1881); Hudson v. Dismukes, 77 Va. 242 (1883); see Burgoon v. Lavezzo, 68 App.D.C. 20, 23, 24, 92 F.2d 726, 729, 730, 113 A.L.R. 944 (1937). See also 14 N.Car.L.Rev. 295, 297 (1936); 15 Col.L.Rev. 171 (1915). Contra: Hayden v. Huff, 60 Neb. 625, 83 N.W. 920 (1900) affirmed 63 Neb. 99, 88 N.W. 179 (1900), negligence in failure to examine records; cf. Storer v. Warren, 99 Ind.App. 616, 192 N.E. 325 (1934).

13. Kahn v. McConnell, 37 Okl. 219, 220, 131 P. 682, 47 L.R.A.,N.S., 1189 (1913); Clute v. Emmerich, 99 N.Y. 342, 2 N.E. 6

WESTLAW REFERENCES
mortgag** /p grantee /p subject assign! assum! discharg*** /p interven! prior! /p subrogat***

§ 10.8 Compelling an Assignment

Subrogation is similar to an assignment of the mortgage creditor's rights, but since it is only an equitable right, it does not give as complete protection as does an assignment.[1] Therefore, frequently one who has a right to be subrogated upon payment of the mortgage debt desires instead a formal assignment. The question arises whether he is entitled to it.

The objection to compelling a mortgage creditor to execute an assignment under such circumstances is that his only duty under his mortgage agreement is to cancel the debt upon payment and to discharge the mortgage on the land—not to keep the mortgage alive by assigning it. But there are many legal incidents which attach to a relationship regardless of the agreement between the parties, simply because equity courts have believed it desirable and fair. In certain circumstances where the claimant shows a substantial need for an assignment as opposed to subrogation an assignment should be compelled.[2] The burden on the mortgagee under an assignment as compared to subrogation is not onerous and the duty to transfer the debt and mortgage without recourse imposes no additional risk on him.

While courts have given varying answers on the question of compelling an assignment,[3] most of the cases have granted it if the person paying the mortgage debt stands in the relation of surety for its payment.[4] Some courts have gone beyond this and granted it where the person paying did so to protect an interest[5] and even in favor of

---

(1885); cf. Weidner v. Thompson, 69 Iowa 36, 28 N.W. 422 (1886).

§ 10.8

1. Liberty Mutual Insurance Co. v. Thunderbird Bank, 113 Ariz. 375, 555 P.2d 333, (1976). See § 10.1, supra. See also Pardee v. Van Anken, N.Y., 3 Barb. 534, 541 (1848). "When there is an assignment of an entire claim there is complete divestment of all rights from the assignor and a vesting of those same rights in the assignee; but, in a case of subrogation, only an equitable right passes to the subrogee and the legal right to the claim is not removed from subrogor." Cantor v. Union Mutual Life Insurance Co., 547 S.W.2d 220, 225 (Mo.App.1977).

2. "[W]here justice requires, the payment of a mortgage note will be considered not as a discharge, but as an assignment of both instruments; [particularly if] it is the intention of the person making payment to take an assignment of the instruments for

his own protection." United States v. Boston and Berlin Transportation Co., 237 F.Supp. 1004, 1008 (D.N.H.1964).

3. For collections of authorities, see Ann.Cas.1914B, 562; 2 A.L.R. 242 (1919) (chattel mortgage); 93 A.L.R. 89 (1934).

4. E.g., Johnson v. Zink, 51 N.Y. 333 (1873). See 93 A.L.R. 89, 99 (1934).

5. Tenant who held valuable long term lease which was subordinate to second mortgage was entitled upon payment or tender of amount due on mortgage to demand an assignment of bond and mortgage from its holder. Global Realty Corp. v. Charles Kannel Corp., 9 Misc.2d 241, 170 N.Y.S.2d 16 (1958). Where remainderman tendered payment he could compel life tenant's execution and delivery of an assignment of mortgage rather than a discharge. Payne v. Foster, 284 App.Div. 1058, 135 N.Y.S.2d 819 (1954). E.g., Averill v. Taylor, 8 N.Y. 44 (1853). In Simonson v. Lauck, 105 App.Div. 82, 93 N.Y.S. 965

lenders who are entitled to subrogation.[6] On the other hand some courts deny the assignment even though the payment was made to protect an interest in the property [7] or when the payor was in the position of a surety.[8]

 WESTLAW REFERENCES
366k31 /p mortgage

B. MARSHALING

§ 10.9 General Principles

Marshaling is an equitable principle applied by the courts to adjust the rights of the various parties having an interest in mortgaged property.[1]

Frequently a single tract of land consisting of several lots or parcels is mortgaged to secure one debt. Or it may be that two or more separate tracts are subject to a single mortgage debt. The various lots or tracts may then be sold or mortgaged to different parties either simultaneously or successively and one or more of the lots or tracts may be retained by the mortgagor. In such cases there are two or more pieces of property as security for the same debt and more than one person has an interest in the properties under the mortgage. For

(1905), the mortgagor, owner of the fee simple as tenant-in-common with four others, obtained an assignment to a third person who had tendered payment of the entire mortgage at the request of the mortgagor. Roberson, 133 Ala. 630, 32 So. 225 (1902), accord. Cf. Fears v. Albea, 69 Tex. 437, 6 S.W. 286, 5 Am.St.Rep. 78 (1887). In Bayles v. Husted, N.Y., 40 Hun. 376 (1886), the widow of a deceased mortgagor tendered to the mortgagee the amount of the secured debt and demanded that the mortgage be assigned to X. Held, the mortgagee should be compelled to make the assignment.

6. French v. Grand Beach Co., 239 Mich. 575, 215 N.W. 13 (1927), noted 12 Minn.L.Rev. 189 (1927). Cf. Arant, Suretyship, 360–367; 34 Harv.L.Rev. 792 (1921); 20 Va.L.Rev. 917 (1934). Lackawanna Trust & Safe Deposit Co. v. Gomeringer, 236 Pa. 179, 84 A. 757 (1912) is contra.

7. Lamb v. Montague, 112 Mass. 352 (1873); Butler v. Taylor, 71 Mass. (5 Gray) 455 (1855); Hamilton v. Dobbs, 19 N.J.Eq. 227 (1868). Cf. Holland v. Citizens, etc., Bank, 16 R.I. 734, 19 A. 654, 8 L.R.A. 553 (1890). See Updike, Mortgages, in 1954 Annual Survey of American Law, 30 N.Y. U.L.Rev. 805, 812 (1955), noting Marine View Savings & Loan Association v. An-

drulonis, Ch., 31 N.J.Super. 378, 106 A.2d 559 (1954).

8. Fitcher v. Griffiths, 216 Mass. 174, 103 N.E. 471 (1913). Cf. Heighe v. Evans, 164 Md. 259, 164 A. 671, 93 A.L.R. 81 (1933).

§ 10.9

1. Marshaling is "the ranking or ordering of several estates or parcels of land for the satisfaction of a judgment or mortgage to which all are liable." 1 Black, Judgments, § 440. For collections of authorities on various aspects of the problem of marshaling see, 5 L.R.A. 280 (1889); 12 L.R.A.,N.S. 965 (1908); id. 359 (1912); id. 302 (1914); Ann.Cas.1914A., 715; id. 1916D, 1119; 35 A.L.R. 1307 (1925); 44 id. 608 (1926); 77 id. 371 (1932); 101 id. 618 (1936); 106 id. 1102 (1937); 110 id. 65 (1937); 119 id. 1109 (1939); 131 A.L.R. 4 (1941). This last is a long and comprehensive survey of the inverse order of alienation rule.

While marshaling originated in realty mortgage cases, it is often applied in modern times to personal property security as well; see Labovitz, Marshaling Under the U.C.C.: The State of the Doctrine, 99 Banking L.J. 440 (1982).

convenience in the following discussion the foregoing situation may be stated in hypothetical terms in which R is the mortgagor and E the mortgagee of the single tract, Blackacre, which is composed of three lots, X, Y and Z. T–1 and T–2 represent later purchasers or second mortgagees, as the case may be, of lots X and Y. Lot Z remains in the hands of R. If the transfers of X and Y are by sale, T–1 and T–2 may have bought in any one of three types of transactions: they may have assumed the mortgage, taken subject to it, or paid the full value of the parcel with R bound to pay off the mortgage on it. Or there may be agreements apportioning the debt in specified amounts or percentages among the various parcels transferred or retained by the mortgagor. The transfer to T–1 may or may not have been recorded. T–2, whether he is purchaser or mortgagee, may have actual notice of the prior transfer to T–1.

If there were no principles of marshaling, in the event of a default on the mortgage, E could proceed against the three parcels in any order he wished. This would endow him with the power, to be exercised at his whim, of wiping out the interest of T–1, T–2, or R in the parcel held by one or another of them by going against it rather than against another or all of them. The purpose and effect of marshaling is to prevent this result.

The term marshaling is used to cover two principles which are commonly given the separate titles of the "inverse order of alienation" rule and the "two funds" doctrine.[2] Under the inverse order of alienation rule, a mortgagee holding a paramount lien on an entire tract of land which has been sold successively in separate parcels must satisfy his debt out of the land retained by the mortgagor-grantor, if possible, and if that is insufficient must resort to the parcels aliened in the inverse order of their alienation.[3] The rule has been traced back to Coke in England,[4] and was first enunciated in this country by Chancellor Kent[5] and later approved by the great weight of authority.[6]

2. See Fidelity & Casualty Co. v. Massachusetts Mutual Life Insurance Co., 74 F.2d 881 (C.C.A.1935); Restatement, Second, Restitution § 44 (Tent.Draft No. 2, 1984). For applications of the principles of marshaling in subdivision financing, see Melli, Subdivision Control in Wisconsin, Wis.L.Rev. 389 (1953). See also Green, Marshaling Assets in Texas, 34 Texas L.Rev. 1054 (1956). For a discussion of subdivision financing problems, see Storke and Sears, Subdivision Financing, 28 Rocky Mt.L.Rev. 1 (1956). See Note, The Rights of a Junior Lienholder in Wisconsin, 43 Marq.L.Rev. 89, 94 (1959). There is limited authority in bankruptcy cases for marshaling to protect unsecured creditors; see Comment, 1983 B.Y.U.L.Rev. 639.

3. Mobley v. Brundidge Banking Co., 347 So.2d 1347 (Ala.1977); Bartley v. Pike-ville National Bank & Trust Co., 532 S.W.2d 446 (Ky.App.1976); Seasons, Inc. v. Atwell, 86 N.M. 751, 527 P.2d 792 (1974); Broughton v. Mount Healthy Flying Service, Inc., 104 Ohio App. 479, 143 N.E.2d 597 (1957).

4. Harbert's Case, 3 Co.Rep. 11b (1584). Cf. Lord Eldon in Aldrich v. Cooper, 8 Ves. 382 (1803), and Sugden, in Averall v. Wade, L1. & G. 252 (1825), on the "two funds" doctrine. See Clowes v. Dickenson, N.Y., 5 Johns.Ch. 235 (1821). See also Sanford v. Hill, 46 Conn. 42 (1878); National Savings Bank of District of Columbia v. Creswell, 100 U.S. 630, 25 L.Ed. 713 (D.C.1880).

5. In Clowes v. Dickenson, supra note 4.

6. Brown v. Simons, 44 N.H. 475 (1863); Cumming v. Cumming, 3 Ga. 460 (1847); Clowes v. Dickenson, note 4, supra; San-

The two funds rule requires that where two creditors have claims upon the assets of a common debtor and one of the creditors can resort to two funds but the other can reach only one, the doubly secured creditor must first seek satisfaction out of the fund which he alone can reach before resorting to the fund upon which both creditors have claims.[7] For example, lots X and Y are mortgaged to E. T–1 then takes a second mortgage on lot X. Unless lot X is sufficient to pay both mortgages, if E should foreclose by taking payment out of it first there will be nothing left for T–1 and he will be reduced to the status of an unsecured creditor. On the other hand, if E takes his payment out of Y first before resorting to X, some or all of the latter is likely to be available for T–1. To prevent the caprice of the doubly secured creditor, E, from determining where the loss shall fall in such a case, the "two funds" rule may be invoked by T–1 to compel E to realize first on Y.[8]

In application the two rules are not always clear and separable. The doctrine of inverse alienation, while generally thought of in situations where the mortgagor-owner has sold parcels successively, may also apply in other circumstances. As one court noted, it "not only applies to a vendee, but to any one having a substantial and valuable interest in any of the separate parcels of land. It has been applied in favor of the wife's dower and her homestead right. It has been applied in favor of judgment creditors, and in fact to almost all the transactions of business in which the rights of creditors, mortgagees, grantees, and lienees are involved before a court of equity."[9] There are times when the court discusses the "two funds" rule but, where more than one junior mortgagee is involved, may consider the inverse order of their encumbrances.[10] The court may recognize the inverse order rule as

---

ford v. Hill, note 4, supra; National Savings Bank v. Creswell, note 4, supra; see Iglehart v. Crane & Wesson, 42 Ill. 261, 265, 269 (1866). See 5 L.R.A. 276, 282 (1889); Ann.Cas.1916D, 1119.

7. All American Holding Corp. v. Elgin State Bank, 17 B.R. 926 (Bkrtcy.Fla.1982); Shedoudy v. Beverly Surgical Supply Co., 100 Cal.App.3d 730, 733, 161 Cal.Rptr. 164 (1980); Pongetti v. Bankers Trust Savings & Loan Association, 368 So.2d 819 (Miss. 1979); Community Bank v. Jones, 278 Or. 647, 566 P.2d 470 (1977); Bartley v. Pikeville National Bank & Trust Co., 532 S.W.2d 446 (Ky.App.1976); Waff Brothers, Inc. v. Bank of North Carolina, N.A., 289 N.C. 198, 221 S.E.2d 273 (1976); In re Beacon Distributors, Inc., 441 F.2d 547 (1st Cir. 1971); 76 A.L.R.3d 327 fn. 2 (1977).

The debtor must be identical as to both properties; See SAC Construction Co. v. Eagle National Bank, 449 So.2d 301 (Fla. App.1984). Cf. DuPage Lumber Co. v. Georgia-Pacific Corp., 34 B.R. 737 (Bkrtcy.

Ill.1983); Moser Paper Co. v. North Shore Publishing Co., 83 Wis.2d 852, 266 N.W.2d 411 (1978).

See generally Restatement, Second, Restitution § 44(2) (Tent.Draft No. 2, 1984).

8. "Its purpose is to prevent the arbitrary action of a senior lienor from destroying the rights of a junior lienor or a creditor having less security." Meyer v. United States, 375 U.S. 233, 237, 84 S.Ct. 318, 321, 11 L.Ed.2d 293 (1963). The rule goes back to Culpepper v. Aston, 2 Ch.Cas. 115, 117 (1682). As to the justice of this rule which operates to the prejudice of general creditors, see Duck v. Wells Fargo Bank, 28 B.R. 398 (Bkrtcy. 9th Cir.1983); Langdell, A Brief Survey of Equity Jurisdiction, 15; Note, 43 Harv.L.Rev. 501 (1930).

9. Mack v. Shafer, 135 Cal. 113, 67 P. 40, 41 (1901). See 53 Am.Jur.2d, Marshaling Assets § 61.

10. See § 10.13. Indeed some states have statutes providing that the order of valid between grantees but refuse to apply it between junior mortgagees.[11]

Because of this confusion the orthodox classifications have been criticized and some commentators have suggested that the cases be grouped under the two heads, "Suretyship Marshaling" and "Lien Marshaling". "The first group is made up of cases in which there are two owners of separate tracts liable for the same mortgage debt, with a real suretyship relation existing between the owners. The second group consists of cases in which there are two mortgages, one of whom has a mortgage on two tracts, and the other a junior mortgage on one of these tracts."[12] These commentators recognize that there may be complex cases which would involve both suretyship marshaling and lien marshaling.

Regardless of which of these two marshaling principles is applicable, it is clear that marshaling will not be applied in such a way as to prejudice the rights of the paramount mortgagee to have his debt satisfied. All fractional interests remain bound by the first mortgage. The mortgagor can no more divest a portion of the mortgaged property by conveying it away or giving a second mortgage on it than he can free the entire property by the same means[13] (provided that the first mortgage is properly recorded). And although restrictions may be placed upon E's enforcement of his rights for the purpose of ordering or ranking the relative positions of T–1, T–2 and R, those restrictions must stop short of prejudicing E's paramount rights as first mortgagee.[14]

---

inverse alienation be applied within the two funds rule.

West's Ann.Cal.Civ.Code § 2899 provides that "Where one has a lien upon several things, and other persons have subordinate liens upon, or interest in, some but not all of the same things, the person having the prior lien, if he can do so without risk of loss to himself, or of injustice to other persons, must resort to the property in the following order, on the demand of any party interested:

"1. To the things upon which he has an exclusive lien;

"2. To the things which are subject to the fewest subordinate liens;

"3. In like manner inversely to the number of subordinate liens upon the same thing; and,

"4. When several things are within one of the foregoing classes, and subject to the same number of liens, resort must be had—

"(1) To the things which have not been transferred since the prior lien was created;

"(2) To the things which have been so transferred without a valuable consideration; and,

"(3) To the things which have been so transferred for a valuable consideration in the inverse order of the transfer."

See also 42 Okl.St.Ann. § 17.

11. Bryson v. Newtown Real Estate & Development Corp., 153 Conn. 267, 216 A.2d 176 (1965). See also Platte Valley Bank of North Bend v. Kracl, 185 Neb. 168, 174 N.W.2d 724 (1970).

12. Storke and Sears, Transfer of Mortgaged Property, 38 Corn.L.Q. 185, 201 et seq. (1953).

13. "[E]very portion of the real estate embraced within the mortgage was equally burdened with the debt. No part could be relieved of the burden without consent of the mortgagee." Broughton v. Mount Healthy Flying Service, Inc., 104 Ohio App. 479, 481, 143 N.E.2d 597, 599 (1957).

14. Lincoln First Bank v. Spaulding Bakeries, Inc., 117 Misc.2d 892, 459 N.Y.S.2d 696 (1983); Charles White Co. v. Percy Galbreath & Sons, Inc., 563 S.W.2d 478 (Ky.App.1978); Caplinger v. Patty, 398

Even risk of loss to E will preclude marshaling.[15] It has been held that the junior creditor has the burden to show that the senior creditor has sufficient collateral to satisfy his claims.[16] In some cases the protection to the mortgagee can be accomplished by the decree itself.[17] After directing that the parcels shall be offered for sale in the inverse order of alienation, beginning with that part of the tract still in the hands of the mortgagor, it may then provide that " '[I]f the aggregate amount bid for the said lands so offered in severalty shall be insufficient to satisfy this decree, then the said master shall offer for sale said lots * * * together as one parcel * * *; and if the amount bid for the said lands so offered together shall exceed the aggregate of the amounts bid for said lands when offered in severalty * * * then said master shall sell said lands together' ".[18] It may be that such a procedure would add to the costs of the action. If so, those costs could be allocated to those for whose benefit the marshaling is ordered.

It is generally held that one entitled to marshaling has a right only to require a certain order of realization out of the various parcels under the mortgage when foreclosure occurs. Consequently a grantee or junior encumbrancer who has such a right must properly assert his equity before sale or other foreclosure of his parcel takes place.[19] This he may do by bill in equity if the attempted foreclosure is under power of sale,[20] or by cross-bill, answer or the like, in case of judicial foreclosure.[21] Even where the mortgagee's suit is for strict foreclosure the

F.2d 471 (8th Cir.Ark.1968); First National Bank of Omaha v. First Cadco Corp., 189 Neb. 553, 203 N.W.2d 770 (1973). "The doctrine is never enforced where it will operate to suspend or put in peril the claim of the paramount creditor, or cause him risk of loss, or where the fund to be resorted to is one which may involve such creditors in litigation, especially if final satisfaction is somewhat uncertain." Platte Valley Bank of North Bend v. Kracl, 185 Neb. 168, 174, 174 N.W.2d 724, 729 (1970) citing 55 C.J.S. Marshaling Assets and Securities § 4, p. 963. In S. Lotman & Sons, Inc. v. Southeastern Financial Corp., 288 Ala. 547, 263 So.2d 499 (1972), the court would not require creditor to attempt satisfaction from 3rd mortgage on land where he also held security interest in equipment. See Matter of St. Cloud Tool & Die Co., 533 F.2d 387 (8th Cir.1976), holding that the creditor requesting marshaling must act promptly so as not to prejudice others by inaction.

See generally Restatement, Second, Restitution § 44(4) (Tent.Draft No. 2, 1984).

15. Victor Gruen Association, Inc. v. Glass, 338 F.2d 826 (9th Cir.Cal.1964). See also Matter of Mills, 40 B.R. 72 (Bkrtcy. 1984) (marshalling denied in bankruptcy

where it would affect unsecured creditors adversely.)

16. Id. Pankow Construction Co. v. Advance Mortgage Corp., 618 F.2d 611, 617 (9th Cir.1980); Grise v. White, 355 Mass. 698, 247 N.E.2d 385 (1969) (record did not establish existing collateral.) But see Continental Oil Co. v. Graham, 8 S.W.2d 719 (Tex.Civ.App.1928) where mortgagee failed to show that marshaling would cause hardship.

17. E.g., Hyde Park Thomson-Houston Light Co. v. Brown, 172 Ill. 329, 50 N.E. 127 (1898).

18. Id. This procedure was followed even in the absence of the contractual provision in Conneaut Building and Loan Co. v. Felch, 100 Ohio App. 52, 135 N.E.2d 480 (1955).

19. Monegan v. Pacific National Bank of Washington, 16 Wash.App. 280, 556 P.2d 226 (1976); Vines v. Wilcutt, 212 Ala. 150, 102 So. 29, 35 A.L.R. 1301 (1925).

20. Vines v. Wilcutt, note 19 supra.

21. Black v. Suydam, 81 Wash. 279, 142 P. 700 (1915), Ann.Cas.1916D, 1113. See 35 A.L.R. 1307, 1310 (1924). Control of all of the parcels by the foreclosing court is essential. Hence marshalling cannot be

same result can be obtained. In such an action an equity court will always order a sale if the equities of the junior parties in interest require it. And it has even been held that a grantee of one of two mortgaged tracts, in a proper case for marshaling, may require the mortgagee who is seeking strict foreclosure to confine his remedy to the other tract where the net value of that tract is clearly equal to the mortgage debt.[22]

While the foregoing are the most usual ways in which principles of marshaling are worked out others should be mentioned. One is to utilize the right of subrogation. Instead of having the land sold on foreclosure by the mortgagee in the order to which a subsequent grantee or mortgagee is entitled, such a transferee may elect to pay off the underlying first mortgage and be subrogated to his rights.[23] Those rights are, however, subject to control according to the principles of marshaling just as they were in the hands of the first mortgagee. Another is by an action to redeem, in which the reciprocal rights of the parties may be adjusted by the decree.[24] Or, the mortgagee may be permitted to sell all of the mortgaged property and the subsequent grantee or mortgagee may assert his priority right to the proceeds after the foreclosing mortgagee has been satisfied and before general creditors are paid.

With this much of the problem and principles of marshalling before us we may now turn to specific instances and applications in the following sections. In doing so we shall consider the problem as it arises where subsequent purchasers from the mortgagor are concerned, where junior encumbrancers are interested, where general creditors assert a claim, and the occasional case where the mortgagor himself is seeking protection, e.g., in a homestead subject to the mortgage.

 WESTLAW REFERENCES
di marshaling

marshal*** /s asset /s doctrine rule

"two fund" /s doctrine rule

---

ordered if part of the mortgaged property is outside of the state. Drexler v. Commercial Savings Bank, 5 F.2d 13 (1925), noted, 25 Col.L.Rev. 974 (1925).

22. Markham v. Smith, 119 Conn. 355, 366, 367, 176 A. 880, 885 (1935); New England Mortgage Realty Co. v. Rossini, 121 Conn. 214, 183 A. 744 (1936). "On the other hand, the mortgagor, or a grantee or junior incumbrancer of *both* tracts, not being entitled to marshalling, is denied such relief on the ground that application should have been made to the court for an order of foreclosure by sale, in which

event, by the usual practice, the tracts would have been sold separately, unless used as a whole." Campbell, Cases on Mortgages, 2d ed., 620 n. 7, citing New Haven Bank N.B.A. v. Jackson, 119 Conn. 451, 453, 455, 177 A. 387, 388 (1935).

23. Taylor v. Jones, 285 Ala. 353, 232 So.2d 601 (1970); Sanders v. Lackey, 59 Tenn.App. 207, 439 S.W.2d 610 (1968); Cobb v. Osman, 83 Nev. 415, 433 P.2d 259 (1967). See §§ 10.2, 10.3, 10.7.

24. Taylor v. Jones, note 23 supra. See §§ 7.1–7.3, supra.

§ 10.10 Grantees—Inverse Order Rule

The basis of the inverse order of alienation rule is that each of the successive purchasers has bought his parcel on terms which impose upon the mortgagor and the remaining property in his hands the primary obligation of paying the mortgage debt. The property in the hands of the grantee, although still liable, stands merely in the position of surety.[1] This situation occurs where the full price of the parcel is paid without deduction of the whole or any part of the debt secured by the blanket mortgage.[2] Persons who have notice of the underlying mortgage through searching the records or otherwise [3] would not enter into such a transaction if they possessed business experience or had consulted a competent lawyer.[4] But one having done so has a right to have the remaining property in the hands of the mortgagor exonerate the parcel he bought.

It has sometimes been asserted that the right of grantee to have marshaling is dependent upon having received a deed with covenants of warranty.[5] Historically this has not been true,[6] and indeed this view

§ 10.10

1. Gribble v. Stearman & Kaplan, Inc., 249 Md. 289, 239 A.2d 573 (1968). "[T]he doctrine of marshaling confers upon the grantee * * * an equitable right to require the mortgagee to seek satisfaction of the underlying obligation from the mortgagor's remaining properties which are subject to the blanket mortgage, before resorting to the premises conveyed. This equitable right on the part of the grantee is, of course, independent of and in addition to its rights against the grantor mortgagor." In re Penn Central Transportation Co., 346 F.Supp. 1323, 1326 (E.D.Pa. 1972), motion denied 346 F.Supp. 1333. See also Storke & Sears, Transfer of Mortgaged Property, 38 Cornell L.Q. 185, 202 n. 69 (1953).

2. This is true even though the purchaser does not receive a deed until after sale of a second parcel. The equity attaches when the consideration is paid. Libby v. Tufts, 121 N.Y. 172, 24 N.E. 12 (1890). This equity would be defeated, of course, if the purchaser of the second parcel did not have notice and could qualify as a bona fide purchaser in other respects.

3. Their ignorance is as to the existence of the mortgage, not its legal consequences. It cannot, therefore, be urged against helping them that their plight is the result of a mistake of law. See Note, 23 Va.L.Rev. 298 (1937).

4. In subdivision financing it is customary to provide in the underlying mortgage agreement that the mortgagee is required "to release any lot from the lien of the mortgage on payment of a specified amount * * *. The contract between the subdivision company and the purchaser should contain a clause requiring the former, upon full payment by the latter, to pay the mortgagee the required amount and procure the release of lien. It is unwise to purchase a lot in a subdivision without first checking the mortgage and contract to see that these provisions are present." Storke and Sears, Transfer of Mortgaged Property, 38 Cornell L.Q. 185, 211 (1953). The language of such provisions has not been standardized and in construing them there is a divergence of authority as to whether the partial release privilege is personal to the mortgagor or can be taken advantage of by purchasers of portions of the property. See 31 Col.L.Rev. 894, 895 (1931). Agreement between mortgagee and mortgagor gave grantee mortgagor's rights in Conway v. Andrews, 286 Ala. 28, 236 So.2d 687 (1970).

5. See, e.g., Pomeroy, Equity Juris, 5th ed., § 1225, "This relation * * * results from the form of the conveyance, which, being a warranty deed, or equivalent to a warranty, shows conclusively an intention between the two that the grantor is to assume the whole burden of the encumbrance as a charge upon his own parcel, while the grantee is to take and hold his portion entirely free."

6. "We are unable to find a case deciding, * * * that the equity could not be founded upon a quitclaim deed; * * * neither can we find a case which affirmatively decides that the rule depends upon does not seem proper. Since it is an equitable concept, the vital question is whether the duty of paying off the debt rests upon the mortgagor rather than the grantee.[7] On that question, the presence or absence of covenants in the deed has value as evidence in determining the question of fact,[8] but otherwise it is immaterial.

The agreement of purchase having created an equity of marshaling which attaches to the rest of the property under the mortgage remaining in the mortgagor's hands, that equity will follow it into the hands of anyone who has notice of it.[9] When T-2 buys Y with notice of T-1's equity he will, of course, take subject to it. Thus after T-1 bought parcel X, parcels Y and Z are subject in R's hands to T-1's equity that they shall be applied to E's debt before X is touched. But if T-2 bought on the same terms as T-1, he, in turn, has a similar equity against Z which stays in R's hands. Or, if R sells Z to T-3 who takes with notice, T-3 will take it subject to the prior equitable rights of T-1 and T-2. Thus when E seeks to foreclose, T-1 can compel him to proceed first against Y and Z before seeking to realize on X; and T-2 in turn can demand that, as between Y and Z, Z go first. Thus we have the rule of inverse order of alienation, which is, as was stated earlier, the great weight of authority in the United States.[10]

the existence or nonexistence of covenants of warranty." Biswell v. Gladney, 182 S.W. 1168, 1172 (Tex.Civ.App.1916), modified on other grounds 213 S.W. 256 (1919). In Wadsworth v. Lyon, 93 N.Y. 201, 45 Am. Rep. 190 (1883), in spite of the absence of covenants of title, the grantee of mortgaged property who had paid the full value of the property was held entitled to exoneration. In Wilcox v. Campbell, 106 N.Y. 325, 12 N.E. 823 (1887), although the grantee took a quitclaim deed he was held entitled to marshal against a prior grantee of another parcel who assumed the mortgage.

7. "It [the rule requiring sale in inverse order of alienation] rests chiefly, perhaps, upon the grounds that where one who is bound to pay a mortgage confers upon others rights in any portion of the property, retaining other portions himself, it is unjust that they should be deprived of their rights, so long as he has property covered by the mortgage, out of which the debt can be made. * * * The rule cannot, therefore, depend upon the existence or nonexistence of covenants of warranty. Cooper v. Bigley, 13 Mich. 463, 474 (1865). See 131 A.L.R. 103 (1941).

8. A warranty deed may show intent of the mortgagor to remain liable on the whole mortgage. Seasons, Inc. v. Atwell, 86 N.M. 751, 527 P.2d 792 (1974); Taylor v. Jones, 285 Ala. 353, 232 So.2d 601 (1970).

9. Taylor v. Jones, 285 Ala. 353, 232 So. 2d 601 (1970). "The second purchaser sits

in the seat of his grantor, and must pay the whole value of what he bought towards the extinguishment of the mortgage, before he can call on the first purchaser to pay anything. The first sale having thrown the whole burden on the part reserved, it cannot be thrown back again by the second sale. In other words the second purchaser takes the land he buys subject to all the liabilities under which the grantor held it." Carpenter v. Koons, 20 Pa. 222, 226 (1852). Brown v. Simons, 44 N.H. 475 (1863). National Savings Bank v. Creswell, 100 U.S. 630, 637, 25 L.Ed. 713 (D.C.1879); Clowes v. Dickenson, 5 Johns, Ch. 235 (N.Y.1821). "In the case of the sale by the mortgagor of all the mortgaged property to different purchasers at the same time, their equities must be regarded as equal, and each must contribute ratably to the discharge of the common burthen * * *." Brown v. Simons, 44 N.H. 475, 478 (1863).

10. Seasons, Inc. v. Atwell, 86 N.M. 751, 527 P.2d 792 (1974); Taylor v. Jones, 285 Ala. 353, 232 So.2d 601 (1970); In re Penn Central Transportation Co., 346 F.Supp. 1323 (E.D.Pa.1972); Ellickson v. Dull, 34 Colo.App. 25, 521 P.2d 1282 (1974); In Voltin v. Voltin, 179 N.W.2d 127 (N.D.1970) portion given to wife in divorce decree to go last; Broughton v. Mount Healthy Flying Service, Inc., 104 Ohio App. 479, 143 N.E.2d 597 (1957) (where parcels had been leased, creditor must look first to residue.)

While the courts in Iowa and Kentucky will apply the doctrine of marshaling to the extent that the residue of property remaining in the hands of the mortgagor will be used to exonerate a grantee or second mortgagee, they reject the doctrine which would require that the debt be satisfied out of portions of the property sold or mortgaged in the order of inverse alienation. Instead the debt is pro-rated against the two tracts or their proceeds proportionate to their respective values.[11] The argument in favor of this minority attitude is that "as between two grantees purchasing different parcels of the incumbered premises at different times, there is no more obligation on the one to pay than on the other. Both of them have purchased premises that are alike affected by a lien which neither created nor undertook to pay. The purchased premises are liable to be sold because of the failure of their grantor to discharge his undertaking, and not because of any failure on their part. In such cases, their interest is common, their rights are equal, and there should be equality of burden."[12]

The argument is plausible but there are answers to it. First, a grantee, unless he can qualify as a bona fide purchaser, takes the property subject to the equities held therein by third persons.[13] Thus T–2 takes parcel Y subject to an existing equity in favor of T–1 which arose when T–1 bought X. Second, a mortgagor who by transferring a part of his mortgaged land established an equity in his grantee to have the residue applied first in satisfaction of the debt could divest this equity at pleasure by transferring such residue to another.[14] This would be an undesirable and anomalous result.

Going back to the majority view, if T–2 and T–3 have actual notice there is no question but that the rule operates. If they do not have actual notice will they be charged with constructive notice by reason of the fact that T–1 recorded the conveyance to him? Most states say yes.[15] The rule has been criticized, however, as placing an undue

See 131 A.L.R. 103 at n. 11 for collection of authorities applying the rule.

    "It appears from the precedents and authorities dealing with the Rule of Inverse Order of Alienation that whether jurisdictions have adopted the rule in its entirety or with some modifications, they are virtually unanimous in holding that where a mortgagor conveys a portion and retains a portion of the encumbered property, the property so retained should first be subjected to the payment of the debt before resorting to the portion conveyed." Seasons, Inc. v. Atwell, 86 N.M. 751, 756, 527 P.2d 792, 797 (1974).

11. Bartley v. Pikeville National Bank & Trust Co., 532 S.W.2d 446 (Ky.App.1976); Bronaugh v. Burley Tobacco Co., 212 Ky. 680, 280 S.W. 97 (1926); Bates v. Ruddick, 2 Iowa 423, 2 Clarke 423, 65 Am.Dec. 774 (1856); Huff v. Farwell, 67 Iowa 298, 25 N.W. 252 (1885). "Even in Kentucky mar-

shaling is granted if the mortgagor agreed with the first grantee to confine the mortgage to the retained tract by procuring a release from its operation (Calhoun v. Federal Land Bank, 230 Ky. 460, 465, 20 S.W. 2d 72, 74 [1929]), or, probably, if the mortgagor expressly agreed with him that he might have marshaling, and the subsequent grantee or mortgagee had knowledge of the agreement." Campbell, Cases on Mortgages, 2d ed., 619 n. 6.

12. Bates v. Ruddick, 2 Iowa, 423, 430, 65 Am.Dec. 774, 779 (1856).

13. Huston, Enforcement of Decrees in Equity, 127–131.

14. See Tiffany, Real Prop., 3d ed., § 1446. Cf. Shenkin, Marshaling of Securities, 79 U. of Pa.L.Rev. 785, n. 14 (1931).

15. Brown v. Simons, 44 N.H. 475 (1863); see Iglehart v. Crane & Wesson, 42 burden upon later purchasers, and as being contrary to the spirit of the recording acts.[16] There is an additional objection where the terms of conveyance between the mortgagor and his first grantee did not make clear whether the grantee was entitled to exoneration against the remainder. Should a later purchaser of part or all of the rest of the property be put upon inquiry to find out, at his peril, the real terms of the bargain? If so, and this is applied also to cases where notice of the prior conveyance is only constructive (because the prior conveyance is recorded), the objections stated above become stronger.[17]

Where the first grantee failed to record and T–2 took his land without actual or constructive notice of T–1, it has been held that T–2 has an equity to have X sold before Y.[18] This seems correct if the rule of constructive notice by recordation is accepted. Since T–2 has no notice of a prior conveyance, he has no reason to believe that he is not the first grantee and he would justifiably expect to be exonerated out of the land he believed was a residue in the hands of the grantor.

There is, however, a situation in which it would seem that T–1's failure to record should not cause T–2 to advance to T–1's position. Where E has a mortgage on two separate parcels of land securing one debt and T–1 takes a second mortgage on parcel X, his recording of the lien on X would have nothing to do with parcel Y and would not put T–2 who takes a second mortgage on Y on notice. Therefore the recording acts would not apply to T–1's recording as giving notice to T–2 and if T–1 fails to record, T–2 should not be given a windfall by advancing to T–1's priority position. It would seem that the proper result in this case would be to pro-rate the debt between the two parcels according to their respective values.

 WESTLAW REFERENCES
di inverse order of alienation doctrine
inverse /s order alienation /s doctrine rule

Ill. 261, 265, 269; Ann.Cas.1916D, 1119 (1866).

16. "The court, in effect, is imposing upon C [the subsequent grantee from the mortgagor of a part of the mortgaged property] a duty of running back every chain of title connected with a blanket mortgage, to ascertain whether any latent equities exist. To impose such a duty is contrary to the spirit of our Recording Acts, the policy of which is to remove secret liens. * * * Prospective purchasers or mortgagees of real estate are rightly considered to be on notice of prior liens on the property concerned, but the equity to marshal is one that can only be uncovered after, what may be in some cases, a most exhaustive and unreasonable search." Note, 79 U. of Pa.L.Rev. 782, 787 n. 28 (1931). See Cun-

ningham, Stoebuck & Whitman, Property § 11.11 (1984), at 801–02.

17. See note 16, supra.

18. In Gray v. H.M. Loud & Sons Lumber Co., 128 Mich. 427, 87 N.W. 376, 54 L.R.A. 731 (1901), the lower court had pro rated the mortgage between two tracts, each of which had been sold by warranty deed with each purchaser paying the full value of the property. The first grantee failed to record, and the subsequent grantee had no actual notice of the first. The upper court reversed the decision and held that the entire mortgage should be paid out of the part first sold. Look also at LaFarge Fire Insurance Co. v. Bell, 22 Barb. 54 (N.Y.1856); Bode v. Rhodes, 119 Wash. 98, 204 P. 802 (1922).

§ 10.11 Effect of Assumption or Taking "Subject" to the Mortgage

Where a mortgagor sells part of a mortgaged tract to a grantee who assumes the payment of the mortgage, the parcel conveyed becomes primarily liable for the payment of the mortgage and the part retained is only secondarily liable.[1] The grantee is also personally liable as principal for the payment of the debt and the mortgagor and the rest of the mortgaged land is surety only as to this personal obligation.[2] As a consequence, not only does the inverse order of alienation rule not apply[3] but the rule is reversed. Since not only the grantee but the parcel conveyed to him have the duty to exonerate the residue in the hands of the mortgagor, the mortgagee can be compelled to foreclose first on the parcel transferred to the grantee.[4] Where the mortgagor afterwards sells the remainder of the tract to a subsequent purchaser who pays the full price on the remaining portion, all of the mortgagor's rights with respect to the assuming grantee's duty in respect to this remaining part inure to the benefit of the second purchaser.[5]

These rights give the subsequent purchaser a choice of several courses. In a foreclosure action by the mortgagee he may have the parcel held by the assuming grantee sold before that held by himself.[6]

§ 10.11

1. Sanders v. Lackey, 59 Tenn.App. 207, 439 S.W.2d 610 (1968); Cobb v. Osman, 83 Nev. 415, 433 P.2d 259 (1967); Chancellor of New Jersey v. Towell, 80 N.J.Eq. 223, 82 A. 861, 39 L.R.A.,N.S., 359, Ann.Cas.1914A, 710 (1912); Wilcox v. Campbell, 106 N.Y. 325, 12 N.E. 823 (1887); Reid v. Whisenant, 191 Ga. 503, 131 N.E. 904, 44 A.L.R. 599 (1926).

2. Id. Prudential Savings and Loan Association v. Nadler, 37 Ill.App.3d 168, 345 N.E.2d 782 (1976); Toler v. Baldwin County Savings & Loan Association, 286 Ala. 320, 239 So.2d 751 (1970); Smith v. Olney Federal Savings & Loan Association, 415 S.W.2d 515 (Tex.Civ.App.1967).

3. In re Beacon Distributors, Inc., 441 F.2d 547 (1st Cir.1971); Cobb v. Osman, note 1 supra; Sanders v. Lackey, note 1, supra. See 131 A.L.R. 4, 62 (1941). Where the first grantee of a portion of mortgaged land assumes or takes subject to the mortgage and other parcels are then sold to grantees who pay full value with an agreement that the mortgagor shall pay off the mortgage, although the parcel in the hands of the first grantee is subject to being sold first, the inverse order of alienation rule would apply to the other grantees. Moore v. Shurtleff, 128 Ill. 370, 21 N.E. 775 (1889).

4. Chancellor of New Jersey v. Towell, 80 N.J.Eq. 223, 82 A. 861, 39 L.R.A.,N.S.,

359, Ann.Cas.1914A, 710 (1912); Epperson v. Cappellino, 113 Cal.App. 473, 298 P. 533 (1931). Contra: Ewing v. Bay Minette Land Co., 232 Ala. 22, 26, 166 So. 409, 413 (1936), on ground marshaling cannot be invoked by a debtor. See § 10.14, infra. This right of the mortgagor to marshaling will be available against subsequent transferees from the grantee if they are not bona fide purchasers. E.g., Costa v. Sardinha, 265 Mass. 319, 163 N.E. 887 (1928).

5. Sanders v. Lackey, note 1, supra; Reid v. Whisenant, note 1, supra. See 44 A.L.R. 608 (1926).

6. Wilcox v. Campbell, 106 N.Y. 325, 329, 12 N.E. 823, 826 (1887); Dieckman v. Walser, 114 N.J.Eq. 382, 386, 168 A. 582, 583 (1933); affirming 112 N.J.Eq. 46, 163 A. 284; Union Central Life Insurance Co. v. Cates, 193 N.C. 456, 463, 464, 137 S.E. 324, 327, 328 (1927); Welch v. Beers, 90 Mass. 151 (1864). Although the subsequent grantee may compel the mortgagee to foreclose first on the property held by the assuming grantee, in the event of a deficiency the mortgagee may sell the remainder of the tract in the hands of the mortgagor or subsequent grantee. Vanderspeck v. Federal Land Bank, 175 Miss. 759, 765, 167 So. 782, 783 (1936). See 39 L.R.A.,N.S., 359, 360 (1912).

If the proceeds of this sale are insufficient to pay the mortgage he may, at his option, either pay the balance due upon the mortgage in order to save his land, or let the land be sold.[7] In either event he has an action against the grantee for failing to perform his promise to pay the mortgage.[8] His damages, depending upon which option he selected, would be the amount he paid,[9] or either the value of the parcel in his hands [10] or the amount of the proceeds from its sale that were applied in discharge of the mortgage foreclosure decree.[11]

As stated by one court: "[W]here the mortgagor sells part of the mortgaged property 'subject to' the pre-existing mortgage without an agreement about payment of the mortgage, it is generally held that the mortgage lien remains an equal charge against all the mortgaged tract and that either mortgagor-vender or his vendee may enforce pro-rata application of the separate tracts to the satisfaction of the mortgage." [12] If it were clear that the purchase of the part was subject to the entire amount of the mortgage which was deducted from its purchase price, the part sold would be primarily liable for the entire debt. In such a case the mortgagor and subsequent purchasers for full value of portions of the tract left in the hands of the mortgagor could insist that the mortgagee, on foreclosing, resort first to the parcel sold subject to the mortgage.[13] Or if there is an explicit provision or clear evidence that the conveyance of a parcel is subject to a specified portion of the mortgage, the parties' intent will govern.[14] In many cases, however, there is no evidence of any express or implied agreement about payment of the mortgage. When such is the situation, where one parcel of a mortgaged tract is sold subject to the mortgage and a later portion is also sold subject to the mortgage, the weight of authority is that the debt will be prorated between the two grantees in proportion to the

---

7. See Wilcox v. Campbell, note 6, supra. He might also pay off the entire mortgage before any of the property is sold. In that case he would be subrogated to the rights of the mortgagee and could enforce the mortgage against the assuming grantee and, if the property is insufficient, take a judgment for the deficiency.

8. Sanders v. Lackey, note 1, supra.

9. See Cooley v. Murray, 11 Colo.App. 241, 52 P. 1108 (1898); Wilcox v. Campbell, 106 N.Y. 325, 12 N.E. 823 (1887).

10. Reid v. Whisenant, 161 Ga. 503, 131 N.E. 904, 44 A.L.R. 599 (1926).

11. Wilcox v. Campbell, 106 N.Y. 325, 12 N.E. 823 (1887). The various alternative remedies are not only set forth clearly but the underlying reasons for them are stated accurately by the court in its opinion.

12. Meadowlands National Bank v. Court Development, Inc., 192 N.J.Super.

579, 471 A.2d 801 (1983), certification denied 96 N.J. 303, 475 A.2d 595 (1984); Sanders v. Lackey, 59 Tenn.App. 207, 219, 439 S.W.2d 610, 616 (1968).

13. See 39 L.R.A.,N.S., 361 (1912).

14. Mickle v. Maxfield, 42 Mich. 304, 3 N.W. 961 (1879); Engle v. Haines, 5 N.J. Eq. 186 (1845) 43 Am.Dec. 624, affirmed 5 N.J.Eq. 632; Moore v. Shurtleff, 128 Ill. 370, 21 N.E. 775 (1889); New England Loan & Trust Co. v. Stephens, 16 Utah 385, 52 P. 624 (1898). If such an agreement is put into the mortgage it clearly will be binding upon all later transferees of any part of the property. Mickle v. Maxfield, supra; Maurer v. Arab Petroleum Corp., 134 Tex. 256, 135 S.W.2d 87, 131 A.L.R. 1 (1940). The same result can be accomplished by inserting a common provision in all deeds transferring fractional interests in the property. Moore v. Shurtleff, supra; New England Loan & Trust Co. v. Stephens, supra.

value of their respective lots.[15] And the same has been held where the mortgagor first conveyed one parcel of the mortgaged land to T–1 who assumed the payment of the mortgage and later conveyed another parcel to T–2 subject to it.[16]

 WESTLAW REFERENCES
mortgag** /5 assum! subject /p personal** primar*** second!
/p liable liability

§ 10.12 Gift Conveyances

Where the mortgagor makes a gift conveyance of a portion of a mortgaged tract with no covenants protecting the grantee against the mortgage, it has been held that the donee will take it subject to a primary liability for a proportional part of the mortgage debt.[1] It has been questioned whether this should be true where the grantor is personally liable for the debt.[2] In such cases, it is urged, the presumption should be that the transferor is to pay his own debt and, consequently, the land retained would be primarily liable.[3] If there is a covenant against encumbrances covering the mortgage, this has been held to be sufficient evidence of intention that the land under the gift conveyance shall not be liable for the debt as to throw the primary liability upon the residue in the hands of the grantor.[4]

 WESTLAW REFERENCES
deed /s covenant warrant*** /p unenforceable /p doner
grantee gift voluntary (lack*** no /s consideration)

---

15. Briscoe v. Power, 47 Ill. 447 (1868); Carpenter v. Koons, 20 Pa. 222 (1852); Stephens v. Clay, 17 Colo. 489, 30 P. 43 (1892); Hooper v. Capitol Life Insurance Co., 92 Colo. 376, 384, 20 P.2d 1011, 1014 (1933); Markham v. Smith, 119 Conn. 355, 363, 176 A. 880, 884 (1935); Hall v. Morgan, 79 Mo. 47 (1883); Hog v. Bramhall, 19 N.J.Eq. 563, 97 Am.Dec. 687; Stuyvesant Security Co. v. Dreyer, 103 N.J.Eq. 457, 461, 143 A. 616, 617 (1929), affirmed 105 N.J.Eq. 585, 148 A. 920, values at time of conveyance taken; Dieckman v. Walser, 112 N.J.Eq. 46, 53, 55, 163 A. 284, 287, 288 (1932), affirmed 114 N.J.Eq. 382, 168 A. 582. Cf. Savings Investment & Trust Co. v. United Realty & Mortgage Co., 84 N.J.Eq. 472, 94 A. 588 (1915), Ann.Cas.1916D, 1134, "subject to" clause in second mortgage.

16. Pearson v. Bailey, 177 Mass. 318, 58 N.E. 1028 (1901).

§ 10.12

1. Mills v. Kelley, 62 N.J.Eq. 213, 215, 50 A. 144, 145 (1901) ("Where the conveyance is voluntary, and there are no covenants, then equality is equity. There is no reason why the voluntary grantee should

not take the land with any charge that may rest upon it, except in so far as the parties themselves have otherwise stipulated."); Jackson v. Condict, 57 N.J.Eq. 522, 526, 41 A. 374 (1898). But see 131 A.L.R. 4, 88 (1941).

2. See Tiffany, Real Property, 3d ed., § 1446.

3. Id. In re Darby's Estate, 2 Ch. 465 (1907) (devisees of balance of mortgagor's property denied contribution against donee-grantee of mortgaged property by deed containing no reference to the mortgage and no covenants for title, express or implied).

4. Harrison v. Guerin, 27 N.J.Eq. 219 (1876). See Howser v. Cruikshank, 122 Ala. 256, 25 So. 206, 82 Am.St.Rep. 76 (1898). The covenant would serve only as evidence of intent. See 5 Houston L.Rev. 221 (1967). Since covenants cannot be effective without consideration, a warranty deed without exception is unenforceable and the donee has no recourse against mortgagor should mortgagee foreclose and cut out donee.

§ 10.13   Second Mortgages

Reverting to our hypothetical of Blackacre, if T–1 is a mortgagee rather than a purchaser, T–1 and E are both creditors of a common debtor and this is a situation to which the two funds rule applies.[1] In the simple example where R has made only one conveyance to T–1 or given one second mortgage to T–1 the result is the same, but it is reached by a different rationale. Under the inverse order doctrine it is that the mortgagor who incurred the debt should be the one to pay it. Under the two funds doctrine it is that the senior encumbrancer should not be able to foreclose on the only fund available to T–1. However the equities which really must be considered are not between E and T–1. E will be paid in any case and it does not matter to E whether he proceeds against the property upon which T–1 has a second mortgage or the property upon which he alone holds a mortgage. So the equity to be considered is actually the same as that considered under the inverse rule of alienation—should R, who incurred the debt, bear the burden of paying it off as opposed to T–1, who took the second mortgage as security expecting that R would pay off the first mortgage? Where there are no other junior lienholders involved or where their rights will not be prejudiced, the two funds rule will be applied.[2]

§ 10.13

1. Generally the funds must be in the hands of a common debtor of both creditors. Dixieland Realty Co. v. Wysor, 272 N.C. 172, 158 S.E.2d 7 (1967); Little v. United Investors Corp., 157 Conn. 44, 245 A.2d 567 (1968); Markman v. Russell State Bank, 358 F.2d 488 (10th Cir.1966). See 135 A.L.R. 739–40 for additional cases. But there are exceptions. See Charles Construction Co., Inc. v. Leisure Resources, Inc., 1 Mass.App. 755, 307 N.E.2d 336 (1974); the court found the reasoning underlying the two funds doctrine had equal application where there is only one fund. See also 8 L.R.A.,N.S., 965 (1912).

2. Associates Realty Credit Limited v. Brune, 89 Wash.2d 6, 568 P.2d 787 (1977); In the Matter of Forester, 529 F.2d 310 (9th Cir.1976); Zellerback Paper Co. v. Valley National Bank of Arizona, 18 Ariz.App. 301, 501 P.2d 570 (1972); Charles Construction Co., Inc. v. Leisure Resources, Inc., 1 Mass.App. 755, 307 N.E.2d 336 (1974); In Waff Brothers, Inc. v. Bank of North Carolina, N.A., 289 N.C. 198, 221 S.E.2d 273 (1976) a preliminary injunction was granted so that the trial court could determine whether the creditor did have security in a second fund. In Columbia Bank for Cooperatives v. Lee, 368 F.2d 934 (4th Cir.1966), certiorari denied 386 U.S. 992, 87 S.Ct. 1308, 18 L.Ed.2d 338 (1967), the doubly secured bank was required to satisfy its debt from the stock rather than the real property because the stock was worth more in the bank's hands than it would be in the hands of the competing creditor. In United States v. Herman, 310 F.2d 846 (2d Cir. 1962), certiorari denied 373 U.S. 903, 83 S.Ct. 1291, 10 L.Ed.2d 199 (1963) and United States v. Stutsman County Implement Co., 274 F.2d 733 (8th Cir.1960) the courts refused to subject the government to the requirement to marshal assets in favor of junior lienors. But the court enforced the requirement in United States v. LeMay, 346 F.Supp. 328 (E.D.Wis.1972), citing United States Fidelity & Guaranty Co. v. Long, 214 F.Supp. 307, 319 (D.Or.1963), "In the application of the doctrine, the United States and its agencies are on an equal basis with other creditors."

For an excellent collection of authorities, see 106 A.L.R. 1102 (1937). See Gest, Marshalling Assets with Reference to the Rights of Successive Part Purchasers and Incumbrancers, 27 Am.L.Reg.,N.S., 739 (1888); Strachan, The Marshalling of Mortgages, 22 L.Q.Rev. 307 (1906); See also notes, 79 U. of Pa.L.Rev. 782 (1931); 18 Harv.L.Rev. 453 (1905); 24 Iowa L.Rev. 328 (1939); 106 A.L.R. 1102 (1937); 5 L.R.A. 280 (1889); 12 L.R.A.,N.S., 965 (1908); 119 A.L.R. 1109 (1939).

If there has been a subsequent second mortgage or conveyance to T–2, does T–1 have the same right to marshal as against T–2 that he would have under the inverse order rule if he had paid full value with the agreement that the duty of discharging the mortgage would fall upon the residue of the land retained by R? Where the question involves competing holders of second mortgages or a second mortgagee and a later transferee, two divergent lines of authority have developed. The major difference between the two lines of cases under the two funds rule is the same distinction that has been offered to explain the difference between the inverse order rule and the two funds doctrine.[3] One group of courts holds that T–1 acquires a fixed and established right in equity at the time he takes his second mortgage on lot X to require E to look primarily to lots Y and Z when he forecloses and to sell them before he resorts to lot X held by T–1,[4] provided that E's rights will not be prejudiced by so doing.[5] Or where both lots must be sold to satisfy E's mortgage T–1 will have a right to any surplus from the sale.[6] This equity would be the same as the equity acquired by T–1 if T–1 were a purchaser rather than a second mortgagee, and under this line of authority the inverse order of alienation is applied.[7] Consequently any subsequent taker of lots X or Y by way of purchase for full value or as second mortgagee will take subject to T–1's prior equity unless he can qualify as a bona fide purchaser for value without notice.[8] Courts adopting this view also hold that T–1 can effectively guard against such a possibility by recording his second mortgage on X which will then give constructive notice of his equity to any later taker of Y or Z.[9] If the subsequent taker is not a bona fide purchaser, the priority of

---

3. "[T]he two doctrines are quite distinct. The equity of marshaling, until it is asserted, is a mere inchoate equity subject to displacement, whereas the equity of the purchaser of land subject to a lien to have that lien satisfied out of land remaining in the grantor and then out of the parcels subsequently conveyed in inverse order of alienation, where it exists at all, is a fixed indefeasible right." Fidelity & Casualty Co. v. Massachusetts Mutual Life Insurance Co., 74 F.2d 881, 884 (4th Cir.1935).

4. See note 7, infra.

5. See note 14, § 10.9, supra.

6. Banks-Miller Supply Co. v. Smallridge, 154 W.Va. 360, 175 S.E.2d 446 (1970).

7. Sibley v. Baker, 23 Mich. 312 (1871); Hunt v. Townsend, 4 Sandf. Ch. 510 (N.Y. 1847); Riverside Apartment Corp. v. Capital Construction Co., 107 N.J.Eq. 405, 413, 152 A. 763, 769 (1930), affirmed 110 N.J. Eq. 67, 158 A. 740, probably constructive notice from recording; Fidelity & Casualty Co. v. Mass. Mutual Life Insurance Co., 74 F.2d 881 (4th Cir.1935), paramount tax lien on the various parcels; Bank of Commerce

of Evansville v. First National Bank of Evansville, 150 Ind. 588, 594, 50 N.E. 566, 568 (1898), senior judgment lien on both properties; mortgage on one, followed by conveyance of other to trustee to pay creditors; Sanborn, McDuffie Co. v. Keefe, 88 N.H. 236, 187 A. 97, 106 A.L.R. 1097 (1936); Ingersoll v. Somers Land Co., 82 N.J.Eq. 476, 89 A. 288 (1913); Robeson's Appeal, 117 Pa. 628, 12 A. 51 (1888), senior judgment lien on both properties; recorded mortgage on one followed by mortgage on the other; later mortgagee charged with constructive notice of the earlier. See 76 A.L.R.3d 333, § 4.

8. As to the rule where the transferees of other parcels have not parted with value cf. quotation from Newby v. Fox, note 20, infra, decided in a jurisdiction following the second view in respect to marshaling by a junior mortgagee on the first parcel.

9. Harron v. Du Bois, 64 N.J.Eq. 657, 54 A. 857 (1903); Ingersoll v. Somers Land Co., note 7, supra; Appeal of Robeson, note 7, supra. If T–1 fails to record he cannot invoke the doctrine against one without actual notice. Birch River Boom & Lum-

T–1 over him is said to rest upon the fact that his equity is not only prior in time but that the later equity is inferior to his either by reason of notice or lack of value being given for it.[10] If T–2, the subsequent purchaser or mortgagee of Y or Z, can qualify under the bona fide purchase rule, he would then stand on an equality with T–1 and the paramount mortgage would then be apportioned between them according to the value of their respective lots.[11]

The rule in England[12] and that followed by many cases in this country[13] is that the equity of marshaling acquired by T–1 when he takes his second mortgage on X is not a fixed equitable right when T–1 acquires his lien, but remains inchoate until the right is invoked by actual proceedings to enforce it;[14] and if at that time the rights of third

---

ber Co. v. Glendon Boom & Lumber Co., 71 W.Va. 139, 76 S.E. 167 (1922). Some cases do not even mention notice. See 106 A.L.R. 1102, 1103 (1937).

If the paramount lien arises against each of the two or more parcels by separate instruments, only most exhaustive search of all deeds or mortgages to or from the mortgagor could reveal to T–2 the prior junior mortgage on lot X to T–1. See 5 Duke B.A.J. 35, 39 (1937); such a burden is much too onerous to impose. Green v. Ramage, 18 Ohio 428 (1849).

10. Conrad v. Harrison, Va.1882, 3 Leigh 532 (Va.1882); Ingersoll v. Somers Land Co., 82 N.J.Eq. 476, 89 A. 288 (1913), constructive notice by record and later mortgage of other parcel was to secure pre-existing debt; Harron v. Du Bois, 64 N.J. Eq. 657, 54 A. 857 (1903), later encumbrance was judgment lien acquired with constructive notice of prior recorded mortgage. See Newby v. Fox, 90 Kan. 317, 319, 133 P. 890, 891 (1913); Bank of Commerce v. First National Bank, note 7, supra, second parcel conveyed to trustee to pay creditors; Sanborn, McDuffie Co. v. Keefe, 88 N.H. 236, 187 A. 97, 106 A.L.R. 1097 (1936). See also 106 A.L.R. 1102, 1103 (1937). Cf. Sager v. Tupper, 35 Mich. 133 (1876); Reilly v. Mayer, 12 N.J.Eq. 55 (1858).

11. Cf. Green v. Ramage, 18 Ohio 428 (1849). Of course both T–1 and T–2 would have an equity to have lot Z in the hands of R sold before touching either X or Y. In such a case any deficiency would be prorated between the latter. See Newby v. Fox, quoted n. 20, infra.

12. Aldrich v. Cooper, 8 Ves. 381 (1803); Barnes v. Racster, 1 Younge & C.Ch.Cas. 401 (1842); Bugden v. Bignold, 2 Y. & C.C.C. 377 (1843). "This disposition of the problem * * * is perhaps attributable to the absence of a recording system at the time the law crystallized. This fact kept

the English courts from dealing with the question of presumed notice * * *." Shenkin, Marshaling of Securities, 79 U. of Pa.L.Rev. 782, 784 (1931). See Kay, L.J., in Flint v. Howard, 2 Ch. 54, 73 (1893); Barnes v. Racster, 1 Younge & C.C.C. 401 (1842). See also 106 A.L.R. 1102, 1109 (1937). But cf. Falconbridge, Mortgages, 2d ed., 1931, § 139.

13. "The decided cases in this country are in conflict. Many jurisdictions adopt the English view, while equally as many courts * * * have reached a contrary result, and have practically accorded the equity to marshal the effect of a lien." Shenkin, op.cit. supra note 12.

14. In some cases either of two junior creditors is in a position to demand marshaling. In In the Matter of Forester, 529 F.2d 310 (9th Cir.1976), a junior lienor was competing with the trustee in bankruptcy (in behalf of the mortgagor's creditors) where each had claims against one fund and the bank as paramount mortgagee had claims against two funds. The majority held that the junior lienor's right to marshaling became vested at the point when he demanded that the first mortgagee marshal its liens. The dissent pointed out that the trustee had already demanded of the bank that it marshal its liens in favor of the bankruptcy estate and that the junior lienor should lose the marshaling contest because its demand for marshaling was later in time than the trustee's and its equities were inferior to those of the trustee. The dissent continued: "The demand is an essential step in perfecting a right to marshal, good against a superior lienor or creditor upon whom the demand is made and against others who are also entitled to marshaling, but the demand does not itself create a lien or interest in any asset. A right to marshal does not ripen into an interest in the nature of an equitable lien persons are involved, it will not be enforced to their prejudice.[15] As a consequence, the paramount mortgage is prorated between the two junior mortgagees in proportion to the value of the parcel to which each has claim.[16] In some of the American cases marshaling is refused by simply denying that when T–2 takes his interest in Y he is charged with constructive notice of the inchoate equity of T–1 through his recorded second mortgage on X.[17]

The English courts prorate even though the later second mortgagee of lot Y has actual notice of the prior junior lien on lot X.[18] There is American authority that T–1's prior equity, even though regarded as inchoate, will prevail over T–2 if the latter did not part with value for it.[19] However, if T–2 paid value, doubt has been expressed as to whether T–1 should prevail over him even if he actually knew of the existence of T–1's mortgage but had no reason to anticipate that T–1 would invoke the doctrine of marshaling.[20] Even if T–2 is a purchaser

until the court, applying equitable principles, enforces it." Id. at 319. Both majority and dissent cite Harrington v. Taylor, 176 Cal. 802, 169 P. 690 (1917) which states: "This inchoate right or equity is not a lien, and is therefore subject to defeat at any time before it is attempted to be enforced."

15. Vandever Investment Co., Inc. v. H.E. Leonhardt Lumber Co., 503 P.2d 185, 76 A.L.R.3d 315 (Okl.1972); Platte Valley Bank of North Bend v. Kracl, 185 Neb. 168, 174 N.W.2d 724 (1970); St. Clair Savings Association v. Janson, 40 Ohio App.2d 211, 318 N.E.2d 538, 69 O.O.2d 196 (1974). Two funds denied when it would prejudice general creditors, Langel v. Moore, 119 Ohio St. 299, 164 N.E. 118 (1928); Bronaugh v. Burley Tobacco Co., 212 Ky. 680, 685, 280 S.W. 97 (1926), junior mortgage on one tract, followed by execution lien on other tract; Richards v. Cowles, 105 Iowa 734, 75 N.W. 648 (1898).

16. Omaha National Bank v. Continental Western Corp., 203 Neb. 264, 278 N.W.2d 339 (1979); Vandever Investment Co., Inc. v. H.E. Leonhardt Lumber Co., n. 64, supra; Bryson v. Newtown Real Estate and Development Corp., 153 Conn. 267, 216 A.2d 176 (1965); Conneaut Building & Loan Co. v. Felch, 100 Ohio App. 52, 135 N.E.2d 480, 60 O.O. 15 (1955); Green v. Ramage, 18 Ohio 428, 51 Am.Dec. 458 (1849). See 76 A.L.R.3d 351, § 5 (1977).

17. See Gilliam v. McCormack, 85 Tenn. 597, 4 S.W. 521 (1887); Bronaugh v. Burley Tobacco Co., note 15, supra; Cf. last sentence quoted from Shenkin, note 12, supra.

18. Barnes v. Racster, 1 Younge & C.C.C. 401 (1842). See note 12, supra.

19. E.g., Ingersoll v. Somers Land Co., 82 N.J.Eq. 476, 89 A. 288 (1913), later mortgage of other parcel was to secure preexisting debt; Harron v. Du Bois, 64 N.J.Eq. 657, 54 A. 857 (1903), later encumbrance was judgment lien; Humphries v. Fitzpatrick, 253 Ky. 517, 69 S.W.2d 1058 (1934), attachment creditor as to second parcel; Bank of Commerce of Evansville v. First National Bank of Evansville, 150 Ind. 588, 594, 50 N.E. 566, 568 (1898), later conveyance of second parcel to trustee to pay creditors. See quotation from Newby v. Fox, note 20, infra. General creditors of the mortgagor have been regarded as falling within this class, First National Bank of Boston v. Proctor, 40 F.2d 841 (1930), in spite of a suggestion that this was unfair to them. See Langdell, A Brief Survey of Equity Jurisdiction, 15. Compare Langel v. Moore, 32 Ohio App. 352, 168 N.E. 57 (1928), affirmed 119 Ohio St. 299, 164 N.E. 118, commented on, 43 Harv.L.Rev. 501 (1930). Cf. Shewmaker v. Yankey, 23 Ky. L.Rep. 1759, 66 S.W. 1 (1902), general creditors for whose benefit an assignment has been made; Bronaugh v. Burley Tobacco Co., 212 Ky. 680, 280 S.W. 97 (1926), judgment creditor.

20. "One who acquires title through the debtor without parting with value (as a judgment creditor or a grantee in a voluntary conveyance) cannot thereby gain any superior standing. Even a purchaser for value who becomes such with notice of a proceeding to enforce the right to have the securities marshaled must be deemed to have acted at his peril. But it might unduly extend this merely equitable right to allow its enforcement against one who has bought and paid for the singly mortgaged land, knowing, to be sure, of the existence for value but has notice of a proceeding by T–1 to enforce his equity he will take subject to it.[21]

The doctrine of the first group of cases has been vigorously criticised as a mistaken and improper application of the doctrine of sale in the inverse order of alienation.[22] It is said that a second mortgagee on X, unlike a purchaser of it for full value, does not pay to get the land free and clear of the first mortgage. He merely bargains for a security interest in it subordinate to the first mortgage. So far as other portions of the tract are concerned, since he did not stipulate for any security interest in them, it even has been argued that as to them he should have no better right than general creditors and should come in, *pari passu,* with them.[23] And it is contended that he should have no priority over T–2 who has acquired an interest in those other parcels without notice as purchaser for full value or as mortgagee.

In answer it is urged that "Second mortgages upon portions of mortgaged premises are rarely taken without considering and relying upon the equity which will arise in favor of the second mortgagee to have the first mortgage charged upon the residue of the property; * * *."[24] Furthermore, it has been pointed out that the English rule opens a door to the practice of fraud by the mortgagor-transferor.[25] And apart from this, it has been difficult for one scholar to understand how the right of a second mortgagee to marshaling, which at the time he takes his mortgage exists against his mortgagor and the owner of the paramount mortgage of the whole tract,[26] "can be lost by the intervention of a second mortgagee, over whom, and over the mortgagor, the second mortgagee has no control; nor is it easy to understand why a second mortgagee should be obliged to keep constant watch upon the registry of deeds and assert his equity by litigation against every

of the two mortgages, but having no particular reason to anticipate that the doctrine of marshaling securities will ever be invoked." Newby v. Fox, 90 Kan. 317, 323, 133 P. 890, 892 (1913). Cf. text at note 8, supra.

21. Id.

22. "If this doctrine is applied to successive second mortgages in these cases, and the second lot so mortgaged is sold first on foreclosure of the blanket mortgage to the exoneration of the second mortgage on the first lot, the result is almost surely to destroy altogether the second mortgage on that lot. * * * It should be clear that it never can be applied without such injury where the second parcel has been mortgaged instead of conveyed outright." Walsh & Simpson, Cas. Security Transactions, 376. See also Newby v. Fox, 90 Kan. 317, 325, 113 P. 890, 893 (1913).

23. "As between secured and unsecured creditors, equity clearly ought to favor the

latter class, if either." Langdell, A Brief Survey of Equity Jurisdiction, 15.

24. La Farge Fire Insurance Co. v. Bell, 22 Barb. 54, 65 (N.Y.1856). As to the duty of a mortgagor to pay off a first mortgage for the benefit of a second mortgagee and the latter's justifiable expectation of advancement in that event see § 10.6, supra.

25. "There is nothing to stop him from giving C, a friend, a mortgage on the second property, reducing to that extent the amount that B would otherwise get. Of course, if a court of equity even suspects the presence of fraud in the case, B and C will not be treated equally, but the possibility is still present, and it may be for this reason that a number of American jurisdictions have reached an opposite result." Shenkin, op.cit. supra note 12, 785 n. 14.

26. See note 20, supra.

casual purchaser who records a deed fixing a later lien upon the mortgaged land." [27]

The English rule of pro-ration even though the subsequent second mortgagee of Y had notice of the prior junior mortgage on X seems wrong. Very clearly T–1 did acquire an equity of marshaling against lots Y and Z at the time he took his second mortgage on X. The equity he acquired at that time may well be regarded as "so weak that the rights of a bona fide purchaser for value without notice could displace it, but the equity should be sufficiently virile not to be defeated by the rights of a subsequent taker with notice of its existence." [28] On the other hand, the rule of pro-ration if T–2 takes without notice of any sort seems entirely fair and prevents the caprice of E from determining where any loss shall fall. If notice is only constructive through recordation of T–1's second mortgage, it is difficult to decide between the two results. The preferable solution would seem to be a compromise. Where the "two funds" rule of marshaling is proper it should not be regarded as creating in the first sub-mortgagee of a parcel a fixed indisplaceable equity as does the inverse order of alienation rule in ties having "jarring liens." [29] To this extent there is merit in the attitude of the courts in the second group of cases. So regarded, however, it seems desirable to accept the view of the first group to the extent that T–1's right to marshaling against the other parcels be recognized as the general rule but that relief will be refused in the particular case if it would work injustice.[30] This gives to the "two funds" doctrine to some extent the greater certainty of the inverse order rule and yet preserves to it sufficient flexibility to deal with the individual case, if this should be necessary, at the date the right is invoked by action. This flexibility, unimportant where the inverse rule is properly applicable, i.e., in case of successive purchases of portions of the mortgaged property for full value, is of consequence where sub-mortgages on different parcels are concerned. As has been pointed out, the reason is that the lienor on lot X may be amply secured whereas the lienor on lot Y is insufficiently margined.[31]

The last point has relevancy also where one of the sub-mortgagees of part of the property subject to a paramount mortgage has taken, in addition, a piece of property not under that mortgage.[32] That is, lots X

27. Keigwin, Cas.Morts., 583 n. 49.

28. Shenkin, Marshaling of Securities, 79 U. of Pa.L.Rev. 782, 787 (1931).

29. Shenkin, op.cit. supra note 28, at 785.

30. E.g., Bernhardt v. Lymburner, 85 N.Y. 175 (1881), although recognizing the general rule of marshaling as being established, refused to apply it where it would work injustice. See also, Sternberger v. Sussman, 69 N.J.Eq. 199, 60 A. 195 (1905), affirmed 85 N.J.Eq. 593, 98 A. 1087. Look also at Payne v. Avery, 21 Mich. 524 (1870); Milligan's Appeal, 104 Pa. 503 (1883).

31. Glenn, Morts., § 298. The learned author adds: "The fact that one may have such a case in front of him does not require a general rule that there shall never be marshalling in the case of liens, but it will justify an exception in this case of hardship." Ibid.

32. In general assets will not be marshaled where there are different funds, or the funds are not in the hands of a com-

and Y only are mortgaged to E. T–1 takes a second mortgage on lot X and also takes a first mortgage on lot Z. T–2 then takes a second mortgage on lot Y with knowledge of the situation. T–1 as well as E is a doubly secured creditor and any equity of marshaling he may have as against E and Y would seem to be limited to the excess of his debt over the value of his outside security, Z. T–2, if T–1 is disregarded, has an equity to have E go first against X. The proper solution, therefore, would seem to be that T–2 should be able to have marshaling, limited only by T–1's superior claim to be able to reach X ahead of T–2 as to any deficiency he would have after applying the value of lot Z. If T–1 is amply secured by Z alone, there is authority for the indicated result.[33] Even if he is not, the principle suggested seems properly applicable and could be used without difficulty if T–1's debt was due at the time of E's foreclosure. Even if it was not, T–1 might be protected by requiring clear proof of the minimum amount Z would yield and reserving out of the sale of X an amount equal to the difference until T–1's debt matured.[34]

 WESTLAW REFERENCES
second*** junior /5 mortgage** /p doctrine rule /s (inverse /s order alienation) "two fund" (marshal*** /s asset)

§ 10.14 Marshaling by Mortgagor—Exemptions

In general a debtor is not entitled to invoke the doctrine of marshaling,[1] but there are many circumstances in which the mortgagor can compel a doubly secured creditor to resort to one fund rather than to another. Even where the mortgagor is primarily liable for the debt he can restrict the mortgagee to selling only so much of the property as is necessary to pay off the mortgage.[2] And he can compel the selling of the property by parcels or en masse as will be most advantageous to him.[3] If the mortgagor is only secondarily liable he can force the mortgagee to proceed against the person or property primarily liable if

mon debtor, but there are exceptions to this. See note 1, supra.

33. Worth v. Hill, 14 Wis. 559 (1861). See Glenn, Morts., § 299.

34. Cf. Worth v. Hill, 14 Wis. 559 (1861). The court said that where the adequacy of T–1's outside security could not be tested by sale, the court might nevertheless grant marshaling to T–2 upon testimony of witnesses provided that such testimony clearly established the entire adequacy of lot Z.

§ 10.14

1. See Dolphin v. Aylward, 4 Eng. & Irish.App.L.Rev. 486, 505; Newby v. Fox, 90 Kan. 317, 320, 133 P. 890, 891 (1913); Rogers v. Meyers, 68 Ill. 92, 97 (1873). See

Schwartz, Marshaling Assets for Benefit of Mortgagor, 5 Not.D.Law. 208 (1930); 47 L.R.A.,N.S., 302 (1914).

2. See text at § 7.21 supra.

3. Id. Security Savings Bank v. King, 198 Iowa, 1151, 199 N.W. 166 (1924); McClintic-Marshall Co. v. Scandinavian-American Building Co., 296 F. 601 (9th Cir. 1924).

As to the right of the maker of a negotiable instrument to compel the marshaling of securities in his favor, look at Sowell v. Federal Reserve Bank of Dallas, 268 U.S. 449, 45 S.Ct. 528, 69 L.Ed. 1041 (1925), discussed in note, 39 Harv.L.Rev. 256 (1925). See also note, 34 Col.L.Rev. 779 (1934).

that will not prejudice the mortgagee.[4] Similarly, if the mortgagor in selling part of a mortgaged tract takes back a mortgage on the portion sold so that he now occupies the position of a singly secured creditor as well as being debtor-mortgagor of the doubly secured creditor, he is entitled to marshaling under the two funds doctrine.[5]

Perhaps the most frequent case where the question of a mortgagor's right to marshal has arisen is where one of the mortgaged parcels, X, is subject to a homestead exemption which was waived [6] in favor of E when R gave the mortgage on the entire tract of which X is a part.[7] Later R may have given a second mortgage on parcel Y on which R had no exemption. Where the question arises between the two creditors E and T–1, the weight of authority refuses to apply the usual two funds rule of marshaling in favor of T–1 even though the result may be that E will collect out of Y leaving T–1 unsecured.[8] The justification for this result is found in the policy of protecting homesteads from forced sales. In some states legislation expressly protects the mortgagor and his family in such a situation.[9] There are, however, some cases which have held that T–1 may have marshaling even against X, the homestead parcel, this being the fund to which he had no access.[10]

Where the question arises between the mortgagor and his creditors, E and T–1, the majority rule is that he may compel E on foreclosure to sell first the property to which the homestead exemption does not apply, i.e., that he may have marshaling against T–1.[11] And there are

4. Konoff v. Lantini, 111 R.I. 691, 306 A.2d 176 (1973); Bartley v. Pikeville National Bank & Trust Co., 532 S.W.2d 446 (Ky.App.1976); Cook v. American States Insurance Co., 150 Ind.App. 88, 275 N.E.2d 832 (1971); Sanders v. Lackey, 59 Tenn. App. 207, 439 S.W.2d 610 (1968); Champlain Valley Federal Savings & Loan Association v. Ladue, 35 A.D.2d 888, 316 N.Y.S.2d 19 (1970).

5. Newby v. Fox, note 1, supra.

6. A debtor may waive his homestead in property so far as the mortgage goes when he gives property on which he has declared it as security for a debt. See Thomas v. Wisner, 65 Colo. 243, 180 P. 744 (1919); Cleve v. Adams, 222 N.C. 211, 22 S.E.2d 567 (1942).

7. For discussions and collections of cases, see 46 Harv.L.Rev. 1035 (1933); 12 Tex.L.Rev. 514 (1934); 23 Minn.L.Rev. 692 (1939), reprinted, 23 Or.L.Rev. 204 (1944); 44 A.L.R. 758 (1926); 77 A.L.R. 371 (1932); 17 Ann.Cas. 1061; 47 L.R.A.,N.S., 302, 303 (1913).

8. McLaughlin v. Hart, 46 Cal. 638 (1873), approved on its special facts by Glenn, Mortgages, § 37.3; Bowers v. Norton, 175 Minn. 541, 222 N.W. 71 (1928), T–1 being an attaching creditor; McArthur v.

Martin, 23 Minn. 74 (1876). See 44 A.L.R. 758 (1926); 77 A.L.R. 371 (1932).

9. E.g., Ill.Code Civ.Proc. § 12–904; S.C. Const. Art. 3, § 28 (subsequently amended); Wis.Stat.Ann. 815.20; Iowa Code of 1950, § 561.21. See 44 A.L.R. 758, 761 (1926); 77 A.L.R. 371, 372 (1932).

10. E.g., State Savings Bank of Anderson v. Harbin, 18 S.C. 425 (1883); cf. Plain v. Roth, 107 Ill. 588 (1883). See 44 A.L.R. 758, 761, 762 (1926). Statutory enactments have overcome most of this authority. E.g., White v. Polleys, 20 Wis. 503, 91 Am. Dec. 432 (1866), later nullified by Wis.Stat. Ann. § 272.20.

11. Alston v. Bitely, 252 Ark. 76, 477 S.W.2d 446 (1972). In Sims v. McFadden, 217 Ark. 810, 233 S.W.2d 375 (1950), the state refused to apply marshaling where exemption would be destroyed even though it entailed a loss to general creditors. Boykin v. First State Bank, 61 S.W.2d 126 (Tex.Civ.App.1933), T–1 being a second mortgagee; In re Tucker's Estate, 160 Or. 362, 85 P.2d 1025 (1938); Frick Co. v. Ketels, 42 Kan. 527, 22 P. 580, 16 Am.St. Rep. 507 (1889). See 44 A.L.R. 758, 763 (1926); 77 A.L.R. 371, 373 (1932).

Where there are other interests exempt under state policy or statute, courts will statutory provisions to the same effect.[12]   There is, however, authority that the mortgagor cannot compel marshaling in such a case.[13]

Where the case arises only between R and E, the majority rule permitting R to save his homestead if E can get paid out of non-exempt property seems a desirable result.[14]   Where exercise of the right to compel marshaling will result in saving the mortgaged homestead at the expense of a creditor whose hold is on non-exempt property, the question moves into doubtful area.   Perhaps T–1 should be granted marshaling against a homestead if he is a second mortgagee of Y but not if he acquired his lien by way of judgment or attachment lien.[15]

 WESTLAW REFERENCES

creditor debtor mortgag** /p doctrine rule /s marshal*** /s asset /p compel! forc*** restrict***

§ 10.15   Effect of Release by Mortgagee

The paramount mortgagee of a tract, having knowledge of parcels which have been transferred or mortgaged to persons under circumstances giving to them a right of marshaling against other portions of the property, must not do anything to defeat the rights of such persons.[1] The knowledge must be actual, not constructive through the recordation of subsequent conveyances or mortgages of portions of the mortgaged property.[2]   If the paramount mortgagee does have actual notice

protect such interests held by a mortgagor by refusing to apply the principle of marshaling in favor of a junior lienor. Dower was protected in Alston v. Bitely, supra this note; Bowen v. Brockenbrough, 119 Ind. 560, 20 N.E. 534 (1889); Stokes v. Stokes, 206 N.C. 108, 173 S.E. 18 (1934). Beneficiaries of life insurance policies may have the right to protection, Meyer v. United States, 375 U.S. 233, 84 S.Ct. 318, 11 L.Ed.2d 293 (1963); Barbin v. Moore, 85 N.H. 362, 159 A. 409, 83 A.L.R. 62 (1932). Marshaling was not applied where the effect would have been to defeat rights of survivorship of debtor's widow in mortgaged realty held in tenancy by the entirety; see First National City Bank v. Phoenix Mutual Life Insurance Co., 364 F.Supp. 390 (S.D.N.Y.1973).

12. See note 9, supra. See 44 A.L.R. 758, 766 (1926); 77 A.L.R. 371, 374 (1932).

13. Booker v. Booker, 225 Ala. 626, 144 So. 870 (1932), discussed 46 Harv.L.Rev. 1034 (1933); Searle v. Chapman, 121 Mass. 19 (1876). See 44 A.L.R. 758, 766 (1926).

14. First National Bank v. Powell, —— Mont. ——, 689 P.2d 255 (1984) (R may have marshalling only if she demands it at the foreclosure sale). See 46 Harv.L.Rev. 1035 (1933); 12 Tex.L.Rev. 515 (1934).

15. E.g., in Merchants National Bank v. Stanton, 55 Minn. 211, 56 N.W. 821, 43 Am.St.Rep. 491 (1893), a mortgagee was granted marshaling on the ground that his interest arose by contract and not *in invitum*. But cf. Boykin v. First State Bank, 61 S.W.2d 126, 129 (Tex.Civ.App.1933).

§ 10.15

1. See Broughton v. Mount Healthy Flying Service, 104 Ohio App. 479, 143 N.E.2d 597, 5 O.O.2d 224 (1957). In General Builders Supply Co. v. Arlington Cooperative Bank, 359 Mass. 691, 271 N.E.2d 342 (1971) reformation of release was denied where it would prejudice rights of subsequent lienors.

2. Iglehart v. Crane & Wesson, 42 Ill. 261, 268 (1866); Woodward v. Brown, 119 Cal. 283, 51 P. 2, 63 Am.St.Rep. 108 (1897), modified 119 Cal. 283, 51 P. 542, 63 Am.St. Rep. 108; Ocean County National Bank v. J. Edwin Ellor & Sons, Inc., 116 N.J.Eq. 287, 290, 173 A. 138, 139 (1934); Balen v. Lewis, 130 Mich. 567, 90 N.W. 416, 47 Am. St.Rep. 499 (1902); Bridgewater Roller Mills Co. v. Strough, 98 Va. 721, 37 S.E. 290 (1900); Clarke v. Cowan, 206 Mass. 252, 92 N.E. 474, 138 Am.St.Rep. 388 (1910), accord. See also Stuyvesant v. Hall, 2 Barb.Ch. 151, 158 (N.Y.1847); 110

of subsequent alienations of mortgages of parcels of the mortgaged property he acts at his peril in releasing from the mortgage any part of the property against which the marshaling equity runs.[3] Hence if he releases a part under such circumstances, he must deduct from the debt, before enforcing his lien against the property in the hands of these persons, the value of the property released which they had a right to have him apply to the debt before resorting to the property held by them.[4] If the right was to have the entire parcel applied first, its entire value must be deducted.[5] On the other hand, if the right was only that the released lot should be used to satisfy its pro rata share of the debt, the mortgagee must abate the debt only to such a proportion of it as the value of released parcel bore to the value of the entire tract.[6]

If the property released is one against which there is no right of marshaling, e.g., if it is the parcel first aliened in cases where the inverse order of alienation rule applies, the mortgagee does not have to make any deduction of its value before he can enforce the mortgage against the other parcels.[7] Further, if in giving a release of a parcel the mortgagee received a consideration which he applied upon the mortgage debt, he may enforce the balance of the debt against the

A.L.R. 65, 70 (1937); 131 A.L.R. 4, 109 (1941); Ann.Cas.1916D, 1119, 1133; Bridgewater Roller Mills v. Receivers of Baltimore Building & Loan Association, 124 F. 718 (1903). See 110 A.L.R. 65, 70, 75 (1937).

3. Charles Construction Co., Inc. v. Leisure Resources, Inc., 1 Mass.App. 755, 307 N.E.2d 336 (1974). See Brooks v. Benham, 70 Conn. 92, 97, 38 A. 908, 910, 66 Am.St. Rep. 87 (1897).

See also Green, Marshaling Assets in Texas, 34 Texas L.Rev. 1054 (1956).

4. The discharge has been rested upon an impairment of the grantee or mortgagee's right of subrogation. Brooks v. Benham, note 3, supra. Cf. § 5.19, supra, for the cognate problem where not just a portion, but the entire property has been sold. The doctrine of discharge here rests upon an application of the same basic principles applied, however, pro tanto. A junior encumbrancer is entitled to have proceeds of sale of mortgaged property applied upon the senior indebtedness, even though the property sold was not covered by the junior mortgage. See Continental Supply Co. v. Marshall, 152 F.2d 300 (C.C.A.Okl.1945), certiorari denied 327 U.S. 803, 66 S.Ct. 962, 90 L.Ed. 1028 (1946).

5. Manufacturers & Traders Trust Co. v. Miner Homes, Inc., 71 A.D.2d 826, 419 N.Y.S.2d 381 (1979), appeal denied 48 N.Y.2d 603, 421 N.Y.S.2d 1027, 396 N.E.2d 206 (1979); Pongetti v. Bankers Trust Sav-

ings & Loan Association, 368 So.2d 819 (Miss.1979); Brown v. Simons, 44 N.H. 475 (1863); Hill v. Howell, 36 N.J.Eq. 25 (1882); Schrack v. Shriner, 100 Pa. 451 (1882); New South South & Loan Association v. Reed, 1898, 96 Va. 345, 31 S.F. 514, 70 Am St.Rep. 858 (1898); Schaad v. Robinson, 50 Wash. 283, 97 P. 104 (1908); Deuster v. McCamus, 14 Wis. 307 (1861)—accord. See also Iglehart v. Crane & Wesson, 42 Ill. 261 (1866); Pomeroy, Eq.Jur., 4th Ed., § 1226, note 4; 110 A.L.R. 65, 67, 73 (1937); 131 A.L.R. 4, 108, 109 (1941). Cf. Gaskill v. Sine, 13 N.J.Eq. 400, 78 Am.Dec. 105 (1861); Snyder v. Crawford, 98 Pa. 414 (1881). Contra: McCoy v. Wynn, 215 Ala. 172, 174, 110 So. 129, 130 (1926).

6. Home Unity Savings & Loan Association v. Balmos, 192 Pa.Super. 542, 162 A.2d 244 (1960); Brooks v. Benham, 70 Conn. 92, 97, 38 A. 908, 910, 66 Am.St.Rep. 87 (1897). See Taylor v. Short's Administrator, 27 Iowa 361, 1 Am.Rep. 280 (1869); Parkman v. Welch, 36 Mass. (19 Pick.) 231 (1837).

7. Clark v. Kraker, 51 Minn. 444, 53 N.W. 706 (1892); Lyman v. Lyman, 32 Vt. 79, 76 Am.Dec. 151 (1859). As to the effect of the mortgagee's release of the mortgagor's personal liability, by dealings with a purchaser of part of the mortgaged property who assumed the mortgage debt, upon the lien of the mortgage upon another part which has been conveyed by the mortgagor to a third person, see 101 A.L.R. 618 (1936).

remaining property provided the amount received was equal to the fair value of the lot in question.[8] And if, as is provided in modern mortgages in which subdivisions are contemplated, the mortgagee is given permission to execute partial releases, he may release portions without further liability to other holders if he adheres to the terms of authorization.[9]

 WESTLAW REFERENCES

266k181 (mortgag** /p doctrine rule right /s marshal*** /s asset /p actual /p knowledge notice /p defeat releas*** diminish*** reduc***)

8. Beardsley v. Empire Trust Co., 96 N.J.Eq. 212, 124 A. 457 (1924), noted 24 Col.L.Rev. 804. See Taylor v. Short's Administrator 27 Iowa 361, 362, 1 Am.Rep. 280 (1869).

9. Thompson v. Thomas, 43 Cal.App. 588, 185 P. 427 (1919). See 110 A.L.R. 65, 72, 77 (1937).

§§ 10.16–11.0 are reserved for supplementary material.

Chapter 11

GOVERNMENT INTERVENTION IN THE MORTGAGE MARKET

Table of Sections

---

§ 11.1 The Mortgage Market, Institutional Lenders, and Their Regulators

About thirty percent of the outstanding debt in the United States is secured by real estate mortgages.[1] Because the United States is a nation of homeowners, it is not surprising that more than two-thirds (68%) of this mortgage debt is secured by 1-to-4 family homes. (Loans on buildings containing four or fewer residential units are conventionally lumped together and termed "home loans.") Another 18% of this mortgage debt is secured by commercial properties, 8% by multifamily apartment buildings, and 6% by farm properties. Mortgage financing is particularly important in the development of new real estate projects and those constructed without mortgage debt are relatively rare.

About 61% of the mortgage debt in the United States is held by private institutional lenders. Federally-supported agencies account for

§ 11.1

1. Economic data in this section are derived from Economic Report of the President (1984) at 302–03; U.S. Dep't of Commerce, Statistical Abstract of the United States 516–17 (1984); and current issues of the Federal Home Loan Bank Board Journal (FHLBBJ), each issue of which contains a statistical series. A further useful source is the Savings and Loan Fact Book, published annually by the United States League of Savings Associations. On the demand for mortgage credit, see Markstein, Crowding Out? An Analysis of Credit Supply and Demand, Mortgage Banking, June 1984, at 35; Aldrich & Kopcke, Real Estate Consequences of the New Credit Markets, 12 Real Est.Rev. 25 (No. 4, Winter 1983).

another 23%, with various miscellaneous lenders, including individuals, holding the remainder. Since private lending institutions are so important in the American mortgage market, they and the regulatory agencies under whose rules they operate are the subject of this section; a subsequent section will discuss the federally-supported agencies active in the mortgage market. There are four principal types of institutions active in mortgage lending in the United States. They are listed below, along with the share of total mortgage debt held by each.

1.	Savings and Loan Associations	27%
2.	Commercial Banks	18%
3.	Life Insurance Companies	8%
4.	Mutual Savings Banks	7%
	Total	61%

There are fairly wide differences in the preferences for mortgage investments among these four types of institutions. For example, the proportions of mortgages on 1-to-4 family homes held by commercial banks and mutual savings banks are roughly equal to their shares of the over-all mortgage market listed above. Savings and loan associations, however, exhibit a definite preference for home mortgages (i.e., those on 1-to-4 family dwellings); their loans account for 32% of all home mortgages. Life insurance companies, by comparison, have been steadily withdrawing from the home mortgage market since about 1968, and now account for only about 1.3% of all home loans.

On the other hand, apartment lending has continued to be quite attractive to life insurance companies; they hold about 13% of all loans on multi-family buildings. Mutual savings banks and savings and loan associations are also active in multi-family lending, holding about 12% and 28% of such loans respectively. Commercial banks have been gradually increasing their permanent lending on apartments, and now hold about 12% of all such loans. Institutions exhibit similar preferences for commercial loans as for apartment loans as discussed above, except that savings and loan associations are a much smaller factor in the commercial real estate market.

The foregoing discussion has focused on permanent or long term lending. Construction lending, which ties up the institution's funds for a relatively short time but requires close on-site supervision, is handled by commercial banks and savings associations to a very substantial extent.[2] Real estate investment trusts are also active in the construction lending field, but life insurance companies, lacking the necessary local officers and personnel, are almost totally absent from construction lending.

One type of lending organization not mentioned above is the mortgage banker (sometimes called a mortgage company or mortgage

---

2. See Mason & Leaffer, The Preferences of Financial Institutions for Construction and Permanent Mortgage Lending, 4 Am.Real Est. & Urb.Econ.Ass'n J. 41 (1976).

broker). This sort of company is organized to originate loans, not for retention in its own portfolio, but almost exclusively for sale or assignment to other investors or government-sponsored agencies which will hold the loans for the long term. All of the four types of financial institutions discussed above are active from time to time in transactions with mortgage bankers, as investors purchasing loans which mortgage bankers have originated. They may also act, in effect, as mortgage bankers themselves, originating loans which they do not expect to hold in portfolio, but rather which will be sold to other investors. A number of institutional lenders have also established mortgage banking subsidiaries in recent years.

An important feature of a mortgage banker's activity (as well as that of any other financial institution which happens to be acting in a mortgage banking capacity) is the "servicing" of the loan. Most investors which purchase mortgage loans on the secondary market lack local offices in the area in which the real estate is located. Consequently they usually contract with the originating lender for "servicing" to be provided by that local organization. Servicing includes collecting the regular payments of principal and interest, maintaining an appropriate escrow account for taxes and insurance, following up on any delinquency, and if necessary, arranging for foreclosure. The servicer maintains proper records, remits the loan payments to the investor which holds the loan, and communicates with the investor if problems arise. For performing this work the servicer receives a fee from the investor, commonly an annual amount of three-eighths of one percent of the average outstanding balance of the loan—for example, $150 on a $40,000 loan. Servicing is considered a profitable and attractive activity by mortgage bankers, and they are usually eager to retain servicing when a loan is sold.

The lending activities of mortgage bankers are relatively unregulated; they must, of course, comply with applicable state law, the requirements and guidelines set down by the investor institutions to whom they sell loans, and the requirements of FHA and VA to the extent that they originate loans of those types. However, they are not subject in most jurisdictions to the supervision of any specialized regulatory agency.[3] For the four major types of institutional mortgage holders, the contrary is true. Each of them must comply with the requirements of at least one, and sometimes several, specialized regulatory agencies at the federal or state level. A brief review of this regulatory system follows.

3. Eleven states license mortgage bankers: Arizona, Arkansas, Delaware, Florida, Hawaii, Illinois, Kentucky, Maryland, Nevada, New Jersey, New Mexico, and Puerto Rico. Supervision is typically handled by the Commissioner of Banking or Savings and Loan Associations. Several states exempt mortgage bankers which are approved by FHA, VA, or other federally-related agencies. See Review of State Mortgage Banker Licensing Statutes, Real Estate Finance Today, Nov. 1984, at 20.

Savings and Loan Associations

The Federal Home Loan Bank Board (FHLBB) is the national regulator of savings associations.[4] Such associations may be either federally or state chartered; about half of the associations are of each type. All federal charters are issued by the FHLBB, and federal associations are closely supervised by the FHLBB in virtually all areas of activity. The FHLBB also exercises considerable authority over most state-chartered savings and loan associations by virtue of their membership in the Federal Savings and Loan Insurance Corporation, an entity controlled by the FHLBB which insures depositors against loss up to a statutory maximum, currently $100,000. This deposit insurance is, of course, an extremely attractive drawing card for institutions seeking deposits, so most state-chartered institutions obtain it, as do all federal associations. The scope of the regulations governing state-chartered institutions through the FSLIC is somewhat more limited than the regulations governing federal associations; for example, the FHLBB's regulations governing lending powers apply to federal but not state institutions.[5] Nevertheless, the scope of FHLBB regulation over state-chartered FSLIC-insured associations is significant.

In most states, state-chartered associations are also subject to the supervision of a state banking or savings and loan commission or board. This agency or some applicable state statute often controls lending powers and other operational activities of state-chartered associations which are not governed by the FSLIC regulations. In many states, state-chartered associations are subject to periodic on-site examinations by both the federal and state authorities. In other states, however, a cooperative arrangement has been negotiated under which the state supervisory agency merely receives copies of the federal examiners' reports and does not attempt to perform independent examinations except in unusual or emergency cases.

There are two business forms under which savings and loan associations may operate: stock and mutual. A stock association is much like any other business corporation, but a mutual association has no outstanding stock, and is owned entirely by its depositors and borrowers. Nearly all states charter mutual associations, and about two-thirds of them charter stock associations as well. For many years, however, all federal associations were of the mutual type. In the 1970's the FHLBB began to permit some state stock associations to convert to

---

4. General descriptions of the FHLBB include Comment, Savings and Loan Associations, Securities Activities, and the Glass-Steagall Act, 20 Houst.L.Rev. 1383 (1983); Biederman & Tuccillo, Taxation and Regulation of the Savings and Loan Industry (1975); U.S. Dep't of Housing and Urban Development, Housing in the Seventies 73–74 (1974); Clarke, The Regulatory and Housing Functions of the FHLBB, 26 Bus.Law. 37 (1970). The Annual Report (April) issue of the Federal Home Loan Bank Board Journal will provide a current summary of the FHLBB's activities.

5. See, e.g., 12 CFR 545.33 (lending powers of federal S & L's); see Earthman, Residential Mortgage Lending: Charting a Course through the Regulatory Maze, 29 Vand.L.Rev. 957 (1976); Note, 33 DePaul L.Rev. 783 (1984).

federal charters while retaining their stock form.[6] This was a popular move, since stock ownership creates additional profit opportunities for the management and organizers of a savings association, and arguably provides a broader and more stable capital base as well.

Major changes in this system were brought about by the Garn-St. Germain Depository Institutions Act of 1982.[7] It authorized the FHLBB to allow conversion of any state-chartered association to a federal charter, and at the same time to convert from mutual to stock or vice versa.

Mutual Savings Banks

Until recently, these institutions were exclusively state-chartered and existed in only eighteen states, mostly in the New England and mid-Atlantic regions.[8] But in 1979 the FHLBB began permitting state-chartered MSB's to convert to federal charters,[9] and the Garn-St. Germain Act authorized it, in 1982, to begin issuing *de novo* federal charters to MSB's.[10]

As the name implies, MSB's are owned by their depositors and borrowers, and have no capital stock. They typically have lending powers which are somewhat broader than those of savings and loan associations, and they are apt to engage in somewhat more commercial and consumer lending than S & L's. Nevertheless, many of them are heavy housing lenders.

About two-thirds of the MSB's have their deposits insured with the FDIC, and many of the remainder are insured by the FSLIC. Some MSB's are also members of the federal home loan bank system, permitting them to receive "advances" or loans from their regional Federal Home Loan Bank.

Commercial Banks

The regulation of commercial banks is far more complex than that of any other form of financial institution. Part of the complexity derives from the fact that both federal and state charters are possible, a feature commonly termed the "dual banking" system.[11] More impor-

6. The FHLBB's regulations governing conversion are found in 12 CFR Part 563b. See generally Saba & Robbins, Savings and Loan Associations—Mutual to Stock Conversion Under the Revised Regulations, 17 Ark.L.Rev. 413 (1984); Allen, Capital Adequacy Problems of S & L's—And the Changes Needed to Meet Them, 10 FHLBBJ 2 (Feb. 1977); Allen, Stock Conversions: Where We Are Now, 9 FHLBBJ 2 (Mar. 1976).

7. Pub.L. No. 97.320, §§ 313–14, codified at 12 U.S.C.A. §§ 1464(i), 1725(j).

8. An excellent source of current information on mutual savings banks, published annually by the National Association of Mutual Savings Banks, is the National Fact Book of Mutual Savings Banking.

9. See 12 CFR Part 567, added by 44 Fed.Reg. 36013.

10. Note 7, supra, at §§ 311–13.

11. See Scott, The Dual Banking System: A Model of Competition in Regulation, 30 Stan.L.Rev. 1 (1977); Brown, The Dual Banking System in the United States (American Bankers Assoc. undated), reprinted in Subcomm. on Financial Institutions, Senate Comm. on Banking, Housing and Urban Affairs, Compendium of Issues

tant is the fact that three federal agencies (rather than a single agency as with savings and loan associations) are charged with commercial bank supervision.[12] All federally-chartered (so-called "national") banks are supervised by the Comptroller of the Currency, a division of the U.S. Treasury Department. State-chartered banks which are members of the Federal Reserve System, and are thereby privileged to draw funds at the credit windows of the Federal Reserve Banks, are supervised by the Board of Governors of the Federal Reserve System, commonly called the Federal Reserve Board (FRB) or the "Fed." Many large state banks fall in this category, and all federally-chartered banks are automatically members of the Federal Reserve System. State-chartered banks which are not members of the Federal Reserve System ("non-fed-member" banks) may nonetheless have their deposits insured (currently up to $100,000) by the Federal Deposit Insurance Corporation (FDIC), which in turn exercises supervisory authority over them. The great majority of state-chartered non-fed-member banks are FDIC-insured as are all fed-member banks and national banks.[13]

In addition to this complex federal regulatory structure, state-chartered banks are all at least potentially subject to regulation by a state agency.[14] In some jurisdictions the state supervision is intense, while in others the state regulators rely principally upon the examination and supervision efforts of the relevant federal agencies except with respect to the small number of banks which are not even FDIC-insured.

The banking regulatory system has fairly been called "baffling." [15] It is quite possible, for example, for a fed-member state bank to be subject to the regulations of at least three agencies—the FRB, the FDIC, and the state banking commissioner—with respect to various phases of its operations. Coordination among the multitude of agencies involved is not as extensive as might be desired. The system has obvious inefficiencies built into it, and it is not unusual for an institution to engage in a sort of "agency-shopping", changing its status in order to align itself with a regulatory agency that will better fit its desires.[16]

Relating to Branching by Financial Institutions, 94th Cong., 2d Sess. (1976) at 239.

12. See Mitchell-Lockyer, The Federalization of Banking-Due-on-Sales, A Case in Point, 15 Pac.L.J. 217 (1984); Gorinson & Manishin, Garn-St. Germain: A Harbinger of Change, 40 Wash. & Lee L.Rev. 1313 (1983); Note, Deregulation of the Banking Industry in the 1980's, 86 W.Va.L.Rev. 189 (1983); Via, Some Thoughts on Evaluating the Tripartite Federal Bank Regulatory System, 93 Banking L.J. 509 (1976); Kreider, American Banking: Structure, Supervision, and Strengths, 92 Banking L.J. 437 (1975).

13. See Murane, The FDIC and Bank Regulation, 89 Banking L.J. 483 (1972);

Scott & Mayer, Risk and Regulation in Banking: Some Proposals for Federal Deposit Insurance Reform, 23 Stan.L.Rev. 857 (1971).

14. See Vestner, Trends and Developments in State Regulation of Banks, 90 Banking L.J. 464 (1973); Bell, State Regulation of Commercial Banks, 26 Bus.Law. 109 (1970).

15. See Hackley, Our Baffling Banking System, Part I, 52 Va.L.Rev. 565 (1966); Part II, 52 Va.L.Rev. 771 (1966).

16. See Changing Charters—Did the Bank Switch Rather Than Fight the Fed. Examiners? Wall St.J., Apr. 26, 1976, at p. 1, col. 6.

The mortgage lending powers of national banks were traditionally governed by Section 24 of the Federal Reserve Act.[17] However, in 1982 the Garn-St. Germain Act removed all statutory restrictions on real estate lending by national banks.[18] The Office of Comptroller of the Currency then amended its rules to leave these banks essentially unrestricted.[19] Neither the FRB nor the FDIC regulate lending powers, so lending activities of state banks are subject only to applicable state statutes and regulations. At both the federal and state levels, commercial banks are usually granted greater discretion in real estate lending than are, for example, savings and loan associations. There is, however, wide variation from state to state.

A large number of proposals for reform of the federal banking regulatory system have been made in recent years, although none has been adopted at this writing. The most radical reform would collapse both banking and savings and loan regulators into a single federal agency. Less far-reaching proposals would leave the savings and loan industry separately regulated as at present, but would merge the three banking regulators into one or two agencies.[20] A strong case can be made for such reorganization, but members of the affected industries have been reluctant to embrace changes which, although theoretically desirable, would disturb relationships which they have come to understand and find manageable.

Life Insurance Companies

Of the four principal types of institutional mortgage lenders, only life insurance companies are not depository institutions. Instead, their assets come from premium payments on life policies and various retirement and annuity programs. These comprise a relatively stable and predictable source of funds compared with bank or savings deposits. Hence, they have a preference for long-term large-dollar mortgage loans. Since life companies are regulated only at the state level by insurance commissions or departments, and since the legal constraints on their lending are not very restrictive, they are generally able to make loans of precisely this type. Moreover, in most jurisdictions life companies are permitted to invest in real estate financings other than

---

17. 12 U.S.C.A. § 371.

18. Note 7, supra, at § 403.

19. 12 CFR Part 34, added by 48 Fed. Reg. 40698.

20. See Blueprint for Reform: The Report of the Task Group on Regulation of Financial Services (1984); Report of the President's Commission on Housing 131–33 (1982); Report of the President's Commission on Financial Structure and Regulation (the "Hunt Commission", after its chairman, Reed O. Hunt) (1972), at 87–95; the Federal Bank Commission Act, S. 684, 95th Cong., 1st Sess. (1977), proposing a single federal banking agency. See Note, The Federal Bank Commission Act: A Proposal to Consolidate the Federal Banking Agencies, 25 Cleve.St.L.Rev. 475 (1977); Keeffe and Head, What is Wrong with the American Banking System and What to do About It, 36 Md.L.Rev. 788 (1977); Verkuil, Perspectives on Reform of Financial Institutions, 83 Yale L.J. 1349 (1974). See also Hearings on Financial Institutions and the Nation's Economy (FINE) "Discussion Principles" before the Subcomm. on Financial Institutions, House Comm. on Banking, Currency and Housing, 94th Cong., 1st & 2d Sess., pts. 1–4 (1975).

standard mortgage loans. These include sale-leasebacks, sale-salebacks, leasehold mortgages, and other innovative financing methods. These investments are often called "basket" loans since the applicable law or regulation usually provides for a maximum percentage of assets which can be devoted to these relatively unusual types of financings.[21]

Real Estate Investment Trusts

A real estate investment trust (REIT) is much like a mutual fund, except that it invests in mortgages or equity positions in real estate rather than in securities. If seventy-five percent of the trust's income is derived from real estate, and if 95 percent of its profits are distributed annually to shareholders, the trust is taxed only on its retained earnings; in effect, the profits can be passed through to the shareholders without tax.[22] REIT's became a major factor in the 1970's in construction lending, especially on income properties, but they made few long-term loans. Shares of REIT's are generally traded on the national and regional stock exchanges and are widely held.

During recent history many REIT's which engaged in mortgage lending experienced financial difficulties. To a great extent they employed bank lines of credit as a source of capital from which to make construction loans. Increases in their cost of funds, construction delays and cost overruns, and inability of their developer-borrowers to market the projects they had financed were all important factors in producing losses. While many mortgage trusts became insolvent, those which survived have adopted more conservative practices and are likely to be a long-term force in the mortgage lending industry.[23]

 WESTLAW REFERENCES
di mortgage banker
di mortgage broker
di mortgage company

Savings and Loan Associations
f.h.l.b.b.   /p   f.s.l.i.c.

Mutual Savings Banks
[no queries]

Commercial Banks
"dual banking system" /p competit!

Life Insurance Companies
sale-leaseback /60 realty (real + 1 property estate)

21. See Gunning and Roegge, Contemporary Real Estate Financing Techniques: A Dialogue on Vanishing Simplicity, 3 Real Prop.Prob. & Tr.J. 322, 325 (1968).

22. See Englebrecht and Kramer, Tax Breaks for REITs Under the Tax Reform Act, 7 Real Est.Rev. 33 (No. 1, Spring 1977).

23. See Stevenson, Lessons From the Mortgage Trust Experience, 6 Real Est. Rev. 72 (No. 3, Fall 1976).

Real Estate Investment Trusts

r.e.i.t. (real +1 property estate +1 "investment trust") /60
      construction

§ 11.2 Mortgage Insurers and Guarantors

From the viewpoint of a mortgage lender, each loan represents a potential risk of loss. In order for an actual loss to be sustained, two or perhaps three occurrences must eventuate. First, there must be a default in payment by the mortgagor or his successor which he is unable or unwilling to cure. Second, the foreclosure of the mortgage (and the ultimate marketing of the property by the lender if it is the successful bidder at the foreclosure sale) must produce insufficient funds to cover the outstanding debt, accrued interest, and costs and fees associated with the foreclosure. Third, in jurisdictions in which deficiency judgments are available, the deficiency must be uncollectable or inadequate to cover the loss resulting from foreclosure.[1]

Lenders attempt to assess the risk of loss for each loan they make. This process is termed "underwriting" the loan; it consists of appraising the property, obtaining a prior credit history on the borrower, verifying the borrower's employment and income, and obtaining a variety of other information thought to be useful in predicting risk. While this process is routinized in the offices of most institutional lenders, and while various rules of thumb have been developed to determine whether a proposed borrower is acceptable, the scientific basis for mortgage risk assessment is surprisingly rudimentary. Some factors commonly considered—length of time on the present job or in residence in the community, for example—are probably of marginal relevance. However, the evidence strongly supports the conclusion that the higher the loan-to-value ratio, the greater the risk.[2]

This relation between loan-to-value ratio and risk is intuitively easy to understand. If the borrower has little or no "equity"—that is, excess value above the mortgage debt—in the property, it is relatively easy for him to decide simply to walk away when financial difficulties arise; he has nothing to protect by sticking it out. He is unlikely to attempt to sell the property in the event of trouble, since the sales proceeds would be inadequate, after payment of the mortgage, to cover a brokerage commission and other selling expenses. Finally, if the lender forecloses or obtains a deed in lieu, there is obviously a strong chance that the ultimate marketing of the property will produce

§ 11.2

1. On antideficiency statutes, see generally § 8.3, supra.

2. See, e.g., Aylward, Residential Mortgages: Lining Up the Customers, Mortgage Banking, Mar. 1984, at 20; von Furstenberg & Green, Estimation of Delinquency Risk for Home Mortgage Portfolios, 2 Am.Real Est. & Urban Econ. Ass'n J. 5 (Spring 1974); von Furstenberg, Technical Studies of Mortgage Default Risk (1971); Herzog and Earley, Home Mortgage Delinquency and Foreclosure (1970); Kendall, Anatomy of the Residential Mortgage (1964).

insufficient funds to cover the debt, interest, and expenses. For these reasons, loan-to-value ratio is highly correlated to mortgage risk.

Logically, lenders which make a high volume of mortgage loans might simply charge a somewhat increased interest rate on loans which they judge to be relatively risky, thus hedging against the losses which they expect will result. In modern American mortgage lending, however, lenders attempt to do this only to a modest extent. For reasons of preference and regulation, they tend to a much greater degree to rely on contracts of indemnification with outside entities, usually termed mortgage insurers, to shift the risk of loss.[3] Such insurance contracts are commonly executed on loans in which the loan-to-value ratio exceeds eighty percent, although some lenders employ an even lower threshold ratio. Mortgage insurers charge premiums for executing these contracts, and the cost is usually passed on to the mortgagor, even though the mortgagee is the insured.

Three types of mortgage insurance are commonly written in the United States. The first and oldest is provided by the Federal Housing Administration (FHA), established in 1934 by the National Housing Act[4] and currently a part of the Department of Housing and Urban Development (HUD). The Veterans Administration was given authority to guarantee home loans for GI's by the Servicemen's Readjustment Act in 1944.[5] (Technically, the VA program is termed guaranty rather than insurance, since the agency does not maintain a fund which is actuarially designed to pay future claims.) Finally, private mortgage insurance companies (PMI's) have become a major force, beginning with the chartering of Mortgage Guaranty Insurance Company in Wisconsin in 1957;[6] there are now more than 15 such companies writing mortgage insurance on a national scale. The Farmers Home Administration (FmHA), a division of the Department of Agriculture, also operates home mortgage insurance and guaranty programs.[7] However, FmHA mortgage insurance is available only in towns of 20,000 or less, and the program is relatively small in scale; it will not be discussed in further detail.

FHA's mortgage insurance programs are much more complex than the activities of VA and the PMI's for two reasons. First, VA and PMI's confine themselves almost exclusively to mortgages on homes (i.e., one-to-four family buildings) and condominiums, while FHA has a

3. See generally Rapkin, The Private Insurance of Home Mortgages (1973); Griffith, Mortgage Guaranty Insurance is What?, 48 Cal.B.J. 683 (1973).

4. 12 U.S.C.A. §§ 1701–42.

5. 38 U.S.C.A. §§ 1801 et seq. The VA also has authority to make direct loans to veterans under 38 U.S.C.A. § 1811, but few such loans are made.

6. See Rapkin, supra note 3, at 38ff; The Arthur D. Little Study of the Private Mortgage Insurance Industry (1975); Graaskamp, Development and Structure of Mortgage Loan Guaranty Insurance in the United States, 34 J. Risk & Ins. 47 (1967); Reppe, Why Residential Lenders Like Mortgage Guaranty Insurance, 3 Real Estate Rev. 58 (No. 3, Fall 1973).

7. See Sec. 417, Housing Act of 1949, 42 U.S.C.A. § 1487.

vast range of programs covering homes, condominiums, cooperatives, apartment buildings, hospitals, and other types of real estate. FHA's programs are commonly identified by the relevant sections of the National Housing Act: Section 203(b) for ordinary home loans, Section 207 for apartments, Section 234 for condominiums, and so on. A second reason for FHA's complexity is that congress has given FHA legislative authority to combine mortgage insurance with certain types of housing subsidy programs for low and moderate income families. Perhaps the two best-known examples of this subsidy-mortgage-insurance concept are Section 235 (of the National Housing Act) for assisting moderate income home purchasers, a program created in 1968 which is still operational at this writing, and Section 236, a rental housing subsidy program also created in 1968 and now virtually phased out as to new projects. The details of such subsidy programs are beyond our present scope; they tend to change frequently, and the reader should refer to current HUD literature for further information.[8] In 1974 congress began to move away from the subsidy-mortgage-insurance idea, enacting Section 8 of the U.S. Housing Act of 1937[9] which provides for rental apartment subsidies irrespective of whether the projects assisted by the subsidies are also financed with FHA-insured mortgages or not. Whether subsidies and mortgage insurance will be further disconnected in federal housing policy remains to be seen.[10]

It is instructive to see how the market in home mortgages is divided among the major groups of mortgage insurers.[11] More than three-quarters of the home loans outstanding are "conventional"—that is, neither insured by FHA nor guaranteed by VA. Roughly 30% of all conventional loans have loan-to-value ratios exceeding 80%, and it is probable that the great majority of this group are PMI-insured. FHA and VA insure about 12% and 10% of all outstanding home mortgages respectively. The annual volume of home mortgages insured by FHA and VA has fluctuated widely.

The major classes of institutional lenders have definite preferences for particular types of mortgage insurance. Savings and loan associa-

8. These programs are described in detail in Milgram, Housing the Urban Poor: Urban Housing Assistance Programs, in House Comm. on Banking, Finance & Urban Affairs, Housing—A Reader 114 (98th Cong., 1st Sess. 1983); U.S. Dep't of Housing and Urban Development, Housing in the Seventies 104–18 (1974).

9. 42 U.S.C.A. § 1437f; the reference to the U.S. Housing Act, originally enacted in 1937, is misleading, since Section 8 in its present form is a 1974 creation. On the operation of Section 8, see Comptroller General of the U.S., Major Changes Are Needed in the New Leased-Housing Program (1977); U.S. Dep't of Housing and Urban Development, Office of Policy Development and Research, Lower Income Housing Assistance Program (Section 8): Interim Findings of Evaluation Research (1978).

10. See Milgram, supra note 8, at 98, 114; Whitman, Federal Housing Assistance for the Poor: Old Problems and New Directions, 9 Urb.Law 1 (1977).

11. The data in this paragraph are derived from Economic Report of the President 302 (1984) and monthly data published in the Federal Home Loan Bank Board Journal. The data reflect year-end 1983 conditions, and the reader may readily update them from more recent publications of the same sources. See also Report of the President's Commission on Housing 160–61 (1982).

tions, for example, have generally had little interest in making FHA and VA loans, but have been very active customers of the PMI's. Mortgage bankers, by contrast, have been strong participants in the FHA and VA markets for many years, in part because they sold many mortgages to the Federal National Mortgage Association (FNMA) during the pre-1972 period when it did not purchase conventional loans. In more recent years, mortgage bankers have also become active in PMI useage. Mutual savings banks have been historically strong users of FHA and VA, and have expanded their PMI participation as well.

Lending institutions and particular loans must meet relevant criteria and rules in order to be eligible for mortgage insurance through any of the three main types of insurers. First, the institution must be approved as such by the insurer or insurers with which it wishes to do business. In the case of FHA and VA, this poses little problem for most financial institutions; a minimum net worth of $100,000 must be demonstrated, as well as compliance with certain internal financial procedures.[12] PMI's are usually eager to attract new institutional customers and their requirements for approval are not difficult to meet.

In addition, the particular loan in question must conform to the applicable insurer's guidelines. For example, a single-family FHA loan cannot exceed limits which are published regularly by HUD, and the loan-to-value ratio cannot be greater than 97% of the first $25,000 of value and 95% of the excess above $25,000.[13] VA has no specific limits on loan amount, and loans for 100% of value (i.e., with no down payment) are common. However, the VA's maximum guarantee is the lesser of $27,500 or 60% of the original mortgage amount.[14] For large loans, the $27,500 figure is controlling, and acts in effect as a substitute for the veteran's down payment. Hence, most lenders are unwilling to make a no-down-payment VA loan for more than about $130,000 to $140,000. PMI's may impose maximum loan amounts or loan-to-value ratio limits as a consequence of their own internal policies or the statutes and regulations of the states in which they are chartered and operate.[15] In addition, PMI-insured conventional loans must comply with the regulations governing the financial institutions which make them, and with the guidelines of the purchasing investor if they are sold on the secondary mortgage market. For these reasons, PMI loans are generally limited to 95% loan-to-value ratios or lower.

For many years both FHA and VA fixed a maximum interest rate on the loans they insured or guaranteed. FHA discontinued this practice for most of its programs in 1983, as explained below, but VA continues to set maximum rates;[16] thus, the following explanation

12. 24 CFR 203.3, 203.4.

13. 24 CFR 203.18. If the unit is owner-occupied and its appraised value does not exceed $50,000, the loan may be 97% of the full value; see 50 Fed.Reg. 19924 (May 13, 1985). Mortgage dollar limits are published in the Federal Register; see, e.g. 49 Fed.Reg. 21520.

14. 38 CFR 36.4302.

15. See Rapkin, supra note 3, at 31–37.

16. 38 CFR 36.4311.

continues to be important. The VA rate is changed from time to time as market rates vary, but is consistently set at a level below the market for conventional loans. This policy is said to act as a brake on interest rates when they are generally rising, and it has some political attractiveness. However, lenders would simply refuse to make VA loans under these circumstances unless they had some alternative method of increasing their return on such loans. The method employed is termed the "discount point" system;[17] it works as follows. The lender demands a cash payment as a condition of making the loan. This cash payment effectively reduces the lender's net disbursement of loan proceeds at the closing. Since the monthly payments made by the borrower are based on the full or gross loan amount, they represent a higher effective yield than the stated interest rate and make the loan attractive to the lender. The cash payment is called a "discount", and is commonly stated in terms of "points"—with one point being one percent of the nominal loan amount. VA regulations prohibit the payment of the discount by the borrower-mortgagor,[18] so someone else, usually the seller of the house, pays it.

The following example will illustrate the discount point system in operation. Assume that current mortgage market yields are 13%, but the VA interest ceiling is 12.5%. The mortgagor applies for and is granted a loan of $50,000. The lender informs the seller that a discount of 3 points or $1,500 is required; the seller is in no position to object if he wishes to sell the house with VA financing. At the closing the seller gives the lender a check for $1,500; the lender disburses $50,000 to the borrower, but has incurred a net outlay of only $48,500. The borrower's monthly payments are based on a $50,000 loan at 12.5% interest.

The impact on effective yield which a given discount will have depends on whether and when the loan will be prepaid prior to maturity. The earlier the prepayment, the greater the boost in yield produced by the discount. To visualize the importance of the time of prepayment on the loan's yield, suppose in the example in the preceding paragraph the loan were prepaid, for some reason, only a week after it was made. The lender, who was out-of-pocket only $48,500 when the loan was made, would receive the full $50,000 balance in payment. Thus, the lender would receive a clear $1,500 profit. Of course, very few loans are prepaid within a week after they are made, but on the other hand, few are held to maturity either. It is commonly assumed that the average life of a mortgage loan will be twelve years. Under this assumption, mathematical tables can be derived which will

17. See Hood & Kushner, Real Estate Finance: The Discount Point System and its Effect on Federally Insured Home Loans, 40 U.Mo.K.C.L.Rev. 1 (1971).

18. 38 CFR 36.4312. The borrower may be charged a 1% fee (usually called an "origination fee") which is supposed to cover the lender's cost of originating the loan; the origination fee may be 2% if the loan involves construction advances. The borrower is permitted to pay the discount points if he is building his own house or is refinancing an existing loan, since there is no seller in such cases to pay the points.

show the precise impact of any given discount on the loan's yield.[19] A simple rule of thumb which gives results approximating these tables is this: one discount point will increase the yield by about one-sixth of one percent. Thus in the example above, three discount points ($1,500) would increase the loan's yield by about one-half of one percent, from 12.5% to 13%.

This discount point system permits VA to maintain the fiction of low interest rates while providing actual yields which are high enough to attract institutional investors, but it has several adverse side-effects. Obviously, sophisticated home sellers will attempt to build the expected discount into the price of the house in order to receive the net sale price they desire. Unfortunately, inexperienced sellers may fail to do so, and hence may receive far few dollars than they expected when the sale is completed. The problem is compounded by the fact that many printed sales contract or earnest money forms do not mention payment of the discount points by the seller if the buyer obtains a VA loan; thus, the stage is set for a dispute as to whether the seller is contractually obligated to do so.

The discount point system raises numerous problems. It reduces competition for mortgage funds, since the seller who pays the discount is often not actively involved in negotiating the loan. It confuses appraisals, since they are based on "comparable" sale prices which may have varying amounts of discount built into them. It encourages early foreclosure, since that tends to maximize the lender's yield on the loan. And when VA allows large differences to develop between the administered rate and market rates, discounts may become so large as to be impractical from the viewpoint of builders and sellers, and thus may seriously retard the functioning of the housing market.

The administration of interest ceilings by FHA and VA was much criticized.[20] After years of debate on the point, Congress in 1983 repealed FHA's mandate to fix interest rates on most of its programs.[21] FHA lenders may now offer a wide variety of financing plans, with interest rates and discounts determined by the market. VA, however, continues to set interest ceilings.

19. Such a table is reproduced in Nelson & Whitman, Real Estate Transfer, Finance & Development 716 (1981).

20. See Report of the President's Commission on Housing 164 (1982); U.S. Dep't of Housing and Urban Development, Final Report of the Task Force on Housing Costs 54, 62 (1978); Testimony of Secretary James Lynn, Hearings on Administration's 1973 Housing Proposals before the Senate Banking, Housing, and Urban Affairs Comm., 93d Cong., 1st Sess. (1973), at 8 (recommendation derived from National Housing Policy Review Task Force); Report of the President's Commission on Financial Structure and Regulation 77 (1972); Report of the Commission on Mortgage Interest Rates 10 (1969).

21. § 424(b)(2), Housing and Urban-Rural Recovery Act of 1983, Pub.L. No. 98–181, effective Nov. 30, 1983. The Section 235 subsidized homeownership program was not affected.

Mortgage Insurance Premiums

The premiums charged for mortgage insurance are generally paid by the mortgagor, either in cash at the time the loan is made or divided into equal monthly installments and paid along with the principal and interest payments. For many years FHA charged a mortgage insurance premium (MIP) of ½ percent per year on the average outstanding balance of the loan, divided into 12 installments and paid with each mortgage payment. However in 1983, acting under new authority from Congress,[22] FHA shifted to a system for most of its programs under which the MIP is paid entirely at the loan closing.[23] It established a premium of 3.8% of the initial loan amount for loans with terms of 25 years or more; slightly smaller premiums were fixed for shorter terms. The MIP may be either paid in cash or financed by adding it to the normal mortgage amount. The new system is easier to administer and results in slightly lower monthly payments, even for mortgagors who finance the MIP. If a group of loans has a favorable loss experience, its mortgagors may receive a refund of a portion of the premiums they have paid.

The VA's loan guarantee program operated for many years at no cost to the veteran-mortgagor; its losses were borne by the federal treasury as a veterans' benefit. However, it now charges a "funding fee" of one percent of the loan amount,[24] which is directed to the VA's Home Loan Guaranty Fund. While not necessarily designed to make the VA program actuarially sound, the fee does serve to offset losses from claims.

Premiums charged by the PMI's vary somewhat from one company to another, and also depend on whether the loan-to-value ratio is 85% or below, between 86% and 90%, or between 91% and 95%. Many PMI's give the borrower a choice between a single front-end charge with no payments thereafter, and a combination of front-end and monthly charges. The latter approach is probably more common. A typical premium for a loan with a 90% loan-to-value ratio would be 0.9% at closing and 0.55% per year (in monthly installments) for the next ten years.[25] The advent of graduated-payment loans and adjustable rate loans have caused many PMI's to reevaluate their premium

22. § 201, Omnibus Budget Reconciliation Act of 1982, Pub.L. No. 97–253, amending National Housing Act § 203(c), 12 U.S.C.A. § 1709(c).

23. 24 CFR 203.259a, 203.280 et seq., added by 48 Fed.Reg. 28794. See Herzog, Single Premium Plan Premiere, Mortgage Banking, Apr. 1984, at 84; 50 Fed.Reg. 2779 (Jan. 22, 1985), giving further detail on the calculation of the one-time premium.

24. 38 CFR 36.4312(e).

25. See Rapkin, supra note 3, at 135. Some variation in premium is made by

some insurers depending on whether the top 30% or 25% of the loan is insured; see text at note 33, infra. Rates of most companies in early 1985 for fixed-interest loans were as follows:

91% to 95% loan-to-value, 30% coverage: 1.3% at closing plus 0.7% per year.

86% to 90% loan-to-value, 30% coverage: 0.9% at closing plus 0.55% per year.

81% to 85% loan-to-value, 25% coverage: 0.5% at closing plus 0.5% per year.

schedules, since these new mortgage forms appear to carry significantly greater risk of default and loss. Higher premiums have been established by most companies for such mortgages.

Claims Procedures

The objective of all mortgage lenders in participating in mortgage insurance programs is to shift loss. When default and foreclosure result in a loss, the lender wishes to make sure that the incidence of that loss falls on the insurer. Some claims procedure is necessary to accomplish this. FHA's procedure differs from those of VA and the PMI's; of the three, FHA's is most likely to shift fully even the most severe losses to the insurer. The VA and PMI procedures are similar, and leave open a greater potential for loss by the lender.

In order to make a claim against FHA,[26] the lender under the single-family programs must acquire title to the property (by foreclosure or deed in lieu) and transfer the property to FHA. It will then receive the full loan balance in payment of the claim. Under the project mortgage (e.g., multifamily apartment) programs, the lender may either transfer title, or may assign the unforeclosed mortgage to FHA, leaving it to worry about working out the default or acquiring title. If the lender chooses the latter approach, FHA will pay only 99% of the loan balance.[27] Whether the loan is foreclosed or assigned FHA also pays the expenses of the lender for taxes, assessments, insurance, repairs, and other out-of-pocket costs.[28] FHA also pays two-thirds of the foreclosure expenses if the lender forecloses.

FHA pays claims either in cash or in the form of debentures. Cash payment is more desirable from the lender's viewpoint, since the debentures carry interest rates, fixed by FHA, which are typically lower than those of comparable government obligations; they must therefore be sold by the lender at a discount if it wishes to liquidate them. The option to pay in debentures is intended to help FHA avoid large and unanticipated lump sum cash outflows. At this writing FHA is paying claims on single-family home loans in cash, but that policy is subject to change.

26. 24 CFR 200.155; see generally Note, 49 Bos.U.L.Rev. 717, 722–23 (1969). See also a proposed regulation, 50 Fed.Reg. 1233 (Jan. 10, 1985), under which lenders could elect to retain title and be credited with a "specified amount" similar to that employed by VA; see note 29 infra.

27. Under the single-family programs, FHA will approve an assignment of a mortgage only if the default was due to circumstances beyond the mortgagor's control; 24 CFR 203.350. The apparent purpose of permitting assignment on such facts would be to permit forbearance or recasting of payments under circumstances in which the mortgagee is unwilling to do so. FHA has construed its duty to accept such assignments very narrowly, and several cases have found it to have abused its discretion in refusing to accept assignments; see Ferrell v. Pierce, 743 F.2d 454 (7th Cir. 1984); Butler v. United States Dep't of HUD, 595 F.Supp. 1041 (E.D.Pa.1984); Federal Nat'l Mortg. Ass'n v. Rathgens, 595 F.Supp. 552 (S.D.Ohio 1984).

28. 24 CFR 203.402. Accrued interest is not a direct element of the claim but is accounted for to some extent by the fact that the debentures issued, if any, are backdated to one month following the date of the first delinquent payment. See 24 CFR 203.410, 203.331.

Upon acquiring the property, FHA has the option to hold and rent it, or to place it on the market for sale; the former is generally done only in the case of multifamily projects which are already tenanted, and for which no responsible buyer is immediately available. Single-family homes are usually marketed as rapidly as possible, often at a substantial loss. In theory FHA is subrogated to the lender's right to seek a deficiency judgment against the mortgagor in states where this is permitted, but as a practical matter FHA seldom exercises this right.[28.5]

VA's claim procedure is quite different than FHA's. Upon notification by the lender that it intends to foreclose, VA ordinarily appraises the property and advises the lender of the "specified amount"—that is, VA's estimate of the property's current value.[29] When the lender acquires title by foreclosure or deed in lieu, it may then transfer the property to VA and receive credit in the specified amount; in effect, the lender is selling the property to VA for that amount. VA then pays the lender's claim, which is equal to the entire outstanding balance, accrued interest, and expenses. However, in no event will the VA payment exceed the sum of (1) the specified amount and (2) the maximum VA guarantee, currently the lesser of $27,500 or 60% of the original loan amount.

To illustrate VA's procedure, assume a loan with an original balance of $75,000, a current balance including interest and expenses of $70,000, and a specified amount or property value of $50,000. The VA guarantee would be $27,500 on these facts. Upon conveyance of the property to VA, the lender would receive the full $70,000 claim. On the other hand, suppose the property had been badly vandalized by the mortgagor, and the specified amount were only $40,000. VA's payment to the lender would be limited to $27,500 plus the specified amount, or a total of $67,500; the lender would suffer a net loss of $2,500. Obviously the VA system will result in a loss to the lender only when the property has dropped rather severely in value, but it can happen. Incidentally, the lender is not required to convey the property to VA in order to make a claim; it may instead retain the property and have the claim payment reduced by the specified amount; this would make sense to the lender if it felt that it could market the property at a net sale price greater than the specified amount. However, in most cases the property is conveyed to VA, which then attempts to market it in much the same fashion as FHA.

The VA is not required to fix a "specified amount" on the property, and if it does not do so, it must instead pay the full amount of the guarantee (ordinarily $27,500) to the lender.[30] It is then the lender's job to dispose of the property in whatever manner seems most advantageous to it. Normally VA will take this approach only when, for some

---

28.5 See United States v. Whitney, 602 F.Supp. 722 (W.D.N.Y.1985) (VA subrogation rights).

29. 38 CFR 36.4320.

30. 38 CFR 3620(b).

reason, it does not want the responsibility of marketing the property. In 1984 the Reagan administration recommended legislative changes which would have eliminated entirely VA's activity in acquiring and marketing houses; it would have adopted this latter approach as VA's sole mode of operation.[31] But it was by no means clear to Congress that such a change would save the government money, and it was not enacted. However, Congress did direct the VA to take its probable administrative costs into account in determining "specified amounts," [32] and to make case-by-case determinations as to which method of claims payment would be most economical to the government.

PMI claims procedures are roughly similar to VA's. The maximum PMI loss or guarantee is usually fixed at 25% (or if a higher premium is paid, 30%) of the current loan balance plus costs and expenses.[33] Upon foreclosure or the taking of a deed in lieu, the lender will contact the PMI for further instructions. The PMI has two choices: either to take a conveyance of the property (or authorize the lender to sell it as the PMI's agent) and pay the lender the full loan balance plus costs and expenses, or to pay the guarantee amount and allow the lender to keep the property. Obviously the PMI will elect the latter route only if the lender's total claim exceeds the property's current value plus the guarantee.

While the basic economic decisions which PMI's must make are similar to those of VA, the guarantee amount is usually smaller with PMI insurance. Consequently the potential for unreimbursed losses is greater. In the VA claims example given above, if PMI insurance had been employed instead, the guarantee amount would be only $17,500 (assuming a 25% policy) and the lender would sustain a loss if the property's value dropped below $52,500. Of course, even value diminutions of this magnitude are quite rare in the current inflationary economy, a fact which may explain why most lenders seem to perceive little difference in effective coverage as among FHA, VA, and the PMI's.

In principle, a mortgage insurance system in which the risk is shared between insurer and lender, as is the case to some degree with VA and the PMI's, can reasonably delegate more underwriting responsibility to the lender than can a system like FHA's in which the lender has virtually no risk. This is so because the lender can be expected to exercise more care in appraising, checking credit, and so forth if its determinations bear on its own potential loss. In fact, VA and the PMI's do delegate more underwriting decision-making to mortgagees than does FHA. However, FHA has experimented in recent years with delegation of processing authority and with risk-sharing. Its "direct

---

31. The mortgage banking industry, in particular, objected to the proposed change; it is not well organized to dispose of foreclosed properties, and did not want to have this burden shifted to it. See BNA Hsg. & Devel. Rptr., Feb. 13, 1984, at 797.

32. See Deficit Reduction Act of 1984, Pub.L. No. 98–369, 98 Stat. 494, 1117, amending 38 U.S.C.A. § 1816.

33. See, e.g., Mortgage Guaranty Insurance Corp., Default and Claims Manual.

endorsement" program, instituted in 1983, allows larger, more experienced lenders who meet certain standards to underwrite FHA single-family home loans without prior review of each loan by HUD.[34]   In addition, there are programs under which both single-family [35] and new [36] and existing [37] multifamily mortgages can be co-insured, with the lender assuming a share of the risk of default and have a rather complete delegation of processing authority.

 WESTLAW REFERENCES

digest(mortgage   /3   insur! guarant**   /p   f.h.a. f.m.h.a. h.u.d. #v.a.
    p.m.i.)

Mortgage Insurance Premiums
m.i.p. "mortgage insurance premium"   /p   f.h.a.

Claims Procedures
cite(24   +3   200.163 200.164)

---

§ 11.3 Government-Sponsored Mortgage Market Support Agencies

In an effort to improve the functioning of the market for residential mortgages, the federal government has created several agencies and institutions.   Among these are FHA and VA, discussed in the preceding section; other entities, which do not insure or guarantee mortgages, will be described here.[1]   They include the Federal National Mortgage Association (FNMA or "Fannie Mae") and the Federal Home Loan Mortgage Corporation (FHLMC or "Freddie Mac"), both of which purchase mortgage loans on the secondary market.   This section will

---

34.   24 CFR 200.163–.164a, adopted 48 Fed.Reg. 11928.

35.   24 CFR Part 204. The claim is 90% of the usual FHA claim payment, with the mortgagee assuming the remaining 10%.

36.   24 CFR Part 251, added by 49 Fed. Reg. 32016. For a good overall summary of HUD's coinsurance efforts, see the proposed rule on 24 CFR Part 251, 49 Fed.Reg. 9084. See also Puller, Fuller & Graham, New Financing from Old Programs, Mortgage Banking, Mar. 1985, at 64; McGavin, Overcoming the Risks in FHA Co-insured Mortgage Loans, Nat'l Law J., Oct. 31, 1983, at 15.

37.   24 CFR Part 255; see also 24 CFR Part 250 (coinsurance on multifamily projects of state housing finance agencies).

§ 11.3

1.   Recent discussions of the secondary mortgage market, the principal type of governmental support system, include McNulty, Secondary Mortgage Markets: Recent Trends and Research Results, 17 FHLBBJ 10 (Apr. 1984); Miles, Housing Finance: Development and Evolution in Mortgage Markets, in House Comm. on Banking, Finance & Urban Affairs, Housing—A Reader, 98th Cong., 1st Sess., at 45; Report of the President's Commission on Housing 166–73 (1982); Hendershott & Villani, Secondary Mortgage Markets and the Cost of Mortgage Funds, 8 J.Am.Real Est. & Urb. Econ. Ass'n 50 (1980); Browne, The Private Mortgage Insurance Industry, the Thrift Industry, and the Secondary Mortgage Market: Their Interrelationships, 12 Akr.L.Rev. 631 (1979).

A earlier but highly insightful study is Grebler, The "New System" of Residential Mortgage Finance, Mortgage Banker, Feb. 1972, at 4, reprinted in Federal Reserve Staff Study, Ways to Moderate Fluctuations in Housing Construction 177 (1972).

See also all issues of Secondary Mortgage Markets, a quarterly published by FHLMC, beginning in Feb. 1984; and the annual reports of FNMA, FHLMC, and GNMA (from which most data in the text are taken).

also discuss the Government National Mortgage Association (GNMA or "Ginnie Mae"), which operates several mortgage market assistance programs, and the Federal Home Loan Bank System, which makes loans to its member institutions, primarily savings and loan associations. Finally, state agencies which provide support for the residential mortgage market will be described.[2]

Secondary Market Agencies—FNMA and FHLMC

Both of these agencies are primarily engaged in purchasing on the secondary market residential mortgages originated by local lending institutions. FNMA is by far the older, having been organized in 1938 as a corporation wholly owned and administered by the federal government.[3] In 1954 it became a "mixed ownership" corporation, owned partly by private shareholders.[4] Finally, by the Housing and Urban Development Act of 1968, FNMA was divided into two separate entities, each of which inherited a portion of the original FNMA's duties.[5] One of these was the Government National Mortgage Association (GNMA), which became a pure federal agency within the Department of Housing and Urban Development, and which retained the management of FNMA's pre-1954 mortgage portfolio and took over certain of its "special assistance" functions, as described below. At the same time, FNMA was re-created as a privately owned and managed corporation, although with certain ties to the federal government; its function is to continue to purchase residential and other mortgages from originating institutions.

Two years after the "privatization" of FNMA, FHLMC was created by the Emergency Home Finance Act of 1970.[6] Its mission is substantially similar to that of FNMA, although it carries out its functions in a somewhat different fashion. Both FNMA and FHLMC are expected to improve the operation of the mortgage market in several ways:[7] (1) They facilitate the flow of capital from areas of the country where funds are plentiful to places in which mortgage money is in short supply. (2) By means of the sale of debt paper and other instruments to persons and institutions who would not ordinarily invest in mortgages,

2. Other institutions supporting the mortgage market, not discussed in the text because of their relatively small impact, include the Federal Land Banks, Federal Intermediate Credit Banks, Banks for Cooperatives, and Farmers Home Administration.

3. FNMA's original charter was contained in Title III of the National Housing Act, 48 Stat. 1246 (1938).

4. Title II of the Housing Act of 1954, 68 Stat. 612.

5. Title VIII of the Housing and Urban Development Act of 1968, 82 Stat. 503, 536. The FNMA General Counsel's Office pro-

vides a booklet entitled "Federal National Mortgage Association Charter Act" which contains complete legislative history details of the Association. The charter's present citation is 12 U.S.C.A. § 1716ff. An excellent historical summary of FNMA is found in 43 Fed.Reg. 36200.

6. 12 U.S.C.A. § 1451.

7. See Villani, The Secondary Mortgage Markets: What They Are, What They Do, and How to Measure Them, 1 Secondary Mortgage Markets 24 (Feb. 1984); Federal National Mortgage Ass'n, A Guide to Fannie Mae 9 (1975).

they shift capital investment from other sectors of the national economy into the mortgage market. The instruments they sell typically have term and repayment structures which are different than mortgages, and thus are more attractive to certain types of investors, such as life insurers and pension funds. (3) By issuing advance commitments to purchase mortgages at fixed interest rates or yields, they assist local lenders and homebuilders in hedging against the risk of rising interest rates in the future. (4) By purchasing mortgages when credit is tight and selling them when funds are readily available, they may assist in smoothing the flow of mortgage funds during the extreme cycles of credit fluctuation which have characterized the post-war American economy.

While FNMA and FHLMC are expected to carry out a similar function, the administrative and regulatory relationships which the two agencies have with the federal government are widely different. FNMA is operated largely like a private corporation. It has outstanding more than 66 million shares of common stock, actively traded on the New York and other exchanges. FNMA's board of directors consists of 18 persons, 5 of whom are appointed by the president of the United States and the other 13 elected by the shareholders in the conventional corporate manner. In addition, the Secretary of Housing and Urban Development holds a variety of regulatory powers over FNMA.[8] These include the authority to fix the association's aggregate annual dividends, to approve increases in its total debt and the issuance of particular debt or equity securities, and to promulgate rules and regulations and to require that a reasonable portion of the corporation's mortgage purchases be related to the national goal of providing adequate housing for low and moderate income families. In addition, the debt securities of the corporation are subject to approval by the Secretary of the Treasury.

The regulatory authority of the Secretary of HUD was regarded as having relatively little significance until 1978, when the secretary proposed a set of far-reaching regulations which would, among other things, have operated to allocate a certain portion of FNMA's mortgage purchase activity for inner-city and other low-income areas.[9] FNMA, which had already created certain inner-city programs, vigorously opposed the regulations, and their more objectional features were ultimately withdrawn by HUD.[10] The precise legal scope of HUD's regulatory power over the corporation was thus not tested by litigation, and still remains uncertain.

The federal government's control over FHLMC is much more straightforward. The corporation is under the direct control of the Federal Home Loan Bank Board, and the three members of the board

8. 12 U.S.C.A. § 1723a(h).

9. 43 Fed.Reg. 7659.

10. 24 CFR Part 81, as amended 43 Fed. Reg. 36200.

are by statute the directors of FHLMC.[11] Since the board members are presidential appointees, FHLMC is for most practical purposes considered a direct federal agency. The corporation's common stock, with a par value of 100 million dollars, was originally subscribed and owned by the twelve Federal Home Loan Banks. In 1984 FHLMC issued participating preferred stock with an estimated value of $600 million which was distributed to the FHLB's member institutions in the savings and loan industry. Neither the common nor the preferred stock carries voting or conversion privileges.

The two agencies are quite different in their orientation to the financial community. FHLMC, as a constituent of the Federal Home Loan Bank Board, is strongly concerned with serving the savings and loan industry. From the time of its creation in 1970 until 1979, it was permitted to buy mortgages only from "supervised" lenders—banks, savings and loan associations, and mutual savings banks. Since 1979 mortgage bankers have also been allowed to sell to FHLMC, but it still buys a majority of its mortgages from savings and loans. FNMA, by contrast, has always been heavily oriented toward serving mortgage bankers.

To judge from the relative sizes from their mortgage portfolios, FNMA appears a far larger organization than FHLMC. At the end of 1983, for example, FNMA held nearly 76 billion dollars in mortgage loans, while FHLMC held only $7.6 billion. But this comparison is in part misleading. The accumulation of FNMA's portfolio began in 1955, while FHLMC's commenced in 1970. Moreover, FNMA has sold over the years since 1955 only a tiny proportion of the mortgages it has purchased. Thus, in most years its entire purchase volume has constituted a net addition to its mortgage portfolio. In order to finance this growing volume of mortgage holdings, FNMA has been required to issue an exceptionally large volume of debentures, notes, and other debt securities. Indeed, FNMA is second only to the United States treasury in amount of debt securities issued.

FHLMC has followed a very different policy. After building up a substantial portfolio of mortgages during the 1970–1974 period, it began in 1975 to sell mortgages at approximately the same rate at which it was acquiring them. To a very large extent these sales have been in the form of participation certificates (PC's), each of which represents an undivided interest in a package of mortgages which FHLMC has accumulated. The PC's are unconditionally guaranteed by the corporation, and pass through interest and principal payments monthly as they are received from the mortgagors. FHLMC also sells Guaranteed Mortgage Certificates (GMC's) and Collateralized Mortgage Obligations (CMO's), which also represent ownership in a pool of mortgages. However, they do not pass through monthly payments; instead, they pay interest semi-annually and return a portion of the principal either

11. 12 U.S.C.A. § 1453(a).

annually (in the case of GMC's) or in specific scheduled years (in the case of CMO's). Thus they resemble ordinary corporate bonds. Like PC's, they are guaranteed by the Mortgage Corporation. They are intended to be attractive to institutional investors who are accustomed to purchasing bonds.

For accounting and legal purposes, the mortgages represented by PC's, CMO's, and GMC's are treated as no longer part of FHLMC's portfolio. For this reason, the corporation's mortgage holdings seem rather small in comparison to those of FNMA, but its impact on the mortgage market is very substantial. In 1983, for example, the Mortgage Corporation purchased nearly 24 billion dollars in mortgages and sold an equivalent amount of PC's. It was thus able to outstrip FNMA's $16.6 billion in mortgage purchases during the same period. In 1981 FNMA began to issue Mortgage-Backed Securities, following FHLMC's lead. This program developed rapidly, and by 1985 FNMA had issued more than $40 billion in MBS.[12]

Both FNMA and FHLMC have been authorized to purchase FHA/VA and conventional mortgages since 1970, when FHLMC was created. Prior to that time, FNMA was permitted to purchase only government-insured or -guaranteed mortgages. The authority to purchase conventional loans has had several important consequences. FNMA and FHLMC cooperated during 1970 in developing a set of standard forms for use with conventional mortgages throughout the United States. These forms have gained wide-spread acceptance and are now often used even in transactions in which the lender does not anticipate a sale of the loan to either FNMA or FHLMC.[13] Another consequence has been the reviewing and approval of private mortgage insurance companies by FNMA and FHLMC. Each agency maintains an approved list, an essential activity since weak or unreliable private mortgage insurers could endanger the security of the conventional mortgages which the two secondary market entities purchase. For both agencies, private mortgage insurance is legally essential on any portion of a loan which exceeds an 80% loan-to-value ratio.

As one might expect from an understanding of its constituency, FHLMC has tended to emphasize the purchase of conventional rather than government-guaranteed loans. In recent years, the same has been true of FNMA, although in the pre-1970 period, its purchases were entirely government insured. By 1976, FNMA was purchasing conventional loans at about four times the rate of government-insured mortgages. While the agencies have been criticized for their lack of support for the government loan market, the diminution in their activity in this

---

12. FNMA Annual Report 13 (1984).

13. See Federal National Mortgage Ass'n Public Meeting on Conventional Mortgage Form, Committee Print, Senate Comm. on Banking, Housing and Urban Affairs, 92d Cong., 1st Sess. (1971). In 1978 FNMA and FHLMC proposed an in-teresting revision of their standard mortgage form for New York to comply with that state's "Plain Language Law", Ch. 747, 1977 N. Y. Laws, requiring that consumer agreements be "written in a clear and coherent manner using words with common and every day meanings."

respect is accounted for to a great extent by the increase in GNMA mortgage-backed securities discussed below. Nonetheless, at the end of 1983 nearly 40% of FNMA's portfolio consisted of FHA-insured and VA-guaranteed loans. FNMA has been particularly active in supporting the HUD housing subsidy programs which were operated on a large scale in the early 1970's, and unsubsidized project mortgages as well. Both FNMA and FHLMC purchase multi-family apartment loans as well as home loans. FNMA is also active in purchasing other types of FHA-insured loans, including those on nursing homes, hospitals, and mobile home parks.

Both FNMA and FHLMC have been the subject of a series of legislative reforms which have broadened the scope of their activity. The most recent at this writing is the Secondary Mortgage Market Enhancement Act,[14] passed in 1984. It authorized FNMA and FHLMC to purchase subordinate lien mortgages up to $57,000, made for any purpose on a principal residence. The purchase of second mortgages on multifamily projects was approved, and certain other restrictions on purchase of multifamily mortgages were eliminated. Purchase authority for loans secured by manufactured homes was also liberalized. The Act amended existing federal securities legislation to facilitate issuance of certain types of mortgage-backed securities, and it preempted certain features of state securities acts which might restrain lenders' efforts to issue such securities.

The Government National Mortgage Association (GNMA)

When FNMA was re-organized as a private corporation in 1968, GNMA was created simultaneously to take over the "special assistance" functions which FNMA had previously handled, and also to manage and liquidate the existing FNMA portfolio of special assistance loans.[15] For example, during the 1961–1968 period FNMA had purchased a large number of below-market-interest-rate mortgages under FHA's 221(d)(3) moderate-income subsidized apartment program. These mortgages, most of which bore only a 3% interest rate, were transferred to GNMA, which continues to hold some of them today. GNMA also holds and continues to purchase from time to time mortgages of a variety of types which are deemed important to national housing policy but would have difficulty attracting private investors. These include loans in urban renewal projects, in disaster areas, on Indian reservations, and in Guam.[16]

14. Pub.L. No. 98–440, 98 Stat. 1689. For legislative history, see 1984 U.S.Code, Cong. & Admin.News 2809.

15. See 12 U.S.C.A. § 1717(a)(2)(A).

16. For details, see any current GNMA annual report. During the 1970's GNMA operated another assistance program, known as the "tandem plan." It involved GNMA's purchasing of FHA and VA mortgages, made at below-market interest rates, from originating lenders at relatively small discounts, and then reselling them on the secondary market at the much deeper discounts the market demanded. The resulting loss was absorbed by appropriations from Congress; the result was to keep mortgage interest rates lower and more affordable.

The GNMA activity which has had the greatest impact on the mortgage market in recent years is its program for guaranteeing mortgage-backed securities.[17] These securities are issued by mortgage lending institutions, including thrifts, banks, and mortgage bankers. The securities are in registered form and are actively traded among investors. They represent the obligation of the issuer, collateralized by a pool of FHA-insured, FmHA-insured, or VA-guaranteed mortgages. The GNMA guarantee behind such securities represents the full faith and credit of the United States government, so the securities are considered highly reliable and desirable.

Several types of GNMA-guaranteed securities have been issued, but by far the largest volume has been of the "fully modified pass-through" type. This means that GNMA guarantees that the holders of the securities will receive their respective shares of the regular monthly principal and interest payments which are due and owing on the underlying mortgages, even if the mortgage payments are in fact delinquent or the issuer fails to remit the payments to the holders. All additional payments resulting from the mortgage foreclosures or prepayments are also passed through to the holders immediately. The minimum size of a pass-through issue is one million dollars, with minimum individual security denominations of $25,000.

The mortgages which collateralize a GNMA-backed issue must all be federally insured or guaranteed. Under the original GNMA program (now termed GNMA I) they must all bear the same interest rate, and must have approximately the same maturity. The mortgages themselves are transferred to a bank or trust company to hold as a custodian. In the event the issuer of the securities defaults in payments, the mortgages are transferred to GNMA, which may in turn place them with another lender to manage and service. The diagram below indicates the relationships of the various parties in a GNMA-backed security issue. The great majority of the securities issued thus far have been collateralized by single family mortgages, but multifamily project and mobile home loans have also been used.

See also Note, The GNMA Securities Market: An Analysis of Proposals for a Regulatory Scheme, 9 Ford.Urb.L.Rev. 457 (1980).

17. 12 U.S.C.A. § 1721(g). See Mortgageamerica Corp. v. American National Bank, 651 S.W.2d 851 (Tex.Civ.App.1983), error refused n.r.e., an interesting case growing out of a mortgage company's efforts to market GNMA MBS which it had issued.

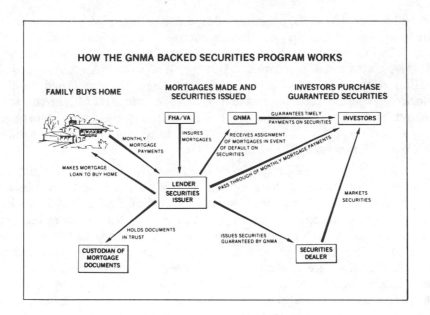

Under GNMA I, the issuing lender deals directly with the investors, remitting the mortgage payments to them monthly. Beginning in 1983, a new program, known as GNMA II, was instituted.[18] It is fundamentally similar to the GNMA I program described above, and does not replace it. But GNMA II is characterized by very large ("jumbo") mortgage pools which are composed of packages of loans from many different originating lenders, as contrasted with GNMA I pools, which are created by a single lender. Loans with different interest rates, within a 1% range, can be mixed in a GNMA II pool. Each individual lender is responsible for marketing a share of the pool's securities based on that lender's contribution to the mortgages in the pool; but the investors who buy the securities are acquiring an interest in the entire pool, which does not correspond to the mortgages originated by any one lender.

Under GNMA II a central paying agent (initially Chemical Bank of New York) handles all processing of the securities, including original issuance, transfers, accounting, payments to investors, and income tax withholding and reporting. Since these functions are centralized, an investor who owns securities in several GNMA II pools receives a single check and payment advice each month. The individual lenders remain responsible for servicing the underlying mortgages and for remitting the loan collections to the paying agent each month. If a lender defaults in doing so GNMA will, of course, step in under its guarantee obligation and make those payments.

18. See Lasko, GNMA II: New Entrees, Mortgage Banking, June 1983, at 19.

The GNMA MBS program's impact has been very great, and it must be regarded as an outstanding success. A very high percentage of all FHA-insured home loans currently originated are funded through GNMA-guaranteed securities. During 1983, GNMA guaranteed 50 billion dollars in these securities, more than the combined total of mortgage-related securities issued by FNMA and FHLMC in the same period, and nearly a quarter of the $223 billion of residential mortgages originated in 1983. In early 1984 the total volume of outstanding GNMA MBS passed $200 billion.

Many of these securities are purchased by institutions which are already in the mortgage lending business, but a major share are bought by pension funds, trusts, profit-sharing plans, and other entities which seldom invest directly in mortgages. In this way the program has been successful in attracting large quantities of new funds to the mortgage market. The fact that the securities carry monthly payments of principal and interest is attractive to many investors, such as pension funds, who have monthly cash flow needs. At the same time, the securities are far simpler investments than mortgages themselves, and require no effort on the part of the investor to satisfy itself with regard to title, appraised value, credit worthiness, or the other factors about which a direct investor in mortgages must be concerned. In addition, the securities are highly liquid, and a secondary market for them is made by many investment banking houses.

The success of the GNMA MBS program has inspired numerous competitors. As mentioned above, both FNMA and FHLMC now issue their own mortgage-backed securities, guaranteeing them directly rather than relying on a GNMA guarantee. Numerous private and public institutional lenders have also experimented with sales of securities collateralized by non-FHA/VA mortgages. Some have been of the pass-through type, but with reliance on the institution's own full faith and credit, private mortgage insurance, or a combination of the two, rather than on GNMA (which is not permitted by law to guarantee conventional mortgage pools). [19]

Since 1983 some lenders (and FHLMC as well) have issued "collateralized mortgage obligations" or CMO's.[20] Like GNMA-guaranteed securities, they are backed by pools of mortgages, but they are not of the pass-through type. Instead, they typically pay interest semiannually, but principal payments from the mortgages are restructured so as to produce several groups of bond-like securities with varying maturities. For example, a CMO might consist of three packages of securities, with maturities of approximately 3, 5, and 10 years. All payments of principal on all of the mortgages would be applied in the early years to

---

19. Budd & Wasserman, The Yankee Mac Mortgage Pass-Through Program, 15 Conn.L.Rev. 385 (1983).

20. See Cholewicki, CMOs Transform Mortgage Credit Markets, Mortgage Banking, Feb.1985, at 61; Street Talk on the CMO, Secondary Mortgage Markets, Feb. 1984, at 45; Use of CMO Structure Grows Rapidly, Freddie Mac Reports, Jan. 1984, at 1.

retire the first group of bonds, then the second group, and so on. The result is a security which is backed by mortgages but closely resembles an industrial bond—an instrument which is attractive to some types of investors who would be disinterested in a pass-through of mortgage payments.

The Federal Home Loan Bank System

The Federal Home Loan Bank System is organized in a manner similar to the Federal Reserve System. It consists of the Federal Home Loan Bank Board, located in Washington D.C., twelve Federal Home Loan Banks located in districts covering the United States, and the 3400 member institutions, most of which are savings and loan associations.[21] The district banks serve as central credit banks for the member institutions and do not do business directly with the public. They are instrumentalities of the federal government, and their basic policies are fixed by the Federal Home Loan Bank Board. However, each of the banks has issued capital stock which is owned by its members. Hence the banks are an unusual hybrid of federal control and private ownership. Each bank has its own staff and board of directors; six of the board members of each bank are appointed by the Federal Home Loan Bank Board to represent the public interest, while the other directors are elected by the member institutions.

The banks provide a variety of benefits to their members, including the acceptance of interest-bearing deposits and the provision of computer services. By far the most important activity of the banks is the making available of credit to their members. Loans from the banks to their members are known as "advances". The savings and loan industry has tended to use these advances as a substitute for funds withdrawn by depositors from savings accounts when tight credit and high interest rates in other markets have resulted in reductions in savings account balances. For this reason the total level of advances has fluctuated widely, tending to reach peak levels when interest rates are highest and dropping off as credit becomes more available. At the close of 1983 nearly 60 billion dollars in advances was outstanding. The banks raise the funds with which to make these advances by the sale of debt obligations in the general capital markets. The instruments sold usually take the form of consolidated obligations of the bank system and are issued by the Bank Board and marketed by its Office of Finance in Washington. Since these obligations are purchased by a wide variety of institutional investors, most of which are not primarily mortgage investors, the bank system has the effect of shifting funds from the general capital markets into the mortgage market. In this respect, and also in its counter-cyclical tendencies, the bank system

---

21. See the Federal Home Loan Bank Act, 47 Stat. 725 (1932), 12 U.S.C.A. § 1421. The system is thoroughly discussed in all recent annual editions of U.S. League of Savings Associations, Savings and Loan Fact Book. Current financial data on the system can be found in all issues of the Federal Home Loan Bank Board Journal.

serves much the same function as FNMA and FHLMC. However, it differs from the secondary market agencies in that no mortgages are actually purchased by the Federal Home Loan Banks from their member institutions. The associations which borrow from the banks continue to hold the mortgages which exist in their portfolios, although these mortgages serve as collateral for advances made.

Many savings and loan associations make relatively little use of the advances, and in the aggregate they have never been as great as 10% of the members' total savings balances. The highest level of advances at the end of any calendar year occurred in 1982, a period of extreme monetary stringency, when 66 billion dollars was outstanding.

State and Local Housing Finance Agencies

The creation by state governments of mortgage market support agencies is a relatively recent phenomenon. In 1960 New York became the first state to do so; by 1970 twelve more states had acted, and now nearly all states have such agencies.[22] The underlying concept of all of the agencies is similar. They sell bonds and other debt issuances which, because of their state government status, are exempt from federal and often state income taxation, and which therefore bear relatively low interest rates. The funds raised by these bond and note sales are then used to finance housing for low-income and moderate-income families and individuals, with the lower interest rates being passed on in the form of lower mortgage interest to the home-buyers (in the case of single-family housing) or sponsors (in the case of rental apartments).

The mechanisms by which the state agencies funnel their money into the residential mortgage market are varied. Some make direct loans to housing developers, sponsors, and individual buyers. Others act as secondary market purchasers, issuing advance commitments to lending institutions to purchase loans which meet prescribed criteria.[22.5] Still others make loans to lending institutions on the condition that the funds be employed in mortgage lending on housing of the type the agency desires to assist. Some employ two or more of the foregoing methods. Whether single-family or multi-family housing is involved, the agencies usually impose limitations on the household income of the occupants and on the cost of the housing.

Other programmatic variations exist. In a few states, legislatures have appropriated subsidy funds which the agencies administer, sometimes employing them to further lower interest rates. In addition, many of the agencies have worked cooperatively with the Department of Housing and Urban Development, supplying mortgage loans for

---

22. See State Housing Finance Agencies: The Iowa Blueprint, 62 Iowa L.Rev. 1524 (1977). The BNA Housing and Development Reporter contains a thorough summary of state agency techniques and a current listing of the individual agencies and the programs they operate.

22.5 See Lupis v. Peoples Mortg. Co., 107 Idaho 489, 690 P.2d 944 (1984).

projects subsidized by HUD under Section 236 or, more recently, the Section 8 program.[23] The advantage of the state agency's lower interest rate when used in conjunction with HUD subsidies is that it may make otherwise infeasible projects feasible by lowering the sponsor's debt service, or may permit the construction of apartment buildings with somewhat greater amenities than would otherwise be possible.

As the success of the state housing finance agencies grew in the late 1970's, cities and counties began to emulate their example, either creating local financing agencies or issuing mortgage-backed bonds themselves. In most of these situations, single-family home loans to owner-occupants were involved. One result of this increased activity was a growing concern on the part of Congress that the implicit federal subsidy was being abused. There were reports of loans to wealthy individuals to buy expensive houses. Since the bonds represented a significant loss of revenue to the federal government, they could hardly be justified in social policy terms except in cases of needy borrowers who could not otherwise afford decent housing.

Congress' objections to this free-wheeling use of tax-free financing found expression in the Mortgage Subsidy Bond Tax Act of 1980,[24] which added Section 103A to the Internal Revenue Code.[25] It deems the interest on mortgage subsidy bonds to be taxable income unless the criteria set out in the Act are met. To qualify, 90% of the mortgage loans in the program must be to first-time homebuyers, and 20% of the funds must be directed to economically distressed areas. Each state is given an annual "quota" in terms of dollar volume of bonds which can be issued;[26] half of this amount is allocated to the state agency, and half to local agencies, unless the state chooses a different allocation. Prices of the homes financed must not exceed certain limits, and the IRS is authorized to publish "safe harbor" figures for these limits.[27]

The authority to issue tax-free bonds under Section 103A lapsed in 1983, but was reinstated through 1987 by the Tax Reform Act of 1984,[28] producing a spate of new bond sales by state and local agencies. But a new twist was added, in an attempt to respond to the long-expressed criticism that tax-exempt bonds are an inherently inefficient and costly technique for subsidizing housing, since much of the lost federal revenue benefits wealthy bond-holders and the various underwriters, lawyers, and other professionals who create and market the bonds. The 1984 Act allows state housing finance agencies to "trade in" a portion

---

23. See Sangster, For Section 8 Housing—New Financing Relationship Between LHA's and State Housing Finance Agencies Proposed, 32 J. Housing 67 (1975).

24. Pub.L. No. 96–499, adding I.R.C. § 103A. On the inefficiency of mortgage subsidy bonds, see U.S. General Acc'tg Office, The Costs and Benefits of Single-Family Mortgage Revenue Bonds: Preliminary Report (Apr. 18, 1983).

25. See I.R.C. Temp.Reg. § 6a.103A.

26. See Rev.Proc. 84–53 for the most recent volume limits at this writing. The 1984 limit for all states totalled $14.854 billion.

27. See Rev.Proc. 84–56 for the most recent "safe harbor" area purchase price limits at this writing.

28. § 611, Pub.L. No. 93–369.

of their unused tax-exempt bond-issuing authority in return for authority to issue taxable bonds tied to "mortgage credit certificates", or MCC's. The MCC's can then be issued to qualified home buyers, and allow them to take a tax *credit* (not merely a deduction) for a portion of the interest they pay on their mortgage loans. The credit may vary from 10% to 50% of the interest paid, and has the obvious effect of reducing the cost of home ownership.[29] Thus, the benefit to the home buyer is economically analogous to that which results from issuance of tax-free bonds. But under the MCC program, the interest on the agency's corresponding bonds is taxable rather than tax-exempt. The program was initially received by the agencies with considerable enthusiasm,[30] although some studies suggested that many lower-income home buyers could not take full advantage of the tax credits.[31]

WESTLAW REFERENCES

Secondary Market Agencies—FNMA and FHLMC
digest(f.n.m.a. f.h.l.m.c. (fannie freddie +1 mae mac) (mortgage +1
    association corporation) % title,synopsis("fannie mae"))

The Government National Mortgage Association (GNMA)
f.n.m.a. g.n.m.a. (fannie ginnie +1 mae) /p f.h.a. #v.a. "farmers
    home" "veterans administration" % title,synopsis("fannie mae"))

The Federal Home Loan Bank System
52k451

State and Local Housing Finance Agencies
state local +1 "housing finance agency"
synopsis,digest(h.u.d. (housing +2 "urban development") /p
    section +1 8 236)

---

§ 11.4 Alternative Mortgage Instruments

The great majority of mortgage loans which have been made in modern times are of the level-payment self-amortizing type described in Section 1.1. Interest is fixed for the life of the loan and payments are the same each month or other period, and fully amortize the debt with no "balloon" payment upon maturity. While this format has resolved the problem of mandatory refinancing which existed in pre-depression mortgage loans, in which only interest was paid monthly,[1] it also has certain disadvantages. The disadvantages fall into two basic categories, as do various proposals for reform.

---

29. See I.R.C. Temp.Reg. 26 C.F.R. 1.25, adopted 50 Fed.Reg. 19344 (May 8, 1985).

30. See BNA Hsg. & Devel.Rptr., Dec. 3, 1984, at 546.

31. See BNA Hsg. & Devel.Rptr., Apr. 22, 1985, at 932.

§ 11.4

1. Pre-depression mortgages were usually written for relatively short periods—five to fifteen years—and made no provision for amortization of principal balance; thus, when the loan matured, the borrower

was expected either to pay the principal out of savings he had accumulated, or to refinance for an additional period with the same or another lender. During the depression many borrowers found both alternatives impossible, and large-scale foreclosures resulted. See Harr, Federal Credit and Private Housing 58 (1960). As Harr describes, the FHA was primarily responsible for popularizing the long-term, level-payment, fully-amortizing loan.

The first troublesome aspect of the standard loan format is its failure to take into account changes in the ability of the mortgagors to make payments over their life spans. For example, young families purchasing a first house are likely to experience significant increases in income as they grow older.[2] Yet the standard loan provides for level payments in terms of nominal dollars; in an inflationary economy, the real value of the monthly payments will decline over time, even though the mortgagors' ability to pay will probably be increasing. Hence their maximum initial loan amount will be fixed by an income which rapidly becomes irrelevant with the passage of time;[3] after a few years they will easily be able to afford payments on a larger home, but can make such a change only through the rather costly method of selling the existing house and buying another.

At the other end of the mortgagors' life span an opposite mismatch occurs. The mortgagors frequently retire and experience a sharp drop in income, but their monthly mortgage payment obligation remains constant despite the fact that principal amortization and inflating house values have combined to produce a very low loan-to-value ratio. The mortgagors might prefer to reduce their payments, or even to stop them entirely, but the standard loan format makes no provision for doing so.

The second major problem with the standard loan relates not to the preferences and incomes of mortgagors, but to the ability of lenders, particularly thrift institutions, to retain deposits and hence to continue lending during periods of sharply increasing interest rates. The United States economy has experienced a series of large fluctuations in interest rates during the post-war period, especially since 1966. These credit cycles are largely produced by the interaction of a complex set of factors, including consumer behavior, federal and state borrowing demands, international trade and economic conditions, and the periodic efforts of the Federal Reserve Board to tighten the supply of money in the economy in order to slow inflation. Interest rate peaks can be clearly discerned in 1966, 1969–70, 1974, 1978, 1981, and 1984. In each case rates have subsequently fallen, but usually not as low as pre-peak levels.[4]

2. Life-cycle incomes are discussed in Weinrobe, Whatever Happened to the Flexible Payment Mortgage?, FHLBBJ, Dec. 1975, at 16. See also Hu, In Search of the Ideal Mortgage, FNMA Seller-Servicer, Apr.-Jun. 1981, at 21.

3. Lenders usually "qualify" borrowers by permitting them to borrow only the amount which can be repaid by monthly installments (including principal, interest, taxes, and insurance) no larger than 25% to 28% of monthly income. See, e.g., FNMA Guide Servicers-Lending, ch. 2, § 102.06 (1984); Federal Home Loan Mortgage Corp., Sellers' Guide Conventional Mortgages § 3.403(a) (1984). FHA uses a guideline of 35% of "net effective income"; see HUD Handbook 4000.2 (1982) at sec. 5-7. Thus income often fixes the maximum amount which a mortgagor can borrow, even if he or she would prefer a larger loan.

4. See the statistical series in any current issue of The Federal Home Loan Bank Board Journal or Mortgage Banking.

The effect of these credit cycles on thrift institutions such as savings and loan associations and mutual savings banks is highly damaging. When short-term rates on alternative investments, such as Treasury bills and commercial paper, rise above the rates being paid on savings deposits by thrift institutions, many sophisticated depositors withdraw their funds from savings accounts and place them in these alternative investments. The institutions may literally run out of money to lend, and the housing market suffers. This phenomenon is known as disintermediation, since it involves the removal of funds from the thrift institutions, which are financial intermediaries.[5] To forestall disintermediation, thrift institutions may attempt to raise the interest rates on their own deposits, thereby inducing investors to keep their funds on deposit. Until recently, one major barrier to such an effort was Regulation Q, under which the Federal Reserve Board and the Federal Home Loan Bank Board set legal limits on deposit interest rates payable by both banks and thrift institutions.[6] In principle, Regulation Q was intended to prevent damaging rate wars among institutions. But whatever the merits of that policy, Regulation Q had the practical effect of keeping rates paid to small savers at below-market levels. Moreover, because it maintained a small interest differential between thrifts and commercial banks (with the former typically being permitted to pay one-fourth percent higher interest), it also served to divert funds into the thrifts, and thus into housing investment.

Regulation Q was persistently criticized by economists as anticompetitive, unfair to small savers, and productive of inefficiency.[7] In the Depository Institutions Deregulation and Monetary Control Act of 1980, Congress directed the financial regulatory agencies to phase out Regulation Q and eliminate all deposit rate ceilings by March 31, 1986.[8] A good deal of this deregulation has already been accomplished at this writing, and it is likely that Regulation Q will indeed pass into history.

But even without Regulation Q, mortgage lenders which have historically been heavy investors in standard mortgages will still have

---

5. Disintermediation and its effects are discussed in The Report of the President's Commission on Housing 118–20 (1982); Klaman, Maintaining Deposit Inflows When Interest Rates Rise: The Impossible Dream, 38 Mortgage Banker 46 (No. 7, Apr. 1978); Gramley, Short-Term Cycles In Housing Production: An Overview of the Problem and Possible Solutions, in Federal Reserve Staff Study: Ways to Moderate Fluctuations in Housing Construction (1972), at 1; Schechter, The Residential Mortgage Financing Problem, Committee Print, House Housing Subcommittee, 92d Cong., 1st Sess., 1971.

6. See 12 U.S.C.A. §§ 3502–09, added by Pub.L. 96–221, §§ 203–210. The repeal of the previous authority of the individual

agencies to fix deposit ceilings is found in 12 U.S.C.A. § 3506. See 12 CFR Part 217 (Federal Reserve Bd.); 12 CFR Part 329 (Federal Deposit Ins. Corp.); 12 CFR Part 526 (Federal Home Loan Bank Bd.). All federally-chartered and federally-insured state-chartered banks and S & L's are controlled by these regulations.

7. See, e.g., The Report of The President's Commission on Financial Structure and Regulation (the "Hunt Commission") (1972) recommending abolition of Regulation Q. Cf. Dunne, Scott & Barrett, The Swan Song of Regulation Q—A Rejoinder, 92 Banking L.J. 219 (1975).

8. See note 6 supra.

difficulty raising their deposit rates to competitive levels during periods of generally rising rates. The reason is that their mortgage portfolios consist of mortgages made in prior years as well as those made in the current year. Even if the institution raises the interest rates on mortgage loans currently being made to very high levels, that action has relatively little impact on the overall yield of the portfolio, since it consists largely of fixed-interest loans made in earlier periods when rates were lower. This "portfolio lag" phenomenon virtually precludes the institutions from raising deposit interest rates quickly, no matter how much they would like to do so. The thrift institutions are caught in a fundamental structural dilemma; by their nature they violate the well-known axiom of finance: "Never borrow short and lend long." In an economy characterized by volatile interest rates, their problem is an acute one.[9]

Two approaches to this problem can be taken, and the thrift institutions and their regulators have moved toward both. The first is to change the maturity structure of the institutions' liabilities—that is, their deposits—in order to make them less volatile. A number of regulatory changes have been made to allow thrifts to offer a broader range of longer-term instruments to savers.[10]

The other approach is to shorten the effective maturity of the institutions' assets, their mortgage loans. Although most home mortgages today have nominal maturities of twenty-five to thirty years, they are typically prepaid in ten to twelve years or less.[11] These early payments are due in part to rapidly inflating housing prices, which tend to make property sales with assumptions and subject-to transfers impractical within a few years after a mortgage loan has been placed on a home. The widespread use of due-on-sale clauses is also an important factor in causing early payoffs. But most portfolio lenders wish to reduce the effective term of the average home mortgage loan a great deal more than the reduction which results from ordinary prepayments associated with home transfers. Hence, since the beginning of the 1980's they have engaged in a major shift away from the standard fixed-rate loan and toward instruments with adjustable rates, with the adjustment indexed to some short-term or medium-term market rate such as that on United State government securities. Such mortgages are viewed as the economic equivalent of short-term loans, even though

---

9. The portfolio lag concept is developed in Ashley, Use of "Due-On" Clauses to Gain Collateral Benefits: A Common-Sense Defense, 10 Tulsa.L.J. 590 (1975). The problem is illustrated by the fact that, in 1980, when current mortgage rates were typically above 15%, 67% of the mortgages held by savings and loan associations carried rates below 10%. See Report of the President's Commission on Housing 129 (1982).

10. See President's Commission on Housing 124–26 (1982); Olin, Changes in Deposit Account Structure, September 1982—March 1983, 16 FHLBBJ 32 (Aug. 1983); regulations cited note 6 supra.

11. See Boykin, Implications of the 12-Year Prepayment Assumption, Mortgage Banker, Nov. 1976, at 38; Kinkade, Mortgage Prepayments and Their Effects on S & L's, FHLBBJ, Jan. 1976, at 12.

their monthly payment schedules might continue to be based on twenty-five or thirty year amortization of principal.

There are, then, two reasons for experimentation in recent years with alternative mortgage instruments: the desire to conform payment schedules to borrowers' abilities to pay, and the desire to make mortgage loans which are not locked into fixed interest yields for long time periods, but on which yields will tend to match those available in the current market from time to time. Certain types of new mortgage formats are associated with each of these two objectives.[12]

Mortgages Which Address The Borrower's Ability to Pay

The *graduated payment mortgage (GPM)* is intended to be attractive to young mortgagors who expect to have rising incomes in the near future. The interest rate on a GPM is fixed, but the payments start out at a relatively low level and gradually rise to a predetermined higher amount. The payments are not keyed to the borrower's actual income, but rather follow a rising schedule which the parties feel he or she will probably be able to meet without difficulty. The objective is to permit the borrower to qualify for a larger loan than would be permitted if the payments were level.[13]

The first federal encouragement for the GPM came in 1974, when the Federal Home Loan Bank Board authorized federal savings and loan associations to make "flexible payment mortgage loans."[14] Such loans were required to be structured so that each payment would cover at least the entire interest due. In addition, by the end of the fifth year the payments had to be high enough for the loan to be fully self-amortizing. The full-interest requirement meant, for example, that the initial payments on an 8.5 percent "flexible payment" mortgage could, at best, be about 8% lower than payments on a standard mortgage. The reduction in payments was not very great, and the program was not widely used.[15]

The enactment of the Housing and Community Development Act of 1974 added a new Section 245 to the National Housing Act,[16] authorizing HUD to insure mortgages "with provisions for varying rates of amortization corresponding to anticipated variations in family income."

12. See generally Iezman, Alternative Mortgage Instruments: Their Effect on Residential Financing, 10 Real Est.L.J. 3 (1981); Thomas, Alternative Residential Mortgages for Tomorrow, 26 Prac.Law 55 (Sept.1980); Federal Home Loan Bank Board, Alternative Mortgage Instruments Research Study (3 vols. 1977) (hereafter cited AMIRS Study); Smith, Reforming the Mortgage Instrument, FHLBBJ, May 1976, at 2; Follain & Struyk, Homeownership Effects of Alternative Mortgage Instru-

ments, 5 Am.Real Est. & Urb.Econ.Ass'n J. 1 (1977).

13. See note 3, supra.

14. 12 CFR 541.14(c); see Cassidy & McElhone, The Flexible Payment Mortgage: An Opportunity for Experimentation by S & L's, FHLBBJ, Aug. 1974, at 7.

15. See Weinrobe, Whatever Happened to the Flexible Payment Mortgage?, FHLBBJ, Dec. 1975, at 16.

16. 12 U.S.C.A. §§ 1715z–10.

After some uncertainty as to how to proceed,[17] HUD in 1976 issued regulations under the authority of Section 245 (now Section 245(a)),[18] approving the insurance by FHA of graduated payment mortgages. The regulations permit monthly payments to be increased in annual steps over the first five years or the first ten years of the loan; under the five-year plan the payments may rise by 2.5%, 5%, or 7.5% each year, while under the ten-year plan payments may increase annually by either 2% or 3%. There is no requirement that all payments cover interest owed, and the FHA program often involves "negative amortization" in the early years. If the early payments do not cover the full interest, the difference is added to principal; thus, it is entirely possible for the outstanding balance to rise rather than be reduced for a few years. The program requires that the outstanding balance never exceed 97% of the original appraised value of the property; to account for the negative amortization, a somewhat larger down-payment than 3% is generally necessary.

To illustrate the operation of the GPM concept, assume the mortgagor borrows $50,000 for a 30-year term at an interest rate of 12%. The monthly payment on a standard level-payment loan would be $514.31. Suppose the mortgagor instead elects a GPM under the most popular of the FHA plans mentioned above—Plan III, which provides for payments increasing at 7.5% per year for the first five years of the loan. Her payments in the first year will be only $395.69, and for the first five years, will rise as follows: [19]

Year 1	395.69 per month
Year 2	425.37 per month
Year 3	457.27 per month
Year 4	491.56 per month
Year 5	528.43 per month

All payments in later years will remain at the same level as the fifth year. The advantages to the borrower in terms of initial qualification for the loan are obvious; the first-year payment is about 23% lower than under a level-payment plan. Of course, this is offset by the higher payments which must be made in years five through thirty, but that is a price which many borrowers are willing to pay.

This example also illustrates the negative amortization which many GPM's produce. Here the $50,000 outstanding balance on the loan does not begin to decline with the first payment, as is the case with level payment mortgages. Instead, because the early payments are insufficient to cover the accrued interest, the balance rises steadily

17. See 40 Fed.Reg. 34625, in which HUD solicited public comments as to what it should do under its Section 245 authority.

18. 12 CFR 203.45, 203.436; condominium financing is also made available under the GPM by virtue of 12 CFR 234.75,

234.259. See McFarlin & Vitek, The HUD GPM Program: An Evaluation, Mortgage Banker, Mar. 1980, at 27.

19. The financial tables from which this example was computed are found in HUD Handbook 4240.2 CHG 2, issued Jan. 29, 1980.

until the 60th month, at which point it "peaks" at $53,935.41. Not until the 151st month does the balance decline below its original level of $50,000. The decline continues, and the loan is fully amortized by the 360th month's payment.

In addition to the Section 245(a) plans described above,[20] Congress permits FHA to insure GPM's with even more liberal terms under Section 245(b), usually termed the Modified Graduated Payment Mortgage or MGPM plan.[21] Monthly payments may rise by 4.6% per year for ten years, or by 7.5% per year for five years. However, eligibility under Section 245(b) is strictly limited. The mortgagor may not have owned a home within the preceding 3 years, and must not qualify under any other FHA mortgage insurance program. The house's appraised value may not exceed 110% of the FHA-determined median prototype housing cost for the area. The mortgage amount may be higher under Section 245(b) than under 245(a), since the "peak" outstanding balance may be as great as the lesser of 113% of the original appraised value of the house, or 97% of appraised value, inflated by 2.5% per year during the period the outstanding balance is rising.

The Veterans Administration has also adopted a GPM plan for VA-guaranteed home mortgages. It is essentially identical to FHA Plan III described above.[22] While the authorizing statute permitted VA to allow negative amortization up to a "peak" of the original appraised value inflated by 2.5% per year (with a maximum of 115% of appraised value),[23] VA did not implement this concept and instead insists that the loan balance never exceed the original appraised value.

The Federal Home Loan Bank Board dramatically revised its mortgage lending regulations for all Federally-insured savings associations in 1983.[24] It eliminated virtually all previous restrictions on the use of GPM's by these lenders. The regulations allow the association to adjust the payment or balance on any real estate loan "as authorized by the contract", which may provide for "the deferral of principal and capitalization of a portion of interest."[25] Payment adjustments must be made "pursuant to a formula, or to a schedule specifying the percentage or dollar change in the payment as set forth in the loan contract."[26] Other than a 40-year maximum loan maturity, the FHLBB imposes no limitations on these contract terms.

20. Section 442 of the Housing and Urban-Rural Recovery Act of 1983, Pub.L. No. 98–181, adds a new Section 245(c) to the National Housing Act. It authorizes FHA to insure graduated payment mortgages on multifamily housing. Such a GPM would have varying rates of amortization corresponding to anticipated variations in project income. FHA has proposed regulations to implement this program; see 49 Fed.Reg. 41068.

21. See 24 CFR 203.46.

22. See 38 CFR 36.4309(e); DVB Circular 26–81–36, published in 46 Fed.Reg. 60124.

23. 38 U.S.C.A. § 1803(d)(2), as amended by the Veterans' Disability Compensation, Housing and Memorial Benefits Amendments of 1981, Pub.L. No. 97–66, 95 Stat. 1026.

24. 48 Fed.Reg. 23032.

25. 12 CFR 545.33(c).

26. 12 CFR 545.33(e)(2).

For national banks, whose lending practices are subject to regulation by the Comptroller of the Currency, the legal environment is even more liberal. In 1983 the Comptroller, responding to the congressional deregulation of bank lending found in the Garn-St. Germain Depository Institutions Act of 1982,[27] eliminated all of its rules and interpretive rulings with respect to amortization and maturity of real estate loans.[28] Hence, a national bank can make virtually any type of GPM loan.

A second type of new mortgage instrument has been proposed for the other end of the life cycle: retirement. Its thesis is that many elderly persons have accumulated large equity values in their homes, but will suffer substantial income reductions upon retirement. Under the *reverse annuity mortgage (RAM)*,[29] the mortgagor in this situation would be given a large cash advance by the lender, and would immediately use this cash to purchase an annuity. The monthly cash flow from the annuity would be used, in part, to pay the interest (and perhaps some principal amortization) on the enlarged mortgage debt; the remainder of the annuity stream would be paid directly to the mortgagor to augment his income.

As an alternative, the mortgagee might make monthly payments directly to the mortgagor, thereby regularly increasing the outstanding balance on the debt; interest would also continue to accrue and be added to principal. Obviously this approach would result at some future point in the reaching of an unacceptable loan-to-value ratio if the mortgagor lived long enough; the lender would demand payoff, presumably achieved only by selling the house, or would foreclose.[30] The advantage of the annuity approach, by contrast, is that it will continue to pay as long as the mortgagor lives, so there is no risk of the mortgagor being forced to vacate the property.

A variety of other variants on the RAM are possible. For example, the lender might offer more favorable terms in return for a share in the property's future appreciation in value. Under another option, the so-called "split equity contract"[31] the homeowner might sell his house to an investor (possibly his mortgagee), reserving a life estate. The sale proceeds could be paid in installments over a number of years, or the

27. § 403, Pub.L. No. 97–320, 96 Stat. 1469, removing all statutory restrictions on real estate lending by national banks.

28. 48 Fed.Reg. 40698. The regulation preempts any state law which would limit national banks as to loan amount, repayment schedule, or term; see 12 CFR Part 34.

29. See Comment, The Effect of Reverse Annuity Mortgages on SSI, 16 U.Cal.Davis L.Rev. 435 (1983); Shaman, New Hope for the Elderly: Home Equity Conversion, Real Estate Today, May 1982, at 36;

Comm. on Aging, U.S. House of Representatives, Home Equity Conversion, 98th Cong., 1st Sess. (1983); Edwards, Reverse Annuity Mortgages, AMIRS Study at XIX; Guttentag, Reverse Annuity Mortgages: How S & L's Can Write Them, AMIRS Study at XVIII.

30. See Quinn, Let the Mortgagor Beware, Forbes, Mar. 20, 1978, at 77, criticizing this type of RAM.

31. See Edwards, Reverse Annuity Mortgages, AMIRS Study, at XIX–5.

vendor might take the proceeds in cash and purchase an annuity. Numerous other permutations may also be conceived.[32]

In recent years most regulatory barriers to the making of RAM loans have been swept away. As mentioned above, the real estate lending powers of national banks are now almost fully deregulated, so they may readily engage in RAM lending.[33] Lending on RAM's by Federally-chartered savings and loan associations is governed by the liberalized regulations issued by the Federal Home Loan Bank Board in 1983; they provide that associations may agree to defer "all interest on loans to natural persons secured by borrower-occupied property and on which periodic advances are being made."[34] Thus the classic RAM, with regular payments to the borrower and accrual of all interest, is authorized. There has also been a good deal of state legislative activity, approving or encouraging the use of RAM's by state-chartered lending institutions.[35] Nevertheless, RAM's continue to be seen as radical or even dangerous by many lenders, and their growth is likely to be slow.

Lack of affordability of housing, especially for young families, has given rise to several other innovative mortgage formats. One of these is the *shared-equity mortgage, or SEM.* It involves at least two parties who are liable on the mortgage loan. One of them will occupy the house; the other is an investor who owns a share of the equity, typically as a tenant in common, and makes a portion of the down payment and monthly payments, but does not occupy the property. Since each contributes a portion of the investment, they are entitled to share, on the basis of agreed percentages, in the proceeds of a subsequent sale or other disposition.

The objective of the SEM is to reduce the owner-occupant's initial down payment and monthly outlays to manageable levels, while providing an investment opportunity for the non-occupant party.[36] There is nothing unique about the mortgage itself, but the agreement between the owning parties is complex and requires careful drafting. FHA has encouraged the development of the SEM by treating the house as

---

32. See Garnett & Guttentag, The Reverse-Shared-Appreciation Mortgage, 3 Housing Fin.Rev. 63 (1984); Chen, Alternative Reverse Mortgages: A Simulation Analysis of Initial Benefits in Baltimore, 2 Housing Fin.Rev. 295 (1983); Note, Reverse Annuity Mortgages and the Due-on-Sale Clause, 32 Stan.L.Rev. 143 (1979).

33. See notes 27–28 supra.

34. 24 CFR 545.33(c). See the previous regulations in 46 Fed.Reg. 51893.

35. See, e.g., N.Y.—McKinney's Banking Law § 6–h; Minn.Stat.Ann. § 47.58(4); Fla.Sess. Laws Ch. 83–311, instructing the Florida Department of Community Affairs to prepare a written report on the feasibility of the RAM in Florida and a set of

recommendations for implementing RAM's. A similar report on "Home Equity Conversion Mortgages", to be prepared by HUD, is required by § 448, Housing and Urban-Rural Recovery Act of 1983, Pub.L. No. 98–181.

36. See Fields, Real Estate Interests as Investment Contracts: An Update and a New Application—the Shared-Equity Program, 12 Real Est.L.J. 307 (1984); Alper, Equity Sharing in Florida, Fla.B.J., Dec. 1984, at 701. If the occupant pays rent to the investor, the latter may claim depreciation on his or her interest in the house; IRC § 280A(d)(3) and proposed IRS Reg. § 1.280A–1.

owner-occupied, and thus eligible for a higher loan-to-value ratio, if the agreement meets certain tests.[37]

Another mortgage technique which has come into common use during the 1980's as a way of improving housing affordability is the "*buy-down*"[38] Here a builder or home-seller makes a substantial payment to the mortgage lender in return for the latter's reducing the interest rate (and hence the monthly payments) on the loan to the buyer. Such a payment is, of course, costly to the seller, but it can be a useful and sometimes powerful tool for marketing the housing. In some cases, the seller requires the buyer to repay in future years the amount advanced to accomplish the buy-down, and may take a junior mortgage on the property to secure this repayment obligation.[39] In most recent buy-down programs, the interest rate reduction has been on the order of 1% to 3%, and has been scheduled to phase out (i.e., to rise to market rate) over a period of one to three years. Such a buy-down is much less costly to the seller than would be the case if the interest rate were to be reduced for the entire life of the loan.

A final innovation described here is the *growing equity mortgage, or GEM*. Unlike the other techniques described above, its primary thrust

---

37. For owner-occupied properties, the usual FHA loan-to-value ratio is 97% of the first $25,000 and 95% of the excess; if the property is not owner-occupied, the loan-to-value ratio is only 85%. 24 CFR 203.18. Under the FHA SEM guidelines, the co-mortgagor's (i.e., the investor-owner's) proportion of the monthly payment obligation must be the same as his share of equity ownership; the occupant must pay at least 55% of the monthly payment; the occupant must have the right to buy out the co-mortgagor on 30 days' notice, with the price to be determined by an FHA-approved appraiser; and either party may sell his interest after giving the other a 30-day option to purchase it. See also FHLMC Sellers' Guide Conventional Mortgages § 3.201(a)(7), providing guidelines for FHLMC purchase of mortgages on shared-equity properties.

38. See Wang and Peterson, Toward Affordability: Buydown and Pledged Account Loans, 42 Mortgage Banking 9 (Aug. 1982). The pledged account is similar to a buy-down, except that the funds needed to reduce the loan interest come from a savings or escrow account rather than being paid in cash. The account balance may be assigned outright to the lender at the closing of the loan, or may be "pledged" or assigned under an agreement by which the lender draws down the funds over a period of time—generally the same period as that during which the interest rate reduction is in effect. See FHLMC Sellers' Guide Con-

ventional Mortgage § 3.201(a)(6), describing FHLMC's policies on purchase of mortgages which have been bought down; where the seller provides the funds, they may not exceed 10% of the original loan amount. See also FNMA Guide Services—Lending, ch. 1, § 417, limiting seller buydowns to 10% of the appraised value of the property if the loan-to-value ratio is 90% or less, and otherwise to 6% of appraised value.

Until deregulation of the FHA interest rate in 1983, see § 11.2 supra at notes 20–21, nearly all FHA loans were made at below-market rates, with the seller compensating the lender by payment of "discount points"—in effect, a buydown of the interest rate. This practice continues with VA loans, which are still subject to VA's regulatory interest ceiling. These buydowns differ from those discussed in the text in that the interest rate remains at the lower level for the entire mortgage term. See Agarwal & Phillips, Mortgage Rate Buydowns: Further Evidence, 3 Housing Fin.Rev. 191, 1984, discussing the extent to which FHA and VA discounts are passed back to home buyers via increased house selling prices.

39. See 49 Fed.Reg. 14113 (proposed amendment to FHA regulation, 24 CFR 203.32, which would authorize such junior mortgages to secure buy-down repayments).

is not the lowering or eliminating of monthly payment amounts; indeed, it increases them. Rather, the objective of the GEM is to produce earlier loan pay-offs, and thus to shorten the effective term of the mortgage. The GEM is similar to a GPM in structure: it involves monthly payments which increase by a prearranged percentage each year for, say, the first five or ten years of the loan. But unlike the GPM, a GEM's first-year payments are identical to those which would be required for a level-payment 30-year mortgage. Since this amount is more than sufficient to cover all accruing interest, the entire added amount of the higher payments in later years is applied to retire the principal of the loan. The result is much more rapid pay-off, typically in the range of 12 to 20 years.[40]

From the mortgagor's viewpoint, the GEM has several advantages. Most obviously, the home will be debt-free at a much earlier date than under a standard mortgage. In addition, because the effective maturity of the debt is shorter, the applicable economic principles encourage lenders to invest at a lower interest rate than would be demanded on a level-payment loan.[41] To the extent that any discount or buy-down is involved, the short effective maturity accentuates its impact in further reducing the interest rate.[42] The result is that a GEM can bear a much more attractive rate to the borrower than a standard loan under the same market conditions. On the other hand, the quick amortization is not always an advantage; after only a few years, if the original mortgagor wishes to sell the property on an assumption basis, the balance on the loan may be too low to be attractive to most buyers.

FHA has approved GEM loans as a variant of the GPM since 1982,[43] and the Government National Mortgage Association (GNMA) is empowered to guarantee mortgage-backed securities which are supported by pools of GEM loans.[44] Like the GPM, the GEM recognizes that many mortgagors will experience ever-higher incomes, and thus increasing ability to pay, over time. By conforming to their expected economic life cycles, it allows them to gain significant economic advantages.

40. See Hill, Growing-Equity Home Loans Are Gaining Popularity Because of Quick Repayments, Wall St.J., Oct. 6, 1982, at 52 col. 1.

41. Under most economic conditions, the "yield curve", which represents interest rates as a function of loan term, slopes upward, indicating the fact that long-term investors usually demand higher rates than short-term investors because their funds are at risk for a longer period. See Weggeland, Understanding the ARMs Indexes, Mortgage Banking, Oct. 1984, at 105.

42. In general, the shorter the loan term, the greater the effect of any discount or buy-down; see Lederman, Pricing Discount ARMs in the Secondary Market, Mortgage Banking, Aug. 1984, at 57.

43. See 49 Fed.Reg. 19451, adding 24 CFR 203.47. The FHA regulations were also amended, in the above Federal Register entry, to make GPM's available for condominium and cooperative share loans.

44. See 24 CFR Part 390, subpart D, as amended by 48 Fed.Reg. 3588.

Mortgages Which Address the Term Mismatch Problem of Portfolio Lenders

As we discussed above, lenders who make or purchase mortgage loan assets to hold in portfolio, and whose capital comes primarily from short-term or medium-term liabilities, such as savings deposits, are faced with a problem of mismatched terms. If rates rise on the liability side of the ledger, the lender's cost of funds may approach or even exceed its earnings from its mortgage portfolio. This happens because so much of the portfolio is comprised of mortgage loans made in earlier years at lower rates.[45] The result is serious financial stress for the lender, and in some cases even insolvency.[46]

At least three types of mortgage formats have been developed in recent years in an attempt to solve this problem. By far the most widely-used and discussed is the *adjustable rate mortgage, or ARM*. It provides for periodic readjustments to the interest rate, based on fluctuations in some external index of rates on financial instruments. Because of these regular rate changes, the lender views the ARM as the approximate economic equivalent of a series of short-term mortgages, each made at a current market rate.

The ARM has a checkered regulatory history. The Federal Home Loan Bank Board was a leader in proposing regulations to authorize ARM's (which were usually termed VRM's, or variable rate mortgages, until the 1980's). But its proposals in 1972[47] and 1975[48] met with strenuous political objection[49] and were withdrawn. Finally in 1978

---

45. For a thorough discussion of these phenomena, see FHLBB, Proposed Amendments Relating to Interest Rate Adjustments, 40 Fed.Reg. 6870.

46. During the early 1980's, the thrift industry suffered from more severe financial trauma than at any time since the Great Depression. The Federal Savings and Loan Insurance Corporation (FSLIC), which bears responsibility for salvaging or liquidating failed S & L's, placed 14 associations in receivership during 1982. All but one of these insolvencies were resolved by mergers with other associationis, and the remaining one was liquidated. In all, there were 210 "supervisory mergers" of financially troubled associations during 1982. Of those, 44 required financial assistance from the FSLIC to compensate for the weakness of one of the merger partners. All of these statistics were higher than for any previous year. See Federal Home Loan Bank Board Annual Report 1982, 16 FHLBBJ, Apr. 1983, at 13–20.

47. 37 Fed.Reg. 16201, withdrawn 38 Fed.Reg. 17023.

48. 40 Fed.Reg. 6870.

49. See Hearings on the Financial Institutions Act of 1975 before the Subcomm. on Financial Institutions, Senate Banking, Housing & Urban Affairs Comm., 94th Cong., 1st Sess. (1975), at 725–49; Hearings on Alternative Mortgages before the Senate Comm. on Banking, Housing & Urban Affairs, 95th Cong., 2d Sess. (1978); Comment, Adjustable Interest Rates in Home Mortgages: A Reconsideration, 1975 Wisc. L.Rev. 742.

During 1984 a new spate of political concern with the risks of ARM's to consumers surfaced; see Adjustable-Rate Mortgage Attacked, Defended at House Panel Hearing, BNA Hsg. & Devel. Rptr., July 2, 1984, at 100; Mortgage Lenders, Others Defend ARMs at Hearing, Legislation Unlikely, BNA Hsg. & Devel. Rptr., Aug. 13, 1984, at 217.

Consumers have seemed a good deal less concerned than politicians; see Consumer Acceptance of ARMs Reported Up; Lenders Concerned about "Payment Shock", BNA Hsg & Devel. Rptr., Apr. 9, 1984, at 978; Thompson, All Quiet on the Western VRM Front, FHLBBJ, Oct. 1978, at 10; Colton, Lessard & Solomon, Borrower Atti-the FHLBB adopted rules allowing such loans by federal savings associations, but they were initially applicable only in states where the Board determined they were necessary to meet competitive pressures from state-chartered associations;[50] California was the initial example. Not until mid-1979 were the geographic limits removed, and adjustable rate lending approved nationwide.[51]

During these years there was considerable concern about the possible adverse impact of ARM's on consumers. Hence the initial FHLBB regulations contained a number of detailed provisions to protect borrowers from unfair or unduly onerous ARM's.[52] They included a minimum time period between rate changes, a maximum percentage rate change per year, a cap on total rate increases over the life of the loan, a minimum adjustment percentage to avoid trivial or harassing changes, a requirement of notice some minimum time before the effective date of any rate adjustment, and detailed disclosure to borrowers before loan closing. In addition, the FHLBB specified the rate index which all ARM's were required to employ.[53]

Over time, virtually all of these restrictions on lender behavior have been relaxed or have disappeared.[54] Under the FHLBB's most recent codification of its lending-power regulations,[55] published in 1983, the remaining restrictions apply only to loans secured by homes owned by borrower-occupants. The index can be any rate which is "readily available to and verifiable by the borrower and is beyond the control of the association." There are no longer any regulated minimum or maximum rate adjustments, either annually or during the loan's life, nor is there any minimum time between adjustments. However, detailed provisions still govern initial disclosure to borrowers and notice prior to rate changes.[56]

---

tudes Toward Alternative Mortgage Instruments, 7 J.Am.Real Est. & Urb.Econ.Ass'n 581 (1979).

50. 43 Fed.Reg. 59336; the geographic restriction was made a part of then 12 CFR 545.6–2(c)(2). This same rule authorized GPM's and RAM's by federal S & L's as well.

51. 44 Fed.Reg. 32199.

52. See Cassidy, Comparison and Analysis of the Consumer Safeguards of Variable Rate and Renegotiable Rate Mortgage Instruments, FHLBB Research Working Paper No. 95 (1980). Note that the regulation itself used the term "VRM." The text here employs "ARM" for the sake of conceptual consistency.

53. In the 1978 geographically-limited regulations, the index was the current cost-of-funds index published by the district Federal Home Loan Bank in which the property was located. When the regulations were applied nation-wide in 1979, the FHLBB's national index of cost of funds to

FSLIC-insured associations was substituted. See 44 Fed.Reg. 32199.

54. See Buckley & Villani, Problems with the Adjustable-Rate Mortgage Regulations, 2 Housing Fin.Rev. 183 (1983), suggesting that the liberalization of federal regulation of ARM's may have gone too far, shifting excessive risk to borrower households. But see Preston v. First Bank of Marietta, 16 Ohio App.3d 4, 473 N.E.2d 1210 (1983), holding unenforceable, as lacking mutuality, an adjustable rate clause with no index rate and no restriction on the lender's power to increase the rate.

55. The publication was occasioned by legislative changes made by the Garn-St. Germain Depository Institutions Act of 1982, Pub.L. No. 97–320, 96 Stat. 1469.

56. See 12 CFR 545.33(e), as amended 48 Fed.Reg. 23032, 23061. See also 50 Fed.Reg. 16094 (Apr. 24, 1985), proposing a requirement that loan applicants be given a standard booklet explaining ARMs.

How does the borrower pay when the rate increases? There are essentially three methods. The most obvious is simply to increase the monthly payments to correspond to the new rate. The only problem with this approach is a practical one: will the borrower be able to afford the higher monthly outlay? In the parlance of the lending industry, will the "rate shock" encourage an unacceptable level of delinquency and ultimate default and foreclosure?

A second alternative is to leave the payment amount at its initial level, but to increase the term of the loan. However, this works only with small rate increases. For example, a fully-amortizing 30-year loan of $50,000, with a 12 percent interest rate, carries monthly payments of $514.31. If the rate is raised to 12.5 percent, the interest alone would amount to $520.83 per month, even if no principal were paid at all. Hence, no conceivable lengthening of the loan's maturity will allow the monthly payment to remain constant with this (relatively small) rate increase. Since most home loans (including ARM's) are made initially with 30-year terms, and 40 years is typically the maximum term permitted under applicable regulations,[57] the greatest rate increase which can be accommodated by lengthening the 30-year maturity is about one-fourth of one percent.

The foregoing assumes that the loan will continue to be self-amortizing despite the rate increase. The third method of accommodating a rate increase does not make this assumption; instead of raising monthly payments to meet the increased interest rate, the payments are held constant and the unpaid interest is simply added to principal, producing "negative amortization" each month in much the same way as do many GPM plans.[58] The difference, of course, is that here there is no specific schedule of rising payments to which the borrower is obligated, and that will eventually "catch up" the capitalized interest. Lenders and regulators have been deeply concerned with this fact, since it raises the prospect that in the event of default the loan may be seriously under-secured by the mortgaged property. Until 1981 the FHLBB did not permit the use of negative amortization in ARM's.[59] Its current rules limit the use of negative amortization: the loan balance may never exceed 125 percent of the original appraised value of the property unless the contract provides for readjustment of the payments at least once every five years, beginning no later than the 10th year of the loan, to a level sufficient to amortize the loan fully over its remaining term at the then-existing interest rate.[60]

Despite questions concerning its long-term impact on consumers and the economy,[61] the ARM has become extremely popular among

57. See, e.g., 12 CFR 545.33(a) (1984) (40 years, federal savings and loan associations); 24 CFR 203.17(d) (35 years, FHA-insured mortgages).

58. See text at notes 18–20 supra.

59. See 46 Fed.Reg. 24148.

60. 12 CFR 545.33(d).

61. See Moser & Whiteley, Short Fuse on ARMs, Mortgage Banking, Aug. 1984, at 22.

lenders.[62] Many consumers find it attractive too, primarily because ARM's carry initial interest rates which are often well below rates on comparable fixed-interest loans. While the Federal Home Loan Bank Board has been the ARM leader among federal regulators, both the Comptroller of the Currency (which regulates lending by national banks)[63] and the National Credit Union Administration[64] also approve ARM lending by the institutions they regulate, as do numerous state banking regulators.[65]

Even more important has been the acceptance by FNMA and FHLMC of ARM's as suitable instruments for purchase.[66] These agencies have been a major force in standardizing ARM's; they have accomplished this by adopting standard forms[67] and identifying the characteristics of instruments they are willing to buy, and the market has responded by creating instruments which meet these specifications. As a result, FMNA and FHLMC have become *de facto* regulators of ARM's.

It is not useful in this book to set out the detailed programs currently being operated by FNMA and FHLMC. In general, they have

---

62. FHLMC performed a survey on a large sample of S & L's, commercial banks, and mortgage bankers in 1983; it determined that 82% of the lenders offered ARM's, and that in the period January-June, 1983, lenders offering ARM's had a mean percentage of 44% ARM originations to total originations. See FHLMC, What Makes an ARM Successful? (1983). See also Colton & Lea, ARMs and the Secondary Markets: The Next Boom?, Secondary Mortgage Markets, May 1984, at 2.

63. 12 CFR 29.1 et seq. Like the FHLBB, the OCC has largely deregulated ARM's except for their disclosure and notice aspects. It expressly authorizes collection of prepayment fees on ARM's; see 12 CFR 29.6. There are no limitations on negative amortization under the OCC rule; cf. note 59 supra. The original OCC rules were much more protective of consumers; see 46 Fed.Reg. 18932. See generally Parks, Adjustable-rate Mortgages—New Regulations for National Banks and Federal Savings and Loan Associations, 70 Ill. B.J. 126 (1981). The preemptive effect of the OCC regulations was upheld in Conference of State Bank Supervisors v. Conover, 710 F.2d 883 (2d Cir.1983).

64. 12 CFR 701.21–6B. The NCUA regulation is somewhat more paternalistic to borrowers than are the FHLBB and OCC; it bars the charging of fees for rate adjustments, prohibits adjustments more often than monthly, and mandates downward adjustment of the loan rate if the index rate declines. Prepayment penalties are

prohibited on all mortgage loans made by federal credit unions; 12 CFR 701.21–6(b) (6). See also the NCUA's proposed relaxation of these rules in 49 Fed.Reg. 30683.

65. See, e.g., West's Ann.Cal.Civ.Code § 1916.5; Minn.Stat.Ann. § 51A.02. See also Note, Alternative Mortgage Instruments: The Oklahoma Experience, 8 Okla. C.U.L.Rev. 121 (1983); Bucki, Variable Rate Instruments in New York State, 54 N.Y.St.B.J. 510 (1982); Note, Variable Rate Mortgages: Texas Savings & Loan Associations Authorized to Offer Flexible Financing Alternatives, 12 St. Mary L.J. 1144 (1981); Washburn, Alternative Mortgage Instruments in California, 12 Akron L.Rev. 599 (1979).

66. See Colton & Lea, ARMs and the Secondary Markets: The Next Boom?, Secondary Mortgage Markets, May 1984, at 2. In 1984, one-third of the $16.7 billion in mortgages purchased by FNMA were ARM's; FNMA Annual Report 15 (1984).

67. See Browne, Development and Practical Application of the Adjustable Rate Mortgage Loan: The Federal Home Loan Mortgage Corporation's Adjustable Rate Mortgage Loan Purchase Program and Mortgage Loan Instruments, 47 Mo.L.Rev. 179 (1982). Eskridge, One Hundred Years of Ineptitude: The Need for Mortgage Rules Consonant with the Economic and Psychological Dynamics of the Home Sale and Loan Transaction, 70 Va.L.Rev. 1083, 1183 (1984). See § 14.7, lawyer's edition of this book.

attempted to encourage ARM's with annual and lifetime caps on interest rate increases, payment increases, or both; to discourage the use of so-called "teaser rates" (in which the initial interest rate on an ARM is made artificially low by means of a buy-down or a rate concession by the lender, raising the possibility of serious "payment shock" to the borrower in later years); to discourage negative amortization; and to adopt fairly conservative standards for qualifying borrowers under ARM's.[68] They have also encouraged experimentation with ARM conversion options—loans which begin life as ARM's, but which may be converted to fixed-rate mortgages at the borrower's option on a specified date.[69] The converted mortgage may bear interest at the then-prevailing rate, an average of rates which have prevailed since the ARM was made, or some combination of the two.

The Federal Housing Administration was a late-comer to ARM activity; its Congressional authority to insure ARM's was not granted until 1983,[70] and was limited by statute to ten percent of the aggregate number of mortgages insured by FHA in any fiscal year. Unlike the financial regulatory agencies discussed above, which elected to approve a broad spectrum of ARM formats for institutional lenders, FHA defined the parameters of its ARM rather strictly.[71] This is an understandable approach, since FHA ultimately bears the full risk of default on loans it insures.[72]

Under FHA's interim ARM rules, adjustments must be made annually, and may not result in rate increases of more than one percent.[73] The rate may not change more than 5 percent (up or down)

---

68. See Freddie Mac Announces New ARM, GPM Purchase Programs, BNA Hsg. & Devel.Rptr, Feb. 11, 1985, at 726; Thomas, Freddie Mac ARM Guidelines, Mortgage Banking, Oct. 1984, at 85; Lederman, Pricing Discount ARMs in the Secondary Market, Mortgage Banking, Aug. 1984, at 57; Standard Rate-Capped ARMs Announced by Fannie Mae, BNA Hsg. & Devel. Rptr., Oct. 22, 1984, at 430; Thomas, Pricing and Analysis of Adjustable Rate Mortgages, Mortgage Banking, Dec. 1984, at 61.

69. See Young & Matthiesen, The Long, Strong ARM: Legal Issues Attendant to Negative Amortization, ARM Loans with Conversion Options, 38 Consumer Fin.L.Q. Rpt. 43 (1984).

70. See § 443, Housing and Urban-Rural Recovery Act of 1983, Pub.L.No. 98–181.

71. See interim rule, 49 Fed.Reg. 23560, codified in 24 CFR 203.49; FHA Mortgagee Letter 84–16, July 18, 1984, summarized in BNA Hsg. & Devel. Rptr., July 30, 1984, at 189; Bak, Introduction to the FHA ARM, Mortgage Banking, Nov. 1984, at 24.

72. See § 11.2, supra, at notes 26–27.

73. The adjustment in the mortgage rate under the FHA rule must be the same as the *absolute* change in the index (subject to the 1% per year and 5% lifetime caps, of course); it is not based on the *proportionate* change in the index. To illustrate, assume the initial mortgage rate is 12% and the initial index rate is 11%. On the date of the first adjustment, the index rate has risen to 11.75%. The mortgage rate will then be adjusted to 12.75%.

Some non-FHA ARM's are adjusted on the basis of proportionate changes in the index. Under such a system, using the numbers in the preceding example, the index would have risen from 11% to 11.75%, a proportionate increase of .06818. The mortgage interest would then be adjusted upward by .06818 of its original 12% level, or to 12.8172%. Hence, the absolute change in the mortgage rate under this method is greater than the absolute change in the index.

over the life of the loan. The index selected by FHA is the weekly average yield on U.S. Treasury securities, adjusted to a constant maturity of one year. While the statute allows rate changes to be paid by increased monthly payments, extensions of loan maturity up to 40 years, or increases in principal balance, FHA's interim rule permits only payment increases. This eliminates any possibility of negative amortization, which FHA obviously felt would be unacceptably risky. However, the rule allows the lender to "carry over" index changes which would produce a rate increase greater than one percent, and apply them in a future year. The rule also contains provisions on disclosure and notice of adjustment.

Many of the conventional ARM loans made in recent years have incorporated a GPM feature; that is, the documents contain a schedule of rising monthly payments for the first five or ten years of the loan, which must be followed irrespective of any interest rate changes.[74] The FHA ARM, however, appears not to contemplate such a feature, but instead provides for payment changes only in accordance with fluctuations in the index rate.[75]

The advent of the FHA ARM set the stage for introduction of an ARM mortgage-backed security guaranteed by the Government National Mortgage Association (GNMA).[76] (GNMA is empowered to guarantee only securities backed by FHA and VA mortgages, and thus could take no action on conventional ARM loans.)[77] GNMA introduced its ARM security program in 1984, thus making a full complement of secondary market mechanisms available for ARM's.[78]

A second new type of mortgage instrument which is intended to help lenders shift interest rate risk to borrowers, and thus to hedge against the prospect of mismatched short-term and long-term rates, is the *shared appreciation mortgage, or SAM.*[79] In a SAM, the lender

---

74. The FHLBB at one point adopted a specific regulation approving loans with both graduated payments and adjustable rates; it was termed the Graduated Payment Adjustable Mortgage Loan (GPAML). See 46 Fed.Reg. 37625 (July 22, 1981). The present FHLBB rule, however, treats ARM's, GPM's, and a variety of other instruments under the same section of the regulations (12 CFR 545.33), allows great flexibility in combining features, and avoids such distinctions in terminology entirely.

On GPARM's, see generally Cortes, Everything You Always Wanted to Know About ARMs, Mortgage Banking, June 1984, at 21; Hu, In Search of the Ideal Mortgage, FNMA Seller/Servicer, Apr.-Jun. 1981, at 21, discussing the design of graduated payment adjustable rate loans.

75. See 24 CFR 203.49(b) (interim rule), adopted 49 Fed.Reg. 23584 (Jun. 6, 1984);

FHA Mortgagee Letter 84–16, July 18, 1984 (ARM's may be originated only under National Housing Act Sections 203(b) (1–4 family fixed payment), 203(k) (rehabilitated housing), and 234(c) (condominiums)). There is no provision for origination under Section 245 (graduated payment).

76. See 24 CFR Part 390, Subpart D, added by 49 Fed.Reg. 23580 (Jun. 6, 1984) (interim rule).

77. See § 11.3 supra at note 17.

78. The ARM program was established under the GNMA type II plan, which involves the creation of large national pools of mortgages by GNMA, with participation by many different lenders. See Carrel, The GNMA Adjustable Rate Security, Mortgage Banking, Oct. 1984, at 99.

79. See generally Friend, Shared Appreciation Mortgages, 34 Hast.L.J. 329 (1982); Comment, The Shared Appreciacharges both fixed interest and contingent interest. The fixed component of interest is typically a good deal lower than current market rates on standard mortgages. The contingent interest is computed as a percentage (perhaps in the range of 10% to 40%) of the amount of price appreciation in the property. The contingent interest is not paid until the property is sold or transferred by the borrower, or until the loan matures at some specified date, say ten years from its inception.[80]

From the borrower's viewpoint, the SAM's advantage is its lower monthly payment level, and thus easier qualification for the loan; in return, the borrower gives up some of the expectation of possible profit which might otherwise have been experienced upon resale of the property. From the lender's viewpoint, if a period of high inflation ensues while the loan is outstanding, the contingent interest will be substantial. Since there is generally a rough correspondence between the inflation level and interest rates, the lender's right to a share of inflation in the property's value may be an attractive substitute for a higher fixed contract interest. On the other hand, the rate of return to the lender on a SAM is obviously speculative, since future inflation cannot be predicted. Moreover, the SAM provides a much lower cash flow to the lender prior to maturity than does a standard loan of the same amount; this is disadvantageous to institutions which have large cash needs.

The FHLBB proposed a specific rule authorizing SAM's in 1980;[81] it was never made final, but the present broader FHLBB lending regulations clearly permit federal savings associations to make SAM loans.[82] The FHA was authorized by Congress in 1983 to insure SAM's on both one-to-four-family housing and multifamily housing.[83]

tion Mortgage: A Clog on the Equity of Redemption?, 15 J.Marsh.L.Rev. 131 (1982); Iezman, The Shared Appreciation Mortgage and the Shared Equity Program: A Comprehensive Examination of Equity Participation, 16 Real Prop. Prob. & Tr.J. 510 (1981); Angell & Wardrep, Evaluating the Shared Appreciation Mortgage, Mortgage Banker, Apr. 1981, at 31; Hu, How to Build a SAM, FNMA Seller/Servicer, Apr.-Jun. 1981, at 30.

Note that we have elsewhere discounted the notion, raised in the law review comment above, that the SAM may constitute a clog on the equity of redemption; see § 3.1 supra.

80. If there is no sale at the time the loan must be paid, the appreciation is normally determined by an appraisal. If the loan is paid at maturity, there will usually be a substantial "balloon" payment due, since the loan term is typically ten years while monthly payments are based on a 30-year amortization schedule. If no sale of the property occurs at that time, the docu-

ments may obligate the lender to refinance the loan, typically with a new fixed-interest mortgage; otherwise, there is no assurance that the borrower will have funds available to make the cash payment. Moreover, if there has been substantial appreciation, the payments on the new loan may be sharply higher than under the old SAM; see Iezman, Alternative Mortgage Instruments: Their Effect on Residential Financing, 10 Real Est.L.J. 3 (1981).

81. See 45 Fed.Reg. 66801 (Oct. 8, 1980).

82. A federal savings association "may receive a portion of the consideration for making a real estate loan in the form of a percentage of the amount by which the current market value of the property, during the loan term or at maturity, exceeds the original appraised value." 12 CFR 545.32(b)(3).

See also West's Ann.Calif.Civ.Code §§ 1917.010 et seq., authorizing investment

83. See note 83 on page 794.

The SAM does not make the lender an equity owner of the property. An arrangement doing so is quite possible, of course, but they have not been much used to finance owner-occupied housing. On the other hand, in commercial real estate lending the taking by the lender of an equity participation interest in the property has been common for many years.[84] The fundamental difference between such a loan and a SAM is that the contingent return on the SAM is based solely on appreciation above the original price of the real estate,[85] while an equity participation loan gives the lender a share of the entire property value at the time the loan is paid.[86]

The third, and in many ways, most interesting of the new efforts to shift interest rate risk to the borrower is the *price-level adjusted mortgage, or PLAM,* sometimes termed the *indexed mortgage, or IM.* To understand it, one must begin with the notion that mortgage interest rates are a composite of two factors: a *real* rate, which represents the return a lender would demand on this sort of investment (given the perceived risk of nonpayment, the supply of and demand for lendable funds, and other relevant market conditions) in a non-inflationary economy; and an *inflation premium* which reflects the lender's expectation about probable inflation in price levels over the life of the loan. The real rate is generally assumed to be about 3% to 4.5% for residential first mortgages.[87] Any amount beyond this represents the inflation premium, the purpose of which is to take account of the fact that the loan will be repaid in dollars which have less purchasing power than those lent. Of course, the lender cannot predict future inflation with certainty, and the inflation premium may in fact turn out to be higher or lower than the actual inflation which occurs.

The problem with standard fixed-payment loans (as PLAM proponents view them) is that the monthly payments, from the outset, are based on an interest rate that includes the inflation premium. If inflation actually occurs, the real value of the monthly payments will

in SAM's by pension funds and containing detailed rules regarding their structure.

83. See §§ 444–45, Housing and Urban-Rural Development Act of 1983, Pub.L. No. 98–181, adding §§ 252–53 to the National Housing Act.

84. See Comment, Lender Participation in the Borrower's Venture: A Scheme To Receive Usurious Interest, 8 Hous.L.Rev. 546 (1971); Comment, Equity Participation in Real Estate Finance, 7 N.C.Cent.L.J. 387 (1976).

85. Of course, SAM mortgages generally give the mortgagor credit, against the appreciation, for any improvements he or she has made during the term of the loan,

such as construction of a swimming pool, an added room, or the like.

86. See Gallagher, Computing the Lender's Yield on an Equity Participation Mortgage, Mortgage Banker, Feb. 1981, at 33.

87. See Note, Alternative Mortgage Instruments: Authorizing and Implementing Price Level Adjusted Mortgages, 16 U.Mich.J.L.Reform 115, 121 n. 28 (1982); Barnes, A Proposal for "Indexed" Mortgage Financing, Mortgage Banker, Oct. 1980, at 32; Cassidy, Price-Level Adjusted Mortgages Versus Other Mortgage Instruments, 14 FHLBBJ 3 (1981).

steadily decline, despite the fact that the borrower's income in real terms may be static or rising.

Under a PLAM, the lender charges only the real rate by way of contract interest. However, the outstanding principal balance on the loan is adjusted periodically (say, annually) to reflect actual changes in the overall price levels of the nation. In the United States, the U.S. Department of Labor's Consumer Price Index could be used for this purpose.[88] The result is that payments are very low in the early years of the mortgage, since they are based on the real rate of only, say, 4.5%. If actual inflation occurs, however, nominal payments will rise each year because the 4.5% rate will be applied to a higher outstanding balance than would otherwise be the case, and the payments must be increased to the level needed to fully amortize the new balance over the remaining term.

PLAM's are very widely used in countries, such as Brazil and Israel, in which inflation is rampant. Whether they will be attractive to American consumers is still unclear, as they have been very little used in residential finance in this country. They present the possibility of extremely sharp increases in nominal dollar payment levels in their later years, although in real terms the payments are constant, and should not pose a problem for mortgagors whose incomes rise as rapidly as inflation. For young borrowers with strong potential for increased earnings, the PLAM may be even more attractive than the GPM in solving the "life cycle" problem and permitting earlier home ownership. At the same time, it has the effect, even more directly than the ARM, of shifting the risk of inflation from lender to borrower. If high inflation ensues, the PLAM probably presents a greater default risk than the ARM or any other plan discussed in this section.

The FHLBB's lending regulations clearly approve of PLAM's,[89] and in 1983 Congress authorized the FHA to insure PLAM mortgages, which it referred to as "indexed mortgages." The FHA's proposed rule implementing this authority contains a thoughtful analysis of the policy issues raised by PLAM's. It also describes the possibility of a modified PLAM, in which the contract rate consists of the real rate plus a "buffer rate" of an additional, say, 5 percent. Only inflation which exceeds the "buffer rate" will be reflected in adjustments to the loan's balance. The result is an instrument which carries a much higher initial payment than a "pure" PLAM (although still much lower than a standard mortgage), but in which the impact of future inflation on later-year payments is greatly ameliorated.

88. This is in fact the index proposed by FHA; see 49 Fed.Reg. 23063 (Jun. 4, 1984).

89. "Adjustments to the payment and the loan balance ∗ ∗ ∗ may be made if (i) the adjustments reflect a change in a national or regional index that measures the rate of inflation or the rate of change in consumer disposable income, is readily available to and verifiable by the borrower, and is beyond the control of the association." 12 CFR 545.33(e)(2).

The PLAM presents an unusual legal problem.[90] In Aztec Properties, Inc. v. Union Planters National Bank,[91] the Tennessee Supreme Court held the PLAM concept violated the Gold Clause Resolution, by which Congress in 1933 prohibited loan clauses requiring payment in a particular form of currency or coin. The Gold Clause Resolution was surely not intended to prohibit indexing of mortgage loan principals, and the case seems wrongly decided, but it represents a litigation risk to any lender considering the use of a PLAM.[92] This legal cloud, when added to the problems of gaining consumer acceptance of PLAM's, probably means that their widespread use is not likely in the near future in the United States.

The Priority of Alternative Mortgage Instruments

As we have seen above, several types of newly-developed mortgage instruments, including the GPM, RAM, ARM, SAM, and PLAM may involve negative amortization—the process of adding unpaid interest to the loan's original balance. Lenders have a practical concern about negative amortization, since it may reduce their margin of security and, in extreme cases, leave them with a loan balance which exceeds the property's value. But negative amortization also raises a difficult priority issue in mortgage law. In substance, capitalizing unpaid interest is the equivalent of making the debtor an additional loan with which to pay the accrued interest. Thus, it can be viewed as a future advance. In general, a future advance loses priority as against any intervening lien (one created between the date of the original mortgage and the date of the advance in question) if the lender had no contractual obligation to make the advance and, at the time it was made, had notice of the intervening lien.[93]

In some types of alternative mortgages the negative amortization is the contractual obligation of the lender, and hence seems to be in no danger of loss of priority. This is most obviously the case with the GPM and RAM, in which the original mortgage documents set out the

---

90. There are other problems. For example, it is quite likely that a PLAM note cannot be negotiable. U.C.C. § 3–104(1)(b) requires a sum certain, and U.C.C. § 3–106 provides that the sum is certain even though it is to be paid with a stated rate of interest. Query whether the interest can be said to be "stated" where it depends on future inflation. See Note, Alternative Mortgage Instruments: Authorizing and Implementing Price Level Adjusted Mortgages, 16 U.Mich.J.L.Reform 115, 128–29 (1982); Dawson & Coultrap, Contracting by Reference to Price Indices, 33 Mich.L.Rev. 685 (1935). On the other hand, it is not particularly obvious that negotiability is essential to a well-functioning primary or secondary mortgage market; see § 5.29 supra.

91. 530 S.W.2d 756 (Tenn.1975), certiorari denied 425 U.S. 975, 96 S.Ct. 2175, 48 L.Ed.2d 799 (1976), noted in 11 Tulsa L.J. 450 (1976), and discussed in Hyer & Kearl, Legal Impediments to Mortgage Innovation, 6 Real Est.L.J. 211, 228–31 (1978).

92. It seems fairly clear that this argument would be inapplicable to the FHA indexed mortgage, since it is directly authorized by Congress. Whether the same is true of PLAM's made under the authority of the FHLBB regulation, see note 89 supra, is less certain. It is quite arguable that the Alternative Mortgage Parity Act, infra notes 107–114, preempts the Gold Clause argument for any PLAM loan made under the authority of the FHLBB regulations.

93. See generally § 12.7 infra.

disbursement and payment schedules precisely, so that there can be no doubt from the outset about the amount of negative amortization which will occur. Suppose, however, that the lender under a RAM reserves discretion to discontinue disbursements to the borrower if it becomes dissatisfied with the property's condition or if the borrower places junior liens on the property. Under these circumstances, further disbursements (and resulting increments to the loan balance) might well be considered optional, and thus to suffer a priority loss.[94] Lenders generally have a tendency to give themselves broad discretion in their loan documents, but in this situation such discretion is extremely dangerous.

With ARM's and PLAM's, the amount of negative amortization which will occur over the loan's life is obviously not predictable when the loan is made, since it will depend on future economic conditions. But this fact alone is insufficient to render the negative amortization "optional", and thus to risk loss of priority. Rather, the question is whether the lender has discretion to add to the loan principal. For example, under an ARM, if the *borrower* has the right to determine whether increased interest will be capitalized or will be covered by increased monthly payments, the lender's priority is not in jeopardy; but if it is the *lender* which is empowered by the documents to make this decision, the risk to priority is raised.[95] Similarly, an ARM lender may believe that it is doing the borrower a favor by permitting negative amortization under documents which do not compel the lender to do so; but the favor may be a costly one, for it may place the lender's priority at risk. The lender is safe only if the documents compel the lender to use negative amortization, either automatically or at the borrower's option.

With the SAM, the problem is somewhat different. The contingent interest does not accrue until the loan is paid off. If the lender is obligated to refinance with a new (non-SAM) loan at that point, there should be no priority problem.[96] If the lender is under no duty to refinance, but does so anyway, it may attempt to rely, for priority purposes, on the doctrine that treats replacement mortgages as retaining the priority of their predecessors.[97] However, it is unclear whether

---

94. This problem would not exist if the RAM were of the type involving immediate disbursement by the lender of the full loan balance, which is then used to purchase a commercial annuity for the borrower. See Brodkey, AMIs: Let The Lawyers Work Out The Details, 45 Legal Bull. 133, 139–41 (1979).

95. See Hyer & Kearl, Legal Impediments to Mortgage Innovation, 6 Real Est. L.J. 211, 232–34 (1978). Earlier versions of the FHLBB's and Comptroller's regulations on ARM's appeared virtually to force their constituent lenders into an optional position; they provided explicitly that the

lender could elect whether or not to implement rate increases. See 12 CFR 545.6–2(a)(2)(i) (FHLBB); 12 CFR 29.5(c)(1) (OCC). These provisions have been deleted from the current versions of the regulations.

96. The FHLBB's proposed SAM regulations did require the lender to refinance; see 45 Fed.Reg. 66801 (Oct. 8, 1980). The present broader FHLBB rule, however, does not. Of course, the lender may undertake a refinancing duty in the original SAM documents, whether compelled to do so by regulation or not.

97. See § 9.4 supra.

the courts will treat the "predecessor" here as the SAM's balance before or after the addition of the contingent interest.

All of these priority problems, of course, could be resolved by statute. But they are issues of state law, and the current federal statutes do not appear to preempt them. Neither do the federal banking agencies' regulations; in the case of ARM's, they provide that the federally-chartered lenders may *make* ARM loans notwithstanding contrary state law,[98] but it is very hard to read into such language any intent to preempt state priority rules,[99] particularly now that the former federal rules confining the lenders to first lien investments have been largely eliminated. In a few states the legislatures have addressed this issue,[1] but preemptive federal legislation would be a useful and desirable addition.[2]

Federal Income Tax Issues With Alternative Mortgage Instruments

Nearly all mortgage borrowers wish to deduct their interest payments for federal income tax purposes. Yet because of the unusual ways in which interest is paid under some forms of alternative mortgages discussed above, questions arise as to the timing of the deduction.

The Internal Revenue Service dealt in 1977 with interest deductibility on a negatively-amortized GPM.[3] For cash-basis taxpayers, it ruled that interest is deductible only when actually paid. In the early years of a GPM all payments typically are applied to interest, and hence are fully deductible. However, interest which is unpaid during these years and is therefore added to principal is not deductible at the time it accrues. In later years of the GPM, when monthly payments exceed the interest which is currently accruing, the IRS will attribute the excess payments to retirement of the previously-capitalized interest. The net effect is to defer some of the deductions to later years, in comparison to a fixed-payment mortgage. Similar reasoning would presumably be applied to any other mortgage format which involved capitalization of unpaid interest.[4]

To what extent is the contingent interest paid on a SAM deductible to the borrower?[5] Under a 1983 ruling of the Internal Revenue

98. See 12 CFR 29.2 (OCC) (ARM's only); 12 CFR 545.2 (FHLBB) (all lending authority); 12 CFR 701.21–6B(b)(2) (NCUA) (ARM's only).

99. Interestingly, the former FHLBB regulation governing GPM's contained an explicit statement that capitalization of interest would not result in a loss of first-lien status; see 12 CFR 545.6–4(b)(3). See Broadkey, AMI's—Let the Lawyers Work Out the Details, 45 Legal Bull. 133, 139 n. 20 (1979). This language was dropped in the FHLBB's 1982 amendments.

1. See, e.g., S.C.Code § 29–3–50.

2. It is arguable that the Alternative Mortgage Transaction Parity Act accomplishes such a preemption; see text at notes 13–15, infra.

3. Rev.Rul. 77–135, 1977–1 Cum.Bull. 133.

4. See Clauretie & Marts, Alternative Mortgages Have Hidden Costs, 14 Real Est. Rev. 69 (No. 1, Spring 1984), comparing the after-tax present values of a variety of alternative mortgage formats.

5. See Mooradian & Rosenblatt, Characterization of Contingent Payments on

Service,[6] the borrower-homeowner may deduct the contingent interest in the year it is actually paid—that is, when the loan is paid off as a result of maturity, prepayment, or sale of the property. However, if the borrower refinances the SAM by executing a new note and mortgage with the same lender, the IRS concluded that the refinancing transaction does not give rise to any deduction on account of the contingent interest. Instead, the payments on the new loan are deductible to the extent that they are allocable to the contingent interest which was due on the SAM. The IRS also cautioned that it might not treat the contingent interest as deductible in cases in which the lender held an equity position in the property or was, in some other respect, more than a mere creditor of the homeowner. Note that, for a high-bracket taxpayer, the treatment of the SAM outlined in the ruling above can be extremely disadvantageous, since it may defer deductibility of the contingent interest for many years.[7]

The Alternative Mortgage Transaction Parity Act of 1982

In 1982 Congress addressed the problem of inconsistency between state and federal regulation of institutional lending on alternative mortgage instruments. It enacted the Alternative Mortgage Transaction Parity Act,[8] which permits state-chartered lenders to "make, purchase, and enforce alternative mortgage transactions" on the same basis as the analogous federally-chartered institutions. Thus, state banks may follow the regulations of the Comptroller of the Currency, state credit unions may follow the NCUA's regulations, and all other lenders (including savings and loan associations and mortgage bankers) may lend under the rules of the Federal Home Loan Bank Board.[9] Any conflicting state law or regulation is preempted. On the other hand, a state-chartered lender which prefers to follow state law is free to do so; lenders may select whichever regulatory scheme is most liberal.

The definition of "alternative mortgage" is very broad, and includes adjustable-rate loans, renegotiable loans with balloon payments, and loans:

> "involving any similar type of rate, method of determining return, term, repayment, or other variation not common to traditional fixed-rate, fixed-term transactions, including without limitation, transactions that involve the sharing of equity or appreciation." [10]

This seems to cover every sort of new mortgage format discussed above, as well as many others not yet devised.

Shared Appreciation Mortgages, 57 J.Tax. 20 (July 1982).

6. Rev.Rul. 83–51, 1983–1 Cum.Bull. 48.

7. See Clauretie & Marts, supra note 4.

8. See Title VIII, Garn–St. Germain Depository Institutions Act of 1982, Pub.L.

No. 97–320, enacting 12 U.S.C.A. §§ 3801 et seq.

9. See 12 U.S.C.A. § 3803.

10. 12 U.S.C.A. § 3802(1).

A state may opt out of the federal preemption scheme by statute or initiative vote adopted prior to October 15, 1985.[11] Several states have done so, and thus have "recaptured" control of mortgage lending by non-federally-chartered institutions within their borders.[12]

Perhaps the most interesting legal question raised by the Parity Act is whether it preempts state priority rules. As discussed above, a mortgage which involves negative amortization raises the risk that priority will be lost if the additions to principal are deemed optional future advances.[13] The Parity Act gives non-federally-chartered lenders the power "to enforce" mortgages "made in accordance with regulations governing alternative mortgage transactions as issued by" the applicable federal agencies.[14] If a mortgage conforms to the relevant federal regulation, does the Parity Act mean that it can be "enforced" with first priority, notwithstanding contrary state law relating to future advances? Such an argument is tenuous, both because the Parity Act says nothing about priority *per se,* and also because to override state priority rules would actually give such mortgages more than *parity;* it would grant them a sort of "super priority" which identical mortgages made by federally-chartered lenders would not have, since their federal regulators have not attempted to preempt state priority rules.[15] This is neither a likely nor a plausible interpretation. Of course, the federal regulators may well amend their regulations in the future to accomplish just such a preemption, and if they do so the Parity Act will obviously bring the state-chartered lenders within that umbrella.

 WESTLAW REFERENCES
"regulation q"

Mortgages Which Address the Borrower's Ability to Pay
[no queries]

Mortgages Which Address the Term Mismatch Problem of Portfolio Lenders
variable adjustable   +1 "rate mortgage"

The Priority of Alternative Mortgage Instruments
266   +p   topic(priority)

Federal Income Tax Issues with Alternative Mortgage Instruments
cite(77–135 83–51)

The Alternative Mortgage Transaction Parity Act of 1982
prelim("alternative mortgage transaction")

---

11. 12 U.S.C.A. § 3804.

12. See, e.g., 9–A Maine Rev.Stat.Ann. § 1–110; New York—McKinney's Banking Law § 6–g.

13. See text at notes 93–2 supra.

14. 12 U.S.C.A. § 3803.

15. See notes 98–99 supra.

§ 11.5   Discrimination in Mortgage Lending

A wide range of federal statutes prohibit racial discrimination in mortgage lending. Some of these statutes also bar discrimination on other bases, such as sex, as well; the coverage of each will be described in turn. The oldest statutory provisions are those of the Civil Rights Act of 1866, now codified in 42 United States Code at Sections 1981 and 1982. Section 1982 provides that "all citizens * * * shall have the same right * * * as is enjoyed by white citizens * * * to inherit, purchase, lease, sell, hold and convey real and personal property." Section 1981 makes similar provisions regarding the right to make and enforce contracts. Until 1968 it was generally assumed that these statutes applied only to actions of the federal or state governments, but in Jones v. Alfred H. Mayer Co.,[1] the Supreme Court held them applicable to private acts of discrimination as well. There is little question that the language of these sections would ban racial discrimination by a mortgage lender.[2] They apply to all transactions, not merely those relating to housing; a commercial mortgage loan, for example, would be covered. However, they provide no administrative enforcement mechanism, and a suit for damages or conceivably an injunction would be the only remedy. Note also that they apply only to discrimination based on race.

Two more recent enactments also prohibit racial discrimination in the provision of mortgage financing. Section 805 of the Civil Rights Act of 1968 (the "Fair Housing Act")[3] makes illegal the discriminatory denial of a loan or discrimination in respect to loan amount, interest rate, duration, or other terms or conditions. Under the original version of the statute, only discrimination based on race, color, religion, or national origin was barred, but a 1974 amendment[4] included sex as well, and also required all persons making "federally related mortgage loans" to married couples to "consider without prejudice the combined income of both husband and wife for the purpose of extending mortgage credit." This last clause was inserted to stop the prevalent practice of

§ 11.5

1. 392 U.S. 409, 88 S.Ct. 2186, 20 L.Ed. 2d 1189 (1968).

2. See Baker v. F & F Investment Co., 489 F.2d 829 (7th Cir.1973).

3. 42 U.S.C.A. § 3605. Discriminatory enforcement of mortgages, as by selective foreclosure, is also illegal; Harper v. Union Savings Association, 429 F.Supp. 1254 (N.D.Ohio 1977). Whether the Fair Housing Act is violated by the discriminatory withholding of services which are ordinarily essential to the securing of mortgage financing is still unclear; compare Mackey v. Nationwide Insurance Co's, 724 F.2d 419 (4th Cir.1984) (hazard insurer's "red-

lining" of minority neighborhoods is not within Fair Housing Act) with Dunn v. Midwestern Indemnity Mid-American Fire & Casualty Co., 472 F.Supp. 1106 (S.D.Ohio 1979) (redlining by insurer violates Fair Housing Act, since it makes housing "unavailable.") See also United States v. American Inst. of Real Estate Appraisers, 442 F.Supp. 1072 (N.D.Ill.1977), appeal dismissed 590 F.2d 242 (7th Cir.1978) (settlement agreement of Dep't of Justice with real estate appraisers' organization.)

4. § 808, Housing and Community Development Act of 1974, Pub.L.No. 93–383, 88 Stat. 633, 728, adding § 527 to the National Housing Act.

discounting a working wife's income in determining the amount of loan for which the couple was qualified.

Section 805 does have certain inherent limitations. It applies only to institutional lenders and others in the business of making real estate loans. In addition, the loan in question must be "for the purpose of purchasing, constructing, improving, repairing, or maintaining a dwelling." Thus, non-housing loans are not covered. The statute expressly directs all federal agencies to administer their programs in a manner which will further the objectives of the law,[5] and it gives the Department of Housing and Urban Development authority to administer the act and to receive, investigate, and attempt to resolve complaints of violations.[6] United States district courts are given jurisdiction over suits for violations,[7] and the Attorney General is empowered to file injunctive actions when he has reasonable cause to believe a person or group is engaged in a pattern or practice of resistance to the act.[8]

A third statute explicitly prohibiting mortgage credit discrimination is the Equal Credit Opportunity Act (ECOA).[9] Originally enacted in 1974 to prohibit discrimination based on sex or marital status, it was expanded in 1976[10] to cover race, color, religion, national origin, and age discrimination as well. Unlike the Fair Housing Act, ECOA is not confined to housing finance, but applies to all extensions of credit, whatever the purpose. Violations may result in civil liability in federal or state courts. The Federal Reserve Board is given the general power to enact regulations under ECOA, and the principal enforcement power is given to the Federal Deposit Insurance Corporation and the Federal Home Loan Bank Board with respect to banks and savings associations respectively.[11] Only persons and institutions which "regularly" extend or renew credit and their assignees are covered by ECOA.

Under the three statutes discussed above, both racial and sex discrimination in lending are broadly prohibited, and it is likely that in their most overt forms they have to a great extent disappeared from the American scene. Two significant issues remain, however. The first is the general problem of loan underwriting criteria which are facially neutral but which in fact have a disproportionate impact on one race or sex; the second is the problem of refusals by institutional lenders to make loans, or the willingness to make loans only on more onerous terms, in certain geographic areas, a practice often termed "disinvestment" or "redlining." The second issue is sometimes an illustration of

---

5. § 1808(d), Fair Housing Act, 42 U.S. C.A. § 3608(d).

6. §§ 808, 810, Fair Housing Act, 42 U.S.C.A. §§ 3608, 3610.

7. § 810(d), Fair Housing Act, 42 U.S. C.A. § 3610(d).

8. § 813, Fair Housing Act, 42 U.S.C.A. § 3613; see, e.g., United States v. American Institute of Real Estate Appraisers, 442 F.Supp. 1072 (N.D.Ill.1977) (suit by

Dep't of Justice; settlement agreement; discriminatory appraisal practices violate Fair Housing Act.)

9. 15 U.S.C.A. § 1691ff.

10. Equal Credit Opportunity Act Amendments of 1976, Pub.L. 94–239, 90 Stat. 251.

11. § 704, Equal Credit Opportunity Act, 15 U.S.C.A. § 1691c.

the first, for a refusal to lend in an area of residential concentration by a minority racial group will plainly have a disproportionate impact on members of a particular race, but redlining may also be considered objectionable as a consequence of its impact on the housing stock and property values, even when no minorities are affected.

The concept that a disproportionate racial *effect* may be illegal, even absent intent to discriminate, is derived from Griggs v. Duke Power Co.,[12] in which the Supreme Court in 1971 considered certain intelligence and aptitude tests administered by an employer to its employees as a condition of promotion. Black employees generally made lower scores on the tests than whites, and hence were not promoted as frequently, but there was no evidence that the employer intended to use the tests to screen out blacks. In response to an attack based on Title VII of the Civil Rights Act of 1964, the Court held that a violation had been made out. The Court's opinion articulated what is commonly called the "effects test": if the plaintiffs can show that the defendant's practices have the effect of disproportionately barring minorities in a substantial manner, the burden shifts to the defendant to show that those practices are required by "business necessity" or "genuine business need."[13] Later cases have generally held that to make a successful defense, the defendant must show that no other procedure with a lesser discriminatory impact could be used to accomplish the same business goal.[14]

For some time after *Griggs* there was doubt as to whether it applied to the Fair Housing Act or other non-employment discrimination statutes,[15] but in 1977 the Supreme Court resolved that issue affirmatively.[16] However, there are still few reported cases dealing

---

12. § 401 U.S. 424, 91 S.Ct. 849, 28 L.Ed.2d 158 (1971).

13. 401 U.S. at 432.

14. See, e.g., Williams v. Matthews Co., 499 F.2d 819 (C.A.Ark.1974), certiorari denied 419 U.S. 1021, 95 S.Ct. 495, 42 L.Ed.2d 294 (1974): to rely on the "business necessity" defense the defendant must show "the absence of any acceptable alternative that will accomplish the same business goal with less discrimination."

15. Compare United States v. City of Black Jack, 508 F.2d 1179 (8th Cir.1974), certiorari denied 422 U.S. 1042, 95 S.Ct. 2656, 45 L.Ed.2d 694, rehearing denied 423 U.S. 884, 96 S.Ct. 158, 46 L.Ed.2d 115 (1975) and Stingley v. City of Lincoln Park, 429 F.Supp. 1379 (E.D.Mich.1977) (applying *Griggs* to housing discrimination) with Boyd v. Lefrak Organization, 509 F.2d 1110 (2d Cir.1975), certiorari denied 423 U.S. 896, 96 S.Ct. 197, 46 L.Ed.2d 129 (1975), (*Griggs* inapplicable to housing). See Note, Applying the Title VII Prima Facie Case to

Title VIII Litigation, 11 Harv.Civ.Rts—Civ. Lib.L.Rev. 128 (1976).

16. In Metropolitan Housing Development Corp. v. Village of Arlington Heights, 429 U.S. 252, 97 S.Ct. 555, 50 L.Ed.2d 450 (1977), the town had refused to rezone certain land on which the plaintiffs proposed to build a low-income housing project. The evidence showed no discriminatory purpose or intent on the part of the town, but it did show a discriminatory impact, since 40% of the population eligible for the project were black, as opposed to only 18% of the overall area population. The Court held that the Fourteenth Amendment did not prohibit municipal actions with such discriminatory effects unless intent were also shown, citing its previous opinion in Washington v. Davis, 426 U.S. 229, 96 S.Ct. 2040, 48 L.Ed.2d 597 (1976). However, it remanded the case for further consideration as to the application of the Fair Housing Act to the town's action, thus clearly implying that a racial effect could form the basis for a Fair Housing Act complaint.

directly with loan underwriting practices which have a discriminatory impact.[17] Clearly many common underwriting rules do so, including the usual 28% housing expense-to-income ratio and probably such requirements as previous homeownership, a specific time in the present residence or on the present job, and the like. The relatively lower incomes and higher mobility of minorities in the United States mean that such criteria will result in more loan rejections than will be experienced by whites. The issue then becomes the nature of the proof which a lender must offer to rebut the prima facie case. Virtually all of the underwriting guidelines now in use have *some* predictive validity in assessing risk of future default, but some of them are far weaker than others.[18] No one alone or in combination is perfectly accurate, of course.

A court confronting this issue is faced with serious problems. Should the judicial standard of business necessity be implemented by inquiring whether the underwriting standards in question are "reasonably predictive" of default, or some such test?[19] What is a reasonably acceptable level of default risk? Suppose it is shown that use of a few relatively noncontroversial criteria, such as loan-to-value ratio, income, and credit rating, provide reasonably adequate predictability, but the addition of other, more objectionable factors such as those mentioned in the preceding paragraph make the underwriting process more accurate. What is called for here is the drawing of fine lines based on complex empirical evidence—a task for which administrative agencies are much better equipped than courts. Yet the most comprehensive federal regulations on the subject, promulgated by the Federal Home Loan Bank Board (FHLBB) and applicable to all federally-insured savings and loan associations, stop short of drawing the necessary lines. Instead, they merely warn that lenders should "take into consideration" the fact that some common underwriting standards, including favoring previous homeowners, those with high educational attainments, those with stable job or residence histories, and those who have previously done business with the lender, may be legally questionable.[20] The

---

See 558 F.2d 1283 (7th Cir.1977) (on remand to Seventh Circuit Court of Appeals), holding that the town's action may violate the Act if certain additional facts are shown, and applying *Griggs*. See also Resident Advisory Board v. Rizzo, 564 F.2d 126 (3d Cir.1977).

17. See Miller v. American Express Co., 688 F.2d 1235 (9th Cir.1982) (applying effects test to sex discrimination under ECOA); Cherry v. Amoco, 490 F.Supp. 1026 (N.D.Ga.1980) (recognizing possible application of effects test to a zip-code credit scoring system, but finding evidence insufficient). See also United States v. American Future Systems, 743 F.2d 169 (3d Cir.1984).

18. Id. The Arthur D. Little Study of the Private Mortgage Insurance Industry (summary 1975), at 11–14.

19. See Mass.Gen.Laws Ann. c. 183, § 64: Lenders shall not discriminate "on a basis that is arbitrary or unsupported by a reasonable analysis of the lending risks," but may exercise "the judgment and care * * * which men of prudence, discretion and intelligence exercise in the management of their affairs. Cf. Bishop v. Pecsok, 431 F.Supp. 34 (N.D.Ohio 1976), holding that criteria imposed by a landlord on tenant applicants must be "reasonable measure of the applicant's ability to be a successful tenant."

20. 12 CFR 531.8(c)(5), added by 43 Fed. Reg. 22338 (May 25, 1978). Compare the guidance provided by the regulations on these points is ambiguous, although they might conceivably provide some evidence of improper practices in a litigated case. The lenders themselves would probably have preferred a clear cut statement of permissible and impermissible practices. The validity of many frequently-employed standards is still open to doubt. The FHLBB's regulation is, however, quite helpful in another way; for the first time, it requires lenders to prepare written loan underwriting standards, review them annually, and make them available to the public.[21]

The regulations promulgated by the California Savings and Loan Commissioner provide an instructive point of comparison with those of the FHLBB. The "effects test" is explicitly stated in the California regulations,[22] and an accompanying set of guidelines[23] lists a number of common practices which are deemed to have a disproportionate racial impact and to lack business justification, and hence to be impermissible. These include the rejection of persons who have had isolated credit problems in the past, those with prior arrest records, those who have not previously owned a home, and those below a certain minimum income or who are buying houses below a specific purchase price or loan amount. Housing expense-to-income ratios below 25% are prohibited, and income from overtime, part-time or other usual work or from alimony or child support payments may not arbitrarily be disregarded. Some ambiguities exist in the California regulations, but they have rather explicit coverage and appear to be readily enforceable.

Redlining

Much of the thrust of recent legislation and regulation has been to combat geographically-based discrimination or redlining.[24] This issue is complicated by the difficulty of separating cause and effect. To some extent, withdrawal by mortgage lenders is a cause of neighborhood deterioration and ultimate abandonment, for the lack of mortgage financing impedes market sales transactions and makes maintenance

regulations issued by the Federal Reserve Board under ECOA, which recognize the "effects test" but make no effort to implement it; 12 CFR 202.6(a), footnote 7. This footnote is retained in the FRB's most recent proposed redraft of the ECOA rules; see 50 Fed.Reg. 10890, 10902 (Mar. 18, 1985). See NCUA regulations, 12 CFR 701.31(e)(1).

21. 12 CFR 528.2a(b), added by 43 Fed. Reg. 22335 (May 25, 1978); see also Mich. Comp.Laws Ann. § 445.1601.

22. 10 Cal.Admin.Code § 245.2(c); the regulation imposes upon the lender employing an underwriting policy with a discriminatory effect the burden to "demonstrate that such * * * policy * * * is required to achieve an overriding legitimate business purpose."

23. 10 Cal.Admin.Code § 246.3.

24. See generally Lucey, The Redlining Battle Continues: Discriminatory Effect v. Business Necessity Under the Fair Housing Act, 8 Bos.Coll.Env.Aff.L.Rev. 357 (1979); Redlining, Disinvestment and the Role of Mutual Savings Banks: A Survey of Solutions, 9 Ford.Urb.L.J. 89 (1980); Givens, The "Antiredlining" Issue: Can Banks Be Forced to Lend?, 95 Banking L.J. 515 (1978); Wisniewski, Mortgage Redlining (Disinvestment): The Parameters of Federal, State and Municipal Regulation, 54 U.Det.J.Urb.L. 367 (1977); Comment, Redlining in Mortgage Lending: California's Approach to Getting the Red Out, 8 Pac.L.J. 699 (1977).

and rehabilitation more difficult. But other factors also operate to cause neighborhood decline: crime and social disorder, lack of maintenance of public services and facilities such as street cleaning and lighting, trash removal, schools and parks, and the general aging of a housing stock which may have been substandard even when constructed. Some areas which lenders have abandoned are sound and attractive (although now threatened by the lack of mortgage funds), while others are so dilapidated and dangerous that lending on properties there would be insane. In an era in which the supply of mortgage funds has rarely been adequate to meet demand, lenders have generally preferred "safe" loans in the suburbs to loans of even moderate and manageable risk in inner-city neighborhoods.

Further complicating the picture is the fact that lenders may withdraw investment from a neighborhood for reasons which have nothing to do with the characteristics of the housing or its residents. For example, they may identify other markets, perhaps hundreds of miles away, where mortgage interest rates are higher, or they may shift out of residential lending in favor of commercial or consumer loans.

The articulation of a workable distinction between reasonable and unreasonable geographic discrimination in mortgage lending is no simple matter, and it is doubtful that any existing law or regulation has yet done so successfully. Some principles, however, are clear. One of these is that a refusal to lend because of the race of the neighborhood's occupants is illegal; this follows from the Fair Housing Act and from a number of state statutes as well.[25] In Laufman v. Oakley Building and Loan Co.,[26] the lender declined to loan to a white applicant because the neighborhood in which he proposed to live was racially integrated. The court found violations of both Section 805 of the Fair Housing Act, discussed above, and Section 804, which prohibits the making "unavailable" of housing because of race. The point is virtually incontestible that racially-motivated redlining, if proveable, is prohibited.

In many cases, however, no evidence of the type of racial motivation shown in Laufman will be available, and the plaintiff will be left with an argument based on the "effects test"; the area being excluded "happens" to be populated by minorities, but it is also characterized by deteriorated or abandoned housing or other structures, poor public facilities, and the like. Refusal to lend in such an environment, absent a showing of racial motives, has not yet been tested judicially in any reported case. Presumably the lender would be obliged to offer business justifications for its decision, and the court would be faced with deciding whether they were sufficiently compelling to justify the with-

---

25. See, e.g., Ill.—Smith-Hurd Ann. ch. 95 ¶ 301 et seq.; West's Ann.Cal.Health & Safety Code § 35812; Mass.Gen.Laws Ann. c. 183 § 64; Mich.Comp.Laws Ann. § 445.1601.

26. 408 F.Supp. 489 (S.D.Ohio 1976). See also Harrison v. Heinzeroth, 414 F.Supp. 66 (N.D.Ohio 1976).

drawal of financing. Again, the question "how compelling? " is presently unresolved.[27]

Both the FHLBB and several state legislatures or regulatory agencies have promulgated rules which attempt to deal with the redlining problem. Their thrust is generally to prohibit discrimination based on property age or location, and to require lenders to focus on the particular real estate which will secure the proposed loan, rather than on the characteristics of the neighborhood as a whole. In simplistic terms, then, a lender may be expected to make a loan on a good house in a bad neighborhood. But the problem is more complex, for it is well known that neighborhood factors have a strong influence on the value of any given parcel of land, and neighborhood trends can reasonably be expected to bear on its future value.

A comparison of the FHLBB and California regulations on this issue is enlightening. The FHLBB specifically prohibits discrimination based on the age or location of the dwelling, but it concedes that numerous neighborhood factors may properly be considered in appraising the dwelling:

> Loan decisions should be based on the present market value of the property offered as security (including consideration of specific improvements to be made by the borrower) and the likelihood that the property will retain an adequate value over the term of the loan. Specific factors which may negatively affect its short-range future value (up to 3-5 years) should be clearly documented. Factors which in some cases may cause the market value of a property to decline are recent zoning changes or a significant number of abandoned homes in the immediate vicinity of the property. However, not all zoning changes will cause a decline in property values, and proximity to abandoned buildings may not affect the market value of a property because of rehabilitation programs or affirmative lending programs, or because the cause of abandonment is unrelated to high risk. Proper underwriting considerations include the condition and utility of the improvements, and various physical factors such as street conditions, amenities such as parks and recreation areas, availability of public utilities and municipal services, and exposure to flooding and land faults. However, arbitrary decisions based on age or location are prohibited, since many older, soundly constructed homes provide housing opportunities which may be precluded by an arbitrary lending policy.[28]

The terms of the California regulation, now adopted by statute in that state, are considerably stronger:

27. See Lucey, supra note 24.

28. 12 CFR 531.8(c)(6), as amended, 43 Fed.Reg. 22338 (May 25, 1978).

No financial institution shall discriminate in the availability of, or in the provision of, financial assistance for the purpose of purchasing, constructing, rehabilitating, improving, or refinancing housing accommodations due, in whole or in part, to the consideration of conditions, characteristics, or trends in the neighborhood or geographic area surrounding the housing accommodation, unless the financial institution can demonstrate that such consideration in the particular case is required to avoid an unsafe and unsound business practice.[29]

The California Savings and Loan Commissioner's regulations interpret the "unsafe or unsound business practice" rather narrowly:

> If an association can document that one or more factors relating to the geographic area closely surrounding the security property are such that, even assuming the availability of nondiscriminatory financing in the geographic area, it is probable that such factors will cause the fair market value of the security property to decrease during the early years of the mortgage term, then the association, in determining whether and under what terms and conditions to grant a mortgage loan may do either or both of the following:
>
> (1) Make an adjustment in the loan to value ratio it considers appropriate for the property; or
>
> (2) Require that a shorter term to maturity be used.
>
> Provided, however, that no adjustment or requirement made pursuant to this subsection shall exceed the minimum required for the security property to continue to be a reasonable security for the loan.[30]

Further guidelines [31] discuss the necessary documentation to establish the probability of value declining over time, the radius within which negative neighborhood factors may be considered, the availability of federal, state, or local rehabilitation or neighborhood improvement programs, and other such matters. Great emphasis is placed on obtaining comparable sales prices on similar properties as the basis for a sound appraisal. The overall tone is strongly oriented toward disregarding neighborhood influences which are not clearly and demonstrably related to the property's value.

The other financial regulatory agencies at the federal level have promulgated regulations prohibiting racial discrimination in lending,[32] and several other states have statutes or regulations dealing with discrimination and redlining.[33] None of these, however, are as comprehensive and explicit as the FHLBB and California rules discussed

29. West's Ann.Cal.Health & Safety Code § 35810.

30. 10 Cal.Admin.Code § 245.3(b).

31. 10 Cal.Admin.Code § 246.1.

32. See 12 CFR 701.31 (Nat'l Credit Union Admin.); 12 CFR Part 338 (FDIC); 12 CFR Part 27 (Office of Comptroller of the Currency). See sources cited note 24 supra.

33. See note 25 supra.

above. These latter rules are particularly significant because they do not rely on proof of racial motivation or even disproportionate racial impact, but are based on appraisal and underwriting concepts which are, on their face, racially neutral.

Two federal statutes enacted in the mid-1970's also bear on the redlining problem. The first is the Home Mortgage Disclosure Act,[34] which requires depository financial institutions to maintain and publish records showing, by census tract, the locations of the properties which secure their residential loans. The Act's thesis is that local citizens and groups will, by analyzing this data, be able to identify lenders guilty of redlining and will apply the pressures of publicity and deposit withdrawals to bring them into line. Whether this will turn out to be effective, and whether it may produce undesirable overreactions in some cases, remains to be seen.[35] The data are also useful to the federal and state agencies which examine depository institutions,[36] and complement the requirements of the Community Reinvestment Act of 1977.[37] This statute requires the federal financial regulatory agencies to consider, in their examinations and in evaluating applications by lenders for new deposit facilities, the institution's record in meeting the credit needs of its entire community, including low- and moderate-income neighborhoods. Presumably lenders who have been guilty of unjustifiable redlining will be subject to criticism by the federal examiners, and may not be able to get permission to open new branches, close offices, or take other actions they desire.[38] But the statute and the regulations of the federal banking agencies have been criticized as vague and ineffectual.[39]

A number of states have statutes prohibiting lending discrimination and redlining, and imposing record-keeping and disclosure duties on lenders. Both the substantive standards and procedural duties

---

34. 12 U.S.C.A. § 2801ff. The HMDA was scheduled to expire on June 28, 1980, but was made permanent by § 318, Pub.L. No. 96–399, 94 Stat. 1659 (1980).

35. See An Analysis of the Effectiveness of the Home Mortgage Disclosure Act of 1975, 28 Case W.Res.L.Rev. 1074 (1978); The Home Mortgage Disclosure Act of 1975: Will It Protect Urban Consumers from Redlining?, 12 N.Eng.L.Rev. 957 (1977); Red-lining and The Home Mortgage Disclosure Act of 1975: A Decisive Step Toward Private Urban Redevelopment, 25 Emory L.J. 667 (1976).

36. Each of the principal federal financial regulatory agencies imposes specific record-keeping duties on the institutions it supervises. These data, which are available for review by the agency's examiners, are much more detailed than those which the institutions must release to the public under the HMDA; they involve logs of individual loan applications, showing the

applicant's race and the characteristics of the proposed loan. See 12 CFR Part 27 (Comptroller of the Currency); 12 CFR Part 203 (Federal Reserve Board); 12 CFR 338.4 (FDIC); 12 CFR 528.6 (FHLBB). See 49 Fed.Reg. 35758 (Sept. 12, 1984), eliminating the FDIC's requirement that certain banks under its supervision keep records on *inquiries* (as distinct from *applications*) concerning home loans.

37. 12 U.S.C.A. § 2901ff.

38. For the applicable regulations under the CRA, see 12 CFR Part 25 (Comptroller of the Currency); 12 CFR 345 (FDIC); 12 CFR Part 563e (FHLBB).

39. McCluskey, The Community Reinvestment Act: Is It Doing the Job?, 100 Bank.L.J. 33 (1983). See also Community Reinvestment Act Regulations: Another Attempt to Control Redlining, 28 Cath.U.L. Rev. 635 (1979).

under state law may vary from those imposed by the federal agencies.[40] The HMDA itself provides that state-chartered financial institutions are exempt from state disclosure rules, but only to the extent that they are inconsistent with the federal act.[41] However, the HMDA is silent on the question whether federally-chartered institutions (national banks and federal savings and loan associations) are required to follow state law. The case law on this issue has regarded the federal regulations as pervasive and fully preemptive so far as record-keeping, reporting, disclosure, and discipline are concerned; the institutions are free to disregard state law with respect to such matters. With regard to the substantive rules of state law, such as those prohibiting discrimination or redlining, the cases hold that their application and enforcement is exclusively a matter for the relevant federal agencies to determine. Any state enforcement mechanisms are inapplicable.[42]

Other approaches to the redlining problem have developed. One of the more promising is the notion of a "mortgage review board," composed of community representatives and lending institution employees, which considers appeals of loan denials. In some cities lenders have cooperated voluntarily in forming such groups, and in others they have done so under pressure from legislation or state regulators.[43] The board may have authority to order the loan granted, or it may refer the applicant to a central pool of funds set up by the lenders of the area for the purpose of making higher-risk loans.[44] Exhaustion of the appeal

40. See note 36 supra.

41. 12 U.S.C.A. § 2805.

42. National State Bank v. Long, 630 F.2d 981 (3d Cir.1980); Conference of Federal Savings and Loan Associations v. Stein, 604 F.2d 1256 (9th Cir.1979), affirmed 445 U.S. 921, 100 S.Ct. 1304, 63 L.Ed.2d 754; Glen Ellyn Savings & Loan Association v. Tsoumas, 71 Ill.2d 493, 17 Ill.Dec. 811, 377 N.E.2d 1 (1978), certiorari denied 439 U.S. 927, 99 S.Ct. 311, 58 L.Ed. 2d 320 (1978). See also Michigan Savings & Loan League v. Francis, 683 F.2d 957 (6th Cir.1982) (where lenders asserted federal law as a defense to a suit enforcing state anti-redlining statute, there was no federal court jurisdiction.)

See Annot., 57 A.L.R. Fed. 322 (1982); Lechner, National Banks and State Anti-redlining Laws: Has Congress Preempted the Field?, 99 Bank.L.J. 388 (1982) (arguing that the panoply of federal legislation constitutes a complete preemption of state law, both substantive and procedural, for federally-chartered institutions); Federal Preemption of the Illinois Financial Institutions Disclosure Act, 28 DePaul L.Rev. 805 (1979); State Regulation of Federally Chartered Financial Institutions: Washington's Anti-redlining Act, 54 Wash.L. Rev. 339 (1979).

43. The Michigan and Massachusetts statutes expressly authorize the creation of such review boards; Mass.Gen.Laws Ann. c. 167, § 73; Mich.Comp.Laws Ann. § 445.1609(1). The Boston Board is described in Comment, The Home Mortgage Disclosure Act of 1975: Will It Protect Urban Consumers From Redlining?, 12 N.Eng.L.Rev. 957, 988 (1977).

44. The Neighborhood Housing Services concept, in which a local office provides some financing to high-risk borrowers and assists others in finding and qualifying for commercially-available loans, is also a promising approach to the red-lining problem. The Urban Reinvestment Task Force, a federal entity sponsored by HUD, the FHLBB, and other agencies, assists and funds the creation of Neighborhood Housing Services offices. See Hood & Neet, Redlining Practices, Racial Resegregation, and Urban Decay: Neighborhood Housing Services as a Viable Alternative, 7 Urban Law. 510 (1975).

may also be a prerequisite to the filing of suit by the disappointed applicant.[45]

WESTLAW REFERENCES
Redlining
redlining

§ 11.6 Federal Preemption of State Mortgage Law

Under the Supremacy Clause of the United States Constitution, federal law which is validly adopted and within the constitutional power of the federal government is the supreme law of the land and supersedes state law.[1] This preemption concept has several applications in mortgage law. The most clearcut is the situation in which a congressional enactment or a valid regulation of a federal agency speaks directly to the point. Numerous illustrations may be cited. The Home Mortgage Disclosure Act requires institutional lenders to assemble and release to the public certain data on the amounts and locations of their residential loans.[2] The Fair Housing Act limits lenders' discretion in rejecting loan applicants because of race or sex,[3] and the Federal Home Loan Bank Board's regulations supplement the Act by requiring the maintenance of records on loan applications and by delimiting the criteria which can be employed by savings associations in screening applicants and properties.[4] The Truth-In-Lending Act[5] mandates that certain disclosures concerning interest and finance charges be made to borrowers, and the Real Estate Settlement Procedures Act (RESPA)[6] requires disclosures concerning settlement charges, prescribes a standard form of settlement statement, and prohibits certain types of kickbacks and rebates between mortgage lenders and other providers of settlement services. In 1973 Congress considered, but did not enact, a comprehensive federal mortgage foreclosure

45. See Mass.Gen.Laws Ann. c. 183, § 64.

§ 11.6

1. U.S. Const. Art. VI, § 2; see McCulloch v. Maryland, 17 U.S. (4 Wheat.) 316, 4 L.Ed. 579 (1819).

2. 12 U.S.C.A. § 2801; see Comment, The Home Mortgage Disclosure Act of 1975: Will It Protect Urban Consumers From Redlining?, 12 N.Eng.L.Rev. 957 (1977); § 11.5, supra, at note 34. See also Glen Ellyn Savings & Loan Association v. Tsoumas, 71 Ill.2d 493, 17 Ill.Dec. 811, 377 N.E.2d 1 (1978).

3. 42 U.S.C.A. § 3605; § 11.5, supra, at note 4. See also Equal Credit Opportunity Act, 15 U.S.C.A. § 1691 et seq.

4. 12 CFR 528.6, as amended, 43 Fed. Reg. 22335 (May 25, 1978); § 11.5, supra, at note 36. The preamble to the regulations states that federal savings associations are not required to observe more stringent state law regarding lending discrimination.

5. 15 U.S.C.A. §§ 1601 et seq.; 12 CFR Part 226.

6. 12 U.S.C.A. §§ 2601 et seq.; 24 CFR, Part 3500. See generally Field, RESPA in a Nutshell, 11 Real Prop.Prob. & Trust J. 447 (1976); Payne, Conveyancing Practice and the Feds: Some Thoughts About RESPA, 29 Ala.L.Rev. 339 (1978).

bill which would have applied to all federally-owned, -insured, or -guaranteed loans;[7] the bill would have preempted state foreclosure procedures in numerous respects, and would perhaps have represented the high-water mark in this area.[8] A somewhat similar bill, but with a much narrower scope, was enacted in 1981.[9] It authorizes nonjudicial power-of-sale foreclosure of mortgages held by the Department of Housing and Urban Development on multifamily housing projects. The act specifically preempts any state law granting post-foreclosure redemption rights.

Beginning in 1980 Congress enacted three statutes which preempt state law in a particularly direct and forceful manner. Each was a product of the extremely high interest rates which prevailed in the early 1980's, and of the resultant financial stress with which mortgage lenders were beset. The first, effective March 31, 1980, preempted state usury laws for all "federally-related" loans secured by first liens on residential real estate.[10] Interest rate ceilings as well as restrictions on discount points and other finance charges were covered. Second, Congress passed Section 341 of the Garn-St. Germain Depository Institutions Act of 1982.[11] Effective October 15, 1982, it preempted (with certain exceptions) state law which restricted exercise by lenders of due-on-sale clauses in mortgage instruments.[12]

The third prong of this preemptive effort was the Alternative Mortgage Transactions Parity Act of 1982, also effective October 15, 1982.[13] It authorized state-chartered financial institutions to make alternative forms of mortgage loans which were approved by the federal financial regulatory agencies, even though such loans might be contrary to state law.[14]

In each of these preemptive statutes, Congress attempted to mitigate the inevitable political objections to federal intrusion into what were traditionally matters exclusively of state concern. It did so by

7. The Federal Mortgage Foreclosure Act, Title IV, S. 2507, 93d Cong., 1st Sess., 1973.

8. See Pedowitz, Current Developments in Summary Foreclosure, 9 Real Prop. Prob. & Trust J. 421, 422–25 (1974).

9. The Multifamily Mortgage Foreclosure Act of 1981, 12 U.S.C.A. §§ 3701–3717. For HUD's regulations implementing the Act, see 24 CFR Part 27. See the more extended discussion, § 7.19 supra, at notes 13–20.

10. § 501, Depository Institutions Deregulation and Monetary Control Act of 1980, Pub.L. No. 96–221, 94 Stat. 161, as amended, §§ 308, 324, Pub.L. No. 96–399, 94 Stat. 1641, 1647–48, codified at 12 U.S.

C.A. § 1735f–7. The FHLBB regulations issued under authority of the statute are found in 12 CFR Part 590. See McInnis v. Cooper Communities, Inc., 271 Ark. 503, 611 S.W.2d 767 (1981), recognizing the validity of the federal act.

11. Pub.L. No. 97–320, 96 Stat. 1505, codified at 12 U.S.C.A. § 1701j–3.

12. For an extended discussion, see §§ 5.22–5.24 supra.

13. Title VIII of the Garn-St. Germain Depository Institutions Act of 1982, Pub.L. No. 97–320, 96 Stat. 1545, codified at 12 U.S.C.A. §§ 3801 et seq.

14. For an extended discussion see § 11.4, supra, at notes 109–114.

permitting state law-makers to adopt, within a limited time period (three years from the federal law's effective date),[15] statutes or constitutional provisions rejecting the federal preemption and recapturing state control.[16] With respect to each of the three, some states took advantage of this opportunity;[17] thus, the federal preemption is not entirely uniform across the nation.

In addition to these statutes, several federal agencies issue regulations governing the operation of federally-chartered financial institutions. Many of these rules (which have the same weight as statutes for preemption purposes) directly contradict state law. The most significant of these are promulgated by the Federal Home Loan Bank Board (FHLBB)[18] and apply to federally-chartered savings and loan associations. It is well-established that federal law governs the internal affairs of such associations "from the cradle to the grave",[19] fully occupying the field. If there is no specific regulation on a matter affecting the internal governance of an association, such as branching,[20] proxy solicitations,[21] employment of officers,[22] or directors' fi-

15. With respect to the preemption of usury ceilings, the states' power to reregulate discount points and other loan charges is not limited by time; see § 501(b)(4), Pub. L. No. 96–221. Such reregulation may apparently be accomplished by considerably less specific language than a reregulation of interest rates.

16. In the case of the due-on-sale preemption, a state was empowered only to continue its restrictions on due-on-sale enforcement which had operated prior to adoption of the federal law. States with no such previous restrictions could not adopt them subsequently and thereby override the federal preemption. See Nelson & Whitman, Congressional Preemption of Mortgage Due-on-Sale Law: An Analysis of the Garn-St. Germain Act, 35 Hast.L.J. 241, 296–98 (1983).

17. See notes 12, 14 supra.

18. See generally § 11.1 supra, at notes 4–7; Bartlett, The Federal-State Preemption Conflict, 44 Legal Bull. 1 (1978).

19. See Meyers v. Beverly Hills Federal Savings & Loan Association, 499 F.2d 1145 (9th Cir.1974). When state courts "deal with the internal affairs of federal savings and loan associations * * * they are nonetheless applying federal law." Mur-

phy v. Colonial Federal Savings and Loan Association, 388 F.2d 609, 612 (1967). See Community Title Co. v. Roosevelt Federal Savings & Loan Association, 670 S.W.2d 895, 903 (Mo.App.1984).

On the FHLBB's control of S & L mergers, see Federal Home Loan Bank Board: Preemptive Rights or Unbridled Powers?, 12 Cap.U.L.Rev. 529 (1983).

20. Lyons Savings & Loan Association v. Federal Home Loan Bank Board, 377 F.Supp. 11 (N.D.Ill.1974); Washington Federal Savings and Loan Association v. Balaban, 281 So.2d 15 (Fla.1973); Springfield Institute for Savings v. Worcester Federal Savings & Loan Association, 329 Mass. 184, 107 N.E.2d 315 (1952), certiorari denied 344 U.S. 844, 73 S.Ct. 184, 97 L.Ed. 684 (1952).

21. Kupiec v. Republic Federal Savings & Loan Association, 512 F.2d 147 (7th Cir. 1975); Murphy v. Colonial Federal Savings & Loan Association, 388 F.2d 609 (2d Cir. 1967); City Federal Savings & Loan Association v. Crowley, 393 F.Supp. 644 (E.D.Wis. 1975).

22. Community Federal Savings & Loan Association v. Fields, 128 F.2d 705 (8th Cir.1942).

duciary duties,[23] the federal courts will supply a rule of federal common law.[24]

In external transactions, such as the content and enforcement of mortgages and notes, however, state law governs unless there is an explicit FHLBB regulation. In recent years the FHLBB has been quite active in attempting to resolve by regulation certain controversial issues in mortgage law as applied to federal associations. Its regulations concerning prepayment penalties [25] and interest on tax escrow accounts [26] on home loans were held to prevail over contrary state law, as were its rules preempting state due-on-sale law for federal associations [27] until Congress fully occupied that field.[28] And of course its regulations governing types of loans, repayment schedules, and the like supersede state law.[29]

There is some authority that the FHLBB has completely occupied the field of relations with borrowers, thereby making state law respecting the content of notes and mortgages inapplicable. In Kaski v. First Federal Savings and Loan Association,[30] the plaintiffs were borrowers who sought to have a variable interest rate clause in their mortgage declared invalid under the Wisconsin statute regulating such clauses.[31] The loan had been made prior to the 1972 FHLBB regulatory amendments which effectively prohibited variable rate clauses,[32] and the parties conceded that there was no FHLBB regulation dealing with the subject. Nonetheless, the Wisconsin Supreme Court held that the

---

23. First Hawaiian Bank v. Alexander, 558 F.Supp. 1128 (D.Haw.1983); Rettig v. Arlington Heights Federal Savings & Loan Association, 405 F.Supp. 819 (N.D.Ill.1975); City Federal Savings and Loan Association v. Crowley, 393 F.Supp. 644 (E.D.Wis.1975).

24. In Murphy, supra note 19, the court was obliged to devise a common-law rule regarding the availability of lists of members to persons planning a proxy fight; by the time Kupiec, supra note 21, was decided, the FHLBB had promulgated a regulation on the point, thereby superseding the Murphy court's common-law rule.

25. Toolan v. Trevose Federal Savings & Loan Association, 501 Pa. 477, 462 A.2d 224 (1983); Meyers v. Beverly Hills Federal Savings and Loan Association, 499 F.2d 1145 (9th Cir.1974); see generally § 6.4, supra.

26. Olsen v. Financial Federal Savings & Loan Association, 105 Ill.App.3d 364, 61 Ill.Dec. 253, 434 N.E.2d 406 (1982); First Federal Savings & Loan Association v. Greenwald, 591 F.2d 417 (1st Cir.1979); see generally § 4.19 supra. Cf. Derenco, Inc. v. Benjamin Franklin Federal Savings &

Loan Association, 281 Or. 533, 577 P.2d 477 (1978), certiorari denied 439 U.S. 1051, 99 S.Ct. 733, 58 L.Ed.2d 712 (1978).

27. Fidelity Federal Savings & Loan Association v. de la Cuesta, 458 U.S. 141, 102 S.Ct. 3014, 73 L.Ed.2d 664 (1982). See also Haugen v. Western Federal Savings & Loan Association, 633 P.2d 497 (Colo. App.1981), affirmed 649 P.2d 323 (Colo. 1982).

28. See § 5.24 supra.

29. See Beal v. First Federal Savings & Loan Association, 90 Wis.2d 171, 279 N.W.2d 693 (1979). See also Conference of State Bank Supervisors v. Conover, 710 F.2d 878 (D.C.Cir.1983) (OCC regulation on adjustable rate mortgages is a valid preemption of state law).

30. 72 Wis.2d 132, 240 N.W.2d 367 (1976).

31. Wis.Stat.Ann. 138.055.

32. See 12 CFR 541.14(a), as amended 37 Fed.Reg. 5118 (Mar. 10, 1972). The loan in the Kaski case was made in 1967.

scheme of federal regulations was pervasive and fully occupied the field, thereby making the Wisconsin statute inapplicable. Virtually all of the cases cited by the court involved the internal governance of associations rather than relationships with borrowers, but the court thought the two spheres of activity were intimately tied together: "The regulation of loan practices directly affects the internal management and operations of federal associations and therefore requires uniform control. The present litigation ought, therefore, be resolved as a matter of federal law." [33] The case was remanded for a determination of the content of the federal (presumably common) law and an assessment of whether exhaustion of FHLBB remedies, if any, should be required.

Kaski is anomalous and should not be followed. The FHLBB regulations governing dealings between associations and borrowers are far from comprehensive,[34] and actually reflect ad hoc responses by the Board to a few specific issues. They do not purport to exhaust the field, and leave far more issues uncovered than covered. State law has customarily governed such matters as the interpretation of notes and mortgages, the negotiability of notes, and procedures for foreclosure, redemption, and collection of deficiencies by federal associations. To invent federal common law to control all of these issues would require extensive litigation and introduce great uncertainty, and it would be entirely unnecessary. There is no significant need for uniformity in such matters, since most federal associations originate few loans across state lines, and their secondary market purchasing activity is generally quite modest in scope. The training of employees and the education of customers are both likely to be simplified by the application of state law. To infer a new legal basis for nearly one-sixth of all home loans made in the United States from the FHLBB's silence is absurd.[35] Federal law should prevail only when there is an applicable FHLBB regulation.[36]

33. 240 N.W.2d at 373.

34. The principal regulations are those discussed in the sources cited at notes 25 through 29 supra, and those dealing with security property, loan-to-value ratios, and maturities; see 12 CFR 545.32–.53.

35. S & L's hold 32% of all home loans, and federal S & L's have about half of the assets of all associations; see 17 Fed.Home Bank Board J., Apr. 1984, at 54.

36. The FHLBB's position on the scope of its preemption of state mortgage law is ambiguous. In Schott v. Mission Federal Savings & Loan Association, Civ. 75–366, D.Cal.1975 (unreported), the plaintiffs attacked the due-on-sale clause in a federal association's mortgage; at that time there was no express FHLBB regulation on the subject. The Board filed an advisory opinion with the court arguing that the topic was preempted because it related to the "internal" affairs of the association. This assertion was based principally on the view that only by use of due-on-sale clauses could federal associations provide the maximum amount of financing at reasonable interest rates to credit-worthy borrowers, thus fulfilling the purpose of their charters. The case was settled, and the FHLBB subsequently issued regulations explicitly preempting the due-on clause issue, so the particular issue is moot. The Board's distinction between internal and external affairs, as expressed in its adviso-

This conclusion is consistent with the United States Supreme Court's opinion in de la Cuesta v. Fidelity Federal Savings and Loan Association,[37] in which the Court upheld the validity and preemptive effect of the FHLBB's due-on-sale regulation. The California Court of Appeal had held that the Board's regulation was outside the authority granted it by Congress under the Home Owners Loan Act,[38] insofar as it purported to preempt state due-on-sale law. In this respect the Court of Appeal was wrong, and the Supreme Court properly reversed it.

But the lender also argued that the existence of the Board's plenary authority to regulate federal associations amounted to an "occupation of the field", superseding all state law even as to matters of real property and mortgages.[39] The Court of Appeal correctly rejected this view, observing that it was contrary to longstanding practice and that it would require the development of a vast body of federal common law which does not now exist.[40] The Supreme Court did not contradict this conclusion. While it cited the *Kaski* court's conclusion that regulation of loan practices affects internal operations and "therefore requires uniform federal control," [41] it did so in a context in which the FHLBB had issued a specific regulation on the subject in controversy. The Court's use of the *Kaski* phraseology is unfortunate, but it cannot fairly be understood to endorse the notion that federal common law governs all real property and mortgage issues for federal savings associations when there is no federal regulation on the point. Only

ry opinion in *Schott,* is nonetheless interesting:

> We are discussing here only Board regulation and control over the affairs, business, business powers and authority, internal and external expansion, supervisory matters, internal operations and affairs, *relationships between the association, its management and its members,* and all similar and related matters respecting federal associations. The Board does not seek to regulate wholly unrelated matters of purely local concern, such as zoning for federal association property, methods of recording title, etc., which are left by the Board to state and local authorities, since they do not impinge upon the regulatory areas under Board control, or interfere with the Board's overall regulatory scheme. (italics added)

As a statement of the delineation between preempted and non-preempted matters, the foregoing is inept and offers little meaningful guidance for the courts. Since the Board can readily preempt any matter within its competence merely by issuing a regulation (as it ultimately did regarding due-on-sale clauses), it can hardly expect the courts to read its collective mind and to decide matters which the Board itself has not articulated. It is hard to avoid the conclusion that the Board's position in the Schott case was inconsistent with its own statement quoted above, and was merely result-oriented; that is, that it had concluded that due-on-sale clauses were desirable by the time the litigation was filed.

For sources of the foregoing materials, see Bartlett, The Federal-State Preemption Conflict, 44 Legal Bull. 1, 8–13 (1978).

37. 458 U.S. 141, 102 S.Ct. 3014, 73 L.Ed.2d 664 (1982), reversing 121 Cal.App. 3d 328, 175 Cal.Rptr. 467 (1981). See § 5.23 supra.

38. 12 U.S.C.A. §§ 1461–1468.

39. 121 Cal.App.3d at 335–36, 175 Cal. Rptr. at 471.

40. 121 Cal.App.3d at 337, 175 Cal.Rptr. at 472.

41. 458 U.S. 152, 170 n. 23, 102 S.Ct. 3015, 3031 n. 23.

on matters of corporate governance does this sort of occupation of the field prevail.

The matter is well put in Shea v. First Federal Savings and Loan Association,[42] in which an attorney sued the savings association for violations of the Connecticut antitrust laws. The association had distributed to its loan customers a list of closing attorneys which it considered acceptable, thereby allegedly steering clients away from the plaintiff. While there were some FHLBB regulations touching the matter of attorney representation in closings, the court concluded that they did not directly treat the problem at hand. It rejected the notion of total "occupation of the field", and held that since this was not a question of internal governance, federal associations were bound by state law unless "compliance actually conflicts with federal law, jeopardizes congressional purposes, or Congress or a federal regulatory body unmistakably indicates otherwise."[43]

Federally-held Mortgages

Perhaps the most perplexing cases in which federal preemption of state mortgage law is asserted are those in which the United States is a party, usually as holder and forecloser of the mortgage. Often the government appears in the guise of the Federal Housing Administration (FHA), the Veterans Administration (VA) or the Small Business Administration (SBA); the mortgage may have been originally made to the federal agency, or it may have been assigned to the agency upon the mortgagor's default. It is well-settled that the federal courts have jurisdiction to foreclose mortgages held by the government.[44] The question arises, however, to what extent state rules governing such matters as appointment of receivers, redemption following sale, and protection against deficiency judgments are binding against the government, which frequently would prefer to be unfettered by them.

The preemption concept asserted by federal agencies in these cases originated in Clearfield Trust Co. v. United States,[45] in which the government sought recovery from Clearfield on account of a check, issued by the United States and drawn on the Treasury, which Clearfield had collected. An endorsement had been forged on the check, but under state law the government had not given notice of the forgery in a timely fashion after its discovery, and hence would have been barred from recovery against Clearfield. The Supreme Court, however, held that the federal common law preempted the state rule:

42. 184 Conn. 285, 439 A.2d 997 (1981).

43. 439 A.2d at 1005.

44. See 28 U.S.C.A. § 1345 (jurisdiction over cases in which the United States is a plaintiff); United States v. Belanger, 598 F.Supp. 598 (D.Me.1984), adopting state foreclosure process as the federal rule.

45. 318 U.S. 363, 63 S.Ct. 573, 87 L.Ed. 838 (1943).

The application of state law, even without the conflict of laws rules of the forum, would subject the rights and duties of the United States to exceptional uncertainty. It would lead to great diversity in results by making identical transactions subject to the vagaries of the laws of the several states. The desirability of a uniform rule is plain.[46]

The *Clearfield Trust* holding was first applied to a mortgage transaction in 1959 in United States v. View Crest Garden Apartments, Inc.[47] There an FHA mortgage had been assigned to the government after default. The government filed an action in federal court to foreclose the mortgage and sought the appointment of a receiver pending foreclosure. The trial court held that under the law of Washington State, no sufficient showing had been made to justify a receiver, but the Ninth Circuit reversed. It held that after default the question of remedies should be determined by federal law, and remanded the case for a determination as to whether federal law would justify appointment of a receiver. The court purported to reach its conclusion by weighing the policies underlying the state and federal rules, but it strongly emphasized the federal need to protect the treasury and promote the security of the federal investment, and it gave little weight to the policies underlying the Washington law of receiverships.

For a time, it appeared that state law respecting mortgage remedies was entirely preempted by the federal government when acting as mortgage holder. However, the seeds of a reconsideration of this trend were sown in 1966 in United States v. Yazell,[48] in which the SBA had made a disaster loan secured by a chattel mortgage to a Texas couple. Upon default and foreclosure, the wife claimed that the Texas law of coverture insulated her separate property from execution by the government to satisfy the deficiency. The Supreme Court agreed, rejecting the SBA's claim that federal common law (which presumably would not recognize the coverture defense) should apply. The Court relied to some extent on the fact that the loan had been individually negotiated with specific reference to state law, and that the documents gave no clue that the government would attempt to overcome the coverture doctrine; in this way it distinguished the *View Crest* case. But the Court's principal rationale involved a weighing of the respective interests of state and federal governments. It held the state law was a significant manifestation of Texas' overall allocation of family property rights and obligations, and noted that the coverture doctrine could hardly be a serious impediment to SBA collections generally, since it

---

46. Id. at 367.

47. 268 F.2d 380 (9th Cir.1959), certiorari denied 361 U.S. 884, 80 S.Ct. 156, 4 L.Ed.2d 120 (1960); see also United States v. Queen's Court Apartments, Inc., 296 F.2d 534 (9th Cir.1961); United States v. Mountain Village Co., 424 F.Supp. 822 (D.Mass.1976).

48. 382 U.S. 341, 86 S.Ct. 500, 15 L.Ed. 2d 404 (1966).

was obsolete in most states. The Court thus concluded that Texas law should apply, although it declined to decide whether through adoption into federal common law or by virtue of the fact that the parties contracted with reference to it.[49]

The balancing approach of *Yazell* was further developed and formalized in 1979 by the Supreme Court in United States v. *Kimbell Foods, Inc.*[50] The *Kimbell* opinion involved two consolidated cases in which federal agencies (the Farmers Home Administration and the Small Business Administration) asserted lien priority in personal property against competing private lienholders.[51] The Court reaffirmed that federal law invariably applies to cases in which the government is asserting or foreclosing a lien, but it articulated a three-pronged test for determining whether the courts should adopt state law as the federal rule of decision. In summary form, the test is as follows: (1) Is the nature of the federal program such that a nationally-uniform rule of law is needed? (2) Would the application of the state rule frustrate specific objectives of the federal program? (3) Would application of a federal rule disrupt commercial relationships which are predicated on state law?

On the facts of *Kimbell,* the Court determined that state law provided an appropriate rule. It emphasized that the federal agencies involved were already organized to take account of and comply with state law, and that their handbooks and procedures made abundant references to state rules. If they had used greater care in lending, they could readily have protected themselves from the losses they suffered under state law. Thus, the state rules would not generally frustrate the objectives of the programs in question. On the other hand, to substitute new federal rules would be highly disruptive, the Court concluded.

---

49. See Note, The Role of State Deficiency Judgment Law in FHA Insured Mortgage Transactions, 56 Minn.L.Rev. 463 (1972), arguing that in such cases state law should be deemed "selectively incorporated" into federal law rather than applied of its own force.

50. 440 U.S. 715, 99 S.Ct. 1448, 59 L.Ed. 2d 711 (1979), on remand 600 F.2d 478 (5th Cir.1979).

51. Neither case involved real estate security. In one case, the debtor had given Kimbell Foods a chattel mortgage containing a dragnet clause; later it executed a security agreement to a bank on the same property, in return for an SBA-guaranteed loan. The District Court held that under Texas law the SBA would prevail because the dragnet mortgage was not "choate" until Kimbell reduced its claim to judg-

ment. 401 F.Supp. 316, 324–35 (N.D.Tex. 1975). The Court of Appeals held that under Texas law the dragnet security given to Kimbell would have priority; but instead of following Texas law, it created a federal common law rule which reached the same result; 557 F.2d 491, 503–05 (5th Cir.1977).

In the other case, the debtor gave FmHA a security interest in his tractor. Later he had the tractor repaired by a mechanic who, when unpaid, asserted a possessory lien on it. The Court of Appeals held that, under Georgia law, the FmHA's lien was unperfected because the description of the tractor was inadequate. However, it adopted a federal common law rule which limited the priority of the mechanic's lien to only a portion of the total repair bill. See 563 F.2d 678 (5th Cir.1977).

If the Court believed that its new test provided enough specificity to produce consistent results in the lower federal courts, it was mistaken. Consider the cases which have dealt with post-sale statutory redemption and antideficiency legislation, features of mortgage foreclosure in many states which the federal mortgage-holding agencies usually find objectionable.[52] The Ninth Circuit has been extremely active in deciding preemption cases of these types. In 1970 in United States v. Stadium Apartments, Inc., it had refused to recognize Idaho's post-sale redemption statute as controlling in an FHA foreclosure.[53] But even before *Kimbell* it had begun to retreat from this position, adopting state antideficiency and statutory redemption rules in an SBA foreclosure[54] and distinguishing *Stadium Apartments* on the ground that the documents there were non-negotiated "boilerplate" which included a waiver by the debtor of the state-law protections.[55]

Later Ninth Circuit cases seemed to suggest that choice-of-law clauses or waivers of state protective rules in the documents themselves were highly significant, and perhaps controlling.[56] And in a case in which no clause in the documents bore on the issue, the Ninth Circuit devised a federal rule allowing the FHA to recover for waste following its foreclosure of an apartment building;[57] such an action would have been barred under the California antideficiency statute,[58] which the

52. See generally §§ 8.4–8.8 supra (statutory redemption); § 8.3 (antideficiency legislation). On the pre-*Kimbell* cases, see Note, Federal Housing Loans: Is State Mortgage Law Preempted?, 19 Santa Clara L.Rev. 431 (1979).

53. United States v. Stadium Apartments, Inc., 425 F.2d 358 (9th Cir.1970), certiorari denied 400 U.S. 926, 91 S.Ct. 187, 27 L.Ed.2d 926 (1970). The decision was based principally on the high cost to the government of holding the property, with little practical opportunity to dispose of it, during the redemption period. The court also emphasized the meager value of the redemption right to the debtor, in its view.

54. United States v. MacKenzie, 510 F.2d 39 (9th Cir.1975). The court opined that the state rules actually tended to fulfill the federal program's goal of helping small businesses—a conclusion which must have astonished the SBA itself, normally considered the best authority on how its programs should be administered.

55. This distinction between individually-negotiated and boilerplate documents was unconvincing to Judges Ely and Browning, concurring in *MacKenzie;* they asserted that *Stadium Apartments* had been effectively overruled.

56. See United States v. Stewart, 523 F.2d 1070 (9th Cir.1975) (California antideficiency rule applied, where documents stated that California law governed the transaction); United States v. Gish, 559 F.2d 572 (9th Cir.1977), certiorari denied 435 U.S. 996, 98 S.Ct. 1648, 56 L.Ed.2d 85 (1978) (rejecting application of the Alaska antideficiency statute, where documents stated that federal law would control). See also United States v. Pastos, 595 F.Supp. 1013 (D.Mont.1984) (regulations and documents adopted federal law).

But the documents have not always been controlling; see United States v. Crain, 589 F.2d 996 (9th Cir.1979), in which the SBA sued guarantors on a note. Arizona law required creditors to exhaust their remedies against the principal debtor, but a clause in the guarantee purported to waive those rights. The court declined to follow the documents, and adopted state law, again asserting, as in *MacKenzie,* supra note 54, that it was consistent with the SBA's goals of protecting small businesses.

57. United States v. Haddon Haciendas, Inc., 541 F.2d 777 (9th Cir.1976).

58. See Cornelison v. Kornbluth, 15 Cal.3d 590, 125 Cal.Rptr. 557, 542 P.2d 981 (1975).

court felt would have interfered with the FHA's goals of eliminating substandard housing. In its only post-*Kimbell* case, United States v. Ellis,[59] the Ninth Circuit embraced the Washington state statutory redemption process in a Farmers Home Administration foreclosure. It refused to follow *Stadium Apartments* despite the fact that the documents in *Ellis*, like those in *Stadium*, were standard forms with no individualized negotiation. It held that the "overriding federal purpose is not adversely affected, and may even be advanced, by adopting state law." [60]

But while the Ninth Circuit moved toward increased recognition of state law, the Eighth Circuit, in United States v. Victory Highway Village, refused to recognize the Minnesota statutory redemption scheme in an FHA foreclosure.[61] The court simply cited pre-*Kimbell* holdings to the same effect and avoided even mentioning *Kimbell*, much less analyzing the case under the *Kimbell* test! [62] The Sixth Circuit employed similarly disappointing judicial craftsmanship in United States v. Scholnick,[63] reaching an identical conclusion with no thoughtful *Kimbell* analysis.

Cases on other legal issues have been much more consistent in adopting state law as the rule of decision. Where the question is lien priority, the courts have followed *Kimbell* faithfully,[64] although often with little analysis.[65] The Fifth Circuit held that the SBA must follow the Georgia rule requiring judicial confirmation of foreclosure sales; [66] in another case it applied Georgia law to determine the standard of reasonableness which SBA must meet in disposing of a leasehold upon

---

59. 714 F.2d 953 (9th Cir.1983). See also United States v. Hargrove, 494 F.Supp. 22 (D.N.M.1979) (semple).

60. *Stadium Apartments* was distinguished on the rather unconvincing ground that it had involved the National Housing Act, the primary objective of which was to maximize the amount of housing produced, while *Ellis* involved a direct loan to a farmer from the Farmers Home Administration, which presumably had differing (but unstated) objectives.

61. 662 F.2d 488 (8th Cir.1981).

62. See John Hancock Mutual Life Insurance Co. v. Bruening Farms Corp., 537 F.Supp. 936 (N.D.Iowa 1982), following *Victory Highway Village*, supra note 61. See also United States v. Curry, 561 F.Supp. 429 (D.Kan.1983), following *Victory Highway Village* and refusing to adopt Kansas law prohibiting waivers of statutory redemption, but nonetheless giving the debtors an equitable period of redemption as is allowed under Kansas law.

63. 606 F.2d 160 (6th Cir.1979). The level of the court's analysis is aptly represented in its dictum: "Local rules that limit the effectiveness of remedies available to the United States are not to be adopted." One could scarcely imagine a statement more out of character with the spirit of *Kimbell*.

64. See, e.g., More v. United States, 505 F.Supp. 612 (N.D.Fla.1980) (FmHA); Sims v. Smith, 502 F.Supp. 609 (N.D.Fla.1980) (FmHA).

65. But see United States v. Dansby, 509 F.Supp. 188 (N.D.Ohio 1981), applying Ohio law to recognize the priority of a state property tax lien, as against an FmHA mortgage, and carefully analyzing FmHA's decentralized administration and capacity to operate efficiently without a uniform federal rule.

66. United States v. Dismuke, 616 F.2d 755 (5th Cir.1980).

which it holds a lien.[67] Here the Court took *Kimbell* seriously, discussing the test at length and commenting particularly on the local title difficulties which would ensue if a new federal rule were constructed.

One of the best-crafted opinions is that of the First Circuit in Chicago Title Insurance Co. v. Sherred Village Associates.[68] There a mortgage on a multifamily housing project was insured by, and subsequently assigned to, the Department of Housing and Urban Development. During construction a subcontractor on the project was unpaid, and it subsequently filed a mechanics' lien. Under Maine law, such liens relate back for priority purposes to the date of the claimant's contract,[69] which was earlier than the HUD-held mortgage. HUD argued strenuously for a federal common law rule of "first in time, first in right", which would have negated the relation back of the lien. But the First Circuit concluded that HUD's program, which is administered on a local basis with careful case-by-case scrutiny of mortgage insurance applications, would not be burdened significantly by the state rule, while employment of a federal rule would seriously interfere with the expectations of local contractors.[70]

State law has also been adopted in recent cases in the face of arguments by government agencies urging federal common law treatment of dragnet clause enforcement,[71] general mortgage foreclosure procedure,[72] and rights of the Federal Deposit Insurance Corporation to collect the debts of insolvent banks.[73] On the other hand, federal common law has been held to control the HUD Secretary's right to become a mortgagee in possession,[74] and (prior to the Congressional preemption of the matter) to preempt state law limiting enforcement of a due-on-sale clause by FmHA.[75]

It is not easy to find a thread of consistency in the preemption decisions. The strongest cases for adoption of state law as the rule of decision are those involving lien priority, as in *Kimbell* itself. In most

---

67. United States v. Irby, 618 F.2d 352 (5th Cir.1980).

68. 708 F.2d 804 (1st Cir.1983).

69. See 10 Maine Rev.Stat.Ann. § 3251; § 12.4 supra.

70. Id. at 810–813.

71. United States v. Vahlco Corp., 720 F.2d 885 (5th Cir.1983).

72. Johnson v. United States Department of Agriculture, 734 F.2d 774 (11th Cir.1984).

73. Federal Deposit Insurance Corp. v. Braemoor Associates, 686 F.2d 550 (7th Cir.1982), certiorari denied 461 U.S. 927, 103 S.Ct. 2086, 77 L.Ed.2d 297 (1983); Federal Deposit Insurance Corp. v. Lattimore Land Corp., 656 F.2d 139 (5th Cir.1981). But see Gunter v. Hutcheson, 674 F.2d 862 (11th Cir.1982), certiorari denied 459 U.S. 826, 103 S.Ct. 60, 74 L.Ed.2d 63 (1982), rehearing denied 459 U.S. 1059, 103 S.Ct. 477, 74 L.Ed.2d 624 (1982) adopting a federal common law rule immunizing the FDIC from a bank debtor's fraud defense when FDIC has acquired the debtor's obligation in good faith by taking over an insolvent bank.

74. United States v. St. Paul Missionary Public Housing, Inc., 575 F.Supp. 867 (N.D.Ohio 1983).

75. United States v. Med O Farm, Inc., 701 F.2d 88 (9th Cir.1983).

such instances state law is neither pro-debtor nor pro-creditor,[76] and in no sense discriminates against the government. It is essentially neutral, and merely establishes ground rules involving filing, possession, and notice which the government can observe as readily as any private party. Moreover, displacement of state priority rules by rules invented by a federal court can be extremely disruptive to local businesses. For these reasons, *Kimbell* makes excellent sense on its facts.

But extending *Kimbell* to other areas of mortgage law, such as statutory redemption and antideficiency legislation, which are quite overtly pro-debtor, is a harder question, as the diversity of judicial decisions illustrates. The government would like to collect its money, and these rules stand in its way. Is preemption "needed"? Will state law frustrate the objectives of the federal program? Only in the sense that the public fisc will suffer added losses, and private debtors will be benefitted, if there is no preemption.[77]

The question is fundamentally one of policy, and it ought to be resolved by the political branches—the Congress and the agencies which administer the programs. It is within their power to preempt state law by statute or regulation, and in some instances they have done so.[78] It makes little sense for federal judges to speculate about how obnoxious the state rule is to a federal program, when those who devised and administer the program can decide for themselves and announce the extent to which state law should govern it.[79] Unless they have done so, or the impairment of the program is obvious and egregious, state law should be followed by the courts.

76. One exception, arguably, is the mechanics' lien relation back doctrine involved in the *Sherred Village* case, supra note 68, which seems inherently adverse to the interest of the government in its capacity as assignee of an institutional lender. But even here there are numerous methods by which the government can minimize or eliminate its risk.

77. Thus, the Ninth Circuit's effort to predicate different preemption results on a distinction, for example, between the objectives of the SBA (to aid small businesses), which are advanced by antideficiency and redemption statutes, and those of HUD (to clear slums and build housing), which are retarded by antideficiency and redemption statutes, is wholly unconvincing. See text at notes 53–60 supra. Both agencies are fundamentally in the business of making federal credit available to the private sector, and both have an equal interest in being repaid.

78. For example, the Multifamily Mortgage Foreclosure Act, 12 U.S.C.A. §§ 3701–3717 specifically preempts any state post-sale redemption rights following a foreclosure under the Act. See United States v. Shimer, 367 U.S. 374, 81 S.Ct. 1554, 6 L.Ed.2d 908 (1961) (VA regulations fully pre-empt inconsistent state foreclosure rules); Cf. United States v. Whitney, 602 F.Supp. 722 (W.D.N.Y.1985). See also notes 10–17 supra, discussing other preemptive federal statutes.

79. We suggest that the announcement ought to be by way of statute or regulation, and not merely by language in the documents. This will encourage consistency in administration, and will subject the decision to public scrutiny in a way that document drafting does not.

There is a further question, not yet answered in the cases, concerning the extent to which the preemption doctrines discussed above should apply when the mortgage is held by a federally-sponsored entity, such as the Federal National Mortgage Association (FHMA) or the Federal Home Loan Mortgage Corporation (FHLMC), rather than by a direct federal agency. Rust v. Johnson [80] provides some guidance, although its facts are distinguishable. There FNMA held a mortgage on realty which was the subject of a city's lien foreclosure action for a delinquent street improvement assessment. The Ninth Circuit held that FHMA was a "federal instrumentality", and thus was entitled to "protection of the federal interest" in its defense against the city's foreclosure. This result seems inconsistent with the cases holding that FNMA is not sufficiently "governmental" to be subject to the burdens of the Due Process Clause when foreclosing mortgages by power of sale.[81] Nevertheless, Rust v. Johnson strongly suggests that FNMA and FHLMC will be treated as direct instrumentalities of the federal government when their mortgage foreclosures come into conflict with state law.

Some of the cases discussed above have considered significant, in deciding whether to adopt state law, the extent to which an agency's programs are administered at the local level, so that it would not be burdensome to impose local law upon them.[82] But it is doubtful that any federal agency's programs are so fully centralized that compliance with state law would present difficult burdens. FHMA and FHLMC illustrate the point well. One can hardly imagine more centralized operations. They deal with thousands of lenders and have purchased millions of mortgages, while employing relatively small staffs operating only at the national and regional levels.[83] Yet they have at the same time been acutely conscious of the variations in mortgage law from one state to another, and have meticulously drafted state-by-state versions of their "standard" instruments in order to comply with those variations.[84] When spread over so many transactions, the cost of this individualization cannot be very great. Arguments by other agencies that they need not do as much, or that the federal courts ought to protect them from their own lack of careful drafting of loan documents and regulations, are not particularly persuasive.

80. 597 F.2d 174 (9th Cir.1979), certiorari denied 444 U.S. 964, 100 S.Ct. 450, 62 L.Ed.2d 376 (1979).

81. See § 7.28 supra.

82. See, e.g., Chicago Title Insurance Co. v. Sherred Village Associates, 708 F.2d 804, 810–11 (1st Cir.1983); United States v. Dansby, 509 F.Supp. 188 (N.D.Ohio 1981).

83. Cf. United States v. Dansby, id., distinguishing FmHA's highly localized operations from FNMA's centralized ones.

84. See Randolph, The FHMA/FHLMC Uniform Home Improvement Loan Note: The Secondary Market Meets the Consumer Movement, 60 N.C.L.Rev. 365 (1982); Browne, Development of the FHMA/FHLMC Plain Language Mortgage Documents—Some Useful Techniques, 14 Real Prop.Prob. & Tr.J. 696 (1979).

WESTLAW REFERENCES

360k4.14 (pre-empt*** supersede* /s federal /s state) /p
     mortgag**

Federally-held Mortgages

title("united states" ("federal housing" veterans "small business" +1
     administration) +p v.) & synopsis, digest(foreslos*** /s
     mortgage)

---

§§ 11.7–12.0 are reserved for supplementary material.

Chapter 12

FINANCING REAL ESTATE
CONSTRUCTION

Table of Sections

§ 12.1 Construction Lending—An Overview

The purpose of a construction loan is to provide funds with which the owner of a parcel of land can construct improvements upon it.[1] The construction loan is superficially similar to a long-term mortgage loan; the borrower's obligation to repay will be represented by a promissory note or similar document, and will be secured by a mortgage, deed of trust, or comparable instrument. In addition, the lender and borrower will usually enter into a construction loan agreement, spelling out the obligations of each with regard to the construction process. The borrower (who is usually the owner of the land on which

---

§ 12.1

1. See generally U.S. League of Sav. Associations, Constr. Lending Guide; Livingston, Current Business Approaches—Commercial Construction Lending, 13 Real Prop.Prob. & Tr.J. 791 (1978); Storke & Sears, Subdivision Financing, 28 Rocky Mt. L.Rev. 549 (1956); Albright, Processing the Constr. Mortgage, 3 Real Est.Rev. 72 (No. 3, Fall 1973); Gallaher, Protecting the Construction Loan, 5 Real Est.Rev. 114 (No. 1, Spring 1975); Tockarshewsky, Reducing the Risks in Construction Lending, 7 Real Est.Rev. 59 (No. 1, Spring 1977); Hall, How to Build Lender Protection into Construction Loan Agreements, 6 Real Est.L.J. 21 (1977).

the project will be built) may perform the construction himself—acting, in effect, as his own general contractor. Alternatively, he may employ a separate general contractor with whom he enters into a construction contract. The discussion below will refer to the borrower as a "developer," and will assume that no separate general contractor is involved unless specifically mentioned. Most of this chapter is equally applicable to construction projects which will be sold upon completion (such as detached-house subdivisions) and to projects which the developer will retain upon completion, either for his own use (such as an individual's own home or a business warehouse or office) or for rental purposes (such as the usual apartment building). Where distinctions among these types of projects are important, they will be noted.

Construction lending is far more critical and exacting, and presents far greater risks to the mortgagee, than does lending on completed structures. This is so because the value of the real estate for security purposes is entirely dependent upon the happening of a future event: the completion of the building or project as agreed by the parties. If the construction is not completed by the mortgagor, or is completed late or defectively, or if the project's value upon completion is less than anticipated, the construction lender may find itself in the unhappy position of being inadequately secured. Such a situation is viewed even more seriously by junior lienors, such as the vendor from whom the present owner purchased the land (and who has not yet been fully paid), or claimants under mechanics and materialmen's liens. These parties are frequently present in construction lending situations, and their roles will be discussed subsequently. Because of their junior security position, their risk of being wiped out by the mortgagor's failure to complete the project as agreed, or the project's lack of value despite its completed status, is even more serious than that of the construction lender.

A critical concern of every construction lender (and of knowledgeable junior lienors as well) is that the funds disbursed by the lender actually find their way into labor and materials used in the project. To some extent this is a matter for negotiation between the borrower and lender; in addition to covering the "hard costs," such as materials and direct labor, the construction lender may be willing to cover certain "soft costs" such as legal and accounting services directly related to the project, insurance, real estate taxes, and possibly even interest on the construction loan itself, as well as charges made by permanent lenders for their commitments. Other negotiable points include whether the construction loan will cover any portion of the land acquisition or site development costs, such as the extension of utility lines, roads and streets, storm and sanitary sewers, and the like to the project. The most conservative position, taken by many construction lenders, is to insist that all land acquisition, site development, and "soft" costs be covered by the developer through cash outlays or other financing separate from (and junior to) the construction loan. In some cases the lender is required by law to limit its construction loans to "hard" construction costs.[2]

The construction lender will be particularly concerned that no construction loan funds be diverted to other uses. Such diversions often occur, and can obviously be devastating to the construction lender, since they greatly increase the probability that the property's security value will be less than the indebtedness it secures. Diversion of funds by a developer does not always imply outright dishonesty. In some cases, the developer may have other projects under construction which are in serious trouble, and he may be tempted to "rob" one project in order to "bail out" another. Diversion of funds is almost always a sign of serious trouble to the construction lender, and wise lenders take careful precautions to insure that it does not occur.

Institutional Construction Lenders

Construction lending cannot be successfully handled by remote control. The lender must be intimately familiar with local circumstances and practices, and must be represented by an on-site inspector. In addition, construction loans tend to be of relatively short duration, since the construction periods for most types of real estate projects are measured in months or small numbers of years. Finally, construction lending tends to be risky but profitable, with fees and interest rates significantly higher than are normally expected on long-term loans on completed real estate developments. Given these constraints, it is not surprising that the two principal types of local lending institutions, commercial banks and savings and loan associations, together account for nearly 90% of all construction lending in the United States.[3] Commercial banks make more than half of all construction loans, displaying some preference for loans on commercial property, while savings and loan associations have a somewhat heavier activity in the residential construction area. The remaining construction lending has been attributable largely to real estate investment trusts in recent years, although these entities have often suffered significant losses on such loans, largely as a consequence of poor underwriting and inspection.[4]

National banks. The authority of national banks to make real estate construction loans is derived from Section 24 of the Federal Reserve Act.[5] For many years this section imposed rather rigid limitations on loan-to-value ratios, amortization, and other features of real

---

2. See, e.g., Sharp Lumber Co. v. Manus Homes, Inc., 189 N.E.2d 447, 90 O.L.A. 421 (Ohio App.1961), holding a construction loan valid despite its noncompliance with an applicable regulation limiting such loans to construction costs.

3. See U.S. Dep't of Commerce, Statistical Abstract of the United States 516 (1984) (commercial banks held 58% of all construction loans in 1982; savings and loan associations held 29%.)

4. See, e.g., Stevenson, Lessons from the Mortgage Trust Experience, 6 Real Est. Rev. 72 (No. 3, Fall 1976).

5. 12 U.S.C.A. § 371. For the former regulations under this section, see 12 CFR 7.2000 et seq.

estate loans, but it was amended by the Garn-St. Germain Depository Institutions Act of 1982[6] to provide that such loans are now subject only to whatever regulatory limitations may be imposed by the Comptroller of the Currency; the Comptroller, in turn, removed all such regulatory requirements in 1983.[7] Hence, national banks are subject only to their own internal policies in determining what construction loans they will make.[8]

Federal savings and loan associations. The regulations of the Federal Home Loan Bank Board govern construction lending by savings and loan association. They have been substantially liberalized in recent years, and impose maximum terms for such loans ranging from two years for a single-family dwelling to six years for nonresidential buildings and eight years for land development loans.[9] The loan's amount may not exceed the market value of the security property.[10]

State-chartered lenders. Each state regulates the lending powers of state-chartered banks and savings and loan associations, as well as mutual savings banks in those states in which they are authorized. The construction lending powers of these institutions vary considerably from one jurisdiction to another.

FHA and VA. Neither the Federal Housing Administration (FHA) nor the Veterans Administration (VA) normally insures or guarantees construction loans to developers of single-family homes. However, under Title X of the National Housing Act,[11] enacted in 1965, FHA may insure land development loans to finance the installation of such improvements as water and sewer systems, other utilities, street paving, and facilities for public or common use by the residents of the development. Such loans must be secured by first mortgages, although FHA will permit the existence of junior financing, such as a subordinated lien representing the unpaid acquisition cost of the land. Title X cannot be used to finance the construction of dwelling units; the developer must obtain a separate construction loan for that purpose, and it will usually be necessary to release lots from the Title X mortgage as they are placed within the coverage of the construction loan, since most construction lenders require that their loans be secured by first liens.

FHA also insures construction loan mortgages on multi-family housing projects under many of its programs.[12] In such cases, a single

6. Pub.L. 97–320, § 403.

7. See 48 Fed.Reg. 40698 (Sept. 30, 1983), repealing 12 CFR 7.2000–7.2700 and adopting 12 CFR Part 34.

8. Indeed, construction loans are not considered real estate loans at all if they have a maturity of no more than 60 months and there is a take-out commitment from a financially responsible party; 12 CFR 34.3(f).

9. 12 CFR 545.36.

10. 12 CFR 545.32(d).

11. 12 U.S.C.A. § 1749aa et seq. See 24 CFR Part 205.

12. These include Section 207 (unsubsidized rental projects); Section 213 (cooperative housing projects); Section 221(d)(2) and 221(d)(4) (moderate-income rental projects); and Section 236 (subsidized rental projects for lower-income families). The numbers refer to sections of the National Housing Act.

set of mortgage documents is frequently used for both the construction and permanent loan periods. In FHA's terminology, the agency's activity during the construction period is known as "insurance of advances." Generally, developers (or "sponsors," as they are called by FHA) who wish the advantages of permanent financing under one of the FHA multi-family programs may elect insurance of advances or not, as they choose.

Despite the fact that FHA does not insure construction loans on housing subdivisions which are to be owner-occupied, the agency nonetheless is sometimes heavily involved in the construction of such projects. This occurs because, under applicable statutes, a house is eligible for a permanent FHA-insured loan with a 97% loan-to-value ratio on the first $25,000 and 95% on the excess *only* if it was "approved for mortgage insurance prior to the beginning of construction" unless it is covered by a HUD-approved warranty plan or is more than one year old.[13] The maximum loan-to-value ratio for a house which has not received such approval is only 90%. Thus, if a builder wishes the advantage of offering his customers high-ratio FHA financing, he must obtain advance approval of his development, with its attendant paperwork (which is substantial) and FHA inspections during construction. The advent of 95% privately-insured conventional permanent financing has made FHA a less attractive approach to many developers,[14] but some are still willing to seek the FHA's "conditional commitment" and concomitant involvement.

The Farmers Home Administration (FmHA), a division of the U.S. Department of Agriculture, operates several programs to finance both single-family and multi-family housing in rural areas.[15] FmHA guarantees loans made by other institutional lenders, and also makes some direct loans. FmHA will provide necessary construction financing for developers, although it strongly prefers that construction loans be made by other institutions.[16]

Underwriting Construction Loans

From the mortgagee's point of view, successful construction lending depends on the interplay of several activities, including thorough underwriting of the proposed loan, inspection during the construction period, and the use of careful controls to insure that disbursed funds are not diverted away from the construction project. "Underwriting," as used in this context, means a careful evaluation of all of the factors which could result in a risk of loss to the construction lender. Not all of these factors are legal in nature, although many have legal ramifica-

13. National Housing Act § 203(b)(2), 12 U.S.C.A. § 1709(b)(2).

14. In 1982 FHA-insured home loans comprised only about 13% of all outstanding home loans; see U.S. Dep't of Commerce, Statistical Abstract of the United States 516 (1984).

15. The principal programs are Section 502 (rural home loans) and Section 515 (rural rental project loans) of the Housing Act of 1949, 42 U.S.C.A. §§ 1472, 1485.

16. 7 CFR 1822.7(g), 1822.94(a).

tions. Underwriting a construction project is complex, and the material given here should be taken only as a brief summary of the items with which the lender will be concerned.

The proposed borrower's reputation, experience, credit rating, and capitalization are highly important to the lender. Success in previous smaller projects is usually a prerequisite to obtaining financing for a major enterprise. If the borrower is a closely-held corporation, its shareholders will usually be asked to take personal liability for the debt. Most lenders will require that the borrower put a substantial amount of his own cash—in many cases on the order of ten percent of the project's construction cost—rather than borrowing the entire amount. This cash investment requirement may be a result of the regulations applicable to the particular lender, or it may derive from the lender's internal policies; in either event, the assetless developer or one whose assets are illiquid (such as other land holdings) does not present an attractive risk.

The marketability of the project is also critical. If the completed structures will be sold or rented, the lender needs some assurance that they will be in demand. A careful market survey will usually be required for a large project.[17] In the case of a project which can be leased to an identifiable business tenant prior to construction (as is often the case with large store space in shopping centers), the lender will usually wish to verify the tenant's credit worthiness.

The architectural and engineering design and the soil tests for the project will be carefully reviewed by the construction lender to make sure that they are technically sound, in compliance with local codes, and will result in a marketable project. The lender will perform an appraisal of the project prior to granting the construction loan, and will carefully analyze the developer's proposed budget and schedule of costs to determine that the project can be completed with the available funds. The lender will also give close scrutiny to the developer's proposed timing and completion date.

A variety of legal matters will be of direct interest to the construction lender, including the quality of the developer's title and his compliance with local zoning and building codes, environmental regulations, and all other local, state, and federal laws which might bear on the construction. The lender will usually require a survey and a plot plan to verify that the property's location and size are as represented by the developer and that the project will comply with any applicable set-back lines.

Finally, the lender will wish to review other documents associated with the project, including the construction contract if the developer is not serving as his own general contractor, the lease forms if the project

---

17. See White, How to Plan and Build a Major Office Building, 10 Real Est.Rev. 87 (No. 1, 1980); Siegelaub & Meistrich, How the Professional Shopping Center Developer Obtains a Mortgage, 9 Real Est.Rev. 50 (No. 1, 1979).

is to be rented after completion, the forms of any bonds required, and the permanent loan commitment if the construction lender is not also to carry the permanent financing.

Of course, not all construction lenders are as uniformly careful and deliberate as the foregoing list suggests. Some are willing to take underwriting shortcuts when dealing with developers with whom they have had prior good experience. But failure to consider any of these details increases the potential risk.

Documentation

When the underwriting process has been completed and the construction lender has determined to make the loan, it will usually execute, with the developer, three basic documents: a promissory note or bond, a construction loan mortgage or deed of trust, and a construction loan agreement. This agreement [18] will generally incorporate by reference the entire plans and specifications for the project, will contain a budget to which the developer agrees to adhere, and will fix a completion date for the project.[19] The specific "hard" and "soft" costs which the loan will cover are identified. It will explain the method of disbursing funds as construction progresses; events which may constitute a default on the part of the borrower will be set forth in detail, and the agreement will specify the lender's remedies for such defaults. The developer's responsibility for such matters as bonds, insurance, and permits from government agencies will be spelled out in detail. The lender's draw inspector may be identified and his right of access to the project assured.

The agreement will usually create a construction loan account out of which funds will be disbursed as construction moves forward; [20] the developer may also be required to deposit an agreed amount of his own cash in this account, as discussed above. From the lender's viewpoint, it is essential that the account, including the loan amount plus the developer's deposit, contain sufficient funds at the commencement of construction to complete the project, and that this sufficiency continue throughout the construction period. The agreement may contain language requiring the borrower to deposit additional funds at any time if the account becomes inadequate to complete construction. The account

18. Examples of two construction loan agreements are reprinted in J. Krashowiecki, Housing and Urban Development Cases and Materials 30, 82 (1969). See also ALI–ABA, Modern Real Estate Transactions 284 (5th ed. 1984); Florida Bar, I. Florida Real Property Practice § 17.56 (1965); Calif.Cont.Ed. of Bar, California Land Security and Development § 30.29 (1960).

19. See American National Bank v. Norris, 368 So.2d 897 (Fla.App.1979), certi-orari denied 378 So.2d 342 (1979) (time was not of the essence of construction loan agreement).

20. Lenders sometimes attempt to charge interest on the funds they have placed in the account, including the portion not yet disbursed. This can raise a serious usury issue; see Hoffman v. Key Federal Savings & Loan Association, 286 Md. 28, 416 A.2d 1265 (1979).

itself will usually be assigned to the lender as additional security for the loan.

Control of Disbursements

Several methods have been developed by which the construction lender may insure that the funds being disbursed under the loan are in fact being used for improvements in the project.[21] Perhaps the oldest method, now commonly used alone only for the construction of detached houses, is the "progress payment" method under which some previously agreed fraction of the funds is disbursed as each stage of construction is completed. The stages of "progress" may be defined either as percentages of total construction cost or as phases of the building's completion: grading, foundation, framing, roof, etc. Either approach requires periodic inspections by the lender.

A more sophisticated method, termed the voucher system, requires the lender to disburse funds only when presented with bills or vouchers for work actually done on the site. The lender may require the developer to pay the bills directly and may issue a single check, say monthly, to the developer to cover them, or it may issue separate checks to the suppliers and subcontractors directly. On large projects, the voucher system is usually supplemented by site inspections by the lender or an inspecting architect employed by the lender. None of these methods is foolproof, but they tend to discourage attempts by the developer to divert loan funds to non-construction uses.

 WESTLAW REFERENCES
developer contractor borrower /p construction /s loan
cite(12 +3 34.3 545.32 545.36)

---

§ 12.2   Construction Contracts and Bonds

Both of the topics covered in this section are very broad and can be treated only briefly here. They are mentioned primarily because of their relation to financing issues and in order to present a reasonably comprehensive picture of the construction process.

Construction Contracts

It is very rare for a landowner to have the skills and the personnel to construct substantial improvements on his land. Occasionally an owner will build his own house, but for larger projects, some form of

21. See Ridloff, Smoothing Out the Mechanics of Construction Loan Advances, 10 Real Est.Rev. 83 (No. 1, 1980); Hall, How to Build Lender Protection into Construction Loan Agreements, 6 Real Est.L.J. 21 (1977); Halper, People and Property: Controlling Construction Contractors, 10 Real Est.Rev. 74 (No. 1, 1980); Livingston, Current Business Approaches—Commercial Construction Lending, 13 Real Prop. Prob. & Tr.J. 791, 799–800 (1978); Walker v. First Pennsylvania Bank, 518 F.Supp. 347 (E.D.Pa.1981).

construction contracting is almost always necessary.[1] A principal decision which the owner must make is whether he should delegate total responsibility for construction to a single entity—a prime or general contractor—or whether he has the skill and time to assume overall management and should enter into separate contracts with those who will perform the major elements of work, such as structural, electrical, plumbing and heating, and the like. The separate contract system has several advantages: (1) The owner is given the opportunity to select individual firms which are, in his opinion, best qualified; (2) he can pay them directly for their work or arrange for disbursements to them from the construction lender, thereby obviating the possibility that the funds will be diverted by a general contractor; and (3) he need not be concerned that a general contractor will attempt to "squeeze" them to do more work for less money, increasing the general contractor's profits at the expense of quality.

Despite these advantages, the single contract system, involving a general contractor, is much more widely used. As suggested, the primary reason is that it permits full delegation of responsibility to a single entity to whom the owner can look in the event there are problems. If the general contractor is honest, competent, and financially responsible, the owner can sign the contract and then forget about the project until it is finished—in theory, at least. In major projects, the owner's architect or engineer will inspect the work frequently, call discrepancies to the general contractor's attention, and inform the owner if they are not corrected. Thus, the single contract system isolates the owner fairly well from continual administrative concerns with the construction work.

Pricing and Bidding

By far the most widely used pricing system is the fixed price or "lump sum" contract. The general contractor contracts that the project will be built for an agreed dollar figure. If the work costs less than anticipated, the contractor pockets the savings; if it costs more, his profits are reduced and he may ultimately sustain a loss. In principle, this provides maximum protection to the owner; in practice, however, if cost overruns threaten to force the general contractor into insolvency or induce him to abandon the project, the owner may be virtually compelled to increase the contract price; a lawsuit, particularly against a financially disabled contractor, is a poor substitute for a completed building.

§ 12.2

1. The discussion here draws upon J. Sweet, Legal Aspects of Architecture, Engineering, and the Construction Process 428–94 (3d Ed.1985). See also Sweet, Your First Construction Contract, 21 Prac.Law. 27 (No. 2, Mar. 1975); E. Colby, Practical Legal Advice for Builders and Contractors 19 (1972); Prac.L.Inst., Construction Contracts 1–58 (1977); Prac.L.Inst., Real Estate Construction Current Problems 45–174 (1973); Simpkin & Nielsen, The Rise of Project/Construction Management, 6 Real Est.Rev. 46 (No. 4, Winter 1977).

An alternative form of contract in fairly wide use is the "guaranteed maximum," in which the owner cannot be charged more than an agreed amount, but if the contractor's costs are lower than estimated, the owner and contractor share in the savings according to some agreed percentage—often 50–50. This gives the contractor an incentive to hold costs down, and at the same time protects the owner to some degree against extravagant overruns.

Another approach is the "cost-plus" contract, in which the owner agrees to pay the contractor's costs plus some agreed percentage or dollar amount. This sort of arrangement is rarely used in real estate development; unless coupled with some maximum or "upset" price it obviously has the potential for wreaking financial devastation on the owner, since it gives the contractor no incentive to watch his costs carefully. The cost-plus contract is usually found only in projects which are so unusual or technologically innovative that no reasonable advance estimate of their costs can be made.

All of the types of contracts discussed above may be entered into either through bidding or negotiation. Normally negotiation is feasible only if the owner or his staff are themselves quite skilled in construction matters; otherwise they will have difficulty in knowing whether the contractor's proposed price is a reasonable one. The competitive aspect of bidding tends to eliminate this problem. On the other hand, bidding has its disadvantages. It is often slower and requires more administrative effort to get the contract executed. Additionally, bidders may tend to reduce their bids below feasible levels in order to get the job, anticipating that they will be able to get additional money from the owner when it becomes apparent that the work cannot be completed for the original price. Nonetheless, in large projects bidding is more widely used than negotiation.

The owner usually solicits bids through some sort of invitation or advertisement. Often he will limit the invitations to contractors who, on the basis of reputation, experience, and financial position, appear to have the capacity to do the job well. Each prospective bidder will be given a package consisting of the complete plans, specifications, and drawings for the project; the proposed construction contract; and a set of rules outlining the bidding process itself—telling when bids are due, whether the owner is obligated to select the lowest (or any) bid, etc. Bidders may be required to post some security to assure that they will actually enter into the contract if their bid is accepted. All of these matters are often covered by statutes on public contracts, frequently in rather inflexible terms.

Obviously, bidding a general contract requires that detailed plans and specifications have first been developed. This is less true in a negotiated contract, in which the prospective contractor may actually work with the owner's architects and engineers in producing the final plans and specifications. A radically different approach is the "package" or "turnkey" contract, in which the owner provides merely a set of general performance specifications. The contractor is responsible for the detailed design as well as the construction of the buildings. In such a transaction he may even supply the land and may be expected to obtain his own financing during construction. In effect, the owner is purchasing a completed building which meets his needs and which was designed especially for him.

Construction bonds—An Introduction

Construction is a volatile and uncertain business; perhaps more than any other, it follows Murphy's Law: If anything can go wrong, it will.[2] Some types of problems are clearly attributable to the contractor: weak capitalization, poor planning or management, and outright dishonesty are illustrative. Other perils are beyond the contractor's control: strikes, shortages, natural disasters, concealed soil problems, changes in government regulations—all may slow construction or make it more costly. In many cases general contractors are financially weak and are unable to respond in damages even when it is clear that they have breached their contracts. Thus, owners and lenders frequently seek the participation of some financially responsible third party who can step in to rectify the contractor's breach or compensate them for the damage it causes.[3]

The third party is usually a commercial surety company, and the instrument which binds it is a surety bond. Several types of surety bonds are commonly used in construction. These are described below, but first some basic terminology is necessary.[4] In the usual case, it is the general contractor whose default is to be protected against;[5] he is termed the *principal*. The owner of the land on which the project is to be constructed, and who employs the contractor, is the *obligee*, for it is to him that the principal's obligation is owed. The *surety* is obligated to perform if the principal does not,[6] or to pay damages instead. The bond

---

2. An axiom of engineers and scientists whose origin is obscure; see American Heritage Dictionary of the English Language 863 (1973).

3. Bonds are often required by statute on public projects, but seldom on private work; an exception is Utah Code Ann. § 14–2–1.

4. See generally J. Sweet, Legal Aspects of Architecture, Engineering, and the Construction Process 363 (1970); Prac.L.Inst., Construction Default: The Contractor's Bond (1976); Surety Ass'n of America, Bonds of Suretyship (1959); R. Kratovil & R. Werner, Modern Mortgage Law & Practice § 25.27(f) (2d ed. 1981); G. Osborne, Law of Suretyship (1966); L. Simpson, Suretyship (1950); Hart & Kane, What Every Real Estate Lawyer Should Know About Payment and Performance Bonds, 17 Real Prop.Prob. & Tr.J. 674 (1982).

5. On a large project, the general contractor may also insist that the major subcontractors obtain bonds to protect him; in that case, the general contractor is the obligee and the subs are principals.

6. Technically, a surety's obligation may or may not be conditioned upon the default of the principal; if it is so conditioned, it is properly termed a guaranty. See L. Simpson, Suretyship §§ 4–6 (1950). The typical construction bond is conditioned upon the principal's default; see, e.g., American Institute of Architects Document A311, Performance Bond and Labor and Material Payment Bond, Feb. 1970 edition, reprinted in Prac.L.Inst., Real Estate Construction Current Problems 525–28 (1973).

will contain a *"penal sum,"* the maximum amount the surety company will be obliged to pay out. The amount is usually as high as the price affixed to the underlying contract between owner and contractor, but it may be less—perhaps only 50 percent or 25 percent. This is a point of negotiation between the contracting parties, except in some public or governmentally-financed projects, in which it is fixed by statute or regulation.[7]

Construction bonds are generally purchased directly by the contractor, who pays the premium (a lump sum amount) and who usually selects the surety (although the construction contract may give the owner a veto or approval power). The premium is usually stated as a percentage of the contract amount, which may vary with the size and type of project, as well as other factors, including the surety company's perception of the risk the particular contractor presents.[8] From the contractor's viewpoint, the bond premium is a cost of constructing the project, and he will therefore take it into account in preparing his bid on the job. The owner thus pays it indirectly. Some contractors may be deemed so unreliable, inexperienced, or financially weak that they cannot qualify for a bond from any company at any price; indeed, this is usually the case with small homebuilding companies, which consequently are seldom required by their customers to obtain bonds. In a project of substantial size, however, a prospective contractor's inability to obtain a bond is an important warning signal to the owner.[9]

Three principal types of bonds are used in the modern construction industry: the bid bond, the performance bond, and the payment bond. Each of these is explained briefly below.[10]

The bid bond. The purpose of this bond is to pay the damages if the contractor who is awarded the contract does not enter into it or if

7. See, e.g., the Miller Act, 40 U.S.C.A. § 270a–d (1964), requiring both a payment and a performance bond in federal construction projects; the amount of the latter is in the discretion of the contracting officer, but the payment bond is fixed by statute at 50 percent of the contract amount for contracts under $1 million, 40 percent for contracts between $1 million and $5 million, and $2.5 million for larger contracts.

8. A typical fee is 1 percent of the first $100,000 (of contract amount), 0.65 percent of the next $2.4 million, and 0.525 percent of the next $3.5 million. On this basis the fee for a $5 million bond would be $29,725. Both payment and performance bonds would be provided for this single fee; a bid bond, if required, would be priced and obtained separately. See Prac.L.Inst., Real Estate Construction Current Problems 231 (1973).

9. See Miller v. Safeco Title Ins. Co., 758 F.2d 364 (9th Cir.1985), in which the builder was unable to qualify for a commercial bond and gave a deed of trust on his home instead.

Sometimes an owner will attempt to save the expense of the bond by requiring that the contractor qualify for it and then waiving it. The thesis is that if the contractor qualifies, he is sufficiently responsible that the bond itself adds little to the owner's protection. If the surety's evaluation was incorrect in such a case, however, the owner will have learned a costly lesson. Id. at 213.

10. An excellent summary of these types of bonds and their legal aspects is Pierce, Rights and Responsibilities of the Contractor's Surety—What Happens When the Contractor Defaults, in Prac.L.Inst., Construction Contracts 435 (1977); see also Rodimer, Use of Bonds in Private Construction, 7 Forum 235 (1972).

he is unable to obtain the other bonds required for the job. In some cases a bid bond is not used; instead each bidder is required to post a cash deposit to assure that he will enter into the contract if he is selected. The bond, however, has the added advantage of serving as a screening mechanism, since bidders who are seriously underqualified probably will not be able to obtain bonds.

The amount of the claim which the owner may make in the event of a default varies with the provisions of the bond. In some cases the bond or the applicable statute provides that the entire penalty amount is forfeited, irrespective of the owner's ability to show actual damages in that amount.[11] Other bond forms limit the owner to actual damages,[12] with the penal sum as a maximum.[13]

In some circumstances the law will excuse a bidder from liability for an inadvertent mistake in his bid. Typically, the courts require proof that the mistake was unintentional and of substantial size, that the owner was notified of the mistake as early as possible, and that he will not be irreparably injured by the court's excusing the bidder.[14] In such cases, the owner is usually denied recovery, both against the bidder himself, and also upon the bid bond.[15] Such holdings follow the general rule that a surety can raise all defenses which would have been available to the principal.[16] From the owner's viewpoint, however, this doctrine makes the bid bond less satisfactory and inclusive than he would prefer.

The performance bond. In the event that the contractor fails to complete the project as agreed, the surety under a performance bond must make good his default. The surety usually has the option of taking over the construction and completing it (usually hiring a new general contractor) or of paying for the completion by the owner or a new general contractor hired by him.[17] The surety's liability, of course,

11. See, e.g., City of Lake Geneva v. States Improvement Co., 45 Wis.2d 50, 172 N.W.2d 176 (1969), holding valid as liquidated damages both bond and statutory clauses which provided for forfeiture of the full bond amount, irrespective of actual damages.

12. See Board of Education v. Sever-Williams Co., 22 Ohio St.2d 107, 258 N.E.2d 605 (1970), in which the bond's terms limited the obligee's recovery to its actual damages, measured by the difference between the bid amount and the amount of the contract ultimately entered into with another contractor.

13. The claim cannot exceed the penal sum, even if actual damages are greater. Bolivar Reorg. School District No. 1 v. American Surety Co., 307 S.W.2d 405 (Mo. 1957).

14. Ruggiero v. United States, 190 Ct. Cl. 327, 420 F.2d 709 (1970). See Smith &

Lowe Construction Co. v. Herrera, 79 N.M. 239, 442 P.2d 197 (1968); M. F. Kemper Construction Co. v. City of Los Angeles, 37 Cal.2d 696, 235 P.2d 7 (1951). Grimes & Walker, Unilateral Mistakes in Construction Bids: Methods of Proof and Theories of Recovery—A Modern Approach, 5 B.C. Indus. & Com.L.Rev. 213 (1964); Annot., 52 A.L.R.2d 792 (1957). Cf. Board of Education v. Sever-Williams Co., supra note 12.

15. White v. Berenda Mesa Water Dist., 7 Cal.App.3d 894, 87 Cal.Rptr. 338 (1970); See Boise Jr. College District v. Mattefs Construction Co., 92 Idaho 757, 450 P.2d 604 (1969).

16. See L. Simpson, Suretyship §§ 52–62 (1950).

17. But the owner can recover on the bond even if he does not in fact complete the project or correct the defects; see Lake View Trust v. Filmore Construction Co., 74

does not exceed the bond's penal sum. In addition, the surety has a legal right to the undisbursed portion of the contract price;[18] otherwise the owner would get a windfall, having his building completed without paying the price he originally agreed upon.

Common types of contractor defaults which will trigger the performance surety's obligation include serious delays in the scheduled progress of the work, deviation from the contract's plans and specifications,[19] abandonment by the contractor, and failure to pay for labor and materials in order to keep the property lien-free. Since the surety is only obligated to the performance originally agreed to by the contractor, not all problems in construction will necessarily give rise to bond claims. The construction contract or applicable law, for example, may excuse the builder (and the surety) for defaults resulting from natural calamities[20] or undisclosed subsoil conditions which make the project more costly.[21] The surety may have a defense based on the owner's fraud,[22] the illegality of the contract,[23] or most other standard contract defenses. The owner may also be denied recovery on the bond if he has failed to perform conditions precedent to the contractor's duties[24] or has made advances to the contractor without the surety's consent for work not yet done.[25] Such premature or excessive payments, particularly if they are not actually used in the construction work, harm the surety's position, both by reducing the contractor's incentive to perform and by diminishing the fund which will be available to complete the building if the contractor defaults.

Another defense available to the surety is the existence of facts, known to the owner and not revealed to the surety, which materially increase the risk of default. If the owner should have perceived the

Ill.App.3d 755, 30 Ill.Dec. 678, 393 N.E.2d 714 (1979).

18. Henningsen v. United States Fidelity & Guar. Co., 208 U.S. 404, 28 S.Ct. 389, 52 L.Ed. 547 (1908); Mid-Continent Cas. Co. v. First National Bank & Trust Co., 531 P.2d 1370 (Okl.1975).

19. See, e.g. Carrols Equities Corp. v. Villnave, 57 A.D.2d 1044, 395 N.Y.S.2d 800 (1977), appeal denied 42 N.Y.2d 810, 399 N.Y.S.2d 1026, 369 N.E.2d 775 (1977).

20. See Barnard-Curtiss Co. v. United States, 257 F.2d 565 (10th Cir.1958), certiorari denied 358 U.S. 906, 79 S.Ct. 230, 3 L.Ed.2d 227, and 358 U.S. 906, 79 S.Ct. 233, 3 L.Ed.2d 227 (1958); cf. Barnard-Curtiss Co. v. United States, 157 Ct.Cl. 103, 301 F.2d 909 (1962).

21. See Scherrer Construction Co. v. Burlington Memorial Hospital, 64 Wis.2d 720, 221 N.W.2d 855 (1974).

22. See United Bonding Insurance Co. v. Donaldson Engineering, Inc., 222 So.2d 447 (Fla.App.1969).

23. See Wheaton v. Ramsey, 92 Idaho 33, 436 P.2d 248 (1968); Medina v. Title Guaranty & Surety Co., 152 App.Div. 307, 136 N.Y.S. 786 (1912), affirmed 211 N.Y. 24, 104 N.E. 1118 (1914).

24. See Kanters v. Kotick, 102 Wash. 523, 173 P. 329 (1918).

25. National American Bank v. Southcoast Contractors, Inc., 276 So.2d 777 (La.App.1973), writ refused 279 So.2d 694 (La.1973); Gibbs v. Hartford Accident & Indemnity Co., 62 So.2d 599 (Fla.1952); Pacific Coast Engineering Co. v. Detroit Fidelity & Surety Co., 214 Cal. 384, 5 P.2d 888 (1931). The more recent cases tend to discharge the surety only pro tanto, to the extent of the harm caused by the advance payment; see Restatement, Security § 128(b)(ii) (1941); L. Simpson, Suretyship § 78 (1950). Some cases treat advance payments as a species of the contract modification problem (see text at note 27, infra), but this may be misleading; the discharge occurs even if the overpayment was unilateral and voluntary.

increased risk, realized that the facts were unknown to the surety, and had a reasonable opportunity to reveal them, his inaction may bar his recovery on the bond.[26]

A recurring problem in the enforcement of performance bonds is the modification of construction contracts as work progresses. In every large project numerous changes are made as a result of unavailability of materials, impracticalities in the original design, or innovations which will improve the building's usefulness. Traditionally the law of suretyship provided for a complete release of the surety in the event of any unconsented material alteration in the principal's contract with the obligee.[27] In theory, the modification increased the surety's risk unjustifiably. Courts today have grown less receptive to this doctrine. Only major changes in the scope of work are likely to result in a release of the surety, and even then, it will probably be held a pro tanto release, only to the extent that the change caused damage to the surety, rather than a complete discharge.[28] Additionally, many performance bonds contain language which expressly permits changes in details of the project, so long as the overall concept remains the same.[29]

The performance bond should not be confused with the completion bond, an instrument which is now largely obsolete. The completion bond differs in two important respects.[30] First, the surety is absolutely bound to complete the project; it has no option to pay a penal amount to the obligee instead. Second, completion bonds are normally written in favor of lending institutions and obligate the surety irrespective of the performance or good faith of the owner himself. Thus, the surety is bound even if the owner has squandered or diverted the construction funds. The obvious risks associated with this sort of instrument have led most commercial sureties to discontinue issuing them.

The payment bond. This is an undertaking by the surety that all persons supplying labor or materials to the project will be paid. It is

---

26. See Sumitomo Bank v. Iwasaki, 70 Cal.2d 81, 73 Cal.Rptr. 564, 447 P.2d 956 (1968); Rocky Mountain Tool & Machine Co. v. Tecon Corp., 371 F.2d 589 (10th Cir. 1966).

27. See United States v. Freel, 186 U.S. 309, 22 S.Ct. 875, 46 L.Ed. 1177 (1902); William J. Morris, Inc. v. Lanzilotta & Teramo Construction Corp., 63 A.D.2d 969, 405 N.Y.S.2d 508 (1978), affirmed 47 N.Y.2d 901, 419 N.Y.S.2d 494, 393 N.E.2d 488 (1979).

28. See, e.g., Carrols Equities Corp. v. Villnave, supra note 19; McLaughlin Electric Supply v. American Empire Insurance Co., 269 N.W.2d 766 (S.D.1978); Zuni Construction Co. v. Great American Insurance Co., 86 Nev. 364, 468 P.2d 980 (1970); Verdugo Highlands, Inc. v. Security Insurance Co., 240 Cal.App.2d 527, 49 Cal.Rptr. 736 (1966); Hochevar v. Maryland Casual-

ty Co., 114 F.2d 948 (6th Cir.1940); cf. Brunswick Nursing & Convalescent Center, Inc. v. Great American Insurance Co., 308 F.Supp. 297 (S.D.Ga.1970). See Restatement, Security § 128(b) (1941).

29. See, e.g., the unusually pro-obligee language in the performance bond appearing at Prac.L.Inst., Real Estate Construction Current Problems 522–25 (1973):

The Surety hereby waives notice of any and all modifications, omissions, additions, changes and advance or deferred payments in and about the Agreement and agrees that the obligations of this Bond shall not be impaired in any manner by reason of any such modifications, omissions, additions, changes or advanced or deferred payments.

30. Id. at 224, 229–30.

arguable that the contractor's duty to pay such persons is a part of his obligation under the construction contract and hence is guaranteed by the performance bond.[31] However, the payment bond obviates the need for this argument and also makes it clear that subcontractors and material suppliers themselves may bring an action on the bond.[32] Thus the bond serves two purposes: it assures the owner a lien-free project, and it induces suppliers and subcontractors to accept work on the project, perhaps at a lower price, because of the assurance that they will be paid. Since no additional charge is generally made for a payment bond when a performance bond is being purchased, the two are usually issued simultaneously.

In public projects, in which the filing of mechanics and materialmen's liens is usually prohibited, the payment bond is even more important and is frequently required by statute.[33] It provides a fund for payment if the general contractor has been dishonest, and thus avoids petitions by subcontractors to legislative bodies for more money to cover the contractor's default.

It is necessary for the payment bond to define the extent of its coverage in terms of layers of subcontractors and suppliers. The 1970 AIA form, for example, defines a "claimant" as "one having a direct contract with the Principal or with a Subcontractor of the Principal for labor, material, or both * * *."[34] Thus, second-tier claimants (sub-subs) are covered, while third-tier claimants (sub-sub-subs) are not.

The payment bond surety is generally entitled to raise as against the owner-obligee the various defenses discussed above in connection with performance bonds. Against third-party beneficiaries of the bond, such as subcontractors and suppliers, however, it is likely that only defenses as to which the claimant has some fault can be asserted. For example, a subcontractor can generally maintain an action on a payment bond despite the fraud of the general contractor or the owner in inducing the surety to write the bond, or the default of the owner in complying with the bond's terms.[35]

---

31. See Cretex Companies v. Construction Leaders, Inc., 342 N.W.2d 135 (Minn. 1984); Dealers Electrical Supply v. United States Fidelity & Guaranty Co., 199 Neb. 269, 258 N.W.2d 131 (1977); Amelco Window Corp. v. Federal Insurance Co., 127 N.J.Super. 342, 317 A.2d 398 (1974); Restatement, Security § 166 (1941).

32. See R. C. Mahon Co. v. Hedrich Construction Co., 69 Wis.2d 456, 230 N.W.2d 621 (1975); Byler v. Great American Insurance Co., 395 F.2d 273 (10th Cir. 1968); Restatement, Security § 165 (1941). There is no necessity that the claimant even knew of the bond at the time he supplied his work or materials; Air Temperature, Inc. v. Morris, 469 S.W.2d 495 (Tenn.App.1970). See also Sukut-Coulson,

Inc. v. Allied Canon Co., 85 Cal.App.3d 648, 149 Cal.Rptr. 711 (1978) (public project).

33. See Cedar Vale Co-op Exch. v. Allen Utilities, Inc., 10 Kan.App.2d 129, 694 P.2d 903 (1985); note 7, supra.

34. See note 6, supra.

35. See United States Fidelity & Guaranty Co. v. Borden Metal Products Co., 539 S.W.2d 170 (Tex.Civ.App.1976); Guin & Hunt, Inc. v. Hughes Supply, Inc., 335 So. 2d 842 (Fla.App.1976); Filippi v. McMartin, 188 Cal.App.2d 135, 10 Cal.Rptr. 180 (1961); Williams v. Baldwin, 228 S.W. 554 (Tex.Comm.App.1921); Culligan Corp. v. Transamerica Insurance Co., 580 F.2d 251 (7th Cir.1978).

The dual obligee bond. Construction lenders sometimes feel a need for the same type of protection which performance and payment bonds afford to owners. The dual obligee bond, which names both the lender and the owner as obligees, accomplishes this.[36] However, nearly every dual obligee bond contains a so-called "savings clause" or "Los Angeles clause," which in substance provides that any default by either obligee will release the surety from its obligation to both.[37] The surety's main concern here is the same as that which led to the disuse of the completion bond—that one of the obligees will interfere with the flow of funds to the contractor. The surety fears that the construction lender might refuse to make proper disbursements, or the owner might intercept disbursements and divert them. The consequence of the savings clause is that the dual obligee bond protects the lender against the defaults of the contractor, but not those of the owner. This fact has great impact, since trouble on the job may well lead the owner to commit a technical default as well: he may advance funds to the contractor prematurely, or may grant a contract modification or extension of time without the surety's consent. Although there are few cases,[38] it seems probable that under the savings clause this sort of behavior will discharge the surety (at least pro tanto, and perhaps absolutely) as to both obligees. To the lender, then, the dual obligee bond does not constitute very adequate protection.[39]

Surety's priority in undisbursed funds. Space does not permit comprehensive treatment here of another common problem with con-

---

36. Other parties may also be made obligees, although the practice is infrequent: a title company, a major tenant of the project, or a permanent lender. See Leake, Contract Bond Co-obligees—Rights and Responsibilities, 37 Ins.Counsel J. 554 (1970).

37. A simple, although quite ambiguous, form of the clause states:

Any default by either or both of the obligees will automatically relieve the principal and the surety from the performance of the contract.

A more comprehensive form is:

The surety shall not be liable under this bond to the obligees, or either of them unless the said obligees, or either of them, shall make payments to the principal, strictly in accordance with the terms of said contract as to payments and shall perform all other obligations to be performed under said contract at the time and in the manner therein set forth.

The latter clause above was used in the bond litigated in New Amsterdam Casualty Co. v. Bettes, 407 S.W.2d 307 (Tex.Civ.App. 1966). See R. Kratovil & R. Werner, Mod-

ern Mortgage Law & Practice § 25.27(f)(1) (2d ed. 1981); Robinson, The Multiple Obligee Construction Bond: A Problem for the Surety, 15 So.Tex.L.J. 181 (1974); Franklin, Dual Obligee Bond—What Constitutes "Default" of an Obligee, 17 Federation Ins. Coun.Q. 51 (No. 4, Summer 1967).

38. In New Amsterdam Casualty Co. v. Bettes, 407 S.W.2d 307 (Tex.Civ.App.1966), the court held that the owner's knowledge that funds were being disbursed to the contractor on the basis of falsified affidavits would not be attributable to the lender; thus, the lender's rights against the surety on the dual obligee bond were preserved.

39. See Kratovil & Werner, Mortgages for Construction and the Lien Priorities Problem—the "Unobligatory" Advance, 41 Tenn.L.Rev. 311, 321 (1974); sources cited note 37, supra.

The loss of coverage is only as to the performance aspect of the bond, and not as to the payment aspect; see Aetna Insurance Co. v. Maryland Cast Stone Co., 254 Md. 109, 253 A.2d 872 (1969); Elliott, Dual Obligee Bonds—Some Practical and Legal Considerations, 11 The Forum 1229 (1976).

struction bonds: the priority as between the surety and other claimants with respect to the undisbursed construction funds. Frequently the other claimant is a lending institution (not the construction lender) which has advanced money to the contractor. The issue may arise as follows. The contractor is midway through the project and finds that, despite the receipt of regular progress payments from the owner or construction lender, he is unable to meet his obligations to his workers or suppliers. To solve this problem he obtains a bank loan, assigning as security for its repayment the payments he expects to receive in the future from the owner. Subsequently he is unable to complete the job or to pay his subcontractors, and the surety steps in and does so. As between the surety and the bank, which is entitled to first priority in the remainder of the contract price, as represented by the balance in the construction loan account?

In Prairie State Bank v. United States,[40] the Supreme Court held for the surety on similar facts, reasoning that the surety was subrogated to the rights of the owner against the defaulting contractor, and that this subrogation dated, in effect, from the time the contract and bond were signed, thus being prior to the bank's assignment.[41] The bank's argument, however, is also appealing, particularly if it can show that the loan it made was used to pay for labor or materials on the job, and perhaps was even required by the bank to be so used. On these facts, the bank loan has reduced the surety's potential liability. This argument, however, is typically rejected on the ground that the bank was a mere volunteer in this role, while the surety was contractually bound by its bond.

While the federal courts have followed *Prairie* quite consistently,[42] state courts have shown more variability. Surveying these cases, one commentator concluded that "while the surety generally wins, assignee banks prevail just often enough to maintain the flow of litigation."[43] It

---

40. 164 U.S. 227, 17 S.Ct. 142, 41 L.Ed. 412 (1896). See also Henningsen v. United States Fidelity & Guaranty Co., 208 U.S. 404, 28 S.Ct. 389, 52 L.Ed. 547 (1908) and Pearlman v. Reliance Ins. Co., 371 U.S. 132, 83 S.Ct. 232, 9 L.Ed.2d 190 (1962), reaffirming the rule of *Prairie*. The development of the law in the federal courts is well summarized in American Fidelity Fire Insurance Co. v. Construcciones Werl, 407 F.Supp. 164, 191–97 (D.St.Croix 1975). See also Mungall, The Buffeting of the Subrogation Rights of the Construction Contract Bond Surety by United States v. Munsey Trust Co., 46 Ins.Couns.J. 607 (1979); Dauer, Government Contractors, Commercial Banks, and Miller Act Bond Sureties— A Question of Priorities, 14 B.C.Indus. & Com.L.Rev. 943 (1973); Rudolph, Financing on Construction Contracts Under the Uniform Commercial Code, 5 B.C.Indus. & Com.L.Rev. 245 (1964); Jordan, The Rights

of a Surety Upon the Default of its Contractor-Principal, 41 Ore.L.Rev. 1 (1961).

41. The bond or bond application will frequently contain language by which the contractor purports to assign to the surety the funds he expects to receive under the contract, but even in the absence of such language the subrogation theory of *Prairie* still obtains.

42. See, e.g., Great American Insurance Co. v. United States, 203 Ct.Cl. 592, 492 F.2d 821 (1974); Framingham Trust Co. v. Gould-National Batteries, Inc., 427 F.2d 856 (1st Cir.1970); American Fidelity Fire Insurance Co. v. Construcciones Werl, supra note 40 and cases cited therein.

43. Rudolph, Financing on Construction Contracts Under the Uniform Commercial Code, 5 B.C.Indus. & Com.L.Rev. 245 (1964); see First Vermont Bank v. Village now is settled that the surety need not file a financing statement under the Uniform Commercial Code, even if the competing creditor does so.[44] Cases sometimes turn on whether the surety knew of or approved the obtaining of the bank loan, whether the fund being contested consists of percentage retainages or of earned but undisbursed progress payments, whether the bank insisted that its loan be used on the job, or whether the project is public or private.[45] Since both claimants are innocent, and both have contributed to the completion of the work, a choice between them is difficult.

The surety may sometimes find itself in a contest with others for the undisbursed contract funds. Mechanic's and materialmen's lien claimants may assert a priority, particularly in those states which give such claimants a statutory right in the undisbursed contract funds.[46] Other creditors of the contractor may make similar claims; even the owner himself may seek a setoff against the contract price, perhaps because of defective work done or damage caused by the contractor.[47] Again, these cases defy generalization, and the reader is referred to detailed discussions of them in the literature.[48]

 WESTLAW REFERENCES

construction   /s   bid contract agreement   /p   mistake

construction   /s   contract agreement bond   /s   performance bid
       payment "dual obligee"   /p   default*** damag***   /p   surety
       subrogat***

---

of Poultney, 134 Vt. 28, 349 A.2d 722 (1975).

44. See First Alabama Bank v. Hartford Accident & Indemnity Co., Inc., 430 F.Supp. 907 (N.D.Ala.1977); Finance Co. of America v. United States Fidelity & Guaranty Co., 277 Md. 177, 353 A.2d 249 (1976); Argonaut Insurance Co. v. C and S Bank of Tipton, 140 Ga.App. 807, 232 S.E.2d 135 (1976); cf. United States Fidelity & Guaranty Co. v. Leach, 438 F.Supp. 295 (M.D. Ga.1977). See Note, Equitable Subrogation—Too Hardy a Plant to be Uprooted by Article 9 of the U.C.C.? 32 U. of Pitts.L.R. 580 (1971).

45. See Rudolph, supra note 43 at 248–49. See, e.g., Fidelity & Casualty Co. of New York v. Central Bank of Birmingham, 409 So.2d 788 (Ala.1982); Himes v. Cameron County Construction Corp., 289 Pa. Super. 143, 432 A.2d 1092 (1981), affirmed 497 Pa. 637, 444 A.2d 98 (1982); First National Bank v. McHasco Electric, Inc., 273 Minn. 407, 141 N.W.2d 491 (1966). In National Surety Co. v. State National Bank,

454 S.W.2d 354 (Ky.App.1970), the court held for the assignee bank on the ground that the surety had acquiesced in the contractor's seeking the bank loan, which occurred after the surety had taken over the project.

46. See General Acrylics v. United States Fidelity & Guaranty Co., 128 Ariz. 50, 623 P.2d 839 (App.1980); § 12.4, infra.

47. In United States v. Munsey Trust Co., 332 U.S. 234, 67 S.Ct. 1599, 91 L.Ed. 2022 (1947), the Court held that the set-off claim of the United States as owner had priority over the claim of the surety; see Mungall, supra note 40; see also Fireman's Insurance Co. v. New York, 91 Misc.2d 183, 397 N.Y.S.2d 524 (1977), affirmed 65 A.D.2d 241, 412 N.Y.S.2d 206 (1979); Safeco Insurance Co. v. State, 89 Misc.2d 864, 392 N.Y.S.2d 976 (1977); American Fidelity Fire Insurance Co. v. Construcciones Werl, supra note 40 and cases cited therein.

48. See sources cited note 40 supra.

§ 12.3   Mortgage Loan Commitments

A loan commitment is a promise by a lender to make a loan at some future time. Both construction and permanent loans are frequently preceded by written commitments.[1] For the developer of a new project, the construction loan commitment is a signal that the search for construction financing is over. Before the commitment is issued, the developer has usually completed most or all of the other arrangements for construction, including land acquisition, basic project design, and the preliminary negotiation of the construction contract. Construction will typically commence within a short time after the commitment is issued, after the developer has made whatever modifications and final touches the committing lender requires.

The permanent loan commitment, a promise by a lender to make a long-term loan on the property when construction is completed, is of critical importance. From the developer's viewpoint, it represents assurance that marketing of the project can be financed (if sales-type development, such as a residential subdivision, is involved), or that funds will be available to pay the construction loan when it is due at the time of completion. This sort of assurance is at least as important to the construction lender as to the developer. As a result of regulatory requirements,[2] internal policies, or both, the great majority of construction lenders will not issue *their* commitment until a permanent or "take-out" loan commitment has first been obtained.[3] The permanent commitment may call either for payoff of the construction loan

---

§ 12.3

1. Calif.Cont.Ed. of Bar, California Real Estate Sales Transactions § 10.42 (1967). A writing is probably required under the Statute of Frauds in most jurisdictions; compare United of Omaha Life Insurance Co. v. Nob Hill Associates, 450 So.2d 536 (Fla.App.1984), petition for review dismissed 458 So.2d 273 (1984), petition for review denied 458 So.2d 274 (1984) and Fremming Construction Co. v. Security Savings & Loan Ass'n, 115 Ariz. 514, 566 P.2d 315 (1977), with Martyn v. First Federal Savings & Loan Association, 257 So.2d 576 (Fla.App.1971). See also Silverdale Hotel Associates v. Lomas & Nettleton Co., 36 Wm.App. 762, 677 P.2d 773 (1984) (parol testimony admitted to supplement written agreement). Even an oral commitment may be used by the borrower to show that the terms of the written note and mortgage differ from the parties' actual agreement and hence are unenforceable; see Peoples Trust & Savings Bank v. Humphrey, — Ind.App. —, 451 N.E.2d 1104 (1983).

The person issuing the commitment must be authorized to do so; Labor Discount Center, Inc. v. State Bank & Trust Co., 526 S.W.2d 407 (Mo.App.1975). In

Walter Harvey Corp. v. O'Keefe, 346 So.2d 617 (Fla.App.1977), the construction lender advanced an additional $450,000, over and above its original loan commitment, in order to cover cost overruns. Even this amount was not sufficient to complete the project, and the developer claimed that the lender was legally obligated to advance even more funds. The court held that the making of one optional advance did not impliedly obligate the lender to make another, and that the lender was entitled to foreclose.

2. See, e.g., N.Y.—McKinney's Banking Law § 103:4(c)(3)(iv); § 12.1 at notes 5–10 supra.

3. See Texas Bank v. Lone Star Life Insurance Co., 565 S.W.2d 353 (Tex.Civ. App.1978); Ridloff, A Construction Lender Looks at Permanent Loan Commitments, 10 Real Est.Rev. 60 (No. 2, 1980); Haggerty, Procedures, Forms and Safeguards in Construction Lending with a Permanent Takeout, 85 Bank.L.J. 1035 (1968). Alternatively, the construction lender may accept a commitment from a high-credit purchaser to *buy* the project (not merely the mortgage) upon completion.

and execution of a new note and mortgage, or for the permanent lender to purchase the construction loan, under a "buy-sell agreement", when construction is completed.[4]

The permanent loan commitment will usually be based on the same underwriting considerations as the construction loan: the borrower's credit, the project's design and technical feasibility, an appraisal of its completed value and marketability, and the satisfaction of various title and other legal requirements.[5] Neither the construction nor permanent lender can afford to leave the evaluation of these matters to the other; both must do a thorough underwriting job if they are prudent, since it is impossible to tell at the commitment stage which of them might eventually foreclose on the property. The requirements of the two lenders must not be inconsistent, and the construction commitment will usually require that the developer comply with all terms of the permanent commitment.

In most cases the construction lender will seek to have the permanent loan commitment assigned to it. Ideally, the construction lender would prefer this assignment to be sufficiently broad that, in the event the construction loan is foreclosed and it winds up owning and completing the project, it will be able to enforce the permanent loan commitment and demand funding of the permanent loan. The permanent lender, however, may resist approving such an assignment. Even a less extensive assignment is useful, since it can ensure that no renegotiation of the permanent loan commitment occurs without the construction lender's approval. The assignment may also have the effect of allowing the construction lender to cure any default by the borrower, a very useful right if the default would otherwise excuse the permanent lender from its commitment.[6]

Loan commitments are usually hedged with numerous conditions to protect the lender's interests.[7] In a sales-type project such as a subdivision or a condominium, the evaluation of the credit-worthiness of the future purchasers of the units is impossible at the outset of construction; thus the permanent loan commitment for such a project

---

4. See text at notes 36–38 infra; Douglas v. United States, 217 Ct.Cl. 97, 576 F.2d 887 (1978); BA Mortgage Co. v. Unisal Development, Inc., 469 F.Supp. 1258 (D.Colo.1979). For an illustrative buy-sell agreement, see ALI–ABA, Modern Real Estate Transactions 324 (5th ed. 1984); Berks Title Ins. Co. v. Haendiges, 591 F.Supp. 879 (N.D.Ohio 1984).

5. See United California Bank v. Prudential Insurance Co., 140 Ariz. 238, 681 P.2d 390 (1983); § 12.1 at note 17 supra.

6. See Ridloff, A Checklist for the Construction Lender's Attorney, 11 Real Est. Rev. 103 (No. 4, 1982); Ridloff, A Sample Construction Loan Commitment, 10 Real Est.Rev. 87 (No. 4, 1981). Cf. American

Fletcher Mortgage Co. v. First American Investment Corp., 463 F.Supp. 186 (N.D. Ga.1978) (construction lender is not third-party beneficiary of standby commitment and cannot recover for its breach).

7. See Walsh, A Practical Guide to Mortgage Loan Commitments, 8 Real Est. L.J. 195 (1980); Garfinkel, Negotiation of Construction and Permanent Loan Commitments, 25 Prac.Law 13 (Mar.1979), 37 (Apr.1979); R. Kratovil, Modern Real Estate Documentation 185–197 (1975); ALI–ABA, Modern Real Estate Transactions 267 (5th ed. 1984) (document prepared by Noel R. Nellis); Ridloff, A Sample Construction Loan Commitment, supra note 6.

is invariably conditioned upon the purchasers' compliance with the lender's customary standards (which may be articulated in the commitment itself), or the standards of the Federal Housing Administration or other insurance or guaranty agency.[8] Other common conditions include submission to the lender of final plans and specifications (if the commitment is issued on the basis of preliminary versions or if the lender has required changes) and submission of other documentation, including the executed construction contract, the documents creating the developer entity (if a corporation, partnership, or trust), leases executed by the major tenants, the title insurance report and binder, the permanent loan commitment if a construction loan is being made, fire and hazard insurance policies, the building permit, and perhaps an opinion of counsel respecting the validity of the developer entity's creation, its power to undertake the project, and the validity of the other documents. In a permanent loan commitment on a project to be built, lien-free completion in accordance with the agreed plans and specifications will be made a condition.[9]

The permanent commitment on a rental project, such as an apartment building or office building, may also be conditioned upon some specified fraction of the project being rented. More complex arrangements are sometimes used, so that a portion of the permanent loan will be funded at a given rental level (the "floor"), and the remainder when a higher rental level (the "ceiling") has been achieved.[10] Obviously a permanent commitment conditioned upon rent-up is less satisfactory to the construction lender than an unconditional commitment, but such conditions are commonly accepted. If the construction lender demands payment before a sufficient number of tenants has been found to meet the permanent lender's rent roll requirements, the developer may be able to obtain an interim or "bridge" loan to carry him through the rent-up period.

A permanent loan commitment will often be conditioned on the developer's continued solvency during the construction period, or that

8. The FHA itself issues conditional commitments to insure permanent loans based on its approval of plans and specifications and its inspections as houses are constructed. The relevant form, FHA 2800–5, provides:

> "The mortgage amount and term set forth in the heading are the maximum approved for this property assuming a satisfactory owner-occupant mortgagor. The maximum amount and term in the heading may be changed depending upon FHA's rating of the borrower, his income and credit. * * * A firm commitment to insure a loan will be issued upon receipt of an Application for Credit Approval, FHA form 2900, executed by an approved mortgagee and a borrower satisfactory to the Commissioner."

9. See United California Bank v. Prudential Insurance Co., supra note 4, construing the commitment to require only a title insurance policy insuring a first lien, rather than a first lien in fact.

In general, substantial rather than strict performance is sufficient; see First National State Bank v. Commonwealth Federal Savings & Loan Association, 610 F.2d 164 (3d Cir.1979); Whalen v. Ford Motor Co., 475 F.Supp. 537 (D.Md.1979). See Ridloff, supra note 3, at 61.

10. See Brown-Marx Associates v. Emigrant Savings Bank, 703 F.2d 1361 (11th Cir.1983) (strict rather than substantial performance of rental levels required.)

his financial condition not suffer any "material adverse change." [11] The commitment will, of course, fully identify the project and the parties, including the general contractor, if any. It will state the amount of the loan and the period within which the loan closing must occur. The plans and specifications, the construction loan agreement, and the form of note and mortgage which the lender proposes to require will usually be incorporated by reference in the commitment on a construction loan. The interest rate and fees to be charged for the loan will be specified, as well as the fee for the commitment itself. Such fees vary with the duration, type, and amount of the commitment, but are frequently in the 1 to 2 percent range. In some cases permanent loan commitments on residential subdivisions are issued and are acceptable to construction lenders without stipulation of the interest rate. Since such commitments do not shift the risk of fluctuating rates to the permanent lender, they may be obtained at a lower cost than is usually charged for a fixed-interest commitment and may even be issued free or at a nominal charge.

Many lenders who issue fixed-interest permanent loan commitments on housing do so on the basis of commitments which they, in turn, have obtained from the Federal National Mortgage Association (FNMA) or the Federal Home Loan Mortgage Corporation (FHLMC). Both of these federally-chartered organizations give advance commitments to local lenders to purchase mortgages in the future. A lender who has such commitments can make equivalent commitments to its loan customers, secure in the knowledge that the mortgages, when originated, can be resold immediately on the secondary market at a known price.[12]

FNMA and FHLMC issue both mandatory commitments, under which the originating lender is contractually bound to deliver the mortgages to the secondary market purchaser, and optional commitments, under which the lender is under no obligation to deliver the loans. The optional commitments extend over longer time periods, and are mainly intended to allow the lender to offer commitments to residential builders to cover purchase loans for their home-buying customers.

In the past both FNMA and FHLMC have used a "free market auction" system for determining the yields (or effective interest rates) [13]

---

11. See Mellon Bank v. Aetna Business Credit, Inc., 619 F.2d 1001 (3d Cir.1980); Ridloff, supra note 3.

12. For a more complete discussion of these agencies and their operations in the secondary mortgage market, see § 11.3 supra; Garrett, How Home Builders Use Conventional Forward Take-out Commitments, 10 Real Est.Rev. 72 (No. 4, Winter 1981).

13. Note that this effective yield is normally higher than the contract interest rate shown on the face of the promissory note signed by the borrower. The loan will ordinarily be sold to FNMA or FHLMC at a discount—that is, an amount lower than the loan's original or outstanding balance. The effect of the discount is to raise the effective yield to FNMA or FHLMC above the contract rate. A standard formula is used to convert yields on loans sold on the secondary market into equivalent discount prices. The prices are often expressed as percentages of face amount. Thus, if at which they will make commitments. These auctions were conducted on announced days at regular intervals by telephone; lenders called and offered to sell mortgages at specified yields, and the secondary market agency then decided how many such offers to accept, starting, of course, with those carrying the highest yields. Neither FHMA nor FHLMC is presently using an auction system; instead, both agencies simply establish and announce periodically the yields at which they will issue commitments to buy mortgage loans of various types.

The agencies offer commitments under a variety of programs. Since they change frequently, the descriptions below are somewhat simplified and should be taken only as illustrative. FHLMC issues mandatory delivery commitments for periods of 30 to 120 days; required yields are announced and offers are accepted daily. No commitment fee is charged. FHLMC also offers optional delivery commitments for 120 to 240 days. Yields are announced and offers accepted weekly, and a commitment fee must be paid.[14]

FNMA has a similar set of commitment programs.[15] Those requiring mandatory delivery may run for periods of 30 or 60 days, or 3 or 4 months in the case of adjustable rate loans (ARM's). Four-month commitments are also available for ARM's on an optional delivery basis. In addition, FNMA offers 9-month or 12-month "stand-by" commitments, designed mainly for home-builders, which have no specific interest yield attached to them. Any part or all of such a commitment can be converted by the lender to a mandatory delivery commitment of the types described above at any time during the 9 month or 12 month period. The yield in effect for the particular type of mortgage at

FNMA pays a price of 95 on a $80,000 mortgage, the dollar price would be $76,000 and the loan is said to be sold at a "five point" discount. The conversion formula for most loan programs is based on the assumption that the loan will be prepaid in 12 years from the date its first payment is due.

To illustrate formula's operation, assume a 30-year fixed-rate loan of $80,000 is made at a contract interest rate of 12%. Such a loan will require monthly payments of $822.89, and after 12 years will have an outstanding balance of 72,697. Assume also that the yield required by FNMA when it purchases the loan is 13%. The applicable formula simply computes the present value (at a 13% rate) of (a) the right to receive the regular monthly payments on the loan until it is 12 years old, plus (b) the right to receive the outstanding balance on the loan when it is 12 years old. Thus:

Present value of right to receive $822.89 per month for 12 years	= $59,863
Present value of right to receive $72,697 12 years in the future	= $15,405
TOTAL price paid by FNMA	= $75,268

Thus, in this example the discount would be $4,732, or 5.92 "points" on the $80,000 loan. The procedure for computing secondary market prices on adjustable rate loans is somewhat more complex. See generally FNMA, Selling Guide § 301 (1984). The originating lender normally does not absorb the discount, but instead passes it on (along with any commitment fee it has paid) to the borrower, builder, or seller of the property. For a discussion of legal limitations on the imposition of the discount on the borrower in VA-guaranteed loans, see § 11.2, supra.

14. See FHLMC, Freddie Mac Essentials (Publication No. 14, 1983).

15. See FNMA, Selling Guide §§ 202, 304, 504 (1984).

the time of the conversion becomes applicable. Commitment fees are charged by FNMA for all of its types of commitments.

The standby commitment concept is not limited to FNMA or to home loans on subdivision tracts. In commercial or income-producing properties as well, the developer may seek a standby commitment from an interim lender on very onerous terms in order to give himself more time to locate permanent financing.[16] The standby commitment will often carry a costly fee, as much as 3 to 5 percent of the amount committed, and will bear a high interest rate and a short maturity if it is ever actually funded. But its real purpose is to satisfy the construction lender's requirement that a take-out commitment exist; the developer has no intention of using it. He may well feel that more attractive permanent financing will be available when construction is completed, either because of changes in money market conditions or because the building will then be fully built and rented and thus appear less risky to a permanent lender. The standby lender's position is obviously risky, and this fact accounts for the high cost of his involvement. Sometimes a construction lender will itself issue a standby commitment as well; in substance, this is its way of contracting for substantially increased interest and fees if the construction loan is not paid off immediately upon completion.[17]

Lender's fees and enforcement rights. The cost to the prospective borrower of obtaining a loan commitment varies widely. On permanent commitments for existing owner-occupied houses, some lenders charge nothing and others charge only an appraisal fee of, say $50 to $200. At the other extreme are construction and permanent loan commitments on large income-producing properties where the borrower will usually be required to cover all of the lender's out-of-pocket costs, such as the appraiser's, attorney's, architect's and engineer's fees. These fees are typically nonrefundable, irrespective of whether a satisfactory commitment is ever issued or a loan ever made. Since such fees can add up substantially, a developer is often well-advised to obtain the appraisal as early as possible, so that he can seek other financing without much loss if the appraisal is too low to make possible an attractive loan.[18]

Another type of fee, which must be paid by the borrower upon the issuance of the commitment, is the nonrefundable commitment fee. Its apparent purpose is to compensate the lender for the opportunity cost and administrative burden of underwriting the loan and holding the funds available for the borrower's use.[19]

---

16. See, e.g., B.F. Saul Real Est. Inv. Trust v. McGovern, 683 S.W.2d 531 (Tex.App.1984); Hidalgo Properties, Inc. v. Wachovia Mortgage Co., 617 F.2d 196 (10th Cir.1980); Prac.L.Inst., Real Estate Financing: Contemporary Techniques 313 (No. 14, 1973).

17. See Prac.L.Inst., Real Estate Construction 225 (No. 5, 1969).

18. R. Kratovil, Modern Real Estate Documentation § 434 (1975).

19. See First National Mortgage Co. v. Arkmo Lumber & Supply Co., 277 Ark. 298, 641 S.W.2d 31 (1982), holding such a

Finally, many lenders, especially permanent lenders on new income properties, require that the borrower post a "good faith deposit," sometimes termed a "security" or "standby" deposit, when the commitment is issued.[20] If the loan is actually made, the deposit is refunded or applied against the borrower's obligations toward interest and loan fees; but if the borrower does not draw down the loan, the deposit will be forfeited. Obviously, the deposit is intended to discourage the borrower from "walking away"—i.e., seeking financing from another source on more attractive terms.

The commitment-related fees just discussed should not be confused with interest and fees on the loan itself.[21] In many cases the lender will charge a "processing fee" or "origination fee" if and when the loan is made, ostensibly to cover the administrative cost and overhead of putting the loan "on the books." In some cases, however, these fees substantially exceed the lender's costs, and amount to a form of prepaid interest, raising the lender's overall yield on the loan. Such fees are common in a wide range of loan types, from single-family residences to large commercial projects. In addition, in VA-guaranteed home loan transactions, in which the face interest rate on the note is limited to a below-market level by government regulation, the lender will usually charge "discounts" or "points" to the builder or seller in order to raise the effective yield on the loan to a competitive level.[22]

A loan commitment usually makes it clear that the lender is legally obligated to loan in the event all of the stated conditions are fulfilled. Rather surprisingly, many commitments are so poorly drafted that they leave unclear whether the borrower has a corresponding obligation to follow through and obtain the loan. In most single-family home loan commitments, certain commitments issued to lenders by FNMA and FHLMC,[23] and in standby commitments,[24] it is apparent

---

free interest for usury purposes. Cf. Stedman v. Georgetown Savings & Loan Association, 595 S.W.2d 486 (Tex.1979).

20. See Prac.L.Inst., Real Estate Construction 327–31 (No. 5, 1969); Douglas v. United States, 217 Ct.Cl. 97, 576 F.2d 887 (1978). Efforts of loan applicants who ultimately did not draw the loan to recover these deposits have generally been unsuccessful; see B.F. Saul Real Est. Inv. Trust v. McGovern, 683 S.W.2d 531 (Tex.App.1984); Joseph v. Lake Michigan Mortgage Co., 106 Ill.App.3d 988, 62 Ill. Dec. 637, 436 N.E.2d 663 (1982); First Fed. Savings & Loan Association v. Sailboat Key, Inc., 375 So.2d 625 (Fla.App.1979), certiorari denied 386 So.2d 641 (1980); Walker v. First Pennsylvania Bank, 518 F.Supp. 347 (E.D.Pa.1981); Annot., 93 A.L.R.3d (1979); Levenson v. Barnett Bank of Miami, 330 So.2d 192 (Fla.App.1976); White Lakes Shopping Center, Inc. v. Jefferson Standard Life Insurance Co., 208

Kan. 121, 490 P.2d 609 (1971). Of course, recovery of the fee is an appropriate remedy if the lender breaches the commitment; see Hidalgo Properties, Inc. v. Wachovia Mortgage Co., 617 F.2d 196 (10th Cir.1980). See Annot., supra.

21. The distinction between commitment fees and loan fees was significant for usury purposes in Gonzales County Savings & Loan Association v. Freeman, 534 S.W.2d 903 (Tex.1976), holding the former outside the usury statute. See also People v. Central Federal Savings & Loan Association, 46 N.Y. 2241, 412 N.Y.S.2d 815, 385 N.E.2d 555 (1978); 1980 Op.Wis.Att'y Gen. No. 9–80, reported in 1974–80 CCH Cons. Cred.Guide ¶ 97,553; Meadow Brook National Bank v. Recile, 302 F.Supp. 62 (E.D. La.1969).

22. See note 13, supra; § 11.2 infra.

23. See text of notes 12–15 supra.

---

24. See note 24 on page 852.

that the party receiving the commitment has no obligation to use it; in effect, the commitment gives the prospective mortgagor an option to borrow. But in loans on income properties, it is often ambiguous whether the borrower has an obligation to borrow the funds.[25]

If a developer to whom a commitment has been issued declines to borrow (presumably because he has found a better deal elsewhere), what remedies can the lender assert? If the loan applicant has deposited fees which by the commitment's terms are nonrefundable, the courts have uniformly allowed the lender to retain them.[26] But if the lender seeks additional relief, he has several barriers to overcome. First, he must persuade the court that the borrower has an affirmative obligation to borrow, and not merely an option; this is typically a matter of construction of the commitment.[27] Second, he may be faced with the argument that the "good faith deposit" is, in substance, a liquidated damages clause, and that its retention is the sole valid remedy at law for the prospective borrower's default. The situation is arguably analogous to a buyer's "earnest money deposit" in a contract to purchase a house; if the seller reserves the right to retain the deposit, it is often held that he can recover no additional damages.[28] In principle, this

24. See Prac.L.Inst., Real Estate Financing: Contemporary Techniques 177–78 (No. 14, 1973).

25. See, e.g., Lowe v. Massachusetts Mutual Life Insurance Co., 54 Cal.App.3d 718, 127 Cal.Rptr. 23 (1976); Goldman v. Connecticut General Life Insurance Co., 251 Md. 575, 248 A.2d 154 (1968). Both cases hold the commitment to be an option to the borrower, but with no clear language in the documents to support the conclusion. A set of letters which reads much like a construction loan commitment was held too vague to be enforced in Willowood Condominium Association, Inc. v. HNC Realty Co., 531 F.2d 1249 (5th Cir. 1976); see also Wheeler v. White, 385 S.W.2d 619 (Tex.Civ.App.1964) reversed 398 S.W.2d 93 (1965).

26. B.F. Saul Real Est. Inv. Trust v. McGovern, 683 S.W.2d 531 (Tex.App.1984); Lowe v. Massachusetts Mutual Life Insurance Co., 54 Cal.App.3d 718, 127 Cal.Rptr. 23 (1976); Suitt Construction Co. Inc., v. Seaman's Bank for Savings, 30 N.C.App. 155, 226 S.E.2d 408 (1976), holding the applicable law is that of the place at which the lender receives the borrower's signed acceptance of the commitment. Other cases are collected in Groot, Specific Performance of Constructs to Provide Permanent Financing, 60 Cornell L.Rev. 719, 729 n. 49. In Levenson v. Barnett Bank of Miami, 330 So.2d 192 (Fla.App.1976), the court held that the developer could recover his "standby" deposit if he could show that

the lender had not in fact been able and prepared to make the loan, since the very purpose of that deposit had been to compensate the lender for holding itself "in readiness." The court distinguished and denied the developer's attempt to recover his commitment fee, which the agreement expressly made nonrefundable; it found that this fee's purpose was to compensate the lender for its time and expense in underwriting the loan.

27. The "option" interpretation has been adopted frequently; see Financial Federal Savings & Loan Association v. Burleigh House, Inc., 305 So.2d 59 (Fla.App. 1974) certiorari denied 429 U.S. 1042, 97 S.Ct. 742, 50 L.Ed.2d 754; D & M Development Co. v. Sherwood & Roberts, Inc., 93 Idaho 200, 457 P.2d 439 (1969); cases cited note 25, supra. But see Lincoln Nat'l Life Ins. Co. v. NCR Corp., 603 F.Supp. 1393 (N.D.Ind.1984), admitting parol evidence and finding an enforceable promise to borrow, but finding no damages in light of the general upward trend of interest rates which occurred following the borrower's breach.

28. See, e.g., Brewer v. Myers, 545 S.W.2d 235 (Tex.Civ.App.1976); Coca-Cola Bottling Works (Thomas) Inc. v. Hazard Coca-Cola Bottling Works, Inc., 450 S.W.2d 515 (Ky.App.1970); Alois v. Waldman, 219 Md. 369, 149 A.2d 406 (1959); Andreason v. Hansen, 8 Utah 2d 370, 335 P.2d 404 (1959); C. McCormick, Damages § 152 (1935). Of course, this conclusion is easy if issue is also a matter of interpretation of the commitment agreement,[29] but if the good faith deposit is substantial, it would not be surprising for a court to hold it is the lender's exclusive remedy. It appears that no reported case deals with this point.[30]

Assuming the lender can overcome these barriers, he is rather clearly entitled to damages against the defaulting commitment-holder. Presumably damages can be shown only if mortgage market conditions have changed so that the lender must place the loan funds with another borrower at lower interest or fees. Damages would then be computed as the difference between the discounted present values of the stream of loan fees and payments the lender would have received if the original loan had been made and the stream of such fees and payments it will be able to earn on alternate investments available at the time of the breach.[30.5] Discounting should be at the interest rate prevailing in the relevant mortgage market at the date of the breach.[31] Interest on the sum thus computed should be added, again preferably at prevailing mortgage market rates, to the date of judgment.[32] The formulation

the contract provides that the vendor's sole damages remedy is retention of the deposit, as is usually the case in California, see Calif.Cont.Ed. of Bar, California Real Estate Sales Transaction §§ 4.67, 11.50 (1967), or if the contract provides that the vendor must elect between retention and other remedies, and he in fact retains the deposit, see G.H. Swope Building Corp. v. Horton, 207 Tenn. 114, 338 S.W.2d 566 (1960); McMullin v. Shimmin, 10 Utah 2d 142, 349 P.2d 720 (1960). See generally Cunningham, Stoebuck & Whitman, Property § 10.4 (1984) at 651–53; M. Friedman, Contracts and Conveyances of Real Property § 12.1(c) (3d ed. 1975); D. Dobbs, Remedies § 12.5 (1973), at 825.

29. In well-drafted commitments, language is employed to clarify the existence of additional remedies (usually in favor of their existence, since the lender is generally the drafter). For example:

> It is understood that the foregoing provision for retention of the deposit shall not constitute an option on Borrower's part not to complete the Loan transaction herein contemplated, but that Lender reserves any and all rights which it may have in law or in equity, including but not limited to specific performance.

ABA Sec. of Real Prop., Probate & Trust Law, The Lawyer's Role in Financing the Real Estate Development 36 (Probate & Prop. Cassette Series, Vol. 1, No. 3, 1975). See also Goldman v. Connecticut General Life Ins. Co., 251 Md. 575, 248 A.2d 154 (1968).

30. See Groot, Specific Performance of Contracts to Provide Permanent Financing, 60 Cornell L.Rev. 718, 730 n. 50 (1975).

30.5 Lincoln Nat'l Life Ins. Co. v. NCR Corp., 603 F.Supp. 1393 (N.D.Ind.1984).

31. The cases which deal with discounting of future income streams contribute little on the appropriate discount rate. See generally D. Dobbs, Remedies 178 (1973). Some courts use statutory or arbitrary rates, but when the breach is so intimately tied to a particular money market, it seems fairest to use the rate prevailing in that market. One may think of the lender as receiving his damages award at the moment of breach and immediately investing it at the then-available rate. In addition, the rate at the date of breach will usually be lower than the rate specified in the commitment (the fall in rates frequently being the very reason for the commitment-holder's breach); the lower rate will produce a larger measure of damages for the lender, which seems reasonable, since the lender is the non-breaching party. Cf. Groot, supra note 30, at 732, advocating interest at mortgage market rates as of the date of judgment.

32. The damages in this sort of case are sufficiently analogous to "liquidated" damages that a court should have no difficulty in awarding interest on them from the date of breach to the date of judgment; see D. Dobbs, Remedies 165–74 (1973). Again, the prevailing rate for mortgages of the type involved should be used in computing interest on the damages, since this is precisely how the lender would have invested suggested here presumes that the lender has mitigated its damages by re-lending at prevailing rates the money which the original loan applicant did not draw down; whether the lender actually re-lends at inferior rates, or not at all, is immaterial. The lender can presumably claim its out-of-pocket expenses, such as legal and architect's fees, as additional damages, but it must obviously offset against this claim all such amounts paid to or for it by the loan applicant.

The fact that damages are readily computable suggests that specific performance will not be available to the lender; [33] its remedy at law is usually entirely adequate.[34] The lender might argue that it had bargained for an interest in land, and that by analogy to land contract cases which hold every parcel of realty to be unique, specific performance should be granted.[35] But the situations are not analogous, for the lender's concern is only with the land's value as security, and not with its individual characteristics as such. Even an express clause in the commitment making it enforceable in specie is unlikely to impress an equity court. Perhaps the only situation imaginable in which specific performance should be awarded is upon a showing by the lender that no comparable investment alternatives were available to it at the time of the breach. If this is the case (which is exceedingly improbable), damages will be more difficult to compute and specific performance arguably the only feasible remedy. Even here, specific performance is both literally impossible and nonsensical if the developer has actually obtained a permanent first mortgage loan from another lender, so that the original lender cannot have the prior lien for which it contracted, or if the project has been abandoned prior to completion, so that the conditions of the original commitment cannot be fulfilled.

Lenders rarely sue holders of loan commitments for breach. The right to recover is tenuous under many commitment forms, the fees and deposits retained by lenders are often adequate recompense for their damages, and in the case of incompleted projects, the prospective borrowers are usually insolvent. In an effort to avoid the necessity of suit, while maximizing the probability that the permanent loan will actually be drawn down, some lenders enter into a "buy-sell agreement" rather than issuing a loan commitment.[36] The buy-sell agree-

---

the funds if he had been awarded them on the date of breach.

33. An argument that the good faith deposit is a liquidated damages clause, and thus bars other remedies, will be unavailing as a defense to a specific performance suit by the lender; only damage actions are barred by this theory. See cases cited note 87, supra; D. Dobbs, Remedies § 12.5 (1973), at 825.

34. See Groot, supra note 30, at 727–36; Annot., 82 A.L.R.3d 1116 (1978); cf. Draper, The Broken Commitment: A Modern View of the Mortgage Lender's Remedy, 59 Cornell L.Rev. 418 (1974). Groot effective-

ly dispatches Draper's arguments that damages are an inadequate remedy.

35. See D. Dobbs, Remedies § 12.10 (1973); Kitchen v. Herring, 42 N.C. 190 (1851). Cf. Centex Homes Corp. v. Boag, 128 N.J.Super. 385, 320 A.2d 194 (1974), denying specific performance to the vendor-builder of a unit in a large condominium project on the ground that the property was not unique.

36. See Haggarty, Procedures, Forms and Safeguards in Construction Lending with a Permanent Takeout, 85 Banking L.J. 1035, 1053 (1968); Prac.L.Inst., Real Estate Construction 327 (No. 5, 1969). The ment contemplates that upon completion of construction, the construction loan itself will begin to require regular payments of interest and amortization and will be purchased by the permanent lender from the construction lender. The permanent lender has the added advantage of a priority dating from the commencement of construction, which in most states means that any mechanics' liens filed during construction will be subordinate if all construction advances have been obligatory.[37] There is thus no opportunity for the developer to find better permanent financing during the construction period; he is locked into the agreement contained in the original documents. If the permanent lender must sue, it will do so to recover on the note or to foreclose the mortgage; a "walk away" by the developer is most unlikely. From the construction lender's viewpoint, the buy-sell agreement is as satisfactory as a permanent loan commitment in most respects, although it does mean that the construction loan documents must be fully acceptable to the permanent lender. There is rarely a problem of unwillingness of the construction lender to sell the loan upon completion since most construction lenders have little desire to get into the long-term loan business. Finally, it should be noted that loan commitments and buy-sell agreements are fundamentally different types of contracts, and a court is unlikely to rewrite the former to make it the latter.[38] The permanent lender should make it perfectly clear whether it is promising to make a new loan or purchase an existing one.

Borrower's enforcement rights. Suppose a lender, despite having issued a loan commitment to a borrower, refuses to make the loan. Assuming that the borrower has met all conditions in the commitment, so that the refusal constitutes a breach, what remedies are available to the borrower?[39] The answer seems to depend on whether the borrower has obtained another loan from an alternate source. If he has done so, and if the interest and fees on the new loan are not higher than under the old commitment, the borrower needs no remedy, aside from possible compensation for incidental or consequential damages. More frequently, however, the new loan will carry higher interest and fees, a reflection of the fact that market rates have risen since the commitment was issued—the very fact which may have induced the committing lender to breach. On these facts damages are an appropriate and adequate remedy. Their computation is similar to the calculation of

---

buy-sell agreement is executed by the construction and permanent lenders, and is usually endorsed by the borrower. Such an agreement is illustrated in Equity Associates v. Society for Savings, 31 N.C.App. 182, 228 S.E.2d 761 (1976) certiorari denied 291 N.C. 711, 232 S.E.2d 203, in which the permanent lender refused to purchase the loan.

37. See Selective Builders, Inc. v. Hudson City Savings Bank, 137 N.J.Super. 500, 349 A.2d 564 (1975); § 12.7, infra.

38. See Exchange Bank & Trust Co. v. Lone Star Life Insurance Co., 546 S.W.2d 948 (Tex.Civ.App.1977).

39. The borrower is not the only possible plaintiff. In Silverdale Hotel Associates v. Lomas & Nettleton Co., 36 Wn.App. 762, 677 P.2d 773 (1984), a general contracter recovered damages from a defaulting construction lender on a promissory estoppel theory.

lender's damages discussed above: the difference between the present values of the payments the borrower would have made under the original commitment and those he must make under reasonable alternative financing.[40] Obviously, the terms of the actual substitute loan obtained will usually be excellent evidence of what is reasonably available in the market, particularly if the borrower shopped diligently for it.

The cases dealing with consequential damages suffered by erstwhile borrowers display a surprising diversity. Each element of damages must meet three initial tests: (1) it must have been "foreseeable" or "within the contemplation" of the parties to the loan commitment, (2) it must have been caused by the lender's breach, and (3) it must be provable with reasonable precision. Clearly the borrower should recover commitment fees already paid to the breaching lender. Direct expenditures related to obtaining a substitute loan, such as architects', abstract, and title attorneys' fees, recording and notary charges, etc., usually qualify without difficulty.[41] Lost rents or profits have been allowed,[42] but usually only upon rather convincing proof that they

40. See text at notes 90–91, supra; Bridgkort Racquet Club, Inc. v. University Bank, 85 Wis.2d 706, 271 N.W.2d 165 (1978); United of Omaha Life Insurance Co. v. Nob Hill Associates, 450 So.2d 536 (Fla.App.1984), petition for review dismissed 458 So.2d 273 (1984), petition for review denied 458 So.2d 274 (1984); Pipkin v. Thomas & Hill, Inc., 298 N.C. 278, 258 S.E.2d 778 (1979); Annot., 4 A.L.R.4th 682, 690 (1981); 36 A.L.R. 1408 (1925); 44 A.L.R. 1486 (1926). Many of the cases state the measure of damages too loosely, as the "difference in the interest rates" or the "increased interest," and provide no discussion of the present value aspect of the computation. See, e.g., Rubin v. Pioneer Federal Savings & Loan Association, 214 Neb. 364, 334 N.W.2d 424 (1983); Consolidated American Life Insurance Co. v. Covington, 297 So.2d 894 (Miss.1974); Archer-Daniels-Midland Co. v. Paull, 188 F.Supp. 277 (W.D.Ark.1960) reversed 293 F.2d 389 (8th Cir.1961), on remand 199 F.Supp. 319 (D.Ark.1961), affirmed 313 F.2d 612 (8th Cir.1963); Annot., 36 A.L.R. 1408 (1925). At least one opinion expressly approves discounting the stream of damages to present value, but provides no indication of the appropriate interest rate or method; Financial Federal Savings & Loan Association v. Continental Enterprises, Inc., 338 So.2d 907 (Fla.App.1976); see particularly the dissent of Pearson, J., arguing that the discount should not be at the statutory rate, but at a rate which is fair and just under the circumstances, taking

into account current rates in the relevant money market.

If the lender's breach has caused the owner to lose his equity in the land, as by foreclosure of a construction loan, the measure of damages is the lost value; see United California Bank v. Prudential Insurance Co., 140 Ariz. 238, 681 P.2d 390, 447–48 (App.1983). See also Lincor Contractors, Ltd. v. Hyskell, 39 Wn.App. 317, 692 P.2d 903 (1984) (damages in amount of equity which borrower would have had in building never built due to construction lender's breach.)

41. Pipkin v. Thomas & Hill, Inc., 298 N.C. 278, 258 S.E.2d 778 (1979); Coastland Corp. v. Third National Mortgage Co., 611 F.2d 969 (4th Cir.1979) (damages for breach of construction loan commitment include amount developer paid for permanent loan commitment, which was never used due to defendant's breach); Culp v. Western Loan & Building Co., 124 Wash. 326, 214 P. 145 (1923) affirmed 127 Wash. 249, 220 P. 766. See Annot., 4 A.L.R.4th 682, 695–98 (1981). Note that if the borrower seeks damages, he is not entitled to recover his commitment fee on the original loan as well, since he is affirming the contract; see Rubin v. Pioneer Federal Savings & Loan, 214 Neb. 364, 334 N.W.2d 424 (1983).

42. W–V Enterprises, Inc. v. Federal Savings & Loan Insurance Corp., 234 Kan. 354, 673 P.2d 1112, 1123 (1983) (also awarding punitive damages for fraud); Pasadena Associates v. Connor, 460 S.W.2d 473 (Tex.

would have been earned if the loan had been granted.[43]   More remote damages,[44] such as the loss of favorable relations with subcontractors, damage to the borrower's credit standing, loss of a contractor's license, and even mental suffering,[45] are conceivable, though difficult to prove.

If the prospective borrower has been unable or unwilling to obtain another loan, his remedial picture is quite different.   He may, of course, seek damages, and they will presumably be measured in the same fashion as described above.[46]   It is more probable, however, that he will pray for specific performance of the commitment, hoping thereby to salvage his interest in the property.   Manifold authorities hold that this remedy is unavailable for breach of a loan commitment, the remedy at law being fully adequate,[47] but in fact numerous cases have granted specific performance.   Nearly all of these can be explained by the fact that the lender had already closed the loan, recorded his mortgage, and even made some disbursements before closing his credit window.[48]   On such facts, the lender's actions will have made alternative first mortgage financing impossible; the mortgage encumbers the borrower's title, and no other lender will be able to secure a prior lien until the old mortgage is satisfied.   Several of these cases have involved construction loans, with the attendant difficulty of refinancing a partially completed project.   If the borrower is precluded from access to the mortgage market, the traditional measure of damages, which requires proof of the availability and cost of alternative

Civ.App.1970) refused n.r.e.; Archer-Daniels-Midland Co. v. Paull, 188 F.Supp. 277 (W.D.Ark.1960), reversed in part, 293 F.2d 389 (8th Cir.1961), order on remand affirmed 313 F.2d 612 (8th Cir.1963). See Annot., 4 A.L.R.4th 682, 698–708 (1981).

43.   The evidence has often been unconvincing to the courts; see First Mississippi Bank v. Latch, 433 So.2d 946 (Miss.1983); Coastland Corp. v. Third National Mortgage Co., 611 F.2d 969, 977–78 (4th Cir. 1979); Davis v. Small Business Investment Co., 535 S.W.2d 740 (Tex.Civ.App.1976); Stanish v. Polish Roman Catholic Union, 484 F.2d 713 (7th Cir.Ind.1973); St. Paul at Chase Corp. v. Manufacturers Life Insurance Co., 262 Md. 192, 278 A.2d 12 (1971), certiorari denied 404 U.S. 857, 92 S.Ct. 104, 30 L.Ed.2d 98 (1971); Archer-Daniels-Midland Co. v. Paull, note 42 supra. See also A.M.R. Enterprises v. United Postal Savings Association, 567 F.2d 1277 (5th Cir. 1978) (construction loan commitment breached; developer can recover fees paid and costs paid toward construction).

44.   See Bank of New Mexico v. Rice, 78 N.M. 170, 429 P.2d 368 (1967), modified after remand, 79 N.M. 115, 440 P.2d 790 (1968).

45.   See Westesen v. Olathe State Bank, 78 Colo. 217, 240 P. 689, 44 A.L.R. 1484 (1925).

46.   See text at note 40, supra.

47.   The classic case is Rogers v. Challis, 54 Eng.Rep. 68 (Ch.1859). See Investment Service Co. v. Smither, 276 Or. 837, 556 P.2d 955 (1976); Kent v. Walter E. Heller Co., 349 F.2d 480 (5th Cir.1965); Steward v. Bounds, 167 Wash. 554, 9 P.2d 1112 (1932), modified 170 Wash. 698, 15 P.2d 1119 (1932).   See Annot., 82 A.L.R.3d 1116 (1978).

48.   Vandeventer v. Dale Construction Co., 271 Or. 691, 534 P.2d 183 (1975) appeal after remand 277 Or. 817, 562 P.2d 196 (1977); Cuna Mutual Insurance Society v. Dominguez, 9 Ariz.App. 172, 450 P.2d 413 (1969); Southhampton Wholesale Food Terminal, Inc. v. Providence Produce Warehouse Co., 129 F.Supp. 663 (D.Mass. 1955); Jacobson v. First National Bank, 129 N.J.Eq. 440, 20 A.2d 19, affirmed, 130 N.J.Eq. 604, 23 A.2d 409 (1941); Columbus Club v. Simons, 110 Okl. 48, 236 P. 12 (1925).

loans, becomes meaningless, and specific performance is entirely appropriate.

Even if the prospective borrower has not executed a mortgage to the committing lender, he might be able to obtain a decree of specific performance if his efforts to obtain an alternate loan have been unsuccessful. It is difficult to apply the traditional measure of damages with confidence on these facts. Moreover, if the breached commitment is for a permanent loan at the completion of construction, the lender's default may result in consequential damages which will be difficult to quantify but are nonetheless harsh, including the besmirching of the developer's reputation and credit, and the possible inability of subcontractors and materials suppliers to collect for their contributions to the project.[49] Several recent cases have recognized these factors [50] and granted specific performance when no mortgage had been executed to the lender.[51]

Not many specific performance cases have been decided, probably because the remedy is usually unattractive from the borrower's viewpoint. The delay inherent in litigation suggests that it is economically feasible only if the borrower has access to some interim financing while the case is pending (such as a construction loan which can be extended until the permanent financing becomes available as a result of the court's decree.) [52] Generally, an alternative loan and a suit for damages are more appealing, and if the project or the borrower is so weak that no other financing can be obtained, a court might infer that a decree of specific performance would also be inefficient and bad policy, constituting a futile effort to shore up an economically fatal situation;

---

49. See generally Groot, Specific Performance of Contracts to Provide Permanent Financing, 60 Cornell L.Rev. 718, 741 (1975). Other damages in this situation, such as the loss of the project due to construction loan foreclosure, and a possible deficiency judgment, are more readily measurable. See St. Paul at Chase Corp. v. Manufacturers Life Insurance Co., 262 Md. 192, 278 A.2d 12 (1971), certiorari denied 404 U.S. 857, 92 S.Ct. 104, 30 L.Ed.2d 98 (1971).

50. First National State Bank v. Commonwealth Federal Savings & Loan Association, 610 F.2d 164 (3d Cir.1979); Selective Builders, Inc. v. Hudson City Savings Bank, 137 N.J.Super. 500, 349 A.2d 564 (1975). Specific performance of a sales contract is routinely granted to the purchaser, even when the contract calls for the seller to finance the sale by taking back a purchase-money mortgage; see Turley v. Ball Associates Limited, 641 P.2d 286 (Colo.App.1981).

51. In Leben v. Nassau Savings & Loan Association, 40 A.D.2d 830, 337 N.Y.S.2d 310 (1972), affirmed 34 N.Y.2d 671, 356

N.Y.S.2d 46, 312 N.E.2d 180 (1974), the permanent lender insisted on a higher interest rate at closing than had been agreed to in the commitment. The borrower signed the documents, but sought and obtained judicial reformation to readjust the interest rate downward. Some dicta in the opinion might be read as approving specific performance, but on the facts the case is similar to those cited in note 47, supra, with reformation of future payments as a substitute for damages. See Groot, supra note 49, at 725–27.

52. Compare Selective Builders, Inc. v. Hudson City Savings Bank, 137 N.J.Super. 500, 349 A.2d 564 (1975), in which the construction lender gave such an extension, making a specific performance suit feasible, with St. Paul at Chase Corp. v. Manufacturers Life Insurance Co., 262 Md. 192, 278 A.2d 12 (1971), certiorari denied 404 U.S. 857, 92 S.Ct. 104, 30 L.Ed.2d 98 (1971), in which the construction lender foreclosed and purchased the project, leaving the developer with only a suit for damages against the reneging permanent lender.

this risk would have to be balanced against the arguments favoring specific performance mentioned in the preceding paragraph.

The Securities and Exchange Act of 1934

In United States v. Austin,[53] the Tenth Circuit Court of Appeals considered a charge of criminal fraud against a lender based on the antifraud provisions of Section 10(b) of the Securities and Exchange Act of 1934.[54]   In substance, the government argued that the lender had issued a mortgage loan commitment and charged a commitment fee with no intention of ever making the loan.   The court concluded that the commitment letter was a "security" within the meaning of the Act, and upheld the defendants' conviction.   If the holding were sound, civil remedies would be available as well.[55]

The decision, however, is of dubious validity, and its logical implications would cut a wide swath indeed: virtually every executory bilateral contract in which one party pays money consideration in return for the other's future performance would be a security.   Plainly the commitment fee paid by a loan applicant is in no sense an "investment"; the applicant does not expect "profits to come solely from the efforts" of the lender.[56]   Indeed, the lender's performance of its commitment will ordinarily be entirely independent of its internal profitability during the commitment period.   The commitment will yield the applicant neither capital appreciation nor a participation in earnings, but only a loan of money upon previously agreed terms.   Any profits earned by the borrower will be attributable to his own entreprenurial and managerial efforts, not those of the lender.[57]

The Tenth Circuit appears to have repented of its holding in *Austin*.   In McGovern Plaza Joint Venture v. First of Denver Mortgage Investors,[58] it held that neither the construction loan nor permanent loan commitments on hotel construction project were securities, lamely distinguishing *Austin* on the ground that it involved a "large-scale, advance fee loan swindle" in which the "entire procedure was fraudulent."   It is difficult to see the relevance of the scale or gravity of the fraud in determining whether a security is being sold.   *Austin* must be regarded as overruled,[59] but it contains a useful lesson.   The issuance of

---

53.   462 F.2d 724 (10th Cir.1972), certiorari denied 409 U.S. 1048, 93 S.Ct. 518, 34 L.Ed.2d 501 (1972).

54.   15 U.S.C.A. § 78j(b) (1970).

55.   See J.I. Case v. Borak, 377 U.S. 426, 84 S.Ct. 1555, 12 L.Ed.2d 423 (1964); Kardon v. National Gypsum Co., 73 F.Supp. 798 (E.D.Pa.1947), supplemented 83 F.Supp. 613 (D.Pa.1947).

56.   S.E.C. v. W. J. Howey Co., 328 U.S. 293, 301, 66 S.Ct. 1100, 1104, 90 L.Ed. 1244 (1946).

57.   See United Housing Foundation, Inc. v. Forman, 421 U.S. 837, 95 S.Ct. 2051,

44 L.Ed.2d 621 (1975), rehearing denied 423 U.S. 884, 96 S.Ct. 157, 46 L.Ed.2d 115 (1975) and 423 U.S. 884, 96 S.Ct. 157, 46 L.Ed.2d 115 (1975).   See generally Sonnenschein, Federal Securities Law Coverage of Note Transactions: The Antifraud Provisions, 35 Bus.Law 1567 (1980).

58.   562 F.2d 645 (10th Cir.1977).

59.   The *Austin* holding is rejected explicitly by Cocklereece v. Moran, 532 F.Supp. 519 (N.D.Ga.1982); Lee v. Navarro Savings Association, 416 F.Supp. 1186 (N.D.Tex.1976), reversed on other grounds 597 F.2d 421 (5th Cir.1979), affirmed 446

a loan commitment may well be fraud under state law, if at the time of issuance the lender intends to breach. Both criminal and civil penalties may be applicable in many jurisdictions.

 WESTLAW REFERENCES

build*** construct*** /s loan /p commitment reliance rely*** relied assur!

§ 12.4 Mechanics' Liens

Mechanics' and materialmen's liens, created by statute, give unpaid contractors, workers, and materials suppliers a security interest in the real estate which they have improved; they may foreclose such liens as an aid to the recovery of the payment owed them. Although the legal scholar can find authority that a form of mechanics' lien existed in the Roman law,[1] was well developed in the civil law [2] and was incorporated in the Code Napoleon,[3] it was unknown in England, either at common law or in equity [4] and, so far as our present laws are concerned, is of native origin in the United States, dating back to the Maryland statute of 1791.[5] Today in every state in the Union such legislation exists,[6] but because the liens are wholly statutory, because the laws creating them are extremely varied both in their provisions

U.S. 458, 100 S.Ct. 1779, 64 L.Ed.2d 425 (1980); and FBS Financial, Inc. v. Clevetrust Realty Investors, CCH Fed.Secur. Rptr.Par. 96,341 (1977), and implicitly by United States v. Namer, 680 F.2d 1088, 1096 n. 16 (5th Cir.1982) and McClure v. First National Bank, 352 F.Supp. 454 (N.D. Tex.1973), affirmed 497 F.2d 490 (5th Cir. 1974), certiorari denied 420 U.S. 930, 95 S.Ct. 1132, 43 L.Ed.2d 402 (1975). See also Sanders v. John Nuveen & Co., Inc., 463 F.2d 1075 (7th Cir.1972), certiorari denied 409 U.S. 1009, 93 S.Ct. 443, 34 L.Ed.2d 302 (1972); First Federal Savings & Loan Association v. Mortgage Corp. of the South, 467 F.Supp. 943 (N.D.Ala.1979), affirmed on the other grounds 650 F.2d 1376 (5th Cir. 1981).

§ 12.4

1. Mackeldy, Handbook of the Roman Law, Dropsie's Translation, 274.

2. See Canal Co. v. Gordon, 73 U.S. (6 Wall.) 561, 571, 18 L.Ed. 894 (1867). Jones v. Great Southern Fireproof Hotel Co., 86 F. 370, 386 (6th Cir.1898), reversed 177 U.S. 449, 20 S.Ct. 690, 44 L.Ed. 842 (1900); 1 Domat, Civil Law, 1861 ed., 681–4, arts. 1736, 1741–5.

3. Code Napoleon, Privileges and Mortgages, § 2 (2103).

4. See Canal Co. v. Gordon, supra note 2; Van Stone v. Stillwell & Bierce Manufacturing Co., 142 U.S. 128, 136, 12 S.Ct.

181, 183, 35 L.Ed. 961 (1891); Durling v. Gould, 83 Me. 134, 137, 21 A. 833 (1890).

5. Acts of General Assembly of Maryland, c. 45, § 10 (1791). "The origin of such laws, in America, arose from the desire to establish and improve, as readily as possible, the city of Washington. In 1791, at a meeting of the commissioners appointed for such purpose, both Thomas Jefferson and James Madison were present, and a memorial was adopted urging the General Assembly of Maryland to pass an act securing to *master-builders,* a lien, on houses erected, and land occupied. The requested law was enacted December 19, 1791." Moore-Mansfield Const. Co. v. Indianapolis New Castle & Toledo Railway Co., 179 Ind. 356, 369, 101 N.E. 296, 44 L.R.A.,N.S. 816, Ann.Cas.1915D, 917 (1913). See Barry Properties v. Fick Bros., 277 Md. 15, 353 A.2d 222 (1976). The next statute was in Pennsylvania in 1803. Act of April 1, 1803, P.L. 791; see Cushman, Proposed Mechanics' Lien Law, 80 U.Pa.L.Rev. 1083 n. 3 (1932).

6. See Armour & Co. v. Western Const. Co., 36 Wash. 529, 78 P. 1106 (1905). In at least two states mechanics' liens are provided for by constitution. West's Ann.Cal. Const. Art. 14 § 3; Vernon's Ann.Tex. Const. Art. 16, § 37; see Youngblood, Mechanics' and Materialmen's Liens in Texas, 26 Sw.L.J. 665, 687 (1972).

and in the courts' construction of them, and because legislatures have been prolific with amendments, generalizations are extremely difficult and always must be checked against local enactments.[7] Furthermore, case law is unreliable in the field because the decisions are meaningful only with reference to the particular statute under which each arose and the precise language of the act at that time. This variability has been justified on the ground that the problems involved are dissimilar in different parts of the country,[8] even perhaps from state to state. This assertion is dubious, but efforts to secure the adoption of uniform legislation on the subject have thus far failed.[9] Because of the resulting state-by-state complexity, a comprehensive treatment of mechanics' liens is impossible here. However, the principal groups of statutes and their general features can be outlined.

The basic idea of the mechanics' lien is that those whose work or materials go into an improvement to real estate [10] should be permitted, in fairness, to satisfy their unpaid bills out of that real estate.[11]

---

7. General (and necessarily cursory) summaries of mechanics' lien law from a national perspective include Introductory Comment, Art. 5, Uniform Simplification of Land Transfers Act, 14 Uniform Laws Annot. 271 (1980); Comment, Mechanics' Liens and Surety Bonds in the Building Trades, 68 Yale L.J. 138 (1968); Report of the Standard State Mechanics' Lien Act Committee of the U.S. Dept. of Commerce 19–25 (1932). Numerous articles and comments analyze the mechanics' lien laws of particular states. Among these (omitting title and author for the sake of brevity) are: 6 Cumb.L.Rev. 243 (Ala.1975); 7 Ariz. L.Rev. 296 (Ariz.1966); 25 Hast.L.J. 1043 (Cal.1974); 47 L.A.Bar.Bull. 299 (Cal.1972); 9 Santa Clara L. 101 (Cal.1968); 39 U.Colo. L.Rev. 105 (Colo.1966); 29 U.Fla.L.Rev. 411 (Fla.1977); 47 Chi-Kent L.Rev. 157 (Ill. 1970); 36 Ind.L.J. 526 (Ind.1921); 51 Iowa L.Rev. 862 (Iowa, 1966); 47 Iowa L.Rev. 144 (Iowa 1961); 62 Ky.L.J. 278 (Ky.1972); 44 Tul.L.Rev. 326 (La.1970); 6 U.Balt.L. Rev. 180 (Md.1977); 28 Md.L.Rev. 225 (Md. 1968); 37 Miss.L.J. 385 (Miss.1966); 42 Mo. L.Rev. 53 (Mo.1976); 12 Wake For.L.Rev. 283 (N.C.1976); 38 Ohio St.L.J. 3 (Ohio 1977); 3 Akron L.Rev. 1 (Ohio 1969); 29 Ohio St.L.J. 917 (Ohio 1968); 74 Dick.L. Rev. 740 (Pa.1970); 35 U.Pitt.L.Rev. 265 (Pa.1963); 25 S.C.L.Rev. 817 (S.C.1974); 6 Memph.St.L.Rev. 519 (Tenn.1976); 5 Memph.St.L.Rev. 359 (Tenn.1975); 26 Southwest L.J. 665 (Tex.1972); Ut.L.Rev. 181 (Utah 1966); 49 Wash.L.Rev. 685 (Wash.1974).

8. See Glenn, Mortgages § 351.

9. The proposed Uniform Mechanics' Lien Law, drafted by the Commissioners on Uniform State Laws in 1932, was adopted only by Florida, and was withdrawn in 1943; see Handbook of Comm. on Uniform State Laws 150 (1943); Cushman, The Proposed Uniform Mechanics' Lien Law, 80 U.Pa.L.Rev. 1083 (1932); the Florida law, which persists today with modifications, is discussed in Note, Lien Rights and Construction Lending: Responsibilities and Liabilities in Florida, 29 U.Fla.L.Rev. 411 (1977). In 1976 the Commissioners on Uniform State Laws promulgated the Uniform Simplification of Land Transfers Act, Article 5 of which deals with "construction liens," and is partially based, in turn, on the Florida statute. This new proposal contains some of the features of the 1932 Act, including a requirement that the lien claimant give notice to the owner of his potential claim. It has been adopted only in Nebraska at this writing; see Neb.Rev.' Stat. §§ 52–125 to 52–159.

10. Even work done off-site may be lienable if it directly benefits the property; see Northlake Concrete Products, Inc. v. Wylie, 34 Wn.App. 810, 663 P.2d 1380 (1983) (sewer line).

11. This does not necessarily mean the contract price can be recovered; if the work was done badly or improperly, the lien may be for less, or even zero. See Ed Hackstaff Concrete, Inc. v. Powder Ridge Condominium "A" Owners' Association, 679 P.2d 1112 (Colo.App.1984); Tighe v. Kenyon, 681 P.2d 547 (Colo.App.1984). And if a valid contract is proved, the contractor may get a personal judgment even though he failed properly to perfect his lien; Paro v. Biondo, 105 App.Div.2d 577, 481 N.Y.S.2d 518 (1984).

Beginning with the original Maryland statute, "[t]hese laws grew, and their validity became established, as the courts held that the building business did not have the protection inherent in the widespread distribution of credit risk common to other businesses, and therefore needed this broader and special protection. Contractors, subcontractors, materialmen, and other building groups were frequently obliged to extend credit in larger amounts, and for longer time, than other businesses. Such parties might have their entire capital, or a substantial part of it, tied up in one or two, or ten or twenty, projects under construction." [12]

To begin with only general contractors or master-builders were given protection under the acts.[13] But by a process of amendment and enlargement of the similar acts that were passed in other states, today "practically every segment composing the construction industry—including contractors, subcontractors, material dealers, laborers, artisans, architects, landscape architects, engineers, surveyors—is granted liens of varying extent under varying conditions for the labor, services, or materials furnished or contracted to be furnished for the particular improvement." [14]

If the mechanics' lien were limited to those with whom the owner dealt with directly, little question would arise as to the amount of the lien upon the property—it would be for the unpaid amount still owing under the contract. When the acts extended the coverage to persons who had no direct dealings with the owner, the statutes divided into two main classes. One, generally designated the "Pennsylvania" type,[15] gives the subcontractor or materialman a direct right of his own regardless of the existence of any indebtedness between the owner and

12. Stalling, Mechanics' Lien Laws As They Exist Today, 4 F.H.L.B.Rev. 232 (1938); see Cook v. Carlson, 364 F.Supp. 24 (D.S.D.1973).

13. Acts of General Assembly of Maryland, c. 45, § 10 (1791).

14. Stalling, supra note 12; Survey of Illinois Law, 1951–1952: Mechanics Liens—Fixtures, 31 Chi.Kent L.Rev. 71 (1952). See Kenneth D. Collins Agency v. Hagerott, ___ Mont. ___, 684 P.2d 487 (1984) (architect may have lien only if building is constructed); Branecky v. Seaman, 688 S.W.2d 117 (Tex.Civ.App.1984) (same); Stratford v. Boland, 306 Pa.Super. 475, 452 A.2d 824 (1982) (architect may have lien only if he supervises construction.)

As to the right to mechanic's lien as for "labor" or "work" in case of preparatory or fabricating work done on materials intended for use and used in particular building or structure, see 25 A.L.R.2d 1370 (1952). In Nolte v. Smith, 189 Cal.App.2d 140, 11 Cal.Rptr. 261 (1961), a civil engineer who surveyed, planned and prepared a subdivision map for recording and erected permanent markers and monuments on the property was held to be entitled to a mechanic's lien. See also Torkko/Korman/Engineers v. Penland Ventures, 673 P.2d 769 (Alaska 1983). Engineers' and architects' liens are sometimes provided by statute; see, e.g., Utah Code Ann § 38–1–3 (1981).

Compare Anderson v. Breezy Point Estates, 283 Minn. 490, 168 N.W.2d 693 (1969) (surveyor may not have lien for cutting brush and staking lots) and Johnson v. Barnhill, 279 S.C. 242, 306 S.E.2d 216 (1983) (same) with Midland Mortgage Co. v. Sanders England Investments, 682 P.2d 748 (Okl.1984) (surveying work is lienable). See also Big S Trucking Co. v. Gervais Favrot, Inc., 450 So.2d 369 (La.App.1983) (lien allowed for hauling away trash or dirt). See Annot., 32 A.L.R.4th 1130 (1984).

15. See 49 Pa.Stat. § 1301. Approximately 30 states adopt the Pennsylvania approach; see Comment, Mechanics' Liens and Surety Bonds in the Building Trades, 68 Yale L.J. 138, 144 n. 30 (1958); Annot., 75 A.L.R.3d 505 (1977).

general contractor [16] and measured by the value of his contribution. Conceivably,[17] under such statutes the claims of the ancillary contractors could exceed the contract price or could still exist even though the owner had paid the general contractor in full; nevertheless they are generally upheld when attacked as unconstitutional.[18] The other type of statute, usually referred to as the "New York" system, measures the liability of the owner's property by the price stated in the original contract with the general contractor less payments properly made to the contractor.[19] The theory of these statutes is that all lien rights are based directly or derivatively upon the contract between the owner and general contractor.[20]

The procedure which a lien claimant must follow varies widely, but he is typically required to file a notice of his claim within some fixed period of time, commonly 60 to 180 days, after completing his work.[21] The notice is usually required to be recorded, served personally on the owner, published in a newspaper, or made effective by some combination of these methods. If the claim is not paid within some additional period, the claimant must usually bring a judicial action to foreclose the lien in a manner similar to mortgage foreclosures.[22]

16. Cf. Baldwin Locomotive Works v. Edward Hines Lumber Co., 189 Ind. 189, 125 N.E. 400 (1919), holding that an express stipulation between owner and general contractor could negative a direct lien.

17. Statutes usually fix the contract price as the uppermost limit for such claims. See Prince v. Neal-Millard Co., 124 Ga. 884, 53 S.E. 761, 4 Ann.Cas. 615 (1906).

18. E.g., Jones v. Great Southern Fireproof Hotel Co., 86 F. 370, 30 C.C.A. 108 (1898), certiorari granted 173 U.S. 704, 19 S.Ct. 885 (1899), reversed 177 U.S. 449, 20 S.Ct. 690, 44 L.Ed. 842 (1900); Hightower v. Bailey, 108 Ky. 198, 56 S.W. 147, 22 Ky. Law Rep. 88, 49 L.R.A. 255, 94 Am.St.Rep. 350 (1900); Becker v. Hopper, 22 Wyo. 237, 138 P. 179, Ann.Cas.1916D, 1041 (1914), affirmed on rehearing 23 Wyo. 209, 147 P. 1085, Ann.Cas.1918B, 35 (1915). But, contra, Selma Sash, Door & Blind Factory v. Stoddard, 116 Ala. 251, 22 So. 555 (1897).

19. See N.Y.Cons.Laws, Cahill, c. 34, §§ 4, 14 (now N.Y.—McKinney's Lien Law, §§ 4, 14). West's Fla.Stat.Ann. § 713.06(1); Official Code Ga.Ann. § 44–14–361(b). See Sewer Viewer, Inc. v. Shawnee Sunset Developers, Inc., 454 So.2d 701 (Fla.App.1984) (statute's limitation does not apply if there is no specific price stated in general contract).

20. See Electric City Concrete Co. v. Phillips, 100 A.D.2d 1, 473 N.Y.S.2d 608 (1984). Commonly there are additional provisions making it the duty of the owner, on notification to him of unpaid obligations by the contractor to subcontractors, to withhold payments to the contractor for the benefit of the notifying lien claimant. Other statutes make it the duty of the owner, on making payments under the contract, to require a statement under oath from the contractor of the sums owed to subcontractors and then to withhold those sums.

21. See First Federal Savings & Loan Association v. Connelly, 97 Ill.2d 242, 73 Ill.Dec. 454, 454 N.E.2d 314 (1983); Wavetek Indiana, Inc. v. K.H. Gatewood Steel Co., ___ Ind. ___, 458 N.E.2d 265 (1984); AAA Electric & Neon Serv., Inc. v. R-Design Co., 364 N.W.2d 869 (Minn.App.1985). The date of completion is not always easy to determine. Suppose the owner calls the mechanic back to correct defective workmanship which has been discovered after nominal completion? See Southwest Paving Co. v. Stone Hills, 206 Cal.App.2d 548, 24 Cal.Rptr. 48 (1962). See also Daily v. Mid-America Bank, 130 Ill.App.3d 639, 85 Ill.Dec. 828, 474 N.E.2d 788 (1985). A sale of the property was held not tantamount to completion in Anderson v. Taylor, 55 Wn.2d 215, 347 P.2d 536, 78 A.L.R.2d 1161 (1959). See Hartman, Creditors' Rights and Security Transactions, 8 Vand.L.Rev. 989 (1955).

22. See Bonner Building Supply, Inc. v. Standard Forest Products, Inc., 106 Idaho 682, 682 P.2d 635 (1984).

When the lien is perfected by the giving of appropriate notice, however, its date for priority purposes generally relates back to some earlier time. This concept is critically important to mortgagees, who frequently must attempt to establish their own priority as against competing mechanics' liens.[23] Nearly half of the states treat the lien as taking its priority from the time of commencement of the building.[24] In theory this rule seems unobjectionable, since an inspection of the property will presumably disclose whether construction has begun or not.[25] As a practical matter, however, commencement is often an ambiguous event, with courts disagreeing as to whether it has occurred when lumber is piled on the property,[26] clearing of trees and brush or grading has begun,[27] or an electrical service pole and box are erected.[28] Well-advised construction lenders often photograph the property on the date they record their mortgages in order to establish that construction has not commenced; thus they hope to ensure their priority over mechanics' liens which might be filed later.[29]

The second most popular priority date is the time at which the particular lienor begins his service or furnishing of materials.[30] The difficulties under such statutes of determining commencement of services or supplies are considerably greater than those of being sure when

The action is ordinarily filed in state court, but may be in federal bankruptcy court; RDC, Inc. v. Brookleigh Builders, Inc., 309 N.C. 182, 305 S.E.2d 722 (1983).

23. The priority date of the mortgage is normally the date it was recorded; see Blue Spot, Inc. v. Rakower, 120 Misc.2d 150, 465 N.Y.S.2d 493 (1983). However, it may lose priority if the mortgagee had notice of the claim of lien when taking the mortgage; see Palmer v. Forrest, Mackey & Associates, 251 Ga. 304, 304 S.E.2d 704 (1983). Similarly, actual notice of an unrecorded mortgage may defeat the priority of a lienor; see Jadwin v. Kasal, 318 N.W.2d 844 (Minn.1982).

24. See Kratovil, Modern Mortgage Law and Practice § 214 (1972); Republic Bank v. Bohmar Minerals, Inc., 661 P.2d 521 (Okl.1983); Durant Construction Co. v. Gourley, 125 Mich.App. 695, 336 N.W.2d 856 (1983); Dixie Heating & Cooling Co. v. Bank of Gadsden, 437 So.2d 576 (Ala.Civ. App.1983). Under this view, it is immaterial whether the particular lienor did his work before or after the mortgage was recorded; see Barker's Inc. v. B.D.J. Development Co., 308 N.W.2d 78 (Iowa 1981). Cf. Strouss v. Simmons, __ Hawaii __, 657 P.2d 1004 (1982) (if mortgage recites it is for construction, it has priority over liens if recorded any time before completion).

25. A common, but not universal, requirement is that the work of improvement must be "visible"; see Strouss v. Simmons, __ Hawaii __, 657 P.2d 1004 (1982); Security Bank v. Pocono Web Press, Inc., 295 Pa.Super. 455, 441 A.2d 1321 (1982). Kloster-Madsen, Inc. v. Tafi's, Inc., 303 Minn. 59, 226 N.W.2d 603 (1975); Cook v. Carlson, 364 F.Supp. 24, 29 D.S.D. (1973).

26. Compare James v. Van Horn, 39 N.J.L. 353, 363 (1877), with Kansas Mortgage Co. v. Weyerhauser, 48 Kan. 335, 29 P. 153 (1892).

27. See Diversified Mortgage Investors v. Gepada, Inc., 401 F.Supp. 682 (S.D.Iowa 1975); Clark v. General Electric Co., 243 Ark. 399, 420 S.W.2d 830 (1967); Rupp. v. Earl H. Cline & Sons, Inc., 230 Md. 573, 188 A.2d 146, 1 A.L.R.3d 815 (1963).

28. Jim Walter Homes, Inc. v. Bowling, 521 S.W.2d 828 (Ark.1975).

29. See Jesco, Inc. v. Home Life Ins. Co., 357 N.W.2d 123 (Minn.App.1984). A similar issue may arise if a bona fide purchaser buys the property; see Starek v. TKW, Inc., 410 So.2d 35 (Ala.1982).

30. See Comment, Mechanics' Liens and Surety Bonds in the Building Trades, 68 Yale L.J. 138, 152 n. 69 (1968); Geiser v. Permacrete, Inc., 90 So.2d 610, 612 (Fla. 1956); Hickey v. Polachek, 63 Or.App. 784, 666 P.2d 294 (1983); In re Williamson, 43 B.R. 813, 827 (Bkrtcy.Utah 1984).

the whole building operation started. There is also the possibility of an intervening mortgage dividing the lien claimants into prior and subsequent groups, creating a problem of concern where the mechanics' lien statute provides that all lien claimants shall, as among themselves, be on a parity.[31] In third place come some half dozen jurisdictions that make the lien attach from the time of filing the claim. In a few states the liens attach at the date of the general contract, or the lienor's contract,[32] or when a notice of the contract is recorded. In some states the liens attach at different times depending upon various factors involved. In Missouri, all construction loans are apparently subordinate to mechanics' liens, regardless of the dates of commencement or recording.[33]

The statutes usually provide that property is lienable only if the improvements were constructed with the consent of the owner.[34] "Owner" is variously defined, and often a lease-holder or life tenant will not have the requisite power to consent.[35] With respect to "consent", it is obviously present if the owner has signed a construction contract, but some courts hold that no formal contract is required, and that the owner's acquiescence or even mere knowledge of the construc-

31. Pacific States Savings, Loan & Building Co. v. Dubois, 11 Idaho, 319, 83 P. 513 (1905); Ward v. Yarnelle, 173 Ind. 535, 91 N.E. 7 (1910); Henry & Coatsworth Co. v. Fisherdick, Administrator, 37 Neb. 207, 55 N.W. 643 (1893), and Meister v. J. Meister, Inc., 103 N.J.Eq. 78, 142 A. 312 (1928), permit the intervening encumbrance to create two different classes of mechanics' liens. See, accord, Conn.Pub. Acts, 3905–6, (now Conn.G.S.A. § 49–33) (1925). Gardner v. Leck, 52 Minn. 522, 54 N.W. 746 (1893), preferred all the lien claimants to the mortgagee. Cf. Finlayson v. Crooks, 47 Minn. 74, 49 N.W. 398, 645 (1891), rehearing denied 47 Minn. 74, 49 N.W. 645 (1891).

32. Chicago Title Insurance Co. v. Sherred Village Associates, 708 F.2d 804 (1st Cir.1983) (Maine law).

33. The theory is that, by making a construction loan, the mortgagee has waived its priority; see Kranz v. Centropolis Crusher Inc., 630 S.W.2d 140 (Mo. App.1982). But see Union Electric Co. v. Clayton Center Limited, 634 S.W.2d 261 (Mo.App.1982), suggesting that the waiver will not necessarily be found in every case.

34. See R. Powell, Real Property, ¶ 486 (1977). Under some statutes the owner's consent is presumed if he has knowledge of the work, unless he posts or records a "notice of non-responsibility"; see Falcon Holdings, Limited v. Isaacson, 66 Or.App. 614, 675 P.2d 501 (1984).

35. Express language in the lease may authorize the tenant to consent for the landlord, see American Seating Co. v. Philadelphia, 434 Pa. 370, 256 A.2d 599 (1969), or the court may imply such authority from the fact that the lease requires the tenant to construct the improvements, see Lentz Plumbing Co. v. Fee, 235 Kan. 266, 679 P.2d 736 (1984); Ott Hardware Co. v. Yost, 69 Cal.App.2d 593, 159 P.2d 663 (1945); cf. Dunlap v. Hinkle, ___ W.Va. ___, 317 S.E.2d 508 (1984) (mere authority in lease for tenant to construct improvements is insufficient to impose lien on lessor); Harner v. Schecter, 105 A.D.2d 932, 482 N.Y.S.2d 124 (1984) (owner's consent implied from course of conduct); Christensen v. Idaho Land Developers, Inc., 104 Id. 458, 660 P.2d 70 (1983); Landas Fertilizer Co. v. Hargreaves, 206 N.W.2d 675 (Iowa 1973); see note, 1952 Wash.U.L.Q. 453 (1952). The lien may well be valid against the limited interest of the tenant, even absent the landlord's consent; see Lentz Plumbing Co. v. Fee, 235 Kan. 266, 679 P.2d 736 (1984); Tropic Builders, Limited v. United States, 52 Hawaii 298, 475 P.2d 362 (1970). Cabana, Inc. v. Eastern Air Control, Inc., 61 Md.App. 609, 487 A.2d 1209 (1985). See also Carolina Builders Corp. v. Howard-Veasey Homes Inc., 72 N.C.App. 224, 324 S.E.2d 626 (1985) (contract vendee has sufficient interest to be considered "owner").

tion will suffice.[36] A number of these latter jurisdictions incorporate procedures under which an owner who has not contracted for the improvement may, within some fixed time after commencement of construction, file of record or post on the property a notice or disclaimer of responsibility.[37] The effect of such a notice, depending on the statute, may be to shift to the lienor the burden of proving actual consent, or entirely to bar the filing of liens on the owner's interest.[38]

Waivers of mechanics' liens are widely permitted, but must be analyzed in two separate contexts. The first is the purported waiver or "no-lien" clause in the original general contract. States which follow the derivative theory of lien liability generally enforce such clauses, treating them as barring liens filed both by the general contractor and by subcontractors and materialmen.[39] States which follow the direct liability approach usually treat no-lien clauses as unenforceable against the latter groups,[40] reasoning that since their rights are not derived from the general contract, it cannot adversely affect them. However, the results in both groups of jurisdictions are frequently affected by specific statutes, which often validate no-lien clauses against subcontractors and materialmen if the contract is filed for record. An intermediate group of states recognizes the validity of the no-lien clause

36. See Crowley Brothers v. Ward, 322 Ill.App. 687, 54 N.E.2d 753 (1944); cf. Petrillo v. Pelham Bay Park Land Co., 119 Misc. 146, 196 N.Y.S. 124 (1922).

37. See, e.g., Minn.Stat.Ann. § 514.06; similar provisions are found in California, Nevada, New Mexico, Oregon, and South Dakota. See comment, supra note 30, at 158 n. 99; Calif.Cont.Ed. of Bar, California Mechanics' Liens §§ 6.4–6.10 (1972); Annot., 123 A.L.R. 7. In some states, such as California, the owner is aided in learning of the proposed construction by the requirement that subcontractors and materials suppliers send him written notice of their activities within 20 days after commencement of the work or supplying of materials; West's Ann.Calif.Civ.Code, § 3097; see Calif.Cont.Ed. of Bar, California Mechanics' Liens §§ 3.8–3.15 (1972); Note, 21 Hast.L.J. 216 (1969). See also C&C Tile & Carpet Co. v. Aday, 697 P.2d 175 (Okl.App. 1975) (special notice to owners who reside on the liened property).

38. Under some statutes, however, the lienor may be permitted to remove the improvement notwithstanding the owner's notice of nonresponsibility; in effect, this may compel the owner to pay for the improvement in order to keep it. See, e.g., American Transit Mix Co. v. Weber, 106 Cal.App.2d 74, 234 P.2d 732 (1951).

39. Jurisdictions recognizing such contractual waivers include Connecticut, Illinois, Indiana, Iowa, Maryland, Minnesota, Missouri, Nebraska, Oregon, Pennsylvania, and Wisconsin. Such clauses are binding as to subcontractors but not as to the general contractor in Idaho, Illinois, and Massachusetts. See Wavetek Indiana, Inc. v. K.H. Gatewood Steel Co., ___ Ind.App. ___, 458 N.E.2d 265 (1984); Comment, supra note 30, at 158 n. 102; Annot., 75 A.L.R.3d 505, 543–48 (1977); Annot., 76 A.L.R.2d 1097 (1961).

New Jersey law permits the owner to avoid all liens merely by filing for record his contract and specifications. However, subcontractors and suppliers may file "notices of intention" to furnish materials or labor, and the owner is then legally bound to ensure that such claimants receive what is due them from each construction disbursement. See Solondz Bros. Lumber Co. v. Piperato, 28 N.J.Super. 414, 101 A.2d 33 (1953). A similar procedure is followed in Florida, although recordation of the contract is not required; see Fla.Stat. § 713.06; Note, Lien Rights and Construction Lending: Responsibilities and Liabilities in Florida, 29 U.Fla.L.Rev. 411, 417–21 (1977).

40. See Annot., 75 A.L.R.3d 505, 533–43 (1977), listing Alabama, Arkansas, Montana, Nebraska, and Ohio cases as following this view.

as binding the contractor, but as having no effect upon subcontractors or materialmen unless they have clearly assented to be bound by it.[41]

Waivers given by individual lien claimants during the course of construction are unquestionably valid,[42] and are extremely useful to owners and construction lenders. It is a wise and common practice for the owner to insist upon a sworn list of subcontractors and suppliers from the general contractor, and to require partial lien waivers from each party on the list prior to each disbursement of construction funds. Construction lenders also usually require such waivers,[43] which serve to indicate that the prospective claimant has been fully paid for work done or materials furnished to that date. When construction of the project is completed, the owner will usually require a final waiver, the effect of which will be to bar the filing of any lien on the project, even if the particular subcontractor must return to the site later to correct defects in his workmanship, for example.[44]

Sometimes waivers obtained during the course of construction are broadly worded to cover not only work performed to date but also all work to be done in the future. The cases are divided on the validity of such prospective waivers; some courts readily hold them valid,[45] while others construe them strongly against the party obtaining the waiver [46] or hold them unenforceable as against public policy.[47]

 WESTLAW REFERENCES

topic("mechanics' lien")

topic("mechanics' lien") (mechanic material! /s lien) /p secur*** /s interest /p foreclos***

---

41. See Steel Suppliers, Inc. v. Ehret, Inc., 486 A.2d 32 (Del.Super. 1984); Aetna Casualty & Surety Co. v. United States, 228 Ct.Cl. 146, 655 F.2d 1047 (1981) (Calif. law); Con Co., Inc. v. Wilson Acres Apartments, Limited, 56 N.C.App. 661, 289 S.E.2d 633 (1982), certiorari denied 306 N.C. 382, 294 S.E.2d 206 (1982); Higby v. Hooper, 124 Mont. 331, 221 P.2d 1043 (1950).

42. See Anchor Concrete Co. v. Victor Savings & Loan Association, 664 P.2d 396 (Okl.1983); Durant Construction, Inc. v. Gourley, 125 Mich.App. 695, 336 N.W.2d 856 (1983). Some courts regard the recitation of nominal consideration as adequate support for a lien waiver; see Ramsey v. Peoples Trust and Savings Bank, 148 Ind. App. 167, 264 N.E.2d 111 (1970). In jurisdictions in which this is not sufficient, the cases are divided as to whether a waiver is valid in favor of the owner of the property if the subcontractor has not actually been paid; compare Gerard C. Wallace Co. v. Simpson Land Co., 267 Md. 702, 298 A.2d 881 (1973) (waiver valid) with Cook v. Metal Building Products Inc., 297 Minn. 330,

211 N.W.2d 371 (1973) (waiver invalid absent detrimental reliance). Most courts would probably hold the waiver valid in favor of the construction lender on detrimental reliance grounds if it released funds on the basis of the waiver.

43. See First National Bank v. Smith, 331 N.W.2d 120 (Iowa 1983), narrowly construing a waiver as against a construction lender; cf. Frank Maio General Contractor, Inc. v. Consolidated Electric Supply, Inc., 452 So.2d 1092 (Fla.App.1984).

44. See R. Kratovil, Modern Mortgage Law and Practice § 214 (1972).

45. Townsend v. Barlow, 101 Conn. 86, 124 A. 832 (1924).

46. Southwestern Electrical Co. v. Hughes, 139 Kan. 89, 30 P.2d 114 (1934); Bruce Construction Corp. v. Federal Realty Corp., 104 Fla. 93, 139 So. 209 (1932).

47. Boise Cascade Corp. v. Stephens, 572 P.2d 1380 (Utah 1977); Brimwood Homes v. Knudsen Builders Supply Co., 14 Utah 2d 419, 385 P.2d 982 (1963).

§ 12.5 Mechanics' Liens—Constitutionality

Several courts have examined the constitutionality of mechanics' lien statutes; most have held them constitutional. In recent years, constitutional attacks on these statutes have featured a due process analysis of the variety involved in the line of Supreme Court cases beginning with Sniadach v. Family Finance Corp.[1] and running through North Georgia Finishing, Inc. v. Di-Chem, Inc.[2] However, mechanics' lien statutes were subjected to constitutional scrutiny long before *Sniadach*. The older cases generally found the statutes to be constitutional[3] as against a variety of constitutional objections, including ones based on due process,[4] equal protection,[5] freedom of contract,[6] and

§ 12.5

1. 395 U.S. 337, 89 S.Ct. 1820, 23 L.Ed. 2d 349 (1969).

2. 419 U.S. 601, 95 S.Ct. 719, 42 L.Ed.2d 751 (1975). The other cases in the series of Supreme Court decisions articulating notice and hearing standards in the debtor-creditor context are Fuentes v. Shevin, 407 U.S. 67, 92 S.Ct. 1983, 32 L.Ed.2d 556 (1972), rehearing denied 409 U.S. 902, 93 S.Ct. 177, 34 L.Ed.2d 165 (1972), and Mitchell v. W. T. Grant Co., 416 U.S. 600, 94 S.Ct. 1895, 40 L.Ed.2d 406 (1974). As to the issue of state action, see also Flagg Brothers, Inc. v. Brooks, 436 U.S. 149, 98 S.Ct. 1729, 56 L.Ed.2d 185 (1978).

3. Cases holding mechanics' lien statutes constitutional include: Jones v. Great Southern Fireproof Hotel Co., 86 F. 370 (C.C.A.Ohio 1898), reversed on other grounds 177 U.S. 449, 20 S.Ct. 690, 44 L.Ed. 842 (1900); Hollenbeck-Bush Planing Mill Co. v. Amweg, 177 Cal. 159, 170 P. 148 (1917); Stimson Mill Co. v. Nolan, 5 Cal. App. 754, 91 P. 262 (1907); Chicago Lumber Co. v. Newcomb, 19 Colo.App. 265, 74 P. 786 (1903); State v. Tabasso Homes, Inc., 42 Del. (3 Terry) 110, 28 A.2d 248 (1942); State v. Chillingworth, 126 Fla. 645, 171 So. 649 (1937); Summerlin v. Thompson, 31 Fla. 369, 12 So. 667 (1893); Prince v. Neal-Millard Co., 124 Ga. 884, 53 S.E. 761 (1906); Boyer v. Keller, 258 Ill. 106, 101 N.E. 237 (1913); Barrett v. Millikan, 156 Ind. 510, 60 N.E. 310 (1901); Smith v. Newbaur, 144 Ind. 95, 42 N.E. 40 (1895), rehearing denied 144 Ind. 95, 42 N.E. 1094 (1896); Aalfs Wall Paper & Paint Co. v. Bowker, 179 Iowa 726, 162 N.W. 33 (1917); Stewart v. Gardner-Warren Implement Co., 70 S.W. 1042 (Ky.1902) 24 Ky.Law Rep. 1216; Hightower v. Bailey, 108 Ky. 198, 56 S.W. 147 (1900); Bardwell v. Mann, 46 Minn. 285, 48 N.W. 1120 (1891); Chears Floor & Screen Co. v. Gidden, 159 Miss. 288, 131 So. 426 (1930);

Colpetzer v. Trinity Church, 24 Neb. 113, 37 N.W. 931 (1888); Baldridge v. Morgan, 15 N.M. 249, 106 P. 342 (1910); Gardner & Meeks Co. v. New York, Central & Hudson River Railroad Co., 72 N.J. Law 257, 62 A. 416 (1905); Chapel State Theatre Co. v. Hooper, 123 Ohio St. 322, 175 N.E. 450, affirmed 284 U.S. 588, 52 S.Ct. 137, 76 L.Ed. 508 (1931); Title Guarantee & Trust Co. v. Wrenn, 35 Or. 62, 56 P. 271 (1899); Cole Manufacturing Co. v. Falls, 90 Tenn. 466, 16 S.W. 1045 (1891); Spokane Manufacturing & Lumber Co. v. McChesney, 1 Wash. 609, 21 P. 198 (1889); Mallory v. La Crosse Abattoir Co., 80 Wis. 170, 49 N.W. 1071 (1891).

Cases finding provisions of mechanics' lien statutes unconstitutional include: Selma Sash, Door & Blind Factory v. Stoddard, 116 Ala. 251, 22 So. 555 (1897); Stimson Mill Co. v. Braun, 136 Cal. 122, 68 P. 481 (1902); Santa Cruz Rock Pavement Co. v. Lyons, 117 Cal. 212, 48 P. 1097 (1897); Cameron-Schroth-Cameron Co. v. Geseke, 251 Ill. 402, 96 N.E. 222 (1911); Kelly v. Johnson, 251 Ill. 135, 95 N.E. 1068 (1911); John Spry Lumber Co. v. Sault Savings Bank, Loan & Trust Co., 77 Mich. 199, 43 N.W. 778 (1889); Meyer v. Berlandi, 39 Minn. 438, 40 N.W. 513 (1888); Masterson v. Roberts, 336 Mo. 158, 78 S.W.2d 856 (1934); Waters v. Wolf, 162 Pa. 153, 29 A. 646 (1894).

4. See, e.g., Stimson Mill Co. v. Nolan, 5 Cal.App. 754, 91 P. 262 (1907); State v. Chillingworth, 126 Fla. 645, 171 So. 649 (1937); Baldridge v. Morgan, 15 N.M. 249, 106 P. 342 (1910).

5. See, e.g., Hollenbeck-Bush Planing Mill Co. v. Amweg, 177 Cal. 159, 170 P. 148 (1917); Barrett v. Milliken, 156 Ind. 510, 60 N.E. 310 (1901).

6. See, e.g., Jones v. Great Southern Fireproof Hotel Co., 86 F. 370 (C.C.A.Ohio 1898), reversed on other grounds 177 U.S.

impairment of contractual obligations.[7] The early due process cases are perhaps the most interesting. Typically it was asserted that allowing a subcontractor not in contractual privity with the landowner to assert a lien on the owner's property amounted to an unauthorized deprivation of property in violation of due process. Cases holding the statutes constitutional frequently responded that authorization was implicit in the owner's formation of the original construction contract, with statute becoming in effect part of the contract.[8]

Some of these early cases did find certain statutory provisions unconstitutional. In Kelly v. Johnson,[9] for example, the statute was held unconstitutional as depriving a landowner of liberty of contract to the extent it vested a subcontractor with the right to a lien despite a lien waiver agreement in the construction contract. In Meyer v. Berlandi,[10] a provision of Minnesota's statute was held unconstitutional that conclusively presumed the landowner's consent to a subcontractor's work if the landowner failed to enjoin the work. The court reasoned that the provision violated due process because it permitted a lien to be filed even when no actual consent to work had been given. In Selma Sash, Door & Blind Factory v. Stoddard,[11] the Alabama statute was found violative of due process because it permitted subcontractors to have a lien on property even when the owner fulfilled his contractual duties to the general contractor.

Notwithstanding these holdings, the vast majority of the older cases upheld the validity of lien statutes. Regardless of the results, however, the older cases have had little precedential impact on recent court considerations of the constitutionality of mechanics' liens. The reason for this is that modern attacks on constitutionality have exclusively featured a due process analysis unknown in earlier years. Between 1969 and 1975, the Supreme Court examined statutory prejudgment procedures in the debtor-creditor context and established notice and hearing standards that must be met for such procedures to comport with due process. In three of these cases—Sniadach v. Family Finance Corp.,[12] Fuentes v. Shevin,[13] and North Georgia Finishing, Inc. v. Di-Chem Inc.[14]—prejudgment procedures were found violative of due process. In one case—Mitchell v. W. T. Grant Co.[15]—due process standards were found to be met. There is considerable uncertainty as to the

449, 20 S.Ct. 690, 44 L.Ed. 842 (1900); Boyer v. Keller, 258 Ill. 106, 101 N.E. 237 (1913).

7. See, e.g., State v. Tabasso Homes, Inc., 42 Del. (3 Terry) 110, 28 A.2d 248 (1942); Colpetzer v. Trinity Church, 24 Neb. 113, 37 N.W. 931 (1888); Chapel State Theatre Co. v. Hooper, 123 Ohio St. 322, 175 N.E. 450, affirmed 284 U.S. 588, 52 S.Ct. 137, 76 L.Ed. 508 (1931).

8. See, e.g., Stimson Mill Co. v. Nolan, 5 Cal.App. 754, 91 P. 262 (1907).

9. 251 Ill. 135, 95 N.E. 1068 (1911).

10. 39 Minn. 438, 40 N.W. 513 (1888).

11. 116 Ala. 251, 22 So. 555 (1897).

12. 395 U.S. 337, 89 S.Ct. 1820, 23 L.Ed. 2d 349 (1969).

13. 407 U.S. 67, 92 S.Ct. 1983, 32 L.Ed. 556 (1972), rehearing denied 409 U.S. 902, 93 S.Ct. 177, 34 L.Ed.2d 165 (1972).

14. 419 U.S. 601, 95 S.Ct. 719, 42 L.Ed. 2d 751 (1975).

15. 416 U.S. 600, 94 S.Ct. 1895, 40 L.Ed. 2d 406 (1974).

precise state of the law in this area—even among justices of the Court [16]—but at least this much seems clear: absent extraordinary circumstances, statutory prejudgment creditor remedies which deprive a debtor of a significant property interest without notice and a prior opportunity for hearing are unconstitutional unless sufficient safeguards are present to ensure that the debtor's interests are protected.[17]

The U.S. Supreme Court has not yet issued an opinion on the application of these due process standards to mechanics' liens; [18] consequently, it is not entirely clear what safeguards would be required. Other courts, however, have struggled with the constitutional issue. Most have upheld the statutes examined,[19] but two have held otherwise.[20] To some extent, of course, the differences in result reflect differences in the statutes examined, but they also reflect differences in approach. A brief survey of prominent cases will make this clear.[21]

16. Compare North Georgia Finishing, Inc. v. Di-Chem, Inc., 419 U.S. 601, 608–09, 95 S.Ct. 719, 723, 42 L.Ed.2d 751 (1975) (concurring opinions) with Mitchell v. W. T. Grant Co., 416 U.S. 600, 623–29, 629–36, 94 S.Ct. 1895, 1907–10, 1910–14, 40 L.Ed.2d 406 (1973) (concurring and dissenting opinions).

17. See, e.g., North Georgia Finishing, Inc. v. Di-Chem, Inc., 419 U.S. 601, 95 S.Ct. 719, 42 L.Ed.2d 751 (1975); Catz & Robinson, Due Process and Creditor's Remedies: From Sniadach and Fuentes to Mitchell, North Georgia and Beyond, 28 Rutgers L.Rev. 541 (1975).

18. The Court did, however, summarily affirm the decision of a three judge district court upholding the constitutionality of Arizona's mechanics' lien statute. See Spielman-Fond, Inc. v. Hanson's, Inc., 379 F.Supp. 997 (D.Ariz.1973) (per curiam), affirmed 417 U.S. 901, 94 S.Ct. 2596, 41 L.Ed. 2d 208 (1974). The degree to which this summary affirmance should be binding on other courts has been the subject of considerable discussion. See, e.g., B & P Development v. Walker, 420 F.Supp. 704 (W.D. Pa.1976); Bankers Trust Co. v. El Paso Pre-Cast Co., 560 P.2d 457 (Colo.1977); Barry Properties, Inc. v. Fick Brothers Roofing Co., 277 Md. 15, 353 A.2d 222 (1976).

19. See B & P Development v. Walker, 420 F.Supp. 704 (W.D.Pa.1976); In re Thomas A. Cary, Inc., 412 F.Supp. 667 (E.D.Va.1976); Ruocco v. Brinker, 380 F.Supp. 432 (S.D.Fla.1974); Spielman-Fond, Inc. v. Hanson's Inc., 379 F.Supp. 997 (D.Ariz.1973) (per curiam), affirmed 417 U.S. 901, 94 S.Ct. 2596, 41 L.Ed.2d 208 (1974); Cook v. Carlson, 364 F.Supp. 24 (D.S.D.1973); Nelson-American Developers, Limited v. Enco Engineering Corp., 337 So.

2d 729 (Ala.1976); Connolly Development, Inc. v. Superior Court, 17 Cal.3d 803, 132 Cal.Rptr. 477, 553 P.2d 637 (1976), appeal dismissed 429 U.S. 1056, 97 S.Ct. 778, 50 L.Ed.2d 773 (1977); Bankers Trust Co. v. El Paso Pre-Cast Co., 560 P.2d 457 (Colo.1977); Tucker Door & Trim Corp. v. Fifteenth Street Co., 235 Ga. 727, 221 S.E.2d 433 (1975); Carl A. Morse, Inc. v. Rentar Industrial Development Corp., 56 A.D.2d 30, 391 N.Y.S.2d 425 (1977); Silverman v. Gossett, 553 S.W.2d 581 (Tenn.1977); Home Building Corp. v. Ventura Corp., 568 S.W.2d 769 (Mo.1978); Keith Young & Sons Construction Co. v. Victor Senior Citizens Housing, Inc., 262 N.W.2d 554 (Iowa 1978); Williams & Works, Inc. v. Springfield Corp., 81 Mich.App. 355, 265 N.W.2d 328 (1978), reversed on other grounds 408 Mich. 732, 293 N.W.2d 304 (1980); South Central District of the Pentecostal Church v. Bruce-Rogers Co., 269 Ark. 130, 599 S.W.2d 702 (1980); Mobile Components, Inc. v. Layon, 623 P.2d 591 (Okl.1980), certiorari denied 454 U.S. 963, 102 S.Ct. 502, 70 L.Ed.2d 378 (1981); Kloos v. Jacobson, 30 B.R. 965 (Bkrtcy.Idaho 1983).

20. Roundhouse Construction Corp. v. Telesco Masons Supplies Co., 168 Conn. 371, 362 A.2d 778 (1975), vacated and remanded 423 U.S. 809, 96 S.Ct. 20, 46 L.Ed. 2d 29 (1975), reaffirmed 170 Conn. 155, 365 A.2d 393 (1976), certiorari denied 429 U.S. 889, 97 S.Ct. 246, 50 L.Ed.2d 172 (1976); Barry Properties Inc. v. Fick Brothers Roofing Co., 277 Md. 15, 353 A.2d 222 (1976).

21. Some commentators have discussed the issue. See Frank & McManus, Balancing Almost Two Hundred Years of Economic Policy Against Contemporary Due Process Standards—Mechanics' Liens in Maryland after Barry Properties, 36 Md.L.

The leading case upholding the constitutionality of a mechanics' lien is Spielman-Fond, Inc. v. Hanson's, Inc.[22] In that case, a three-judge district court evaluated the Arizona mechanics' lien statute in light of *Sniadach* and *Fuentes*. The court focused on whether the filing of a mechanics' lien constituted a constitutionally cognizable deprivation of property that would require proper notice and hearing. While the court conceded that a mechanics' lien reduced the owner's ability to alienate his property, it ruled that lien filing did "not amount to a taking of a significant property interest."[23] Accordingly, said the court, due process was not violated by the absence of notice and hearing prior to lien filing. The Supreme Court summarily affirmed the ruling of this three-judge panel.[24]

Several cases have followed the *Spielman-Fond* decision in finding that a mechanics' lien filing does not involve the taking of a significant property interest.[25] For example, in Carl A. Morse Inc. v. Rentar Industrial Development Corp.,[26] the due process challenge to the New York statute was asserted by a landowner whose property was subjected to lien claims of over a million dollars. The court analyzed the *Sniadach* line of cases through *North Georgia*, focusing particularly on how the New York statutory scheme differed from the one invalidated in the *North Georgia* case. The court averred that the New York provision effected no deprivation of use or possession of property. Although it admitted that a mechanics' lien impinges on the economic interests of a landowner, the court found this insufficient to bring the Fourteenth Amendment into play. It was, said the court, a "minimal intrusion." In addition, the court reasoned that even though the value of the property is diminished by the amount of a lien, the loss is offset by the value of the improvements contributed by a lienor. The court also examined the particular provisions of the lien statute, and found them to constitute a constitutional accommodation of the competing interest of owners, materialmen, and purchasers. Among the safe-

Rev. 733 (1977); Levine, Due Process of Law in Pre-Judgment Attachment and the Filing of Mechanics' Liens, 50 Conn.B.J. 335 (1976); Note, The Constitutional Validity of Mechanics' Liens Under the Due Process Clause—A Reexamination after Mitchell and North Georgia, 55 B.U.L.Rev. 263 (1975); Note, Mechanics' Liens Subject to Fourteenth Amendment Guarantees, 26 Cath.U.L.Rev. 129 (1976); 8 Conn.L.Rev. 744 (1976).

22. 379 F.Supp. 997 (D.Ariz.1973) (per curiam), affirmed 417 U.S. 901, 94 S.Ct. 2596, 41 L.Ed.2d 208 (1974).

23. Id. at 999.

24. 417 U.S. 901, 94 S.Ct. 2596, 41 L.Ed. 2d 208 (1974).

25. See B & P Development v. Walker, 420 F.Supp. 704 (W.D.Pa.1976); In re

Thomas A. Cary, Inc., 412 F.Supp. 667 (E.D.Va.1976); Ruocco v. Brinker, 380 F.Supp. 432 (S.D.Fla.1974); Bankers Trust Co. v. El Paso Pre-Cast Co., 560 P.2d 457 (Colo.1977); Tucker Door & Trim Corp. v. Fifteenth Street Co., 235 Ga. 727, 221 S.E.2d 433 (1975); Carl A. Morse, Inc. v. Rentar Industrial Development Corp., 56 A.D.2d 30, 391 N.Y.S.2d 425 (1977); Silverman v. Gossett, 553 S.W.2d 581 (Tenn.1977).

A pre-*Spielman-Fond* decision upheld the constitutionality of the South Dakota mechanics' lien provisions on the grounds that the deprivation of property was de minimus. See Cook v. Carlson, 364 F.Supp. 24 (D.S.D.1973).

26. 56 A.D.2d 30, 391 N.Y.S.2d 425 (1977).

guards contained within these provisions, the court noted that the lienor was required in filing the lien to state under oath the facts giving rise to his claim, that the owner could discharge the lien by posting a bond, that the owner could compel an expeditious determination on the merits by demanding foreclosure, and that the lien could remain in force no longer than a year from filing unless a foreclosure action were commenced or a continuance granted.[27]

A different analytical approach to the due process question was taken by the California Supreme Court in Connolly Development, Inc. v. Superior Court.[28] The statutory scheme under attack in *Connolly* required a potential lienor to follow certain procedures in order to obtain a lien. One such requirement was the filing of a preliminary notice of claim with the owner, general contractor, and construction lender within twenty days of furnishing materials. In addition, the actual lien claim had to be recorded within ninety days after completion of the improvement or within thirty days after recordation of a notice of completion of the project. The lien could be released if the owner posted a bond, and it was discharged unless a foreclosure suit was begun within ninety days of recordation. These particular provisions ultimately convinced the court to conclude that a constitutional accommodation of competing interests was achieved by the California lien provisions.

Unlike the two cases discussed earlier, the court in *Connolly* determined that a constitutionally cognizable taking of property was involved in the recordation of a mechanics' lien. "A deprivation," said the court, "need not reach the magnitude of a physical seizure of property in order to fall within the compass of the due process clause."[29] Here, the constraints imposed on the owner's ability to sell or encumber his property were held sufficient to constitute a taking under the Fourteenth Amendment.

Having crossed this threshold, the court was then forced to decide whether state action was present. The court had no difficulty finding state action—a mechanics' lien is a creature of statute, and it can only be recorded and enforced under the power of the state.

The final question before the court was whether the statutory provisions comported with due process. The court held that they did. In reaching this conclusion, the court noted that California law provided more safeguards than the Arizona statute upheld in *Spielman-Fond*.[30] It also observed that the problematic garnishment provisions

27. The court did not mention the fact that a lien could be filed up to four months following completion of the contract or the furnishing of materials. Id. at 35–36, 391 N.Y.S.2d at 432 (dissenting opinion).

28. 17 Cal.3d 803, 132 Cal.Rptr. 477, 553 P.2d 637 (1976), appeal dismissed 429 U.S. 1056, 97 S.Ct. 778, 50 L.Ed.2d 773 (1977). The case also deals with the consti-

tutionality of California's statutory "stop notice" provision.

29. Id. at 812, 132 Cal.Rptr. at 483, 553 P.2d at 643.

30. One such protection is the California requirement that the lien claimant give a preliminary notice to the "owner or reputed owner" within 20 days of commencing work. The court acknowledged invalidated in *North Georgia* were different from the provisions of California law. In this regard, the court emphasized that the California statute did not effect a total deprivation of the owner's property, that the lienor had a legitimate interest in that property, and that the landowner had adequate statutory protection. The court noted that modern due process analysis was flexible, basically constituting a consideration of affected interests. In light of the statutory safeguards, the balance of interest weighed in favor of constitutionality.

Two courts have held mechanics' lien provisions unconstitutional under due process analysis. The first decision was that of the Supreme Court of Connecticut in Roundhouse Construction Corporation v. Telesco Masons Supplies Company.[31] The Maryland Supreme Court decided the second in Barry Properties Inc. v. Fick Bros. Roofing Company.[32] Each of these decisions merits discussion.

Beginning its analysis in *Roundhouse,* the Connecticut court reviewed the statutory provisions under attack. These provisions required that, in order to have a valid lien, a potential lienor must file a sworn statement of amount claimed with the town clerk within sixty days after his work. The provisions also required subcontractors and materialmen not privy to the original construction agreement to give notice to the owner against whose property liens are claimed. The owner could apply for dissolution of the lien by filing a bond, or request a discharge on grounds of invalidity. If the request were not honored within thirty days, the owner could then bring a court action for discharge. In no case could a lien remain in force longer than four years unless the lienor commenced a foreclosure action within two years of filing.

The court found that these provisions failed to meet due process hearing standards. Although acknowledging that an early post-taking hearing instead of a prior hearing seemed acceptable after *North Georgia,* the court was concerned that it was possible for a lien to continue for two years without any hearing at all. This was different, said the court, from the Arizona statute upheld in *Spielman-Fond,* under which the lien could last no longer than six months without a foreclosure action. "Such a provision," said the court, "would seem to offer the bare minimum of due process protection consistent with the extent of deprivation present."[33] On the issue of deprivation itself the court noted that even though a mechanics' lien does not prevent the

---

that the owner would not always get actual notice. See Brown Co. v. Superior Court, 148 Cal.App.3d 891, 196 Cal.Rptr. 258 (1983).

31. 168 Conn. 371, 362 A.2d 778, vacated and remanded 423 U.S. 809, 96 S.Ct. 20, 46 L.Ed.2d 29 (1975), reaffirmed 170 Conn. 155, 365 A.2d 393 (1976), certiorari denied 429 U.S. 889, 97 S.Ct. 246, 50 L.Ed.2d 172 (1976).

32. 277 Md. 15, 353 A.2d 222 (1976).

33. 168 Conn. at 381, 362 A.2d at 783. The court was also concerned that the lien statute permitted the ex parte filing, without judicial supervision, of a conclusory statement and that there was no requirement of posting a bond by the lienor.

alienation of property, it does restrict the opportunity to alienate. This was sufficient, according to the court, to constitute a significant taking of property.[34]

A similar analysis pointed to unconstitutionality in *Barry Properties*. The Maryland statutory provisions under attack allowed for creation of a mechanics' lien by a general contractor without prior notice to the owner. Although a subcontractor was required to give the owner a notice of intent to make a lien claim, the claim could be filed before the notice was given. In any case, this notice had to be given within ninety days after furnishing work or material.[35] No hearing was required concerning the lien prior to foreclosure. After recordation, the lien could last for one year, unless enforcement were sought within that period. During this year, the owner could sue to compel the claimant to prove the lien's validity or he could post a bond and secure a release. The court, in reasoning reminiscent of *Connolly*, found that state action was involved and that there was a significant taking of property.[36] The only remaining question was whether the statutory scheme provided "protections such as those discussed in *Mitchell* and *North Georgia Finishing* or is deemed to be within the 'extraordinary circumstances' exception." [37]

The court noted that there was no requirement of a sworn statement by the creditor, setting forth facts upon which the lien was based, that there was no requirement of a bond to protect the debtor, nor was there an opportunity for a prompt post-lien hearing. The owner's opportunity to compel the claimant to prove the lien's validity was subject to the usual strictures of the trial calendar. In view of these findings, the court said the requirements of *Mitchell* and *North Georgia* were unmet. It also concluded that the extraordinary circumstances exception did not apply. *Spielman-Fond* was distinguishable, said the court, because the Arizona statute provided for safeguards not reflected in Maryland law.[38]

---

34. The Connecticut statute was subsequently amended to give the owner notice and the right to a prompt hearing; see Conn.Gen.Stat.Ann. § 49–33 et seq. It has been held constitutional as to owners, but may be invalid as to general contractors, who must post bond to obtain a hearing. See General Electric Supply Co. v. Southern New England Telephone Co., 185 Conn. 583, 441 A.2d 581 (1981).

35. A general contractor was not required to give any such notice, but had to file a lien claim within 180 days of the completion of work or the furnishing of materials. 277 Md. at 19–20, 353 A.2d at 226.

36. The court said that the existence of a lien diminishes an owner's equity, severely impairs alienability of property, and makes additional financing problematical.

After *Barry Properties* was decided, the Maryland legislature revised the statute to require notice to the owner and a judicial hearing before attachment of the lien. See 1976 Md.Laws ch. 349, amending Md.Code, Real Prop., §§ 9–101 to 9–113; Cabana, Inc. v. Eastern Air Control, Inc., 61 Md.App. 609, 487 A.2d 1209 (1985); Tyson v. Masten Lumber & Supply, Inc., 44 Md. App. 293, 408 A.2d 1051 (1979); Note, 6 U.Balt.L.Rev. 181 (1976).

37. 277 Md. at 31, 353 A.2d at 232.

38. The court specifically referred to the Arizona provisions requiring that the claimant make a sworn statement upon filing his lien claim, that the owner be notified within a reasonable time of the filing, that the claimant institute enforcement proceedings within six months of filing, and permitting the owner to discharge

Modern due process challenges to statutory provisions have usually failed, either because courts have been unwilling to find a significant deprivation of property or because appropriate constitutional accommodations have been found within the statutory scheme itself. Some well reasoned recent opinions, however, have discerned a significant deprivation of property in the imposition of mechanics' liens. Once this threshold is crossed, state action is easily found; the remaining question is whether adequate safeguards exist. Precisely what safeguards will be found adequate is not clear, but it appears that a statute may be in constitutional trouble if it permits a potential lienor to file without notice long after work's completion or if it allows a lien to subsist beyond six months without requiring a hearing. The *Spielman-Fond* case has become something of a standard in this area; courts have thus far been unwilling to invalidate statutory provisions like those upheld in that case.

 WESTLAW REFERENCES
topic("mechanics' lien") /p constitutional***

§ 12.6   The Stop Notice and the Equitable Lien

The mechanics' lien, the traditional refuge of unpaid subcontractors and suppliers, is often useless to them in construction projects. Increasingly construction lenders have learned to record their mortgages before any work is done,[1] and to avoid optional advances;[2] under these circumstances the mechanics' lien claimants are almost certain to be subordinate to the construction loan, and its foreclosure will seldom produce any surplus for them. An alternative source of payment to the subcontractors and suppliers is the payment bond, but its use is generally confined to large commercial projects and those being built with public funds.[3] In residential subdivisions and small apartment projects, neither the lien nor the bond is likely to be available.

At least ten states have attempted to provide another route to the unpaid subcontractors and suppliers: the stop notice.[4] In essence, it is a right to make and enforce a claim against the construction lender (or

---

the lien by filing a bond. Id. at 34, 353 A.2d at 233–34.

§ 12.6

1. Mechanics' liens generally relate back in priority to the time the work was commenced; if the construction loan mortgage is recorded first, it will have priority over such liens. See § 12.4, supra, at notes 23–29.

2. An optional advance under a construction loan, if made by a lender having actual notice of intervening liens, will generally be subordinate to them. See § 12.7, infra.

3. See § 12.2, supra, at notes 31–35.

4. Ala.Code 1975, § 35–11–210; West's Cal.Civ.Code, §§ 3156–72; Colo.Rev.Stat. § 38–22–102; Burns Ind.Ann.Stat. § 32–8–3–9; Miss.Code 1972, § 85–7–181; N.C. Gen.Stat. § 44A–18; N.J.S.A. 2A:44–77, 78; Vernon's Texas Code Ann., Property Code §§ 53.081–.084; Wis.Stat.Ann. § 779.036; West's Rev.Code Wash.Ann. § 60.04.210. See generally Comment, Mechanics Liens: The "Stop Notice" Comes to Washington, 49 Wash.L.Rev. 685, 694 (1974); Comment, California's Private Stop Notice Law: Due Process Requirements, 25 Hast.L.J. 1043, 1054–57 (1974).

in some states, the owner) [5] for a portion of the undisbursed construction loan proceeds, if any. It is somewhat like a garnishment of the loan funds, although the analogy is not entirely accurate; a stop notice may be effectively filed, for example, even if the borrower-developer has defaulted and is therefore not entitled to any further construction draws.[6] Obviously the stop notice is effective only if some funds remain in the lender's or owner's hands.[7] The remedy is statutory, and specific time requirements must be met; [8] often the claimant must file a bond to indemnify the lender against damages which might result from a wrongful claim.[9] The lender may simply pay the claim and discharge the stop notice,[10] but if the claim is disputed or there are insufficient funds to pay all stop notice claims, litigation may be necessary.[11]

The statutes commonly deny availability of the stop notice if a payment bond has been filed, and some also do so if conventional mechanics' lien recovery is available.[12] Thus the foreclosure of the construction loan is not a bar to the assertion of a stop notice, and in some states may actually be helpful by establishing that the mechanics' lien has been destroyed.

One effect of the stop notice remedy is generally to make lenders more careful in administration of construction loans. There are two reasons for this. One is that if claimants are unpaid and therefore file

---

5. See, e.g., West's Ann.Cal.Civ.Code, §§ 3158–59; under California law, the claimant need not file a bond if his notice is directed to the owner. See also Matter of Hull, 19 B.R. 501 (Bkrtcy.Ind.1982) (Indiana statute confers personal right against owner, but not a lien on funds); Matter of Valaireo, Inc., 9 B.R. 289 (Bkrtcy.N.J.1981) (New Jersey, semple); Exchange Savings & Loan Association v. Monocrete Pty, Limited, 629 S.W.2d 34 at 37 (Tex.1982).

Some of the statutes also provide for the filing of stop notices against governmental entities for whom public works projects are being constructed.

6. See A–1 Door & Materials Co. v. Fresno Guarantee Savings & Loan Association, 61 Cal.2d 728, 40 Cal.Rptr. 85, 394 P.2d 829 (1964).

7. See International Telephone & Telegraph Corp. v. Envirco Services, Inc., 144 N.J.Super. 31, 364 A.2d 549 (1976) (owner not liable on stop notice where general contractor's breach has terminated owner's liability on contract.)

8. See, e.g., Moss, The Stop Notice Remedy in California—Updated, 47 L.A.Bar. Bull. 299 (1972). Under the California statute, the claimant must give a notice to the construction lender within 20 days after commencing work, or it is ineligible to file a stop notice; see Romak Iron Works v.

Prudential Insurance Co., 104 Cal.App.3d 767, 163 Cal.Rptr. 869 (1980).

9. E.g., West's Ann.Cal.Civ.Code, § 3083. In order to free up the funds which the stop notice has frozen, the lender or owner can file a corresponding bond and discharge the stop notice; id. at § 3171.

10. The lender or owner is generally personally liable if he fails to set aside, from the construction loan account, the amount claimed by the stop notice (or the amount set by the statute, if different from the claim; see West's Rev.Code Wash.Ann. 60.04.210(4), setting forth a rather complex and confusing formula for determining the amount to be withheld; see, Comment, Wash.L.Rev., supra note 4, at 697 n. 68.) See Flintkote Co. v. Presley of Northern California, 154 Cal.App.3d 458, 201 Cal. Rptr. 262 (1984).

11. The stop notice claimants usually share pro-rata if the funds are insufficient to pay all claims. The statutes may provide a procedure for adjudication of disputed claims; see, e.g., West's Ann.Cal.Civ. Code, §§ 3172–73.

12. See Colorado, New Jersey, and Wisconsin statutes, supra note 4. Cf. Cordell v. Regan, 23 Wn.App. 739, 598 P.2d 416 (1979) (claimant may simultaneously file stop notice and foreclose mechanics lien).

stop notices, they may bring the entire project to a halt; [13] this is especially true if it is necessary to litigate the validity of the claims and there are many of them, for they may tie up the entire construction loan account for a long period.[14] A second reason is that negligent or wrongful disbursal of funds may come back to haunt the lender; the stop notice claimants may assert that such money should be regarded, for stop notice purposes, as still held in the hands of the lender and amenable to the claims.[15] Lenders in stop notice jurisdictions are likely to take a fairly active role in project supervision, and often use the voucher or direct-payment system of loan disbursement rather than the looser progress-payments system.[16] By this they hope to make certain that all subcontractors and suppliers are paid on time, and that no funds are diverted to non-construction uses.

Since the stop notice amounts to a garnishment of funds without a prior notice or hearing, it might be held a violation of due process under the *Sniadach-North Georgia* line of cases discussed in Section 12.5, supra. The California Supreme Court held its state's statute valid against such an attack in Connolly Development, Inc. v. Superior Court.[17] While the court conceded that the stop notice resulted in more than *de minimis* takings of property, and that it involved state action, it concluded that the interest of stop notice claimants in a rapid and efficient remedy outweighed the relatively limited deprivation visited upon the owner. In other states, however, this issue may yet be resolved differently.

The Equitable Lien

It often happens that neither the stop notice nor the mechanics' lien provides an adequate remedy to one who has supplied labor or materials to a construction project. As we have already indicated, foreclosure of the construction loan mortgage will usually wipe out the mechanics' lien, and the stop notice may be unavailable in the jurisdiction or the claimant may have omitted some essential procedural

13. See Idaco Lumber Co. v. Northwestern Savings & Loan Association, 265 Cal. App.2d 490, 71 Cal.Rptr. 422 (1968); Ilyin, Stop Notice—Construction Loan Officer's Nightmare, 16 Hast.L.J. 187 (1964).

14. See Note, 13 Cal.West.L.Rev. 489, 531–33 (1977). The California statute provides a speedy summary procedure for litigating the validity of stop notices on public projects, but it does not apply to private projects; West's Ann.Cal.Civ.Code, §§ 3197–3205. In Connolly Development, Inc. v. Superior Court, 17 Cal.3d 803, 132 Cal.Rptr. 477, 553 P.2d 637 (1976), appeal dismissed 429 U.S. 1056, 97 S.Ct. 778, 50 L.Ed.2d 773 (1977), the court expressed approval of the summary procedure and suggested that the statute might be amended to cover private work as well, but conclud-

ed that its unavailability on private projects did not make the stop notice unconstitutional; id. at 17 Cal.3d 828 n. 26, 132 Cal.Rptr. at 494 n. 26.

15. See Moss, The Stop Notice Remedy in California—Updated, 47 L.A. Bar Bull. 299, 303–04 (1972); Miller v. Mountain View Savings & Loan Association, 238 Cal. App.2d 644, 48 Cal.Rptr. 278 (1965).

16. See Lubell, Changes in Construction Lenders' Policies—1958–1969, A Lender's Viewpoint, 44 L.A.Bar Bull. 346 (1969).

17. 17 Cal.3d 803, 132 Cal.Rptr. 477, 553 P.2d 637 (1976), appeal dismissed, 429 U.S. 1056, 97 S.Ct. 778, 50 L.Ed.2d 773 (1977). See Note, 13 Cal.West L.Rev. 489 (1977).

element in his filing or may be outside the scope of the statute. For example, he may be a remote materialman (one who has supplied materials to another materialman), an architect (in a jurisdiction in which architects are protected by neither mechanics' liens nor stop notices, as is common), or a general contractor [18] (a class not covered by most stop notice laws).

On such facts, the claimant who has supplied materials or labor may assert an equitable lien on either the land itself or the undisbursed portion of the construction loan funds, if any.[19] Several barriers exist which may cause this claim to fail, however. One is the argument that the mechanics' lien and stop notice statutes were intended by the legislature to constitute the sole remedies for such claimants, and that any extra-statutory remedy is out of order.[20] This argument is sound if the legislature has said as much,[21] but in most jurisdictions there is no indication that the statutory remedies are intended to be exclusive, and such a result should not be easily inferred.[22]

To analyze the other barriers to recovery on an equitable lien theory, we must focus on lien claims to the undisbursed loan funds.[23] While claims to a lien on the land itself are also entirely possible,[24] they are analytically much simpler and will be discussed later. Courts dealing with lien claims to the loan funds have explained the lien as based on either of two theories: the equitable concept of unjust enrichment [25] or the contract doctrine of third-party beneficiary,[26] with the lien claimant as the beneficiary of the construction loan agreement.

18. General contractors are usually within the class of persons who can claim equitable liens of the type described in the text below; see Swinerton & Walberg Co. v. Union Bank, 25 Cal.App.3d 259, 101 Cal. Rptr. 665 (1972).

19. See Reitz, Construction Lenders' Liability to Contractors, Subcontractors, and Materialmen, 130 U.Pa.L.Rev. 416 (1981); Lefcoe & Schaffer, Construction Lending and the Equitable Lien, 40 So.Cal.L.Rev. 439 (1967); Smith & Cobbe, Questions of Priority Between Mechanics' Lienors and Construction Loan Mortgages, 38 Ohio St. L.J. 3, 15–17 (1977).

20. R.M. Shoemaker Co. v. Southeastern Pennsylvania Economic Development Corp., 275 Pa.Super. 594, 419 A.2d 60 (1980).

21. See West's Ann.Cal.Civ.Code § 3264, enacted in 1967, which expressly declares the stop notice the exclusive remedy as against undisbursed construction loan funds, thereby wiping out a long line of California equitable lien cases; see Boyd & Lovesee Lumber Co. v. Modular Marketing Corp., 44 Cal.App.3d 460, 118 Cal.Rptr. 699 (1975); Pankow Construction Co. v. Advance Mortgage Co., 618 F.2d 611 (9th Cir.1980); Gutierrez, California Civil Code

Section 3264 and the Ghost of the Equitable Lien, 30 Hast.L.J. 493 (1979).

22. See Crane Co. v. Fine, 221 So.2d 145 (Fla.1969), conformed to 222 So.2d 36, recognizing the equitable lien as an alternative to the mechanics' lien.

23. See Aetna Casualty & Surety Co. v. United States, 228 Ct.Cl. 146, 655 F.2d 1047 (1981) (Court of Claims has no jurisdiction of claimed equitable lien against HUD as assignee of construction loan). Cf. Bor-Son Building Corp. v. Heller, 572 F.2d 174 (8th Cir.1978) (federal district courts have jurisdiction of such claims.) But see Marcus Garvey Square, Inc. v. Winston Burnett Construction Co., 595 F.2d 1126 (9th Cir.1979).

24. See note 33, infra.

25. S.S. Silberblatt, Inc. v. East Harlem Pilot Block, 608 F.2d 28 (2d Cir.1979); Irwin Concrete, Inc. v. Sun Coast Properties, Inc., 33 Wn.App. 190, 653 P.2d 1331 (1982); In re Monroe County Housing Corp., 18 B.R. 741 (Bkrtcy.Fla.1982); Cf. Taylor Woodrow Blitman Construction Co. v. Southfield Gardens Co., 534 F.Supp. 340 (D.Mass.1982) (no unjust enrichment, where owner was solvent and where a val-

26. See note 26 on page 879.

Some courts have dealt with these concepts separately while others have merged them together, sometimes adding a dose of estoppel; the cases are difficult to synthesize. Depending on which of these theories is employed, the equitable lien claimant may be required to satisfy one or more of the criteria discussed below.

Commonly, the courts will recognize an equitable lien only if the construction lender has made some representation to the claimant during the course of construction.[27] One type of representation usually considered sufficient is an assurance that the claimant will be paid, or that he will be "made whole" or "taken care of."[28] Such a statement seems to satisfy the supposed requirement, in third-party-beneficiary law, that the parties have intended the claimant to have the benefits of the contract.[29] Yet this test reflects a misconception, for the modern majority view is that only the obligee to whom the direct promise was made must have intended that the third party be benefitted by it;[30] under this view the intent of the obligor—the construction lender in the present discussion—is immaterial, and his statements to the lien claimant should be deemed irrelevant. Since in virtually every case all of the parties understand from the outset that the owner or developer

id mechanics lien could be filed by contractor); Van-Tex v. Pierce, 703 F.2d 891 (5th Cir.1983) (no unjust enrichment where owner was solvent); Mursor Builders, Inc. v. Crown Mountain Apartment Associates, 467 F.Supp. 1316, 1334–35 (D.V.I.1978) (same).

26. Cf. Knight Construction Co. v. Barnett Mortgage Trust, 572 S.W.2d 381 (Tex. Civ.App.1978), error refused n.r.e., rejecting the third party beneficiary approach on the ground that contractor was merely an incidental beneficiary; Merchants National Bank v. Professional Constructors, Inc., 579 S.W.2d 100 (Ky.1979).

27. See Swansea Concrete Products, Inc. v. Distler, 126 Ill.App.3d 927, 81 Ill. Dec. 688, 467 N.E.2d 388 (1984); Watson Construction Co. v. Amfac Mortgage Corp., 124 Ariz. 570, 606 P.2d 421 (App.1979).

28. See F.W. Eversley & Co. v. East New York Non-Profit HDFC, Inc., 409 F.Supp. 791 (S.D.N.Y.1976); J.G. Plumbing Service Co. v. Coastal Mortgage Co., 329 So.2d 393 (Fla.App.1976), certiorari dismissed 339 So.2d 1169 (Fla.1976); Gee v. Eberle, 279 Pa.Super. 101, 420 A.2d 1050 (1980); In re Monroe County Housing Corp., 18 B.R. 741 (Bkrtcy.Fla.1982); First National State Bank v. Carlyle House, Inc., 102 N.J.Super. 300, 246 A.2d 22, affirmed 107 N.J.Super. 389, 258 A.2d 545 (1969); Wahl v. Southwest Savings & Loan Association, 12 Ariz.App. 90, 467 P.2d 930 (1970) vacated in part 106 Ariz. 381, 476 P.2d 836 (1970) (representations by borrower not

sufficient; lender must make representations to lien claimant); Liberty National Bank v. Kaibab Industries, Inc., 591 P.2d 692 (Okl.1978) (same); United Plumbing v. Gibralter Savings & Loan Association, 7 Ariz.App. 540, 441 P.2d 575 (1968); G.L. Wilson Building Co. v. Leatherwood, 268 F.Supp. 609 (W.D.N.C.1967); Demharter v. First Federal Savings & Loan Association, 412 Pa. 142, 194 A.2d 214 (1963).

Cf. Morgen-Oswood & Associates, Inc. v. Continental Mortgage Investors, 323 So.2d 684 (Fla.App.1975), certiorari dismissed 342 So.2d 1100 (1977) (equitable lien imposed with no discussion of lender's representations); Spring Construction Co. v. Harris, 614 F.2d 374 (4th Cir.1980) (lien imposed despite lack of evidence that contractors were "lulled" into continuing work). Compare Chase Manhattan Bank v. S/D Enterprises, Inc., 353 So.2d 131 (Fla. App.1977), appeal after remand 374 So.2d 1121 (1979), in which a statement of precisely this type was held to be insufficient to establish a lien; see also Rinker Materials Corp., v. Palmer First National Bank, 361 So.2d 156 (Fla.1978); Coke Lumber Co. v. First National Bank, 529 S.W.2d 612 (Tex.Civ.App.1975).

29. Cf. United States v. Chester Heights Associates, 406 F.Supp. 600, 604 (D.S.C.1975).

30. Williston, Contracts § 356A (3d Ed. 1959).

plans to contract for the construction of the improvements and to pay for them with borrowed funds, it is crystal clear that the owner intends to benefit the contractor and his subcontractors and suppliers.[31] No further demonstration of intent should be required.

Other courts tend to focus on whether the construction lender has made some false statement to the lien claimant which has misled him to continue to furnish labor or materials.[32] The usual statement of this type is an assurance that sufficient funds remain in the construction loan account to complete the project or to pay the claimant.[33] Such a statement, if false, seems to satisfy the "unjust" element of the unjust enrichment concept. Here again, however, the lender's statement is quite arguably irrelevant. The essence of unjust enrichment is that the lender is receiving something (in this case, the improvements on the real estate, upon foreclosure) for which he has not paid (as is shown by the presence of undisbursed loan funds.) The enrichment, it would seem, is equally unjust whether the lender duped the lien claimant or not. The equitable lien claim should not be dependent upon a showing of false communications by the lender to the contractors or suppliers.

If the third-party-beneficiary theory is employed by the court, the lien claim may be barred by the owner-borrower's default. Such a default—for example, failure to obtain a permanent loan commitment or failure to pay interest on the construction loan when due—may permit the lender to argue that he no longer has any obligation to make additional disbursements of loan funds; since this is true as against the owner-borrower, the lender will assert it is also true of third party beneficiaries, since their rights are derivative of the owner-borrower's.[34] This defense by the lender is a formidable one. Some courts have thought it inapplicable if the lien claimant completed his work before the borrower's default, so that the right to payment could be said to have "vested."[35] If the lender has encouraged the contractors and suppliers to continue with their work on the project despite the default, the court might find that the lender waived the default, at

---

31. The later California cases took this position; see McBain v. Santa Clara Sav. & Loan Association, 241 Cal.App.2d 829, 51 Cal.Rptr. 78 (1966); but see note 21, supra. See also Trans-Bay Engineers & Builders, Inc. v. Hills, 551 F.2d 370 (D.C.Cir.1976) (no express representation, but "expectation" of lien claimant was reasonable); United States v. Mill Association, Inc., 480 F.Supp. 3 (E.D.N.Y.1978) (intent to benefit contractor inferred from statement in building loan agreement that, in compliance with N.Y. lien law, lender would hold funds in trust for contractor).

32. The contractor's false statements to the lender, on the other hand, may cause a court to charge him with "unclean hands" and deny an equitable lien; see Mursor Builders, Inc. v. Crown Mountain Apart-

ment Associates, 467 F.Supp. 1316, 1334–35 (D.V.I.1978).

33. Chase Manhattan Bank v. S/D Enterprises, Inc., 353 So.2d 131 (Fla.App. 1977); Hall's Miscellaneous Iron Works, Inc. v. All South Investment Co., 283 So.2d 372 (Fla.App.1973) (lien on land imposed; misrepresentations by general contractor.)

34. Van-Tex Inc. v. Pierce, 703 F.2d 891 (5th Cir.1983); Trans-Bay Engineers & Builders, Inc. v. Hills, 551 F.2d 370 (D.C. Cir.1976); Pioneer Plumbing Supply Co. v. Southwest Savings & Loan Association, 102 Ariz. 258, 428 P.2d 115 (1967).

35. See Trans-Bay Engineers & Builders, Inc., supra note 34; Travelers Indemnity Co. v. First National State Bank, 328 F.Supp. 208 (D.N.J.1971).

least so far as the lien claimants are concerned.[36] And at least one court has quite consciously disregarded the borrower's default and granted a lien on a third-party-beneficiary theory.[37] Yet it must be conceded that such a default is in general a serious impediment to the establishment of a lien on this theory. By comparison, the unjust enrichment theory is not impaired by the borrower's default, so long as it can be shown that the foreclosing lender will nonetheless get more than he has paid for while the lien claimants go unpaid.

Some Florida courts have imposed the requirement that the project have been substantially completed as a condition of imposing a lien on the loan funds.[38] The rationale seems to be that if the project is incomplete, the lender will be forced to foreclose and liquidate the property at a loss; hence he will not be enriched at all, and no lien should be imposed.[39] This analysis is far too simplistic, however. In some cases, the lender will himself complete the project before liquidating it, and may eventually earn a tidy profit from doing so. And even if the project is immediately resold by the lender at a price below the outstanding balance on the debt, that by no means establishes that the lender has not been enriched; but for the labor or materials contributed by the lien claimant, the project would almost certainly have sold for an even lower price, and the lender would have sustained a greater loss. In effect, the lender is mitigating his loss at the expense of the unpaid contractor or supplier. It may well be that the lender's enrichment is less than the unpaid bill, and perhaps the former figure should serve as an upper limit of the lien, but the fact that the project is uncompleted should not act as an absolute barrier to imposition of the lien.[40]

The foregoing discussion assumes that the lender has not disbursed the funds which would have gone to pay the lien claimant. Suppose the lender has in fact done so, but the disbursement was made in a fashion which allowed the owner-borrower or some other person, such as the general contractor, to divert the money. On these facts, one of two innocent parties must bear the loss. Neither the lender nor the lien claimant is at fault. It might be argued that the lender has a better opportunity to control the ultimate disposition of the funds or to select reliable borrowers, or that he should have employed a more

---

36. Spring Construction Co. v. Harris, 562 F.2d 933 (4th Cir.1977); 614 F.2d 374 (4th Cir.1980).

37. Bennett Construction Co. v. Allen Gardens, Inc., 433 F.Supp. 825 (W.D.Mo. 1977).

38. Giffen Industries v. Southeastern Associates, Inc., 357 So.2d 217 (Fla.App. 1978); J.G. Plumbing Service Co. v. Coastal Mortgage Co., 329 So.2d 393 (Fla.App. 1976). See also Urban Systems Development Corp. v. NCNB Mortgage Corp., 513 F.2d 1304 (4th Cir.1975), discussed in Urban, Future Advances Lending in North

Carolina, 13 Wake For.L.Rev. 297, 339–43 (1977). The California courts rejected this requirement; Miller v. Citizens Savings and Loan Association, 248 Cal.App.2d 655, 56 Cal.Rptr. 844 (1967); McBain v. Santa Clara Savings & Loan Association, 241 Cal. App.2d 829, 51 Cal.Rptr. 78 (1966). But see note 12, supra.

39. See Mortgage Associates, Inc. v. Monona Shores, Inc., 47 Wis.2d 171, 177 N.W.2d 340 (1970).

40. See S.S. Silberblatt, Inc. v. East Harlem Pilot Block, 608 F.2d 28, 40–41 (2d Cir.1979).

reliable (although probably more costly) disbursement system—perhaps the voucher system rather than progress payments. Still, it is hard to maintain that unjust enrichment of the lender has occurred. Perhaps the lien should still be imposed, in effect throwing the loss onto the lender's shoulders, in order to encourage lenders to use the best feasible methods of controlling funds and to mitigate damages in the event of default. Yet some authors have argued that lenders are likely to be little influenced in either respect by the decisions of the courts in this matter.[41] In cases in which the lender has not been enriched, and where a default bars the third-party-beneficiary theory, the imposition of the lien should probably depend on whether the lender acted in accordance with reasonable standards in administering the loan; if he did, no lien should be found to exist. From a policy viewpoint, this case is much like that of the priority dispute between the construction lender and the mechanics' lien claimant, discussed in § 12.7, below.

As indicated above, equitable liens can also be asserted against the improved real estate.[42] In this context the equitable lien is merely being employed as a substitute for a conventional mechanic's lien. The analysis is relatively straightforward, since in most cases there is a contractual relationship between the owner of the land and the lien claimant or those with whom he dealt. So long as the debt is proved and the land which was improved is identifiable, no great difficulty should be experienced in obtaining a judgment imposing the lien. The problems arise in determining its priority. As against bona fide purchasers of the land, the equitable lien is not discoverable through the public records and must consequently take a subordinate position.[43] As against the construction lender, the lien is also likely to be subordinate unless there is evidence that the lender's statements or assurances of payment induced the claimant to refrain from filing an ordinary mechanic's lien,[44] and that such a lien, if filed, would have had priority.

 WESTLAW REFERENCES

"stop notice"

build*** construct*** /s loan /p material*** mechanic equit! /s lien /p represent! misrepresent!

---

41. Lefcoe & Schaffer, Construction Lending and the Equitable Lien, 40 So.Cal. L.Rev. 439 (1967).

42. See Architectronics v. Salem-American Ventures, Inc., 350 So.2d 581 (Fla.App. 1977); Syring v. Sartorious, 28 Ohio App. 2d 308, 277 N.E.2d 457, 57 O.O.2d 477 (1971). See generally Note, The Equitable Lien Alternative in Ohio, 44 U.Cin.L.Rev. 265 (1975).

43. Divine Homes, Inc. v. Gulf Power Co., 352 So.2d 115 (Fla.App.1977); Jacobsen v. Conlon, 14 Ill.App.3d 306, 302 N.E.2d 471 (1973).

44. Architectronics v. Salem-American Ventures, Inc., 350 So.2d 581 (Fla.App. 1977); Hall's Miscellaneous Ironworks, Inc. v. All South Investment Co., 283 So.2d 372 (Fla.App.1973). In Indiana Mortgage & Realty Investors v. Peacock Construction Co., 348 So.2d 59 (Fla.App.1977), the lender's telephone statement to the contractor that sufficient funds remained in the construction loan account to complete the project was held insufficient to give the contractor an equitable lien on the property superior to that of the lender.

§ 12.7 Future Advances

There are many transactions in which it is desirable from a business viewpoint for the parties to enter into a present mortgage even though some portion of the loan funds is not to be advanced to the mortgagor until some future date.[1] The most common examples are construction loans and other loans to improve real property, in which the funds are advanced in installments as work progresses and the property becomes more valuable security.[2] Another illustration is the "open-end" mortgage, typically a permanent home loan in which the lender reserves the option, after the principal balance has been partially reduced, to advance additional funds up to the original balance to pay for needed remodeling of the house or other purposes.[3] Other transactions involving future advances include mortgages to secure prospective indorsements, guarantees, or accommodations of commercial paper to be issued by the mortgagor;[4] fluctuating balances under lines of credit established with an institutional lender, such as a bank;[5] and as security for a corporate bond issue, or series of issues.[6]

The advantages of such arrangements, in which the borrower takes only a fraction of the loan to begin with but will receive more in the future, are substantial. The mortgagor saves interest on the surplus until he is ready to use it, and escapes the burden of proper investment of it for the interim. Both parties avoid the expense and paperwork inherent in refinancing the initial loan, or in executing a series of junior mortgages. Particularly with construction loans, the mortgagee has the advantage of seeing that construction is progressing satisfactorily before committing larger sums of money to the project, and of

---

§ 12.7

1. See Comment, Future Advances Under the ULTA and USLTA: The Construction Lender Receives a New Status, 34 Wash. & Lee L.Rev. 1027 (1977); Urban, Future Advances Lending in North Carolina, 13 Wake For.L.Rev. 297 (1977); Comment, Mortgages to Secure Future Advances: Problems of Priority and the Doctrine of Economic Necessity, 46 Miss. L.J. 433 (1975); Comment, The Priority Problem Between Construction Mortgages and Mechanics' Liens in Alabama, 6 Cumb. L.Rev. 243 (1975); Kratovil & Werner, Mortgages for Construction and the Lien Priorities Problem—The "Unobligatory" Advance, 41 Tenn.L.Rev. 311 (1974); Meek, Mortgage Provisions Extending the Lien to Future Advances and Antecedent Indebtedness, 26 Ark.L.Rev. 423 (1973); Note, Mortgages for Future Advances: The Need for Legislation in Wisconsin, 1965 Wisc.L. Rev. 175 (1965); Blackburn, Mortgages to Secure Future Advances, 21 Mo.L.Rev. 209 (1956).

2. See § 12.1, supra; Lefcoe & Schaffer, Construction Lending and the Equitable Lien, 40 So.Cal.L.Rev. 439 (1967).

3. See Note, the Open-End Mortgage—Future Advances: A Survey, 5 DePaul L.Rev. 76 (1955); Note, Refinements in Additional Advance Financing: The "Open End" Mortgage, 38 Minn.L.Rev. 507 (1954). See also FNMA-FHLMC 1 to 4 family mortgage, clause 21, for future advances language not limited to the original principal amount of the loan.

4. See Ackerman v. Hunsicker, 85 N.Y. 43, 39 Am.Rep. 621 (1881); Robinson v. Williams, 22 N.Y. 380 (1860).

5. McDaniels v. Colvin, 16 Vt. 300, 42 Am.Dec. 512 (1844). See Ill.Rev.Stat.1977, ch. 17 § 6405, a provision aimed at facilitating the use of mortgages to secure revolving lines of consumer credit.

6. Reed's Appeal, 122 Pa. 565, 16 A. 100 (1888); Claflin v. South Carolina Railway Co., 8 F. 118, 4 Hughes 12 (C.C.S.C.1880); In re Sunflower State Refining Co., 183 F. 834 (D.Kan.1911); 11 Col.L.Rev. 459.

making sure that the growth in value represented by the construction is reasonably adequate to secure the additional advances.

Ideally, construction loans and other mortgages to secure future advances should state explicitly the amount initially advanced, the amounts of additional advances to be made in the future, and the terms and conditions on which those advances will be made. Frequently, however, neither the mortgage nor the bond or note is so specific. Instead, two other forms are common. (1) The mortgage may name a certain total sum as if it were being advanced simultaneously with the execution of the mortgage, although in reality (and as may be shown by extrinsic, perhaps oral, evidence) some of the funds are not intended to be advanced until a later time. (2) The mortgage may name only the amount of the initial advance but state that it secures future advances as well, although their amounts and the conditions on which they will be made are left indefinite. One common version of the latter type is the "dragnet" or "anaconda" clause, which purports to make the mortgaged land security for "all debts, past, present, or future, which the mortgagor may owe to the mortgagee." Dragnet clauses are discussed in the next section. In construction lending, there will commonly be a separate written construction loan agreement which fills in the terms and conditions of the future advances which both of these forms omit.

The first form, which seems to pretend that the whole amount has already been advanced, is misleading. Nevertheless, in the absence of fraud, it is clearly enforceable between the parties, although only for the amount actually advanced plus interest, of course.[7] It is valid even as against third party creditors or encumbrancers.[8] This makes sense with respect to subsequent creditors; they can hardly complain of the fact that the mortgage overstated the debt, since the usual effect will have been to make them even more conservative in giving the mortgagor further credit. On the other hand, there is a real danger to pre-existing unsecured creditors; because the recorded mortgage gives them the misimpression that the mortgagor's property is fully encumbered, they may forego efforts to obtain judgment liens or otherwise improve their position.[9] Nonetheless, the law has generally disregarded this problem and upheld the mortgage as against all creditors.

7. See Note, Future Advance Clauses in Tennessee—Construction and Effect, 5 Memphis St.L.Rev. 586 (1975); Note, 23 U.Kan.L.Rev. 745 (1975).

8. Hemmerle v. First Federal Savings & Loan Association, 338 So.2d 82 (Fla.App. 1976).

9. Shirras v. Caig, 11 U.S. (7 Cranch) 34, 3 L.Ed. 260 (1812); Griffin v. New Jersey Oil Co., 11 N.J.Eq. 49 (1855); Whelan v. Exchange Trust Co., 214 Mass. 121, 100 N.E. 1095 (1913); Witczinski v. Everman, 51 Miss. 841 (1876); Kramer v. Trust-

ees of Farmers' & Mechanics' Bank of Steubenville, 15 Ohio 253 (1846); Savings & Loan Society v. Burnett, 106 Cal. 514, 39 P. 922 (1895) (trust deed); Tully v. Harloe, 35 Cal. 302, 95 Am.Dec. 102 (1868); Straeffer v. Rodman, 146 Ky. 1, 141 S.W. 742, Ann.Cas.1913C, 549 (1911); Merchants' State Bank of Fargo v. Tufts, 14 N.D. 238, 103 N.W. 760, 116 Am.St.Rep. 682 (1905)—accord. Cf. Youngs v. Wilson, 27 N.Y. 351 (1863); Winchell v. Coney, 54 Conn. 24, 5 A. 354 (1886) (contra.)

The second format, which states no total debt at all, might be thought open to attack on grounds of its vagueness. However, the courts have been abundantly willing to admit extrinsic documents (i.e., a construction loan agreement) or parol evidence in order to clarify the parties' obligations, and to enforce the mortgage as the parties are found to have intended.[10] One reason for the courts' willingness to enforce such broad mortgage language is that it is often difficult to predict at the outset the exact amount which will be needed in a complex construction job; the same is true of mortgages given to secure performance of public obligations, such as those given by land developers to local governments to guarantee completion of street paving and other required improvements. Moreover, the very vagueness of the mortgage is a warning to third party creditors that they had better inquire of the mortgagee about the status of the debt. Hence, there is little or no risk that they will be misled.

The courts' liberality with regard to the validity of mortgages securing future advances is not boundless, however. If the mortgage neither states the full amount (including future advances) nor warns that future advances are contemplated, it will probably be held unenforceable, at least as against third party creditors.

Optional vs. obligatory advances. Thus far we have not discussed whether advances made in the future under a mortgage are obligatory or optional. Certainly the mortgage itself or collateral documents (such as a construction loan agreement) can be drafted to read either way. If the mortgagee has no contractual duty, but may elect to make the additional advances and include them within the security of the mortgage if he chooses, they are said to be optional. The distinction seems simple, but in practice it is often hard to draw, as will be seen below.

So far as enforcement between the parties is concerned, the obligatory-optional distinction is irrelevant. Even if the advance is clearly optional, its acceptance by the mortgagor signifies his willingness to have it included in the mortgage. However, when a subsequent third-

---

10. The courts are liberal in construing the parties' agreement as including future advances. See House of Carpets Inc. v. Mortgage Investment Co., 85 N.M. 560, 514 P.2d 611 (1973); Industrial Supply Corp. v. Bricker, 306 So.2d 133 (Fla.App.1975); Potwin State Bank v. J.B. Houston & Son Lumber Co., 183 Kan. 475, 327 P.2d 1091 (1958); McDaniels v. Colvin, 16 Vt. 300, 42 Am.Dec. 512 (1844); Citizens' Savings Bank v. Kock, 117 Mich. 225, 75 N.W. 458 (1898); Huntington v. Kneeland, 102 App. Div. 284, 92 N.Y.S. 944 (1905), affirmed 187 N.Y. 563, 80 N.E. 1111 (1907); Blackmar v. Sharp, 23 R.I. 412, 50 A. 852 (1901); Lamoille County Savings Bank & Trust Co. v. Belden, 90 Vt. 535, 98 A. 1002 (1916).

Cf. Hendricks v. Webster, 159 F. 927, 87 C.C.A. 107 (1908); First National Bank v. Manser, 104 Me. 70, 71 A. 134 (1908). See also 1 A.L.R. 1586 (1919). Parol evidence may be used to show that future advances are included. Langerman v. Puritan Dining Room Co., 21 Cal.App. 637, 132 P. 617 (1913).

See Mortgages for Future Advances: The Need for Legislation in Wisconsin, 1965 Wis.L.Rev. 175, 179; Thomson, Titles as Affected by Liens: Open-End Mortgages and Mortgages to Secure Future Advances, 28 Tenn.L.Rev. 354 (1961); Comment, The Extent of the Debts Secured By a Mortgage in Arkansas, 9 Ark.L.Rev. 45 (1954). A few cases are contra; see Akron Savings & Loan Co. v. Ronson Homes, Inc., 15 Ohio St.2d 6, 238 N.E.2d 760, 44 O.O.2d 4 (1968); Matz v. Arick, 76 Conn. 388, 56 A. 630 (1904).

party creditor enters the picture, it becomes critically important to determine whether the advance is obligatory or not. The rule widely followed in the United States is this: if the advance is obligatory, it takes its priority from the date of the original mortgage, and the subsequent creditor is junior to it.[11] (This is, of course, subject to the operation of the recording acts; it is assumed in this discussion that the mortgage was recorded immediately upon execution.) However, if the advance is optional, and if the mortgagee has notice when the advance is made that a subsequent mortgagee or lienor has acquired an interest in the land, then the advance loses its priority to that creditor.[12] "Notice", as used here, is a concept requiring further explanation and will be discussed later.[13]

How can this rule be explained? Some earlier decisions and texts employed a highly formalistic approach: in a mortgage to secure future advances, each advance is in reality a separate mortgage which would normally take its priority only from the date it was made, but an equitable "relation back" will occur to the date of the original mortgage if the advance was obligatory or if the mortgage lacked notice of the intervening creditor.[14] This explanation is highly dubious; realistical-

11. Kemp v. Thurmond, 521 S.W.2d 806 (Tenn.1975); House of Carpets, Inc. v. Mortgage Investment Co., 85 N.M. 560, 514 P.2d 611 (1973); Earnshaw v. First Federal Savings & Loan Association of Lowell, 109 N.H. 283, 249 A.2d 675 (1969); Western Mortgage Loan Corp. v. Cottonwood Construction Co., 18 Utah 2d 409, 424 P.2d 437 (1967); Thompson v. Smith, 420 P.2d 526 (Okl.1966); Potwin State Bank v. J.B. Houston & Son Lumber Co., 183 Kan. 475, 327 P.2d 1091 (1958); The English roots of the doctrine are found in Lord Chancellor Campbell's opinion in Hopkinson v. Rolt, 9 H. of L. 514, 11 Eng.Rep. 829 (1861). See generally Annot., 80 A.L.R.2d 179 (1961). See the excellent discussion in Korngold, Construction Loan Advances and the Subordinated Purchase Money Mortgagee: An Appraisal, a Suggested Approach, and the ULTA Perspective, 50 Ford.L.Rev. 313, 329–39 (1981).

12. Poulos Investment, Inc. v. Mountainwest Savings & Loan Association, 680 P.2d 1073 (Wyo.1984) (doctrine inapplicable to accrued interest); Wilson v. Ripley County Bank, ___ Ind.App. ___, 462 N.E.2d 263 (1984); Watson Construction Co. v. Amfac Mortgage Co., 124 Ariz. 570, 606 P.2d 421 (App.1979) (dictum); Liberty National Bank v. Kaibab Industries, Inc., 591 P.2d 692 (Okl.1978); Percy Galbreath & Son, Inc. v. Watkins, 560 S.W.2d 239 (Ky. App.1977); Idaho First National Bank v. Wells, 100 Idaho 256, 596 P.2d 429 (1979); Trustees of C.I. Mortgage Group v. Stagg of Huntington, Inc., 484 Pa. 464, 399 A.2d 386

(1979); National Bank of Washington v. Equity Investors, 81 Wn.2d 886, 506 P.2d 20 (1973), appeal after remand 83 Wn.2d 435, 518 P.2d 1072; J.I. Kislak Mortgage Corp. v. William Matthews Builder, Inc., 287 A.2d 686 (Del.Super.1972), affirmed 303 A.2d 648 (Del.1973); Colonial Mortgage Service Co. v. Southard, 56 Ohio St.2d 347, 304 N.E.2d 250 (1978); Wayne Building & Loan Co. v. Yarborough, 11 Ohio St.2d 195, 228 N.E.2d 841, 40 O.O.2d 182 (1967); Housing Mortgage Corp. v. Allied Construction, Inc., 374 Pa. 312, 97 A.2d 802 (1953); Yost-Linn Lumber Co., v. Williams, 121 Cal.App. 751, 9 P.2d 324 (1932); Home Savings & Loan Association v. Sullivan, 140 Okl. 300, 284 P. 30 (1929).

13. See text at notes 33–34, infra.

14. Ladue v. Detroit & Milwaukee Railroad Co., 13 Mich. 380, 87 Am.Dec. 759 (1865), is probably the leading authority for this view. See also Ter-Hoven v. Kerns, 2 Pa. 96 (1845) ("Every future advancement is, in reality, a new debt * * *"); Walsh, Mortgages, 77 (Mortgages given to secure advances to be made in the future create no lien either at law or in equity until such advances are made. As money is advanced under a mortgage of this kind of lien arises thereunder to the extent of the advance actually made. This lien relates back in equity to the original date of the mortgage * * *."); 4 Pomeroy, Eq.Juris. 594; Bank of Montgomery County's Appeal, 36 Pa. 170, 3 Grant 300 (1860); Alexandria Savings Institution ly, there is only one mortgage involved.[15] But more important, the "relation back" concept provides no policy rationale. Why should obligatory advances be treated as relating back, while optional ones are not? What does notice to the mortgagee have to do with whether relation back will occur?

Perhaps the best explanation attributes the rule permitting the ending of the first mortgagee's priority as to later advances to a concern over the marketability of the mortgagor's title, either for the purpose of obtaining loans from additional mortgagees by others or of sale. This concern is compounded by the traditional solicitude of the courts for the mortgagor as a person who needs unusual protection, the deepseated policy in favor of free alienability of land, and, most of all, by a desire to make the mortgage device an effective one in securing the various economic and business advantages for which it was invented.

On this last matter, it is pointed out that if optional advances had an absolute preference, the mortgagor, although having no right to demand the contemplated additional loan funds, would be unable to obtain financing elsewhere for no one else would lend on a security which could be cut down by subsequent action by the first mortgagee. And, for like reason, the mortgagor would be unable to sell the property. It is true that even if the advances are obligatory he may find himself with a claim which is quite empty practically. Nevertheless he does have a legal right to performance by the mortgagee and as great, or probably a far greater actual probability of getting it from his mortgagee than he would from another lender even though this other were given power to end the priorities of the first. So long as the mortgagor and his property constitute a good risk, the mortgagee will fulfill his contract; when the risk becomes so bad that the mortgagee refuses to continue, the chance of successful financing elsewhere would be remote.

While this argument has much merit, it is a bit difficult to apply in the context in which the optional-obligatory dispute most often arises: a contest between a construction lender who recorded before work commenced, but has made some optional advances, and a group of unpaid subcontractors or suppliers who have filed mechanics' liens. In effect, the lien claimants have supplied credit to the mortgagor, albeit in the form of labor and materials rather than cash. They have usually done so with full knowledge that there is a prior construction mortgage on record, and with no expectation that the lender would take any action which would subordinate his mortgage to their liens. In

v. Thomas, 70 Va. (29 Grat.) 483 (1877) are to the same effect. See also 11 Col.L.Rev. 459 (1911). Similarly, Second National Bank of Warren v. Boyle, 155 Ohio St. 482, 99 N.E.2d 474, 44 O.O. 440 (1951), noted, 13 U. of Pitt.L.Rev. 431 (1952), took the position that a mortgage for optional future advances was only an offer to provide security if and when such advances were made. Further, such advances must be made in reliance upon the mortgage.

15. See Osborne, Mortgages 114–17 (2d Ed. 1970).

effect they have, to paraphrase the argument of the preceding paragraph, lent on a security which they knew could be cut down by subsequent action by the first mortgagee. Why are they willing to assume such a risk? The answers are several: custom in the industry dictates it; they trust the developer's honesty and business judgment; and they expect that the construction lender will carefully supervise the job and the loan disbursements to guard against difficulty. When they are disappointed in these expectations, perhaps because the developer and lender underestimated costs or construction problems, or because the developer was able to divert funds away from the project, they try to advance their priority by showing that some of the loan advances were optional. If they succeed in finding such evidence, they thereby enhance their chances of collecting on their lien claims. Yet this success can only be regarded as a windfall—indeed, a fluke. It is most improbable that its eventuation was a factor in inducing them to work on the project in the first place, or that the owner would have been in a weaker position to obtain labor and materials for his project if the law gave original priority to all construction loan advances, optional or not.

Most construction lenders and their title insurers, as might be expected, despise the optional advance doctrine.[16] They argue that it tends to drive out construction capital and thereby to discourage needed real estate development. It is hard to show that this is so in the real world, however; the legal interpretations of the doctrine in particular states do not appear to have much bearing on the decisions of financial institutions to make or not to make construction loans there.

The one feature of the doctrine that cannot be doubted is its uncertainty in application; as will be seen below, it is often hard to tell whether an advance is obligatory or not, and litigation frequently results. Professor Grant Gilmore has argued that this very uncertainty is the principle virtue of the rule:

> Nevertheless, the conceptually nonsensical distinction between "obligatory" and "voluntary" has had the result (which is not in the least nonsensical) of preserving (or creating) a wide area of judicial discretion. There are few, if any, future advance clauses which an astute judge cannot, at will, classify on one side or the other of the line between obligatory and voluntary. When he has picked his label, he has also picked his priority rule. The distinction amounts to an absence of rule; the judges are invited to pick and choose, case by case, ad hoc or ad hominem. This is a recurrent phenomenon in a common law system when the arguments for or against a given position balance each other exactly. There is much to be said

---

16. See Skipworth, Should Construction Lenders Lose Out on Voluntary Advances If a Loan Turns Sour?, 5 Real Est.L.J. 221 (1977); Kratovil & Werner, Mortgages for Construction and the Lien Priorities Problem—The "Unobligatory" Advance, 41 Tenn.L.Rev. 311 (1974).

for giving the mortgagee an absolute priority. There is much to be said for allowing other creditors a chance at the assets (or the debtor's equity in the assets). There is much to be said for allowing the mortgagor freedom to choose new sources of financing and for allowing new lenders to come in with secure liens. Only a very wise or a very foolish man would be willing to state, categorically, where truth lies and to propose a rule for application in all possible situations. There is, then, much to be said for having no rule at all, or only a make-believe rule, and for letting the judges decide: judges are not necessarily wiser than other people, but they are paid to decide things.[17]

Gilmore's argument is appealing but ultimately unconvincing. The cost of learning the answer in a particular case, stated in terms of attorneys' fees, court costs, and the time of witnesses, is far too high. A rule which could be applied with certainty, whatever its content, would be preferable.

As between construction lenders and mechanics' lien claimants, there is really no ground for a strong preference; each is usually innocent of any wrongdoing, and each is a potential victim of the poor judgment, bad luck, or dishonesty of the developer/mortgagor. The lender is usually in a better position to guard against these misfortunes,[18] but on the other hand if he has made advances which were genuinely optional, he has typically done so in a good faith effort to stave off the developer's default and the foreclosure of the mortgage, an effort which surely redounds to the benefit of the prospective lien claimants as well. In an ideal world perhaps the law would grant the lienors and the lender equal priority, allowing them to share pro-rata in the foreclosure proceeds,[19] but no American statute or case seems to take this view. An arbitrary rule favoring either the lender or the lien claimants, irrespective of the obligatory character of the advances, would be much more desirable than the unpredictability and ultimate fortuity of the present system.

What is an "optional" advance? Construction lenders frequently attempt, by language in their construction loan agreements, to reserve fairly broad discretion in making later determinations as to whether a mortgagor/developer is making satisfactory progress on the project. While lenders are generally not eager to cut off further payments or to foreclose, they often prefer to have the apparent right to do so if they sense trouble developing. This is well illustrated in National Bank of Washington v. Equity Investors,[20] in which the agreement made the

---

17. G. Gilmore, Security Interests in Personal Property § 35.4 (1965).

18. But see Skipworth, supra n. 16, at 224; Lefcoe & Schaffer, Construction Lending and the Equitable Lien, 40 So.Cal.L. Rev. 439, 447–49 (1967); First Nat. State Bank of N.J. v. Carlyle House, Inc., 102 N.J.Super. 300, 246 A.2d 22 (1968), af-

firmed without opinion 107 N.J.Super. 389, 258 A.2d 545 (1969).

19. This suggestion is advanced in Comment, The Priority Problem Between Construction Mortgages and Mechanics' Liens in Alabama, 6 Cumb.L.Rev. 243 (1975).

20. 81 Wn.2d 886, 506 P.2d 20 (1973), appeal after remand 83 Wn.2d 435, 518 bank's duty to advance the construction loan conditional upon a current appraisal, retention of an architect, and progress on the project, all of which were to be "satisfactory" to the bank. Moreover, funds were "to be advanced at such times and in such amounts as the Lender shall determine." No advance was due unless, in the judgment of the lender, all work which the advance covered had been done in a good and workmanlike manner. The Washington Supreme Court concluded that under this language the bank had no definite obligation to advance *any* funds; hence all advances were optional. By reserving too much discretion, the bank had defeated its own priority. The discretionary language may have represented sound banking practice, but the court found it legally insufficient to obligate the bank.[21]

A different problem is represented by J.I. Kislak Mortgage Corp. v. William Matthews Builder, Inc.,[22] in which the lender's agreement provided that it was not obligated to make construction advances unless the mortgagor provided evidence that all of the preceding advances had actually been disbursed to subcontractors or materialmen. Notwithstanding this language, the lender made advances without requiring receipts or other such evidence; the court held that these advances were optional and consequently subordinate to filed mechanics' liens.

These and similar cases can be synthesized into three principles which a construction lender should carefully observe. First, he must not reserve too much discretion, but must have a genuine contractual obligation to lend; if he makes the obligation conditional, the conditions must be objectively defined and not subject to the lender's control or whim.[23] Second, the lender must use the controls and assert the conditions which he has reserved for himself in the loan agreement. Even if those procedural controls and conditions are far more restrictive than most prudent lenders require, so that his failure to assert them could in no wise be regarded as negligence, he may still be charged with making optional advances if he does not make the mortgagor hew to the line.[24] Third, the lender must make no further advances after the occurrence of any event which is defined by the documents as a default of the mortgagor; if the lender has the *right* to cease making advances, he had better exercise it.[25] Since the construc-

P.2d 1072 (1974). The rule was subsequently reversed by statute in Washington; see West's Rev.Code Wash.Ann. 60.04.220.

21. See Moore, Seeking Firmer Ground: Mortgages to Secure Future Advances and the Priorities Quagmire, 12 Suff.L.Rev. 445, 463 (1978).

22. 287 A.2d 686 (Del.Super.1972), affirmed 303 A.2d 648 (Del.1973); see also Trustees of C.I. Mortgage Group v. Stagg of Huntington, Inc., 247 Pa.Super. 336, 372 A.2d 854 (1977), reversed 484 Pa. 464, 399 A.2d 386 (1979).

23. See, e.g., the construction loan agreement in Irwin Concrete, Inc. v. Sun

Coast Properties, Inc., 33 Wn.App. 190, 653 P.2d 1331 (1982) (advances held to be obligatory).

24. For example, if progress payments are made ahead of schedule, they are optional; Housing Mortgage Corp. v. Allied Construction, Inc., 374 Pa. 312, 97 A.2d 802 (1953).

25. Central Pennsylvania Savings Association v. Carpenters of Pennsylvania, Inc., 298 Pa.Super. 250, 444 A.2d 755, affirmed 502 Pa. 17, 463 A.2d 414 (1983); New York & Suburban Federal Savings & Loan Association v. Fi-Pen Realty Co., 133 N.Y.S.2d 33 (Sup.Ct.1954); Planters' Lumber Co. v.

tion loan agreements frequently contain broad and ambiguous pro-lender language, it is frighteningly easy to make, in the ordinary course of business, what turns out to be an optional advance. Better drafting may help, but it is only a partial solution.[26]

The lender may be put to an extremely difficult choice even if it is obvious that any further advances will be optional. If construction is only partially completed and the construction loan account has been exhausted, it may make excellent business sense for the lender to provide further funds in the hope of getting the building completed; the increment in value which can be added by the investment of further money may far outstrip the amount invested. Moreover, completing the project so that it can be marketed is in everyone's interest if it can be accomplished at a reasonable added cost; the developer, the lender, prospective lien claimants, and the public at large will be benefitted. But if the optional/obligatory rule induces the lender to foreclose at that point the lien claimants will be wiped out (as will the developer), to no one's advantage. Hence, the net result of the rule which deprives optional advances of their priority may well be to give a few lien claimants windfalls (in cases in which the lender is ignorant of the rule or misjudges its applicability), but to harm the great majority of lien claimants by encouraging knowledgable lenders to foreclose immediately when a default occurs or the loan account is exhausted.

In a case in which further (albeit optional) advances represent the only sensible course to the lender, he may argue that those advances

Griffin Chapel M.E. Church, 157 Miss. 714, 128 So. 76 (1930). Cf. N.C.Gen.Stat. § 45–70(a), defining an advance as obligatory even though it might have been withheld because of the borrower's default. See Urban, Future Advances and Title Insurance Coverage, 15 Wake For.L.Rev. 329, 356 n. 97 (1979).

It is quite likely that any advance made after exhaustion of the originally-committed construction funds will be held optional, even in the absence of relevant contractual language, since the law does not obligate the lender to fund the building to completion; Walter Harvey Corp. v. O'Keefe, 346 So.2d 617 (Fla.App.1977); Kinner v. World Savings & Loan Corp., 57 Cal.App.3d 724, 129 Cal.Rptr. 400 (1976). See also First Federal Savings & Loan Association of Rochester v. Green-Acres Building Corp., 38 Misc.2d 149, 236 N.Y.S.2d 1009 (1963), holding that a charge against the loan account to cover interest or fees on the loan is *per se* optional, since the lender could not sue itself for them. Cf. Mortgage Guarantee Co. v. Hammond Lumber Co., 13 Cal.App.2d 538, 57 P.2d 164 (1936).

26. One approach is to provide in the construction loan agreement that no de-

fault will be deemed to exist until the lender sends a formal notice of default to the borrower; another is to provide that all advances reasonably made by the lender to complete the improvements or to protect his security are deemed obligatory. The success of either of these techniques is problematic; see Urban, supra note 25; Skipworth, supra note 16, at 226–27.

Still another approach is to place the entire construction loan amount in an escrow or trust account, thus giving the appearance that the lender has made only a single obligatory advance; the trustee or escrowee is then charged with administration of the loan. The Maryland courts have accepted this technique enthusiastically, probably as a reaction to the extremely restrictive Maryland statute regarding future advance mortgages which prevailed until 1972; see Toney Schloss Properties Corp. v. Union Federal Saving & Loan Association, 233 Md. 224, 196 A.2d 458 (1964); text at notes 45–48 infra. However, if the lender has effective control of the trustee, the ruse is so obvious that its success in other jurisdictions is doubtful.

are economically if not contractually obligatory,[27] and should therefore retain their priority. Some support for this view may be drawn from the cases which hold that advances to cover delinquent property taxes or insurance, or to pay for necessary repairs, are deemed obligatory because they are essential to protect the lender's security.[28] Over-budget advances to complete construction might conceivably be viewed in a similar light.[29] One commentator has even recommended that before a construction lender makes an optional advance, he should obtain an appraisal of the property in order to show that the advance does make business sense and is in effect economically compelled.[30] Unfortunately, most courts which have considered the economic compulsion argument have rejected it.[31] If a lender acts in an economically reasonable manner to protect or enhance the security by making further advances, and makes them by means of a non-negligent mechanism—that is, one reasonably calculated to ensure that the funds are actually employed in improvements to the realty—the courts ought to protect loan's priority irrespective of the optional nature of the advances. Such a rule would better serve all parties, although only a few cases thus far support it.[32]

Notice. An optional advance loses its priority only to intervening liens of which the mortgagee has notice at the time the advance is

27. See Skipworth, supra note 16; Comment, Mortgages to Secure Future Advances: Problems of Priority and the Doctrine of Economic Necessity, 47 Miss.L.J. 433 (1975).

28. See United States v. Seaboard Citizens National Bank, 206 F.2d 62 (4th Cir. 1953); Blackburn, Mortgages to Secure Future Advances, 21 Mo.L.Rev. 209, 220–21 (1956); Gilmore, Security Interests in Personal Property 929 (1965); but see Heller v. Gate City Building & Loan Association, 75 N.M. 596, 408 P.2d 753 (1965).

29. A few cases adopt this view; see Central Pennsylvania Savings Association v. Carpenters of Pennsylvania, Inc., 502 Pa. 17, 463 A.2d 414 (1983); First National Bank v. Zook, 50 N.D. 423, 196 N.W. 507 (1923); Hyman v. Hauff, 138 N.Y. 48, 33 N.E. 735 (1893); Rowan v. Sharps Rifle Manufacturing Co., 29 Conn. 282 (1860). But see Poulos Investment Co. v. Mountainwest Savings & Loan Association, 680 P.2d 1073 (Wyo.1984). There are also numerous cases upholding the priority of optional advances to farmers to prevent loss of growing crops; see Cedar v. W.E. Roche Fruit Co., 16 Wn.2d 652, 134 P.2d 437 (1943); Hamilton v. Rhodes, 72 Ark. 625, 83 S.W. 351 (1904); Comment, supra note 27, at 446–47.

30. Skipworth, supra note 16, at 238–39.

31. See, e.g., Elmendorf-Anthony Co. v. Dunn, 10 Wn.2d 29, 116 P.2d 253 (1941); Althouse v. Provident Mutual Building Loan Association, 59 Cal.App. 31, 209 P. 1018 (1922).

32. The Mississippi cases require that the mortgagee use reasonable diligence to ensure that the funds advanced actually pay for improvements to the property, but this requirement is in addition to, not in lieu of, the requirement that they be obligatory; see Wortman & Mann, Inc. v. Frierson Building Supply Co., 184 So.2d 857 (Miss.1966); Southern Life Insurance Co. v. Pollard Appliance Co., 247 Miss. 211, 150 So.2d 416 (1963); Comment, supra note 27 at 458–60. Under the Arkansas rule, the lender must disburse the advances for construction purposes, but has no absolute duty to ensure that they are so used; see House v. Scott, 244 Ark. 1075, 429 S.W.2d 108 (1968). The California statute gives even optional advances on a construction loan priority if they are applied against filed mechanics' lien claims or actually used to pay for improvements to the realty; West's Ann.Cal.Civ.Code, § 3136; see Turner v. Lytton Savings & Loan Association, 242 Cal.App.2d 457, 51 Cal.Rptr. 552 (1966). Concerning the general duty of construction lenders to use reasonable care in disbursing advances, see § 12.10, infra.

made. By the weight of authority, the notice must be actual;[33] in the case of mechanics' liens, this presumably means not merely knowledge that contractors have done work or supplied materials to the site, but that they are unpaid and their bills are overdue.[34] A minority view holds that the mortgagee is also charged with constructive notice from the public records, so that recordation of the appropriate form of notice of lien would postpone the priority of all further advances whether the lender had actual knowledge or not.[35] The basic policy choice regarding notice is whether it is more reasonable to impose on the lender the burden of searching the records before each disbursement which might be deemed optional, or to impose on the intervening lienor the duty to inform the lender of this claim? Technical arguments, based on whether each advance is the equivalent of a new mortgage, are of only academic interest, and do not assist in the resolution of the policy question.

From the viewpoint of the intervening lienor, it may be observed that the title search which the lender would be required to make before each advance under the minority rule is not a very extensive one; he would need only to update his examination from the date of the previous advance. Moreover, there may be cases in which the junior lienor cannot readily locate the senior in order to give him actual notice, so that recording is the only practical alternative. Such cases must, however, be quite rare; the vast majority of mortgages to secure future advances, and particularly construction loans, are made by institutional lenders to whom notice may readily be given. From the lender's perspective, there can be no doubt that there is a real cost implicit in the necessity of making even a partial title search. The burden is magnified by the difficulty of knowing whether an advance is optional, probably causing most conservative lenders to obtain such searches before every advance in minority rule states.[36] The cost, of course, will be passed on to the developer and ultimately to the public.

33. See Central Pennsylvania Savings Association v. Carpenters of Pennsylvania, Inc., 298 Pa.Super. 250, 444 A.2d 755 (1982), affirmed 502 Pa. 17, 463 A.2d 414 (1983); Idaho First National Bank v. Wells, 100 Idaho 256, 596 P.2d 429 (1979); Security Trust Co. v. Graney, 89 Misc.2d 290, 391 N.Y.S.2d 46 (1977); McMillen Feed Mills, Inc. v. Mayer, 265 S.C. 500, 220 S.E.2d 221 (1975); Alston v. Bitely, 252 Ark. 76, 477 S.W.2d 446 (1972); Pike v. Tuttle, 18 Cal. App.3d 746, 96 Cal.Rptr. 403 (1971); Leche v. Ponca City Production Credit Association, 478 P.2d 347 (Okl.1970); Biersdorff v. Brumfield, 93 Idaho 569, 468 P.2d 301 (1970); Rochester Lumber Co. v. Dygert, 136 Misc. 292, 240 N.Y.S. 580 (1930); Annot., 138 A.L.R. 566 (1942). The Ohio statute requires written notice; see Ohio Rev. Code § 5301.232; Four Seasons Developers, Inc. v. Security Federal Savings & Loan Association, 8 Ohio App.3d 300, 456 N.E.2d 1344 (1983).

34. See Grider v. Mutual Federal Savings & Loan Association, 565 S.W.2d 647 (Ky.1978) (" * * * mortgagee must know that there are unpaid claims for which a lien may be asserted and that the debtor is unable to pay such claims or that the claimant intends to file a lien.")

35. See, e.g., Lincoln Federal Savings & Loan Association v. Platt Homes, Inc., 185 N.J.Super. 457, 449 A.2d 553 (1982); People's Savings Bank v. Champlin Lumber Co., 106 R.I. 225, 258 A.2d 82 (1969), following Ladue v. Detroit & Milwaukee Railroad Co., 13 Mich. 380, 87 Am.Dec. 759 (1865).

36. See Note, Mortgages for Future Advances: The Need for Legislation in Wisconsin, 1965 Wisc.L.Rev. 175, 181 (1965).

A more even-handed rule would require that actual notice be given except in cases in which the junior lienor could show inability to locate the lender by a reasonable effort; the needs of both parties would thereby be accommodated.

Waiver and Estoppel. Even if the advances made by a construction lender are clearly obligatory, several cases indicate that the lender's priority may be lost if he makes statements to prospective lien claimants which mislead them with respect to potential problems with the project.[37] For example, suppose a subcontractor, in the midst of construction, inquires of the lender about the economic soundness of the project, and is told that sufficient funds remain in the construction loan account to permit completion; in fact, the account is badly depleted and it is unlikely that the project can be completed with the funds available. Relying on the false impression he has been given, the subcontractor continues his work, in effect throwing good money after bad. On such facts, it is hard to deny that the liens ultimately filed[38] should have priority over advances made after the misleading statement. A duty of candor to junior lienors should accompany the right of priority which the law awards to the construction lender.

Statutory modifications. A number of states have reversed the traditional doctrine by legislation and permit future advances to take the same priority as the original mortgage regardless of their optional character.[39] Most of these statutes also require a definite statement in the mortgage of the maximum amount which will be advanced under it, and withdraw priority for advances which exceed the amount stipulated together with costs, fees, and accrued interest.[40] The statutes usually

37. See Trout's Investments, Inc. v. Davis, 482 S.W.2d 510 (Mo.App.1972); H.B. Deal Construction Co. v. Labor Discount Center, Inc., 418 S.W.2d 940 (Mo.1967). Cases recognizing the principle, but finding no estoppel on the facts, include Liberty National Bank v. Kiabab Industries, Inc., 591 P.2d 692 (Okl.1978); Palmer First National Bank v. Rinker Materials Corp., 348 So.2d 1234 (Fla.App.1977); Gancedo Lumber Co. v. Flagship First National Bank, 340 So.2d 486 (Fla.App.1976); First National State Bank v. Carlyle House, Inc., 102 N.J.Super. 300, 246 A.2d 22 (1968), affirmed without opinion 107 N.J.Super. 389, 258 A.2d 545 (1969); Utah Savings & Loan Association v. Mecham, 12 Utah 2d 335, 366 P.2d 598 (1961).

38. The representations may be so convincing that the subcontractors or suppliers do not file their liens until after the applicable statutory period has run; they should nonetheless be granted liens (and priority) as against the construction lender. See also § 12.6, supra, regarding the possibility of such lien claimants being awarded equitable liens on any undisbursed construction loan funds.

39. West's Ann.Cal.Civ.Code, § 3136; Conn.Gen.Stat.Ann. § 49–3; 25 Del.Code § 2118(a); West's Fla.Stat.Ann. § 697.04; Official Code Ga.Ann. § 44–14–2; Ill.Rev. Stat. 1977, ch. 30, § 37a; Kan.Stat.Ann. § 58–2336, analyzed in Fidelity Savings Association v. Witt, 8 Kan.App. 640, 665 P.2d 1108 (1983); Md. Real Property Code § 7–102 (1974); 9B Maine Rev.Stat.Ann. § 436; Mont.Codes Ann. § 71–1–206; V.A.M.S. § 443.055, noted 49 Mo.L.Rev. 103 (1984); Neb.Rev.Stat. § 76–238.01; New Mex.Stat. Ann.1978, § 61–7–9; Ohio Rev.Code § 5301.232 (preserving common-law optional-obligatory distinction); S.C.Code 1976, § 29–3–50; West's Rev.Code Wash.Ann. § 60.04.220.

40. Most of the statutes cited supra, n. 39 require some binding statement of the maximum loan amount. Under the Connecticut statute, however, the parties may amend the advances schedule (including, presumably, the maximum amount) at any future time. The Florida statute appears exalt the mortgage above all types of intervening liens; the California statute appears on its face to grant priority only over mechanics' liens, but has been held to give a construction loan priority over a vendor's purchase money mortgage as well.[41] While some of the statutes apply only if the future advances are for improvements to the real estate or for similar purposes,[42] others make no requirement concerning the use of the advances.[43]

The Florida, Maine, Missouri, and Nebraska statutes [44] are particularly interesting; they permit the mortgagor to file a notice limiting the amount of the advances having priority to not less than the amount which has actually been disbursed to him to date. These statutes provide an ingenious answer to the argument, discussed previously, that if optional advances are given priority the debtor may be entirely foreclosed from obtaining additional financing, having no right to demand more funds from the original mortgagee and no apparent equity to pledge as security with a new lender. The borrower in the states mentioned who finds himself in such a predicament can file the applicable notice, thereby freeing his equity in the property for junior financing.

Another feature shared by the Maine and Nebraska statutes is their provision that written notice be given to the mortgagee by persons furnishing labor or materials to the realty. All optional advances made after the receipt of such notice are deemed inferior to resulting mechanics' or materialmen's liens. This provision roughly codifies the common law with respect to a particular type of intervening lien, while clarifying the nature of the notice required. However, the statutes do not define "optional" and consequently leave construction lenders in much the same dilemma discussed previously.

The Maryland statute has a fascinating and checkered history. It was originally enacted in 1825,[45] apparently because of serious abuses of the future advances mortgage. Language in such mortgages was so broad as to permit the mortgagee to acquire the mortgage, then proceed to buy up at depreciated prices debts owed by the mortgagor to third parties, and assert them against the mortgagor's land.[46] The statute, which was modified numerous times, in effect held that no future

---

to require an express statement that the mortgage is given for future advances, but a mortgage referring only to a stated principal sum, with no reference to further advances, was given priority over intervening liens in Snead Construction Co. v. First Federal Savings & Loan Association, 342 So.2d 517 (Fla.App.1977). For a general review of the Florida law, see Silver Waters Corp. v. Murphy, 177 So.2d 897 (Fla. App.1965).

41. Turner v. Lytton Savings & Loan Association, 242 Cal.App.2d 457, 51 Cal. Rptr. 552 (1966).

42. E.g., Conn., Cal., Ga.

43. E.g., Fla., Me., Md., S.C.

44. See note 39, supra; Green, Search Real Estate Records Before Making Future Advances, Fla. B.J., Dec. 1984, at 704.

45. Md.Laws, 1825, c. 50; Md.Code, 1957, Art. 66, §§ 2, 3 (repealed).

46. Watkins, Maryland Mortgages for Future Advances, 4 Md.L.Rev. 111 (1940); comment, Md.Ann. Real Property Code § 7–102 (1974).

advance, optional or obligatory, would have priority but from the date it was made. By its terms the law did not apply to Baltimore or Prince George's counties, and in the rest of the state a practice grew up among construction lenders, sanctioned by the courts, of evading the statute by depositing the entire loan amount into an escrow or trust account from which the escrowee or trustee would administer the disbursements.[47] Finally in 1972 the statute was repealed and replaced with an express endorsement of priority for all future advances, irrespective of their obligatory character.[48] The Maryland statute thus shifted from one of the most restrictive (although easily evaded) in the country to one of the most liberal.

All of these statutes represent legislative recognition of the economic compulsion concept [49] and the need for reasonable discretion on the part of lenders in making optional advances to protect their interests in construction projects. These same concepts are carried over, although with greater precision and complexity, to the Uniform Land Transactions Act (ULTA) and the Uniform Simplification of Land Transfers Act (USLTA), adopted by the National Conference of Commissioners on Uniform State Laws.[50] As these uniform acts are organized, it is necessary to consider mortgages for future advances in three distinct contexts: (1) as between mortgagee and mortgagor; (2) as between mortgagee and intervening claimants other than those claiming "construction liens" (the term ULTA and USLTA use for mechanics' and materialmen's liens); and (3) as between mortgagee and intervening construction lien claimants.

As between the mortgagor and mortgagee, mortgages for future advances are valid, but are limited to the maximum aggregate amount stated in the mortgage unless the advance is made to protect the security (as by paying property taxes, etc.) or to complete the improvements under a construction agreement,[51] in which cases the stated maximum amount may be exceeded.[52] There is no requirement that the mortgage state that it secures future advances.[53]

47. See, e.g., Toney Schloss Properties Corp. v. Union Federal Savings & Loan Association, 233 Md. 224, 196 A.2d 458 (1964); Comment, Md.Ann. Real Property Code § 7–102 (1974).

48. Md.Ann Real Property Code § 7–102 (1974).

49. Comment, Md.Ann Real Property Code § 7–102 (1974).

50. See Benfield, The Future Advances Lender: Status Under Present Illinois Law and Under ULTA and USOLTA, 1981 S.I. U.L.Rev. 451; Comment, Future Advances Under the ULTA and the USLTA: The Construction Lender Receives a New Status, 34 Wash. & Lee L.Rev. 1027 (1977).

51. U.L.T.A. § 3–205(e).

52. U.L.T.A. § 3–205(c).

53. This statement is clearly correct with respect to construction advances and advances to protect the security; U.L.T.A. § 3–205(e). Whether it is also true of other types of future advances is unclear under the ULTA; the matter would presumably be governed by the common law, which has generally permitted such advances notwithstanding the lack of reference to them in the mortgage. See text at notes 7–10, supra.

When a contest arises between the mortgagee and intervening claimants other than those claiming construction liens, the issue is one of priority. The ULTA grants full priority to the mortgagee who advances funds to complete improvements under a construction loan; the lender's knowledge of the intervening lien, the maximum amount stated in the mortgage, and the obligatory or optional nature of the advance are all irrelevant.[54] If the loan is for any other purpose, the lender will have priority only if the advance is made to protect the security,[55] or is made or committed to before he receives actual notice of the intervening lien.[56] In the language of the ULTA, an advance is made "pursuant to a commitment" if the lender has promised to advance the funds, even though a default by the borrower or some other extrinsic condition may excuse or has excused him from his legal duty to do so.[57] Thus, even on a non-construction loan, the lender may well have priority over intervening liens despite the fact that they were disbursed after the borrower's default. However, if the advance is not for completion of improvements or protection of the security, it can have priority only to the extent that it does not exceed the maximum amount stated in the mortgage.[58]

Finally, a somewhat different scheme of priorities is established as between the mortgagee and construction lien claimants. Such liens take priority over all future advances under non-construction loans, even if the lender has made the advance or commitment before learning of the lien.[59] However, they are inferior to advances under construction loans if the advances are paid toward improvements on the real estate, the discharge of prior construction liens, or protection of the security interest (again, such as payment of taxes.)[60] Even if none of these three criteria are met, the construction loan will have priority to the extent of advances made before the lender had actual knowledge that a mechanics' lien had attached.[61]

In sum, the ULTA and USLTA give construction lenders considerable advantages not made available to other lenders of future advances. The construction lender is not limited to the maximum amount stated in the mortgage; this provision is reasonable, since inflating construction costs can make the parties' original cost estimate inadequate even though additional advances to complete the project are socially highly desirable. Construction loan advances made to enable completion of the improvements have priority over most types of intervening liens, even if they are clearly optional. Even as against mechanics' liens, construction loan advances are given priority if they are "made in payment of the price of the agreed improvements."[62] This last phrase

---

54. U.L.T.A. § 3–301(b)(4).

55. U.L.T.A. § 3–301(b)(3).

56. U.L.T.A. § 3–301(b)(1)(2).

57. U.L.T.A. § 1–201(14).

58. U.L.T.A. § 3–301(b)(1), (2).

59. U.S.L.T.A. § 5–209(a).

60. U.S.L.T.A. § 5–209(c).

61. U.S.L.T.A. § 5–209(b).

62. U.S.L.T.A. § 5–209(c)(1). Comment 2 (Supp. 1985) appears to confirm that the lender's duty to apply the funds to construction is absolute.

may have important connotations, for it can be read to impose an absolute duty on the part of the lender to make certain that the funds are not diverted to non-construction purposes. Compare the language employed in describing the priority of construction loan advances over *non*-mechanics' lien claims: "made * * * to enable completion of the agreed improvement." [63] This terminology does not seem to require that the funds in fact be used to purchase the improvements, but only that they be advanced to the owner or developer with that purpose in mind. Diversion of the funds would not, under this view, be fatal to the lender's priority.[64]

Whether any distinction along these lines was intended by the Commissioners is hard to say. It is not easy to see why a mechanics' lien claimant should be entitled to a higher standard of care or performance from the construction lender than, say, a junior mortgagee or a subordinated purchase-money vendor. In any event, to impose absolute liability on the lender seems excessively harsh; a standard of reasonable care in selecting and implementing a method of disbursal of funds would give adequate protection for all types of intervening lienors. However, speaking generally, the Commissioners have achieved a reasonable balance between the needs of construction lenders and other claimants, and they have acted wisely in granting construction lenders the flexibility they need to complete troubled projects without undue fear of loss of priority.

 WESTLAW REFERENCES
build*** construct*** /s loan /p advance

---

§ 12.8 Dragnet Clauses

The dragnet clause is a mortgage provision which purports to make the real estate security for other, usually unspecified, debts which the mortgagor may already owe or may owe in the future to the mortgagee. The clause is not functionally related to construction lending and is discussed at this point only because it is conceptually a mortgage to secure future advances. In a sense the dragnet clause is just the opposite of a construction loan; the lender usually has no particular future advances in mind, and merely "throws in" the clause in the hope that it might come in handy later.

A simple form of dragnet clause reads as follows:

"This mortgage is given to secure the payment of a promissory note (described in detail), and also the payment of any

---

63. U.L.T.A. § 3–301(b)(4).

64. But see Benfield, supra note 50, at 480–81 n. 82, suggesting that the same standard applies whether or not the intervening lien is a mechanics' lien—namely, that the advance must actually be used for construction, rather than merely have been intended for such use.

additional sums and interest thereon now or hereafter due or owing from mortgagor to mortgagee." [1]

A more carefully-drafted form, which attempts to resolve some questions implicit in the foregoing clause, is:

> "This mortgage is given to secure the payment of a promissory note (described in detail), and any other indebtedness or obligation of the mortgagor, or any of them, and any present of future demands of any kind or nature which mortgagee or its successor may have against the mortgagor or any of them, whether created directly, or acquired by assignment, whether absolute or contingent, whether due or not, whether otherwise secured or not, or whether existing at the time of the execution of this instrument or arising thereafter." [2]

Dragnet clauses are frequently included in the printed language of mortgages drafted by mortgagees. They are seldom the subject of negotiation, and may go entirely unnoticed by the mortgagor until the mortgagee asserts them. The rule making optional advances subordinate to intervening liens [3] is highly relevant in this context. Advances secured by dragnet clauses are almost never obligatory; the only factual issue is generally whether the mortgagee had the requisite notice of intervening liens, and this is usually not hard to determine. [4] Moreover the rule, which was severely criticized in the preceding section as applied to construction loans, makes rather good sense in the dragnet clause case; in its absence, a mortgagor might naively execute upon his house a mortgage containing a dragnet clause and consequently find himself locked to that particular lender for the rest of his life. [5]

Dragnet clauses are generally upheld, [6] but because their apparent coverage is so broad, and because the mortgagor is often unaware of

---

§ 12.8

1. The language is adapted from Union Bank v. Wendland, 54 Cal.App.3d 393, 126 Cal.Rptr. 549 (1976). See Emporia State Bank & Trust Co. v. Mounkes, 214 Kan. 178, 179, 519 P.2d 618, 620 (1974); Note, Future Advance Clauses in Tennessee— Construction and Effect, 5 Memph.St.L. Rev. 586 (1975).

2. Wong v. Beneficial Savings & Loan Association, 56 Cal.App.3d 286, 128 Cal. Rptr. 338 (1976).

3. See § 12.7, supra, at notes 11–15.

4. See Bank of Ephriam v. Davis, 559 P.2d 538 (Utah 1977), requiring actual notice on the part of the lender to subordinate its lien deriving from a dragnet clause. Since no such notice was shown, the lender was held to have priority despite the optional nature of the advances. Under some statutes, a future advances clause may never have priority for more than the original balance, irrespective of

notice of intervening liens; see New Mexico Bank v. Lucas Brothers, 92 N.M. 2, 582 P.2d 379 (1978).

5. See Dicus v. Ripley County Bank, ___ Ind.App. ___, 471 N.E.2d 1257 (1984); Meek, Mortgage Provisions Extending the Lien to Future Advances and Antecedent Indebtedness, 26 Ark.L.Rev. 485 (1973).

6. Fazio v. Alan Sinton, Limited, 41 B.R. 865 (Bkrtcy.Pa.1984); Clovis Nat'l Bank v. Harmon, 102 N.M. 166, 692 P.2d 1315 (1984); O'Neill Production Credit Association v. Mitchell, 209 Neb. 206, 307 N.W.2d 115 (1981); North Park Bank v. Nichols, 645 P.2d 620 (Utah 1982); Whiteway Finance Co. v. Green, 434 So.2d 1351 (Miss.1983); Smith v. Union State Bank, ___ Ind.App. ___, 452 N.E.2d 1059 (1983); First National Bank v. Rozelle, 493 F.2d 1196 (10th Cir.1974); Lammey v. Producers Livestock Credit Corp., 463 P.2d 491 (Wyo.1970). See generally Annot. 3 A.L.R. 4th 690 (1980).

their presence or implications, the courts tend to construe them narrowly against the mortgagee.[7] Generalizations are difficult, since the language of the particular clause may be a decisive factor. However, the following illustrations show numerous ways in which the courts have narrowed the application of dragnet clauses. Sometimes such holdings are said to be based on the intention of the parties, but in reality they usually represent the court's conceptions of fairness and equity.[8] These illustrations are not intended to represent any majority rule, as there are many conflicting or contrary cases. They merely show the sort of judicial treatment dragnet clauses often receive.

1. The mortgage will only secure advances made or debts incurred in the future. If the mortgagor already owes debts to the mortgagee at the time the mortgage is executed, it would supposedly be easy enough to identify those existing debts specifically; if they are not so identified, it is assumed that the parties did not intend to secure them.[9]

2. Only debts of the same type or character as the original debt are secured by the mortgage.[10] For example, if the original loan is for

7. In re Bonner, 43 B.R. 261 (Bkrtcy. Ala. 1984); Badger State Agri-Credit & Realty, Inc. v. Lubahn, 122 Wis.2d 718, 365 N.W.2d 616 (1985); Everett Credit Union v. Allied Ambulance Serv., Inc., 12 Mass.App. 343, 424 N.E.2d 1142 (1981); First v. Byrne, 238 Iowa 712, 28 N.W.2d 509 (1947); Annot., 172 A.L.R. 1072 (1948). The courts of Tennessee tend to be an exception, construing dragnet clauses rather consistently in favor of the lender; see Note, Future Advances Clauses in Tennessee—Construction and Effect, 5 Memph.St.L.Rev. 586 (1975).

8. See Justice, Secured Transactions—What Floats Can Be Sunk, 24 Vill.L.Rev. 867, 896–99 (1979).

9. First National Bank v. Lygrisse, 231 Kan. 595, 647 P.2d 1268 (1982); Durham v. First Guaranty Bank, 331 So.2d 563 (La. App.1976), writ denied 334 So.2d 431; National Bank v. Blankenship, 177 F.Supp. 667 (E.D.Ark.1959), affirmed sub nom. National Bank v. General Mills, 283 F.2d 574 (8th Cir.1960); First v. Byrne, 238 Iowa 712, 28 N.W.2d 509 (1947); Bank of Searcy v. Kroh, 195 Ark. 785, 114 S.W.2d 26 (1938); Farmer's National Bank v. DeFever, 177 Okla. 561, 61 P.2d 245 (1936); Iser v. Mark Building Corp., 253 N.Y. 499, 171 N.E. 757 (1930). Cf. Guilmette v. Peoples Savings Bank, 12 B.R. 799 (Bkrtcy.R.I. 1981); Clovis Nat'l Bank v. Harmon, 102 N.M. 166, 692 P.2d 1315 (1984); Badger State Agri-Credit & Realty, Inc. v. Lubahn, supra note 7; Mercer v. Daoran Corp., 662 S.W.2d 382 (Tex.App.1983), judgment reversed 676 S.W.2d 580 (1984); Tryck, Nyman & Hayes, Inc. v. Ficke, 591

P.2d 104. (1979); United States v. Automatic Heating & Equipment Co., 181 F.Supp. 924 (E.D.Tenn.1960), affirmed 287 F.2d 885 (6th Cir.1961). See also Ram Co. v. Estate of Kobbeman, 236 Kan. 75, 696 P.2d 936 (1985) (dragnet clause covers preexisting advances growing out of same transaction).

10. In re Continental Resources Corp., 43 B.R. 658 (Bkrtcy. Okl.1984) (Okl. law); Trapp v. Tidwell, 418 So.2d 786 (Miss.1982) (clause does not cover claims in tort); Canal National Bank v. Becker, 431 A.2d 71 (Me.1981); First Security Bank v. Shiew, 609 P.2d 952 (Utah 1980) (quoting treatise); Security Bank v. First National Bank, 263 Ark. 525, 565 S.W.2d 623 (1978); Garnett State Savings Bank v. Tush, 232 Kan. 447, 657 P.2d 508 (1983); Emporia State Bank & Trust Co. v. Mounkes, 214 Kan. 178, 519 P.2d 618 (1974), noted 23 U.Kan.L.Rev. 745 (1975) (original mortgage loan apparently to purchase realty; note signed eight years later to buy car and start son in restaurant business not covered by dragnet clause); Airline Commerce Bank v. Commercial Credit Corp., 531 S.W.2d 171 (Tex.Civ.App. 1975), error refused n.r.e.; Akamine & Sons, Limited v. American Security Bank, 50 Hawaii 304, 440 P.2d 262 (1968); Hendrickson v. Farmers' Bank & Trust Co., 189 Ark. 423, 73 S.W.2d 725 (1934).

Cf. Financial Acceptance Corp. v. Garvey, 6 Mass.App.Ct. 610, 380 N.E.2d 1332 (1978) (dragnet clause, in mortgage securing note made by mortgagor, also secures later note guaranteed by mortgagor); Fleming v. First American Bank, 171 Ga. App. 295, 319 S.E.2d 119 (1984) (semple);

home repairs, a future loan or advance for more repairs would be secured by the mortgage but a loan for an automobile purchase would not. It is easy to imagine grey areas in such a test. For example, what if the second loan were for adding a room to the house? The resolution of the matter is made easier if the documents on the second loan state that it is to be secured under the dragnet clause of the existing mortgage.

3. As an extension of the foregoing concept, it is sometimes held that the dragnet clause will cover future debts only if the documents evidencing those debts specifically refer back to the clause.[11]

4. If the future debt is separately secured, whether by another mortgage or by a personal property security agreement, it may be assumed that the parties did not intend that it also be secured by the dragnet mortgage.[12]

5. The clause is inapplicable to debts which were originally owed by the mortgagor to third parties, and which were assigned to or purchased by the mortgagee.[13]

6. If there are several joint mortgagors, only future debts on which all of the mortgagors are obligated [14] (or at least of which all were aware) [15] will be covered by the dragnet clause.

Wong v. Beneficial Savings & Loan Association, 56 Cal.App.3d 286, 128 Cal.Rptr. 338 (1976); First National Bank v. Rozelle, 493 F.2d 1196 (10th Cir.1974); In re Dorsey Electric Supply Co., 344 F.Supp. 1171 (E.D. Ark.1972); Murdock Acceptance Corp. v. Jones, 50 Tenn.App. 431, 362 S.W.2d 266 (1961); Thorp Sales Corp. v. Dolese Brothers Co., 453 F.Supp. 196 (W.D.Okla.1978).

11. Stockyards National Bank v. Capitol Steel & Iron Co., 201 Kan. 429, 441 P.2d 301 (1968); First National Bank v. Lygrisse, 231 Kan. 595, 647 P.2d 1268 (1982); Uransky v. First Federal Savings & Loan, 684 F.2d 750 (11th Cir.1982). North Carolina follows this rule by statute; see N.C.Gen.Stat. § 45–68(2); Matter of Mills, 39 B.R. 564 (Bkrtcy.N.C.1984). Cf. Cabot, Cabot & Forbes Land Trust v. First National Bank, 369 So.2d 89 (Fla.App.1979).

12. Vaughn & Co., Limited, v. Saul, 143 Ga.App. 74, 237 S.E.2d 622 (1977); Moran v. Gardemeyer, 82 Cal. 102, 23 P. 8 (1889); Second National Bank v. Boyle, 155 Ohio St. 482, 99 N.E.2d 474, 44 O.O. 440 (1951). Cf. United States v. Vahlco Corp., 720 F.2d 885, 892 n. 14 (5th Cir.1983).

13. Pongetti v. Bankers Trust, 368 So. 2d 819 (Miss.1979); Wood v. Parker Square State Bank, 400 S.W.2d 898 (Tex.1966); Thorp Sales Corp. v. Dolese Brothers Co., note 10 supra. Cf. Georgia Railroad Bank v. McCullough, 241 Ga. 456, 246 S.E.2d 313 (1978) (clause may be enforced by bank

into which original mortgagee is merged.) See also Bowen v. Kicklighter, 124 Ga.App. 82, 183 S.E.2d 10 (1971) (assignee of mortgage may not assert dragnet clause to secure advances made to mortgagor before assignment.) See Ga.Code Ann. § 44–14–1(b) (clause limited to debts arising " * * * between the original parties to the security agreement.")

14. Farmers Trust v. Manning, 311 N.W.2d 285 (Iowa 1981); Bank of Woodson v. Hibbitts, 626 S.W.2d 133 (Tex.App.1981), error refused n.r.e.; O'Neill Production Credit Association v. Mitchell, 209 Neb. 206, 307 N.W.2d 115 (1981); Mohler v. Buena Vista Bank, 42 Colo.App. 4, 588 P.2d 894 (1978); Holiday Inns, Inc. v. Susher-Schaefer Investment Co., 77 Mich.App. 658, 259 N.W.2d 179 (1977); United States v. American National Bank, 255 F.2d 504 (5th Cir.1958), certiorari denied 358 U.S. 835, 79 S.Ct. 58, 3 L.Ed.2d 72 (1958), rehearing denied 359 U.S. 1006, 79 S.Ct. 1135, 3 L.Ed.2d 1034 (1959); First v. Byrne, 238 Iowa 712, 28 N.W.2d 509 (1947). Cf. Citizens Bank v. Gibson, ___ Ind.App. ___, 463 N.E.2d 276 (1984); Sutton v. Atlantic Bank, 167 Ga.App. 861, 307 S.E.2d 746 (1983); Willis v. Rabun County Bank, 249 Ga. 493, 291 S.E.2d 715 (1982); Newton County Bank v. Jones, 299 So.2d 215 (Miss.1974); Wright v. Lincoln County

15. See note 15 on page 902.

7. Once the original debt has been fully discharged, the mortgage is extinguished and cannot secure future loans.[16]

8. If the real estate is transferred by the mortgagor to a third party, any debts which the original mortgagor incurs thereafter are not secured by the mortgage.[17] This is the position taken by the drafters of the Uniform Land Transfer Act.[18]

9. If the real estate is transferred by the mortgagor to a grantee, advances subsequently made by the mortgagee to the grantee are not secured by the mortgage, even if the grantee expressly assumed the mortgage.[19]

In addition to these judicial limitations, most of the statutes relating to future advances discussed in the preceding section [20] limit the amount of such advances to the maximum amount stated in the original mortgage. This limitation is important in the construction of dragnet clauses since the clauses on their face are usually unlimited as to amount.

While the dragnet clause is usually regarded as advantageous to mortgagees, that is not necessarily the case. One reason is that the types of judicial limitations on the clause discussed above are very much open to debate and further development in most states; in this sense, the clause is an invitation to litigation. Moreover, even if the clause is held to be valid, it may be turned against the mortgagee. Union Bank v. Wendland,[21] a California intermediate appellate decision, provides an interesting example. Somewhat simplified, the Wendlands borrowed a sum from the bank and gave a deed of trust (containing a dragnet clause) on their house as security. Subsequently, they borrowed an additional amount from the same bank to remodel the house, giving a second note and another deed of trust on the same real estate. Upon their default the bank foreclosed the first deed of trust by power of sale. It then brought a suit upon the second note. The antideficiency statute, by its terms, barred any personal judgment on a

Bank, 62 Tenn.App. 560, 465 S.W.2d 877 (1970); Martin v. First National Bank, 279 Ala. 303, 184 So.2d 815 (1966).

15. Lomanto v. Bank of America, 22 Cal.App.3d 663, 99 Cal.Rptr. 442 (1972); Gates v. Crocker-Anglo National Bank, 257 Cal.App.2d 857, 65 Cal.Rptr. 536 (1968).

16. Underwood v. Jarvis, 358 So.2d 731 (Ala.1978); Tedesco v. CDC Federal Credit Union, 167 Ga.App. 337, 306 S.E.2d 397 (1983) (debtor may have mortgage cancelled only if he gives up right to any further advances); Jacobs v. City National Bank, 229 Ark. 79, 313 S.W.2d 789 (1958); cf. Padgett v. Haston, 279 Ark. 367, 651 S.W.2d 460 (1983); State Bank of Albany v. Fioravanti, 51 N.Y.2d 638, 435 N.Y.S.2d 947, 417 N.E.2d 60 (1980); Central Production Credit Association v. Page, 268 S.C. 1,

231 S.E.2d 210 (1977) (dragnet clause remains valid even after principal debt is fully paid.)

17. Trapp v. Tidwell, 418 So.2d 786 (Miss.1982) (mortgagee gave permission for grantee to assume loan; is estopped to assert dragnet clause); Vaughn v. Crown Plumbing & Sewer Service, Inc., 523 S.W.2d 72 (Tex.Civ.App.1975), error refused n.r.e.

18. U.L.T.A. § 3–205(d).

19. Uransky v. First Federal Savings & Loan Association, 1 B.R. 640 (Bkrtcy.Fla. 1979); Walker v. Whitmore, 165 Ark. 276, 262 S.W. 678 (1924).

20. § 12.7, supra, at notes 39–48.

21. 54 Cal.App.3d 393, 126 Cal.Rptr. 549 (1976).

note secured by a deed of trust which had been foreclosed by power of sale.[22] The Wendlands argued, and the court held, that the second note was in fact secured by the first deed of trust (through the operation of its dragnet clause) and thus could not be collected by way of personal suit.

Dragnet clauses can also be dangerous to title insurers. In Southwest Title Insurance Co. v. Northland Building Corp.,[23] the title company issued a policy which specifically excepted two existing mortgages which the company's search had disclosed. The policy language recited that those mortgages secured certain specific promissory notes which were carefully identified in the policy. However, the mortgages also contained dragnet clauses which caused them to secure other loans made to the mortgagors as well, a fact not mentioned in the policy. The Texas Supreme Court held that, as to the loans covered by the dragnet clauses, the policy exceptions were ineffective and the title company was liable. More careful drafting of the policy exceptions could probably have produced a different result, but the case illustrates how dragnet clauses can have unanticipated and undesired results.

 WESTLAW REFERENCES
(dragnet +1 clause provision) anaconda /s mortgage

§ 12.9   Subordination Agreements

By subordination agreements mortgagees may agree to alter the relative priorities that the applicable law and documents would otherwise give their mortgages.[1] Subordination agreements are subject to recording statutes and are used in many kinds of transactions.[2] It is well established that parties may use a subordination agreement to establish the priority of mortgages executed on the same property at the same time.[3] And a senior mortgage can be subordinated to specific

22. West's Ann.Cal.Civil Proc.Code, § 580(d); see § 8.3, supra.

23. 552 S.W.2d 425 (Tex.1977).

§ 12.9

1. A mortgagee must personally agree to be subordinated. The trustee under a trust deed has no power to subordinate without the consent of the beneficiary unless the trust instrument so provides. Tuscarora, Inc. v. B.V.A. Credit Corp., 218 Va. 849, 241 S.E.2d 778 (1978); First Funding Corp. v. Birge, 220 Va. 326, 257 S.E.2d 861 (1979); Belknap Savings Bank v. Lamar Land and Canal Co., 28 Colo. 326, 64 P. 212 (1901). See also Fierst v. Commonwealth Land Title Insurance Co., 499 Pa. 68, 451 A.2d 674 (1982). Persons dealing with a trustee must take notice of the scope of his authority. But if the trustee has power to subordinate, a third party acting in good faith is protected unless apprised of facts that should reasonably put him on notice that a breach of trust is involved. Dye v. Lincoln Rochester Trust Co., 40 A.D.2d 583, 334 N.Y.S.2d 402 (1972), affirmed 31 N.Y.2d 1012, 341 N.Y.S.2d 619, 294 N.E.2d 207 (1973).

2. Like other contracts, a subordination agreement will be unenforceable if made without consideration; see Dugan v. First National Bank, 227 Kan. 201, 606 P.2d 1009 (1980); Cameron v. Churchill Mortgage Corp., 249 Ga. 362, 290 S.E.2d 474 (1982). The Statute of Frauds is also applicable; see Troj v. Chesebro, 30 Conn.Sup. 30, 296 A.2d 685 (1972).

3. Gautney v. Gautney, 253 Ala. 584, 46 So.2d 198 (1950); Collins v. Home Savings & Loan Association, 205 Cal.App.2d 86, 22 Cal.Rptr. 817, 822 (1962); Hagen v. Butler, 83 Idaho 427, 363 P.2d 712 (1961).

junior mortgage.[4] A subordination may be for an indefinite time, or may be limited to a fixed period.[5] It may be made subject to the fulfillment of certain conditions, and will then be ineffective if they are not met.[6] If a first mortgage is subordinated to a third mortgage, the first mortgage also becomes subordinate to the second mortgage.[7] In general, an agreement to subordinate a mortgage to another mortgage to be made in the future is enforceable,[8] but enforcement may be denied if the future mortgage is not sufficiently described.

Subordination of Vendors to Construction Lenders

Subordination agreements are frequently used in mortgages relating to new real estate developments because they make it possible for developers to finance subdivisions and other construction projects without investing large amounts of their own capital. First, the developer persuades the original land seller to accept a purchase money mortgage or trust deed for all or a large part of the purchase price.[9] Then, using the land as security, the developer arranges a construction loan from an institutional lender to finance the construction of the houses, apartments, or condominiums that he plans. A subordination agreement with the seller makes this financing scheme possible by reordering the lien priorities between the purchase money mortgage and the construction loan. Institutional lenders are often required by law or their own

4. Conshohocken Federal Savings & Loan Association v. Period & Country Homes, Inc., 287 Pa.Super. 520, 430 A.2d 1173 (1981); Olds Bros. Lumber Co. v. Marley, 72 Ariz. 392, 236 P.2d 464 (1951); State Savings & Loan Association v. Kauaian Dev. Corp., 50 Hawaii 540, 445 P.2d 109 (1968).

5. Williams v. Vestman, 668 P.2d 957 (Colo.App.1983); Campanella v. Rainier National Bank, 26 Wn.App. 418, 612 P.2d 460 (1980) (party given priority by subordination for one year must complete foreclosure within the year).

6. See Riggs National Bank v. Wines, 59 Md.App. 219, 474 A.2d 1360 (1984), certiorari denied 301 Md. 43, 481 A.2d 802 (1984); Life Savings & Loan Association v. Bryant, 125 Ill.App.3d 1012, 81 Ill.Dec. 577, 467 N.E.2d 277 (1984). See also Guarantee Bank v. Magness Construction Co., 462 A.2d 405 (Del.1983) (agreement to subordinate to a loan to be made to a corporation does not subordinate to a loan made to a related individual.)

7. Old Stone Mortgage & Realty Trust v. New Georgia Plumbing, Inc., 239 Ga. 345, 236 S.E.2d 592 (1977); Shaddix v. National Surety Co., 221 Ala. 268, 128 So. 220 (1930); Ladner v. Hogue Lumber & Supply Co., 229 Miss. 505, 511, 91 So.2d 545, 547 (1956).

A contrary result may follow if the subordination agreement is limited expressly to a specific junior lien; see Colorado Nat'l Bank v. F.E. Biegert, 165 Colo. 78, 438 P.2d 506 (1968).

Moreover, once the junior lien to which the mortgage was subordinated has been discharged, the mortgage resumes its original priority as against any intermediate liens. See Commercial Bank v. Stratford, 149 Ga.App. 736, 256 S.E.2d 69 (1979).

8. Ray Thomas Enterprises v. Fox, 128 Cal.App.3d 361, 180 Cal.Rptr. 253 (1982).

9. Sellers are often willing to accept a purchase money mortgage because of the tax benefits from receiving payments spread over a number of years (I.R.C. § 453). Sellers will subordinate their purchase money mortgages if they are convinced that the sale depends upon the developer being able to obtain first lien construction financing. And usually sellers are compensated by receiving a higher purchase price. See generally Note, The Subordination of Purchase-Money Security, 52 Cal.L.Rev. 157 (1964). See Statland Holliday, Inc. v. Stendig Development Corp., 46 A.D.2d 135, 362 N.Y.S.2d 2 (1974).

internal policies to secure real estate loans with first liens,[10] but in the absence of an explicit reversal of priorities, the law presumes that the purchase money mortgage is intended to have priority.[11] The purchase money mortgage is usually recorded first, as well, so an enforceable subordination agreement is necessary to give the institutional lender the first lien.[12]

Much of the recent litigation relating to subordination agreements has centered on their enforceability, especially in relation to indefiniteness.[13] The validity and effectiveness of subordination agreements have been challenged at two points in the transaction: (1) while the agreement is still executory and (2) after the construction loan has been made and a contest over priority develops between the seller and the construction lender as a result of the developer's default.

The most common way for litigation to arise while the agreement is still executory is for a developer to bring suit against a seller seeking specific performance of a contract for the sale of land. The problem arises because it is not feasible to negotiate the terms of the construction loan at the time the contract for the purchase of the land is entered into. The clause in the contract, or in the purchase-money mortgage, may either be phrased as a promise to execute a subordination agreement in the future, or may be a self-sufficient subordination which requires no further documentation.[14] In either case, the clause is more or less indefinite concerning the terms of the construction loan to be obtained. Then the seller reneges on the whole transaction or refuses to enter into a specific subordination agreement that would subordinate his lien to the particular loan that the purchaser has arranged.[15] When the purchaser seeks specific performance of the contract, the seller usually attempts to avoid performance by showing

---

10. Until recently, National banks were required to take first liens under 12 U.S. C.A. § 1371, and federal savings and loans under 12 U.S.C.A. § 1464(c).

While these requirements have now been repealed, state-chartered institutions may be bound by similar rules. Many lenders demand first liens as a matter of internal policy.

11. See § 9.1 supra; West's Ann.Cal. Civ.Code, § 2898. This presumption may be rebutted by an intentional recording of the construction mortgage before the purchase-money mortgage; see Carolina Builders Corp. v. Howard-Veasey Homes, Inc., 72 N.C.App. 224, 324 S.E.2d 626 (1985).

12. See McNamara, Subordination Agreements as Viewed by Sellers, Purchasers, Construction Lenders, and Title Companies, 12 Real Est.L.J. 347 (1984); Dreckshage v. Community Federal Savings & Loan Association, 555 S.W.2d 314 (Mo. 1977), enforcing subordinations although the developer lied about the content of the

agreements and the vendors never read them.

13. See generally, Lambe, Enforceability of Subordination Clauses, 19 Real Prop. Prob. & Tr.J. 631 (1984); Annotation, Requisite Definiteness of Provision in Contract for Sale or Lease of Land, that Vendor or Landlord Will Subordinate His Interest to Permit Other Party to Obtain Financing, 26 A.L.R.3d 855 (1969); Miller, Starr and Regalia, Subordination Agreements in California, 13 U.C.L.A.L.Rev. 1298 (1966).

14. See Rockhill v. United States, 288 Md. 237, 418 A.2d 197 (1980).

15. "The agreement altering priority may be contained in a separate writing or it may be set forth in the recorded security instrument. In either case the provisions of the subordination agreement are regulated, in part, by statute, and it must be recorded in order to impart constructive notice of its contents. By the terms of the 'automatic' subordination agreement the seller's lien is recorded with an agreement that the subordination clause is too vague and indefinite to be enforced. In the cases in which the courts have ruled for the seller, the entire contract has been held unenforceable, since the clause is considered a material part of the contract. However, it has been suggested that an absolute and unconditional waiver of the subordination clause by the purchaser could save the rest of the contract.[16]

When the subordination agreement is challenged after a default has occurred and a contest over priority has developed, sellers attempt to raise these same arguments. But because the contract has been at least partially performed, other issues prevent the question from being decided simply by determining if the contract is indefinite or unjust and unreasonable on its face.

Actions to Enforce Executory Subordination Agreements

In California, where most of the litigation related to subordination agreements has occurred, the courts have been sympathetic to the seller, generally regarding him as an unsophisticated party in need of protection. They have held that "an enforceable subordination clause must contain terms that will define and minimize the risk that the subordinating lien will impair or destroy the seller's security."[17] Although the California courts have not specified a minimum set of terms that will make a subordination agreement enforceable, they have provided some guidance.[18]

In 1967 the California Supreme Court was asked to decide in Handy v. Gordon if a subordination clause specifying maximum loan amounts per unit, maximum interest rates, and maximum loan periods could be enforced by specific performance. In addition to arguing that the subordination clause was too indefinite to enforce, the seller raised

---

that the lien of a subsequent lender will automatically be senior to the seller's lien without further acts on his part. By the terms of the other common form, the seller promises to execute a subsequent instrument which will subordinate his lien to that of the lender. However, even under the 'automatic' subordination agreement, a title company will usually require the seller to execute another document at the time the new lien is recorded, in order specifically to subordinate the seller's lien to the new lien." Miller, Starr and Regalia, Subordination Agreements in California, 13 U.C.L.A.L.Rev. 1298, 1299 (1966).

16. Spellman v. Dixon, 256 Cal.App.2d 1, 4, 63 Cal.Rptr. 668, 671 (1967).

17. Handy v. Gordon, 65 Cal.2d 578, 55 Cal.Rptr. 769, 422 P.2d 329, 26 A.L.R.3d 848 (1967). See Stockwell v. Lindeman, 229 Cal.App.2d 750, 40 Cal.Rptr. 555 (1964); Magna Development Co. v. Reed, 228 Cal.App.2d 230, 39 Cal.Rptr. 284

(1964); Burrow v. Timmsen, 223 Cal.App. 2d 283, 35 Cal.Rptr. 668, 100 A.L.R.2d 544 (1963); Roven v. Miller, 168 Cal.App.2d 391, 335 P.2d 1035 (1959).

18. In Stockwell v. Lindeman, supra note 17, a California court of appeals held that a subordination clause which specified a maximum loan amount and a maximum interest rate and provided that repayment should be made upon the terms required by the lender, could be enforced by specific performance. The court said that the terms of repayment could be supplied by the lender or by custom but that the contract would not be valid if the terms of repayment were left for future agreement between the parties themselves. Although Stockwell is cited with apparent approval in Handy v. Gordon, supra note 17, Stockwell's reliance on custom or the future loan agreement to supply additional terms providing essential protection to the vendor is of questionable validity after *Handy.*

a defense based upon a statute [19] which prohibited the enforcement of a contract by specific performance if the contract is not just and reasonable to the party against whom enforcement is sought. The court denied the suit for specific performance, saying that the contract was not fair and reasonable to the seller because it did not adequately define and minimize his risk. Specifically, the clause did not limit the buyer's use of the loan proceeds to construction on the land. Nor did it provide assurance that the amounts of the loans would not exceed the value which the improvements added to the land; the loan maximums were expressed in terms of absolutes and did not limit the loan amounts to percentages of the building costs. Finally, the loan limits were maximums per lot and the developer had discretion to determine the number of lots.

While the court in Handy v. Gordon appeared to decide the case on the basis of whether the contract was just and reasonable to the seller, it would seem that the subordination clause was not just and reasonable because it was too indefinite. Thus in subordination agreement cases it probably makes no difference that the statutory defense relied upon in Handy v. Gordon technically applies only to suits for specific performance: if a subordination agreement is so indefinite that it is unfair to require a seller to perform under it, it probably would not be definite enough to support a suit for damages.

In Malani v. Clapp [20] the Supreme Court of Hawaii followed reasoning like that of *Handy,* holding that a subordination agreement must adequately protect the subordinating party. There a lessor sued a lessee for breach of contract, and the lessee tried to avoid the contract by showing that the subordination clause [21] was too indefinite to enforce. The subordination agreement limited the term of subordination to two years, required the lessee to be personally liable to the lessor, and required the lessee to show an aggregate net worth of $2,000,000. In addition to the clause itself, the court looked at the entire context of the transaction to determine if the lessor was adequately protected. The court felt that because of the protections in the subordination

19. West's Ann.Cal.Civ.Code, § 3391(2). See also West's Ann.Cal.Civ.Code, §§ 2953.1–2953.5 which provides that where the secured loan to be subordinated is less than $25,000, the subordination agreement or clause must contain a prominent warning that the agreement may subordinate the holder of the note to another security which would normally have a lower priority. If the warning is not given and the subordinating party has no actual knowledge of the subordination, he can void the agreement anytime within two years by recording notice.

20. 56 Hawaii 507, 542 P.2d 1265 (1975).

21. Under this agreement the lessor would subordinate her fee estate to a construction loan to be procured by the lessee. While this type of agreement is commonly called a subordination agreement, it is technically inaccurate to call it such. In reality the "subordination clause" is an agreement by the lessor to join in the lessee's mortgage, thereby subjecting the fee title to the mortgage. See Committee on Leases, Ground Leases and Their Financing, 4 Real Prop.Prob. & Trust J. 437 (1969).

clause and because the type of construction was specified in a building permit, the lessor was adequately protected.[22]

Most of the other courts which have been asked to decide the validity of subordination agreements have similarly held that terms limiting the seller's risk are necessary to make the agreement enforceable. While these courts have not uniformly designated certain terms as essential, the terms which they most often mention are maximum loan amounts, maximum interest rates, maximum loan periods, and requirements that the loan proceeds be used for improvements on the land.[23] Despite the general trend toward requiring terms of limitation in subordination agreements, there are a few recent cases in which courts have ruled that construction loans do not have to be described in detail.[24]

Action to Reverse Priorities After a Default

A contest over priorities after a default is quite different from an action to enforce an executory subordination agreement. First, the parties usually have executed a second subordination agreement describing the specific construction loan, thus curing any indefiniteness in the original agreement.[25] Miller v. Citizens Savings and Loan Association [26] provides an example of such a situation. This case revolved around a term limiting the use of the loan proceeds that was in the first agreement but not in the second. The court merged the agreements and enforced the clause in the first agreement that required the construction loans to be used only for certain purposes.[27] But even absent the first agreement, the court noted that "a subordination agreement should be construed, unless it expressly provides otherwise, as permitting the loan proceeds to be used only for * * *" purposes which will improve the seller's security position.[28] The seller

22. The court might not have been so willing to find that the lessor was adequately protected if it had been the lessor who was trying to avoid the contract.

23. Stenehjem v. Kyn Jin Cho, 631 P.2d 482 (Alaska 1981); American Savings & Loan Association v. Orenstein, 81 Mich. App. 249, 265 N.W.2d 111 (1978); Lahaina-Maui Corp. v. Tau Tet Hew, 362 F.2d 419 (9th Cir.1966); Troj v. Chesebro, 30 Conn. Sup. 30, 296 A.2d 685 (1972); Hux v. Raben, 74 Ill.App.2d 214, 219 N.E.2d 770 (1966), affirmed 38 Ill.2d 223, 230 N.E.2d 831 (1967); Grooms v. Williams, 227 Md. 165, 175 A.2d 575 (1961).

24. Hyatt v. Maryland Federal Savings & Loan Association, 42 Md.App. 623, 402 A.2d 118 (1979); Rivers v. Rice, 233 Ga. 819, 213 S.E.2d 678 (1975); Ideal Realty Co., v. Reese, 122 Ga.App. 707, 178 S.E.2d 564 (1970); White & Bollard, Inc. v. Goodenow, 58 Wn.2d 180, 361 P.2d 571 (1961).

25. In Roberts v. Harkins, 292 So.2d 603 (Fla.App.1974), certiorari denied 302 So.2d 417 (Fla.1974), a later specific subordination was held to supersede an earlier promise to subordinate which was much more protective of the subordinating mortgagee's interests.

26. 248 Cal.App.2d 655, 56 Cal.Rptr. 844 (1967). See discussion in The California Supreme Court 1966–1967: X. Secured Transactions A. Subordination Agreements, 1967, 55 Cal.L.Rev. 1184–1187.

27. But see Fandel, Inc. v. First of Denver Mortgage Investors, 522 S.W.2d 721 (Tex.Civ.App.1975).

28. Miller v. Citizens Savings and Loan Association, 248 Cal.App.2d 655, 663, 56 Cal.Rptr. 844, 851 (1967). See also B.J.I. Corp. v. Larry W. Corp., 183 N.J.Super. 310, 443 A.2d 1096 (1982), taking a similar approach; Ban-Co. Investment Co. v. Loveless, 22 Wn.App. 122, 587 P.2d 567 (1978);

was granted reestablishment of the superiority of his lien over that part of the construction loan not used for authorized purposes.[29]

Even when a second agreement has not cured indefiniteness, courts have held that the seller was estopped from asserting that the subordination agreement was invalid. In First Connecticut Small Business Investment Co. v. Arba[30] the seller contended that a subordination agreement violated the Statute of Frauds because it contained neither the interest rate nor the maturity date of the construction loan. Although Connecticut courts had earlier accepted the Statute of Frauds as a defense against the enforcement of a similar subordination agreement,[31] in *Arba* the court held that the seller was estopped because the agreement had been executed and a lender had relied to his detriment on the subordination.[32] Similarly, in Republic National Life Insurance Co. v. Lorraine Realty Corp.,[33] the Minnesota Supreme Court upheld the validity of a rather vague subordination agreement because all of the parties had operated under it without questioning it for fourteen years.

Drafting Subordination Agreements in Sales to Developers

The developer will want a self-executing subordination agreement that contains enough terms to be enforceable. To be safe the developer should see that the agreement includes (1) the maximum loan amount both as an absolute and as a percentage of the cost of construction, (2) the maximum interest rate, (3) the payment provisions and the minimum and maximum terms of years over which the construction loan is to be repaid, and (4) a clause stating the purposes for which the loan will be used. The terms should not be so restrictive that the developer cannot obtain financing meeting the conditions described.

The seller will want all of the terms mentioned above, and he may also bargain for other safeguards that will protect him from unreasonable risk. He should consider prohibiting refinancing, future advances,

---

Finest Investments v. Security Trust Co., 96 A.D.2d 227, 468 N.Y.S.2d 256 (1983), affirmed 61 N.Y.2d 897, 474 N.Y.S.2d 481, 462 N.E.2d 1199 (1984).

See Schneider v. Ampliflo Corp., 148 Cal. App.3d 637, 196 Cal.Rptr. 172 (1983), upholding a subordination which very clearly provided that the proceeds of the loan gaining priority need not be used for improvements on the subject property.

But see Back v. Union Life Insurance Co., 5 Ark.App. 176, 634 S.W.2d 150 (1982) (if subordinating vendor wishes proceeds of senior loan to go to improvements on land, he must so provide in the agreement.); Hyatt v. Maryland Federal Savings & Loan Association, 42 Md.App. 623, 402 A.2d 118 (1979); Grenada Ready-Mix Concrete, Inc. v. Watkins, 453 F.Supp. 1298 (N.D.Miss. 1978).

29. For a more thorough discussion of diversion of funds see § 12.10, infra. See also Connecticut Gen. Life Ins. Co. v. Dredge, 746 F.2d 1420 (10th Cir.1984), reversing the priorities set up in a subordination agreement because it was procured by an agent who had a conflict of interest and who withheld pertinent information from the subordinating vendors.

30. 170 Conn. 168, 365 A.2d 100 (1976).

31. Troj v. Chesebro, supra note 2.

32. See also American Century Mortgage Investors v. Unionamerican Mortgage and Equity Trust, 355 A.2d 563 (D.C.App. 1976).

33. 279 N.W.2d 349 (Minn.1979).

dragnet clauses and assignments of the senior loan. He will certainly wish to require that all proceeds be used for permanent improvements on the land.[34] He may want to require that all documents, plans and specifications be submitted for his approval, and that the lender make all disbursements through a voucher or progress payment system that assures that the funds pay only for materials and labor that improve the land. The seller may want to reserve the right to inspect the premises or the records of the other parties at any time. He may also want to require the construction lender to give him some reasonable notice—say, 30 days—before the lender files a notice of default, thus giving the seller an opportunity to cure the default. The seller should make sure that the subordination agreement is recorded in full, and he should try to get the construction lender to sign it. In general, he should investigate the project thoroughly and bargain for any safeguards that will insure the project's successful completion.

Subordination of Vendees' Rights

A contract purchaser of real estate may make a claim against the land in the event the seller breaches the contract. This claim may be either for specific performance, or for foreclosure of his equitable "vendee's lien" as an aid to restitution of his down payment or earnest money.[35] If improvements are to be constructed on the land after the contract of sale is entered into, the seller/developer may place a construction loan mortgage on the land to finance this development activity. In the event of a subsequent default by the developer on both the sale contract and the construction loan, the question arises whether the lender's or vendee's rights have priority.

The question may be approached by straight-forward application of the recording acts. Typically the sales contract is unrecorded, while the subsequent construction mortgage is placed of record. Thus, the mortgagee is in a position to claim priority over the vendee if it has the characteristics of a bona fide purchaser for value.[36] However, in most cases the lender will be fully informed of any preexisting sales contract, and hence will have no priority claim based on the recording act.[37]

34. A lawyer was successfully sued by the seller he had represented for failing to draft a subordination agreement that required that all loan proceeds be used for permanent improvements on the property. Starr v. Mooslin, 14 Cal.App.3d 988, 92 Cal. Rptr. 583 (1971).

If funds are diverted and the condition is thereby breached, the subordinating party will be restored to priority to that extent. See National Mortgage Co. v. American Title Insurance Co., 299 N.C. 369, 261 S.E. 2d 844 (1980), refusing to hold the construction lender's title insurer liable for such loss of priority.

35. See R. Cunningham, W. Stoebuck & D. Whitman, Property (1984), at § 10.5 (specific performance), § 10.8 (vendee's lien).

36. Id.; Garcia v. Atmajian, 113 Cal. App.3d 516, 169 Cal.Rptr. 845 (1980) (vendee's lien vs. optional advance under prior mortgage); Hillblom v. Ivancsits, 76 Ill. App.3d 306, 395 N.E.2d 119 (1979) (vendee's lien); Cohen v. Thomas & Son Transfer Line, Inc., 196 Colo. 386, 586 P.2d 39 (1978) (specific performance).

37. See State Savings & Loan Association v. Kauaian Development Co., 50 Hawaii 540, 445 P.2d 109 (1968). In a later

Construction lenders may attempt to solve this problem by insisting that developers with whom they do business employ subordination clauses in their sale contracts. One form of clause provides that:

> The Purchaser agrees that all terms and provisions of this contract are and shall be subject and subordinate to the lien of any building loan mortgage heretofore or hereafter made and any advances heretofore or hereafter made * * *." [38]

Such a clause is at least potentially enforceable.[39] However, the sort of broad language quoted, which contains no limitations on the amount, interest rate, or use of funds from the loan to which the contract is subordinated, may be subject to the same sort of objections on the basis of fairness and specificity discussed above in connection with subordinations by land vendors.[40]

Subordination Between Mortgages and Leases

The priority relationship that exists between a lease and a mortgage usually depends upon the order in which they are recorded,[41] unless their priorities have been altered by a subordination agreement.[42] In large developments such as shopping centers that involve mortgages and leases, subordination agreements are frequently negotiated carefully because the priorities of the mortgages and leases are very important to the parties involved. For instance, an institutional lender may insist on having a first lien on the property securing his mortgage, and while a lease is an encumbrance rather than a lien, the lender may still consider it unacceptable for the mortgage to be junior to a lease. On the other hand, because foreclosure of a senior mortgage

decision in the same case, 62 Hawaii 188, 613 P.2d 1315 (1980), the court held the construction lender to be subordinate to the rights of vendees who entered into contracts of purchase *after* the construction mortgage was recorded. It construed language in the mortgage, reciting that it was "subject to" the condominium declaration, as making the mortgage subordinate to the rights of all condominium unit purchasers.

38. Olympic Towers Purchase Agreement, reprinted in 1A P. Rohan & M. Reskin, Condominium Law & Practice ¶ 118.17 (Appendix 1976).

39. State Savings & Loan Association v. Kauaian Development Co., 50 Hawaii 540, 445 P.2d 109 (1968), expressly endorses such use of subordination clauses. See also Dunson v. Stockton, Whatley, Davin & Co., 346 So.2d 603 (Fla.App.1977), holding that an owner who deeds land to a developer to build him a house, with the understanding that the developer will obtain a construction loan mortgage, impliedly subordinates to the construction lender his contract right to repurchase the property;

Life Savings & Loan Association v. Bryant, 125 Ill.App.3d 1012, 81 Ill.Dec. 577, 467 N.E.2d 277 (1984) (subordination clause in purchase contract was ineffective, since its conditions were never fulfilled.)

40. See B.J.I. Corp. v. Larry W. Corp., 183 N.J.Super. 310, 443 A.2d 1096 (1982) holding that, under such a broad clause, a court might deny priority as to advances which were not actually used to benefit the property, unless the purchaser understood and bargained for the clause.

41. Notice also plays a role in determining priorities, of course. A recorded mortgage may not have priority over an unrecorded prior lease if the mortgagee has notice of the lease. Republic National Life Insurance Co. v. Marquette Bank and Trust Co., 251 N.W.2d 120 (Minn.1977).

42. Wright v. Home Beneficial Life Insurance Co., 155 Ga.App. 241, 270 S.E.2d 400 (1980); Prudential Insurance Co. v. Bull Market, Inc., 66 Ohio Misc. 9, 420 N.E.2d 140 (1979).

will usually destroy all leases subordinate to it,[43] a major tenant in a shopping center may have a great deal to lose if its lease is subordinate to a mortgage.

In some states the mortgagee has the option of keeping junior leases in force by omitting joinder of the lessees in the foreclosure proceeding.[44] In these states it is never a disadvantage to a mortgagee to be senior to important leases.[45] But in other states where foreclosure permits omitted junior lessees to terminate, it may be a serious detriment to a mortgagee to have his mortgage senior to important leases. The leases of major tenants often form a very important part of the security value of a shopping center. A mortgagee may desire to have his mortgage subordinate to important leases so that he can foreclose without losing these leases. It is possible for a mortgagee to agree with a tenant to subordinate his mortgage to a lease after the mortgagor is in default,[46] but the mortgagee cannot accomplish this result unilaterally.

Before a mortgagee chooses to have his mortgage subordinate to a lease on the mortgaged premises, he should examine the lease carefully to be sure that it does not contain onerous duties for the landlord to perform.[47] He should also be sure that the lease does not give the lessee an option to buy that will cut off his mortgage if the option is exercised.

If the lender does assume priority, whether by order of recording or by agreement, he can insure that he will have the option of keeping the leases in force by having the mortgagor procure attornment agreements from the lessees. In an attornment agreement the lessee agrees to accept the purchaser at a foreclosure sale as his landlord and to be bound to him by the lease. Yet attornment agreements usually do not bind the mortgagee or the sale purchaser to refrain from cancelling junior leases.

It is a simple matter for the lessor to put a subordination clause and an attornment clause in the form leases signed by minor tenants

43. See id; T.D. Bickham Corp. v. Hebert, 432 So.2d 228 (La.1983).

44. See § 7.12, supra; Hyde, The Real Estate Lease as a Credit Instrument, 20 Bus.Law. 359, 389 (1965).

45. Anderson, The Mortgagee Looks at the Commercial Lease, 10 U. of Fla.L.Rev. 484, 495 (1957).

46. Landau v. Western Pennsylvania National Bank, 445 Pa. 217, 282 A.2d 335 (1971).

47. If the mortgagee feels that some of the landlord's covenants in the lease would be objectionable, he may be able to reach an agreement with the tenant that those clauses will not be enforceable against the mortgagee if he takes possession, or against a buyer at the mortgage foreclosure sale. The tenant, in turn, may bargain with the mortgagee for notice of the landlord's default and some reasonable time period in which the tenant may cure it, thus minimizing the risk of default to the tenant. This right to cure, however, is attractive to the tenant only if the debt service on the mortgage plus the other operating and carrying costs of the building do not exceed the rent which the tenant is obligated to pay under the lease. Moreover, the right to cure is binding against the landlord only if he expressly agrees to it in the lease or in a later agreement. Anderson, supra note 45, at 495.

who have little bargaining power. But it is more difficult to negotiate an attornment clause or subordination clause in a lease with a major tenant. Nonetheless it is often less expensive to negotiate the clauses into the original lease than to get a lease amendment from a powerful tenant.[48] In order for the mortgagor to get a subordination agreement from a major tenant he may have to get the mortgagee to agree to a nondisturbance clause which guarantees that as long as the lessee conforms to the lease he will be allowed to remain in possession of the property even if a foreclosure occurs. If the lessee is given a nondisturbance clause, the mortgagee should make sure that the lessee also has an obligation to remain bound by the lease after a foreclosure.[49]

As was mentioned earlier, a major tenant may lose a great deal if his lease is destroyed by a foreclosure, especially if he has made expensive improvements on the property. If the tenant is powerful enough, he may be able to demand that his lease be prior to all mortgages on the property. But if it is not practical for the tenant to negotiate priority he can protect himself to a considerable extent by agreeing to subordinate his lease only to mortgages that meet certain standards. In this way he can prevent his lease from becoming subordinate to a mortgage so onerous that foreclosure is assured. If the lessee is a tenant of the entire premises, he may seek to limit prior mortgages to those which have annual requirements including taxes and operating costs that do not exceed gross rent.[50] If he has a clause in his lease which allows him to cure defaults, he will then be able to prevent a foreclosure.

Another way that the lessee can protect himself, as suggested above, is by obtaining a nondisturbance clause [51] protecting him from eviction after a foreclosure as long as he honors the lease. Depending upon the wording of the agreement, he may have the option to remain under the lease or to treat it as destroyed. If the lessee has this option, he may prefer this position to having his lease superior to the mortgage. However, a mortgage which is technically senior will still have priority over conflicting provisions in the lease. For example, the lease may require the landlord to use fire insurance proceeds for rebuilding, while under the provisions of the mortgage the proceeds could be used to pay off part of that mortgage. The lessee should make sure that the

---

48. See Committee on Leases, Drafting Shopping Center Leases, 2 Real Property, Probate and Trust Journal 222, 247 (No. 2 Summer 1967).

49. Hyde, The Real Estate Lease as a Credit Instrument, 20 Bus.Law. 359, 392 (1965).

50. M. Friedman, Preparation of Leases, 61 (1962).

51. See KVR Realties, Inc. v. Treasure Star, Inc., 58 N.Y.2d 793, 58 N.Y.2d 793,

445 N.E.2d 641 (1983). A lease covenant of quiet enjoyment will not keep the foreclosure of a superior mortgage from cutting off the lessee's right of possession. 220 West 42 Associates v. Ronbet Newmark Co., 53 A.D.2d 829, 385 N.Y.S.2d 304 (1976), modified 40 N.Y.2d 1000, 391 N.Y.S.2d 107, 359 N.E.2d 701 (1976). Only a clause to which the mortgagee is a party will guarantee nondisturbance.

agreements in the lease with regard to fire insurance, condemnation awards and removal of fixtures will be honored by the mortgagee.[52]

Often subordination clauses in form leases state only that the lease will be subordinate to all present and future mortgages on the property. Earlier, this section pointed out that, under many decisions, a subordination agreement in a purchase money mortgage must define the terms of future construction loans with considerable specificity in order to be enforceable. Reasoning by analogy from the purchase money situation, a court might require that a subordination agreement in a lease contain language limiting future mortgages to terms which the lessor-mortgagor is reasonably likely to be able to perform. If a lease contains a clause subordinating the lease to a future mortgage which is not adequately described or limited, the tenant may be able successfully to attack the subordination clause on the grounds that it is (1) too indefinite to enforce, (2) unjust and unreasonable, or (3) invalid under the Statute of Frauds.[53]

There are two points in time at which a tenant may be able to attack a subordination clause in his lease: while the lease is still executory, and after a foreclosure. If the tenant successfully attacks the subordination clause while the lease is still executory, the court might declare the lease void. After a foreclosure, the only reason a tenant will wish to attack the clause will be to restore the priority of his lease so that it will not be cut off by the foreclosure. If the subordination clause is so indefinite that it has exposed the tenant to unreasonable risk, a court may be willing to reinstate the priority of the tenant's lease.[54] The tenant may be more likely to succeed if he was required to sign a form lease. If he had the opportunity to bargain for the terms of his lease with the help of counsel, the court may not be as sympathetic to his cause. The value of his leasehold may also make a difference in whether the court considers the subordination clause a material term.[55]

 WESTLAW REFERENCES
subordination /s contract agreement loan mortgage

§ 12.10 Improper Disbursement of Loan Proceeds

Once a construction loan is obtained, the distribution of loan funds becomes a critical concern of all parties interested in the project, since

52. M. Friedman, supra note 50 at 64; Committee on Leases, supra note 48 at 247.

53. See text at notes 9 to 33, supra.

54. Such an argument was rejected, despite an extremely vague lease clause, in T.D. Bickham Corp. v. Hebert, 432 So.2d 228 (La.1983).

55. In valuing a leasehold on commercial property many factors must be considered, including the bonus value of the lease (the present value of the difference between the fair market value of the lease and the rent), the value of the location to the tenant's business, and the value of the improvements which the tenant has made on the property.

improper disbursement can result in non-payment of subcontractors and material suppliers and the collapse of the entire project. The potential for severe economic loss emphasizes the importance of care on the part of the construction lender.

Suppose, for example, that the construction lender fails to supervise the course of construction and advances more money than the construction progress warrants. Suppose also that the owner or general contractor who receives the advances diverts them to other projects or to personal use. If the amount of the construction loan accurately reflected the cost of construction, diversion of funds will cause the project to go unfinished and the subcontractors to go unpaid. When the owner-borrower defaults on the loan, the lender may foreclose. In the usual case, the lender's lien will be superior to the mechanics' liens filed by unpaid subcontractors and the lender will take the proceeds of the sale.[1] The lender will also have priority over any land vendor or ground lessor who subordinated his interest to enable the developer to secure a construction loan.[2] Other parties may be injured as well. The surety on the performance bond (if any) will be liable for the losses resulting from the non-completion.[3] Purchasers of interests in the project may be unable to realize their expectations. Finally, any guarantors on the construction loan may be liable to the lender for the default.

Given the catastrophic consequences that can result from improper disbursement of the funds by construction lenders, the question of lender liability naturally arises. In a preceding section of this chapter it was observed that lenders can suffer a partial loss of priority in many jurisdictions if their loan disbursements are found to be "optional" instead of "obligatory."[4] This theory is helpful in some cases, but its application depends on such subtle vagaries of interpretation of the construction loan agreement and the conduct of the parties that it is at best an unreliable basis for reversal of priorities.[5] This section will focus on other theories used by courts to grant relief to parties injured by improper loan distributions.[6] It should be observed, however, that cases denying relief to injured parties are numerous; unless express covenants of the loan agreement or conditions of a subordination agreement have been breached by the lender, most jurisdictions are unwilling to impose liability for wrongful distribution of loan proceeds in the absence of fraud or collusion.[7]

§ 12.10

1. See § 12.7, supra.

2. See § 12.9, supra.

3. See § 12.2, supra.

4. § 12.7, supra.

5. See Korngold, infra note 7, at 329–39: "Too crude a vehicle for the task."

6. See Smith & Cobbe, Questions of Priority Between Mechanics' Lienors and Construction Loan Mortgagees, 38 Ohio St.L.J. 3, 13–18 (1977).

7. See e.g., Carlsberg Resources Corp. v. Cambria Savings & Loan Association, 413 F.Supp. 880 (W.D.Pa.1976), affirmed 554 F.2d 1254 (3d Cir.1977); Weiss v. Brentwood Savings & Loan Association, 4 Cal. App.3d 738, 84 Cal.Rptr. 736 (1970); Gill v. Mission Savings & Loan Association, 236 Cal.App.2d 753, 46 Cal.Rptr. 456 (1965); Drobnick v. Western Federal Savings &

Express Agreement

The most widely accepted basis for lender liability for improper disbursements is the lender's breach of an express agreement to disburse the loan in a particular manner. Such agreements are not easy to find, since most construction loan documents are drafted by the lender and carefully avoid imposing specific duties upon it. But where an agreement can be made out, it is a powerful weapon.

The concept is illustrated by Modesto Lumber Co. v. Wylde.[8] In extending a building loan to the owners of residential property, the lender guaranteed that no claim would become a lien on the property and that the construction contractor would not be paid until all claims for labor and materials were satisfied. In fact, the lender disbursed funds directly to the contractor, instructing him to apply the funds to the accounts of materialmen. The contractor did not do so and the materialmen were not paid. In the ensuing litigation, a trial court awarded damages to the materialmen and allowed them to have two liens against the owner's property. The landowners were granted a personal judgment against the lender. On appeal, the court discharged one lien and reduced the amount of the other, but upheld the lender's liability to the owner to the extent of the materialman's lien. The court reasoned that "the loan association accepted a trusteeship to disburse these funds first to the laborers and materialmen and the balance to the contractor. It fairly appears that the loan association paid sums direct to the contractor."[9]

The utility of this approach is quite limited. Even if the construction loan agreement contains provisions which obligate the lender to employ a specific type of disbursement or to use a certain level of care, the borrower who signs that agreement may not be the party principal-

---

Loan Association, 479 P.2d 393 (Colo.App. 1970); First Connecticut Small Business Investment Co. v. Arba, Inc., 170 Conn. 168, 365 A.2d 100 (1976); Roberts v. Harkins, 292 So.2d 603 (Fla.App.1974), certiorari denied 302 So.2d 417 (1974); Hyatt v. Maryland Federal Savings & Loan Association, 42 Md.App. 623, 402 A.2d 118 (1979); Kennedy v. Betts, 33 Md.App. 258, 364 A.2d 74 (1976); Conshohocken Federal Savings & Loan Association v. Period & Country Homes, Inc., 287 Pa.Super. 520, 430 A.2d 1173 (1981); Forest Inc. v. Guaranty Mortgage Co., Inc., 534 S.W.2d 853 (Tenn. App.1975); Fandel, Inc. v. First of Denver Mortgage Investors, 522 S.W.2d 721 (Tex. Civ.App.1975) (per curiam); Tuscarora, Inc. v. BVA Credit Corp., 218 Va. 849, 241 S.E.2d 778 (1978); National Bank of Washington v. Equity Investors, 81 Wn.2d 886, 506 P.2d 20 (1973), appeal after remand 83 Wn.2d 435, 518 P.2d 1072 (1974); 42 Yale L.J. 980 (1933); Grenada Ready-Mix Concrete, Inc. v. Watkins, 453 F.Supp. 1298 (N.D.Miss.1978). See generally Korngold, Construction Loan Advances and the Subordinated Purchase Money Mortgagee: An Appraisal, A Suggested Approach, and the ULTA Perspective, 50 Ford.L.Rev. 313, 319–328 (1981).

8. 217 Cal. 421, 19 P.2d 238 (1933). See also Prudential Insurance Co. v. Executive Estates, Inc., 174 Ind.App. 674, 369 N.E.2d 1117 (1977) (lender's employee orally promised borrower "there would be no liens or encumbrances on that real estate because Prudential would take care of it."); Falls Lumber Co. v. Heman, 114 Ohio App. 262, 181 N.E.2d 713 (1961); Dunson v. Stockton, Whatley, Davin & Co., 346 So.2d 603 (Fla. App.1977). But see Laight v. Idaho First Nat'l Bank, ___ Ind.App. ___, 697 P.2d 1225 (1985), refusing to find lender liability where the loan agreement explicitly relieved the lender from any responsibility for payment to subcontractors.

9. Id. at 428, 19 P.2d at 240.

ly harmed by improper disbursal. Indeed, in the typical case, it is subordinating vendors [10] and subcontractors who have the most to lose when improper disbursements are made. Yet since they are not parties to the construction loan agreement, they find it difficult to use it as a basis for recovery.[11] In such cases an argument based on the third party beneficiary concept may be availing. Basically, the theory permits a third person to enforce a promise made for his benefit even though he is a stranger to the contract.[12]

The plaintiff most likely to benefit from an attempted use of the third party beneficiary theory is a subordinated land vendor. While several courts have doubted whether parties to a construction loan agreement *intend* to benefit a subordinating vendor,[13] it is clear that the vendor is, in practical terms, a beneficiary of such agreement. Given the circumstances and equities involved in a typical subordination situation, it is likely that some courts would be responsive to the theory's use. Certainly those courts which have accepted the "common enterprise" view of the subordination agreement could approve of this theoretical approach.

It should be observed that no court has yet granted recovery on a third party beneficiary theory to a party injured by lender negligence. Several have rejected the theory's application when asserted by an injured contractor or materialman.[14] One typical opinion observed that successful assertion of such a third party claim required a demonstration that the "contracting parties intended to create a direct, not incidental or consequential benefit to the third party."[15] The court did not find such a demonstration. While this obstacle may be difficult to overcome in many jurisdictions, it would not appear to be impossible, particularly for a subordinating vendor. At least one case has suggested the legitimacy of such a cause of action.[16]

We suggest that the courts have been excessively parsimonious in applying the third party beneficiary concept. It is clear that subordinated vendors and mechanics' lien claimants rely heavily on the

---

10. Cambridge Acceptance Corp. v. Hockstein, 102 N.J.Super. 435, 439, 246 A.2d 138, 140 (1968) (per curiam).

11. See, e.g., United States v. Chester Heights Associates, 406 F.Supp. 600 (D.S.C.1976); Ross v. Continental Mortgage Investors, 404 F.Supp. 922 (E.D.La.1975); Lampert Yards, Inc. v. Thompson-Wetterling Construction & Realty, Inc., 302 Minn. 83, 223 N.W.2d 418 (1974); Forest, Inc. v. Guaranty Mortgage Co., Inc., 534 S.W.2d 853 (Tenn.App.1975).

12. See Restatement (Second) of Contracts § 302 (1981), defining a beneficiary as "intended" and therefore able to enforce the contract " * * * if recognition of the right to performance in the beneficiary is appropriate to effectuate the intention of the parties and * * * the circumstances

indicate that the promisee intends to give the beneficiary the benefit of the promised performance."

13. See Chicago Title & Trust Co. v. First Arlington National Bank, 118 Ill. App.3d 401, 73 Ill.Dec. 626, 454 N.E.2d 723 (1983); Rockhill v. United States, 288 Md. 237, 418 A.2d 197 (1980); United States v. Chester Heights Associates, 406 F.Supp. 600 (D.S.C.1976).

14. See cases cited note 13, supra.

15. See United States v. Chester Heights Associates, supra note 13, at 606–07.

16. See Middlebrook-Anderson Co. v. Southwest Savings & Loan Association, 18 Cal.App.3d 1023, 1038, 96 Cal.Rptr. 338, 347 (1971).

construction lender's care and competence, and the lender and borrower are usually fully aware of their reliance. It is hard to see why the need exists for any further evidence that the borrower and lender intend these parties to be benefitted by the lender's agreement to disburse funds in a particular manner or with particular care.

Conditional Subordination

A second theoretical approach to the problem of improper disbursements stresses the notion of conditional subordination. Under this theory, the focus is on the agreement by which a land vendor subordinates his interest to that of a subsequent lender. If the agreement is conditioned on application of loan proceeds to construction costs, some courts will protect the lender's priority only to the extent disbursements go to construction. When the condition is spelled out in sufficiently explicit terms in the subordination agreement, this theory is very widely accepted,[17] although it is obviously difficult to apply it in favor of those who were not parties to the subordination agreement, such as mechanics lien claimants.[18]

An example of conditional subordination can be seen in the 1962 decision in Collins v. Home Savings & Loan Association.[19] There a land vendor agreed to subordinate his interest to a "construction loan for the purpose of constructing on each lot a dwelling house with the usual appurtenances."[20] This provision was contained in the seller's deed of trust, which was recorded before the construction loan was obtained. At the request of the title company the vendor signed a subsequent subordination provision that identified more accurately the trust deeds to which his interest was subordinated. However, the second provision did not contain the limiting language of the provision in the vendor's trust deed. When the project failed, the construction lender foreclosed and sold the property to third parties. The subordinating vendor then sued the lender, alleging that three of the disbursements were for nonconstruction purposes and therefore not within the terms of the subordination agreement. The lender's defense was that there was no requirement in the later subordination agreement that disbursements go to any particular purpose. Despite the failure of the second subordination provision to repeat the conditions of the first, judgment was for the vendor. The court observed that the lender had actual as well as constructive knowledge of the language in the earlier subordination clause. It also suggested that the two subordination provisions were "executed contemporaneously" and should be read together. Finally,

---

17. Some courts refuse to allow the vendor to recover under this theory when the subordination conditions appear in the vendor's trust deed, but not in the lender's trust deed. See e.g., Gill v. Mission Savings & Loan Association, 236 Cal.App.2d 753, 46 Cal.Rptr. 456 (1965); Fandel, Inc. v. First of Denver Mortgage Investors, 522 S.W.2d 721 (Tex.Civ.App.1975) (per curiam).

18. See discussion at notes 12–16 supra.

19. 205 Cal.App.2d 86, 22 Cal.Rptr. 817 (1962).

20. Id. at 89, 22 Cal.Rptr. at 819.

the court noted that it was possible to infer "that the only reason for respondents' subordination of their lien was the expectation that if payments were advanced by the appellant solely for construction purposes, the liens superior to their own would increase in value only as the property under development enjoyed a corresponding increase in value because of the accompanying progress in the work of construction." [21] The court concluded that subordination conditions were unsatisfied and that the vendor's lien retained its priority. Because the property had been sold to third parties, damages were allowed against the lender for the principal amount of the vendor's deed of trust plus interest. It is noteworthy that this result was not one of partial priority; rather, the vendor's entire lien was held superior to that of the lender for purposes of awarding damages.[22]

A later California case, Miller v. Citizens Savings & Loan Association,[23] went further in liberalizing the construction of subordination agreements; it held that even without an explicit reference in the agreement to the construction use of the funds, it "should be construed, unless it expressly provides otherwise, as permitting the loan proceeds to be used only for such purposes." [24]

Additional complexities arise when the subordination agreement is implicit—as when the vendor purposefully postpones the recordation of his interest until the lender's lien is recorded. In such a circumstance, any conditions to the "agreement" are implicit as well. What should be the consequences of the lender's disbursement of loan proceeds to nonconstruction purposes? This was the issue facing the court in Middlebrook-Anderson Co. v. Southwest Savings & Loan Association.[25] There the plaintiff agreed to sell 28 lots to developers, with part of the purchase price to be secured by a deed of trust. It was understood that the deed of trust was to be second to a construction loan the developers would obtain. In order to have first priority, the lender recorded its trust deeds first. When the developer abandoned the project, the lender foreclosed, purchasing the property itself.[26] The vendor was "wiped out" by the foreclosure, and brought suit, complaining that the lender had permitted the developers to use $300,000 of the loan disbursements for non-construction purposes. In consequence, the vendor argued, it was entitled to a restoration of priority and damages. The

21. Id. at 99, 22 Cal.Rptr. at 825.

22. The court did not reveal the reason for this particular result, but it did point out that the amount of the improper disbursements was greater than the value of the vendor's deed of trust. As a general proposition, absolute priority or damages would appear to be in order when partial priority results in no benefit to the vendor, i.e., when the foreclosure sale would provide no excess over that portion of the lender's lien given priority under the terms of the conditional subordination.

23. 248 Cal.App.2d 655, 56 Cal.Rptr. 844 (1967).

24. Id. at 663–664, 56 Cal.Rptr. at 851.

25. 18 Cal.App.3d 1023, 96 Cal.Rptr. 338 (1971). For discussions of this case see Lambe, Enforceability of Subordination Agreements, 19 Real Prop.Prob. & Tr.J. 631, 639–47 (1984); Note, Purchase Money Subordination Agreements in California: An Analysis of Conditional Subordination, 45 So.Cal.L.Rev. 1109 (1972).

26. Ultimately, the property was sold to third parties.

cause of action depended, of course, on a conclusion that the agreement to take a second trust deed was the equivalent of a subordination agreement—otherwise there was no priority to be restored. The court ruled "that the duties owed by a lender to a seller under a formal subordination agreement do not differ from the duties owed by a lender to a seller when the lender obtains priority over the seller under an agreement by the seller to record after the lender." [27] The lender's main defenses were that it had no duty to supervise the loan distributions and that there was no privity of contract between it and the vendor. These defenses, held the court, were insufficient to prevent a trial on the merits.

The court was persuaded that there were "strong public policy reasons to protect the seller in subordination situations." [28] To be enforceable, a subordination clause "must contain terms that will define and minimize the risk that the subordinating liens will impair or destroy the seller's security." [29] Given the lender's superior ability to prevent loan misappropriations and its greater ability to absorb loss, the court ruled that an implied agreement to disburse loan proceeds for construction purposes "should be spelled out from the lender's alleged actual knowledge of the provisions of the seller's lien in general, and of the subordination therein in particular." [30] Furthermore the court said:

> "In the superior position of a financial institution constantly engaged in professional construction lending, Southwestern had no reason to believe their trust deed conferred any lien to which the fee was subordinate other than to the extent of money spent for construction purposes. Its loan under the circumstances cannot be viewed other than as subject to the fair application of the construction funds. Accordingly, we conclude that such lien as the trust deed might have conferred on the lender should not be advanced or preferred over the seller." [31]

27. 18 Cal.App.3d at 1029, 96 Cal.Rptr. at 341. For a contrary view, see Spaziani v. Millar, 215 Cal.App.2d 667, 30 Cal.Rptr. 658 (1963); Miller, Regalia & Starr, Subordination Agreements in California, 13 U.C. L.A.L.Rev. 1298 (1966).

28. 18 Cal.App.3d at 1036, 96 Cal.Rptr. at 346. In United States Cold Storage of California v. Great Western Sav. & Loan Ass'n, 165 Cal.App.3d 1214, 212 Cal.Rptr. 232 (1985), the court expressly limited *Middlebrook's* implied subordination theory to construction loans. In a subsequent case the public policy requiring protection of subordinating sellers persuaded a California Court to rule that lender and borrower may not make modifications in their loan agreement without the knowledge and consent of the subordinating seller if the modi-

fications materially affect his rights. Gluskin v. Atlantic Savings & Loan Association, 32 Cal.App.3d 307, 108 Cal. Rptr. 318 (1973).

29. 18 Cal.App.3d at 1036, 96 Cal.Rptr. at 346; Handy v. Gordon, 65 Cal.2d 578, 55 Cal.Rptr. 769, 422 P.2d 329 (1967); see § 12.9, supra.

30. Id. at 1038, 96 Cal.Rptr. at 347.

31. Id. A subsequent decision carved out an exception to the *Middlebrook-Anderson* rule when the subordinating vendor is also a part owner of the purchaser and participates in the construction project. Woodworth v. Redwood Empire Savings & Loan Association, 22 Cal.App.3d 347, 99 Cal.Rptr. 373 (1971).

The approach taken by the court in *Middlebrook-Anderson* is far more activist than many courts can swallow. It has been followed by some [32] and explicitly rejected by others.[33]

Breach of Duty of Care

The theories of recovery considered thus far have focused on lender liability arising out of the breach of express agreements or reversal of priority for failure to meet conditions in subordination agreements. These theories are not helpful, of course, when there has been no express agreement or facts giving rise to conditional subordination. A third approach has been taken by some courts: lenders have occasionally been found liable for improper disbursals because they have breached a duty of care, evidently arising in tort. This is a fairly radical step, and some courts have been unwilling to take it.[34]

One variation on the breach of duty theme may be seen in Fikes v. First Federal Savings & Loan Association.[35] The case involved a foreclosure action by the lender of a construction loan. Fikes, who owned an unrecorded equitable interest [36] in the project, challenged the lender's priority on the ground that the developer diverted loan disbursements to other projects during the course of construction, and did so with the lender's knowledge. The court recognized the validity of the equitable interest asserted, and found that the lender had knowledge of Fikes' existence before construction funds were loaned. The central issue facing the court was whether a lender has a duty to protect such third party interests of which it has knowledge.[37] The lender argued that no such duty existed because there was no privity of

---

32. See B.J.I. Corp. v. Larry W. Corp., 183 N.J.Super. 310, 443 A.2d 1096 (1982) (implying conditions in subordination clause in purchase contract); Peoples Bank v. L & T Developers, Inc., 434 So.2d 699 (Miss.1983), judgment corrected 437 So.2d 7 (1983) (approving *Middlebrook* but adopting a direct "duty" approach).

33. See Tuscarora, Inc. v. B.V.A. Credit Corp., 218 Va. 849, 241 S.E.2d 778 (1978); Rockhill v. United States, 288 Md. 237, 418 A.2d 197 (1980); Conshohocken Federal Savings & Loan Association v. Period & Country Homes, Inc., 287 Pa.Super. 520, 430 A.2d 1173 (1981); Grenada Ready-Mix Concrete, Inc. v. Watkins, 453 F.Supp. 1298 (N.D.Miss.1978).

34. Courts frequently hold that a lender owes no duty of care in loan disbursements to parties lacking contractual privity or a fiduciary relationship with the lender. See, e.g., Rockhill v. United States, supra note 33; Shankle Equipment Co. v. Liberty National Bank, 569 P.2d 965 (Okl.1977); Armetta v. Clevetrust Realty Investors, 359 So.2d 540 (Fla.App.1978), certiorari de-nied 366 So.2d 879 (1978); Ross v. Continental Mortgage Investors, 404 F.Supp. 922 (E.D.La.1975); Lampert Yards, Inc. v. Thompson-Wetterling Construction & Realty Inc., 302 Minn. 83, 223 N.W.2d 418 (1974); Forest Inc. v. Guaranty Mortgage Co. Inc., 534 S.W.2d 853 (Tenn.App.1975). See also Grenada Ready-Mix Concrete, Inc. v. Watkins, 453 F.Supp. 1298 (N.D.Miss. 1978), rejecting a duty of care to a "subordinated" ground lessor.

35. 533 P.2d 251 (Alaska 1975). See also Big Land Investment Corp. v. Lomas & Nettleton Financial Corp., 657 P.2d 837, 839 n. 5 (Alaska 1983); Stenehjem v. Cho, 631 P.2d 482, 488 (Alaska 1981).

36. The equitable interest arose out of an earnest money agreement between Fikes and the property owner's agent. Fikes allowed the developer to have legal title in order to facilitate construction financing. The arrangement was entered into on the lender's advice. Id. at 256.

37. Id. at 260.

contract between it and Fikes. The court rejected his contention and held that a duty did exist. It founded the duty in equity.

The court observed that when the plaintiff allowed the developer to take legal title to the property, Fikes had the reasonable expectation that First Federal would perform its role as interim construction lender in a conventional manner. If First Federal had disbursed the construction loan proceeds according to normal secured-lending practices, the property which Fikes had contracted to buy would have been enhanced in value.[38] By failing to follow such ordinary disbursement procedures, First Federal breached its duty to Fikes.[39] In consequence of this breach, the court ruled that the lender's security interest encompassed only those funds spent for construction.

A similar result was reached in Cambridge Acceptance Corp. v. Hockstein.[40] In that case the subordinated ground lessor challenged a foreclosure action brought by the construction lender's assignee, alleging that the loan disbursements were expended for nonconstruction purposes. Unable to find an agreement between owner and lender that limited subordination to funds advanced for construction, the court said that there was at most an "intent and expectation" on the owner's part that the subordination would be to a construction loan. The court then noted the general view that "absent an express stipulation between the subordinator and the construction lender conditioning the scope of the subordination, diversion of construction money by the borrower from its contemplated use will not dislodge the advanced lienor from his bargained-for priority in the absence of collusion with the mortgagor in diverting the money from its purpose."[41] Despite the general rule, judgment was for the landowner. Equitable principles, said the court, required the construction lender "to make and administer the loan in the conventional manner of a construction lender rather than mask what is essentially a loan on the general credit and reliability of the borrower and the security of the land value as a construction loan, and act accordingly in disbursing the funds."[42] The lender failed to observe this standard. It was "totally oblivious of and seemingly disinterested in what the borrower actually did with the money."[43] Because the landowner was equitably entitled to rely on the expectation that the lender would comply with conventional practices, the lender's failure to do so estopped it from asserting the subordination of the owner's interest.

The Mississippi courts have imposed a direct duty of reasonably careful disbursement on construction lenders, in favor both of mechanics lien claimants[44] and subordinated land vendors.[45] In the latter

---

38. Id. at 261.

39. Id.

40. 102 N.J.Super. 435, 246 A.2d 138 (1968) (per curiam).

41. 102 Id. at 438, 246 A.2d at 140.

42. Id. at 440, 246 A.2d at 141.

43. Id. 246 A.2d at 141.

44. Cook v. Citizens Savings & Loan Association, 346 So.2d 370 (Miss.1977).

45. Peoples Bank v. L & T Devel., Inc., 434 So.2d 699 (Miss.1983), noted 53 Miss.L. Rev. 691 (1983), remanded for determina-

situation, the Mississippi Supreme Court described the rule recently in these terms:

> "Absent an express agreement to the contrary, a construction lender owes a duty to the landowner who subordinates his purchase money deed of trust. That duty is to exercise reasonable diligence to see that the funds loaned are in fact used in the construction project. If the construction lender fails to exercise reasonable diligence in this regard, its deed of trust will be prior in right to the landowner's purchase money deed of trust only to the extent that proceeds of the construction loan actually went into the construction project." [46]

Several other cases have adopted a breach of duty analysis.[47] One in particular deserves mention. In Commercial Standard Insurance Co. v. Bank of America [48] the court focused more on the policy considerations and the need to protect the plaintiff than on any strict search for duty. The issue was whether the lender could be liable to the surety on a performance bond for improperly disbursing loan proceeds to a construction contractor. The surety, which was forced to cover the losses on the project when the contractor defaulted, sought to be subrogated to the landowner's claims against the lender for negligent disbursement of loan proceeds. The court held that the surety could be subrogated to the owner's claims. It also found that inasmuch as the lender had agreed to disburse loan proceeds in accordance with the value of construction progress, the lender owed the owner a duty to exercise reasonable care. The lender contended, however, that even if it owed a duty to the owner, it owed none to the surety. The court's examination of this duty question reflected a negligence analysis founded in policy considerations. "Duty" observed the court "is not sacrosanct in itself, but only an expression of the sum total of those considerations of policy which lead the law to say that the particular plaintiff is entitled to protection." [49] The policy considerations considered were:

> "the foreseeability of harm to the plaintiff, the degree of certainty that the plaintiff suffered injury, the closeness of the

tion of property values, 437 So.2d 7 (Miss. 1983).

46. Id. at 713. Some earlier Mississippi case law appeared to impose an absolute duty to prevent diversion of loan proceeds; see Weiss, Dreyfous & Seiferth, Inc. v. Natchez Investment Co., 166 Miss. 253, 260, 140 So. 736, 738 (1932). But it is now clear that only reasonable care is required; see Guaranty Mortgage Co. v. Seitz, 367 So. 2d 438 (Miss.1979); Southern Life Insurance Co. v. Pollard Appliance Co., 247 Miss. 211, 150 So.2d 416 (1963).

47. See, e.g. Essex Savings Bank v. Leeker, 2 Conn.App. 98, 476 A.2d 1071 (1984); Prudential Insurance Co. v. Executive Estates, Inc., 174 Ind.App. 674, 369 N.E.2d 1117 (1977); Radunich v. Basso, 235 Cal.App.2d 826, 45 Cal.Rptr. 824 (1965); Westland Homes Corp. v. Hall, 193 Neb. 237, 226 N.W.2d 622 (1975); Western Mortgage Loan Co. v. Cottonwood Construction Co., 18 Utah 2d 409, 424 P.2d 437 (1967) (dictum).

48. 57 Cal.App.3d 241, 129 Cal.Rptr. 91 (1976).

49. Id. at 248, 129 Cal.Rptr. at 95 (quoting Dillon v. Legg, 68 Cal.2d 728, 734, 69 Cal.Rptr. 72, 76, 441 P.2d 912, 916 (1968)).

connection between the defendant's conduct and the injury suffered, the moral blame attached to the defendant's conduct, the policy of preventing future harm, the extent of the burden to the defendant and consequences to the community of imposing a duty to exercise care with resulting liability for breach, and the availability, cost, and prevalence of insurance for the risk involved." [50]

After analyzing these factors in the context of the facts alleged, the court imposed a duty on the lender, running to the surety, to exercise reasonable care in disbursing loan proceeds.

Several courts have used a principal-agent theory to find a duty of careful disbursement in the construction lender.[51] Since lenders generally insist on supervising the disbursements themselves rather than permitting their borrowers to do so, the lender can be viewed as the borrower's agent for this purpose, with a corresponding fiduciary obligation to see that the funds are distributed with due care.

It may be possible to find in state statutes a standard of care in disbursement of construction loan proceeds. For example, the Ohio code provides that no payment may be made by a lending institution to a contractor unless the latter has given the lender its affidavit setting forth any unpaid claims of subcontractors, materials suppliers, and laborers. This duty obviously runs to the borrower,[52] but in Takach v. Williams Homes,[53] the Ohio Supreme Court held that it also ran in favor of a party who had contracted to buy the property upon completion of construction, and who had obtained a long-term loan commitment from the same lender.

Note that even if a duty of reasonable care is found, it may not provide a remedy for every diversion of construction funds. In Daniels v. Big Horn Federal Savings & Loan Association,[54] the lender conceded it owed a duty of due care. However, since it was not common at that time for construction lenders in Wyoming to obtain lien waivers from subcontractors before making each disbursement, the court held that the defendant's failure to do so gave rise to no liability.

Assuming that lenders must use reasonable care to ensure that the loan funds find their way into improvements to the land, questions can

50. Id., 129 Cal.Rptr. at 95 (quoting Rowland v. Christian, 69 Cal.2d 108, 70 Cal.Rptr. 97, 443 P.2d 561 (1968)).

51. See Prudential Insurance Co. v. Executive Estates, Inc., 174 Ind.App. 674, 369 N.E.2d 1117 (1977); Falls Lumber Co. v. Heman, 114 Ohio App. 262, 181 N.E.2d 713 (1961). Cf. Gardner Plumbing, Inc. v. Cottrill, 44 Ohio St.2d 111, 117, 338 N.E.2d 757, 760–61 (1975), noted 45 U.Cin.L.Rev. 492 (1976).

52. See Plumbing Supply Co. v. Kostelnik, 69 Ohio Misc. 11, 430 N.E.2d 1340, 23 O.O.3d 77 (1980).

53. 6 Ohio St.3d 357, 453 N.E.2d 656 (1983).

54. 604 P.2d 1046 (Wyo.1980). See also Spurlock v. Fayette Federal Savings & Loan Association, ___ Ind.App. ___, 436 N.E.2d 811, 30 A.L.R.4th 125 (1982) (lender had no duty to avoid mechanics liens, where all disbursements were made directly to borrower); Essex Savings Bank v. Leeker, 2 Conn.App. 98, 476 A.2d 1071 (1984) (construction lender is not required to be an expert on modular housing, but only to use reasonable care in disbursement).

arise as to what items constitute "improvements." There is obviously no difficulty with labor and materials expended on the site, and most courts would have little difficulty approving off-site infrastructure, such as extension of water and sewer lines, storm drains, and roads leading to the site.[55] Architects' and engineers' fees are more debatable, since the work products of these professionals may or may not enhance the property's value, depending on their quality and whether or not they can be used in completing the project after default and foreclosure.[56] Even more dubious are fees or interest on the construction loan and payments on junior financing, ground lease rentals, and the like.[57] Obviously, it is desirable to cover these details in a carefully-drafted construction loan agreement or subordination clause.

On the whole, a modest trend to hold construction lenders to a standard of reasonable care in disbursement now seems to be developing. Several factors argue for the soundness of this approach. One is the enormous power which such lenders hold, by virtue of their priority position, to wreak economic havoc on owners, purchase-money mortgagee, and mechanics lienors if they act irresponsibly in making disbursements.[58] Another is the common understanding of these junior parties that the construction lender will use good practices to protect itself, and that they too will be benefitted by these practices.[59] Arguably these considerations apply only where the lender has notice of the junior parties' existence and potential claims, but that is nearly always the case.

Adoption by the courts of a general duty of reasonable care has the advantage of avoiding the vagaries of interpretation of construction loan agreements and subordination agreements, and the uncertainties of the third party beneficiary doctrine, discussed earlier in this section. It also benefits junior parties who do not have the sophistication and knowledge of construction loan practices which would lead them to insist on contractual protection from sloppy disbursements. In light of the construction lender's broad legal and economic control of the entire transaction, imposition of this sort of duty is reasonable and commendable.

55. See B.J.I. Corp. v. Larry W. Corp., 183 N.J.Super. 310, 443 A.2d 1096 (1982) (approving house, off-site roads, gutter, sewers); Hyatt v. Maryland Federal Savings & Loan Association, 42 Md.App. 623, 402 A.2d 118 (1979) (approving preliminary engineer and architectural work, water and sewer systems).

56. See Hyatt v. Maryland Federal Savings & Loan Association, id.; G. Credit Co. v. Mid-West Land Development, Inc., 207 Kan. 325, 485 P.2d 205 (1971) (approving engineers' and architects' plans and specifications, construction loan interest, and rental payments on ground lease).

57. See Hyatt v. Maryland Federal Savings & Loan Association, id.; cf. Ban-Co Investment Co. v. Loveless, 22 Wn.App. 122, 587 P.2d 567 (1978) (disapproving prepayment of rent on ground lease and payments for developer's overhead and profit).

58. See Korngold, Construction Loan Advances and the Subordinated Purchase Money Mortgagee: An Appraisal, A Suggested Approach, and the ULTA Perspective, 50 Ford.L.Rev. 313, 354–56 (1981).

59. Id. at 357.

WESTLAW REFERENCES
construct*** build*** /s contract agreement loan /p disburse!
distribut*** /p proceed /p junior lien*** mechanic materialm*n

§ 12.11 Lender Liability for Construction Defects or Other Wrongful Acts of Contractors

If a lender becomes more than ordinarily involved in a construction project, its additional activities may form the basis for liability for negligent or illegal acts which the builder commits. The seminal case in this regard is Connor v. Great Western Savings and Loan Association.[1] This 1969 decision by the California supreme court, which generated considerable concern and commentary,[2] held a construction lender liable to subdivision home purchasers for construction defects in their homes. In *Connor* an inexperienced and undercapitalized construction company borrowed construction funds from Great Western Savings and Loan. In addition to lending these funds, Great Western "warehoused" the land upon which the subdivision was to be constructed, purchasing it in bulk and reselling it to the developer as he was able to use it. The lender was also granted a right of first refusal to make the permanent loans to subdivision homebuyers. The agreement between lender and developer provided that if Great Western met the terms of a competing lender and still lost the loan, the developer would have to pay Great Western the fees it otherwise would have earned.[3] Great Western reviewed the developer's plans, but failed to follow its usual procedure and examine the foundation specifications. When the defectively constructed foundations later cracked, the purchasers brought suit against several defendants, including Great Western. In reversing a judgment of nonsuit against Great Western, the California supreme court said:

> Great Western became much more than a lender content to lend money at interest on the security of real property. It became an active participant in a home construction enterprise. It had the right to exercise extensive control of the enterprise. Its financing, which made the enterprise possible,

§ 12.11

1. 69 Cal.2d 850, 73 Cal.Rptr. 369, 447 P.2d 609 (1969).

2. See e.g., Annot., Financing Agency's Liability to Purchaser of New Homes or Structures for Consequences of Construction Defects. 39 A.L.R.3d 247 (1971); Note, the Expanding Scope of Enterprise Liability, 69 Colum.L.Rev. 1084 (1969); Comment, New Liability in Construction Lending: Implications of Connor v. Great Western Sav. & Loan, 42 So.Cal.L.Rev. 353 (1969); Comment, Liability of the Institutional Lender for Structural Defects in New Housing, 35 U.Chi.L.Rev. 739 (1968); 6 Houston L.Rev. 580 (1969); 5 Real Property, Prob. & Tr.J. 495 (1970).

3. This sort of referral arrangement may be an illegal tying agreement under the Sherman Act; see Fortner Enterprises, Inc. v. United States Steel Corp., 394 U.S. 495, 89 S.Ct. 1252, 22 L.Ed.2d 495 (1969).

took on ramifications beyond the domain of the usual money lender.[4]

Because of this extensive involvement in the subdivision project, the court found that the lender had a duty to purchasers to exercise reasonable care in preventing defective construction. In so ruling, the court created a new theory of construction lender liability.

In a few cases decided after *Connor,* the courts have found highly intimate connections between developer and lender, and thus have imposed liability. For example, in Central Bank v. Baldwin,[5] the Nevada supreme court noted that the lender's wholly-owned subsidiary owned half of the developer corporation's stock, provided it with a generous line of credit, and inspected all of its construction work. This sort of involvement seems even more extensive than that in *Connor,* and was sufficient to support a judgment against the lender for defective construction.

In Dunson v. Stockton, Whatley, Davin & Co.,[6] *Connor* was used as the basis for a reordering of normal mortgage priorities. A housing developer had contracted to sell a completed house to the Dunsons. Ordinarily, the developer's construction loan mortgage on the property would have had priority over the Dunsons' contract rights, and its foreclosure would have destroyed their interest.[7] However, prior to foreclosure the lender had become so concerned about the developer's shaky operation that it assumed control of the partially completed construction, placing its own employee in charge of the project. Because of this close tie between developer and lender, the court held that all advances made after the lender had taken control were subordinate to the vendee's interest.

Connor has also been a factor in some cases which would otherwise probably have been decided against the landowner. For example, ordinarily a construction lender's policy of making routine inspections during the course of construction is assumed to be for the lender's benefit alone, and does not form the basis for a claim by the owner if the inspection is carelessly done,[8] even if the owner has paid an "inspection fee." However, a combination of the *Connor* theory and an

---

4. 69 Cal.2d at 864, 73 Cal.Rptr. at 376, 447 P.2d at 616 (1969).

5. 94 Nev. 581, 583 P.2d 1087 (1978). But see Starfish Condominium Association v. Yorkridge Service Corp., 295 Md. 693, 458 A.2d 805 (1983), refusing to hold the lender liable on very similar facts, and summarily dismissing *Connor* as having "no application," 458 A.2d at 819.

6. 346 So.2d 603 (Fla.App.1977).

7. The Dunsons had initially conveyed the lot by deed to the developer in order to facilitate its arrangement of construction financing; the court took this conveyance to be the equivalent of a voluntary subordination of the Dunsons' interest to the construction loan. On subordination by vendees generally, see § 12.9, supra, at notes 35–40; § 13.3, infra.

8. See, e.g., Goodman v. Pate Construction Co., 305 Pa.Super. 147, 451 A.2d 464 (1982); Butts v. Atlanta Federal Savings & Loan Association, 152 Ga. 40, 262 S.E.2d 230 (1979); Meyers v. Guarantee Savings & Loan Association, 79 Cal.App.3d 307, 144 Cal.Rptr. 616 (1978); Rice v. First Federal Savings & Loan Association, 207 So.2d 22 (Fla.App.1968).

explicit promise by the lender produced a contrary result in Rudolph v. First Southern Federal Savings and Loan Association.[9] While the court did not find the sort of general control by the lender which existed in *Connor,* it noted a statement by an officer of the lender to the owners that the lender "had its own inspector who would not approve a draw * * * until the work was performed properly." [10] The court thought this a sufficient basis for allowing the jury to decide whether the lender had assumed a duty to make inspections for the owner's benefit, and thus would be liable for substandard work by the contractor.

However, the great majority of recent cases have distinguished *Connor,* permitting lender defendants to avoid liability.[11] The distinction has usually been based on the lack of extensive involvement of the lender in the project,[12] although neither *Connor* nor its progeny make it very clear just how far a lender's activity must go to move within the zone of liability. Perhaps most courts would track the facts of *Connor* itself, requiring both land warehousing and a permanent loan referral scheme, or some similarly intimate involvement. Although one court has suggested that the *Connor* theory represents a minority view,[13] several decisions have adopted the *Connor* rationale—or at least suggested that it might be applied—to subject lenders to liability in a variety of circumstances not involving physical defects in new construction as *Connor* did.

9. 414 So.2d 64 (Ala.1982).

10. Id. at 71. Cf. Butts v. Atlanta Federal Savings & Loan Association, 152 Ga. 40, 262 S.E.2d 230 (1979), rejecting, on the basis of the parol evidence rule, a similar claim deriving from the statement of the lender's officer "that all work would be checked and approved for good workmanship before any funds were disbursed."

11. Drake v. Morris Plan Co., 53 Cal. App.3d 208, 125 Cal.Rptr. 667 (1976) (no lender liability for wrongful death for financing sale of automobile for incompetent unlicensed driver); Fox & Carskadon Financial Corp. v. San Francisco Savings & Loan Association, 52 Cal.App.3d 484, 125 Cal.Rptr. 549 (1975) (no lender liability to apartment building purchaser who lost equity in foreclosure); Skerlec v. Wells Fargo Bank National Association, 18 Cal.App.3d 1003, 96 Cal.Rptr. 434 (1971) (no lender liability in tort to plaintiff injured in collision where lender knew automobile purchaser could not comply with financial responsibility laws); Bradler v. Craig, 274 Cal.App.2d 466, 79 Cal.Rptr. 401 (1969) (no liability in lender for construction defects in house in the absence of extraordinary lender involvement in the project); Callaizakis v. Astor Development Co., 4 Ill.App.

3d 163, 280 N.E.2d 512 (1972) (no lender liability to condominium purchasers for structural defects in the absence of *Connor*-like facts); Bill Stremmel Motors, Inc. v. IDS Leasing Corp., 89 Nev. 414, 514 P.2d 654 (1973) (financing agent not liable for acts of equipment seller unless knows of wrongful acts and induces others to utilize services of the seller); L.A. Christiansen v. Philcent Corp., 226 Pa.Super. 157, 313 A.2d 249 (1973) (no lender liability to home purchasers for construction defects in absence of *Connor*-like facts). See also Flamingo Drift Fishing, Inc. v. Nix, 251 So.2d 316 (Fla.App.1971) (lender's employment of inspector to supervise construction of fishing vessel did not impose obligation on bank toward the purchaser).

12. Allison v. Home Savings Association, 643 S.W.2d 847 (Mo.App.1982); Clark v. Grover, 132 Mich.App. 476, 347 N.W.2d 748 (1984); Wierzbicki v. Alaska Mutual Savings Bank, 630 P.2d 998 (Alaska 1981); Murry v. Western American Mortgage Co., 124 Ariz. 387, 604 P.2d 651 (1979); Butts v. Atlanta Federal Savings & Loan Association, 152 Ga.App. 40, 262 S.E.2d 230 (1979).

13. See Wright v. United States, 428 F.Supp. 782, 789 (D.Mont.1977), affirmed 599 F.2d 304 (9th Cir.1979).

In Jemison v. Montgomery Real Estate and Co.[14] a Michigan home purchaser who had abandoned her home as uninhabitable sued the real estate broker and the mortgagee for fraudulent misrepresentation in the sale. The plaintiff alleged that the lender knew she was on welfare and knew that she was relatively uneducated and commercially inexperienced. She further alleged that the lender both knew that the realtor was unscrupulous and was aware of facts giving rise to the fraud. Relying on *Connor,* the plaintiff concluded that since the lender "knew or should have known all of these facts, it made itself an integral and necessary part of the fraudulent transaction when it entered into the mortgage loan agreement with plaintiff." [15] Reversing the appellate court, the Michigan supreme court indicated that these allegations stated a cause of action against the lender.

Another application of the *Connor* rule was suggested in Morroco v. Felton.[16] In that case, a New Jersey landlord brought a summary dispossession action against several tenants. The tenants responded by filing to remove the dispossession action and by suing the landlord and mortgagees for breach of an implied warranty of habitability. The court focused on procedural matters, but it observed by way of dicta that, under the *Connor* rationale, liability for maintaining decent dwellings may extend to the lender. "[I]t may well be necessary," said the court, "to join third parties. Especially where the property in question is heavily mortgaged, some determination on the mortgagee's liability appears appropriate." [17]

Without explicitly relying on *Connor,* a federal court ruled that construction lenders can be liable for fraud in connection with the purchase of subdivision lots. In Timmrock v. Munn,[18] 328 plaintiffs alleged fraud in the sale of subdivision lots, arguing that investment contracts were involved and that a violation of federal securities laws had occurred. They also claimed violations of the Interstate Land Sales Full Disclosure Act.[19] The plaintiffs alleged that the bank which had financed the project's construction had entered into an accord with the developers and had allowed itself to be held out to the public as the financial backer of the project. In moving to dismiss the action under the Disclosure Act, the bank contended that section 1709 of the Act limited actions to those brought against developers and their agents. The bank claimed it was neither. Responding to this defense, the court noted that a bank would not be subject to the Act in the normal course of its business, but that if it went beyond this, the bank could be liable.[20] The court ruled that the "plaintiffs are therefore entitled to

---

14. 396 Mich. 106, 240 N.W.2d 205 (1976). The facts are reported at 47 Mich. App. 731, 210 N.W.2d 10 (1973).

15. 210 N.W.2d at 15 (dissenting opinion).

16. 112 N.J.Super. 226, 270 A.2d 739 (1970).

17. 270 A.2d at 743.

Nelson & Whitman, Real Est.Fin. Law, 2d Ed. HB—31

18. 433 F.Supp. 396 (N.D.Ill.1977).

19. 15 U.S.C.A. § 1701 et seq. (1970).

20. Essentially the same rule was suggested in Zachery v. Treasure Lake of Georgia, Inc., 374 F.Supp. 251 (N.D.Ga. 1974). In *Zachery,* the court found that only a lender-borrower relationship existed between the lender and the developer.

attempt to show that the Bank exceeded the normal scope of financing practices and actively participated in and aided the advancement of a fraudulent scheme, or otherwise assisted in the luring of purchasers for an allegedly dubious project." [21]

Lender liability could arise in other contexts as well.[22] Tort actions might be brought against lenders heavily involved in construction projects when construction defects contribute to personal injuries.[23] Governmental agencies might cite lenders for building code violations if they go beyond the usual scope of financing in connection with a non-complying structure. Creative plaintiffs could imagine other approaches. The potential for lender liability under a *Connor* theory is real.[24] Even though the case has been frequently distinguished, its theory has been occasionally applied to impose liability on financial institutions who operate outside the scope of normal lending activity.

Government Agency Liability for Construction Defects

When government agencies, such as the Federal Housing Administration (FHA), Veterans Administration (VA), and Farmers Home Administration (FmHA), are asked to make direct loans to home buyers, or to guarantee or insure loans made by private lenders,[25] they generally inspect the property to ensure that it meets their construction standards. Since the agency in question may well end up owning the

---

The lender was therefore not liable for misrepresentation under the Interstate Land Sales Full Disclosure Act. It is noteworthy that even a public financing agency can be found to be a developer. See California Housing Finance Agency v. Elliot, 17 Cal.3d 575, 131 Cal.Rptr. 361, 551 P.2d 1193 (1976).

21. 433 F.Supp. at 406.

22. A similar theory of close-connectedness has been used to prevent financial institutions from achieving holder in due course status. See, e.g., Commercial Credit Corp. v. Orange County Machine Works, 34 Cal.2d 766, 214 P.2d 819 (1950); see § 5.29 supra.

23. For a case rejecting application of the *Connor* rule in such a situation, see Wright v. United States, 428 F.Supp. 782 (D.Mont.1977), affirmed 599 F.2d 304 (9th Cir.1979).

24. The California legislature made a somewhat ambiguous attempt to reverse or limit *Connor:*

A lender who makes a loan of money [for construction purposes] * * * shall not be held liable to third persons for any loss or damage occasioned by a defect in the * * * property * * * unless such loss or damage is a result of an act of the lender outside the scope of the

activities of a lender of money or unless the lender has been a party to misrepresentations with respect to such * * * property.

West's Ann.Cal.Civ.Code, § 3434. The statute may be read as merely restating the result in *Connor,* but if this is its intent it is superfluous. In any event it is hardly a model of legislative drafting, and adds nothing to the clarity of the law in California.

See Gutierrez, Liability of a Construction Lender Under Civil Code Section 3434: An Amorphous Epitaph to Connor v. Great Western Savings & Loan Association, 8 Pac.L.J. 1 (1977).

Equally opaque is Nev.Rev.Stat. 41.590, also apparently enacted as a response to *Connor.* It provides that a construction lender shall not be liable for construction defects "unless the loss or damage is the result of some other action or activity of the lender than the loan transaction." See also V.A.M.S. § 369.264; U.L.T.A. § 2–310 (construction lender is not liable, "solely by reason of making the loan," for construction defects).

25. See generally § 11.2, infra, concerning the mortgage insurance and guaranty functions of these agencies.

property and attempting to market it,[26] this concern with physical quality is entirely logical as a matter of self-protection. However, the buyer of the property may also claim that she relied on the government inspection, and if it was done carelessly or improperly, may bring an action against the agency for damages in the amount necessary to correct the defects which the inspection should have disclosed.

Until recently, such actions nearly always failed. The agencies' defenses were generally based on (1) the notion that the government's inspections were only made on its own behalf, and were not intended to benefit the buyer;[27] and (2) that the Federal Tort Claims Act (FTCA),[28] which provides a limited waiver of sovereign immunity for actions against the Federal government, contains an exception for torts based on misrepresentation, and that claims for inadequate inspection fell within that exception.[29]

However, two theories developed in recent years have the potential for overcoming these objections. One of them is based on a contract, inferred from the agency's regulations, to make the necessary inspections in a proper manner. For a claim sounding in contract, the FTCA and its limitations are irrelevant.[30] However, only the regulations of FmHA have been held to comprise such a contract,[31] and even those regulations have subsequently been amended to negate the contract theory quite effectively.[32]

A more fruitful attack may be based on the tort of negligent performance of an assumed duty, the so-called "Good Samaritan" doctrine. Even though the agency has no duty to inspect, if it undertakes to do so voluntarily, it may be liable for negligence in carrying out the inspection.[33] In Block v. Neal,[34] the Supreme Court held that

26. In the case of an insured or guaranteed loan, the agency will usually pay the claim and take title to the property from the foreclosing lender; it will then attempt to remarket the property. Obviously construction defects may impair the agency's ability to sell for a high price.

27. See, e.g., Davis v. Romney, 490 F.2d 1360 (3d Cir.1974); Stanley v. Veterans Administration, 454 F.Supp. 9 (E.D.Pa. 1978); Baker v. Surman, 361 N.W.2d 108 (Minn.App.1985).

28. 28 U.S.C.A. § 2680.

29. The landmark case is United States v. Neustadt, 366 U.S. 696, 81 S.Ct. 1294, 6 L.Ed.2d 614 (1961). See also Scott v. First Investment Co., 556 F.Supp. 782 (W.D.Pa. 1983); Provencal v. Michel Construction Corp., 505 F.Supp. 770 (W.D.Mich.1980). See generally Annot., 30 A.L.R.Fed. 421.

30. For contract claims, the relevant waiver of sovereign immunity is the Tucker Act, 28 U.S.C.A. § 1346. Claims thereunder must be brought in the Court of

Claims if the amount in controversy exceeds $10,000.

31. Kipf v. United States, 501 F.Supp. 110 (D.Mont.1980). See also Navarro v. United States, 586 F.Supp. 799 (D.V.I.1984), apparently acknowledging the contract claims but declining jurisdiction because they exceeded the $10,000 Tucker Act limit. Cf. Scott v. First Investment Corp., 556 F.Supp. 782 (W.D.Pa.1983), distinguishing the HUD regulations from those of FmHA and rejecting the contract theory of agency liability.

32. See 7 CFR 1924.9, effective June 12, 1980; the amended regulations state explicitly that "FmHA's inspections are not to assure the borrower that the house is built in accordance with the plans and specifications. The inspections create or imply no duty or obligation to the particular borrower * * *."

33. See Restatement (Second) of Torts § 323 (1965).

34. See note 34 on page 932.

the gravamen of this sort of tort claim lay in the faulty performance of the inspection rather than in faulty communication to the borrower of its results. Hence, it was not barred by the FTCA's exception for misrepresentation.

However, the victory for plaintiffs signalled by Block v. Neal seems to have been shortlived. The 1980 amendments to the FmHA regulations mentioned above [35] appear to exclude quite expressly any duty of careful inspection, whether based on tort or contract, and several lower federal courts have so held.[36] Similar tort claims against FHA or VA may still be viable.

Other barriers stand in the way of aggrieved plaintiffs as well. A claim under the FTCA must be filed within a defined period after it arises, in written form, and with specific supporting evidence.[37] Moreover, Congress has enacted provisions giving monetary relief to homebuyers who purchase new houses under the principal federal programs and discover that they have serious structural defects.[38] There are many constraints on recovery under these provisions, and no judicial review is available. Several decisions have held that if a claim is within their scope, they constitute the exclusive remedy and no action for improper inspection will lie.[39] The Supreme Court expressly left this issue undecided in Block v. Neal. Ideally, it should be resolved by Congress.

 WESTLAW REFERENCES

construct*** build*** /s contract agreement loan /p lender bank
association /p liability liable /p defect*** wrong*** /p
vicarious fiduciary trust! (duty +s care)

---

34. 460 U.S. 289, 103 S.Ct. 1089, 75 L.Ed. 2d 67 (1983). See also Martin v. Block, 571 F.Supp. 1180 (D.V.I.1983); Park v. United States, 517 F.Supp. 970 (D.Or.1981). The doctrine applies only if the plaintiff actually relied on the faulty inspection; see Kynerd v. United States Dep't of HUD, 607 F.Supp. 117 (S.D.Miss.1985).

35. See note 32 supra.

36. Moody v. United States, 585 F.Supp. 286 (E.D.Tenn.1984); Cash v. United States, 571 F.Supp. 513 (N.D.Ga.1983).

37. See 28 CFR Part 14; Navarro v. United States, 586 F.Supp. 799 (D.V.I.1984), rejecting a claim against FmHA because it was not filed with agency within the prescribed 2 year period.

38. See 12 U.S.C.A. § 1735b (FHA); 38 U.S.C.A. § 1827 (VA); 42 U.S.C.A. § 1479(c) (FmHA). See Note, Federal Compensation for Victims of the "Homeownership for the Poor" Program, 84 Yale L.J. 294 (1974).

39. See Summers v. United States, 510 F.2d 123 (8th Cir.1975), certiorari denied 423 U.S. 851, 96 S.Ct. 95, 46 L.Ed.2d 75 (1975). Cf. Martin v. Block, 571 F.Supp. 1180 (D.V.I.1983), suggesting that the compensation scheme is not the exclusive remedy.

§§ 12.12–13.0 are reserved for supplementary material.

Chapter 13

FINANCING CONDOMINIUMS AND COOPERATIVES

Table of Sections

---

§ 13.1 An Overview of Condominiums and Cooperatives

This chapter will deal with legal problems relating to the financing of condominiums and cooperatives. While space does not permit a detailed treatment of the non-financing aspects of these forms of ownership, a rudimentary overview of the legal relationships involved will preface discussion of the central topic.[1]

Both condominiums and cooperatives are legal formats for "unit ownership"—that is, the ownership of a physically defined portion of a larger parcel of (usually improved) real property. In the majority of cases, the "unit" is a residential apartment in a multifamily housing project. Condominiums are much more tightly controlled by state legislation than are cooperatives, and in recent years many states have amended their condominium statutes to permit the creation of condominiums in non-residential property, including commercial and industrial buildings, and even on unimproved land.[2] There are no signifi-

---

§ 13.1

1. The most complete and useful treatment of such non-financing areas is P. Rohan & M. Reskin, Condominium Law & Practice (1976). Other works include D. Clurman & E. Hebard, Condominiums and Cooperatives (1969); A. Ferrer & K. Stecher, Law of Condominium (1967); P. Rohan & M. Reskin, Cooperative Housing Law and Practice (1975); and K. Romney, Condominium Development Guide (1974). Law journal symposia on condominium issues include 55 Fla.B.J. (Feb.1981); 10 Wm.Mitch.L.Rev. 1 (1984); and 48 St. John's L.Rev. 677 (1974).

2. The model act on which many early American statutes were based used the term "apartment", presumably implying cant legal barriers to non-residential cooperative ownership, although it is quite rare.

In most cases the owner of a condominium or cooperative unit is also a participant in some organization of owners which has responsibility for the operation, maintenance, and management of the "common areas"—features of the building or project which are used or available for use by all unit owners, such as exterior walls, roofs, lobbies, stairwells, elevators, grounds and landscaping, and often recreational facilities. The principal distinctions between condominiums and cooperatives are discussed below.

The Condominium

The term "condominium" is variously used to refer to the underlying concept, the building, or the individual unit; in this chapter, it refers to the building. In a condominium, each owner holds fee simple title to his unit directly. In addition, he and his fellow unit owners each own undivided fractional shares in the common areas of the project as tenants in common.[3] Management and maintenance of these common facilities are performed by an owners' association, which may be incorporated or unincorporated.[4] The fractional shares in the common areas and the vote of each member of the association are assigned on some equitable basis, such as the number of square feet in the unit or its proportionate share of the original value of all units.[5] The association may assert a lien on each unit to enforce the owner's obligation to pay his share of the assessments levied by the association

residential use; see Federal Housing Administration, Model Statute for the Creation of Apartment Ownership § 2(a), reprinted in G. Nelson & D. Whitman, Real Estate Transfer, Finance and Development 901 (1981) [hereinafter cited as FHA Model Act]. Examples of much broader definitions which permit non-residential uses include Uniform Condominium Act ("U.C.A.") § 1–103(25) (1980); Alaska Stat. 34.07.450(1); 60 Okl.Stat.Supp.1976, § 503(b); Va.Code 1950, § 55–79.2(a). See P. Rohan & M. Reskin, Condominium Law and Practice § 5.01[2] (1976). On non-residential condominiums, see generally, D. Clurman, The Business Condominium (1973); Note, Commercial Condominiums: Statutory Roadblocks to Development, 34 U.Fla.L.Rev. 432 (1982); Lundquist, Mixed Use Condominiums under the Minnesota Uniform Condominium Act, 10 Wm.Mitch. L.Rev. 97 (1984).

Condominiums on raw land are still problematic under some statutes; see Bonner Properties, Inc. v. Planning Board, 185 N.J.Super. 553, 449 A.2d 1350 (1982); Prestwick Landowners' Association v. Underhill, 69 Ohio App.2d 45, 429 N.E.2d 1191 (1980).

3. This distinguishes the condominium from the planned unit development ("P.U.D."), in which the owners association holds title to the common areas. See Country Greens Village One Owner's Association v. Meyers, 158 Ga.App. 609, 281 S.E.2d 346 (1981).

4. The present trend seems to be incorporation of associations. See Hyatt, Condominium and Home Owner Associations: Formation and Development, 24 Emory L.J. 977 (1975); Jackson, Why You Should Incorporate a Homeowners Association, 3 Real Est.L.J. 311 (1975); Krasnowiecki, Townhouses with Homes Association: A New Perspective, 123 U.Pa.L.Rev. 711 (1975).

5. See Reichman, Residential Private Governments: An Introductory Survey, 43 U.Chi.L.Rev. 253 (1976). Under the Uniform Condominium Act, expenses, voting rights, and common area ownership can each be based on a different formula; see U.C.A. § 2–107 (1980).

for management, maintenance, insurance, reserves for replacements, and the like.[6]

There is little question that a form of unit ownership similar to the condominium concept can be developed by careful structuring of documents in the absence of an authorizing statute. This has been done in many countries and continues today in England.[7] However, every jurisdiction in the United States has enacted a condominium statute which attempts to regularize procedures, spell out the duties and obligations of the unit owners and the association, provide for such eventualities as damage, destruction, and condemnation of the condominium, and provide legal confirmation of the association's lien rights against delinquent unit owners. The statutes also provide for separate property tax assessment on each unit and prohibit partitioning of the common areas. Most American statutes were enacted during the 1960–1970 period, and were based heavily on model legislation drafted by the Federal Housing Administration.[8] The statutes were helpful in standardizing relationships and protecting unit owners from some forms of overreaching, but they were unnecessarily restrictive in many respects and a "second generation" of statutes, which generally provide far greater flexibility in the legal structuring of the development, as well as more extensive consumer protection, has begun to be enacted.[9] In 1977 the Commissioners on Uniform Laws promulgated the Uniform Condominium Act, a second-generation statute which has attracted widespread interest.[10]

The Cooperative

In a cooperative the entire project, including the individual units and the common areas, is owned by a single corporation (often organ-

6. See Jackson, Homeowners Associations: Remedies to Enforce Assessment Collections, 51 L.A.B.J. 423 (1976).

7. See 1 P. Rohan & M. Reskin, Condominium Law and Practice, ch. 4 (1976); Leyser, The Ownership of Flats—A Comparative Study, 7 Int'l & Comp.L.Q. 31 (1958).

8. See note 2 supra.

9. Leaders in this movement include West's Fla.Stat.Ann. §§ 718.101–.508, discussed in Comment, 8 U.Mich.J.L.Ref. 387 (1975) and 27 U.Miami L.Rev. 451 (1973); Utah Code Ann.1953, 57–8–1 through 57–8–36; Va.Code §§ 55–79.39–.103, discussed in Comment, 9 U.Richmond L.Rev. 135 (1974) and Johnakin, A Second Generation of Condominium Statutes, Lawyers Title News, May–June 1974, at 3. See generally Cannella, Recent Innovations in State Condominium Legislation, 48 St.John's L.Rev. 994 (1974).

10. The 1977 version of the UCA has been adopted in Minnesota, Pennsylvania, and West Virginia. A revised version of the UCA was promulgated in 1980, and has been adopted in Maine, Missouri, New Mexico, and Rhode Island. In addition, several states have "borrowed" the UCA's treatment of specific issues and incorporated it into their existing statutes.

The Commissioners on Uniform Laws also adopted the Uniform Planned Community Act ("UPCA", intended to govern P.U.D.'s) in 1980 and the Model Real Estate Cooperative Act ("MRECA") in 1981. See Fisher, The Model Real Estate Cooperative Act: A Critique, 12 Real Est.L.J. 53 (1983). In 1982 they adopted the Uniform Common Interest Ownership Act ("UCIOA"), which was intended as a consolidation of all three of the previous acts mentioned. The UCIOA has been adopted in Connecticut.

ized on a non-profit basis).[11] Persons who purchase units in the cooperative receive, as evidence of their interests, two documents: a "proprietary lease", indicating the member's right of possession in the particular apartment, and a stock certificate, evidencing ownership of a share or shares in the corporation. The documents usually provide that ownership of the stock and the tenant's interest in the proprietary lease are inseparable.

In most cooperatives, each apartment's owners have a single vote, rather than a vote apportioned by value or size as with condominiums. The functions of the corporation are similar to those of the owners' association in a condominium, but are more extensive. Since the cooperative corporation owns the project, it will normally be the mortgagor on one or more blanket mortgages covering the building. The "rent" paid by tenants under their proprietary leases must be sufficient to cover the cost of servicing this debt and the property taxes on the project in addition to such management, maintenance, and other expenses and reserves as would be expected in a condominium. Both condominium[12] and cooperative unit owners are entitled to deduct the portion of their monthly payments attributable to mortgage interest and real estate taxes, although this privilege is available to cooperative members only if at least 80% of the gross income of the corporation is derived from payments by tenant-stockholders.[13]

---

11. Although corporate ownership of cooperatives is by far the most common format, trust or tenancy-in-common ownership are also possible and have been used occasionally. See Future Federal Savings & Loan Association v. Daunhauer, 687 S.W.2d 871 (Ky.App.1985); P. Rohan & M. Reskin, Cooperative Housing Law and Practice § 201 (1975). I.R.C. § 216(b)(1)(c), which permits deduction of mortgage interest and property taxes by cooperative owners, is satisfied only if "no stockholder * * * is entitled to receive any distribution not out of earnings and profits of the corporation except on a complete or partial liquidation of the corporation." See the description of Co-op City by the Court in United Housing Foundation, Inc. v. Forman, 421 U.S. 837, 840, 95 S.Ct. 2051, 2054, 44 L.Ed.2d 621 (1975), rehearing denied 423 U.S. 884, 96 S.Ct. 157, 46 L.Ed.2d 115 (1975) and 423 U.S. 884, 96 S.Ct. 157, 46 L.Ed.2d 115 (1975).

For a readable brief history of the cooperative housing movement in New York, see Gray, The 'Revolution' of 1881 Is Now In Its 2d Century, New York Times, Oct. 28, 1984, at 61.

12. Rev.Rul. 64–31, 1964–1 C.B. 300.

13. See I.R.C. § 216, which imposes numerous other requirements on co-ops in addition to the 80% test; Miller, The Impact of a Housing Cooperative's "Bad" Income on

Its Members' Section 216(a) Deduction, Now and Under Proposed Legislation, 10 J.Real Est.Tax. 99 (1983). The treatment of the portion of a co-op member's monthly payment which is attributable to amortization on the blanket mortgage raises difficult tax problems. Often the co-op and its members will agree that this amount is to be treated as additional contribution to capital, and hence not income to the corporation; this is attractive, since the corporation is a taxable entity, and may otherwise owe federal tax on its income. This approach has been successful in avoiding tax at the corporate level in several cases; see, e.g., Lake Forest, Inc. v. Commissioner, 22 T.C.M. 156 (CCH) (1963). However, the members may also wish to assert that the amorization component of each monthly payment is income for purposes of the 80% rule, thus maximizing the amount of income the co-op can receive from outside sources (e.g., commercial rental space, vending and laundry machines) while still qualifying under § 216. The Court of Claims has held that the co-op and its members can agree to either capital or income treatment of the amortization payments but cannot have it both ways; see Eckstein v. United States, 452 F.2d 1036 (Ct. Cl.1971). See Miller, Tax Problems of the Housing Cooperative under the 80% Income Rule, 18 Prac.Law. 81 (No. 4, Apr. 1972), which also discusses the other requirements

For federal tax purposes a cooperative member is treated much like the owner of a condominium or a detached house, assuming the requirements of I.R.C. section 216 are met. But for many other purposes the question remains: Is the cooperator's interest real or personal property? Since the cooperative is a unique kind of hybrid,

which § 216 imposes on the legal structure of co-ops.

A radically different approach was used by the Tax Court in Park Place, Inc. v. Commissioner, 57 T.C. 767 (1972), which held that mortgage amortization, property tax, maintenance, and apparently mortgage interest components of payments made by co-op members to the corporation are not taxable income to it—and that the corporation has no offsetting deduction when it pays out these items—despite the fact that the same items *are* income for purposes of the 80% rule of § 216. The Tax Court thus gave the members the best of both worlds; whether this view will prevail over *Eckstein* remains to be seen.

This issue may become somewhat less important as a result of an amendment to I.R.C. § 216(c), made by § 2101(b) of the Tax Reform Act of 1976, which expressly authorizes cooperatives to claim depreciation deductions on their real estate; the Tax Court had rejected such a claim in *Park Place.* Apparently this deduction is available even if individual tenant-shareholders are also claiming depreciation on their own units because they are being used in a trade or business or for the production of income. See Feuer, Calculating Allowable Depreciation for Tenant-Stockholders of Cooperatives, 60 J.Tax. 288 (1984). At least in the early years of ownership of new buildings, depreciation will usually more than offset mortgage amortization thus minimizing or eliminating taxable income even if the amortization payments are regarded as income. For older and long-held buildings, the conflict between *Eckstein* and *Park Place* will still require resolution.

Condominiums have no 80% test to meet, and they normally make no assessments upon members for mortgage interest or amortization. However, both cooperatives and condominium associations may collect general operating reserves or reserves for future replacements or improvements in amounts exceeding the offsetting deductions of the current year's expenditures. Several theories have been developed (and accepted by the Commissioner) under which these reserves may escape taxation at the association or corporate level; one such theory is that, if

earmarked specifically for replacements or improvements rather than general operations or repairs, they are contributions to capital; another is that the association is merely an agent of the members in holding these funds until they need to be expended. See Concord Village, Inc. v. Commissioner, 65 T.C. 142 (1975); Rev.Rul. 75–370, 1975–2 C.B. 25; Rev.Rul. 75–371, 1975–2 C.B. 52; Miller, Amounts Collected from Unit Owners: Are They Subject to Income Tax, 9 J.Real Est.Tax 351 (1982); Frank, IRS Takes Harsh Position on Exempting Condominium and Homeowners' Associations, 44 J.Taxation 306 (1976).

It may also be possible for a condominium or cooperative corporation to qualify for tax-exempt status under I.R.C. § 501(c) (4) as a "civic league." However, in Rev. Rul. 74–99, 1974–1 C.B. 131, the Commissioner seems to have limited application of § 501(c)(4) to associations which (1) bear a reasonably recognizable relationship to an area recognizable as a governmental subdivision or a district thereof; (2) perform no exterior maintenance on privately-owned residences; and (3) own and maintain only facilities which are used and enjoyed by the general public, such as streets and parks. Obviously, many associations far exceed these limited activities, and hence will not be deemed tax-exempt.

I.R.C. § 528, added by § 2101 of the Tax Reform Act of 1976, allows homeowners associations in condominiums and planned unit developments to elect a limited form of tax-exempt status. Cooperatives are not eligible for this election, and a variety of limiting criteria must be met. Moreover, if the election is made, only "exempt function income", defined as membership dues, fees, and assessments, is exempt. Income from use charges for facilities, such as swimming pools, and from other sources is taxable, and the corporate surtax exemption is denied to electing associations. Thus the election could be quite disadvantageous in some cases, and non-electing associations will presumably be relegated to the pre-1976 arguments discussed above if they wish to shelter their excess income from taxation. See Cowan, Working With New Rules for Condominiums, Cooperatives, and Homeowners Associations, 46 J.Taxation 204 (1977).

answers to this question vary, depending on the view the courts take of the underlying policies. The characterization of the interest may be relevant for a wide variety of reasons, including the doctrine of restraints on alienation, rent control, ad valorem taxes, transfer taxes, conveyancing doctrines, construction of wills and of intestacy and judgment lien statutes, availability of title insurance, institutional financing,[14] summary eviction proceedings against members, and determination of the proper procedures for registering or recording transfers and creations of security interests, whether under the Uniform Commercial Code or realty recording acts. The answers of the courts in these contexts are far from uniform,[15] although there is no reason why the interest of a cooperative member should not be treated on a par with a condominium unit owner—as the owner of real property—for most purposes.

It is apparent that each member of a cooperative is somewhat more reliant upon the financial strength and honesty of his or her fellow members than is a condominium unit owner. If many members of a cooperative default, it may be impossible to meet the regular debt service payments on the blanket mortgage, which may consequently be foreclosed. In a condominium, by contrast, each unit owner arranges his own permanent financing on his apartment, and defaults by one's neighbors in the payment of monthly assessments, while possibly endangering the solvency of the owners' association, cannot directly trigger foreclosure by a lender of the unit belonging to a non-delinquent owner. On the other hand, it is probably easier for the member's organization to evict a delinquent owner and to realize on the security of his unit for unpaid assessments in a cooperative than in a condominium.[16]

---

14. Whether cooperative financing involves real or personal property under the rules of financial regulatory agencies, and the procedures for perfecting liens on cooperative members' interests, are discussed in the text accompanying § 13.6, notes 14–28 infra.

15. See Comment, Legal Characterization of the Individual's Interest in a Cooperative Apartment: Realty or Personalty, 73 Colum.L.Rev. 250 (1973); P. Rohan & M. Reskin, Cooperative Housing Law and Practice, § 2.01[5] (1975). See Weiss v. Karch, 62 N.Y.2d 849, 477 N.Y.S.2d 615, 466 N.E.2d 155 (1984) (UCC governs measure of damages for breach of contract of sale of cooperative apartment). Cf. California Coastal Commission v. Qvanta, Investment Corp., 113 Cal.App.3d 579, 170 Cal. Rptr. 263 (1980) (cooperative conversion is a "division of land.").

There is a further question: is the cooperative member a tenant or an owner? See, e.g., Linden Hill No. 1 Cooperative Corp. v. Kleiner, 124 Misc.2d 1001, 478 N.Y.S.2d 519 (1984) (statute protecting tenant ownership

of pets applies to cooperative member); Penokie v. Colonial Townhouses Cooperative, Inc., 140 Mich.App. 740, 366 N.W.2d 31 (1985) (statute governing refunds of tenants' security deposits does not apply to cooperative member).

16. The cooperative can treat the delinquent member as a tenant and use unlawful detainer or other summary process to evict him; Martin v. Villa Roma, Inc., 131 Cal.App.3d 362, 182 Cal.Rptr. 382 (1982); Sun Terrace Manor v. Municipal Court, 33 Cal.App.3d 739, 108 Cal.Rptr. 307 (1973); Green v. Greenbelt Homes, Inc., 232 Md. 496, 194 A.2d 273 (1963). See Rohan, Cooperative Housing: An Appraisal of Residential Controls and Enforcement Procedures, 18 Stan.L.Rev. 1323 (1966), questioning whether such a severe remedy should be available for minor defaults or violations of the co-op's rules. In a condominium, by contrast, the usual remedy is foreclosure of the association's lien on the unit, an action which normally enjoys no calendar preference and may take many months to complete. In either case, of

Condominiums and cooperatives share many of the same economic and social advantages: economies of scale in the initial cost and maintenance of recreation, parking, and other community facilities, the potential for competent management of the common areas, and the advantages of security and social contact which result from relatively high-density occupancy, as well as the concomitant problems.[17] Since the advent of condominium statutes in most American jurisdictions, lending institutions and developers (and consequently consumers) have tended to prefer condominiums in most jurisdictions, and except in New York, relatively few new cooperatives are being built.

WESTLAW REFERENCES
"uniform condominium act"
89ak1 89ak2 89ak3

The Condominium
di condominium

The Cooperative
di cooperative
co-op cooperative   /s   housing unit apartment

§ 13.2   Financing Condominiums and Cooperatives

Condominium and cooperative financing differ from one another in important respects. A condominium project is much like a subdivision of detached houses; financing of construction is usually independent of the permanent or long-term financing of the sales of individual units.[1] The construction loan is typically secured by a blanket mortgage on the entire property, with provision for the release of each individual unit from that mortgage as the units are sold by the developer to customers; the "partial release clause" in the construction mortgage will spell out the circumstances under which units will be released and the amount which must be applied toward retirement of the construction indebtedness for each unit sold.[2] The permanent mortgages placed on individu-

course, the association must follow its own rules and bylaws, and may also be subject to local statutes or ordinances; see Clydesdale, Inc. v. Wegener, 372 A.2d 1013 (D.C.1977).

17. See Shlopack, Condominium or Cooperative: Issues Facing the Developer, 55 Fla.B.J. 105 (1981); Comment, Community Living Condominium Style: Bed of Roses—Or Bed of Thorns?, 6 Univ.W.L.A.L.Rev. 121 (1974).

13.2

1. See Pfeiler, Condominium Financing: Some Legal Basics, 38 Legal Bull. 249, 255–62 (1972) [hereinafter cited as Pfeiler]. Like most subdivision lenders, the condominium construction lender will usually require that a "take-out" or permanent

loan commitment be obtained from another lender (or the permanent loan department of the same institution) before approving the construction loan. See Fegan, Condominium Financing, 48 St.John's L.Rev. 799 (1974) [hereinafter cited as Fegan].

2. A common provision requires "presales" (executed contracts of sale to customers) on some fixed percentage of the units (say, 35% to 75%) before the construction lender will release the lien on any of the units. See Vishny, Financing the Condominium, 1970 Ill.L.F. 181 (1970). Similarly, the permanent lender may refuse to disburse funds until a specified percentage of the units have been presold; Fegan, supra note 1. The FNMA and

al units by their purchasers are usually arranged by the developer through a single lender, which may or may not be the mortgagee on the construction loan.[3]

In the early years of American condominium development, it was often difficult for a unit purchaser to obtain a long-term loan from any lender other than the one with whom the developer had arranged the original permanent financing, since institutions were generally reluctant to undertake an extensive review of the complex documents unless they were certain that they could place numerous loans as a result.[4] However, since 1978, both the Federal National Mortgage Association (FNMA) and the Federal Home Loan Mortgage Corporation (FHLMC) have greatly simplified and streamlined their requirements for condominium loan purchases.[5] Once a project has been approved by these agencies, many lenders are usually willing to make loans on individual units in that project, since a secondary market for them is assured. Thus, the FNMA/FHLMC guidelines have become a *de facto* standard for permanent loans on condominium units.

Cooperatives are also financed with construction mortgages, but there are generally no individual loans to those who purchase the units when construction is completed.[6] Instead, the construction loan may simply be converted to a permanent loan by the mortgagee—which means that it will begin to draw regular (usually monthly) payments of amortization and interest. At that point the construction loan may also be sold by the original mortgagee to another investor, particularly if the construction lender is a type of institution that prefers to avoid long-term mortgages. Alternatively, the cooperative corporation may obtain a new blanket loan from a permanent lender and use the proceeds to discharge the construction loan. In either event, the permanent mortgage on a cooperative project is a blanket mortgage

---

FHLMC guidelines generally require 51% to 75% presales; see note 5 infra.

In imposing such requirements, lenders are concerned that they not be committed to financing the project as a condominium until they have substantial evidence of consumer demand; if the demand does not materialize, they may insist that the building be converted to rental use.

3. As an alternative to financing unit sales with new permanent mortgages, it is theoretically possible for the construction lender to take a separate mortgage on each unit, and to convert those mortgages to permanent status by loan assumptions as the units are sold to customers. This procedure is fairly common in some areas of the nation with subdivision development, but is not widely used with condominiums. It arguably violates § 14 of the FHA Model Act, which provides: "At the time of the first conveyance of each apartment, every mortgage and other lien affecting such

apartment * * * shall be paid and satisfied of record * * *." There is no policy reason to prohibit assumptions of construction loans by unit purchasers, and the Model Act should not be so construed.

4. See Gose, Strum & Zinman, Real Estate Financing Techniques: What Now?, 9 Real Prop., Prob. & Tr.J. 617, 634 (1974). This lack of support from other institutions made it difficult for the original permanent lender to diversify its portfolio by declining to make resale loans as the units turned over later.

5. See FHMLC Sellers Guide § 3.207; FNMA Lending Guide ch. 3. See generally Rosenthal, Condominium and P.U.D. Projects: Steps to Approval, Mortgage Banker, May 1984, at 57.

6. Berger, Condominium: Shelter on a Statutory Foundation, 63 Colum.L.Rev. 987 (1963).

covering the entire property. Unit purchasers make down payments equal to the difference between the unit's market sales value and its pro-rata share of the blanket mortgage; in effect, they assume their shares of the mortgage.

The subsequent resale of an individual unit by one occupant to another also involves different treatment in condominiums than in cooperatives. In a condominium unit sale the existing mortgage may be assumed, taken subject to, or paid off by the unit purchaser with the proceeds of a new loan he has arranged, just as in the sale of a detached house. By contrast, the sale of a cooperative unit amounts to an implicit "assumption" by the purchaser of that unit's pro rata share of the blanket mortgage on the project. Hence the cash paid by the purchaser of a resale cooperative unit may represent three components: (1) the amortization of the blanket mortgage which has occurred since payments were commenced on it; (2) the original unit purchaser's down-payment; and (3) any increase in value which may have occurred since the project was completed due to inflation or to improvements.[7]

Obviously, the longer the project is occupied the higher the cash required by a resale purchaser is likely to be, and the greater the difficulty the seller can anticipate in finding a buyer with sufficient cash and a willingness to invest it in the unit. The seller may be willing to take a promissory note from the purchaser in lieu of some part of this cash, and may be able to secure such a note with an interest in some real or personal property belonging to the purchaser. But an installment sale by the unit owner may jeopardize the standing of the purchaser under I.R.C. section 216.[8]

---

7. Some cooperatives limit the resale price by bylaw to the original down payment made by the seller, and others allow him to recoup only his improvements, his share of the mortgage amortization achieved, and some cost-of-living adjustment factor. These projects are usually termed "limited equity" cooperatives. The FHA insists on such resale price limits on the cooperatives whose mortgages it insures under some programs. The New York Supreme Court upheld these limits in Katz v. Nostrand Gardens Cooperative, Inc., May 2, 1984, reported in BNA Hsg & Devel. Rptr 1145 (May 21, 1984). See FHA Model Form of Bylaws § 8(d), reproduced in J. Krasnoweicki, Housing and Urban Development 317, 323 (1969); National Comm'n. on Urban Problems, Building the American City 137 (1968). Many cooperatives impose no restrictions on resale prices at all.

8. I.R.C. § 216(b)(2) defines a "tenant-shareholder" as one "whose stock is fully paid-up in an amount" reasonably related to the unit's share of the corporation's equity in the project. The applicable regulation,

Treas.Reg. § 1.216–1(e), appears to say that this relationship is to be determined "as of the date of the original issuance of the stock". Arguably, an installment sale would qualify if the purchaser made a cash payment equal to the unit's share of the original equity, but this is not clear. Alternatively, the purchaser might structure the transaction so as to "fully pay" for the *stock* with cash, but to pay some additional amount, by way of a promissory note, for the assignment of the *proprietary lease*. The difficulty with this argument is that the stock and lease are invariably required by their own terms or the applicable corporate charter or bylaws to be held by the same person. In sum, whether any installment sale can qualify under § 216 is problematic. This is unfortunate, since there seems to be no policy reason whatever to make the tax benefits of § 216 hinge on an all-cash sale. See Miller, Tax Problems of the Housing Cooperative Under the 80% Income Rule, 18 Prac.Lawyer 81 (No. 4, Apr.1972); Jacobs & Kurfist, Cooperative Apartment Living and Loving—Part I, 7 J.Real Est.Tax. 307 (1980).

The alternative, of course, is institutional financing for the resale purchaser. For a number of reasons, chiefly relating to questions about their statutory authority to do so, institutional lenders were traditionally reluctant to make loans on individual cooperative apartments. Starting with the New York legislation in 1971, a number of states have clarified that authority, and such loans are now widely available.[9]

Whether the financing is provided by a financial institution or the seller of the unit, the creditor will normally desire a security interest in the unit. The usual approach involves a pledge of the proprietary lease and the stock—a transaction analogous to a mortgage on real estate. Since the blanket mortgage on the project cannot be disturbed, any security interest in an individual unit is economically analogous to a second mortgage. However, the legal effect of such a pledge is still uncertain on several points.[10]

It is quite possible that the corporation might decide to refinance the original blanket mortgage on the project; this might be done because the original mortgage is of the balloon type and has reached maturity,[11] because lower interest rates have become available, or because additional cash is needed for repairs or improvements. This last objective might also be achieved by the placement of a second blanket mortgage on the property without disturbing the first. It is apparent that either refinancing or additional financing can result in higher monthly assessments on the members than they anticipated when they joined the cooperative. If an appropriate vote of the directors or members is forthcoming, the added assessments will be imposed on all members, whether they agree with the decision or not.[12]

Since an installment purchaser is arguably not a "tenant-shareholder" it is entirely conceivable that a single installment sale could so reduce the total income from tenant-shareholders that the cooperative would cease to qualify under the 80% test of § 216.

9. See Goldstein, Institutional Purchase Money Financing of Cooperative Apartments, 46 St.Johns L.Rev. 632 (1972); § 13.6, infra.

10. See § 13.6, infra; P. Rohan & M. Reskin, Cooperative Housing Law & Practice § 5A.08[3] (1984).

11. While most buildings newly constructed for cooperative use are financed with fully-amortized mortgages, it is not unusual to find a balloon mortgage on a building which is converted from ordinary rental to co-op use. Indeed, if the interest rate on the existing mortgage is significantly below current rates at the time of conversion, it would be foolish to refinance at the time of conversion notwithstanding the balloon feature of the old loan. See Offering Statement, 72–84 Barrow Street,

reprinted in 2A P. Rohan & M. Reskin, Cooperative Housing Law and Practice, at 245, 288 app. (1975).

12. For example, the Standard Form Cooperative Bylaws published by the New York Attorney General provide, at Art. III, sec. 7:

The Board of Directors shall have discretionary power to * * * determine the cash requirements of the Corporation to be paid as aforesaid by the shareholder-tenants under their respective proprietary leases. Every such determination by the Board of Directors shall be final and conclusive as to all shareholder-tenants * * *.

See P. Rohan & M. Reskin, Cooperative Housing Law and Practice § 24.67 app. (1975). Similar language is found in most proprietary leases. The decision-making power of the Board is generally very broad, and could even extend to a resolution to sell the project and distribute the proceeds to the members. See Anderson, Cooperative Apartments in Florida: A Legal Analysis, 12 U.Miami L.Rev. 13, 35 (1957).

Thus, each member's financial future lies to some extent in the hands of his neighbors, a situation which some might think uncomfortable, and which is largely avoided by the condominium form of ownership.[13]

One should not assume that permanent financing is always essential to the sale of either condominiums or cooperatives. Especially in retirement developments, all-cash purchases are quite common, since many buyers have just sold larger detached houses, often at substantial gains. Retirees usually wish to reinvest these funds and find the purchase of a condominium or cooperative unit a convenient way of doing so. In addition, some costly cooperatives operate under bylaws which require apartment purchasers to invest substantial cash, perhaps 30% to 50%, and sometimes as much as 100%.

 WESTLAW REFERENCES

condominium /p financ!

"security interest" /p condominium

tenant shareholder /p condominium cooperative

§ 13.3   Construction Financing of Condominiums

Although the financing of condominium construction is much like subdivision financing, there are important differences.[1] The documentation of a condominium project is much more complex, its marketability more speculative (at least, from the perspective of many institutional lenders), and the risk of loss it presents in the event of failure correspondingly greater.

Every new condominium project begins with site selection and acquisition. Developers commonly use their own capital to pay the cost of necessary land options. Before applications for institutional financing can be made, however, other costs must be incurred; surveys, engineering and market studies, and architects' fees, for example. These may be financed by use of the developer's cash or the contributions of his or her business associates, or through unsecured debt. In some cases these expenses are reimbursed out of the first draw of funds on the construction loan.

Upon exercise of the land option, the developer may be expected to pay the full cash price of the land to the seller. Often, however, the seller can be persuaded to sell on an installment basis and to accept a

---

13. But not completely. Even in a condominium, it is possible for the owners' association to levy larger-than-expected assessments to cover extravagant improvements to the recreational facilities or other common areas. Since title to common areas is held by the unit owners in tenancy in common, the association cannot mortgage them. Nonetheless, the assessments themselves are liens on the units, whether particular owners approve of the expendi-

tures or not. In some cases, condominium bylaws may place an upper limit on assessment amounts.

§ 13.3

1. Good general discussions of condominium construction financing include K. Romney, Condominium Development Guide ch. 7 (1974); Fegan, supra § 13.2 n. 1; Pfeiler, supra § 13.2 n. 1.

minimal initial cash payment. This installment indebtedness will usually be secured by a mortgage, and it will be necessary for the seller to subordinate his lien to that of the construction loan,[2] since virtually all construction lenders, as a matter of policy or the requirements of their governmental regulatory agencies, insist on first priority for the construction mortgage. Unless it is to be paid off from the proceeds of the construction loan, the land seller's subordinated mortgage (like the construction mortgage) must contain a partial release clause enabling the sale of individual units free of the lien.

When the land has been optioned and the necessary background studies completed, the developer is ready to apply for a construction loan. This submission is usually more comprehensive than would be expected in a detached-house subdivision, and the developer may seek the assistance of a mortgage loan broker in preparing and presenting it to prospective construction lenders. Prospective lenders will be particularly interested in the developer's own financial position, prior condominium experience, and reputation; they will also analyze the market demand information, architectural and engineering work, and general demographic and locational data submitted by the developer. In many cases the construction lender will make no commitment until permanent financing has been arranged for the sales of units; hence, the developer will make a similar submission of information to prospective permanent lenders, who are generally concerned with the same factors. The permanent financing commitment is not only a prerequisite to construction financing in many cases, but comprises a powerful marketing tool as well, especially if it ties the permanent lender to a fixed interest rate in a rising interest market.

A project does not become a condominium until some basic document—usually termed a master deed, declaration, or plan of unit ownership—is executed by the owners of the real estate and filed for record. This master deed describes the project, the individual units, and the common areas; it assigns weights to each unit for voting and assessment purposes; it provides for a lien on the units to secure the assessments; and it may contain such covenants as a right of first refusal upon resale by a unit owner.[3] The master deed may be filed whenever the owners desire, but in many cases the construction lender will insist that filing be delayed until some fixed percentage of the units have been "presold"—that is, until prospective unit purchasers have paid earnest money deposits and signed purchase agreements on them. On the other hand, no conveyances by deed of units can occur until the

---

2. Subordination by vendors is discussed in Note, Purchase Money Subordination Agreements in California: An Analysis of Conditional Subordination, 45 S.Cal. L.Rev. 1109 (1972); see § 12.9, supra.

3. Some writers have questioned whether such a clause may constitute an unreasonable restraint on alienation or may violate the Rule Against Perpetuities. Neither result seems justifiable or probable. See 1 (pt. 2) P. Rohan & M. Reskin, Condominium Law and Practice § 10.03 (1976). The FHA approved form of master deed does not contain a right of first refusal.

master deed has been filed.[4] Given these constraints, the filing usually occurs sometime towards the end of the construction period.

Construction loan mortgages on condominium projects can be insured by the Federal Housing Administration (FHA) under section 234(d) of the National Housing Act.[5] This insurance coverage, which is not generally available on construction loans in detached-house subdivisions, is not particularly attractive to most developers. The principal amount of the loan may be as high as 90% of the "replacement cost" of the project,[6] in substance, this means the actual cost of land and improvements.[7] By contrast, conventional construction loans are rarely made for more that 75% or 80% of value, but "value" as calculated by the conventional lender may be as high as the total retail sale price of the units, and will generally exceed the project's cost by a substantial margin.[8] Thus, conventional construction financing may actually be for as much or more money than FHA-insured financing. The only other significant advantage of an FHA-insured construction mortgage is that the developer is assured that FHA mortgage insurance will also be available immediately on the permanent loans on individual units as they are sold.[9]

Unfortunately FHA-insured construction loans have numerous disadvantages. FHA regulations impose dollar limits on the mortgage amount per unit, and in many areas effectively eliminate luxury or even high-middle-income projects.[10] The developer must enter into a regulatory agreement with FHA which may significantly limit his discretion in managing the construction and marketing of the project.[11] FHA mortgage insurance premiums must be paid in addition to interest, fees, and discounts charged by the lending institution. Moreover, FHA processing of multifamily mortgage insurance applications has the reputation of being slow and cumbersome, and FHA minimum property standards with respect to some construction features may appear excessive to some developers. In light of these problems, it is not surprising that there has been relatively little construction lending under the section 234 program.

Developers of condominium projects sometimes do not complete construction. Failure to do so may result from poor planning and management of the construction work, inadequate budgeting, unanticipated increases in costs, weather problems, strikes, or weak market

---

4. See 24 CFR 234.26(d)(1) (F.H.A.-insured condominium mortgages).

5. 12 U.S.C. § 1715. Applicable regulations are found at 24 CFR 234.1ff.

6. 12 U.S.C.A. § 1715y(e)(2).

7. 24 CFR 234.505(h).

8. See K. Romney, Condominium Development Guide § 7.04 (1974).

9. Loans on individual units in a project not previously covered by an FHA blanket mortgage are insurable by FHA only if the project contains eleven or fewer units, or has been completed for more than one year. See National Housing Act § 234(c), 12 U.S.C.A. § 1715y(c); 24 C.F.R. 234.26(a).

10. The limits have been increased on several occasions. At this writing the basic limit is $67,500. In high-cost areas this is adjusted upward, typically to $74,900. Hawaii has the highest limit, $101,250. See 24 C.F.R. 234, App. A.

11. 24 CFR 234.26(f).

acceptance of the project. Abandonment will invariably constitute a default under the terms of the construction loan mortgage, and the lender may elect to foreclose. In this setting there are usually unpaid workmen, subcontractors, or suppliers who are entitled to file mechanics' liens. In addition, the prospective purchasers of units in the project will have signed contracts of sale and made down payments or earnest money deposits with the developer; some such contracts may have been executed before construction began, and some afterward. These three groups, the construction lender, mechanics' lienors, and vendees often find themselves adverse to one another in respect to rights in the real estate.

Such problems are not unique to condominium developments; they also occur with speculative subdivisions and other types of construction. We discuss them here because condominiums have frequently been defaulted upon during construction in recent years, and because condominium statutes sometimes contain provisions which bear on these disputes. The problem of priorities as between construction lenders and mechanics' lien claimants has been discussed earlier in this book.[12] We focus here on the rights of purchase contract vendees vis-à-vis the construction lender and mechanics' lien claimants.

Priority as Between Construction Lender and Vendees

A difficult conflict may arise with respect to earnest money deposits or down payments (the terms are used here synonymously) collected from intended unit vendees before and during the construction period. If these funds, which may be very substantial, are available for current use by the developer, they may help him solve serious cash shortage problems, but at high risk to the vendees.[13] The FHA [14] and the statutes of some states [15] require that such deposits be escrowed pending completion and transfer of title of the individual units, making them inaccessible to the developer. Such provisions are highly desirable. Where this is not the law, a problem arises in situations in which the developer has invaded the deposits and subsequently abandons the project prior to completion; the unit purchasers may well be left with only their personal rights of action against the developer (who is often insolvent). Even if the construction lender forecloses and completes

12. See §§ 12.4, 12.7, & 12.9 supra.

13. See Damian, Condominium Development: Representing the Developer, in Condominium Development 35, 61 (Prac. Law Inst.1971).

14. See FHA Subscription and Purchase Agreement Form No. 3279, cl. 1, reprinted in 1 P. Rohan & M. Reskin, Condominium Law and Practice § 9.04[6] (1976).

15. See, e.g., U.C.A. § 4–110; Va.Code § 55–79.95 (Supp.1977); Fla.Stat.Ann. § 718.202 (Supp.1977) (permitting the de-

veloper to use the money to defray construction costs if the contract of sale so provides). See Note, Recent Innovations in State Condominium Legislation, 48 St. John's L.Rev. 994, 999 (1974); Note, Florida Condominiums—Developer Abuses and Security Law Implications Create a Need For a State Regulatory Agency, 25 U.Fla.L. Rev. 350, 358 (1973). The better approach is to prohibit by statute all developer use of deposit funds; the significance of contract language permitting the developer's use of deposits is unlikely to be understood by lay purchasers.

construction, the original unit subscribers may have neither the right to complete their purchases by paying the remainder of the original contract price, nor the right to a return of their deposits.

This issue may be characterized as one of priority as between the purchase contracts and the construction mortgage. The contract vendee has, under the law of most states, both a right to specific performance and an equitable lien on the realty to secure the return of his down payment if the vendor fails to complete the contract.[16] The difficulty is that enforceability of these rights is constrained in two respects: first, they may be subordinate to pre-existing liens, such as the construction mortgage, if they arise after that mortgage is recorded; and second, they are not enforceable even against a subsequent mortgagee or purchaser who has no notice of the existence of the vendee's contract.[17] The latter constraint may not be a serious problem in most cases; seldom will a construction lender grant a loan without first asking about preconstruction sales activity, and the developer will ordinarily be eager to inform the lender of the contracts which have been signed.[18] The matter is more difficult if the purchase contract is signed after the construction mortgage has been recorded. In State Savings and Loan Association v. Kauaian Development Co.,[19] the Hawaii Supreme Court drew a distinction between subscription agreements entered into before and after the creation of the construction mortgage. Agreements executed after the mortgage were obviously subordinate to it, the court thought, apparently because of the constructive notice the public records imparted to vendees,[20] while those executed before the mortgage recordation had priority.[21] However, the court

---

16. Gribble v. Stearman & Kaplan, Inc., 249 Md. 289, 239 A.2d 573 (1968). See generally Cunningham, Stoebuck & Whitman, Property §§ 10.5, 10.8 (1984); Annot., 43 A.L.R.2d 1384 (1954).

17. Glynn v. Marquette, 152 Cal.App.3d 277, 199 Cal.Rptr. 306 (1984); Carson v. Isabl Apartments, Inc., 20 Wn.App. 293, 579 P.2d 1027 (1978) (specific performance); Hillblom v. Irancsits, 76 Ill.App.3d 306, 395 N.E.2d 119 (1979); National Indemnity Co. v. Banks, 376 F.2d 533 (5th Cir.1967); Mihranian, Inc. v. Padula, 134 N.J.Super. 557, 342 A.2d 523 (1975) affirmed 70 N.J. 252, 359 A.2d 473 (1976) (vendee's lien).

18. See Wayne Building & Loan Co. v. Yarborough, 11 Ohio St.2d 195, 228 N.E.2d 841 (1967); Palmer v. Crews Lumber Co., Inc., 510 P.2d 269 (Okla.1973). These cases suggest that it is sufficient that the subsequent lender knows a contract has been executed, whether or not he is aware of the terms of the contract, the vendee's identity, or the amount of any downpayment made.

19. 50 Hawaii 540, 445 P.2d 109 (1968).

20. The Hawaii Supreme Court revised this view of the case in State Savings & Loan Association v. Kauaian Development Co., 62 Haw. 188, 613 P.2d 1315 (1980). Since the construction mortgage stated that it was "subject to" the condominium declaration, the court held that the mortgage was subordinate to the equitable liens of the unit purchasers who signed their contracts *after* as well as before recordation of the construction mortgage. In effect, the "subject to" language was treated as a subordination of the mortgage to the contracts of sale.

See also Palmer v. Forrest, Mackey & Associates, 251 Ga. 304, 304 S.E.2d 704 (1983) (where construction mortgage is recorded before contract of sale is executed, the contract vendee is on constructive notice of the mortgage and is subordinate to it.)

21. See also Hinsdale Federal Savings & Loan Association v. Gary-Wheaton Bank, 100 Ill.App.3d 746, 56 Ill.Dec. 558, 427 N.E.2d 963 (1981), adopting a similar position, but granting only a vendee's lien and not specific performance against the observed that even prior subscription agreements could be made subordinate to the mortgage by express language of subordination, which could be placed in the purchase contract or in a separate document signed by the vendee. The court did not discuss the degree of specificity that would be necessary in such clauses, nor whether it would require that they be intelligible to the laymen signing them.

As a consequence of the *Kauaian* reasoning, most purchase agreements in use now probably contain subordination language.[22] A foreclosing construction lender would thus appear to be free to disregard the agreement and sell the unit to another purchaser and would have no obligation to return the deposit to the contract vendee.

However, the enforceability of such subordination clauses may be open to serious doubt. The purchaser will ordinarily be entirely unsophisticated, and is unlikely to have any concept of the significance of the clause. In addition, the clause will seldom contain details of the proposed construction financing to which the vendee is being asked to subordinate. By analogy to the cases involving so-called "automatic" subordination of purchase-money financing by land vendors to develop-

foreclosing construction lender. It is unclear why specific performance was denied. The contract was unrecorded, but the lender had actual knowledge of it. The court gave the vendees priority for all payments made before they acquired actual knowledge of the construction loan; evidently, it thought that mere recordation of the construction mortgage would not give the vendees constructive notice, once they had entered into the contract. To the same effect is Wayne Building & Loan Co. v. Yarborough, supra note 18. This conclusion is reasonable, since it would be entirely unrealistic to expect a vendee to examine the record title before making each payment under the contract; see Giorgi v. Pioneer Title Insurance Co., 85 Nev. 319, 454 P.2d 104 (1969); Cunningham, Stoebuck & Whitman, Property § 11.10 nn. 67–68 (1984).

See also Waldorff Insurance & Bonding Co. v. Eglin National Bank., 453 So.2d 1383 (Fla.App.1984) (lender is subordinate because it had constructive notice of vendee's rights from his possession of condominium unit at the time developer executed mortgage); Stahl v. Roulhac, 50 Md.App. 382, 438 A.2d 1366 (1982); Fikes v. First Federal Savings & Loan Association, 533 P.2d 251 (Alaska 1975); Tucson Federal Savings & Loan Association v. Sundell, 106 Ariz. 137, 472 P.2d 6 (1970). But see Nelson v. Great Northwest Federal Savings & Loan Association, 37 Wn.App. 316, 679 P.2d 953

(1984), in which the court awarded priority to a construction deed of trust which was made and recorded *after* the execution of the contract of sale of a condominium unit. Inexplicably, the court concluded that the contract conveyed to the purchasers no interest in the realty; thus, they were denied specific performance against the lender, which had acquired title to the project by foreclosure. The case seems egregiously wrong.

22. See, e.g., Olympic Towers Purchase Agreement, reprinted in 1A P. Rohan & M. Reskin, Condominium Law and Practice, 118.17 app. (1976):

The Purchaser agrees that all terms and provisions of this contract are and shall be subject and subordinate to the lien of any building loan mortgage heretofore or hereafter made and any advances heretofore or hereafter made thereon and any payments or expenses already made or incurred or which hereafter may be made or incurred, pursuant to the terms thereof, or incidental thereto, or to protect the security thereof, to the full extent thereof without the execution of any further legal documents by the Purchaser. This subordination shall apply whether such advances are voluntary or involuntary and whether made in accordance with the building loan schedule.

ers, it might well be argued that such subordinations by contract vendees are too vague or too unfair to enforce.[23]

Even a contract vendee who signed his contract after the construction mortgage was recorded, or who has executed a valid subordination clause, might nonetheless manage to persuade a court of his priority. If the developer's default is traceable in part to the failure of the construction lender to monitor and supervise the progress of the project as its documents gave it the right to do, or if the lender negligently permitted the developer to divert loan funds away from the project, the vendee might argue that such behavior breaches a duty to the vendee, and that the proper remedy for the lender's breach is a loss of priority for the construction loan.[24] Depending on the facts, an argument against the lender's priority may also be based on estoppel. If the lender has reviewed and approved the sales price schedule and the purchase agreement forms, has supplied the developer with criteria for qualifying prospective purchasers in respect to income, credit worthiness, and the like, and has mandated the pre-completion sale of some fixed number of units as a condition of the construction loan agreement, a court might well find the lender estopped by its extensive involvement in the vendor-vendee relationship to deny the priority of the vendee's lien.[25]

23. See Tucson Federal Savings & Loan Association v. Sundell, 106 Ariz. 137, 472 P.2d 6 (1970), refusing to enforce a rather ambiguous subordination language in a purchase contract; B.I.J. Corp. v. Larry W. Corp., 183 N.J.Super. 310, 443 A.2d 1096 (1982), construing a broad subordination clause in a purchase contract as ineffective to the extent that disbursements under the mortgage were made for purposes other than improvements to the property. See § 12.9 supra at notes 35–40.

24. See id.; § 12.10, supra, discussing various theories of lender liability. But see Pope Heating & Air Conditioning Co. v. Garrett-Bromfield Mortgage Co., 29 Colo. App. 169, 480 P.2d 602 (1971), holding a subordination agreement unconditional and binding despite diversion of construction loan funds; Forest Inc. v. Guaranty Mortgage Co., 534 S.W.2d 853 (Tenn.Ct. App.1975) (semble); See also Falls Lumber Co. v. Heman, 114 Ohio App. 262, 181 N.E.2d 713 (1961), in which a construction lender was held liable in tort to a contract vendee for its failure to disburse construction funds in accordance with the applicable statute, thereby permitting mechanics' liens to be filed against the property; cf. Gardner Plumbing, Inc. v. Cottrill, 44 Ohio St.2d 111, 338 N.E.2d 757 (1975).

25. See § 12.9 supra. Cf. Fikes v. First Federal Savings & Loan Association, 533 P.2d 251 (Alaska 1975), holding a construc-tion lender's lien limited to funds actually spent on construction and not diverted, as against the claim of a prior contract vendee of which the lender had knowledge; Tucson Federal Savings & Loan Association v. Sundell, 106 Ariz. 137, 472 P.2d 6 (1970) (semble) in which the court relied on the fact that the vendee had no knowledge of the construction mortgage. No cases have been found in which the estoppel argument has been raised by a junior vendee. The tendency of courts to protect contract vendees against the literal language of subordination clauses they have signed is illustrated by First Federal Savings & Loan Association v. Ott, 285 So.2d 695 (Fla.App.1973), in which the developer refinanced the original construction loan with the same lender; the court refused to enforce the subordination agreement in vendee's contract and she was permitted to take free of the refinanced mortgage. In Security National Bank v. Village Mall at Hillcrest, 85 Misc.2d 771, 382 N.Y.S.2d 882, 889 (1976), the Attorney General of New York argued that the construction lender's lien should be subordinated to the liens of contract vendees because the lender had (1) modified the construction loan agreement without recording the modification, (2) participated in a public offering of the condominium project without making the required disclosures to offerees under New York law, (3) participated in a violation of

An alternative approach for the vendee might be based on an analogy to the cases which have permitted subcontractors and materials suppliers to assert an equitable lien on any undisbursed portion of the construction loan funds if the usual mechanics' lien remedies are unavailing to them.[26] In equity, the contract vendee would seem to have as strong a moral claim to these funds as do those who have invested labor and materials, at least if construction has been completed without exhausting the construction loan account and the vendee's deposit has been used for construction purposes. Unfortunately, this argument may be ineffective in those jurisdictions which have codified the equitable lien concept without including contract vendees among its beneficiaries. New York, for example, has created a statutory trust consisting of the down payments of contract vendees. However, they may recover their funds after the developer's default only if they have not been used in improving the property; in addition, the usual classes of mechanics' lien claimants have first priority on the trust funds.[27] This approach seems entirely inadequate to protect the vendees, although it may be better than no protection at all.

As a matter of policy, it is entirely reasonable to impose on the construction lender a duty to return vendees' deposits in cases in which the lender had played an active role in approving or supervising the developer's marketing program. The lender is far better able than the vendee to investigate the developer's solvency, experience, and reliability, and to spread the risk of the developer's default. Moreover, any construction lender wishing to avoid this risk may easily do so merely by requiring that all deposits by vendees be placed in escrow. The law should not permit developers (and construction lenders) to rely upon vendees' down payments as a means of financing construction; doing so is an indicator that the developer is dangerously underfunded, and a lender who actively countenances such a procedure should be held accountable to the vendees for their loss.[28]

---

the statutory provisions allowing vendees' deposits to be used only for improvements, and (4) charged usurious interest rates. The court found that triable issues of fact were involved and denied summary judgment on the merits of these claims.

26. See Reitz, Construction Lenders' Liability to Contractors, Subcontractors, and Materialmen, 130 U.Pa.L.Rev. 416 (1981); § 12.6, supra.

27. New York—McKinney's Lien Law § 71–a. See Security National Bank v. Village Mall at Hillcrest, Inc., 85 Misc.2d 771, 382 N.Y.S.2d 883, 889 (1976); Glazer v. Alison Homes Corp., 62 Misc.2d 1017, 309 N.Y.S.2d 381 (1970). The latter case, though sound in policy, seems to go quite beyond the statutory language and permits contract vendees to assert a lien on funds which were wrongfully diverted by the de-

veloper from construction loan proceeds, although the opinion concedes that mechanics' lienors would have a superior claim to these funds.

28. In some respects the matter is similar to Connor v. Great Western Savings & Loan Association, 69 Cal.2d 850, 73 Cal. Rptr. 369, 447 P.2d 609 (1969), in which a construction lender was held liable to home purchasers for its failure to adequately supervise the construction of houses with serious structural defects. The case of diversion of vendees' downpayments seems an especially appealing one for application of the concept, since developers' marketing programs are so generally superintended by construction lenders, particularly in condominium projects. See § 12.11 supra.

Priority as Between Mechanics' Lien Claimants and Vendees

The rights of mechanics' lien claimants in condominium projects raise problems similar to, but more intricate than, those of claims made on subdivision lots. Even if the work was done or the materials supplied on only a single lot or unit, the matter is not simple. It is clear enough that if the vendee enters into his contract of purchase after the work has been completed and the lien filed of record, the lien will have priority and the vendee will take subject to it.[29] This means that if the developer (or his general contractor) are unavailable for recovery, as is all too common, the unit vendee will suffer the loss unless he is protected by an owner's policy of title insurance.

If the vendee acquires legal title by deed to the unit or lot after the work has been done and the lien has "attached",[30] but before the lien is filed of record, he may be entirely innocent of any actual knowledge of the lien's attachment. A few jurisdictions, mostly in the South, protect bona fide purchasers in this situation, granting them priority over the lien.[31] Most states, however, hold the vendee's interest subject to the lien, either on the ground that even BFP's are subject to mechanics' liens [32] or that the very fact of construction activity on the land imparts notice of the potential filing of liens, and thus negates BFP status.[33] Moreover, owner's title insurance coverage is unlikely to assist the purchaser on these facts; many policies expressly exclude coverage for unfiled liens.

Suppose the vendee's contract of purchase predates the attachment of the lien, even though the conveyance by deed occurs later. May he

29. United Accounts, Inc. v. Larson, 121 N.W.2d 628 (N.D.1963); Annot., 85 A.L.R. 927, 928 (1933).

30. The exact time at which priority attaches varies among jurisdictions. Many fix it as of the day the first work is done on the overall construction project, and others on the date the lien claimant first performed his work. Less popular rules attach the lien at the time the general contract or the claimant's contract is entered into or recorded, or when the notice of lien is filed of record. Under all of these rules except the last-mentioned, a lien may attach without any clear evidence of the claim appearing in the public records. The lien must usually be "perfected" by filing of record within some fixed period after the work is completed, and is then said to "relate back" to the attachment date. See R. Kratovil, Modern Mortgage Law and Practice § 214 (1972); 4 American Law of Property § 16.106F (A. J. Casner ed. 1952). See generally § 12.4, supra.

31. See, e.g., Ky.Rev.Stat. 376.010; Walker v. Valley Plumbing Co., 370 S.W.2d 136 (Ky.1963); First State Bank v. Stacey,

37 Tenn.App. 223, 261 S.W.2d 245 (1953); Wood v. Barnes, 420 S.W.2d 425 (Tex.Ct. App.1967); Comfortcraft Heating, Inc. v. Salamone, 19 App.Div. 760, 241 N.Y.S.2d 581 (1963); Bryant v. Ellenburg, 106 Ga. 510, 127 S.E.2d 468 (1962).

32. Schrader Iron Works, Inc. v. Lee, 26 Cal.App.3d 621, 103 Cal.Rptr. 107 (1972); State Savings & Loan Association v. Kauai-an Devel. Co., 50 Hawaii 540, 445 P.2d 109, 123 (1968); Metropolitan Water Co. v. Hild, 415 P.2d 970 (Okl.1966). See generally G. Thompson, Real Property § 5218 n. 69 (1957).

33. The knowledge of work in progress may be actual or constructive. See Guaranty Pest Control, Inc. v. Commercial Investment & Development Corp., 288 Ala. 604, 264 So.2d 163 (1972); Capital Bank & Trust Co. v. Broussard Paint & Wallpaper Co., 198 So.2d 204 (La.App.1967); Clark Certified Concrete Co. v. Lindberg, 216 Md. 576, 141 A.2d 685 (1958); J. R. Meade Co. v. Forward Construction Co., 526 S.W.2d 21 (Mo.App.1975); H. Tiffany, Real Property § 1578 (1939); Annot., 50 A.L.R.3d 944 (1973).

argue that his vendee's lien created by execution of the contract has chronological, and thus legal, priority over the mechanics' liens? In Wayne Building & Loan Co. v. Yarborough,[34] the Ohio Supreme Court so held, although the vendee was given priority only to the extent of down payments made before the liens attached at the commencement of the work; the vendee had no priority as to further payments he made on the contract after work began. The decision appears to place no emphasis on whether the lien claimants had notice of the executed contract of purchase at the time they began their work, but such notice would presumably strengthen the vendee's position. Thus, in one Texas case the lien claimants were permitted priority for work done up to the time they learned of the executed contract, but not thereafter.[35] However, the existence of the purchase contract has been fatal to the vendee in several decisions in which courts have seen it as clearly establishing the vendee's position as an equitable "owner", and thus a member of the class of persons whose interests were subject to mechanic's liens.[36]

As these cases suggest, the relationship of vendees' and lien claimants' rights is uncertain and confused, although the lienors have usually prevailed. The courts have vacillated between the traditional desire to protect good faith purchasers and to enhance the reliability of the public records, on the one hand, and the wish to construe the lien statutes liberally to aid lien claimants, on the other. One major defect in the system lies in its failure to require potential lien claimants to record some public notice as a condition of *attachment* (rather than mere perfection) of the lien. But even a change in the law in this respect would not fully protect purchasers, since they rarely examine the public records or obtain title reports before signing purchase agreements and making deposits. In essence, the contest is between two claimants neither of whom has taken any formal step to give the world notice of his lien, and each of whom is at least dimly aware of the other's potential existence. On these facts it would be arbitrary to make priorities turn on which interest "attached" first, as by lien claimant's first work or the vendee's execution of a contract. Given the almost universal lack of sophisticated residential unit buyers, and the alternative methods open to lien claimants, who are generally well aware of the risks, to safeguard their interests,[37] the preferable ap-

34. 11 Ohio St.2d 195, 228 N.E.2d 841, 849–50 (1967).

35. Stone v. Pitts, 389 S.W.2d 601 (Tex. Civ.App.1965). The lienor's knowledge of the vendee's interest may also be used to compel him to include the vendee as an "owner" in the notice of lien, and failure to do so may exculpate the vendee. See F. M. Sibley Lumber Co. v. Gottesman, 314 Mich. 60, 22 N.W.2d 72 (1946); cf. Oklahoma Hardware Co. v. Townsend, 494 P.2d 326 (Okl.1972). See Annot., 48 A.L.R.3d 153 (1973).

36. Home Carpet, Inc. v. Bob Antrim Homes, Inc., 210 N.W.2d 652 (Iowa 1973); Toler v. Satterthwaite, 200 Kan. 103, 434 P.2d 814 (1967).

37. Subcontractors and materialmen may verify the developer's credit standing, may contact the construction lender to determine whether the project is on schedule and funds available, may insist on immediate payment in cash, or may confine their business activities to developers who have payment bonds. None of these steps may be completely effective or feasible, but they proach to this dilemma (short of comprehensive legislative reform) is to recognize a prior vendee's lien for all deposits paid prior to the time the purchaser learns not merely that work has been done on the land, but that delinquent payments are owed to potential lien claimants.

Assuming that a condominium unit purchaser is subject to mechanics' liens, other questions arise. If the work was done or the materials supplied for several units, the common areas, or the entire project, what interests are subjected to the lien? Most of the courts which have dealt with the issue have held that the common areas as such are not lienable.[38] Often this result follows from express language in the condominium statutes involved; the common areas have no independent legal existence apart from the units to which they are appurtenant.[39] Hence a lien claimant who has performed work only on common areas would be expected to file the lien on the individual units—presumably all of them—whose owners had rights in the common facilities in question. A further problem for the lien claimant is raised if some of the units have been conveyed by the developer at the time he hires the lien claimant-to-be. The vendees of these units might argue that they cannot be held subject to the lien because they neither contracted for nor consented to the work done.[40] It is likely, however, that they would be held to have consented, or be estopped from denying their consent, if the work in question benefitted common areas in which they had rights and which they expected to use.

If work is performed on numerous units, the common areas, or the project as a whole, is a lien claimant required to apportion the lien among all of the affected units and satisfy it from each of them only on a pro rata basis? If the law does not compel this result, the claimant obviously has power to create great injustice among unit owners by "picking on" some while favoring others. This issue has risen frequently in the subdivision context, and the courts have almost uniformly

place the potential lien claimant in a considerably stronger position than contract vendees.

38. See, e.g., W. H. Dail Plumbing, Inc. v. Roger Baker & Associates, Inc., 64 N.C. App. 682, 308 S.E.2d 452 (1983), review denied, 310 N.C. 152, 311 S.E.2d 296 (1984); Rainier Pacific Supply, Inc. v. Gray, 30 Wn.App. 340, 633 P.2d 1355 (1981); Country Village Heights Condominium v. Mario Bonito Inc., 79 Misc.2d 1088, 363 N.Y.S.2d 501 (1975); Stevens Construction Co. v. Draper Hall, Inc., 73 Wis.2d 104, 242 N.W.2d 893 (1976). But see Plateau Supply Co. v. Bison Meadows Corp., 31 Colo. App. 205, 500 P.2d 162 (1972); E. D. McGillicuddy Construction Co. v. Knoll Recreation Association, 31 Cal.App.3d 891, 107 Cal.Rptr. 901 (1973). The *Rainier Pacific* and *Stevens* cases conclude that liens on the common areas are impermissible even though the lien claimants commenced

their work before the condominium declaration was recorded, and thus at a time when the building was not subject to the condominium statute.

39. FHA Model Act § 9(a). The UCA is apparently to the same effect; UCA § 3–117(c) (1980). See A. Ferber & K. Stecher, Law of Condominium § 117 (1967).

40. See, e.g., Romito Brothers Electric Construction Co. v. Frank A. Flannery, Inc., 40 Ohio St.2d 79, 320 N.E.2d 294 (1974). The New York statute permits the filing of a lien on an individual unit only if the work was requested by the owner of the unit or was for emergency repairs. See Country Village Heights Condominium v. Mario Bonito, Inc., 79 Misc.2d 1088, 363 N.Y.S.2d 501 (1975). See FHA Model Act § 9(b), imputing consent of all unit owners to any work performed on the common area if authorized by the association.

held that, if the lien is susceptible of reasonable apportionment, then apportionment is required.[41] In a condominium, apportionment would seldom be difficult to calculate, since the units are even more likely to be of similar value and have similar construction than subdivision houses. Moreover, many condominium statutes expressly provide that a lien on more than one unit can be satisfied and discharged by pro rata payment by each unit owner.[42] One court has interpreted such language as applicable only when the lien is incurred by one or more individual unit owners, rather than by a developer,[43] but this construction seems strained and inequitable. Whatever the source of the lien, it should be dischargable as to any unit when its owner pays his share; this seems to be the prevalent view.[44]

Pro rata apportionment of the liens among all units does not necessarily mean that all unit owners will bear equal burdens. In Hostetter v. Inland Development Corp.,[45] some units had been sold by the developer, while others remained unsold, at the time the mechanics' liens were foreclosed. The developer had violated the condominium statute by failing to place the purchasers' deposits in escrow and by failing to discharge all liens when selling the units. Hence, the court dictated an equitable foreclosure scheme, analogous to marshalling,[46] under which the units remaining in the developer's hands would be foreclosed before resort could be had to the units sold to consumers.

The creation of a condominium regime often causes confusion among those who wish to file notices of mechanics' liens. It is usually held that a notice of lien which describes the "property" by means of the original description of the land on which the condominium was

41. Apportionment of mechanics' liens was required in Weaver v. Harland, 176 Va. 224, 10 S.E.2d 547 (1940). See also West's Ann.Cal.Civ.Code § 3130; Del.Code tit. 25, § 2713.

42. FHA Model Act, § 9(b); UCA § 3–117(c); A. Ferber & K. Stecher, Law of Condominium § 117 (1967); In re Zachman Homes, 47 B.R. 496, 518 (Bkrtcy.D. Minn.1984) (applying Minn. law).

43. E. D. McGillicuddy Construction Co. v. Knoll Recreation Associates, 31 Cal.App. 3d 891, 107 Cal.Rptr. 901 (1973); the court did not explain why allocation of the lien on a pro rated basis among unit owners was impractical. The opinion seemed to rely upon the fact that all purchasers had owner's title insurance coverage—a consideration which seems both irrelevant and improper.

44. W. H. Dail Plumbing, Inc. v. Roger Baker & Associates Inc., 64 N.C.App. 682, 308 S.E.2d 452 (1983), review denied 310 N.C. 152, 311 S.E.2d 296 (1984); Michael Weller, Inc. v. Aetna Casualty & Surety

Co., 126 Ariz. 323, 614 P.2d 865 (App.1980); Rainier Pacific Supply, Inc. v. Gray, 30 Wn.App. 340, 633 P.2d 1355 (1981); Hostetter v. Inland Development Corp., 172 Mont. 167, 561 P.2d 1323 (1977); United Masonry, Inc. v. Jefferson Mews, Inc., 218 Va. 360, 237 S.E.2d 171 (1977). The last case is particularly interesting, as only one-half of the 264 units had actually been constructed. The court ordered apportionment of the lien for work done on the residential structure among only the 132 units built, but apportioned the lien for work on the common-element clubhouse among all 264 units. See also Southern Colonial Mortgage Co. v. Medeiros, 347 So.2d 736 (Fla. App.1977). Plateau Supply Corp. v. Bison Meadows Corp., supra note 38, is contra, but is based on the preexisting interpretation by the Colorado courts of that mechanics' lien statute as allowing arbitrary apportionment of the lien as among the parcels covered by it.

45. 172 Mont. 167, 561 P.2d 1323 (1977).

46. See § 10.10 supra.

built is ineffective.[47] Similarly, a notice of lien describing the common areas is invalid, as discussed above. The units themselves must be identified in the notice. In Rainier Pacific Supply, Inc. v. Gray,[48] the lienors had commenced their work before the condominium declaration was filed. After it was recorded, they filed notices of lien which contained only the legal description of the land on which the condominium was located. In light of the Washington statute which made mechanics' liens relate back to the date the lienor commenced work, the court held the notices valid; the recording of the declaration, it found, automatically converted the blanket liens into proportional liens on the individual units, with no refiling necessary.

Priority as Between Mechanics' Lien Claimants and the Owners Association's Assessment Lien

There are several situations in which a mechanics lien may compete in priority with the association's lien for unpaid assessments. This may occur when the developer conveys units without paying all contractors, workers, and suppliers of materials; it may also occur when the association hires work done on the common areas or an individual unit owner contracts for work on her unit.

This conflict is usually resolved by reference to the jurisdiction's condominium statute. Many of the statutes, following the FHA Model Act, provide that the assessment lien is superior to all other liens except first mortgages on the units, property taxes, and governmental assessments.[49] This would appear to make mechanics' liens subordinate to the association.[50] In a few states, statutes expressly grant priority to mechanics' liens.[51]

47. See Papa v. Greenwich Green, Inc., 177 Conn. 295, 416 A.2d 1196 (1979); cases cited note 44 supra.

48. 30 Wn.App. 340, 633 P.2d 1355 (1981). A similar result was reached in Southern Colonial Mortgage Co. v. Medeiros, 347 So.2d 736 (Fla.App.1977).

49. FHA Model Act § 9(b); A. Ferber & K. Stecher, Law of Condominium § 117 (1967). See Washington Federal Savings & Loan Association v. Schneider, 95 Misc.2d 924, 408 N.Y.S.2d 588 (1978) (under such a statute, association's lien is superior to second mortgage which was recorded before the association's notice of lien.) The UCA has a similar provision, but also gives priority to liens and encumbrances recorded before the condominium declaration; however, it grants the association's lien priority for the past six months of assessments, even as against a first mortgage. UCA § 3–116 (1980).

50. But see Security National Bank v. Village Mall at Hillcrest, 85 Misc.2d 771, 382 N.Y.S. 882, 896 (1976), appearing to

favor the mechanics' lien claimants under such a statute, on the ground that the association's lien does not come into existence and acquire a priority date until some notice or action to enforce it is filed. This decision seems to contradict the statute. Cf. New York—McKinney's Real Prop. Law § 339–z.

The UCA expressly declares that its provisions on the priority of the assessment lien do not apply against mechanics' liens; on this point it is simply silent. UCA § 3–116(b). However, the UCA provides in general that the "association has a lien" for assessments, that recordation of the declaration is record notice and perfection of the lien, and that no further recordation of a claim of lien for assessments is required. UCA § 3.116(a), (c). From these premises, it may be reasoned that the lien's priority as against a mechanics' lien will be determined merely by the chronological order of recordation of the declara-

51. See note 51 on page 956.

The New York statute expands the rights of mechanics' lien claimants in another fashion as well, granting them, for work done on common areas, a lien on funds collected by the owner's association.[52] This remedy was apparently thought necessary because of the impermissibility of liening the common areas directly, the difficulty of proving that unit owners requested the work done on common areas, and the cumbersomeness of apportionment of the lien among a large number of individual units. From the lienor's viewpoint this remedy is probably superior to merely filing an action to collect the debt owed. In cases in which the association itself requested the work done the procedure is reasonable, but if the work was done at the developer's request, it is difficult to see the fairness of imposing on the association the duty of repaying it.

Special Declarant Rights and Obligations in Foreclosure

When a construction lender forecloses on a condominium project in which not all units have been sold, the foreclosure sale purchaser (typically the lender itself) obviously steps into the developer's shoes as a real property owner of the unsold units. However, questions may arise concerning the extent to which the developer's *other* rights and duties, going beyond mere real estate ownership, are "inherited" by the foreclosing lender.

With respect to the developer's rights, those of greatest interest relate to the marketing program. For example, the developer, as "declarant" of the condominium, may have reserved the right to maintain a sales office and to offer prospective purchasers limited use of the common recreation facilities.[53] He may also have arranged the voting rights in the owners' association so as to give him control for part or all of the marketing period.[54] Will such rights as these pass to the foreclosing lender?

Arguments based on covenants running with the land, or on the specific language of the construction loan mortgage, might be made to support the lender's claim to these rights. The Uniform Condominium Act clarifies the issue, stating that at the lender's request, it

> "succeeds to all special declarant rights related to that real estate held by that declarant, or only to any rights reserved in the declaration ∗ ∗ ∗ and held by that declarant to maintain models, sales offices and signs. The judgment or instrument conveying title shall provide for transfer of only the special declarant rights requested." [55]

tion and the "relation back" date of the mechanics' lien (typically the date work was commenced; see note 30 supra.)

51. See Idaho Code § 55–1518; N.C. Gen.Stat. § 47A–22(a); Wis.Stat.Ann. 703.23(1)(a).

52. New York—McKinney's Real Prop. Law § 339–*l*(2).

53. Such rights are permitted under UCA § 2–115.

54. On declarant control of the executive board, see UCA § 3–103(d).

55. UCA § 3–104(c).

Thus it appears that under the UCA the lender can pick and choose the rights which will pass to it.[56]

The other side of the coin is the lender's liability. There is obviously a possibility that, if the lender has been sufficiently intimately involved in the development of the project, it will be liable for construction defects or other failures by the developer under the doctrine of Connor v. Great Western Savings and Loan Association.[57] But this sort of involvement is extremely rare.[58] In its absence, courts are likely to try to achieve some sort of rough parity between the extent of the lender's assumption of benefits from the original declarant and the corresponding liabilities to be imposed on the lender.

There is little court-developed law in this area yet,[59] but the UCA formalizes the parity concept. Under the UCA, the foreclosing lender's liability depends on which of four choices it makes in assuming the declarant's rights. First, suppose the lender makes no assumption of rights; it will be held to have undertaken no corresponding liabilities (except, presumably, those relating to its own conduct after acquiring title to the unsold units.) The second choice under the UCA permits the lender to assume the declarant's rights solely for the purpose of transferring them to other persons—the buyers of the units thus acquired.[60] Such a lender may still exercise the control over the executive board of the association which could have been asserted by the original developer,[61] but is not liable to the unit owners except for any improper behavior in exercising those particular rights.

A third possibility is for the lender to assume the developer's rights to maintain models, offices, and signs in the project. If this is the lender's decision, its liability is limited to breaches of legal duty associated with those particular facilities, and to the duty to provide the public offering statement to customers required by the UCA.[62]

Finally, a lender which assumes all of the special declarant rights, or any rights other than those specifically mentioned above, becomes broadly liable for breaches of all declarant duties, with certain named exceptions.[63] The exceptions include liabilities associated with the

56. See Note, Special Declarant Rights and Obligations Following Mortgage Foreclosure on Condominium Developments, 25 Wm. & Mary L.Rev. 463 (1984), at 478 n. 103.

57. 69 Cal.2d 850, 73 Cal.Rptr. 369, 447 P.2d 609, (1968), discussed in § 12.11 supra. See Chotka v. Fidelco Growth Investors, 383 So.2d 1169 (Fla.App.1980), in which the foreclosing lender completed the construction work and finished marketing the units; the court held the lender liable for construction defects which resulted from the original developer's poor work.

58. See Roundtree Villas Assoc. v. 4701 Kings Corp., 282 S.C. 415, 321 S.E.2d 46 (1984); Riverview Condominium Corp. v.

Campagna Construction Co., 406 So.2d 101 (Fla.App.1981); First Wisconsin Bank v. Roose, 348 So.2d 610 (Fla.App.1977); § 12.11, supra, at notes 11–12.

59. See Chotka v. Fidelco Growth Investors, supra note 57.

60. UCA § 3–104(e)(4).

61. Such control is authorized (with limitations) by UCA § 3–103(d).

62. UCA § 3–104(e)(3).

63. UCA § 3–104(e)(2). See Roundtree Villas Assoc. v. 4701 Kings Corp., 282 S.C. 415, 321 S.E.2d 46 (1984) (lender liable for repairs it made negligently after it took over and marketed completed project).

misrepresentations, breaches of fiduciary duty in connection with the owner's association, and construction warranty obligations of the previous declarant, and any defaults of the previous declarant occurring after the transfer.[64] In this fashion the UCA attempts to make an even-handed allocation of liability to the original developer's successor. The UCA may well become a guideline for the courts in this area, even in states which have not adopted it by statute.[65]

  WESTLAW REFERENCES

financ*** /p condominium /s construct***

developer /p construction /s loan /p condominium

"master deed" /p condominium

di master deed

construction /s loan /p condominium /p default*** abandon!
    foreclos***

Priority as Between Construction Lender and Vendees

di equitable lien

priority /p condominium /p lien

"equitable lien" /p foreclos*** /p priority

subordinat! /s mortgage /p vendee /p construction

Priority as Between Mechanics' Lien Claimants and Vendees

topic(257) /p condominium

"mechanics lien" /p condominium

lien** /p vendee /p priority

Priority as Between Mechanics' Lien Claimants and the Owners Association's Assessment Lien

association /p lien /p condominium

Special Declarant Rights and Obligations in Foreclosure

foreclos*** /p condominium /p construction

---

§ 13.4 Financing Conversions to Condominium and Cooperative Status

Rental apartment buildings are frequently converted to condominium status. The converter may be the original landlord, or the building may be sold to an intermediary who will handle the conversion and marketing process. Often some remodeling and refurbishing of the apartments, lobby, and recreational facilities is necessary. Such facilities as the heating plant, roof, and plumbing may be replaced. Despite these expenses, the financial rewards of the conversion can be extremely attractive, since buildings often sell for as much as 33 to 40 percent more than their previous value as rental properties.[1] For landlords

---

64. Note that if the successor owner is an "affiliate" of the original declarant, it is subject to all of the liabilities of its transferor, irrespective of the extent of its assumption of rights; UCA § 3–104(e)(1).

65. See also the discussion of Mich. Comp.Laws Ann. §§ 559.235, –237 and Or.

Rev.Stat. 94.097, 94.103, in Note, supra note 56, at 482–85.

§ 13.4

1. See Jaskol, A Lender Looks at Condominium Conversions, 4 Real Estate Rev. 70 (No. 1, 1974). On efforts of converters to achieve capital gain (as distinct from who find themselves beset with rising costs for maintenance and utilities, complaints from tenants, and the growing influence of rent control ordinances, conversion may seem an ideal way out of an uncomfortable position.[2]

At the same time, conversion is a risky business.[3] Marketing of the converted apartments may be slow, especially if numerous other buildings are being converted or new condominiums built in the same market. It is usually desirable to keep the unsold units rented, but vacancies often grow when the tenants know that the building is being converted. On the other hand, in many buildings the existing tenants cannot afford the purchase prices of the converted units, and hence are forced out of their longtime residences; they may oppose the conversion bitterly and in some jurisdictions their opposition will constitute a legal barrier.[4] Detailed discussion of these problems is beyond the scope of the present treatment, but they must be considered carefully by any lender who is asked to finance a conversion.

Occasionally an apartment building owner is able to manage a conversion without resort to new blanket financing, but this can be accomplished only if the existing mortgage lender is agreeable. If the mortgage contains a due-on-sale clause, the lender must waive it. The lender must also be willing to join in the condominium declaration, and must modify the existing mortgage documents by inserting a partial release clause, permitting the sale of individual units free of the blanket lien. Often the lender is uninterested in taking these steps, or will do so only in return for financial concessions which the converter finds unacceptable. The alternate approach for the converter is to obtain an interim loan from a different lender which will contain the necessary language, and whose proceeds will be used to pay off the existing loan. The attractiveness of this technique will depend on numerous factors, including the interest rate and other costs associated with the interim loan, and the prepayment penalty which may be demanded by the old lender.

---

ordinary income) treatment on the gain from conversions, see Boris, Co-ops and Condominiums: Capital Gain on Conversion and Other Problems, 40 N.Y.U.Fed. Tax.Inst. 22–1 (1982); Livsey, Minimizing the Tax Consequences of Condominium Conversions and Other Real Property Development, 39 N.Y.U.Fed.Tax.Inst. 28–1 (1981); Miller, Can A Straight Condominium Conversion Produce A Capital Gain?, 54 J.Tax. 8 (Jan. 1981); Comment, Capital Gains Treatment for Gain Realized in Condominium Conversions, 47 Mo.L.Rev. 269 (1982).

2. 1 P. Rohan & M. Reskin, Condominium Law & Practice § 3A.01 (1984).

3. See Channing, Condominium Conversions: A Developer's View, 55 Fla.B.J. 85 (1981); Moss, Checklist for Successful Con-

dominium Conversions, 5 Real Est.Rev. 116 (No. 3, 1975).

4. See, e.g., New York—McKinney's Gen.Bus.Law § 352–e et seq.; West's Fla. Stat.Ann. § 718.604–.622; 2 P. Rohan & M. Reskin, Cooperative Housing Law & Practice § 6.09 (1983) (summarizing state and local regulations throughout the nation); Comment, Displacement in Gentrifying Neighborhoods: Regulating Condominium Conversion Through Municipal Land Use Controls, 63 Bos.U.L.Rev. 955 (1983); Judson, Defining Property Rights: The Constitutionality of Protecting Tenants from Condominium Conversion, 187 Harv.Civ. Rts-Civ.Lib.L.Rev. 179 (1983); Kamer, Conversion of Rental Housing to Unit Ownership—A Noncrisis, 10 Real Est.L.J. 187 (1982).

Interim loans to finance conversions usually do not require regular principal amortization, but do require the reduction of the principal by some agreed amount for each condominium unit sold, much in the same manner as blanket construction loans on subdivisions.[5] They are usually limited to 75 or 80 percent of the property's value *as a condominium*, but if this would result in a loan approaching 100 percent of the value as a rental project, the interim lender will often require some cash investment by the converter, thus limiting the loan to, perhaps, 90 percent of the rental value. In any event, the "value" on which the loan is based will generally include the cost of the renovations which the converter plans to make. A portion of the interim loan may even be disbursed in installments as these improvements are put in place, as with a construction loan.

The interim lender is intensely concerned with the converter's cash flow projections for the conversion period. The building must generate enough cash to cover interest payments on the interim loan as well as the usual operating, maintenance, and management costs of a rental building, and the converter's obligation to pay assessments to the new owners' association. Since a shortfall can easily result in default and foreclosure of the interim mortgage, the interim lender must be confident that it can complete the conversion successfully if necessary.

Conversion of rental buildings to cooperatives is far less common than conversion to condominiums except in New York, where it is a frequent and intensely regulated occurrence.[6] The motivations for a cooperative conversion are much the same as have been discussed above; avoidance of rent control and high costs, and the opportunity to make a substantial profit.[7] However, the financing problems are much simpler since, absent a due-on-sale clause, the agreement of the existing lender is generally unneeded, and the conversion can proceed without his participation.[8] Often the outstanding balance on the existing financing will be too low to make conversion feasible. In such cases the existing loan may be refinanced, or if its interest rate is so low that it is worth preserving, a wrap-around second mortgage may be arranged to provide cash for refurbishing the building and to lower the required down payments of the apartment purchasers. Separate original, inter-

---

5. See Reppe, Winning Over the Condominium Lender, 5 Real Est.Rev. 104 (No. 2, 1975); Fantini, A Practical Primer for Analyzing Condominium Conversions, 34 Mortgage Banker 48 (Aug. 1973).

6. See New York—McKinney's Gen. Bus.Law § 352–e (conversions in New York State generally), § 352–ee (conversions of nonresidential property), § 352–eee (conversions in municipalities of Westchester, Nassau & Rockland Counties which adopt it), and § 352–eeee (conversions in New York City.) These rules are summarized in 2 P. Rohan & M. Reskin, Cooperative Housing Law & Practice § 6.04 (1983);

Comment, Examining Cooperative Conversion: An Analysis of Recent New York Legislation, 11 Ford.Urb.L.J. 1089 (1982). See Richards v. Kaskel, 32 N.Y.2d 524, 347 N.Y.S.2d 1, 300 N.E.2d 388 (1973).

7. See 2 P. Rohan & M. Reskin, supra note 6, at § 6.09[1] (1983).

8. In Boston Five Cents Sav. Bank v. Pierce, 601 F.Supp. 38 (D.Mass.1984), the court rejected the lender's argument that conversion of a rental building to a co-op was a breach of its preexisting FHA-insured mortgage.

im, and permanent loans are not necessarily required, however; if the existing financing on the rental building is satisfactory, there is usually no reason that it cannot be carried through the conversion period and become the permanent financing for the cooperators.

 WESTLAW REFERENCES
conver! /7 condominium /p financ!

§ 13.5 Permanent Financing of Condominium Units

Permanent mortgage loans on condominium units can generally be made by institutional lenders on the same terms as loans on detached houses or other buildings. However, the permanent lender on a condominium unit must be concerned with many factors which are unimportant or nonexistent in the financing of subdivision houses.[1] Most of these factors are related to the importance of the owner's association and the common areas to the success (and thus the future security value) of the project. While the discussion which follows concentrates on the permanent lender's concerns, construction lenders should also be cognizant of the factors mentioned, since they may be forced into a permanent lending role in the event of the developer's default on the construction loan or the permanent lender's refusal to honor its loan commitment. Indeed, unit purchasers themselves should be equally mindful of these problem areas, although they are often insufficiently sophisticated to realize the potential dangers.

Certain precautions are particularly significant to the permanent lender if it finances the sale of some units while other units or the common areas are still under construction or remain in the developer's hands. Obviously, the unit being financed should itself be completed. To ensure that the project will be successfully marketed as a condominium, many permanent lenders impose a "pre-sale requirement"; that is, they will refuse to close any loans until the developer has entered into binding sale contracts for some fixed percentage of the units.[2] The permanent lender will also be legitimately concerned with the developer's financial ability to complete the project, and may wish to verify that sufficient funds remain in the construction loan account for this purpose.

The payment of assessments to the association for unsold units can also pose a problem. Many statutes make no distinction between sold and unsold units, and require that assessments be collected uniformly

§ 13.5

1. See generally Rosenthal, Condominium and P.U.D. Projects: Steps to Approval, Mortgage Banking, May, 1984, at 57; Jackson, Attorneys for Lenders: What You Should Check in Condominium and PUD Documentations, (pts. 1 & 2) 4 Barrister 47

(Winter), 55 (Spring) (1977) [hereinafter cited as Jackson]; Waldron, Curtain May Soon Rise on Act Two of Condominium Problems, 37 Mortgage Banker 27 (Nov. 1976).

2. See Vishny, Financing the Condominium, 1970 U.Ill.L.F. 181, 190.

from all.[3]   This approach seems unreasonable from the developer's viewpoint, since unoccupied units obviously contribute little or nothing to certain variable costs of the association's operations; for example, they supply no users for the swimming pool, tennis courts, or equestrian trails.   On the other hand there are many fixed costs which are independent of the number of users.   A fair resolution of this problem would be to require a somewhat smaller assessment for units still owned by the developer than are paid for occupied units.   While a two-level assessment system is not permitted under many statutes, the same result may be achieved if the developer pays a full assessment but is entitled to reimbursement of a portion from the other owners under a separate contract.   Alternatively, the developer might pay the full assessment amounts and attempt to recover his outlays through higher sale prices for the later-sold units.[4]   In any event, the permanent lender should ascertain that the developer is obligated to pay a fair share of the costs of operating the association during the marketing period and that he has the financial strength to do so; his default might result in deteriorating physical facilities or a financially weakened or even insolvent association.   The lender may even require a cash deposit from the developer to secure these payments.

The permanent lender must also be concerned with the developer's attempts to retain control over the association until most of the units have been sold.   Often this is accomplished by creating two classes of stock, attached to unsold and sold units respectively, with the former having a greater voting power.   For example, if the first class has three votes per share and the second only one vote per share, the developer can maintain effective control until the project is three-fourths sold. This degree of retention of control is probably reasonable to protect the developer against the enactment of rules or procedures which would retard his sales.[5]   The permanent mortgagee, however, may refuse to lend if the period of developer control will extend past some given percentage of units transferred, and may also insist on the fixing of an outside date by which control must pass to the unit owners irrespective of the number of sales.

Virtually every important aspect of the association's ongoing functions concerns the permanent lender, since operational inadequacies may be reflected in diminished security value of the units.   Questions on which the lender will need to be satisfied include the following: Is membership in the association automatic?   Has a lien for unpaid

3. U.C.A. § 3–115 requires that once any units have been assessed, all units (including those still owned by the developer) must be assessed under the same formula. Until that time, however, the developer is free to pay all common area expenses himself.

4. See Wolfe, How to Set Up a Homeowners Association So It Works For (Not Against) You, House & Home 74 (Sept. 1974).

5. Id. at 83. A few statutes expressly limit the period of developer control; see, e.g., U.C.A. § 3–103; West's Fla.Stat.Ann. §§ 718.301 (condominiums), 719.301 (cooperatives).

assessments been created by proper language in the declaration or master deed? Has the association established a reasonable budget, supported by adequate assessment amounts? Is the assessment delinquency rate reasonably low? Have adequate reserves for repairs and replacements been set up, with provision that they not be used except for specified items? Has a competent management firm been hired if the project is large enough to justify it? Is the project subject to unreasonable management contracts or recreational facility leases? Is an independent annual audit made of the association's books? Has adequate blanket insurance been arranged for the common areas and exteriors of units, with provision for increased coverage to match inflation?

Many permanent lenders insist on certain types of protection in the condominium documentation. For example, the lender may want: notice from the association of default in assessments by any of its mortgagors; exemption (if the lender becomes the owner of a unit through foreclosure) from the usual clause giving the association a right of first refusal or other right to control the subsequent transfer of the unit, and from any restriction on leasing of units; notice of cancellation of any insurance policies on the project; the right to examine the association's books at reasonable times; notice of association meetings and the right to attend; notice of any substantial loss or damage to common areas; and the right to vote on, or even to veto, such major policy decisions as the hiring or firing of a management firm, amendments to the declaration or bylaws, expansion or contraction of the project, or use of hazard insurance proceeds other than for repairs.

Finally, the lender will probably wish to redraft its usual mortgage and note forms to add special provisions relating to condominiums.[6] These revisions will usually include covenants by the mortgagor to pay his association assessments when due, to notify the lender of any delinquency notices received from the association, and to abide by all provisions of the condominium's declaration, bylaws, and rules. The documents may require that assessments be paid to an escrow or impound account. The mortgagor may also be required to covenant not to vote in favor of major policy changes in the project without the mortgagee's consent. Failure of the association to maintain adequate insurance coverage may be made a condition of default, and the lender may reserve the right to pay delinquent assessments and to charge them against the mortgagor's loan balance.

Authority of Lenders, Insurers, and Investors

There is little controversy concerning the power of lenders to make permanent mortgage loans on condominium units. Both federally-

6. Condominium Rider, FNMA/ FHLMC, Uniform Instrument 6/75; Grosser, Making the Loan Commitment, in Community Ass'n Institute, Summary of Proceedings, First Nat. Conference on Community Ass'ns 66 (1976).

chartered and state-chartered institutions are generally permitted to treat them as the equivalent of single-family houses, although the lending powers of state-chartered institutions are a matter of state law and some variations exist.

The Federal Housing Administration (FHA) insures permanent mortgages on condominium units under the same general terms and conditions as mortgages on detached houses, but if the project has more than eleven units, insurance on permanent mortgages is available only if the project has previously been covered by an FHA-insured project mortgage or has been completed for more than one year.[7]

The Veteran's Administration (VA) was first given authority to guarantee loans on condominium units in 1970, but could do so only when at least one unit in the project had been insured by FHA.[8] In 1975 this statutory limitation was dropped, and the VA now guarantees such loans regardless of prior FHA involvement.[9] VA imposes a number of requirements to protect its interests,[10] including a seventy percent presale requirement (which may be reduced in special circumstances), and limitations on reservations of rights by developers (such as the leasing of common areas to the association and the retention of a veto over the association after unit owners obtain majority control). In addition, VA regards projects as unacceptable if they prohibit leasing of units for six months or more, or impose a right of first refusal upon resale.[11] As with FHA, the terms of the VA loan guarantee are identical to those on detached houses.[12]

Both the Federal National Mortgage Association (FNMA) and the Federal Home Loan Mortgage Corporation (FHLMC) purchase permanent mortgage loans on condominium units. If a project has been the subject of an FHA condominium project mortgage, neither of these secondary market agencies is further concerned with the documentation; however, if construction was conventionally financed, FNMA and FHLMC impose a number of stringent requirements on the documentation and on certain operational aspects of the project as well.[13] The two agencies have similar, but not identical, requirements; they are too

---

7. National Housing Act § 234(c), 12 U.S.C.A. § 1715y(c); 24 CFR 234.26(a) (1984).

8. Veterans Housing Act of 1970, § 3, 84 Stat. 1108 (current version at 38 U.S. C.A. § 1810(d)).

9. Veterans Housing Act of 1974, Pub. L. No. 93–569, § 3, 88 Stat. 1863 (adding 38 U.S.C.A. § 1810(a)(6) and repealing 38 U.S. C.A. § 1810(d)).

10. See 38 CFR 36.4356–.4360a, as amended, 50 Fed.Reg. 5975 (Feb. 13, 1985).

11. The latter requirement is imposed only on condominiums established after December 31, 1976; see 38 CFR 36.4358(c) (6).

12. 38 CFR 36.4356.

13. Examples include the completion of common area improvements, the adequacy of reserves for repairs and replacements, 70 percent occupancy by year-round residents, a 70 percent pre-sale requirement (which may be reduced by special approval), freedom for mortgagees from any rights of the association to restrict sales of units, and a power in the association to terminate any management contract upon 90 days notice. See FHLMC, Sellers Guide Conventional Mortgages § 3.207; FNMA, Guide Servicers-Lending, ch. 3, Parts 1–6.

numerous to be summarized here, but generally deal with the issues and concerns discussed earlier in this section.[14]

An obvious concern to permanent lenders is the priority of the mortgage loan as against the lien of the owner's association for unpaid assessments. A large majority of the state statutes follow the FHA Model Act in providing that the lien is subordinate to any "first mortgage of record"; [15] other statutes subordinate the lien to all mortgages.[16] Obviously, under such statutes the mortgagee or other purchaser at a foreclosure sale is not subject to any liability for the assessment delinquencies of the former mortgagor, and mortgage foreclosure wipes out the association lien as to such amounts.[17] However, the real covenant which imposes the lien continues to run with the land, and assessments which accrue after the mortgage foreclosure do become the liability of the foreclosure purchaser, secured by the association's lien.

Subordination of the association's lien to the first mortgage as described above is generally thought advantageous to lenders, and FHLMC, FNMA, FHA and VA all require it.[18] It is clearly undesirable from the viewpoint of the association and its other members, since they will usually have to withstand an unusually heavy assessment to make up the delinquency of the foreclosed unit owners.[19] In the long run, a series of such incidents could endanger the solvency of the association, to the detriment of unit owners and mortgagees alike. At present, however, the preference of mortgagees for priority seems well-established. Little thought seems to have been given to the consequences of a deed in lieu of foreclosure. Such deeds may be construed not to disturb subordinate liens, so the association would appear to emerge entirely unscathed.[20] In a sense this is probably unfortunate, since it serves as an incentive for the lender to employ foreclosure, a decision which is usually more costly and time-consuming for all parties.

In an effort to avoid assessment defaults, some permanent mortgage lenders require their mortgagors to pay their assessments into an

---

14. See text at notes 2–6, supra; see generally sources cited at note 1, supra.

15. FHA Model Act § 23(a), supra § 13.1 note 2; Va.Code § 55–79.85 (first mortgages "securing institutional lenders"). Under the U.C.A., the lien has priority even over first mortgages, to the extent of six months' regular expense assessments; U.C.A. 3–116(b).

16. See, e.g., Utah Code Ann. § 57–8–20; Brask v. Bank of St. Louis, 533 S.W.2d 223 (Mo.App.1976).

17. FHA Model Act § 23(b), supra § 13.1 note 2. But see U.C.A. § 3–116(b), described in note 15 supra.

18. FHLMC Sellers' Guide Conventional Mortgages § 3.207 (recognizing validity of U.C.A. approach, supra note 15); FNMA Guide Servicers-Lending, ch. 3, § 409 (providing that in states following the U.C.A. approach, supra note 15, the declaration must require monthly assessments); 24 CFR 234.55 (FHA); 38 CFR § 36.4352, § 36.4358(b)(4)(iii) (VA administrator has discretion to allow owner's association lien priority).

19. The FHA Model Act § 23(b), supra § 13.1 note 2, specifically authorizes the charging of such deficiencies against all unit owners, but the language is probably unnecessary.

20. See §§ 6.18–.19 supra; Note, 31 Mo. L.Rev. 312 (1966) (discussing priority of deeds in lieu). Cf. Alden Hotel Co. v. Kanin, 88 Misc.2d 546, 387 N.Y.S.2d 948 (1976).

impound, reserve, or escrow account similar to those customarily maintained for taxes and insurance; the lender then remits the sums collected to the association on a regular basis. Many lenders are unenthusiastic about this technique, however, since it involves much more frequent payouts than are necessary for tax and insurance funds, and since the assessment lien, unlike taxes and assessments, is usually subordinate to the mortgage. Nonetheless, collection of assessments by the lender is generally a useful and desirable means of discouraging delinquencies and stabilizing the association's cash flow.

 WESTLAW REFERENCES

"pre-sale requirement"

Authority of Lenders, Insurers, and Investors
condominium /p insur! /p loan
"condominium property act"

§ 13.6 Permanent Financing of Cooperative Units

Traditionally the only permanent financing involving a cooperative project was its blanket mortgage. In most respects lenders have viewed blanket mortgages as similar to loans on rental apartment buildings, although they have been concerned to some extent with the governance, internal procedures, and financial stability of cooperative corporations. Permanent blanket mortgages (as well as construction loans) on cooperative projects can be insured by FHA under section 213 of the National Housing Act.[1] Loan-to-value ratios may be as high as ninety-eight percent, a feature which makes section 213 more attractive than conventional loans, which are generally limited to eighty percent of value. While the time and complexity of processing under section 213 reduce its usefulness, the program was for a time very active in those jurisdictions in which cooperatives are popular.[2]

Federal savings and loan associations are authorized to make blanket loans on cooperatives on the same basis as on other (e.g. rental) projects.[3] The cooperative itself must maintain both general operating reserves and reserves for replacements in the same amounts as are required by the FHA section 213 program.[4]

Beginning with the New York statute enacted in 1971,[5] numerous states have authorized institutional lenders to make loans, often called

§ 13.6

1. 12 U.S.C.A. § 1715e.

2. From the initiation of the § 213 program in 1950 through 1975, project mortgages on 116,155 units were insured. The states in which use of the program was heaviest were (in order of decreasing use) California, New York, Florida, Arizona, Michigan, Illinois and New Jersey. California and New York were roughly equal in participation, and together accounted for 57 percent of the units. See U.S. Dep't of Housing and Urban Development, 1975 Statistical Yearbook 134 (1976). Participation has generally dropped off sharply in recent years.

3. 12 CFR 545.33(g)(1).

4. See 24 CFR 213.30.

5. New York—McKinney's Banking Law §§ 103(5) (banks), 235(8–a) (savings banks), 380(2–a) (savings and loan associa-

"share loans," on the security of individual cooperative units.[6] Prior to this development, lack of institutional financing was a major impediment to the financial success of cooperatives; subsequent purchasers of units were obliged to pay cash, obtain personal loans from external sources, or negotiate installment contracts or promissory notes to unit sellers to cover the non-cash portion of the purchase price.

Institutional financing of individual co-op units was given further impetus by section 4(b) of the Emergency Home Purchase Act of 1974, which added a new subsection (n) to section 203 of the National Housing Act, authorizing FHA to insure individual unit loans in buildings which were subject to blanket mortgages insured under section 213.[7] Under FHA's regulations, the loan must be secured by a first lien on the corporate stock certificate and the "occupancy certificate" or proprietary lease. The loan maturity is limited to thirty years or the remaining term of the blanket mortgage, whichever is less.[8] The FHA regulations recognize that a unit purchaser is always taking, in effect, subject to the blanket mortgage; thus, a lien on the unit is economically analogous to a second mortgage. The regulations limit the share loan to no more than the normal FHA amount, less the unit's pro-rata share of the blanket mortgage.[9]

Several of the other major federal agencies involved in housing have followed FHA's example and included cooperative share loans in their programs. The Federal Home Loan Bank Board has authorized federally-chartered savings and loan associations to make share loans on the same basis as loans on detached housing.[10] The Veterans Administration has authorized share loans under its loan guaranty program, although it has reserved the right to make project-by-project determinations of acceptability, rather than issuing detailed regulations specifying what loans will be approved.[11] The Federal National Mortgage Association [12] has a program for purchasing share loans originated by local lending institutions.[13] In the aggregate, these

tions). These statutes have undergone a series of liberalizing amendments since their enactment in 1981. They now permit maturities and loan-to-value ratios as generous as on loans made to owner-occupants of single-family homes. See generally Goldstein, Institutional Purchase Money Financing of Cooperative Apartments, 46 St.Johns L.Rev. 632 (1972).

6. See, e.g., West's Ann.Cal.Financial Code § 7133.4; Smith-Hurd Ill.Ann.Stat. ch. 32, ¶ 791(d); Mass.Gen.Laws Ann. c. 157B, § 1; Minn.Stat.Ann. § 47.20 subd. 3; N.J.Stat.Ann. 17:2–6.

7. 12 U.S.C.A. § 1709(n). See 24 CFR § 203.43c(f). FHA has proposed a regulatory amendment which will allow share loans where there is no FHA blanket mortgage, as to projects which have been completed for one year or more. See 49 Fed.

Reg. 40188 (Oct. 15, 1984). The proposal will implement § 419 of the Housing and Urban-Rural Recovery Act of 1983, Pub.L. No. 98–181.

8. 24 CFR § 203.43c(h)(4).

9. See 24 CFR § 203.43c(g).

10. 12 CFR § 545.33(g)(2).

11. See 38 CFR § 36.4343.

12. See FNMA Guide Servicers—Lending, ch. 1, Part 8; ch. 2, § 208; ch. 3, Parts 7–11.

13. See also BNA Hsg. & Devel.Rptr., Aug. 27, 1984, at 273, describing a new corporation, the Share Loan Service Corporation (SLSC), which was created to purchase share loans primarily for resale to FNMA. It is likely that the Federal Home Loan Mortgage Corporation (FHLMC) will changes represent a vast increase in institutional borrowing opportunities over those available only a few years earlier.

Creating and Foreclosing Share Loan Security Interests

Despite the great expansion in institutional lending on cooperative apartments, there is still a surprising degree of uncertainty as to the proper method for a lender to acquire, perfect, and foreclose upon a security interest in the stock and proprietary lease. The problem stems from the fact that the cooperator holds two inseparable rights—a share of stock, which seems undeniably personal property, and a leasehold which may be viewed either as realty or personalty.[14] This dichotomy has proven troublesome in a variety of contexts: whether the federal securities laws govern cooperative apartment sales,[15] whether the usual rights and duties associated with landlord-tenant law apply,[16] and whether real estate or personal property concepts govern sales contracts [17] and distribution of decedents' estates.[18]

On the specific problem of perfection of a security interest in a cooperative apartment, the case law is helpful but not fully satisfactory. An analogy can be drawn from cases which involve enforcement of sales contracts on cooperative apartments; they take the position that the principal rights of the cooperative tenant stem from the ownership of shares, and thus that the UCC controls.[19] This suggests that the UCC should govern issues relating to security interests as well. The New York Court of Appeals adopted this view in State Tax Commission v. Shor.[20] It held that, since the cooperative apartment was not to be regarded as realty, a creditor who obtained a judgment against an apartment owner would not thereby acquire an automatic lien on the

---

also establish a share loan purchase program.

14. The leasehold estate was traditionally regarded as a "chattel real", a species of personal property; see R. Cunningham, W. Stoebuck & D. Whitman, Property § 6.11 (1984).

15. They do not; see United Housing Foundation, Inc. v. Foreman, 421 U.S. 837, 95 S.Ct. 2051, 44 L.Ed.2d 621 (1975), rehearing denied 423 U.S. 884, 96 S.Ct. 157, 46 L.Ed.2d 115 (1975).

16. Compare Linden Hill No. 1 Cooperative Corp. v. Kleiner, 124 Misc.2d 1001, 478 N.Y.S.2d 519 (1984) (statute protecting tenant ownership of pets applies to cooperatives) and Suarez v. Rivercross Tenants' Corp., 107 Misc.2d 135, 438 N.Y.S.2d 164 (1981) (implied warranty of habitability for residential tenants applies to cooperatives) with Earl W. Jimerson Housing Co. v. Butler, 97 Misc.2d 563, 412 N.Y.S.2d 560 (1979) (summary possession procedure, normally applicable to landlord-tenant relationship, does not apply to cooperatives.)

17. Silverman v. Alcoa Plaza Associates, 37 A.D.2d 166, 323 N.Y.S.2d 39 (1971) (U.C.C. Art. 2 governs, prohibiting forfeiture of purchaser's earnest money deposit); McManus v. McManus, 83 A.D.2d 553, 440 N.Y.S.2d 954 (1981), affirmed 55 N.Y.2d 855, 447 N.Y.S.2d 708, 432 N.E.2d 601 (1982), dismissed 55 N.Y.2d 605, 447 N.Y.S.2d 1029, 432 N.E.2d 604 (1982) (U.C.C. Art. 2 governs in determination that contract of sale is enforceable despite omission of price term.) See also Stockton v. Lucas, 482 F.2d 979 (T.E.C.A.1973) (stock and lease are personal property for purposes of federal price control legislation.)

18. In re Miller's Estate, 205 Misc. 770, 130 N.Y.S.2d 295 (1954) (cooperative apartment interest treated as personalty). See also Greene v. Levenhar, 24 B.R. 331 (Bkrtcy.N.Y.1982) (cooperative apartment interest is personalty, and hence cannot be held in tenancy by the entirety.)

19. See cases cited note 17 supra.

20. 43 N.Y.2d 151, 400 N.Y.S.2d 805, 371 N.E.2d 523 (1977).

apartment. In dictum, the court asserted that a lender could perfect a security interest in the apartment merely by taking possession of the shares and the lease, in a manner analogous of the taking of a pledge of chattel paper or instruments.[21] No filing of a financing statement would be necessary.[22] A subsequent Federal district court decision has confirmed this view.[23] Under these cases, the shares of stock are viewed as the primary indicium of ownership, with the lease being merely ancillary.

Some lenders are uncomfortable with these conclusions. They may point to UCC Article 9's statement that it is inapplicable to "the creation or transfer of an interest in or lien on real estate, including a lease * * *."[24] To guard against the possibility that their interest in the proprietary lease will be held unperfected, they may obtain and record a real estate mortgage in addition to taking possession of the documents and filing under Article 9.[25] Whether this is necessary is still in doubt. It seems almost irresponsible that this question has not been settled long ago by legislation, at least in New York where cooperatives are of such great economic importance.

A related question arises as to how a creditor can properly foreclose upon a security interest in a cooperative apartment. In FDIC v. Evans,[26] the secured lender, which had taken a possessory pledge of the shares and lease, conducted a nonjudicial sale to a bona fide purchaser, relying on UCC § 9–504's authorization to secured parties to dispose of collateral in a "commercially reasonable" manner. The court found this action proper, and rejected the argument of the preceding paragraph that a security interest in the proprietary lease is excluded from UCC Article 9.[27]

Because of the bifurcated nature of cooperative apartment ownership, these questions are not easily answered within the framework of existing law. Clarifying legislation is badly needed, and until it is

---

21. U.C.C. § 9–305: "A security interest in * * * goods, instruments, * * * or chattel paper may be perfected by the secured party's taking possession of the collateral." See § 5.28 supra at notes 24–42.

22. See U.C.C. § 9–302(1). Note that filing may still be important as a device to protect against federal tax liens and the possible bankruptcy of the cooperator; see Rifkin, Co-op Proprietary Leases, N.Y. State B.J., June 1979, at 290; cf. Superior Financial Corp. v. Haskell, infra note 23.

23. Superior Financial Corp. v. Haskell, 556 F.Supp. 199 (S.D.N.Y.1983) (upholding priority of lender's unfiled security interest in cooperative apartment, perfected by possession of documents, against a subsequently-filed federal tax lien.)

24. U.C.C. 9–104(j).

25. See P. Rohan & M. Reskin, Cooperative Housing Law & Practice § 5A.08(3) (1984). In New York, recording of the mortgage apparently gives rise to liability for the mortgage recording tax, a result to be avoided if possible.

26. No. 75–C–1947 (E.D.N.Y. Apr. 14, 1976), unreported. The opinion is reprinted in full in P. Rohan & M. Reskin, supra note 12, at § 5A.08(3) n. 32 (1984).

27. The court also rejected an argument that the sale was a violation of Due Process because it was held without a prior hearing. This is consistent with the usual attitude of the courts in reviewing power-of-sale foreclosures of real estate mortgages, see §§ 7.23–7.30 supra.

adopted [28] a good deal of wasteful litigation will probably occur. While few cooperatives are now being developed outside of New York, lenders and unit owners in many states would be benefitted by adoption of clear procedures for perfecting and foreclosing interests in existing cooperatives.[29]

 WESTLAW REFERENCES

co-operative co-op /p financ! /p mortgag
12 +4 1715e & court(ny)

Creating and Foreclosing Share Loan Security Interests

co-operative co-op /s apartment house housing unit dwelling /p
      "chattel real" personalty (personal /4 property)

---

28. A Subcommittee on Cooperatives of the Association of the Bar of the City of New York has drafted a proposed amendment to UCC Article 9; in general, it would make clear that Article 9 applies to security interests in cooperative apartments, but that filing, rather than mere possession of documents, is necessary for perfection. At this writing the proposal has not been enacted. See P. Rohan & M.

Reskin, Cooperative Housing Law & Practice § 5A.09 (1984).

29. These problems are largely resolved if the cooperative is of the type in which each owner holds a fractional share in the project as a tenant in common. Such interests are readily mortgagable and may be foreclosed upon. See Future Federal Savings & Loan Association v. Daunhauer, 687 S.W.2d 871 (Ky.App.1985).

Appendix

WESTLAW REFERENCES

I. INTRODUCTION

This informational appendix is designed to aid the reader in the general use of the WESTLAW system and more specifically to demonstrate how WESTLAW can be used in conjunction with this text to help make research in the area of real estate finance law swift and complete.

II. THE WESTLAW SYSTEM

WESTLAW is a computer-assisted legal research service of West Publishing Company. It is accessible through a number of different types of computer terminals. The materials available through WESTLAW are contained in databases stored at the central computer in St. Paul, Minnesota.

To use the WESTLAW service a "query" or search request, is typed into the terminal and sent to the central computer. There it is processed and all of the documents that satisfy the search request are identified. The text of each of these documents is then stored on magnetic disks and transmitted to the user via a telecommunication network. This data then appears on the user's terminal, where it may be reviewed and evaluated. The user must then decide if the displayed documents are pertinent or if further research is desired. If further research is necessary, the query may be recalled for editing, or an entirely new query may be sent. Documents displayed on the terminal may be printed or, on some terminals, the text may be stored on its own magnetic disks.

III. IMPROVING LEGAL RESEARCH WITH WESTLAW

The WESTLAW system is designed for use in conjunction with the more traditional tools of legal research. In principle, WESTLAW works as an index to primary and secondary legal materials. Yet it differs from traditional digests and indices in that more terms can be researched, and more documents retrieved.

Through WESTLAW it is possible to index, or search for any significant term or combination of terms in an almost infinite variety of

971

grammatical relationships by formulating a query composed of those terms. Unlike manual systems of secondary legal sources that reference only a few key terms in each document, WESTLAW is capable of indexing every key word. This enables documents to be located using terms not even listed in manual reference systems.

In addition to its expanded search term capabilities, WESTLAW, through its numerous databases, enables the user to research issues in any and every jurisdiction quickly and efficiently. The queries found in this text are primarily designed to access WESTLAW's state and federal case law databases. However, WESTLAW provides access to many specialized libraries as well. For example, WESTLAW contains separate topical databases for areas of federal and state law such as tax, securities, energy, and government contracts.

WESTLAW also includes the text of the United States Code and the Code of Federal Regulations, the Federal Register, West's INSTA–CITE ™, Shepard's ® Citations, *Black's Law Dictionary* and many other legal sources. Furthermore, because new cases are continuously being added to the WESTLAW databases as they are decided by the courts, the documents retrieved will include the most current law available on any given issue.

In addition, WESTLAW queries augment the customary role of footnotes to the treatise text by directing the user to a wider range of supporting authorities. Readers may use the preformulated queries supplied in this edition "as is" or formulate their own queries in order to retrieve cases relevant to the points of law discussed in the text.

IV. QUERY FORMULATION

a. *General Principles*

The art of query formulation is the heart of WESTLAW research. Although the researcher can gain technical skills by using the terminal, there is no strictly mechanical procedure for formulating queries. One must first comprehend the meaning of the legal issue to be researched before beginning a search on WESTLAW. Then the user will need to supply imagination, insight, and legal comprehension with knowledge of the capabilities of WESTLAW to formulate a useful query. Effective query formulation requires an alternative way of thinking about the legal research process.

Using WESTLAW is a constant balancing between generating too many documents and missing important documents. In general, it is better to look through a reasonable number of irrelevant documents than it is to be too restrictive and miss important material. The researcher should take into consideration at the initial query formulation stage what he or she will do if too many, or not enough documents are retrieved. Thought should be given as to how the query might be narrowed or the search broadened, and what can be done if the initial search retrieves zero documents.

Some issues by their very nature will require more lengthy queries than others; however, it is best to strive for efficiency in structuring the query. Look for unique search terms that will eliminate the need for a lengthy query. Keep in mind that WESTLAW is literal. Consider all possible alternative terms. Especially consider inherent limitations of the computer. It doesn't think, create, or make analogies. The researcher must do that for the computer. The computer is designed to look for the terms in the documents in relationships specified by the query. The researcher should know what he or she is looking for, at least to the extent of knowing how the terms are likely to show up in relevant documents. Always keep in mind the parameters of the system as to date and database content.

The WESTLAW Reference Manual should be consulted for more information on query formulation and WESTLAW commands. The Reference Manual is updated periodically to reflect new enhancements of WESTLAW. It provides detailed and comprehensive instructions on all aspects of the WESTLAW system and offers numerous illustrative examples on the proper format for various types of queries. Material contained in the Reference Manual enables the user to benefit from all of the system's capabilities in an effective and efficient manner.

b. The WESTLAW Query Defined

The query is a message to WESTLAW. It instructs the computer to retrieve documents containing terms in the grammatical relationships specified by the query. The terms in a query are made up of words and/or numbers that pinpoint the legal issue to be researched.

An example of the kind of preformulated queries that appear in this publication is reproduced below. The queries corresponding to each section of the text appear at the end of the section.

The query appearing below is taken from Chapter 7, Section 7.2, and appears at the end of this section of the text.

"junior lienholder" heir devisee lessee (tenant /3 life joint) remainder*** reversion** /s redemption redeem***

This query instructs WESTLAW to retrieve documents containing any of the terms JUNIOR LIENHOLDER, HEIR, DEVISEE, LESSEE, or TENANT within three terms of the word LIFE, or JOINT or a form of the words REMAINDER or REVERSION all within the same sentence as REDEMPTION or a form of the root REDEEM.

This query illustrates what a standard request to WESTLAW looks like—words or numbers describing an issue, tied together by connectors. These connectors tell WESTLAW in what relationships the terms must appear. WESTLAW will retrieve all documents from the database that contain the terms appearing in those relationships.

The material that follows explains the methods by which WESTLAW queries are formulated, and shows how users of *Real Estate Finance Law* can employ the preformulated queries in this publication in their research of real estate finance law. In addition, there are instructions that will enable readers to modify their queries to fit the particular needs of their research.

c. Selection of Terms

After determining the legal issue that is to be researched, the first step in query formulation is to select the key terms from the issue that will be used as search terms in the query. Words, numbers, and various other symbols may be used as search terms.

The goal in choosing search terms is to select the most unique terms for the issue. In selecting such terms it is frequently helpful to imagine how the terms might appear in the language of the documents that will be searched by the query. Moreover, it is necessary to consider the grammatical and editorial structure of the document. This involves a consideration of how the writer of the document (i.e., judge or headnote and synopsis writer) has worded both the factual and legal components of the issue involved in the case.

Although traditional book research generally starts with a consideration of the general legal concepts under which particular problems are subsumed, WESTLAW research starts with a consideration of specific terms that are likely to appear in documents that have addressed those problems. This is so because documents are retrieved from WESTLAW on the basis of the terms they contain. The more precise the terms, the more relevant the search results will be. For example, in researching the effects of transfers by the mortgagor, inclusion of the unique terms "due-on-sale" or "Garn-St. Germain Act" rather than, say, the common term "mortgage" would retrieve more specific, and hopefully more pertinent documents.

Once the initial search terms have been selected for a query, it is important to consider synonyms, antonyms, and other alternatives for the search terms. A space left between each of these alternative terms will be read as an "or" in WESTLAW. (See section d: Query Formulation: Proximity Connectors.) The nature of the legal issue will determine which alternative terms are desirable.

d. The Format of Search Terms

Once the key search terms have been selected, it is necessary to consider the proper form in which the terms should appear in the query. As WESTLAW is literal in its search for terms, and as a term may appear in a variety of ways, derivative forms of each search term must be considered. There are two devices available on WESTLAW for automatically generating alternative forms of search terms in a query. The first of these is the Unlimited Root Expander, the symbol (!). Placement of the ! symbol at the end of the root term generates other forms containing the same root. For example, adding the ! symbol to "forfeit" in the following query:

    forfeit!   /s   constitutional

instructs the computer to generate the words FORFEIT, FORFEITS, FORFEITURE, FORFEITED, and FORFEITURES as search terms for the query. Yet time and space are saved by not having to include each of these alternatives in the query.

The second device used to automatically generate alternative forms of search terms is the Universal Character, the symbol (*). This symbol permits the generation of all possible characters by placing one or more asterisks at the location in the term where the universal character is desired. For example, placing two asterisks on the root MORTGAG in the following query:

    mortgag**   /3   right

instructs the computer to generate all forms of the root term with up to two additional characters. Thus, the terms MORTGAGE, MORTGA- GOR, MORTGAGEE, and MORTGAGED would be generated by this query. The symbol * may also be embedded inside of a term as in the following query:

    s****holder   /s   condominium

This will generate the alternative terms STOCKHOLDER and SHAREHOLDER without the need to enter both synonymous terms. As WESTLAW automatically generates plural forms for search terms (e.g., the endings -s -es and -ies) it is generally unnecessary to use the root expansion devices to obtain plural forms of search terms.

e. *Proximity Connectors*

Once the search terms and alternate search terms have been selected the next consideration is how these terms may be ordered so as to retrieve the most relevant documents. The connectors and their meanings appear below.

1. *Space (or).* A space between search terms is read as an "or" by WESTLAW. For example, leaving a space between the query terms CONDOMINIUM and COOPERATIVE:

    condominium cooperative

instructs the computer to retrieve documents that contain either the word CONDOMINIUM or the word COOPERATIVE or both.

2. *Ampersand (&).* The symbol & means "and." Placing it be- tween two terms instructs the computer to retrieve documents that contain both of the terms without regard to word order. For example, inserting the & between the terms SELLER and DUTY:

    seller & duty

commands the computer to retrieve documents that contain both the term SELLER and the term DUTY anywhere in the text. The amper- sand may also be placed between groups of alternative terms. By

placing an & between SELLER or TRANSFEROR and DUTY or OBLI-
GATION:

> seller transferor & duty obligation

documents containing the terms SELLER and/or TRANSFEROR and
the terms DUTY and/or OBLIGATION may be retrieved.

3. */p (same paragraph).* The /p symbol means "within the same
paragraph." It requests that the terms to the left of the /p appear
within the same paragraph as the terms to the right of the connector.
For example, placing the /p between PRIORITY and SUBROGATION:

> priority /p subrogation

instructs the computer to retrieve documents in which both the terms
PRIORITY and SUBROGATION appear in the same paragraph. The
terms on each side of the /p connector may appear in the document in
any order within the paragraph. As with the & connector the /p may
be placed between groups of alternative terms. Thus, the query

> priority lien /p subrogation contribution

will succeed in retrieving all documents in which the terms PRIORITY
and/or LIEN appear in the same paragraph as SUBROGATION and/or
CONTRIBUTION.

4. */s (same sentence).* The /s symbol requires that the search
terms so connected occur within the same sentence. A /s placed
between SEARCH and TITLE

> search /s title

will retrieve documents that contain the words SEARCH and TITLE in
the same sentence, without regard to which of these terms occur first in
the sentence. As with the previous connectors, the /s may be placed
between groups of alternative terms. Inserting the /s between the
terms SEARCH or EXAMINE and TITLE or ABSTRACT

> search examine /s title abstract

instructs the computer to retrieve documents with the terms SEARCH
and/or EXAMINE and the terms TITLE and/or ABSTRACT regardless
of which terms appear first.

5. *+s (precedes within sentence).* The +s symbol requires that
the term to the left of the +s connector precede the terms to the
right of the connector within the same sentence. The query

> registered +s property

instructs the computer to retrieve all documents in which the word
REGISTERED precedes the word PROPERTY where both words appear
in the same sentence. This connector may also be used between groups
of alternative terms. Thus, the query

> registered torrens +s property land

commands the computer to retrieve all documents in which the terms
REGISTERED and/or TORRENS precedes the terms PROPERTY and/
or LAND in the same sentence.

6. */n (numerical proximity—within n words).* The /n symbol means "within n words," where n represents any whole number between 1 and 255, inclusive. It requests that the term to the left of the /n appear within the designated number of words as terms to the right of the connector. For example, in the following query:

option /5 contract

the computer is instructed to retrieve all documents in which the term OPTION appears within 5 words of the term CONTRACT, without regard to word order. In addition, the + symbol may be used to require that the terms to the left of the numerical proximity connector precede the terms to the right of the connector. Thus, the query above could be altered to require that OPTION precede CONTRACT by no more than 5 words by replacing the /5 connector with the +5 words by replacing the /5 connector with the +5 connector.

option +5 contract

Both the /n and the +n conectors may also be used between groups of alternative search terms. For example:

option +5 contract agreement

instructs the computer to retrieve all documents in which the word OPTION occurs within the five words preceding the words CONTRACT or AGREEMENT.

7. *" "(quotation marks).* The " " (quotation marks) symbol is the most restrictive grammatical connector. When used to enclose search terms it requires that the computer retrieve only those documents in which enclosed terms appear exactly as they do within the quotation marks. For example, placing the following words within quotation marks

"holder in due course"

commands the computer to retrieve all documents in which the terms HOLDER, DUE and COURSE occur in precisely the same order as they do within the quotation marks.

The quotation marks symbol is especially effective when searching for legal terms of art, legal concepts, or legal entities that occur together as multiple terms. Some examples are: "statute of frauds", "parol evidence" and "eminent domain."

8. *% (exclusion/but not).* The % symbol may be translated as "but not." It instructs the computer to exclude documents that contain terms appearing after the percentage symbol. For example, to retrieve documents containing the terms "RECORDING ACT" and NOTICE within the same sentence but not the term RACE, the following query would be used:

"recording act" /s notice % race

Any document containing the word RACE would automatically be excluded in the document search.

The connectors described above may be used in a variety of combinations, enabling the user to fine-tune a query to meet his or her specific research needs.

V. ADVANCED SEARCH TECHNIQUES

a. *The Field Search*

Within any given database a more specialized search may be conducted. Rather than searching the entire text of a case for a designated query term, the search may be limited to specific portions of the case by conducting a "field search." A search may be restricted to a particular field (or portion) of a document by incorporating the field name into the query, followed by the field search terms enclosed in parentheses.

The fields available for WESTLAW case law databases are described below.

1. *Title Field:* The title field may be used to retrieve a particular case on WESTLAW. The ampersand, rather than the v. is used between the names of the parties. Thus, to retrieve the case entitled *Loretto v. Teleprompter Manhattan CATV Corp.* the following query would be used:

    title(loretto & teleprompter)

2. *Citation Field:* The citation field may be used for any document for which a citation exists in the WESTLAW databases. The proper database must first be selected. A numerical proximity connector is then used instead of the publication name to separate volume and page number. For example, to retrieve the case appearing at 102 S.Ct. 3164, the Supreme Court database must be selected. The following query may then be used:

    citation(102 +3 3164)

3. *Court Field:* The court field permits searches for case law to be restricted to particular states, districts, or courts. The correct database in which to conduct the search must be chosen. For example, to restrict a search to cases from the United States District Court in New York the database "dct" must be chosen. The following query might then be used:

    court(ny) & mortgag! /s moratori**

4. *Judge Field:* A search may be limited to the individual or majority opinion of a particular judge. To retrieve all cases in which Justice Powell has authored an opinion the following query would be used:

    judge(powell)

5. *Synopsis Field:* The synopsis field consists of the editorially prepared summary of the case found immediately after the title. By reading the synopsis it may be determined if the decision generally

encompasses the legal issue being researched without reading the entire decision.

The synopsis field search can be especially useful in focusing broad queries which might retrieve too many cases if the entire case was searched. For example, the following query would limit retrieval to cases in which a contract for deed was a key element:

synopsis(contract /2 deed)

6. *Topic Field:* The topic field contains the West topics and Key Numbers assigned to the headnotes in a case. A search in this field may be conducted by using either the West topic name or by using the West Key Number designated for that topic. For example, the West digest topic of Lis Pendens has been given the Key Number 242. Thus, in order to retrieve cases classified under the digest topic Lis Pendens either of these two queries could be used:

topic(lis pendens) /p mortgag** /s notice

or

topic(242) /p mortgag** /s notice

7. *Digest Field:* The digest field contains digest paragraphs prepared by West editors. It includes headnotes, corresponding digest topics and Key Numbers, the title and citation of the case, courts, and year of decision. The digest field can be used to search for terms which are not among the West topic headings. For example, the following query may be used to research real estate finance law even though this is not one of the West topic headings.

digest("real estate" /s financ***)

8. *Headnote Field:* A headnote search limits the search to the language of the headnote, exclusive of the digest topic and Key Number lines and case identification information. Thus, the headnote field is useful in conducting a search where exclusion of the topic name, the key number or the title of the case is necessary to cull only the most pertinent cases. For example, if the query includes statute or rule numbers the digest field can be helpful to exclude unwanted citation and key numbers. The query found below is an illustration of this function. The search, run in federal case law databases will retrieve cases discussing insured mortgages under the National Housing Act.

headnote(12 +10 1701) & insure* /5 mortgag**

9. *Opinion Field:* The opinion field contains the text of the case, court and docket numbers, and the names of the attorneys and judges participating. The opinion field search is useful in retrieving cases in which a particular attorney, judge or witness has been involved. The following format can be used to retrieve this information:

opinion(irving /s younger)

NOTE: Terms may be searched for in clusters of fields by joining any number of field names by commas. This technique is illustrated below:

synopsis,digest("deed of trust" /s mortgag**)

With this query documents containing the terms DEED OF TRUST and MORTGAG** in either the synopsis or digest portions of the case will be retrieved.

b. Field Browsing

The WESTLAW fields listed above may be used in yet another way. This second method, known as field browsing, may be used with any query. Once a search has been completed, the documents retrieved may be scanned by entering the "f" command. A list of fields available for browsing is then displayed. Once a field has been selected, WESTLAW will display only the specified field(s).

The WESTLAW Reference Manual should be consulted for further instruction on using WESTLAW fields for searching or browsing.

c. Date Restrictions

WESTLAW may be instructed to retrieve documents appearing before, after or on a specified date, as well as within a range of dates. To use the date restriction the term DATE, followed in parentheses by the words BEFORE and/or AFTER, or the abbreviations BEF and/or AFT, or the symbols < and > must be included in the query. Note that the month, day and year may be included to further restrict the search. Date restrictions should be placed at the beginning or end of the query and connected to the query by an ampersand. The following are examples of how the date restriction may be used within a query:

```
date(after 1965)  &  clog***  /s  equity  /2  redemption
date(aft 1965)  &  clog***  /s  equity  /2  redemption
clog***  /s  equity  /2  redemption  &  date (> 1965)
```

clog*** /s equity /2 redemption & date (aft may 10, 1965 and bef feb 28, 1981)

d. Key Number Searching

Searches may be performed using West Digest Topic and Key Numbers as search terms. When using this search technique, the query consists of the West Digest Topic Number followed by the letter k (or the ☞ symbol available on WALT keyboards) and then the Key Number classified as a subheading under the Digest Topic and Key Number. For example, to retrieve cases under the Digest Topic classification of Quieting Title (Digest Topic Number 318), and under its subsection or Key Number for mortgagors and mortgagees (Key Number 10(5)), the following queries would be used.

```
318k10(5) or 318 10(5)
```

A complete list of Digest Topics and their numerical equivalents appears in the WESTLAW Reference Manual and is also available on-line in the WESTLAW database directory.

e. The Find Command

The FIND command may be used at any point in a search to retrieve a particular case from WESTLAW. No matter what the database, a case may be displayed by typing FIND followed by the case citation. For example:

  find 54 sct 231

will retrieve the case of *Home Building & Loan Assn. v. Blaisdell.* To return to the original screen the GOBACK command is then entered.

f. The Locate Command

The LOCATE command may be used when viewing documents retrieved by a search query, to find documents within the search results which contain certain words. To locate a term LOCATE or LOC is typed followed by the ENTER key. On the screen which follows the LOCATE terms are then typed. The terms may or may not be words contained in the query. WESTLAW will then search the documents retrieved by the query to find the LOCATE terms. For example, to search the documents retrieved by the query:

  headnote(12   +10   1701) & insur** /5 mortgag**

for those documents containing the term "interest rate," LOCATE, then ENTER would be typed into WESTLAW. The term "INTEREST RATE" would then be typed in from the next screen. Those documents containing the term "INTEREST RATE" will then be displayed.

VI. CITATION RESEARCH WITH WESTLAW

a. Shepard's® Citations on WESTLAW

From any point in WESTLAW, case citations may be entered to retrieve Shepard's listings for those citations. To enter a citation to be Shepardized, the following format is used:

  sh 54 sct 231

or

  sh 54 s.ct. 231

or

  sh 54sct231

When the citation is entered, Shepard's listings for the citation will be displayed. To Shepardize a citation it is not necessary to be in the same database as that of the citation. For example, a Supreme Court citation may be entered from the Pacific Reporter database.

b. WESTLAW as a Citator

It is possible to retrieve new cases citing previous decisions by using WESTLAW itself as a citator. Using WESTLAW as a citator complements Shepard's Citations by retrieving very recent decisions not yet included in Shepard's. Because citation styles are not always uniform, special care must be taken to identify variant forms of citations.

1. *Retrieving Cases that Cite Code and Statute Sections*

Court decisions that cite to sections of codes or statutes are retrievable by including the section or statute number in the query. For example, to retrieve cases that cite section 4399.01 of the Ohio Statutes the following query would be used in the OH–CS (Ohio Cases) database:

```
4399.01
```

As the statute number is a unique term, it is not necessary to include additional search terms in the query.

2. *Retrieving Cases that Cite Other Court Decisions*

WESTLAW can be used as a citator of other court decisions if the title of the decision, its citation, or both, are known. When only the title of the case is known, use the following format:

```
fuentes  /5  shevin
```

This query instructs the computer to retrieve all documents citing the case of *Fuentes v. Shevin*. The /5 numerical connector requires that the term FUENTES occur within five words of the term SHEVIN.

If the citation of the case is known, it may be added to the query to retrieve only those documents citing the correct case name and case citation. For example, to retrieve cases that have referred to the *Fuentes* decision by its citation, 407 U.S. 67, the following format may be used:

```
407  +5  67
```

If both the citation and the case title are known, one or both of the case name terms may be used to retrieve all documents citing this case. The queries below illustrate this format.

```
fuentes  /5  shevin  /15  407  +5  67
```

or

```
fuentes  /15  407  +5  67
```

or

```
shevin  /15  407  +5  67
```

3. *West's INSTA–CITE*™

INSTA–CITE, West Publishing Company's case history system, allows users to quickly verify the accuracy of case citations and the validity of decisions. It contains prior and subsequent case histories in sequential listings, parallel citations and precedential treatment.

Some examples of the kind of direct case history provided by INSTA–CITE are: "affirmed," "certiorari denied," "decision reversed and remanded," and "judgment vacated." A complete list of INSTA–CITE case history and precedential treatment notations appears in the WESTLAW Reference Manual.

The format for entering a case citation into INSTA–CITE consists of the letters IC followed by the citation, with or without spaces and periods:

ic 395 U.S. 337

or

ic 395 us 337

or

ic 395us337

VII. SPECIAL FEATURES

a. Black's Law Dictionary

WESTLAW contains an on-line version of Black's Law Dictionary. The dictionary incorporates definitions of terms and phrases of English and American law.

The dictionary may be accessed at any point while using WESTLAW by typing DI followed by the term to be defined:

di quitclaim

To obtain definitions of a phrase, enter the command DI followed by the phrase without quotation marks:

di quo warranto

If the precise spelling of a term to be defined is not known, or a list of dictionary terms is desired, a truncated form of the words may be entered with the root expansion symbol (!) attached to it:

di sub!

This example will produce a list of dictionary terms beginning with the root SUB. From the list of terms a number corresponding to the desired term can be entered to obtain the appropriate definition of SUBROGATION.

VIII. WESTLAW HORNBOOK QUERIES

a. Query Format

The queries that appear in this publication are intended to be illustrative. They are approximately as general as the material in the Hornbook text to which they correspond.

Although all of the queries in this publication reflect proper format for use with WESTLAW, there is seldom only one "correct" way to formulate a query for a particular problem. The queries reflect a wide range of alternative ways that queries may be structured for effective research. Such variance in query style reflects the great flexibility that the WESTLAW system affords its users in formulating search strategies.

For some research problems, it may be necessary to make a series of refinements to the queries such as the addition of search terms or the substitution of different grammatical connectors, to adequately fit the particular needs of the individual researcher's problem. The responsibility remains with the researcher to "fine-tune" the WESTLAW queries in accordance with his or her own research requirements. The primary usefulness of the preformulated queries in this hornbook is in providing users with a foundation upon which further query construction can be built.

Individual queries in this hornbook may retrieve from one to over a hundred cases, depending on the database to which there are addressed. If a query does not retrieve any cases in a given database, it is because there are no documents in that database which satisfy the proximity requirements of the query. In this situation, to search another database with the same query, enter the letter S followed by the initials DB, followed by the new database identifier. Thus, if a query was initially addressed to the District Courts (dct) database, but retrieved no documents, the user could then search the Courts of Appeals (cta) database with the same query by entering the following command:

    s db cta

The maximum number of cases retrieved by a query in any given database will vary, depending on a variety of factors, including the relative generality of the search terms and proximity connectors, the frequency of litigation or discussion of the issue in the courts and administrative bodies, and the number of documents comprising the database.

b. *Textual Illustrations*

Examples from the text of this edition have been selected to illustrate how the queries provided in this treatise may be expanded, restricted, or altered to meet the specific needs of the reader's research in the area of real estate finance law. A portion of Chapter 9 section 9.1 of this text appears below. The footnotes have been omitted for purposes of brevity.

Purchase Money Mortgage Priority Concepts

It is widely accepted that a purchase money mortgage, executed at the same time with the deed of purchase of land, or in pursuance of agreement as part of one continuous transaction, takes precedence over any other claim of lien attaching to the property through the vendee-mortgagor. This is so even though the claim antedates the execution of the mortgage to the seller. It will also have priority if it is in favor of a third person who advanced the purchase money paid to the vendor, provided the money was loaned for this purpose only.

This excerpt discusses the priority of the holder of a purchase money mortgage. In order to retrieve documents discussing this point of law the following preformulated query is given as a suggested search strategy on WESTLAW:

    266k158 (purchase /3 money /3 mortgage /p priority.)

The headnote illustrated below is one retrieved from the Pacific (pac) database with the above query from the text.

R 1 OF 22   P 9 OF 31   PAC   T

669 P.2d 390

[6]

266K158

MORTGAGES

K. **Priority** of **mortgage** for **purchase money.**

Utah 1983.

Equity and justice justified protection afforded vendor parting with his property on faith that his mortgage or trust deed securing purchase monies loan to vendee was entitled to priority over any preexisting claims against vendee mortgager, and thus Utah Supreme Court adopted doctrine granting special **priority** to **purchase money mortgages.**

Nelson v. Stoker

669 P.2d 390

In the text of the case which follows the paragraph below appears.

R 1 OF 22   P 25 OF 31   PAC   T

669 P.2d 390

One of the frequent and important instances of its superiority is over liens arising under judgments against the grantee-mortgagor under a judgment obtained and docketed or recorded before the **purchase money mortgage** is executed.

IV American Law of Property, supra note 2, S 16.106E at 220–21 (citations omitted). Another leading authority comments as follows:

This rule, of course, is not confined to judgments and attachments; on the contrary, it extends to all liens legal or equitable, that otherwise might clasp the land at and with its acquisition by the mortgagor. All such liens, indifferently, yield to the **purchase money mortgage.**

The query can be altered in a number of ways to tailor it to the needs of the individual researcher. For example, to research the priority of a third party lender in a purchase money mortgage situation the following query could be used:

266k158 (purchase /3 money /3 mortgage /p priority) /p third /3 party person

By adding the terms THIRD, PARTY and PERSON and requiring that these terms appear within the same paragraph as the terms in the original query, more relevant documents will be retrieved. The headnote from one such document found in the Pacific (pac) database appears below.

R 2 OF 2   P 11 OF 27   PAC   T

345 P.2d 1015

202K96

HOMESTEAD

K. Purchase money and lien or mortgage therefor.

Kan. 1959.

Money borrowed from a **third person** by purchaser of a homestead, and paid to the vendor, is purchase money for which purchased property is liable to such **third person** where transaction between the parties to the lending transaction contemplates security for the obligation, and mortgage arising from such transaction takes **priority** over homestead exemption, and it matters not that such **purchase money mortgage** may be an equitable mortgage. Const. art. 15, s 9.

Hill v. Hill.
345 P.2d 1015, 185 Kan. 389.

Just how a query is altered will depend upon the research objectives of the individual.

IX. RANKING DOCUMENTS RETRIEVED ON WESTLAW: AGE AND TERM OPTIONS

Documents retrieved by a query can be ordered in either of two ways. One way is to order documents by their dates, with the most recent documents displayed first. This is ranking by AGE. Using the AGE option is suggested when the user's highest priority is to retrieve the most recent decisions frim a search.

Alternatively, documents can be ranked by the frequency of appearance of query terms. This is ranking by TERMS. When a search is performed with the TERMS option, the cases containing the greatest number of different search terms will be displayed first.

When a database is accessed by entering a database identifier, WESTLAW responds with a screen requesting that the query be entered. At this point the user may select which type or ranking, AGE or TERMS, is desired.

The queries offered in this hornbook were formulated and tested for relevancy with use of the TERMS option. Accordingly, in certain instances use of the AGE option with the preformulated queries may display less relevant, yet more recent cases, first.

X. CONCLUSION

This appendix has demonstrated methods that can be used to obtain the most effective research results in the area of real estate finance law. The addition of WESTLAW references at the end of each section of the text opens the door to a powerful and easily accessed computerized law library.

The queries may be used as provided or they may be tailored to meet the needs of researcher's specific problems. The power and flexibility of WESTLAW affords users of this publication a unique opportunity to greatly enhance their access to and understanding of real estate finance law.

Table of Cases

References are to Pages

C

E

F

H

K

M

N

O

P

S

T

U

V

Index

†